THE AUTHORITY

VOLUME 2

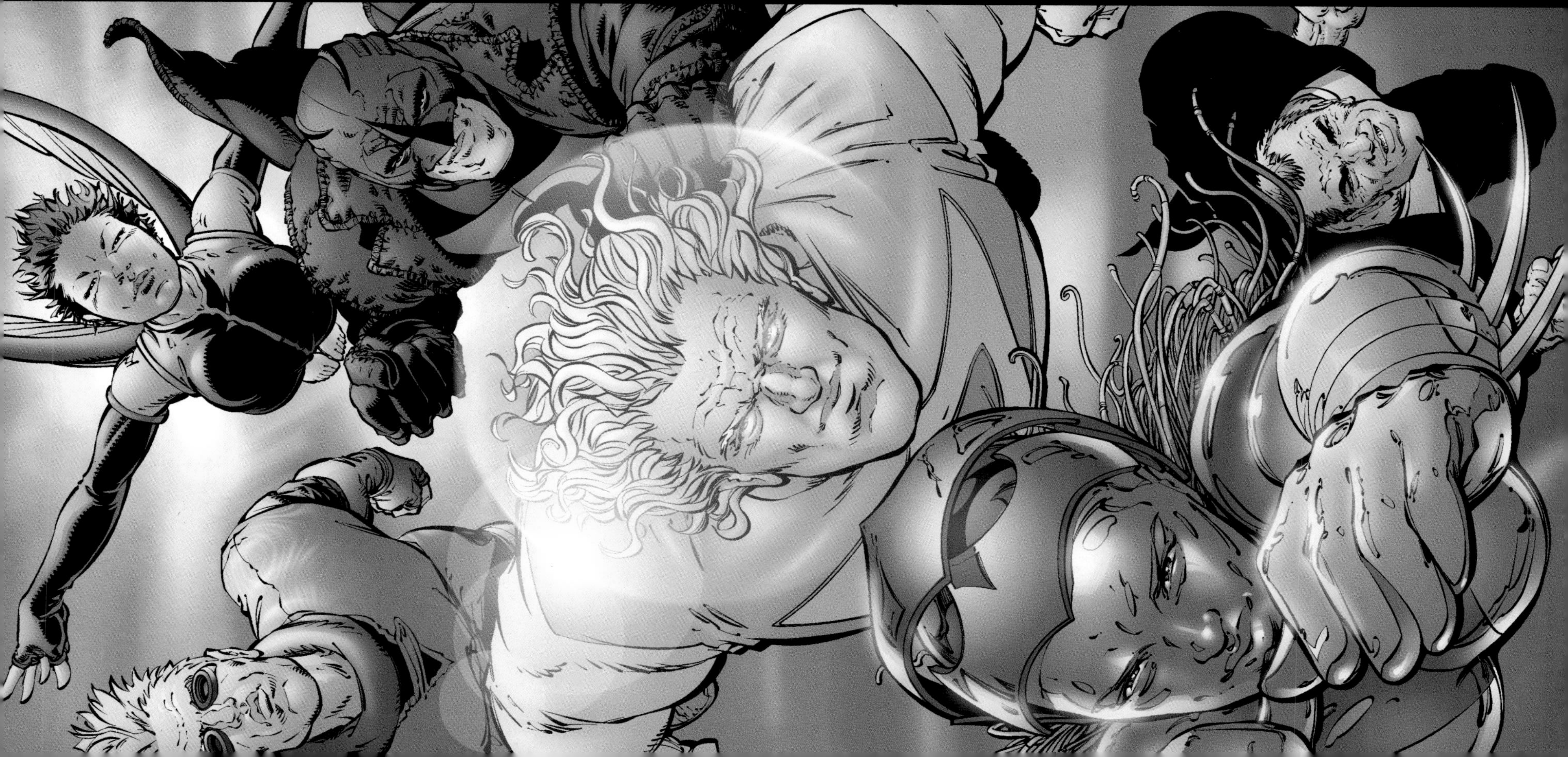

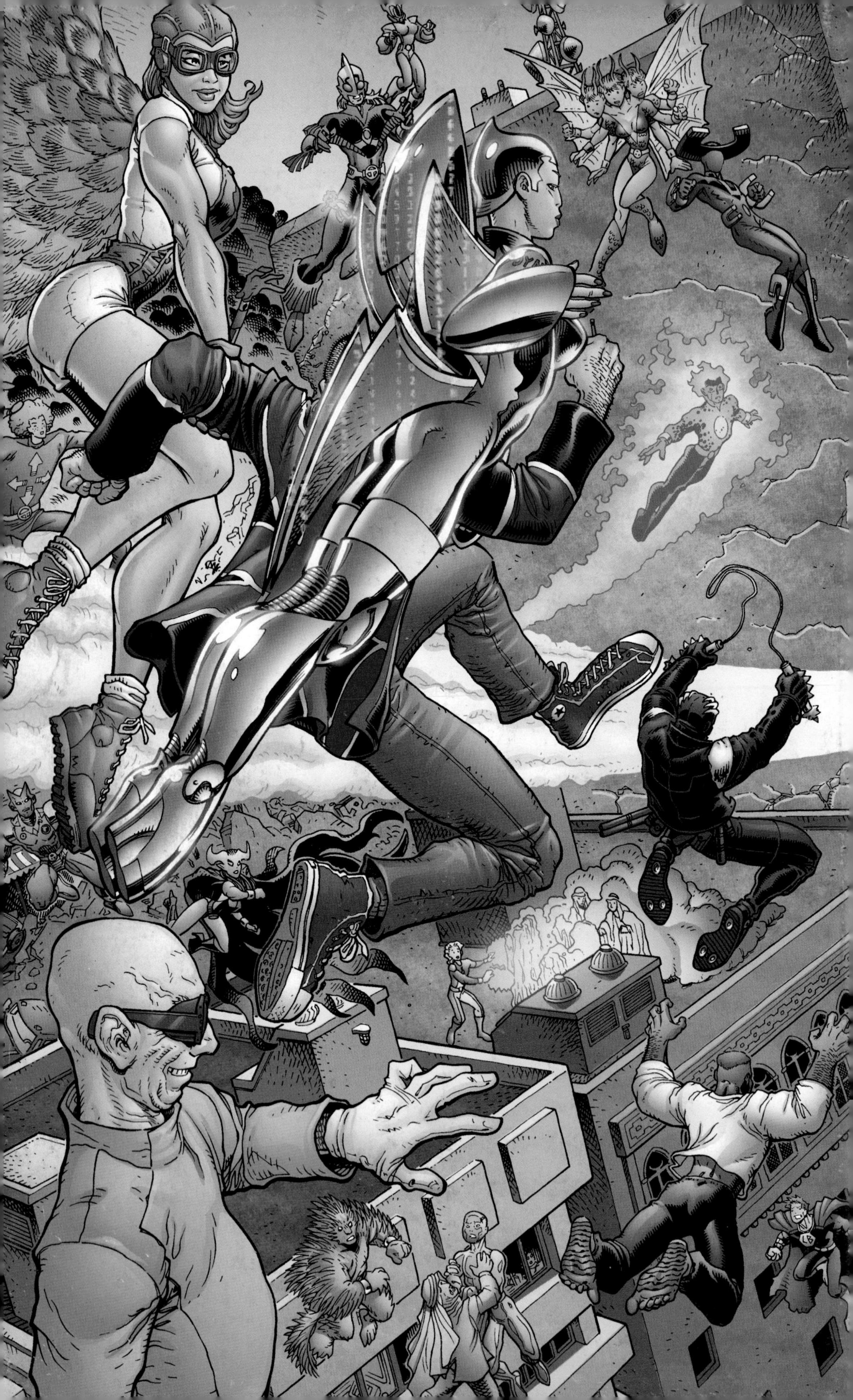

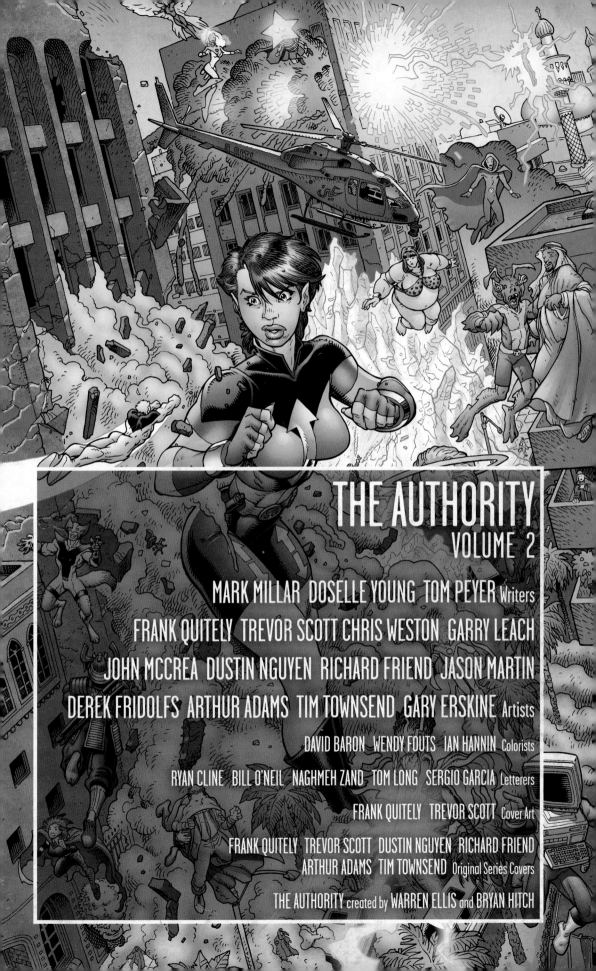

THE AUTHORITY
VOLUME 2

MARK MILLAR DOSELLE YOUNG TOM PEYER Writers

FRANK QUITELY TREVOR SCOTT CHRIS WESTON GARRY LEACH

JOHN MCCREA DUSTIN NGUYEN RICHARD FRIEND JASON MARTIN

DEREK FRIDOLFS ARTHUR ADAMS TIM TOWNSEND GARY ERSKINE Artists

DAVID BARON WENDY FOUTS IAN HANNIN Colorists

RYAN CLINE BILL O'NEIL NAGHMEH ZAND TOM LONG SERGIO GARCIA Letterers

FRANK QUITELY TREVOR SCOTT Cover Art

**FRANK QUITELY TREVOR SCOTT DUSTIN NGUYEN RICHARD FRIEND
ARTHUR ADAMS TIM TOWNSEND** Original Series Covers

THE AUTHORITY created by **WARREN ELLIS** and **BRYAN HITCH**

JOHN LAYMAN RACHELLE BRISSENDEN EDITORS – ORIGINAL SERIES SCOTT NYBAKKEN EDITOR
ROBBIN BROSTERMAN DESIGN DIRECTOR – BOOKS DAMIAN RYLAND PUBLICATION DESIGN

BOB HARRAS SENIOR VP – EDITOR-IN-CHIEF, DC COMICS

DIANE NELSON PRESIDENT DAN DIDIO AND JIM LEE CO-PUBLISHERS GEOFF JOHNS CHIEF CREATIVE OFFICER JOHN ROOD EXECUTIVE VP – SALES, MARKETING
AND BUSINESS DEVELOPMENT AMY GENKINS SENIOR VP – BUSINESS AND LEGAL AFFAIRS NAIRI GARDINER SENIOR VP – FINANCE JEFF BOISON VP – PUBLISHING
PLANNING MARK CHIARELLO VP – ART DIRECTION AND DESIGN JOHN CUNNINGHAM VP – MARKETING TERRI CUNNINGHAM VP – EDITORIAL ADMINISTRATION
ALISON GILL SENIOR VP – MANUFACTURING AND OPERATIONS HANK KANALZ SENIOR VP – VERTIGO AND INTEGRATED PUBLISHING JAY KOGAN VP – BUSINESS AND
LEGAL AFFAIRS, PUBLISHING JACK MAHAN VP – BUSINESS AFFAIRS, TALENT NICK NAPOLITANO VP – MANUFACTURING ADMINISTRATION SUE POHJA VP – BOOK
SALES COURTNEY SIMMONS SENIOR VP – PUBLICITY BOB WAYNE SENIOR VP – SALES

THE AUTHORITY VOLUME 2

PUBLISHED BY DC COMICS. COPYRIGHT © 2013 DC COMICS. ALL RIGHTS RESERVED.

ORIGINALLY PUBLISHED IN SINGLE MAGAZINE FORM IN THE AUTHORITY 13-29. COPYRIGHT © 2000, 2001, 2002 DC COMICS. ALL RIGHTS RESERVED.
ALL CHARACTERS, THEIR DISTINCTIVE LIKENESSES AND RELATED ELEMENTS FEATURED IN THIS PUBLICATION ARE TRADEMARKS OF DC COMICS.
THE STORIES, CHARACTERS AND INCIDENTS FEATURED IN THIS PUBLICATION ARE ENTIRELY FICTIONAL. DC COMICS DOES NOT READ OR ACCEPT UNSOLICITED
SUBMISSIONS OF IDEAS, STORIES OR ARTWORK.

DC COMICS, 1700 BROADWAY, NEW YORK, NY 10019. A WARNER BROS. ENTERTAINMENT COMPANY
PRINTED BY RR DONNELLEY, SALEM, VA, USA. 11/15/13. FIRST PRINTING. ISBN: 978-1-4012-4275-6

LIBRARY OF CONGRESS CATALOGING-IN-PUBLICATION DATA

MILLAR, MARK, AUTHOR.
 THE AUTHORITY VOLUME 2 / MARK MILLAR, FRANK QUITELY.
   PAGES CM
 SUMMARY: "THE AUTHORITY, NOW UNDER JACK HAWKSMOOR'S LEADERSHIP FOLLOWING JENNY SPARKS' DEATH AT THE END OF THE 20TH CENTURY, FACE
MULTIPLE FOES SUCH AS A MAD SCIENTIST AND HIS ARMY OF SUPERHUMANS WHO WANTED TO INFLUENCE THE 21ST CENTURY THROUGH JENNY SPARKS'
SUCCESSOR JENNY QUANTUM, A PREVIOUS DOCTOR WHO MANIPULATED THE EARTH ITSELF, AND A DUPLICATE TEAM OF SUPERHEROES MODELED ON THE
AUTHORITY THAT WAS CREATED AND BACKED BY THE G7 GROUP OF NATIONS. COLLECTS THE AUTHORITY #13-29" — PROVIDED BY PUBLISHER.
 ISBN 978-1-4012-4275-6 (HARDBACK)
 1. GRAPHIC NOVELS. I. QUITELY, FRANK, 1968- ILLUSTRATOR II. TITLE.
 PN6728.A88M56 2013
 741.5'973--DC23
                                  2013031444

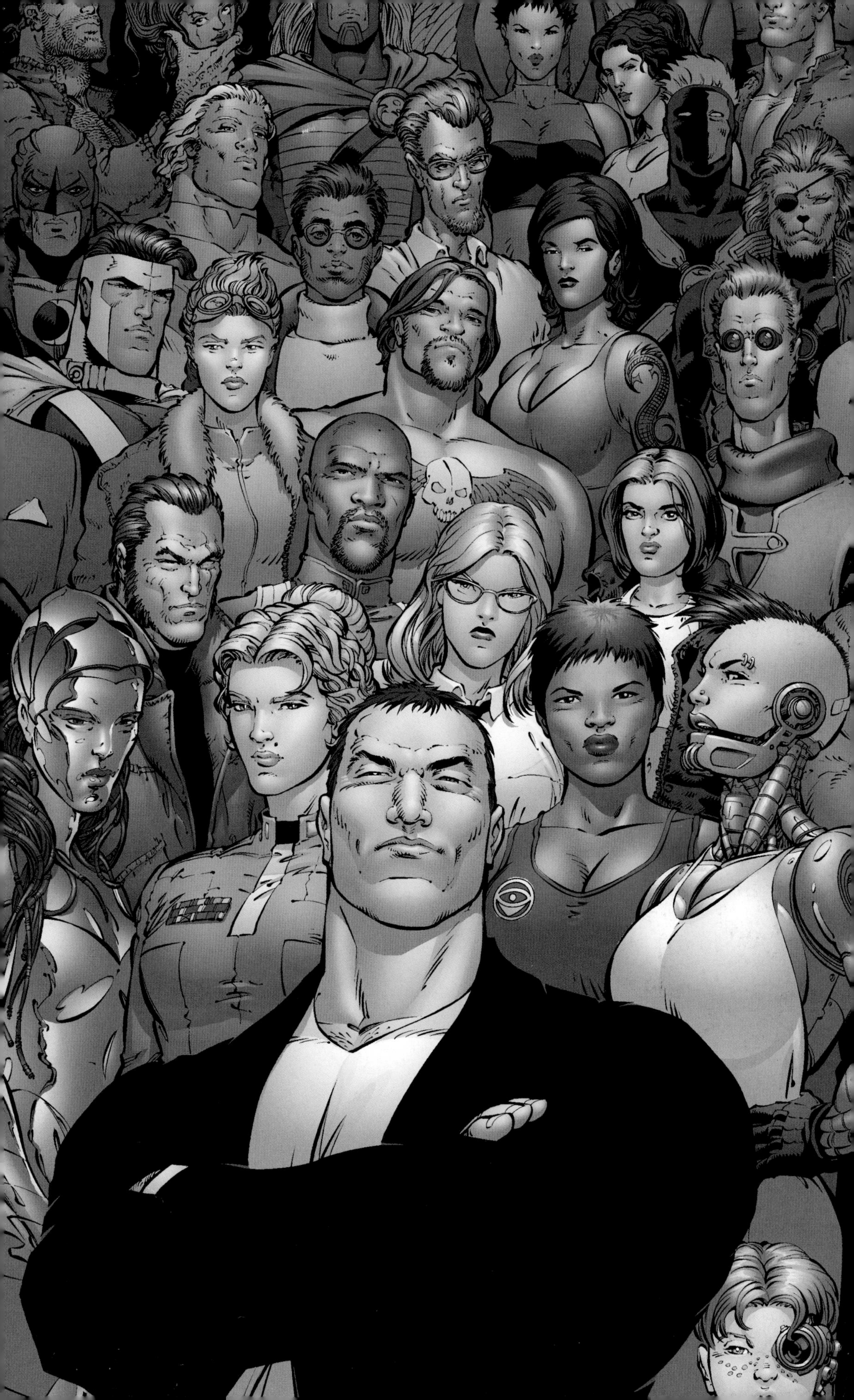

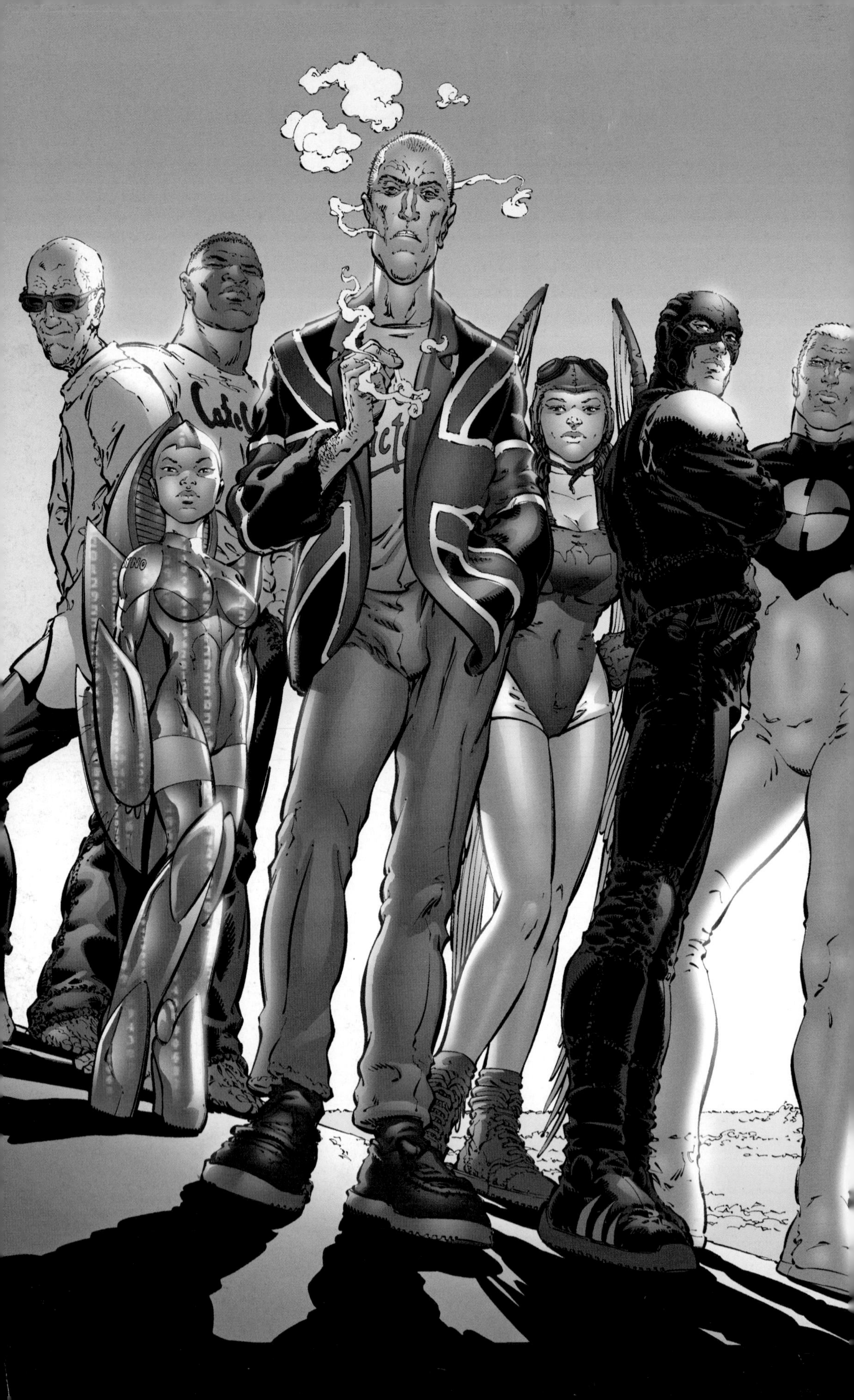

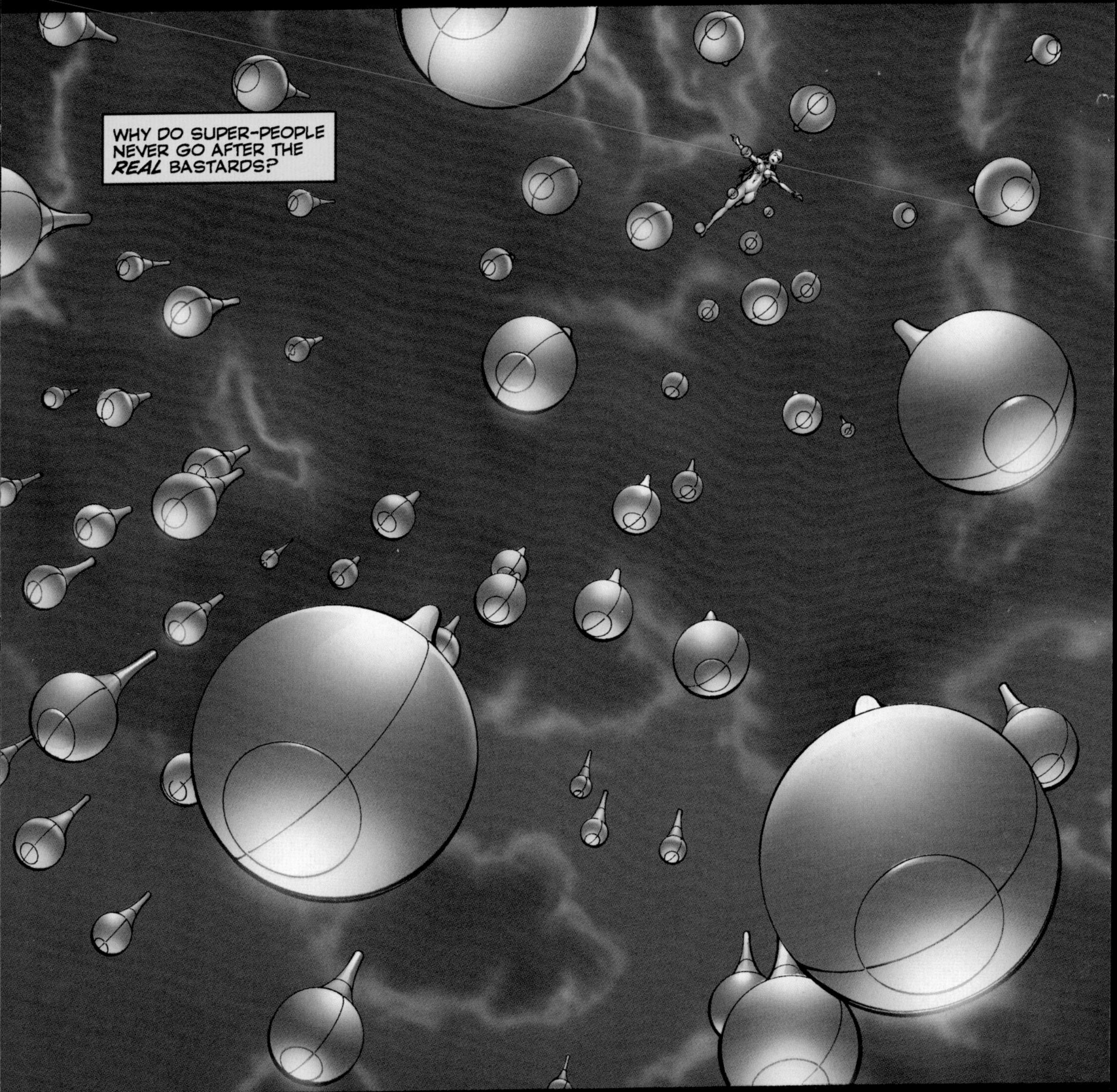
WHY DO SUPER-PEOPLE NEVER GO AFTER THE *REAL* BASTARDS?

The AUTHORITY "THE NATIVITY" ONE of FOUR

MARK MILLAR writer and **FRANK QUITELY** artist with **TREVOR SCOTT** inker

DAVID BARON colorist

RYAN CLINE letterer

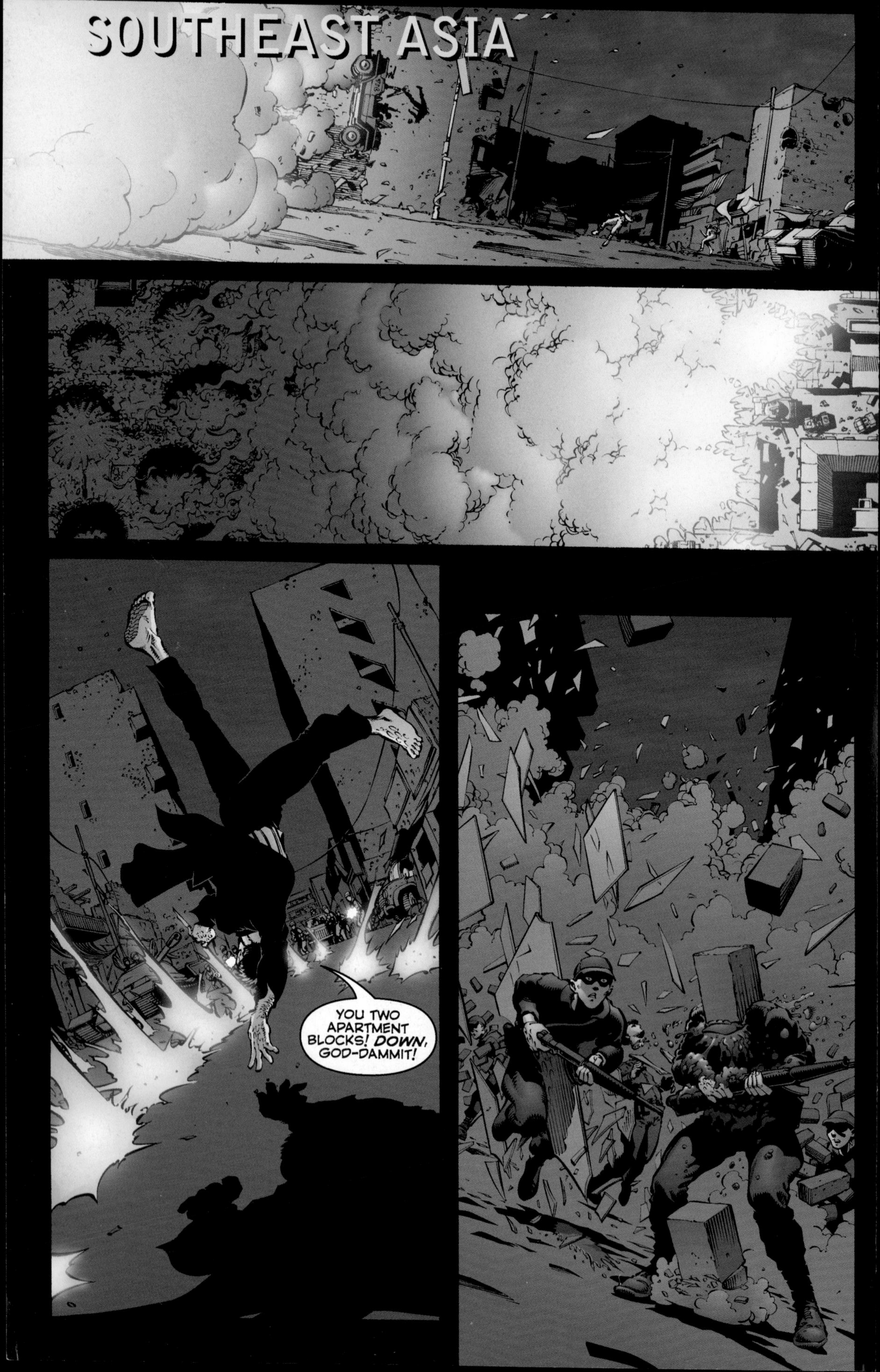
SOUTHEAST ASIA
YOU TWO APARTMENT BLOCKS! DOWN, GOD-DAMMIT!

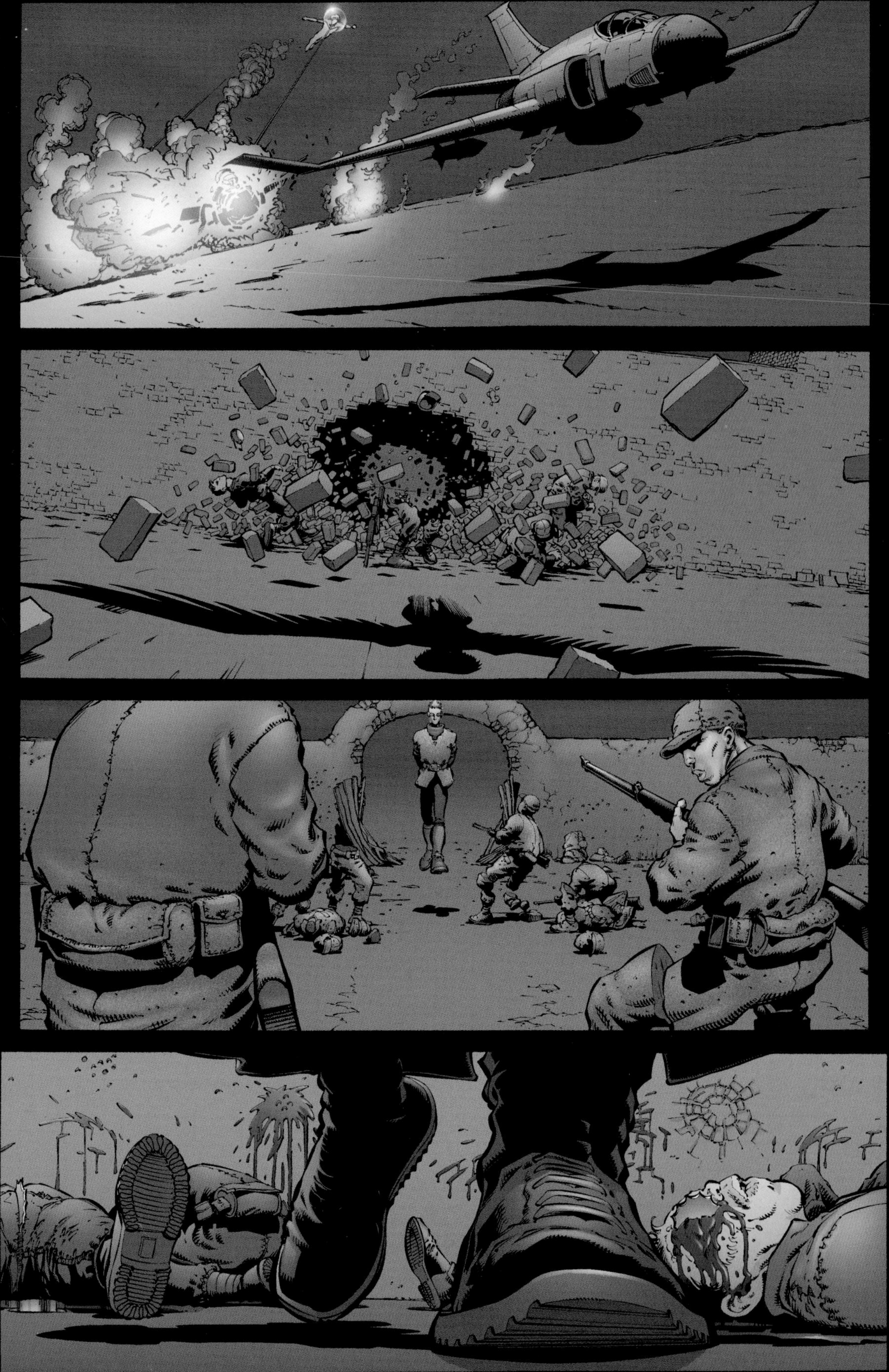

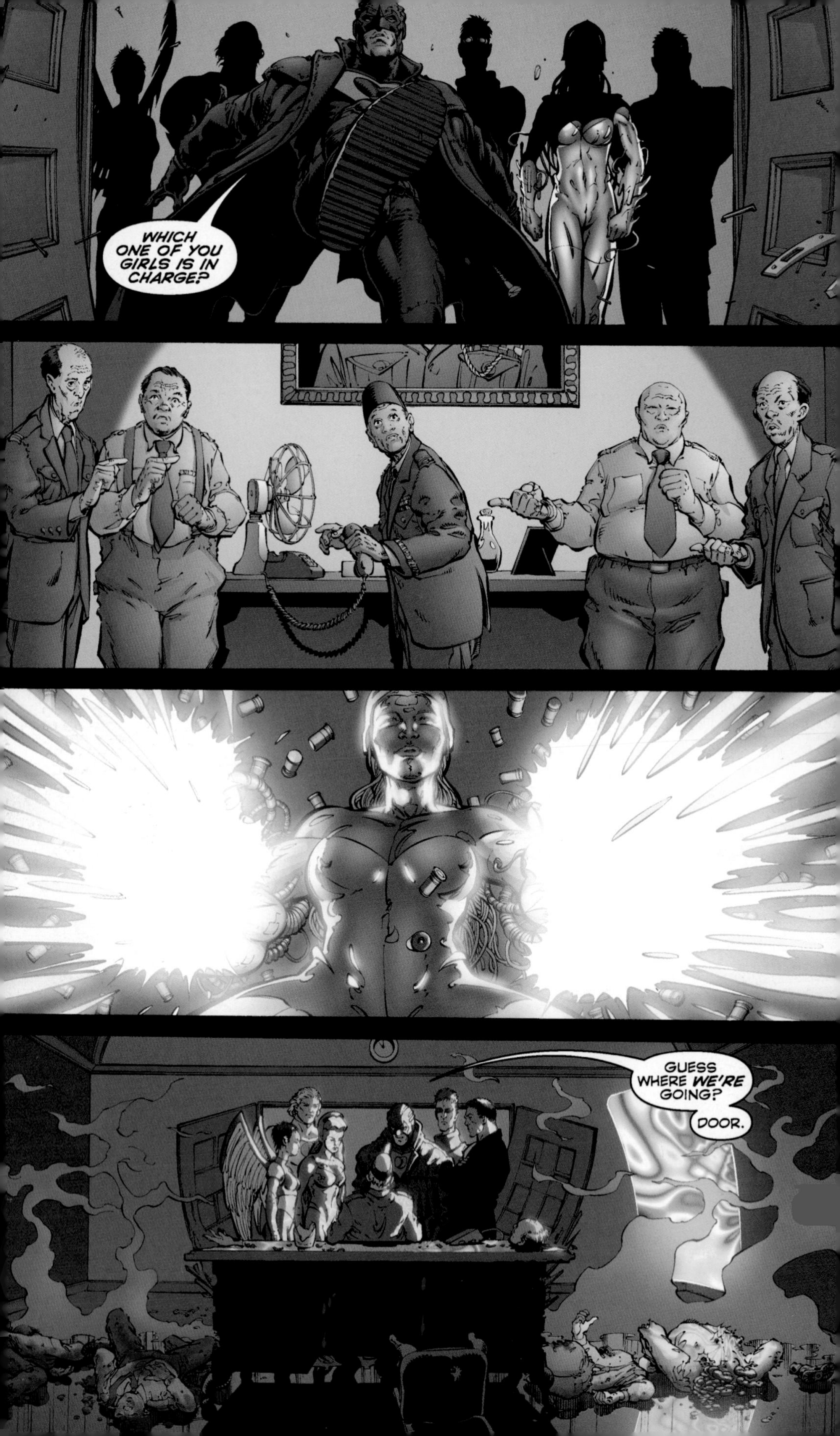
WHICH ONE OF YOU GIRLS IS IN CHARGE?
GUESS WHERE WE'RE GOING?
DOOR.

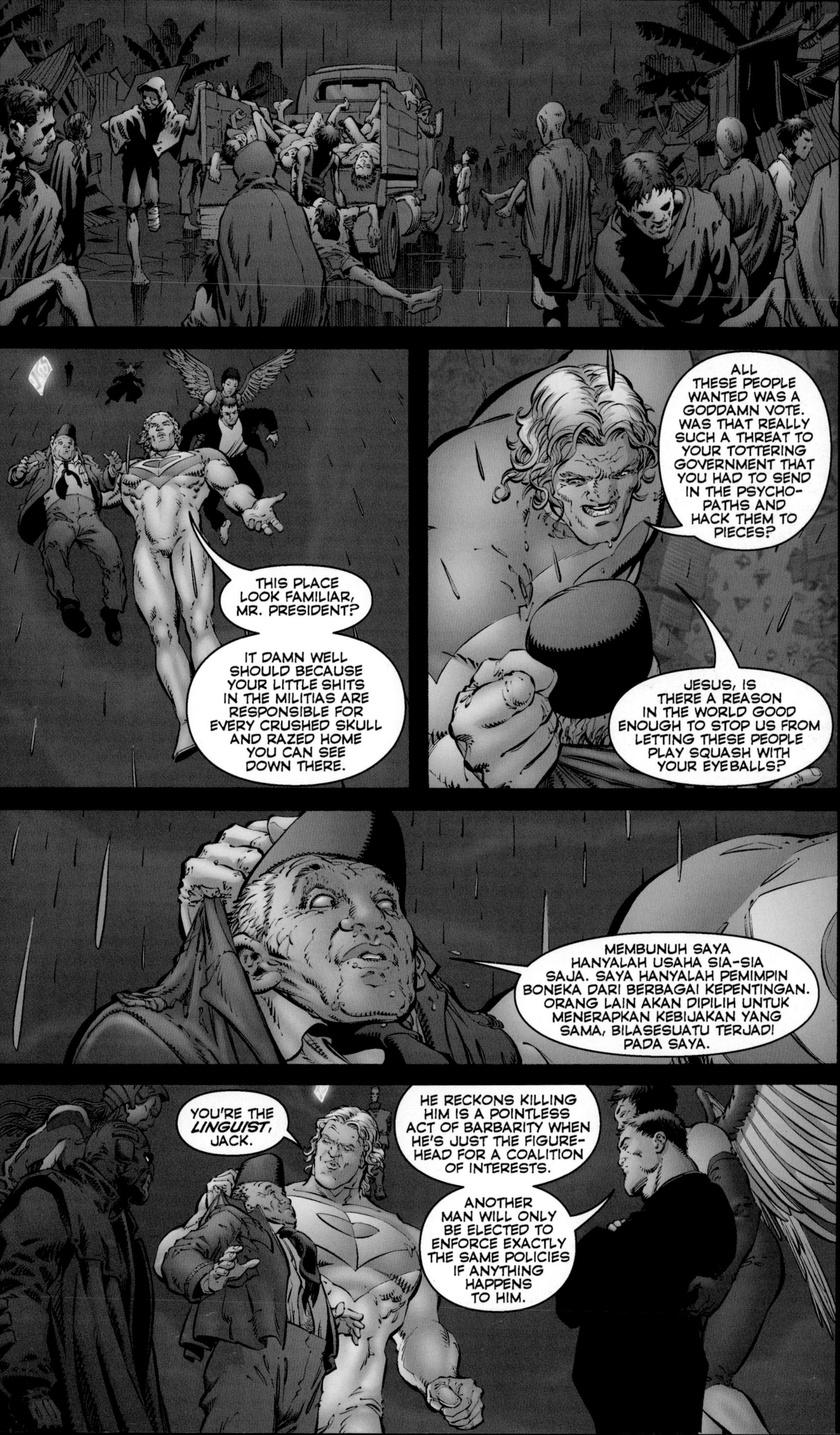
THIS PLACE LOOK FAMILIAR, MR. PRESIDENT?
IT DAMN WELL SHOULD BECAUSE YOUR LITTLE SHITS IN THE MILITIAS ARE RESPONSIBLE FOR EVERY CRUSHED SKULL AND RAZED HOME YOU CAN SEE DOWN THERE.
ALL THESE PEOPLE WANTED WAS A GODDAMN VOTE. WAS THAT REALLY SUCH A THREAT TO YOUR TOTTERING GOVERNMENT THAT YOU HAD TO SEND IN THE PSYCHO-PATHS AND HACK THEM TO PIECES?
JESUS, IS THERE A REASON IN THE WORLD GOOD ENOUGH TO STOP US FROM LETTING THESE PEOPLE PLAY SQUASH WITH YOUR EYEBALLS?
MEMBUNUH SAYA HANYALAH USAHA SIA-SIA SAJA. SAYA HANYALAH PEMIMPIN BONEKA DARI BERBAGAI KEPENTINGAN. ORANG LAIN AKAN DIPILIH UNTUK MENERAPKAN KEBIJAKAN YANG SAMA, BILASESUATU TERJADI PADA SAYA.
YOU'RE THE *LINGUIST*, JACK.
HE RECKONS KILLING HIM IS A POINTLESS ACT OF BARBARITY WHEN HE'S JUST THE FIGURE-HEAD FOR A COALITION OF INTERESTS.
ANOTHER MAN WILL ONLY BE ELECTED TO ENFORCE EXACTLY THE SAME POLICIES IF ANYTHING HAPPENS TO HIM.

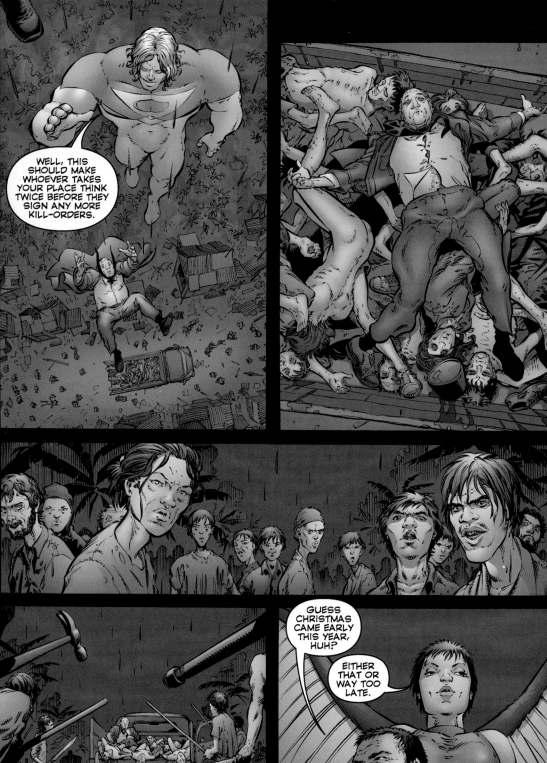

WELL, THIS SHOULD MAKE WHOEVER TAKES YOUR PLACE THINK TWICE BEFORE THEY SIGN ANY MORE KILL-ORDERS.

GUESS CHRISTMAS CAME EARLY THIS YEAR, HUH?

EITHER THAT OR WAY TOO LATE.

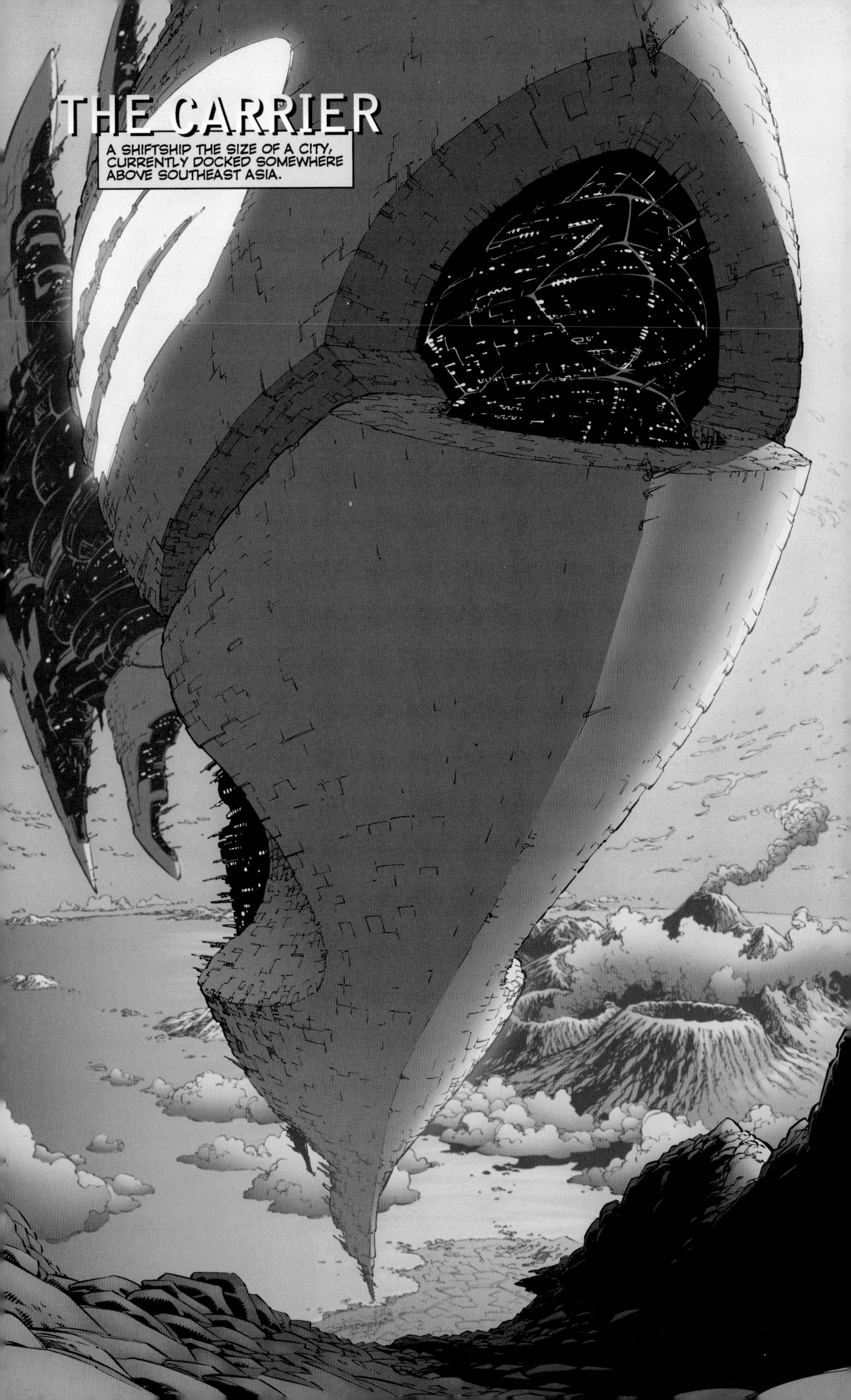
THE CARRIER
A SHIFTSHIP THE SIZE OF A CITY, CURRENTLY DOCKED SOMEWHERE ABOVE SOUTHEAST ASIA.

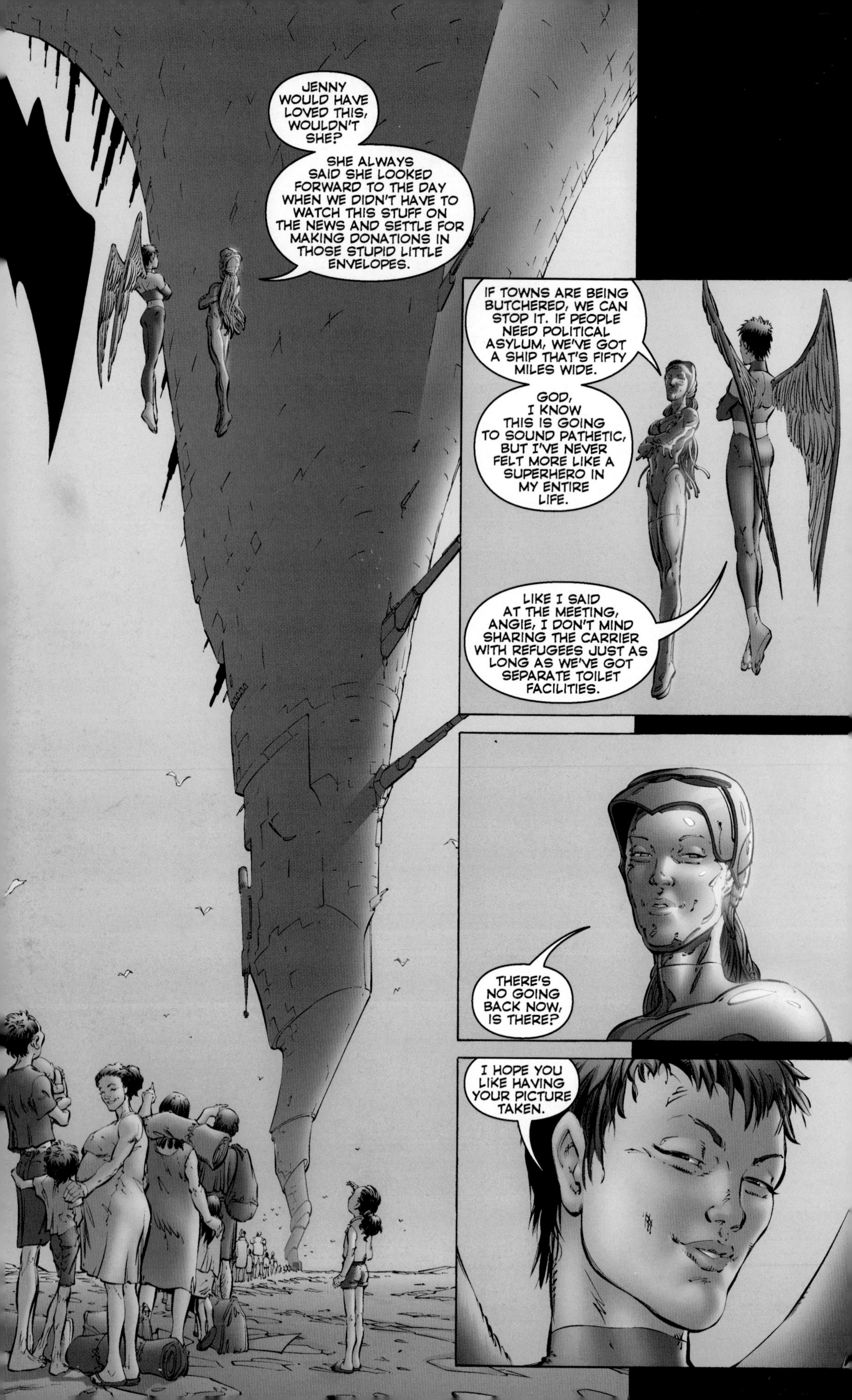

JENNY WOULD HAVE LOVED THIS, WOULDN'T SHE?
SHE ALWAYS SAID SHE LOOKED FORWARD TO THE DAY WHEN WE DIDN'T HAVE TO WATCH THIS STUFF ON THE NEWS AND SETTLE FOR MAKING DONATIONS IN THOSE STUPID LITTLE ENVELOPES.
IF TOWNS ARE BEING BUTCHERED, WE CAN STOP IT. IF PEOPLE NEED POLITICAL ASYLUM, WE'VE GOT A SHIP THAT'S FIFTY MILES WIDE.
GOD, I KNOW THIS IS GOING TO SOUND PATHETIC, BUT I'VE NEVER FELT MORE LIKE A SUPERHERO IN MY ENTIRE LIFE.
LIKE I SAID AT THE MEETING, ANGIE, I DON'T MIND SHARING THE CARRIER WITH REFUGEES JUST AS LONG AS WE'VE GOT SEPARATE TOILET FACILITIES.
THERE'S NO GOING BACK NOW, IS THERE?
I HOPE YOU LIKE HAVING YOUR PICTURE TAKEN.

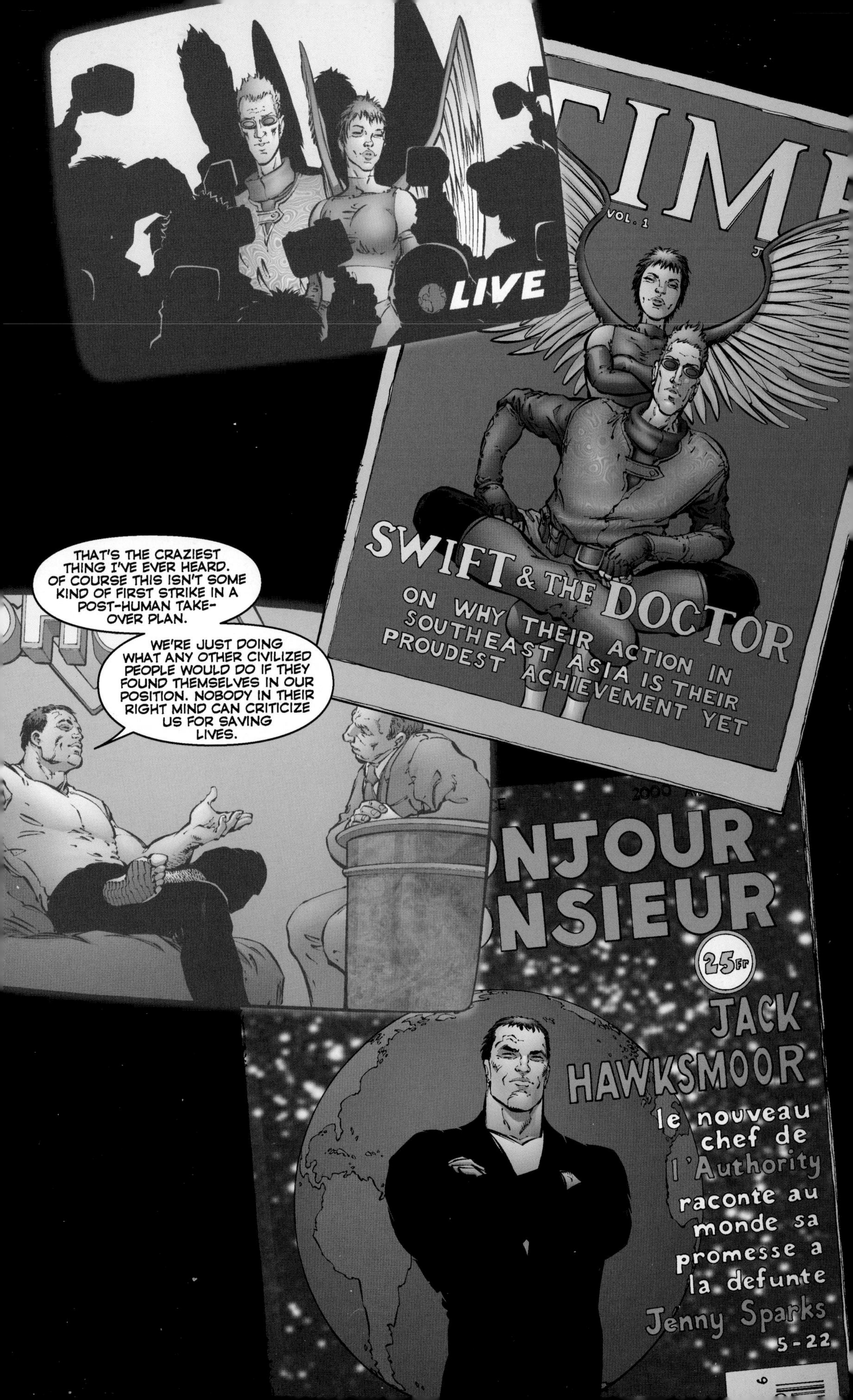
LIVE
TIME
VOL. 1
SWIFT & THE DOCTOR
ON WHY THEIR ACTION IN SOUTHEAST ASIA IS THEIR PROUDEST ACHIEVEMENT YET
THAT'S THE CRAZIEST THING I'VE EVER HEARD. OF COURSE THIS ISN'T SOME KIND OF FIRST STRIKE IN A POST-HUMAN TAKE-OVER PLAN.
WE'RE JUST DOING WHAT ANY OTHER CIVILIZED PEOPLE WOULD DO IF THEY FOUND THEMSELVES IN OUR POSITION. NOBODY IN THEIR RIGHT MIND CAN CRITICIZE US FOR SAVING LIVES.
NJOUR
NSIEUR
25Fr
JACK HAWKSMOOR
le nouveau chef de l'Authority raconte au monde sa promesse a la defunte Jenny Sparks
5-22

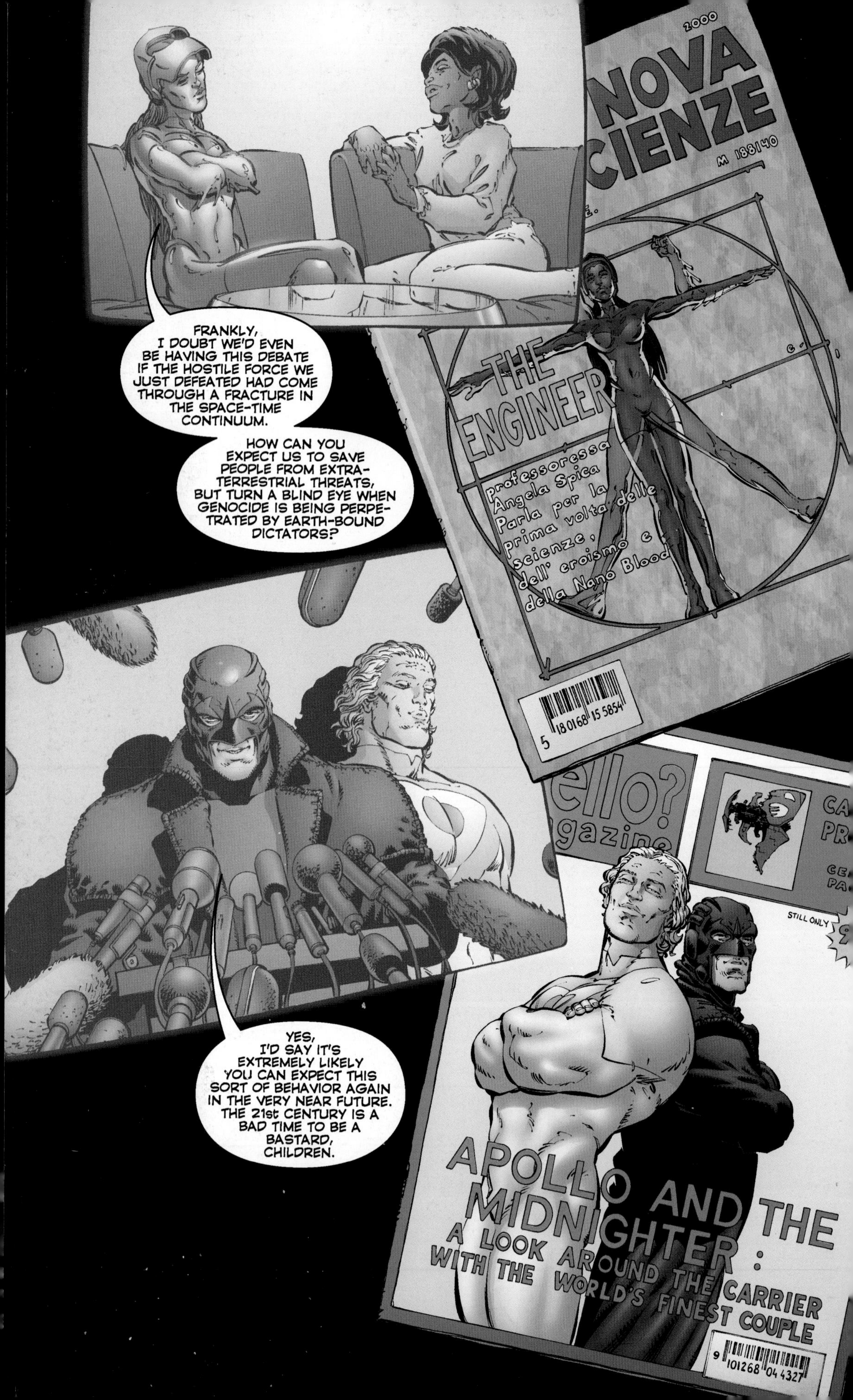
FRANKLY, I DOUBT WE'D EVEN BE HAVING THIS DEBATE IF THE HOSTILE FORCE WE JUST DEFEATED HAD COME THROUGH A FRACTURE IN THE SPACE-TIME CONTINUUM.
HOW CAN YOU EXPECT US TO SAVE PEOPLE FROM EXTRA-TERRESTRIAL THREATS, BUT TURN A BLIND EYE WHEN GENOCIDE IS BEING PERPE-TRATED BY EARTH-BOUND DICTATORS?
2000
NOVA
CIENZE
M 188140
THE ENGINEER
professoressa Angela Spica Parla per la prima volta delle scienze, dell' eroismo e della Nano Blood
YES, I'D SAY IT'S EXTREMELY LIKELY YOU CAN EXPECT THIS SORT OF BEHAVIOR AGAIN IN THE VERY NEAR FUTURE. THE 21st CENTURY IS A BAD TIME TO BE A BASTARD, CHILDREN.
STILL ONLY
APOLLO AND THE MIDNIGHTER
A LOOK AROUND THE CARRIER WITH THE WORLD'S FINEST COUPLE

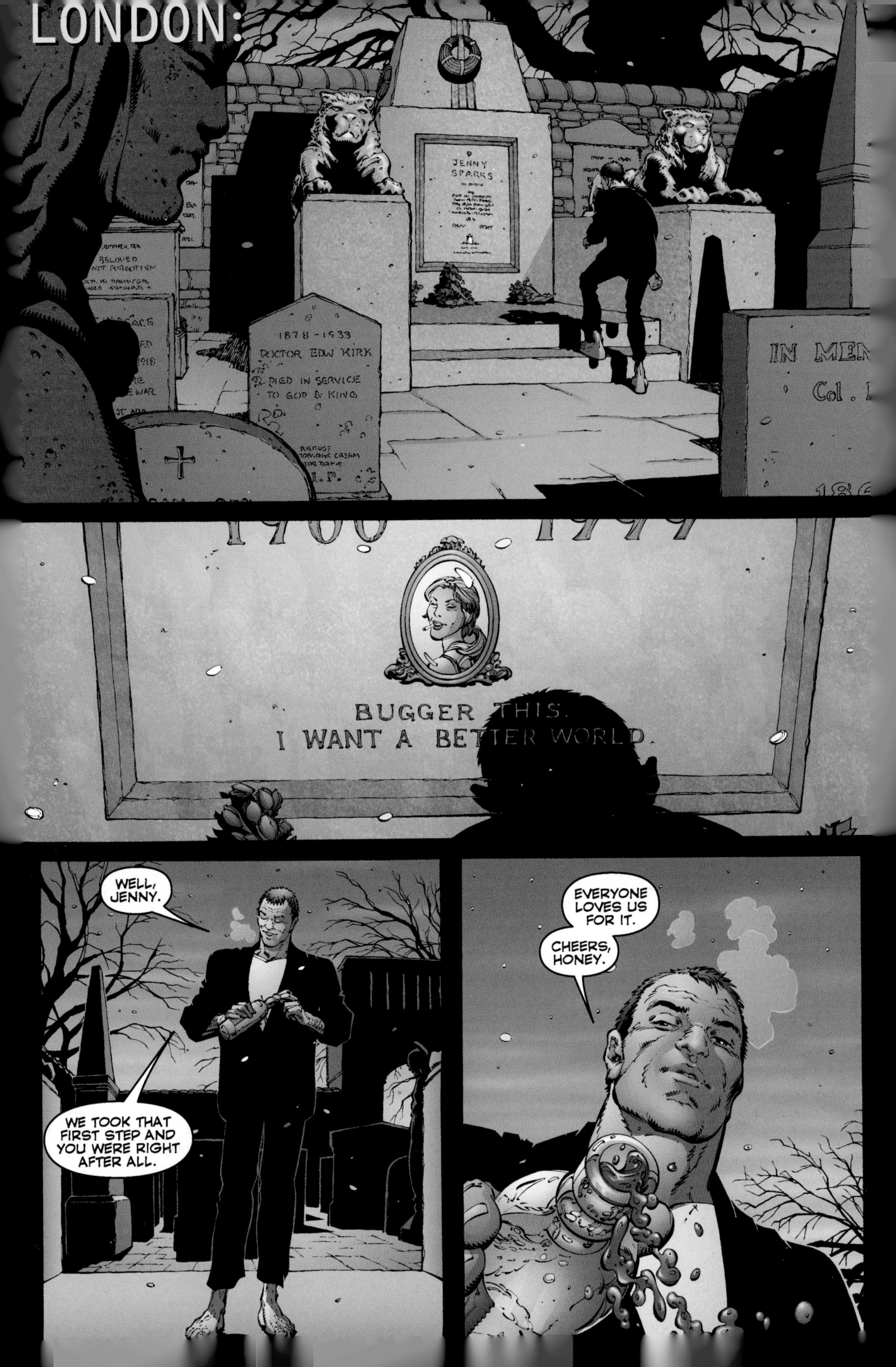
LONDON:
JENNY SPARKS
BELOVED
NOT FORGOTTEN
1878 - 1933
DOCTOR EDW KIRK
DIED IN SERVICE
TO GOD & KING
BUGGER THIS.
I WANT A BETTER WORLD.
WELL, JENNY.
WE TOOK THAT FIRST STEP AND YOU WERE RIGHT AFTER ALL.
EVERYONE LOVES US FOR IT.
CHEERS, HONEY.

I HEARD SOMEWHERE *JENNY'S* MEMORIAL IS BIGGER THAN THE ONE THEY BUILT FOR PRINCESS DIANA.

IT MUST BE WEIRD GOING PUBLIC AFTER ALL THOSE YEARS IN BLACK OPS, JACK. YOU THINK YOU'LL EVER GET USED TO HAVING YOUR OWN FAN CLUB AND POSABLE ACTION FIGURE?

WELL, MAYBE THE FAIRY-TALE PRINCESS SHOULD HAVE DIED SAVING THE WORLD INSTEAD OF ARGUING ABOUT WHO'S PAYING THIS MONTH'S CREDIT CARD BILL IN THE BACK OF A MERCEDES.

BELIEVE IT OR NOT, BEING CHASED DOWN THE STREET BY HORNY TEENAGE GIRLS WAS NEVER MY AMBITION, DOCTOR.

ALL THAT TICKER-TAPE PARADE CRAP REALLY MAKES ME CRINGE, BUT I'VE GOT TO ADMIT I'M SERIOUSLY GETTING INTO THE NEW, PROACTIVE OPERATIONS BEING FAMOUS LETS US GET AWAY WITH IT.

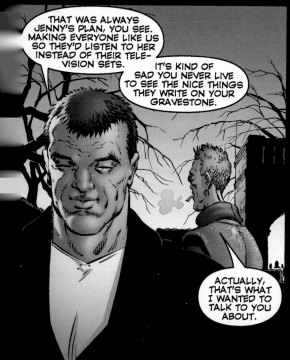

THAT WAS ALWAYS JENNY'S PLAN, YOU SEE. MAKING EVERYONE LIKE US SO THEY'D LISTEN TO HER INSTEAD OF THEIR TELE-VISION SETS.

IT'S KIND OF SAD YOU NEVER LIVE TO SEE THE NICE THINGS THEY WRITE ON YOUR GRAVESTONE.

ACTUALLY, THAT'S WHAT I WANTED TO TALK TO YOU ABOUT.

YOU SEE, JENNY MIGHT NOT ACTUALLY BE AS COMPLETELY DECEASED AS WE ALL ORIGINALLY THOUGHT.

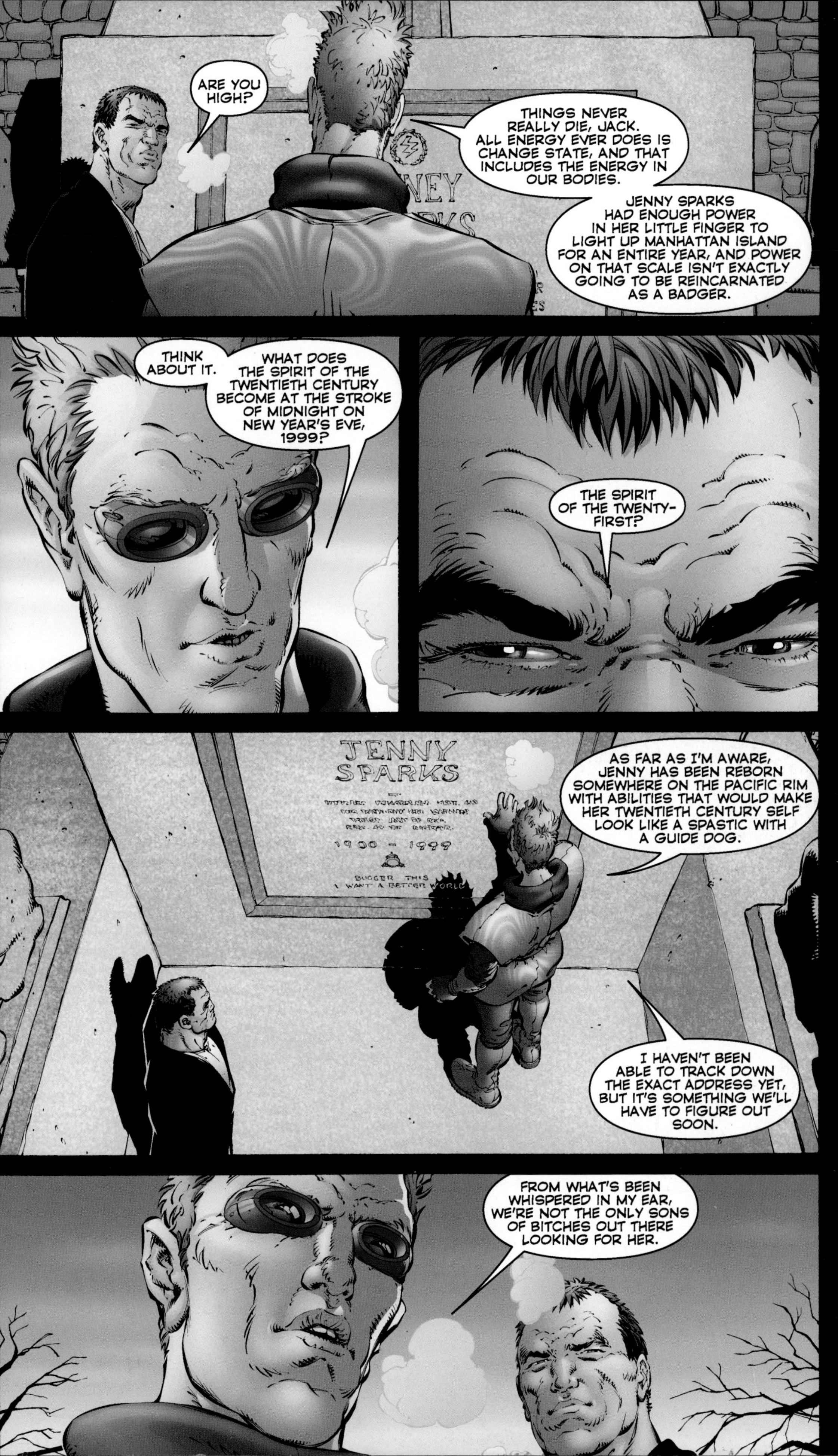
ARE YOU HIGH?
THINGS NEVER REALLY DIE, JACK. ALL ENERGY EVER DOES IS CHANGE STATE, AND THAT INCLUDES THE ENERGY IN OUR BODIES.
JENNY SPARKS HAD ENOUGH POWER IN HER LITTLE FINGER TO LIGHT UP MANHATTAN ISLAND FOR AN ENTIRE YEAR, AND POWER ON THAT SCALE ISN'T EXACTLY GOING TO BE REINCARNATED AS A BADGER.
THINK ABOUT IT.
WHAT DOES THE SPIRIT OF THE TWENTIETH CENTURY BECOME AT THE STROKE OF MIDNIGHT ON NEW YEAR'S EVE, 1999?
THE SPIRIT OF THE TWENTY-FIRST?
JENNY
SPARKS
1900 - 1999
BUGGER THIS
I WANT A BETTER WORLD
AS FAR AS I'M AWARE, JENNY HAS BEEN REBORN SOMEWHERE ON THE PACIFIC RIM WITH ABILITIES THAT WOULD MAKE HER TWENTIETH CENTURY SELF LOOK LIKE A SPASTIC WITH A GUIDE DOG.
I HAVEN'T BEEN ABLE TO TRACK DOWN THE EXACT ADDRESS YET, BUT IT'S SOMETHING WE'LL HAVE TO FIGURE OUT SOON.
FROM WHAT'S BEEN WHISPERED IN MY EAR, WE'RE NOT THE ONLY SONS OF BITCHES OUT THERE LOOKING FOR HER.

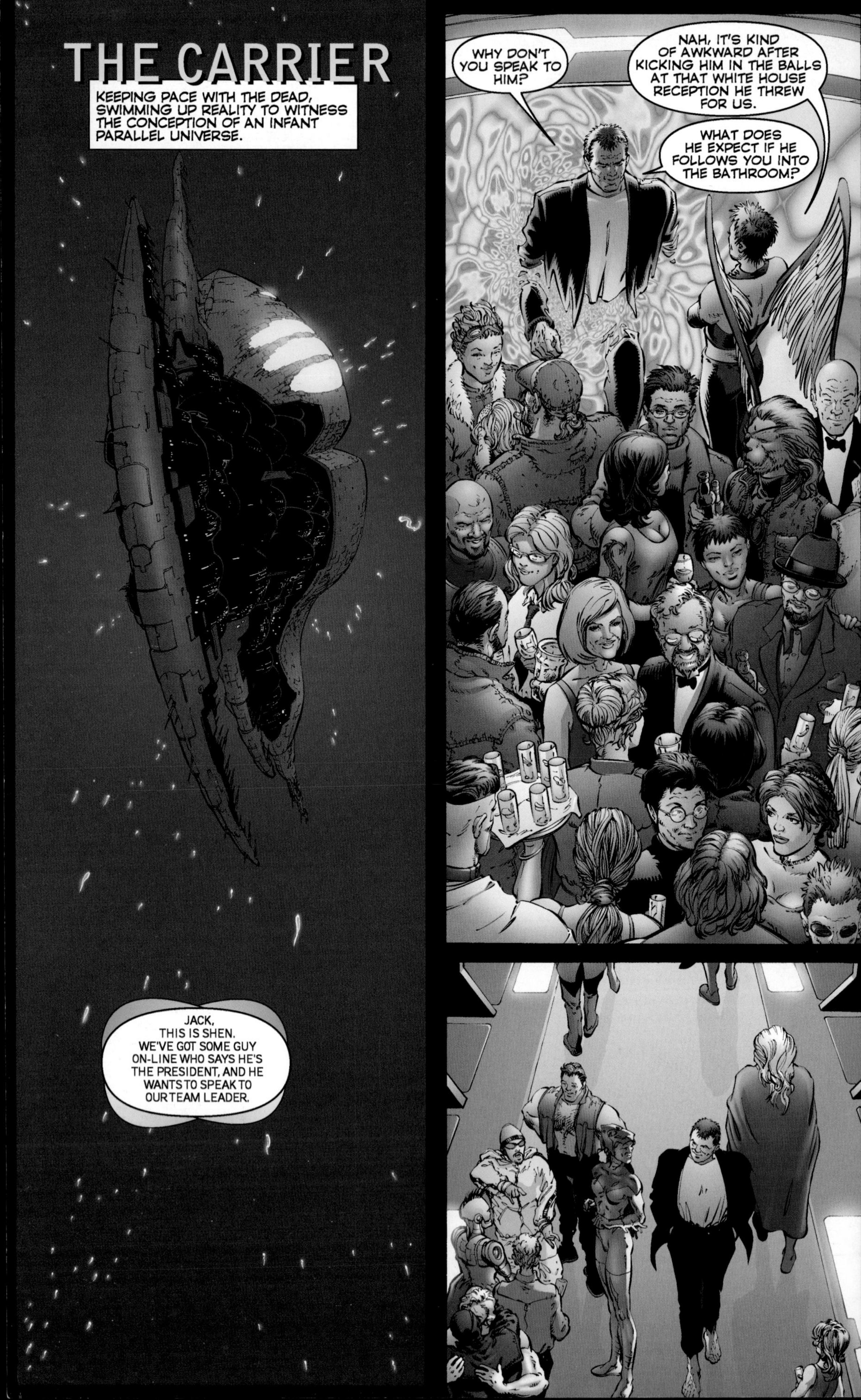
THE CARRIER
KEEPING PACE WITH THE DEAD, SWIMMING UP REALITY TO WITNESS THE CONCEPTION OF AN INFANT PARALLEL UNIVERSE.
JACK, THIS IS SHEN. WE'VE GOT SOME GUY ON-LINE WHO SAYS HE'S THE PRESIDENT, AND HE WANTS TO SPEAK TO OUR TEAM LEADER.
WHY DON'T YOU SPEAK TO HIM?
NAH, IT'S KIND OF AWKWARD AFTER KICKING HIM IN THE BALLS AT THAT WHITE HOUSE RECEPTION HE THREW FOR US.
WHAT DOES HE EXPECT IF HE FOLLOWS YOU INTO THE BATHROOM?

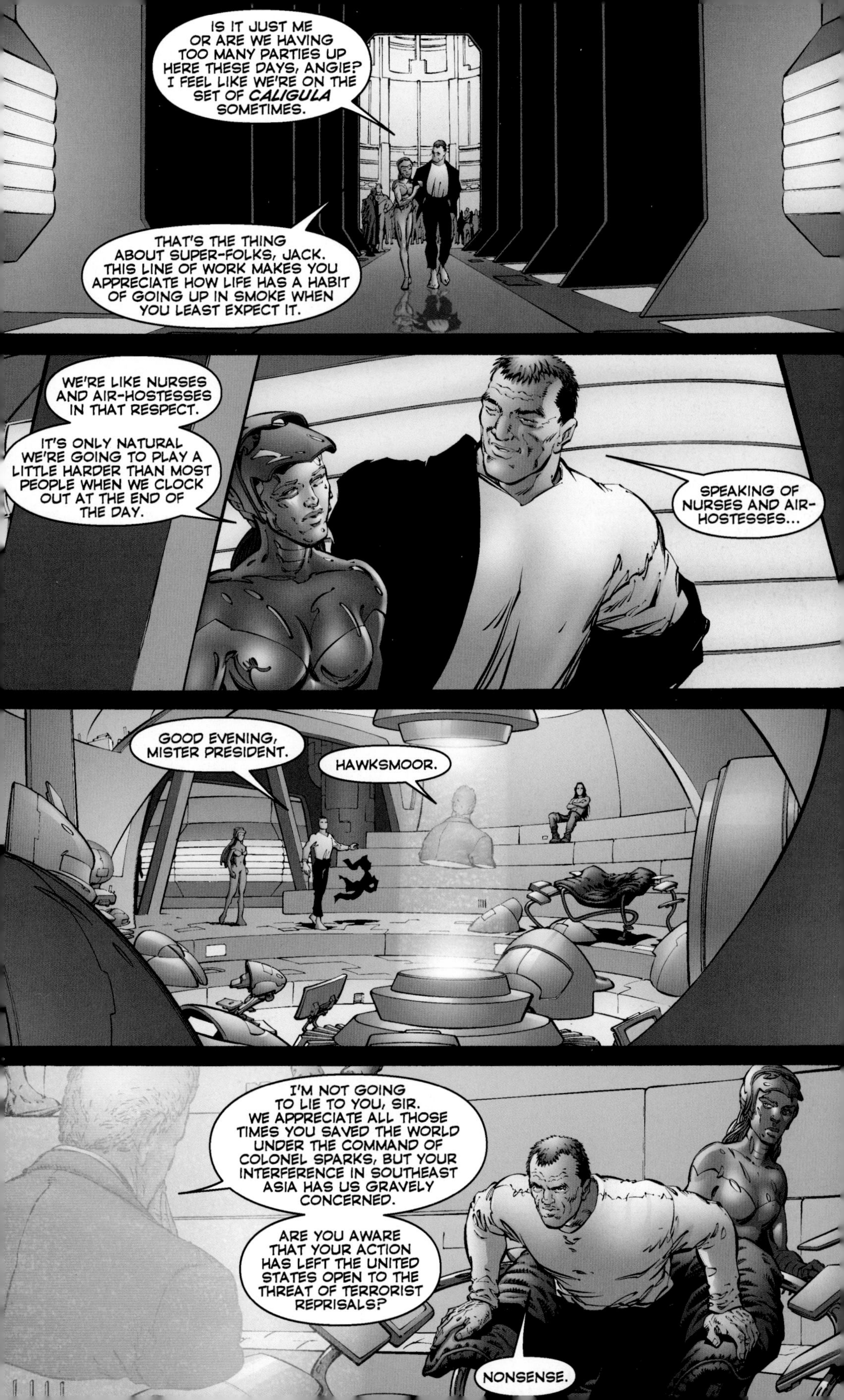
IS IT JUST ME OR ARE WE HAVING TOO MANY PARTIES UP HERE THESE DAYS, ANGIE? I FEEL LIKE WE'RE ON THE SET OF *CALIGULA* SOMETIMES.
THAT'S THE THING ABOUT SUPER-FOLKS, JACK. THIS LINE OF WORK MAKES YOU APPRECIATE HOW LIFE HAS A HABIT OF GOING UP IN SMOKE WHEN YOU LEAST EXPECT IT.
WE'RE LIKE NURSES AND AIR-HOSTESSES IN THAT RESPECT.
IT'S ONLY NATURAL WE'RE GOING TO PLAY A LITTLE HARDER THAN MOST PEOPLE WHEN WE CLOCK OUT AT THE END OF THE DAY.
SPEAKING OF NURSES AND AIR-HOSTESSES...
GOOD EVENING, MISTER PRESIDENT.
HAWKSMOOR.
I'M NOT GOING TO LIE TO YOU, SIR. WE APPRECIATE ALL THOSE TIMES YOU SAVED THE WORLD UNDER THE COMMAND OF COLONEL SPARKS, BUT YOUR INTERFERENCE IN SOUTHEAST ASIA HAS US GRAVELY CONCERNED.
ARE YOU AWARE THAT YOUR ACTION HAS LEFT THE UNITED STATES OPEN TO THE THREAT OF TERRORIST REPRISALS?
NONSENSE.

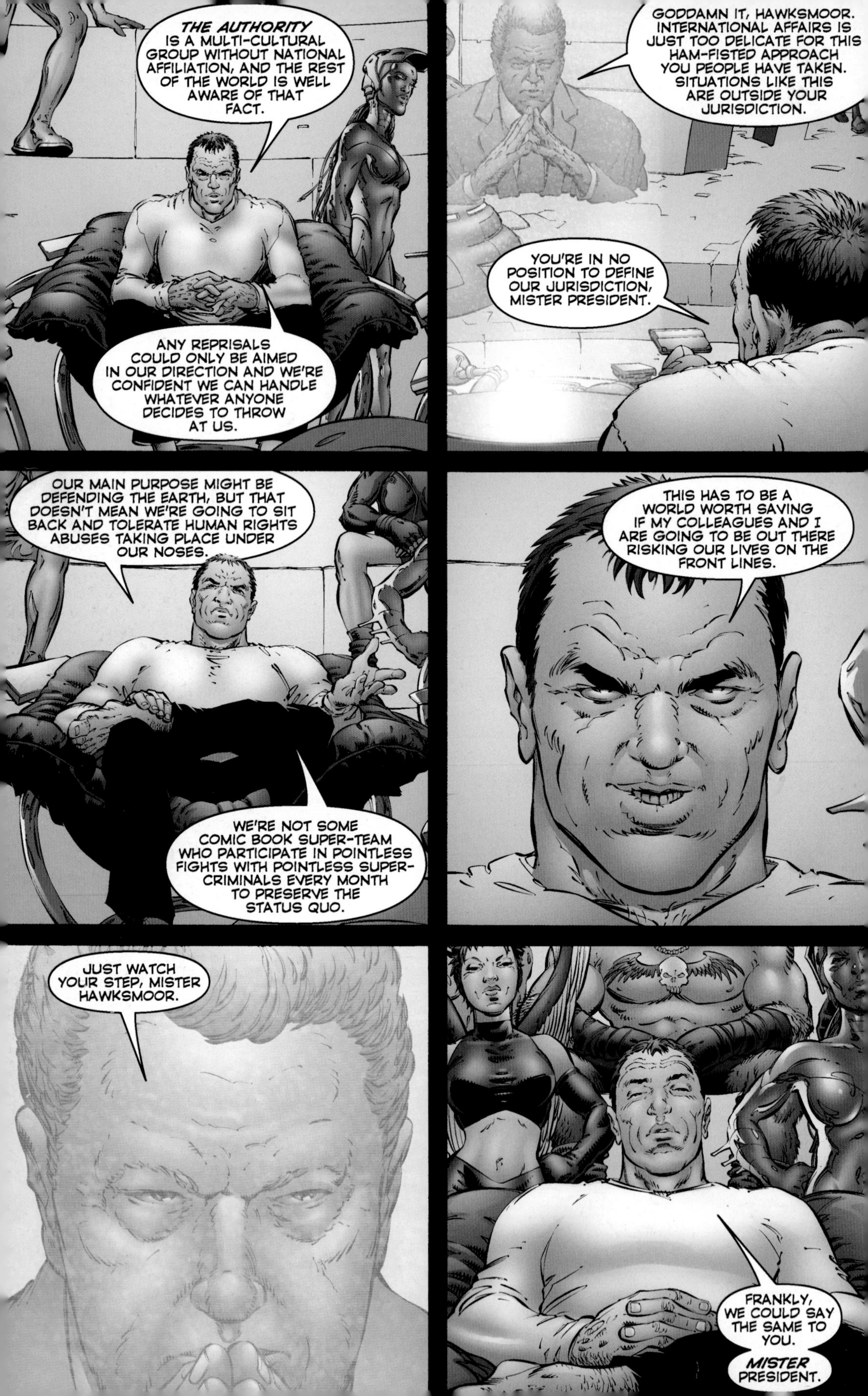
THE AUTHORITY IS A MULTI-CULTURAL GROUP WITHOUT NATIONAL AFFILIATION, AND THE REST OF THE WORLD IS WELL AWARE OF THAT FACT.
ANY REPRISALS COULD ONLY BE AIMED IN OUR DIRECTION AND WE'RE CONFIDENT WE CAN HANDLE WHATEVER ANYONE DECIDES TO THROW AT US.
GODDAMN IT, HAWKSMOOR. INTERNATIONAL AFFAIRS IS JUST TOO DELICATE FOR THIS HAM-FISTED APPROACH YOU PEOPLE HAVE TAKEN. SITUATIONS LIKE THIS ARE OUTSIDE YOUR JURISDICTION.
YOU'RE IN NO POSITION TO DEFINE OUR JURISDICTION, MISTER PRESIDENT.
OUR MAIN PURPOSE MIGHT BE DEFENDING THE EARTH, BUT THAT DOESN'T MEAN WE'RE GOING TO SIT BACK AND TOLERATE HUMAN RIGHTS ABUSES TAKING PLACE UNDER OUR NOSES.
WE'RE NOT SOME COMIC BOOK SUPER-TEAM WHO PARTICIPATE IN POINTLESS FIGHTS WITH POINTLESS SUPER-CRIMINALS EVERY MONTH TO PRESERVE THE STATUS QUO.
THIS HAS TO BE A WORLD WORTH SAVING IF MY COLLEAGUES AND I ARE GOING TO BE OUT THERE RISKING OUR LIVES ON THE FRONT LINES.
JUST WATCH YOUR STEP, MISTER HAWKSMOOR.
FRANKLY, WE COULD SAY THE SAME TO YOU.
MISTER PRESIDENT.

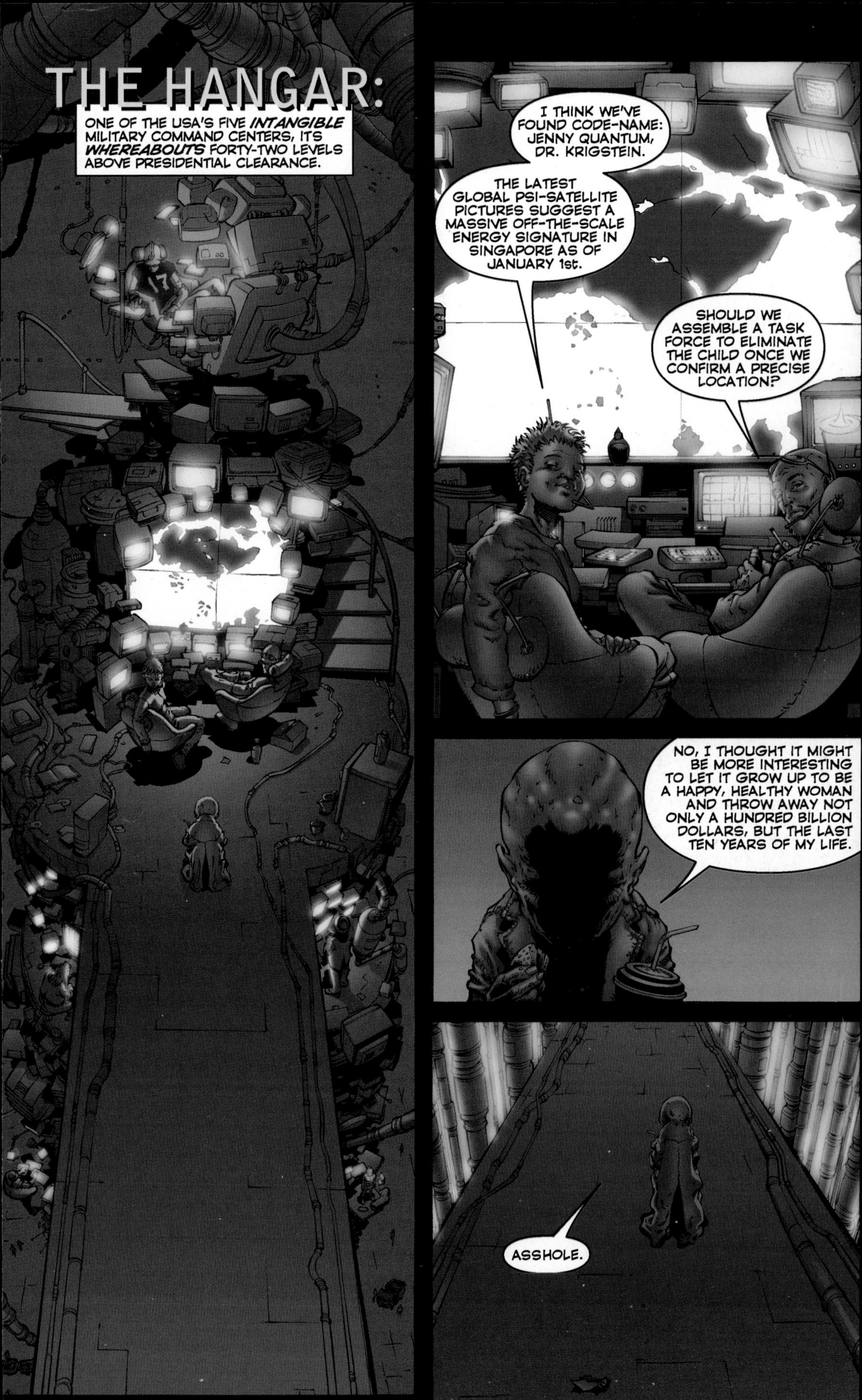
THE HANGAR:
ONE OF THE USA'S FIVE INTANGIBLE MILITARY COMMAND CENTERS, ITS WHEREABOUTS FORTY-TWO LEVELS ABOVE PRESIDENTIAL CLEARANCE.
I THINK WE'VE FOUND CODE-NAME: JENNY QUANTUM, DR. KRIGSTEIN.
THE LATEST GLOBAL PSI-SATELLITE PICTURES SUGGEST A MASSIVE OFF-THE-SCALE ENERGY SIGNATURE IN SINGAPORE AS OF JANUARY 1st.
SHOULD WE ASSEMBLE A TASK FORCE TO ELIMINATE THE CHILD ONCE WE CONFIRM A PRECISE LOCATION?
NO, I THOUGHT IT MIGHT BE MORE INTERESTING TO LET IT GROW UP TO BE A HAPPY, HEALTHY WOMAN AND THROW AWAY NOT ONLY A HUNDRED BILLION DOLLARS, BUT THE LAST TEN YEARS OF MY LIFE.
ASSHOLE.

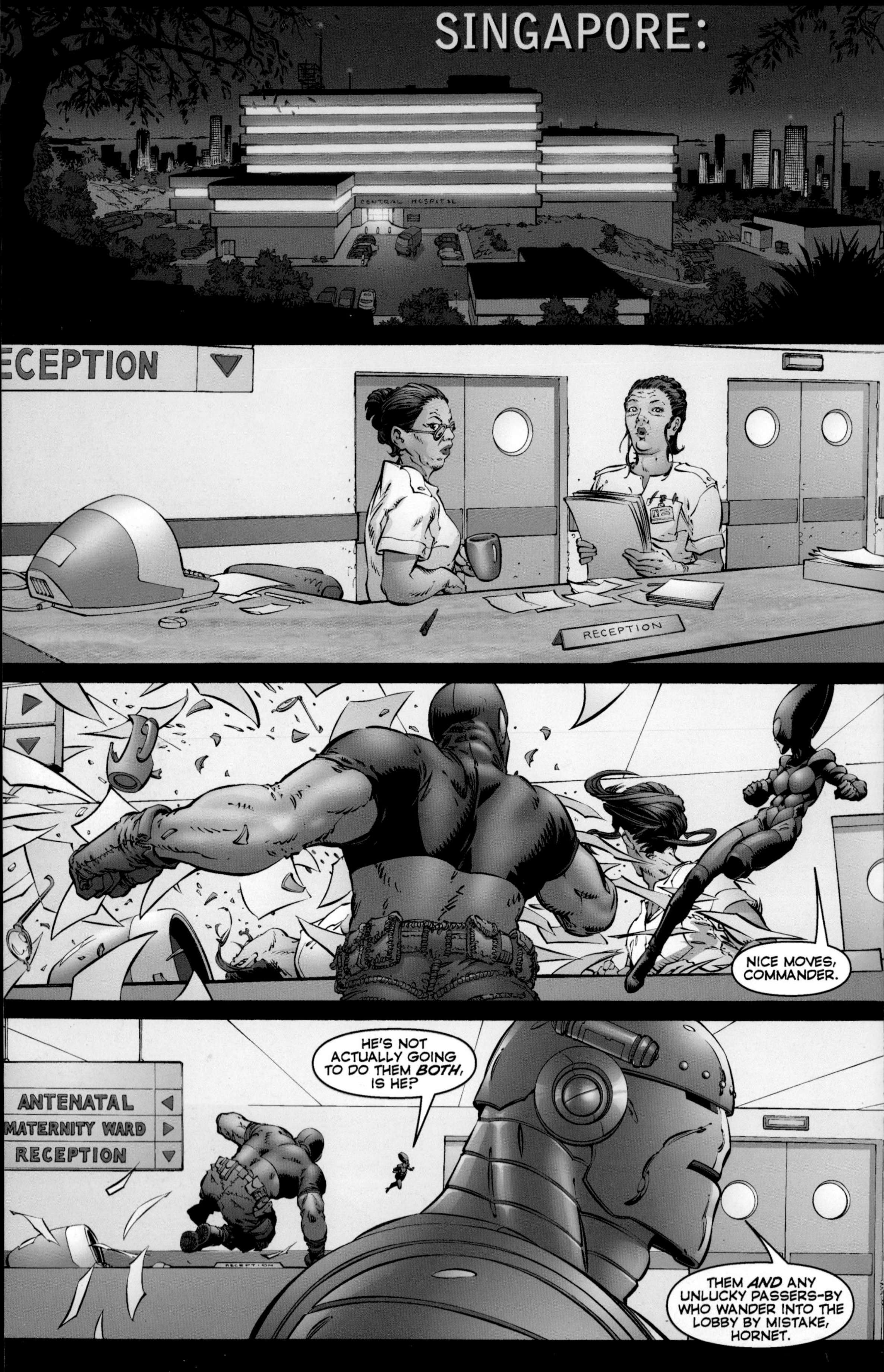
SINGAPORE:
CENTRAL HOSPITAL
RECEPTION
RECEPTION
NICE MOVES, COMMANDER.
ANTENATAL
MATERNITY WARD
RECEPTION
HE'S NOT ACTUALLY GOING TO DO THEM *BOTH*, IS HE?
THEM *AND* ANY UNLUCKY PASSERS-BY WHO WANDER INTO THE LOBBY BY MISTAKE, HORNET.

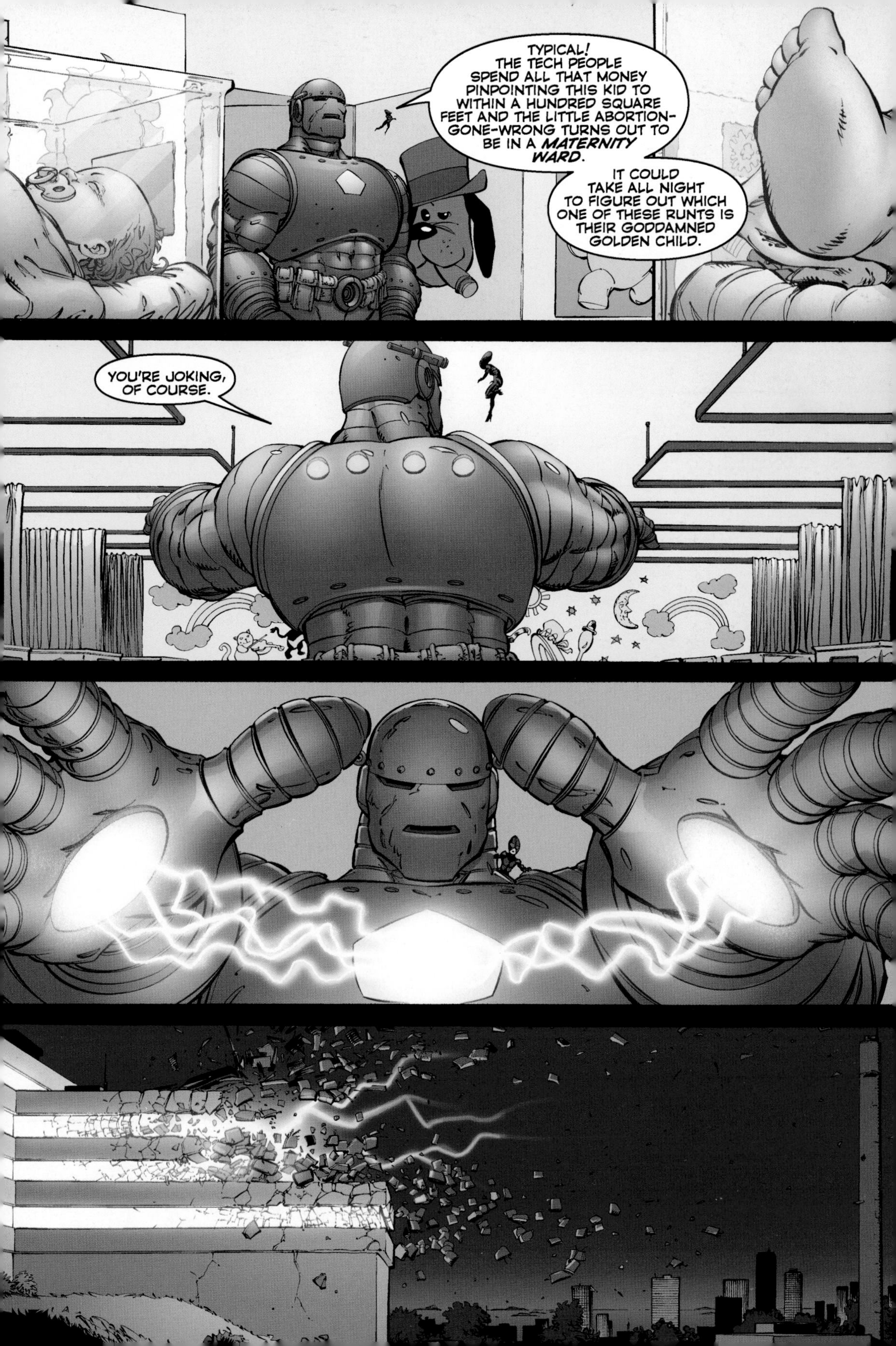
TYPICAL! THE TECH PEOPLE SPEND ALL THAT MONEY PINPOINTING THIS KID TO WITHIN A HUNDRED SQUARE FEET AND THE LITTLE ABORTION-GONE-WRONG TURNS OUT TO BE IN A *MATERNITY WARD*.
IT COULD TAKE ALL NIGHT TO FIGURE OUT WHICH ONE OF THESE RUNTS IS THEIR GODDAMNED GOLDEN CHILD.
YOU'RE JOKING, OF COURSE.

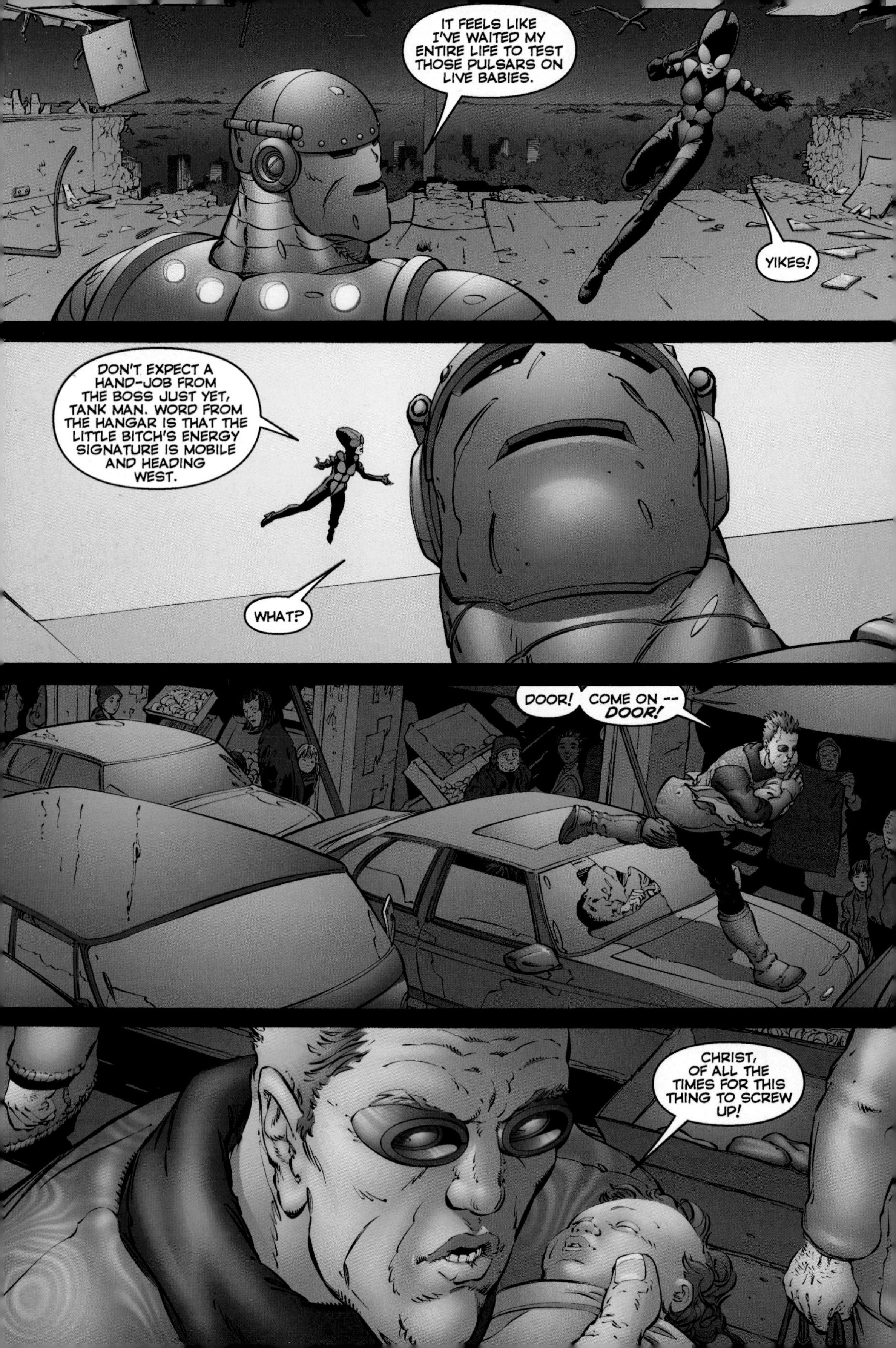
IT FEELS LIKE I'VE WAITED MY ENTIRE LIFE TO TEST THOSE PULSARS ON LIVE BABIES.
YIKES!
DON'T EXPECT A HAND-JOB FROM THE BOSS JUST YET, TANK MAN. WORD FROM THE HANGAR IS THAT THE LITTLE BITCH'S ENERGY SIGNATURE IS MOBILE AND HEADING WEST.
WHAT?
DOOR!
COME ON -- DOOR!
CHRIST, OF ALL THE TIMES FOR THIS THING TO SCREW UP!

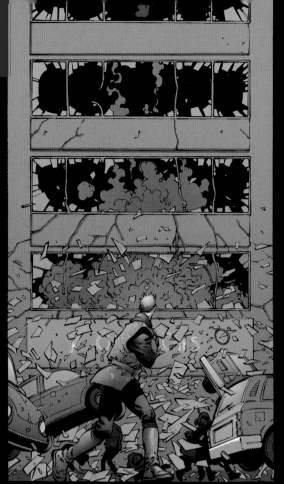

THE CARRIER'S TELEPORTER IS WORKING FINE, DOCTOR.

YOU'VE JUST BEEN DISCONNECTED FROM YOUR TEAM'S RADIO-TELEPATHY AND YOUR OWN QUITE CONSIDERABLE ABILITIES.

ANY LAST WORDS BEFORE WE TEAR OUT YOUR GODDAMN INTESTINES?

ACTUALLY, TWO SPRING TO MIND IMMEDIATELY...

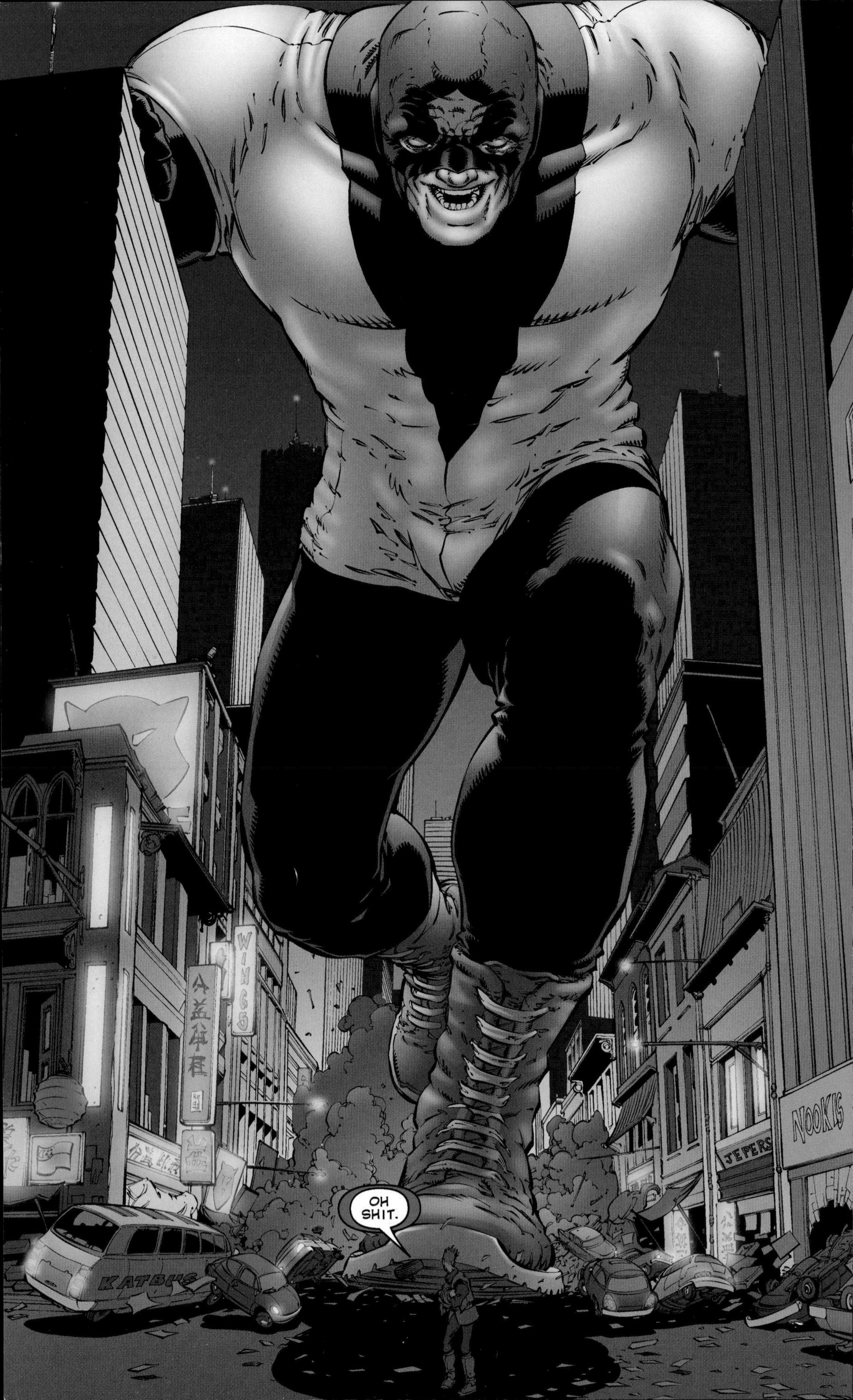
OH SHIT.
WINGS
NOOKIS
JEPERS
KATBUS

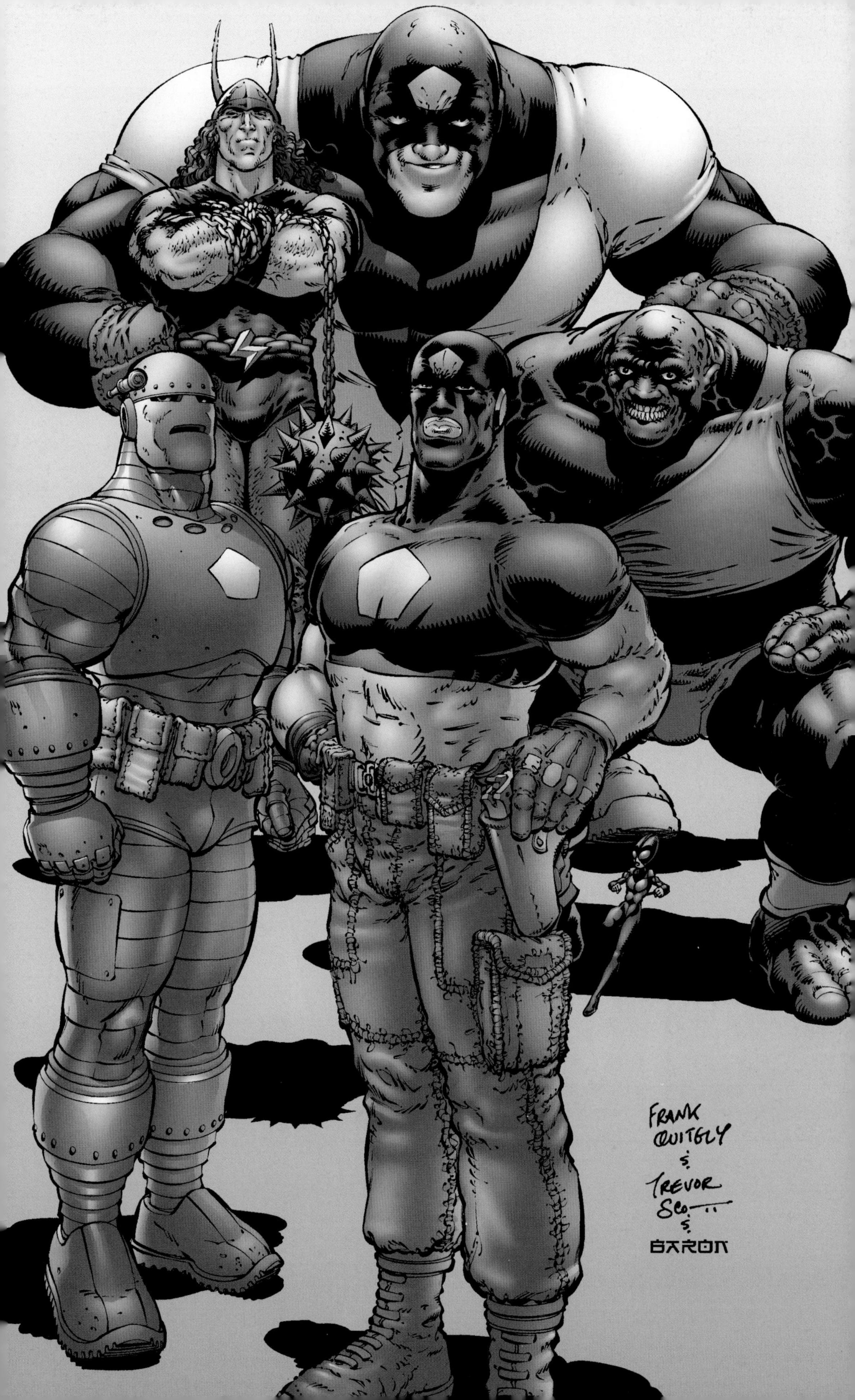
FRANK QUITELY & TREVOR SCOTT & BARON

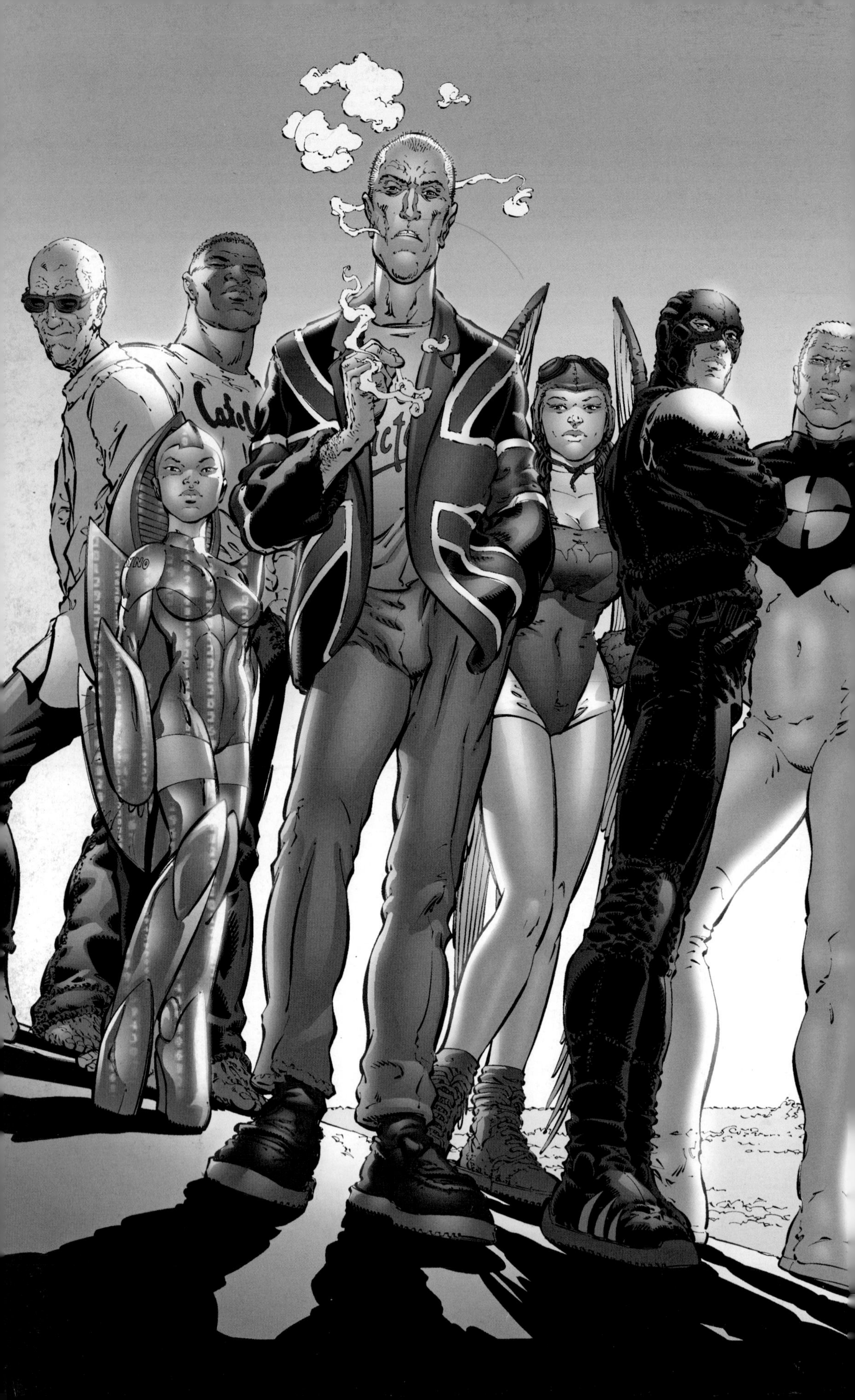

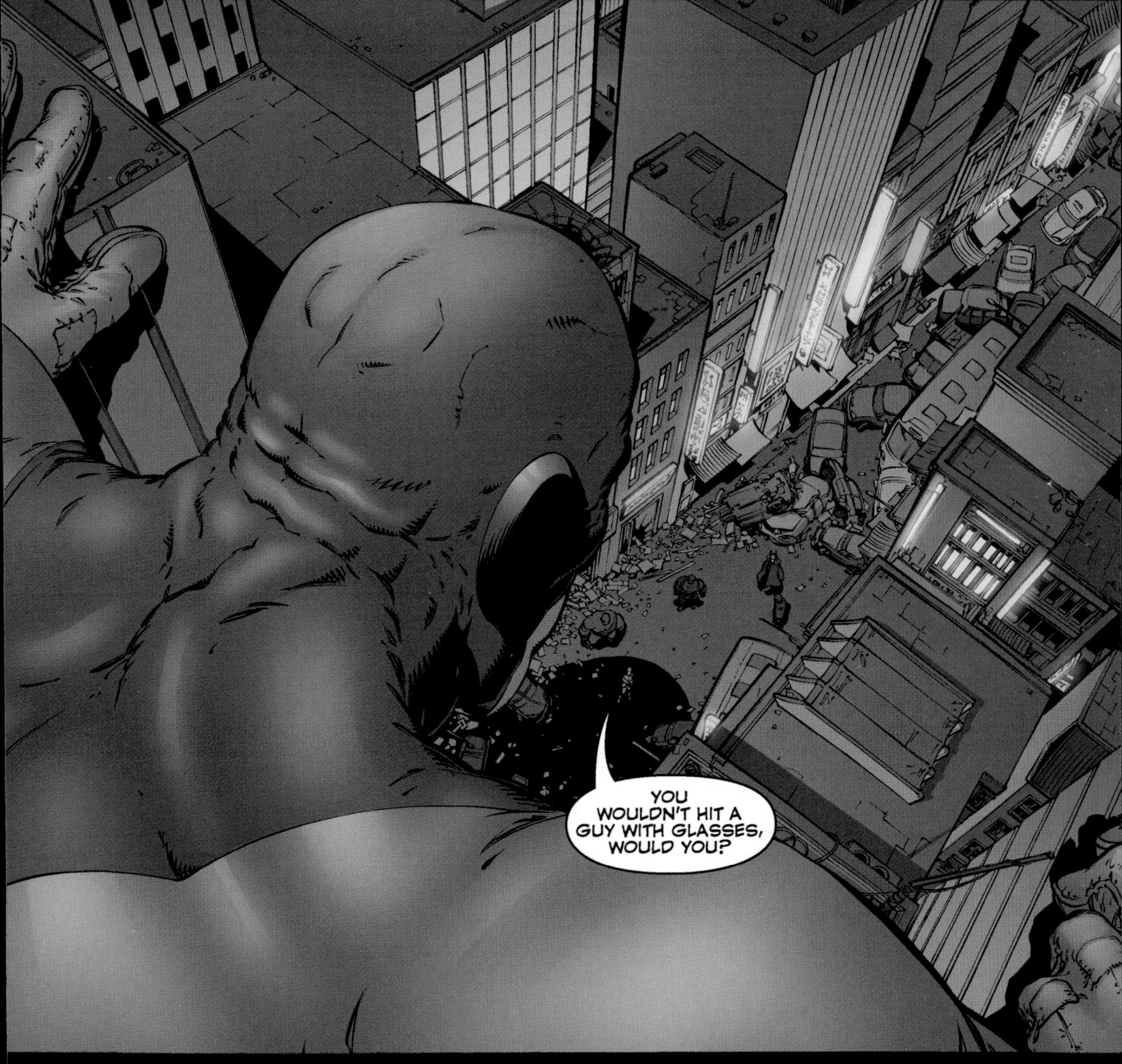
YOU WOULDN'T HIT A GUY WITH GLASSES, WOULD YOU?

The AUTHORITY
"THE NATIVITY"
TWO of FOUR

MARK MILLAR writer and **FRANK QUITELY** artist with **TREVOR SCOTT** inker

DAVID BARON colorist

RYAN CLINE letterer

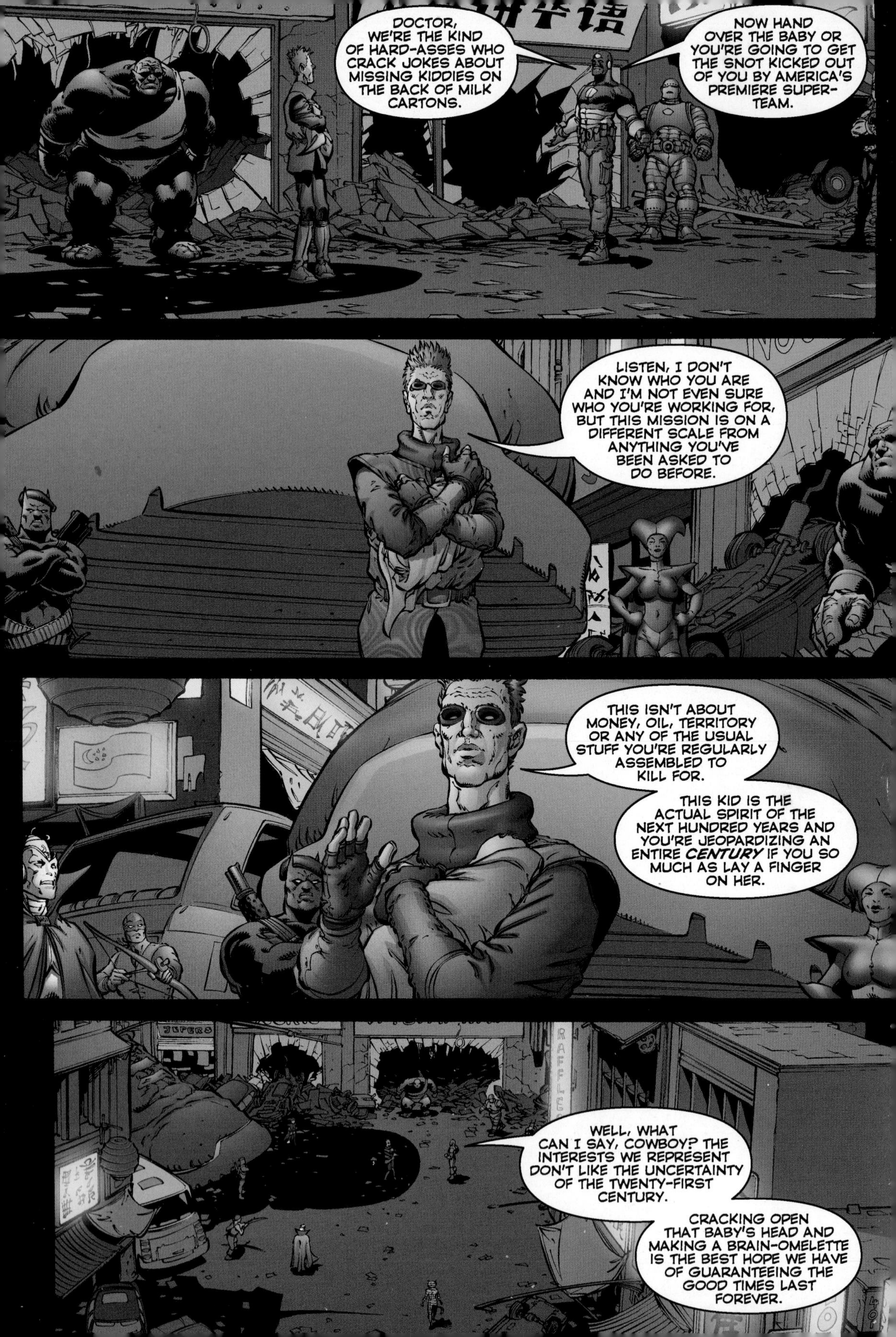
DOCTOR, WE'RE THE KIND OF HARD-ASSES WHO CRACK JOKES ABOUT MISSING KIDDIES ON THE BACK OF MILK CARTONS.
NOW HAND OVER THE BABY OR YOU'RE GOING TO GET THE SNOT KICKED OUT OF YOU BY AMERICA'S PREMIERE SUPER-TEAM.
LISTEN, I DON'T KNOW WHO YOU ARE AND I'M NOT EVEN SURE WHO YOU'RE WORKING FOR, BUT THIS MISSION IS ON A DIFFERENT SCALE FROM ANYTHING YOU'VE BEEN ASKED TO DO BEFORE.
THIS ISN'T ABOUT MONEY, OIL, TERRITORY OR ANY OF THE USUAL STUFF YOU'RE REGULARLY ASSEMBLED TO KILL FOR.
THIS KID IS THE ACTUAL SPIRIT OF THE NEXT HUNDRED YEARS AND YOU'RE JEOPARDIZING AN ENTIRE *CENTURY* IF YOU SO MUCH AS LAY A FINGER ON HER.
WELL, WHAT CAN I SAY, COWBOY? THE INTERESTS WE REPRESENT DON'T LIKE THE UNCERTAINTY OF THE TWENTY-FIRST CENTURY.
CRACKING OPEN THAT BABY'S HEAD AND MAKING A BRAIN-OMELETTE IS THE BEST HOPE WE HAVE OF GUARANTEEING THE GOOD TIMES LAST FOREVER.

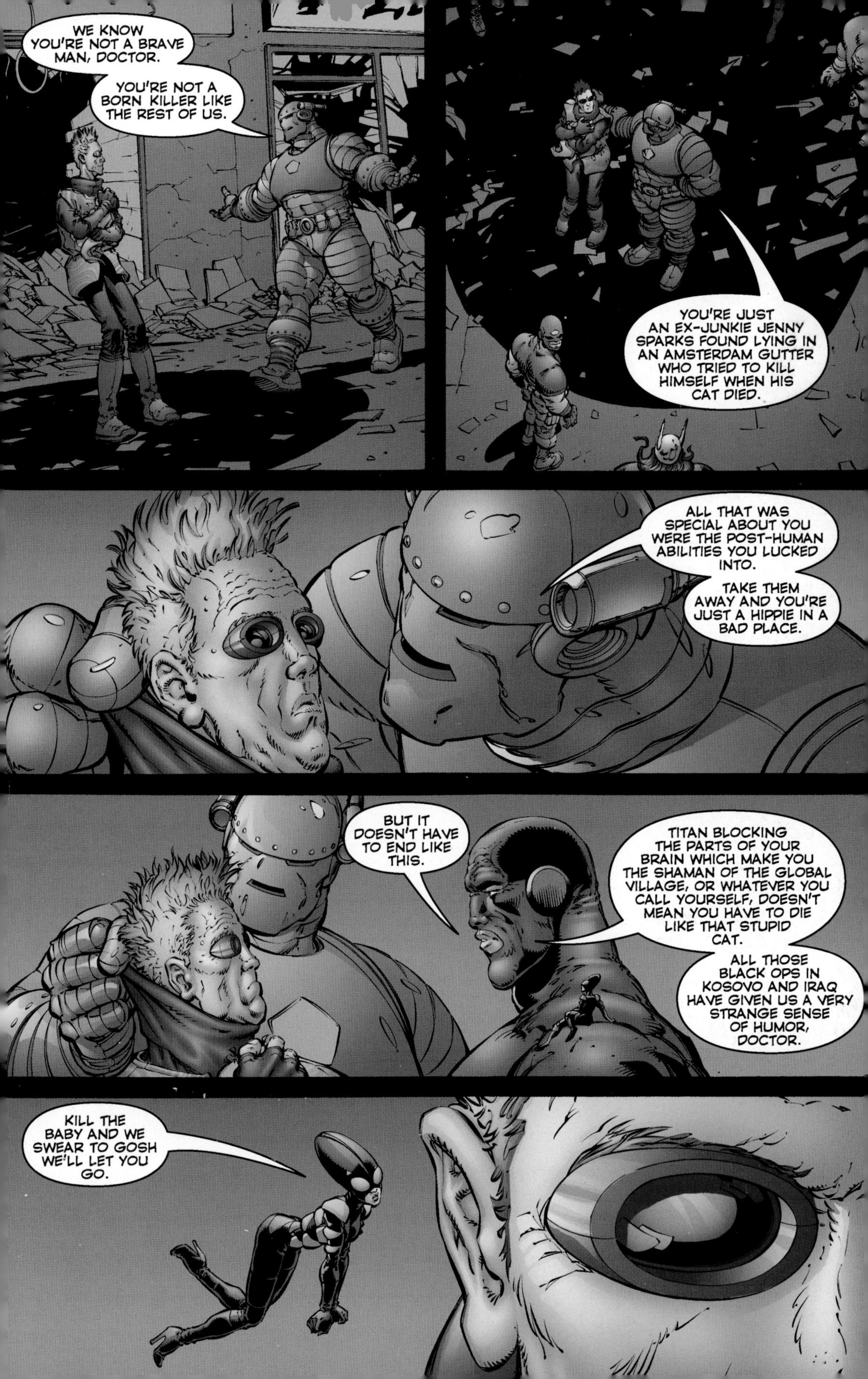

WE KNOW YOU'RE NOT A BRAVE MAN, DOCTOR.
YOU'RE NOT A BORN KILLER LIKE THE REST OF US.
YOU'RE JUST AN EX-JUNKIE JENNY SPARKS FOUND LYING IN AN AMSTERDAM GUTTER WHO TRIED TO KILL HIMSELF WHEN HIS CAT DIED.
ALL THAT WAS SPECIAL ABOUT YOU WERE THE POST-HUMAN ABILITIES YOU LUCKED INTO.
TAKE THEM AWAY AND YOU'RE JUST A HIPPIE IN A BAD PLACE.
BUT IT DOESN'T HAVE TO END LIKE THIS.
TITAN BLOCKING THE PARTS OF YOUR BRAIN WHICH MAKE YOU THE SHAMAN OF THE GLOBAL VILLAGE, OR WHATEVER YOU CALL YOURSELF, DOESN'T MEAN YOU HAVE TO DIE LIKE THAT STUPID CAT.
ALL THOSE BLACK OPS IN KOSOVO AND IRAQ HAVE GIVEN US A VERY STRANGE SENSE OF HUMOR, DOCTOR.
KILL THE BABY AND WE SWEAR TO GOSH WE'LL LET YOU GO.

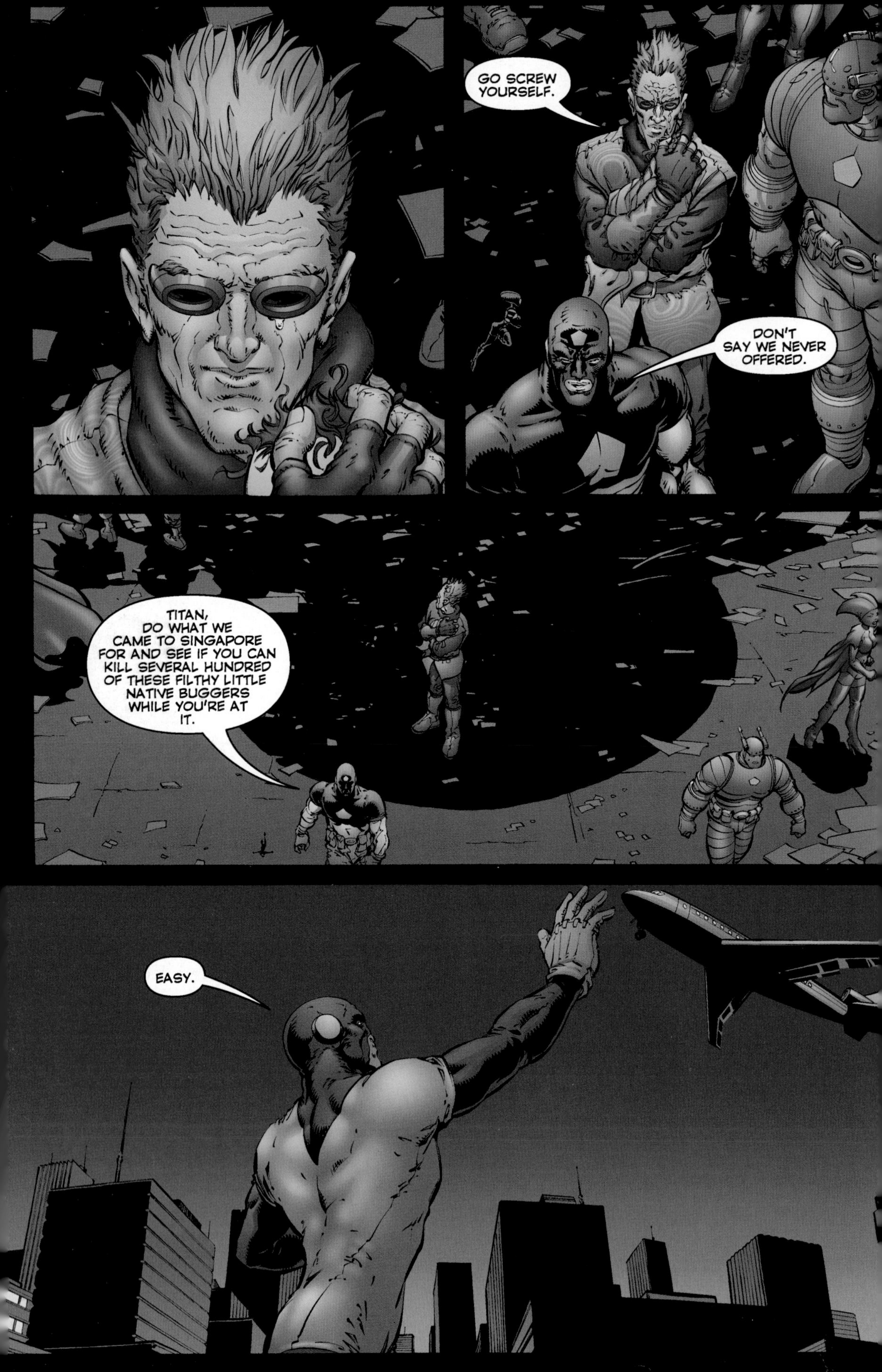
GO SCREW YOURSELF.
DON'T SAY WE NEVER OFFERED.
TITAN, DO WHAT WE CAME TO SINGAPORE FOR AND SEE IF YOU CAN KILL SEVERAL HUNDRED OF THESE FILTHY LITTLE NATIVE BUGGERS WHILE YOU'RE AT IT.
EASY.

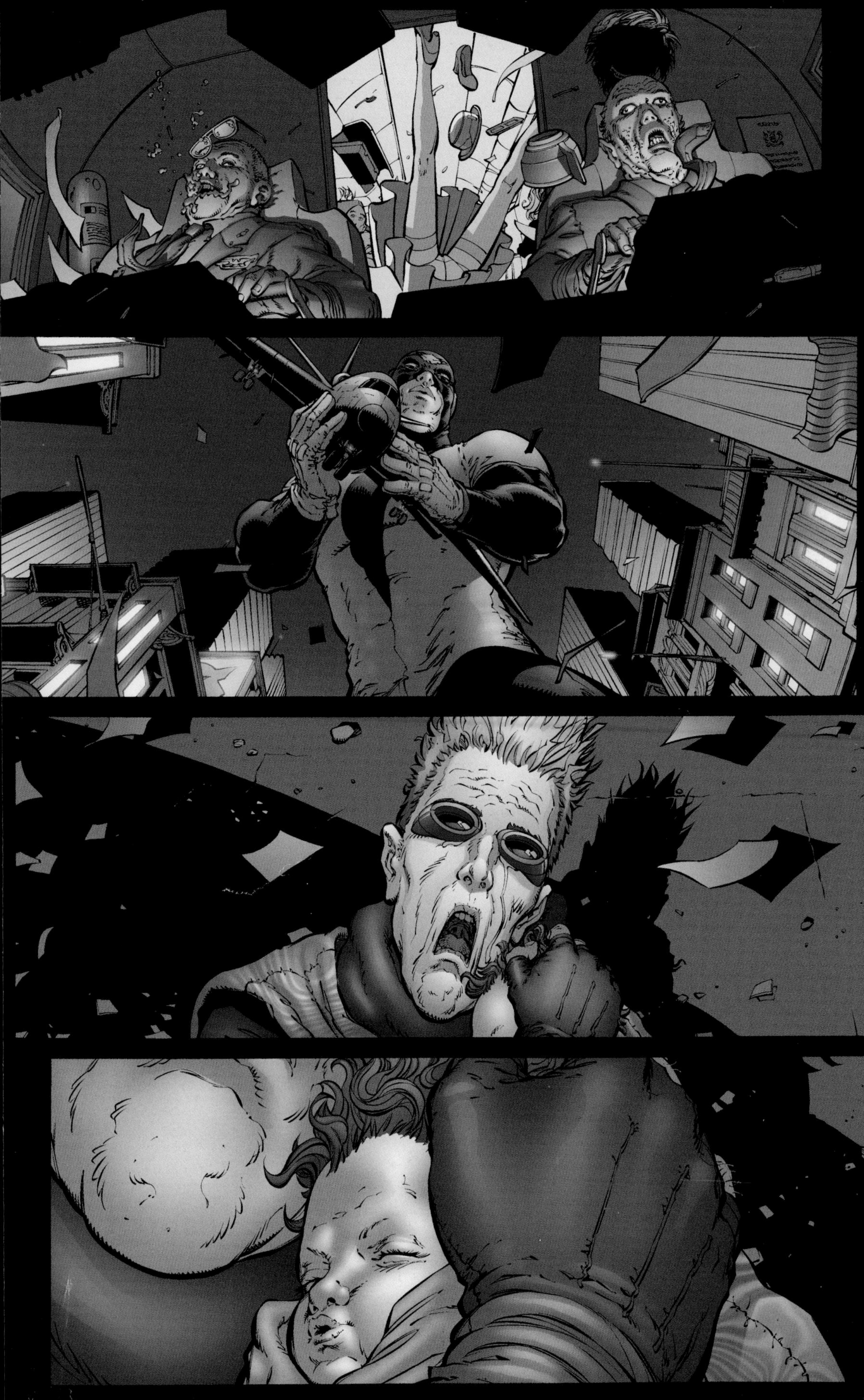

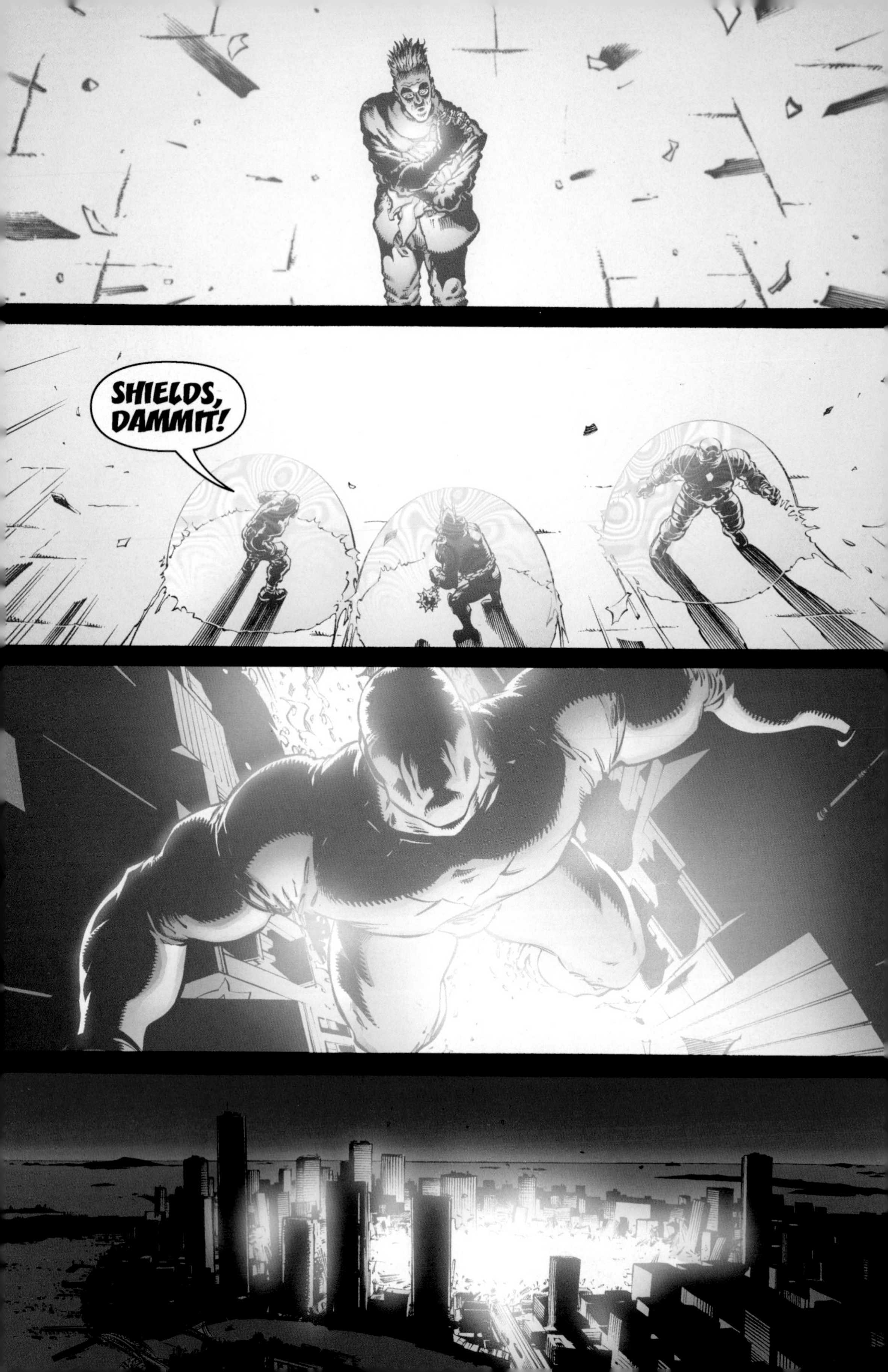
SHIELDS, DAMMIT!

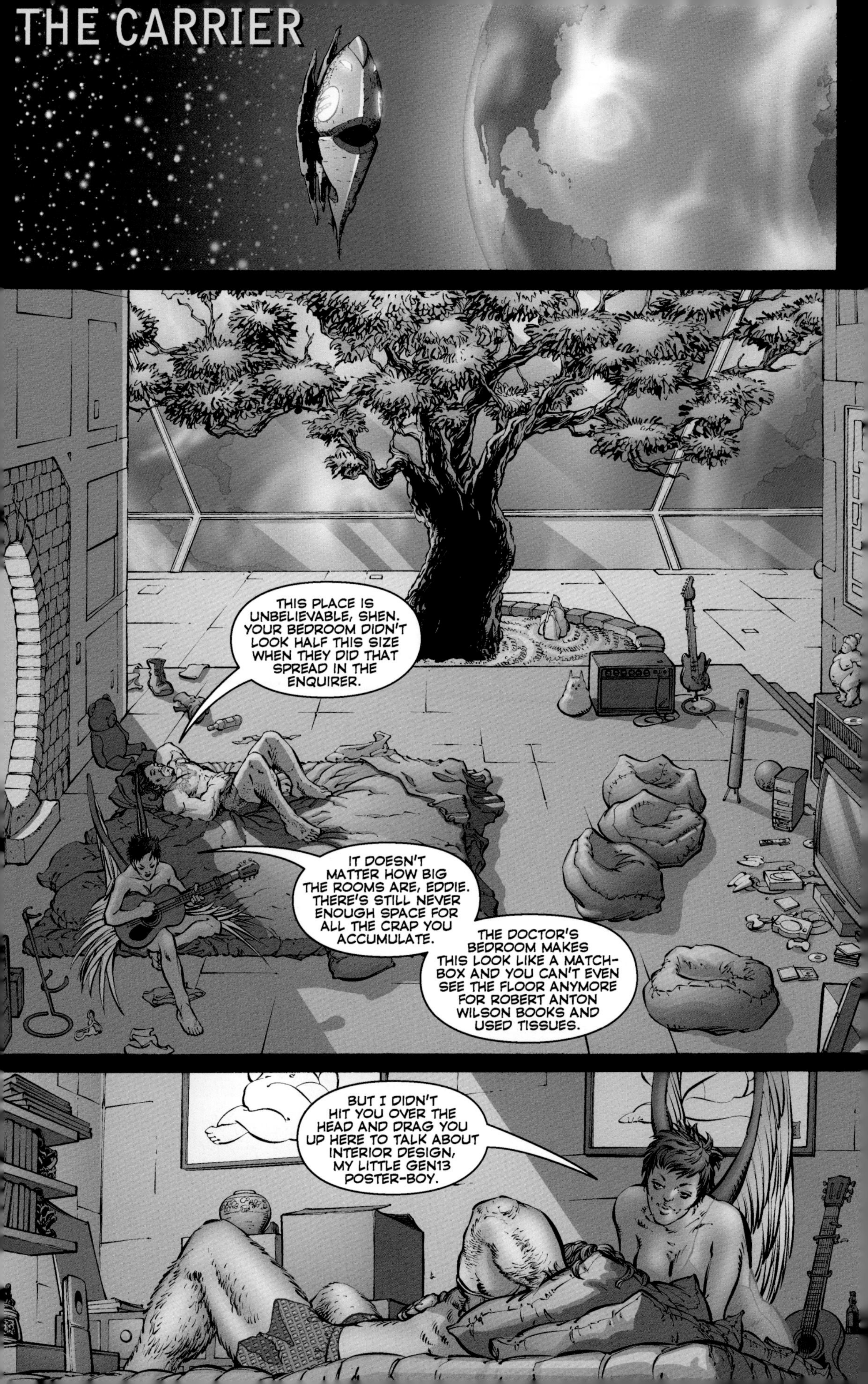
THE CARRIER
THIS PLACE IS UNBELIEVABLE, SHEN. YOUR BEDROOM DIDN'T LOOK HALF THIS SIZE WHEN THEY DID THAT SPREAD IN THE ENQUIRER.
IT DOESN'T MATTER HOW BIG THE ROOMS ARE, EDDIE. THERE'S STILL NEVER ENOUGH SPACE FOR ALL THE CRAP YOU ACCUMULATE.
THE DOCTOR'S BEDROOM MAKES THIS LOOK LIKE A MATCH-BOX AND YOU CAN'T EVEN SEE THE FLOOR ANYMORE FOR ROBERT ANTON WILSON BOOKS AND USED TISSUES.
BUT I DIDN'T HIT YOU OVER THE HEAD AND DRAG YOU UP HERE TO TALK ABOUT INTERIOR DESIGN, MY LITTLE GEN13 POSTER-BOY.

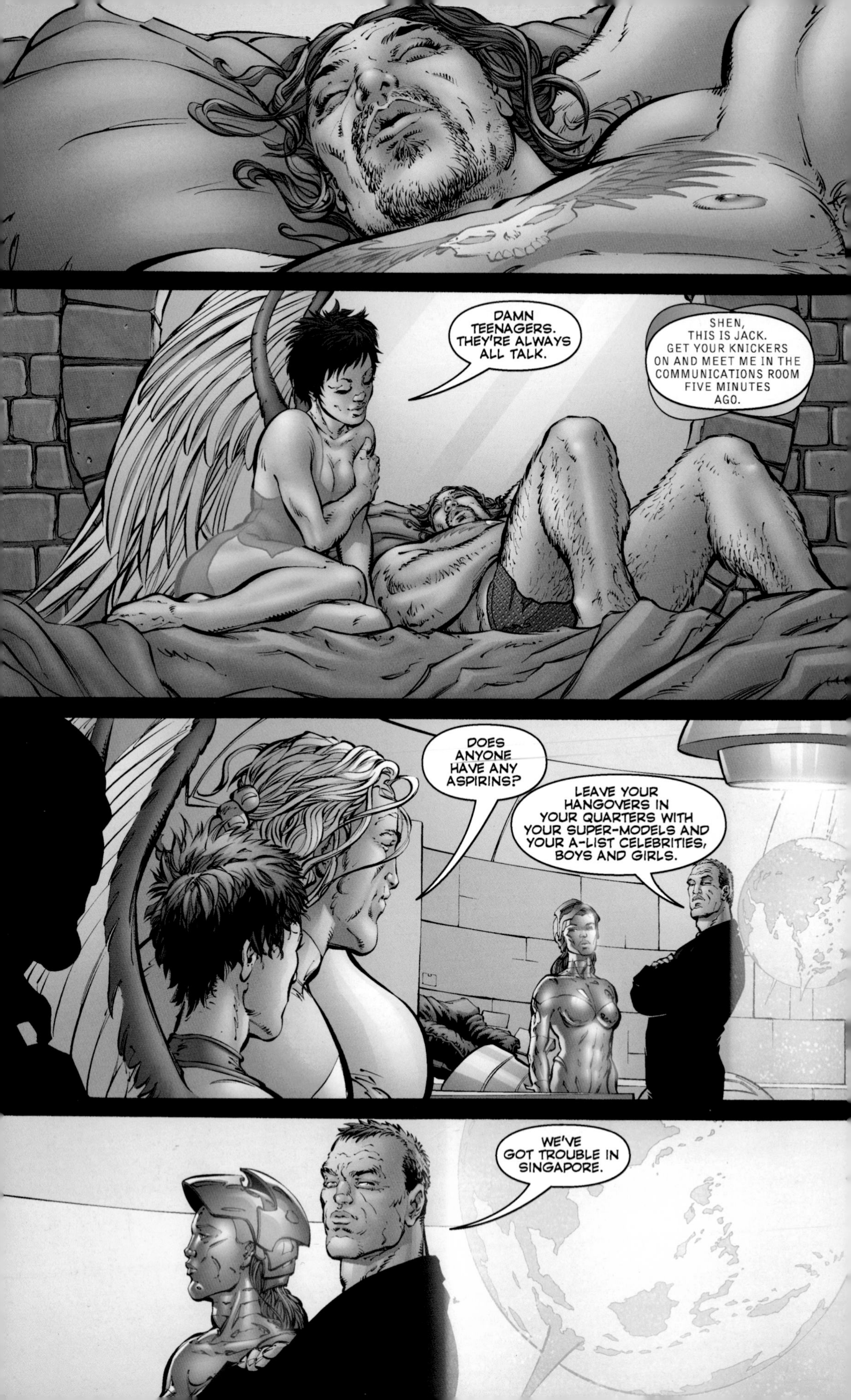
DAMN TEENAGERS. THEY'RE ALWAYS ALL TALK.
SHEN, THIS IS JACK. GET YOUR KNICKERS ON AND MEET ME IN THE COMMUNICATIONS ROOM FIVE MINUTES AGO.
DOES ANYONE HAVE ANY ASPIRINS?
LEAVE YOUR HANGOVERS IN YOUR QUARTERS WITH YOUR SUPER-MODELS AND YOUR A-LIST CELEBRITIES, BOYS AND GIRLS.
WE'VE GOT TROUBLE IN SINGAPORE.

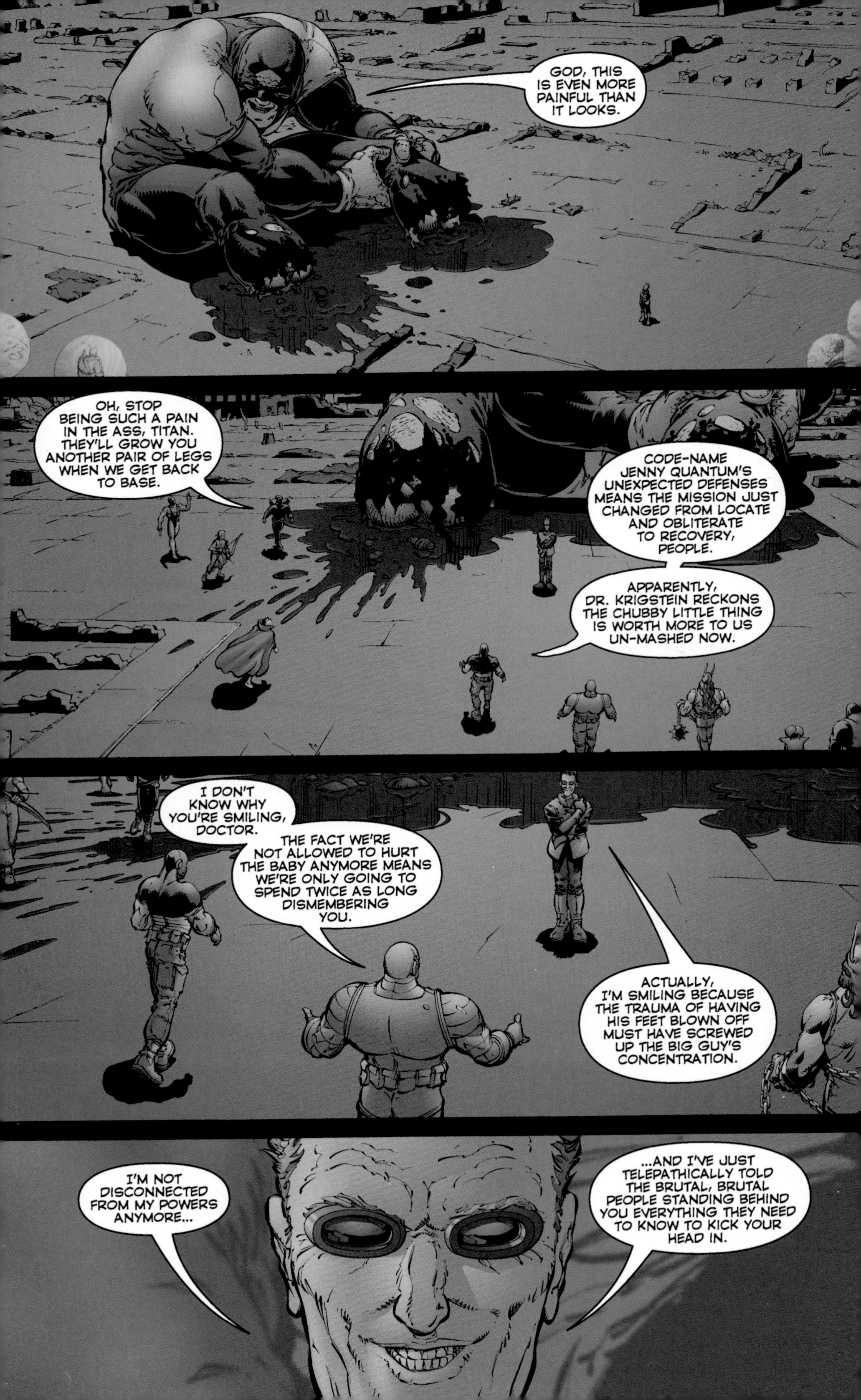
GOD, THIS IS EVEN MORE PAINFUL THAN IT LOOKS.
OH, STOP BEING SUCH A PAIN IN THE ASS, TITAN. THEY'LL GROW YOU ANOTHER PAIR OF LEGS WHEN WE GET BACK TO BASE.
CODE-NAME JENNY QUANTUM'S UNEXPECTED DEFENSES MEANS THE MISSION JUST CHANGED FROM LOCATE AND OBLITERATE TO RECOVERY, PEOPLE.
APPARENTLY, DR. KRIGSTEIN RECKONS THE CHUBBY LITTLE THING IS WORTH MORE TO US UN-MASHED NOW.
I DON'T KNOW WHY YOU'RE SMILING, DOCTOR.
THE FACT WE'RE NOT ALLOWED TO HURT THE BABY ANYMORE MEANS WE'RE ONLY GOING TO SPEND TWICE AS LONG DISMEMBERING YOU.
ACTUALLY, I'M SMILING BECAUSE THE TRAUMA OF HAVING HIS FEET BLOWN OFF MUST HAVE SCREWED UP THE BIG GUY'S CONCENTRATION.
I'M NOT DISCONNECTED FROM MY POWERS ANYMORE...
...AND I'VE JUST TELEPATHICALLY TOLD THE BRUTAL, BRUTAL PEOPLE STANDING BEHIND YOU EVERYTHING THEY NEED TO KNOW TO KICK YOUR HEAD IN.

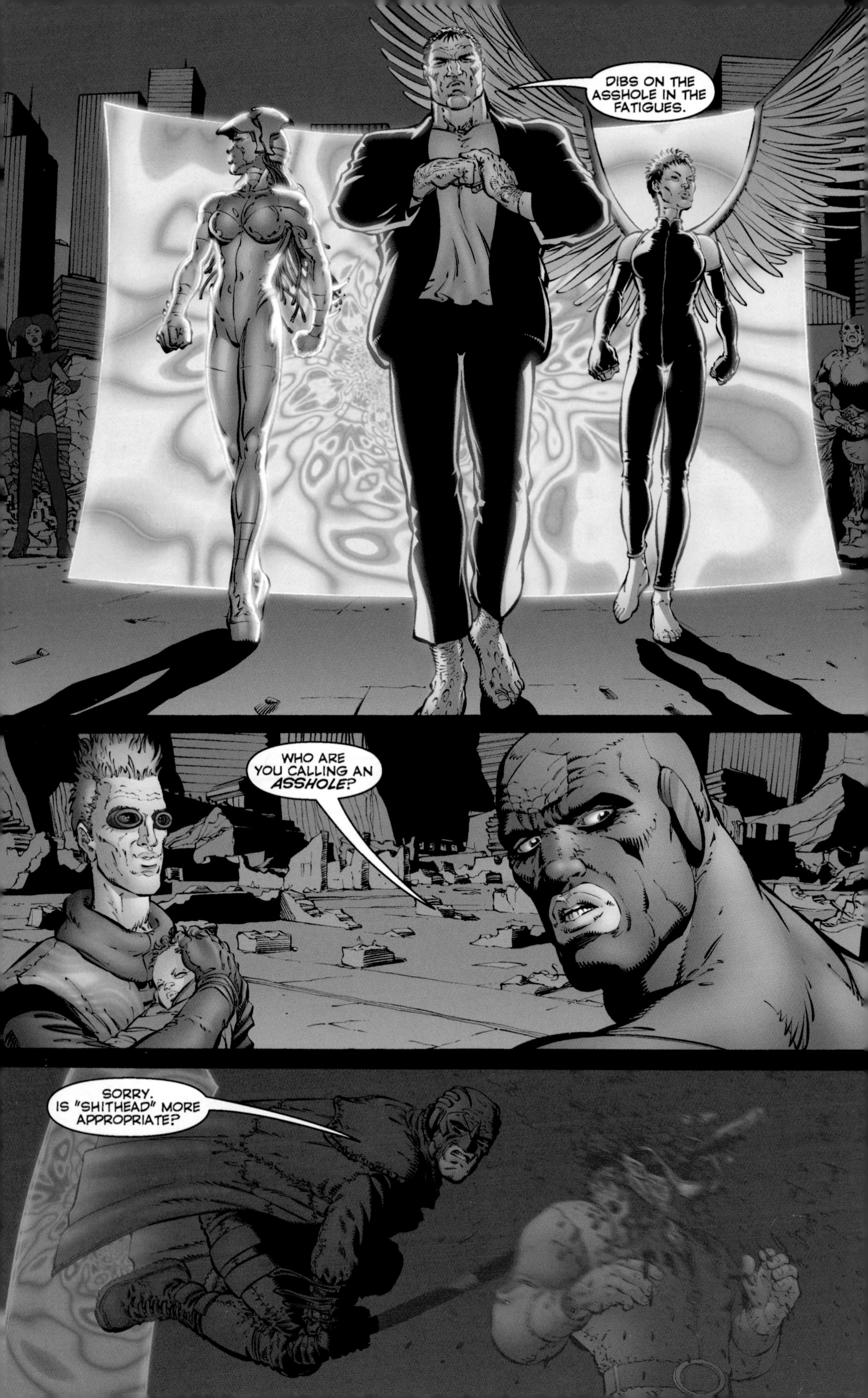
DIBS ON THE ASSHOLE IN THE FATIGUES.
WHO ARE YOU CALLING AN *ASSHOLE*?
SORRY. IS "SHITHEAD" MORE APPROPRIATE?

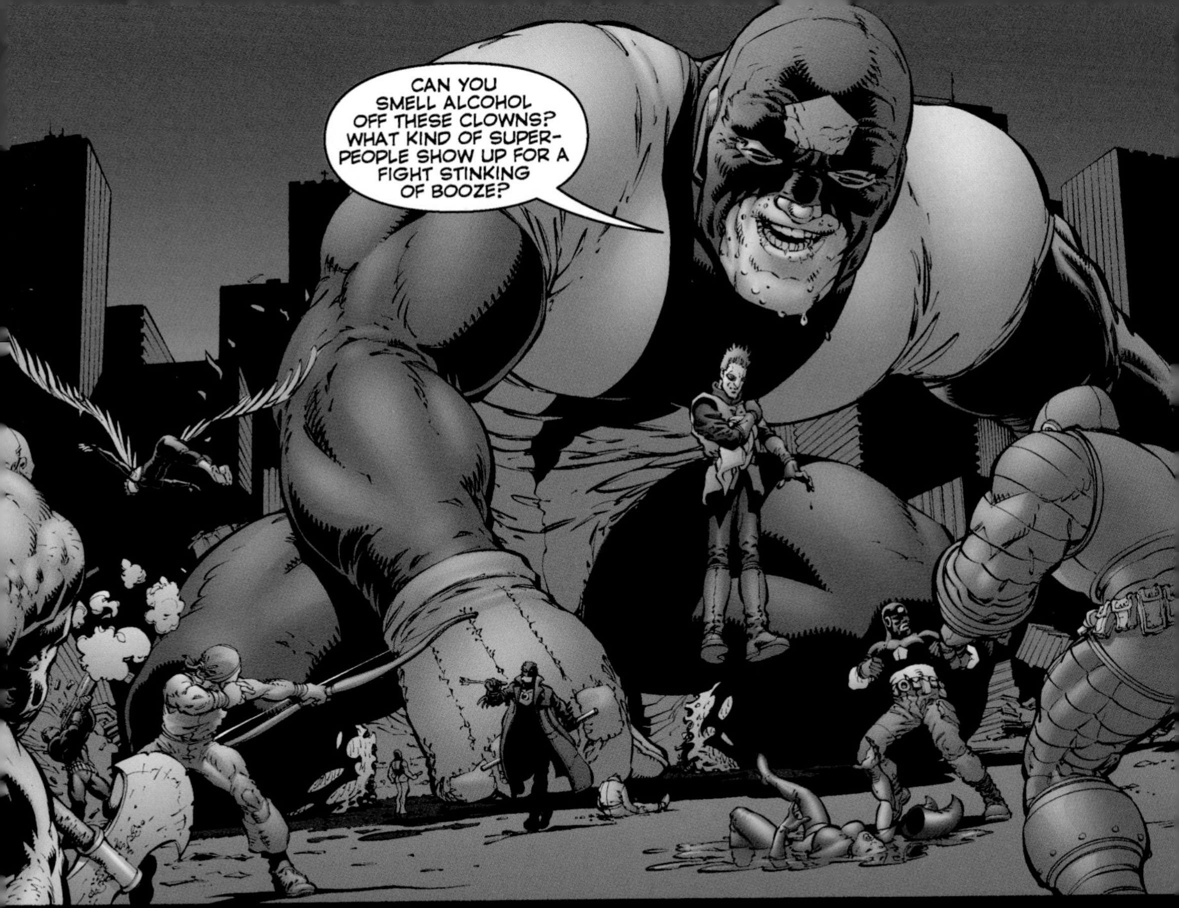
CAN YOU SMELL ALCOHOL OFF THESE CLOWNS? WHAT KIND OF SUPER-PEOPLE SHOW UP FOR A FIGHT STINKING OF BOOZE?

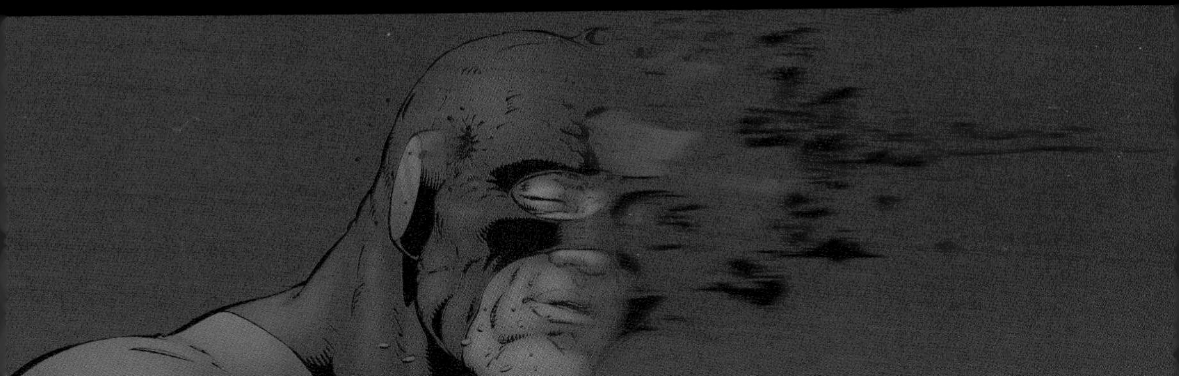

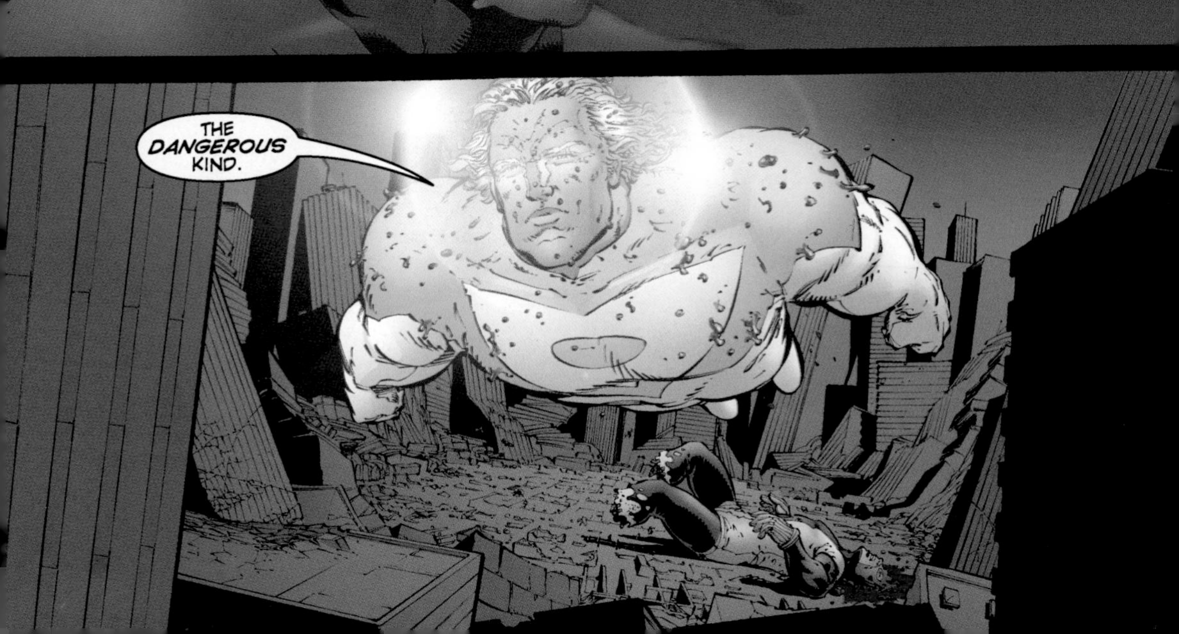
THE *DANGEROUS* KIND.

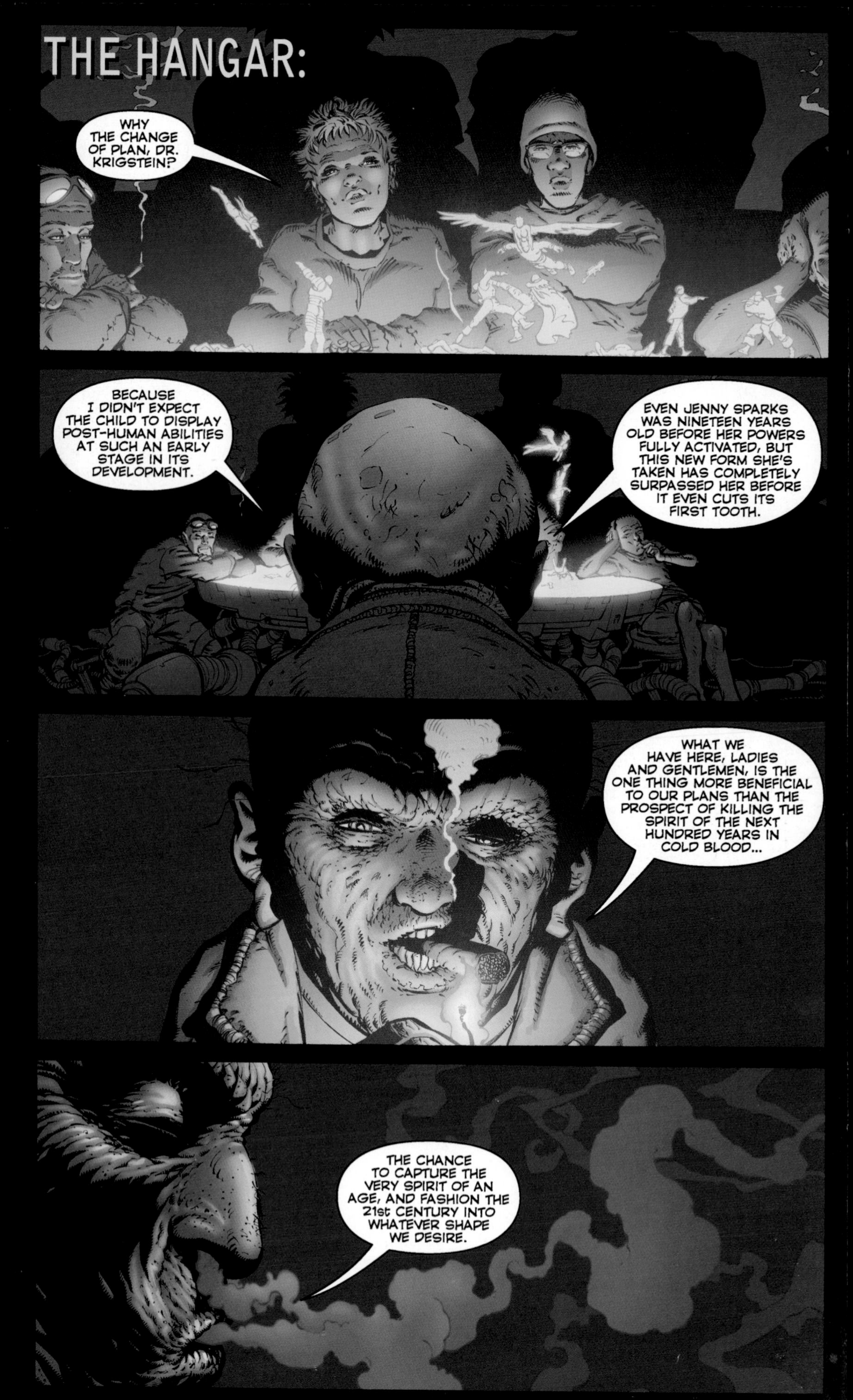
THE HANGAR:
WHY THE CHANGE OF PLAN, DR. KRIGSTEIN?
BECAUSE I DIDN'T EXPECT THE CHILD TO DISPLAY POST-HUMAN ABILITIES AT SUCH AN EARLY STAGE IN ITS DEVELOPMENT.
EVEN JENNY SPARKS WAS NINETEEN YEARS OLD BEFORE HER POWERS FULLY ACTIVATED, BUT THIS NEW FORM SHE'S TAKEN HAS COMPLETELY SURPASSED HER BEFORE IT EVEN CUTS ITS FIRST TOOTH.
WHAT WE HAVE HERE, LADIES AND GENTLEMEN, IS THE ONE THING MORE BENEFICIAL TO OUR PLANS THAN THE PROSPECT OF KILLING THE SPIRIT OF THE NEXT HUNDRED YEARS IN COLD BLOOD...
THE CHANCE TO CAPTURE THE VERY SPIRIT OF AN AGE, AND FASHION THE 21st CENTURY INTO WHATEVER SHAPE WE DESIRE.

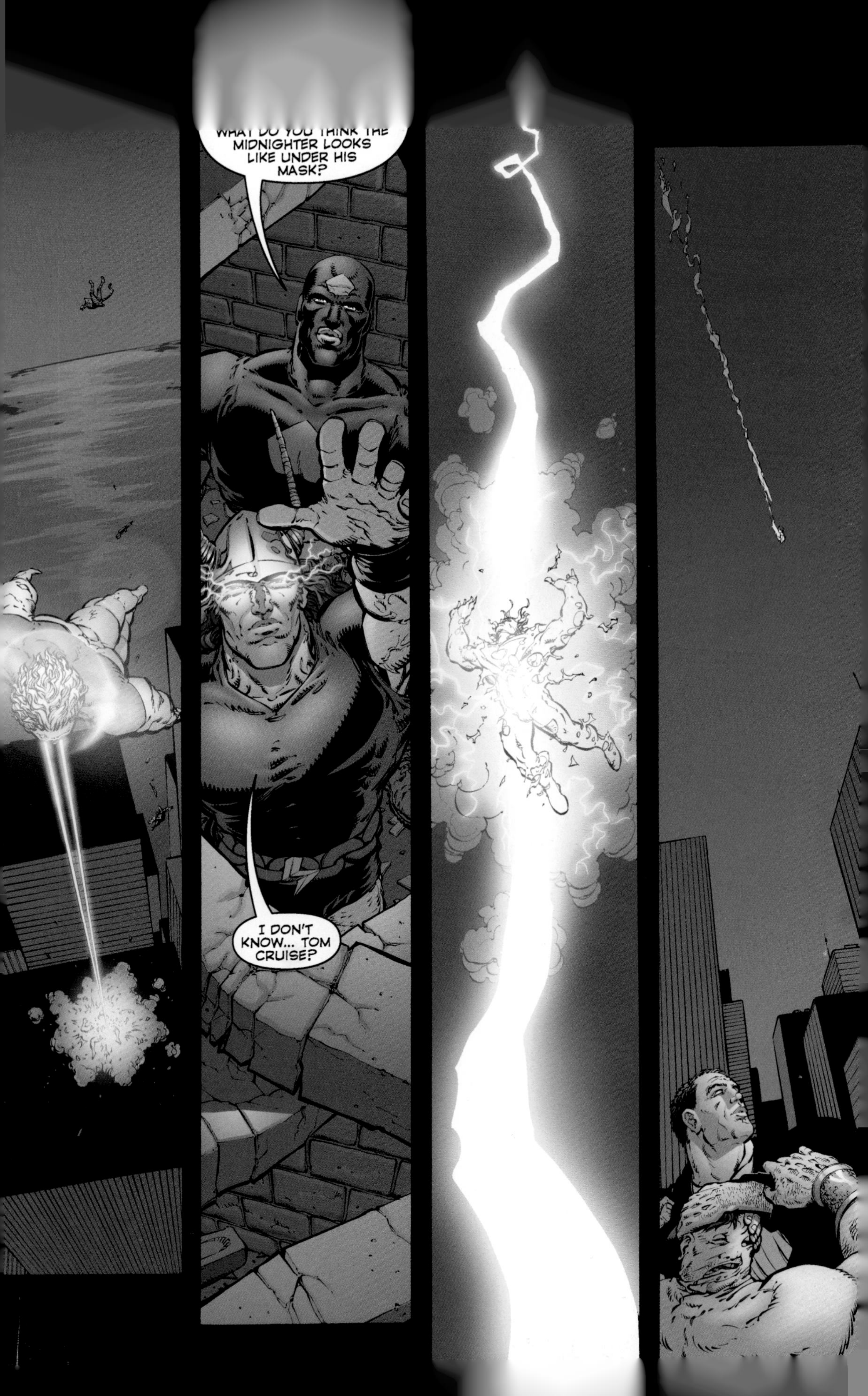
WHAT DO YOU THINK THE MIDNIGHTER LOOKS LIKE UNDER HIS MASK?
I DON'T KNOW... TOM CRUISE?

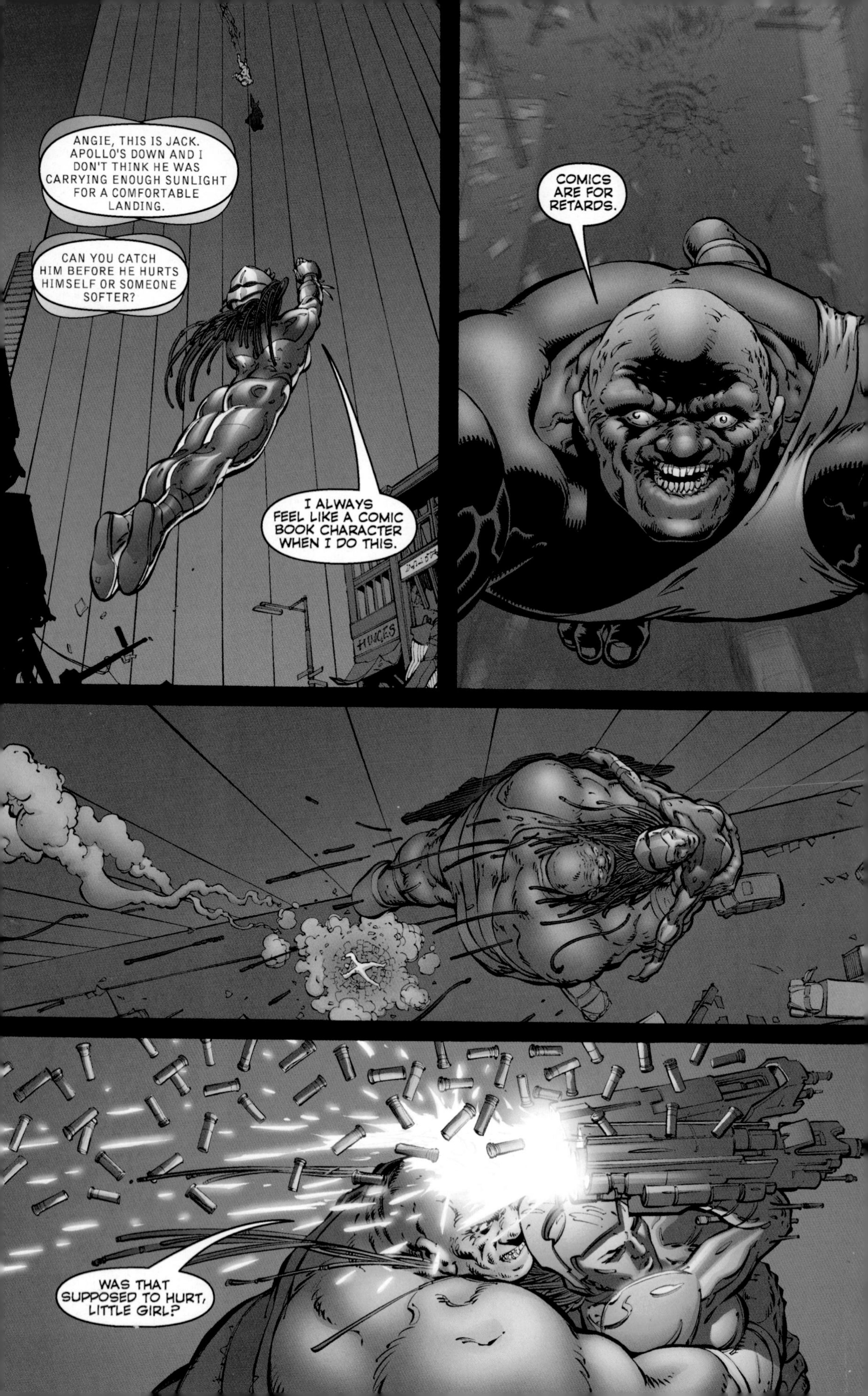
ANGIE, THIS IS JACK. APOLLO'S DOWN AND I DON'T THINK HE WAS CARRYING ENOUGH SUNLIGHT FOR A COMFORTABLE LANDING.
CAN YOU CATCH HIM BEFORE HE HURTS HIMSELF OR SOMEONE SOFTER?
I ALWAYS FEEL LIKE A COMIC BOOK CHARACTER WHEN I DO THIS.
HINGES
COMICS ARE FOR RETARDS.
WAS THAT SUPPOSED TO HURT, LITTLE GIRL?

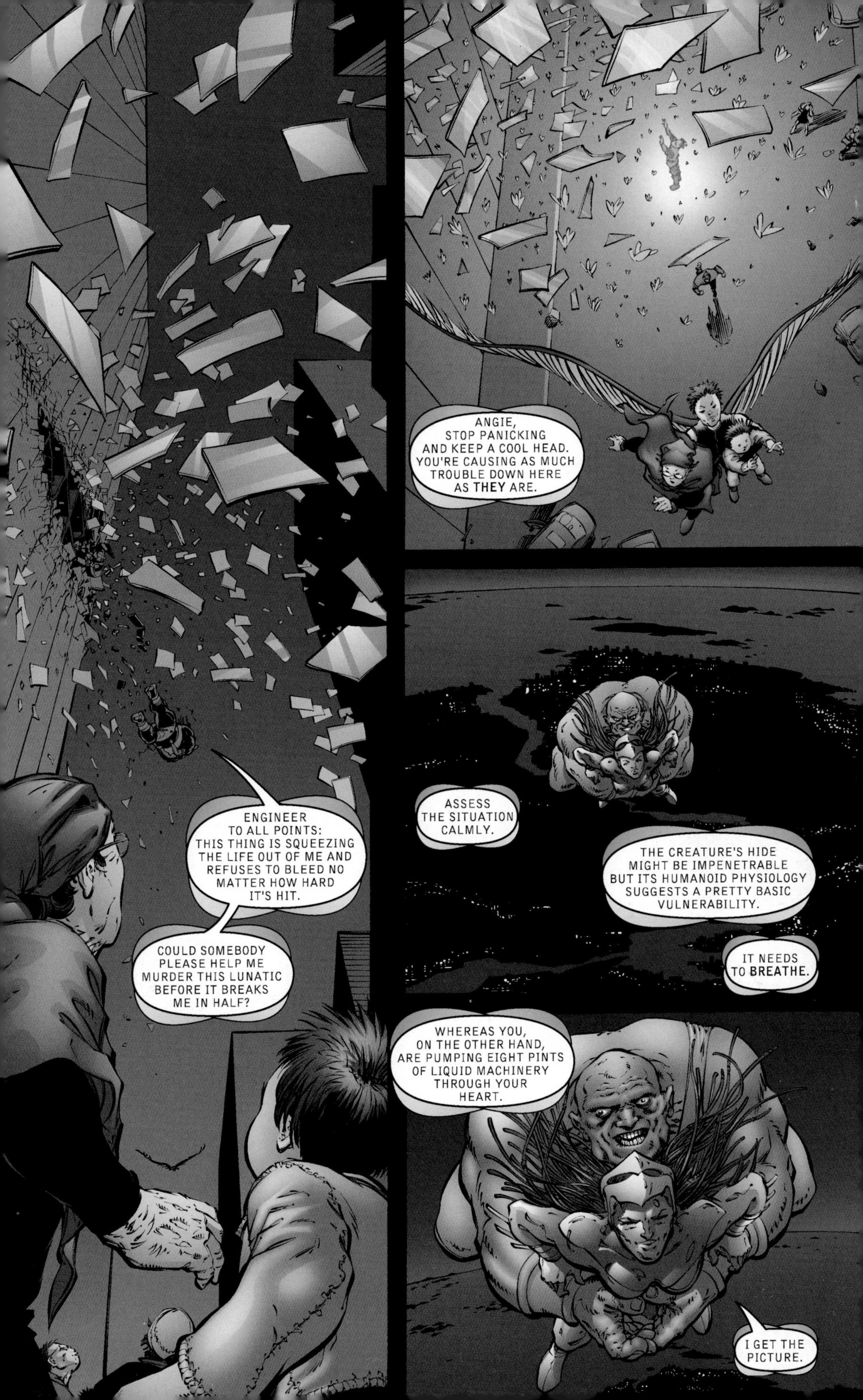
ENGINEER TO ALL POINTS: THIS THING IS SQUEEZING THE LIFE OUT OF ME AND REFUSES TO BLEED NO MATTER HOW HARD IT'S HIT.
COULD SOMEBODY PLEASE HELP ME MURDER THIS LUNATIC BEFORE IT BREAKS ME IN HALF?
ANGIE, STOP PANICKING AND KEEP A COOL HEAD. YOU'RE CAUSING AS MUCH TROUBLE DOWN HERE AS **THEY** ARE.
ASSESS THE SITUATION CALMLY.
THE CREATURE'S HIDE MIGHT BE IMPENETRABLE BUT ITS HUMANOID PHYSIOLOGY SUGGESTS A PRETTY BASIC VULNERABILITY.
IT NEEDS TO **BREATHE.**
WHEREAS YOU, ON THE OTHER HAND, ARE PUMPING EIGHT PINTS OF LIQUID MACHINERY THROUGH YOUR HEART.
I GET THE PICTURE.

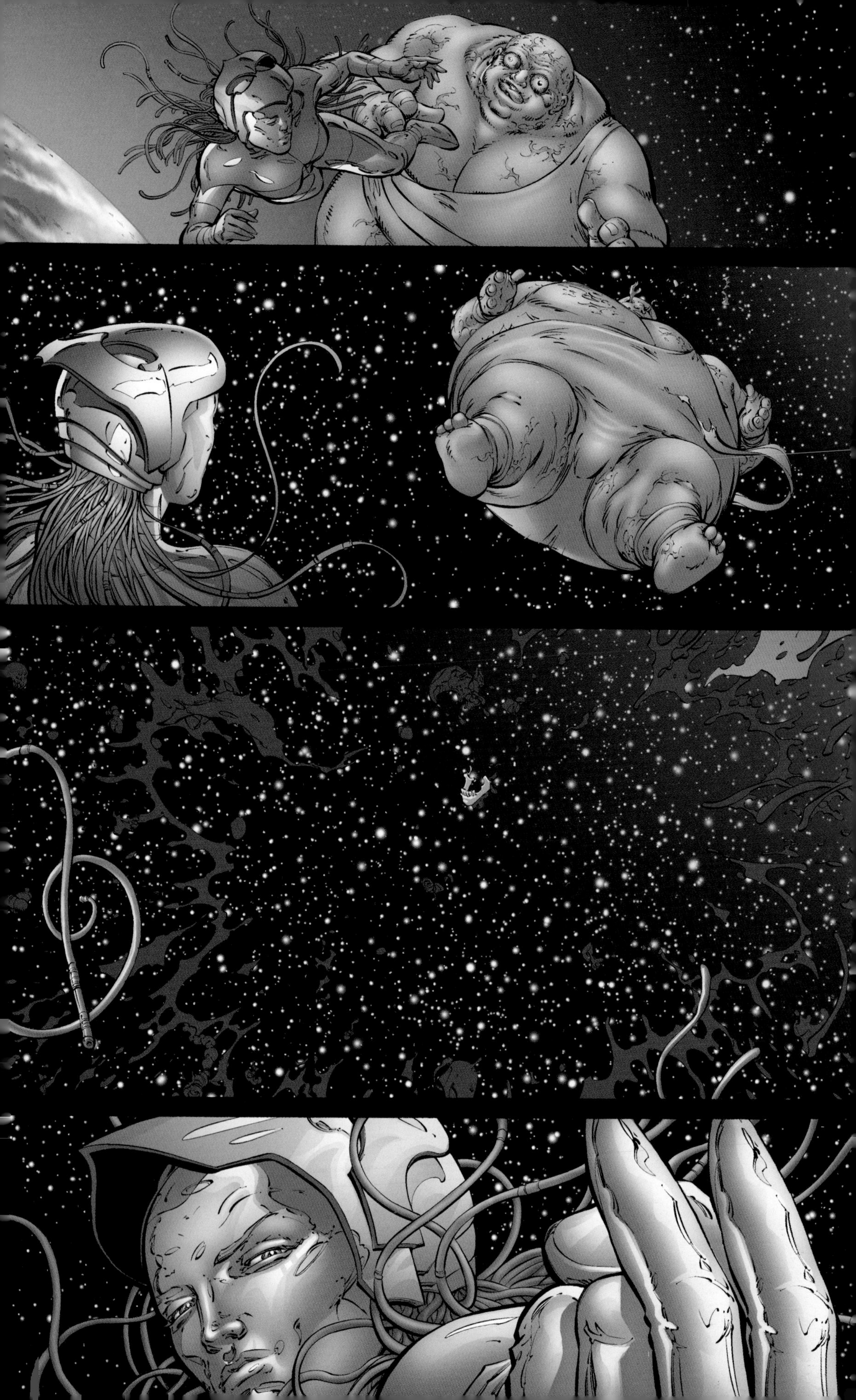

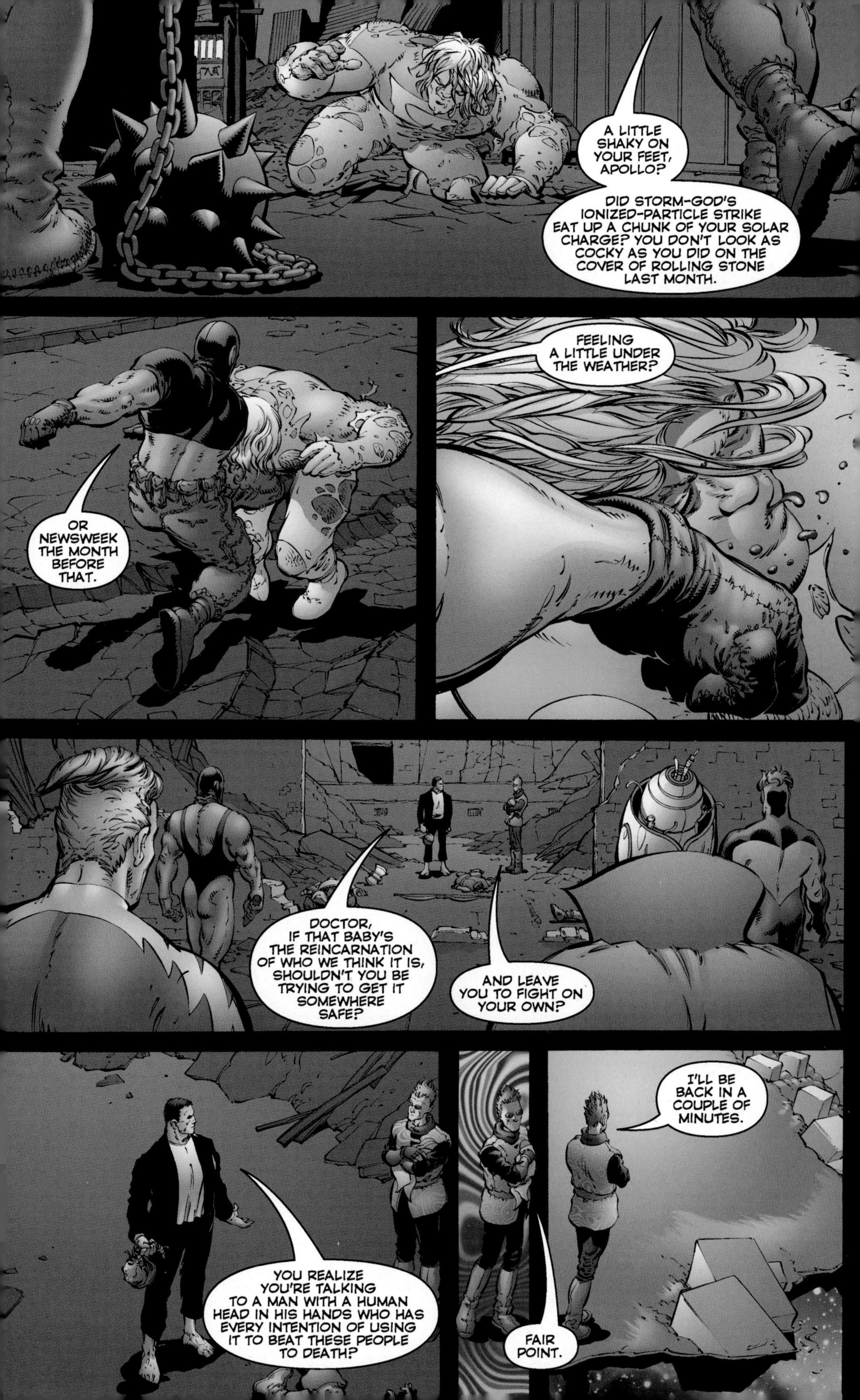
A LITTLE SHAKY ON YOUR FEET, APOLLO?
DID STORM-GOD'S IONIZED-PARTICLE STRIKE EAT UP A CHUNK OF YOUR SOLAR CHARGE? YOU DON'T LOOK AS COCKY AS YOU DID ON THE COVER OF ROLLING STONE LAST MONTH.
OR NEWSWEEK THE MONTH BEFORE THAT.
FEELING A LITTLE UNDER THE WEATHER?
DOCTOR, IF THAT BABY'S THE REINCARNATION OF WHO WE THINK IT IS, SHOULDN'T YOU BE TRYING TO GET IT SOMEWHERE SAFE?
AND LEAVE YOU TO FIGHT ON YOUR OWN?
YOU REALIZE YOU'RE TALKING TO A MAN WITH A HUMAN HEAD IN HIS HANDS WHO HAS EVERY INTENTION OF USING IT TO BEAT THESE PEOPLE TO DEATH?
FAIR POINT.
I'LL BE BACK IN A COUPLE OF MINUTES.

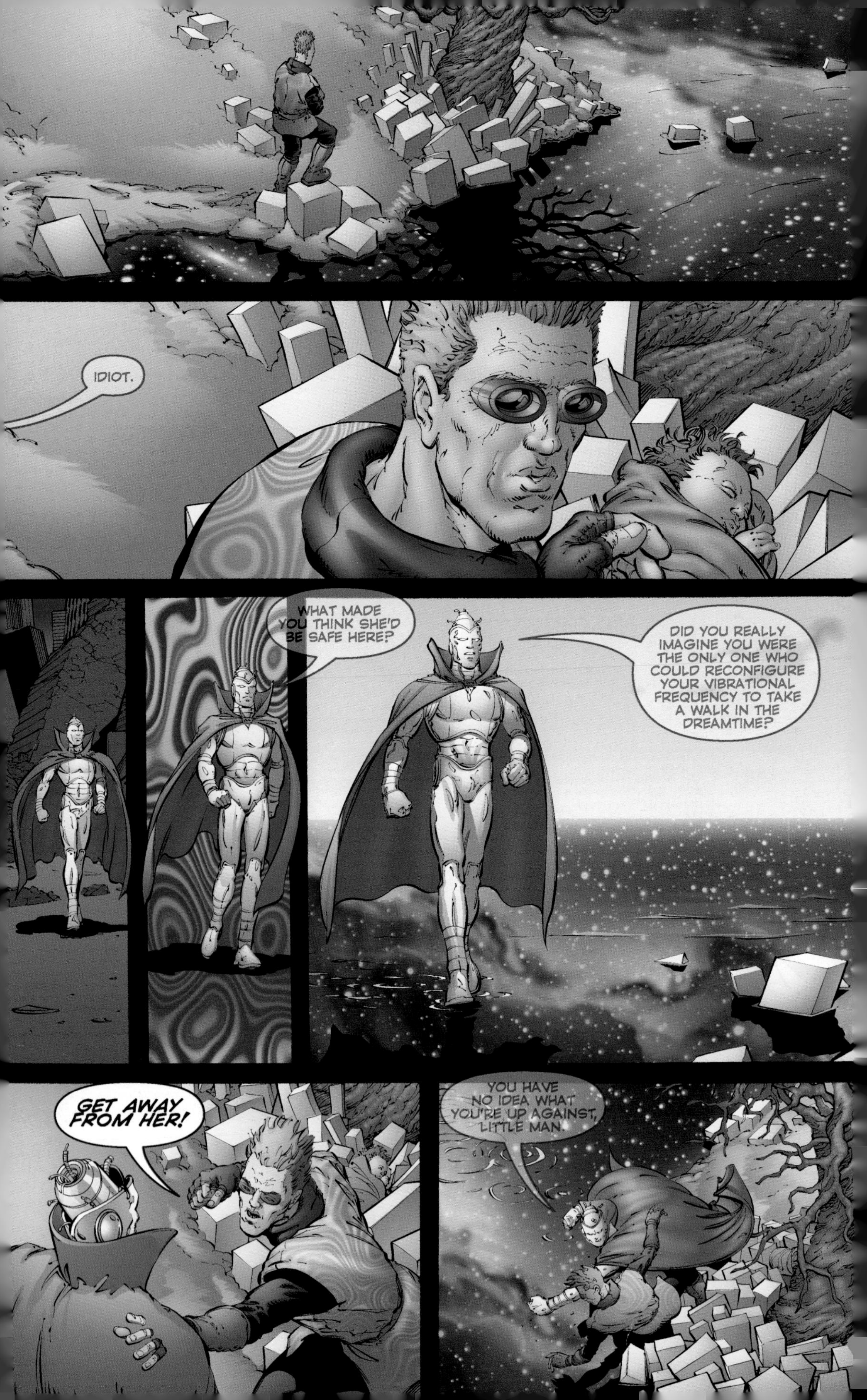
IDIOT.
WHAT MADE YOU THINK SHE'D BE SAFE HERE?
DID YOU REALLY IMAGINE YOU WERE THE ONLY ONE WHO COULD RECONFIGURE YOUR VIBRATIONAL FREQUENCY TO TAKE A WALK IN THE DREAMTIME?
GET AWAY FROM HER!
YOU HAVE NO IDEA WHAT YOU'RE UP AGAINST, LITTLE MAN.

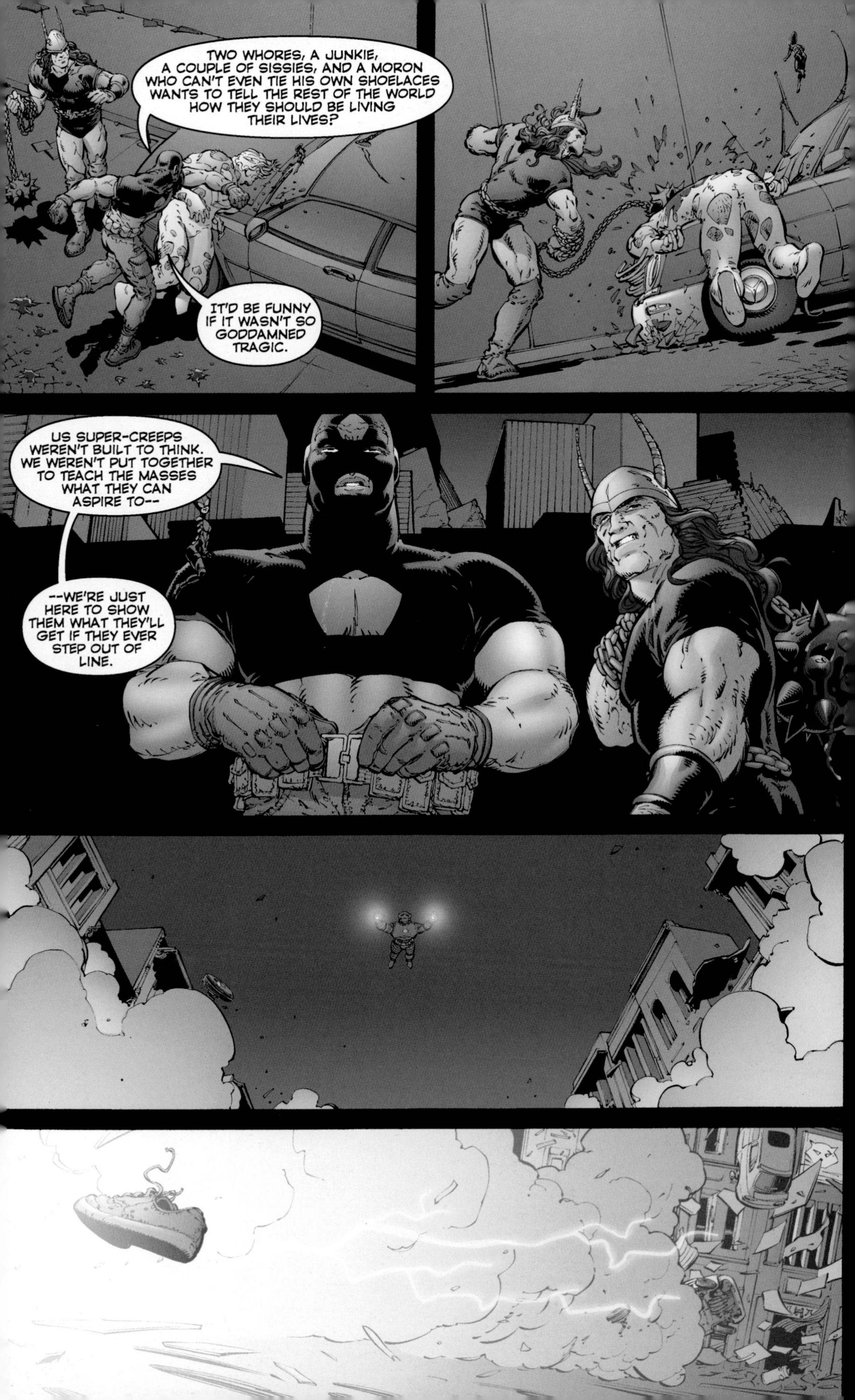
TWO WHORES, A JUNKIE, A COUPLE OF SISSIES, AND A MORON WHO CAN'T EVEN TIE HIS OWN SHOELACES WANTS TO TELL THE REST OF THE WORLD HOW THEY SHOULD BE LIVING THEIR LIVES?
IT'D BE FUNNY IF IT WASN'T SO GODDAMNED TRAGIC.
US SUPER-CREEPS WEREN'T BUILT TO THINK. WE WEREN'T PUT TOGETHER TO TEACH THE MASSES WHAT THEY CAN ASPIRE TO--
--WE'RE JUST HERE TO SHOW THEM WHAT THEY'LL GET IF THEY EVER STEP OUT OF LINE.

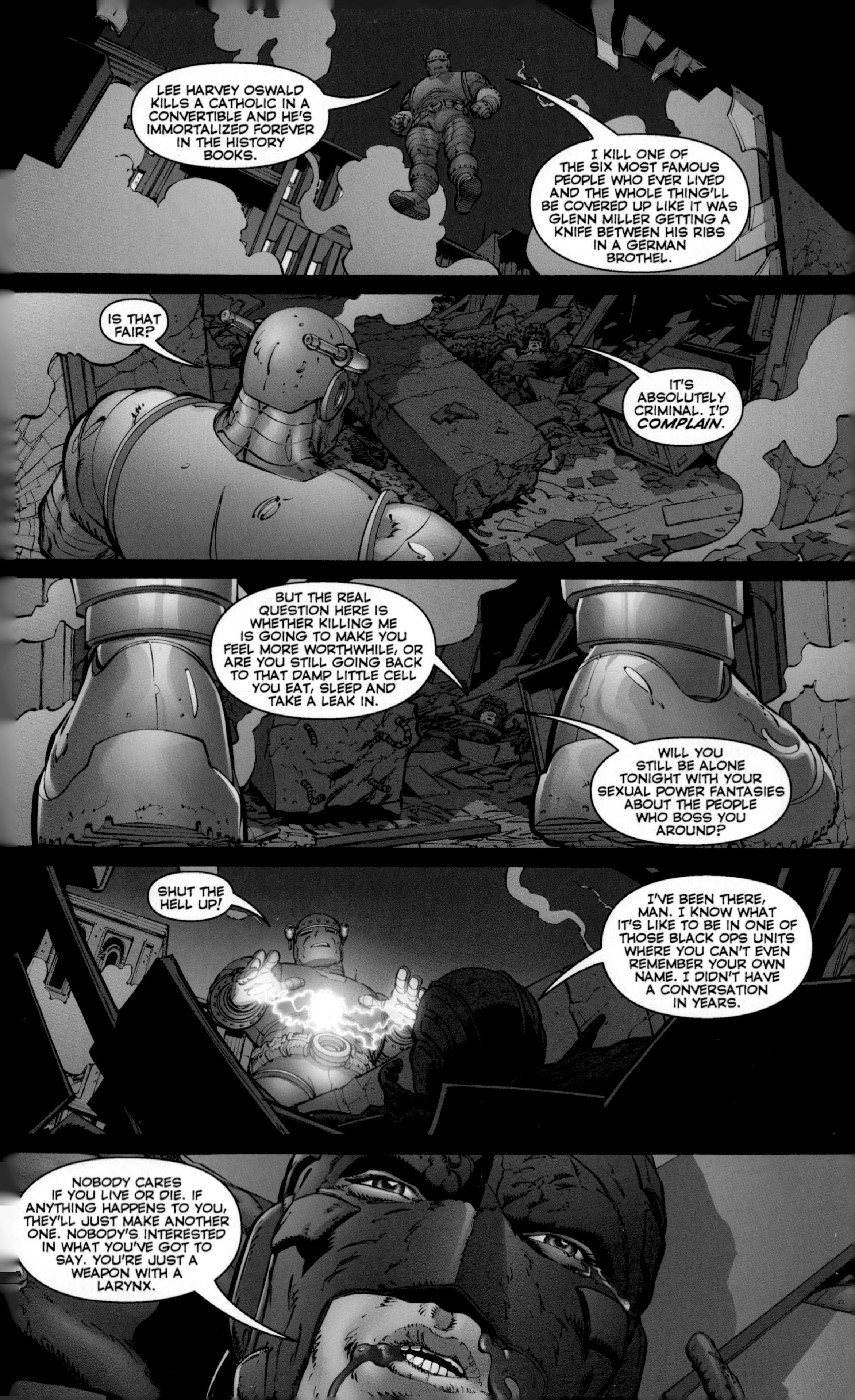
LEE HARVEY OSWALD KILLS A CATHOLIC IN A CONVERTIBLE AND HE'S IMMORTALIZED FOREVER IN THE HISTORY BOOKS.
I KILL ONE OF THE SIX MOST FAMOUS PEOPLE WHO EVER LIVED AND THE WHOLE THING'LL BE COVERED UP LIKE IT WAS GLENN MILLER GETTING A KNIFE BETWEEN HIS RIBS IN A GERMAN BROTHEL.
IS THAT FAIR?
IT'S ABSOLUTELY CRIMINAL. I'D COMPLAIN.
BUT THE REAL QUESTION HERE IS WHETHER KILLING ME IS GOING TO MAKE YOU FEEL MORE WORTHWHILE, OR ARE YOU STILL GOING BACK TO THAT DAMP LITTLE CELL YOU EAT, SLEEP AND TAKE A LEAK IN.
WILL YOU STILL BE ALONE TONIGHT WITH YOUR SEXUAL POWER FANTASIES ABOUT THE PEOPLE WHO BOSS YOU AROUND?
SHUT THE HELL UP!
I'VE BEEN THERE, MAN. I KNOW WHAT IT'S LIKE TO BE IN ONE OF THOSE BLACK OPS UNITS WHERE YOU CAN'T EVEN REMEMBER YOUR OWN NAME. I DIDN'T HAVE A CONVERSATION IN YEARS.
NOBODY CARES IF YOU LIVE OR DIE. IF ANYTHING HAPPENS TO YOU, THEY'LL JUST MAKE ANOTHER ONE. NOBODY'S INTERESTED IN WHAT YOU'VE GOT TO SAY. YOU'RE JUST A WEAPON WITH A LARYNX.

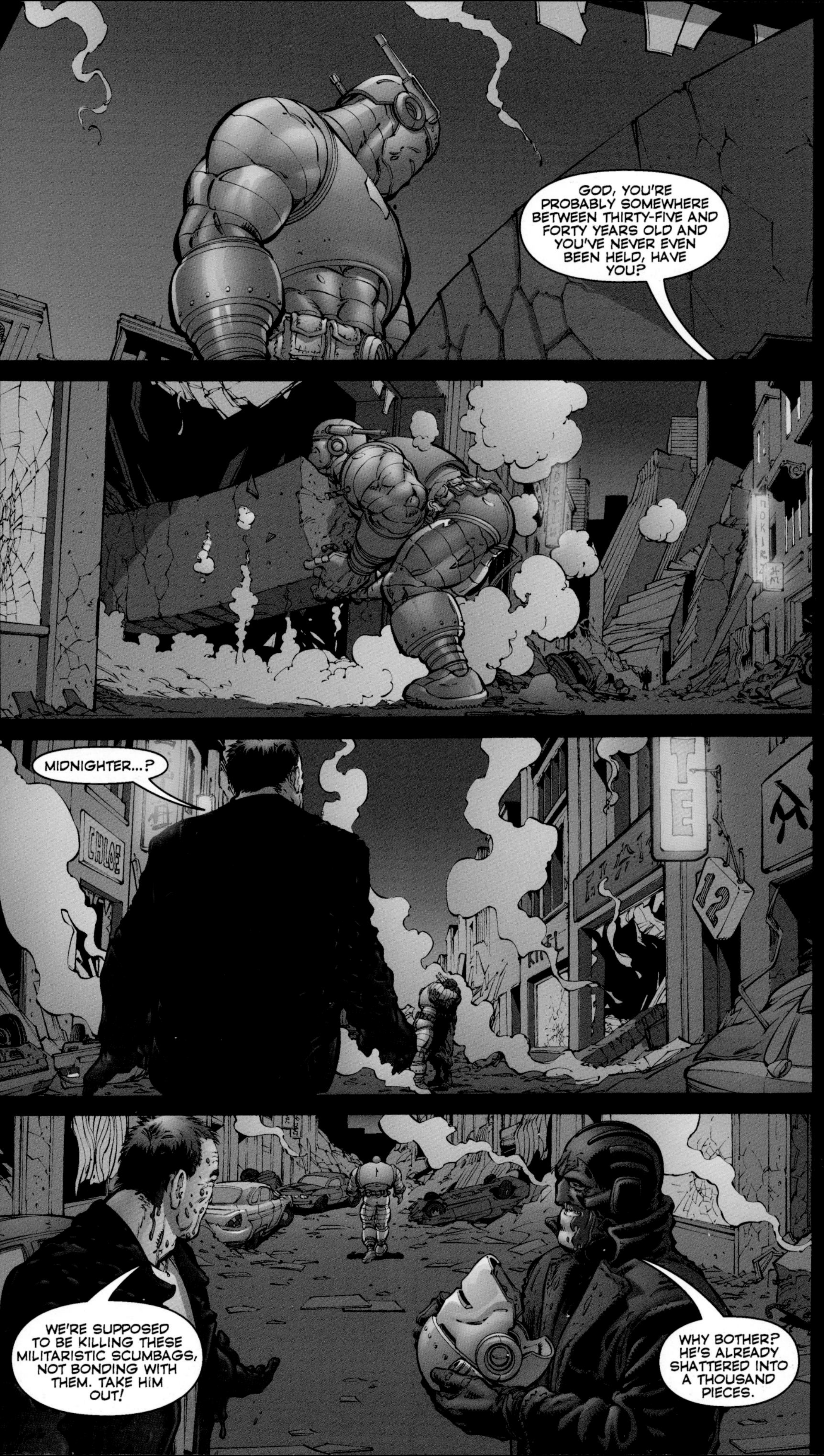
GOD, YOU'RE PROBABLY SOMEWHERE BETWEEN THIRTY-FIVE AND FORTY YEARS OLD AND YOU'VE NEVER EVEN BEEN HELD, HAVE YOU?
MIDNIGHTER...?
WE'RE SUPPOSED TO BE KILLING THESE MILITARISTIC SCUMBAGS, NOT BONDING WITH THEM. TAKE HIM OUT!
WHY BOTHER? HE'S ALREADY SHATTERED INTO A THOUSAND PIECES.

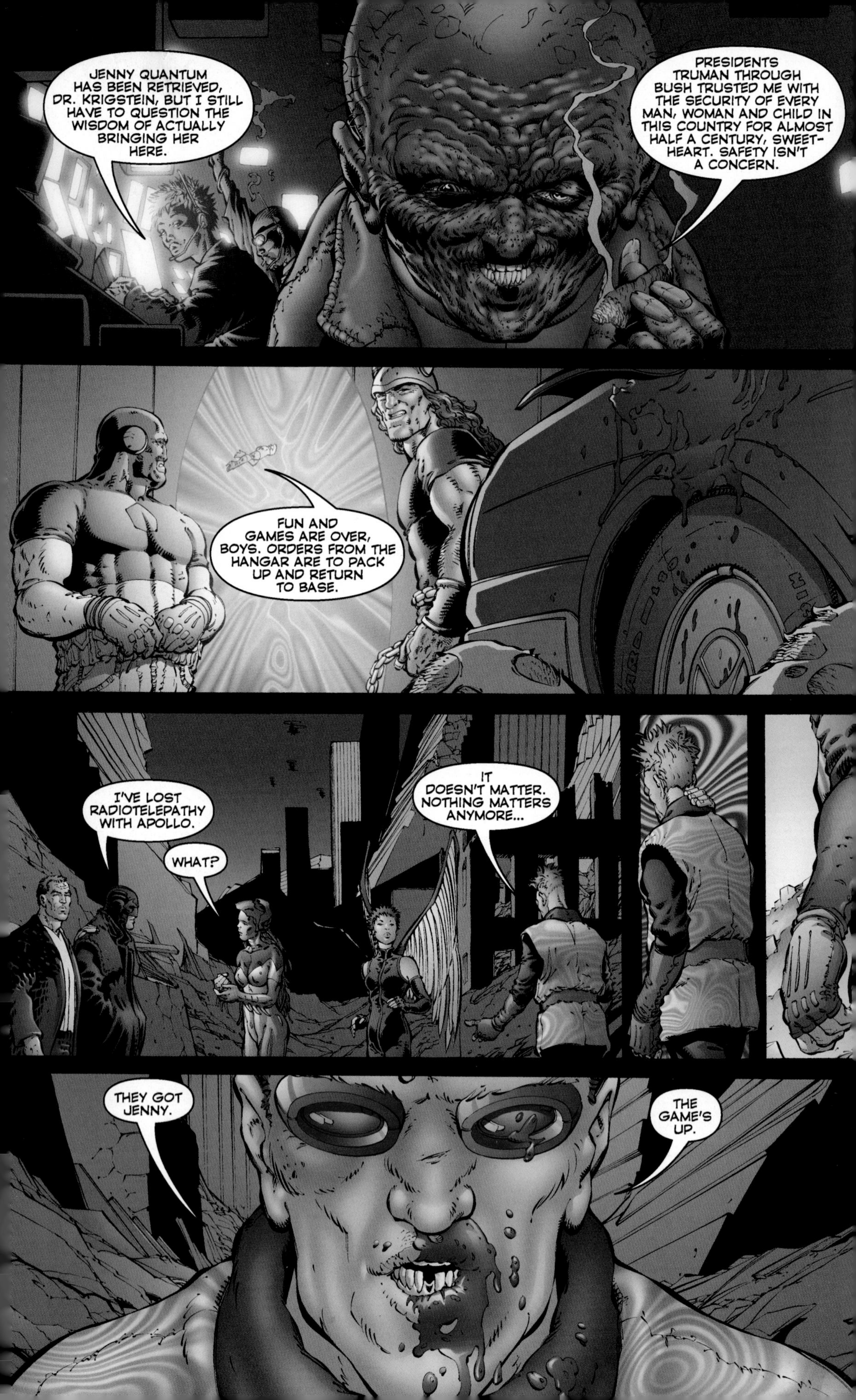

JENNY QUANTUM HAS BEEN RETRIEVED, DR. KRIGSTEIN, BUT I STILL HAVE TO QUESTION THE WISDOM OF ACTUALLY BRINGING HER HERE.
PRESIDENTS TRUMAN THROUGH BUSH TRUSTED ME WITH THE SECURITY OF EVERY MAN, WOMAN AND CHILD IN THIS COUNTRY FOR ALMOST HALF A CENTURY, SWEET-HEART. SAFETY ISN'T A CONCERN.
FUN AND GAMES ARE OVER, BOYS. ORDERS FROM THE HANGAR ARE TO PACK UP AND RETURN TO BASE.
I'VE LOST RADIOTELEPATHY WITH APOLLO.
WHAT?
IT DOESN'T MATTER. NOTHING MATTERS ANYMORE...
THEY GOT JENNY.
THE GAME'S UP.

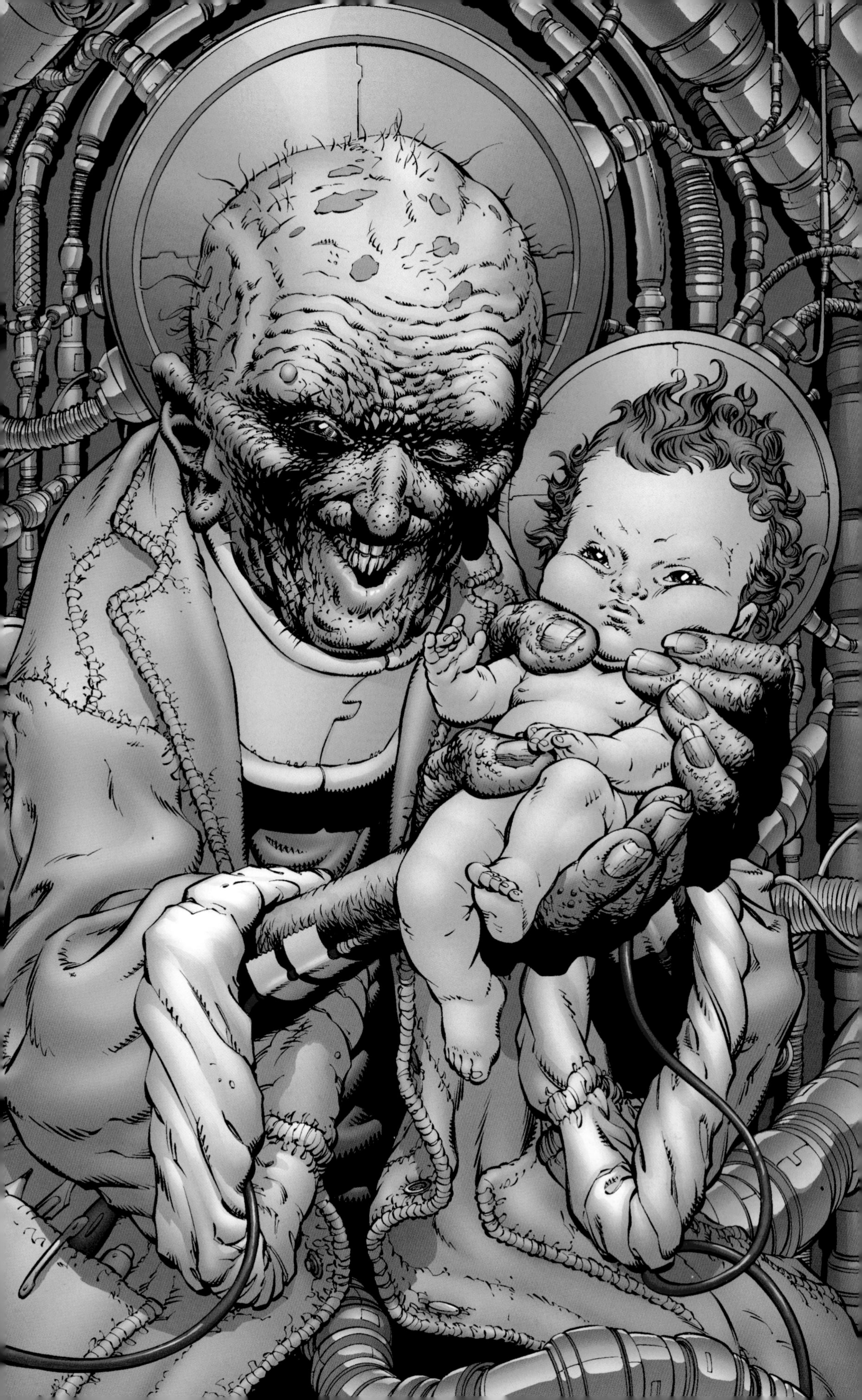

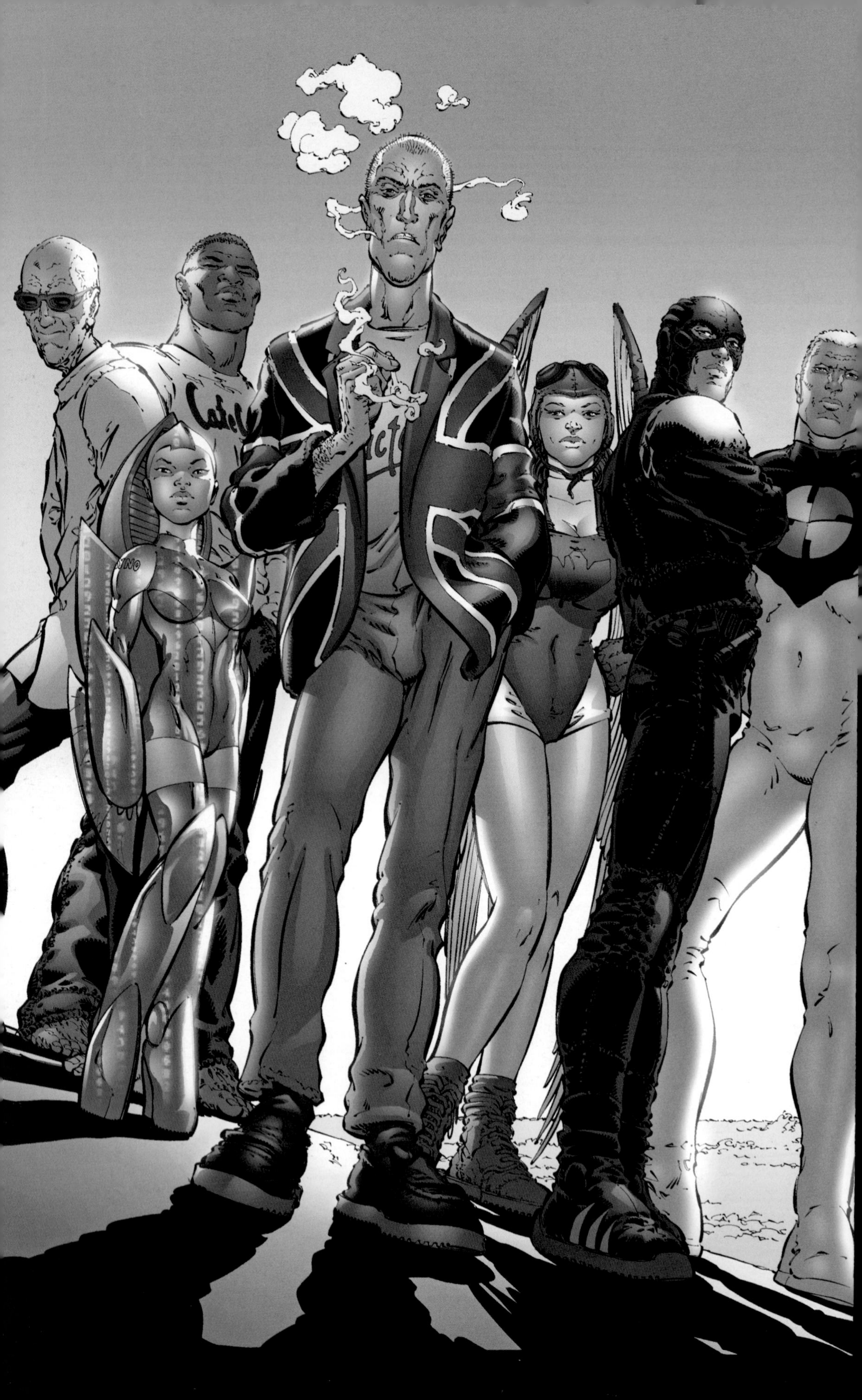

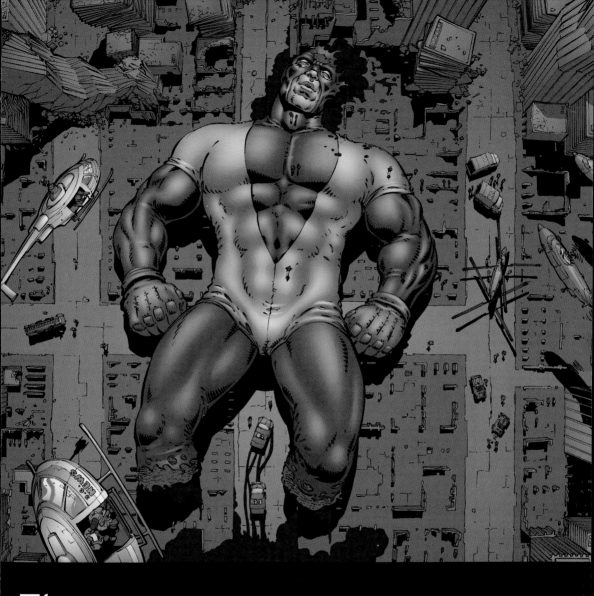

The AUTHORITY
"THE NATIVITY"
THREE of FOUR

MARK MILLAR writer

and

FRANK QUITELY with
artist

TREVOR SCOTT
inker

DAVID BARON
colorist

RYAN CLINE
letterer

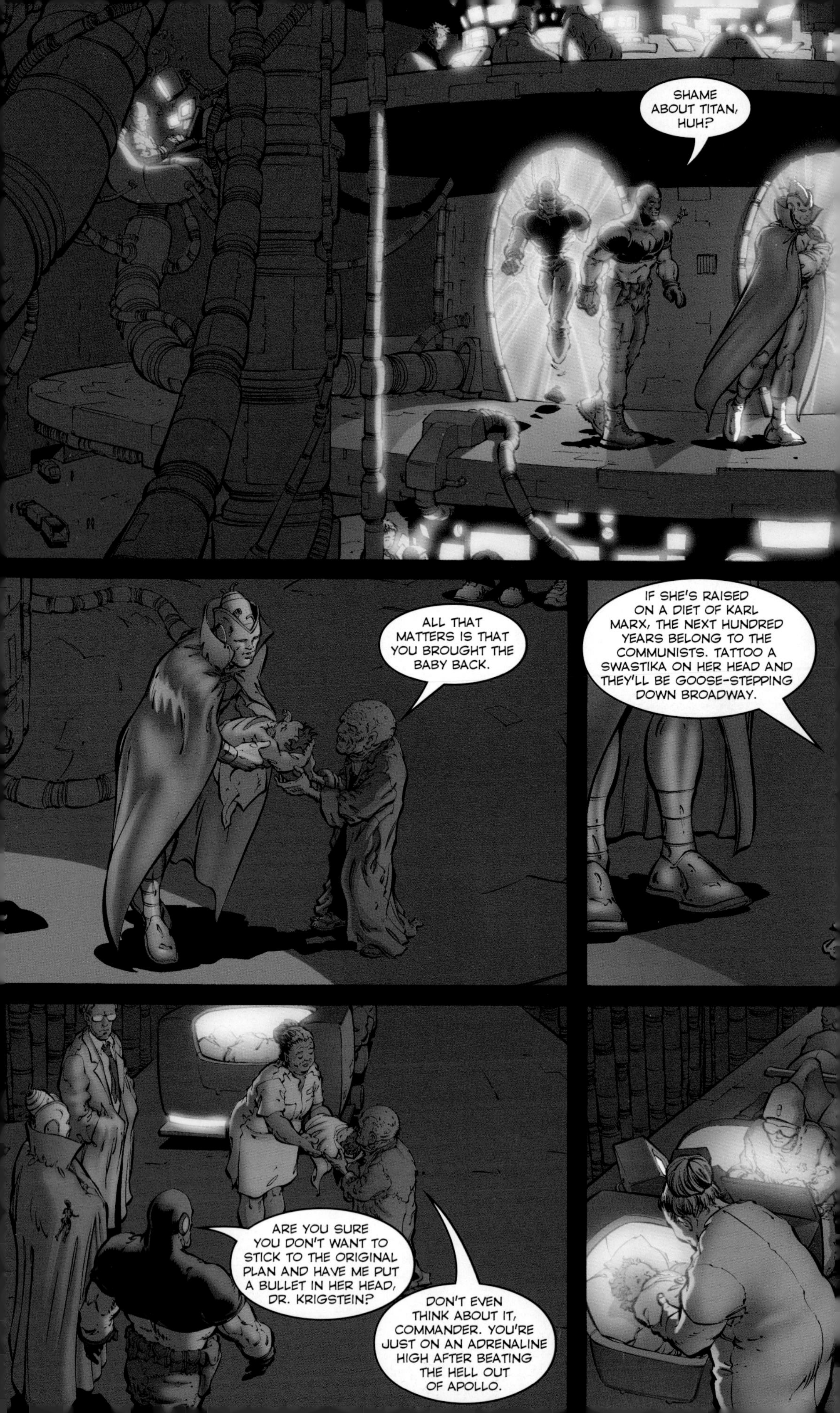
SHAME ABOUT TITAN, HUH?
ALL THAT MATTERS IS THAT YOU BROUGHT THE BABY BACK.
IF SHE'S RAISED ON A DIET OF KARL MARX, THE NEXT HUNDRED YEARS BELONG TO THE COMMUNISTS. TATTOO A SWASTIKA ON HER HEAD AND THEY'LL BE GOOSE-STEPPING DOWN BROADWAY.
ARE YOU SURE YOU DON'T WANT TO STICK TO THE ORIGINAL PLAN AND HAVE ME PUT A BULLET IN HER HEAD, DR. KRIGSTEIN?
DON'T EVEN THINK ABOUT IT, COMMANDER. YOU'RE JUST ON AN ADRENALINE HIGH AFTER BEATING THE HELL OUT OF APOLLO.

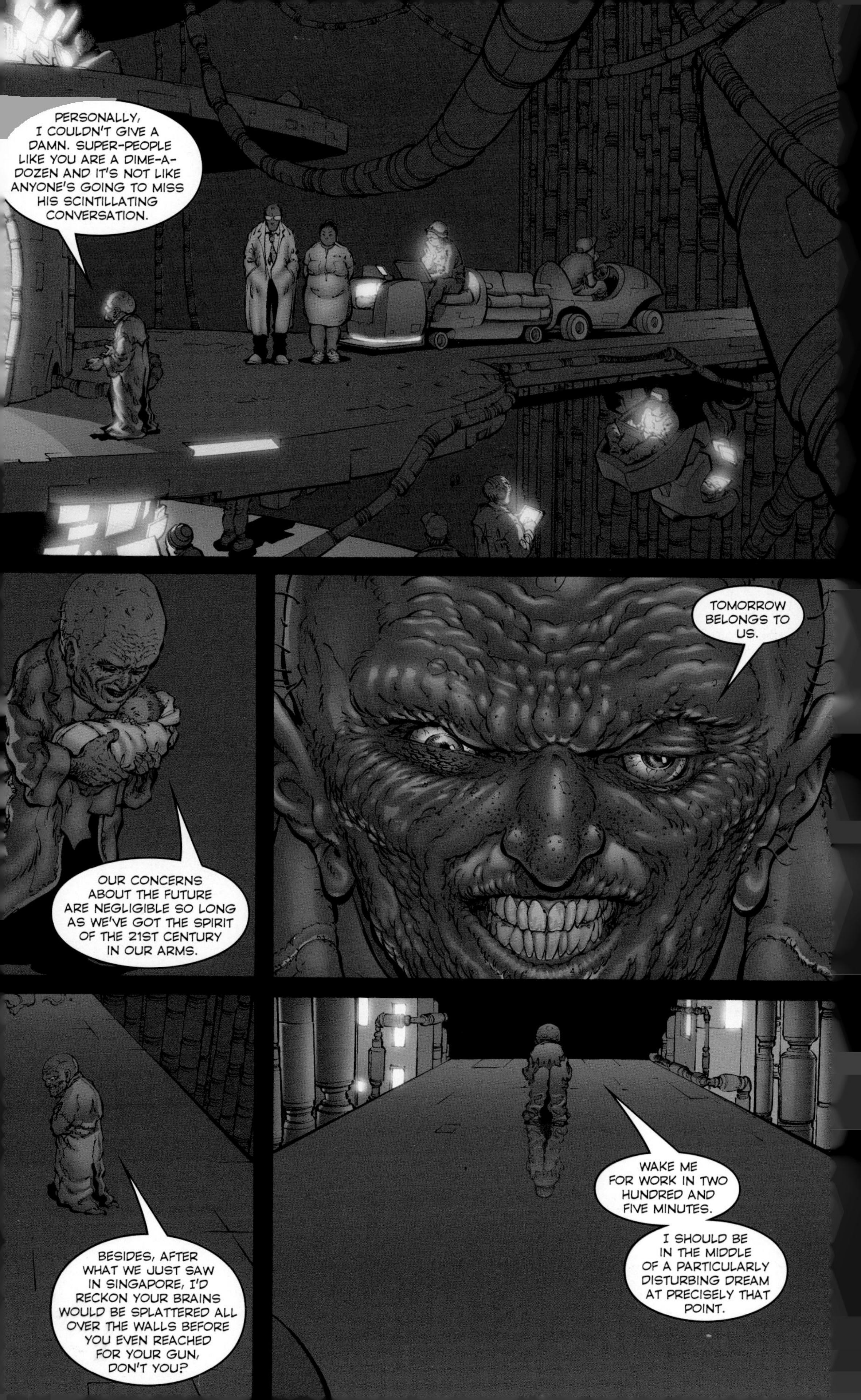
PERSONALLY, I COULDN'T GIVE A DAMN. SUPER-PEOPLE LIKE YOU ARE A DIME-A-DOZEN AND IT'S NOT LIKE ANYONE'S GOING TO MISS HIS SCINTILLATING CONVERSATION.
OUR CONCERNS ABOUT THE FUTURE ARE NEGLIGIBLE SO LONG AS WE'VE GOT THE SPIRIT OF THE 21ST CENTURY IN OUR ARMS.
TOMORROW BELONGS TO US.
BESIDES, AFTER WHAT WE JUST SAW IN SINGAPORE, I'D RECKON YOUR BRAINS WOULD BE SPLATTERED ALL OVER THE WALLS BEFORE YOU EVEN REACHED FOR YOUR GUN, DON'T YOU?
WAKE ME FOR WORK IN TWO HUNDRED AND FIVE MINUTES.
I SHOULD BE IN THE MIDDLE OF A PARTICULARLY DISTURBING DREAM AT PRECISELY THAT POINT.

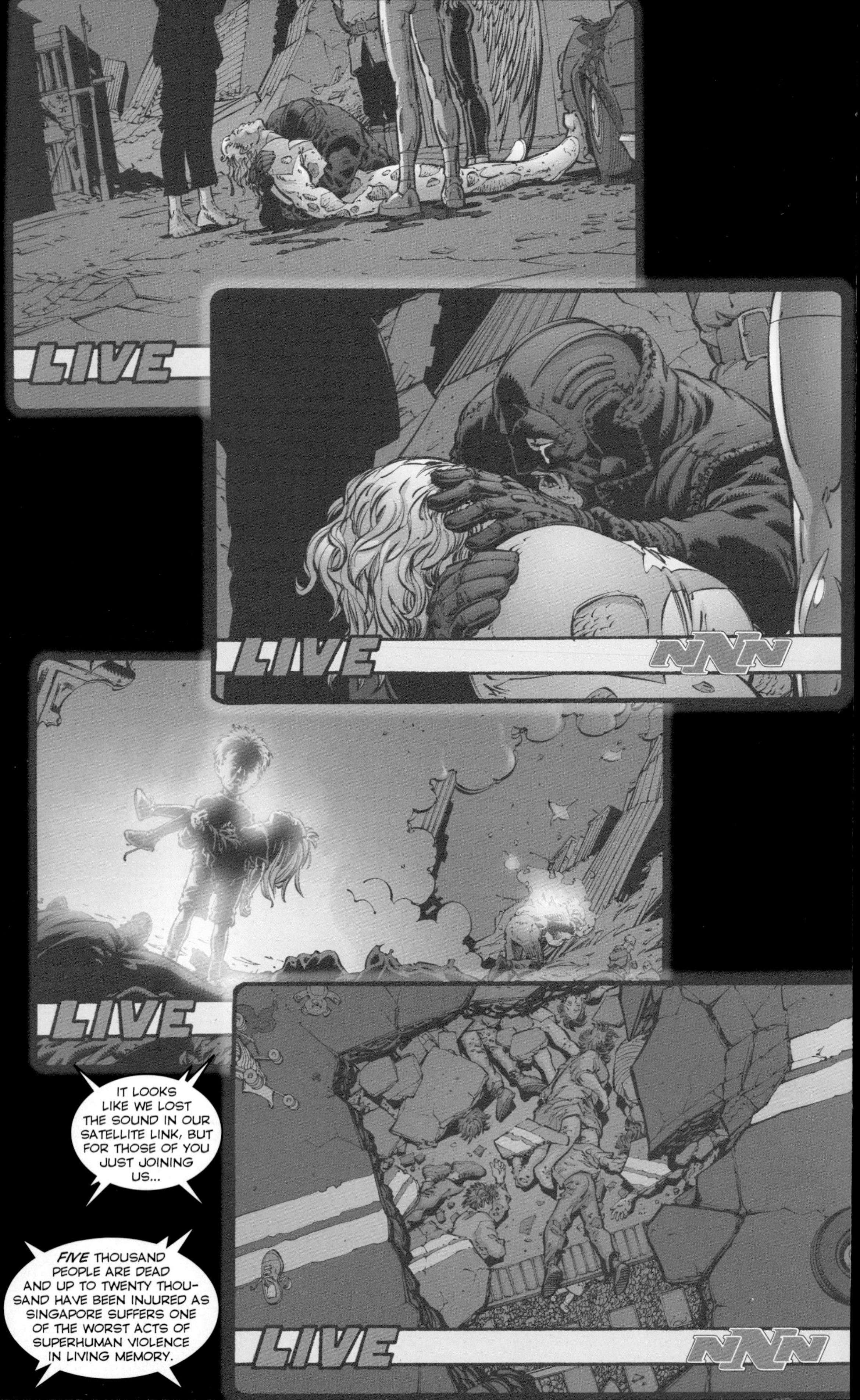
LIVE
LIVE
NNN
LIVE
IT LOOKS LIKE WE LOST THE SOUND IN OUR SATELLITE LINK, BUT FOR THOSE OF YOU JUST JOINING US...
FIVE THOUSAND PEOPLE ARE DEAD AND UP TO TWENTY THOU-SAND HAVE BEEN INJURED AS SINGAPORE SUFFERS ONE OF THE WORST ACTS OF SUPERHUMAN VIOLENCE IN LIVING MEMORY.
LIVE
NNN

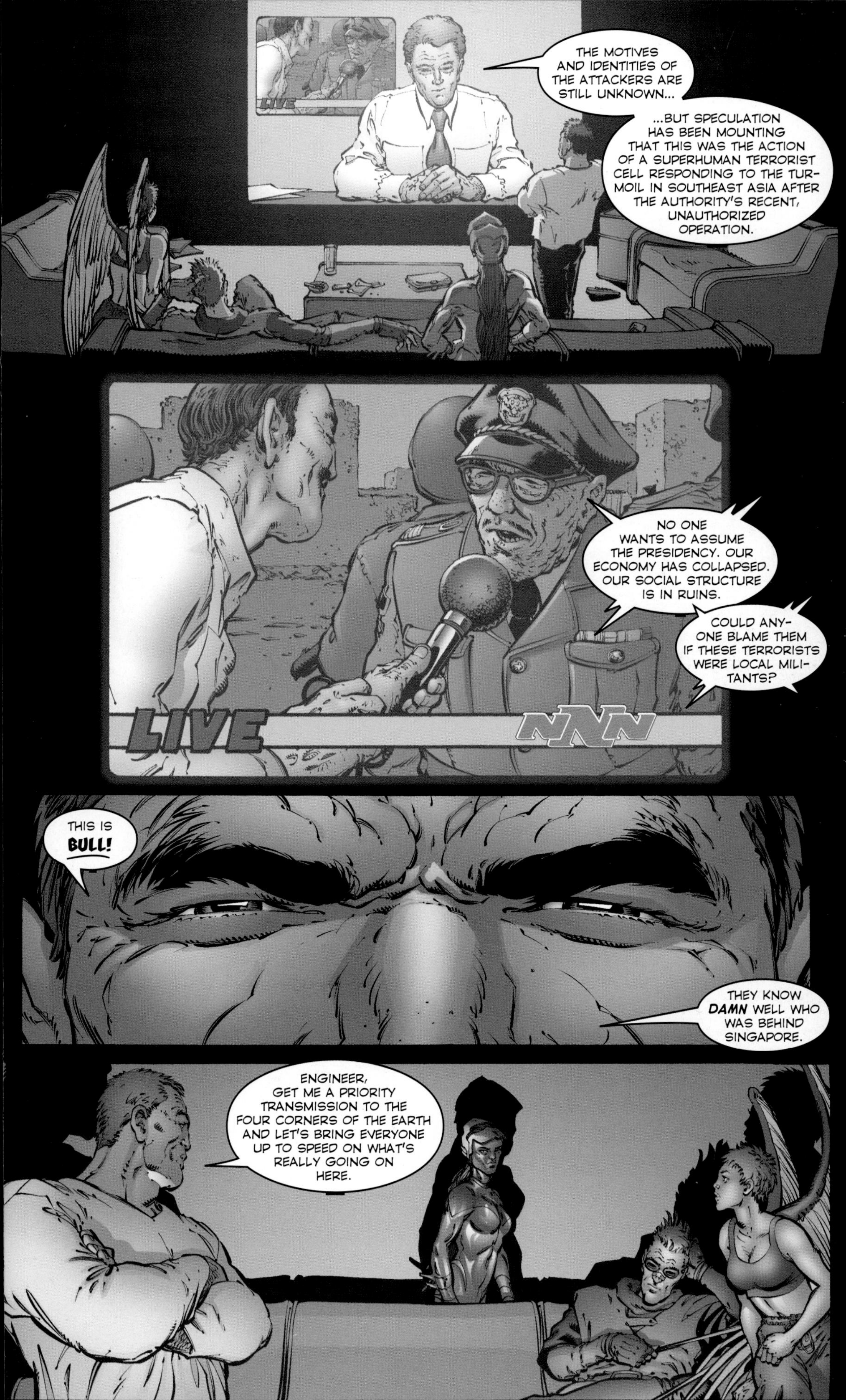
THE MOTIVES AND IDENTITIES OF THE ATTACKERS ARE STILL UNKNOWN...
...BUT SPECULATION HAS BEEN MOUNTING THAT THIS WAS THE ACTION OF A SUPERHUMAN TERRORIST CELL RESPONDING TO THE TURMOIL IN SOUTHEAST ASIA AFTER THE AUTHORITY'S RECENT, UNAUTHORIZED OPERATION.
LIVE
NO ONE WANTS TO ASSUME THE PRESIDENCY. OUR ECONOMY HAS COLLAPSED. OUR SOCIAL STRUCTURE IS IN RUINS.
COULD ANYONE BLAME THEM IF THESE TERRORISTS WERE LOCAL MILITANTS?
LIVE
NNN
THIS IS **BULL!**
THEY KNOW ***DAMN*** WELL WHO WAS BEHIND SINGAPORE.
ENGINEER, GET ME A PRIORITY TRANSMISSION TO THE FOUR CORNERS OF THE EARTH AND LET'S BRING EVERYONE UP TO SPEED ON WHAT'S REALLY GOING ON HERE.

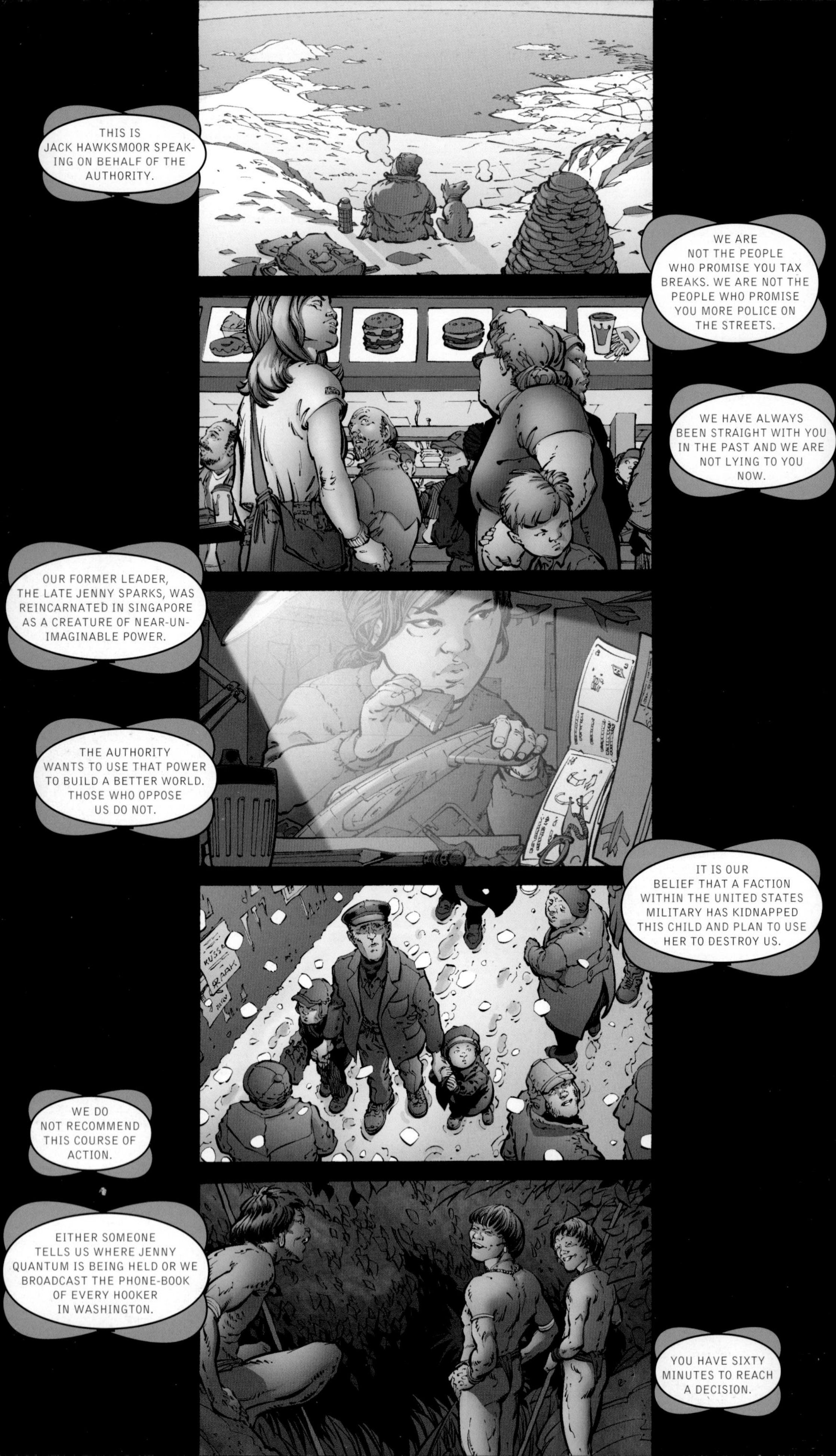
THIS IS JACK HAWKSMOOR SPEAK-ING ON BEHALF OF THE AUTHORITY.
WE ARE NOT THE PEOPLE WHO PROMISE YOU TAX BREAKS. WE ARE NOT THE PEOPLE WHO PROMISE YOU MORE POLICE ON THE STREETS.
WE HAVE ALWAYS BEEN STRAIGHT WITH YOU IN THE PAST AND WE ARE NOT LYING TO YOU NOW.
OUR FORMER LEADER, THE LATE JENNY SPARKS, WAS REINCARNATED IN SINGAPORE AS A CREATURE OF NEAR-UN-IMAGINABLE POWER.
THE AUTHORITY WANTS TO USE THAT POWER TO BUILD A BETTER WORLD. THOSE WHO OPPOSE US DO NOT.
IT IS OUR BELIEF THAT A FACTION WITHIN THE UNITED STATES MILITARY HAS KIDNAPPED THIS CHILD AND PLAN TO USE HER TO DESTROY US.
WE DO NOT RECOMMEND THIS COURSE OF ACTION.
EITHER SOMEONE TELLS US WHERE JENNY QUANTUM IS BEING HELD OR WE BROADCAST THE PHONE-BOOK OF EVERY HOOKER IN WASHINGTON.
YOU HAVE SIXTY MINUTES TO REACH A DECISION.

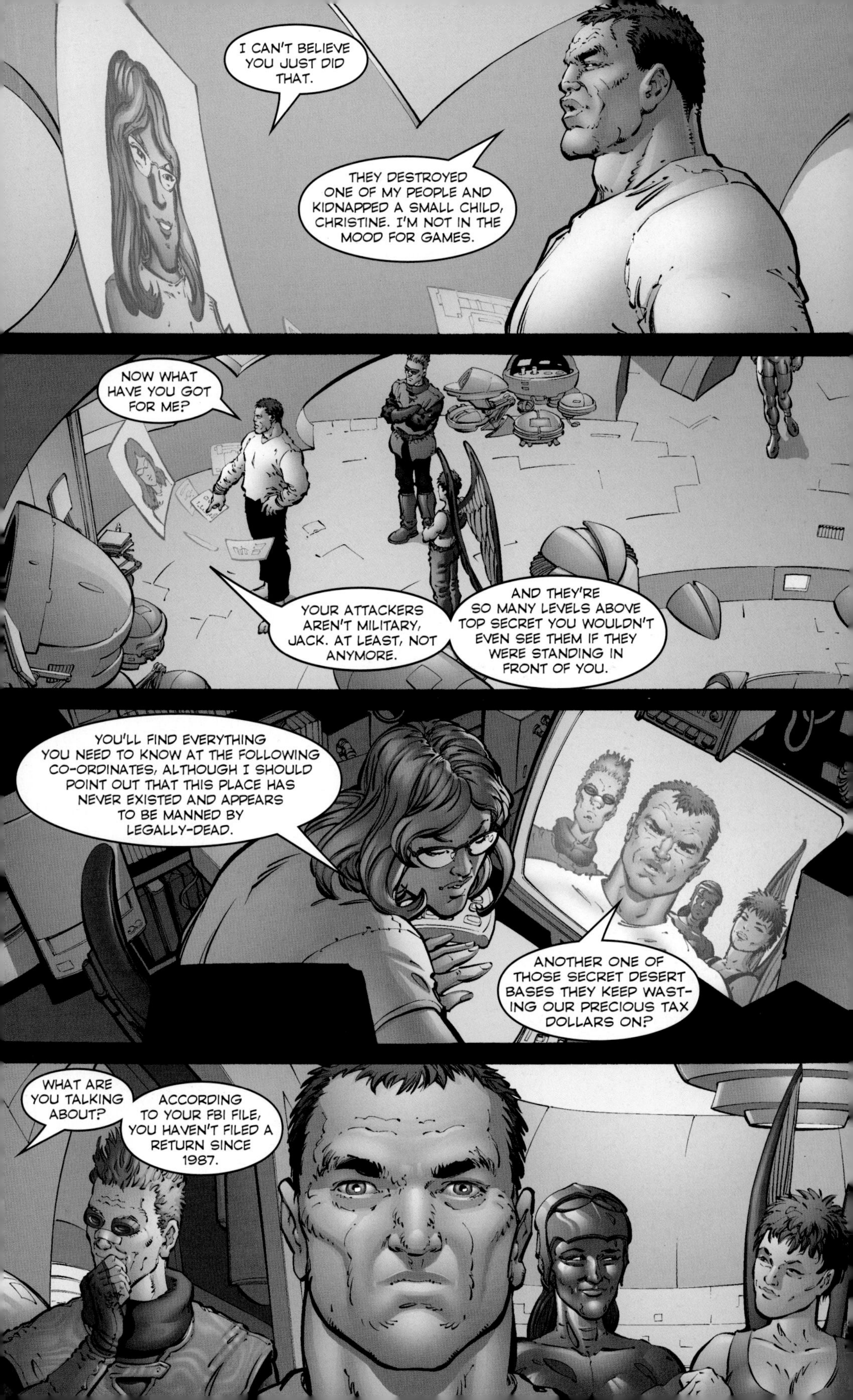
I CAN'T BELIEVE YOU JUST DID THAT.
THEY DESTROYED ONE OF MY PEOPLE AND KIDNAPPED A SMALL CHILD, CHRISTINE. I'M NOT IN THE MOOD FOR GAMES.
NOW WHAT HAVE YOU GOT FOR ME?
YOUR ATTACKERS AREN'T MILITARY, JACK. AT LEAST, NOT ANYMORE.
AND THEY'RE SO MANY LEVELS ABOVE TOP SECRET YOU WOULDN'T EVEN SEE THEM IF THEY WERE STANDING IN FRONT OF YOU.
YOU'LL FIND EVERYTHING YOU NEED TO KNOW AT THE FOLLOWING CO-ORDINATES, ALTHOUGH I SHOULD POINT OUT THAT THIS PLACE HAS NEVER EXISTED AND APPEARS TO BE MANNED BY LEGALLY-DEAD.
ANOTHER ONE OF THOSE SECRET DESERT BASES THEY KEEP WASTING OUR PRECIOUS TAX DOLLARS ON?
WHAT ARE YOU TALKING ABOUT?
ACCORDING TO YOUR FBI FILE, YOU HAVEN'T FILED A RETURN SINCE 1987.

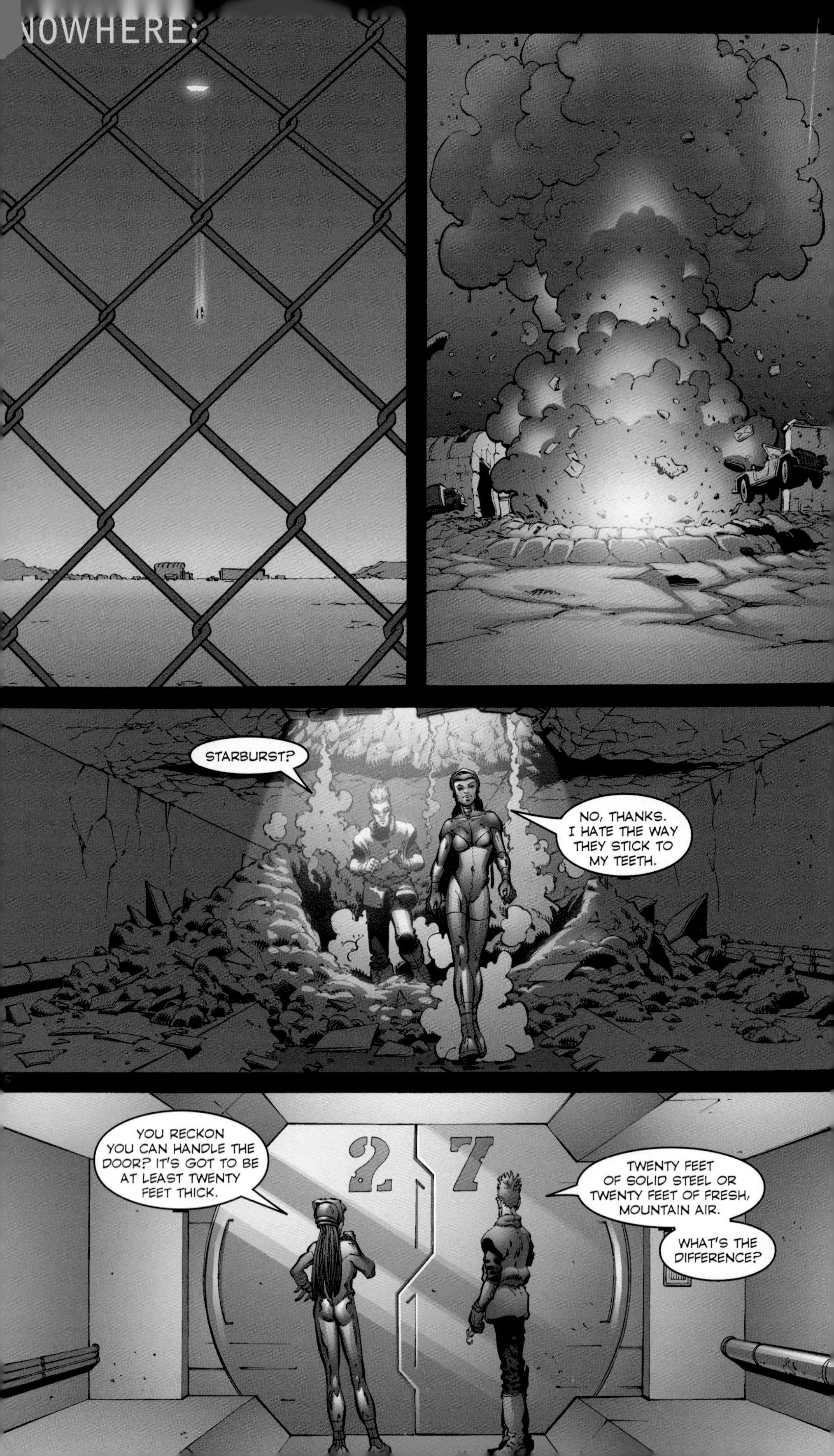
NOWHERE:
STARBURST?
NO, THANKS. I HATE THE WAY THEY STICK TO MY TEETH.
27
YOU RECKON YOU CAN HANDLE THE DOOR? IT'S GOT TO BE AT LEAST TWENTY FEET THICK.
TWENTY FEET OF SOLID STEEL OR TWENTY FEET OF FRESH, MOUNTAIN AIR.
WHAT'S THE DIFFERENCE?

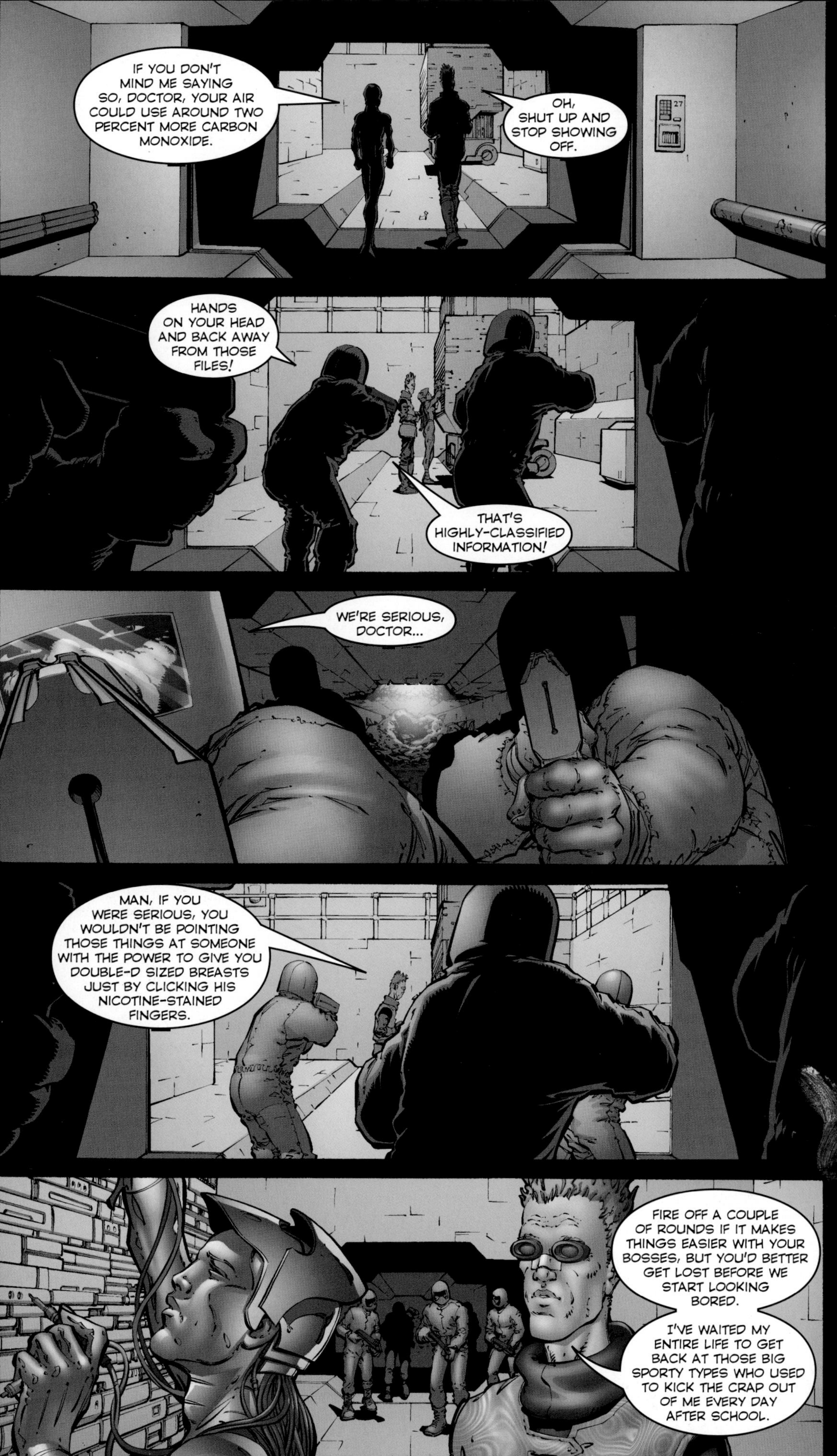
IF YOU DON'T MIND ME SAYING SO, DOCTOR, YOUR AIR COULD USE AROUND TWO PERCENT MORE CARBON MONOXIDE.
OH, SHUT UP AND STOP SHOWING OFF.
HANDS ON YOUR HEAD AND BACK AWAY FROM THOSE FILES!
THAT'S HIGHLY-CLASSIFIED INFORMATION!
WE'RE SERIOUS, DOCTOR...
MAN, IF YOU WERE SERIOUS, YOU WOULDN'T BE POINTING THOSE THINGS AT SOMEONE WITH THE POWER TO GIVE YOU DOUBLE-D SIZED BREASTS JUST BY CLICKING HIS NICOTINE-STAINED FINGERS.
FIRE OFF A COUPLE OF ROUNDS IF IT MAKES THINGS EASIER WITH YOUR BOSSES, BUT YOU'D BETTER GET LOST BEFORE WE START LOOKING BORED.
I'VE WAITED MY ENTIRE LIFE TO GET BACK AT THOSE BIG SPORTY TYPES WHO USED TO KICK THE CRAP OUT OF ME EVERY DAY AFTER SCHOOL.

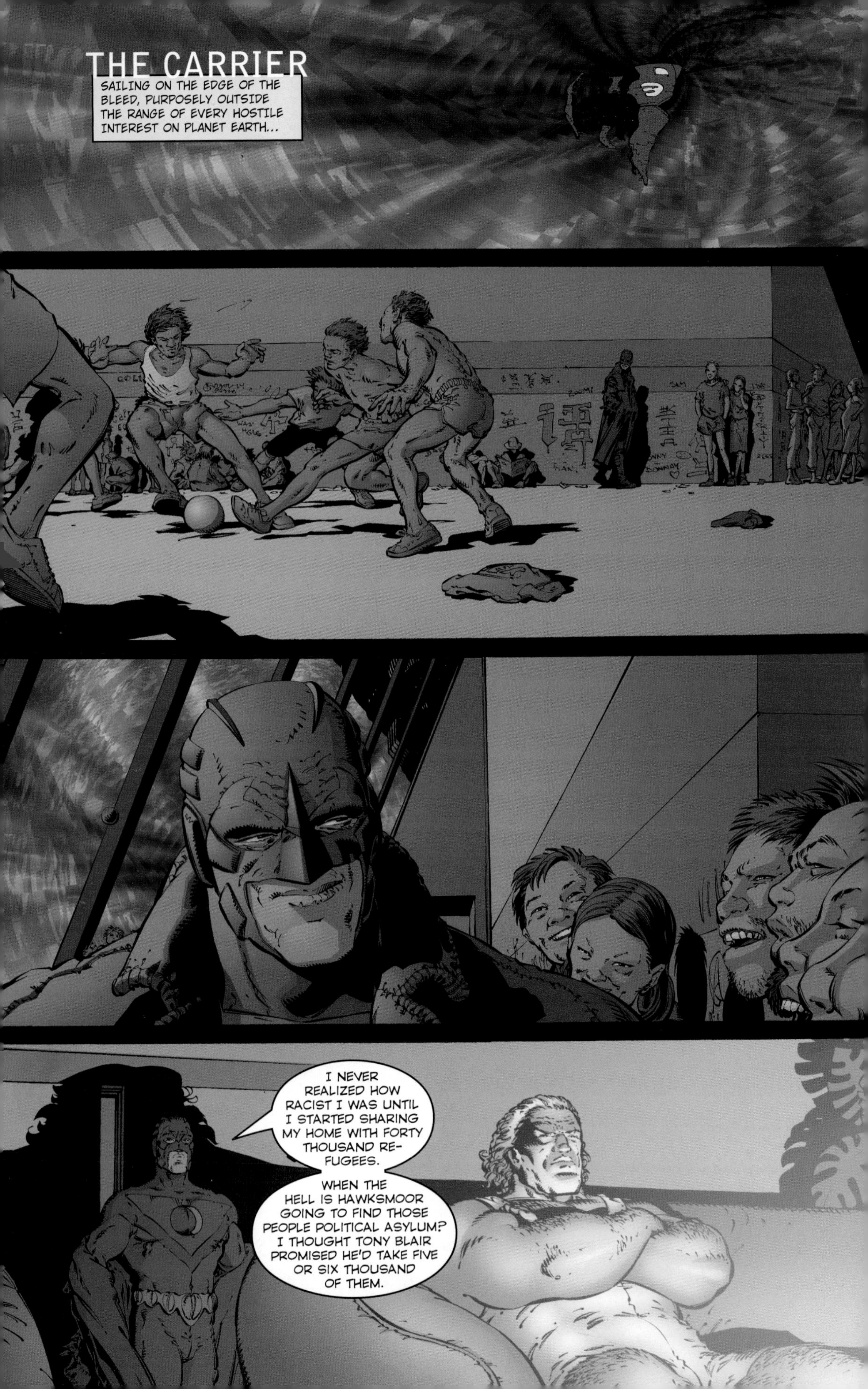
THE CARRIER
SAILING ON THE EDGE OF THE BLEED, PURPOSELY OUTSIDE THE RANGE OF EVERY HOSTILE INTEREST ON PLANET EARTH...
I NEVER REALIZED HOW RACIST I WAS UNTIL I STARTED SHARING MY HOME WITH FORTY THOUSAND REFUGEES.
WHEN THE HELL IS HAWKSMOOR GOING TO FIND THOSE PEOPLE POLITICAL ASYLUM? I THOUGHT TONY BLAIR PROMISED HE'D TAKE FIVE OR SIX THOUSAND OF THEM.

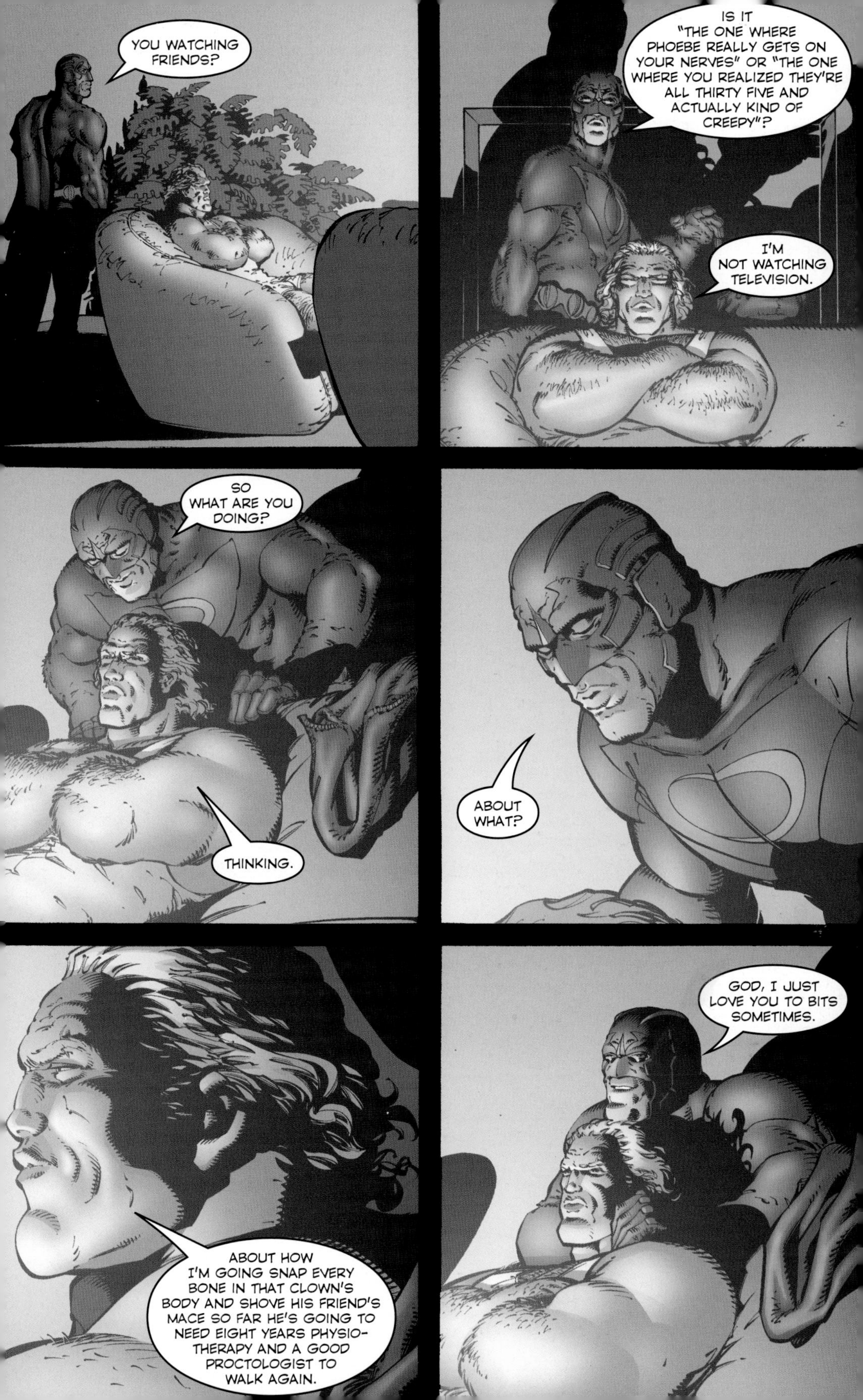
YOU WATCHING FRIENDS?
IS IT "THE ONE WHERE PHOEBE REALLY GETS ON YOUR NERVES" OR "THE ONE WHERE YOU REALIZED THEY'RE ALL THIRTY FIVE AND ACTUALLY KIND OF CREEPY"?
I'M NOT WATCHING TELEVISION.
SO WHAT ARE YOU DOING?
THINKING.
ABOUT WHAT?
ABOUT HOW I'M GOING SNAP EVERY BONE IN THAT CLOWN'S BODY AND SHOVE HIS FRIEND'S MACE SO FAR HE'S GOING TO NEED EIGHT YEARS PHYSIO-THERAPY AND A GOOD PROCTOLOGIST TO WALK AGAIN.
GOD, I JUST LOVE YOU TO BITS SOMETIMES.

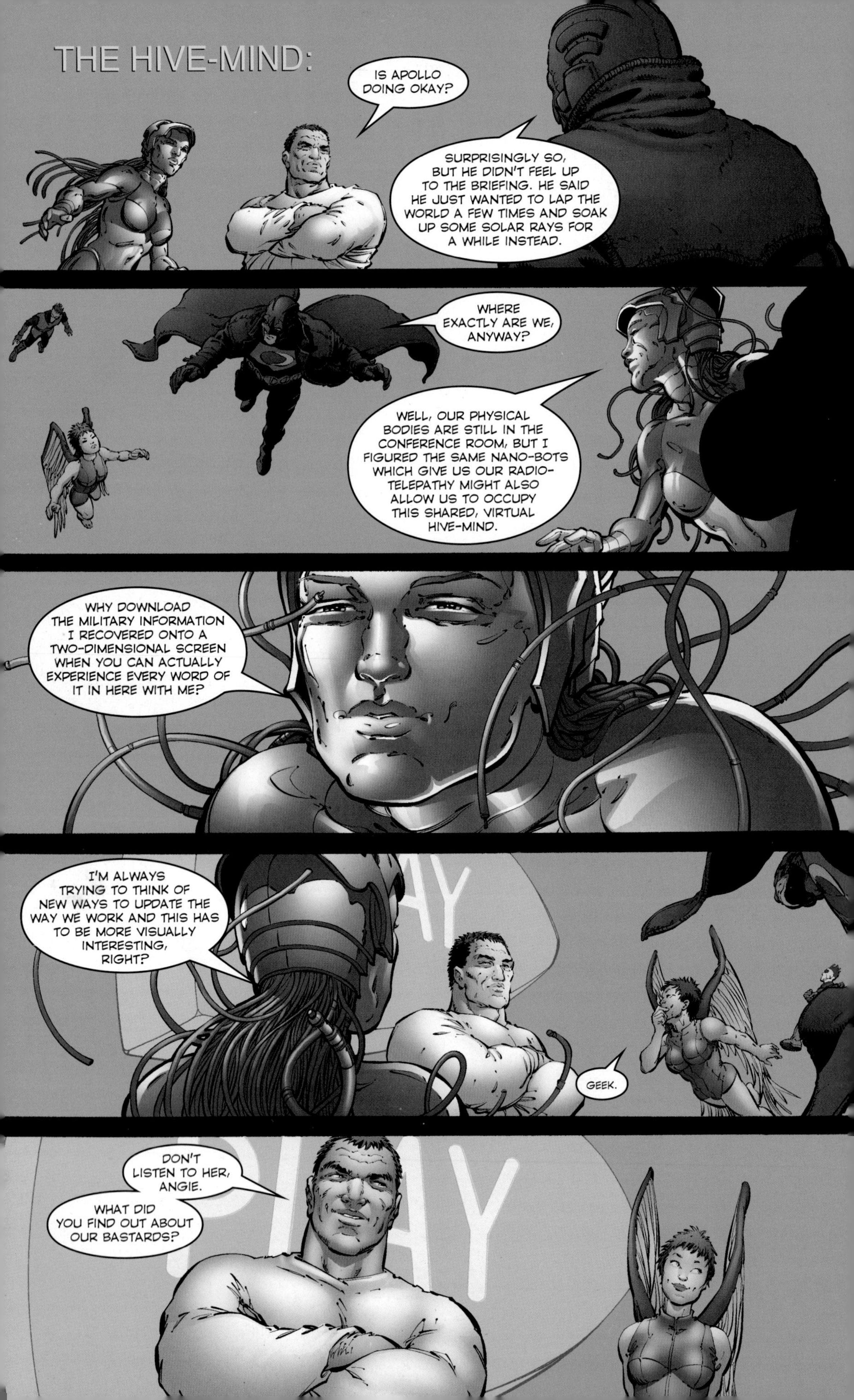
THE HIVE-MIND:
IS APOLLO DOING OKAY?
SURPRISINGLY SO, BUT HE DIDN'T FEEL UP TO THE BRIEFING. HE SAID HE JUST WANTED TO LAP THE WORLD A FEW TIMES AND SOAK UP SOME SOLAR RAYS FOR A WHILE INSTEAD.
WHERE EXACTLY ARE WE, ANYWAY?
WELL, OUR PHYSICAL BODIES ARE STILL IN THE CONFERENCE ROOM, BUT I FIGURED THE SAME NANO-BOTS WHICH GIVE US OUR RADIO-TELEPATHY MIGHT ALSO ALLOW US TO OCCUPY THIS SHARED, VIRTUAL HIVE-MIND.
WHY DOWNLOAD THE MILITARY INFORMATION I RECOVERED ONTO A TWO-DIMENSIONAL SCREEN WHEN YOU CAN ACTUALLY EXPERIENCE EVERY WORD OF IT IN HERE WITH ME?
I'M ALWAYS TRYING TO THINK OF NEW WAYS TO UPDATE THE WAY WE WORK AND THIS HAS TO BE MORE VISUALLY INTERESTING, RIGHT?
GEEK.
DON'T LISTEN TO HER, ANGIE.
WHAT DID YOU FIND OUT ABOUT OUR BASTARDS?

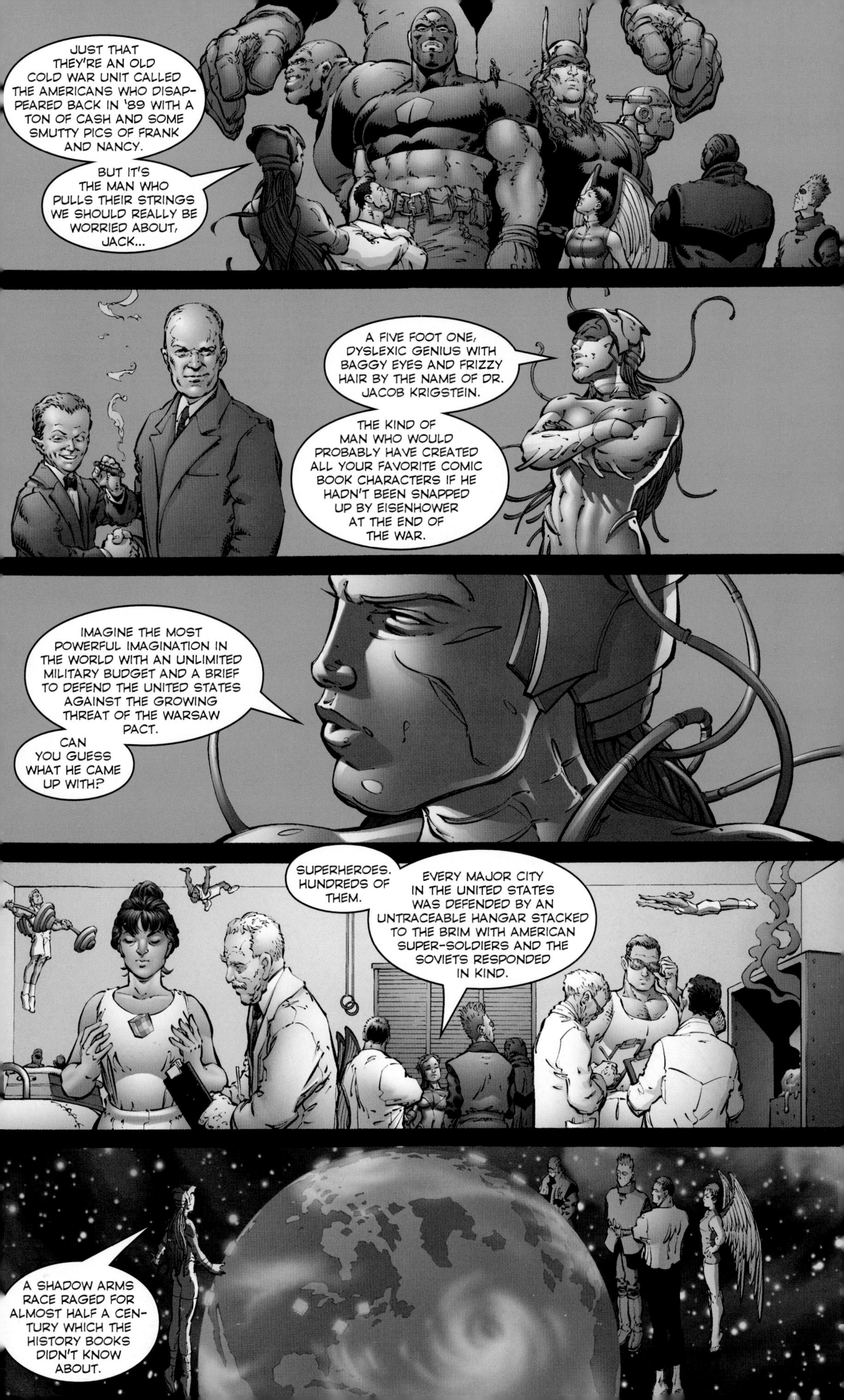
JUST THAT THEY'RE AN OLD COLD WAR UNIT CALLED THE AMERICANS WHO DISAPPEARED BACK IN '89 WITH A TON OF CASH AND SOME SMUTTY PICS OF FRANK AND NANCY.
BUT IT'S THE MAN WHO PULLS THEIR STRINGS WE SHOULD REALLY BE WORRIED ABOUT, JACK...
A FIVE FOOT ONE, DYSLEXIC GENIUS WITH BAGGY EYES AND FRIZZY HAIR BY THE NAME OF DR. JACOB KRIGSTEIN.
THE KIND OF MAN WHO WOULD PROBABLY HAVE CREATED ALL YOUR FAVORITE COMIC BOOK CHARACTERS IF HE HADN'T BEEN SNAPPED UP BY EISENHOWER AT THE END OF THE WAR.
IMAGINE THE MOST POWERFUL IMAGINATION IN THE WORLD WITH AN UNLIMITED MILITARY BUDGET AND A BRIEF TO DEFEND THE UNITED STATES AGAINST THE GROWING THREAT OF THE WARSAW PACT.
CAN YOU GUESS WHAT HE CAME UP WITH?
SUPERHEROES. HUNDREDS OF THEM.
EVERY MAJOR CITY IN THE UNITED STATES WAS DEFENDED BY AN UNTRACEABLE HANGAR STACKED TO THE BRIM WITH AMERICAN SUPER-SOLDIERS AND THE SOVIETS RESPONDED IN KIND.
A SHADOW ARMS RACE RAGED FOR ALMOST HALF A CENTURY WHICH THE HISTORY BOOKS DIDN'T KNOW ABOUT.

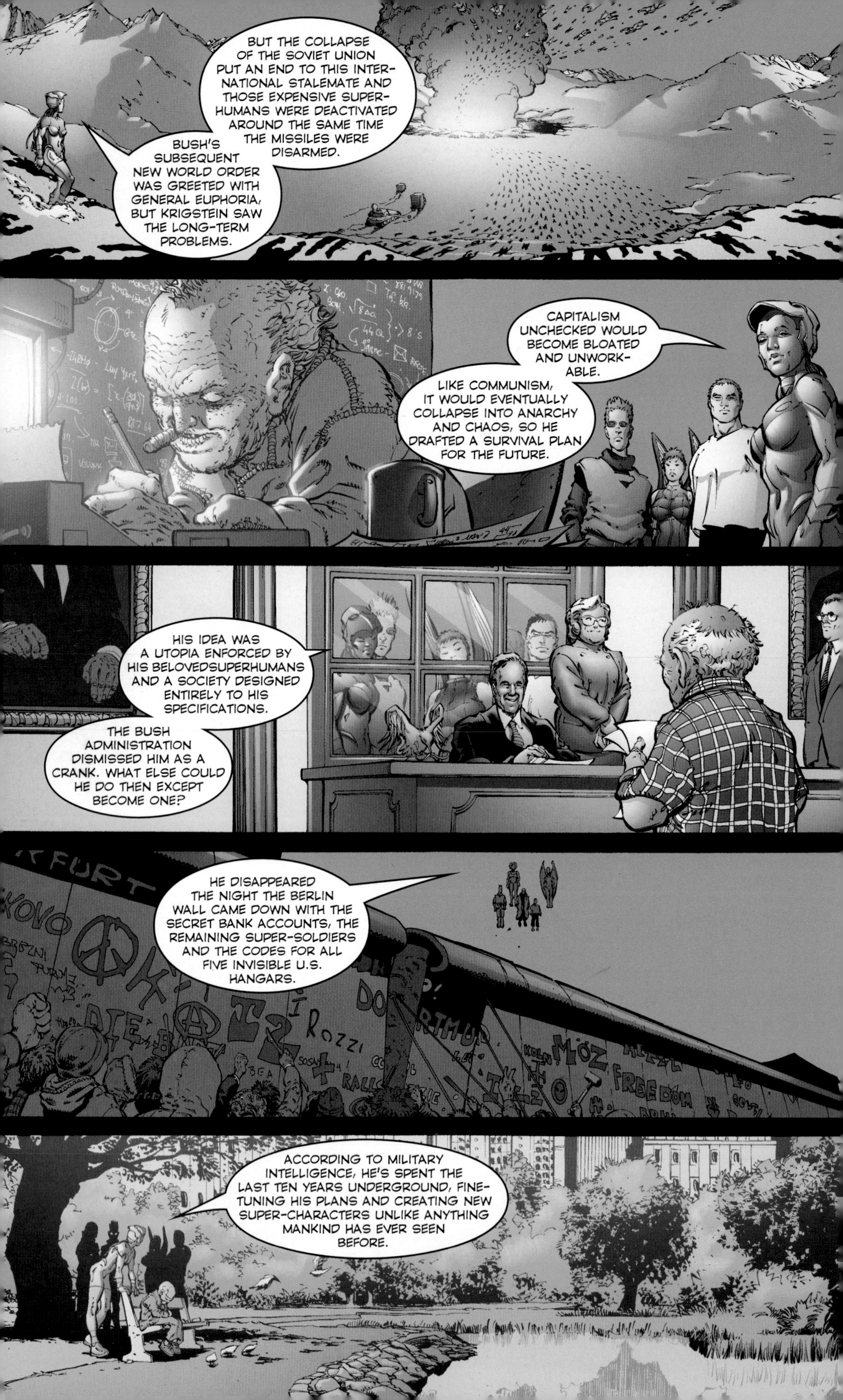
BUT THE COLLAPSE OF THE SOVIET UNION PUT AN END TO THIS INTER-NATIONAL STALEMATE AND THOSE EXPENSIVE SUPER-HUMANS WERE DEACTIVATED AROUND THE SAME TIME THE MISSILES WERE DISARMED.
BUSH'S SUBSEQUENT NEW WORLD ORDER WAS GREETED WITH GENERAL EUPHORIA, BUT KRIGSTEIN SAW THE LONG-TERM PROBLEMS.
CAPITALISM UNCHECKED WOULD BECOME BLOATED AND UNWORK-ABLE.
LIKE COMMUNISM, IT WOULD EVENTUALLY COLLAPSE INTO ANARCHY AND CHAOS, SO HE DRAFTED A SURVIVAL PLAN FOR THE FUTURE.
HIS IDEA WAS A UTOPIA ENFORCED BY HIS BELOVEDSUPERHUMANS AND A SOCIETY DESIGNED ENTIRELY TO HIS SPECIFICATIONS.
THE BUSH ADMINISTRATION DISMISSED HIM AS A CRANK. WHAT ELSE COULD HE DO THEN EXCEPT BECOME ONE?
HE DISAPPEARED THE NIGHT THE BERLIN WALL CAME DOWN WITH THE SECRET BANK ACCOUNTS, THE REMAINING SUPER-SOLDIERS AND THE CODES FOR ALL FIVE INVISIBLE U.S. HANGARS.
ACCORDING TO MILITARY INTELLIGENCE, HE'S SPENT THE LAST TEN YEARS UNDERGROUND, FINE-TUNING HIS PLANS AND CREATING NEW SUPER-CHARACTERS UNLIKE ANYTHING MANKIND HAS EVER SEEN BEFORE.

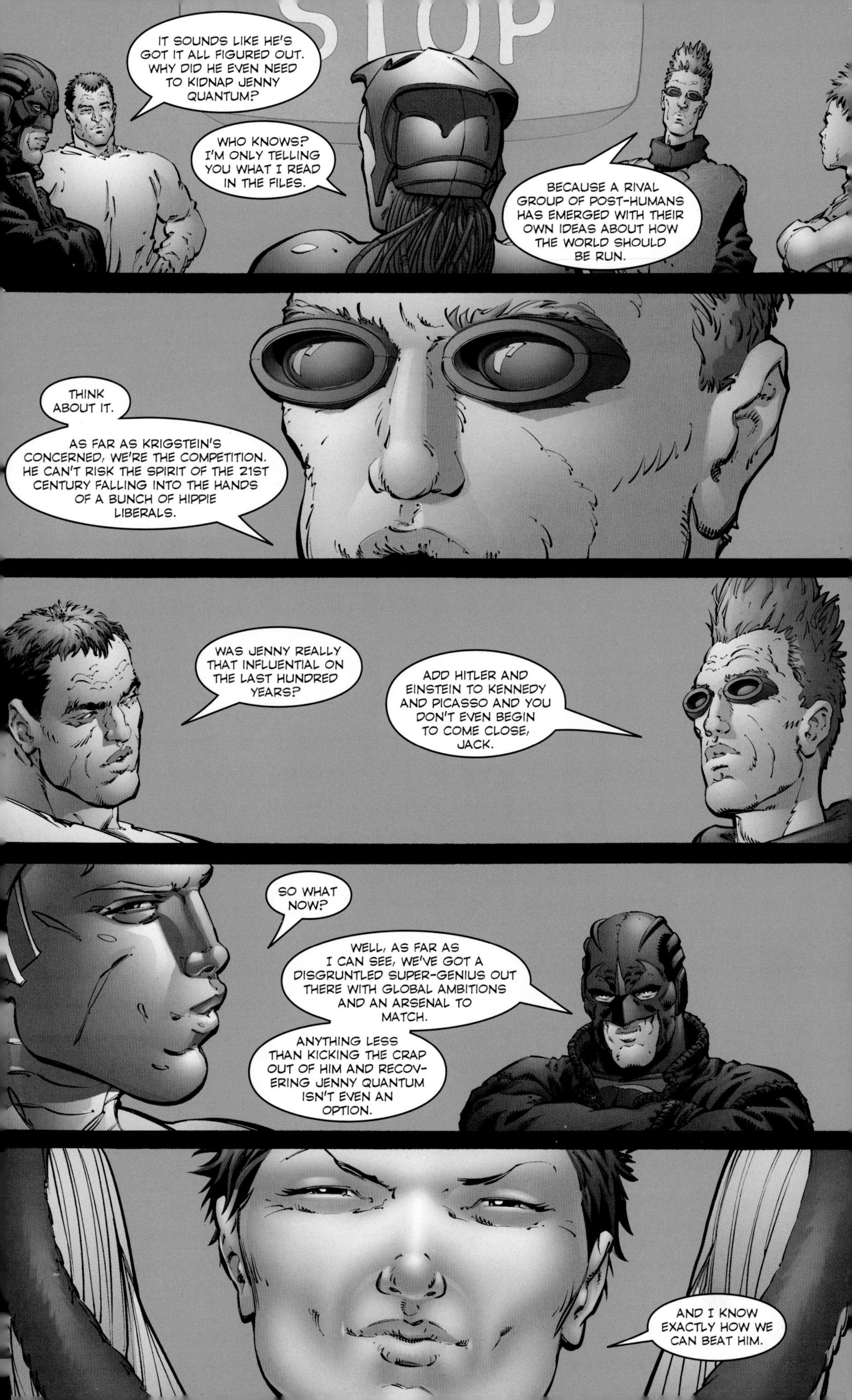
STOP
IT SOUNDS LIKE HE'S GOT IT ALL FIGURED OUT. WHY DID HE EVEN NEED TO KIDNAP JENNY QUANTUM?
WHO KNOWS? I'M ONLY TELLING YOU WHAT I READ IN THE FILES.
BECAUSE A RIVAL GROUP OF POST-HUMANS HAS EMERGED WITH THEIR OWN IDEAS ABOUT HOW THE WORLD SHOULD BE RUN.
THINK ABOUT IT.
AS FAR AS KRIGSTEIN'S CONCERNED, WE'RE THE COMPETITION. HE CAN'T RISK THE SPIRIT OF THE 21ST CENTURY FALLING INTO THE HANDS OF A BUNCH OF HIPPIE LIBERALS.
WAS JENNY REALLY THAT INFLUENTIAL ON THE LAST HUNDRED YEARS?
ADD HITLER AND EINSTEIN TO KENNEDY AND PICASSO AND YOU DON'T EVEN BEGIN TO COME CLOSE, JACK.
SO WHAT NOW?
WELL, AS FAR AS I CAN SEE, WE'VE GOT A DISGRUNTLED SUPER-GENIUS OUT THERE WITH GLOBAL AMBITIONS AND AN ARSENAL TO MATCH.
ANYTHING LESS THAN KICKING THE CRAP OUT OF HIM AND RECOV-ERING JENNY QUANTUM ISN'T EVEN AN OPTION.
AND I KNOW EXACTLY HOW WE CAN BEAT HIM.

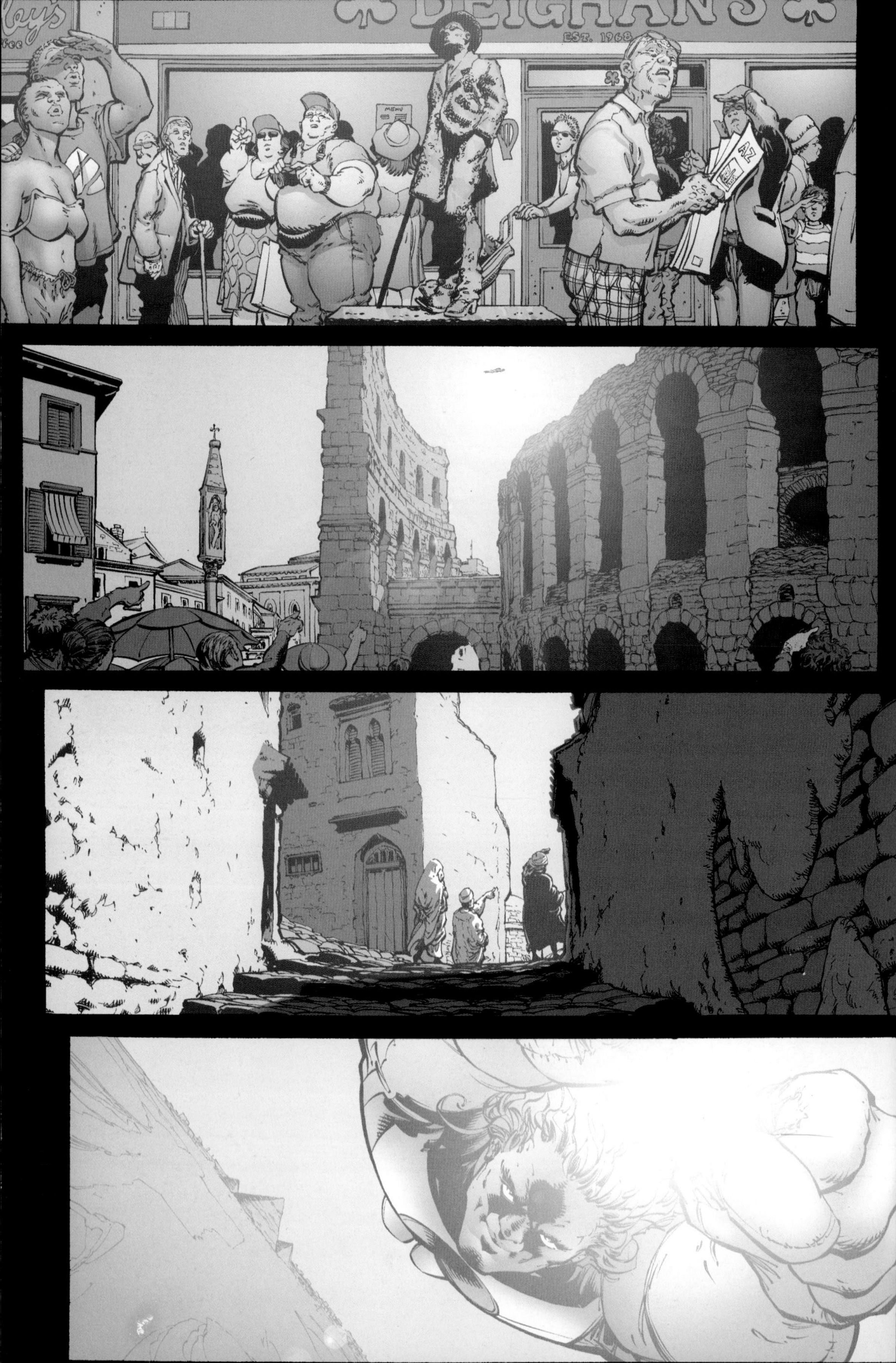
DEIGHAN'S
EST. 1968
MENU
AZ

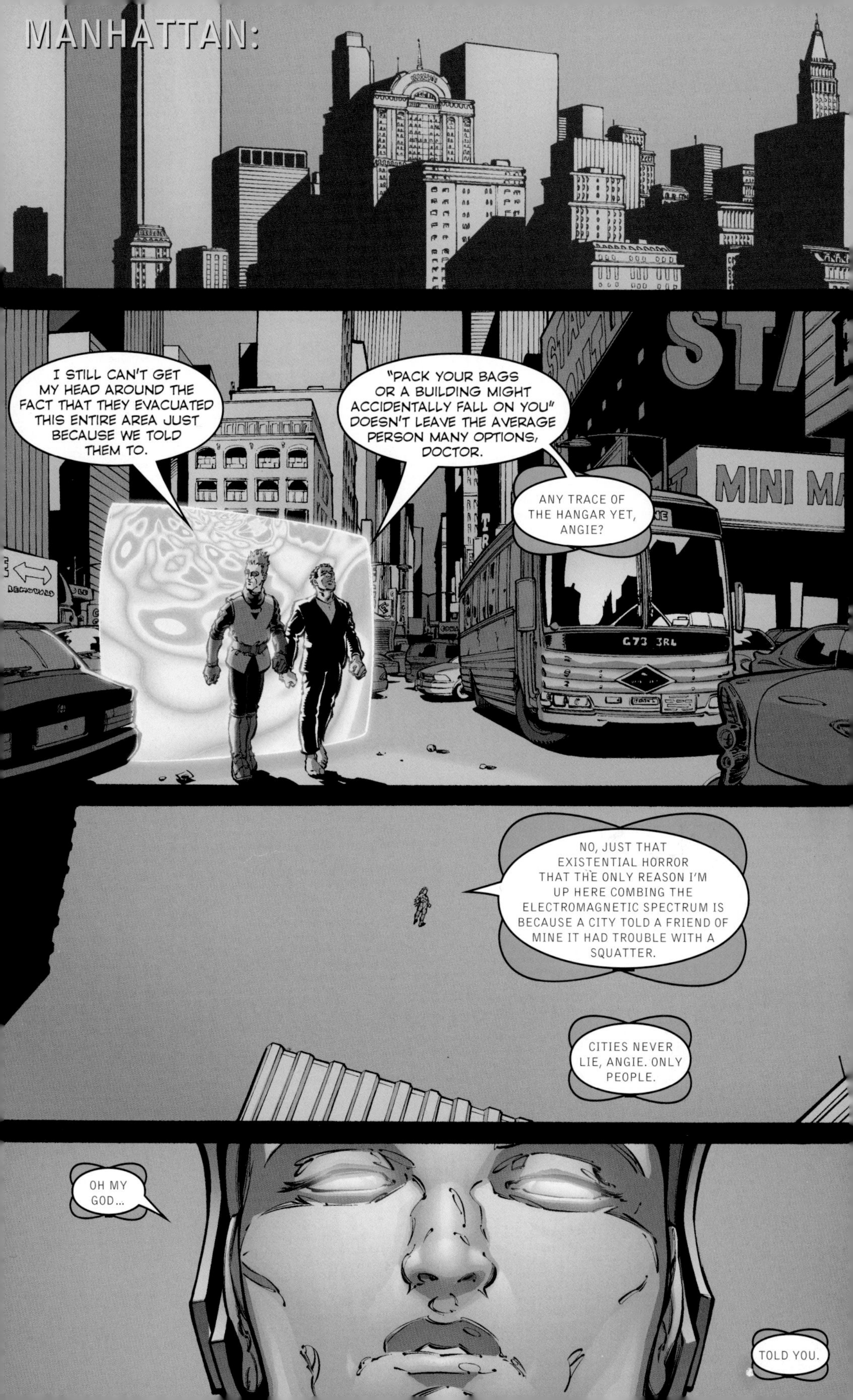
MANHATTAN:
I STILL CAN'T GET MY HEAD AROUND THE FACT THAT THEY EVACUATED THIS ENTIRE AREA JUST BECAUSE WE TOLD THEM TO.
"PACK YOUR BAGS OR A BUILDING MIGHT ACCIDENTALLY FALL ON YOU" DOESN'T LEAVE THE AVERAGE PERSON MANY OPTIONS, DOCTOR.
ANY TRACE OF THE HANGAR YET, ANGIE?
MINI MA
G73 3RL
NO, JUST THAT EXISTENTIAL HORROR THAT THE ONLY REASON I'M UP HERE COMBING THE ELECTROMAGNETIC SPECTRUM IS BECAUSE A CITY TOLD A FRIEND OF MINE IT HAD TROUBLE WITH A SQUATTER.
CITIES NEVER LIE, ANGIE. ONLY PEOPLE.
OH MY GOD...
TOLD YOU.

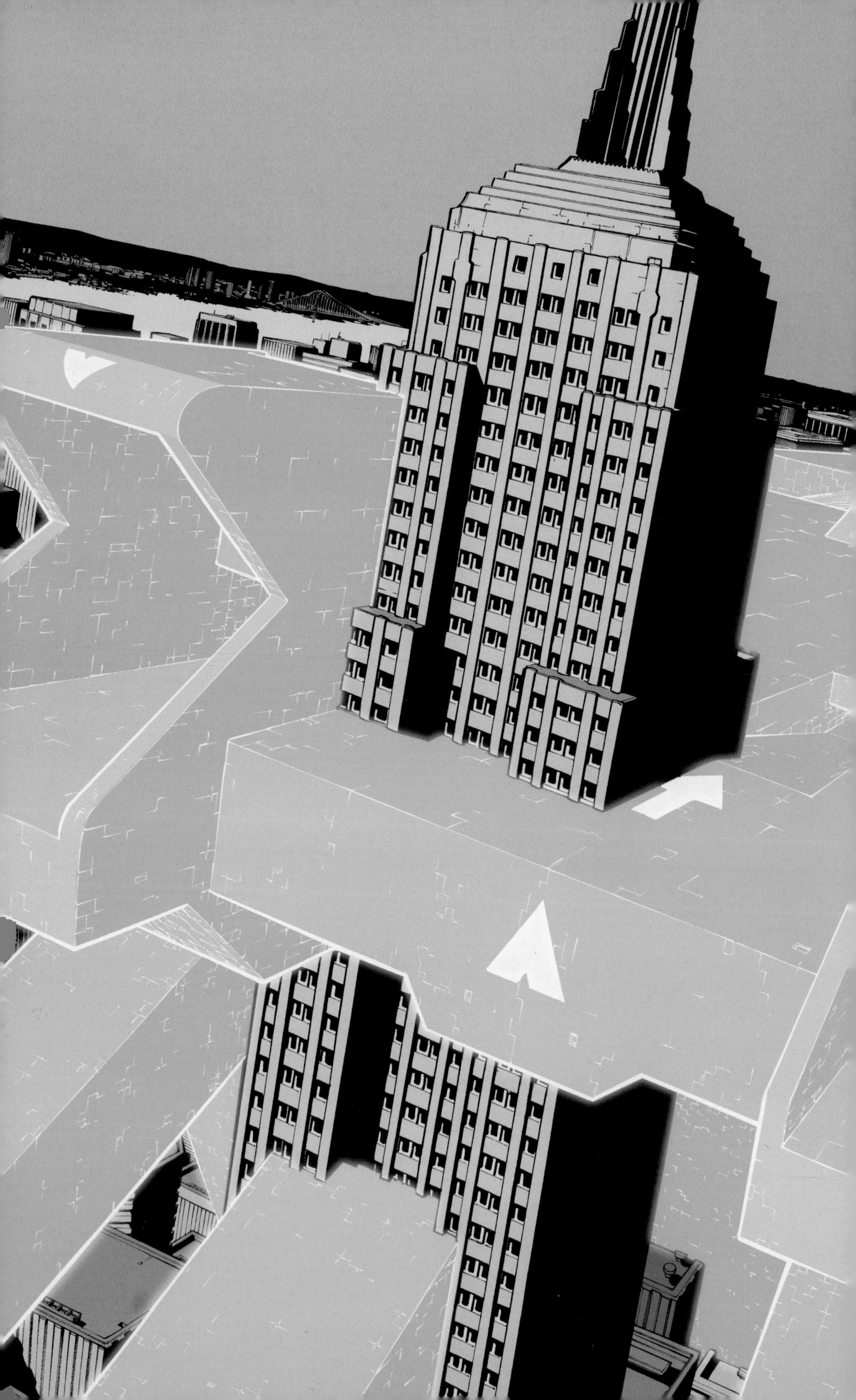

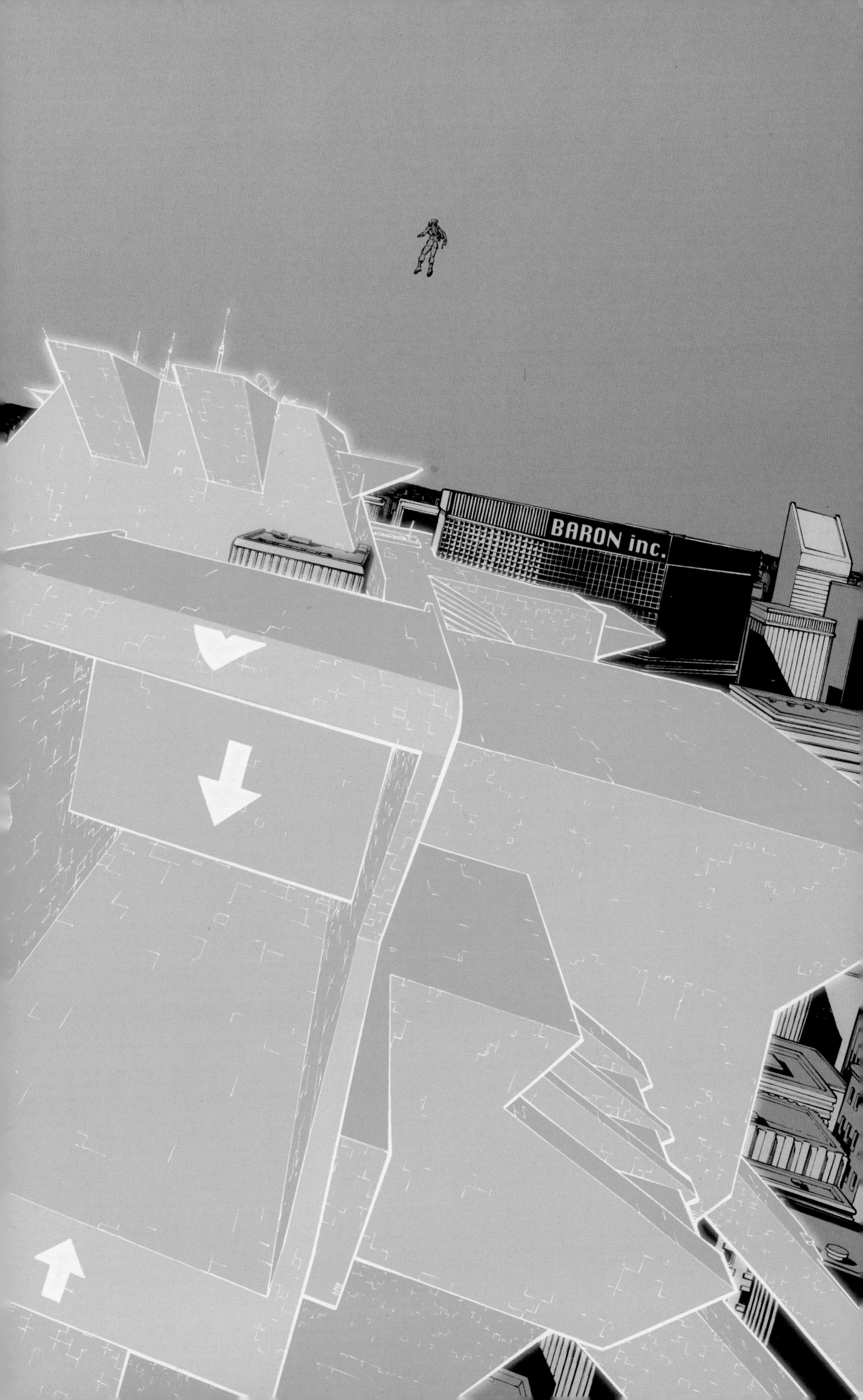
BARON inc.

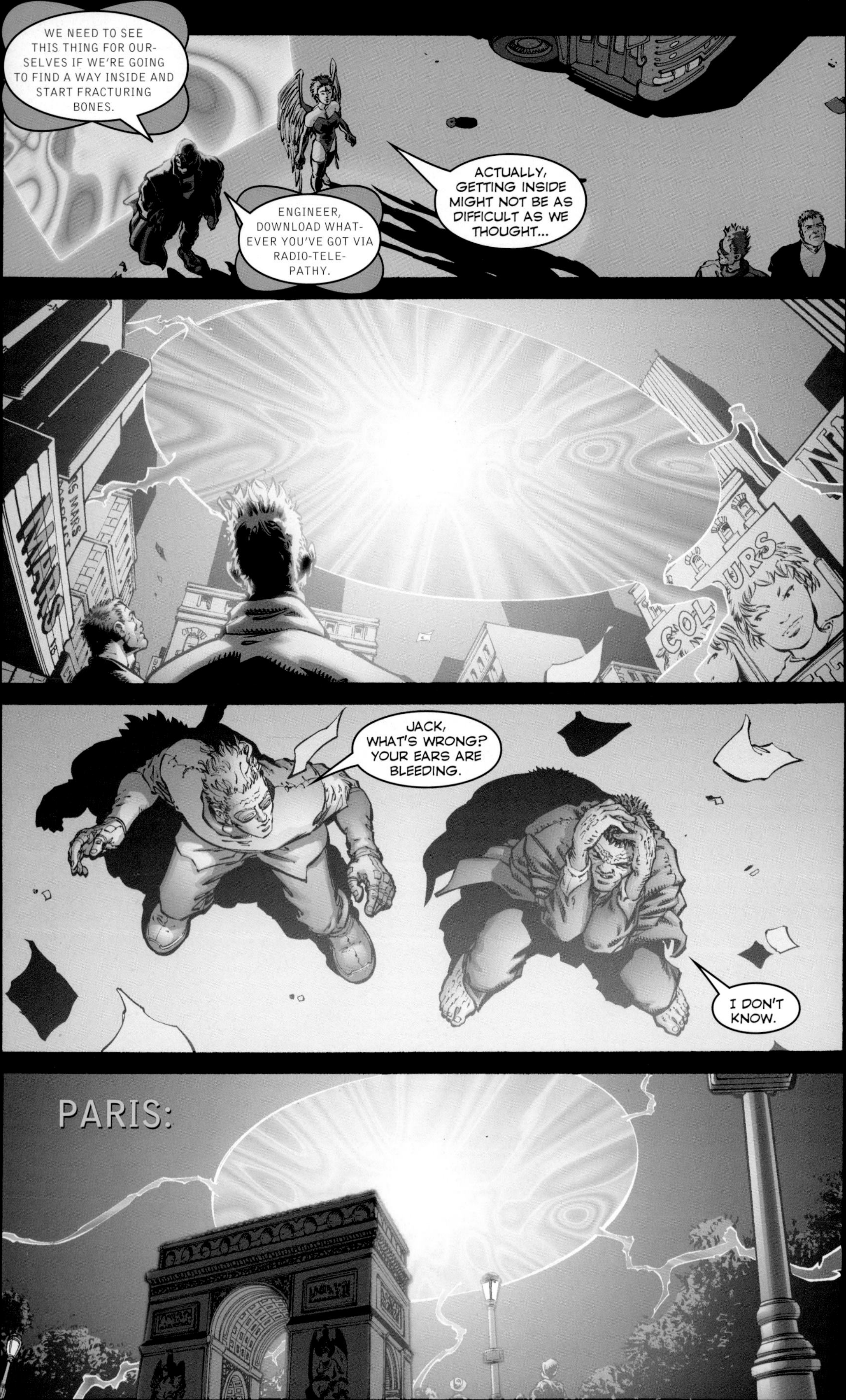

WE NEED TO SEE THIS THING FOR OUR-SELVES IF WE'RE GOING TO FIND A WAY INSIDE AND START FRACTURING BONES.
ENGINEER, DOWNLOAD WHAT-EVER YOU'VE GOT VIA RADIO-TELE-PATHY.
ACTUALLY, GETTING INSIDE MIGHT NOT BE AS DIFFICULT AS WE THOUGHT...
JACK, WHAT'S WRONG? YOUR EARS ARE BLEEDING.
I DON'T KNOW.
PARIS:

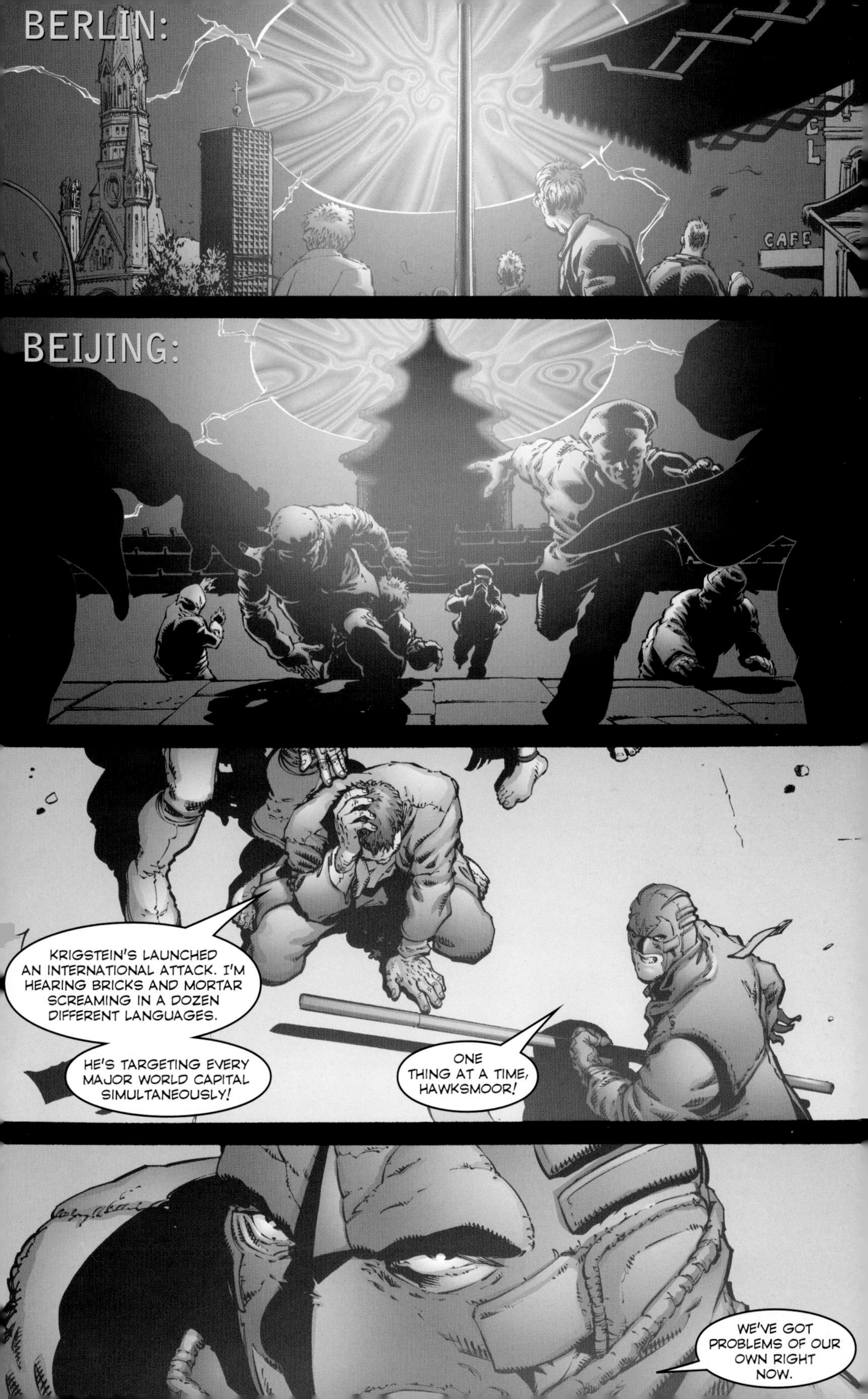
BERLIN:
CAFE
BEIJING:
KRIGSTEIN'S LAUNCHED AN INTERNATIONAL ATTACK. I'M HEARING BRICKS AND MORTAR SCREAMING IN A DOZEN DIFFERENT LANGUAGES.
HE'S TARGETING EVERY MAJOR WORLD CAPITAL SIMULTANEOUSLY!
ONE THING AT A TIME, HAWKSMOOR!
WE'VE GOT PROBLEMS OF OUR OWN RIGHT NOW.

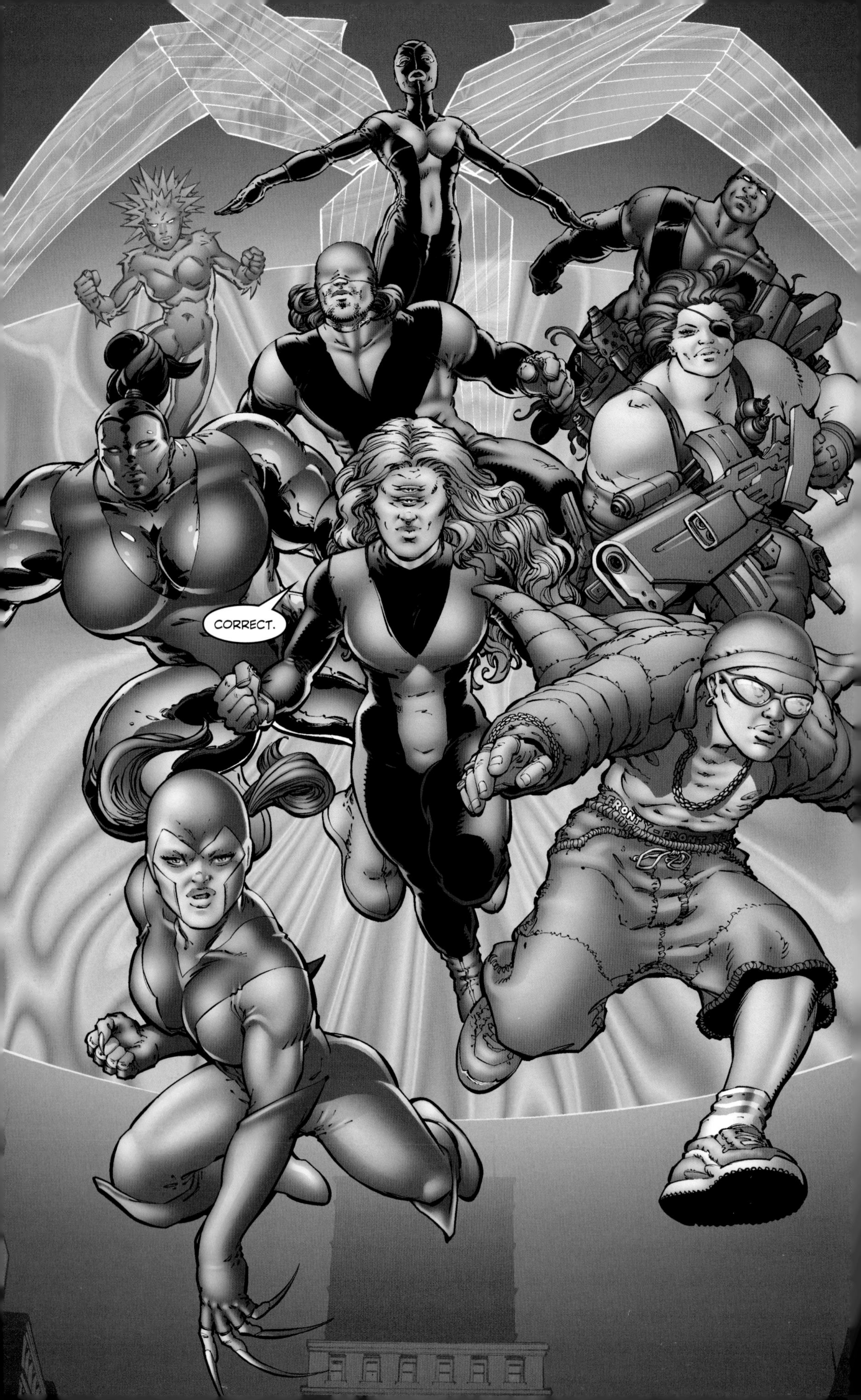
CORRECT.

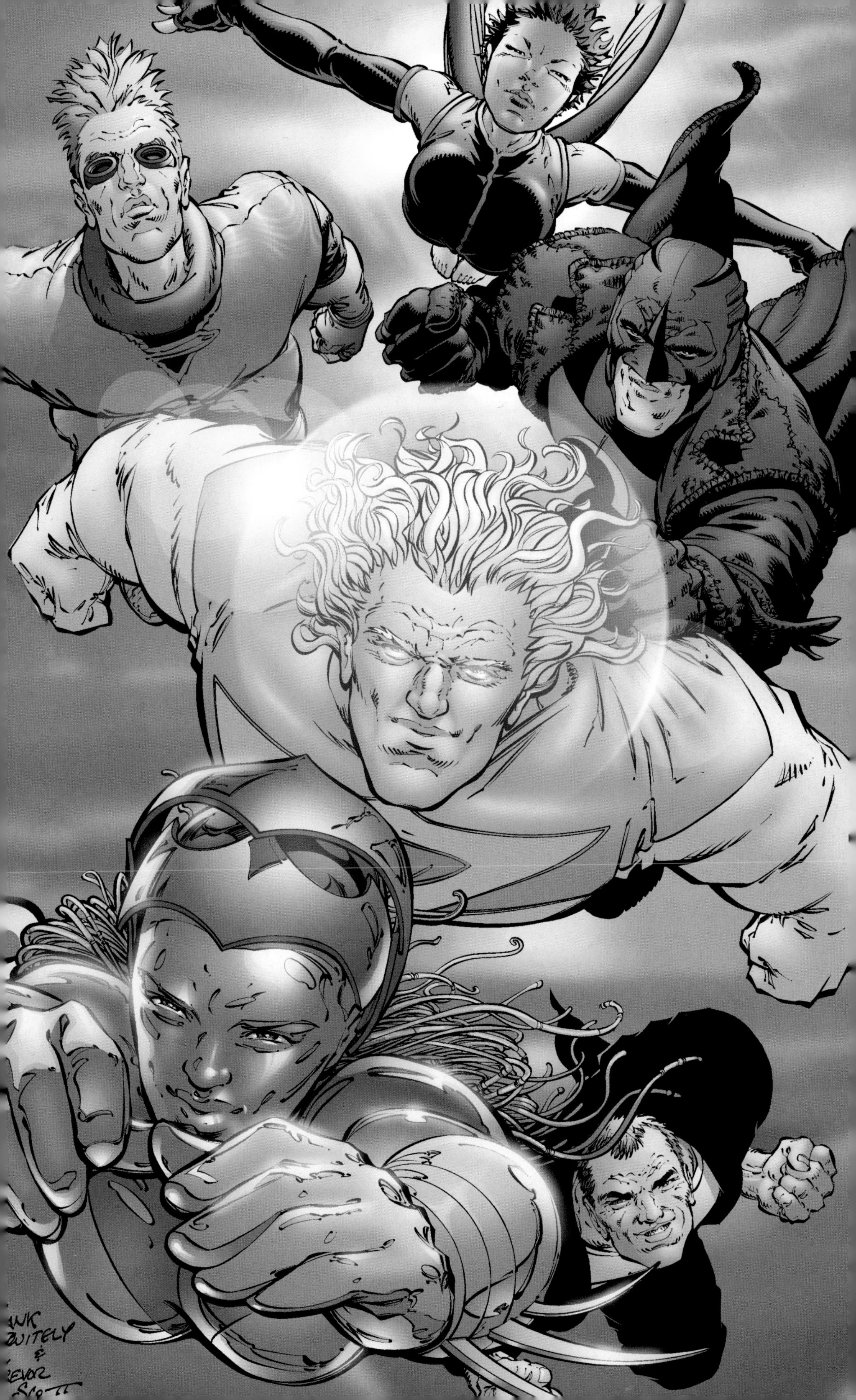

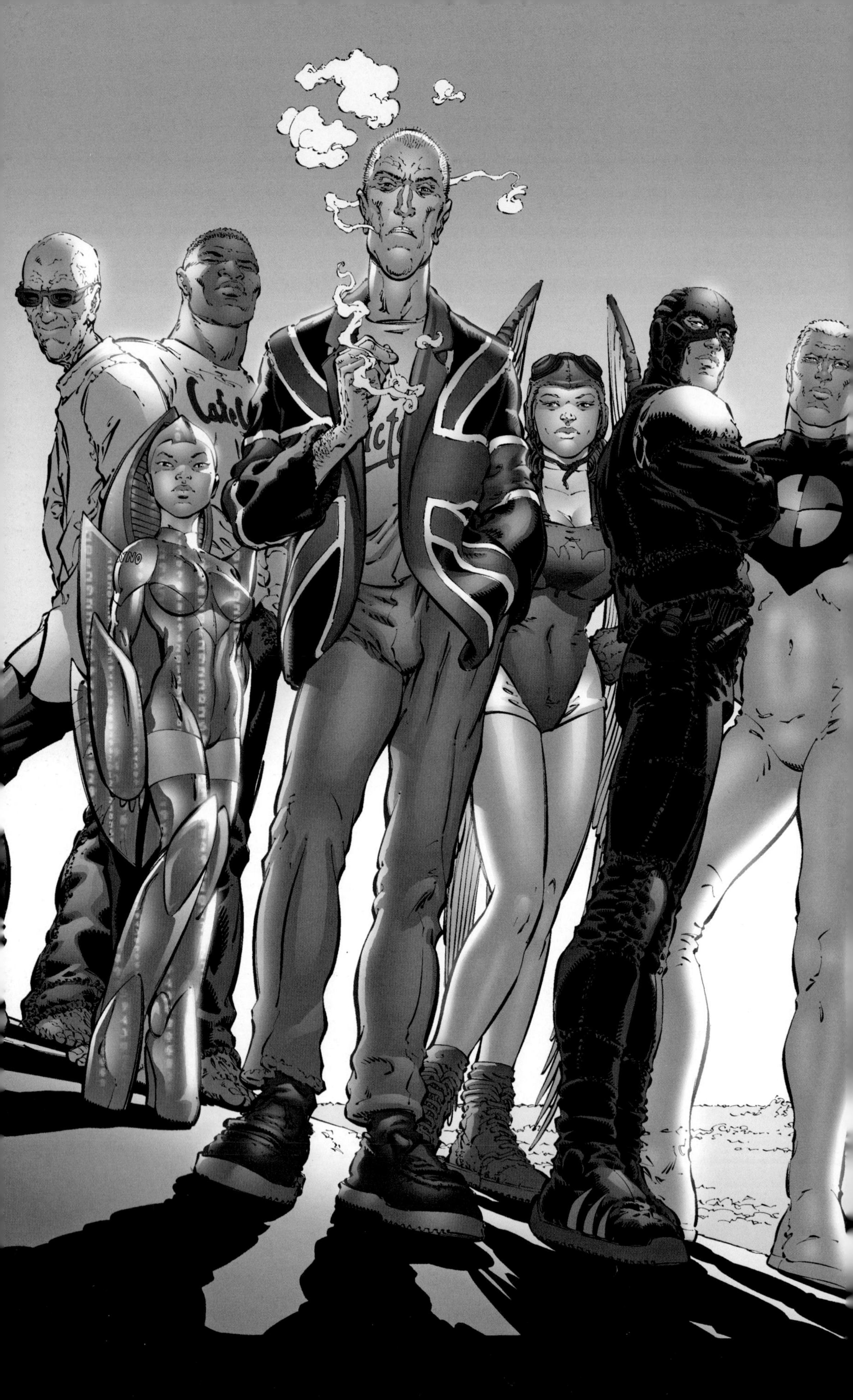

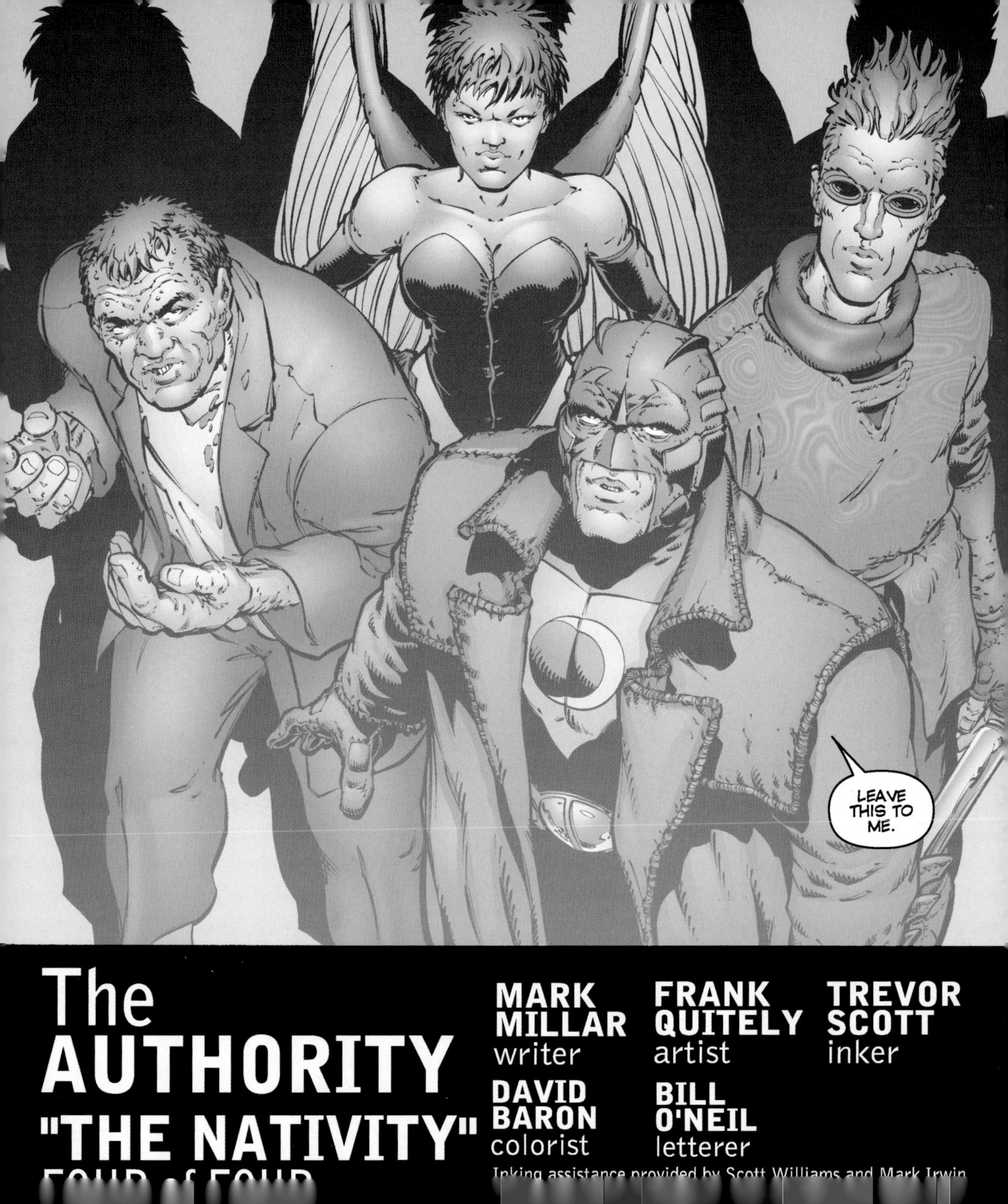
LEAVE THIS TO ME.

The AUTHORITY "THE NATIVITY" FOUR of FOUR

MARK MILLAR writer
FRANK QUITELY artist
TREVOR SCOTT inker
DAVID BARON colorist
BILL O'NEIL letterer

Inking assistance provided by Scott Williams and Mark Irwin

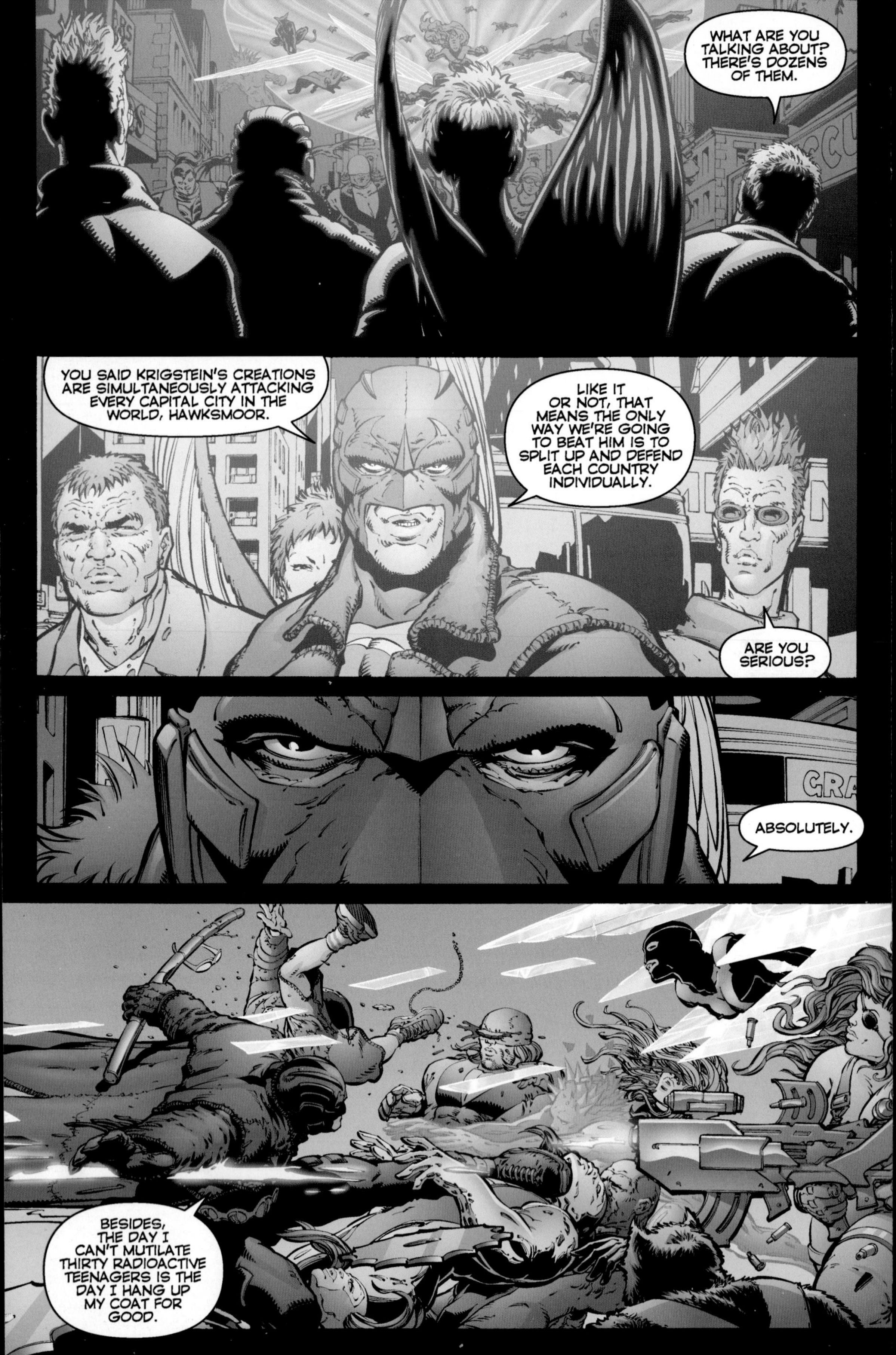

WHAT ARE YOU TALKING ABOUT? THERE'S DOZENS OF THEM.
YOU SAID KRIGSTEIN'S CREATIONS ARE SIMULTANEOUSLY ATTACKING EVERY CAPITAL CITY IN THE WORLD, HAWKSMOOR.
LIKE IT OR NOT, THAT MEANS THE ONLY WAY WE'RE GOING TO BEAT HIM IS TO SPLIT UP AND DEFEND EACH COUNTRY INDIVIDUALLY.
ARE YOU SERIOUS?
ABSOLUTELY.
BESIDES, THE DAY I CAN'T MUTILATE THIRTY RADIOACTIVE TEENAGERS IS THE DAY I HANG UP MY COAT FOR GOOD.

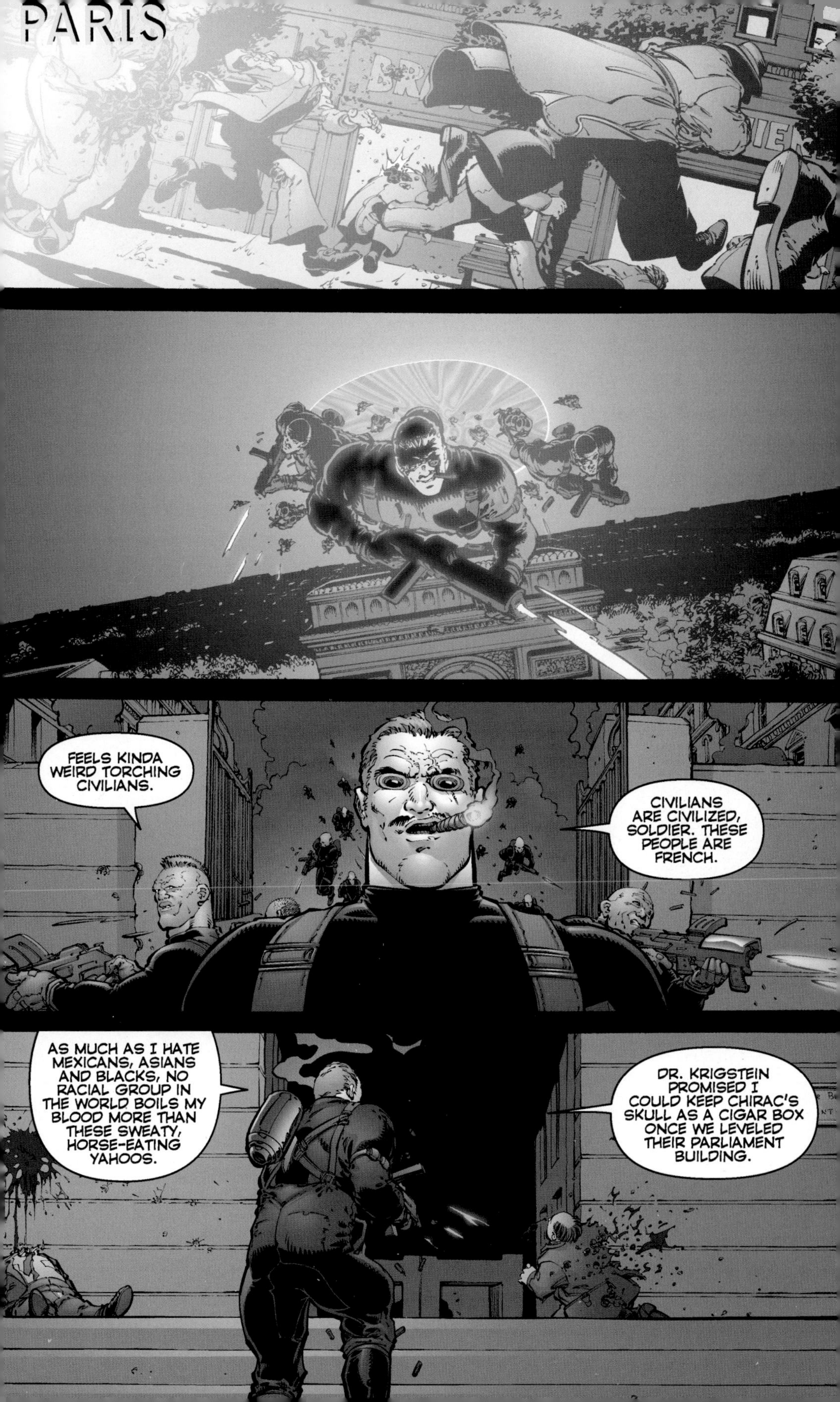

PARIS
FEELS KINDA WEIRD TORCHING CIVILIANS.
CIVILIANS ARE CIVILIZED, SOLDIER. THESE PEOPLE ARE FRENCH.
AS MUCH AS I HATE MEXICANS, ASIANS AND BLACKS, NO RACIAL GROUP IN THE WORLD BOILS MY BLOOD MORE THAN THESE SWEATY, HORSE-EATING YAHOOS.
DR. KRIGSTEIN PROMISED I COULD KEEP CHIRAC'S SKULL AS A CIGAR BOX ONCE WE LEVELED THEIR PARLIAMENT BUILDING.

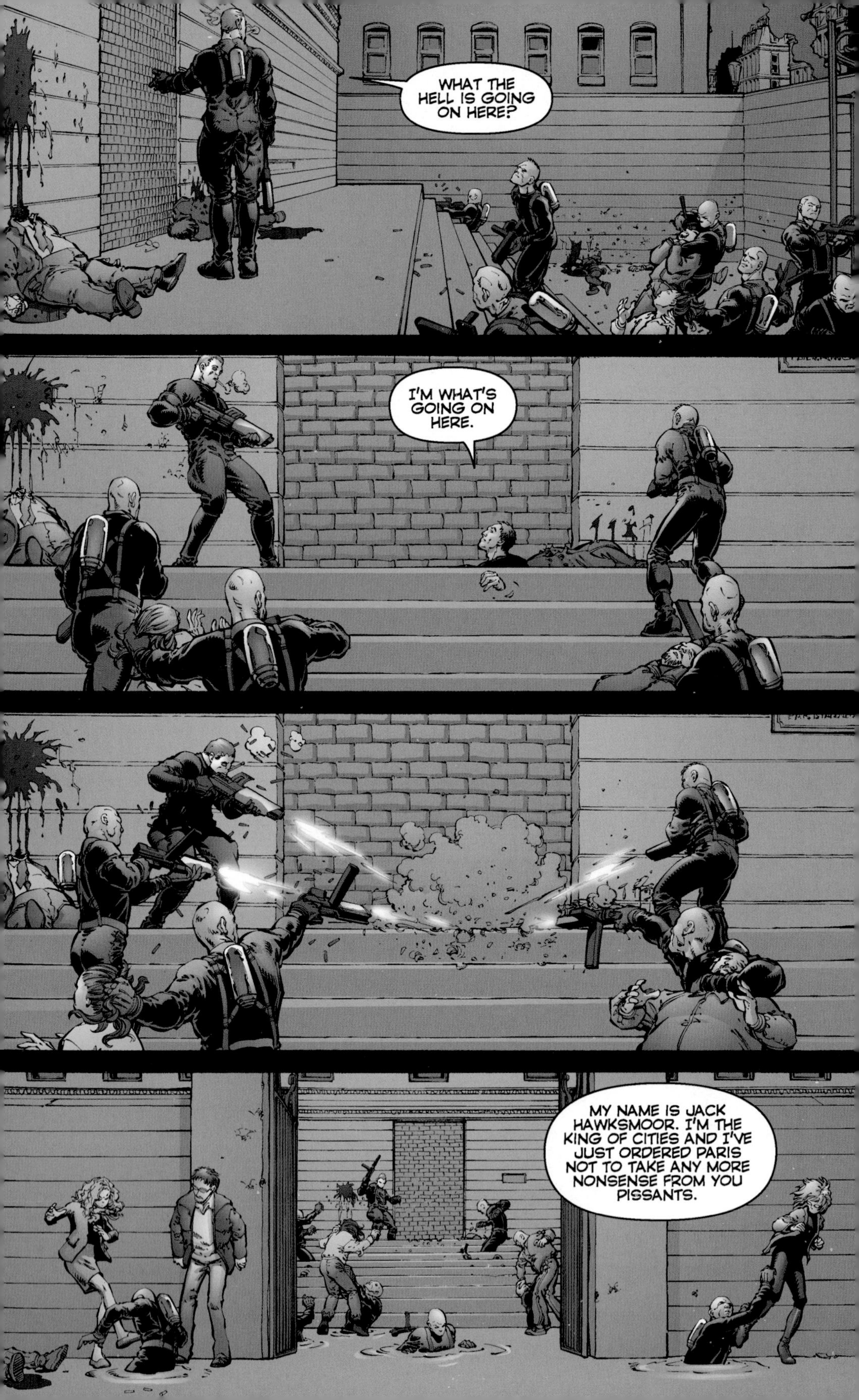
WHAT THE HELL IS GOING ON HERE?
I'M WHAT'S GOING ON HERE.
MY NAME IS JACK HAWKSMOOR. I'M THE KING OF CITIES AND I'VE JUST ORDERED PARIS NOT TO TAKE ANY MORE NONSENSE FROM YOU PISSANTS.

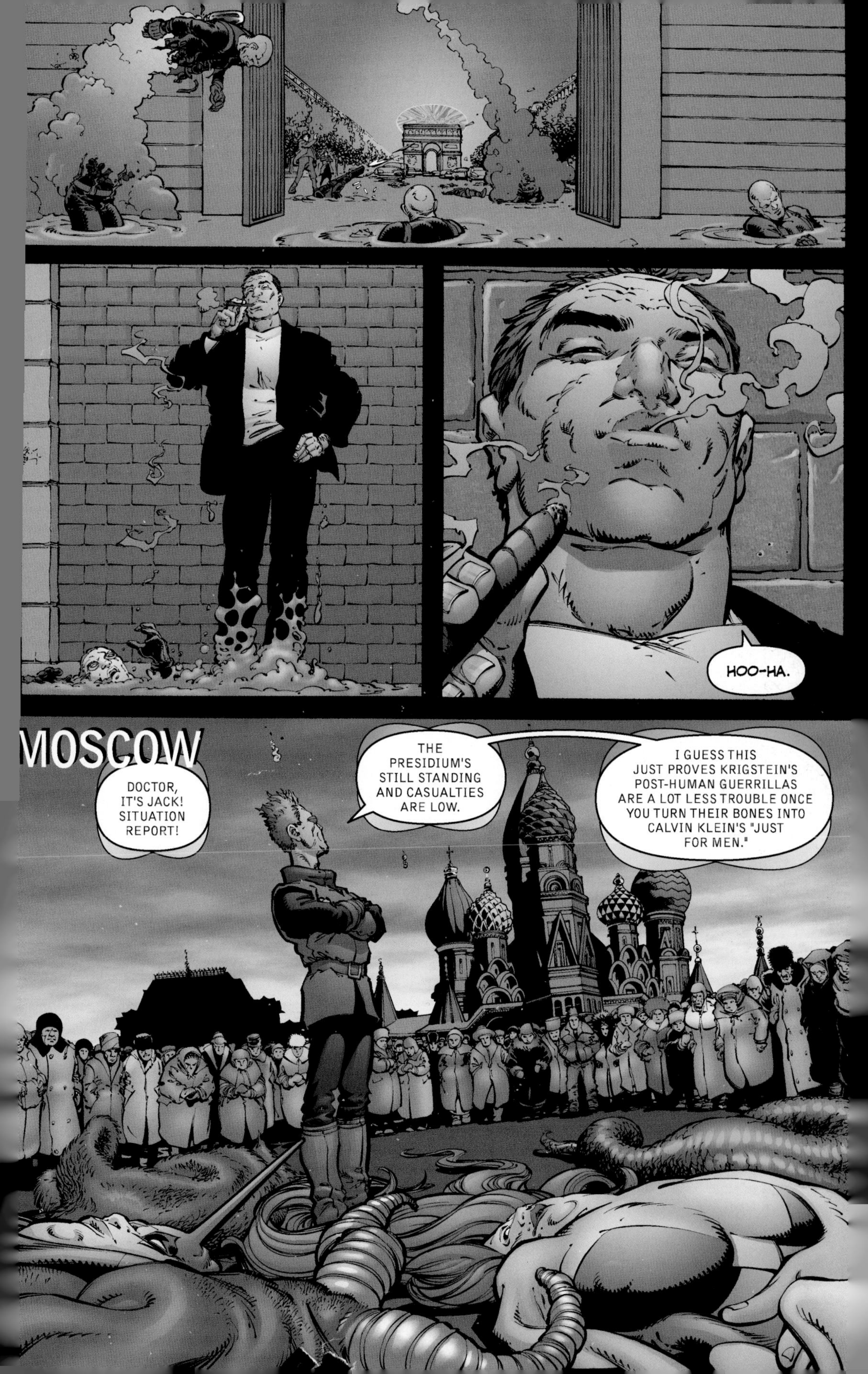
HOO-HA.
MOSCOW
DOCTOR, IT'S JACK! SITUATION REPORT!
THE PRESIDIUM'S STILL STANDING AND CASUALTIES ARE LOW.
I GUESS THIS JUST PROVES KRIGSTEIN'S POST-HUMAN GUERRILLAS ARE A LOT LESS TROUBLE ONCE YOU TURN THEIR BONES INTO CALVIN KLEIN'S "JUST FOR MEN."

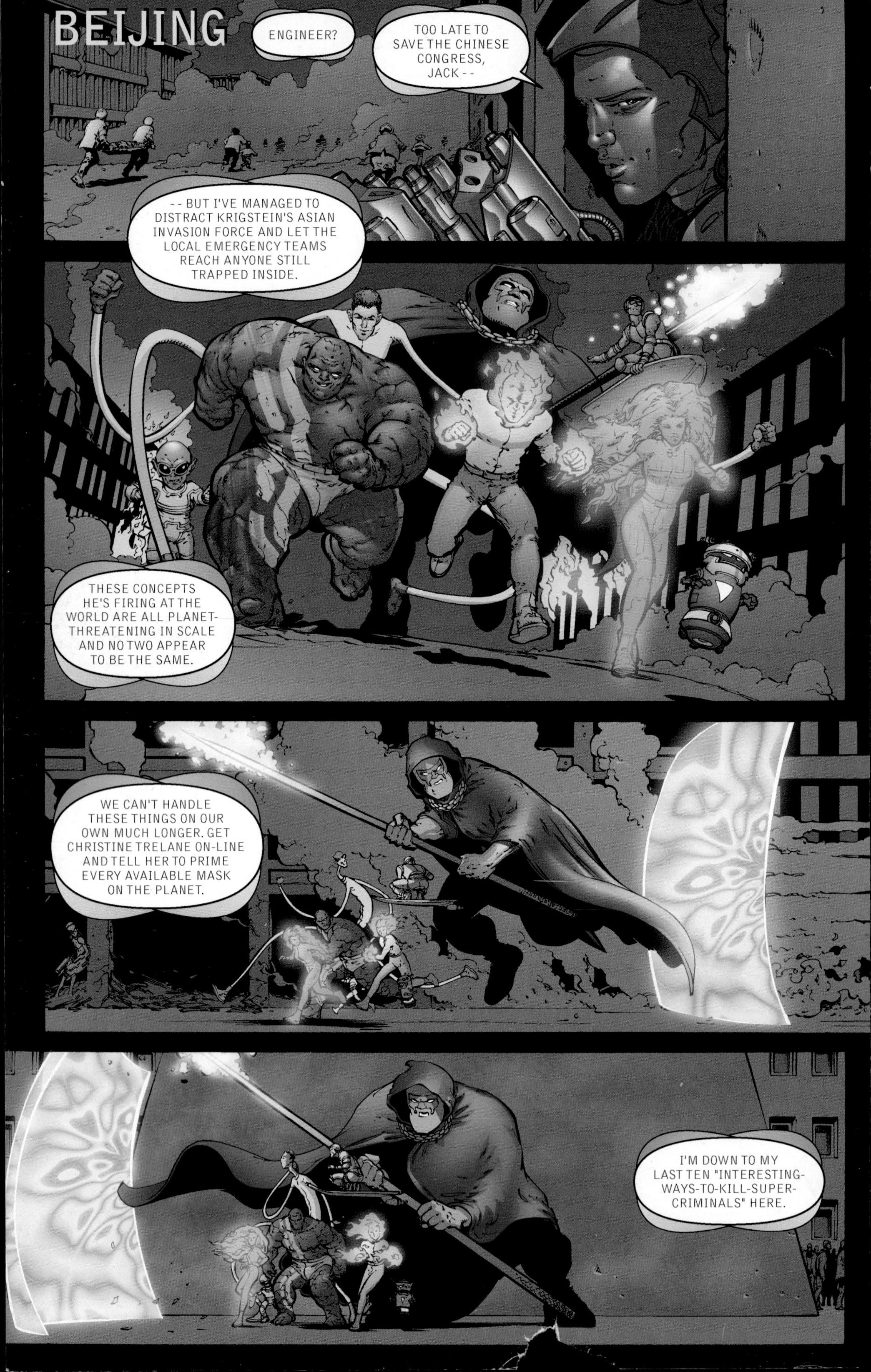
BEIJING
ENGINEER?
TOO LATE TO SAVE THE CHINESE CONGRESS, JACK - -
- - BUT I'VE MANAGED TO DISTRACT KRIGSTEIN'S ASIAN INVASION FORCE AND LET THE LOCAL EMERGENCY TEAMS REACH ANYONE STILL TRAPPED INSIDE.
THESE CONCEPTS HE'S FIRING AT THE WORLD ARE ALL PLANET-THREATENING IN SCALE AND NO TWO APPEAR TO BE THE SAME.
WE CAN'T HANDLE THESE THINGS ON OUR OWN MUCH LONGER. GET CHRISTINE TRELANE ON-LINE AND TELL HER TO PRIME EVERY AVAILABLE MASK ON THE PLANET.
I'M DOWN TO MY LAST TEN "INTERESTING-WAYS-TO-KILL-SUPER-CRIMINALS" HERE.

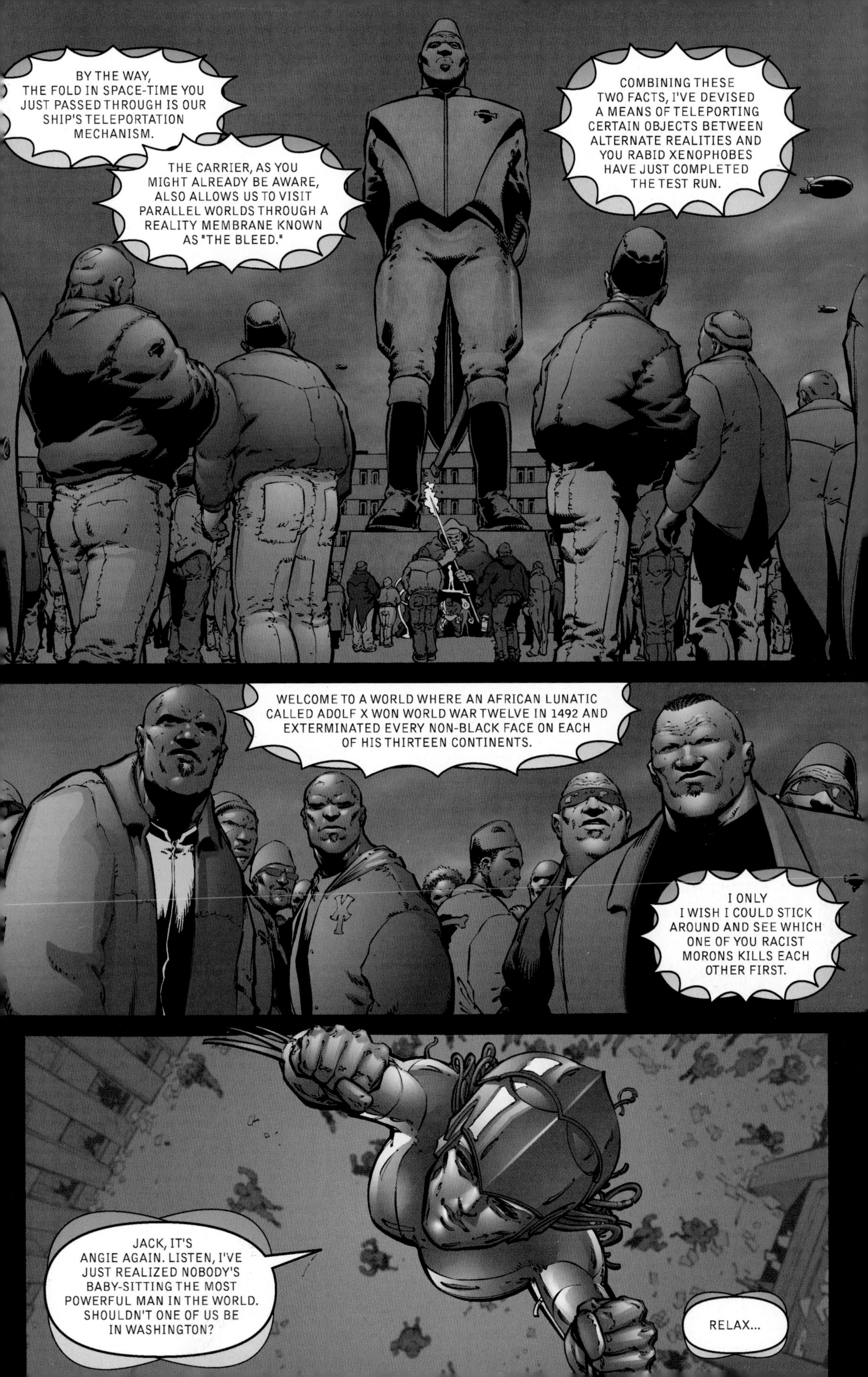
BY THE WAY, THE FOLD IN SPACE-TIME YOU JUST PASSED THROUGH IS OUR SHIP'S TELEPORTATION MECHANISM.
THE CARRIER, AS YOU MIGHT ALREADY BE AWARE, ALSO ALLOWS US TO VISIT PARALLEL WORLDS THROUGH A REALITY MEMBRANE KNOWN AS "THE BLEED."
COMBINING THESE TWO FACTS, I'VE DEVISED A MEANS OF TELEPORTING CERTAIN OBJECTS BETWEEN ALTERNATE REALITIES AND YOU RABID XENOPHOBES HAVE JUST COMPLETED THE TEST RUN.
WELCOME TO A WORLD WHERE AN AFRICAN LUNATIC CALLED ADOLF X WON WORLD WAR TWELVE IN 1492 AND EXTERMINATED EVERY NON-BLACK FACE ON EACH OF HIS THIRTEEN CONTINENTS.
I ONLY I WISH I COULD STICK AROUND AND SEE WHICH ONE OF YOU RACIST MORONS KILLS EACH OTHER FIRST.
JACK, IT'S ANGIE AGAIN. LISTEN, I'VE JUST REALIZED NOBODY'S BABY-SITTING THE MOST POWERFUL MAN IN THE WORLD. SHOULDN'T ONE OF US BE IN WASHINGTON?
RELAX...

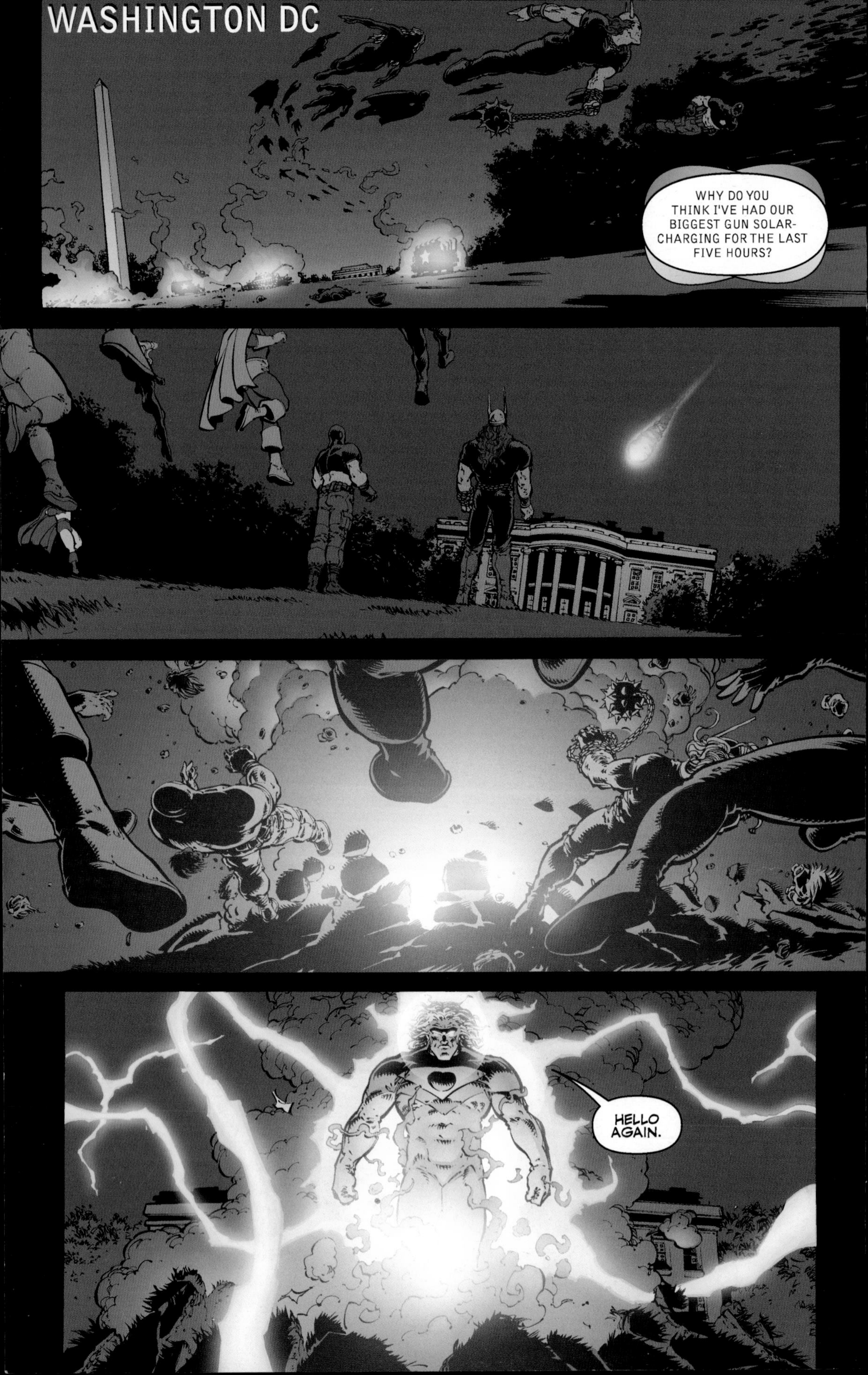
WASHINGTON DC
WHY DO YOU THINK I'VE HAD OUR BIGGEST GUN SOLAR-CHARGING FOR THE LAST FIVE HOURS?
HELLO AGAIN.

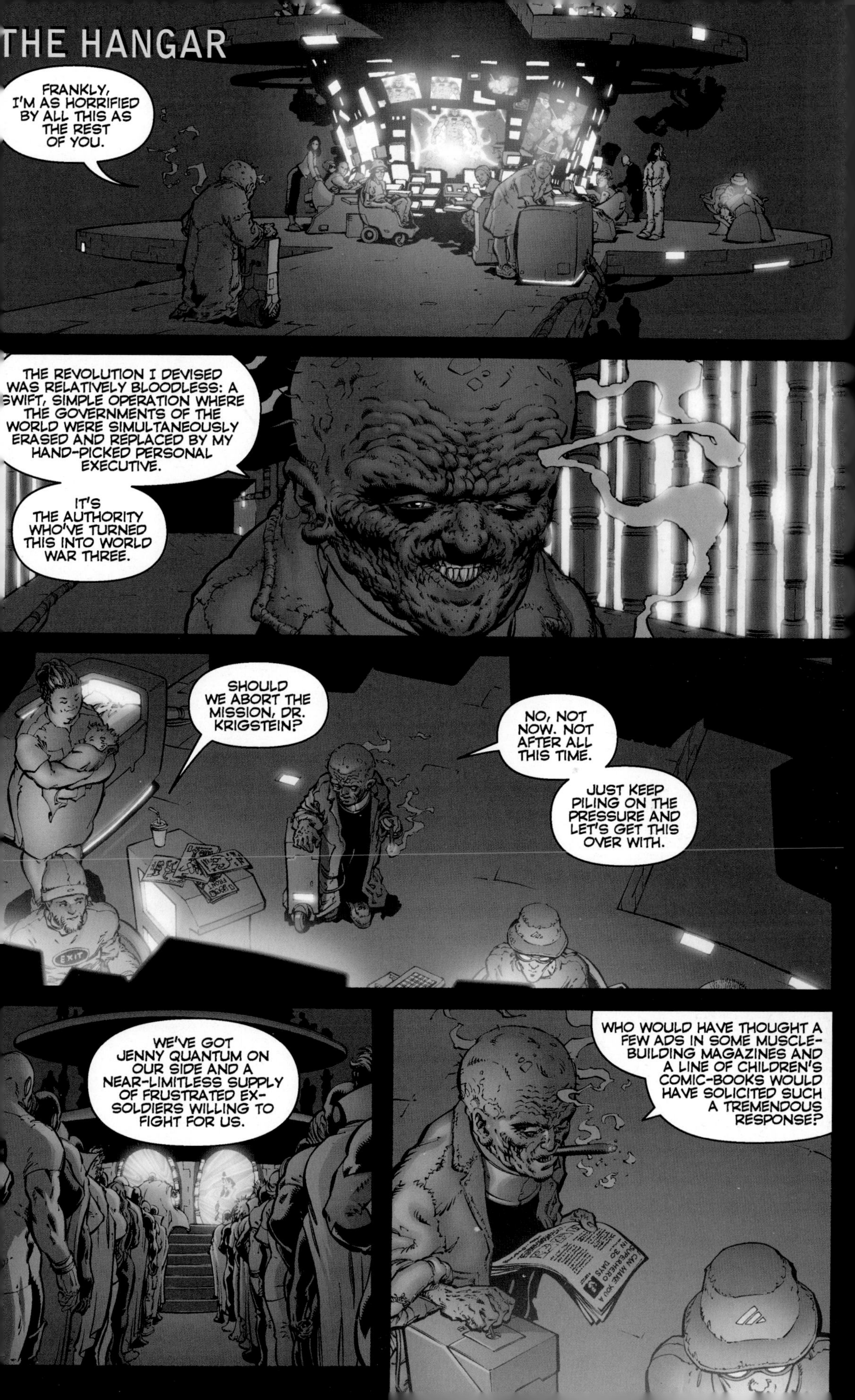
THE HANGAR
FRANKLY, I'M AS HORRIFIED BY ALL THIS AS THE REST OF YOU.
THE REVOLUTION I DEVISED WAS RELATIVELY BLOODLESS: A SWIFT, SIMPLE OPERATION WHERE THE GOVERNMENTS OF THE WORLD WERE SIMULTANEOUSLY ERASED AND REPLACED BY MY HAND-PICKED PERSONAL EXECUTIVE.
IT'S THE AUTHORITY WHO'VE TURNED THIS INTO WORLD WAR THREE.
SHOULD WE ABORT THE MISSION, DR. KRIGSTEIN?
NO, NOT NOW. NOT AFTER ALL THIS TIME.
JUST KEEP PILING ON THE PRESSURE AND LET'S GET THIS OVER WITH.
WE'VE GOT JENNY QUANTUM ON OUR SIDE AND A NEAR-LIMITLESS SUPPLY OF FRUSTRATED EX-SOLDIERS WILLING TO FIGHT FOR US.
WHO WOULD HAVE THOUGHT A FEW ADS IN SOME MUSCLE-BUILDING MAGAZINES AND A LINE OF CHILDREN'S COMIC-BOOKS WOULD HAVE SOLICITED SUCH A TREMENDOUS RESPONSE?

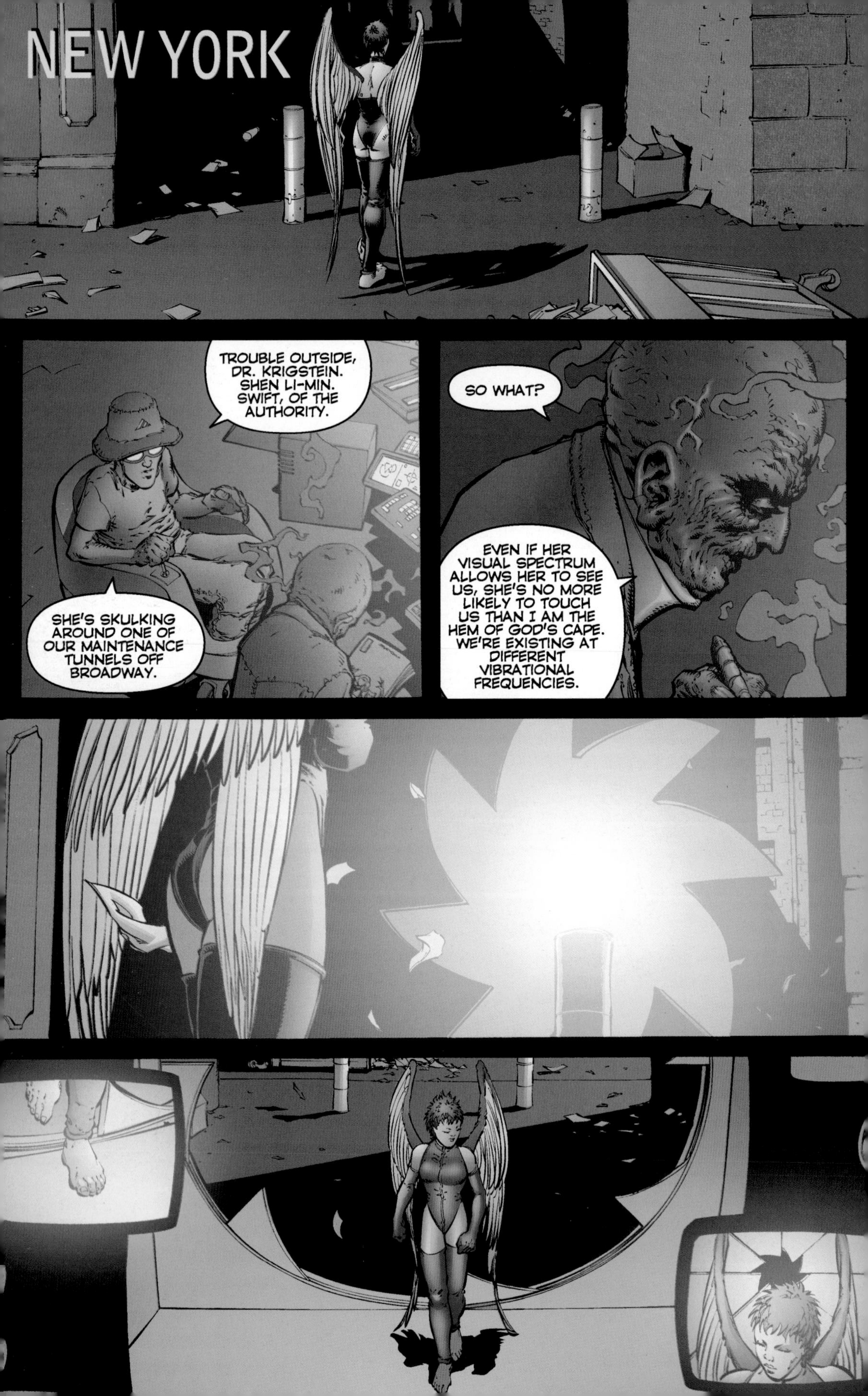
NEW YORK
TROUBLE OUTSIDE, DR. KRIGSTEIN. SHEN LI-MIN. SWIFT, OF THE AUTHORITY.
SHE'S SKULKING AROUND ONE OF OUR MAINTENANCE TUNNELS OFF BROADWAY.
SO WHAT?
EVEN IF HER VISUAL SPECTRUM ALLOWS HER TO SEE US, SHE'S NO MORE LIKELY TO TOUCH US THAN I AM THE HEM OF GOD'S CAPE. WE'RE EXISTING AT DIFFERENT VIBRATIONAL FREQUENCIES.

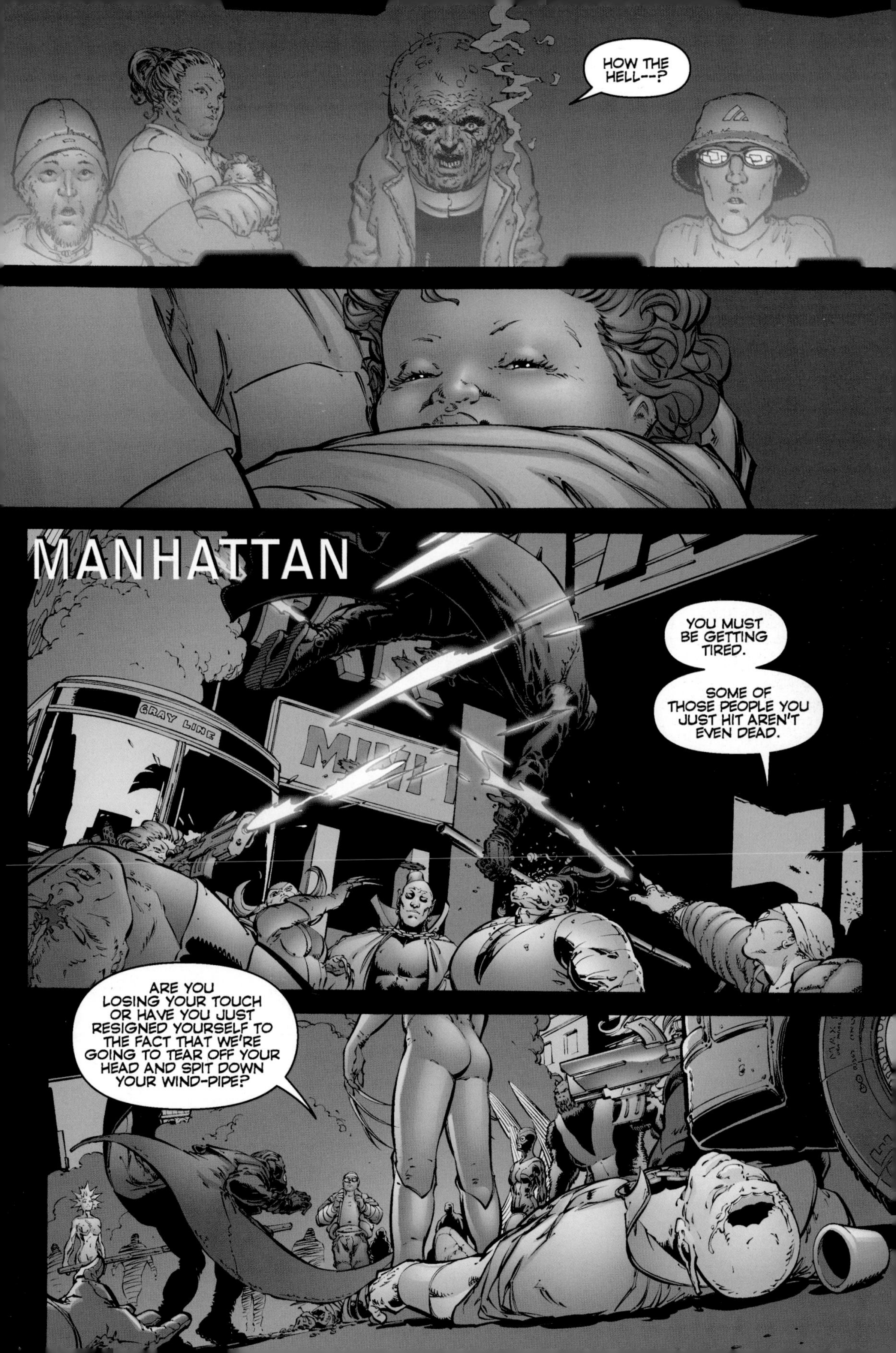
HOW THE HELL--?
MANHATTAN
YOU MUST BE GETTING TIRED.
SOME OF THOSE PEOPLE YOU JUST HIT AREN'T EVEN DEAD.
GRAY LINE
ARE YOU LOSING YOUR TOUCH OR HAVE YOU JUST RESIGNED YOURSELF TO THE FACT THAT WE'RE GOING TO TEAR OFF YOUR HEAD AND SPIT DOWN YOUR WIND-PIPE?

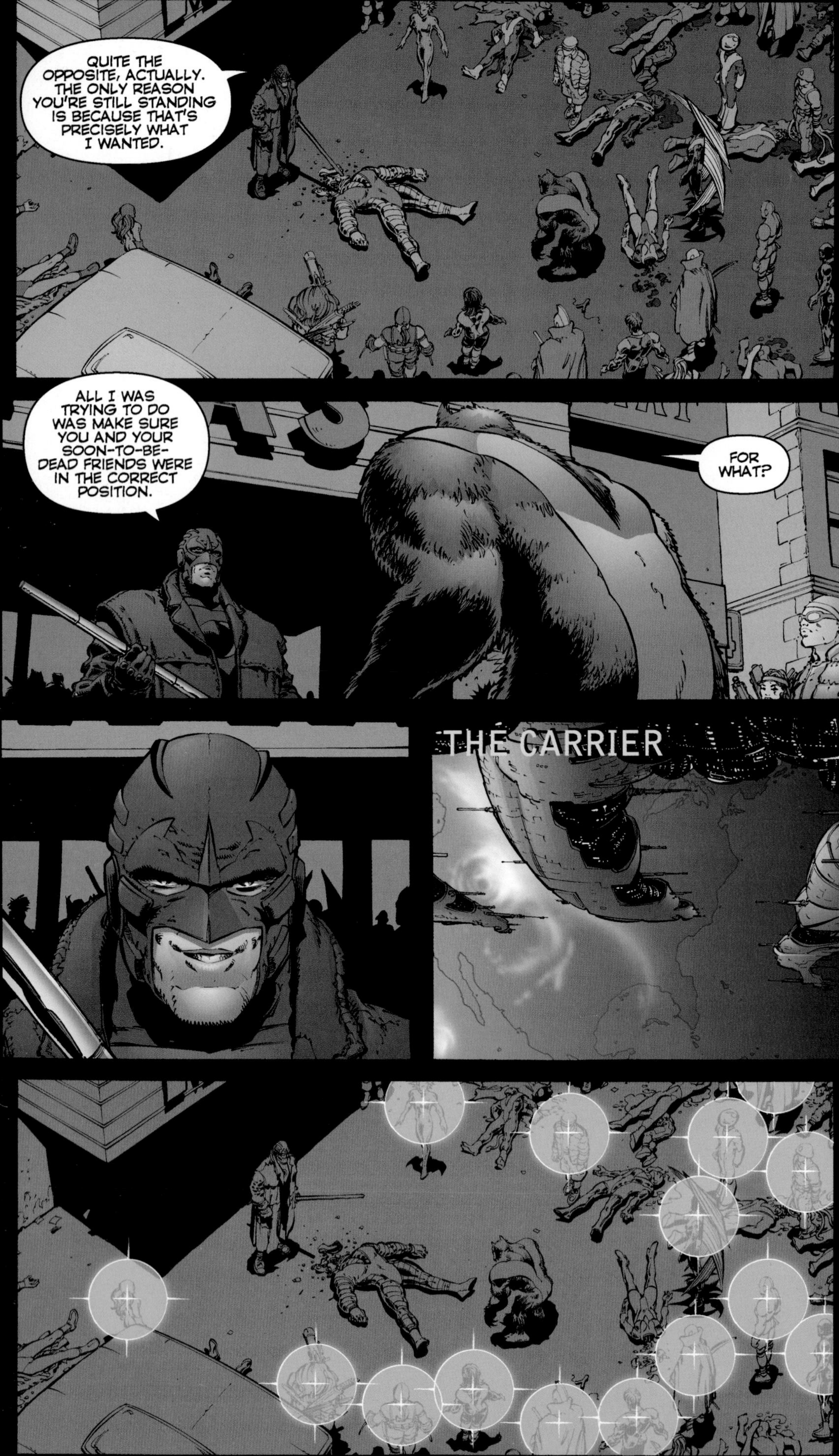
QUITE THE OPPOSITE, ACTUALLY. THE ONLY REASON YOU'RE STILL STANDING IS BECAUSE THAT'S PRECISELY WHAT I WANTED.
ALL I WAS TRYING TO DO WAS MAKE SURE YOU AND YOUR SOON-TO-BE-DEAD FRIENDS WERE IN THE CORRECT POSITION.
FOR WHAT?
THE CARRIER

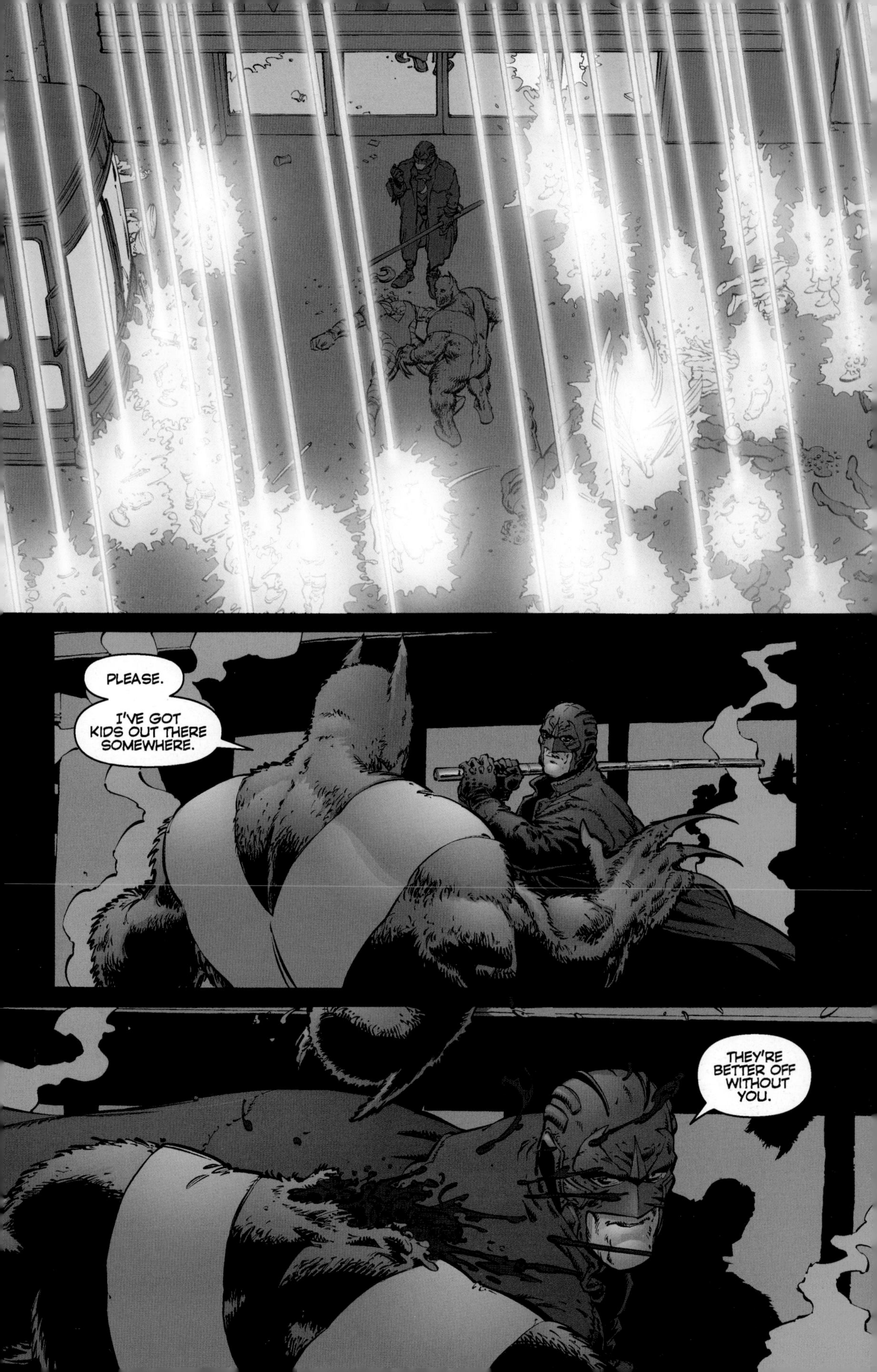
PLEASE.
I'VE GOT KIDS OUT THERE SOMEWHERE.
THEY'RE BETTER OFF WITHOUT YOU.

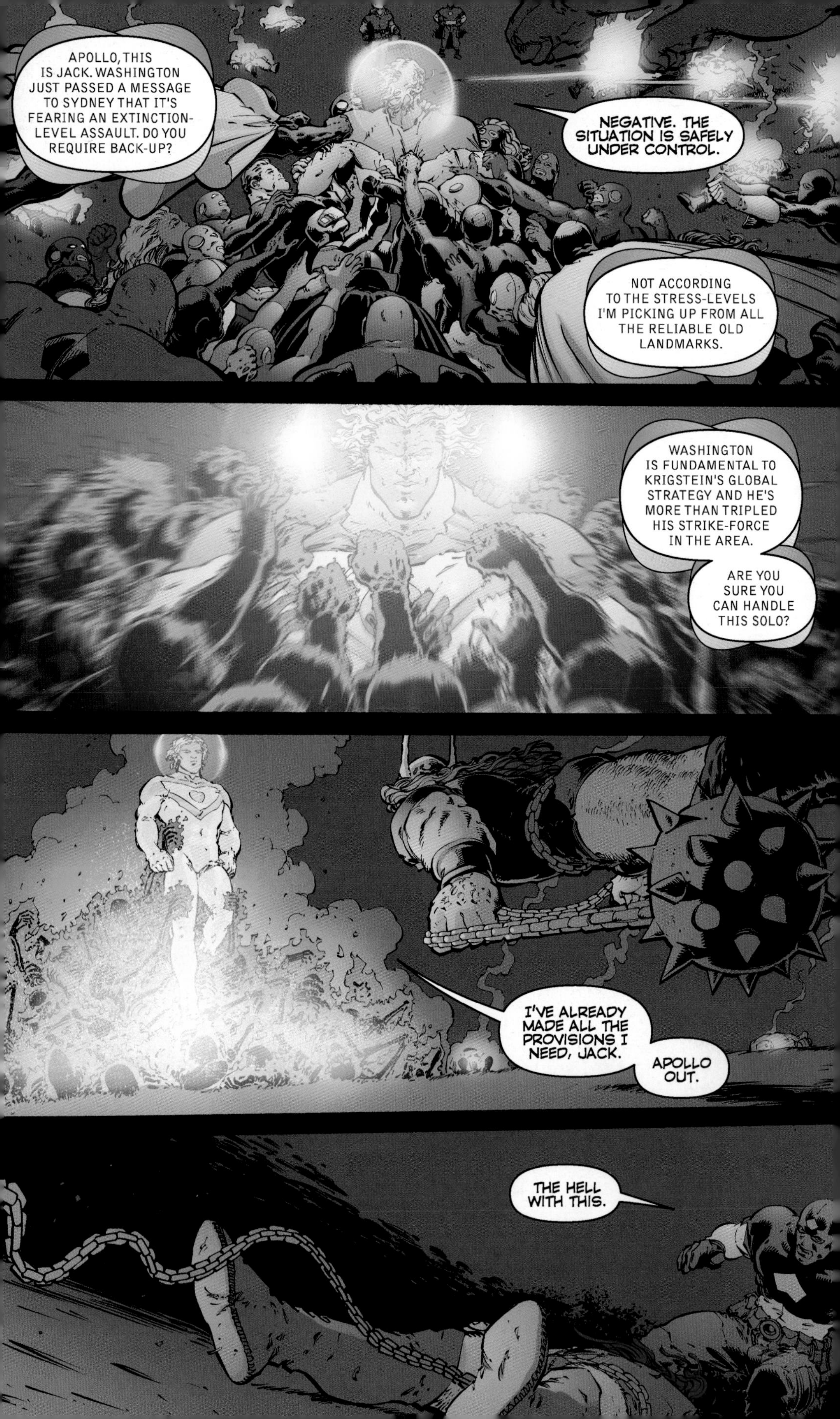
APOLLO, THIS IS JACK. WASHINGTON JUST PASSED A MESSAGE TO SYDNEY THAT IT'S FEARING AN EXTINCTION-LEVEL ASSAULT. DO YOU REQUIRE BACK-UP?
NEGATIVE. THE SITUATION IS SAFELY UNDER CONTROL.
NOT ACCORDING TO THE STRESS-LEVELS I'M PICKING UP FROM ALL THE RELIABLE OLD LANDMARKS.
WASHINGTON IS FUNDAMENTAL TO KRIGSTEIN'S GLOBAL STRATEGY AND HE'S MORE THAN TRIPLED HIS STRIKE-FORCE IN THE AREA.
ARE YOU SURE YOU CAN HANDLE THIS SOLO?
I'VE ALREADY MADE ALL THE PROVISIONS I NEED, JACK.
APOLLO OUT.
THE HELL WITH THIS.

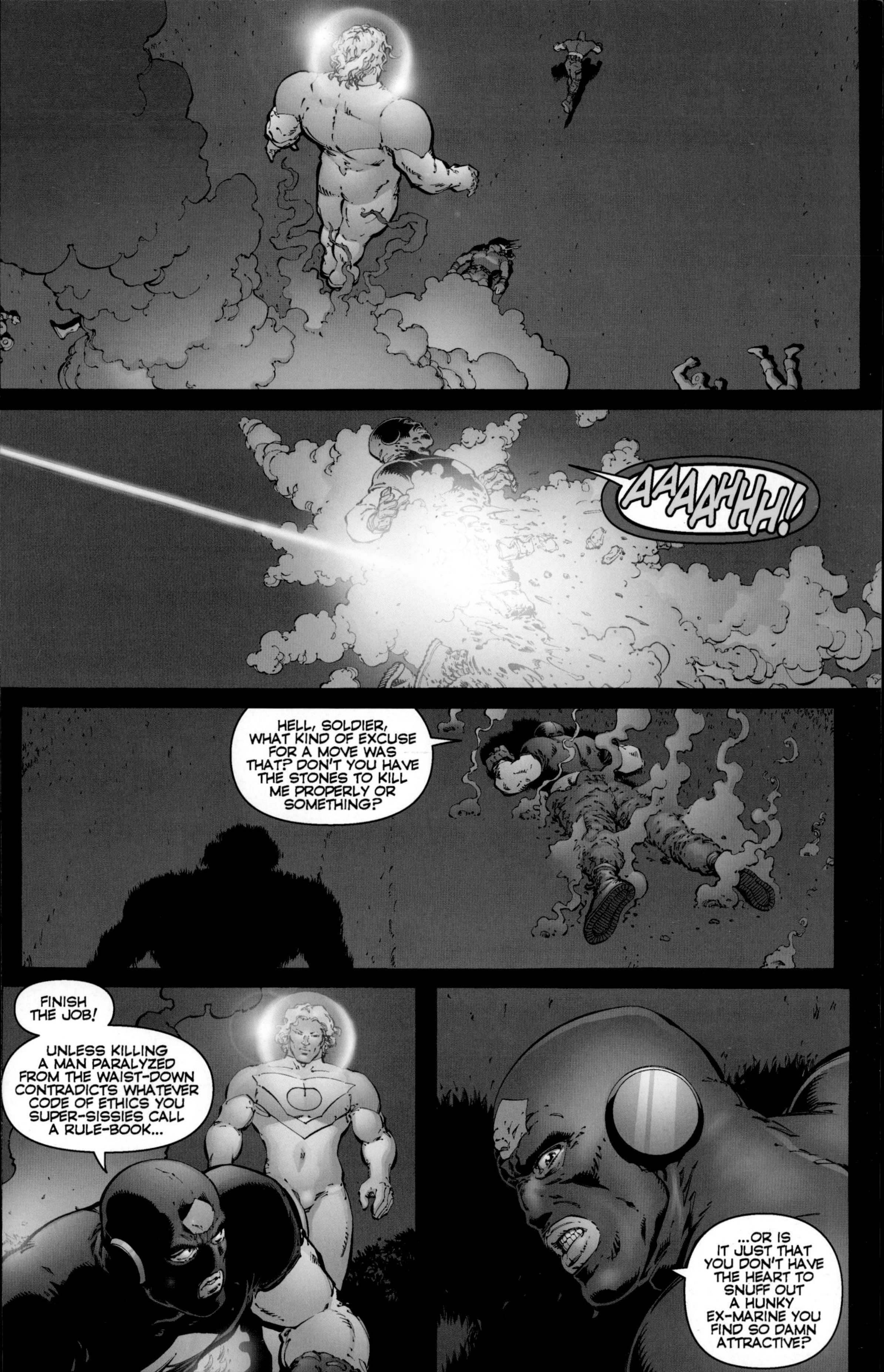
AAAAHHH!
HELL, SOLDIER, WHAT KIND OF EXCUSE FOR A MOVE WAS THAT? DON'T YOU HAVE THE STONES TO KILL ME PROPERLY OR SOMETHING?
FINISH THE JOB!
UNLESS KILLING A MAN PARALYZED FROM THE WAIST-DOWN CONTRADICTS WHATEVER CODE OF ETHICS YOU SUPER-SISSIES CALL A RULE-BOOK...
...OR IS IT JUST THAT YOU DON'T HAVE THE HEART TO SNUFF OUT A HUNKY EX-MARINE YOU FIND SO DAMN ATTRACTIVE?

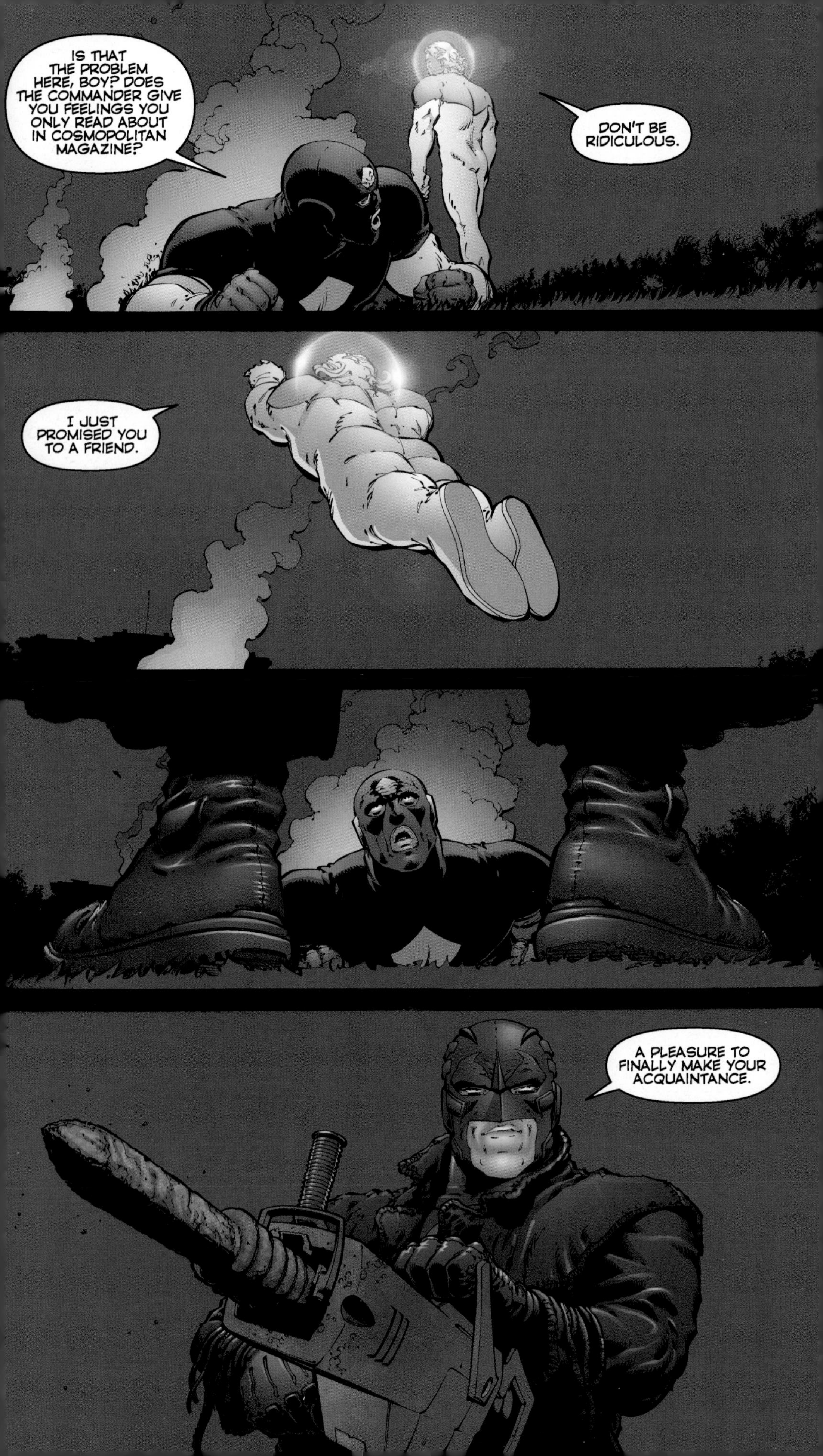
IS THAT THE PROBLEM HERE, BOY? DOES THE COMMANDER GIVE YOU FEELINGS YOU ONLY READ ABOUT IN COSMOPOLITAN MAGAZINE?
DON'T BE RIDICULOUS.
I JUST PROMISED YOU TO A FRIEND.
A PLEASURE TO FINALLY MAKE YOUR ACQUAINTANCE.

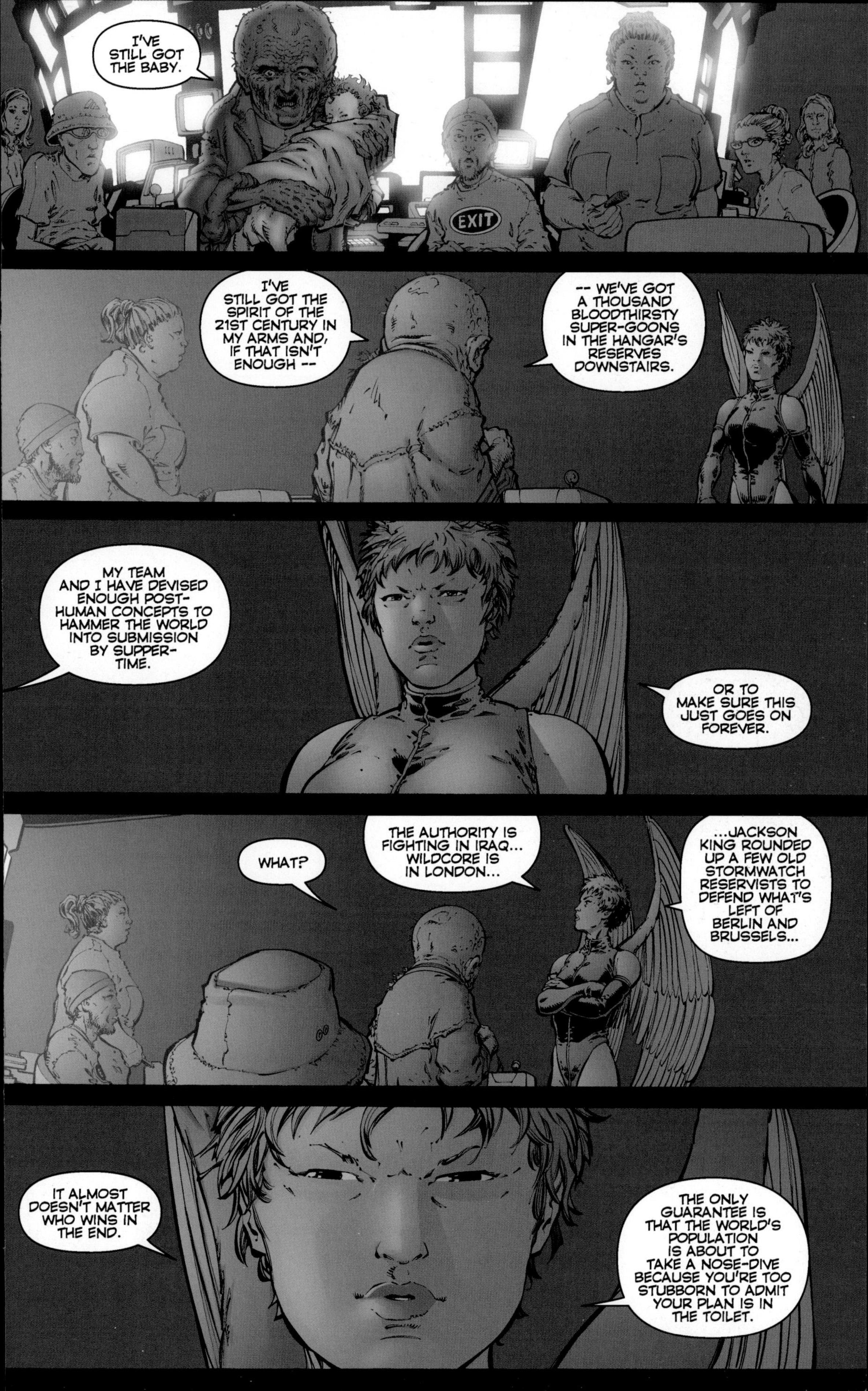
I'VE STILL GOT THE BABY.
I'VE STILL GOT THE SPIRIT OF THE 21ST CENTURY IN MY ARMS AND, IF THAT ISN'T ENOUGH --
-- WE'VE GOT A THOUSAND BLOODTHIRSTY SUPER-GOONS IN THE HANGAR'S RESERVES DOWNSTAIRS.
MY TEAM AND I HAVE DEVISED ENOUGH POST-HUMAN CONCEPTS TO HAMMER THE WORLD INTO SUBMISSION BY SUPPER-TIME.
OR TO MAKE SURE THIS JUST GOES ON FOREVER.
WHAT?
THE AUTHORITY IS FIGHTING IN IRAQ... WILDCORE IS IN LONDON...
...JACKSON KING ROUNDED UP A FEW OLD STORMWATCH RESERVISTS TO DEFEND WHAT'S LEFT OF BERLIN AND BRUSSELS...
IT ALMOST DOESN'T MATTER WHO WINS IN THE END.
THE ONLY GUARANTEE IS THAT THE WORLD'S POPULATION IS ABOUT TO TAKE A NOSE-DIVE BECAUSE YOU'RE TOO STUBBORN TO ADMIT YOUR PLAN IS IN THE TOILET.
EXIT

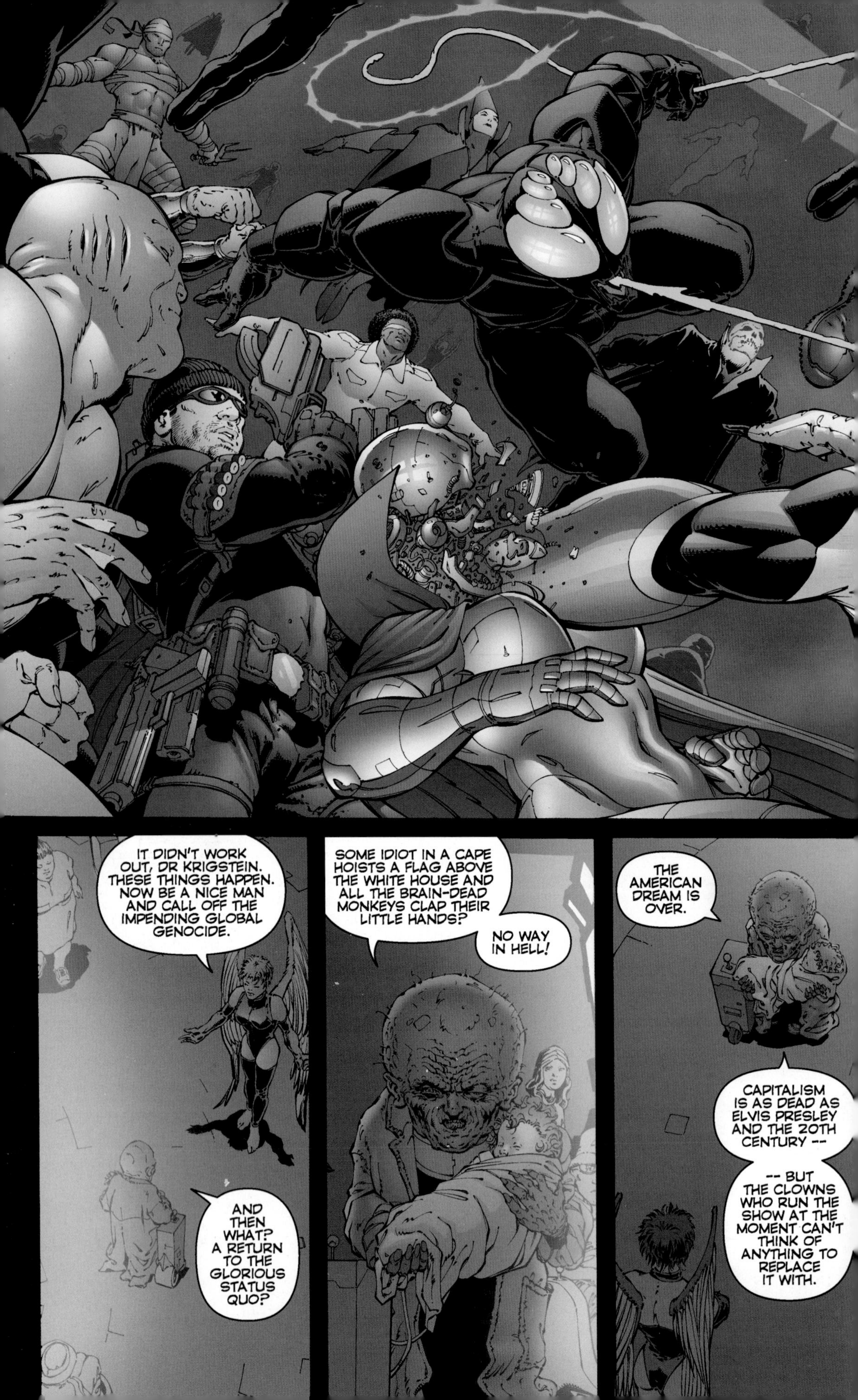
IT DIDN'T WORK OUT, DR KRIGSTEIN. THESE THINGS HAPPEN. NOW BE A NICE MAN AND CALL OFF THE IMPENDING GLOBAL GENOCIDE.
AND THEN WHAT? A RETURN TO THE GLORIOUS STATUS QUO?
SOME IDIOT IN A CAPE HOISTS A FLAG ABOVE THE WHITE HOUSE AND ALL THE BRAIN-DEAD MONKEYS CLAP THEIR LITTLE HANDS?
NO WAY IN HELL!
THE AMERICAN DREAM IS OVER.
CAPITALISM IS AS DEAD AS ELVIS PRESLEY AND THE 20TH CENTURY --
-- BUT THE CLOWNS WHO RUN THE SHOW AT THE MOMENT CAN'T THINK OF ANYTHING TO REPLACE IT WITH.

MY PLANS FOR THE WORLD COULD REVOLUTIONIZE THINGS FOR EVERYONE. THEIR ONLY IDEAS ARE CCTV CAMERAS ON EVERY STREET-CORNER AND DAMN MICRO-CHIPS IN OUR HEADS. I'VE ATTENDED THE SECRET MEETINGS, SWEETHEART. I KNOW WHAT THEY'RE UP TO.

YOU CAN'T KILL A MAN FOR TRYING TO SAVE THE HUMAN RACE FROM NUTRASWEET, POKEMON AND GOVERNOR GEORGE W. BUSH.

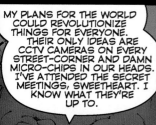

I DIDN'T COME HERE TO EXECUTE YOU, KRIGSTEIN. QUITE THE REVERSE, IN FACT.

WE WANT YOU TO JOIN US.

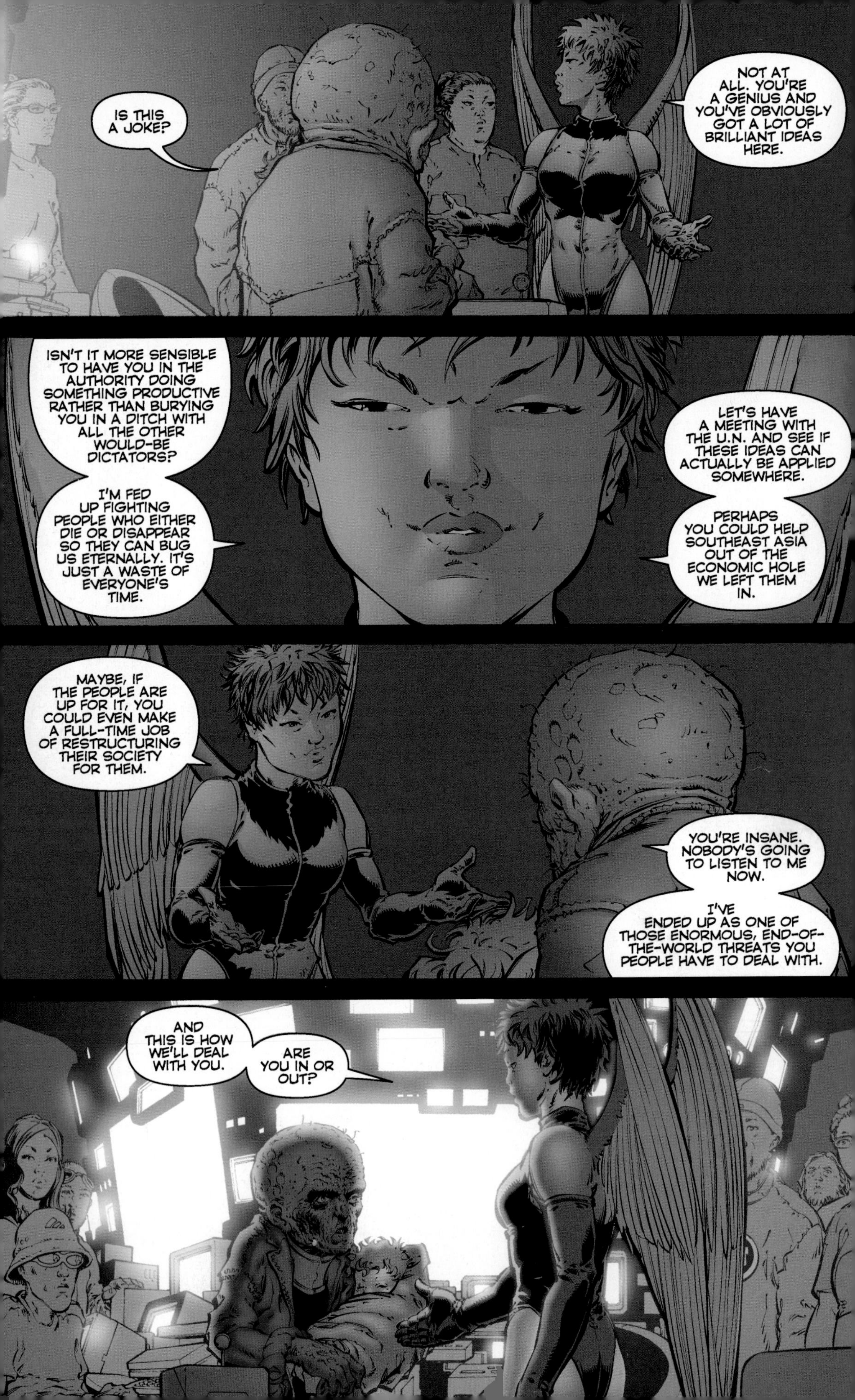
IS THIS A JOKE?
NOT AT ALL. YOU'RE A GENIUS AND YOU'VE OBVIOUSLY GOT A LOT OF BRILLIANT IDEAS HERE.
ISN'T IT MORE SENSIBLE TO HAVE YOU IN THE AUTHORITY DOING SOMETHING PRODUCTIVE RATHER THAN BURYING YOU IN A DITCH WITH ALL THE OTHER WOULD-BE DICTATORS?
I'M FED UP FIGHTING PEOPLE WHO EITHER DIE OR DISAPPEAR SO THEY CAN BUG US ETERNALLY. IT'S JUST A WASTE OF EVERYONE'S TIME.
LET'S HAVE A MEETING WITH THE U.N. AND SEE IF THESE IDEAS CAN ACTUALLY BE APPLIED SOMEWHERE.
PERHAPS YOU COULD HELP SOUTHEAST ASIA OUT OF THE ECONOMIC HOLE WE LEFT THEM IN.
MAYBE, IF THE PEOPLE ARE UP FOR IT, YOU COULD EVEN MAKE A FULL-TIME JOB OF RESTRUCTURING THEIR SOCIETY FOR THEM.
YOU'RE INSANE. NOBODY'S GOING TO LISTEN TO ME NOW.
I'VE ENDED UP AS ONE OF THOSE ENORMOUS, END-OF-THE-WORLD THREATS YOU PEOPLE HAVE TO DEAL WITH.
AND THIS IS HOW WE'LL DEAL WITH YOU.
ARE YOU IN OR OUT?

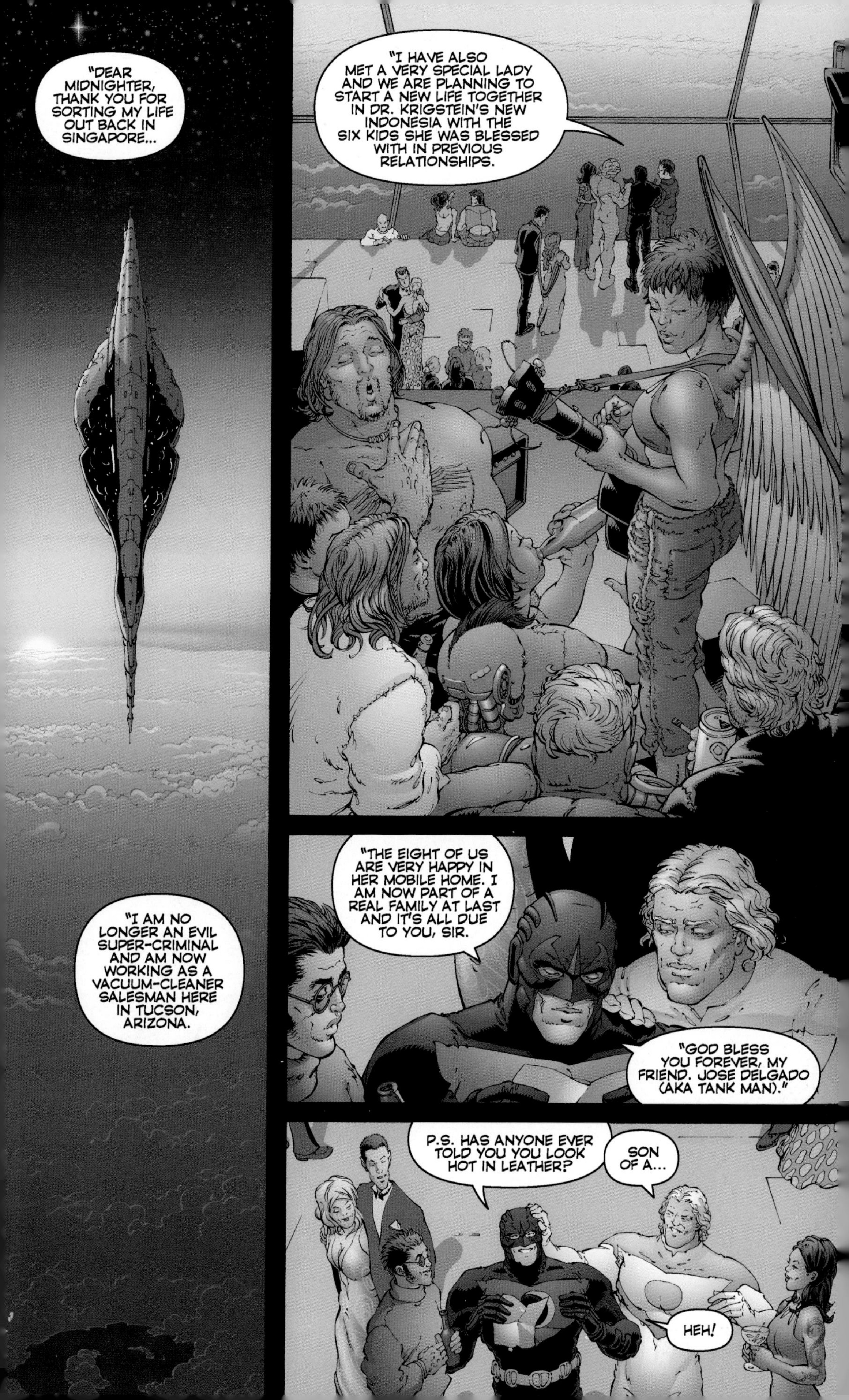
"DEAR MIDNIGHTER, THANK YOU FOR SORTING MY LIFE OUT BACK IN SINGAPORE...
"I AM NO LONGER AN EVIL SUPER-CRIMINAL AND AM NOW WORKING AS A VACUUM-CLEANER SALESMAN HERE IN TUCSON, ARIZONA.
"I HAVE ALSO MET A VERY SPECIAL LADY AND WE ARE PLANNING TO START A NEW LIFE TOGETHER IN DR. KRIGSTEIN'S NEW INDONESIA WITH THE SIX KIDS SHE WAS BLESSED WITH IN PREVIOUS RELATIONSHIPS.
"THE EIGHT OF US ARE VERY HAPPY IN HER MOBILE HOME. I AM NOW PART OF A REAL FAMILY AT LAST AND IT'S ALL DUE TO YOU, SIR.
"GOD BLESS YOU FOREVER, MY FRIEND. JOSE DELGADO (AKA TANK MAN)."
P.S. HAS ANYONE EVER TOLD YOU YOU LOOK HOT IN LEATHER?
SON OF A...
HEH!

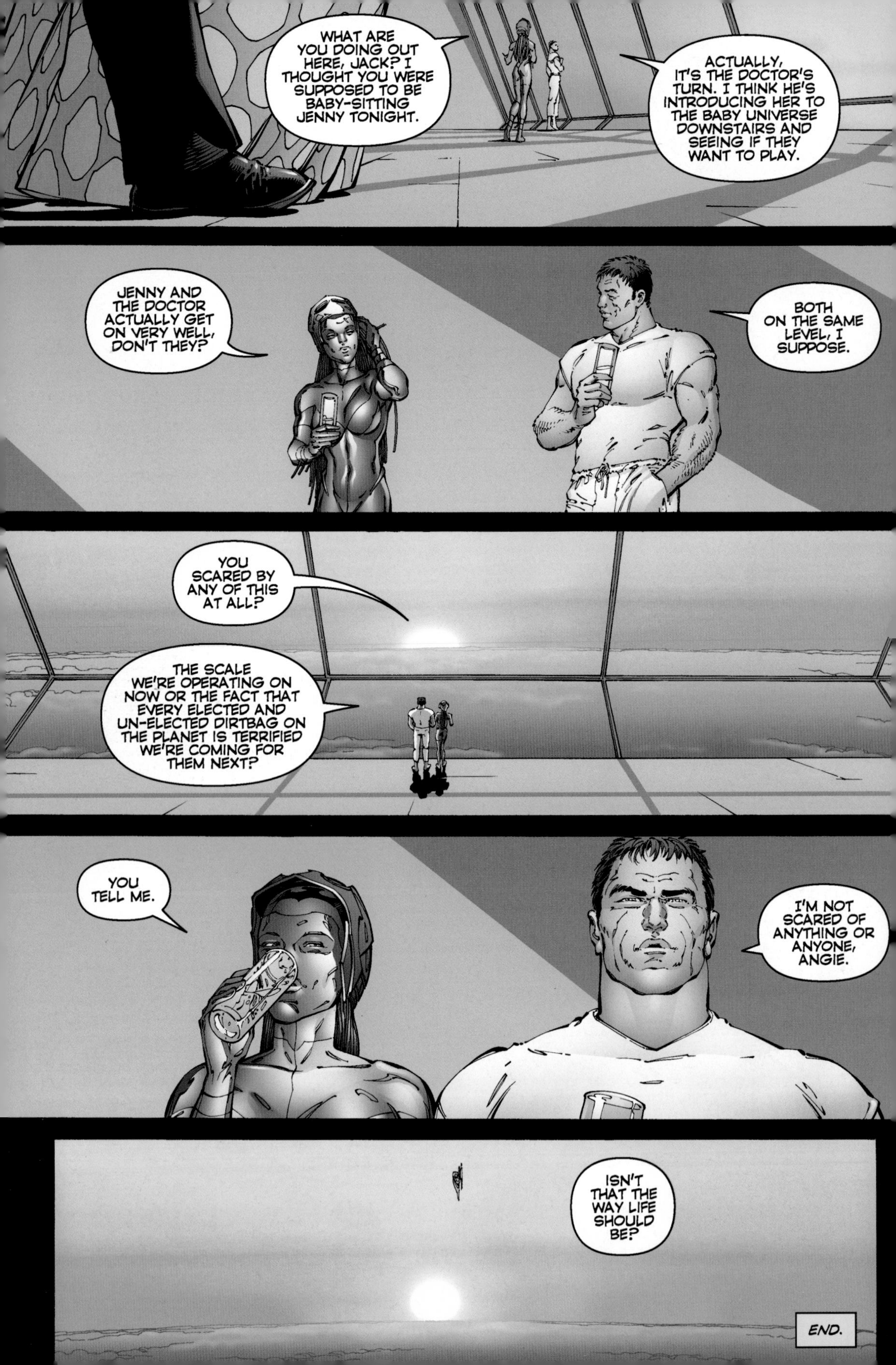
WHAT ARE YOU DOING OUT HERE, JACK? I THOUGHT YOU WERE SUPPOSED TO BE BABY-SITTING JENNY TONIGHT.
ACTUALLY, IT'S THE DOCTOR'S TURN. I THINK HE'S INTRODUCING HER TO THE BABY UNIVERSE DOWNSTAIRS AND SEEING IF THEY WANT TO PLAY.
JENNY AND THE DOCTOR ACTUALLY GET ON VERY WELL, DON'T THEY?
BOTH ON THE SAME LEVEL, I SUPPOSE.
YOU SCARED BY ANY OF THIS AT ALL?
THE SCALE WE'RE OPERATING ON NOW OR THE FACT THAT EVERY ELECTED AND UN-ELECTED DIRTBAG ON THE PLANET IS TERRIFIED WE'RE COMING FOR THEM NEXT?
YOU TELL ME.
I'M NOT SCARED OF ANYTHING OR ANYONE, ANGIE.
ISN'T THAT THE WAY LIFE SHOULD BE?
END.

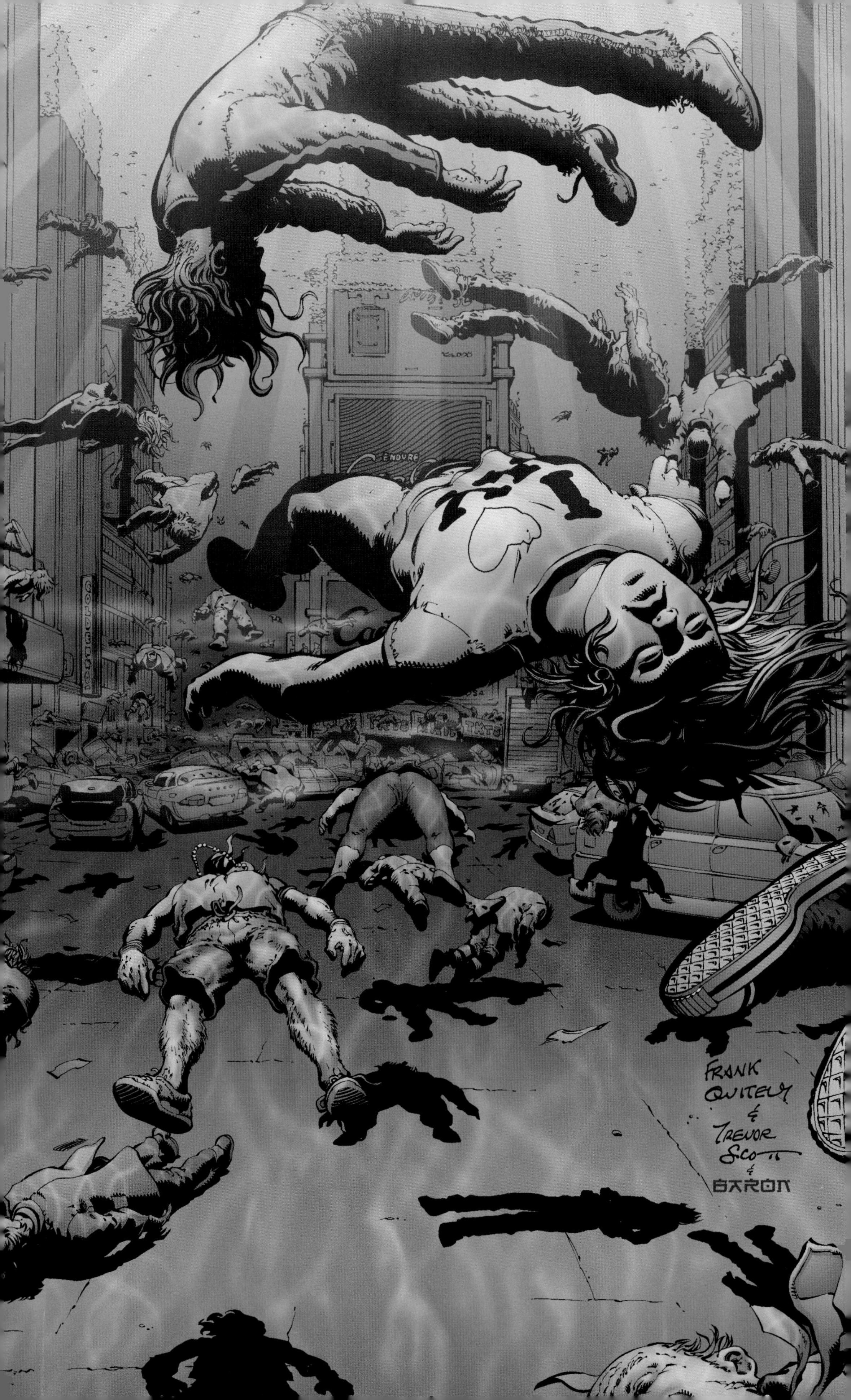
TKTS
FRANK QUITELY & TREVOR SCOTT & BARON

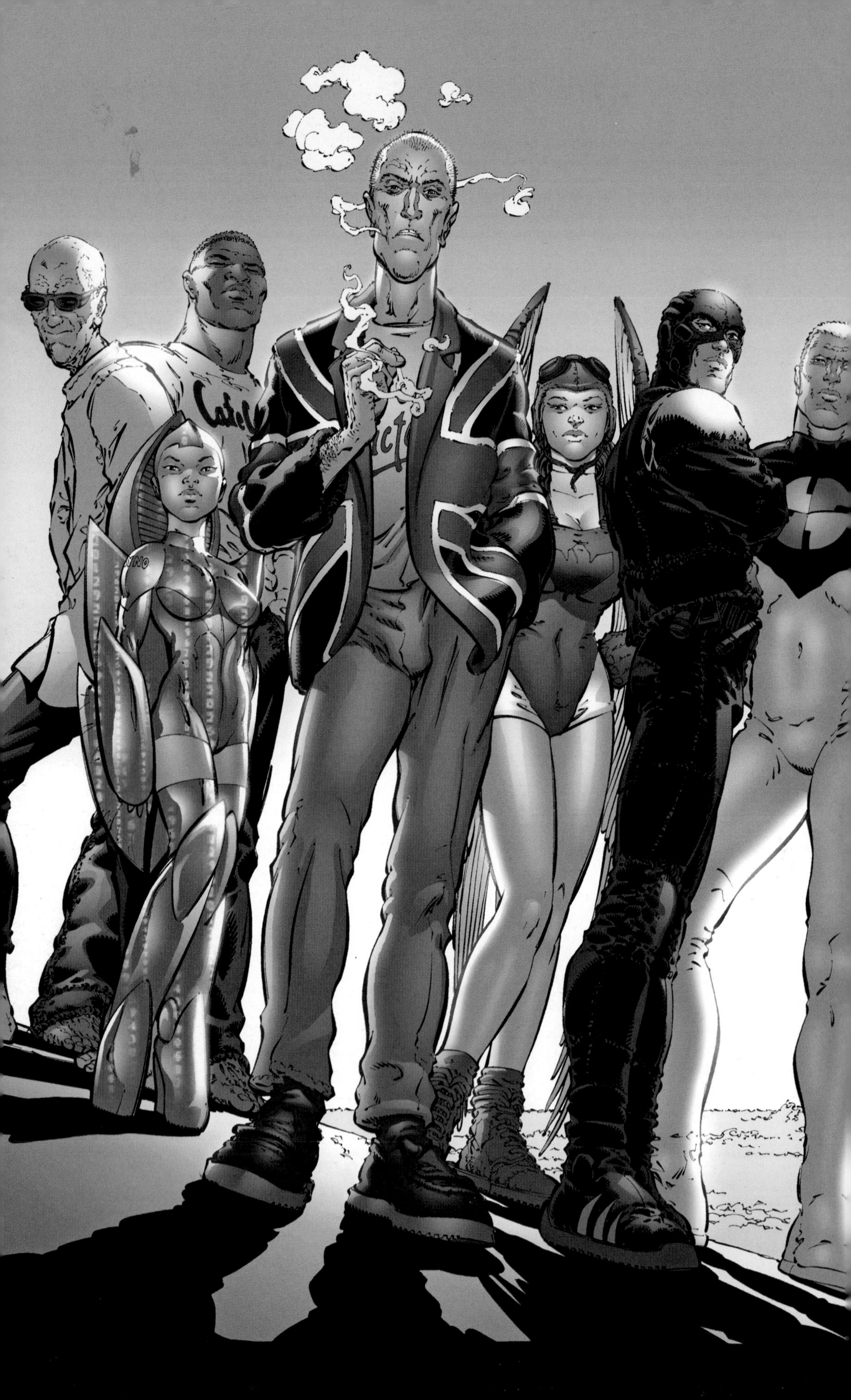

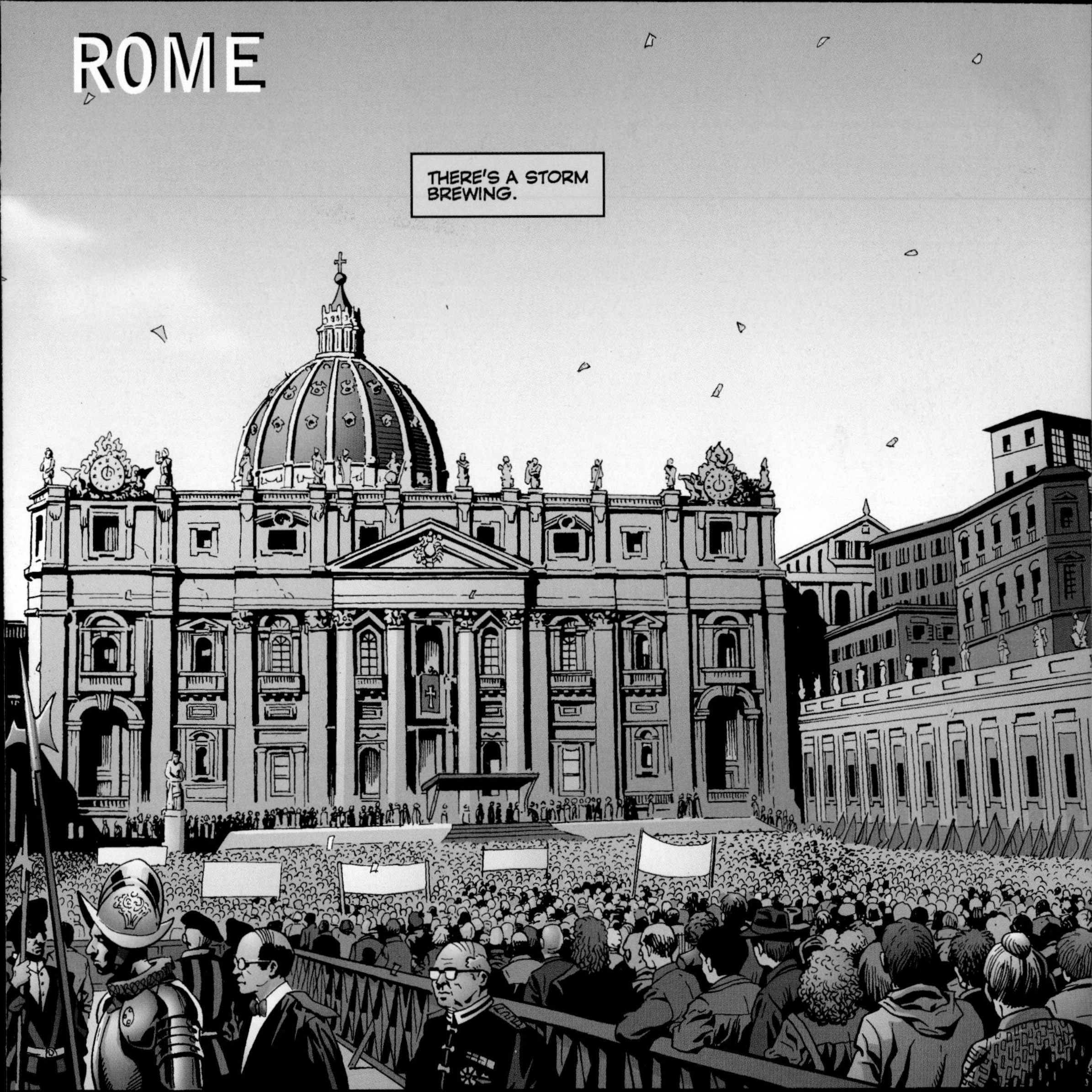

The AUTHORITY "Earth Inferno"

ONE of FOUR

MARK MILLAR writer
CHRIS WESTON artist
GARRY LEACH inker
DAVID BARON w/ Wildstorm FX colorist
BILL O'NEIL letterer

Inking assistance provided by Trevor Scott and Sal Regla

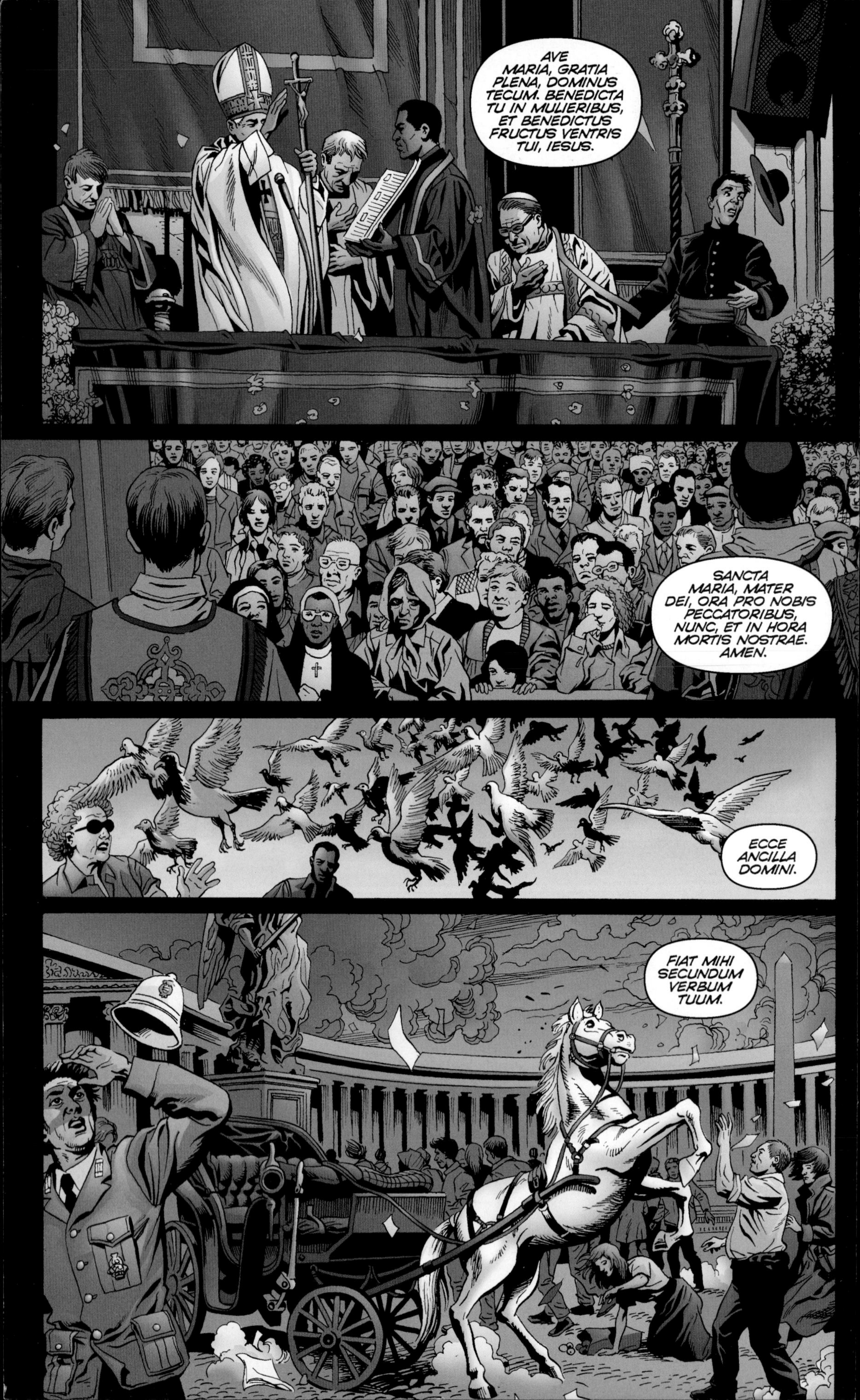
AVE MARIA, GRATIA PLENA, DOMINUS TECUM. BENEDICTA TU IN MULIERIBUS, ET BENEDICTUS FRUCTUS VENTRIS TUI, IESUS.
SANCTA MARIA, MATER DEI, ORA PRO NOBIS PECCATORIBUS, NUNC, ET IN HORA MORTIS NOSTRAE. AMEN.
ECCE ANCILLA DOMINI.
FIAT MIHI SECUNDUM VERBUM TUUM.

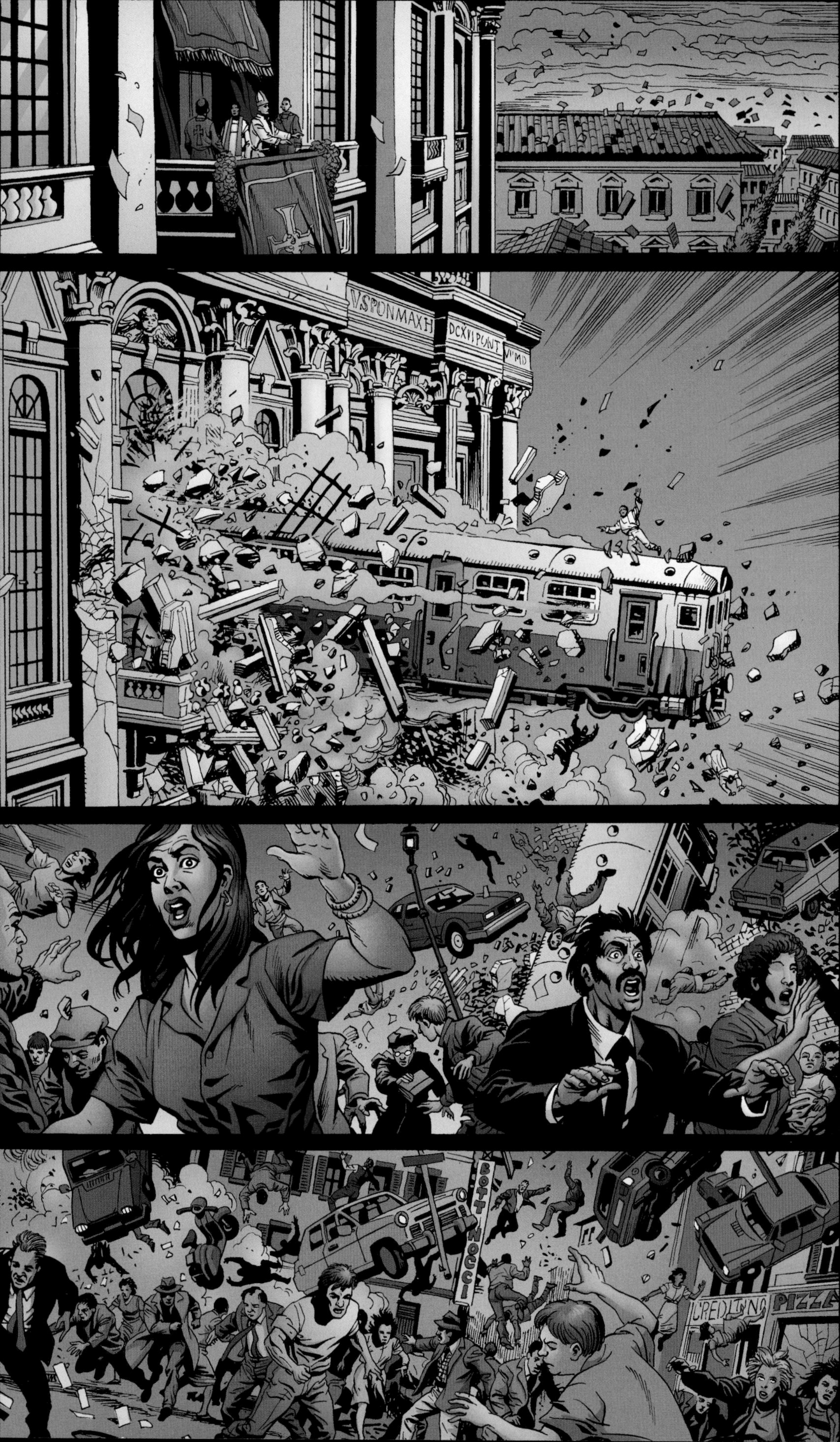
VSPONMAXH
DCXVIPONT
BOTT
NOCCI
PIZZA

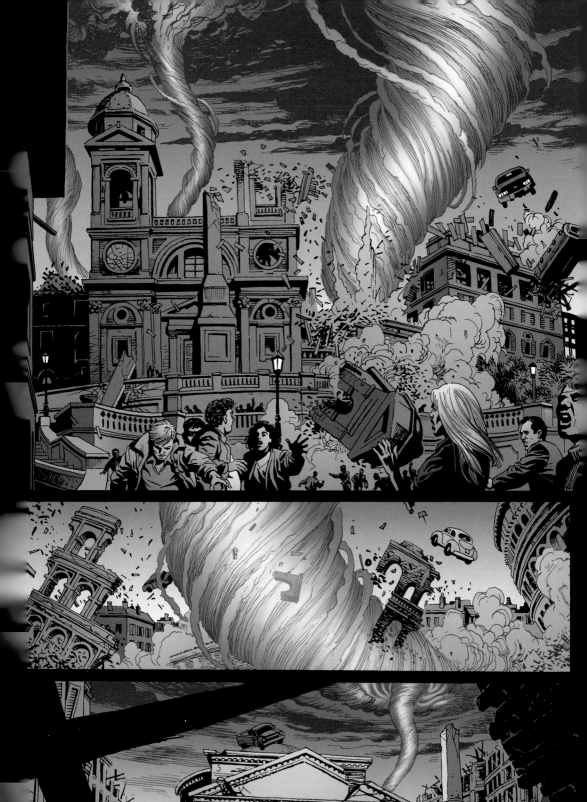

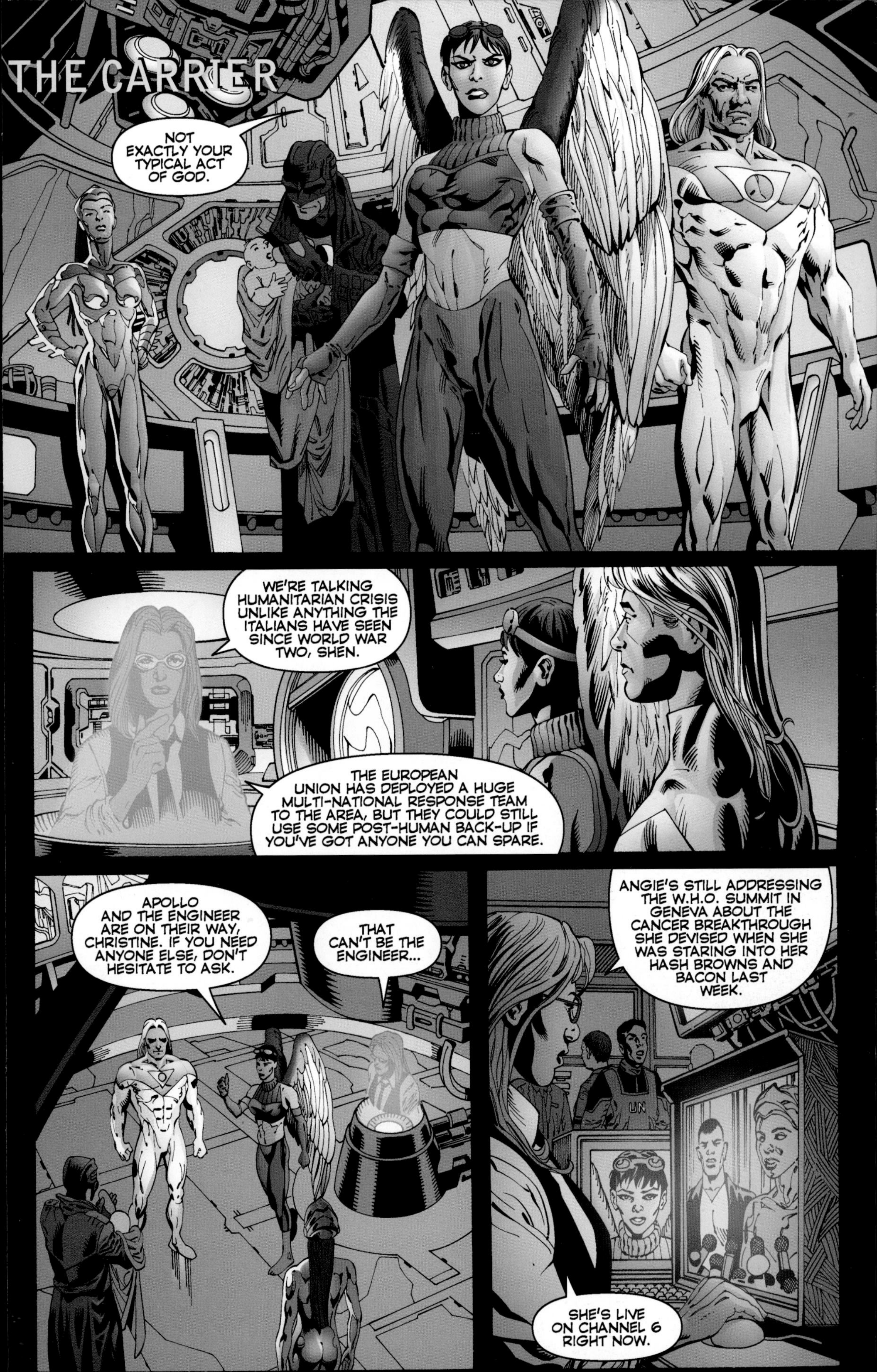
THE CARRIER
NOT EXACTLY YOUR TYPICAL ACT OF GOD.
WE'RE TALKING HUMANITARIAN CRISIS UNLIKE ANYTHING THE ITALIANS HAVE SEEN SINCE WORLD WAR TWO, SHEN.
THE EUROPEAN UNION HAS DEPLOYED A HUGE MULTI-NATIONAL RESPONSE TEAM TO THE AREA, BUT THEY COULD STILL USE SOME POST-HUMAN BACK-UP IF YOU'VE GOT ANYONE YOU CAN SPARE.
APOLLO AND THE ENGINEER ARE ON THEIR WAY, CHRISTINE. IF YOU NEED ANYONE ELSE, DON'T HESITATE TO ASK.
THAT CAN'T BE THE ENGINEER...
ANGIE'S STILL ADDRESSING THE W.H.O. SUMMIT IN GENEVA ABOUT THE CANCER BREAKTHROUGH SHE DEVISED WHEN SHE WAS STARING INTO HER HASH BROWNS AND BACON LAST WEEK.
SHE'S LIVE ON CHANNEL 6 RIGHT NOW.
UN

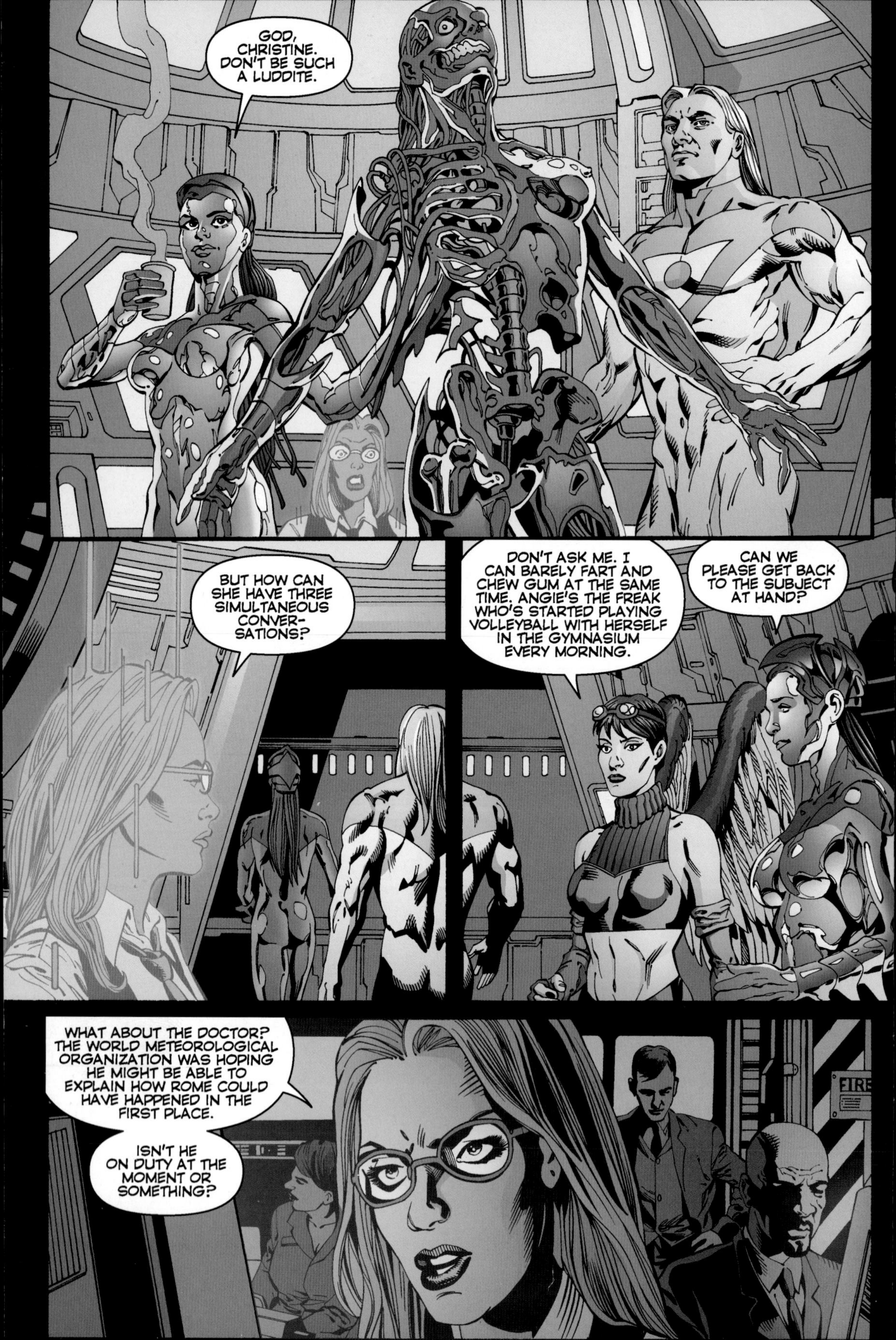
GOD, CHRISTINE. DON'T BE SUCH A LUDDITE.
BUT HOW CAN SHE HAVE THREE SIMULTANEOUS CONVER-SATIONS?
DON'T ASK ME. I CAN BARELY FART AND CHEW GUM AT THE SAME TIME. ANGIE'S THE FREAK WHO'S STARTED PLAYING VOLLEYBALL WITH HERSELF IN THE GYMNASIUM EVERY MORNING.
CAN WE PLEASE GET BACK TO THE SUBJECT AT HAND?
WHAT ABOUT THE DOCTOR? THE WORLD METEOROLOGICAL ORGANIZATION WAS HOPING HE MIGHT BE ABLE TO EXPLAIN HOW ROME COULD HAVE HAPPENED IN THE FIRST PLACE.
ISN'T HE ON DUTY AT THE MOMENT OR SOMETHING?
FIRE

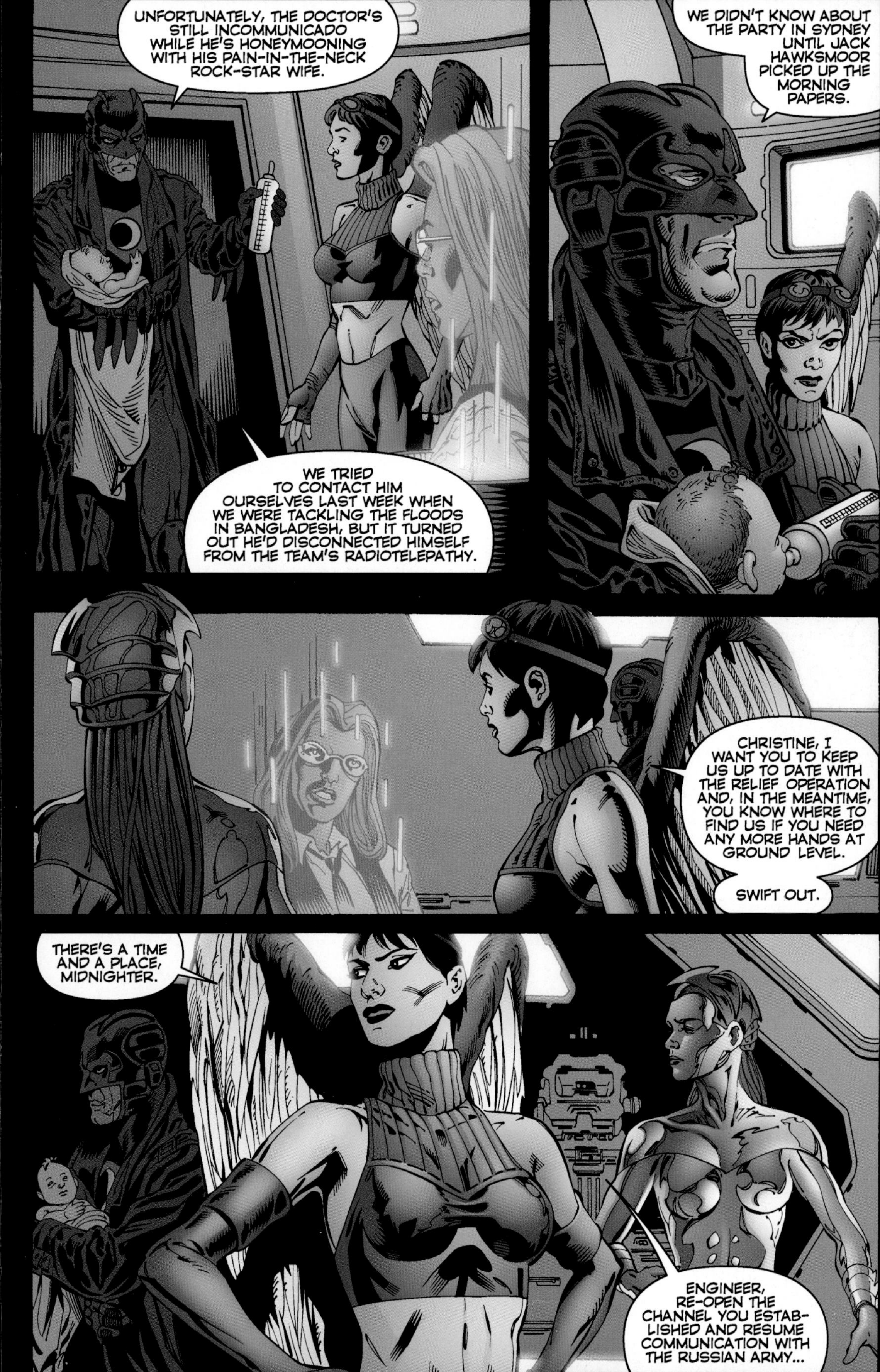
UNFORTUNATELY, THE DOCTOR'S STILL INCOMMUNICADO WHILE HE'S HONEYMOONING WITH HIS PAIN-IN-THE-NECK ROCK-STAR WIFE.
WE TRIED TO CONTACT HIM OURSELVES LAST WEEK WHEN WE WERE TACKLING THE FLOODS IN BANGLADESH, BUT IT TURNED OUT HE'D DISCONNECTED HIMSELF FROM THE TEAM'S RADIOTELEPATHY.
WE DIDN'T KNOW ABOUT THE PARTY IN SYDNEY UNTIL JACK HAWKSMOOR PICKED UP THE MORNING PAPERS.
CHRISTINE, I WANT YOU TO KEEP US UP TO DATE WITH THE RELIEF OPERATION AND, IN THE MEANTIME, YOU KNOW WHERE TO FIND US IF YOU NEED ANY MORE HANDS AT GROUND LEVEL.
SWIFT OUT.
THERE'S A TIME AND A PLACE, MIDNIGHTER.
ENGINEER, RE-OPEN THE CHANNEL YOU ESTAB-LISHED AND RESUME COMMUNICATION WITH THE RUSSIAN ARMY...

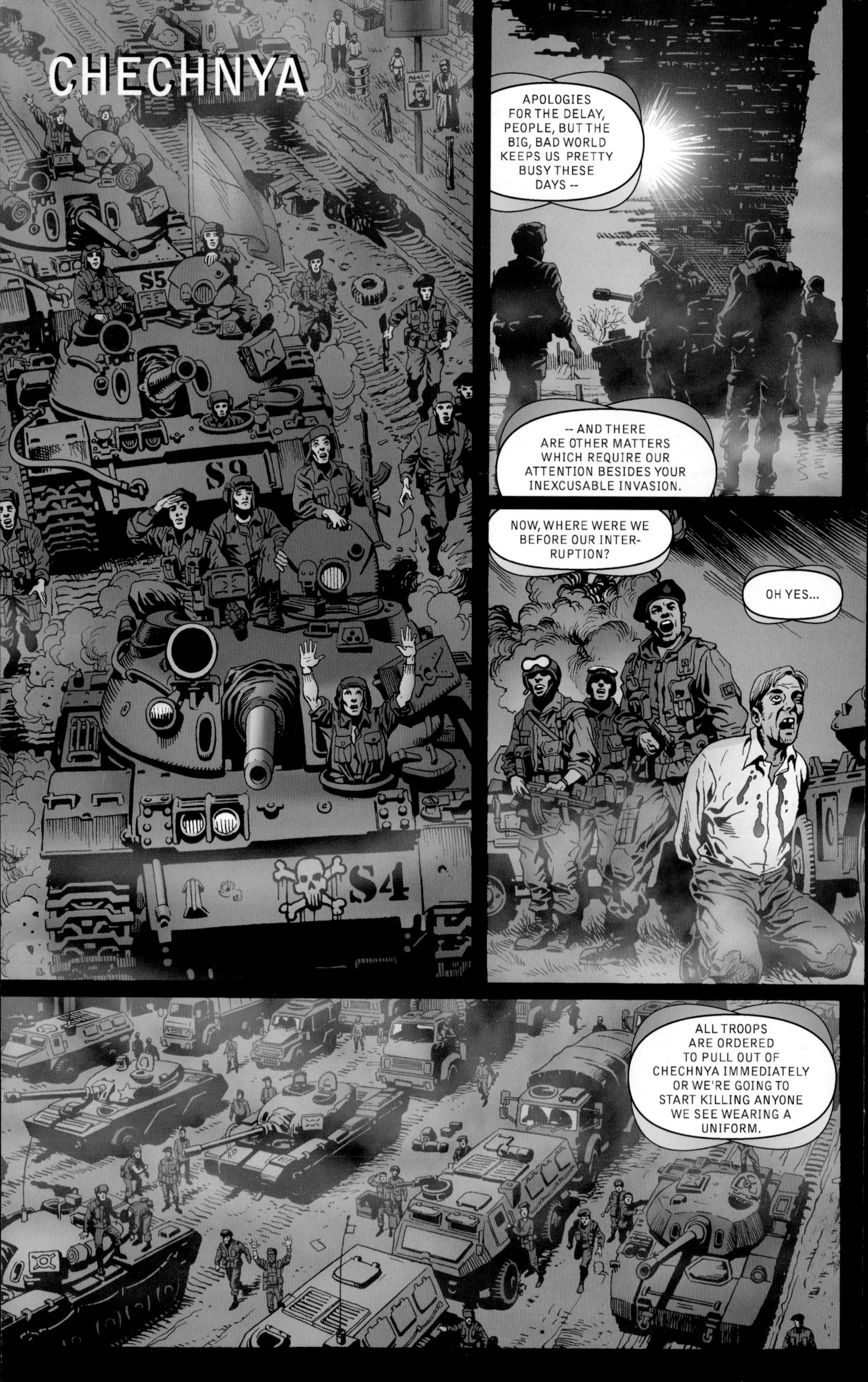
CHECHNYA
APOLOGIES FOR THE DELAY, PEOPLE, BUT THE BIG, BAD WORLD KEEPS US PRETTY BUSY THESE DAYS --
-- AND THERE ARE OTHER MATTERS WHICH REQUIRE OUR ATTENTION BESIDES YOUR INEXCUSABLE INVASION.
NOW, WHERE WERE WE BEFORE OUR INTER-RUPTION?
OH YES...
ALL TROOPS ARE ORDERED TO PULL OUT OF CHECHNYA IMMEDIATELY OR WE'RE GOING TO START KILLING ANYONE WE SEE WEARING A UNIFORM.
S5
S9
S4

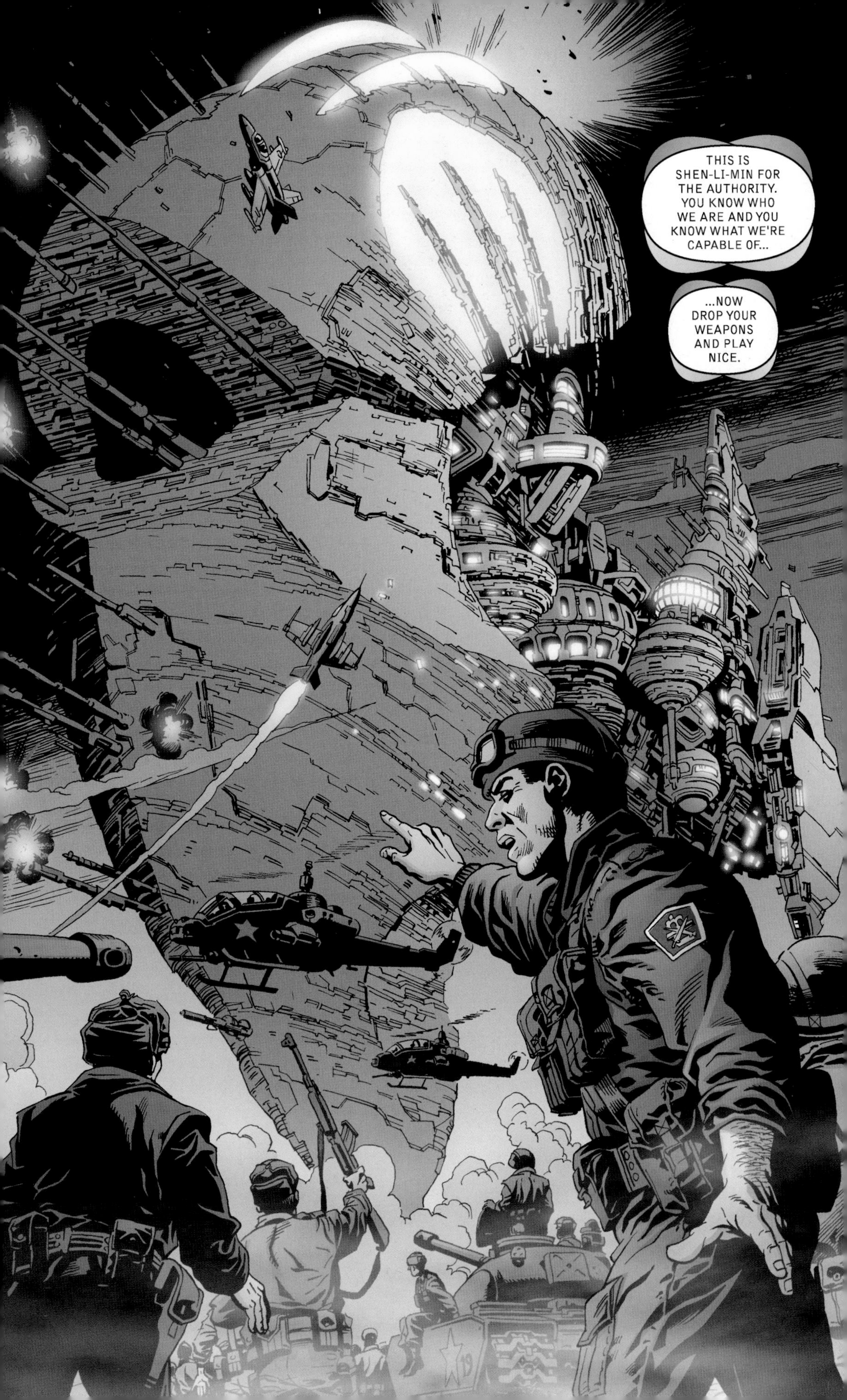
THIS IS SHEN-LI-MIN FOR THE AUTHORITY. YOU KNOW WHO WE ARE AND YOU KNOW WHAT WE'RE CAPABLE OF...
...NOW DROP YOUR WEAPONS AND PLAY NICE.

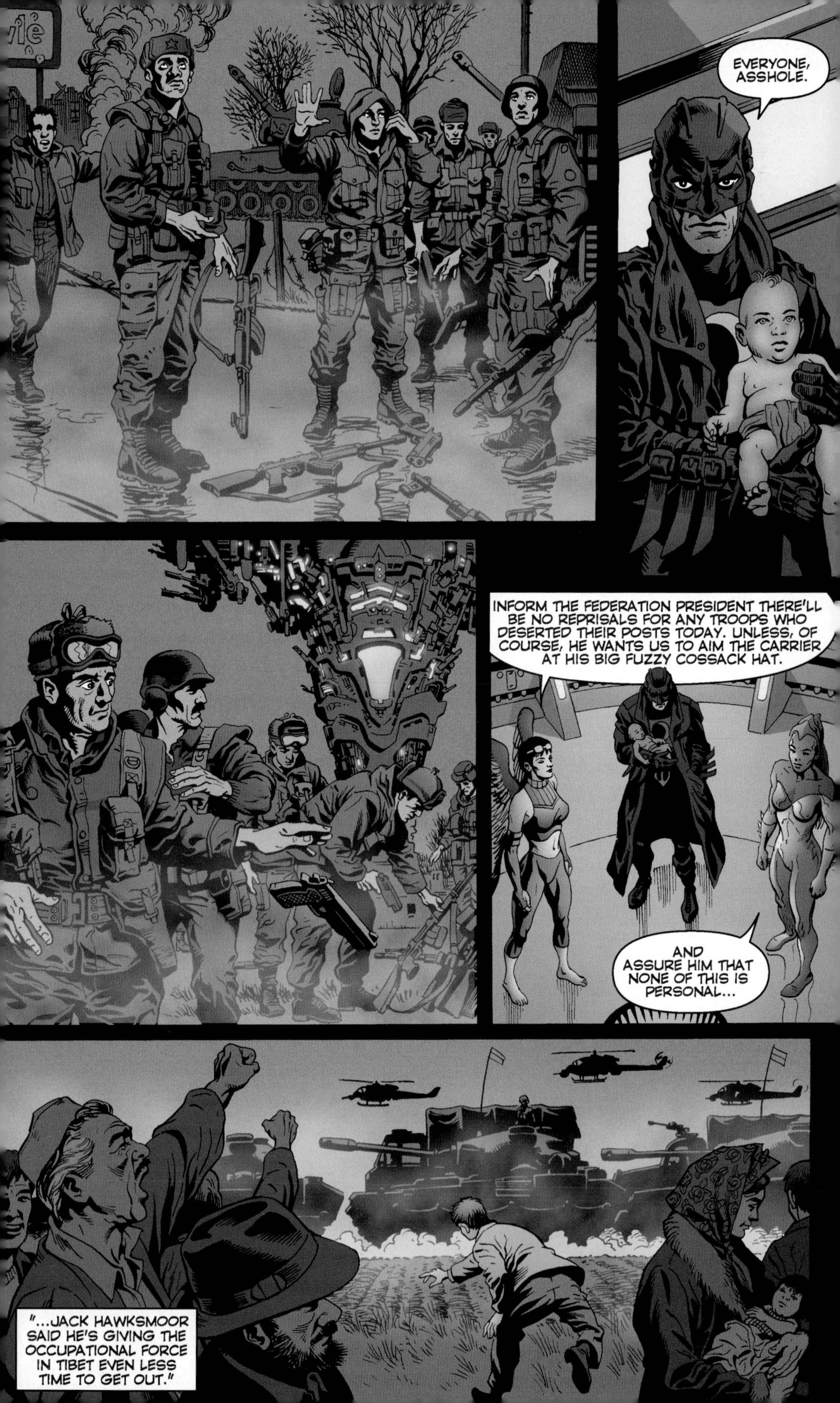
EVERYONE, ASSHOLE.
INFORM THE FEDERATION PRESIDENT THERE'LL BE NO REPRISALS FOR ANY TROOPS WHO DESERTED THEIR POSTS TODAY. UNLESS, OF COURSE, HE WANTS US TO AIM THE CARRIER AT HIS BIG FUZZY COSSACK HAT.
AND ASSURE HIM THAT NONE OF THIS IS PERSONAL...
"...JACK HAWKSMOOR SAID HE'S GIVING THE OCCUPATIONAL FORCE IN TIBET EVEN LESS TIME TO GET OUT."

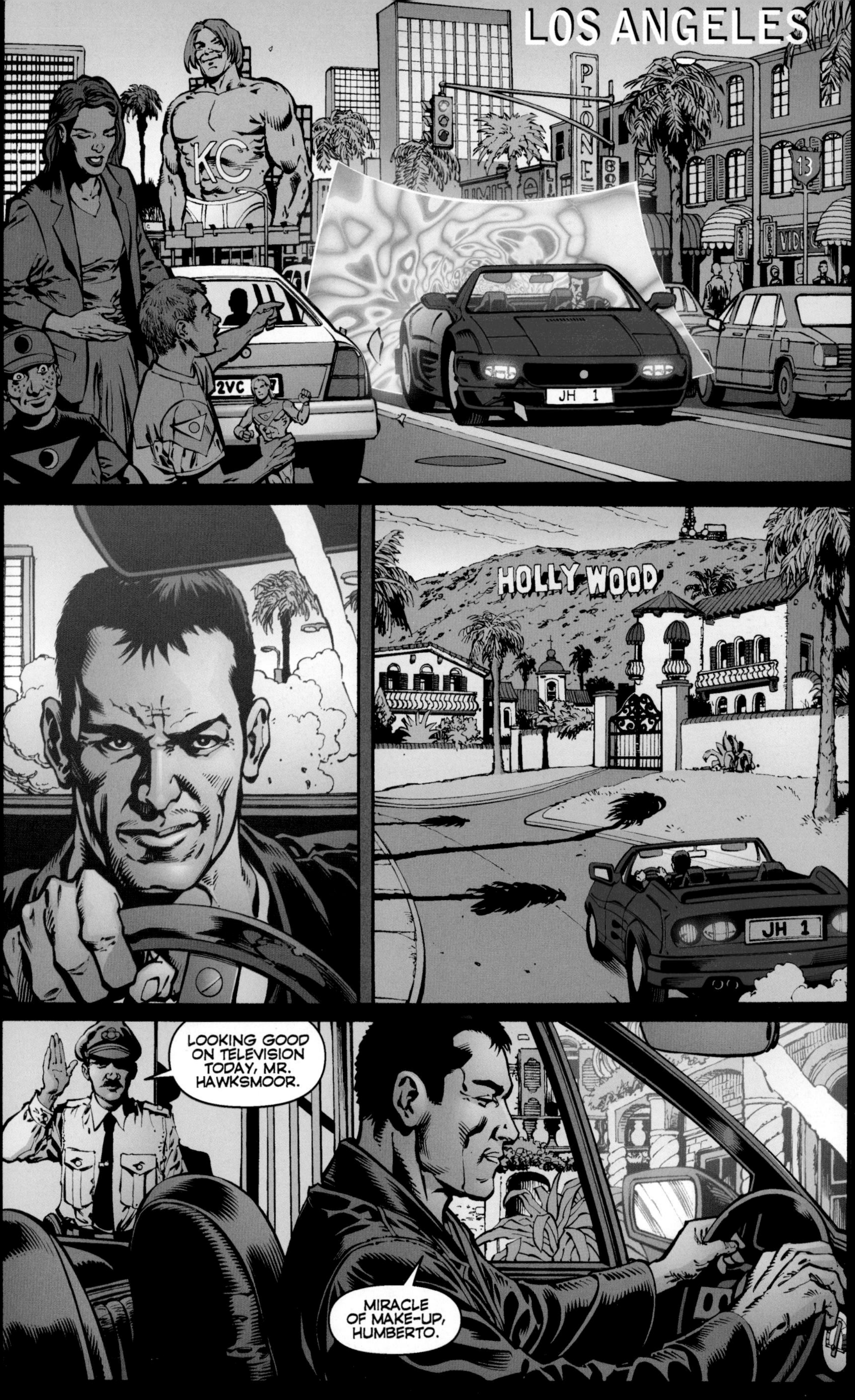
LOS ANGELES
PHONE
KC
2VC
JH 1
HOLLYWOOD
JH 1
LOOKING GOOD ON TELEVISION TODAY, MR. HAWKSMOOR.
MIRACLE OF MAKE-UP, HUMBERTO.

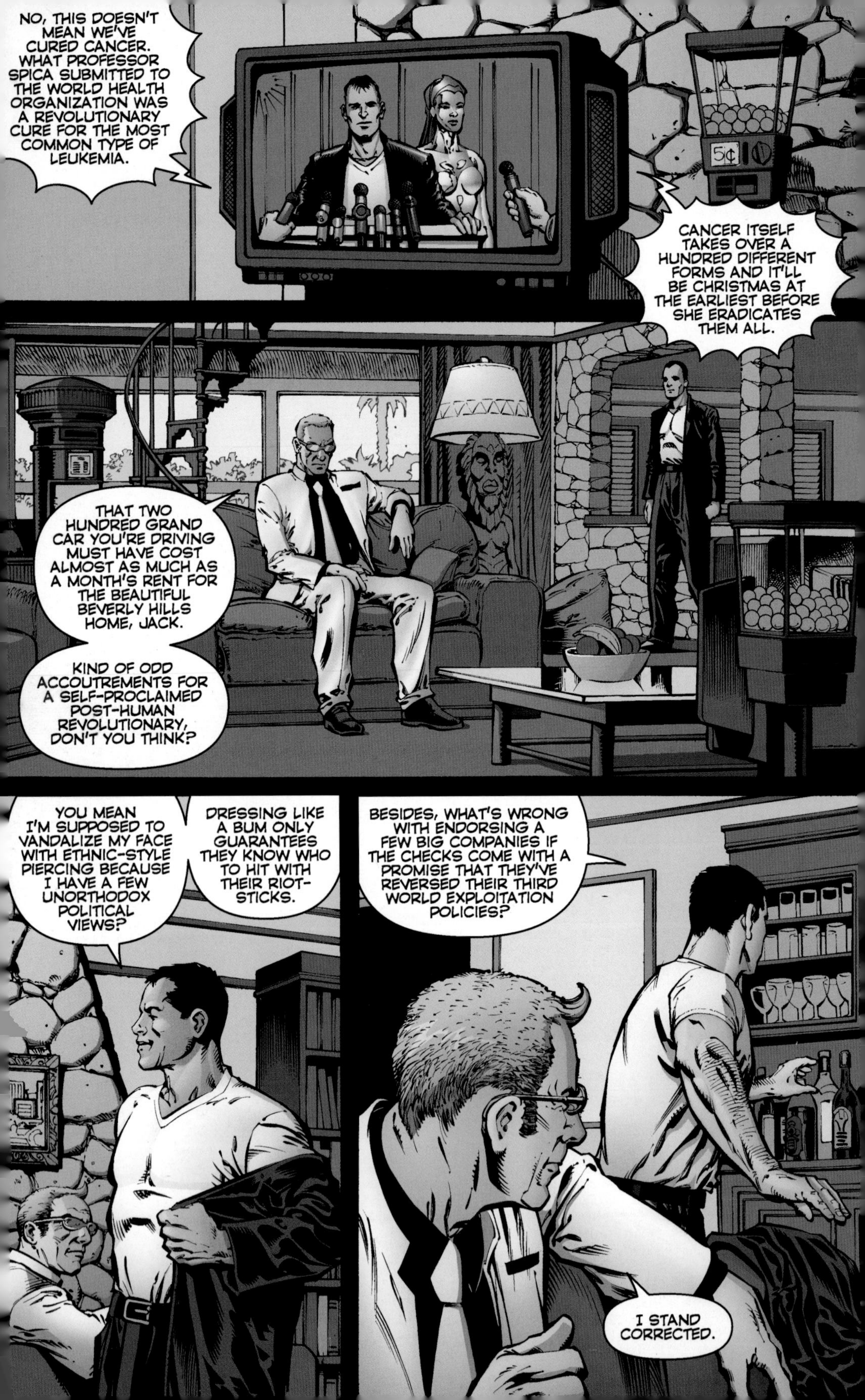
NO, THIS DOESN'T MEAN WE'VE CURED CANCER. WHAT PROFESSOR SPICA SUBMITTED TO THE WORLD HEALTH ORGANIZATION WAS A REVOLUTIONARY CURE FOR THE MOST COMMON TYPE OF LEUKEMIA.
5¢
CANCER ITSELF TAKES OVER A HUNDRED DIFFERENT FORMS AND IT'LL BE CHRISTMAS AT THE EARLIEST BEFORE SHE ERADICATES THEM ALL.
THAT TWO HUNDRED GRAND CAR YOU'RE DRIVING MUST HAVE COST ALMOST AS MUCH AS A MONTH'S RENT FOR THE BEAUTIFUL BEVERLY HILLS HOME, JACK.
KIND OF ODD ACCOUTREMENTS FOR A SELF-PROCLAIMED POST-HUMAN REVOLUTIONARY, DON'T YOU THINK?
YOU MEAN I'M SUPPOSED TO VANDALIZE MY FACE WITH ETHNIC-STYLE PIERCING BECAUSE I HAVE A FEW UNORTHODOX POLITICAL VIEWS?
DRESSING LIKE A BUM ONLY GUARANTEES THEY KNOW WHO TO HIT WITH THEIR RIOT-STICKS.
BESIDES, WHAT'S WRONG WITH ENDORSING A FEW BIG COMPANIES IF THE CHECKS COME WITH A PROMISE THAT THEY'VE REVERSED THEIR THIRD WORLD EXPLOITATION POLICIES?
I STAND CORRECTED.

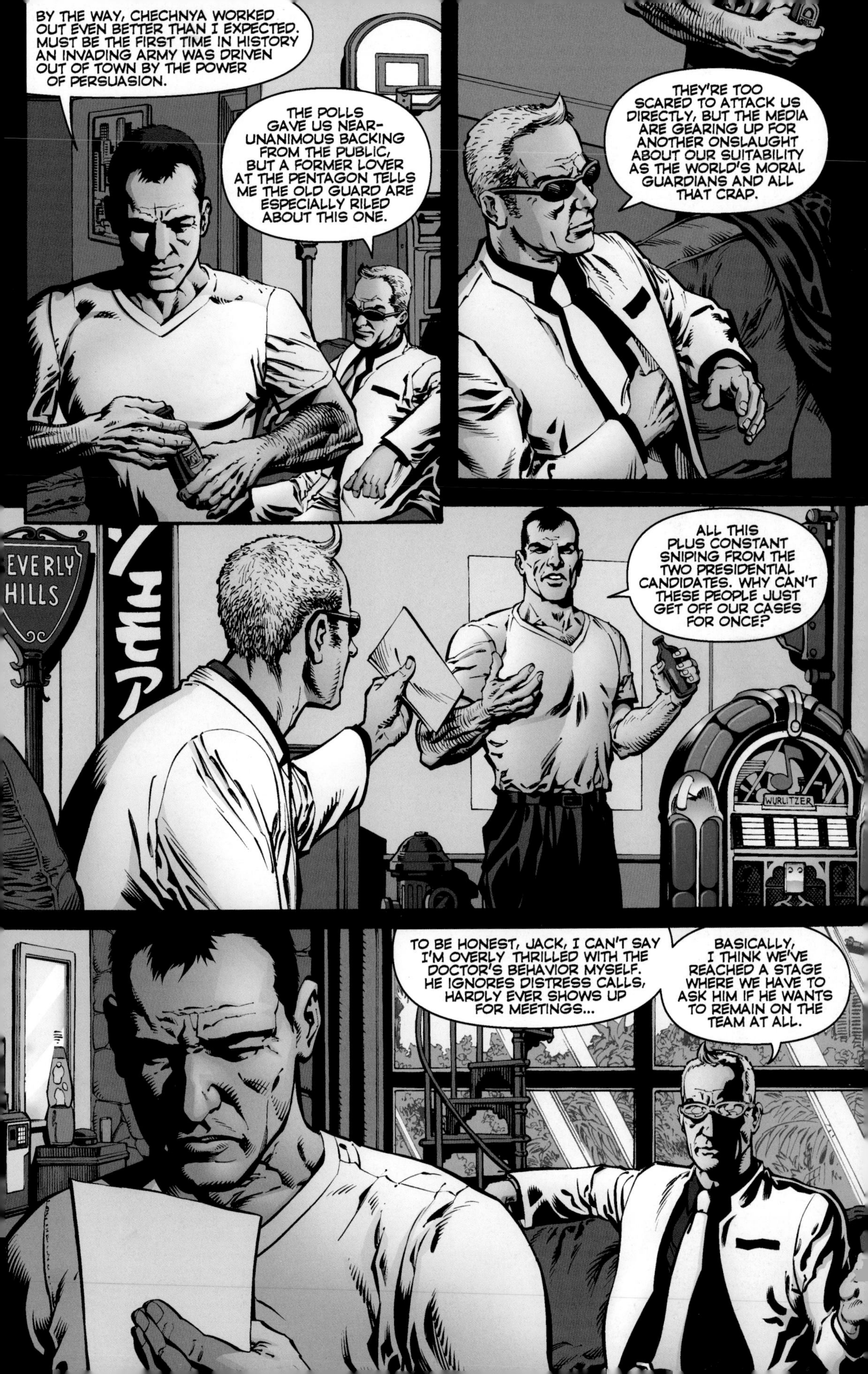
BY THE WAY, CHECHNYA WORKED OUT EVEN BETTER THAN I EXPECTED. MUST BE THE FIRST TIME IN HISTORY AN INVADING ARMY WAS DRIVEN OUT OF TOWN BY THE POWER OF PERSUASION.
THE POLLS GAVE US NEAR-UNANIMOUS BACKING FROM THE PUBLIC, BUT A FORMER LOVER AT THE PENTAGON TELLS ME THE OLD GUARD ARE ESPECIALLY RILED ABOUT THIS ONE.
THEY'RE TOO SCARED TO ATTACK US DIRECTLY, BUT THE MEDIA ARE GEARING UP FOR ANOTHER ONSLAUGHT ABOUT OUR SUITABILITY AS THE WORLD'S MORAL GUARDIANS AND ALL THAT CRAP.
EVERLY HILLS
ALL THIS PLUS CONSTANT SNIPING FROM THE TWO PRESIDENTIAL CANDIDATES. WHY CAN'T THESE PEOPLE JUST GET OFF OUR CASES FOR ONCE?
WURLITZER
TO BE HONEST, JACK, I CAN'T SAY I'M OVERLY THRILLED WITH THE DOCTOR'S BEHAVIOR MYSELF. HE IGNORES DISTRESS CALLS, HARDLY EVER SHOWS UP FOR MEETINGS...
BASICALLY, I THINK WE'VE REACHED A STAGE WHERE WE HAVE TO ASK HIM IF HE WANTS TO REMAIN ON THE TEAM AT ALL.

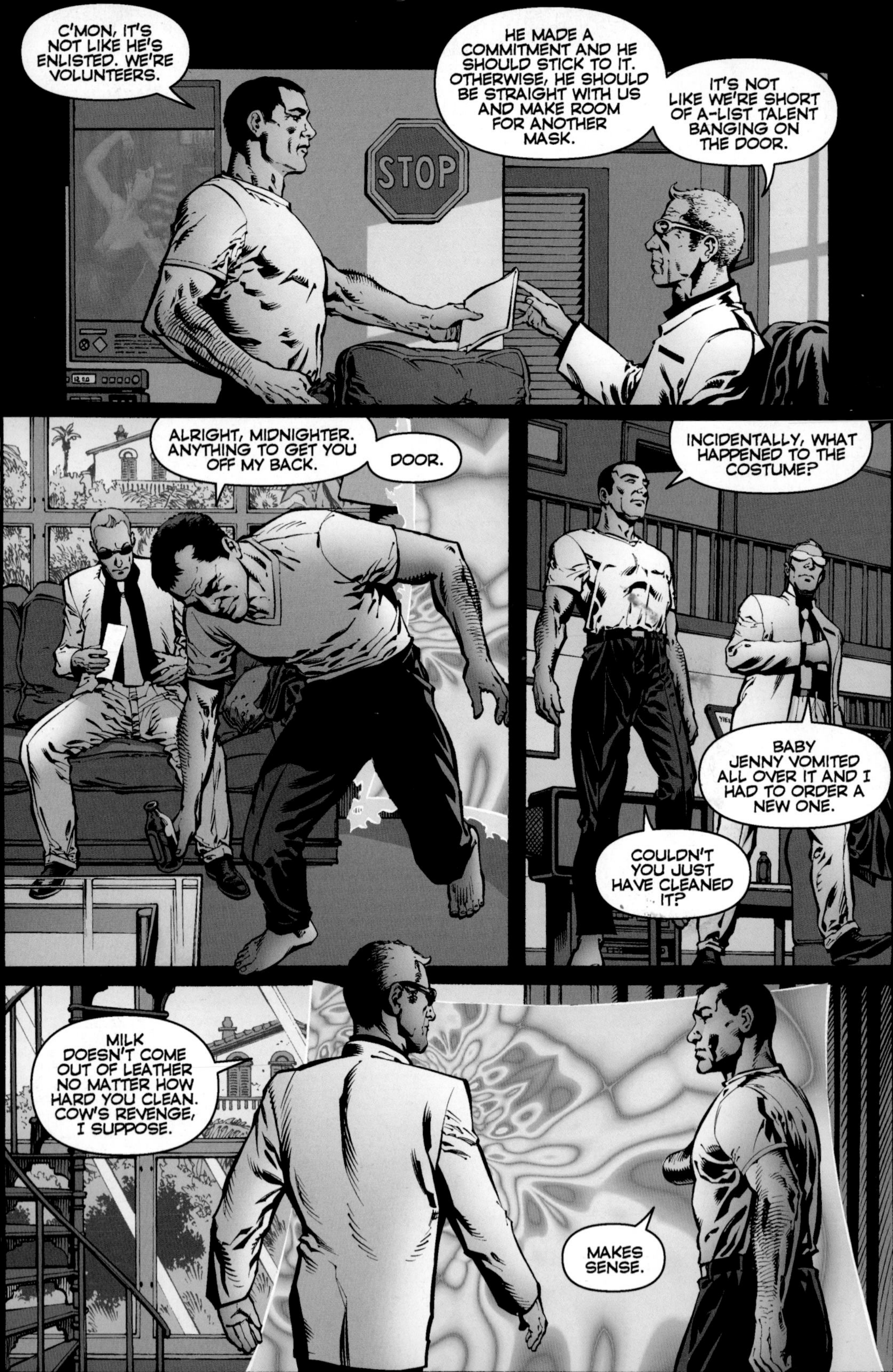
C'MON, IT'S NOT LIKE HE'S ENLISTED. WE'RE VOLUNTEERS.
HE MADE A COMMITMENT AND HE SHOULD STICK TO IT. OTHERWISE, HE SHOULD BE STRAIGHT WITH US AND MAKE ROOM FOR ANOTHER MASK.
IT'S NOT LIKE WE'RE SHORT OF A-LIST TALENT BANGING ON THE DOOR.
STOP
ALRIGHT, MIDNIGHTER. ANYTHING TO GET YOU OFF MY BACK.
DOOR.
INCIDENTALLY, WHAT HAPPENED TO THE COSTUME?
BABY JENNY VOMITED ALL OVER IT AND I HAD TO ORDER A NEW ONE.
COULDN'T YOU JUST HAVE CLEANED IT?
MILK DOESN'T COME OUT OF LEATHER NO MATTER HOW HARD YOU CLEAN. COW'S REVENGE, I SUPPOSE.
MAKES SENSE.

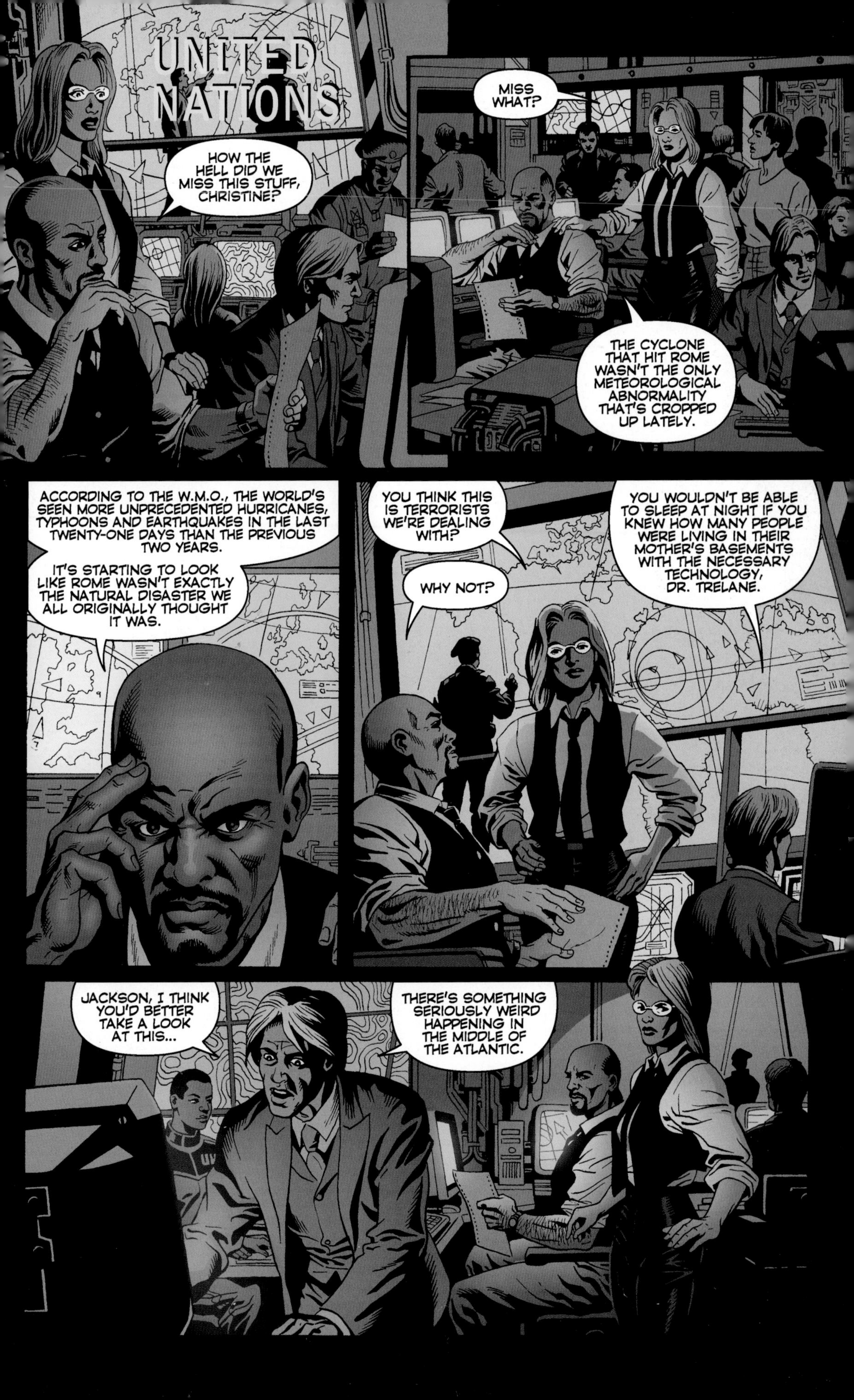
UNITED NATIONS
HOW THE HELL DID WE MISS THIS STUFF, CHRISTINE?
MISS WHAT?
THE CYCLONE THAT HIT ROME WASN'T THE ONLY METEOROLOGICAL ABNORMALITY THAT'S CROPPED UP LATELY.
ACCORDING TO THE W.M.O., THE WORLD'S SEEN MORE UNPRECEDENTED HURRICANES, TYPHOONS AND EARTHQUAKES IN THE LAST TWENTY-ONE DAYS THAN THE PREVIOUS TWO YEARS.
IT'S STARTING TO LOOK LIKE ROME WASN'T EXACTLY THE NATURAL DISASTER WE ALL ORIGINALLY THOUGHT IT WAS.
YOU THINK THIS IS TERRORISTS WE'RE DEALING WITH?
WHY NOT?
YOU WOULDN'T BE ABLE TO SLEEP AT NIGHT IF YOU KNEW HOW MANY PEOPLE WERE LIVING IN THEIR MOTHER'S BASEMENTS WITH THE NECESSARY TECHNOLOGY, DR. TRELANE.
JACKSON, I THINK YOU'D BETTER TAKE A LOOK AT THIS...
THERE'S SOMETHING SERIOUSLY WEIRD HAPPENING IN THE MIDDLE OF THE ATLANTIC.

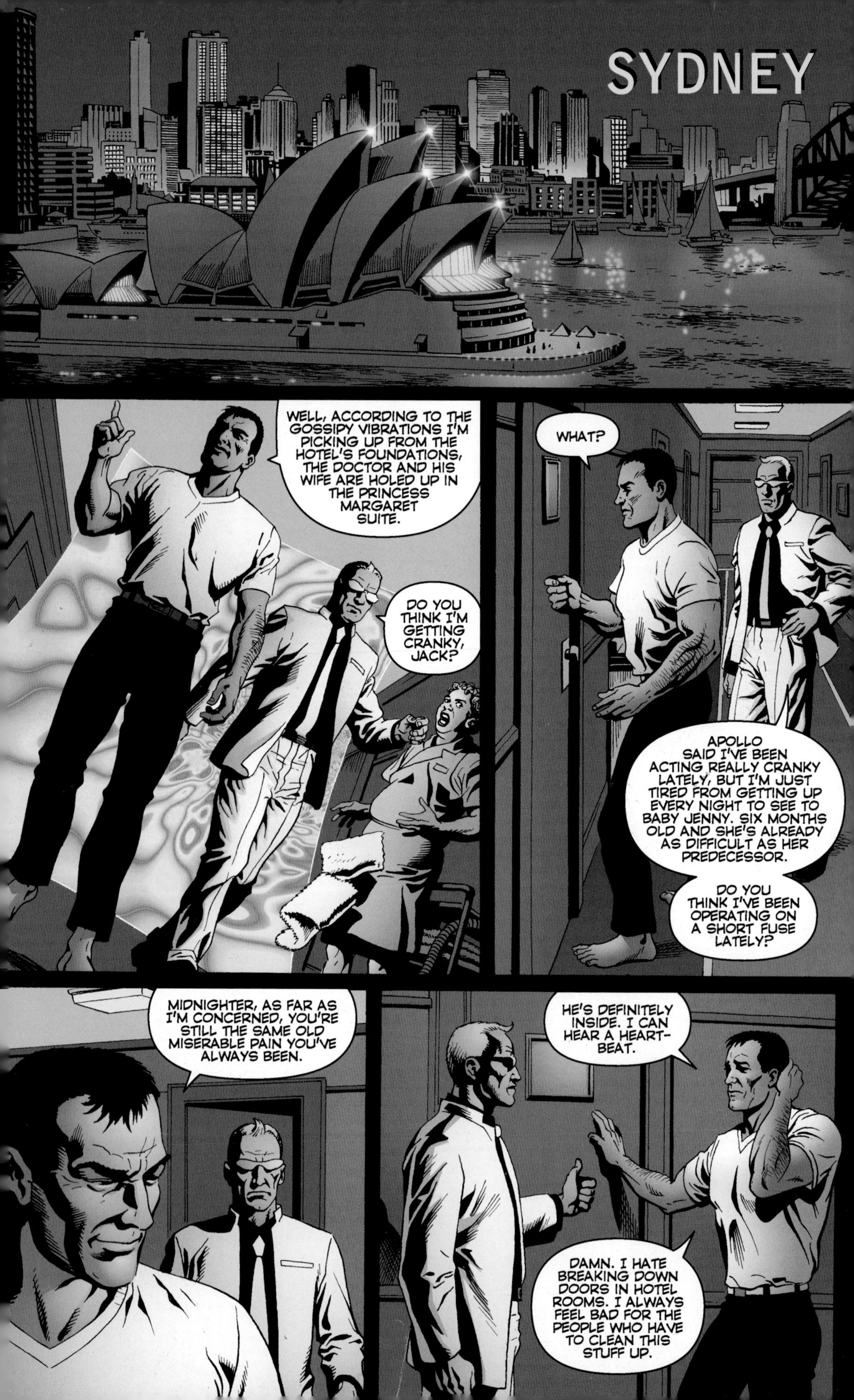
SYDNEY
WELL, ACCORDING TO THE GOSSIPY VIBRATIONS I'M PICKING UP FROM THE HOTEL'S FOUNDATIONS, THE DOCTOR AND HIS WIFE ARE HOLED UP IN THE PRINCESS MARGARET SUITE.
DO YOU THINK I'M GETTING CRANKY, JACK?
WHAT?
APOLLO SAID I'VE BEEN ACTING REALLY CRANKY LATELY, BUT I'M JUST TIRED FROM GETTING UP EVERY NIGHT TO SEE TO BABY JENNY. SIX MONTHS OLD AND SHE'S ALREADY AS DIFFICULT AS HER PREDECESSOR.
DO YOU THINK I'VE BEEN OPERATING ON A SHORT FUSE LATELY?
MIDNIGHTER, AS FAR AS I'M CONCERNED, YOU'RE STILL THE SAME OLD MISERABLE PAIN YOU'VE ALWAYS BEEN.
HE'S DEFINITELY INSIDE. I CAN HEAR A HEART-BEAT.
DAMN. I HATE BREAKING DOWN DOORS IN HOTEL ROOMS. I ALWAYS FEEL BAD FOR THE PEOPLE WHO HAVE TO CLEAN THIS STUFF UP.

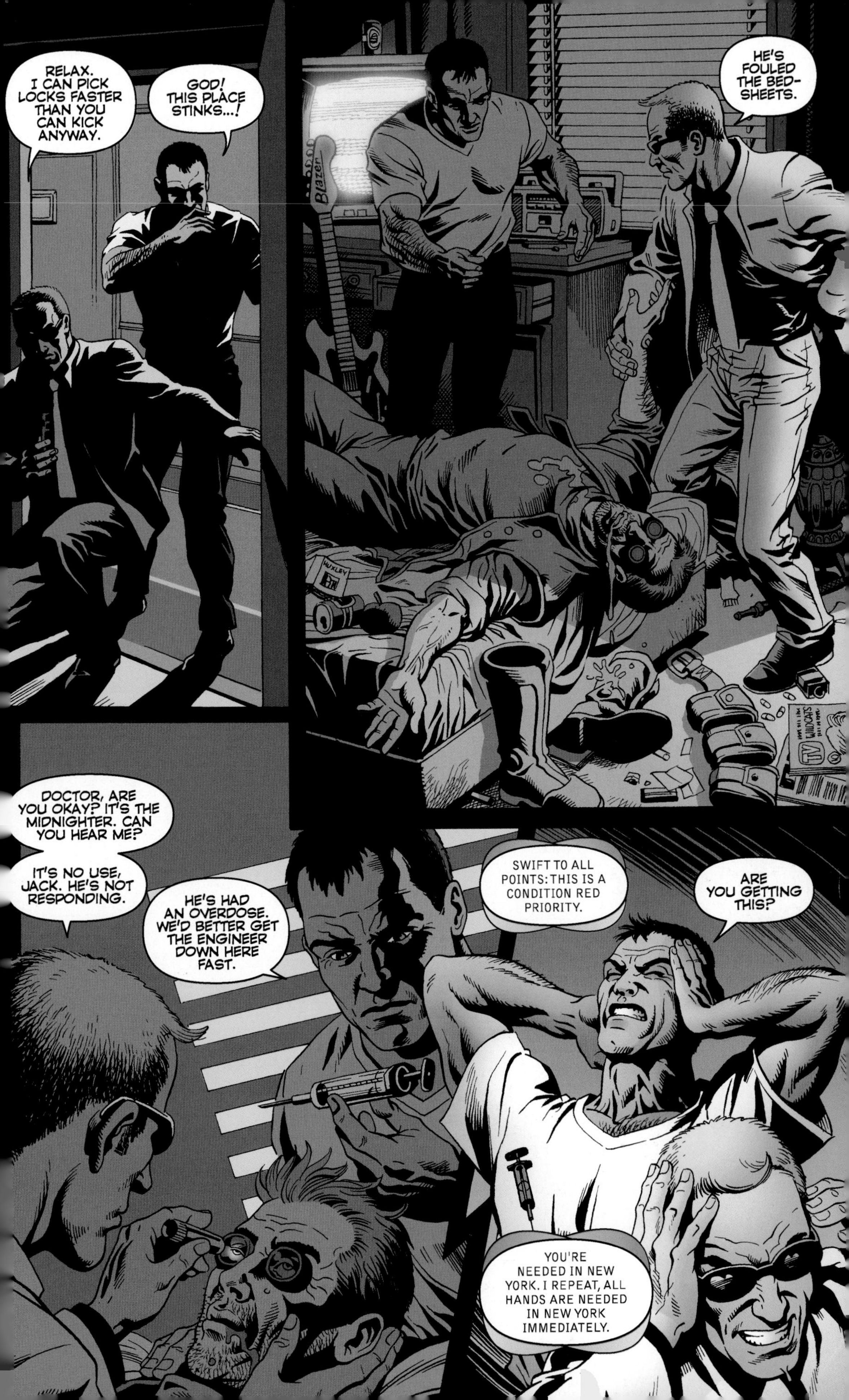
RELAX. I CAN PICK LOCKS FASTER THAN YOU CAN KICK ANYWAY.
GOD! THIS PLACE STINKS...!
HE'S FOULED THE BED-SHEETS.
DOCTOR, ARE YOU OKAY? IT'S THE MIDNIGHTER. CAN YOU HEAR ME?
IT'S NO USE, JACK. HE'S NOT RESPONDING.
HE'S HAD AN OVERDOSE. WE'D BETTER GET THE ENGINEER DOWN HERE FAST.
SWIFT TO ALL POINTS: THIS IS A CONDITION RED PRIORITY.
ARE YOU GETTING THIS?
YOU'RE NEEDED IN NEW YORK. I REPEAT, ALL HANDS ARE NEEDED IN NEW YORK IMMEDIATELY.

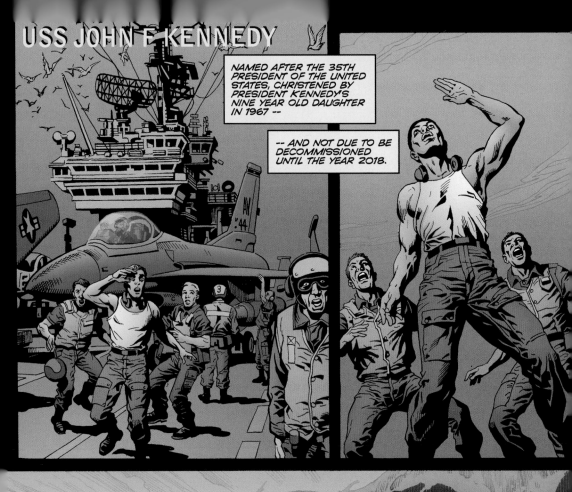

USS JOHN F. KENNEDY

NAMED AFTER THE 35TH PRESIDENT OF THE UNITED STATES, CHRISTENED BY PRESIDENT KENNEDY'S NINE YEAR OLD DAUGHTER IN 1967 --

-- AND NOT DUE TO BE DECOMMISSIONED UNTIL THE YEAR 2018.

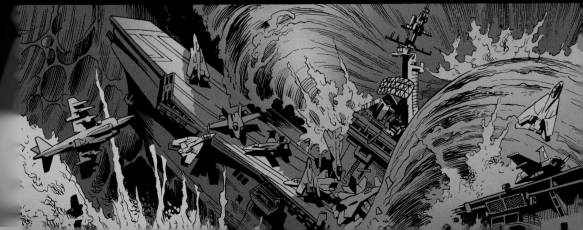

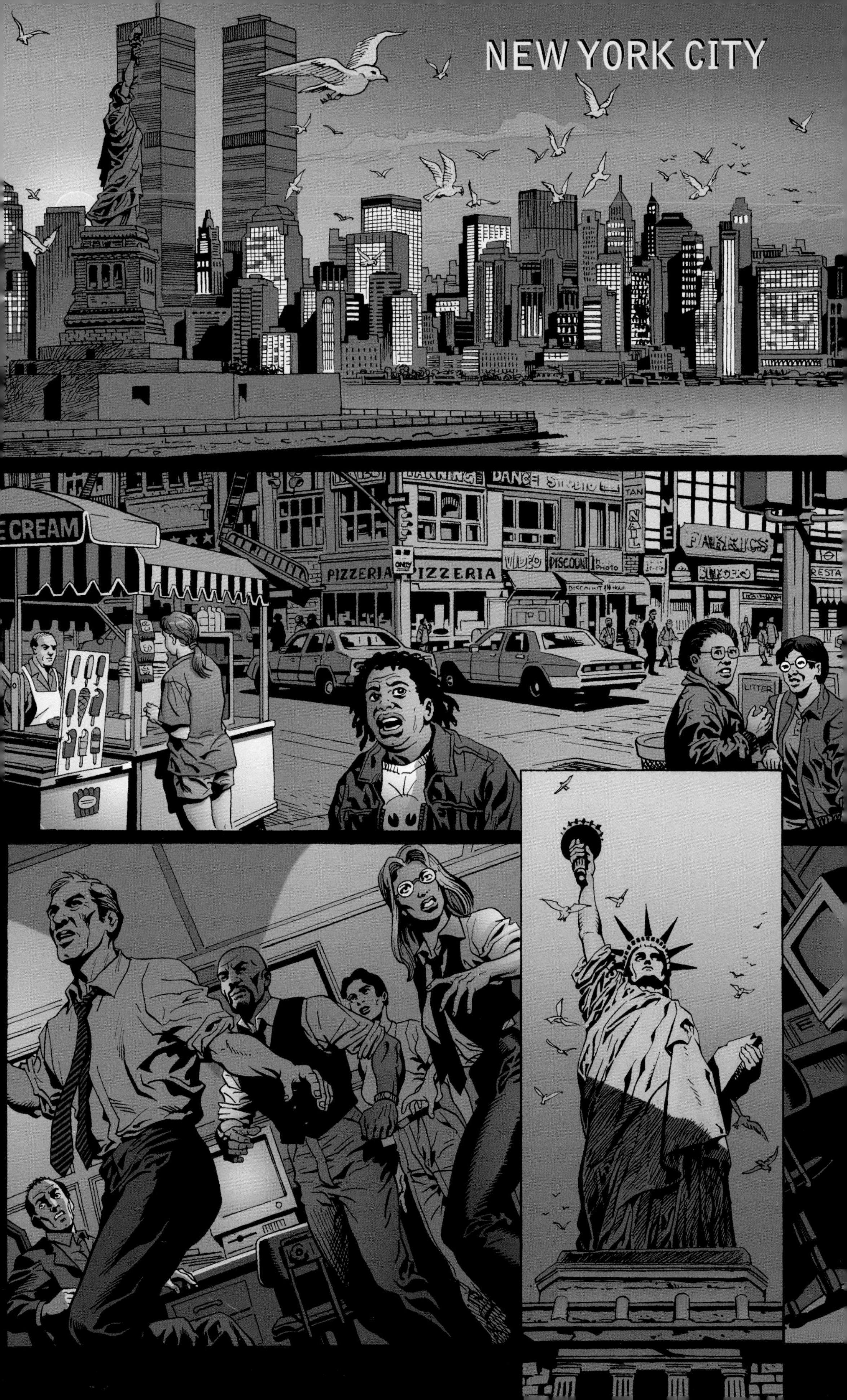
NEW YORK CITY
CREAM
PIZZERIA
PIZZERIA
VIDEO
DISCOUNT
LITTER

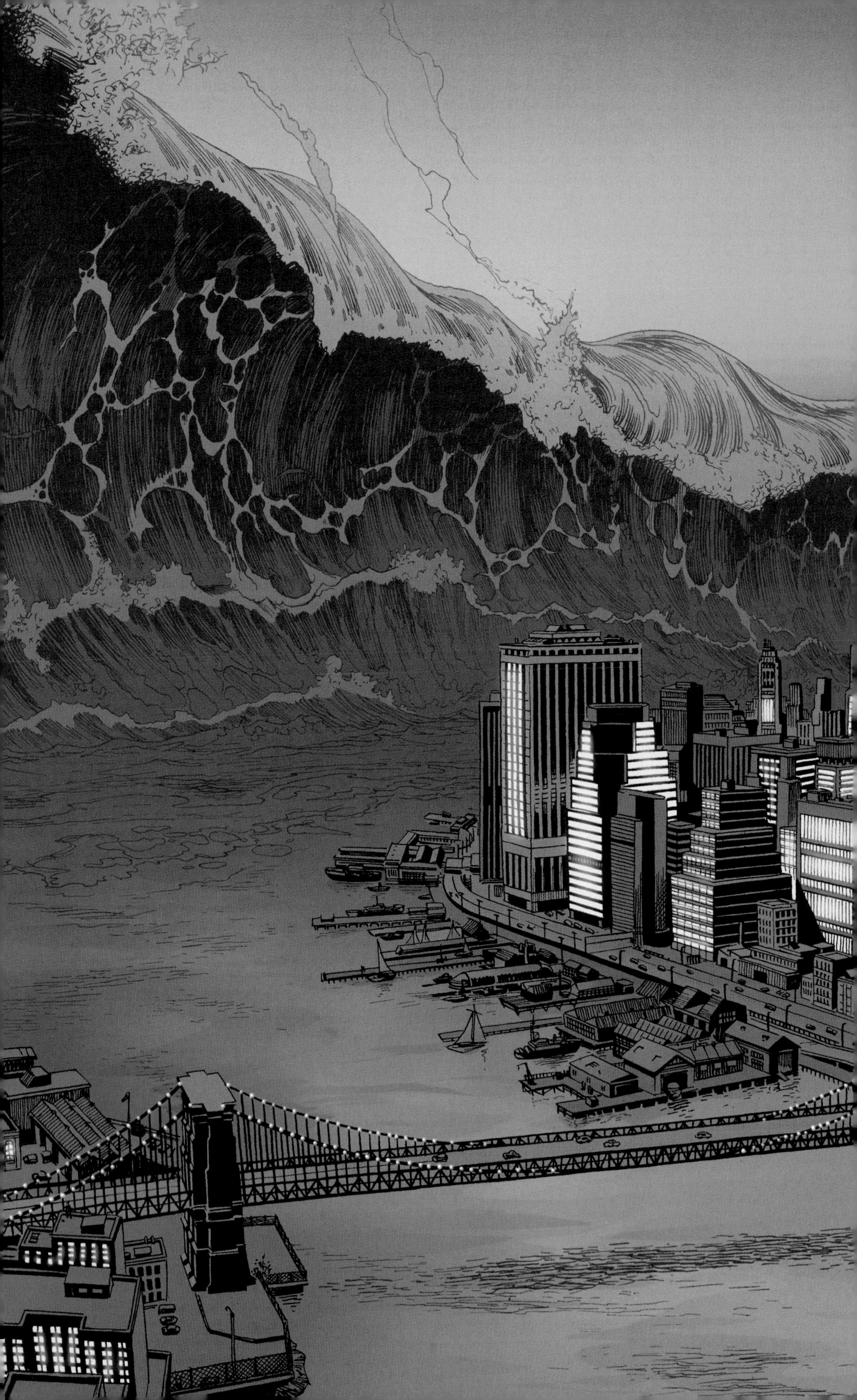

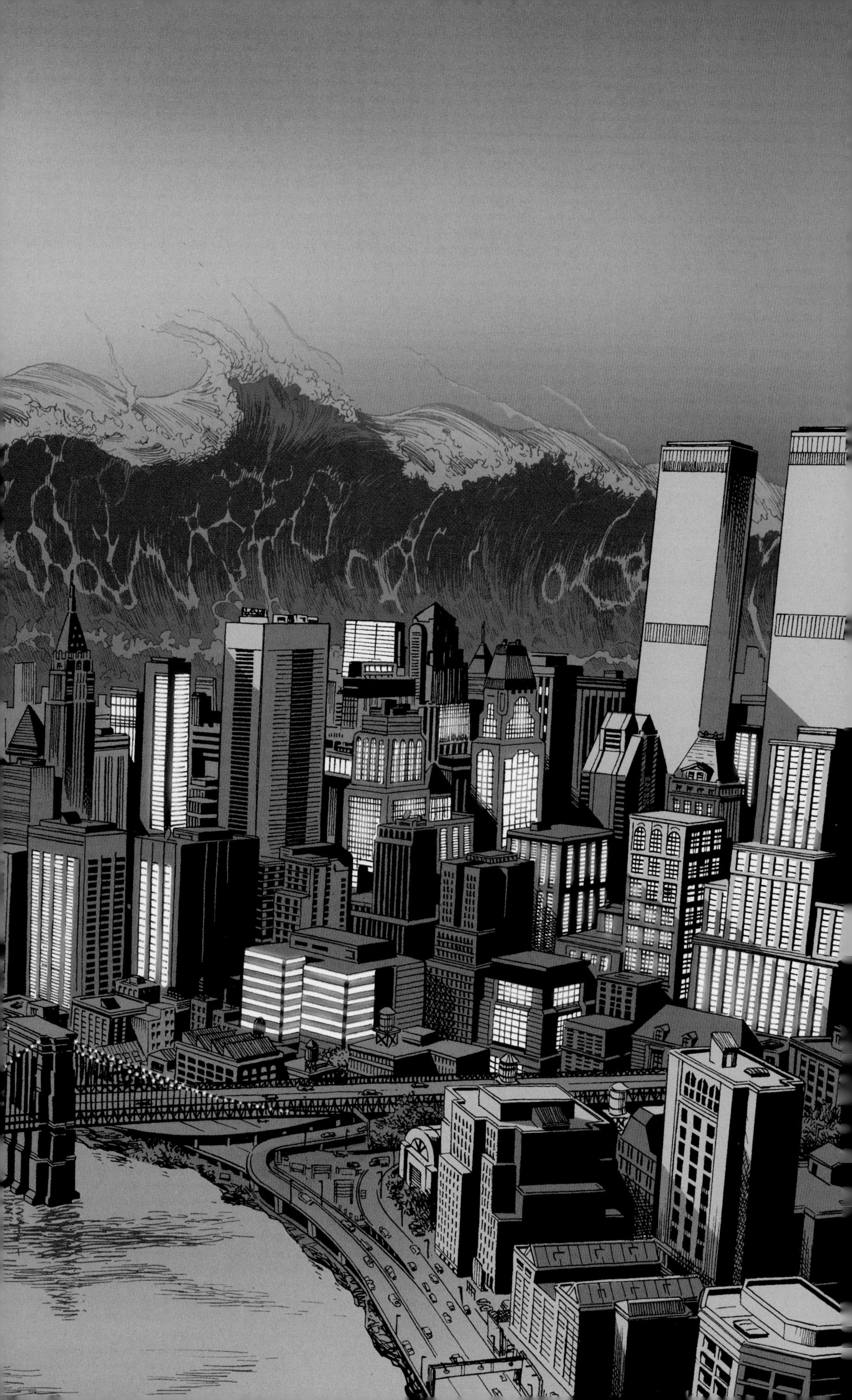

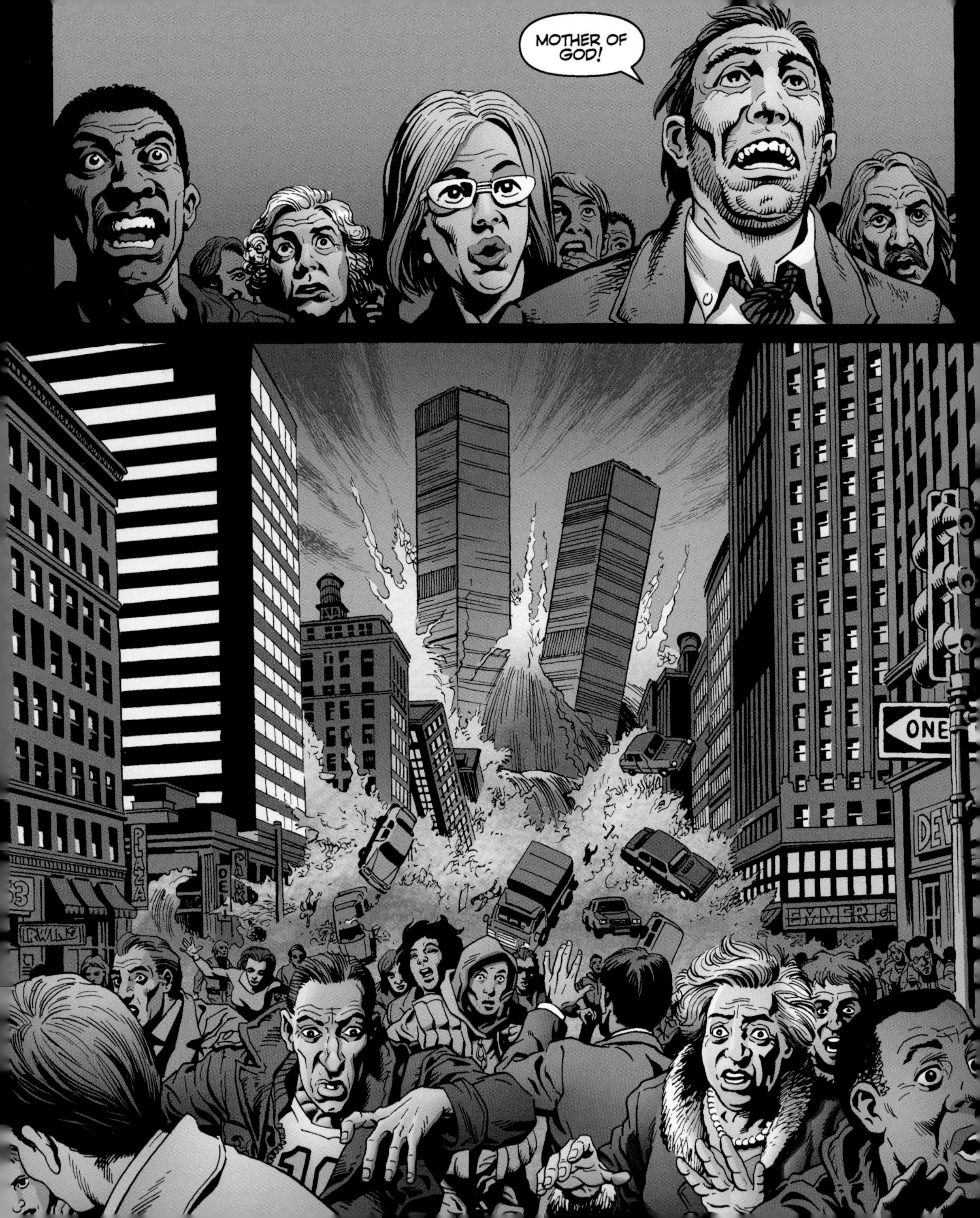
MOTHER OF GOD!
PLAZA
ONE

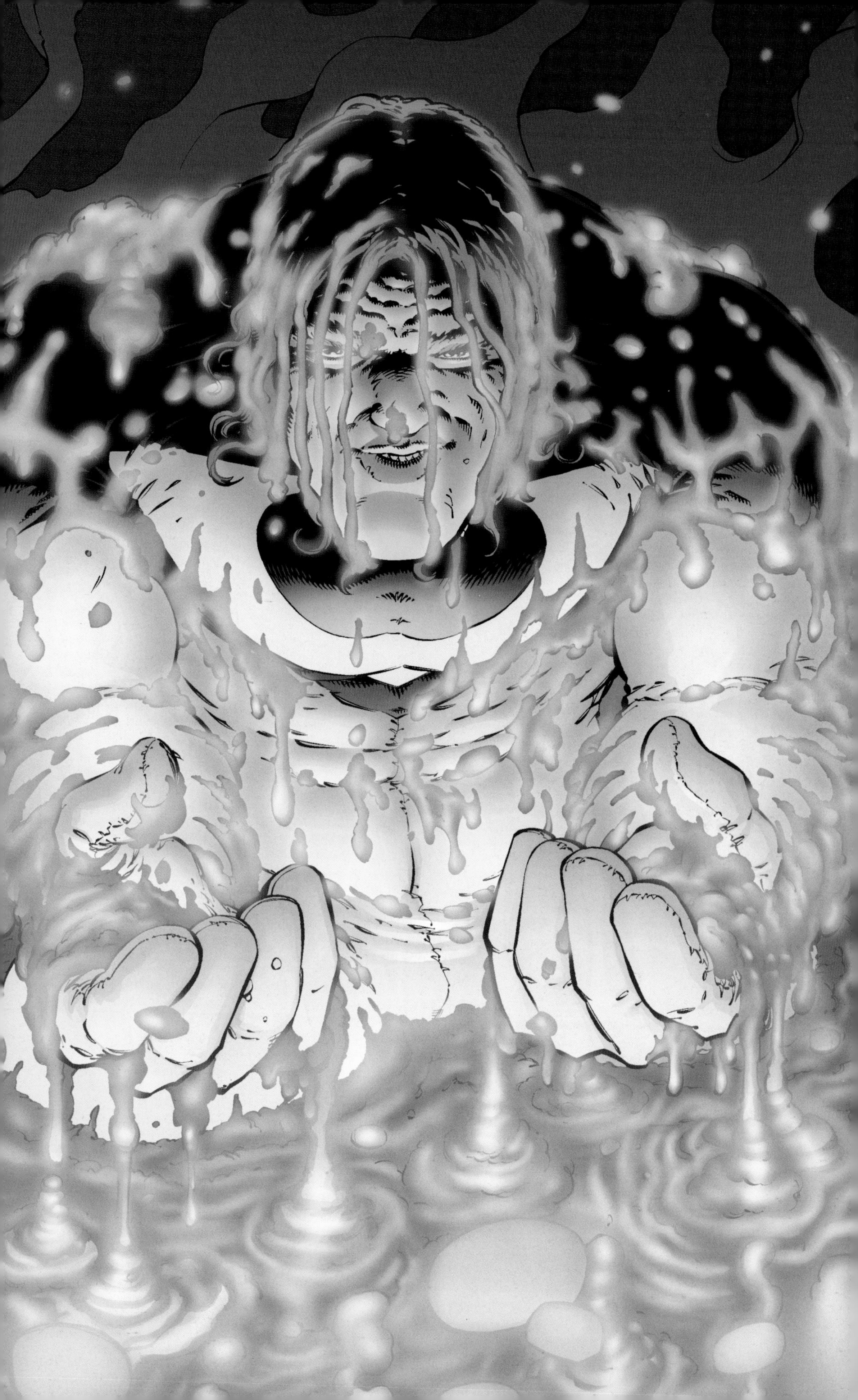

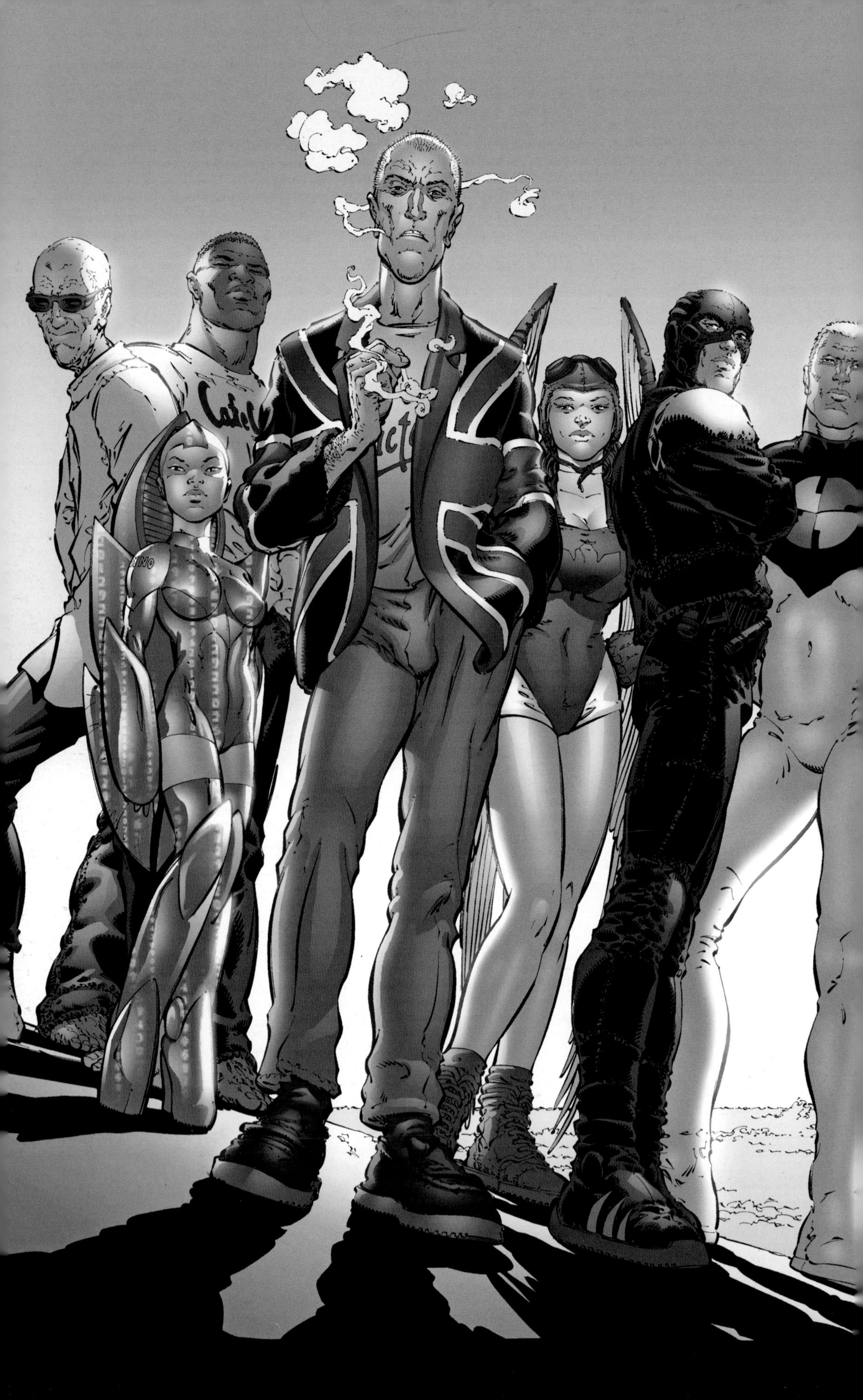

NEW YORK CITY

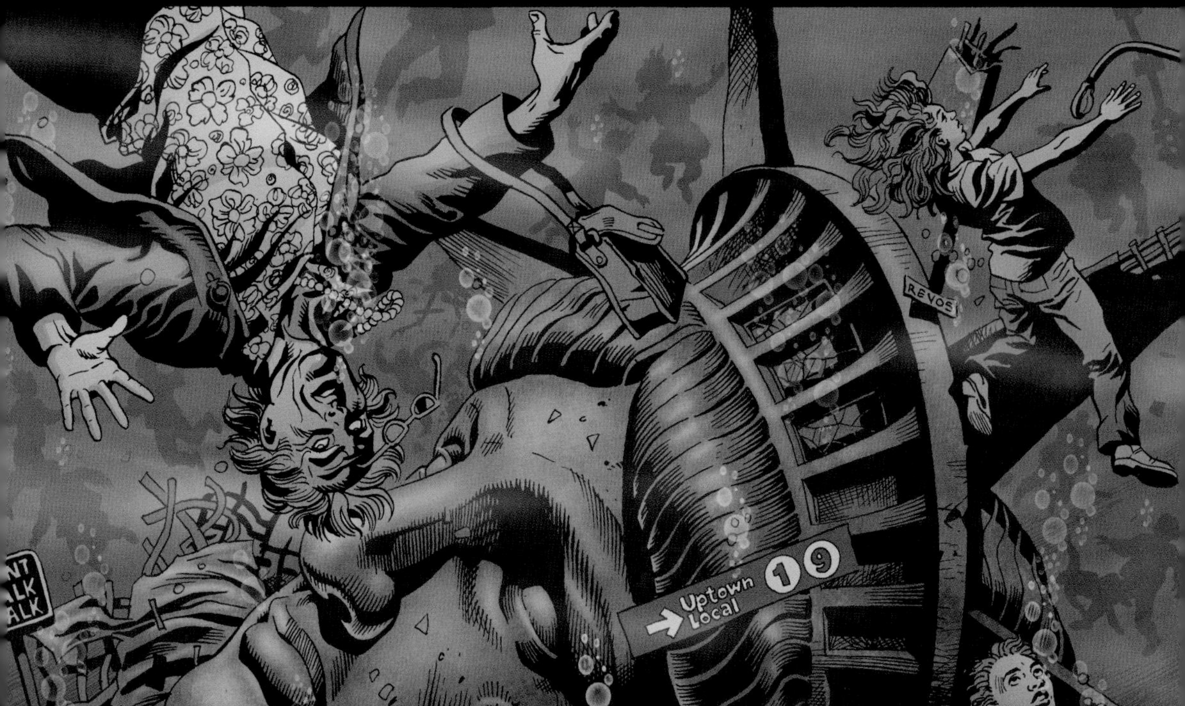

Uptown Local
1 9

The AUTHORITY

"Earth Inferno"

TWO of FOUR

MARK MILLAR writer

CHRIS WESTON artist

GARRY LEACH inker

BARON& FOUTS colorists

BILL O'NEIL letterer

Inking assistance provided by Derek Fridolfs, Sal Regla and Chris Weston.

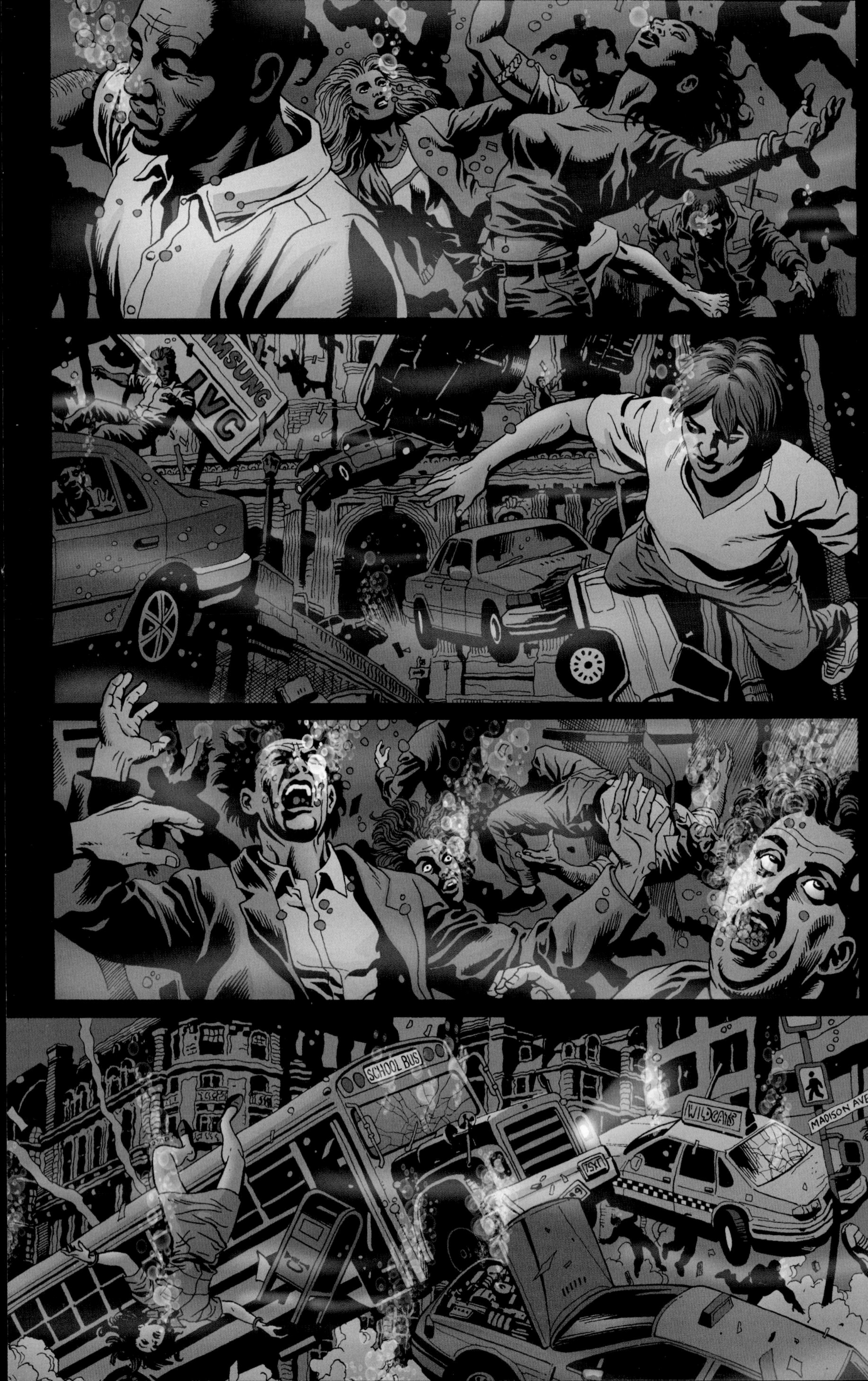
SCHOOL BUS
WILDCATS
MADISON AVE

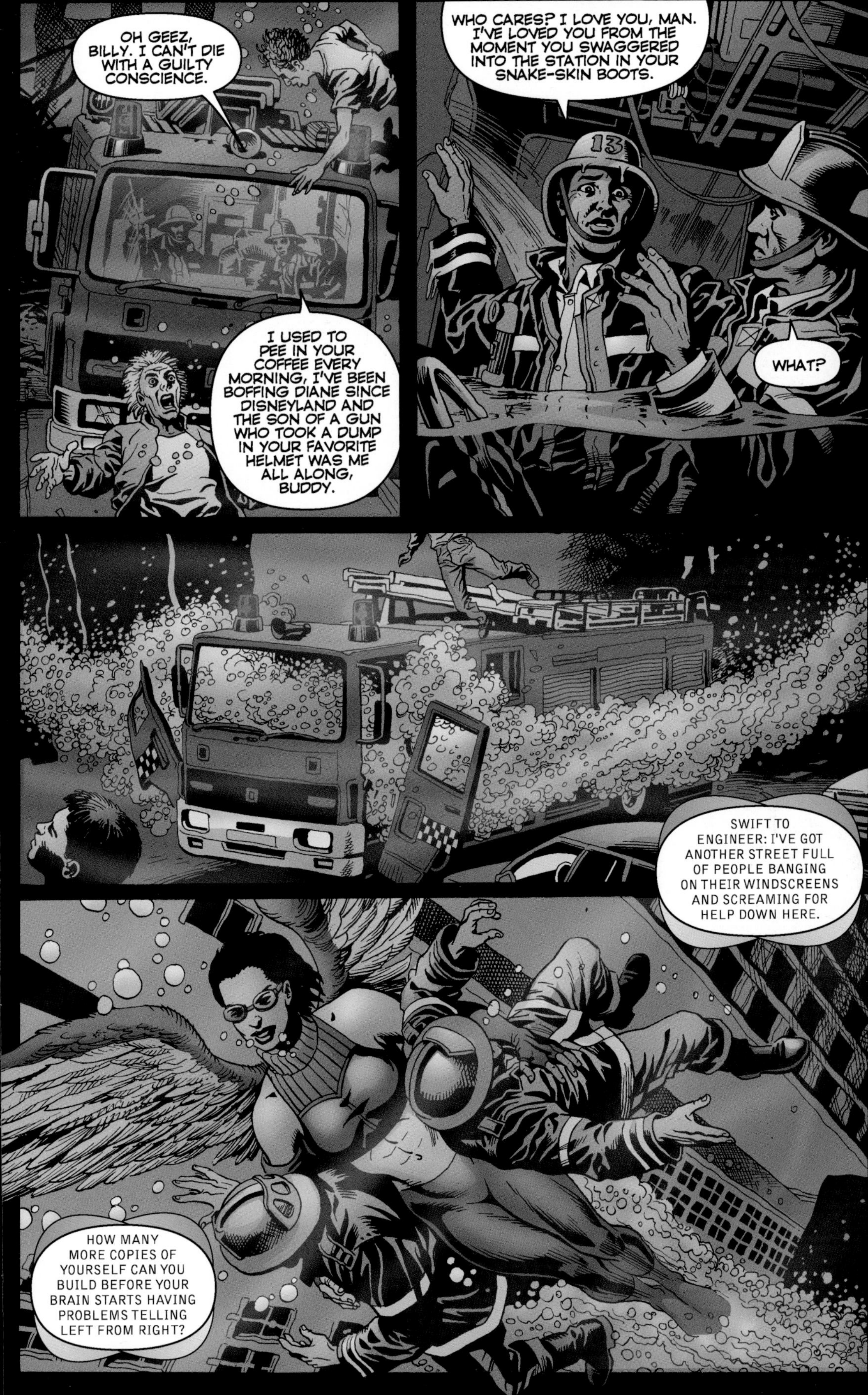

OH GEEZ, BILLY. I CAN'T DIE WITH A GUILTY CONSCIENCE.
I USED TO PEE IN YOUR COFFEE EVERY MORNING, I'VE BEEN BOFFING DIANE SINCE DISNEYLAND AND THE SON OF A GUN WHO TOOK A DUMP IN YOUR FAVORITE HELMET WAS ME ALL ALONG, BUDDY.
WHO CARES? I LOVE YOU, MAN. I'VE LOVED YOU FROM THE MOMENT YOU SWAGGERED INTO THE STATION IN YOUR SNAKE-SKIN BOOTS.
13
WHAT?
SWIFT TO ENGINEER: I'VE GOT ANOTHER STREET FULL OF PEOPLE BANGING ON THEIR WINDSCREENS AND SCREAMING FOR HELP DOWN HERE.
HOW MANY MORE COPIES OF YOURSELF CAN YOU BUILD BEFORE YOUR BRAIN STARTS HAVING PROBLEMS TELLING LEFT FROM RIGHT?

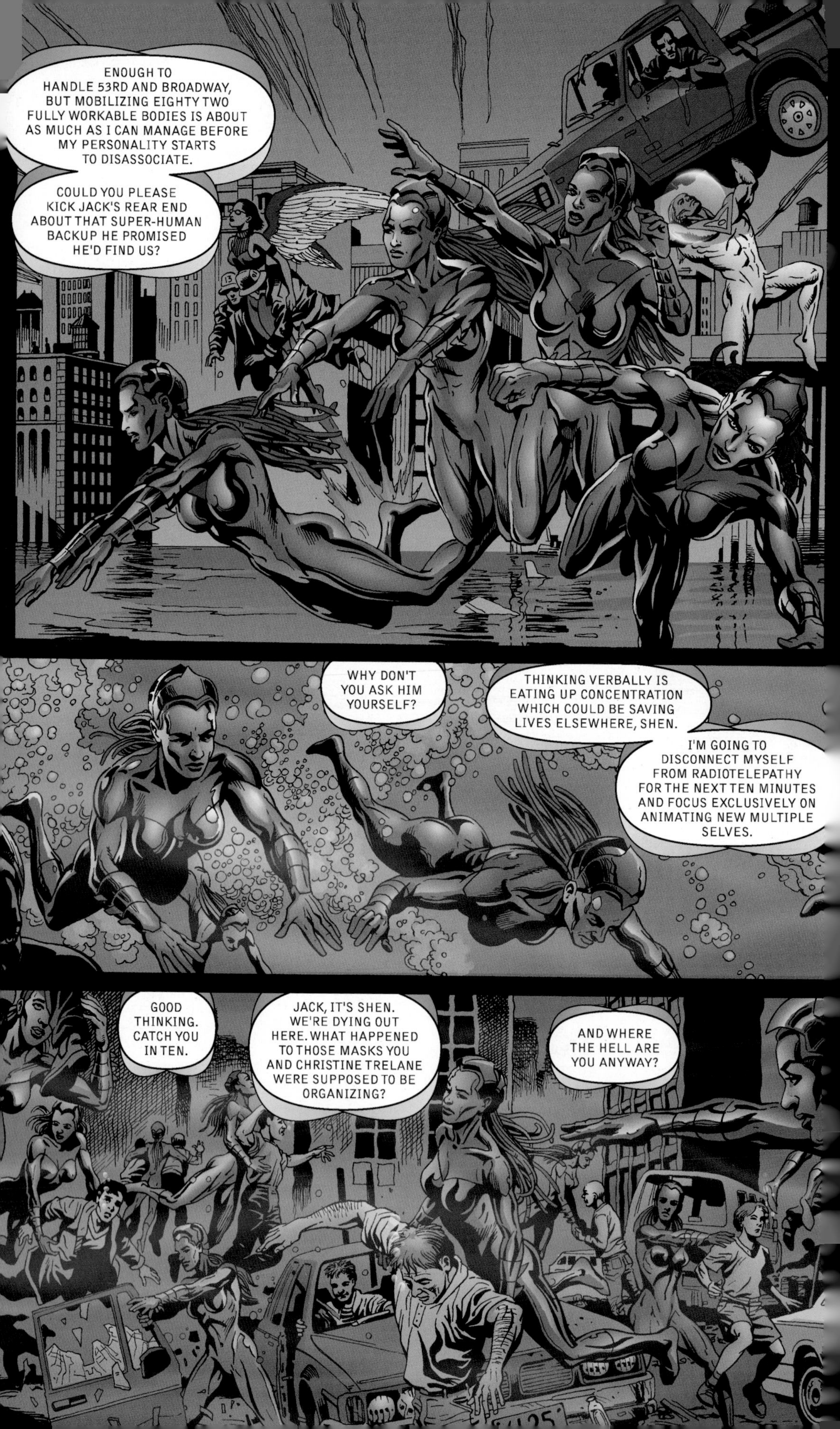
ENOUGH TO HANDLE 53RD AND BROADWAY, BUT MOBILIZING EIGHTY TWO FULLY WORKABLE BODIES IS ABOUT AS MUCH AS I CAN MANAGE BEFORE MY PERSONALITY STARTS TO DISASSOCIATE.
COULD YOU PLEASE KICK JACK'S REAR END ABOUT THAT SUPER-HUMAN BACKUP HE PROMISED HE'D FIND US?
WHY DON'T YOU ASK HIM YOURSELF?
THINKING VERBALLY IS EATING UP CONCENTRATION WHICH COULD BE SAVING LIVES ELSEWHERE, SHEN.
I'M GOING TO DISCONNECT MYSELF FROM RADIOTELEPATHY FOR THE NEXT TEN MINUTES AND FOCUS EXCLUSIVELY ON ANIMATING NEW MULTIPLE SELVES.
GOOD THINKING. CATCH YOU IN TEN.
JACK, IT'S SHEN. WE'RE DYING OUT HERE. WHAT HAPPENED TO THOSE MASKS YOU AND CHRISTINE TRELANE WERE SUPPOSED TO BE ORGANIZING?
AND WHERE THE HELL ARE YOU ANYWAY?

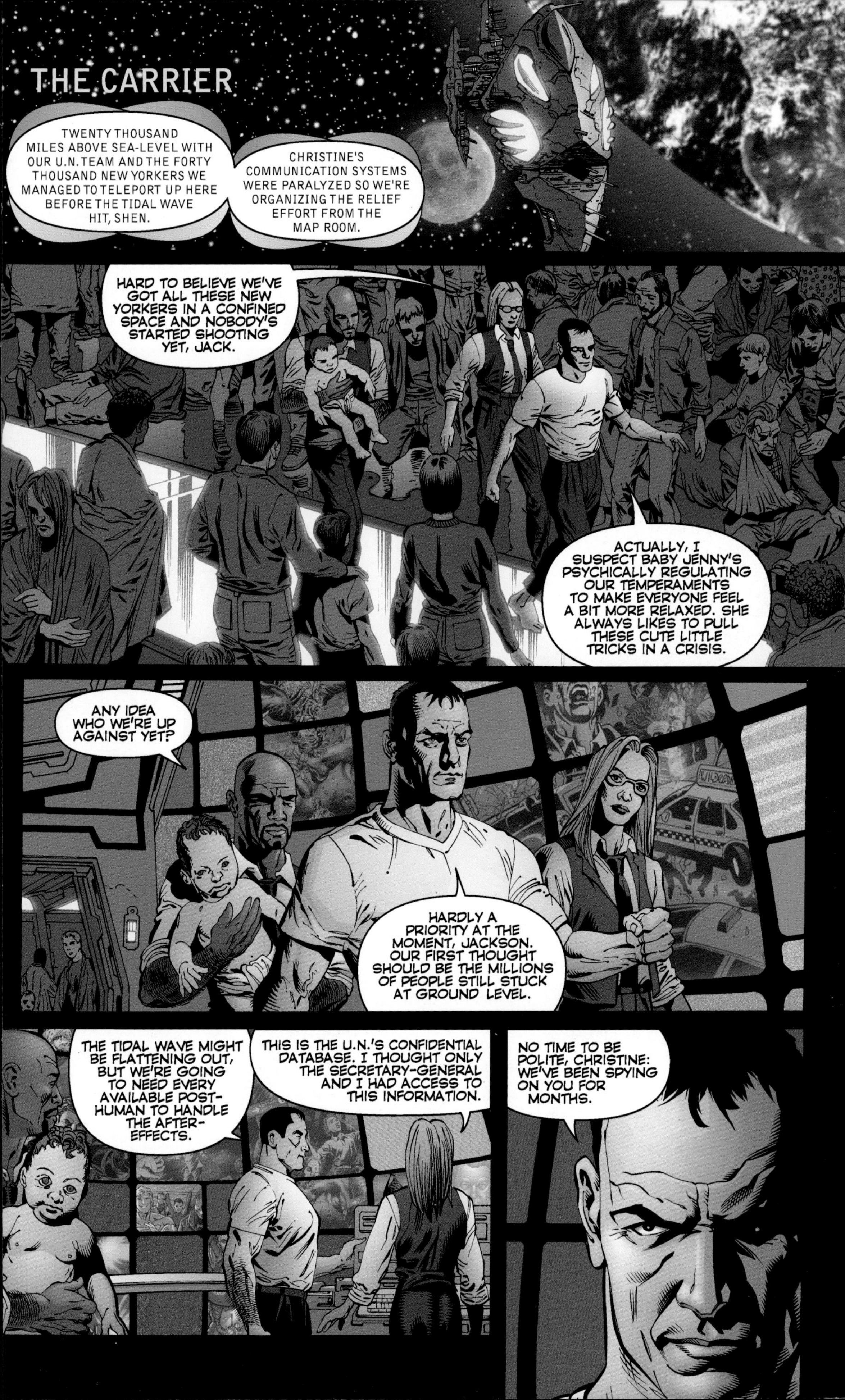
THE CARRIER
TWENTY THOUSAND MILES ABOVE SEA-LEVEL WITH OUR U.N. TEAM AND THE FORTY THOUSAND NEW YORKERS WE MANAGED TO TELEPORT UP HERE BEFORE THE TIDAL WAVE HIT, SHEN.
CHRISTINE'S COMMUNICATION SYSTEMS WERE PARALYZED SO WE'RE ORGANIZING THE RELIEF EFFORT FROM THE MAP ROOM.
HARD TO BELIEVE WE'VE GOT ALL THESE NEW YORKERS IN A CONFINED SPACE AND NOBODY'S STARTED SHOOTING YET, JACK.
ACTUALLY, I SUSPECT BABY JENNY'S PSYCHICALLY REGULATING OUR TEMPERAMENTS TO MAKE EVERYONE FEEL A BIT MORE RELAXED. SHE ALWAYS LIKES TO PULL THESE CUTE LITTLE TRICKS IN A CRISIS.
ANY IDEA WHO WE'RE UP AGAINST YET?
HARDLY A PRIORITY AT THE MOMENT, JACKSON. OUR FIRST THOUGHT SHOULD BE THE MILLIONS OF PEOPLE STILL STUCK AT GROUND LEVEL.
THE TIDAL WAVE MIGHT BE FLATTENING OUT, BUT WE'RE GOING TO NEED EVERY AVAILABLE POST-HUMAN TO HANDLE THE AFTER-EFFECTS.
THIS IS THE U.N.'S CONFIDENTIAL DATABASE. I THOUGHT ONLY THE SECRETARY-GENERAL AND I HAD ACCESS TO THIS INFORMATION.
NO TIME TO BE POLITE, CHRISTINE: WE'VE BEEN SPYING ON YOU FOR MONTHS.

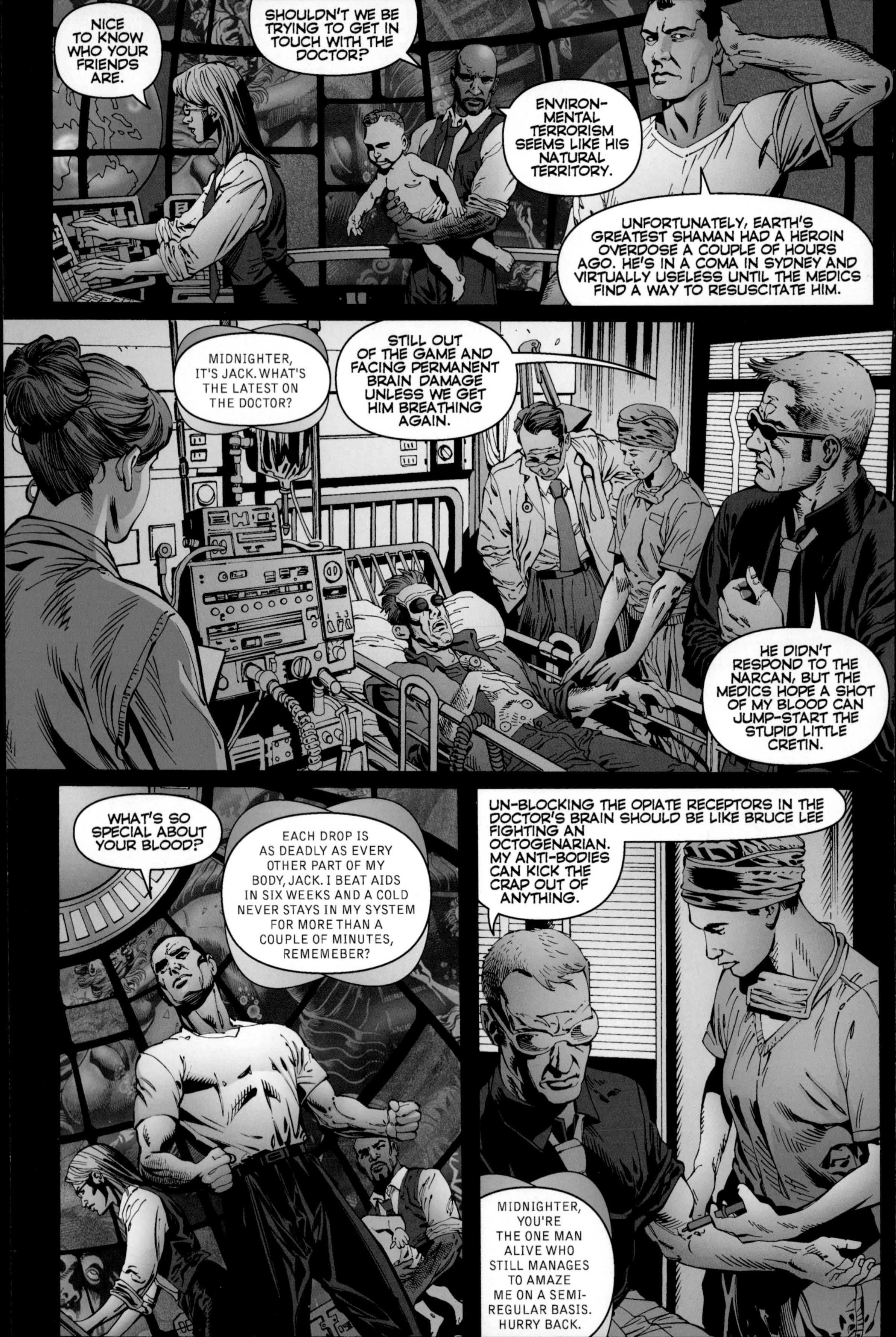
NICE TO KNOW WHO YOUR FRIENDS ARE.
SHOULDN'T WE BE TRYING TO GET IN TOUCH WITH THE DOCTOR?
ENVIRON-MENTAL TERRORISM SEEMS LIKE HIS NATURAL TERRITORY.
UNFORTUNATELY, EARTH'S GREATEST SHAMAN HAD A HEROIN OVERDOSE A COUPLE OF HOURS AGO. HE'S IN A COMA IN SYDNEY AND VIRTUALLY USELESS UNTIL THE MEDICS FIND A WAY TO RESUSCITATE HIM.
MIDNIGHTER, IT'S JACK. WHAT'S THE LATEST ON THE DOCTOR?
STILL OUT OF THE GAME AND FACING PERMANENT BRAIN DAMAGE UNLESS WE GET HIM BREATHING AGAIN.
HE DIDN'T RESPOND TO THE NARCAN, BUT THE MEDICS HOPE A SHOT OF MY BLOOD CAN JUMP-START THE STUPID LITTLE CRETIN.
WHAT'S SO SPECIAL ABOUT YOUR BLOOD?
EACH DROP IS AS DEADLY AS EVERY OTHER PART OF MY BODY, JACK. I BEAT AIDS IN SIX WEEKS AND A COLD NEVER STAYS IN MY SYSTEM FOR MORE THAN A COUPLE OF MINUTES, REMEMEBER?
UN-BLOCKING THE OPIATE RECEPTORS IN THE DOCTOR'S BRAIN SHOULD BE LIKE BRUCE LEE FIGHTING AN OCTOGENARIAN. MY ANTI-BODIES CAN KICK THE CRAP OUT OF ANYTHING.
MIDNIGHTER, YOU'RE THE ONE MAN ALIVE WHO STILL MANAGES TO AMAZE ME ON A SEMI-REGULAR BASIS. HURRY BACK.

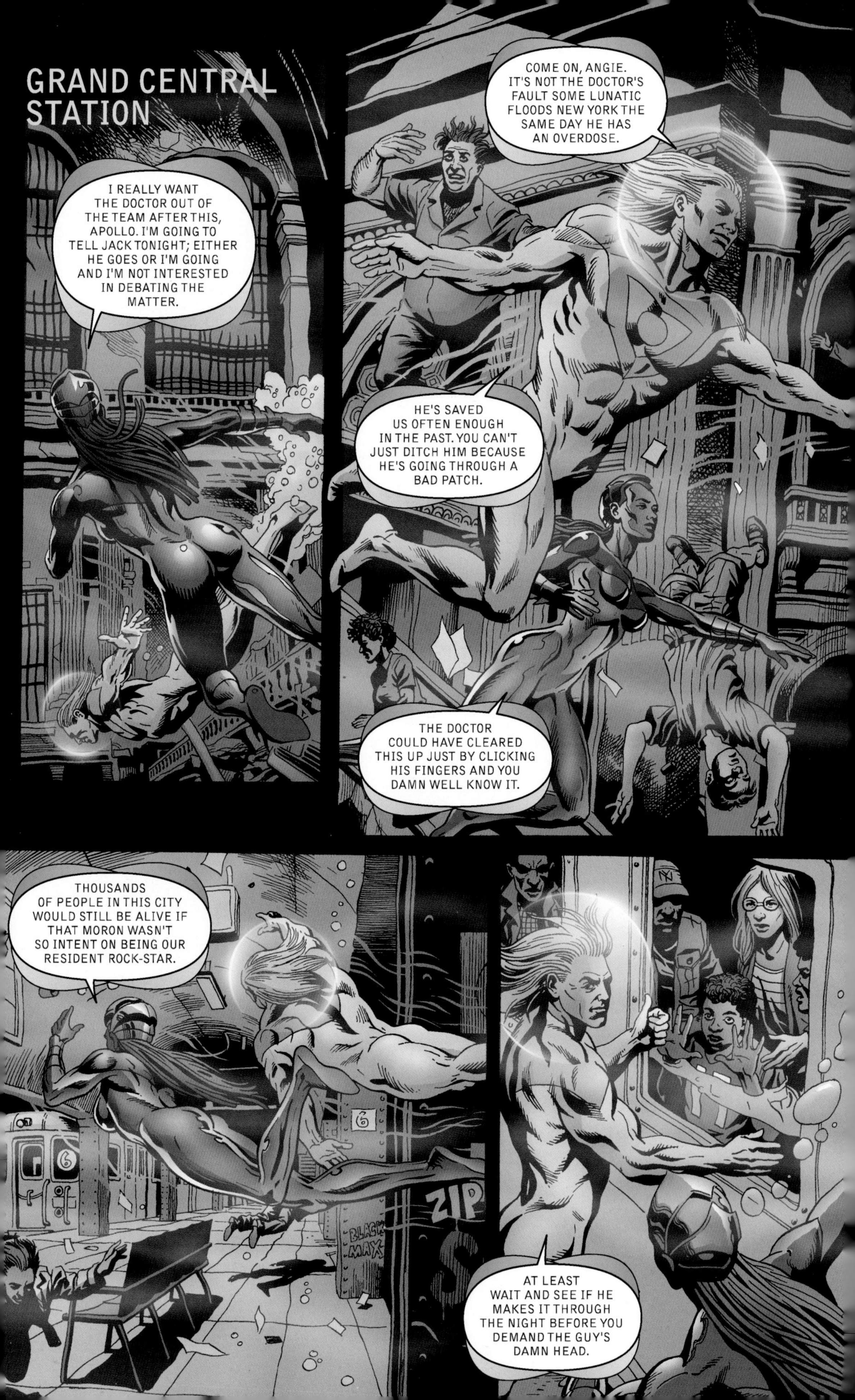
GRAND CENTRAL STATION
I REALLY WANT THE DOCTOR OUT OF THE TEAM AFTER THIS, APOLLO. I'M GOING TO TELL JACK TONIGHT; EITHER HE GOES OR I'M GOING AND I'M NOT INTERESTED IN DEBATING THE MATTER.
COME ON, ANGIE. IT'S NOT THE DOCTOR'S FAULT SOME LUNATIC FLOODS NEW YORK THE SAME DAY HE HAS AN OVERDOSE.
HE'S SAVED US OFTEN ENOUGH IN THE PAST. YOU CAN'T JUST DITCH HIM BECAUSE HE'S GOING THROUGH A BAD PATCH.
THE DOCTOR COULD HAVE CLEARED THIS UP JUST BY CLICKING HIS FINGERS AND YOU DAMN WELL KNOW IT.
THOUSANDS OF PEOPLE IN THIS CITY WOULD STILL BE ALIVE IF THAT MORON WASN'T SO INTENT ON BEING OUR RESIDENT ROCK-STAR.
AT LEAST WAIT AND SEE IF HE MAKES IT THROUGH THE NIGHT BEFORE YOU DEMAND THE GUY'S DAMN HEAD.

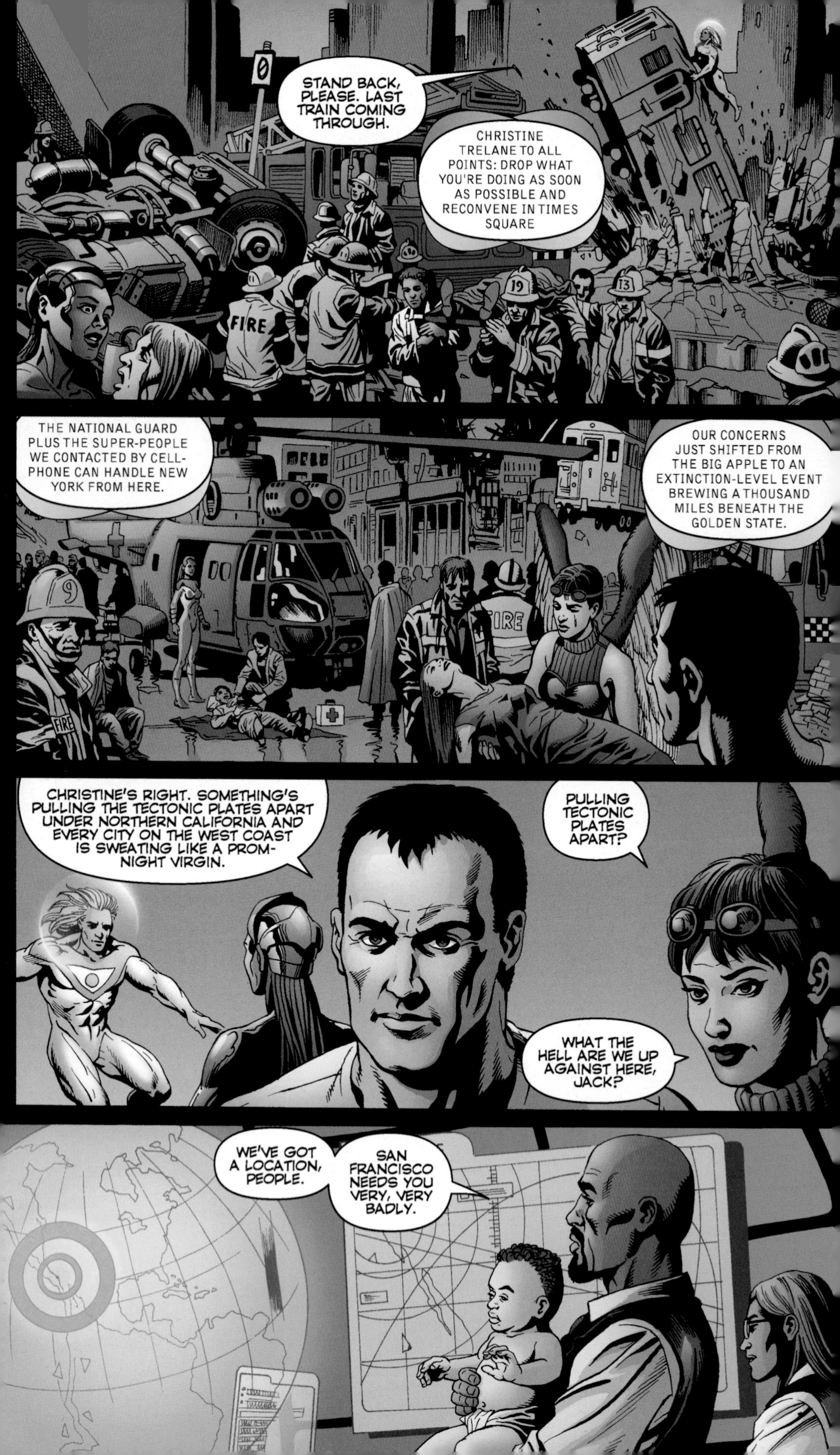
0
STAND BACK, PLEASE. LAST TRAIN COMING THROUGH.
CHRISTINE TRELANE TO ALL POINTS: DROP WHAT YOU'RE DOING AS SOON AS POSSIBLE AND RECONVENE IN TIMES SQUARE
FIRE
19
13
THE NATIONAL GUARD PLUS THE SUPER-PEOPLE WE CONTACTED BY CELL-PHONE CAN HANDLE NEW YORK FROM HERE.
OUR CONCERNS JUST SHIFTED FROM THE BIG APPLE TO AN EXTINCTION-LEVEL EVENT BREWING A THOUSAND MILES BENEATH THE GOLDEN STATE.
9
FIRE
FIRE
CHRISTINE'S RIGHT. SOMETHING'S PULLING THE TECTONIC PLATES APART UNDER NORTHERN CALIFORNIA AND EVERY CITY ON THE WEST COAST IS SWEATING LIKE A PROM-NIGHT VIRGIN.
PULLING TECTONIC PLATES APART?
WHAT THE HELL ARE WE UP AGAINST HERE, JACK?
WE'VE GOT A LOCATION, PEOPLE.
SAN FRANCISCO NEEDS YOU VERY, VERY BADLY.

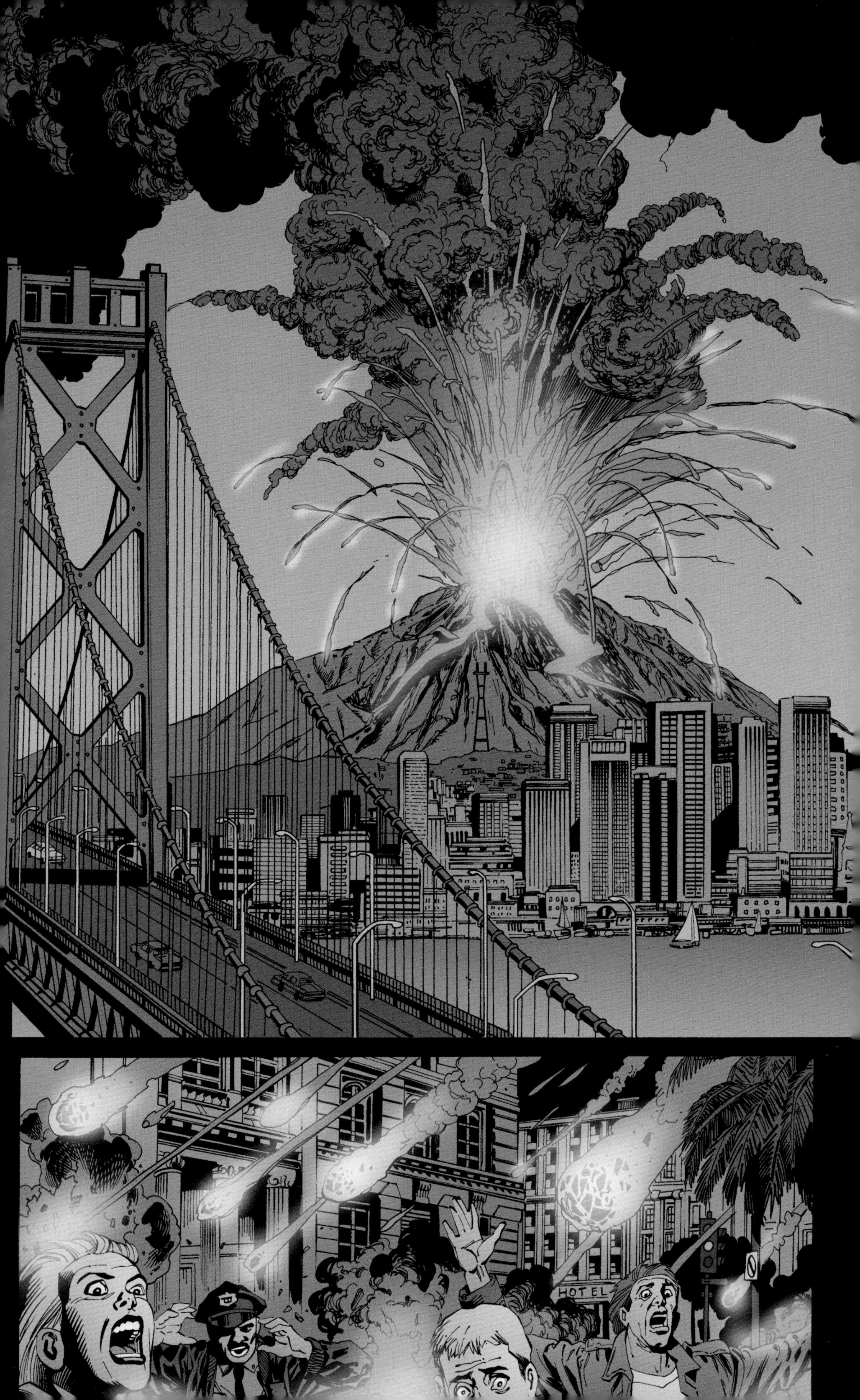
HOTEL

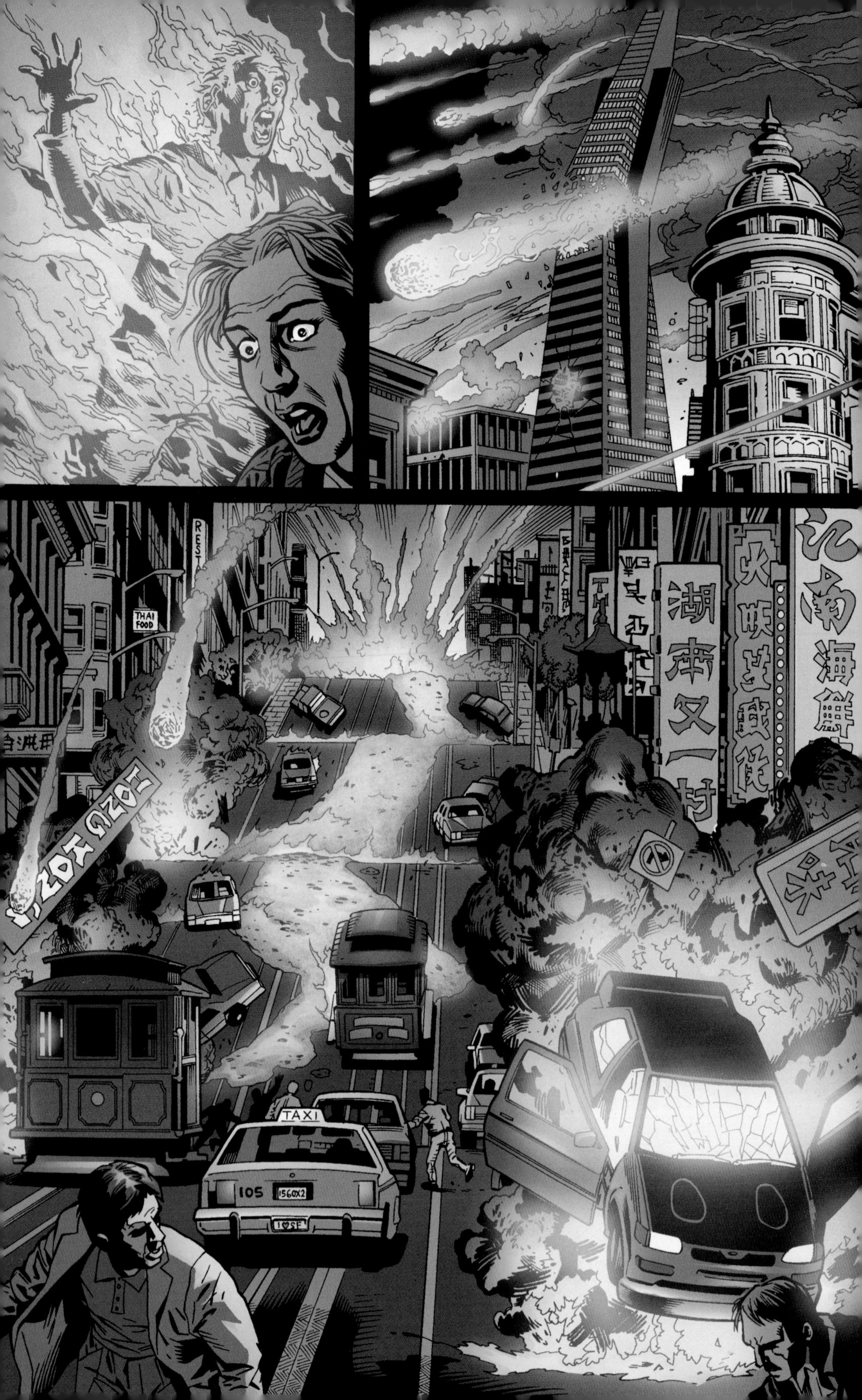

RESTA
THAI FOOD
TAXI
105
1560X2
I♥SF

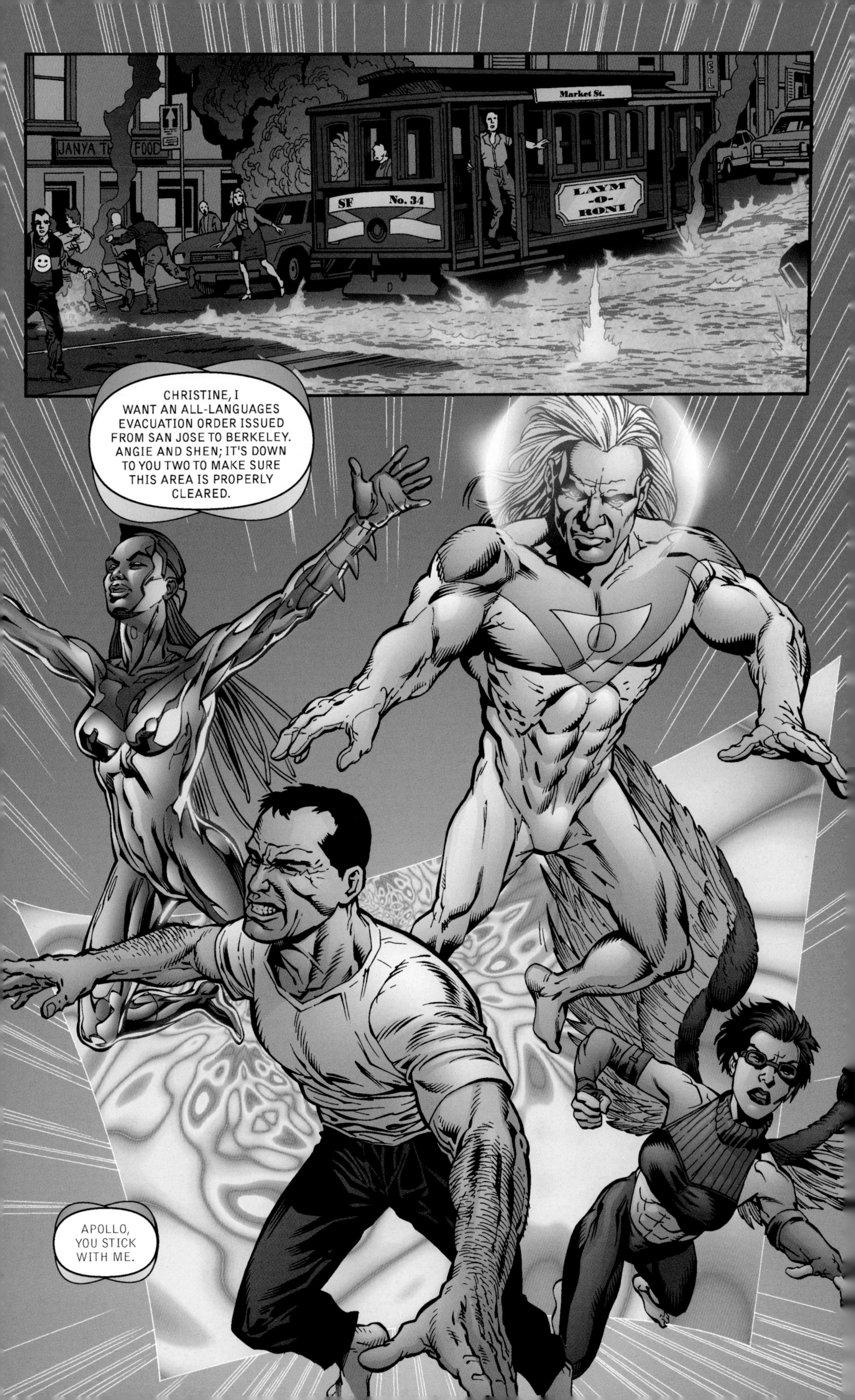
Market St.
JANYA TH
FOOD
SF No. 34
LAYM -O- RONI
CHRISTINE, I WANT AN ALL-LANGUAGES EVACUATION ORDER ISSUED FROM SAN JOSE TO BERKELEY. ANGIE AND SHEN; IT'S DOWN TO YOU TWO TO MAKE SURE THIS AREA IS PROPERLY CLEARED.
APOLLO, YOU STICK WITH ME.

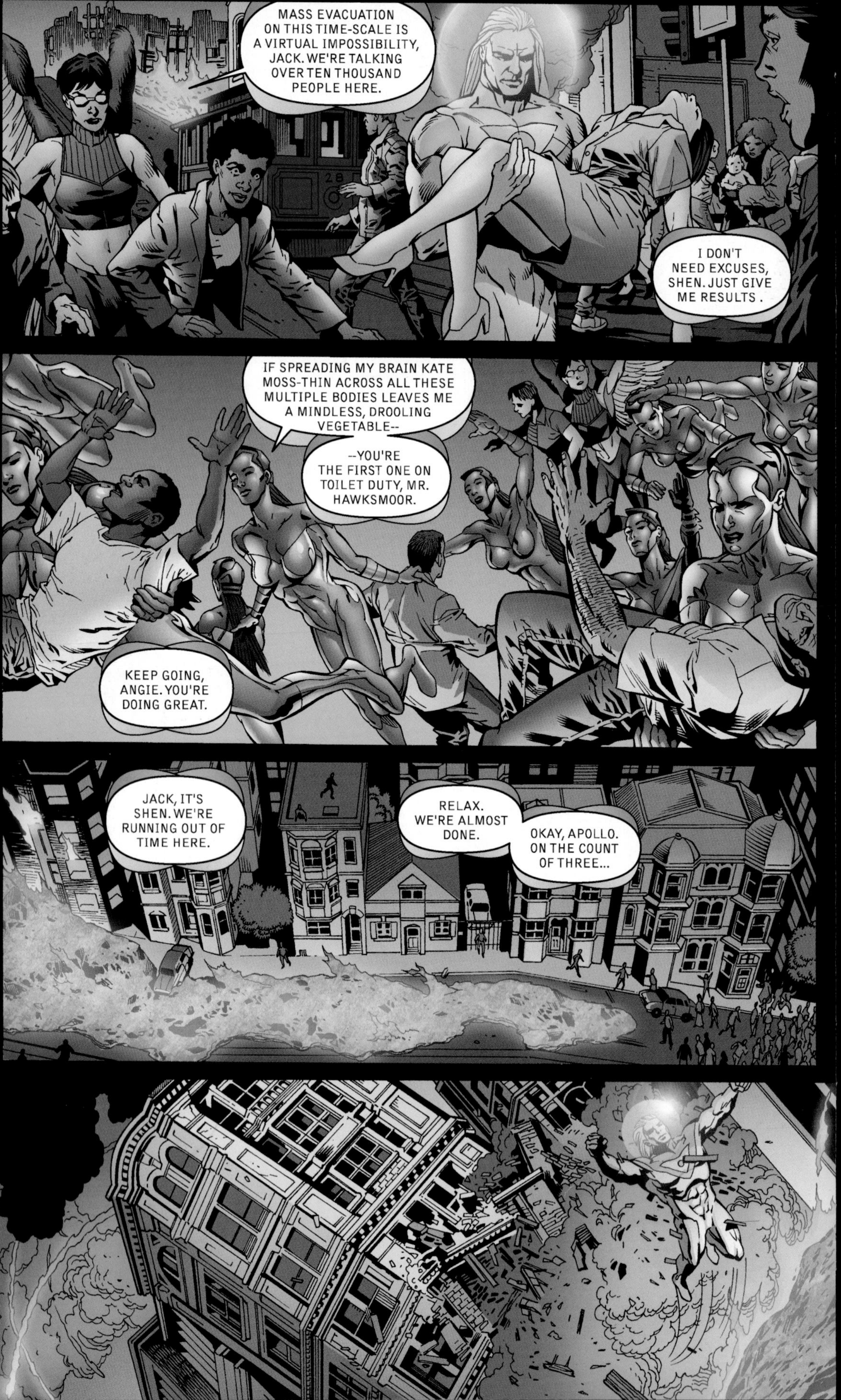
MASS EVACUATION ON THIS TIME-SCALE IS A VIRTUAL IMPOSSIBILITY, JACK. WE'RE TALKING OVER TEN THOUSAND PEOPLE HERE.
I DON'T NEED EXCUSES, SHEN. JUST GIVE ME RESULTS .
IF SPREADING MY BRAIN KATE MOSS-THIN ACROSS ALL THESE MULTIPLE BODIES LEAVES ME A MINDLESS, DROOLING VEGETABLE--
--YOU'RE THE FIRST ONE ON TOILET DUTY, MR. HAWKSMOOR.
KEEP GOING, ANGIE. YOU'RE DOING GREAT.
JACK, IT'S SHEN. WE'RE RUNNING OUT OF TIME HERE.
RELAX. WE'RE ALMOST DONE.
OKAY, APOLLO. ON THE COUNT OF THREE...

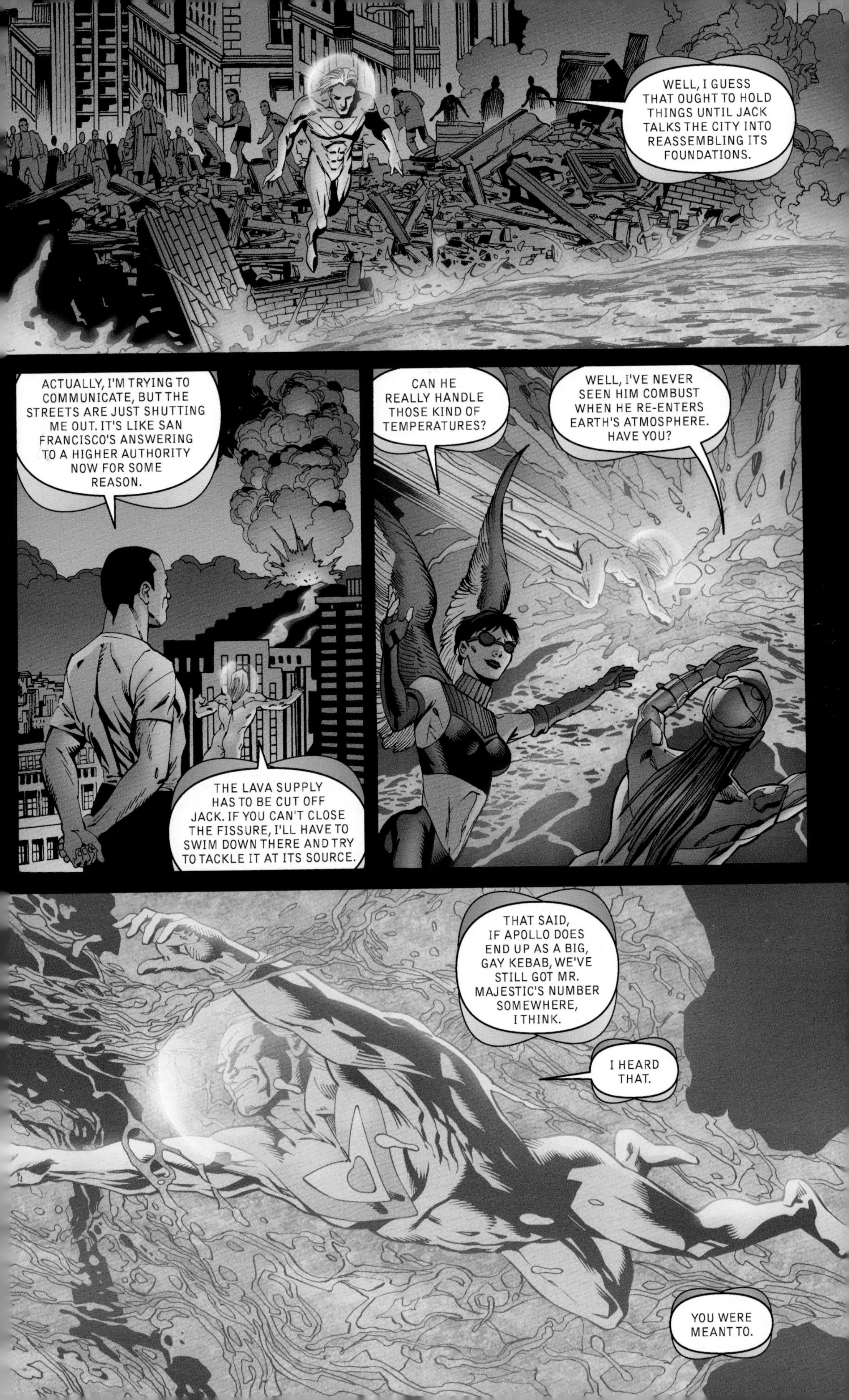
WELL, I GUESS THAT OUGHT TO HOLD THINGS UNTIL JACK TALKS THE CITY INTO REASSEMBLING ITS FOUNDATIONS.
ACTUALLY, I'M TRYING TO COMMUNICATE, BUT THE STREETS ARE JUST SHUTTING ME OUT. IT'S LIKE SAN FRANCISCO'S ANSWERING TO A HIGHER AUTHORITY NOW FOR SOME REASON.
THE LAVA SUPPLY HAS TO BE CUT OFF JACK. IF YOU CAN'T CLOSE THE FISSURE, I'LL HAVE TO SWIM DOWN THERE AND TRY TO TACKLE IT AT ITS SOURCE.
CAN HE REALLY HANDLE THOSE KIND OF TEMPERATURES?
WELL, I'VE NEVER SEEN HIM COMBUST WHEN HE RE-ENTERS EARTH'S ATMOSPHERE. HAVE YOU?
THAT SAID, IF APOLLO DOES END UP AS A BIG, GAY KEBAB, WE'VE STILL GOT MR. MAJESTIC'S NUMBER SOMEWHERE, I THINK.
I HEARD THAT.
YOU WERE MEANT TO.

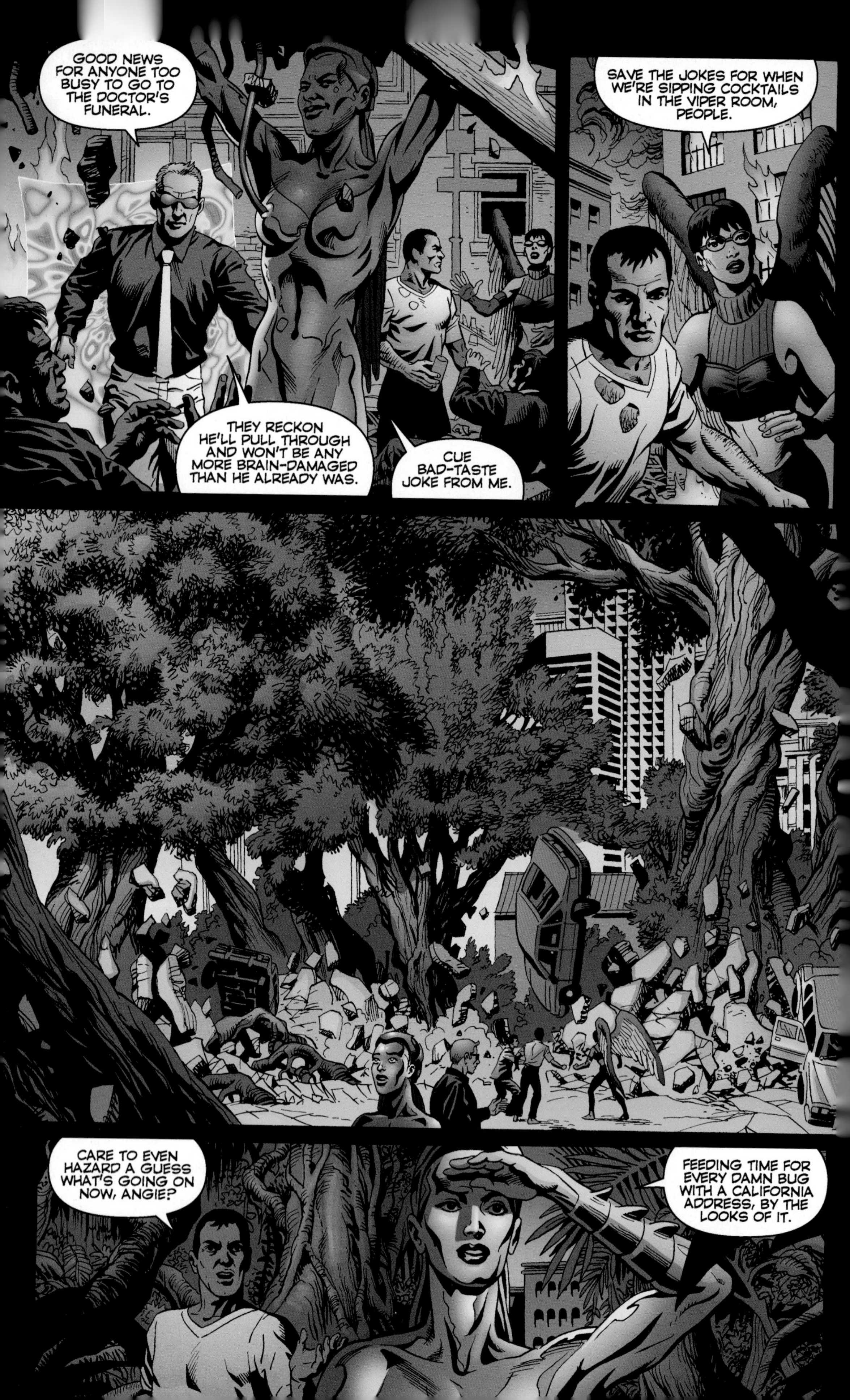
GOOD NEWS FOR ANYONE TOO BUSY TO GO TO THE DOCTOR'S FUNERAL.
THEY RECKON HE'LL PULL THROUGH AND WON'T BE ANY MORE BRAIN-DAMAGED THAN HE ALREADY WAS.
CUE BAD-TASTE JOKE FROM ME.
SAVE THE JOKES FOR WHEN WE'RE SIPPING COCKTAILS IN THE VIPER ROOM, PEOPLE.
CARE TO EVEN HAZARD A GUESS WHAT'S GOING ON NOW, ANGIE?
FEEDING TIME FOR EVERY DAMN BUG WITH A CALIFORNIA ADDRESS, BY THE LOOKS OF IT.

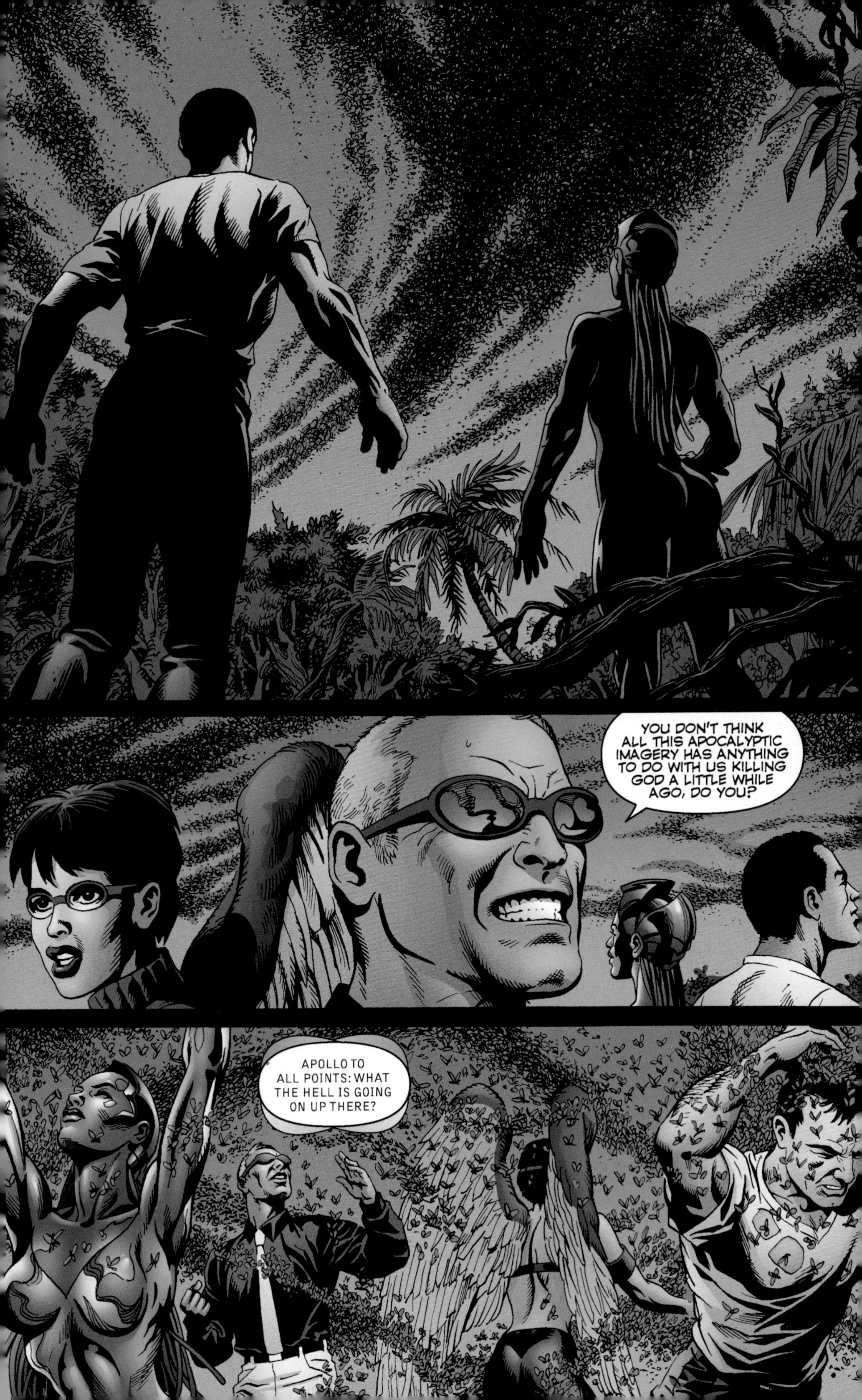
YOU DON'T THINK ALL THIS APOCALYPTIC IMAGERY HAS ANYTHING TO DO WITH US KILLING GOD A LITTLE WHILE AGO, DO YOU?
APOLLO TO ALL POINTS: WHAT THE HELL IS GOING ON UP THERE?

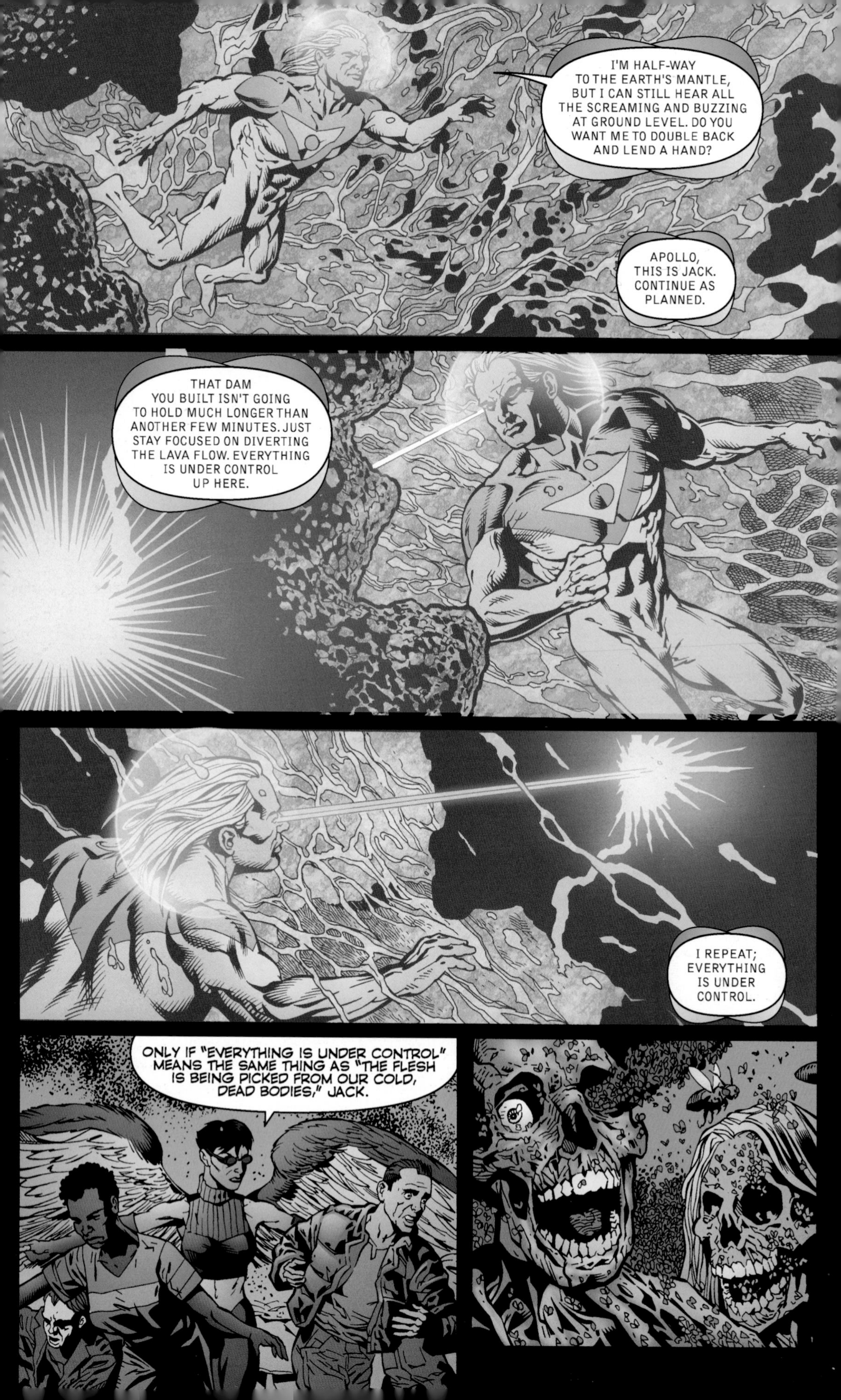
I'M HALF-WAY TO THE EARTH'S MANTLE, BUT I CAN STILL HEAR ALL THE SCREAMING AND BUZZING AT GROUND LEVEL. DO YOU WANT ME TO DOUBLE BACK AND LEND A HAND?
APOLLO, THIS IS JACK. CONTINUE AS PLANNED.
THAT DAM YOU BUILT ISN'T GOING TO HOLD MUCH LONGER THAN ANOTHER FEW MINUTES. JUST STAY FOCUSED ON DIVERTING THE LAVA FLOW. EVERYTHING IS UNDER CONTROL UP HERE.
I REPEAT; EVERYTHING IS UNDER CONTROL.
ONLY IF "EVERYTHING IS UNDER CONTROL" MEANS THE SAME THING AS "THE FLESH IS BEING PICKED FROM OUR COLD, DEAD BODIES," JACK.

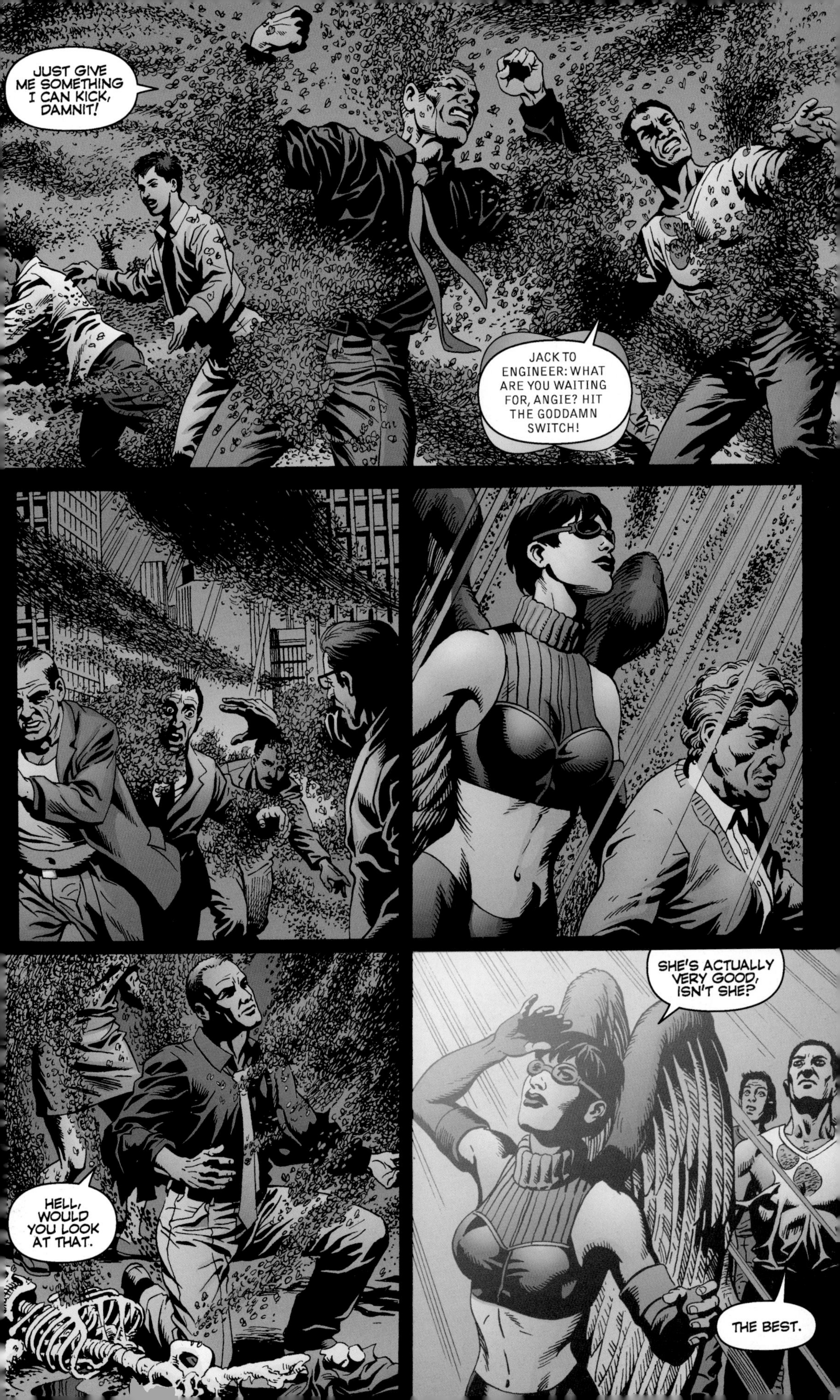
JUST GIVE ME SOMETHING I CAN KICK, DAMNIT!
JACK TO ENGINEER: WHAT ARE YOU WAITING FOR, ANGIE? HIT THE GODDAMN SWITCH!
HELL, WOULD YOU LOOK AT THAT.
SHE'S ACTUALLY VERY GOOD, ISN'T SHE?
THE BEST.

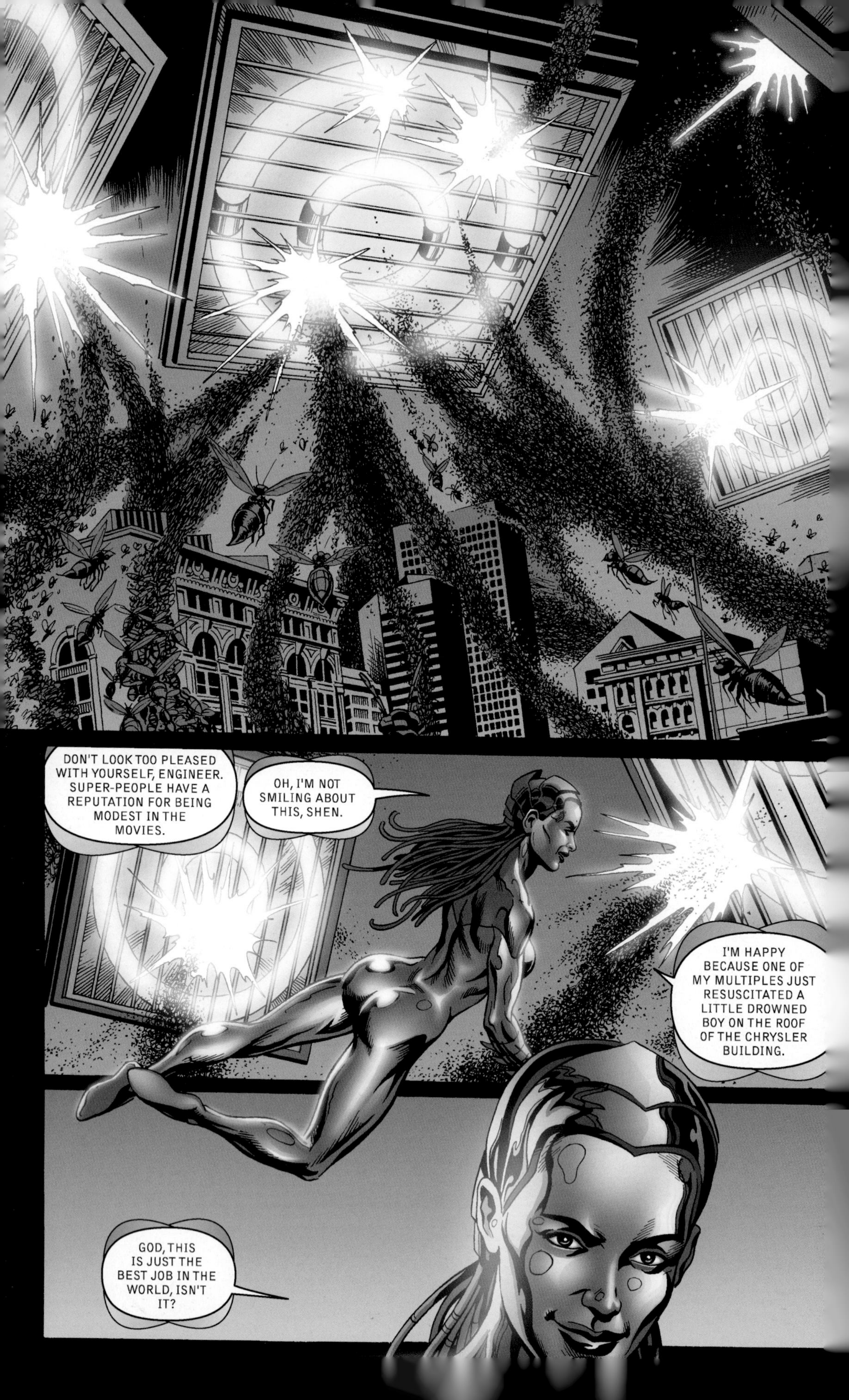
DON'T LOOK TOO PLEASED WITH YOURSELF, ENGINEER. SUPER-PEOPLE HAVE A REPUTATION FOR BEING MODEST IN THE MOVIES.
OH, I'M NOT SMILING ABOUT THIS, SHEN.
I'M HAPPY BECAUSE ONE OF MY MULTIPLES JUST RESUSCITATED A LITTLE DROWNED BOY ON THE ROOF OF THE CHRYSLER BUILDING.
GOD, THIS IS JUST THE BEST JOB IN THE WORLD, ISN'T IT?

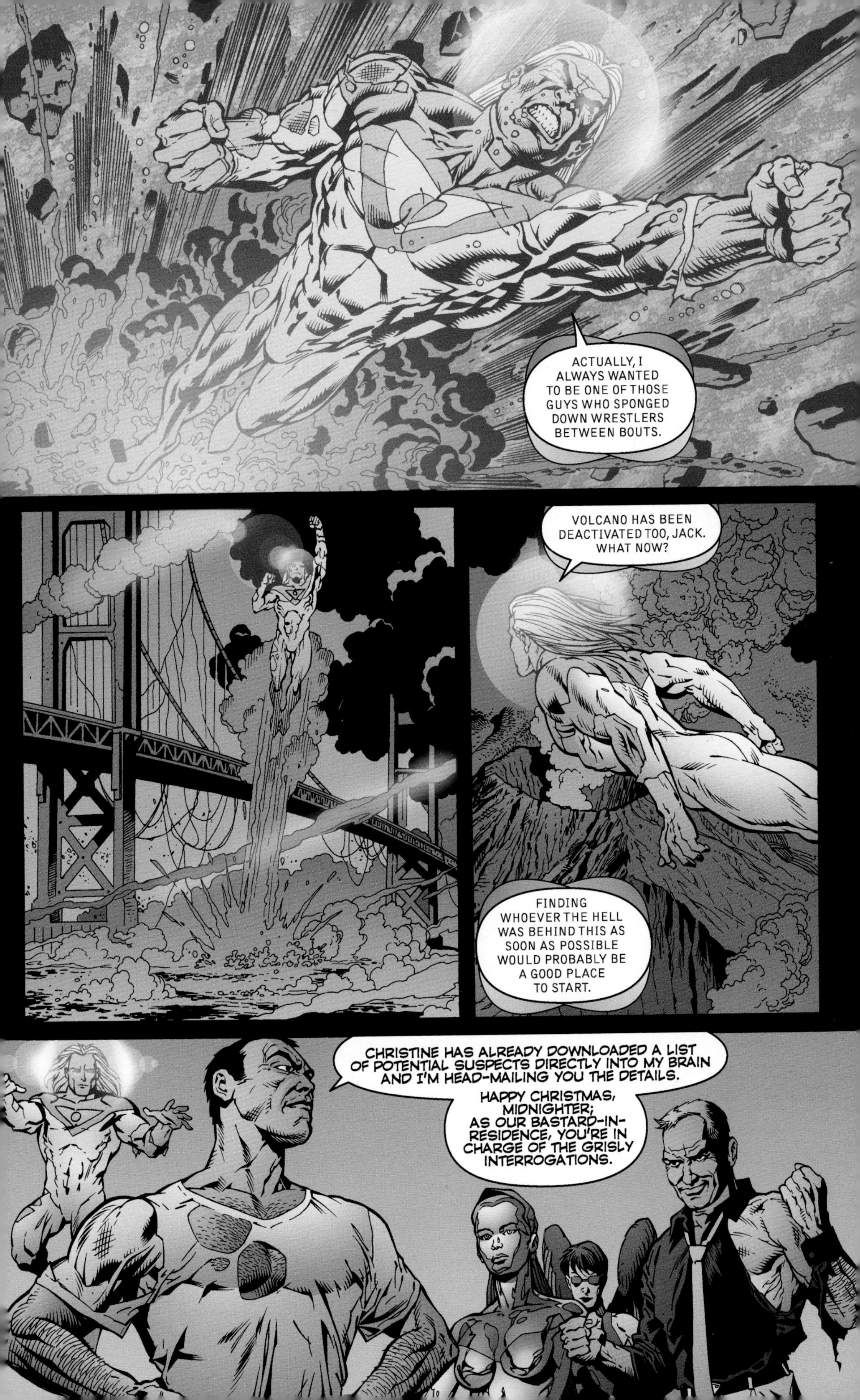
ACTUALLY, I ALWAYS WANTED TO BE ONE OF THOSE GUYS WHO SPONGED DOWN WRESTLERS BETWEEN BOUTS.
VOLCANO HAS BEEN DEACTIVATED TOO, JACK. WHAT NOW?
FINDING WHOEVER THE HELL WAS BEHIND THIS AS SOON AS POSSIBLE WOULD PROBABLY BE A GOOD PLACE TO START.
CHRISTINE HAS ALREADY DOWNLOADED A LIST OF POTENTIAL SUSPECTS DIRECTLY INTO MY BRAIN AND I'M HEAD-MAILING YOU THE DETAILS.
HAPPY CHRISTMAS, MIDNIGHTER; AS OUR BASTARD-IN-RESIDENCE, YOU'RE IN CHARGE OF THE GRISLY INTERROGATIONS.

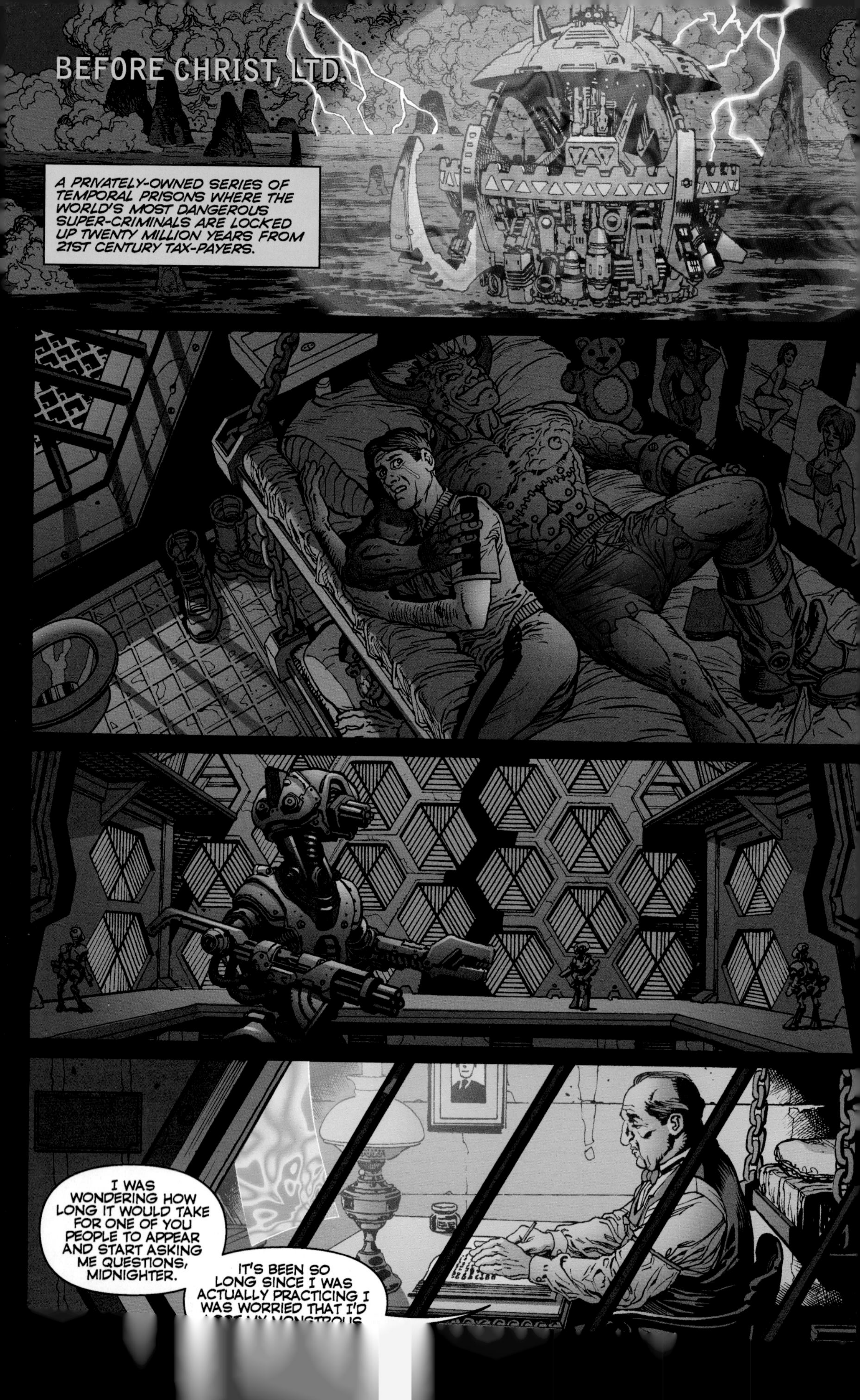
BEFORE CHRIST, LTD.
A PRIVATELY-OWNED SERIES OF TEMPORAL PRISONS WHERE THE WORLD'S MOST DANGEROUS SUPER-CRIMINALS ARE LOCKED UP TWENTY MILLION YEARS FROM 21ST CENTURY TAX-PAYERS.
I WAS WONDERING HOW LONG IT WOULD TAKE FOR ONE OF YOU PEOPLE TO APPEAR AND START ASKING ME QUESTIONS, MIDNIGHTER.
IT'S BEEN SO LONG SINCE I WAS ACTUALLY PRACTICING I WAS WORRIED THAT I'D

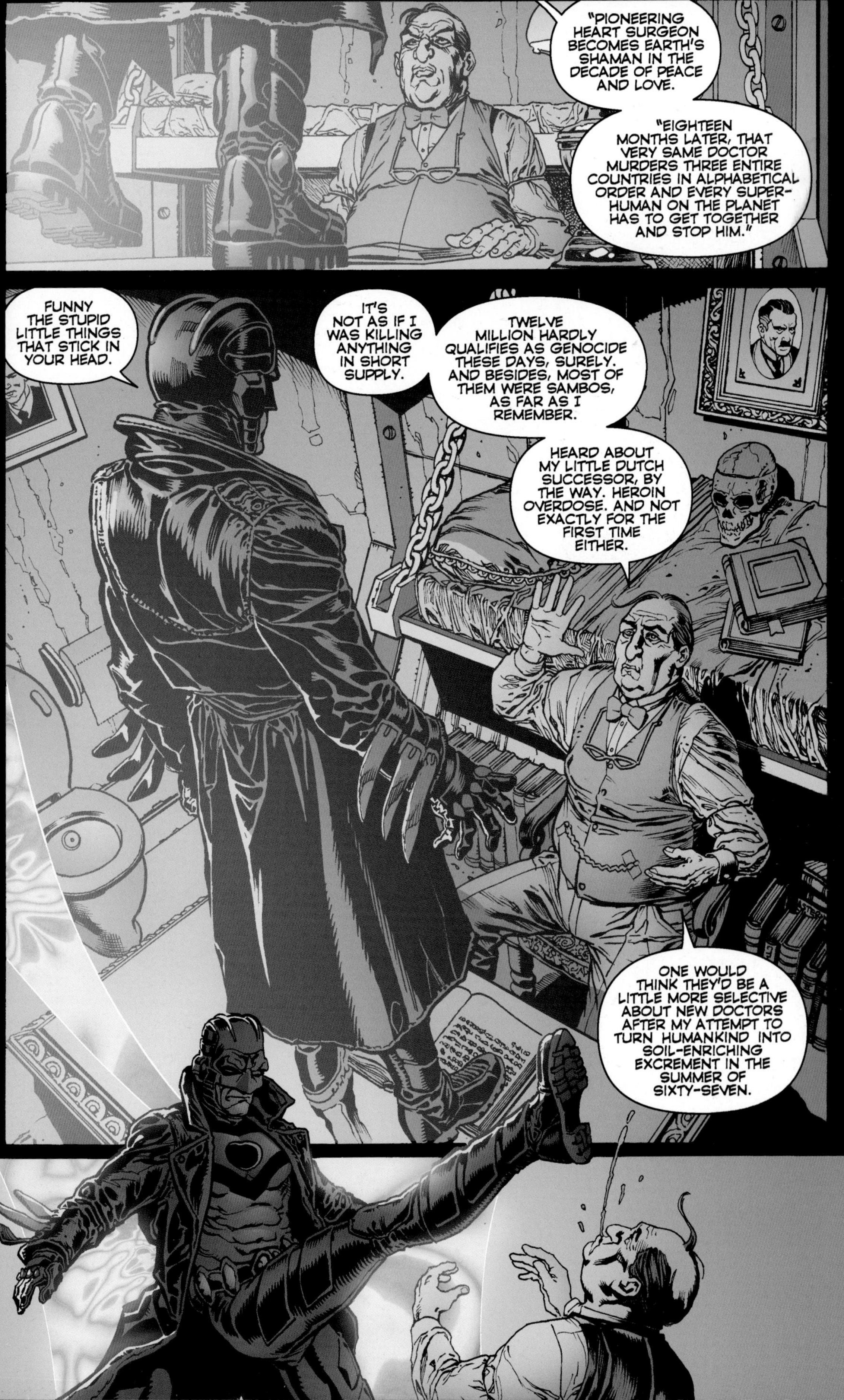

"PIONEERING HEART SURGEON BECOMES EARTH'S SHAMAN IN THE DECADE OF PEACE AND LOVE.
"EIGHTEEN MONTHS LATER, THAT VERY SAME DOCTOR MURDERS THREE ENTIRE COUNTRIES IN ALPHABETICAL ORDER AND EVERY SUPER-HUMAN ON THE PLANET HAS TO GET TOGETHER AND STOP HIM."
FUNNY THE STUPID LITTLE THINGS THAT STICK IN YOUR HEAD.
IT'S NOT AS IF I WAS KILLING ANYTHING IN SHORT SUPPLY.
TWELVE MILLION HARDLY QUALIFIES AS GENOCIDE THESE DAYS, SURELY. AND BESIDES, MOST OF THEM WERE SAMBOS, AS FAR AS I REMEMBER.
HEARD ABOUT MY LITTLE DUTCH SUCCESSOR, BY THE WAY. HEROIN OVERDOSE. AND NOT EXACTLY FOR THE FIRST TIME EITHER.
ONE WOULD THINK THEY'D BE A LITTLE MORE SELECTIVE ABOUT NEW DOCTORS AFTER MY ATTEMPT TO TURN HUMANKIND INTO SOIL-ENRICHING EXCREMENT IN THE SUMMER OF SIXTY-SEVEN.

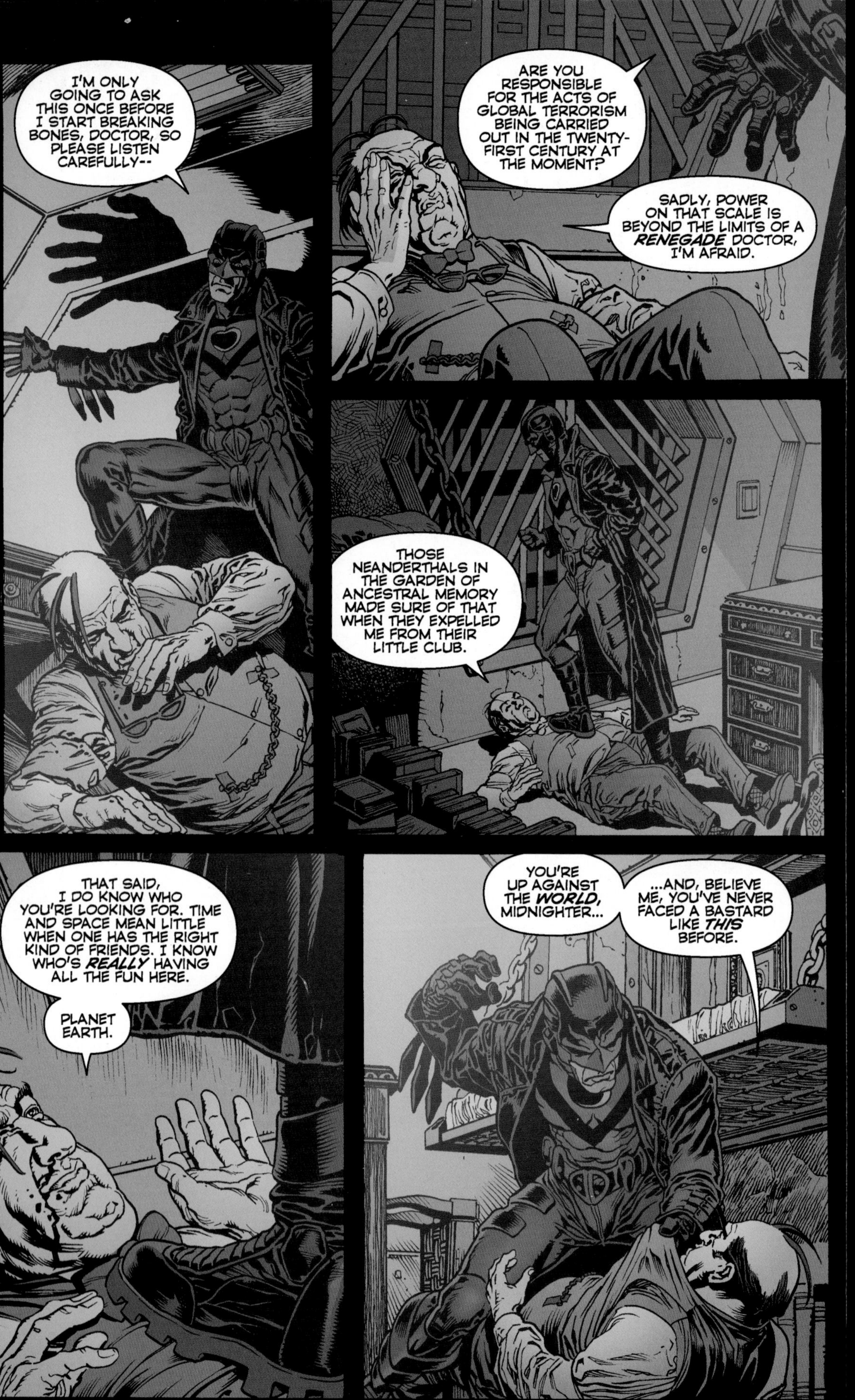
I'M ONLY GOING TO ASK THIS ONCE BEFORE I START BREAKING BONES, DOCTOR, SO PLEASE LISTEN CAREFULLY--
ARE YOU RESPONSIBLE FOR THE ACTS OF GLOBAL TERRORISM BEING CARRIED OUT IN THE TWENTY-FIRST CENTURY AT THE MOMENT?
SADLY, POWER ON THAT SCALE IS BEYOND THE LIMITS OF A *RENEGADE* DOCTOR, I'M AFRAID.
THOSE NEANDERTHALS IN THE GARDEN OF ANCESTRAL MEMORY MADE SURE OF THAT WHEN THEY EXPELLED ME FROM THEIR LITTLE CLUB.
THAT SAID, I DO KNOW WHO YOU'RE LOOKING FOR. TIME AND SPACE MEAN LITTLE WHEN ONE HAS THE RIGHT KIND OF FRIENDS. I KNOW WHO'S *REALLY* HAVING ALL THE FUN HERE.
PLANET EARTH.
YOU'RE UP AGAINST THE *WORLD,* MIDNIGHTER...
...AND, BELIEVE ME, YOU'VE NEVER FACED A BASTARD LIKE *THIS* BEFORE.

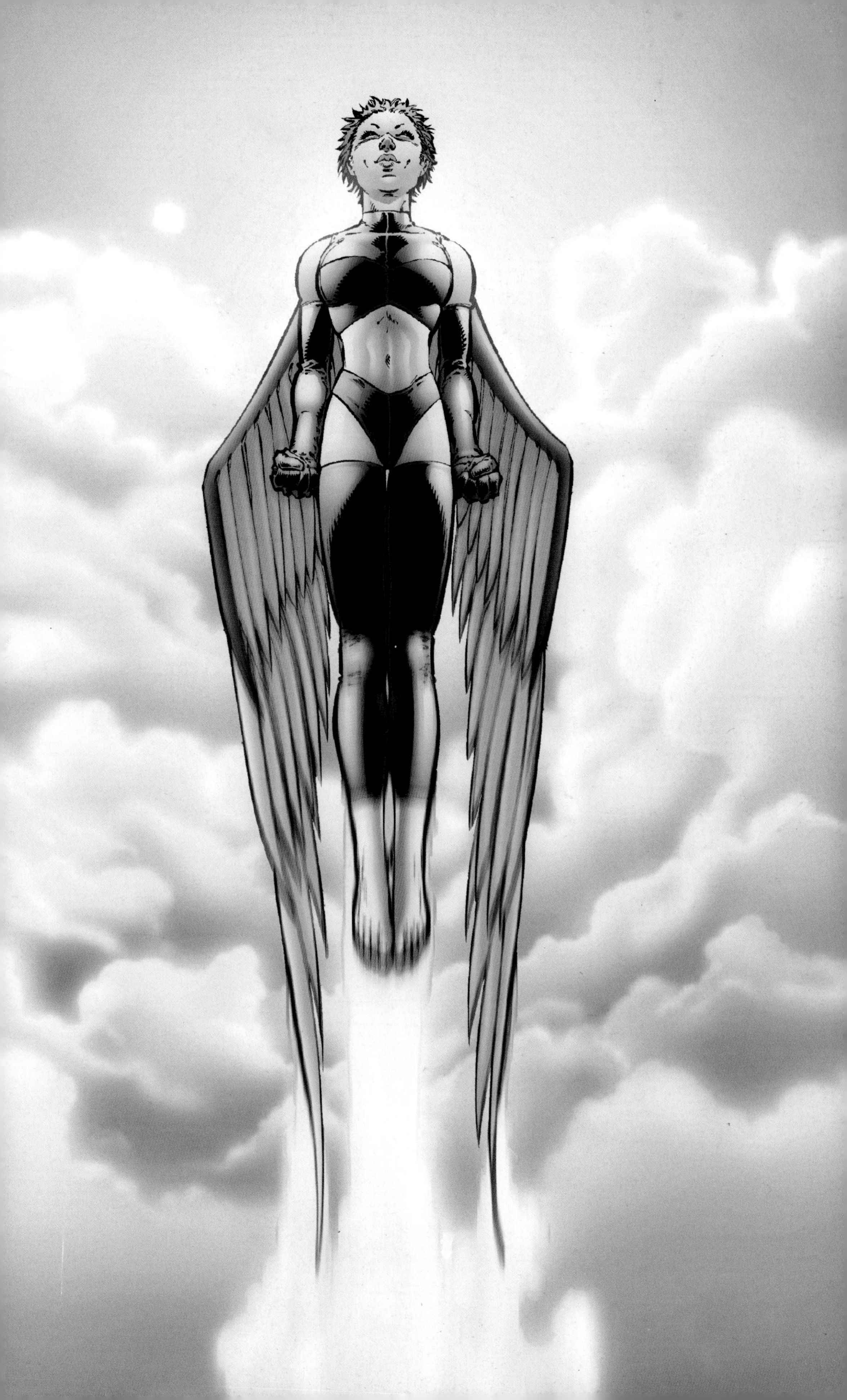

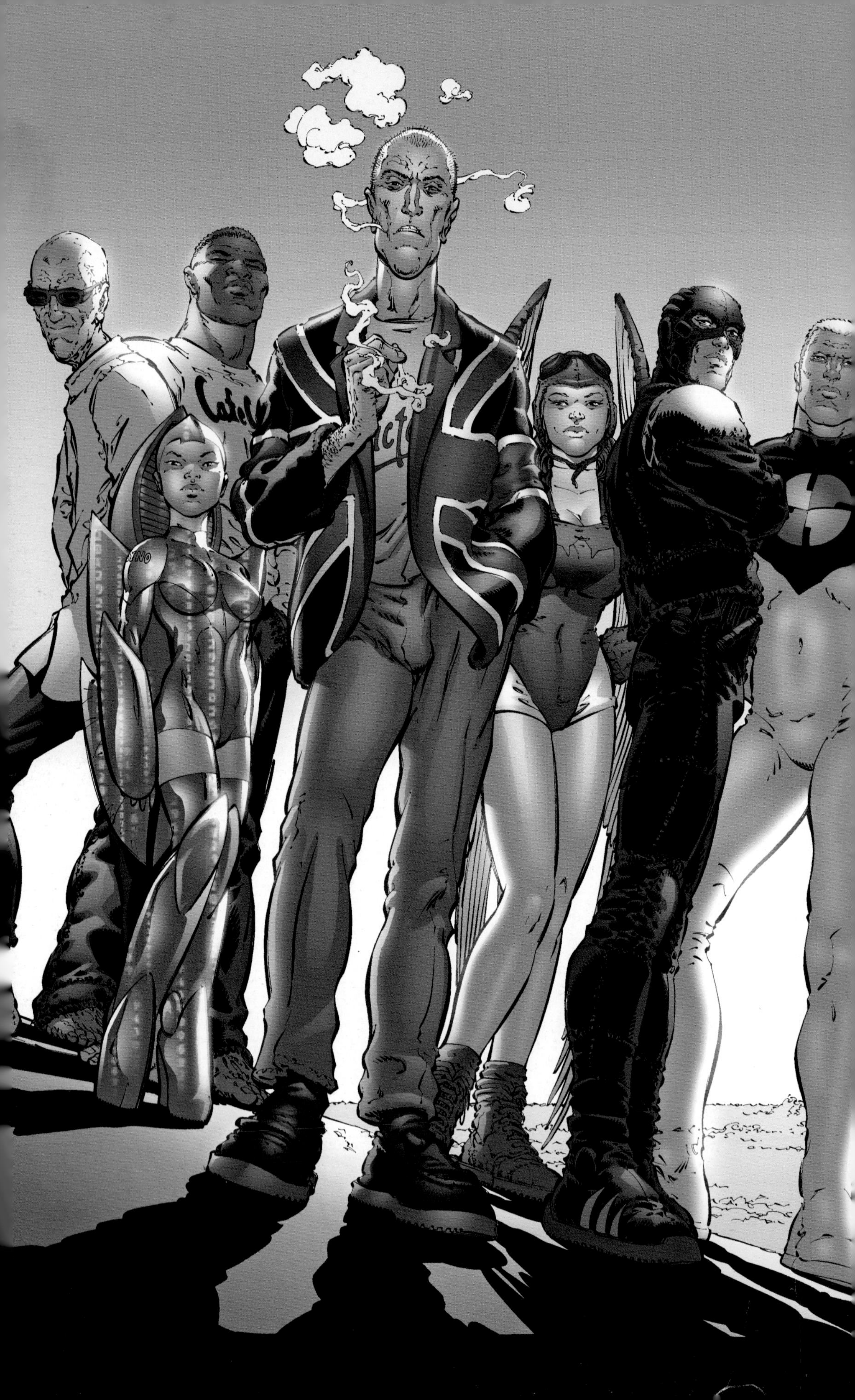

The AUTHORITY

"Earth Inferno"
THREE of FOUR

MARK MILLAR
writer

DAVID BARON
colorist

FRANK QUITELY
artist

BILL O'NEIL
letterer

TREVOR SCOTT
inker

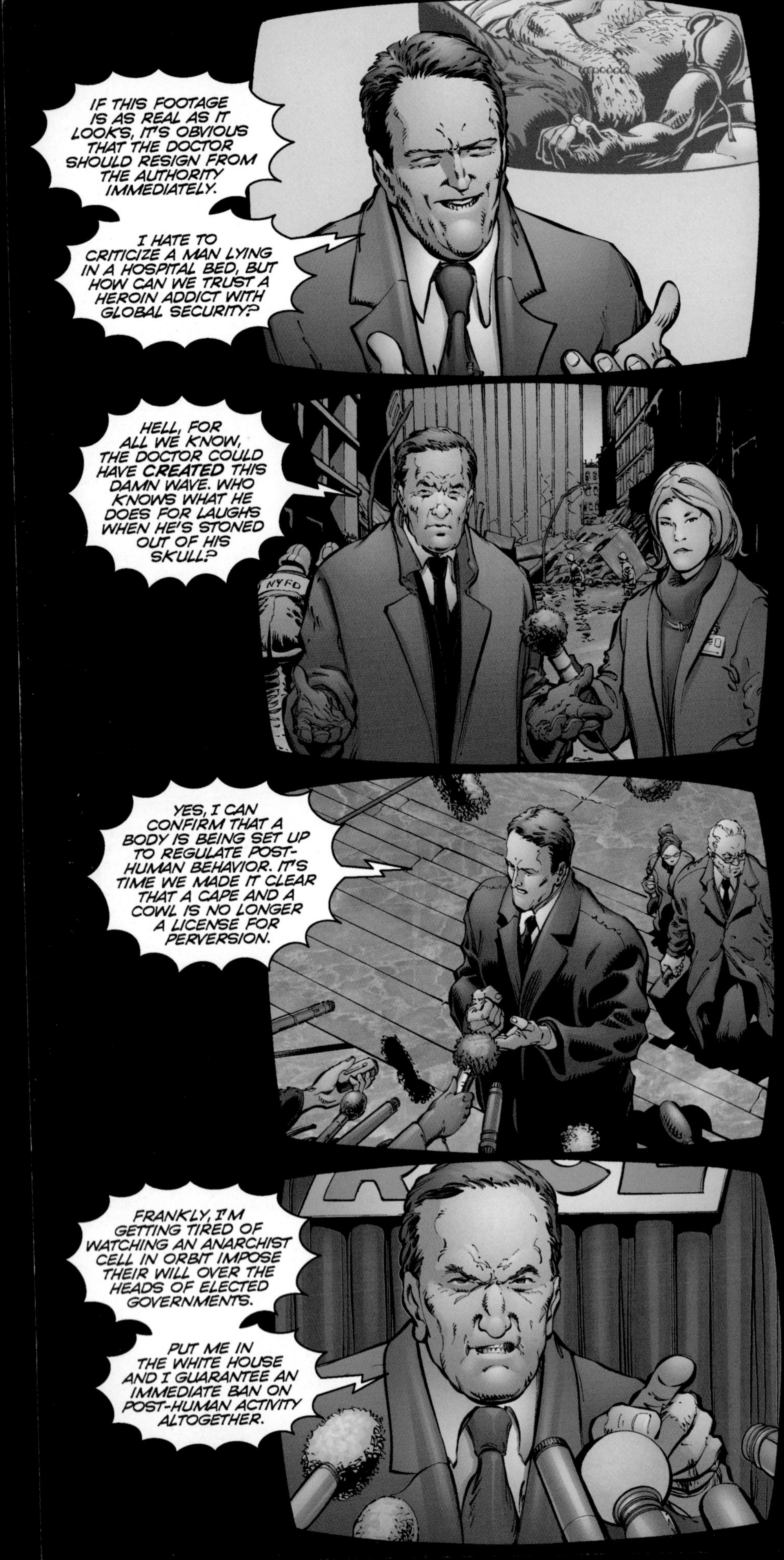
IF THIS FOOTAGE IS AS REAL AS IT LOOKS, IT'S OBVIOUS THAT THE DOCTOR SHOULD RESIGN FROM THE AUTHORITY IMMEDIATELY.
I HATE TO CRITICIZE A MAN LYING IN A HOSPITAL BED, BUT HOW CAN WE TRUST A HEROIN ADDICT WITH GLOBAL SECURITY?
HELL, FOR ALL WE KNOW, THE DOCTOR COULD HAVE CREATED THIS DAMN WAVE. WHO KNOWS WHAT HE DOES FOR LAUGHS WHEN HE'S STONED OUT OF HIS SKULL?
NYFD
YES, I CAN CONFIRM THAT A BODY IS BEING SET UP TO REGULATE POST-HUMAN BEHAVIOR. IT'S TIME WE MADE IT CLEAR THAT A CAPE AND A COWL IS NO LONGER A LICENSE FOR PERVERSION.
FRANKLY, I'M GETTING TIRED OF WATCHING AN ANARCHIST CELL IN ORBIT IMPOSE THEIR WILL OVER THE HEADS OF ELECTED GOVERNMENTS.
PUT ME IN THE WHITE HOUSE AND I GUARANTEE AN IMMEDIATE BAN ON POST-HUMAN ACTIVITY ALTOGETHER.

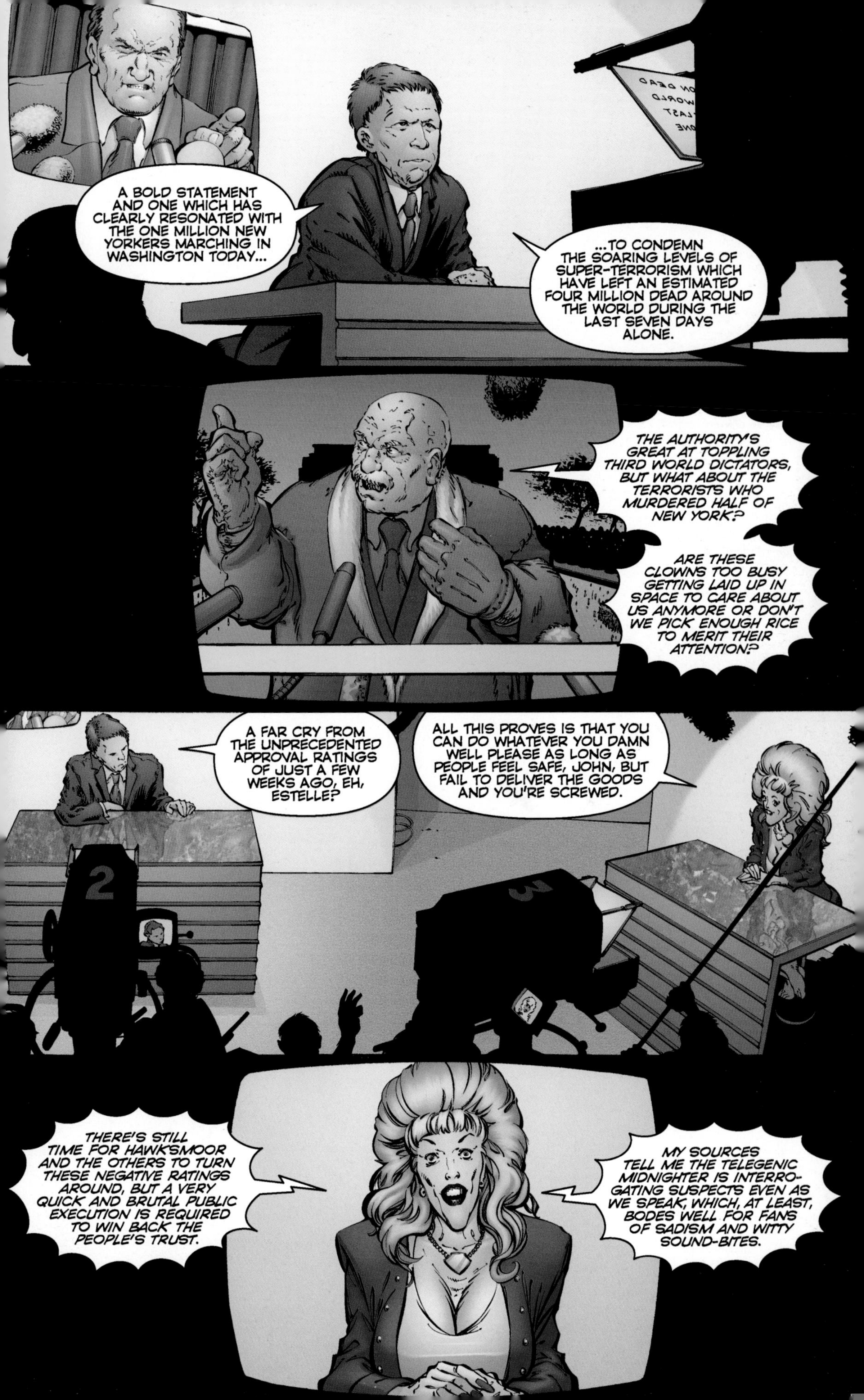

A BOLD STATEMENT AND ONE WHICH HAS CLEARLY RESONATED WITH THE ONE MILLION NEW YORKERS MARCHING IN WASHINGTON TODAY...
...TO CONDEMN THE SOARING LEVELS OF SUPER-TERRORISM WHICH HAVE LEFT AN ESTIMATED FOUR MILLION DEAD AROUND THE WORLD DURING THE LAST SEVEN DAYS ALONE.
THE AUTHORITY'S GREAT AT TOPPLING THIRD WORLD DICTATORS, BUT WHAT ABOUT THE TERRORISTS WHO MURDERED HALF OF NEW YORK?
ARE THESE CLOWNS TOO BUSY GETTING LAID UP IN SPACE TO CARE ABOUT US ANYMORE OR DON'T WE PICK ENOUGH RICE TO MERIT THEIR ATTENTION?
A FAR CRY FROM THE UNPRECEDENTED APPROVAL RATINGS OF JUST A FEW WEEKS AGO, EH, ESTELLE?
ALL THIS PROVES IS THAT YOU CAN DO WHATEVER YOU DAMN WELL PLEASE AS LONG AS PEOPLE FEEL SAFE, JOHN, BUT FAIL TO DELIVER THE GOODS AND YOU'RE SCREWED.
THERE'S STILL TIME FOR HAWKSMOOR AND THE OTHERS TO TURN THESE NEGATIVE RATINGS AROUND, BUT A VERY QUICK AND BRUTAL PUBLIC EXECUTION IS REQUIRED TO WIN BACK THE PEOPLE'S TRUST.
MY SOURCES TELL ME THE TELEGENIC MIDNIGHTER IS INTERROGATING SUSPECTS EVEN AS WE SPEAK, WHICH, AT LEAST, BODES WELL FOR FANS OF SADISM AND WITTY SOUND-BITES.

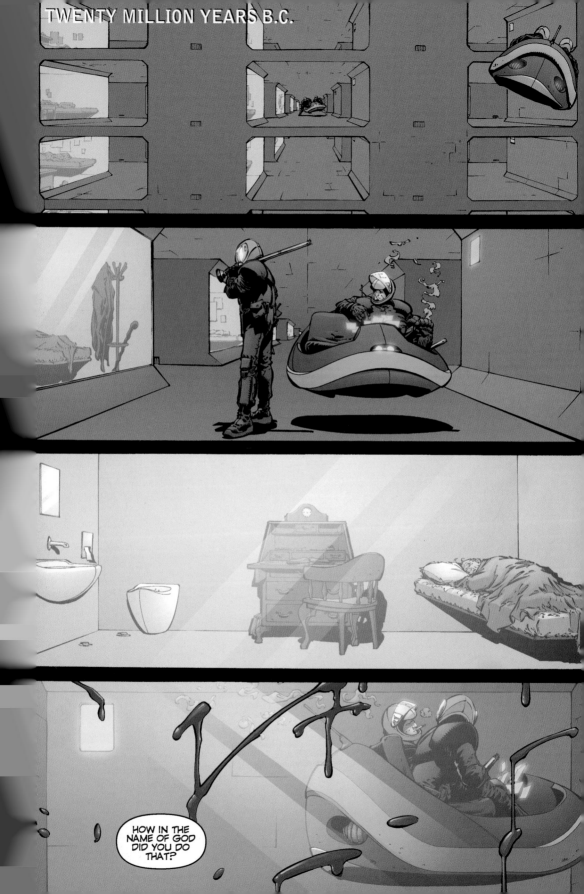

TWENTY MILLION YEARS B.C.

HOW IN THE
NAME OF GOD
DID YOU DO
THAT?

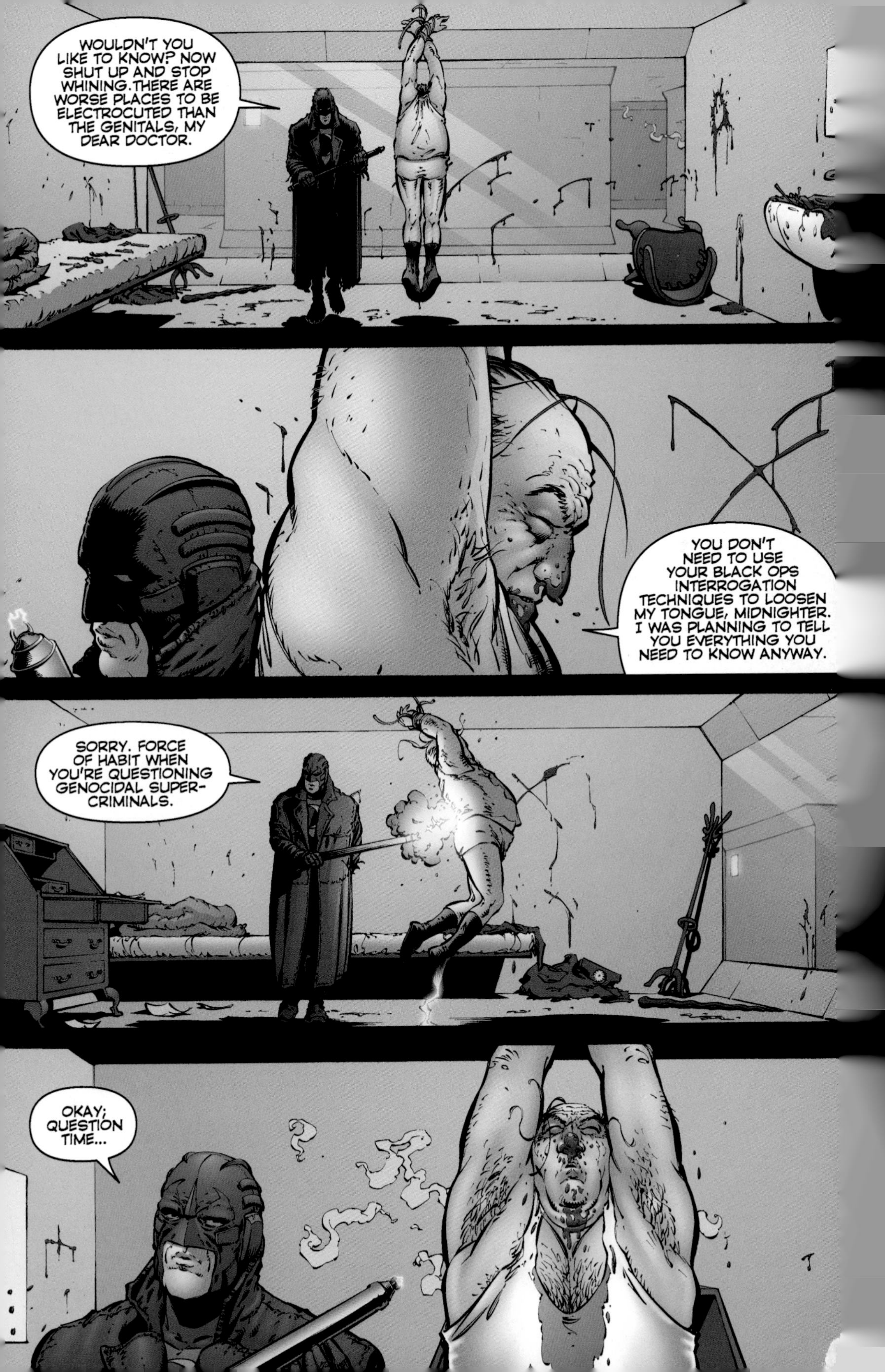
WOULDN'T YOU LIKE TO KNOW? NOW SHUT UP AND STOP WHINING. THERE ARE WORSE PLACES TO BE ELECTROCUTED THAN THE GENITALS, MY DEAR DOCTOR.
YOU DON'T NEED TO USE YOUR BLACK OPS INTERROGATION TECHNIQUES TO LOOSEN MY TONGUE, MIDNIGHTER. I WAS PLANNING TO TELL YOU EVERYTHING YOU NEED TO KNOW ANYWAY.
SORRY. FORCE OF HABIT WHEN YOU'RE QUESTIONING GENOCIDAL SUPER-CRIMINALS.
OKAY; QUESTION TIME...

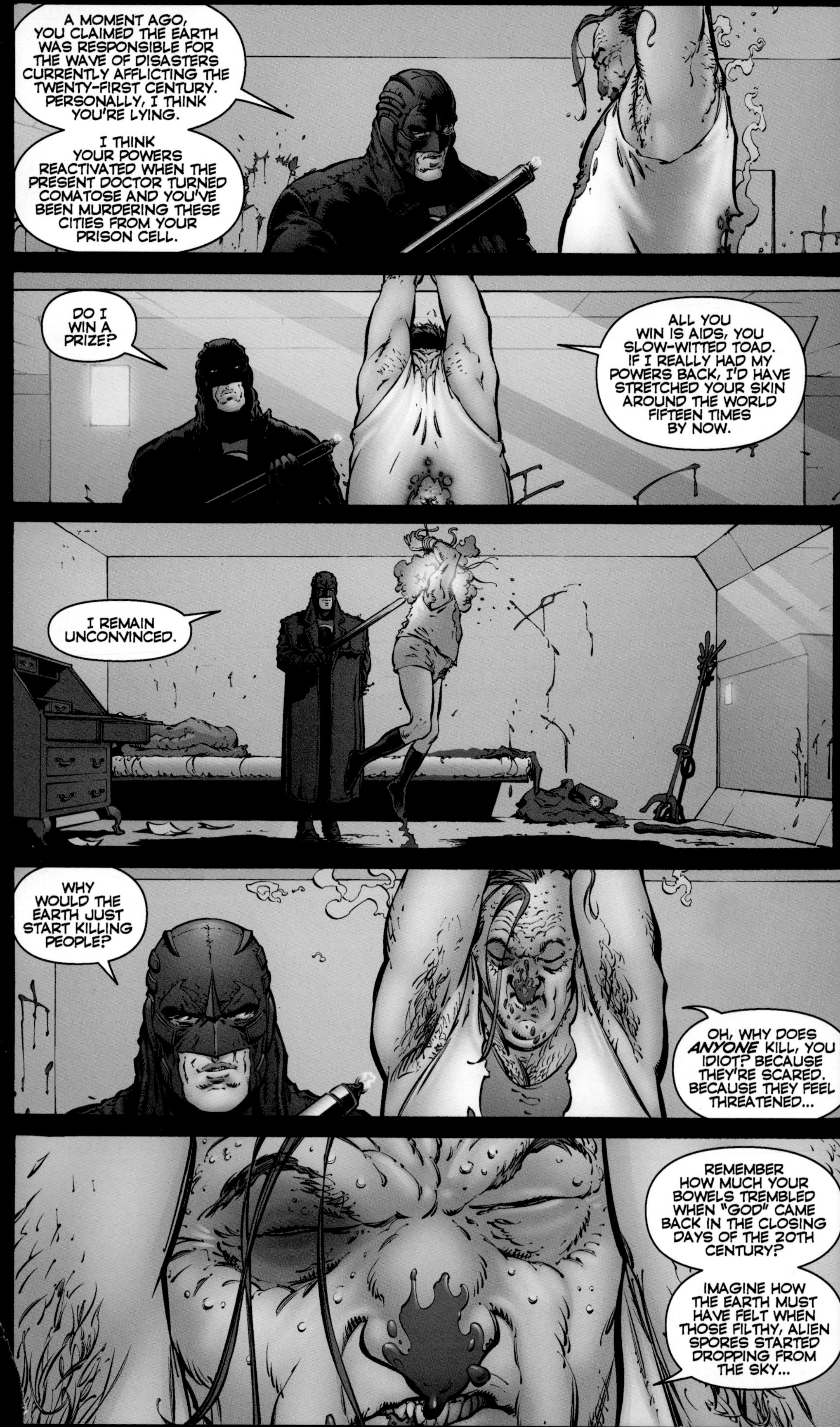

A MOMENT AGO, YOU CLAIMED THE EARTH WAS RESPONSIBLE FOR THE WAVE OF DISASTERS CURRENTLY AFFLICTING THE TWENTY-FIRST CENTURY. PERSONALLY, I THINK YOU'RE LYING.
I THINK YOUR POWERS REACTIVATED WHEN THE PRESENT DOCTOR TURNED COMATOSE AND YOU'VE BEEN MURDERING THESE CITIES FROM YOUR PRISON CELL.
DO I WIN A PRIZE?
ALL YOU WIN IS AIDS, YOU SLOW-WITTED TOAD. IF I REALLY HAD MY POWERS BACK, I'D HAVE STRETCHED YOUR SKIN AROUND THE WORLD FIFTEEN TIMES BY NOW.
I REMAIN UNCONVINCED.
WHY WOULD THE EARTH JUST START KILLING PEOPLE?
OH, WHY DOES *ANYONE* KILL, YOU IDIOT? BECAUSE THEY'RE SCARED. BECAUSE THEY FEEL THREATENED...
REMEMBER HOW MUCH YOUR BOWELS TREMBLED WHEN "GOD" CAME BACK IN THE CLOSING DAYS OF THE 20TH CENTURY?
IMAGINE HOW THE EARTH MUST HAVE FELT WHEN THOSE FILTHY, ALIEN SPORES STARTED DROPPING FROM THE SKY...

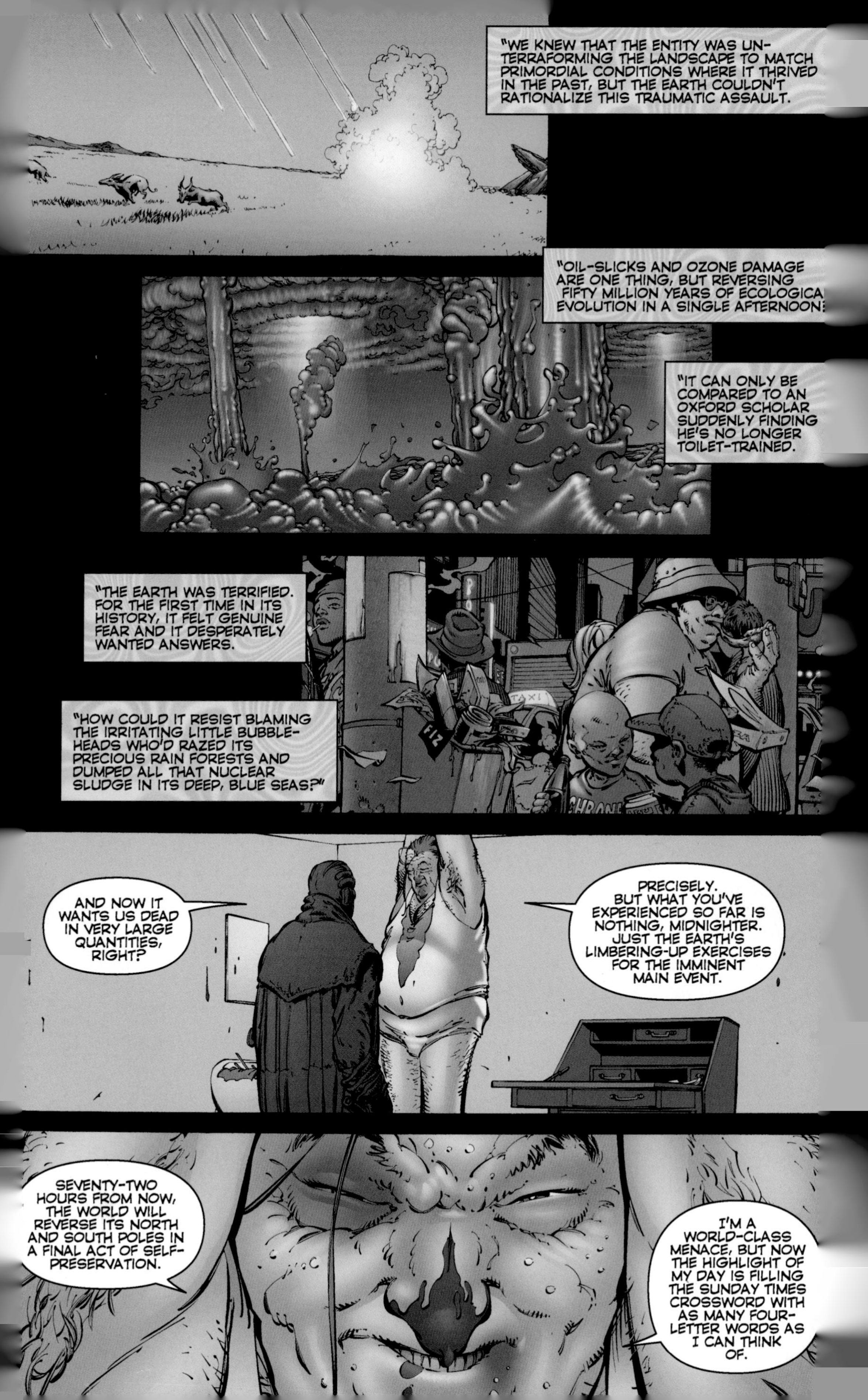
"WE KNEW THAT THE ENTITY WAS UN-TERRAFORMING THE LANDSCAPE TO MATCH PRIMORDIAL CONDITIONS WHERE IT THRIVED IN THE PAST, BUT THE EARTH COULDN'T RATIONALIZE THIS TRAUMATIC ASSAULT.
"OIL-SLICKS AND OZONE DAMAGE ARE ONE THING, BUT REVERSING FIFTY MILLION YEARS OF ECOLOGICAL EVOLUTION IN A SINGLE AFTERNOON?
"IT CAN ONLY BE COMPARED TO AN OXFORD SCHOLAR SUDDENLY FINDING HE'S NO LONGER TOILET-TRAINED.
"THE EARTH WAS TERRIFIED. FOR THE FIRST TIME IN ITS HISTORY, IT FELT GENUINE FEAR AND IT DESPERATELY WANTED ANSWERS.
"HOW COULD IT RESIST BLAMING THE IRRITATING LITTLE BUBBLE-HEADS WHO'D RAZED ITS PRECIOUS RAIN FORESTS AND DUMPED ALL THAT NUCLEAR SLUDGE IN ITS DEEP, BLUE SEAS?"
TAXI
AND NOW IT WANTS US DEAD IN VERY LARGE QUANTITIES, RIGHT?
PRECISELY. BUT WHAT YOU'VE EXPERIENCED SO FAR IS NOTHING, MIDNIGHTER. JUST THE EARTH'S LIMBERING-UP EXERCISES FOR THE IMMINENT MAIN EVENT.
SEVENTY-TWO HOURS FROM NOW, THE WORLD WILL REVERSE ITS NORTH AND SOUTH POLES IN A FINAL ACT OF SELF-PRESERVATION.
I'M A WORLD-CLASS MENACE, BUT NOW THE HIGHLIGHT OF MY DAY IS FILLING THE SUNDAY TIMES CROSSWORD WITH AS MANY FOUR-LETTER WORDS AS I CAN THINK OF.

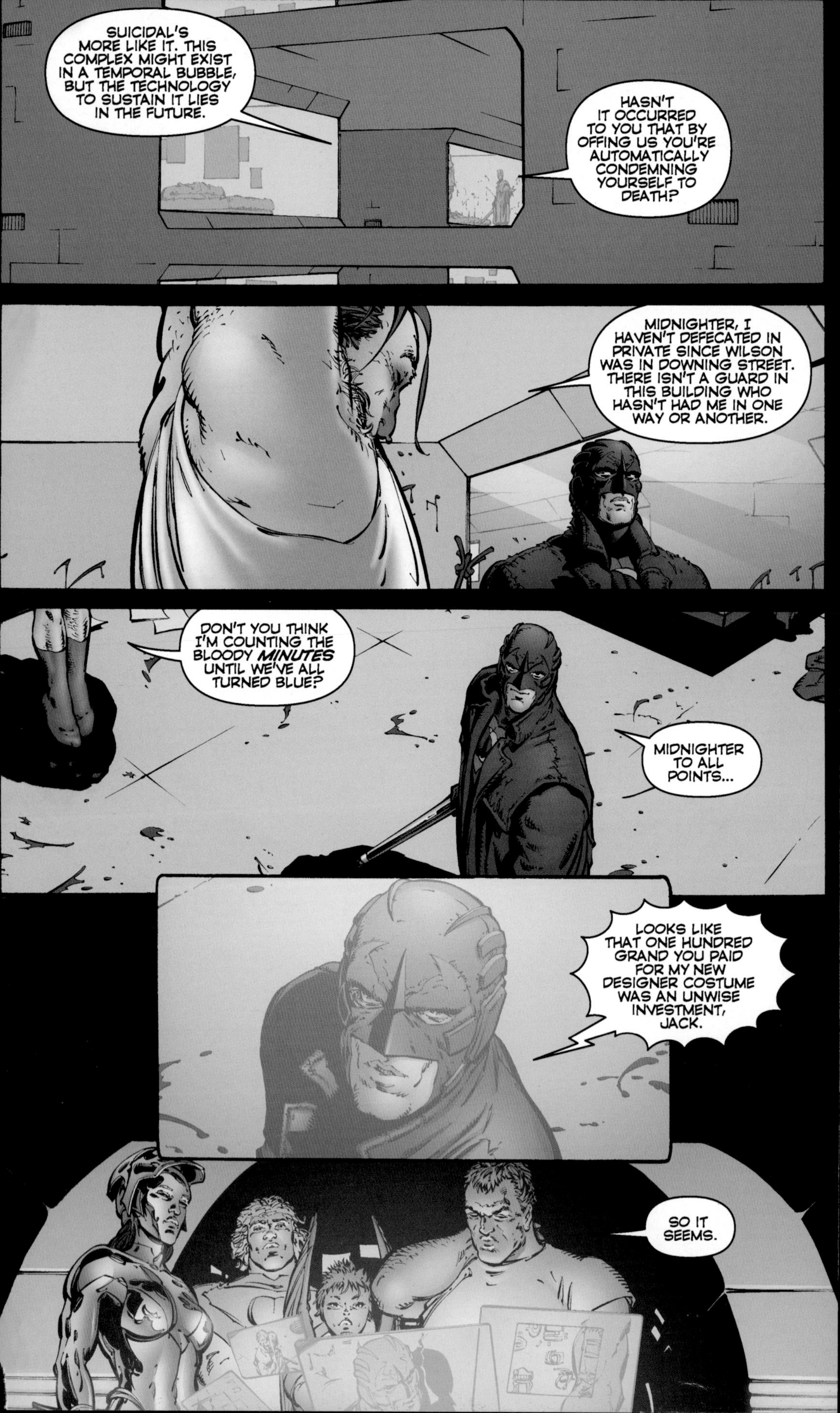
SUICIDAL'S MORE LIKE IT. THIS COMPLEX MIGHT EXIST IN A TEMPORAL BUBBLE, BUT THE TECHNOLOGY TO SUSTAIN IT LIES IN THE FUTURE.
HASN'T IT OCCURRED TO YOU THAT BY OFFING US YOU'RE AUTOMATICALLY CONDEMNING YOURSELF TO DEATH?
MIDNIGHTER, I HAVEN'T DEFECATED IN PRIVATE SINCE WILSON WAS IN DOWNING STREET. THERE ISN'T A GUARD IN THIS BUILDING WHO HASN'T HAD ME IN ONE WAY OR ANOTHER.
DON'T YOU THINK I'M COUNTING THE BLOODY *MINUTES* UNTIL WE'VE ALL TURNED BLUE?
MIDNIGHTER TO ALL POINTS...
LOOKS LIKE THAT ONE HUNDRED GRAND YOU PAID FOR MY NEW DESIGNER COSTUME WAS AN UNWISE INVESTMENT, JACK.
SO IT SEEMS.

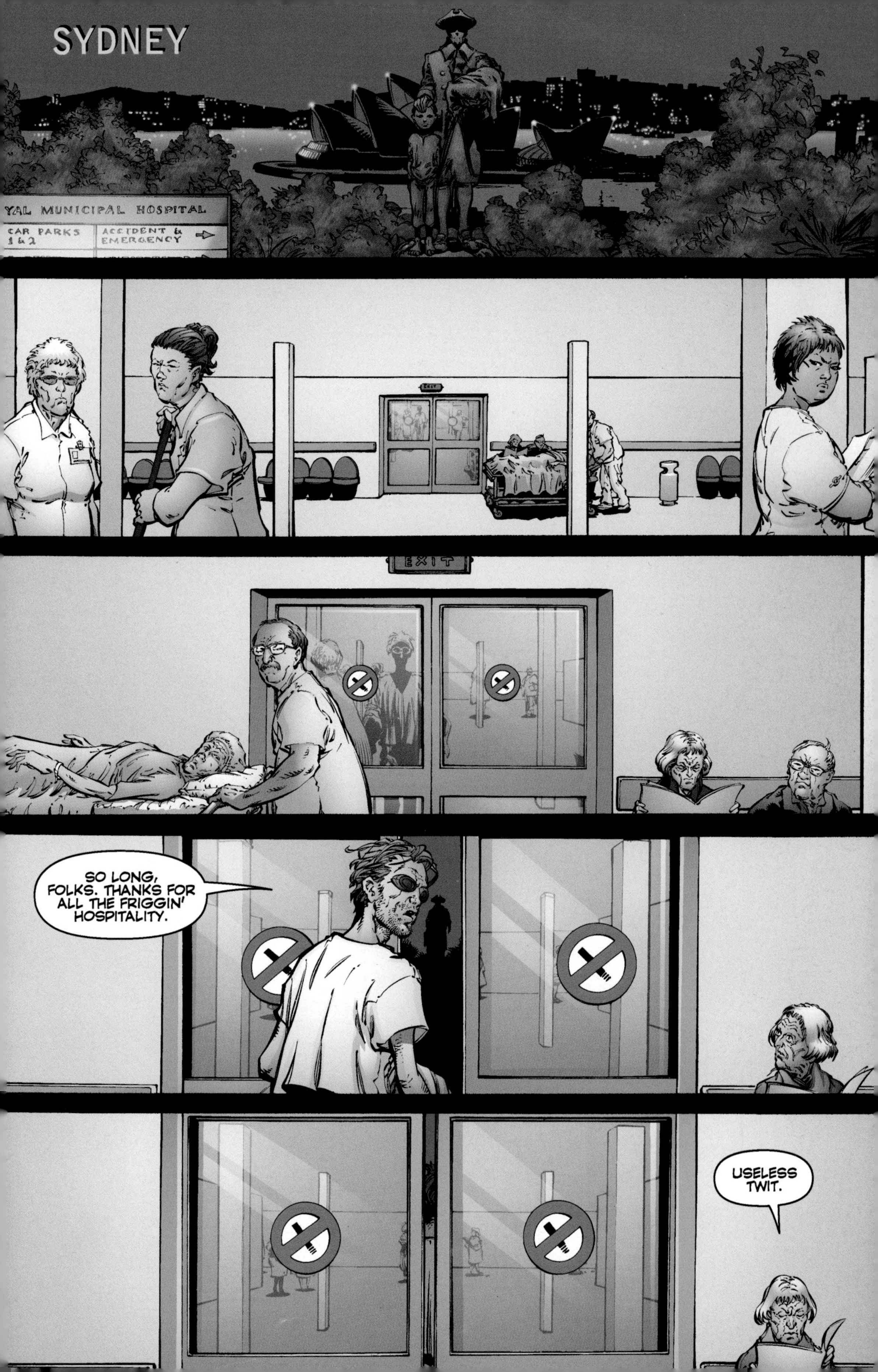
SYDNEY
YAL MUNICIPAL HOSPITAL
CAR PARKS 1 & 2
ACCIDENT & EMERGENCY
EXIT
SO LONG, FOLKS. THANKS FOR ALL THE FRIGGIN' HOSPITALITY.
USELESS TWIT.

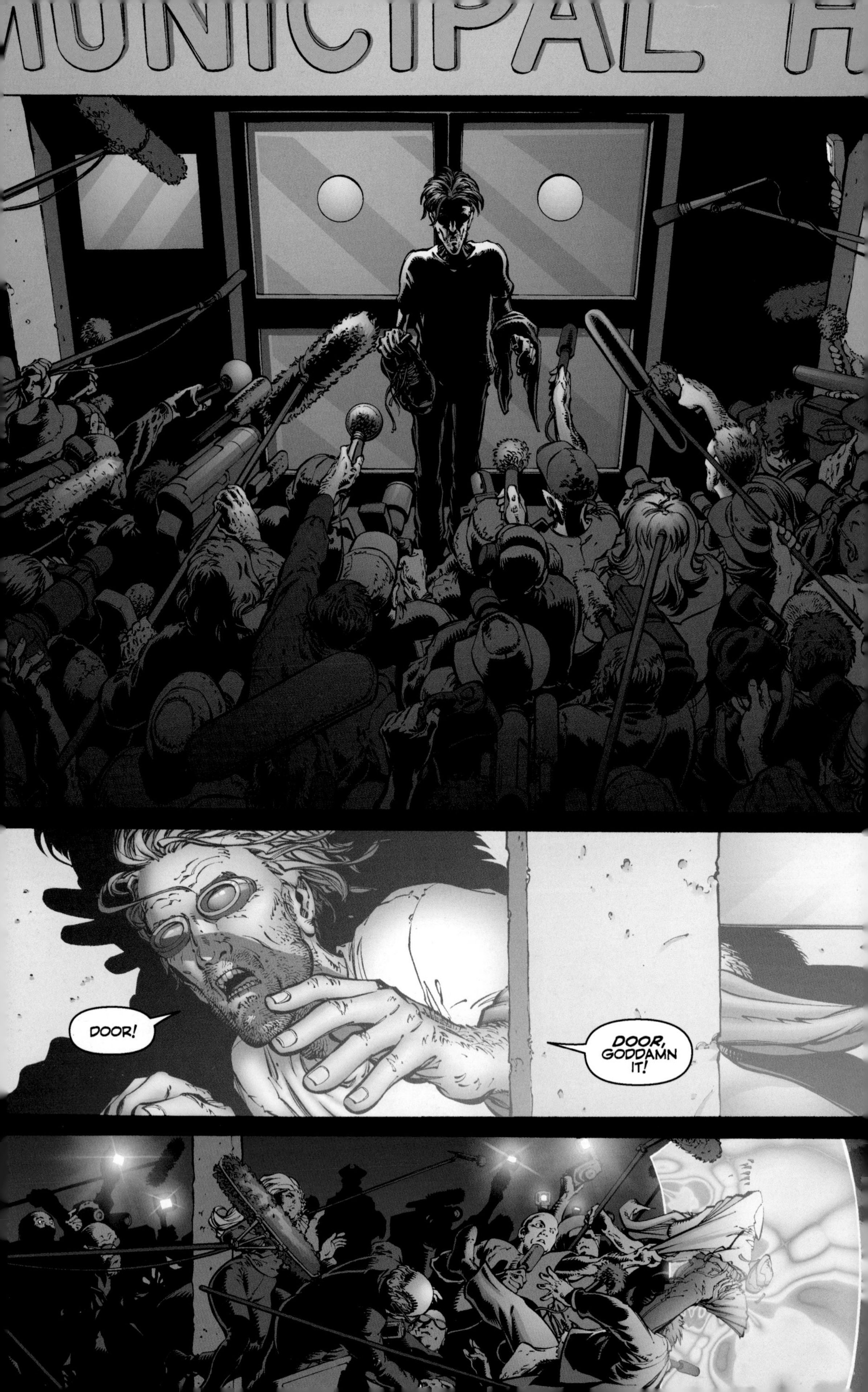
MUNICIPAL H
DOOR!
DOOR, GODDAMN IT!

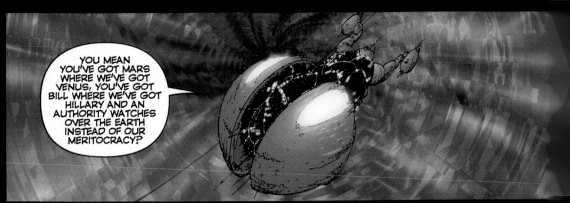

YOU MEAN YOU'VE GOT MARS WHERE WE'VE GOT VENUS, YOU'VE GOT BILL WHERE WE'VE GOT HILLARY AND AN AUTHORITY WATCHES OVER THE EARTH INSTEAD OF OUR MERITOCRACY?

UNBELIEVABLE.

HARD TO IMAGINE LIVING IN AN AMERICA WHERE THE PRESIDENT ISN'T CHASING EVERY LITTLE HIMBO WITH AN ASS-CLEAVAGE.

I DON'T KNOW WHAT THAT MEANS EXACTLY, BUT THIS PLACE IS REALLY STARTING TO GROW ON ME.

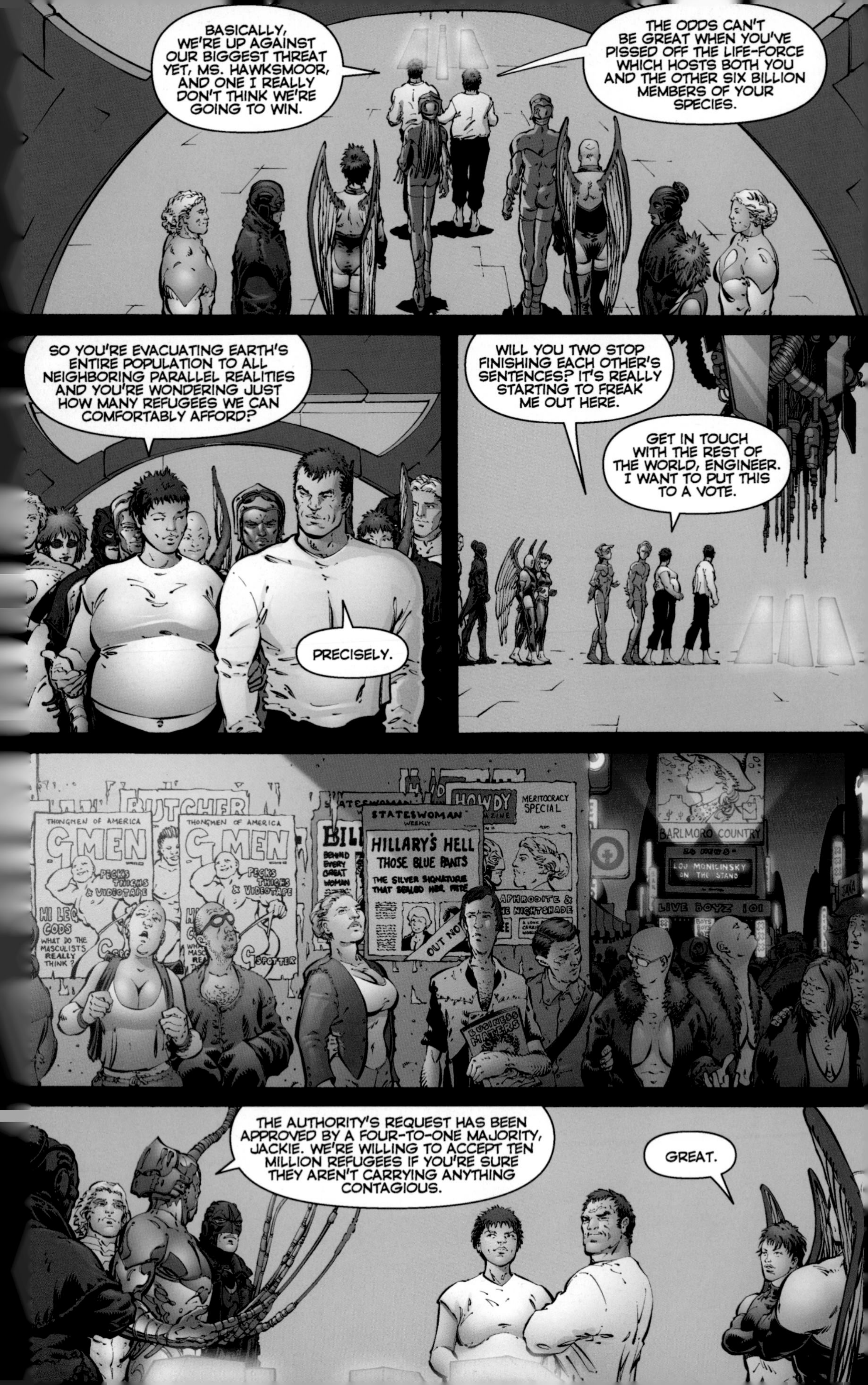
BASICALLY, WE'RE UP AGAINST OUR BIGGEST THREAT YET, MS. HAWKSMOOR, AND ONE I REALLY DON'T THINK WE'RE GOING TO WIN.
THE ODDS CAN'T BE GREAT WHEN YOU'VE PISSED OFF THE LIFE-FORCE WHICH HOSTS BOTH YOU AND THE OTHER SIX BILLION MEMBERS OF YOUR SPECIES.
SO YOU'RE EVACUATING EARTH'S ENTIRE POPULATION TO ALL NEIGHBORING PARALLEL REALITIES AND YOU'RE WONDERING JUST HOW MANY REFUGEES WE CAN COMFORTABLY AFFORD?
PRECISELY.
WILL YOU TWO STOP FINISHING EACH OTHER'S SENTENCES? IT'S REALLY STARTING TO FREAK ME OUT HERE.
GET IN TOUCH WITH THE REST OF THE WORLD, ENGINEER. I WANT TO PUT THIS TO A VOTE.
THONGMEN OF AMERICA
G MEN
PECKS THIGHS & VIDEOTAPE
HI LEG GODS
WHAT DO THE MASCULISTS REALLY THINK?
THONGMEN OF AMERICA
G MEN
PECKS THIGHS & VIDEOTAPE
STATESWOMAN WEEKLY
HILLARY'S HELL
THOSE BLUE PANTS
THE SILVER SIGNATURE THAT SEALED HER FATE
HOWDY
MERITOCRACY SPECIAL
BARLMORO COUNTRY
LOU MONICINSKY ON THE STAND
LIVE BOYZ 101
BUSINESS MATERS
THE AUTHORITY'S REQUEST HAS BEEN APPROVED BY A FOUR-TO-ONE MAJORITY, JACKIE. WE'RE WILLING TO ACCEPT TEN MILLION REFUGEES IF YOU'RE SURE THEY AREN'T CARRYING ANYTHING CONTAGIOUS.
GREAT.

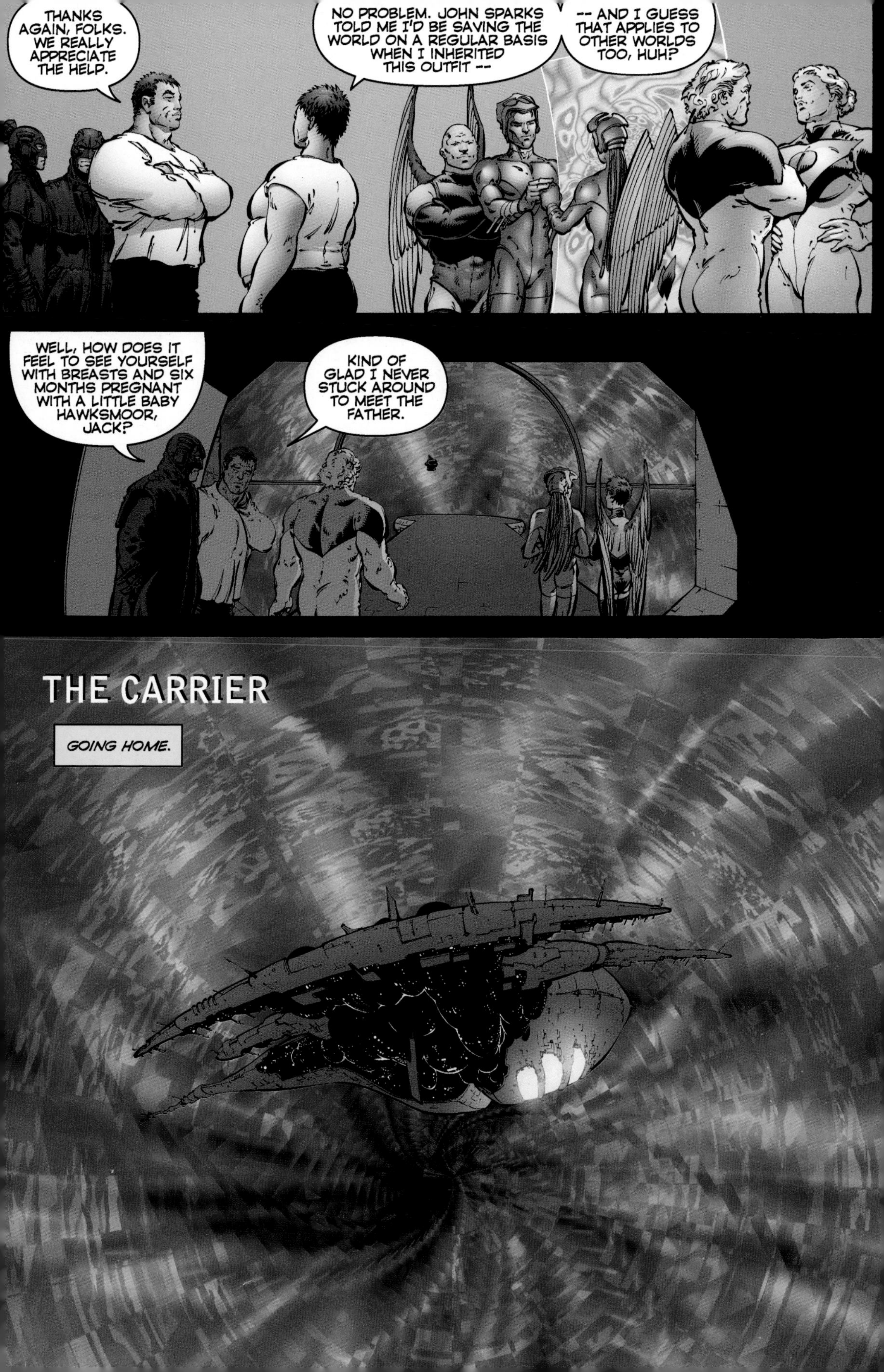
THANKS AGAIN, FOLKS. WE REALLY APPRECIATE THE HELP.
NO PROBLEM. JOHN SPARKS TOLD ME I'D BE SAVING THE WORLD ON A REGULAR BASIS WHEN I INHERITED THIS OUTFIT --
-- AND I GUESS THAT APPLIES TO OTHER WORLDS TOO, HUH?
WELL, HOW DOES IT FEEL TO SEE YOURSELF WITH BREASTS AND SIX MONTHS PREGNANT WITH A LITTLE BABY HAWKSMOOR, JACK?
KIND OF GLAD I NEVER STUCK AROUND TO MEET THE FATHER.
THE CARRIER
GOING HOME.

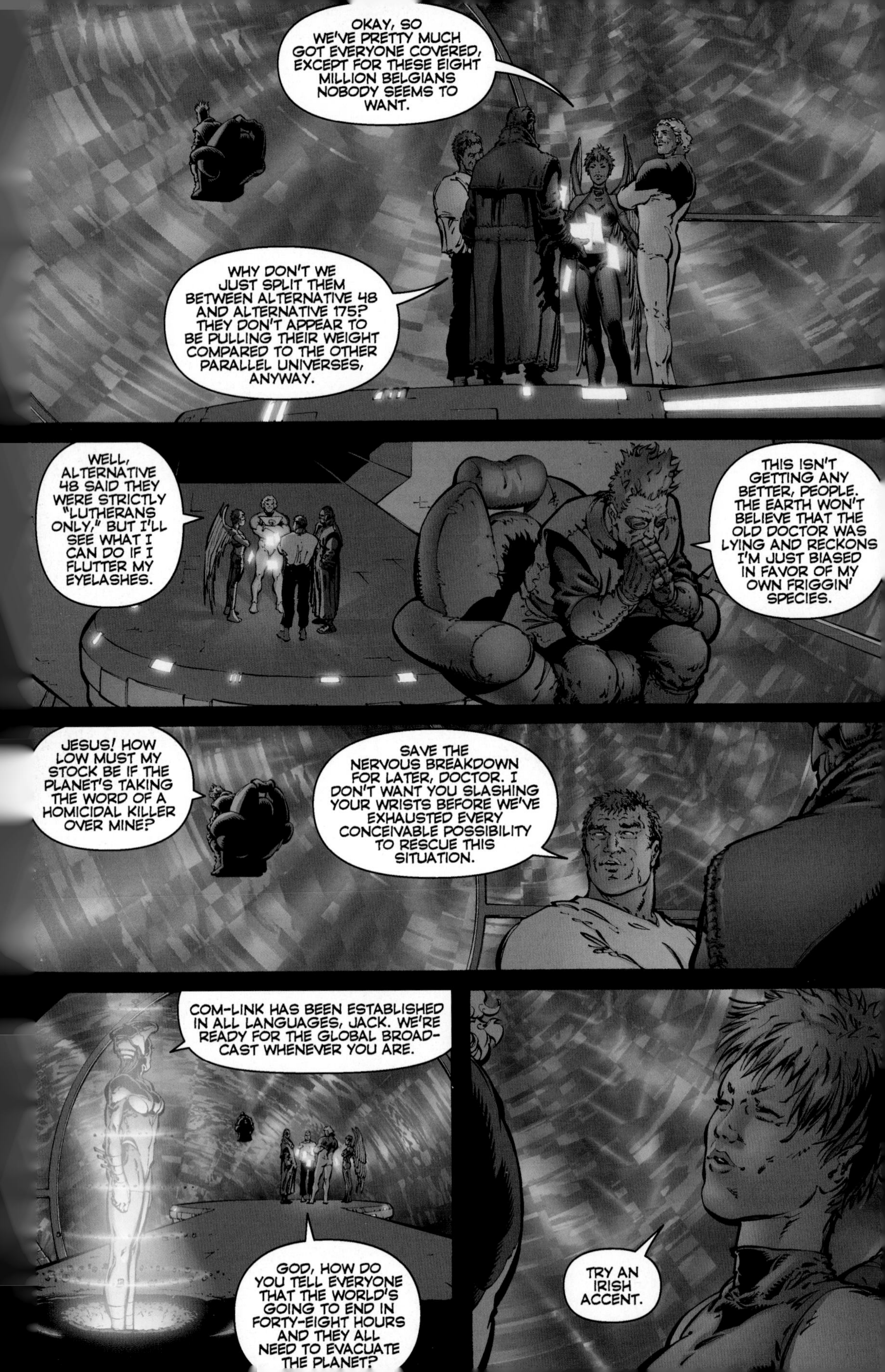
OKAY, SO WE'VE PRETTY MUCH GOT EVERYONE COVERED, EXCEPT FOR THESE EIGHT MILLION BELGIANS NOBODY SEEMS TO WANT.
WHY DON'T WE JUST SPLIT THEM BETWEEN ALTERNATIVE 48 AND ALTERNATIVE 175? THEY DON'T APPEAR TO BE PULLING THEIR WEIGHT COMPARED TO THE OTHER PARALLEL UNIVERSES, ANYWAY.
WELL, ALTERNATIVE 48 SAID THEY WERE STRICTLY "LUTHERANS ONLY," BUT I'LL SEE WHAT I CAN DO IF I FLUTTER MY EYELASHES.
THIS ISN'T GETTING ANY BETTER, PEOPLE. THE EARTH WON'T BELIEVE THAT THE OLD DOCTOR WAS LYING AND RECKONS I'M JUST BIASED IN FAVOR OF MY OWN FRIGGIN' SPECIES.
JESUS! HOW LOW MUST MY STOCK BE IF THE PLANET'S TAKING THE WORD OF A HOMICIDAL KILLER OVER MINE?
SAVE THE NERVOUS BREAKDOWN FOR LATER, DOCTOR. I DON'T WANT YOU SLASHING YOUR WRISTS BEFORE WE'VE EXHAUSTED EVERY CONCEIVABLE POSSIBILITY TO RESCUE THIS SITUATION.
COM-LINK HAS BEEN ESTABLISHED IN ALL LANGUAGES, JACK. WE'RE READY FOR THE GLOBAL BROAD-CAST WHENEVER YOU ARE.
GOD, HOW DO YOU TELL EVERYONE THAT THE WORLD'S GOING TO END IN FORTY-EIGHT HOURS AND THEY ALL NEED TO EVACUATE THE PLANET?
TRY AN IRISH ACCENT.

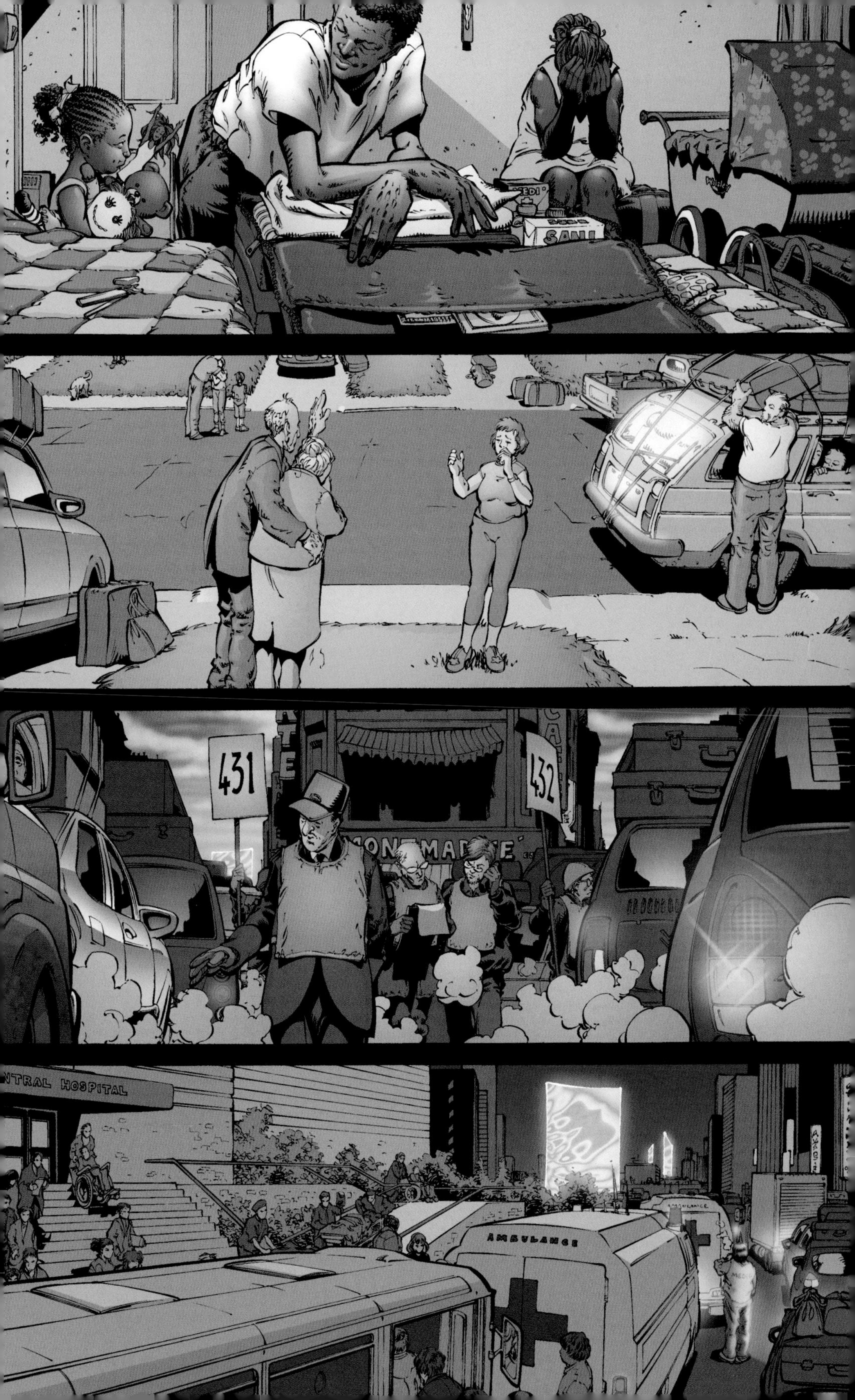
431
432
NTRAL HOSPITAL
AMBULANCE

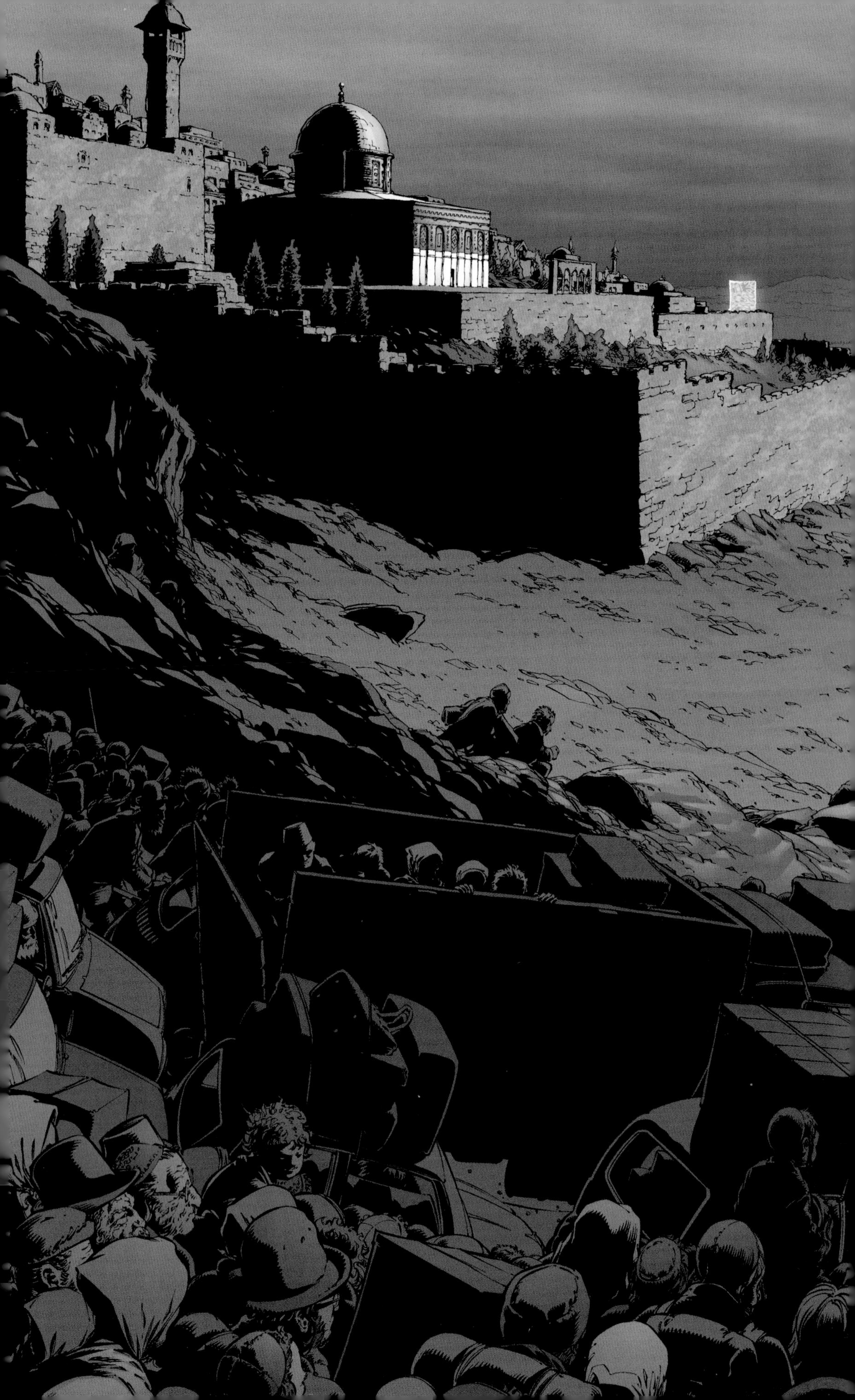

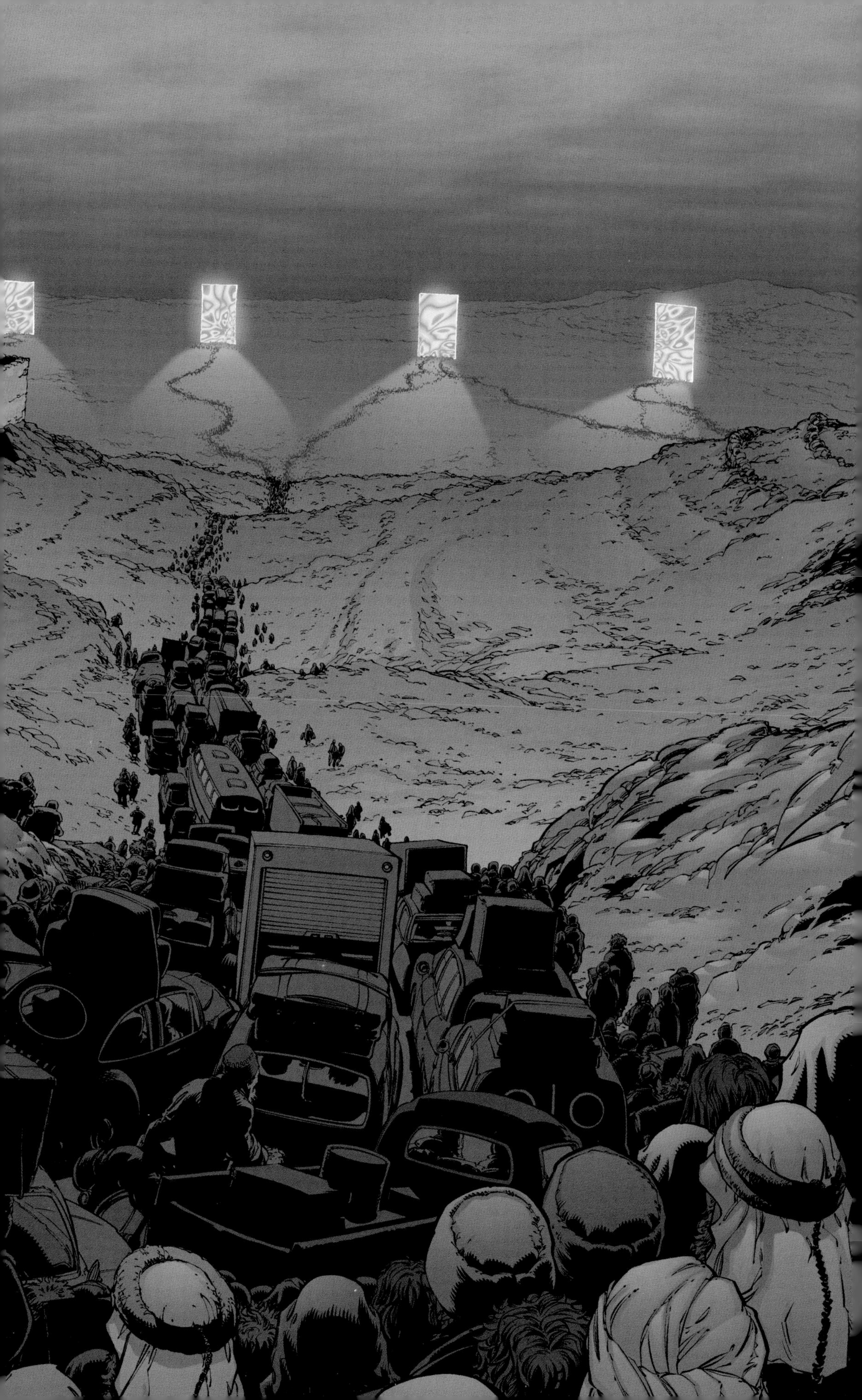

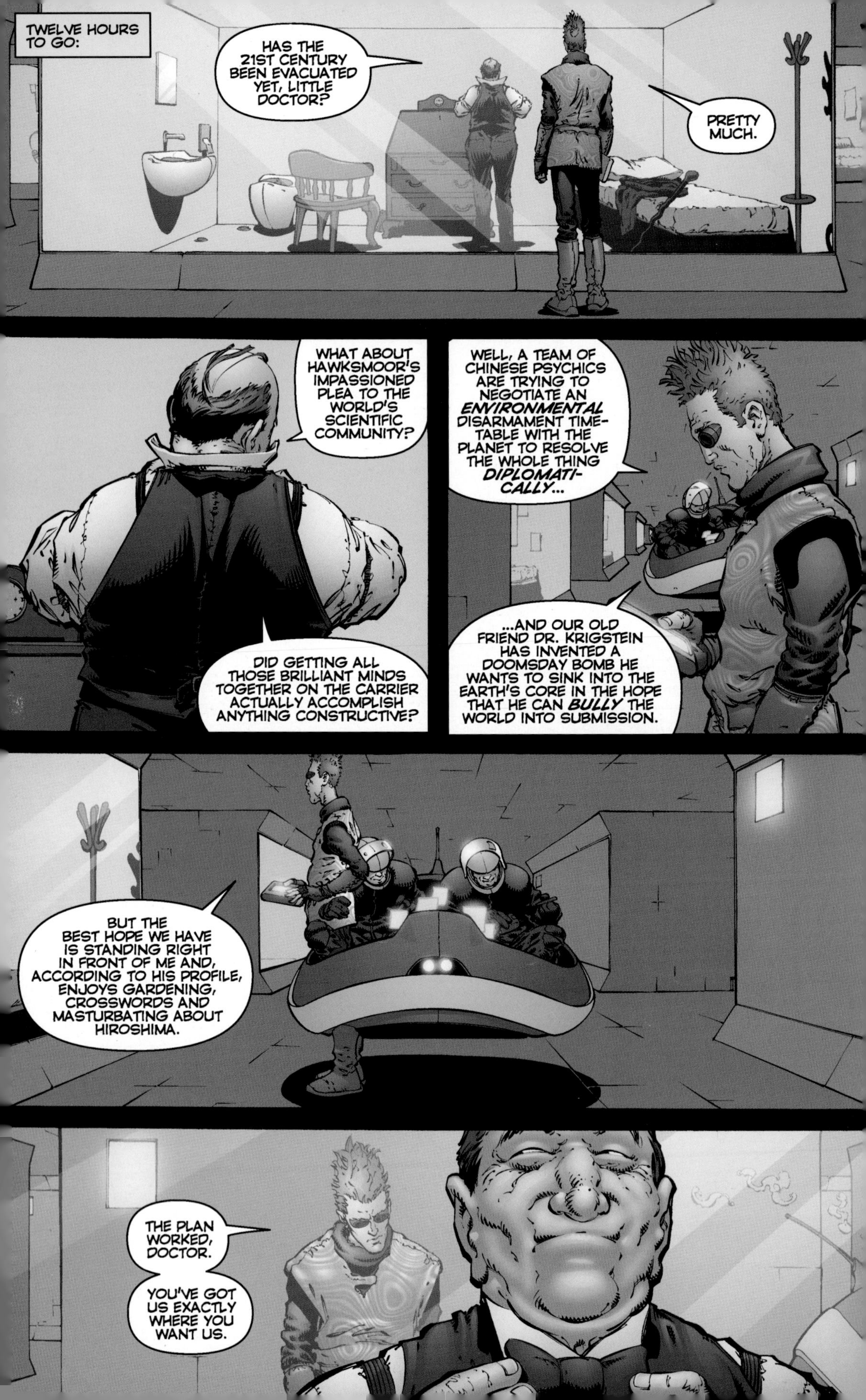
TWELVE HOURS TO GO:
HAS THE 21ST CENTURY BEEN EVACUATED YET, LITTLE DOCTOR?
PRETTY MUCH.
WHAT ABOUT HAWKSMOOR'S IMPASSIONED PLEA TO THE WORLD'S SCIENTIFIC COMMUNITY?
DID GETTING ALL THOSE BRILLIANT MINDS TOGETHER ON THE CARRIER ACTUALLY ACCOMPLISH ANYTHING CONSTRUCTIVE?
WELL, A TEAM OF CHINESE PSYCHICS ARE TRYING TO NEGOTIATE AN ENVIRONMENTAL DISARMAMENT TIME-TABLE WITH THE PLANET TO RESOLVE THE WHOLE THING DIPLOMATI-CALLY...
...AND OUR OLD FRIEND DR. KRIGSTEIN HAS INVENTED A DOOMSDAY BOMB HE WANTS TO SINK INTO THE EARTH'S CORE IN THE HOPE THAT HE CAN BULLY THE WORLD INTO SUBMISSION.
BUT THE BEST HOPE WE HAVE IS STANDING RIGHT IN FRONT OF ME AND, ACCORDING TO HIS PROFILE, ENJOYS GARDENING, CROSSWORDS AND MASTURBATING ABOUT HIROSHIMA.
THE PLAN WORKED, DOCTOR.
YOU'VE GOT US EXACTLY WHERE YOU WANT US.

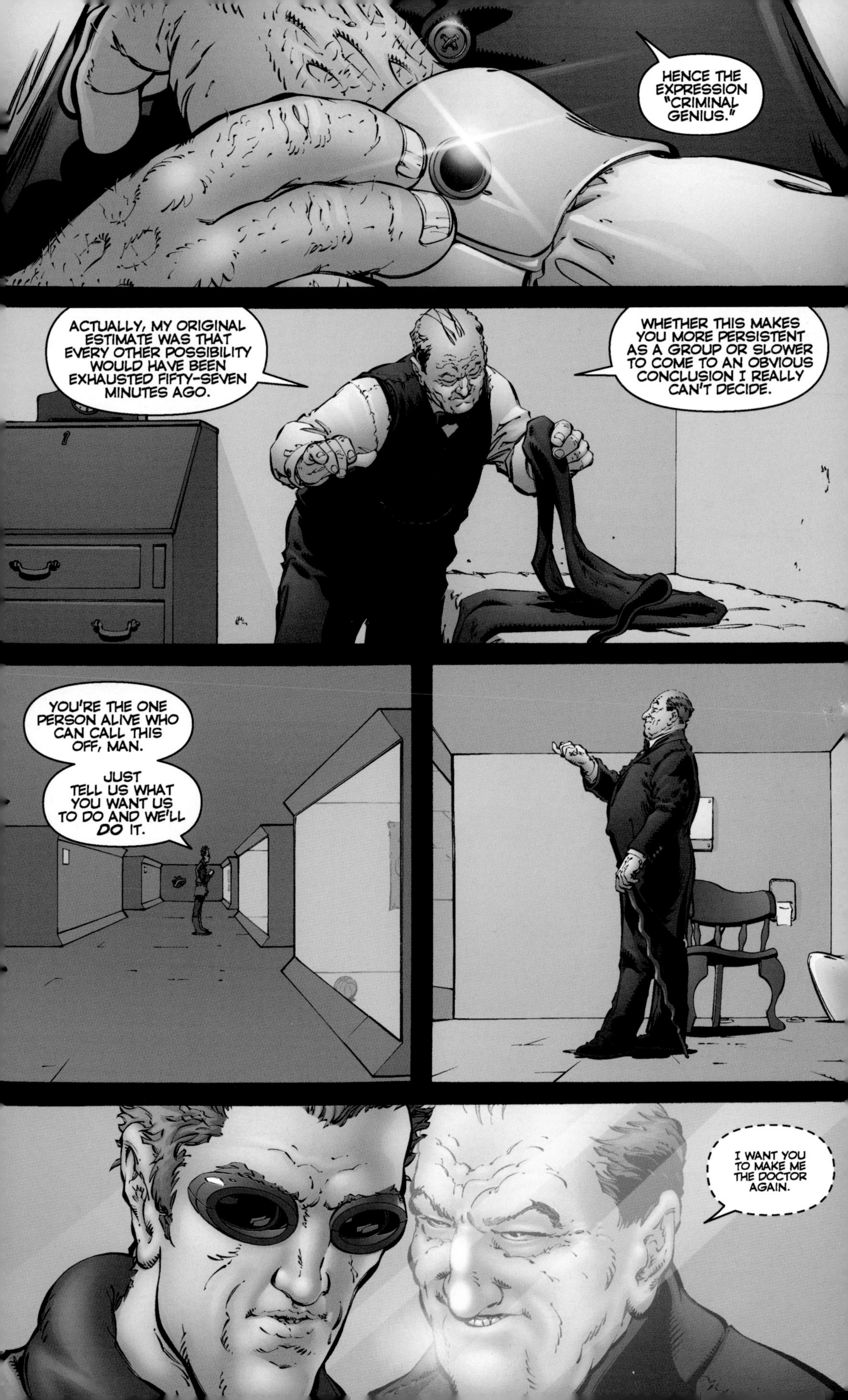
HENCE THE EXPRESSION "CRIMINAL GENIUS."
ACTUALLY, MY ORIGINAL ESTIMATE WAS THAT EVERY OTHER POSSIBILITY WOULD HAVE BEEN EXHAUSTED FIFTY-SEVEN MINUTES AGO.
WHETHER THIS MAKES YOU MORE PERSISTENT AS A GROUP OR SLOWER TO COME TO AN OBVIOUS CONCLUSION I REALLY CAN'T DECIDE.
YOU'RE THE ONE PERSON ALIVE WHO CAN CALL THIS OFF, MAN.
JUST TELL US WHAT YOU WANT US TO DO AND WE'LL DO IT.
I WANT YOU TO MAKE ME THE DOCTOR AGAIN.

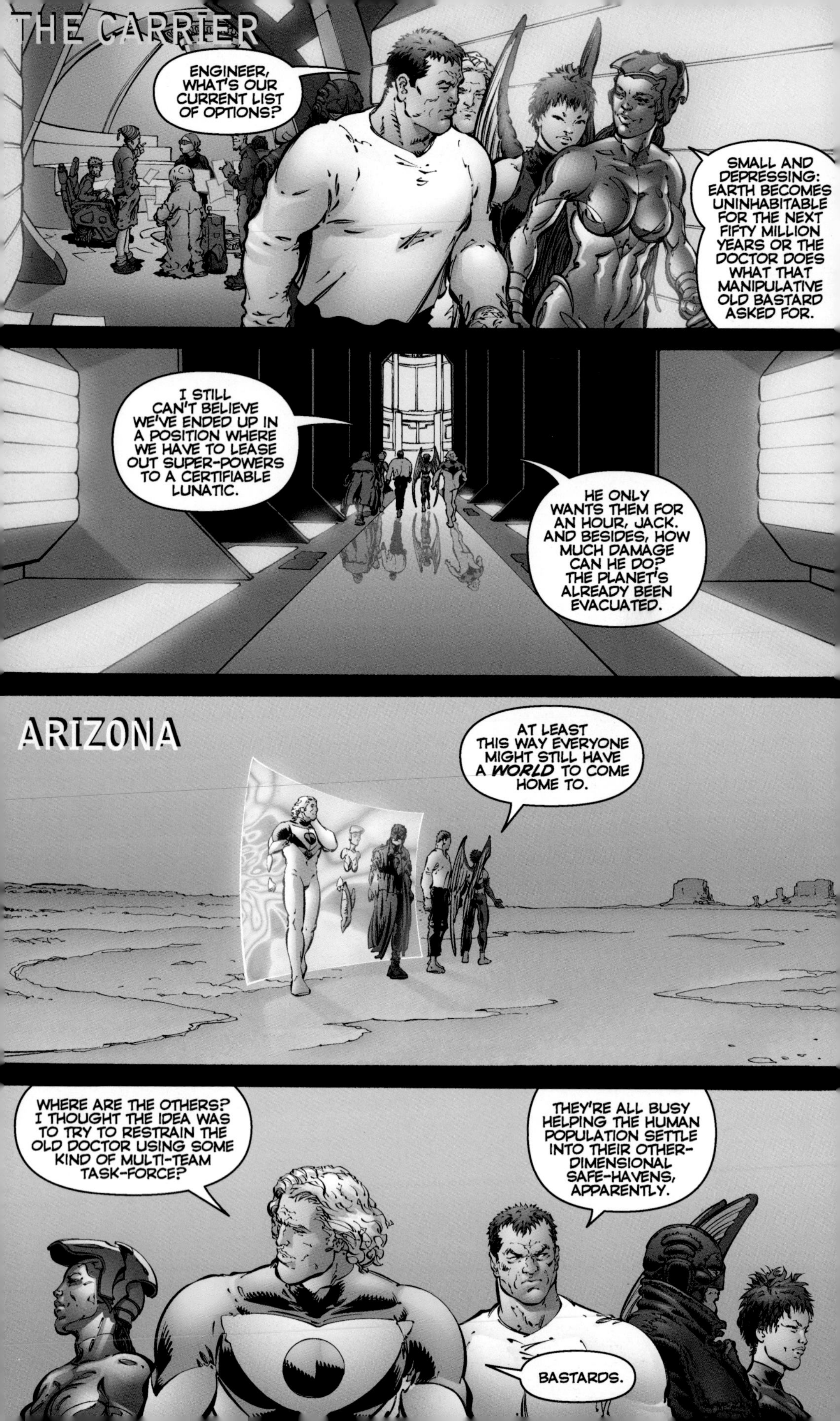
THE CARRIER
ENGINEER, WHAT'S OUR CURRENT LIST OF OPTIONS?
SMALL AND DEPRESSING: EARTH BECOMES UNINHABITABLE FOR THE NEXT FIFTY MILLION YEARS OR THE DOCTOR DOES WHAT THAT MANIPULATIVE OLD BASTARD ASKED FOR.
I STILL CAN'T BELIEVE WE'VE ENDED UP IN A POSITION WHERE WE HAVE TO LEASE OUT SUPER-POWERS TO A CERTIFIABLE LUNATIC.
HE ONLY WANTS THEM FOR AN HOUR, JACK. AND BESIDES, HOW MUCH DAMAGE CAN HE DO? THE PLANET'S ALREADY BEEN EVACUATED.
ARIZONA
AT LEAST THIS WAY EVERYONE MIGHT STILL HAVE A *WORLD* TO COME HOME TO.
WHERE ARE THE OTHERS? I THOUGHT THE IDEA WAS TO TRY TO RESTRAIN THE OLD DOCTOR USING SOME KIND OF MULTI-TEAM TASK-FORCE?
THEY'RE ALL BUSY HELPING THE HUMAN POPULATION SETTLE INTO THEIR OTHER-DIMENSIONAL SAFE-HAVENS, APPARENTLY.
BASTARDS.

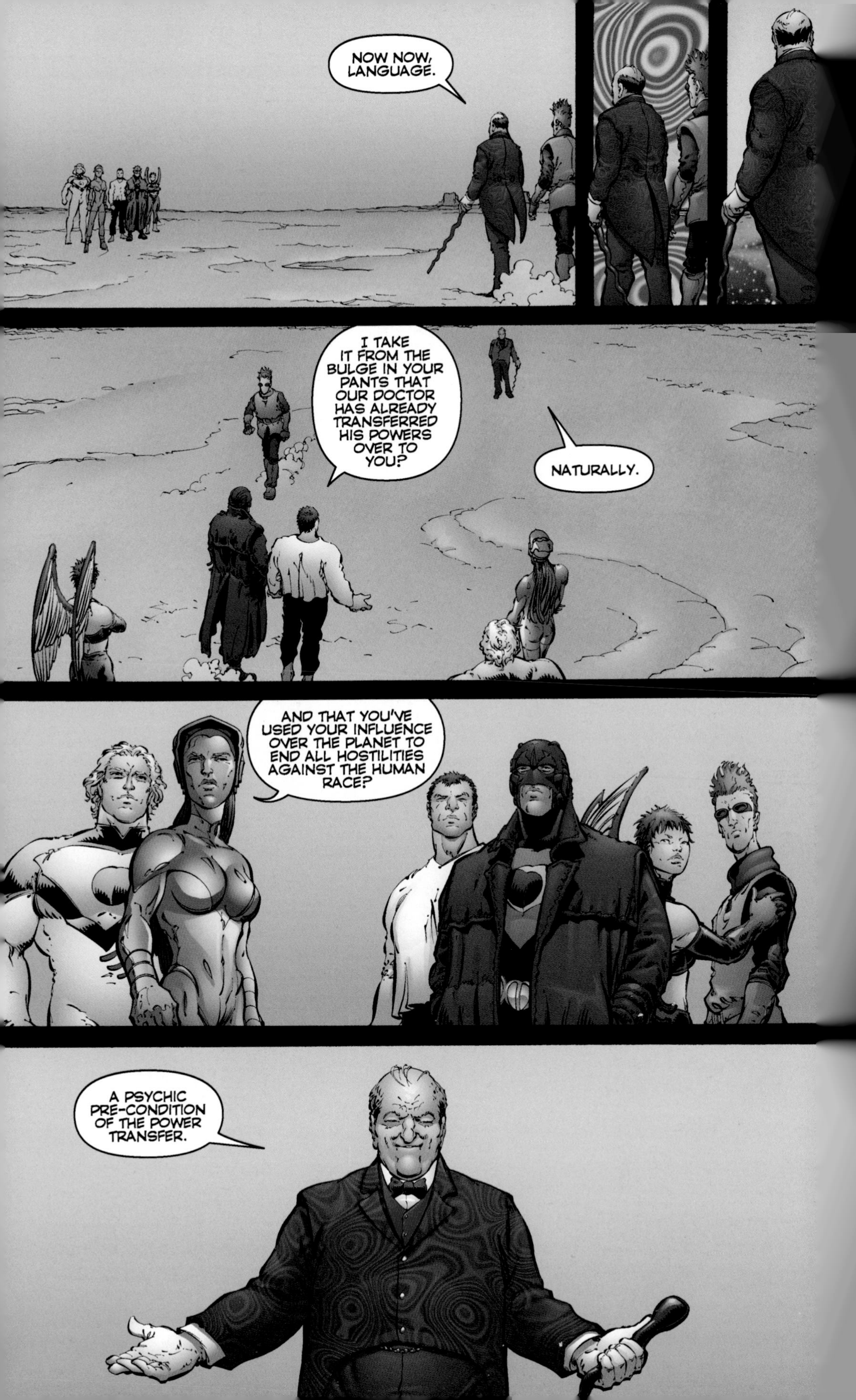

NOW NOW, LANGUAGE.
I TAKE IT FROM THE BULGE IN YOUR PANTS THAT OUR DOCTOR HAS ALREADY TRANSFERRED HIS POWERS OVER TO YOU?
NATURALLY.
AND THAT YOU'VE USED YOUR INFLUENCE OVER THE PLANET TO END ALL HOSTILITIES AGAINST THE HUMAN RACE?
A PSYCHIC PRE-CONDITION OF THE POWER TRANSFER.

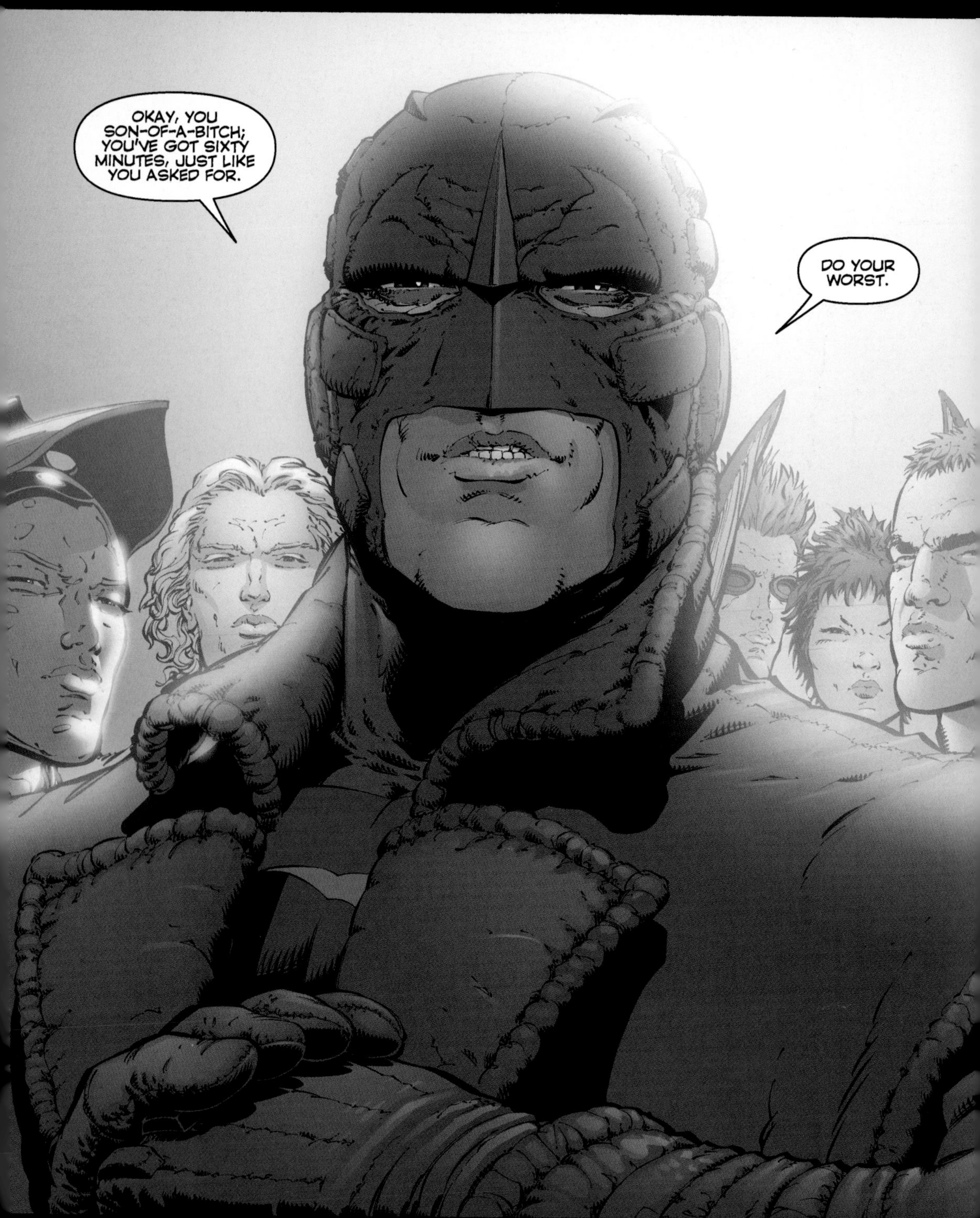
OKAY, YOU SON-OF-A-BITCH; YOU'VE GOT SIXTY MINUTES, JUST LIKE YOU ASKED FOR.
DO YOUR WORST.

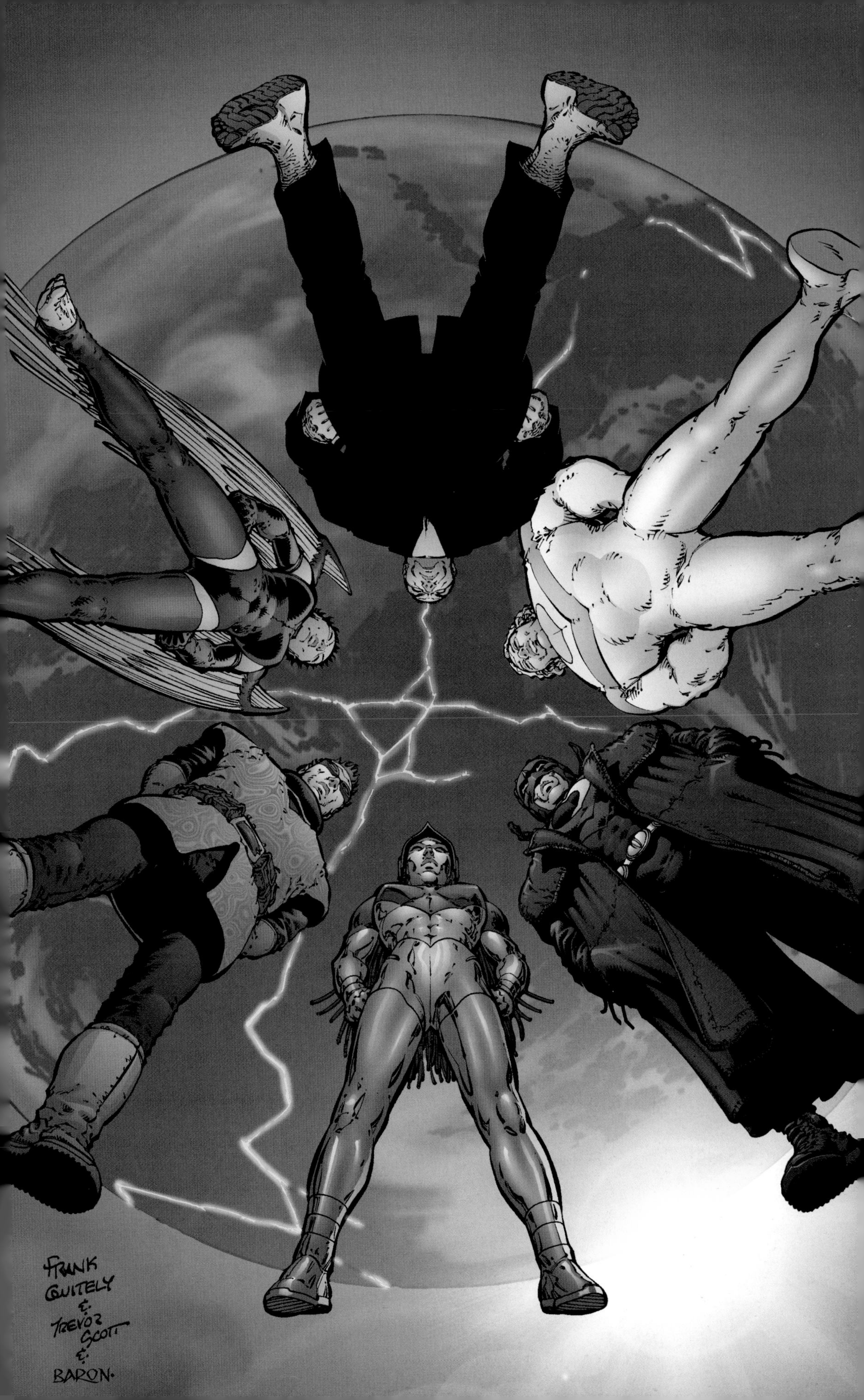
FRANK
QUITELY
&
TREVOR
SCOTT
&
BARON.

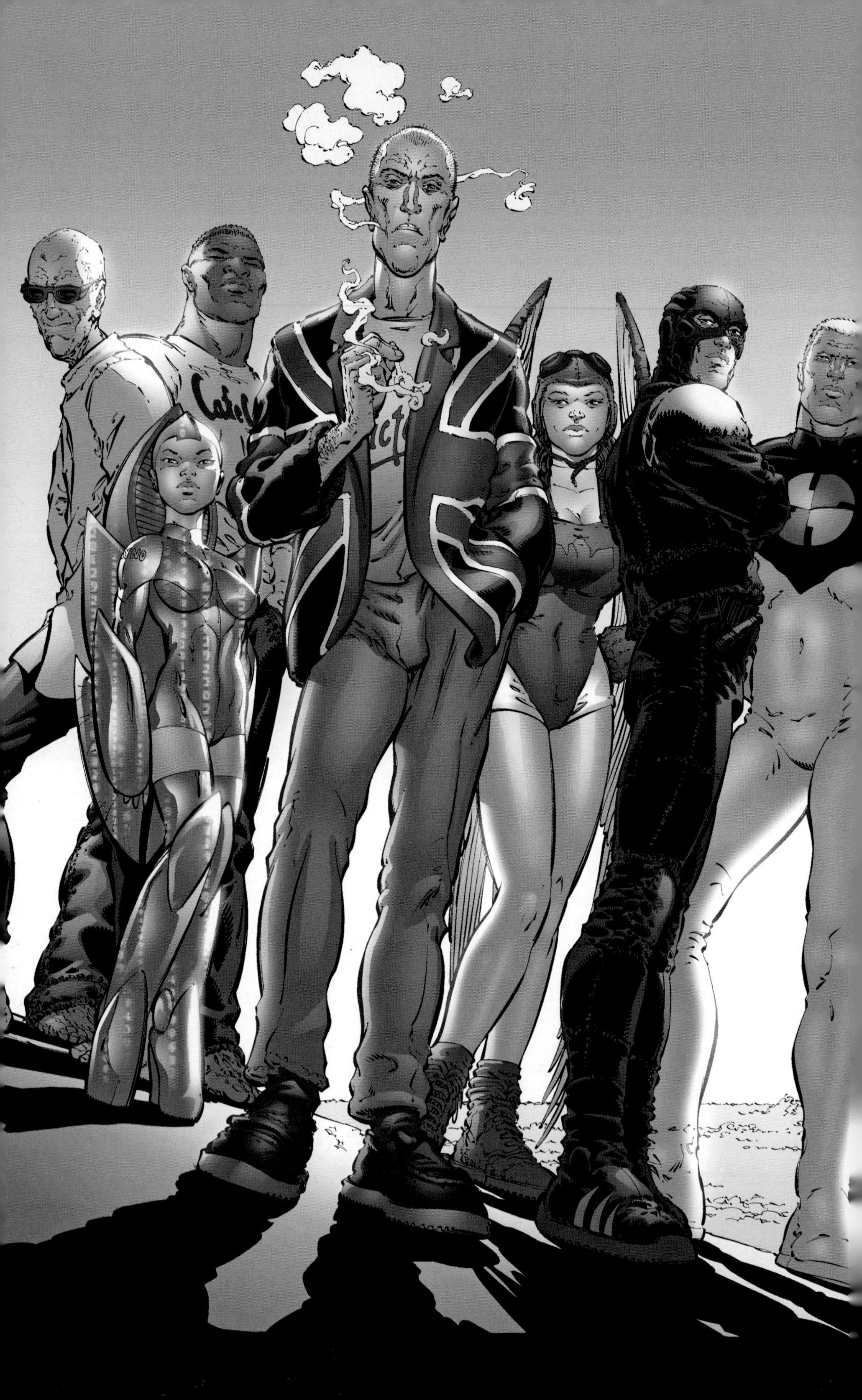

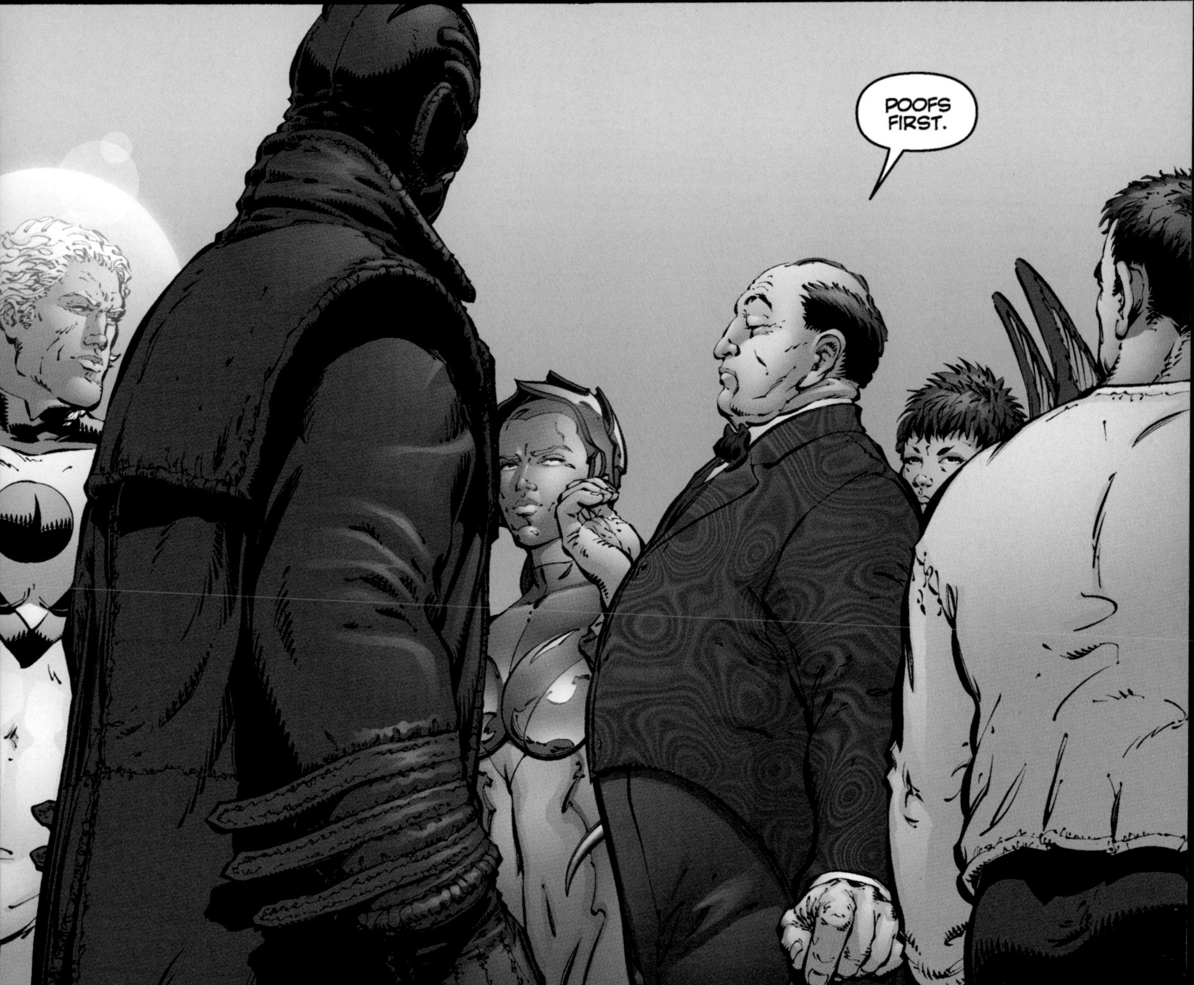
POOFS FIRST.

The AUTHORITY
"Earth Inferno"
FOUR of FOUR

MARK MILLAR writer
FRANK QUITELY artist
TREVOR SCOTT inker
DAVID BARON colorist
BILL O'NEIL letterer

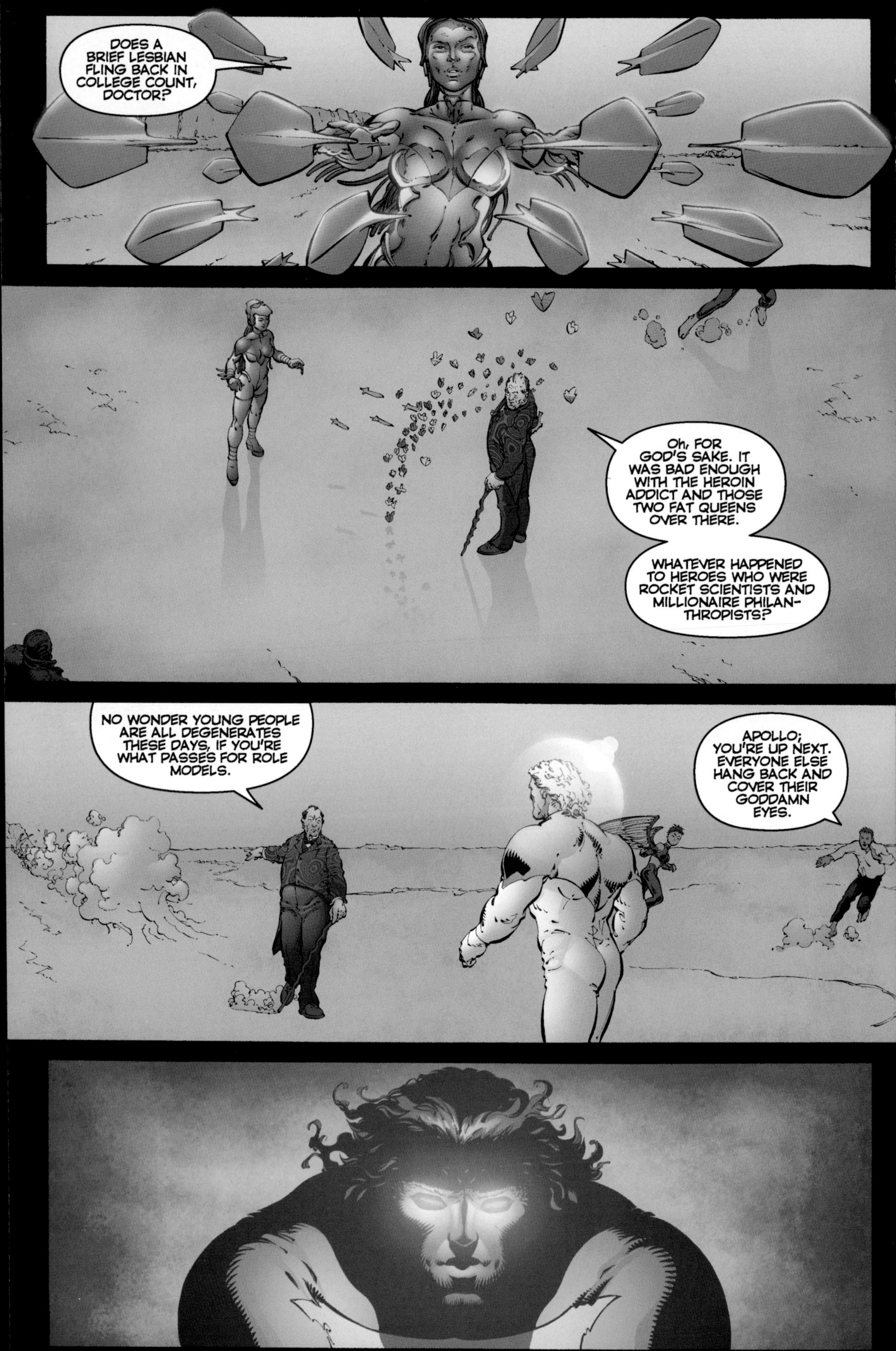
DOES A BRIEF LESBIAN FLING BACK IN COLLEGE COUNT, DOCTOR?
Oh, FOR GOD'S SAKE. IT WAS BAD ENOUGH WITH THE HEROIN ADDICT AND THOSE TWO FAT QUEENS OVER THERE.
WHATEVER HAPPENED TO HEROES WHO WERE ROCKET SCIENTISTS AND MILLIONAIRE PHILAN-THROPISTS?
NO WONDER YOUNG PEOPLE ARE ALL DEGENERATES THESE DAYS, IF YOU'RE WHAT PASSES FOR ROLE MODELS.
APOLLO; YOU'RE UP NEXT. EVERYONE ELSE HANG BACK AND COVER THEIR GODDAMN EYES.

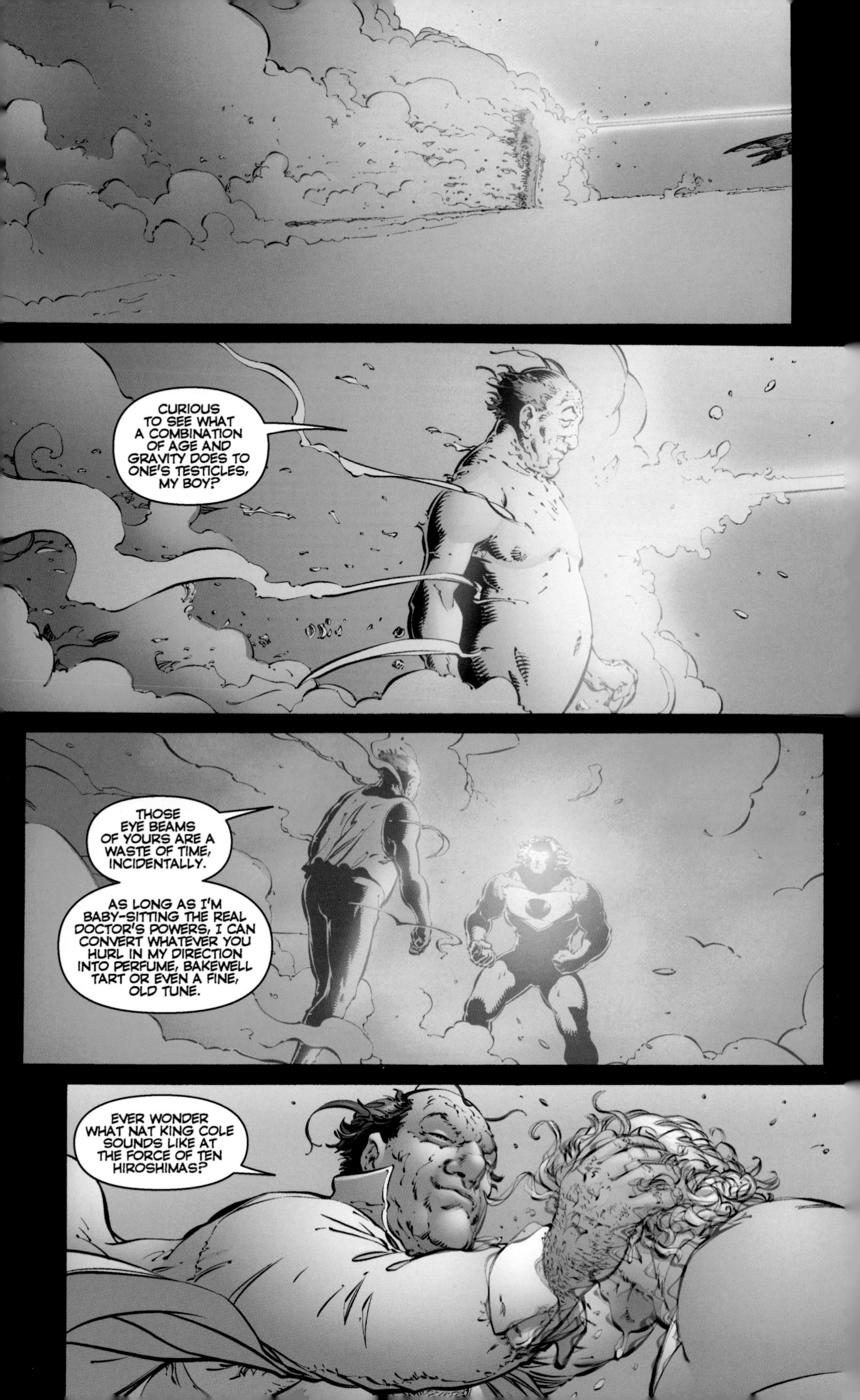
CURIOUS TO SEE WHAT A COMBINATION OF AGE AND GRAVITY DOES TO ONE'S TESTICLES, MY BOY?
THOSE EYE BEAMS OF YOURS ARE A WASTE OF TIME, INCIDENTALLY.
AS LONG AS I'M BABY-SITTING THE REAL DOCTOR'S POWERS, I CAN CONVERT WHATEVER YOU HURL IN MY DIRECTION INTO PERFUME, BAKEWELL TART OR EVEN A FINE, OLD TUNE.
EVER WONDER WHAT NAT KING COLE SOUNDS LIKE AT THE FORCE OF TEN HIROSHIMAS?

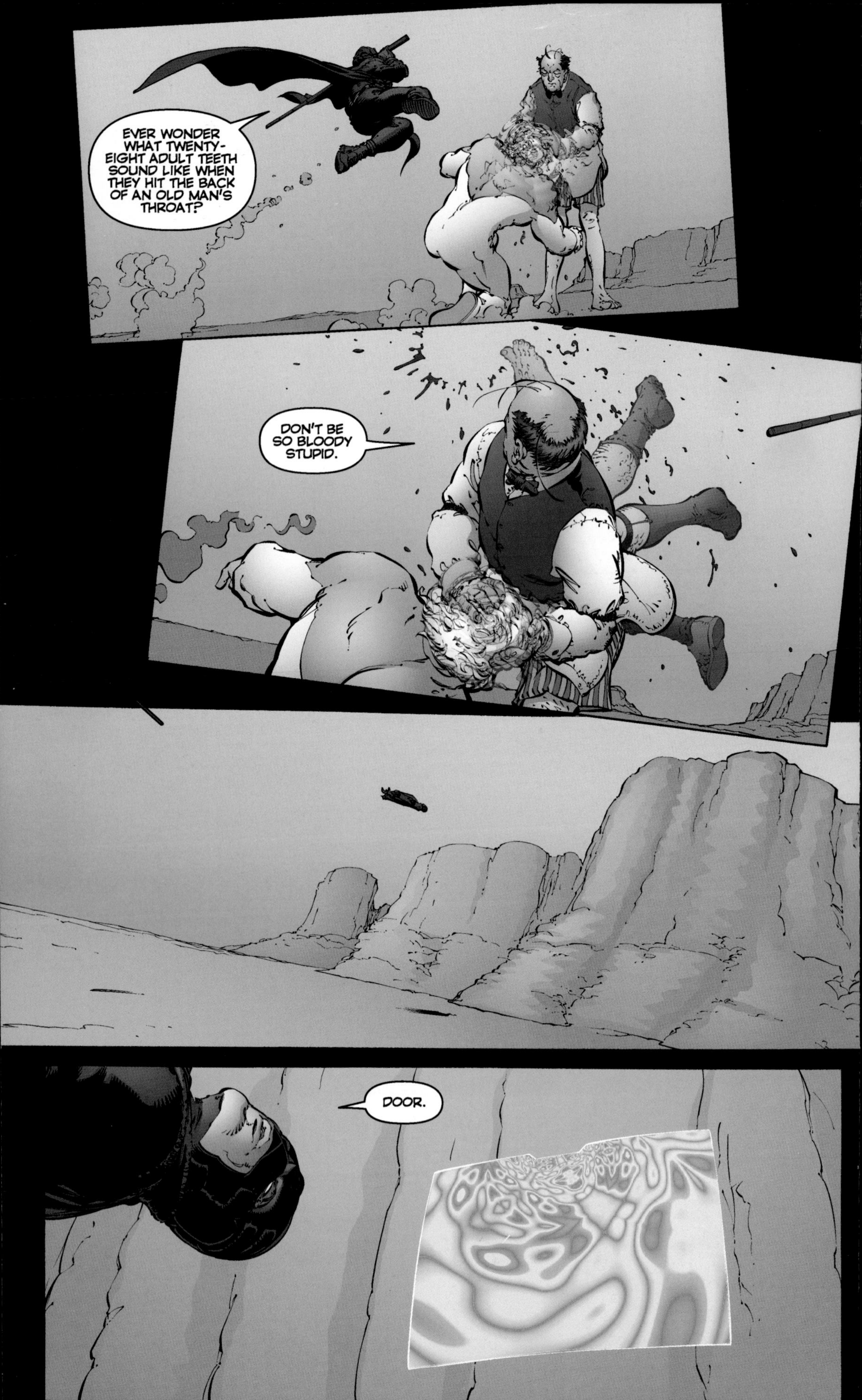
EVER WONDER WHAT TWENTY-EIGHT ADULT TEETH SOUND LIKE WHEN THEY HIT THE BACK OF AN OLD MAN'S THROAT?
DON'T BE SO BLOODY STUPID.
DOOR.

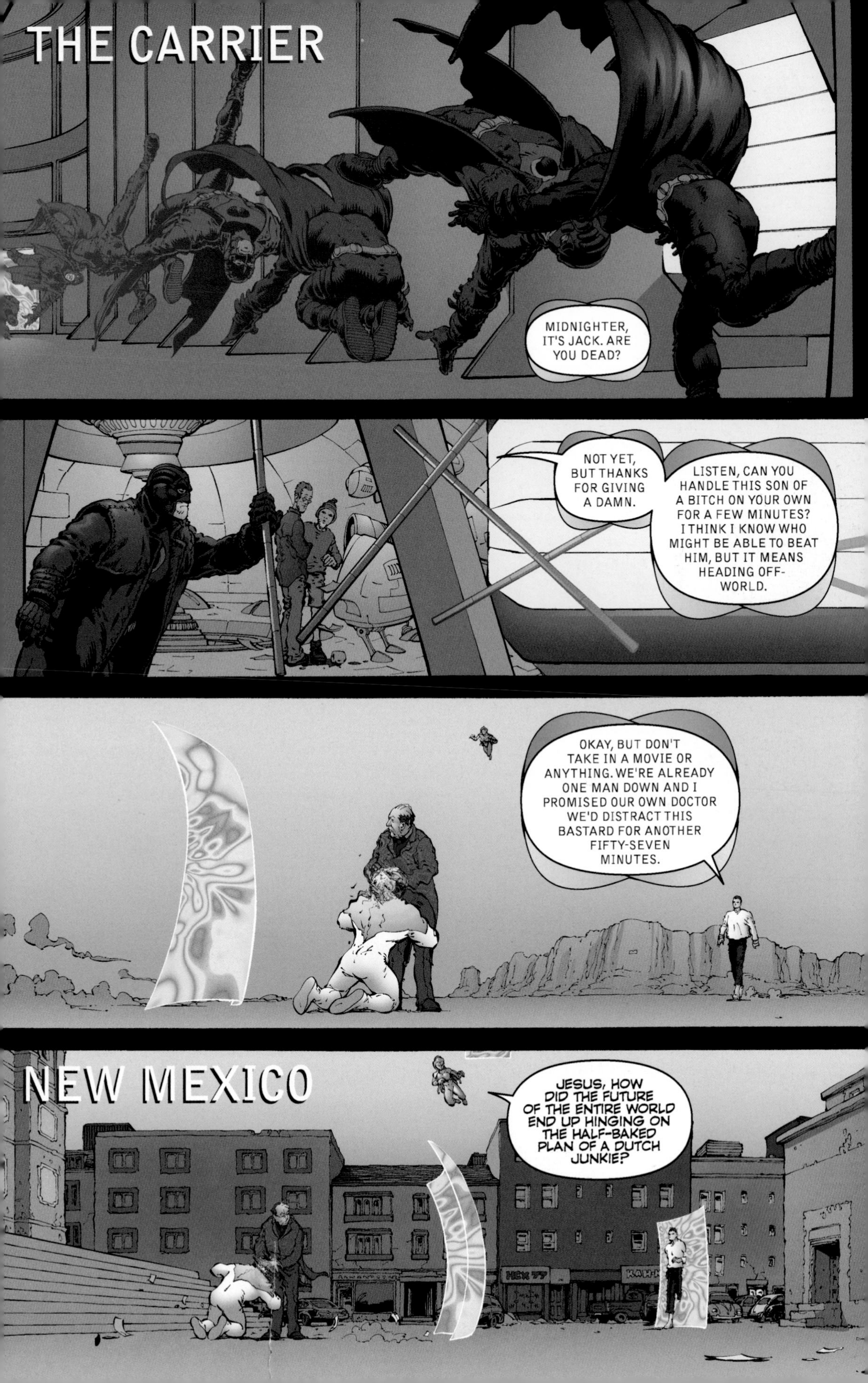
THE CARRIER
MIDNIGHTER, IT'S JACK. ARE YOU DEAD?
NOT YET, BUT THANKS FOR GIVING A DAMN.
LISTEN, CAN YOU HANDLE THIS SON OF A BITCH ON YOUR OWN FOR A FEW MINUTES? I THINK I KNOW WHO MIGHT BE ABLE TO BEAT HIM, BUT IT MEANS HEADING OFF-WORLD.
OKAY, BUT DON'T TAKE IN A MOVIE OR ANYTHING. WE'RE ALREADY ONE MAN DOWN AND I PROMISED OUR OWN DOCTOR WE'D DISTRACT THIS BASTARD FOR ANOTHER FIFTY-SEVEN MINUTES.
NEW MEXICO
JESUS, HOW DID THE FUTURE OF THE ENTIRE WORLD END UP HINGING ON THE HALF-BAKED PLAN OF A DUTCH JUNKIE?

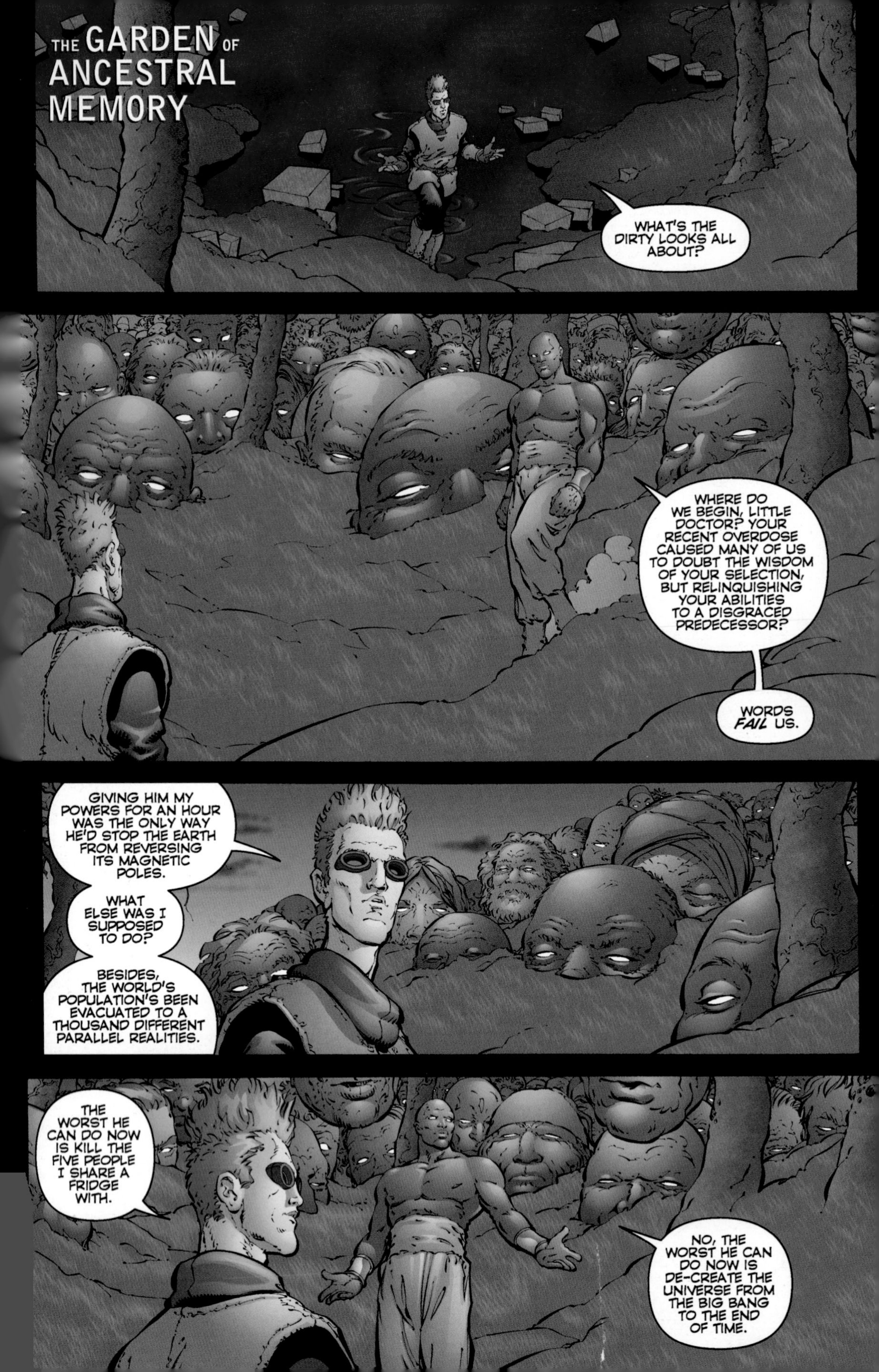
THE GARDEN OF ANCESTRAL MEMORY
WHAT'S THE DIRTY LOOKS ALL ABOUT?
WHERE DO WE BEGIN, LITTLE DOCTOR? YOUR RECENT OVERDOSE CAUSED MANY OF US TO DOUBT THE WISDOM OF YOUR SELECTION, BUT RELINQUISHING YOUR ABILITIES TO A DISGRACED PREDECESSOR?
WORDS FAIL US.
GIVING HIM MY POWERS FOR AN HOUR WAS THE ONLY WAY HE'D STOP THE EARTH FROM REVERSING ITS MAGNETIC POLES.
WHAT ELSE WAS I SUPPOSED TO DO?
BESIDES, THE WORLD'S POPULATION'S BEEN EVACUATED TO A THOUSAND DIFFERENT PARALLEL REALITIES.
THE WORST HE CAN DO NOW IS KILL THE FIVE PEOPLE I SHARE A FRIDGE WITH.
NO, THE WORST HE CAN DO NOW IS DE-CREATE THE UNIVERSE FROM THE BIG BANG TO THE END OF TIME.

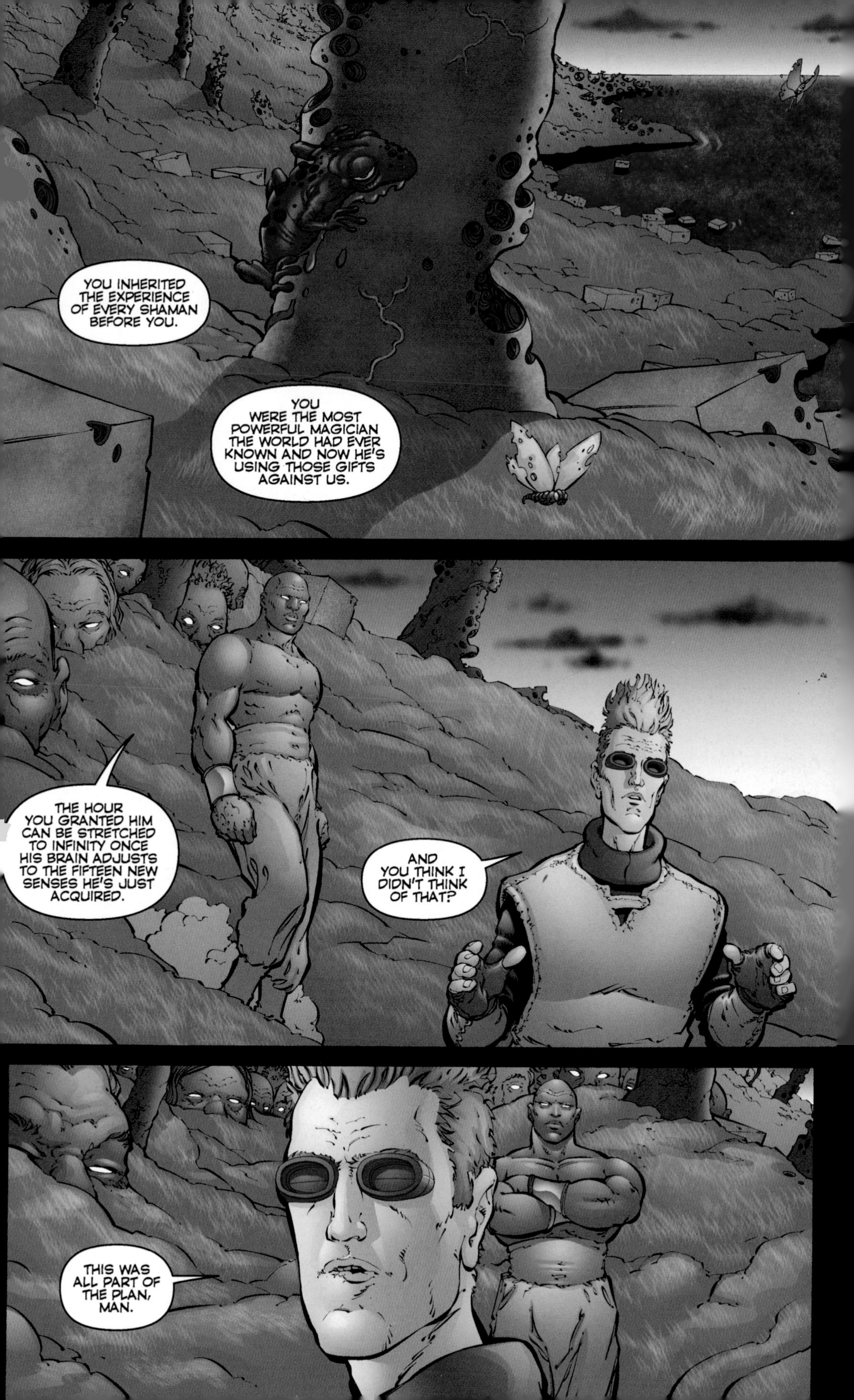
YOU INHERITED THE EXPERIENCE OF EVERY SHAMAN BEFORE YOU.
YOU WERE THE MOST POWERFUL MAGICIAN THE WORLD HAD EVER KNOWN AND NOW HE'S USING THOSE GIFTS AGAINST US.
THE HOUR YOU GRANTED HIM CAN BE STRETCHED TO INFINITY ONCE HIS BRAIN ADJUSTS TO THE FIFTEEN NEW SENSES HE'S JUST ACQUIRED.
AND YOU THINK I DIDN'T THINK OF THAT?
THIS WAS ALL PART OF THE PLAN, MAN.

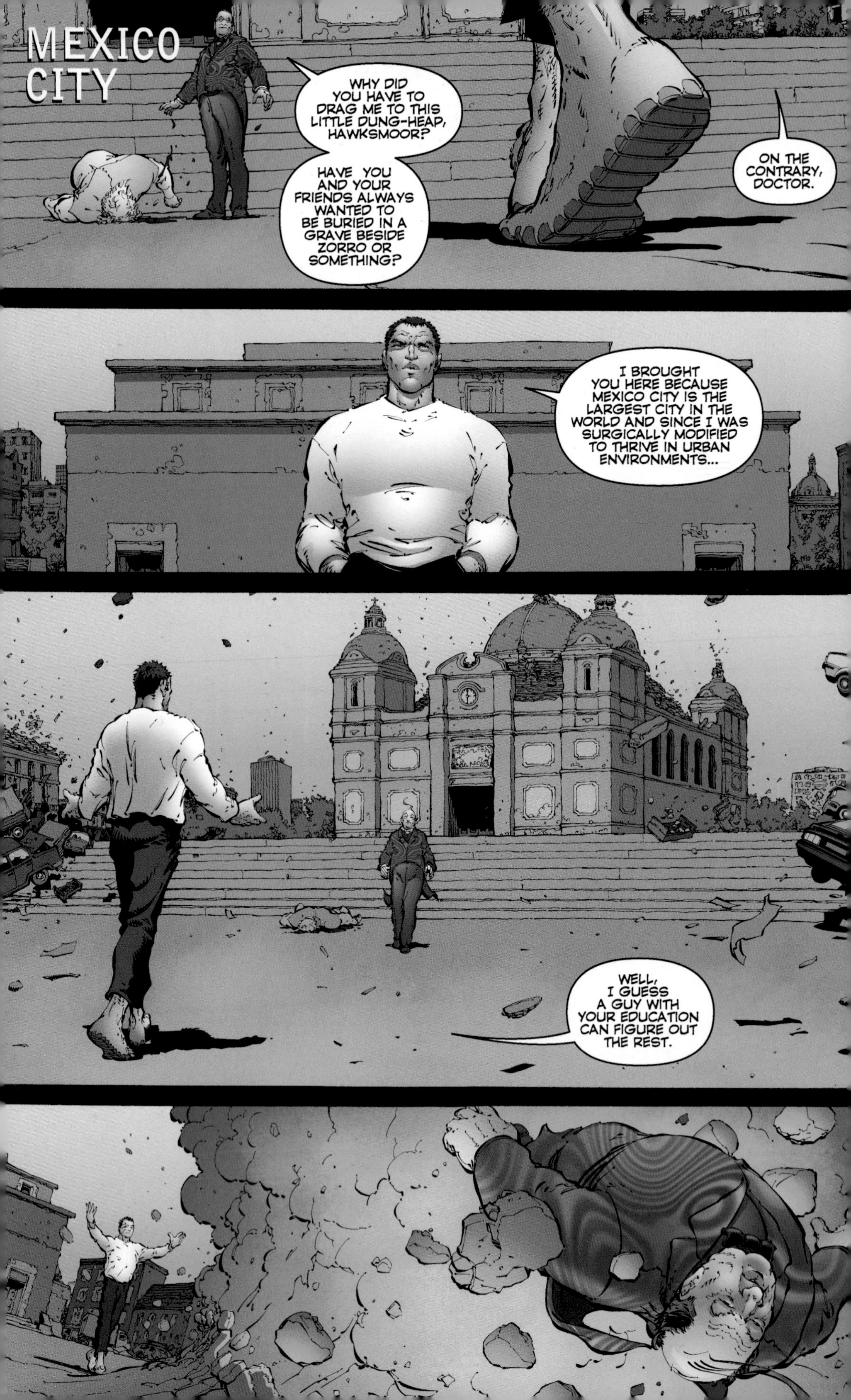
MEXICO CITY
WHY DID YOU HAVE TO DRAG ME TO THIS LITTLE DUNG-HEAP, HAWKSMOOR?
HAVE YOU AND YOUR FRIENDS ALWAYS WANTED TO BE BURIED IN A GRAVE BESIDE ZORRO OR SOMETHING?
ON THE CONTRARY, DOCTOR.
I BROUGHT YOU HERE BECAUSE MEXICO CITY IS THE LARGEST CITY IN THE WORLD AND SINCE I WAS SURGICALLY MODIFIED TO THRIVE IN URBAN ENVIRONMENTS...
WELL, I GUESS A GUY WITH YOUR EDUCATION CAN FIGURE OUT THE REST.

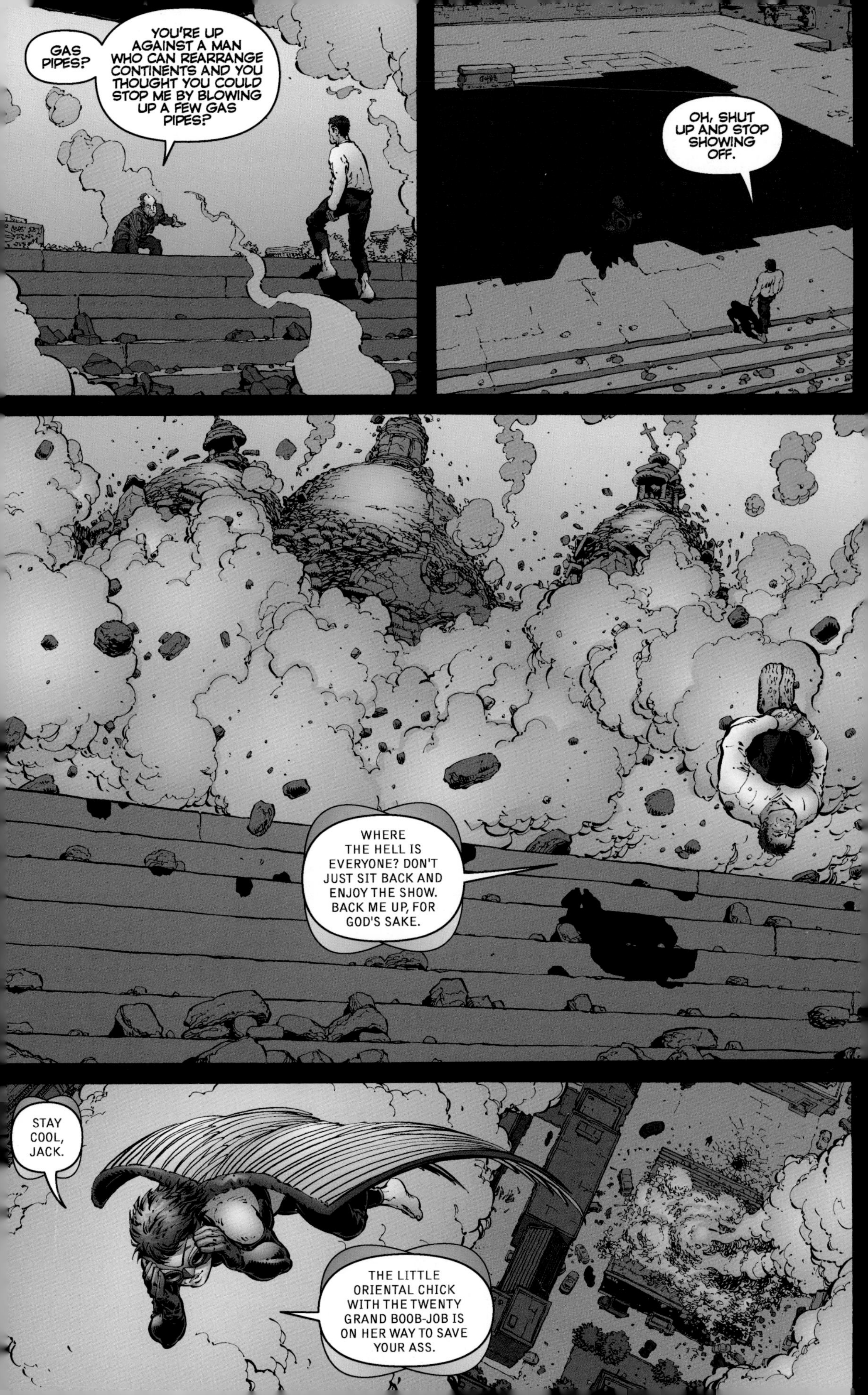
GAS PIPES?
YOU'RE UP AGAINST A MAN WHO CAN REARRANGE CONTINENTS AND YOU THOUGHT YOU COULD STOP ME BY BLOWING UP A FEW GAS PIPES?
OH, SHUT UP AND STOP SHOWING OFF.
WHERE THE HELL IS EVERYONE? DON'T JUST SIT BACK AND ENJOY THE SHOW. BACK ME UP, FOR GOD'S SAKE.
STAY COOL, JACK.
THE LITTLE ORIENTAL CHICK WITH THE TWENTY GRAND BOOB-JOB IS ON HER WAY TO SAVE YOUR ASS.

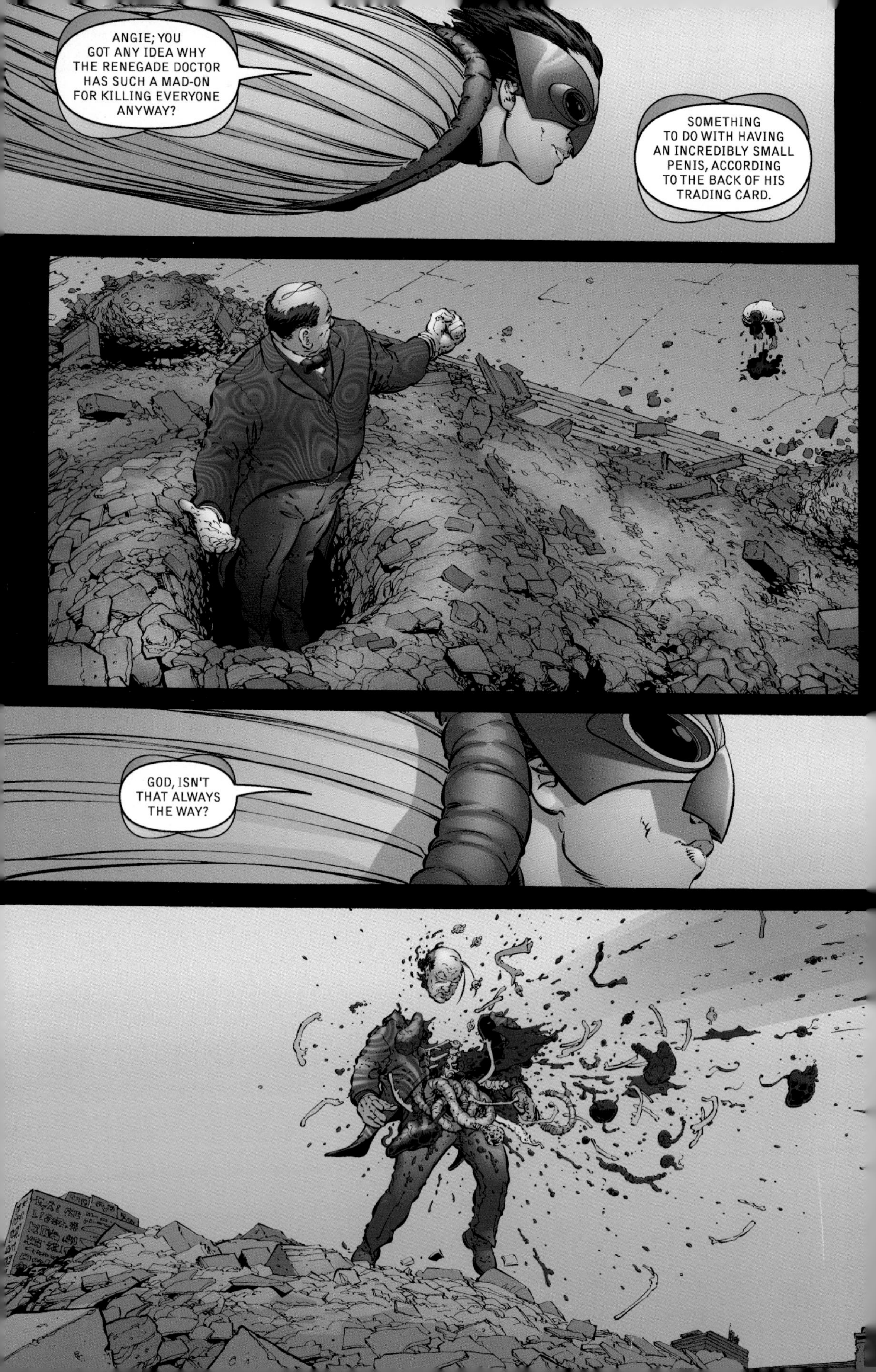
ANGIE; YOU GOT ANY IDEA WHY THE RENEGADE DOCTOR HAS SUCH A MAD-ON FOR KILLING EVERYONE ANYWAY?
SOMETHING TO DO WITH HAVING AN INCREDIBLY SMALL PENIS, ACCORDING TO THE BACK OF HIS TRADING CARD.
GOD, ISN'T THAT ALWAYS THE WAY?

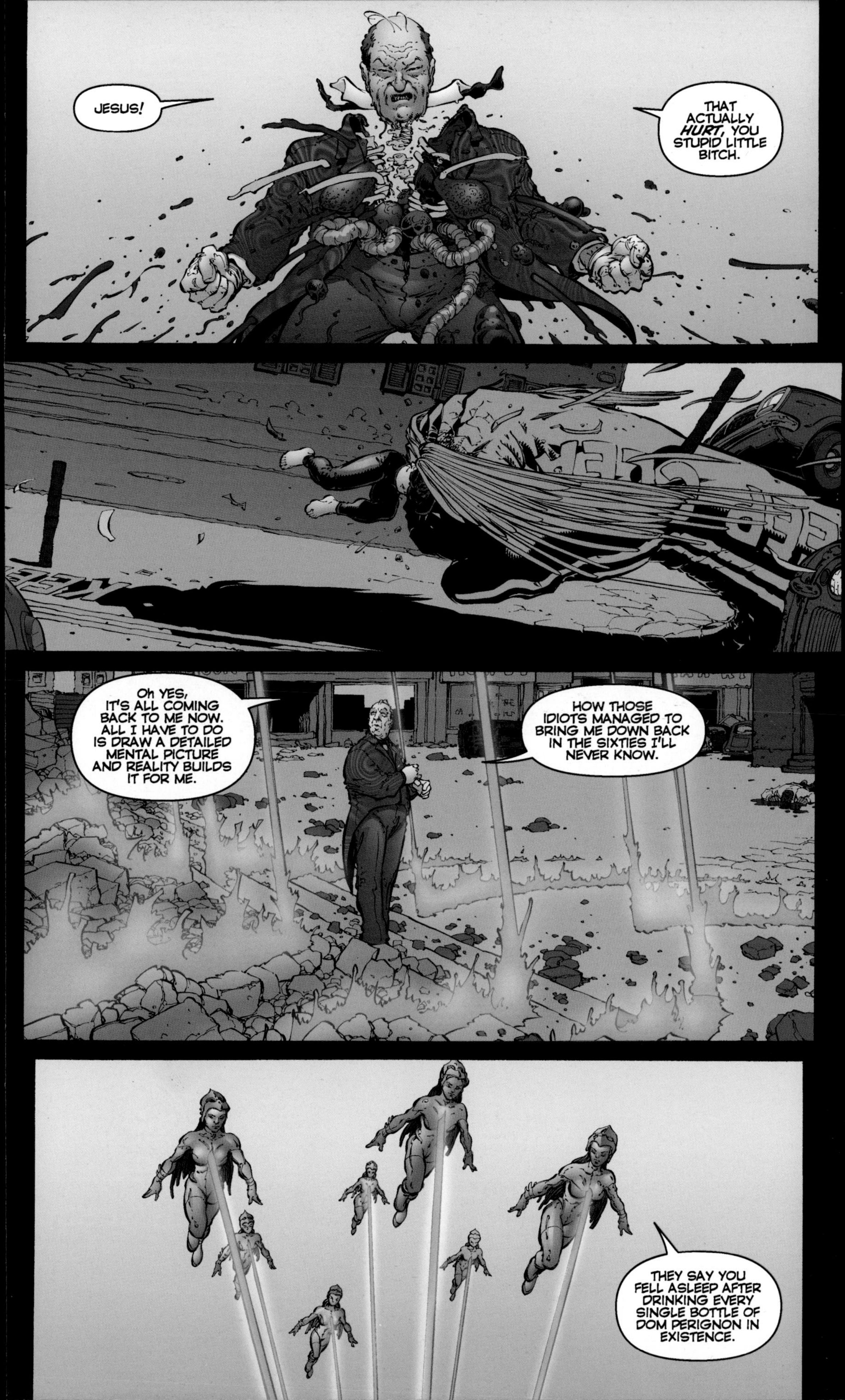
JESUS!
THAT ACTUALLY HURT, YOU STUPID LITTLE BITCH.
Oh YES, IT'S ALL COMING BACK TO ME NOW. ALL I HAVE TO DO IS DRAW A DETAILED MENTAL PICTURE AND REALITY BUILDS IT FOR ME.
HOW THOSE IDIOTS MANAGED TO BRING ME DOWN BACK IN THE SIXTIES I'LL NEVER KNOW.
THEY SAY YOU FELL ASLEEP AFTER DRINKING EVERY SINGLE BOTTLE OF DOM PERIGNON IN EXISTENCE.

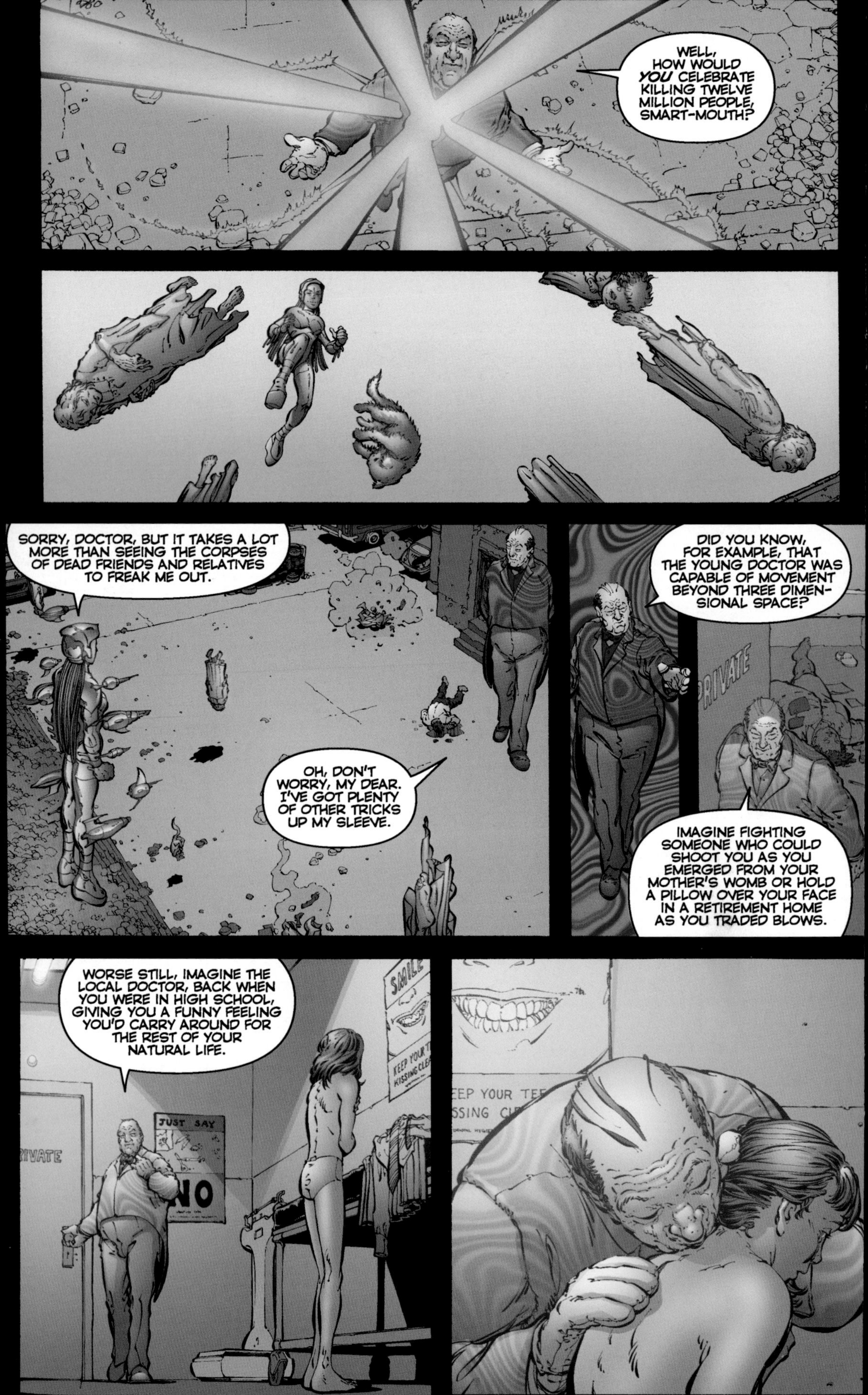
WELL, HOW WOULD YOU CELEBRATE KILLING TWELVE MILLION PEOPLE, SMART-MOUTH?
SORRY, DOCTOR, BUT IT TAKES A LOT MORE THAN SEEING THE CORPSES OF DEAD FRIENDS AND RELATIVES TO FREAK ME OUT.
OH, DON'T WORRY, MY DEAR. I'VE GOT PLENTY OF OTHER TRICKS UP MY SLEEVE.
DID YOU KNOW, FOR EXAMPLE, THAT THE YOUNG DOCTOR WAS CAPABLE OF MOVEMENT BEYOND THREE DIMENSIONAL SPACE?
PRIVATE
IMAGINE FIGHTING SOMEONE WHO COULD SHOOT YOU AS YOU EMERGED FROM YOUR MOTHER'S WOMB OR HOLD A PILLOW OVER YOUR FACE IN A RETIREMENT HOME AS YOU TRADED BLOWS.
WORSE STILL, IMAGINE THE LOCAL DOCTOR, BACK WHEN YOU WERE IN HIGH SCHOOL, GIVING YOU A FUNNY FEELING YOU'D CARRY AROUND FOR THE REST OF YOUR NATURAL LIFE.
SMILE
JUST SAY
NO

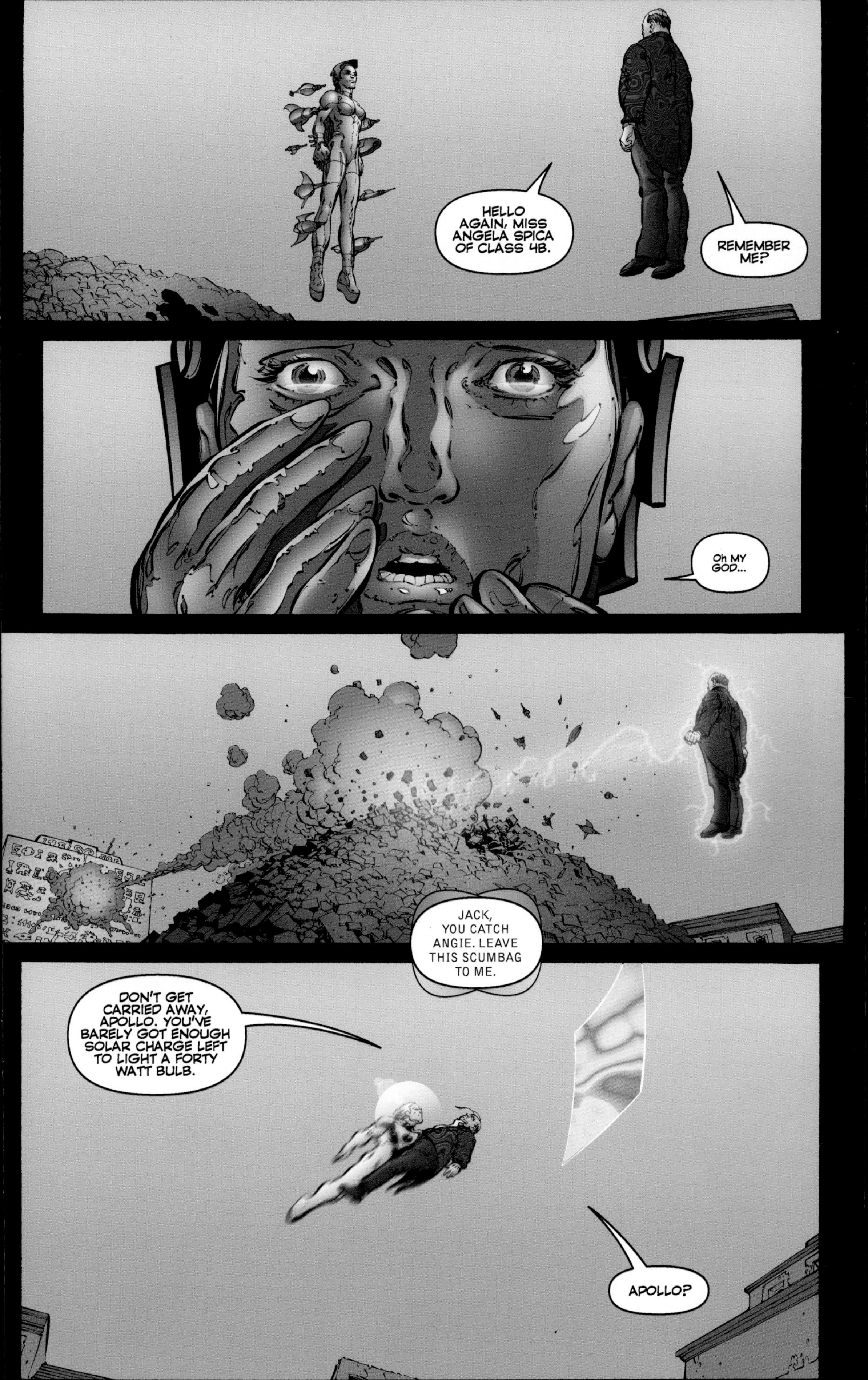
HELLO AGAIN, MISS ANGELA SPICA OF CLASS 4B.
REMEMBER ME?
Oh MY GOD...
JACK, YOU CATCH ANGIE. LEAVE THIS SCUMBAG TO ME.
DON'T GET CARRIED AWAY, APOLLO. YOU'VE BARELY GOT ENOUGH SOLAR CHARGE LEFT TO LIGHT A FORTY WATT BULB.
APOLLO?

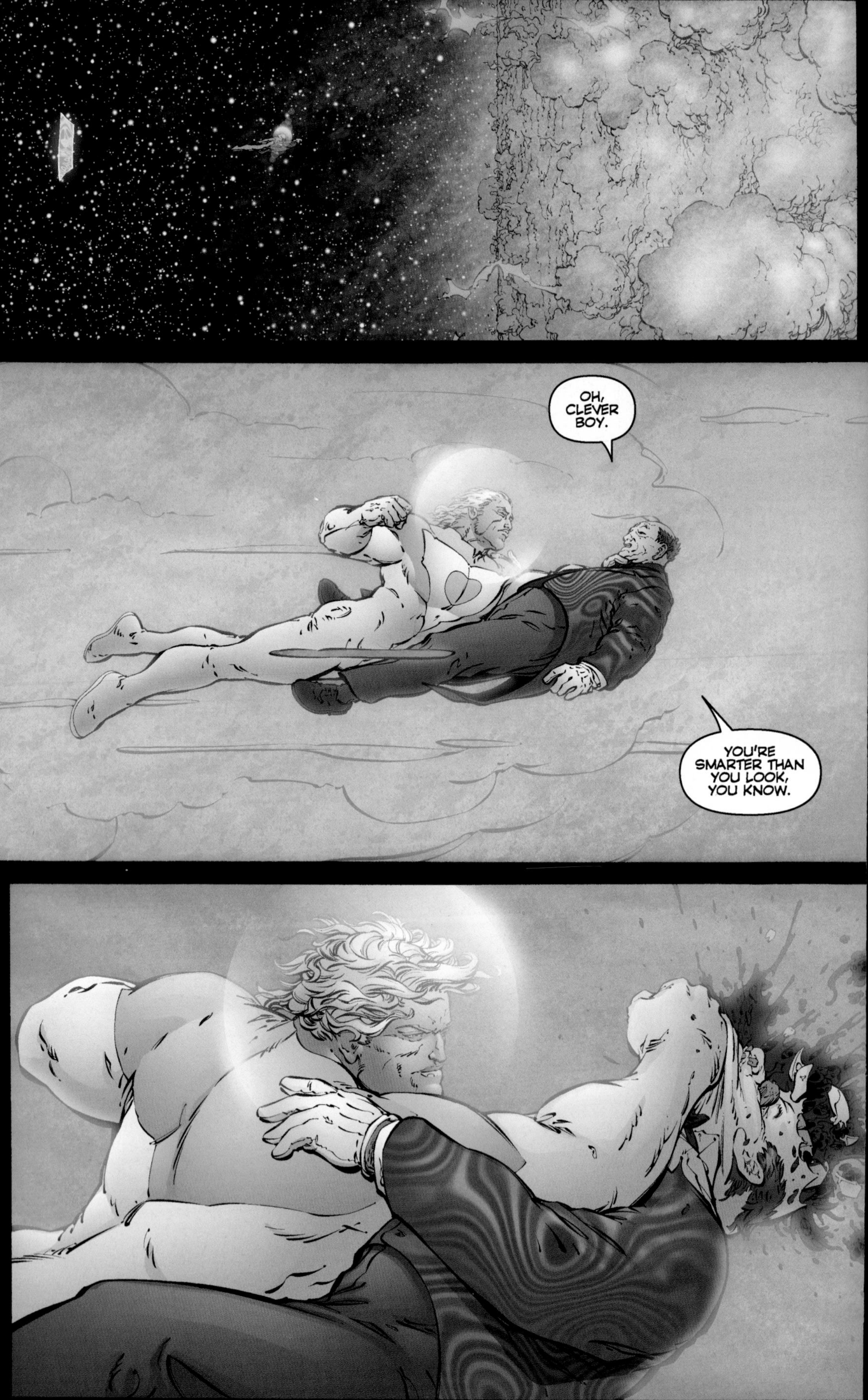
OH, CLEVER BOY.
YOU'RE SMARTER THAN YOU LOOK, YOU KNOW.

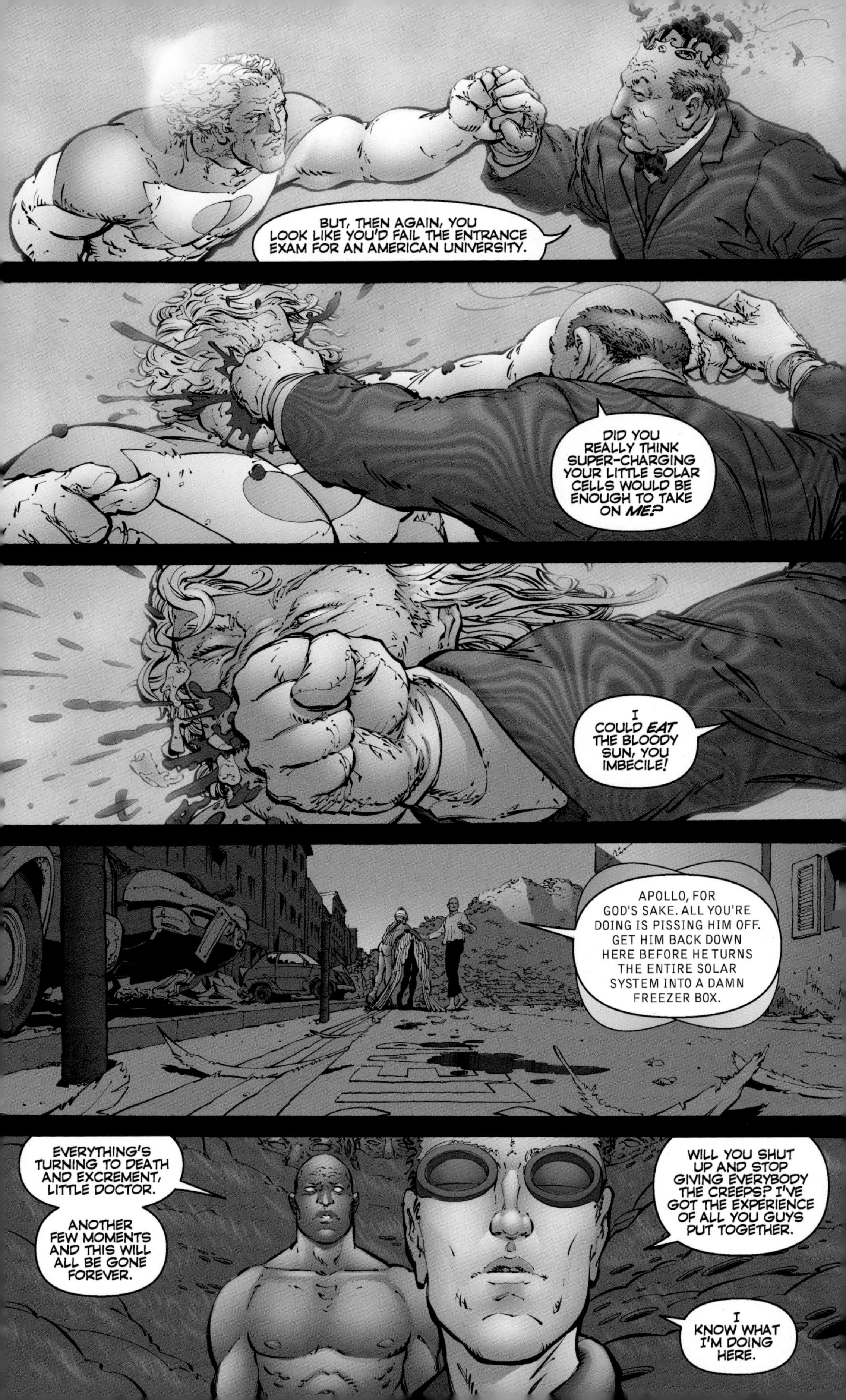
BUT, THEN AGAIN, YOU LOOK LIKE YOU'D FAIL THE ENTRANCE EXAM FOR AN AMERICAN UNIVERSITY.
DID YOU REALLY THINK SUPER-CHARGING YOUR LITTLE SOLAR CELLS WOULD BE ENOUGH TO TAKE ON ME?
I COULD EAT THE BLOODY SUN, YOU IMBECILE!
APOLLO, FOR GOD'S SAKE. ALL YOU'RE DOING IS PISSING HIM OFF. GET HIM BACK DOWN HERE BEFORE HE TURNS THE ENTIRE SOLAR SYSTEM INTO A DAMN FREEZER BOX.
EVERYTHING'S TURNING TO DEATH AND EXCREMENT, LITTLE DOCTOR.
ANOTHER FEW MOMENTS AND THIS WILL ALL BE GONE FOREVER.
WILL YOU SHUT UP AND STOP GIVING EVERYBODY THE CREEPS? I'VE GOT THE EXPERIENCE OF ALL YOU GUYS PUT TOGETHER.
I KNOW WHAT I'M DOING HERE.

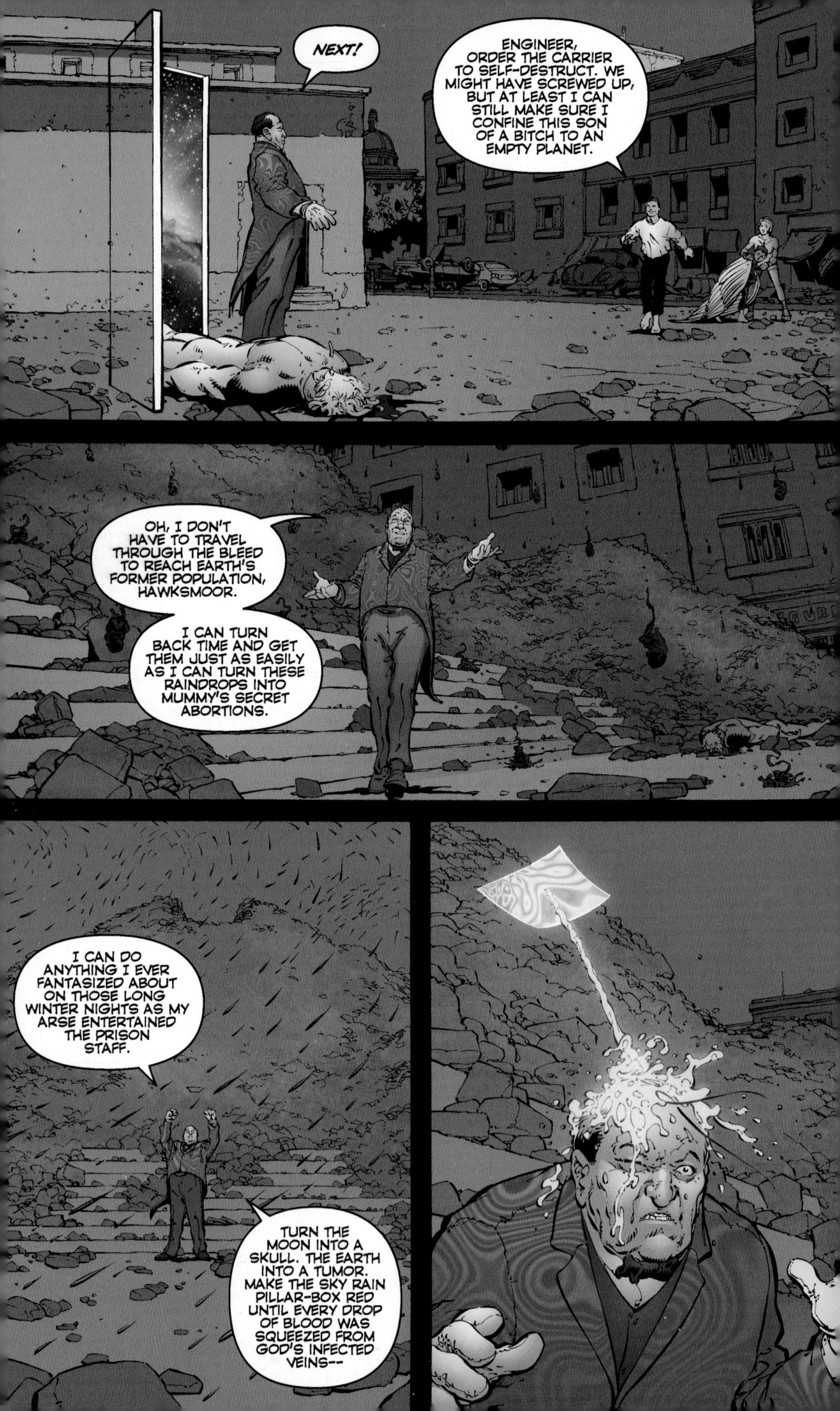
NEXT!
ENGINEER, ORDER THE CARRIER TO SELF-DESTRUCT. WE MIGHT HAVE SCREWED UP, BUT AT LEAST I CAN STILL MAKE SURE I CONFINE THIS SON OF A BITCH TO AN EMPTY PLANET.
OH, I DON'T HAVE TO TRAVEL THROUGH THE BLEED TO REACH EARTH'S FORMER POPULATION, HAWKSMOOR.
I CAN TURN BACK TIME AND GET THEM JUST AS EASILY AS I CAN TURN THESE RAINDROPS INTO MUMMY'S SECRET ABORTIONS.
I CAN DO ANYTHING I EVER FANTASIZED ABOUT ON THOSE LONG WINTER NIGHTS AS MY ARSE ENTERTAINED THE PRISON STAFF.
TURN THE MOON INTO A SKULL. THE EARTH INTO A TUMOR. MAKE THE SKY RAIN PILLAR-BOX RED UNTIL EVERY DROP OF BLOOD WAS SQUEEZED FROM GOD'S INFECTED VEINS--

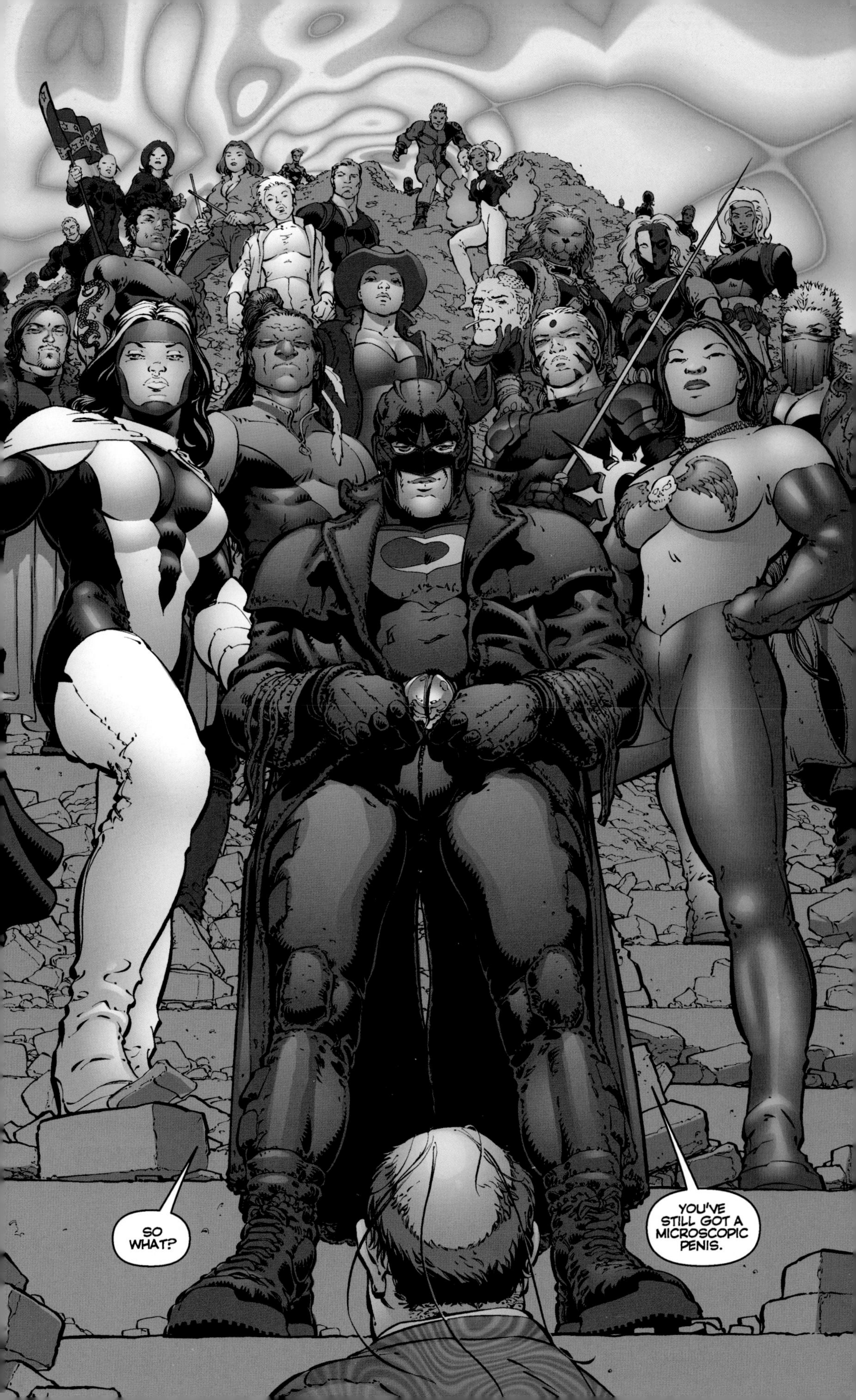
SO WHAT?
YOU'VE STILL GOT A MICROSCOPIC PENIS.

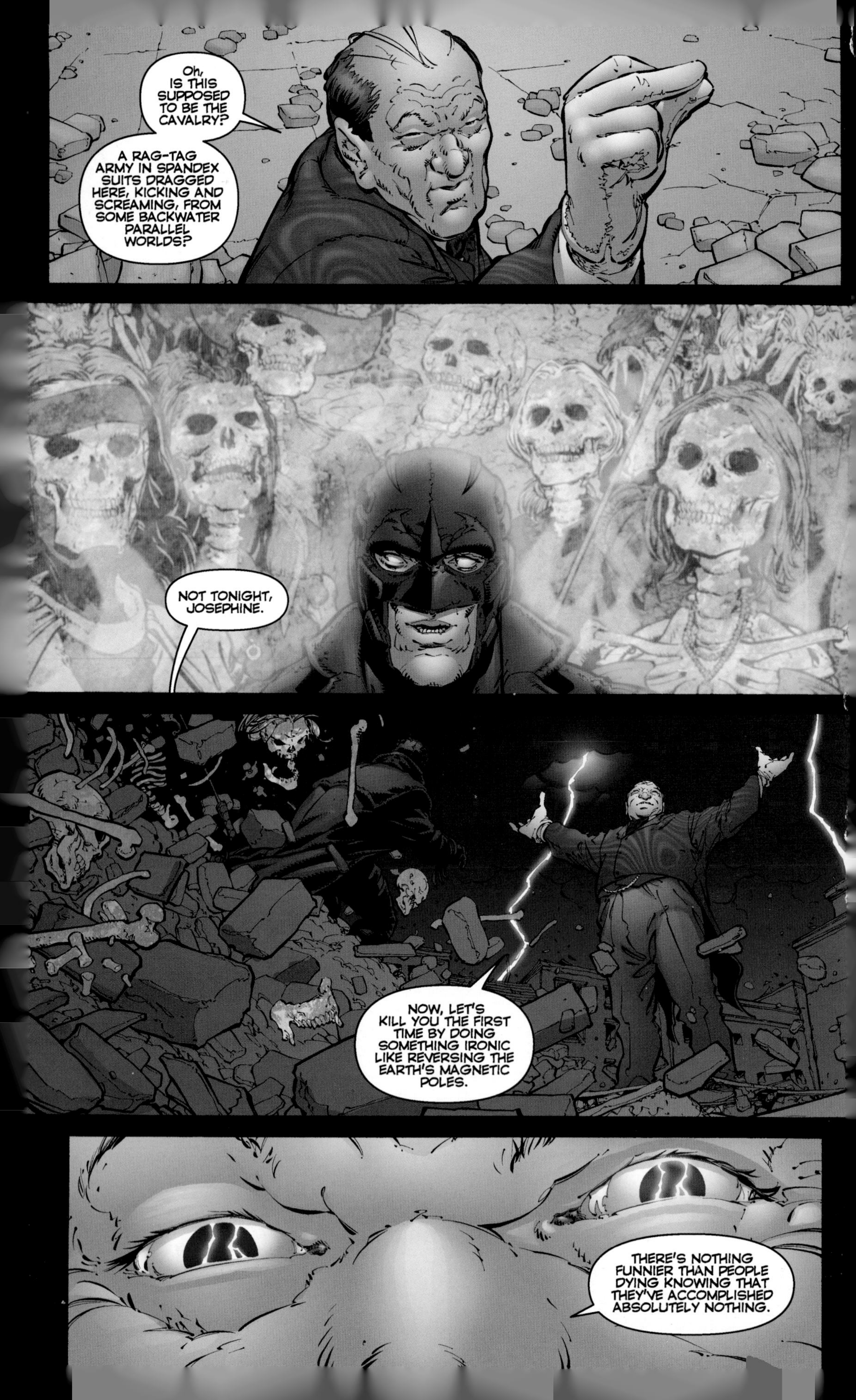
Oh, IS THIS SUPPOSED TO BE THE CAVALRY?
A RAG-TAG ARMY IN SPANDEX SUITS DRAGGED HERE, KICKING AND SCREAMING, FROM SOME BACKWATER PARALLEL WORLDS?
NOT TONIGHT, JOSEPHINE.
NOW, LET'S KILL YOU THE FIRST TIME BY DOING SOMETHING IRONIC LIKE REVERSING THE EARTH'S MAGNETIC POLES.
THERE'S NOTHING FUNNIER THAN PEOPLE DYING KNOWING THAT THEY'VE ACCOMPLISHED ABSOLUTELY NOTHING.

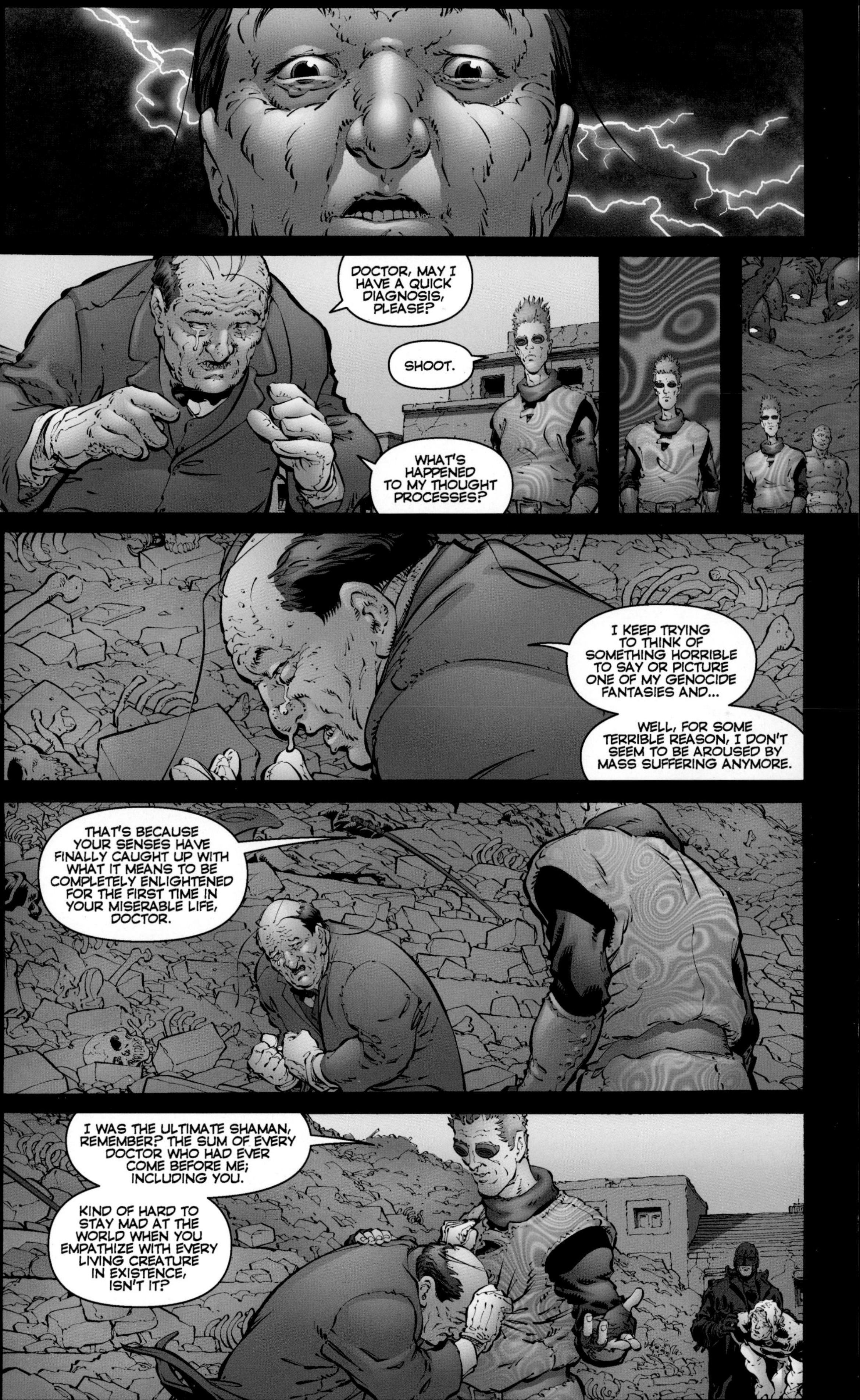
DOCTOR, MAY I HAVE A QUICK DIAGNOSIS, PLEASE?
SHOOT.
WHAT'S HAPPENED TO MY THOUGHT PROCESSES?
I KEEP TRYING TO THINK OF SOMETHING HORRIBLE TO SAY OR PICTURE ONE OF MY GENOCIDE FANTASIES AND...
WELL, FOR SOME TERRIBLE REASON, I DON'T SEEM TO BE AROUSED BY MASS SUFFERING ANYMORE.
THAT'S BECAUSE YOUR SENSES HAVE FINALLY CAUGHT UP WITH WHAT IT MEANS TO BE COMPLETELY ENLIGHTENED FOR THE FIRST TIME IN YOUR MISERABLE LIFE, DOCTOR.
I WAS THE ULTIMATE SHAMAN, REMEMBER? THE SUM OF EVERY DOCTOR WHO HAD EVER COME BEFORE ME; INCLUDING YOU.
KIND OF HARD TO STAY MAD AT THE WORLD WHEN YOU EMPATHIZE WITH EVERY LIVING CREATURE IN EXISTENCE, ISN'T IT?

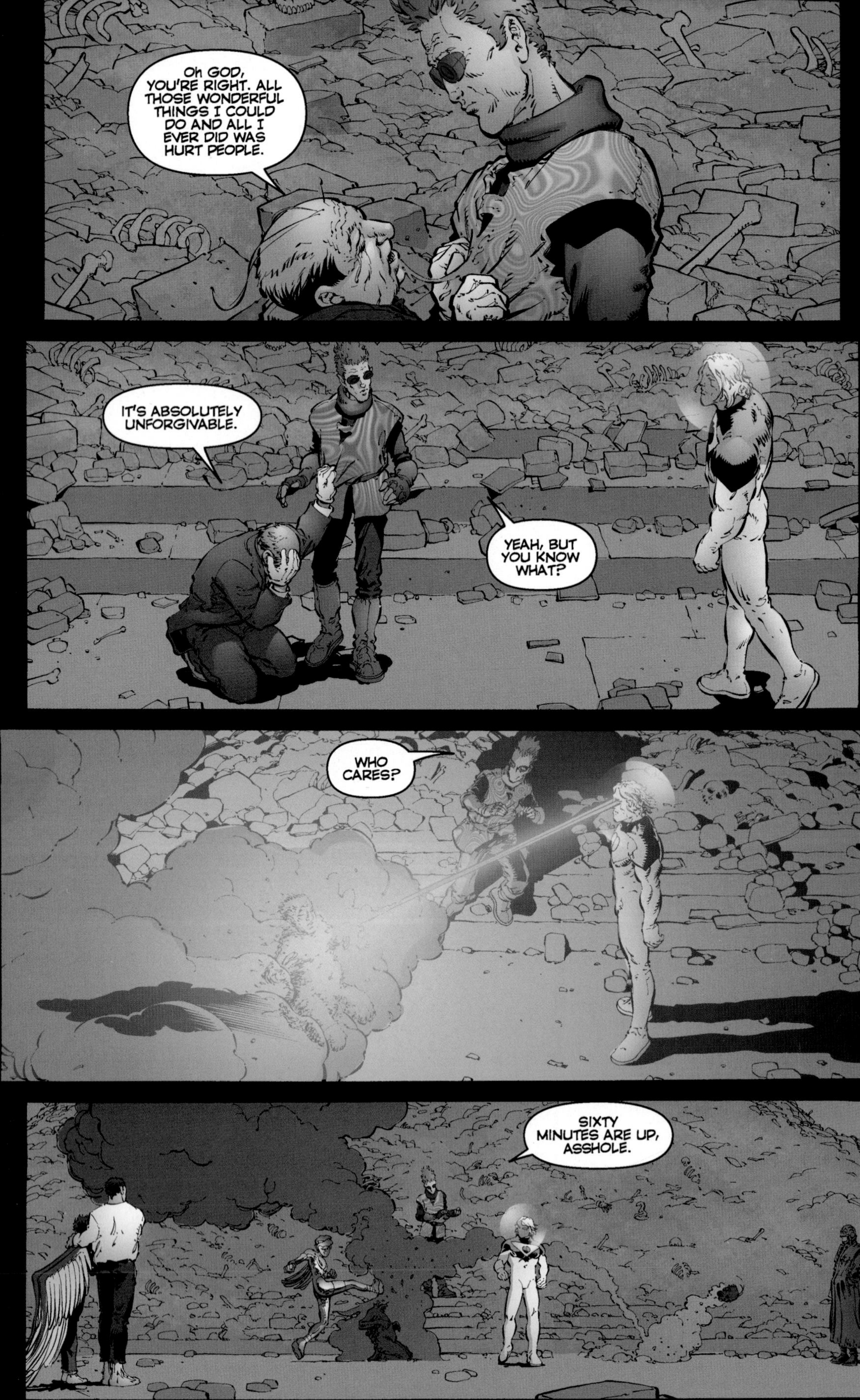
Oh GOD, YOU'RE RIGHT. ALL THOSE WONDERFUL THINGS I COULD DO AND ALL I EVER DID WAS HURT PEOPLE.
IT'S ABSOLUTELY UNFORGIVABLE.
YEAH, BUT YOU KNOW WHAT?
WHO CARES?
SIXTY MINUTES ARE UP, ASSHOLE.

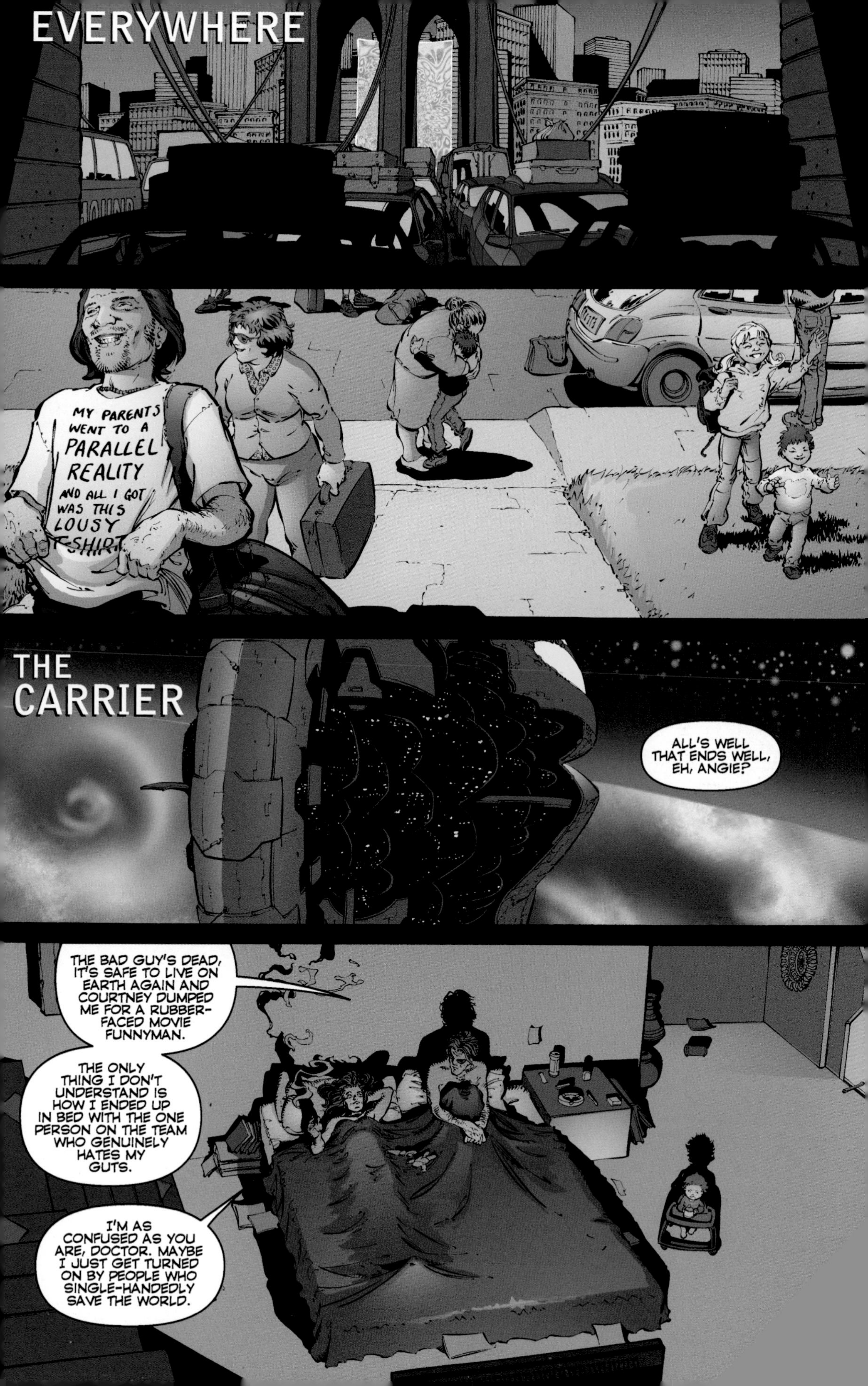
EVERYWHERE
MY PARENTS WENT TO A PARALLEL REALITY AND ALL I GOT WAS THIS LOUSY T-SHIRT
THE CARRIER
ALL'S WELL THAT ENDS WELL, EH, ANGIE?
THE BAD GUY'S DEAD, IT'S SAFE TO LIVE ON EARTH AGAIN AND COURTNEY DUMPED ME FOR A RUBBER-FACED MOVIE FUNNYMAN.
THE ONLY THING I DON'T UNDERSTAND IS HOW I ENDED UP IN BED WITH THE ONE PERSON ON THE TEAM WHO GENUINELY HATES MY GUTS.
I'M AS CONFUSED AS YOU ARE, DOCTOR. MAYBE I JUST GET TURNED ON BY PEOPLE WHO SINGLE-HANDEDLY SAVE THE WORLD.

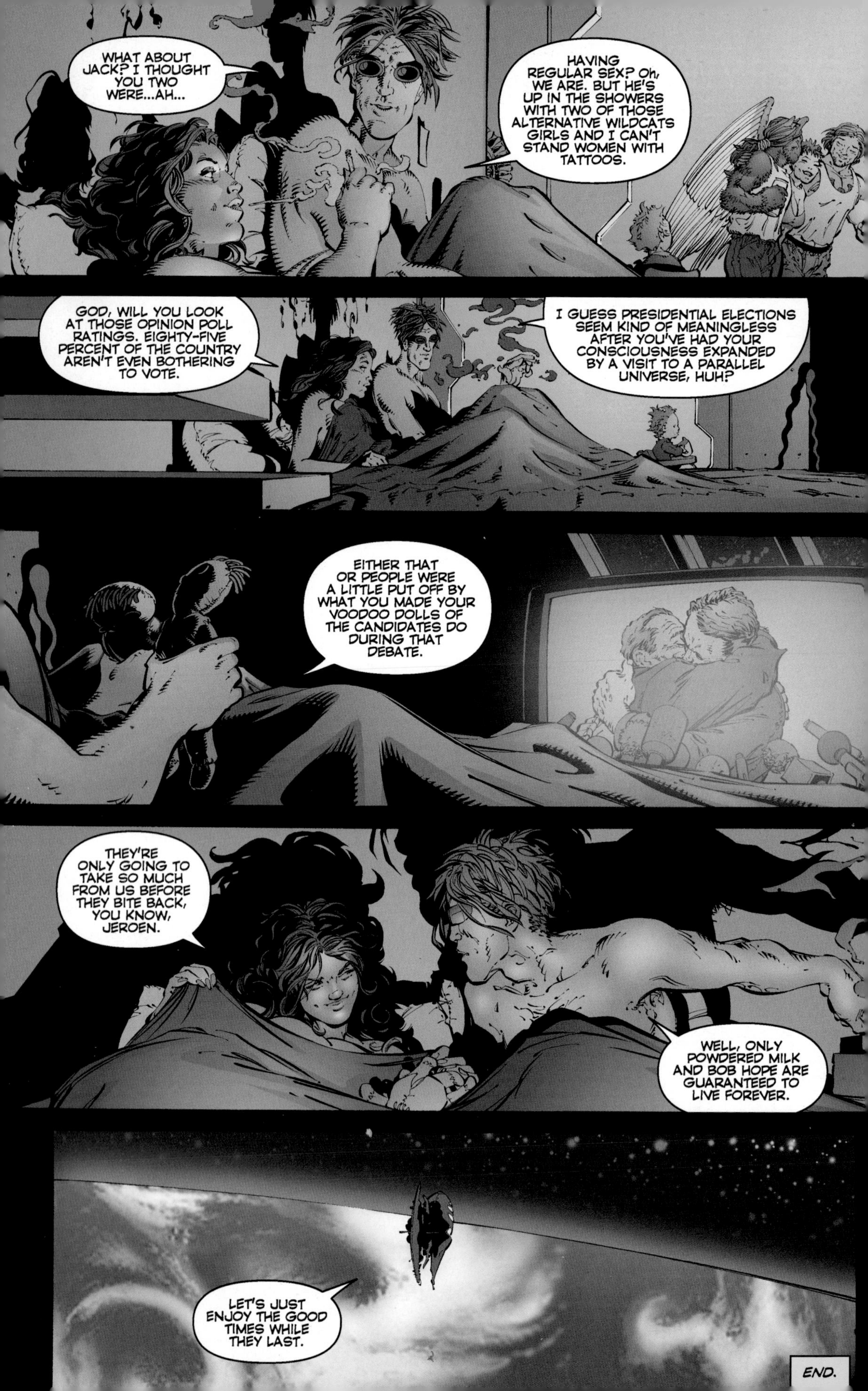
WHAT ABOUT JACK? I THOUGHT YOU TWO WERE...AH...
HAVING REGULAR SEX? Oh, WE ARE. BUT HE'S UP IN THE SHOWERS WITH TWO OF THOSE ALTERNATIVE WILDCATS GIRLS AND I CAN'T STAND WOMEN WITH TATTOOS.
GOD, WILL YOU LOOK AT THOSE OPINION POLL RATINGS. EIGHTY-FIVE PERCENT OF THE COUNTRY AREN'T EVEN BOTHERING TO VOTE.
I GUESS PRESIDENTIAL ELECTIONS SEEM KIND OF MEANINGLESS AFTER YOU'VE HAD YOUR CONSCIOUSNESS EXPANDED BY A VISIT TO A PARALLEL UNIVERSE, HUH?
EITHER THAT OR PEOPLE WERE A LITTLE PUT OFF BY WHAT YOU MADE YOUR VOODOO DOLLS OF THE CANDIDATES DO DURING THAT DEBATE.
THEY'RE ONLY GOING TO TAKE SO MUCH FROM US BEFORE THEY BITE BACK, YOU KNOW, JEROEN.
WELL, ONLY POWDERED MILK AND BOB HOPE ARE GUARANTEED TO LIVE FOREVER.
LET'S JUST ENJOY THE GOOD TIMES WHILE THEY LAST.
END.

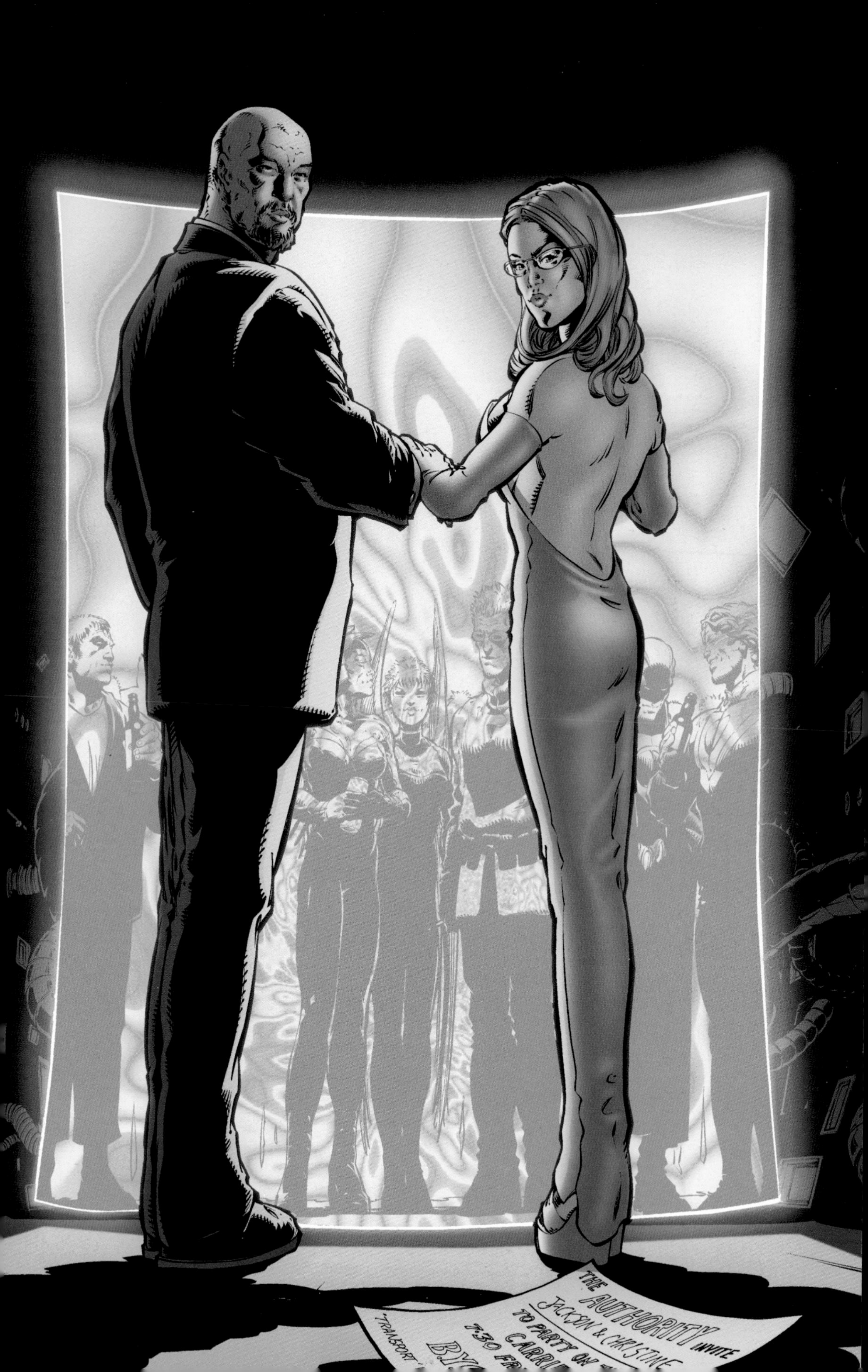
THE AUTHORITY INVITE
JACKSON & CHRISTINE
TO PARTY ON
7.30
"TRANSPORT"

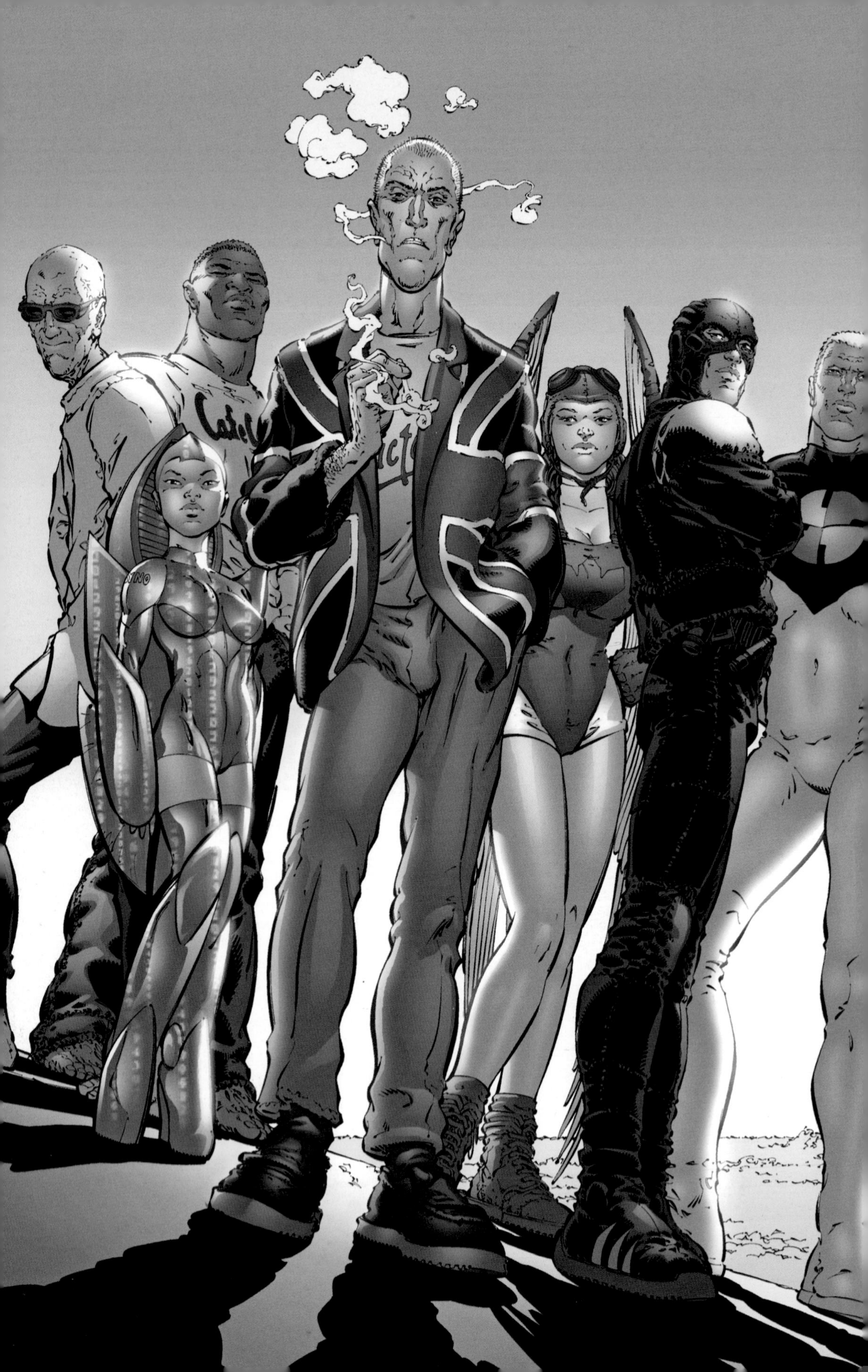

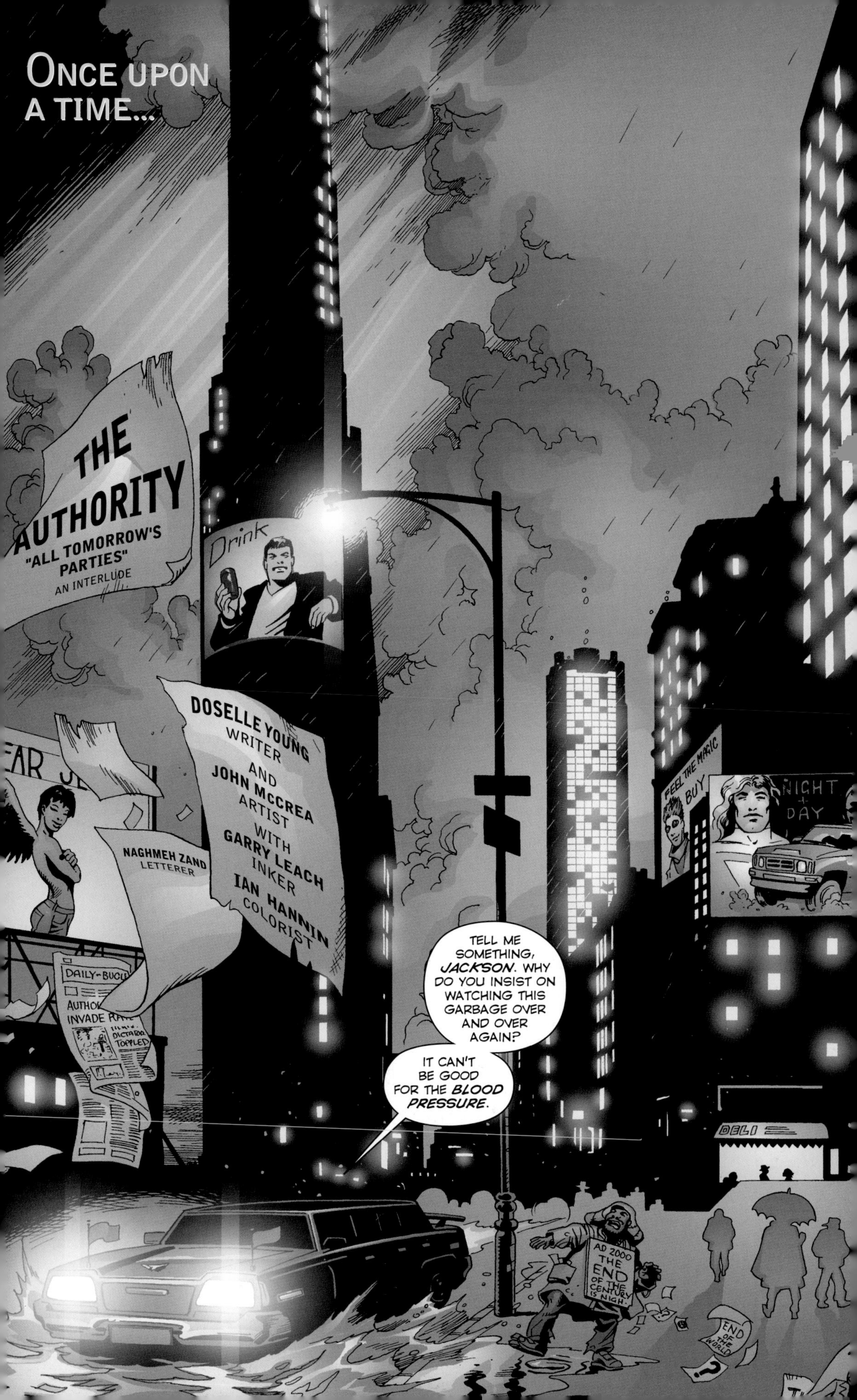
ONCE UPON A TIME...
THE AUTHORITY
"ALL TOMORROW'S PARTIES"
AN INTERLUDE
Drink
DOSELLE YOUNG
WRITER
AND
JOHN McCREA
ARTIST
WITH
GARRY LEACH
INKER
IAN HANNIN
COLORIST
NAGHMEH ZAND
LETTERER
DICTATOR TOPPLED
FEEL THE MAGIC
BUY
NIGHT + DAY
TELL ME SOMETHING, JACKSON. WHY DO YOU INSIST ON WATCHING THIS GARBAGE OVER AND OVER AGAIN?
IT CAN'T BE GOOD FOR THE BLOOD PRESSURE.
DELI
AD 2000 THE END OF THE CENTURY IS NIGH.
END OF THE WORLD

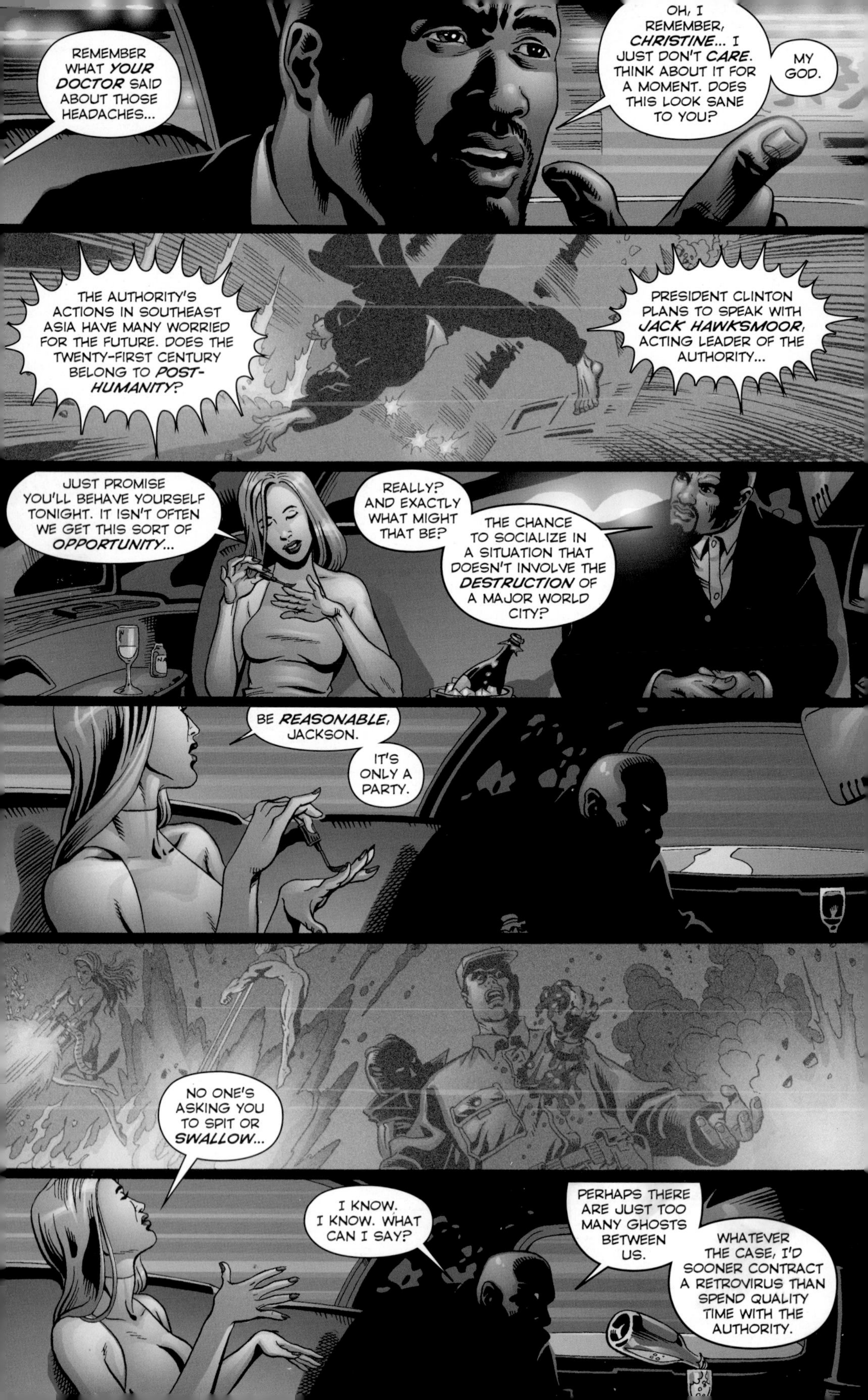
REMEMBER WHAT YOUR DOCTOR SAID ABOUT THOSE HEADACHES...
OH, I REMEMBER, CHRISTINE... I JUST DON'T CARE. THINK ABOUT IT FOR A MOMENT. DOES THIS LOOK SANE TO YOU?
MY GOD.
THE AUTHORITY'S ACTIONS IN SOUTHEAST ASIA HAVE MANY WORRIED FOR THE FUTURE. DOES THE TWENTY-FIRST CENTURY BELONG TO POST-HUMANITY?
PRESIDENT CLINTON PLANS TO SPEAK WITH JACK HAWKSMOOR, ACTING LEADER OF THE AUTHORITY...
JUST PROMISE YOU'LL BEHAVE YOURSELF TONIGHT. IT ISN'T OFTEN WE GET THIS SORT OF OPPORTUNITY...
REALLY? AND EXACTLY WHAT MIGHT THAT BE?
THE CHANCE TO SOCIALIZE IN A SITUATION THAT DOESN'T INVOLVE THE DESTRUCTION OF A MAJOR WORLD CITY?
BE REASONABLE, JACKSON.
IT'S ONLY A PARTY.
NO ONE'S ASKING YOU TO SPIT OR SWALLOW...
I KNOW. I KNOW. WHAT CAN I SAY?
PERHAPS THERE ARE JUST TOO MANY GHOSTS BETWEEN US.
WHATEVER THE CASE, I'D SOONER CONTRACT A RETROVIRUS THAN SPEND QUALITY TIME WITH THE AUTHORITY.

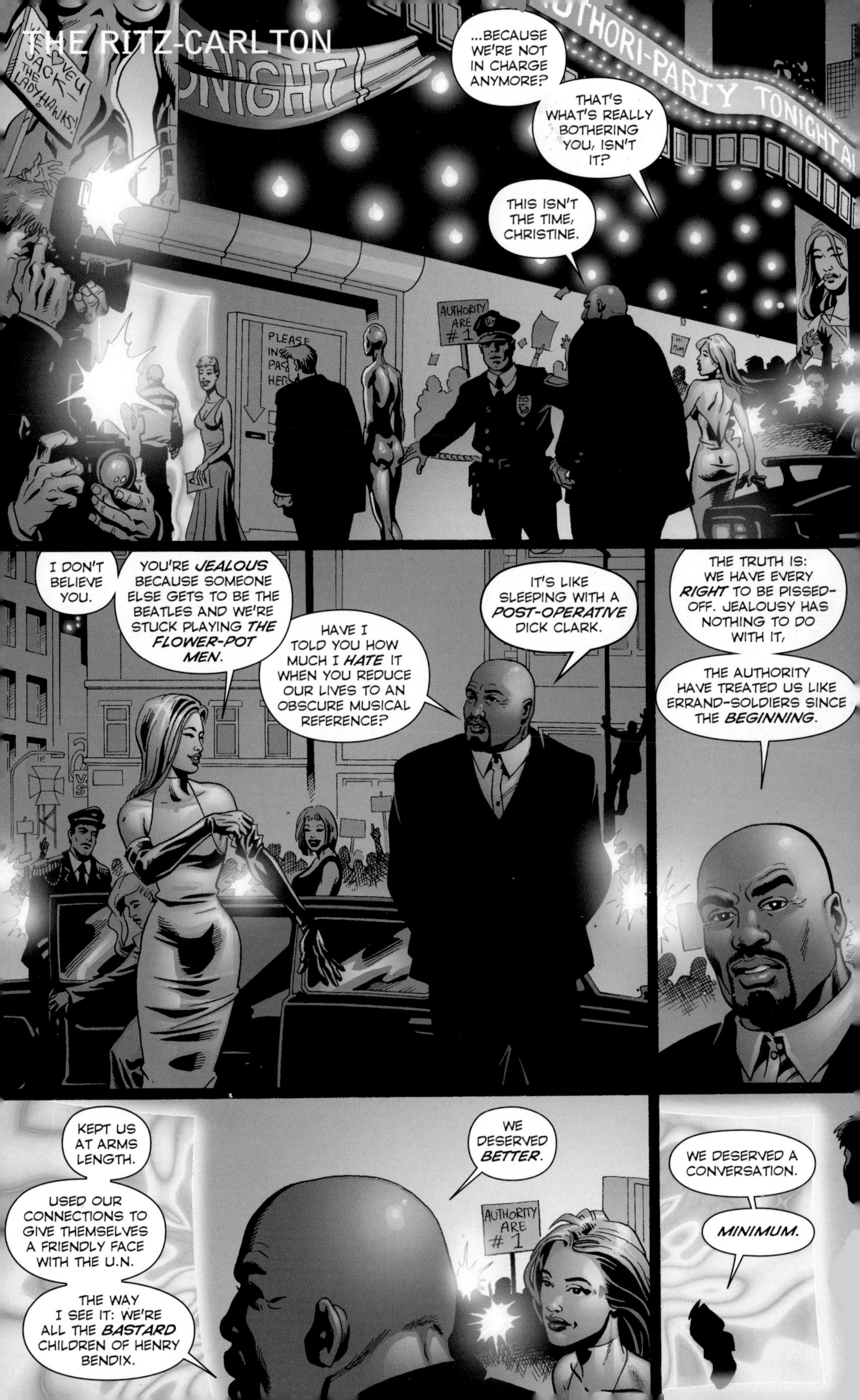
THE RITZ-CARLTON
...BECAUSE WE'RE NOT IN CHARGE ANYMORE?
THAT'S WHAT'S REALLY BOTHERING YOU, ISN'T IT?
THIS ISN'T THE TIME, CHRISTINE.
AUTHORITY ARE #1
I DON'T BELIEVE YOU.
YOU'RE JEALOUS BECAUSE SOMEONE ELSE GETS TO BE THE BEATLES AND WE'RE STUCK PLAYING THE FLOWER-POT MEN.
HAVE I TOLD YOU HOW MUCH I HATE IT WHEN YOU REDUCE OUR LIVES TO AN OBSCURE MUSICAL REFERENCE?
IT'S LIKE SLEEPING WITH A POST-OPERATIVE DICK CLARK.
THE TRUTH IS: WE HAVE EVERY RIGHT TO BE PISSED-OFF. JEALOUSY HAS NOTHING TO DO WITH IT,
THE AUTHORITY HAVE TREATED US LIKE ERRAND-SOLDIERS SINCE THE BEGINNING.
KEPT US AT ARMS LENGTH.
USED OUR CONNECTIONS TO GIVE THEMSELVES A FRIENDLY FACE WITH THE U.N.
THE WAY I SEE IT: WE'RE ALL THE BASTARD CHILDREN OF HENRY BENDIX.
WE DESERVED BETTER.
AUTHORITY ARE #1
WE DESERVED A CONVERSATION.
MINIMUM.

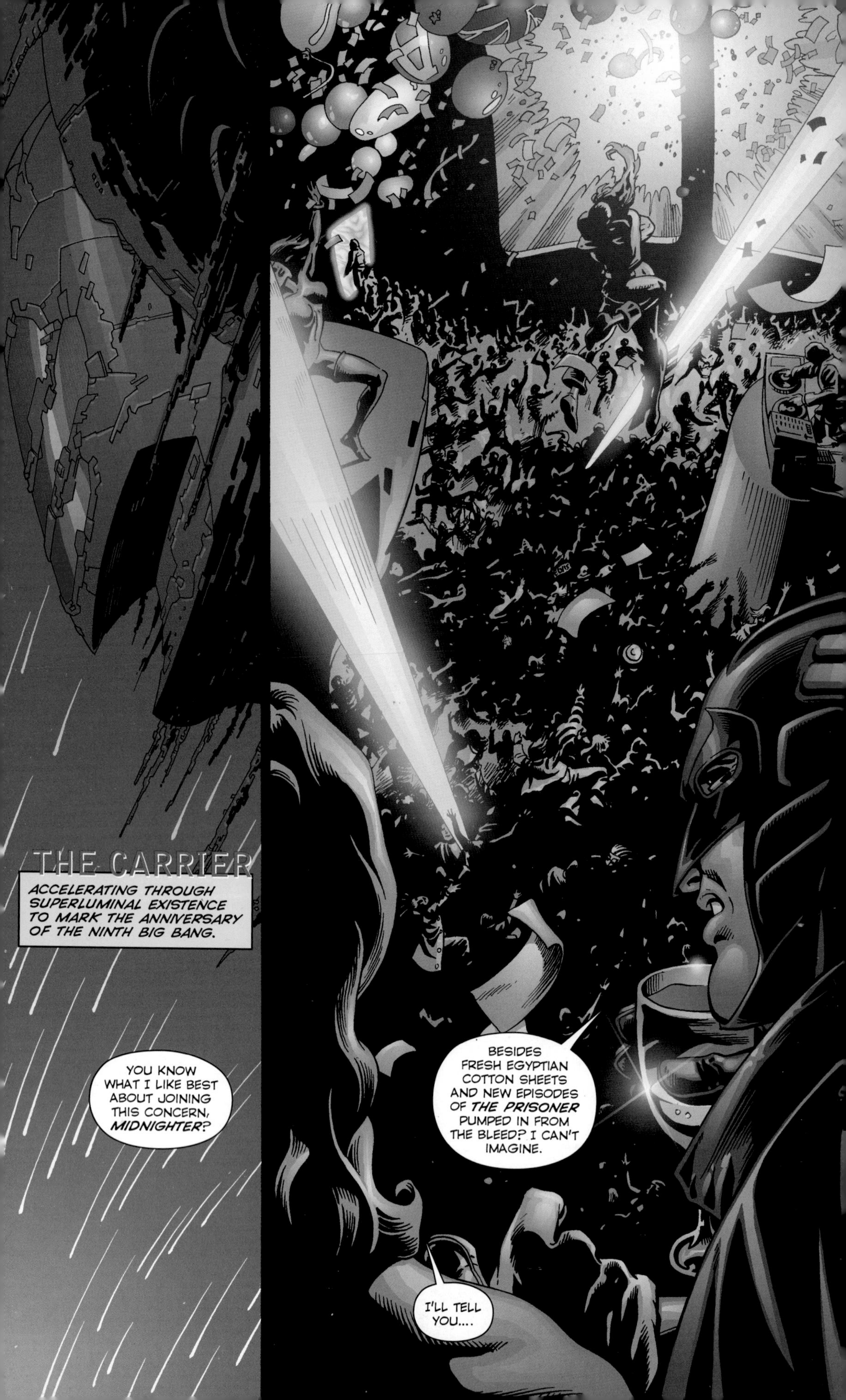
THE CARRIER
ACCELERATING THROUGH SUPERLUMINAL EXISTENCE TO MARK THE ANNIVERSARY OF THE NINTH BIG BANG.
YOU KNOW WHAT I LIKE BEST ABOUT JOINING THIS CONCERN, MIDNIGHTER?
BESIDES FRESH EGYPTIAN COTTON SHEETS AND NEW EPISODES OF THE PRISONER PUMPED IN FROM THE BLEED? I CAN'T IMAGINE.
I'LL TELL YOU....

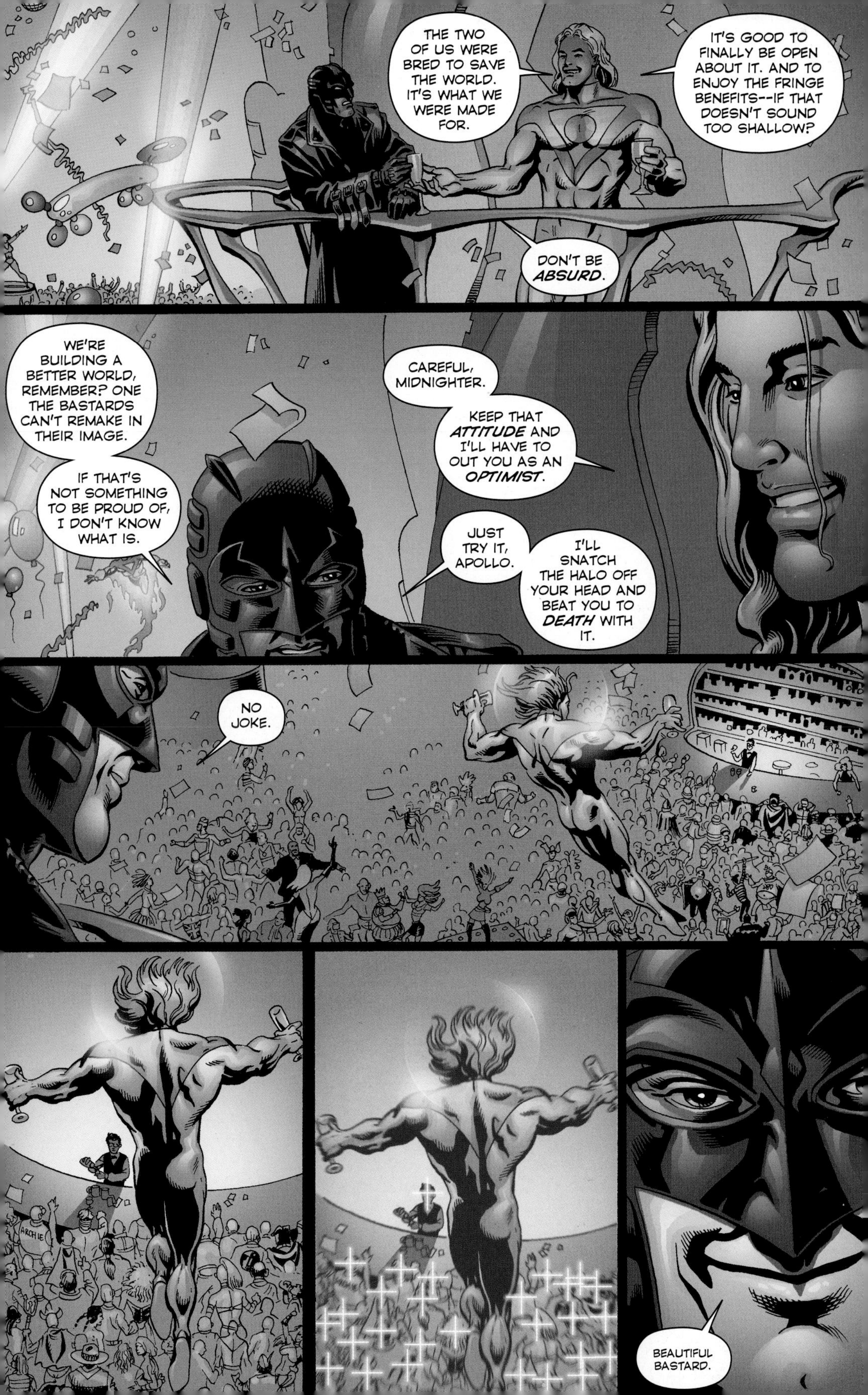
THE TWO OF US WERE BRED TO SAVE THE WORLD. IT'S WHAT WE WERE MADE FOR.
IT'S GOOD TO FINALLY BE OPEN ABOUT IT. AND TO ENJOY THE FRINGE BENEFITS--IF THAT DOESN'T SOUND TOO SHALLOW?
DON'T BE ABSURD.
WE'RE BUILDING A BETTER WORLD, REMEMBER? ONE THE BASTARDS CAN'T REMAKE IN THEIR IMAGE.
IF THAT'S NOT SOMETHING TO BE PROUD OF, I DON'T KNOW WHAT IS.
CAREFUL, MIDNIGHTER.
KEEP THAT ATTITUDE AND I'LL HAVE TO OUT YOU AS AN OPTIMIST.
JUST TRY IT, APOLLO.
I'LL SNATCH THE HALO OFF YOUR HEAD AND BEAT YOU TO DEATH WITH IT.
NO JOKE.
ARCHIE
BEAUTIFUL BASTARD.

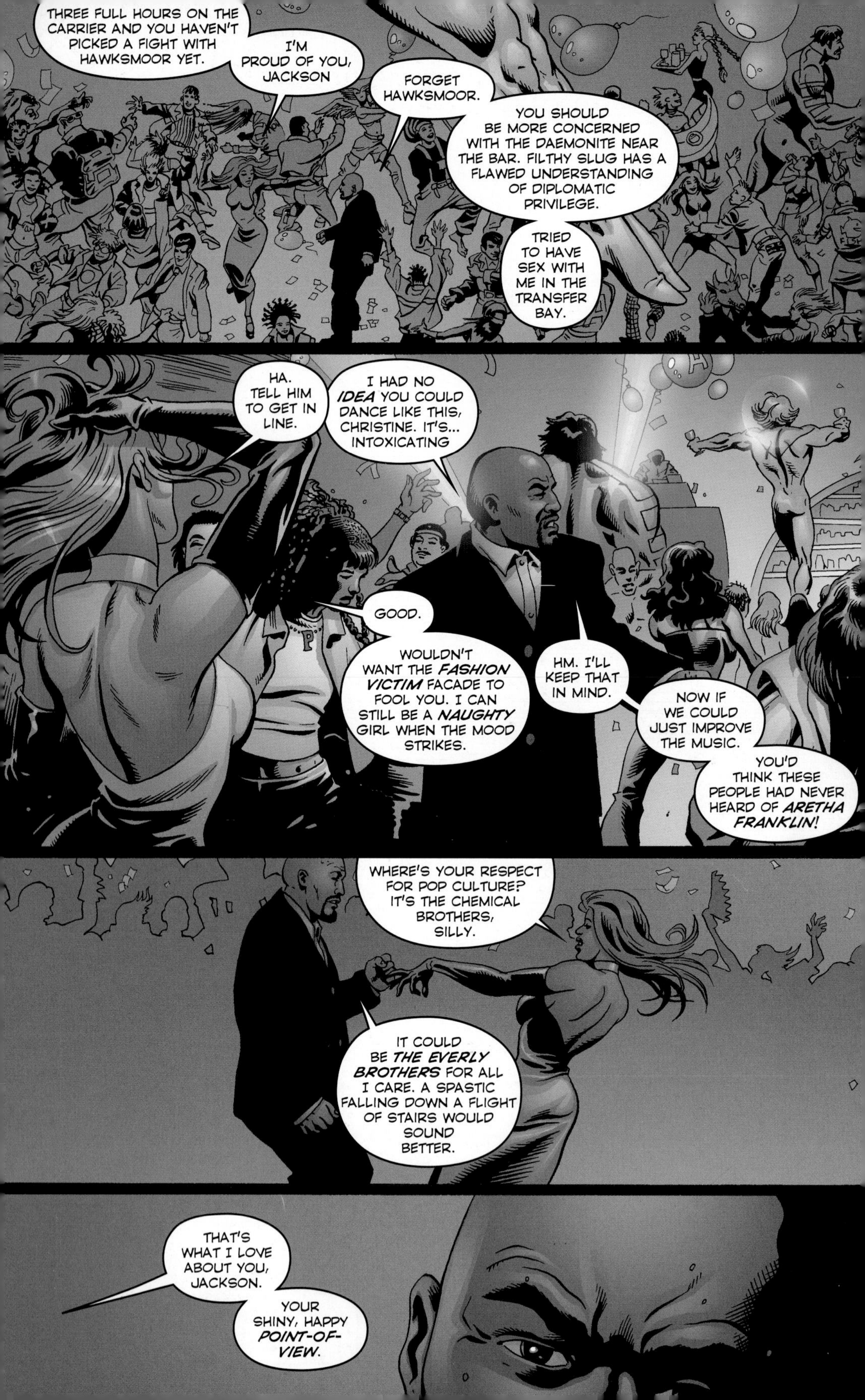
THREE FULL HOURS ON THE CARRIER AND YOU HAVEN'T PICKED A FIGHT WITH HAWKSMOOR YET.
I'M PROUD OF YOU, JACKSON
FORGET HAWKSMOOR.
YOU SHOULD BE MORE CONCERNED WITH THE DAEMONITE NEAR THE BAR. FILTHY SLUG HAS A FLAWED UNDERSTANDING OF DIPLOMATIC PRIVILEGE.
TRIED TO HAVE SEX WITH ME IN THE TRANSFER BAY.
HA. TELL HIM TO GET IN LINE.
I HAD NO *IDEA* YOU COULD DANCE LIKE THIS, CHRISTINE. IT'S... INTOXICATING
GOOD.
WOULDN'T WANT THE *FASHION VICTIM* FACADE TO FOOL YOU. I CAN STILL BE A *NAUGHTY* GIRL WHEN THE MOOD STRIKES.
HM. I'LL KEEP THAT IN MIND.
NOW IF WE COULD JUST IMPROVE THE MUSIC.
YOU'D THINK THESE PEOPLE HAD NEVER HEARD OF *ARETHA FRANKLIN*!
WHERE'S YOUR RESPECT FOR POP CULTURE? IT'S THE CHEMICAL BROTHERS, SILLY.
IT COULD BE *THE EVERLY BROTHERS* FOR ALL I CARE. A SPASTIC FALLING DOWN A FLIGHT OF STAIRS WOULD SOUND BETTER.
THAT'S WHAT I LOVE ABOUT YOU, JACKSON.
YOUR SHINY, HAPPY *POINT-OF-VIEW*.

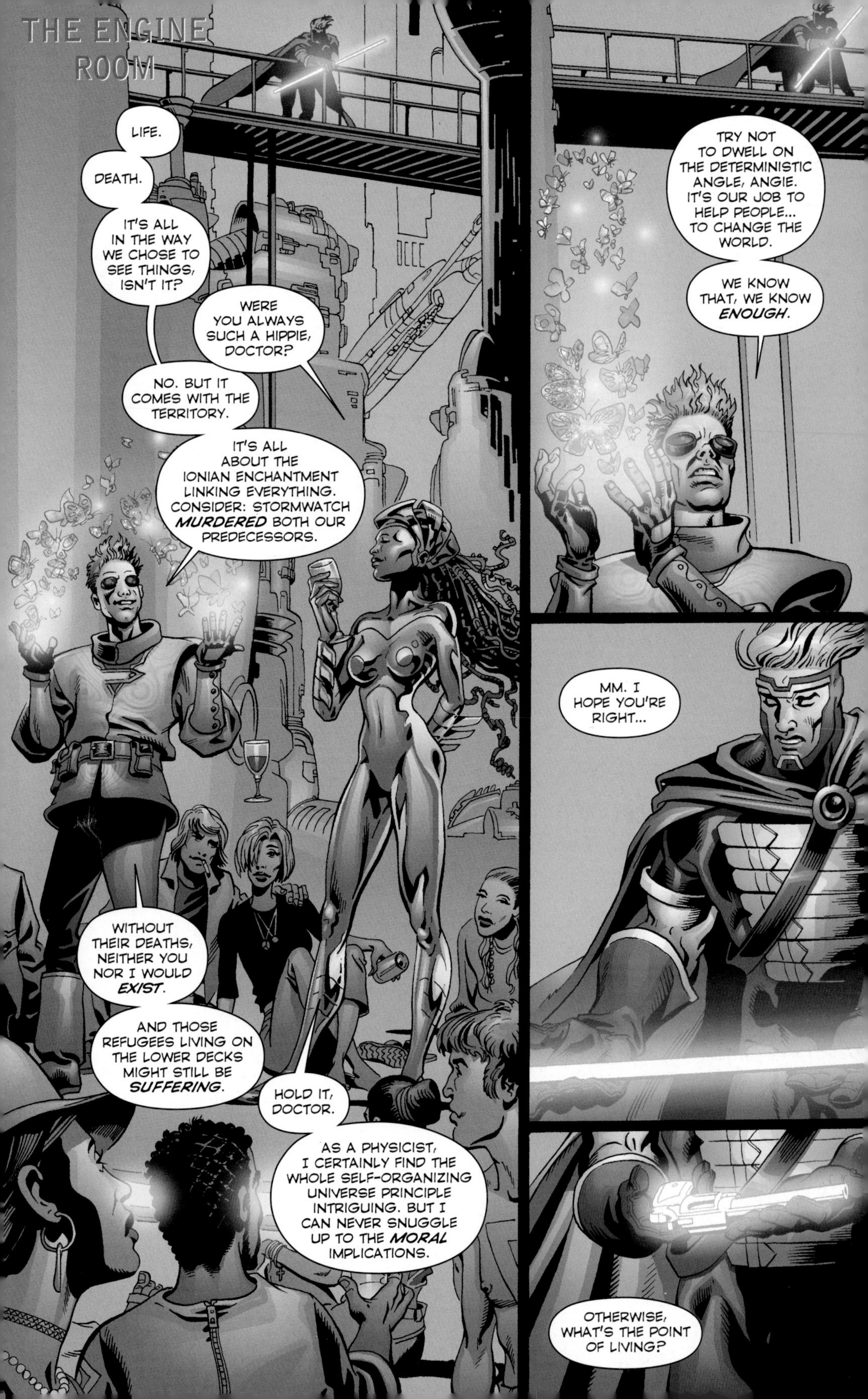
THE ENGINE ROOM
LIFE.
DEATH.
IT'S ALL IN THE WAY WE CHOSE TO SEE THINGS, ISN'T IT?
WERE YOU ALWAYS SUCH A HIPPIE, DOCTOR?
NO. BUT IT COMES WITH THE TERRITORY.
IT'S ALL ABOUT THE IONIAN ENCHANTMENT LINKING EVERYTHING. CONSIDER: STORMWATCH *MURDERED* BOTH OUR PREDECESSORS.
WITHOUT THEIR DEATHS, NEITHER YOU NOR I WOULD *EXIST*.
AND THOSE REFUGEES LIVING ON THE LOWER DECKS MIGHT STILL BE *SUFFERING*.
HOLD IT, DOCTOR.
AS A PHYSICIST, I CERTAINLY FIND THE WHOLE SELF-ORGANIZING UNIVERSE PRINCIPLE INTRIGUING. BUT I CAN NEVER SNUGGLE UP TO THE *MORAL* IMPLICATIONS.
TRY NOT TO DWELL ON THE DETERMINISTIC ANGLE, ANGIE. IT'S OUR JOB TO HELP PEOPLE... TO CHANGE THE WORLD.
WE KNOW THAT, WE KNOW *ENOUGH*.
MM. I HOPE YOU'RE RIGHT...
OTHERWISE, WHAT'S THE POINT OF LIVING?

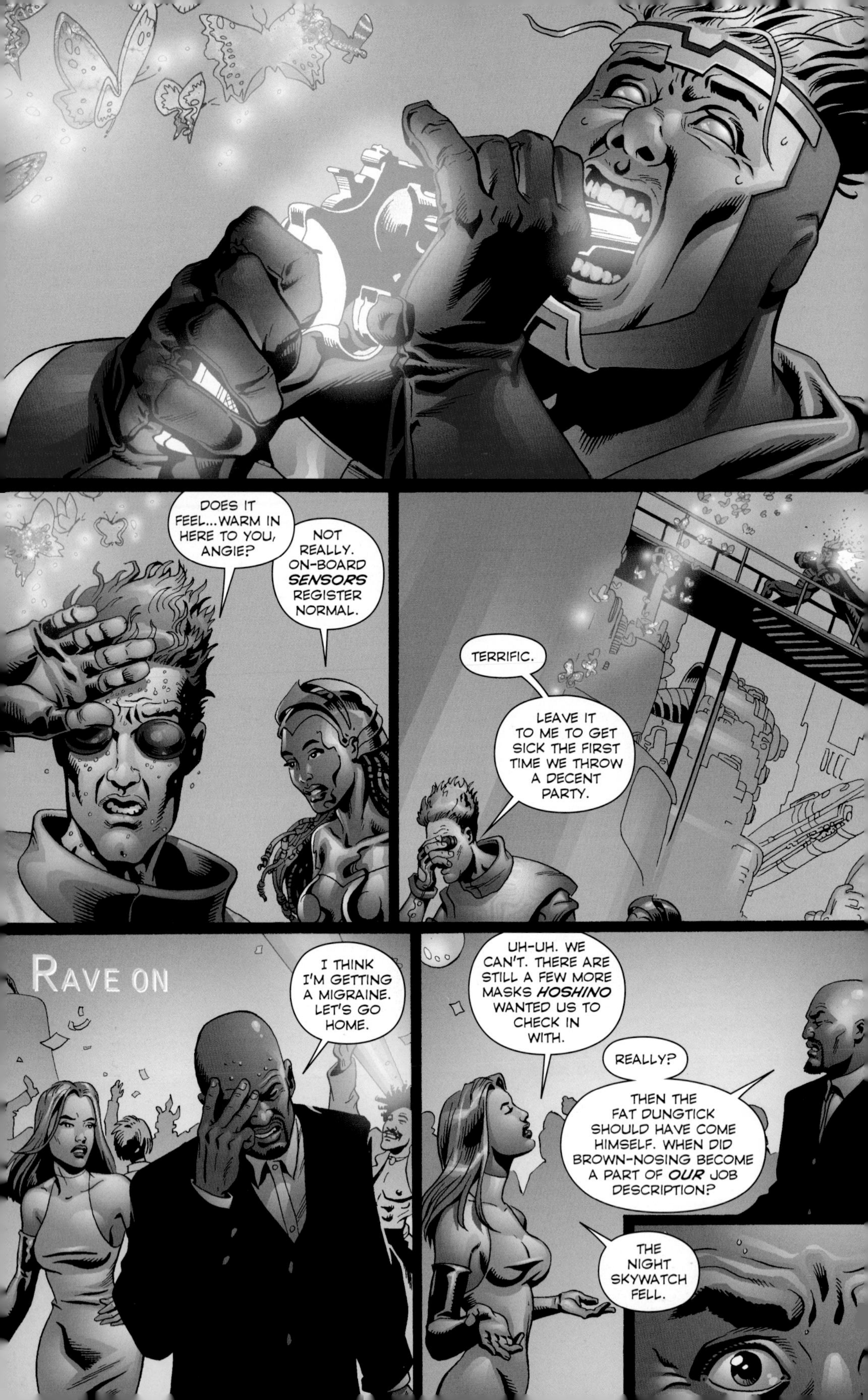
DOES IT FEEL...WARM IN HERE TO YOU, ANGIE?
NOT REALLY. ON-BOARD *SENSORS* REGISTER NORMAL.
TERRIFIC.
LEAVE IT TO ME TO GET SICK THE FIRST TIME WE THROW A DECENT PARTY.
RAVE ON
I THINK I'M GETTING A MIGRAINE. LET'S GO HOME.
UH-UH. WE CAN'T. THERE ARE STILL A FEW MORE MASKS *HOSHINO* WANTED US TO CHECK IN WITH.
REALLY?
THEN THE FAT DUNGTICK SHOULD HAVE COME HIMSELF. WHEN DID BROWN-NOSING BECOME A PART OF *OUR* JOB DESCRIPTION?
THE NIGHT SKYWATCH FELL.

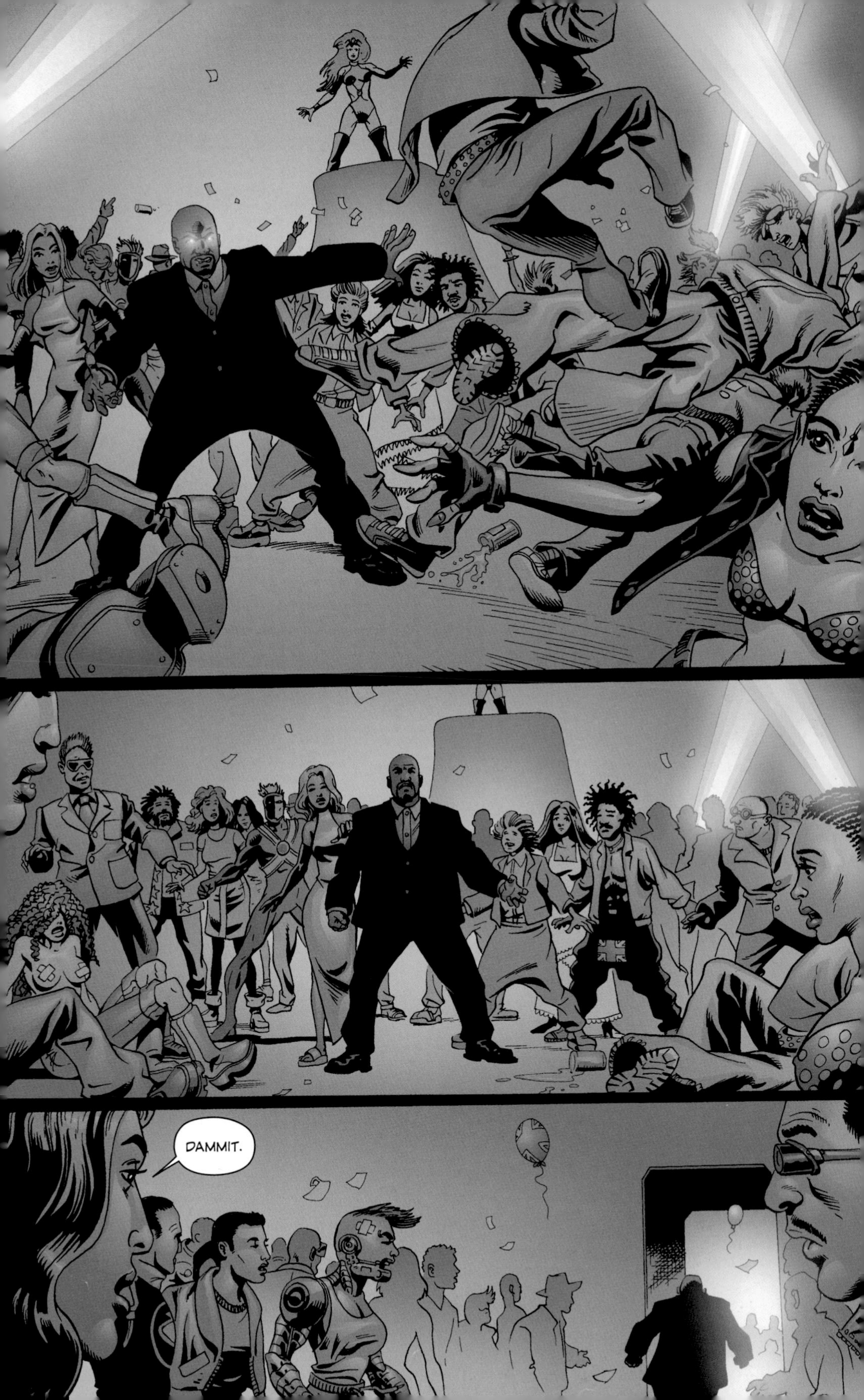
DAMMIT.

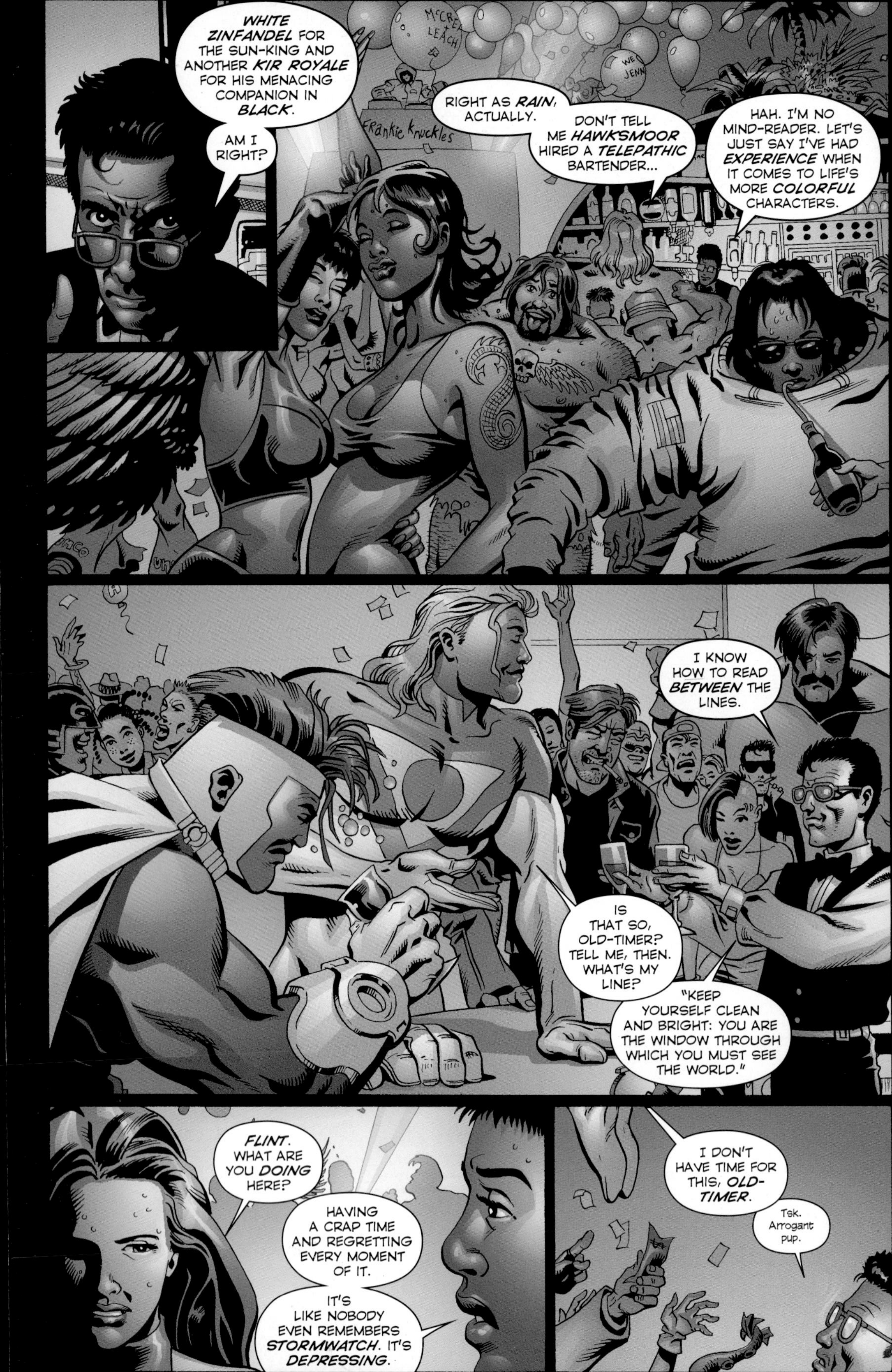
WHITE ZINFANDEL FOR THE SUN-KING AND ANOTHER KIR ROYALE FOR HIS MENACING COMPANION IN BLACK.
AM I RIGHT?
RIGHT AS RAIN, ACTUALLY.
DON'T TELL ME HAWKSMOOR HIRED A TELEPATHIC BARTENDER...
HAH. I'M NO MIND-READER. LET'S JUST SAY I'VE HAD EXPERIENCE WHEN IT COMES TO LIFE'S MORE COLORFUL CHARACTERS.
I KNOW HOW TO READ BETWEEN THE LINES.
IS THAT SO, OLD-TIMER? TELL ME, THEN. WHAT'S MY LINE?
"KEEP YOURSELF CLEAN AND BRIGHT: YOU ARE THE WINDOW THROUGH WHICH YOU MUST SEE THE WORLD."
FLINT. WHAT ARE YOU DOING HERE?
HAVING A CRAP TIME AND REGRETTING EVERY MOMENT OF IT.
IT'S LIKE NOBODY EVEN REMEMBERS STORMWATCH. IT'S DEPRESSING.
I DON'T HAVE TIME FOR THIS, OLD-TIMER.
Tsk. Arrogant pup.

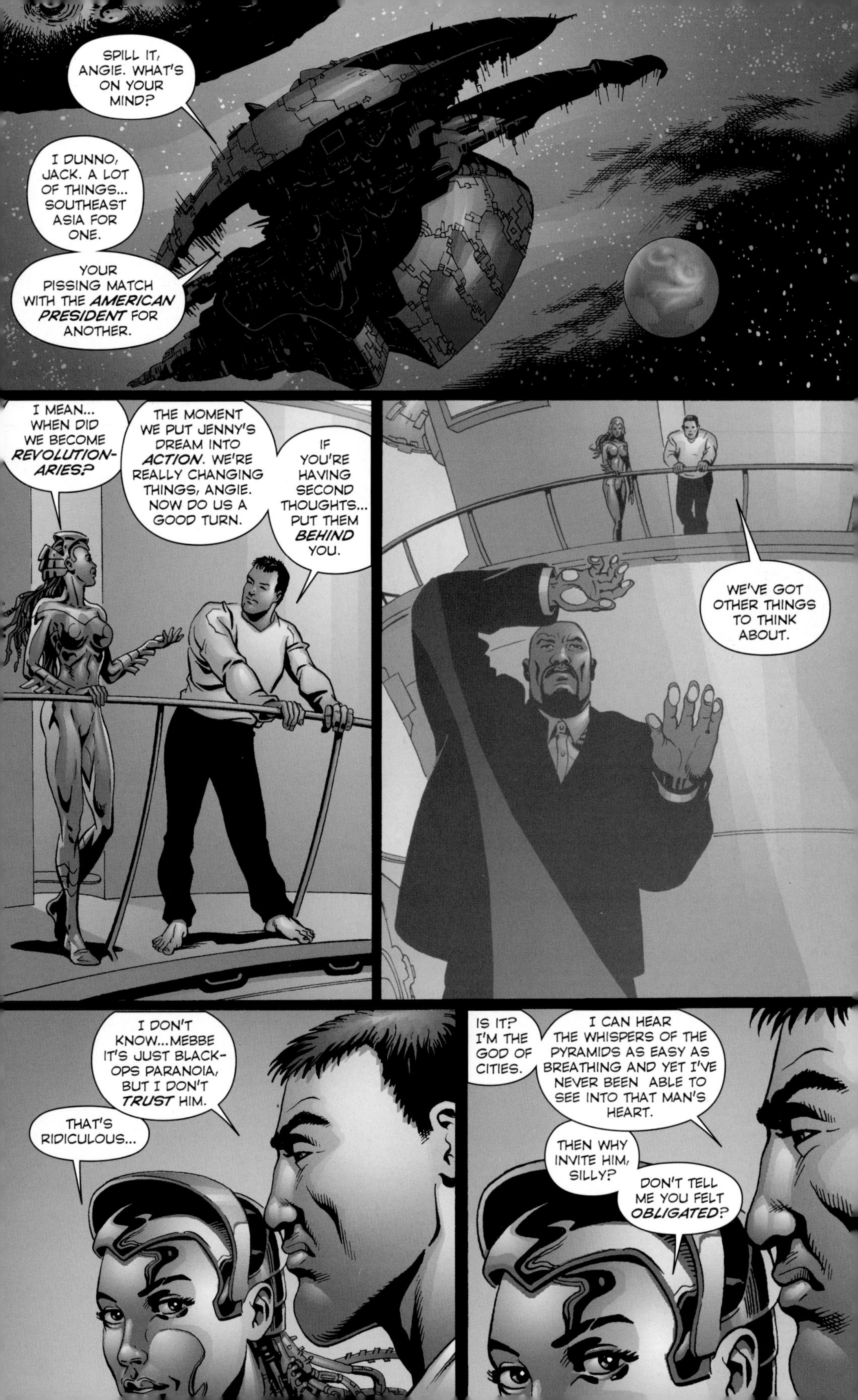

SPILL IT, ANGIE. WHAT'S ON YOUR MIND?
I DUNNO, JACK. A LOT OF THINGS... SOUTHEAST ASIA FOR ONE.
YOUR PISSING MATCH WITH THE AMERICAN PRESIDENT FOR ANOTHER.
I MEAN... WHEN DID WE BECOME REVOLUTION-ARIES?
THE MOMENT WE PUT JENNY'S DREAM INTO ACTION. WE'RE REALLY CHANGING THINGS, ANGIE. NOW DO US A GOOD TURN.
IF YOU'RE HAVING SECOND THOUGHTS... PUT THEM BEHIND YOU.
WE'VE GOT OTHER THINGS TO THINK ABOUT.
I DON'T KNOW...MEBBE IT'S JUST BLACK-OPS PARANOIA, BUT I DON'T TRUST HIM.
THAT'S RIDICULOUS...
IS IT? I'M THE GOD OF CITIES.
I CAN HEAR THE WHISPERS OF THE PYRAMIDS AS EASY AS BREATHING AND YET I'VE NEVER BEEN ABLE TO SEE INTO THAT MAN'S HEART.
THEN WHY INVITE HIM, SILLY?
DON'T TELL ME YOU FELT OBLIGATED?

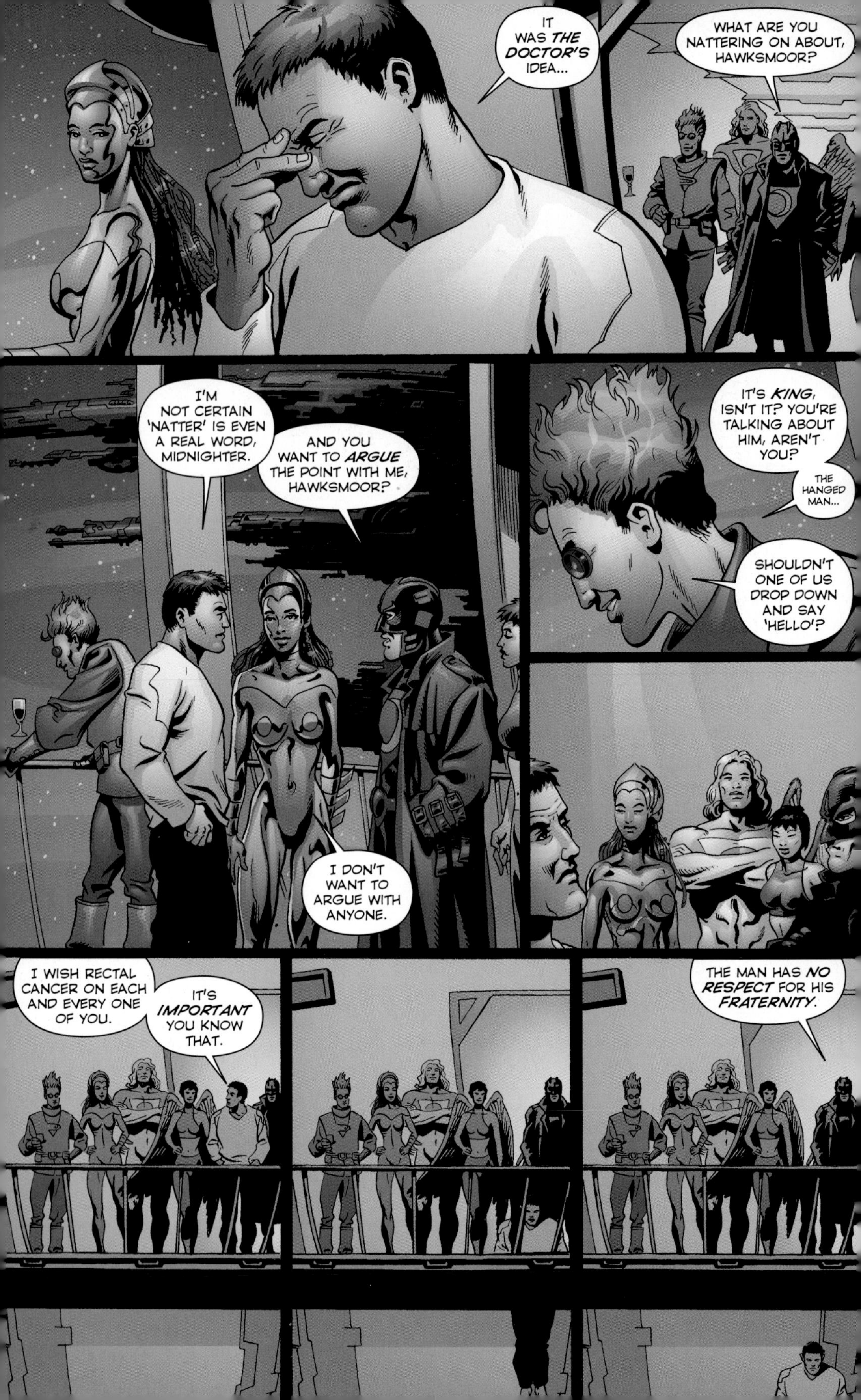
IT WAS THE DOCTOR'S IDEA...
WHAT ARE YOU NATTERING ON ABOUT, HAWKSMOOR?
I'M NOT CERTAIN 'NATTER' IS EVEN A REAL WORD, MIDNIGHTER.
AND YOU WANT TO ARGUE THE POINT WITH ME, HAWKSMOOR?
I DON'T WANT TO ARGUE WITH ANYONE.
IT'S KING, ISN'T IT? YOU'RE TALKING ABOUT HIM, AREN'T YOU?
THE HANGED MAN...
SHOULDN'T ONE OF US DROP DOWN AND SAY 'HELLO'?
I WISH RECTAL CANCER ON EACH AND EVERY ONE OF YOU.
IT'S IMPORTANT YOU KNOW THAT.
THE MAN HAS NO RESPECT FOR HIS FRATERNITY.

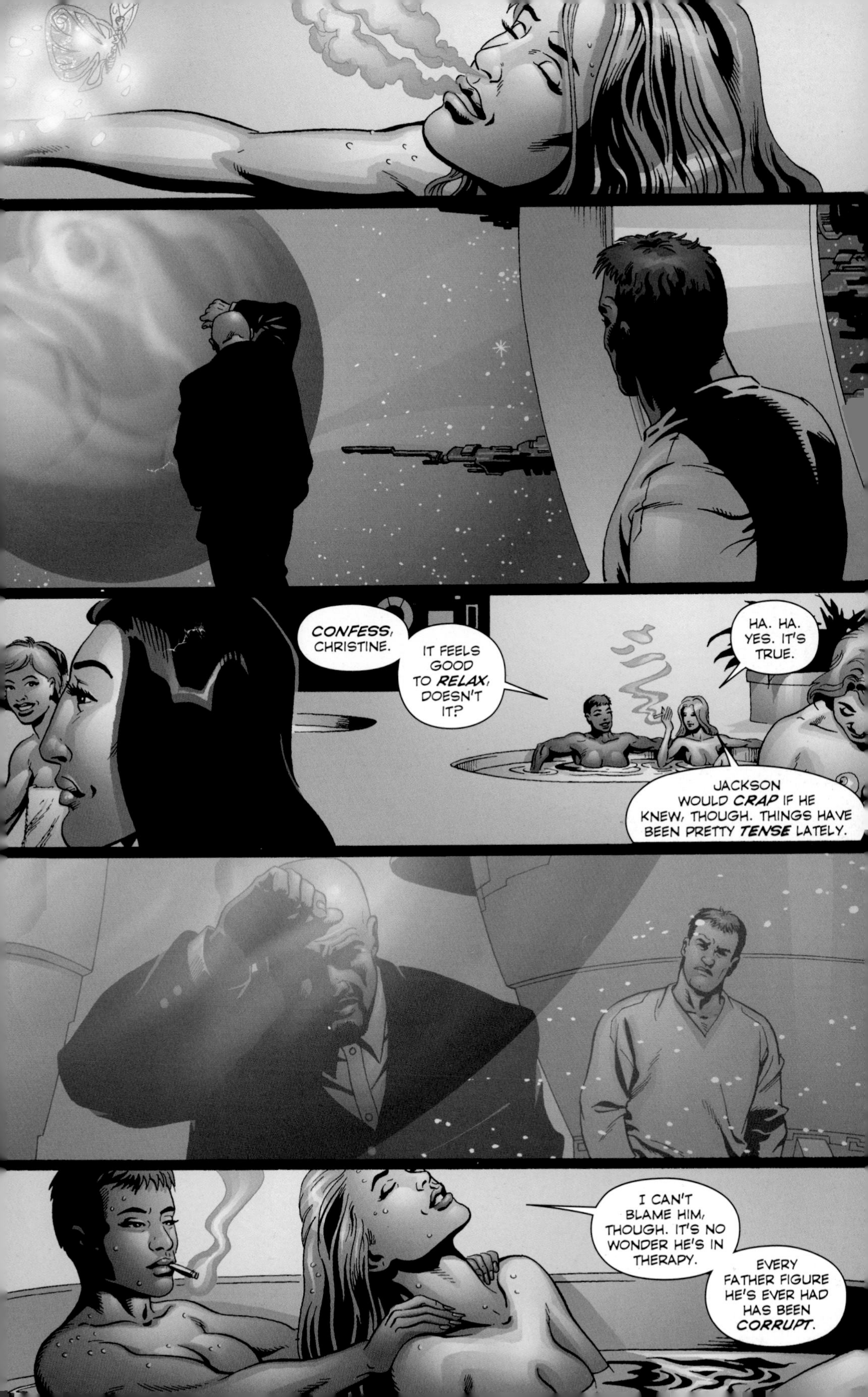
CONFESS, CHRISTINE.
IT FEELS GOOD TO RELAX, DOESN'T IT?
HA. HA. YES. IT'S TRUE.
JACKSON WOULD CRAP IF HE KNEW, THOUGH. THINGS HAVE BEEN PRETTY TENSE LATELY.
I CAN'T BLAME HIM, THOUGH. IT'S NO WONDER HE'S IN THERAPY.
EVERY FATHER FIGURE HE'S EVER HAD HAS BEEN CORRUPT.

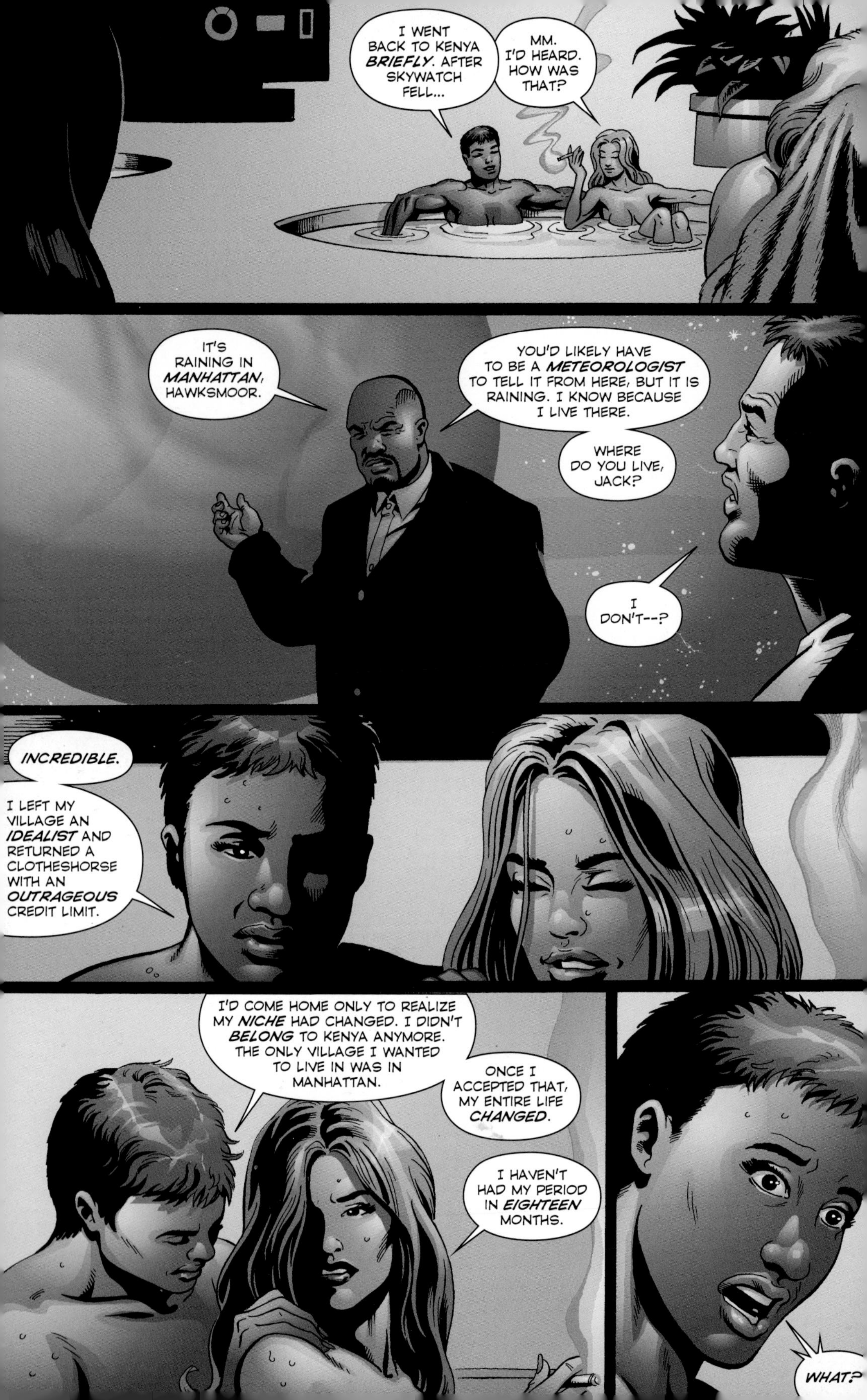
I WENT BACK TO KENYA *BRIEFLY*. AFTER SKYWATCH FELL...
MM. I'D HEARD. HOW WAS THAT?
IT'S RAINING IN *MANHATTAN*, HAWKSMOOR.
YOU'D LIKELY HAVE TO BE A *METEOROLOGIST* TO TELL IT FROM HERE, BUT IT IS RAINING. I KNOW BECAUSE I LIVE THERE.
WHERE DO YOU LIVE, JACK?
I DON'T--?
INCREDIBLE.
I LEFT MY VILLAGE AN *IDEALIST* AND RETURNED A CLOTHESHORSE WITH AN *OUTRAGEOUS* CREDIT LIMIT.
I'D COME HOME ONLY TO REALIZE MY *NICHE* HAD CHANGED. I DIDN'T *BELONG* TO KENYA ANYMORE. THE ONLY VILLAGE I WANTED TO LIVE IN WAS IN MANHATTAN.
ONCE I ACCEPTED THAT, MY ENTIRE LIFE *CHANGED*.
I HAVEN'T HAD MY PERIOD IN *EIGHTEEN* MONTHS.
WHAT?

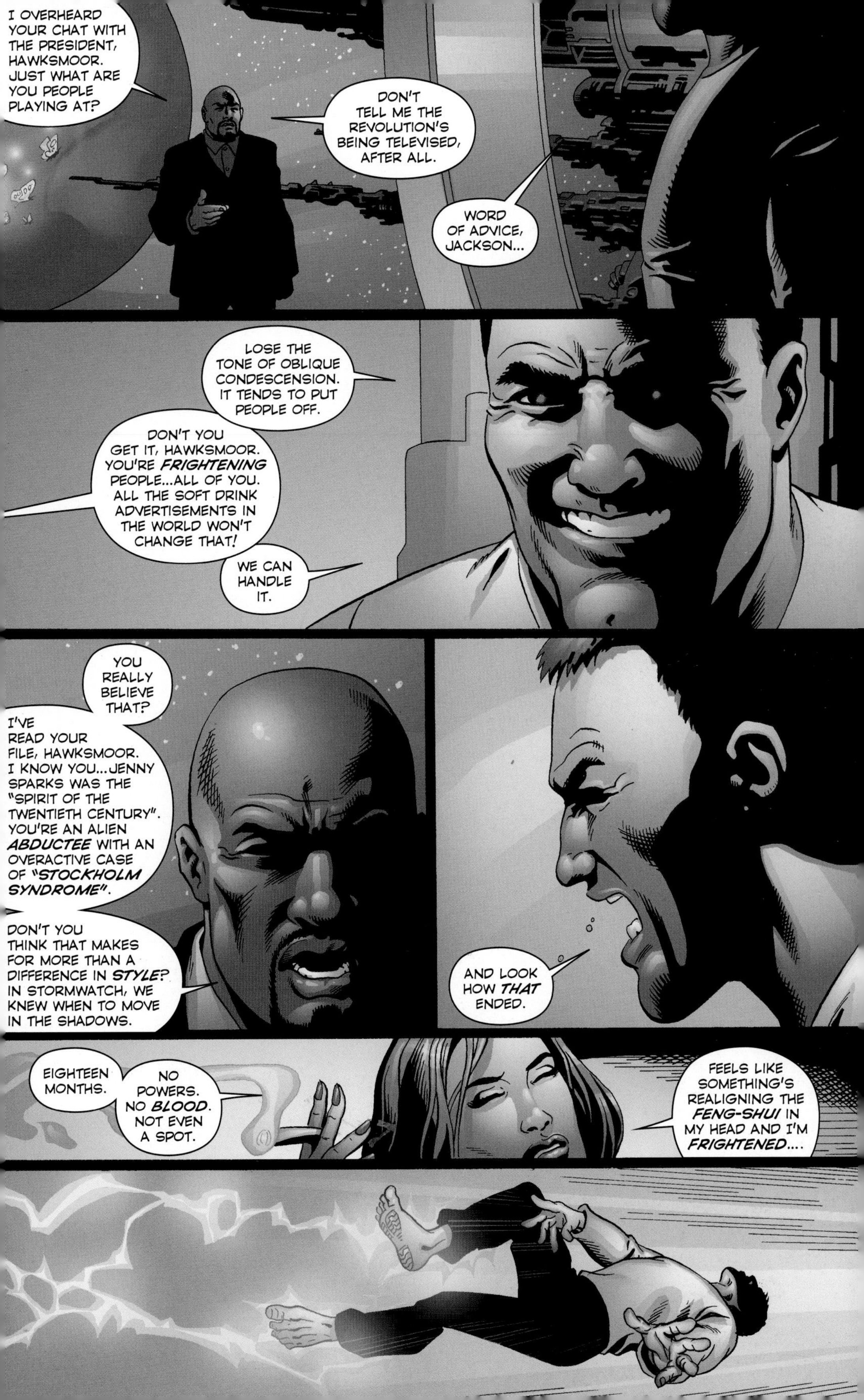
I OVERHEARD YOUR CHAT WITH THE PRESIDENT, HAWKSMOOR. JUST WHAT ARE YOU PEOPLE PLAYING AT?
DON'T TELL ME THE REVOLUTION'S BEING TELEVISED, AFTER ALL.
WORD OF ADVICE, JACKSON...
LOSE THE TONE OF OBLIQUE CONDESCENSION. IT TENDS TO PUT PEOPLE OFF.
DON'T YOU GET IT, HAWKSMOOR. YOU'RE *FRIGHTENING* PEOPLE...ALL OF YOU. ALL THE SOFT DRINK ADVERTISEMENTS IN THE WORLD WON'T CHANGE THAT!
WE CAN HANDLE IT.
YOU REALLY BELIEVE THAT?
I'VE READ YOUR FILE, HAWKSMOOR. I KNOW YOU...JENNY SPARKS WAS THE "SPIRIT OF THE TWENTIETH CENTURY". YOU'RE AN ALIEN *ABDUCTEE* WITH AN OVERACTIVE CASE OF *"STOCKHOLM SYNDROME"*.
DON'T YOU THINK THAT MAKES FOR MORE THAN A DIFFERENCE IN *STYLE*? IN STORMWATCH, WE KNEW WHEN TO MOVE IN THE SHADOWS.
AND LOOK HOW *THAT* ENDED.
EIGHTEEN MONTHS.
NO POWERS. NO *BLOOD*. NOT EVEN A SPOT.
FEELS LIKE SOMETHING'S REALIGNING THE *FENG-SHUI* IN MY HEAD AND I'M *FRIGHTENED*....

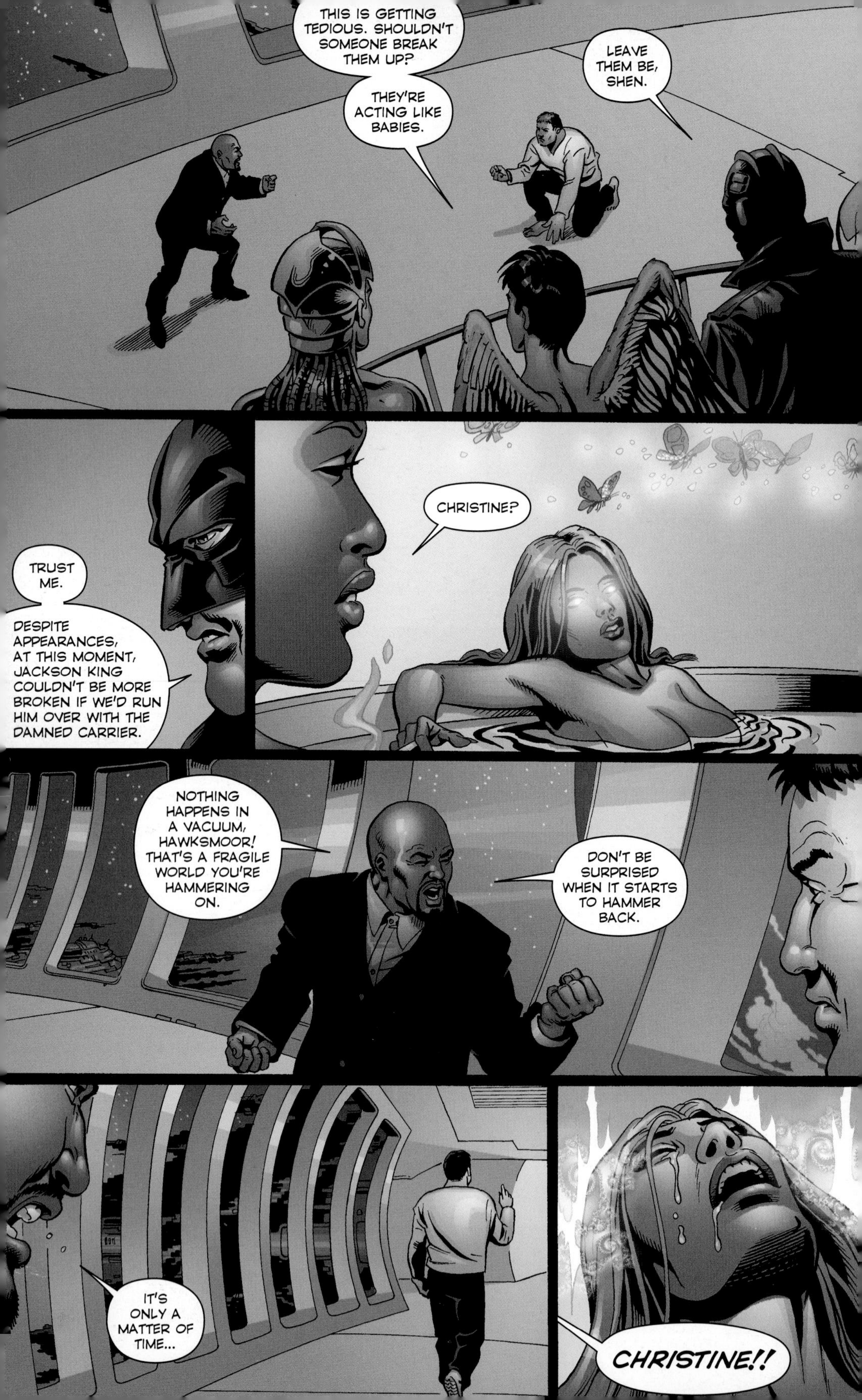
THIS IS GETTING TEDIOUS. SHOULDN'T SOMEONE BREAK THEM UP?
THEY'RE ACTING LIKE BABIES.
LEAVE THEM BE, SHEN.
TRUST ME.
DESPITE APPEARANCES, AT THIS MOMENT, JACKSON KING COULDN'T BE MORE BROKEN IF WE'D RUN HIM OVER WITH THE DAMNED CARRIER.
CHRISTINE?
NOTHING HAPPENS IN A VACUUM, HAWKSMOOR! THAT'S A FRAGILE WORLD YOU'RE HAMMERING ON.
DON'T BE SURPRISED WHEN IT STARTS TO HAMMER BACK.
IT'S ONLY A MATTER OF TIME...
CHRISTINE!!

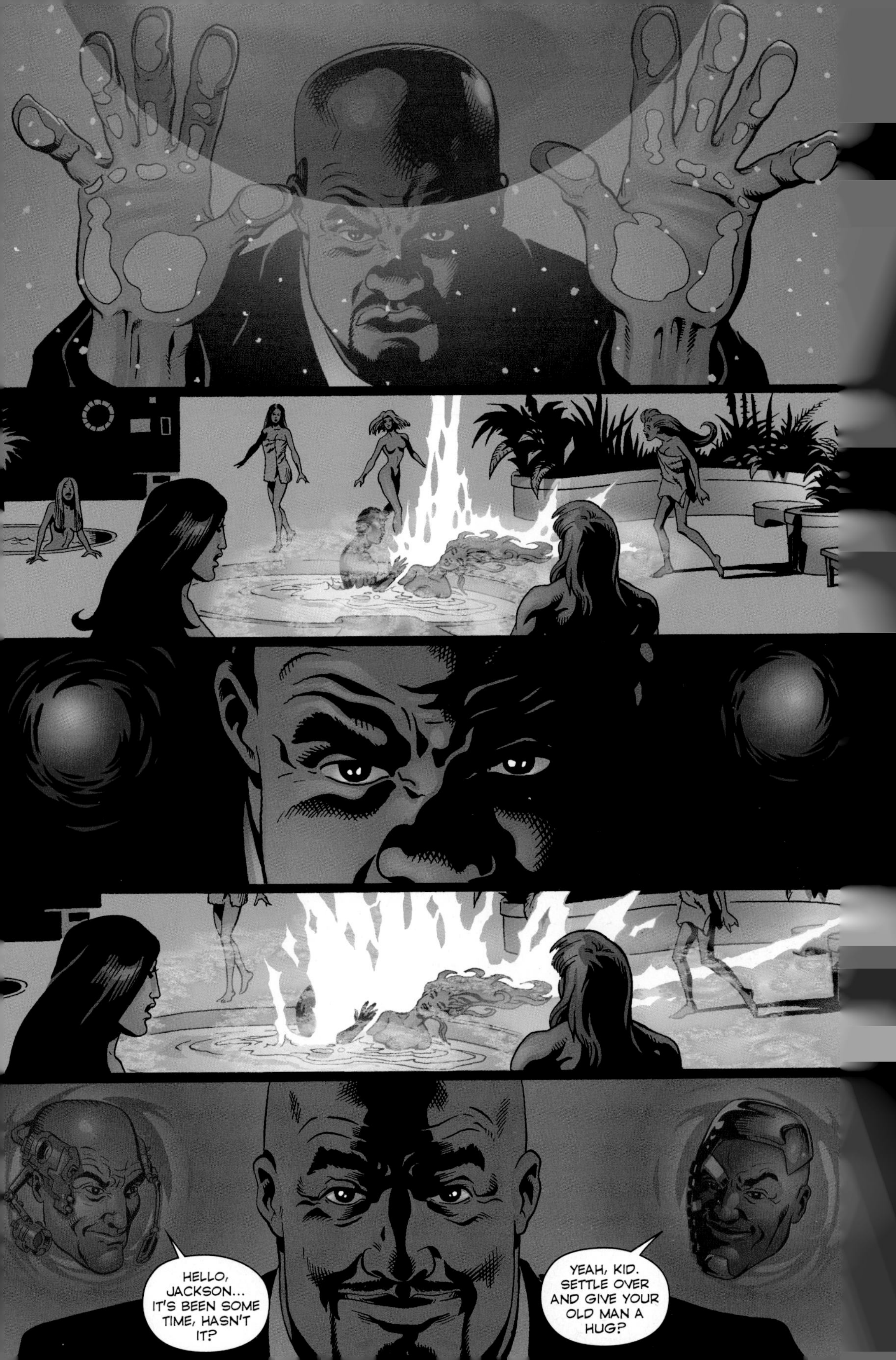
HELLO, JACKSON... IT'S BEEN SOME TIME, HASN'T IT?
YEAH, KID. SETTLE OVER AND GIVE YOUR OLD MAN A HUG?

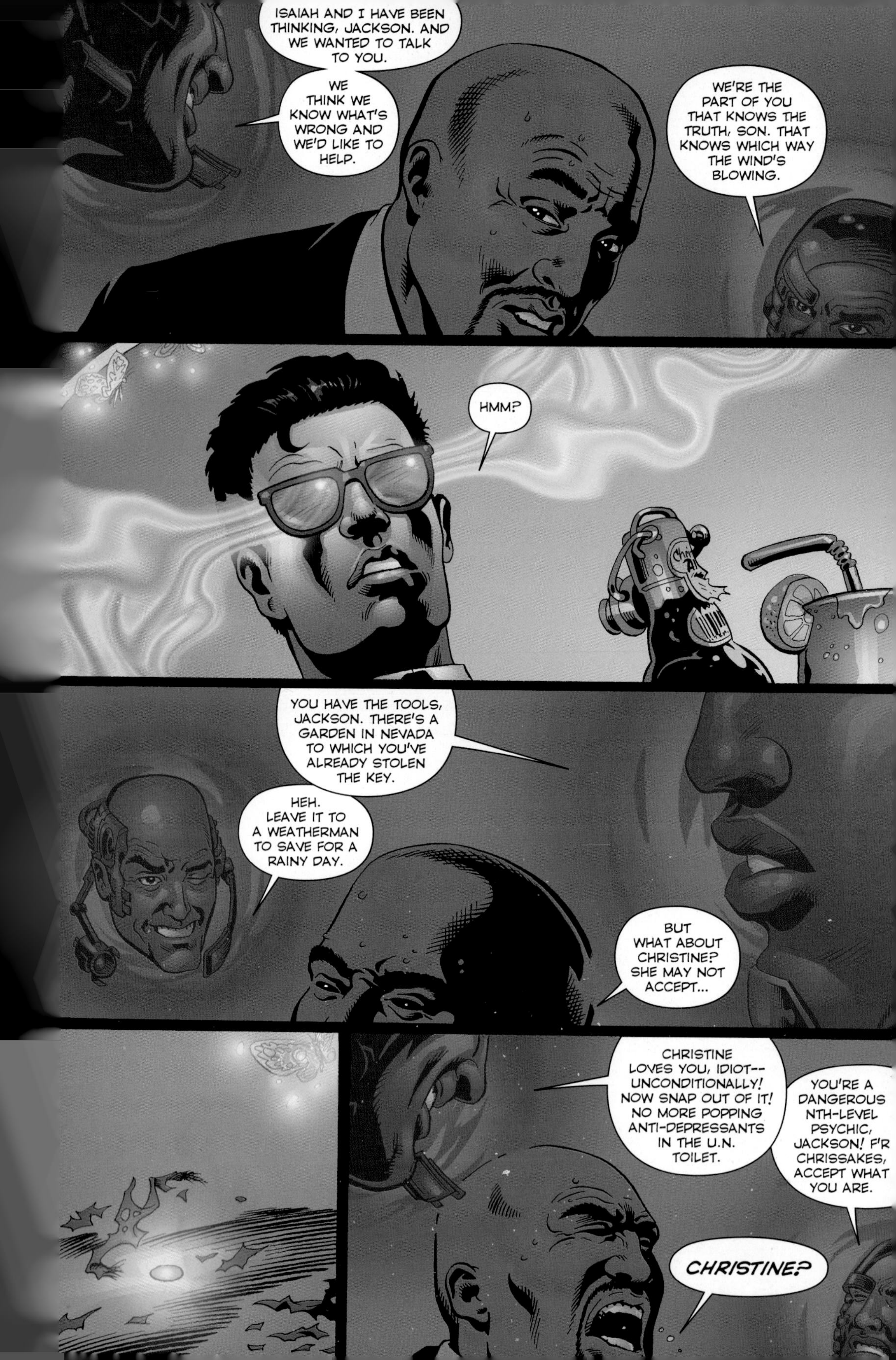
ISAIAH AND I HAVE BEEN THINKING, JACKSON. AND WE WANTED TO TALK TO YOU.
WE THINK WE KNOW WHAT'S WRONG AND WE'D LIKE TO HELP.
WE'RE THE PART OF YOU THAT KNOWS THE TRUTH, SON. THAT KNOWS WHICH WAY THE WIND'S BLOWING.
HMM?
YOU HAVE THE TOOLS, JACKSON. THERE'S A GARDEN IN NEVADA TO WHICH YOU'VE ALREADY STOLEN THE KEY.
HEH. LEAVE IT TO A WEATHERMAN TO SAVE FOR A RAINY DAY.
BUT WHAT ABOUT CHRISTINE? SHE MAY NOT ACCEPT...
CHRISTINE LOVES YOU, IDIOT-- UNCONDITIONALLY! NOW SNAP OUT OF IT! NO MORE POPPING ANTI-DEPRESSANTS IN THE U.N. TOILET.
YOU'RE A DANGEROUS NTH-LEVEL PSYCHIC, JACKSON! F'R CHRISSAKES, ACCEPT WHAT YOU ARE.
CHRISTINE?

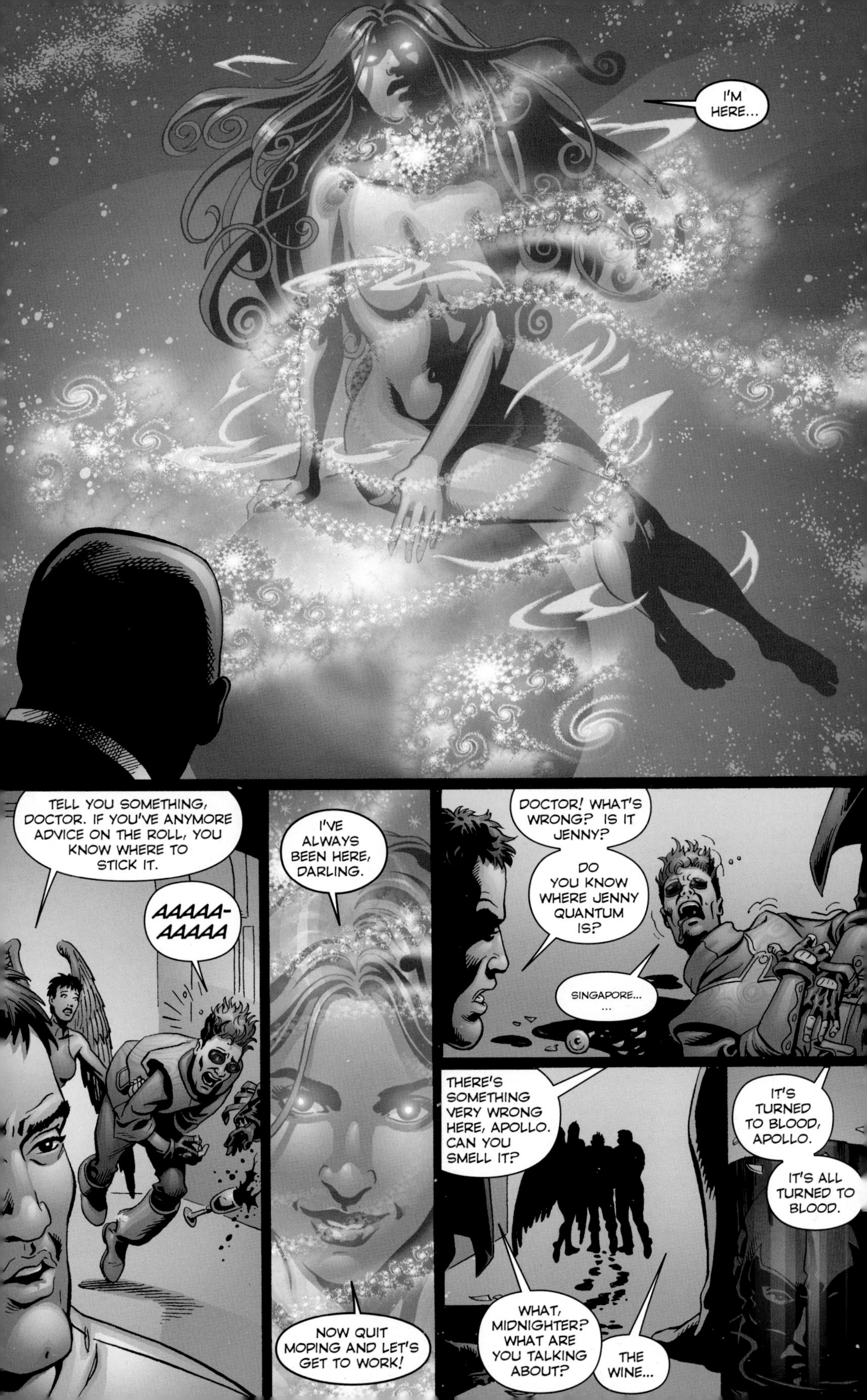
I'M HERE...
TELL YOU SOMETHING, DOCTOR. IF YOU'VE ANYMORE ADVICE ON THE ROLL, YOU KNOW WHERE TO STICK IT.
AAAAA-AAAAA
I'VE ALWAYS BEEN HERE, DARLING.
NOW QUIT MOPING AND LET'S GET TO WORK!
DOCTOR! WHAT'S WRONG? IS IT JENNY?
DO YOU KNOW WHERE JENNY QUANTUM IS?
SINGAPORE... ...
THERE'S SOMETHING VERY WRONG HERE, APOLLO. CAN YOU SMELL IT?
WHAT, MIDNIGHTER? WHAT ARE YOU TALKING ABOUT?
THE WINE...
IT'S TURNED TO BLOOD, APOLLO.
IT'S ALL TURNED TO BLOOD.

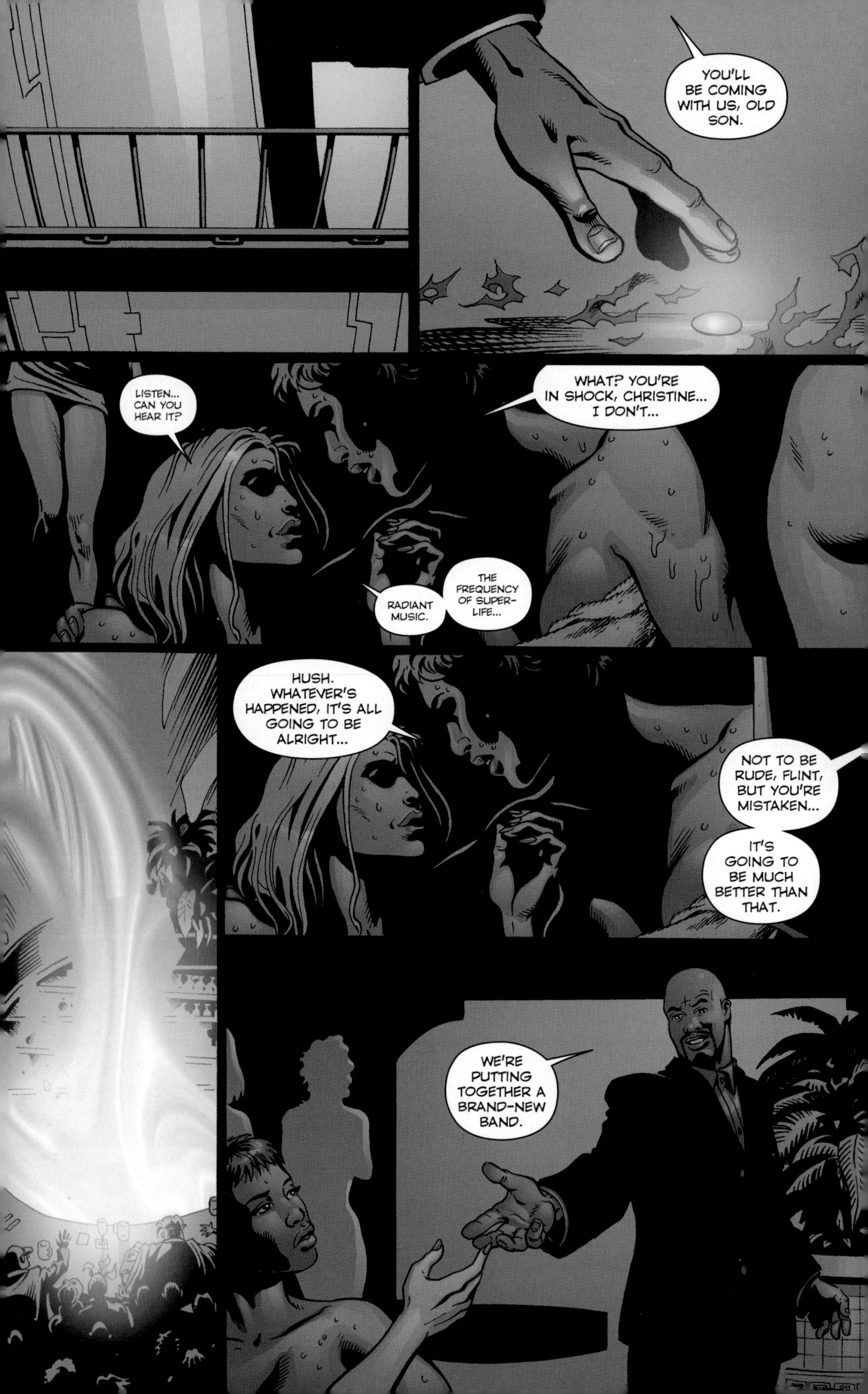

YOU'LL BE COMING WITH US, OLD SON.
LISTEN... CAN YOU HEAR IT?
WHAT? YOU'RE IN SHOCK, CHRISTINE... I DON'T...
RADIANT MUSIC.
THE FREQUENCY OF SUPER-LIFE...
HUSH. WHATEVER'S HAPPENED, IT'S ALL GOING TO BE ALRIGHT...
NOT TO BE RUDE, FLINT, BUT YOU'RE MISTAKEN...
IT'S GOING TO BE MUCH BETTER THAN THAT.
WE'RE PUTTING TOGETHER A BRAND-NEW BAND.

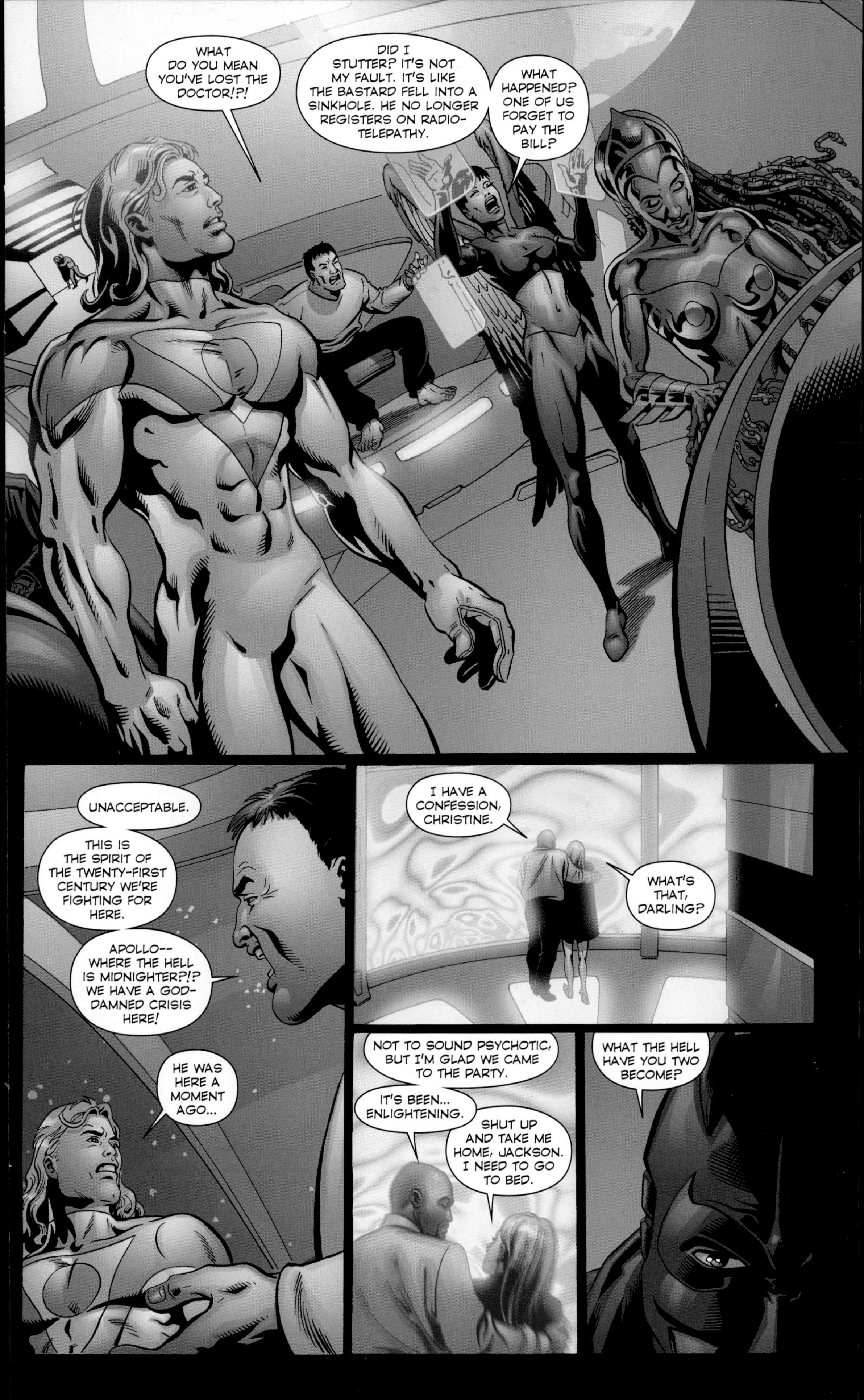
WHAT DO YOU MEAN YOU'VE LOST THE DOCTOR!?!
DID I STUTTER? IT'S NOT MY FAULT. IT'S LIKE THE BASTARD FELL INTO A SINKHOLE. HE NO LONGER REGISTERS ON RADIO-TELEPATHY.
WHAT HAPPENED? ONE OF US FORGET TO PAY THE BILL?
UNACCEPTABLE.
THIS IS THE SPIRIT OF THE TWENTY-FIRST CENTURY WE'RE FIGHTING FOR HERE.
APOLLO-- WHERE THE HELL IS MIDNIGHTER?!? WE HAVE A GOD-DAMNED CRISIS HERE!
HE WAS HERE A MOMENT AGO...
I HAVE A CONFESSION, CHRISTINE.
WHAT'S THAT, DARLING?
NOT TO SOUND PSYCHOTIC, BUT I'M GLAD WE CAME TO THE PARTY.
IT'S BEEN... ENLIGHTENING.
SHUT UP AND TAKE ME HOME, JACKSON. I NEED TO GO TO BED.
WHAT THE HELL HAVE YOU TWO BECOME?

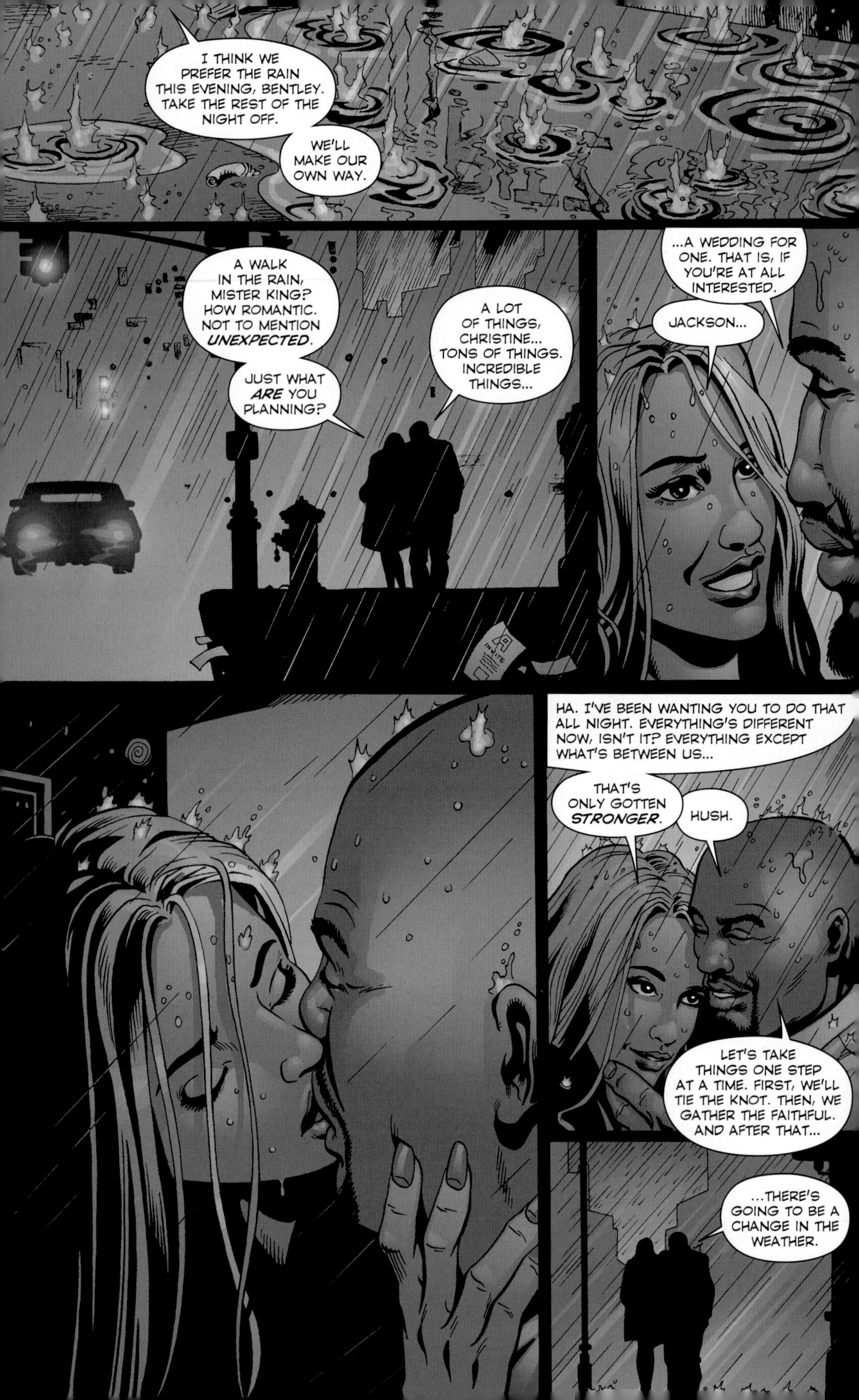
I THINK WE PREFER THE RAIN THIS EVENING, BENTLEY. TAKE THE REST OF THE NIGHT OFF.
WE'LL MAKE OUR OWN WAY.
A WALK IN THE RAIN, MISTER KING? HOW ROMANTIC. NOT TO MENTION *UNEXPECTED*.
JUST WHAT *ARE* YOU PLANNING?
A LOT OF THINGS, CHRISTINE... TONS OF THINGS. INCREDIBLE THINGS...
...A WEDDING FOR ONE. THAT IS, IF YOU'RE AT ALL INTERESTED.
JACKSON...
HA. I'VE BEEN WANTING YOU TO DO THAT ALL NIGHT. EVERYTHING'S DIFFERENT NOW, ISN'T IT? EVERYTHING EXCEPT WHAT'S BETWEEN US...
THAT'S ONLY GOTTEN *STRONGER*.
HUSH.
LET'S TAKE THINGS ONE STEP AT A TIME. FIRST, WE'LL TIE THE KNOT. THEN, WE GATHER THE FAITHFUL. AND AFTER THAT...
...THERE'S GOING TO BE A CHANGE IN THE WEATHER.

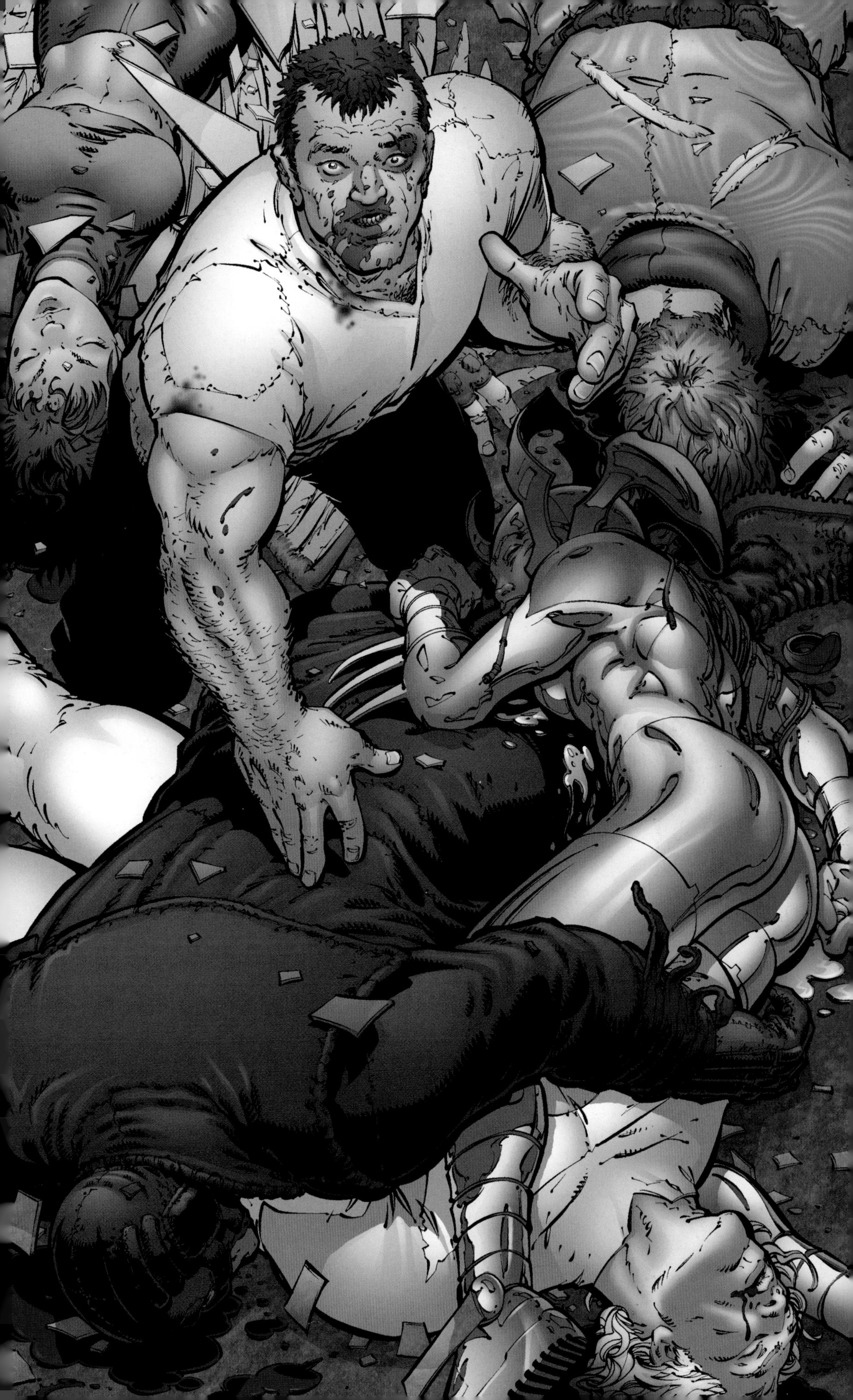

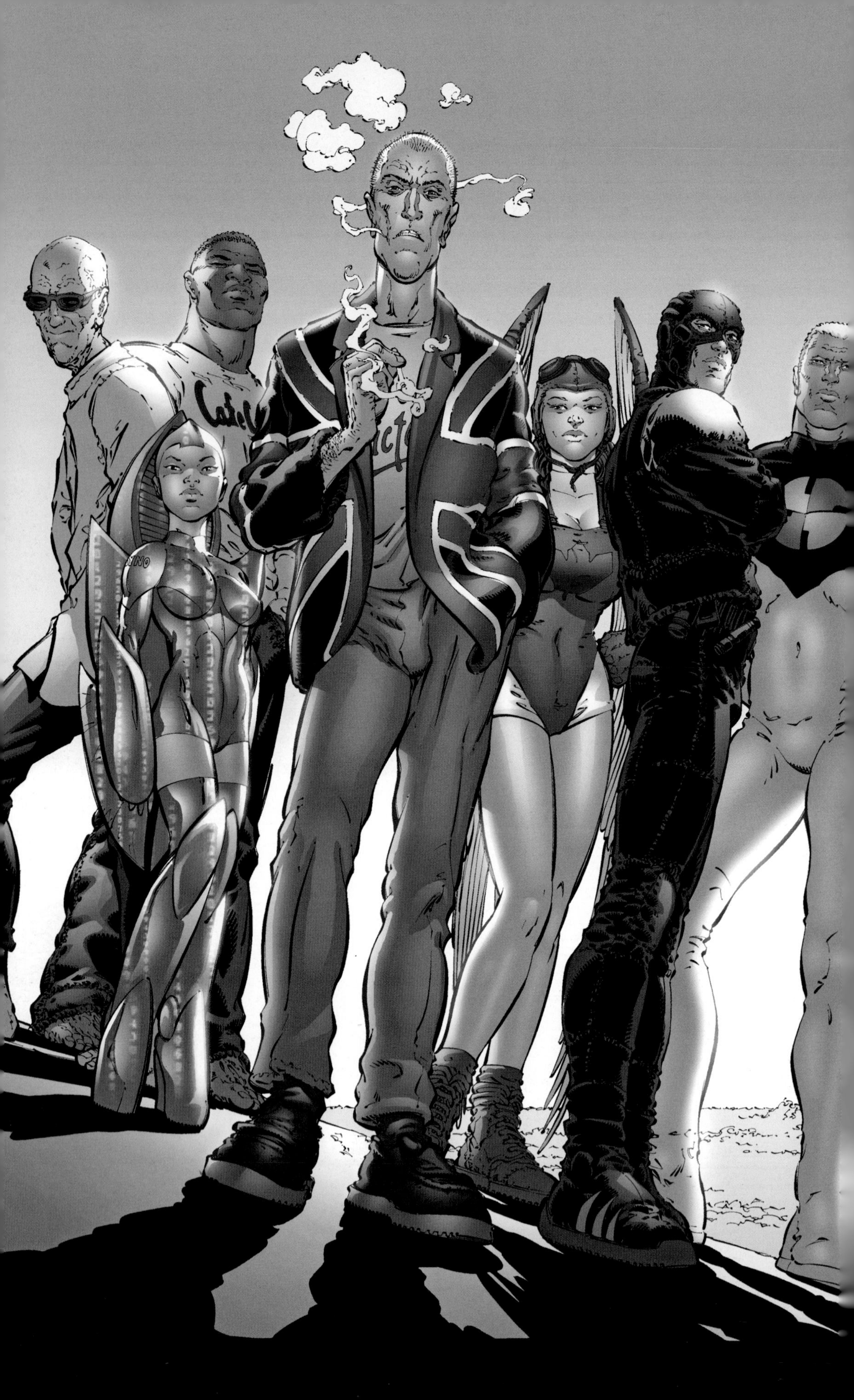

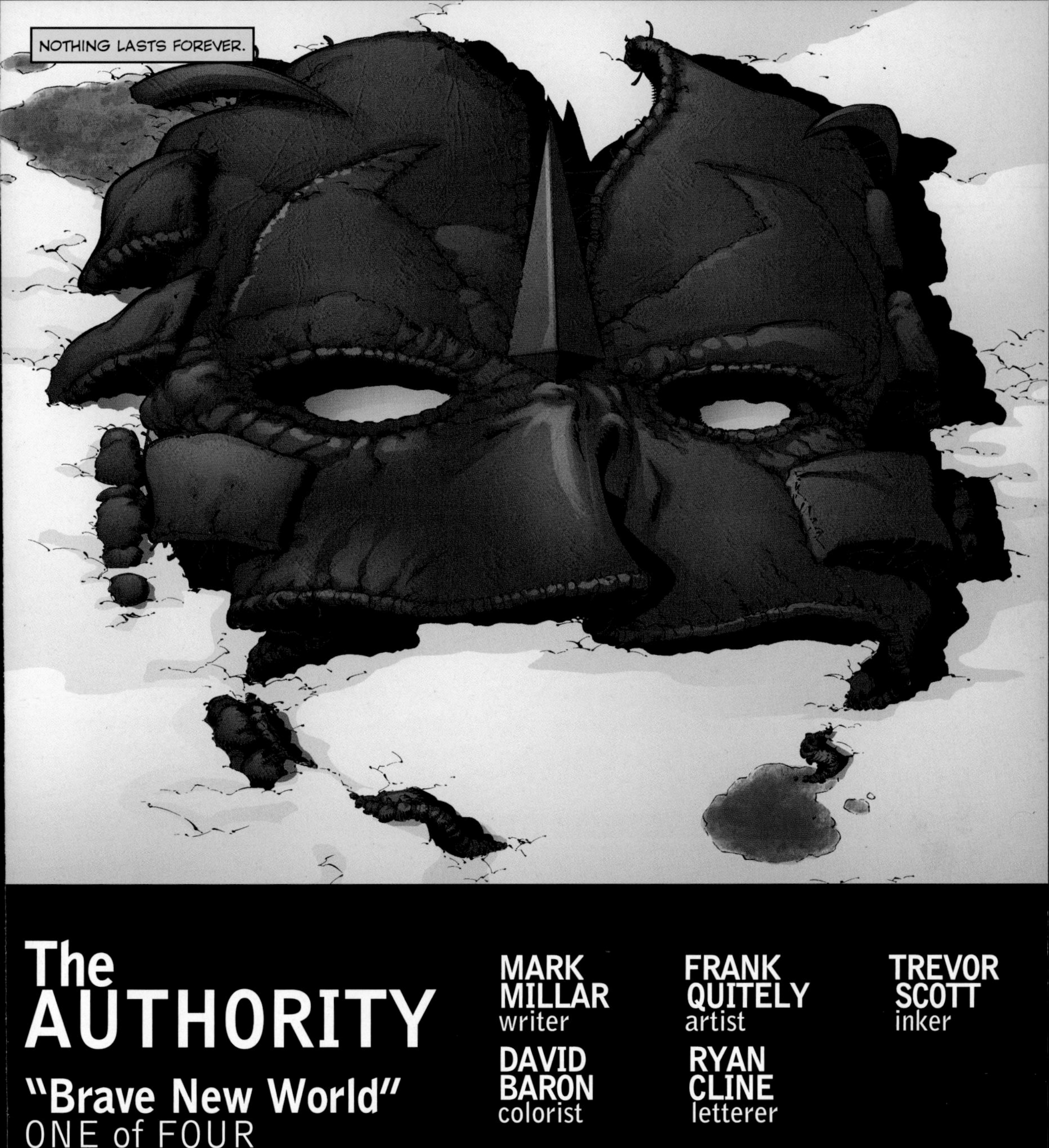
NOTHING LASTS FOREVER.

The AUTHORITY

"Brave New World"

ONE of FOUR

MARK MILLAR writer

FRANK QUITELY artist

TREVOR SCOTT inker

DAVID BARON colorist

RYAN CLINE letterer

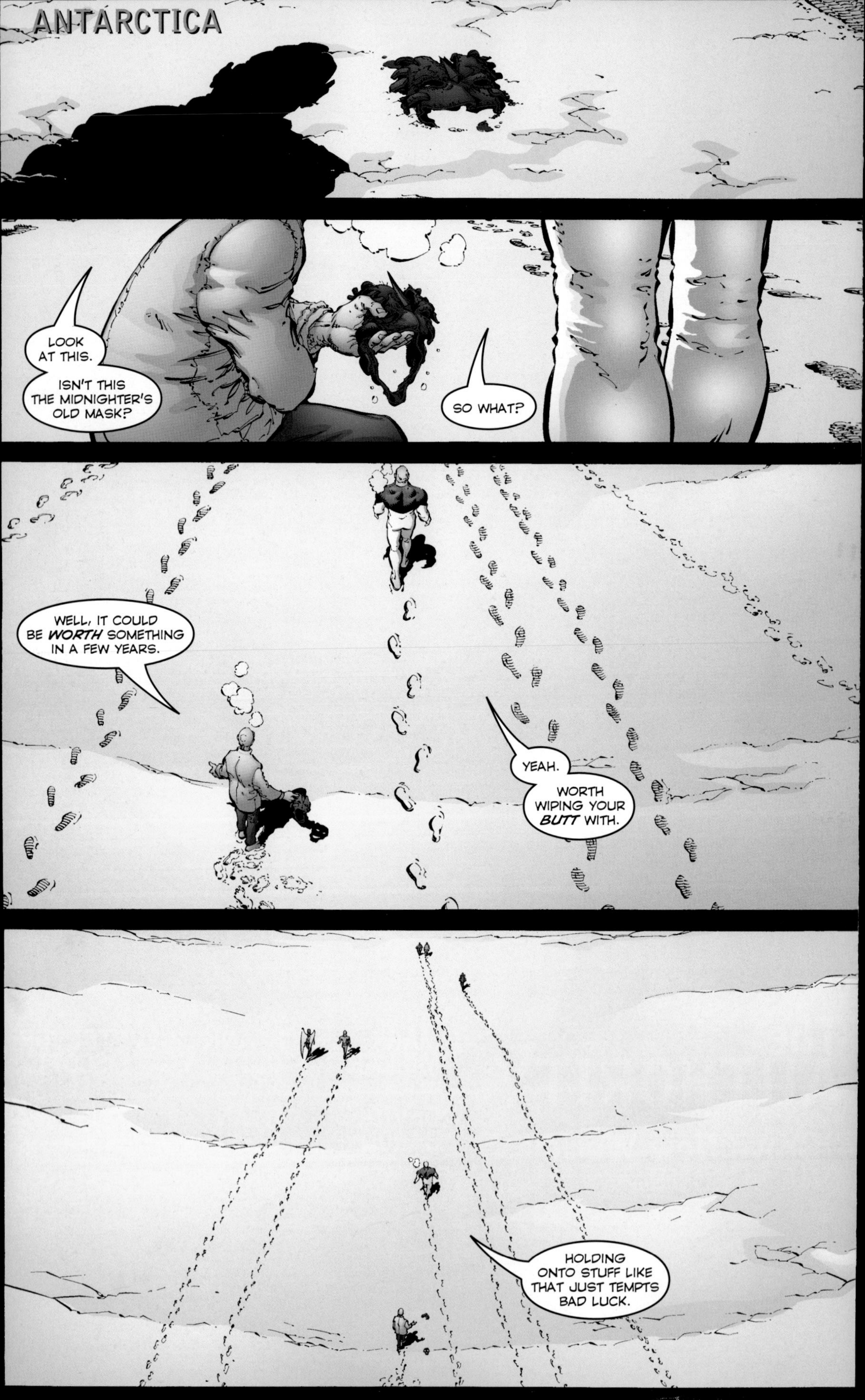
ANTARCTICA
LOOK AT THIS.
ISN'T THIS THE MIDNIGHTER'S OLD MASK?
SO WHAT?
WELL, IT COULD BE *WORTH* SOMETHING IN A FEW YEARS.
YEAH.
WORTH WIPING YOUR *BUTT* WITH.
HOLDING ONTO STUFF LIKE THAT JUST TEMPTS BAD LUCK.

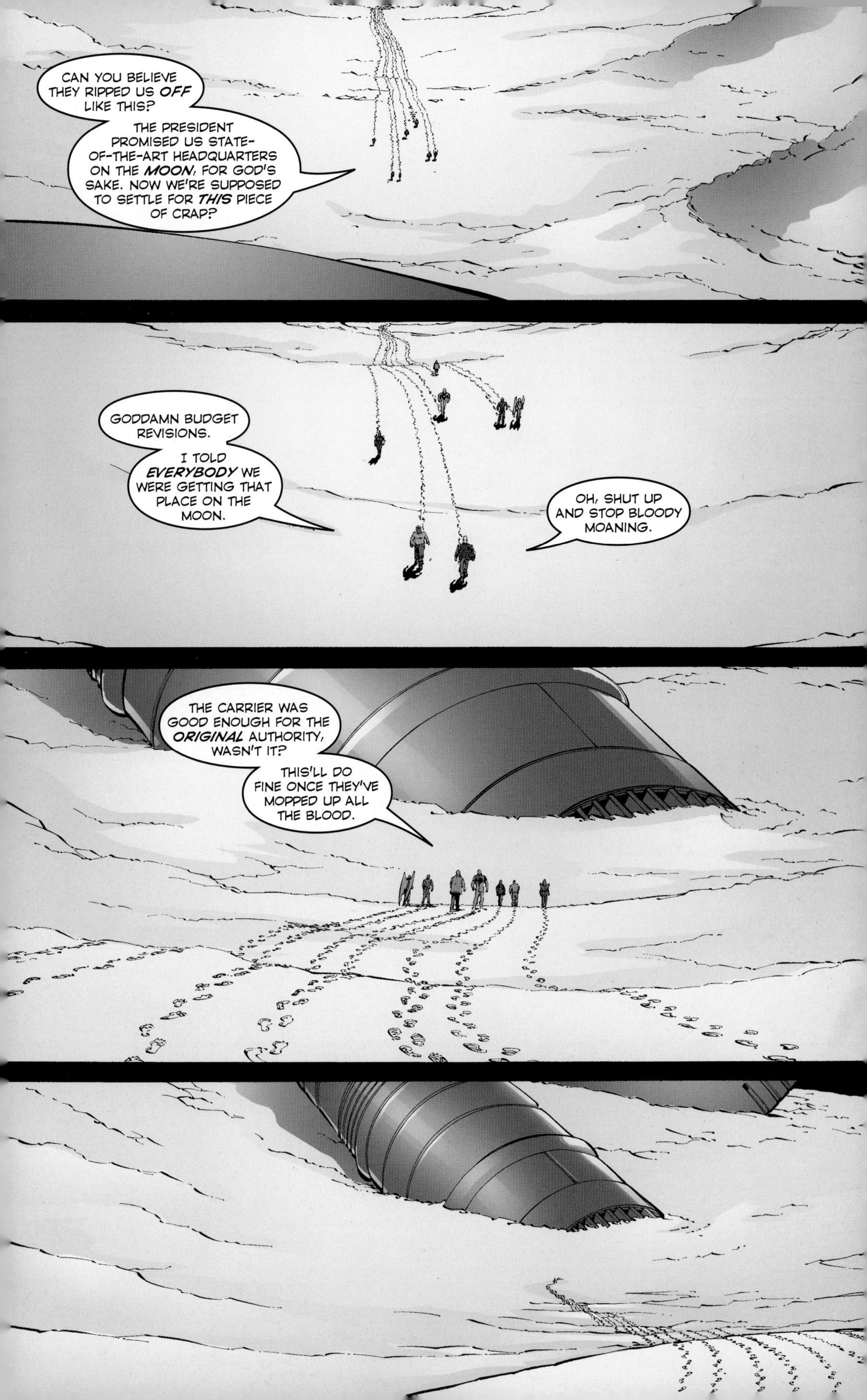
CAN YOU BELIEVE THEY RIPPED US OFF LIKE THIS?
THE PRESIDENT PROMISED US STATE-OF-THE-ART HEADQUARTERS ON THE MOON, FOR GOD'S SAKE. NOW WE'RE SUPPOSED TO SETTLE FOR THIS PIECE OF CRAP?
GODDAMN BUDGET REVISIONS.
I TOLD EVERYBODY WE WERE GETTING THAT PLACE ON THE MOON.
OH, SHUT UP AND STOP BLOODY MOANING.
THE CARRIER WAS GOOD ENOUGH FOR THE ORIGINAL AUTHORITY, WASN'T IT?
THIS'LL DO FINE ONCE THEY'VE MOPPED UP ALL THE BLOOD.

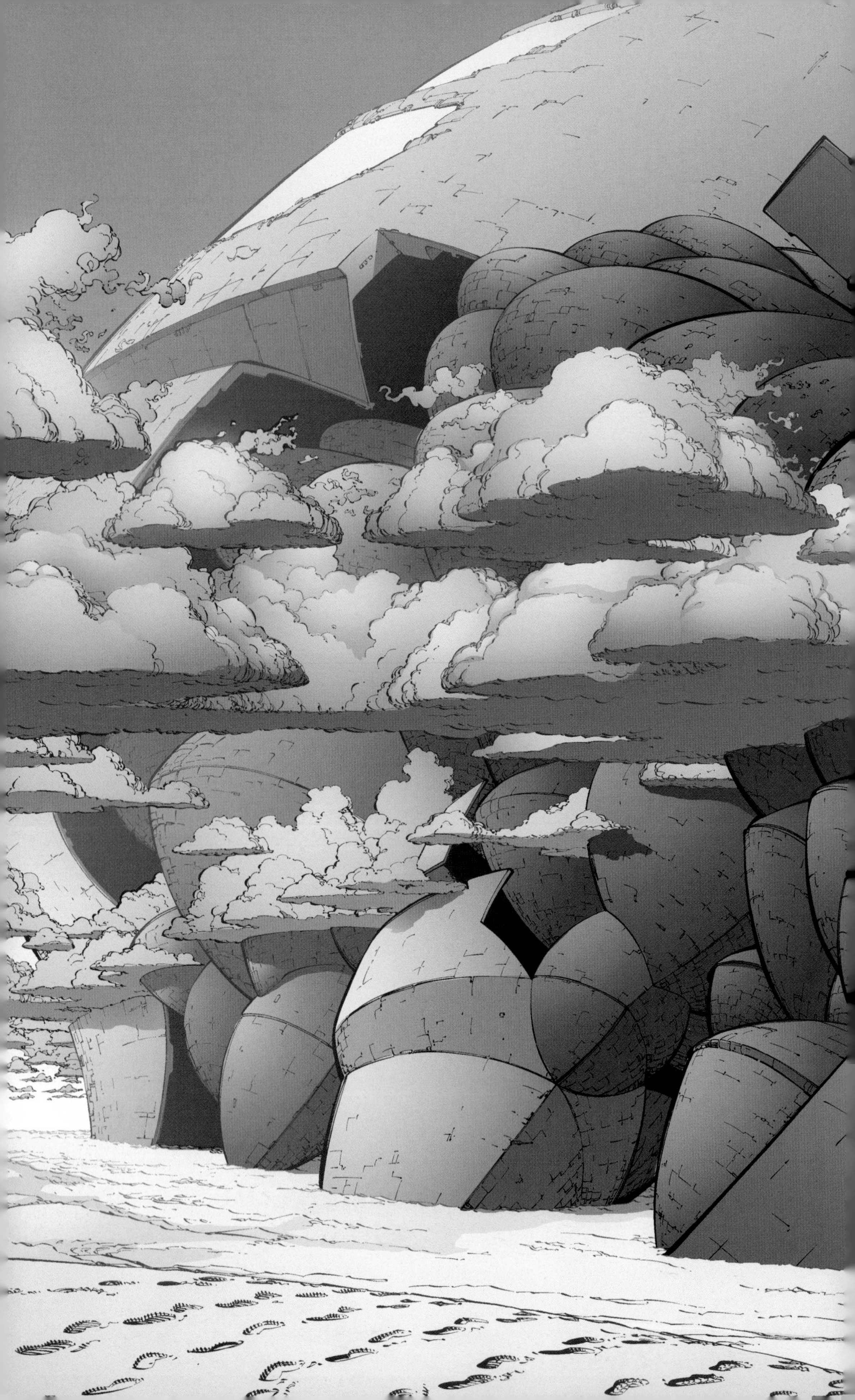

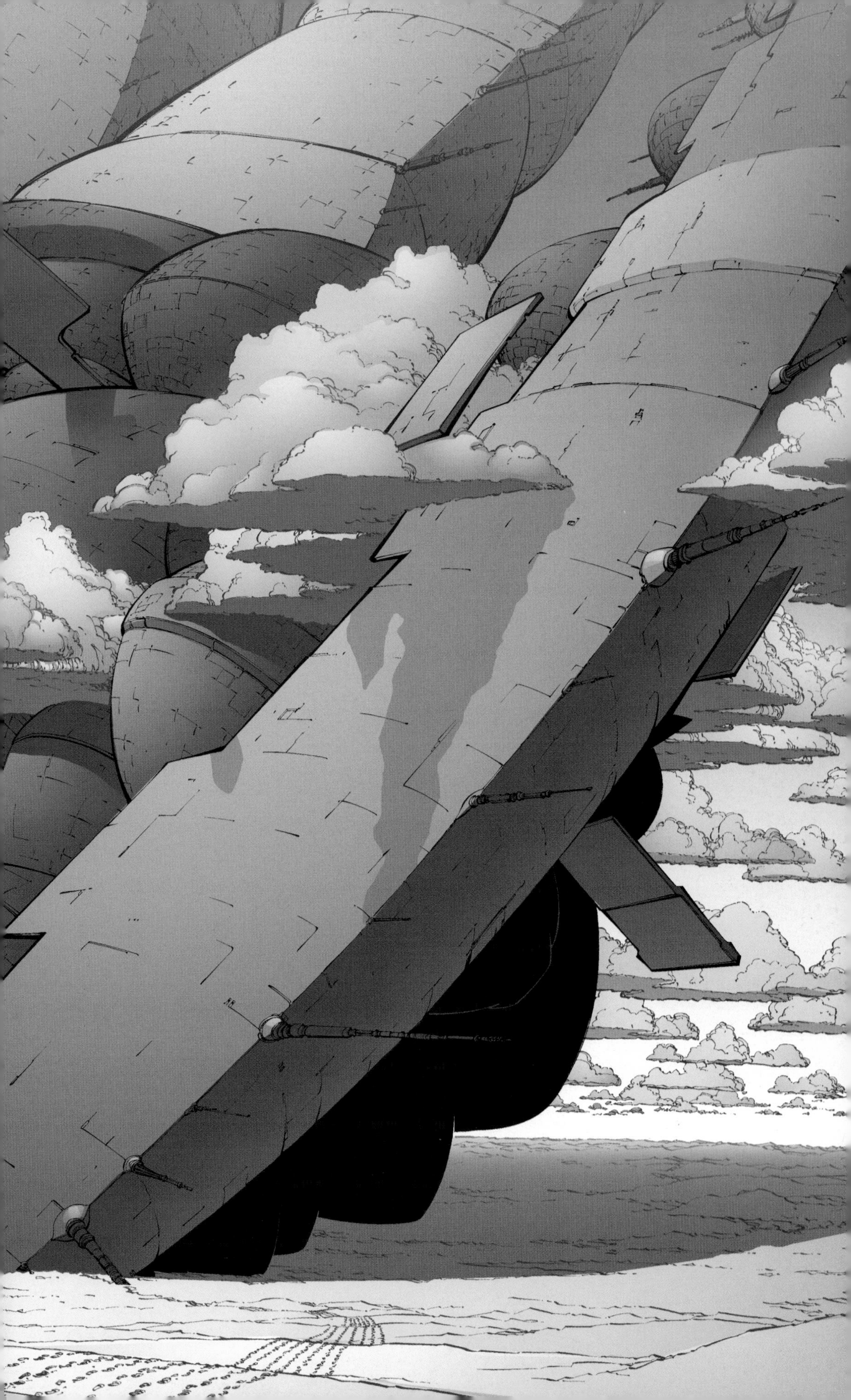

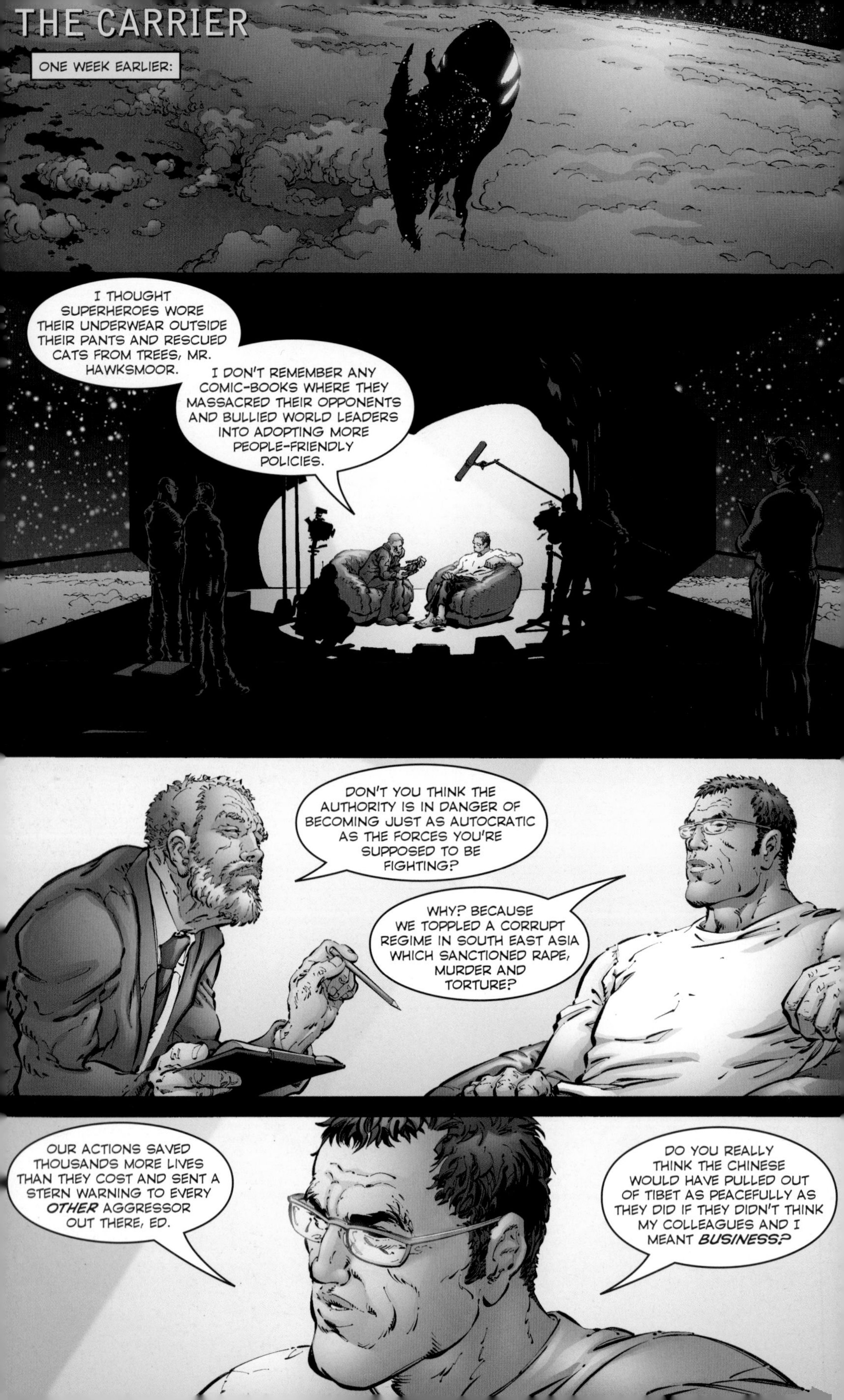
THE CARRIER
ONE WEEK EARLIER:
I THOUGHT SUPERHEROES WORE THEIR UNDERWEAR OUTSIDE THEIR PANTS AND RESCUED CATS FROM TREES, MR. HAWKSMOOR.
I DON'T REMEMBER ANY COMIC-BOOKS WHERE THEY MASSACRED THEIR OPPONENTS AND BULLIED WORLD LEADERS INTO ADOPTING MORE PEOPLE-FRIENDLY POLICIES.
DON'T YOU THINK THE AUTHORITY IS IN DANGER OF BECOMING JUST AS AUTOCRATIC AS THE FORCES YOU'RE SUPPOSED TO BE FIGHTING?
WHY? BECAUSE WE TOPPLED A CORRUPT REGIME IN SOUTH EAST ASIA WHICH SANCTIONED RAPE, MURDER AND TORTURE?
OUR ACTIONS SAVED THOUSANDS MORE LIVES THAN THEY COST AND SENT A STERN WARNING TO EVERY *OTHER* AGGRESSOR OUT THERE, ED.
DO YOU REALLY THINK THE CHINESE WOULD HAVE PULLED OUT OF TIBET AS PEACEFULLY AS THEY DID IF THEY DIDN'T THINK MY COLLEAGUES AND I MEANT *BUSINESS*?

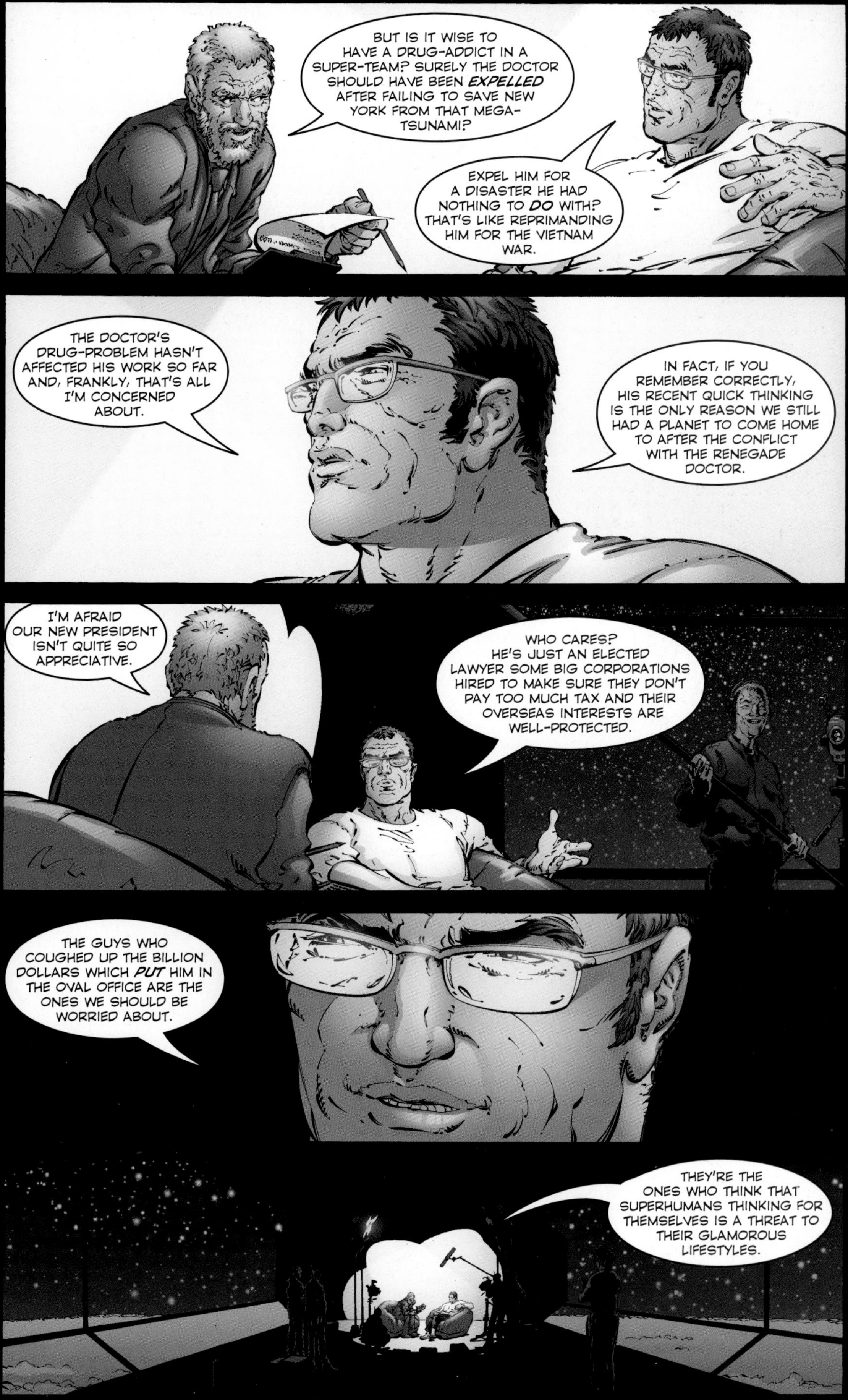

BUT IS IT WISE TO HAVE A DRUG-ADDICT IN A SUPER-TEAM? SURELY THE DOCTOR SHOULD HAVE BEEN *EXPELLED* AFTER FAILING TO SAVE NEW YORK FROM THAT MEGA-TSUNAMI?
EXPEL HIM FOR A DISASTER HE HAD NOTHING TO *DO* WITH? THAT'S LIKE REPRIMANDING HIM FOR THE VIETNAM WAR.
THE DOCTOR'S DRUG-PROBLEM HASN'T AFFECTED HIS WORK SO FAR AND, FRANKLY, THAT'S ALL I'M CONCERNED ABOUT.
IN FACT, IF YOU REMEMBER CORRECTLY, HIS RECENT QUICK THINKING IS THE ONLY REASON WE STILL HAD A PLANET TO COME HOME TO AFTER THE CONFLICT WITH THE RENEGADE DOCTOR.
I'M AFRAID OUR NEW PRESIDENT ISN'T QUITE SO APPRECIATIVE.
WHO CARES? HE'S JUST AN ELECTED LAWYER SOME BIG CORPORATIONS HIRED TO MAKE SURE THEY DON'T PAY TOO MUCH TAX AND THEIR OVERSEAS INTERESTS ARE WELL-PROTECTED.
THE GUYS WHO COUGHED UP THE BILLION DOLLARS WHICH *PUT* HIM IN THE OVAL OFFICE ARE THE ONES WE SHOULD BE WORRIED ABOUT.
THEY'RE THE ONES WHO THINK THAT SUPERHUMANS THINKING FOR THEMSELVES IS A THREAT TO THEIR GLAMOROUS LIFESTYLES.

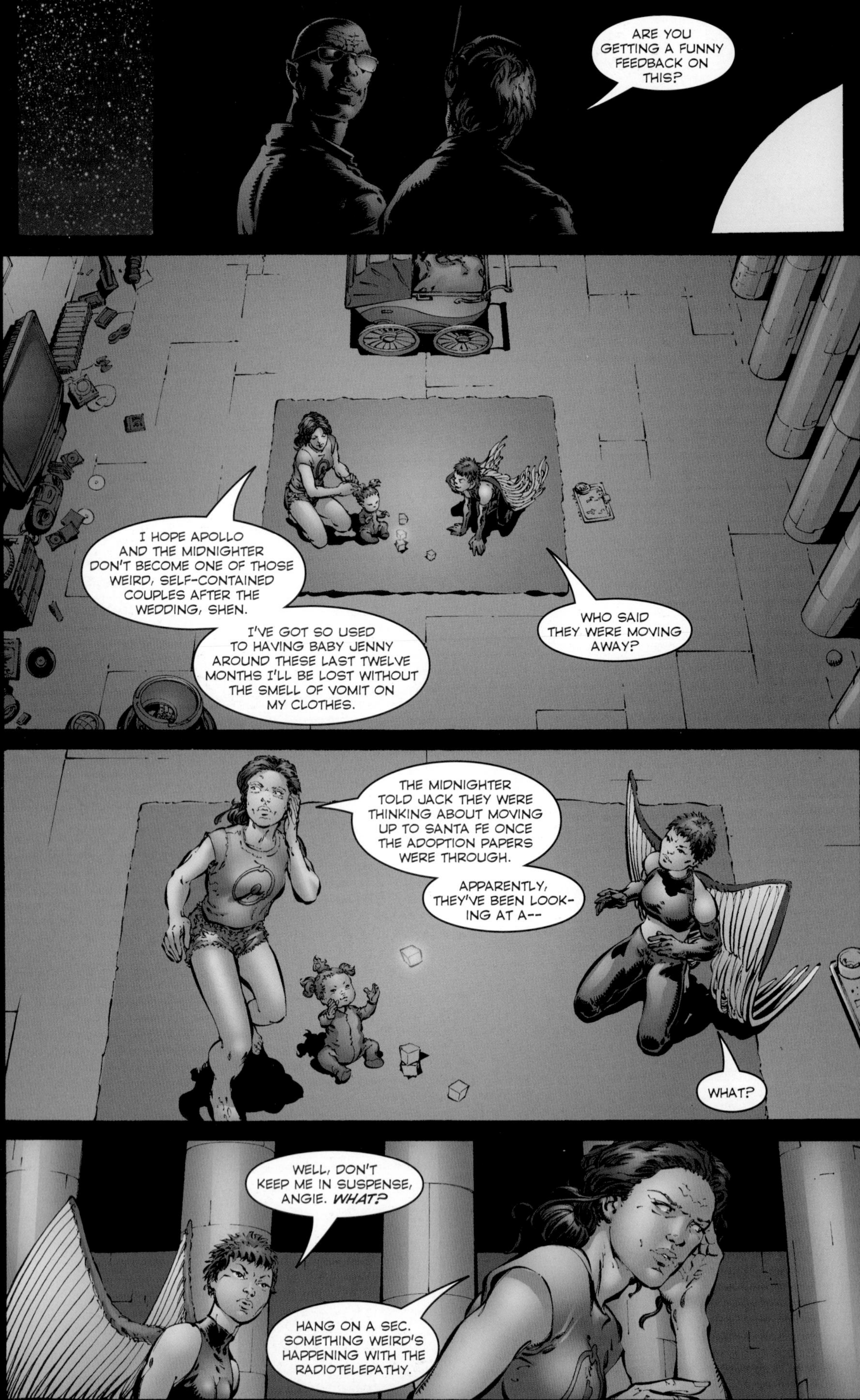
ARE YOU GETTING A FUNNY FEEDBACK ON THIS?
I HOPE APOLLO AND THE MIDNIGHTER DON'T BECOME ONE OF THOSE WEIRD, SELF-CONTAINED COUPLES AFTER THE WEDDING, SHEN.
I'VE GOT SO USED TO HAVING BABY JENNY AROUND THESE LAST TWELVE MONTHS I'LL BE LOST WITHOUT THE SMELL OF VOMIT ON MY CLOTHES.
WHO SAID THEY WERE MOVING AWAY?
THE MIDNIGHTER TOLD JACK THEY WERE THINKING ABOUT MOVING UP TO SANTA FE ONCE THE ADOPTION PAPERS WERE THROUGH.
APPARENTLY, THEY'VE BEEN LOOKING AT A--
WHAT?
WELL, DON'T KEEP ME IN SUSPENSE, ANGIE. *WHAT?*
HANG ON A SEC. SOMETHING WEIRD'S HAPPENING WITH THE RADIOTELEPATHY.

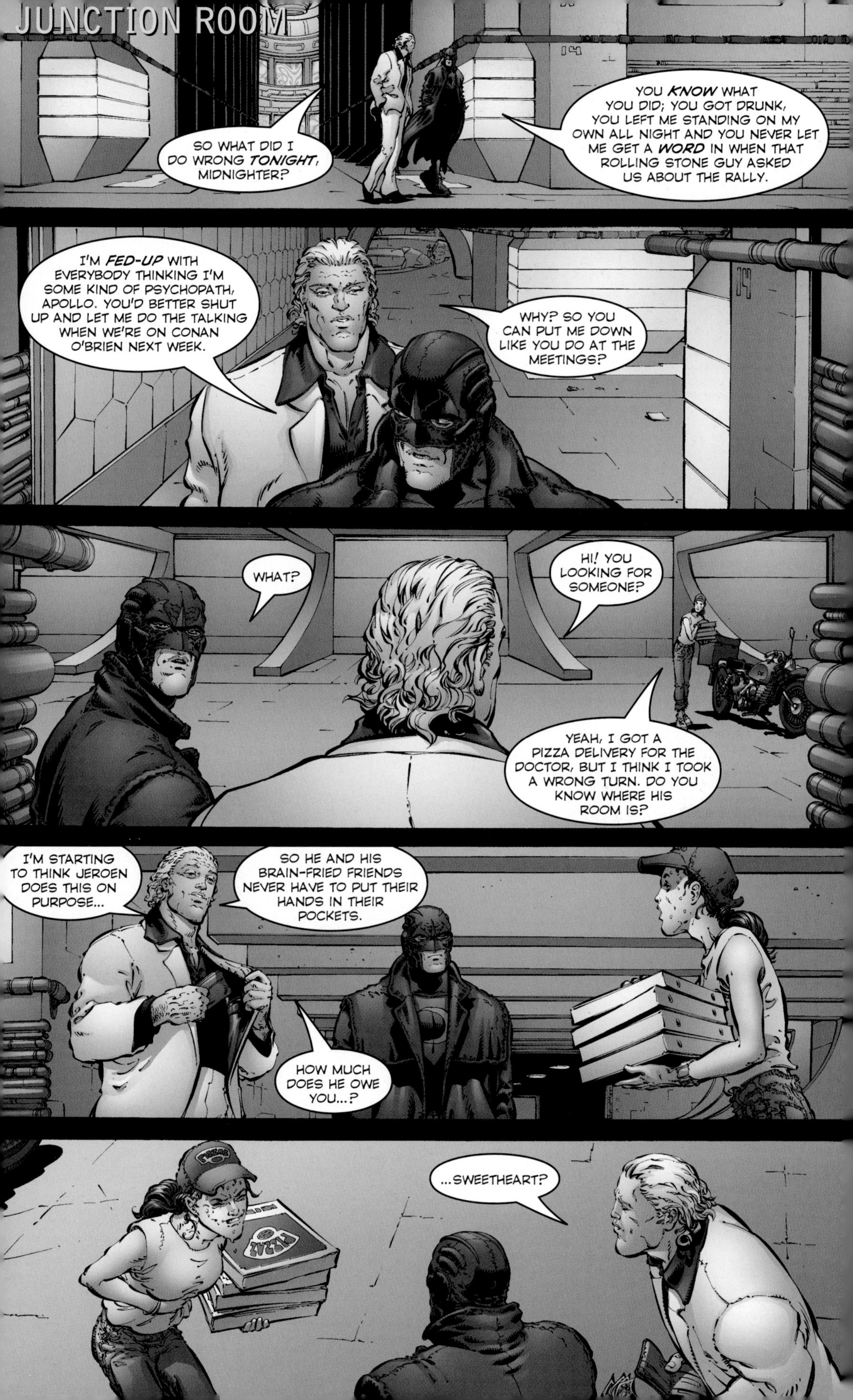
JUNCTION ROOM
SO WHAT DID I DO WRONG *TONIGHT*, MIDNIGHTER?
YOU *KNOW* WHAT YOU DID; YOU GOT DRUNK, YOU LEFT ME STANDING ON MY OWN ALL NIGHT AND YOU NEVER LET ME GET A *WORD* IN WHEN THAT ROLLING STONE GUY ASKED US ABOUT THE RALLY.
I'M *FED-UP* WITH EVERYBODY THINKING I'M SOME KIND OF PSYCHOPATH, APOLLO. YOU'D BETTER SHUT UP AND LET ME DO THE TALKING WHEN WE'RE ON CONAN O'BRIEN NEXT WEEK.
WHY? SO YOU CAN PUT ME DOWN LIKE YOU DO AT THE MEETINGS?
WHAT?
HI! YOU LOOKING FOR SOMEONE?
YEAH, I GOT A PIZZA DELIVERY FOR THE DOCTOR, BUT I THINK I TOOK A WRONG TURN. DO YOU KNOW WHERE HIS ROOM IS?
I'M STARTING TO THINK JEROEN DOES THIS ON PURPOSE...
SO HE AND HIS BRAIN-FRIED FRIENDS NEVER HAVE TO PUT THEIR HANDS IN THEIR POCKETS.
HOW MUCH DOES HE OWE YOU...?
...SWEETHEART?

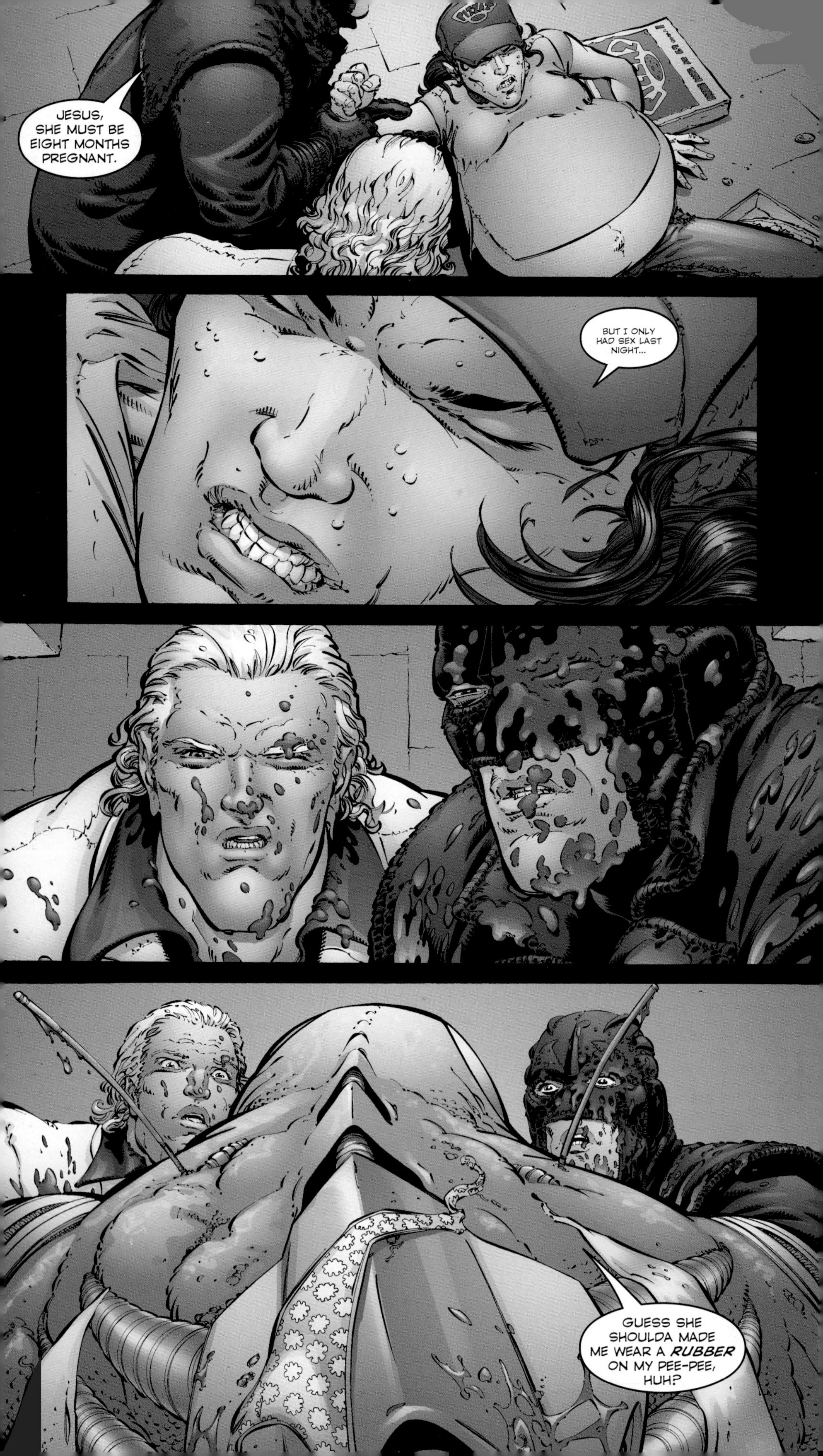
JESUS, SHE MUST BE EIGHT MONTHS PREGNANT.
BUT I ONLY HAD SEX LAST NIGHT...
GUESS SHE SHOULDA MADE ME WEAR A *RUBBER* ON MY PEE-PEE, HUH?

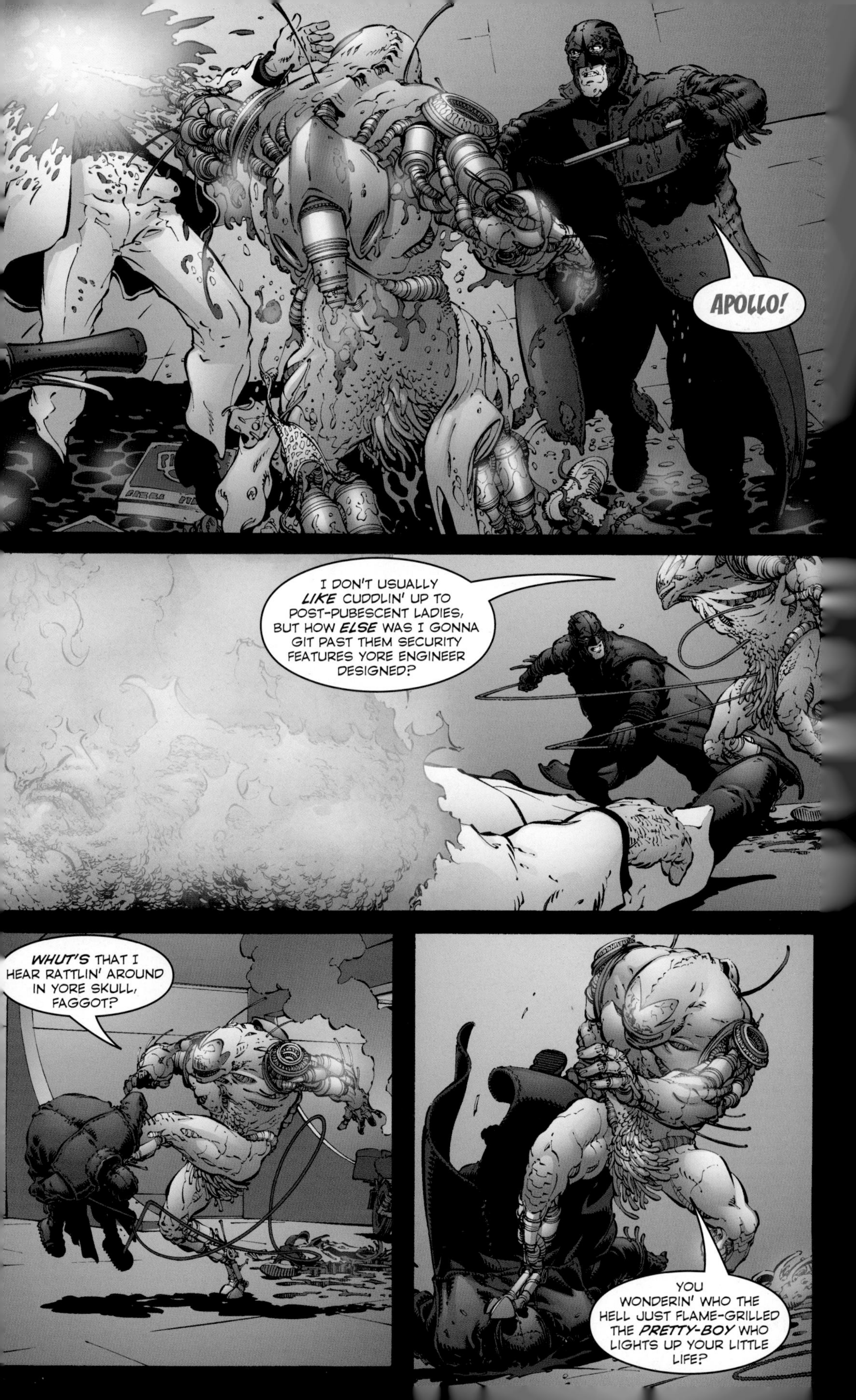
APOLLO!
I DON'T USUALLY *LIKE* CUDDLIN' UP TO POST-PUBESCENT LADIES, BUT HOW *ELSE* WAS I GONNA GIT PAST THEM SECURITY FEATURES YORE ENGINEER DESIGNED?
WHUT'S THAT I HEAR RATTLIN' AROUND IN YORE SKULL, FAGGOT?
YOU WONDERIN' WHO THE HELL JUST FLAME-GRILLED THE *PRETTY-BOY* WHO LIGHTS UP YOUR LITTLE LIFE?

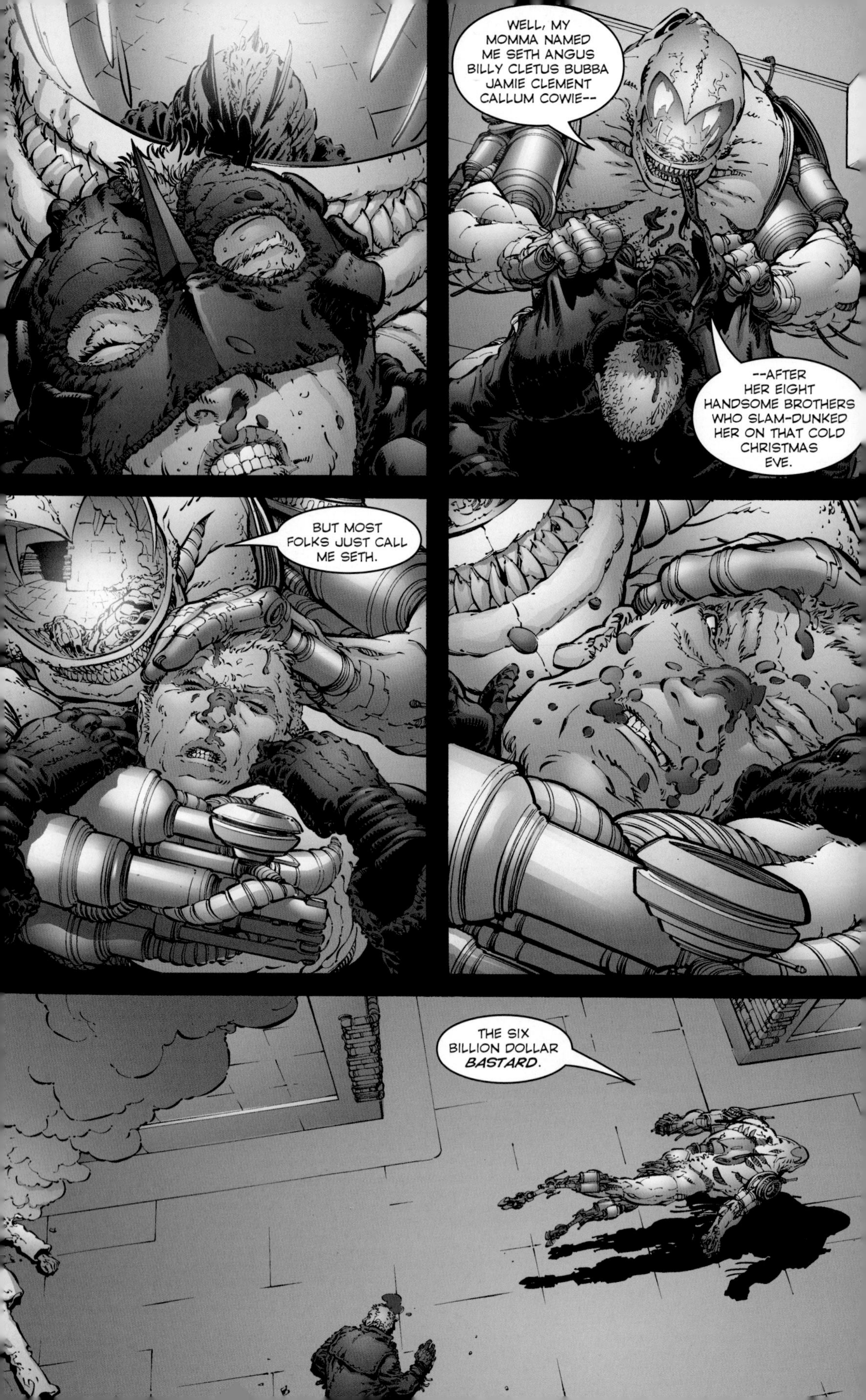
WELL, MY MOMMA NAMED ME SETH ANGUS BILLY CLETUS BUBBA JAMIE CLEMENT CALLUM COWIE--
--AFTER HER EIGHT HANDSOME BROTHERS WHO SLAM-DUNKED HER ON THAT COLD CHRISTMAS EVE.
BUT MOST FOLKS JUST CALL ME SETH.
THE SIX BILLION DOLLAR *BASTARD*.

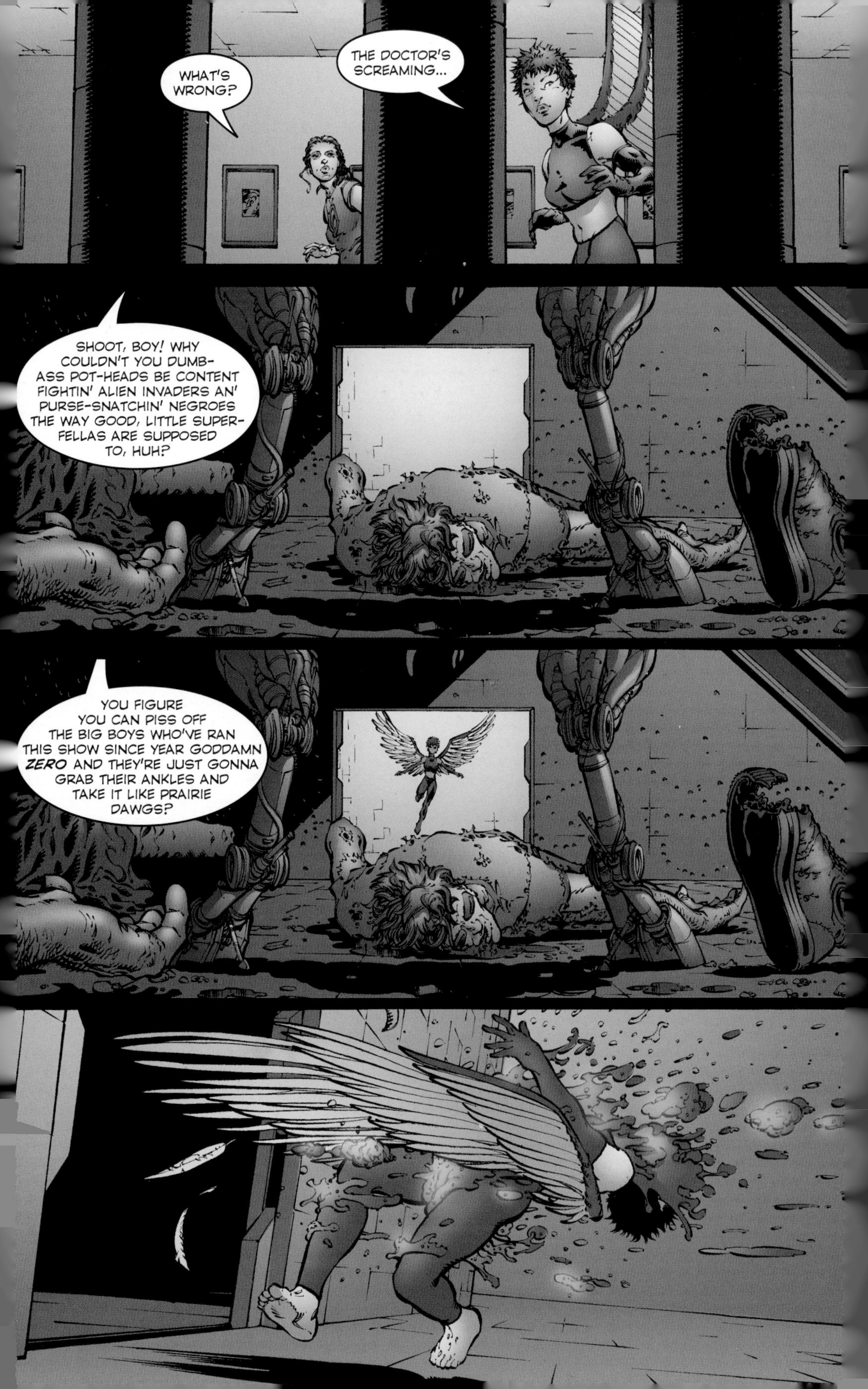
WHAT'S WRONG?
THE DOCTOR'S SCREAMING...
SHOOT, BOY! WHY COULDN'T YOU DUMB-ASS POT-HEADS BE CONTENT FIGHTIN' ALIEN INVADERS AN' PURSE-SNATCHIN' NEGROES THE WAY GOOD, LITTLE SUPER-FELLAS ARE SUPPOSED TO, HUH?
YOU FIGURE YOU CAN PISS OFF THE BIG BOYS WHO'VE RAN THIS SHOW SINCE YEAR GODDAMN ***ZERO*** AND THEY'RE JUST GONNA GRAB THEIR ANKLES AND TAKE IT LIKE PRAIRIE DAWGS?

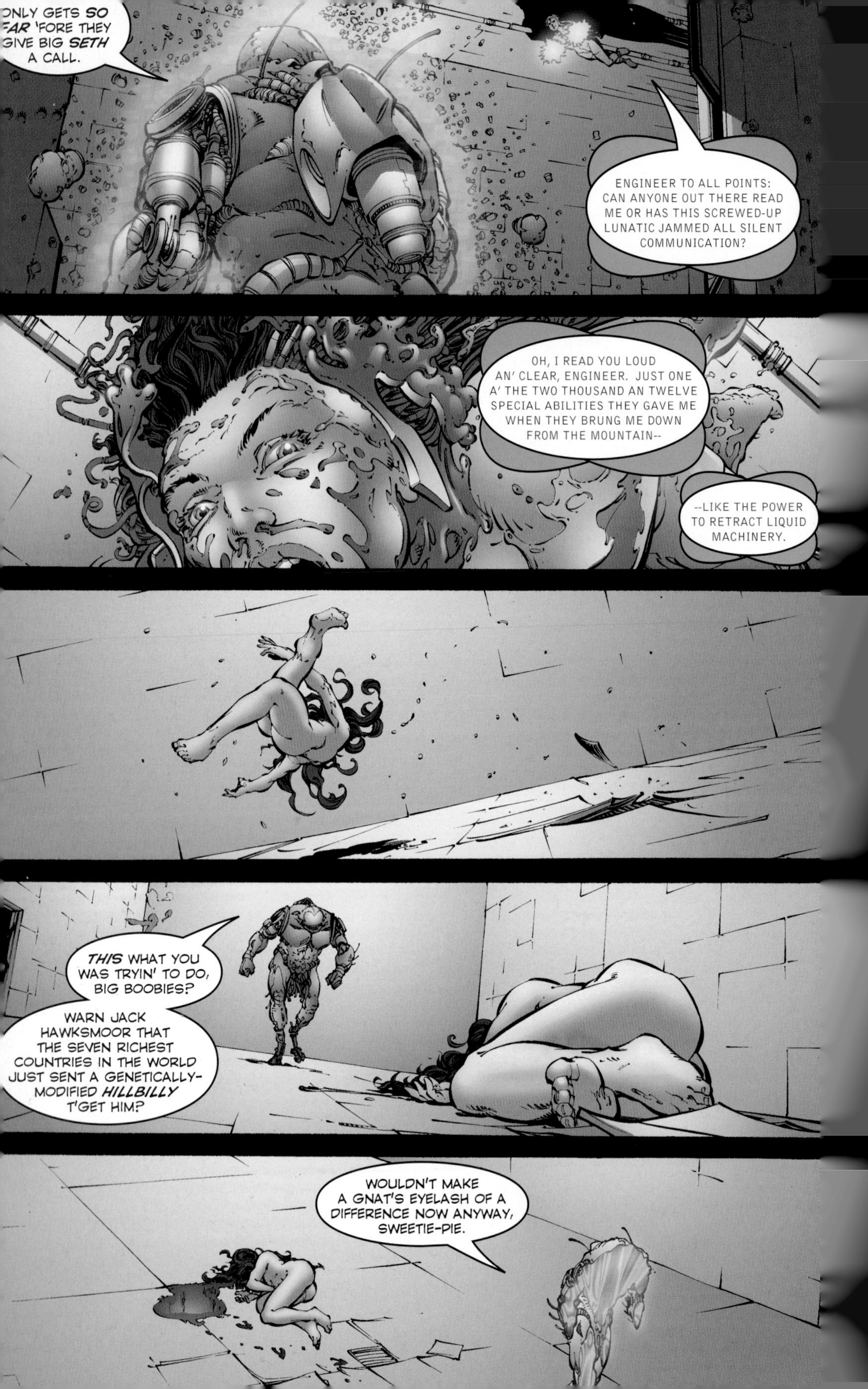

ONLY GETS SO FAR 'FORE THEY GIVE BIG SETH A CALL.
ENGINEER TO ALL POINTS: CAN ANYONE OUT THERE READ ME OR HAS THIS SCREWED-UP LUNATIC JAMMED ALL SILENT COMMUNICATION?
OH, I READ YOU LOUD AN' CLEAR, ENGINEER. JUST ONE A' THE TWO THOUSAND AN TWELVE SPECIAL ABILITIES THEY GAVE ME WHEN THEY BRUNG ME DOWN FROM THE MOUNTAIN--
--LIKE THE POWER TO RETRACT LIQUID MACHINERY.
THIS WHAT YOU WAS TRYIN' TO DO, BIG BOOBIES?
WARN JACK HAWKSMOOR THAT THE SEVEN RICHEST COUNTRIES IN THE WORLD JUST SENT A GENETICALLY-MODIFIED HILLBILLY T'GET HIM?
WOULDN'T MAKE A GNAT'S EYELASH OF A DIFFERENCE NOW ANYWAY, SWEETIE-PIE.

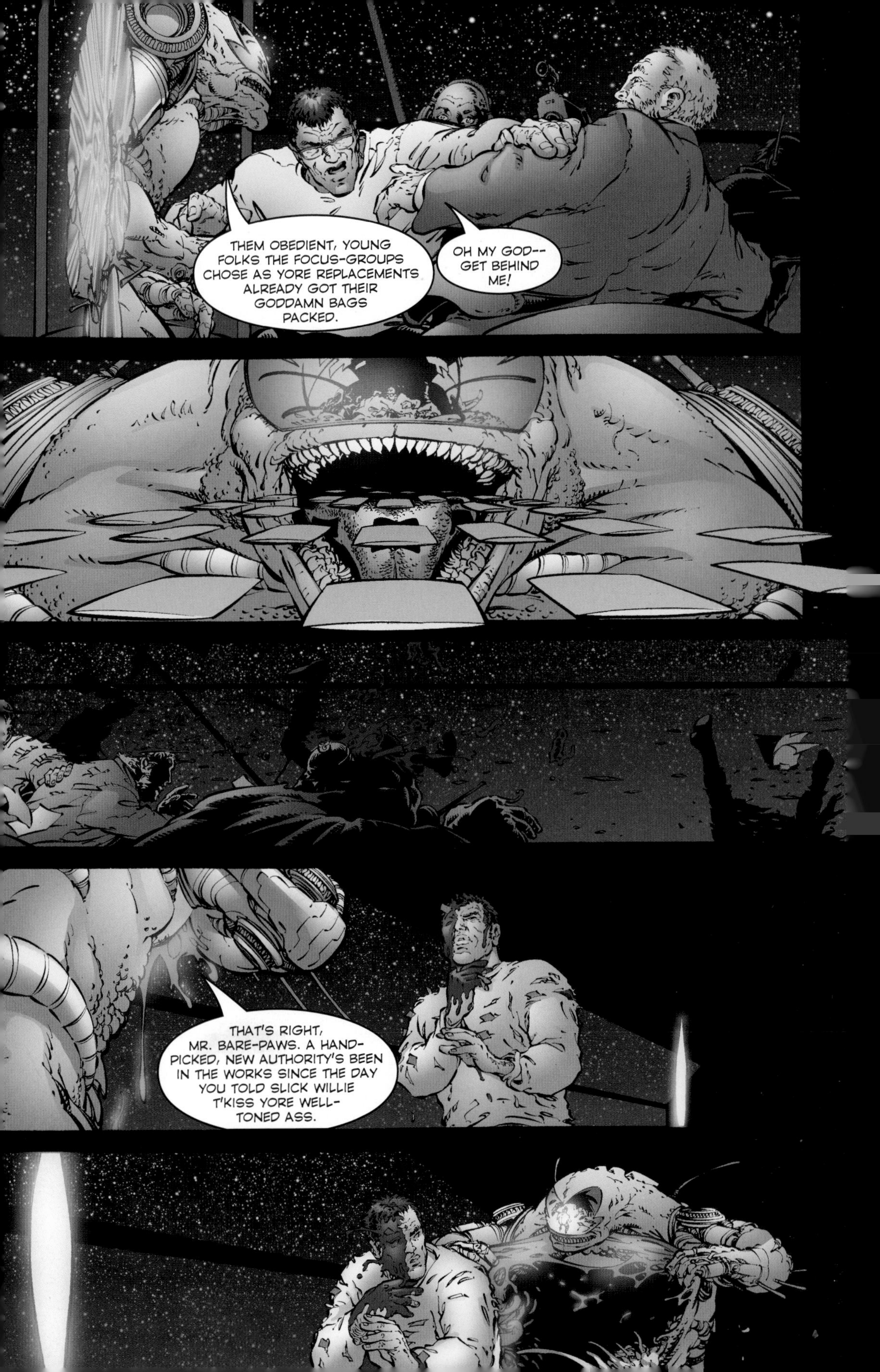
THEM OBEDIENT, YOUNG FOLKS THE FOCUS-GROUPS CHOSE AS YORE REPLACEMENTS ALREADY GOT THEIR GODDAMN BAGS PACKED.
OH MY GOD-- GET BEHIND ME!
THAT'S RIGHT, MR. BARE-PAWS. A HAND-PICKED, NEW AUTHORITY'S BEEN IN THE WORKS SINCE THE DAY YOU TOLD SLICK WILLIE T'KISS YORE WELL-TONED ASS.

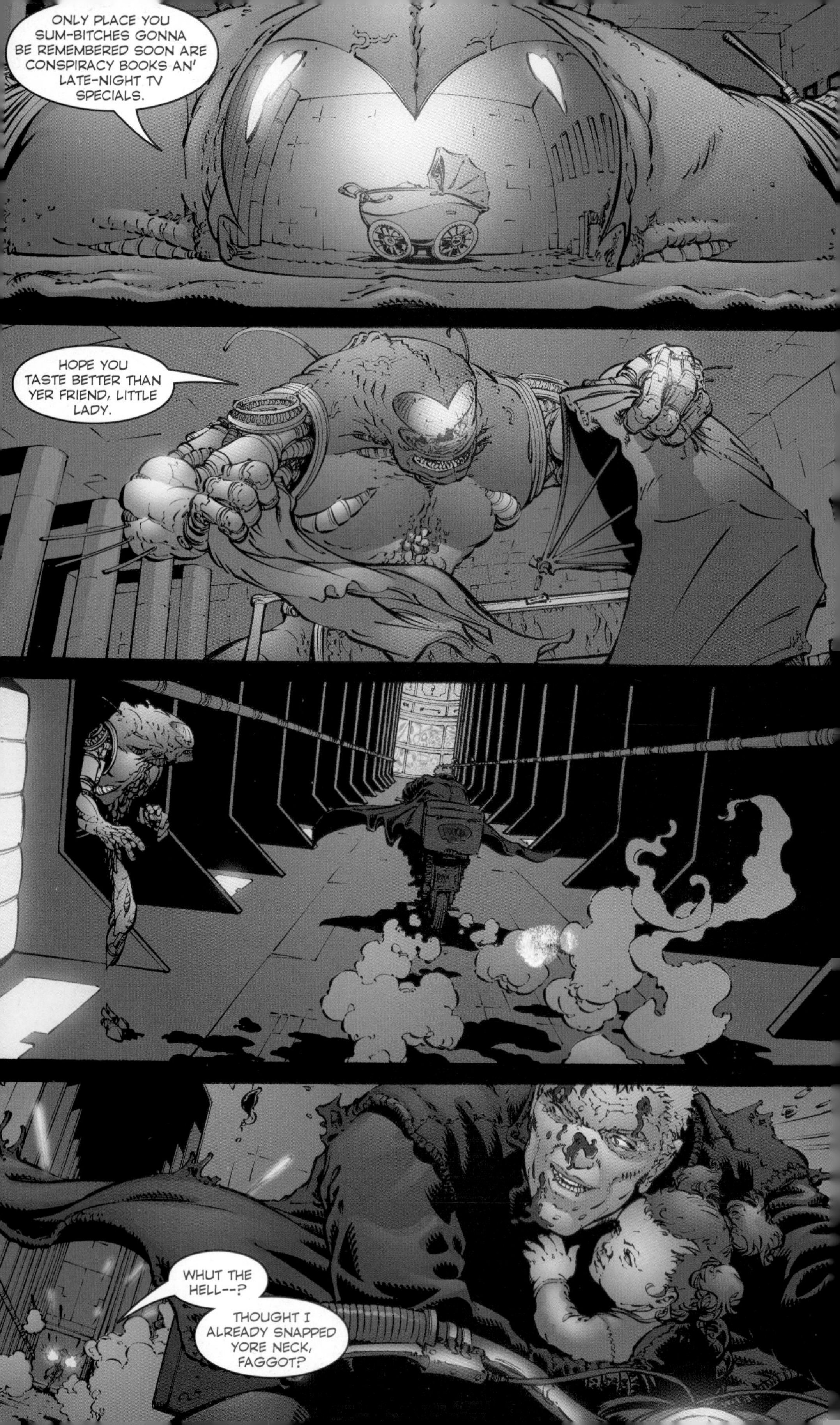
ONLY PLACE YOU SUM-BITCHES GONNA BE REMEMBERED SOON ARE CONSPIRACY BOOKS AN' LATE-NIGHT TV SPECIALS.
HOPE YOU TASTE BETTER THAN YER FRIEND, LITTLE LADY.
WHUT THE HELL--?
THOUGHT I ALREADY SNAPPED YORE NECK, FAGGOT?

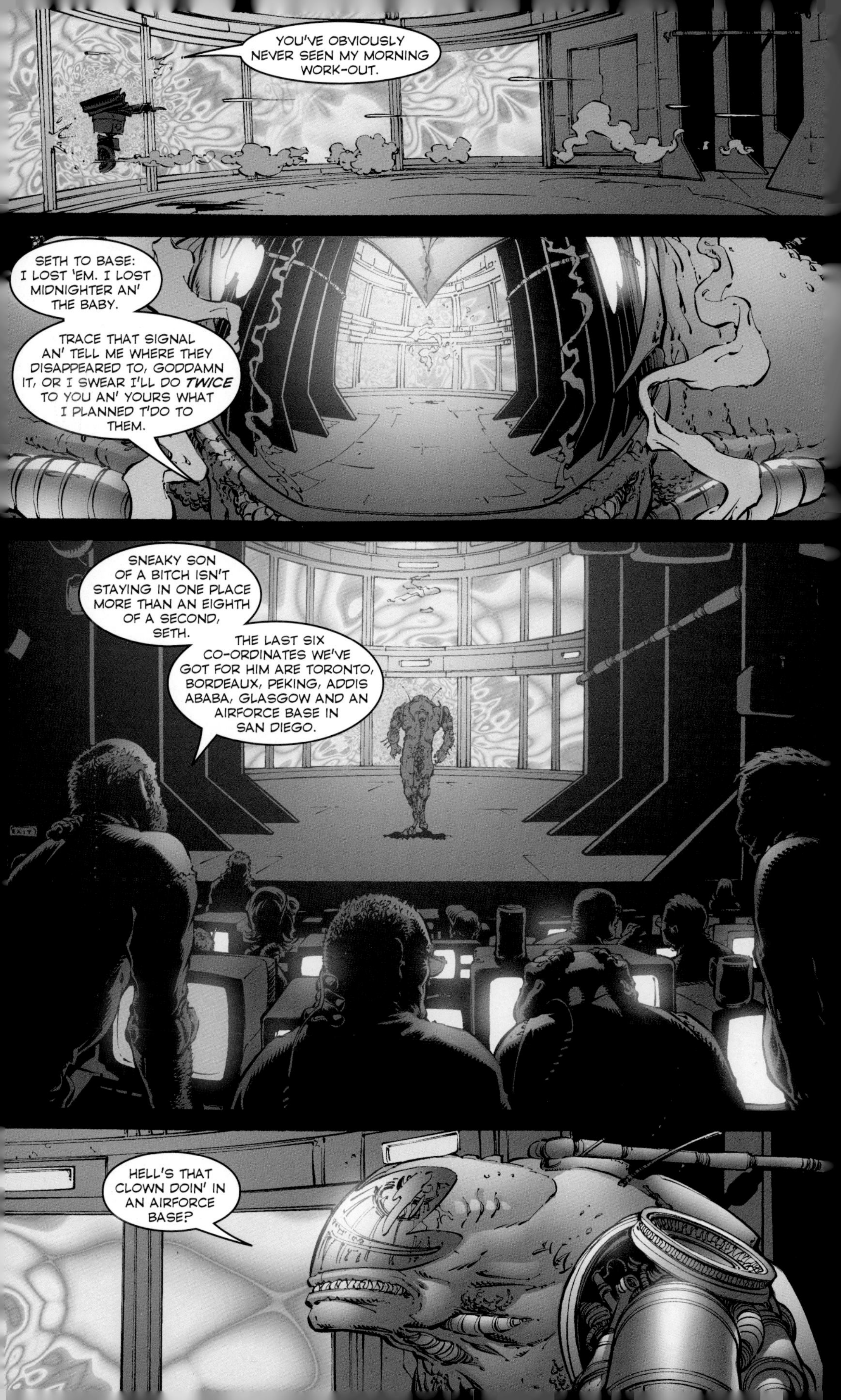
YOU'VE OBVIOUSLY NEVER SEEN MY MORNING WORK-OUT.
SETH TO BASE: I LOST 'EM. I LOST MIDNIGHTER AN' THE BABY.
TRACE THAT SIGNAL AN' TELL ME WHERE THEY DISAPPEARED TO, GODDAMN IT, OR I SWEAR I'LL DO *TWICE* TO YOU AN' YOURS WHAT I PLANNED T'DO TO THEM.
SNEAKY SON OF A BITCH ISN'T STAYING IN ONE PLACE MORE THAN AN EIGHTH OF A SECOND, SETH.
THE LAST SIX CO-ORDINATES WE'VE GOT FOR HIM ARE TORONTO, BORDEAUX, PEKING, ADDIS ABABA, GLASGOW AND AN AIRFORCE BASE IN SAN DIEGO.
HELL'S THAT CLOWN DOIN' IN AN AIRFORCE BASE?

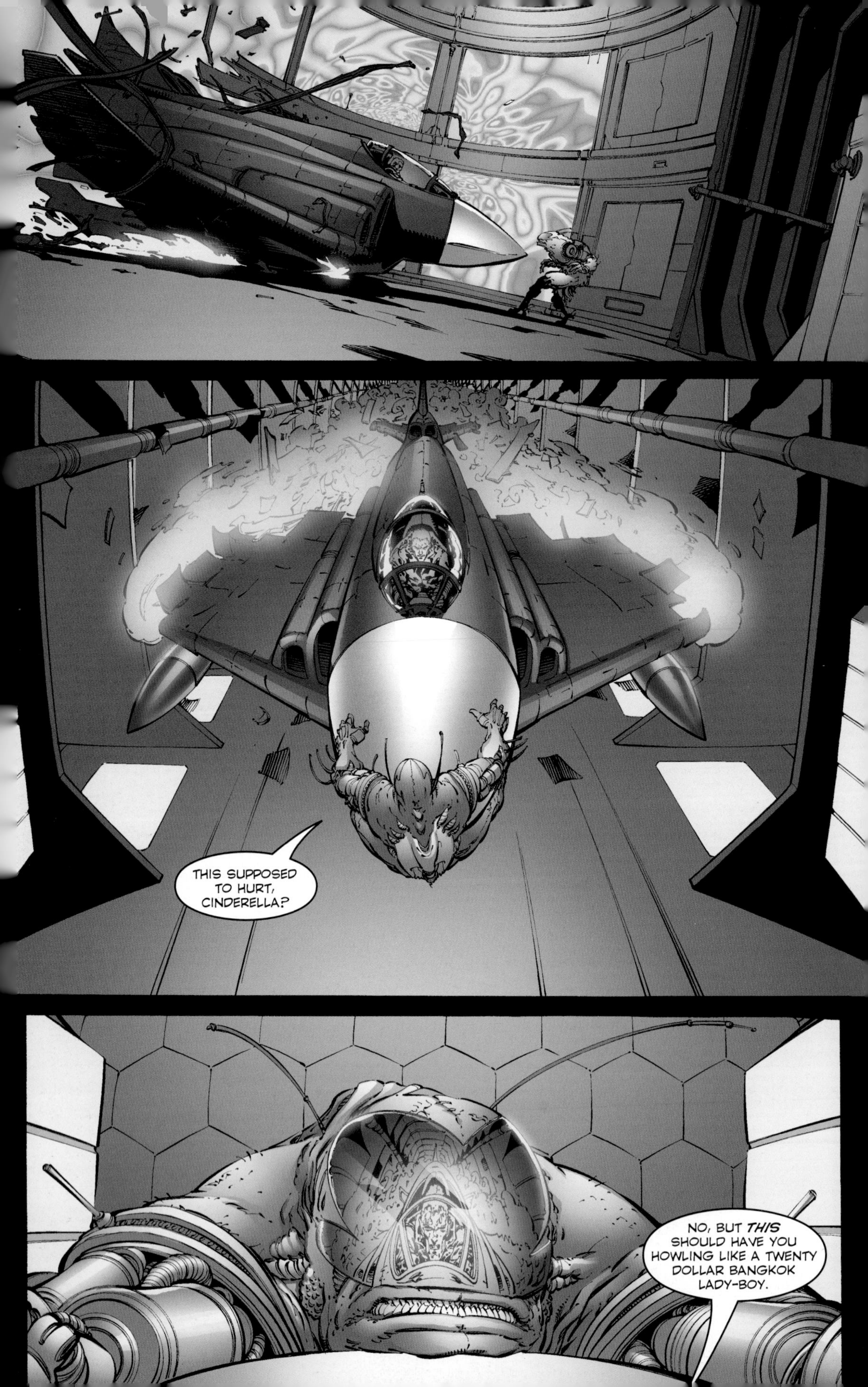
THIS SUPPOSED TO HURT, CINDERELLA?
NO, BUT *THIS* SHOULD HAVE YOU HOWLING LIKE A TWENTY DOLLAR BANGKOK LADY-BOY.

DIE, MOTHER-$@%$&*!

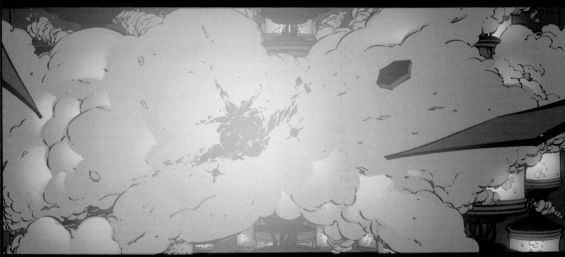

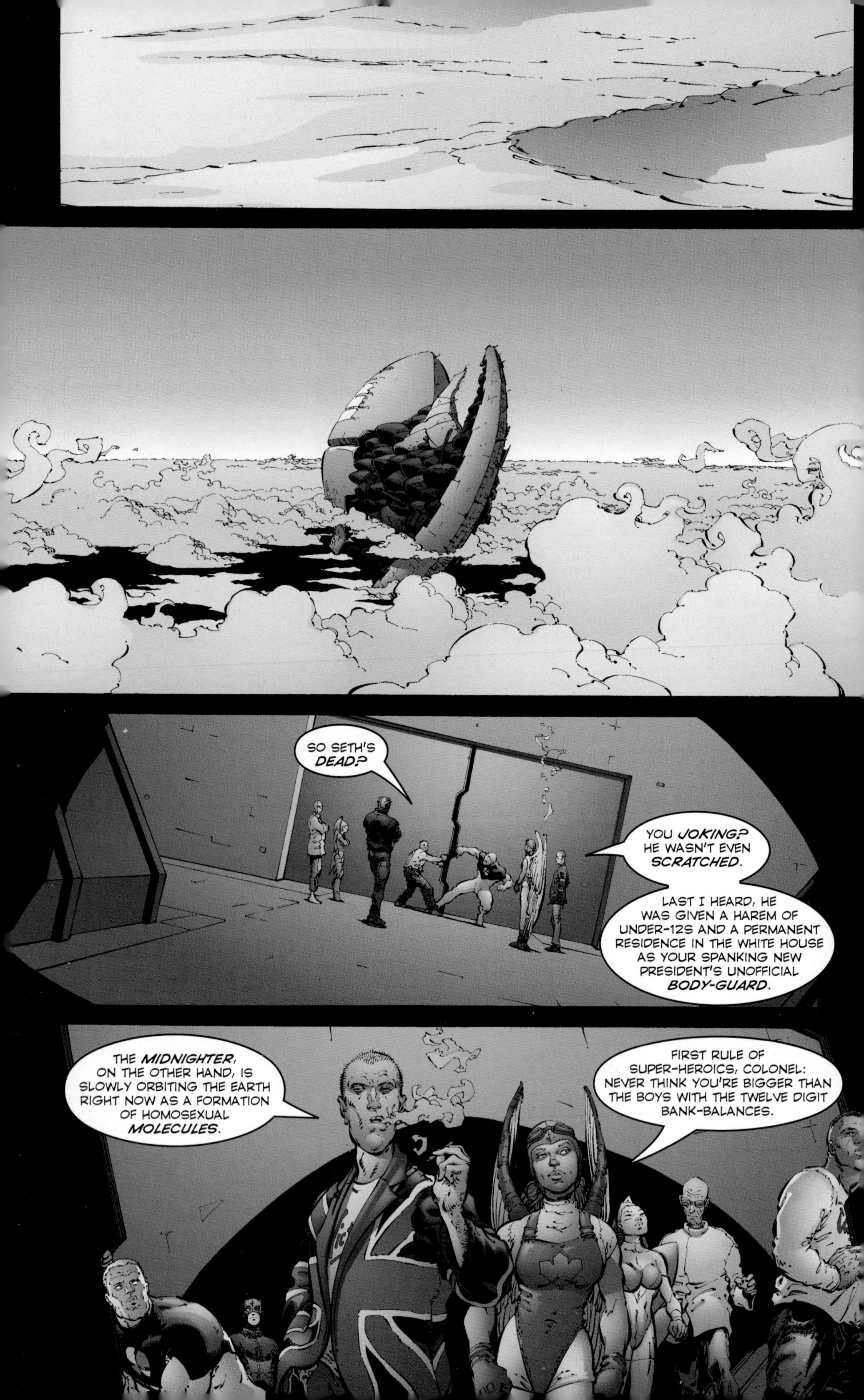
SO SETH'S *DEAD?*
YOU *JOKING?* HE WASN'T EVEN *SCRATCHED*.
LAST I HEARD, HE WAS GIVEN A HAREM OF UNDER-12S AND A PERMANENT RESIDENCE IN THE WHITE HOUSE AS YOUR SPANKING NEW PRESIDENT'S UNOFFICIAL *BODY-GUARD*.
THE *MIDNIGHTER*, ON THE OTHER HAND, IS SLOWLY ORBITING THE EARTH RIGHT NOW AS A FORMATION OF HOMOSEXUAL *MOLECULES*.
FIRST RULE OF SUPER-HEROICS, COLONEL: NEVER THINK YOU'RE BIGGER THAN THE BOYS WITH THE TWELVE DIGIT BANK-BALANCES.

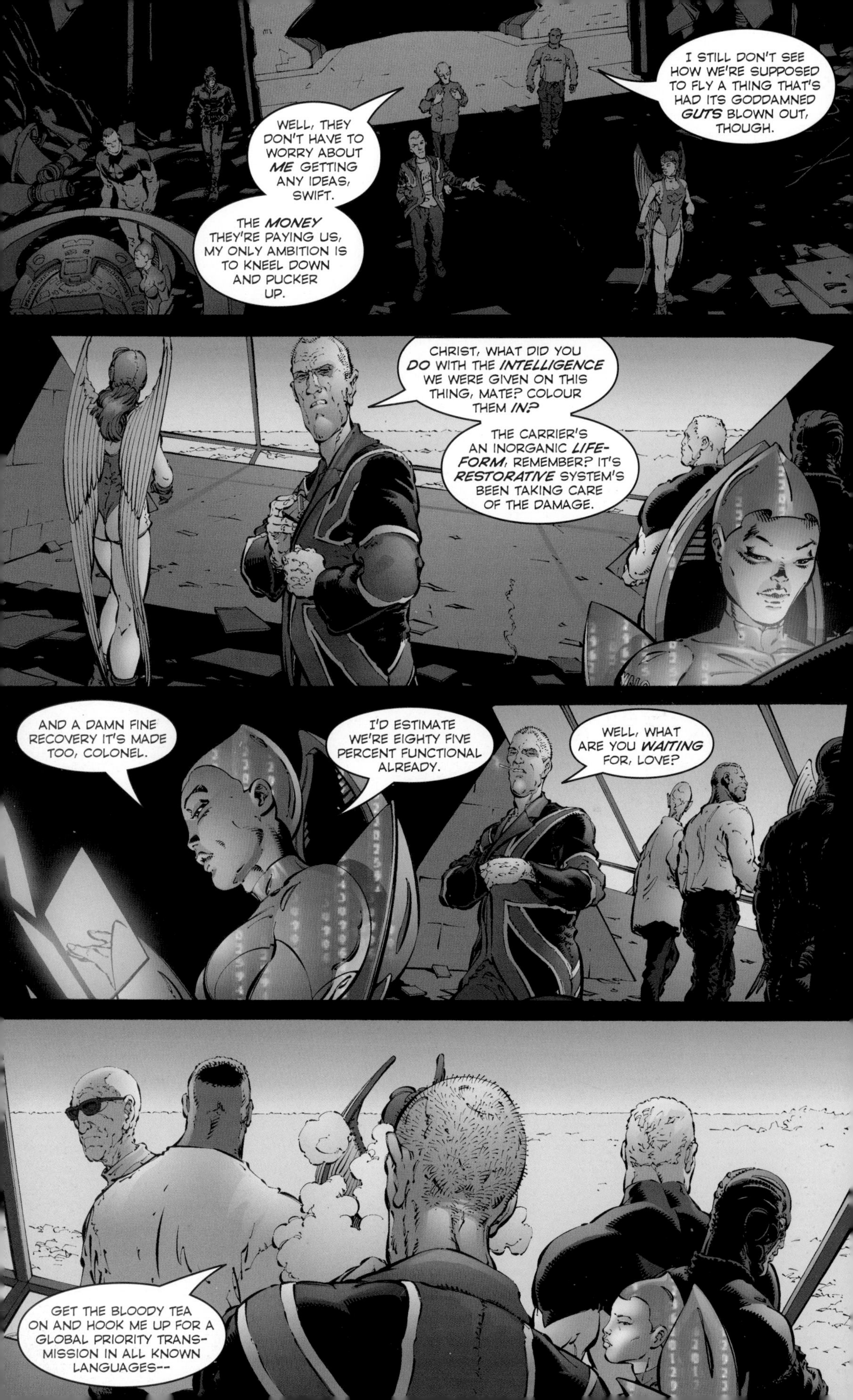
WELL, THEY DON'T HAVE TO WORRY ABOUT ME GETTING ANY IDEAS, SWIFT.
THE MONEY THEY'RE PAYING US, MY ONLY AMBITION IS TO KNEEL DOWN AND PUCKER UP.
I STILL DON'T SEE HOW WE'RE SUPPOSED TO FLY A THING THAT'S HAD ITS GODDAMNED GUTS BLOWN OUT, THOUGH.
CHRIST, WHAT DID YOU DO WITH THE INTELLIGENCE WE WERE GIVEN ON THIS THING, MATE? COLOUR THEM IN?
THE CARRIER'S AN INORGANIC LIFE-FORM, REMEMBER? IT'S RESTORATIVE SYSTEM'S BEEN TAKING CARE OF THE DAMAGE.
AND A DAMN FINE RECOVERY IT'S MADE TOO, COLONEL.
I'D ESTIMATE WE'RE EIGHTY FIVE PERCENT FUNCTIONAL ALREADY.
WELL, WHAT ARE YOU WAITING FOR, LOVE?
GET THE BLOODY TEA ON AND HOOK ME UP FOR A GLOBAL PRIORITY TRANS-MISSION IN ALL KNOWN LANGUAGES--

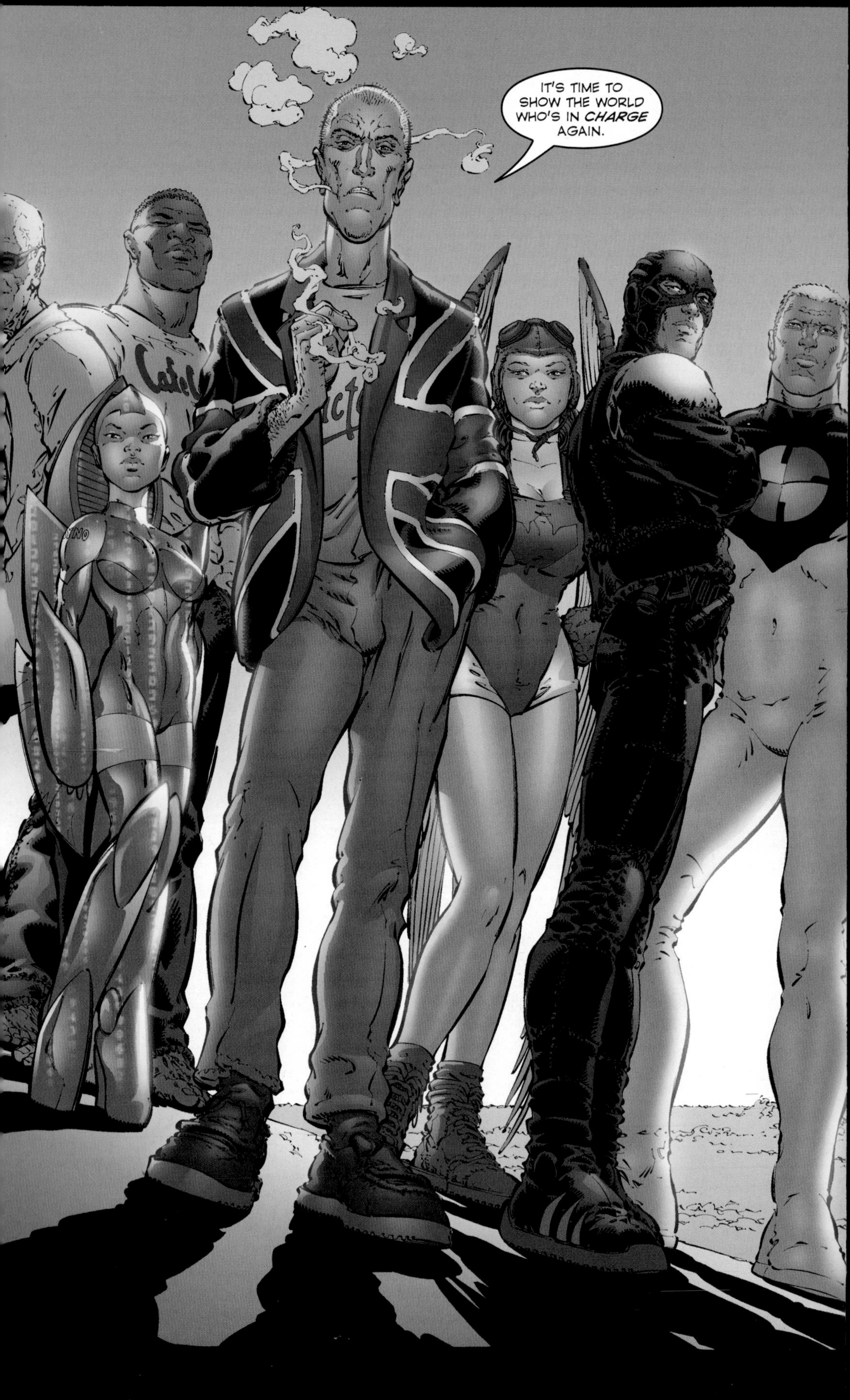
IT'S TIME TO SHOW THE WORLD WHO'S IN *CHARGE* AGAIN.

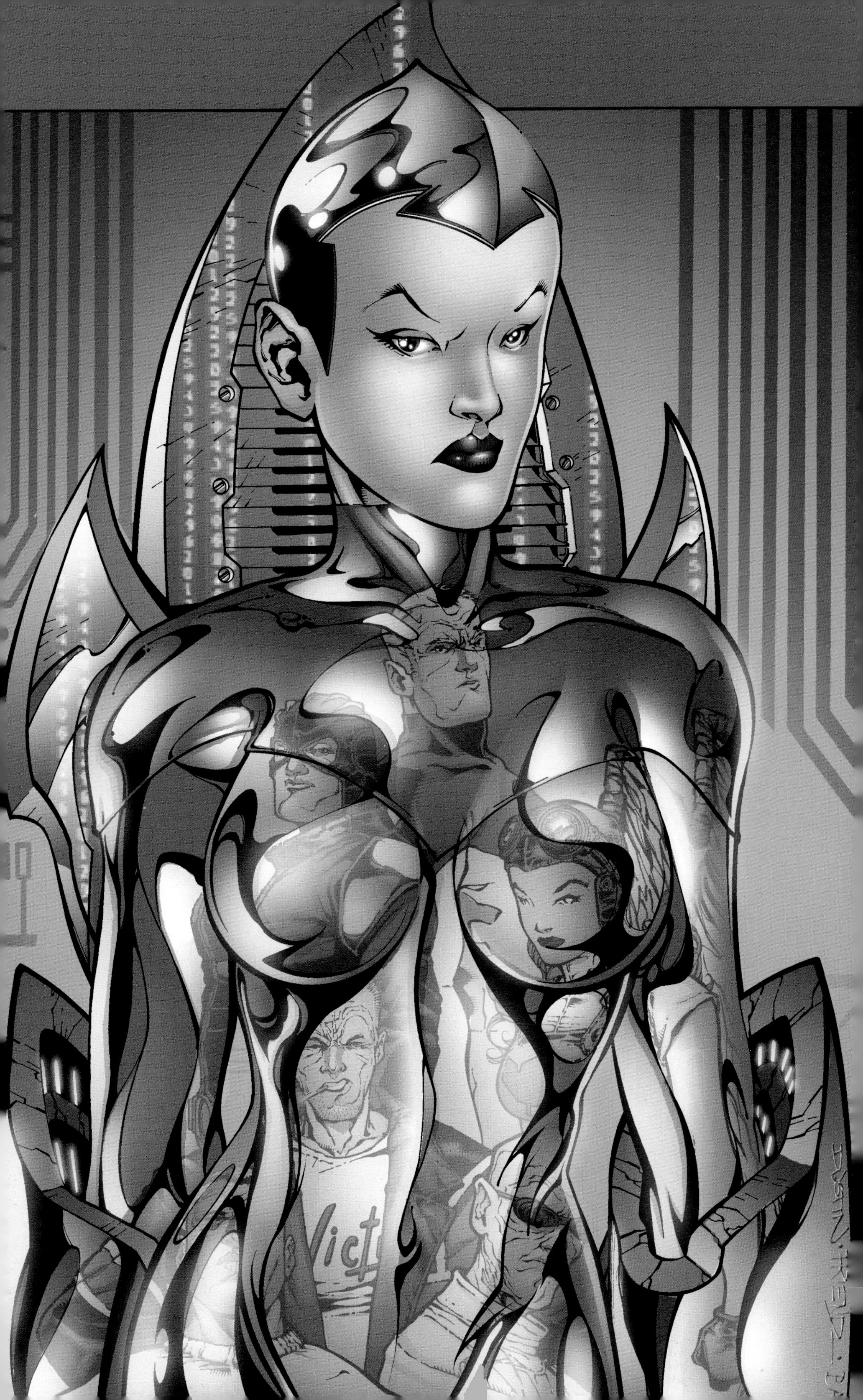

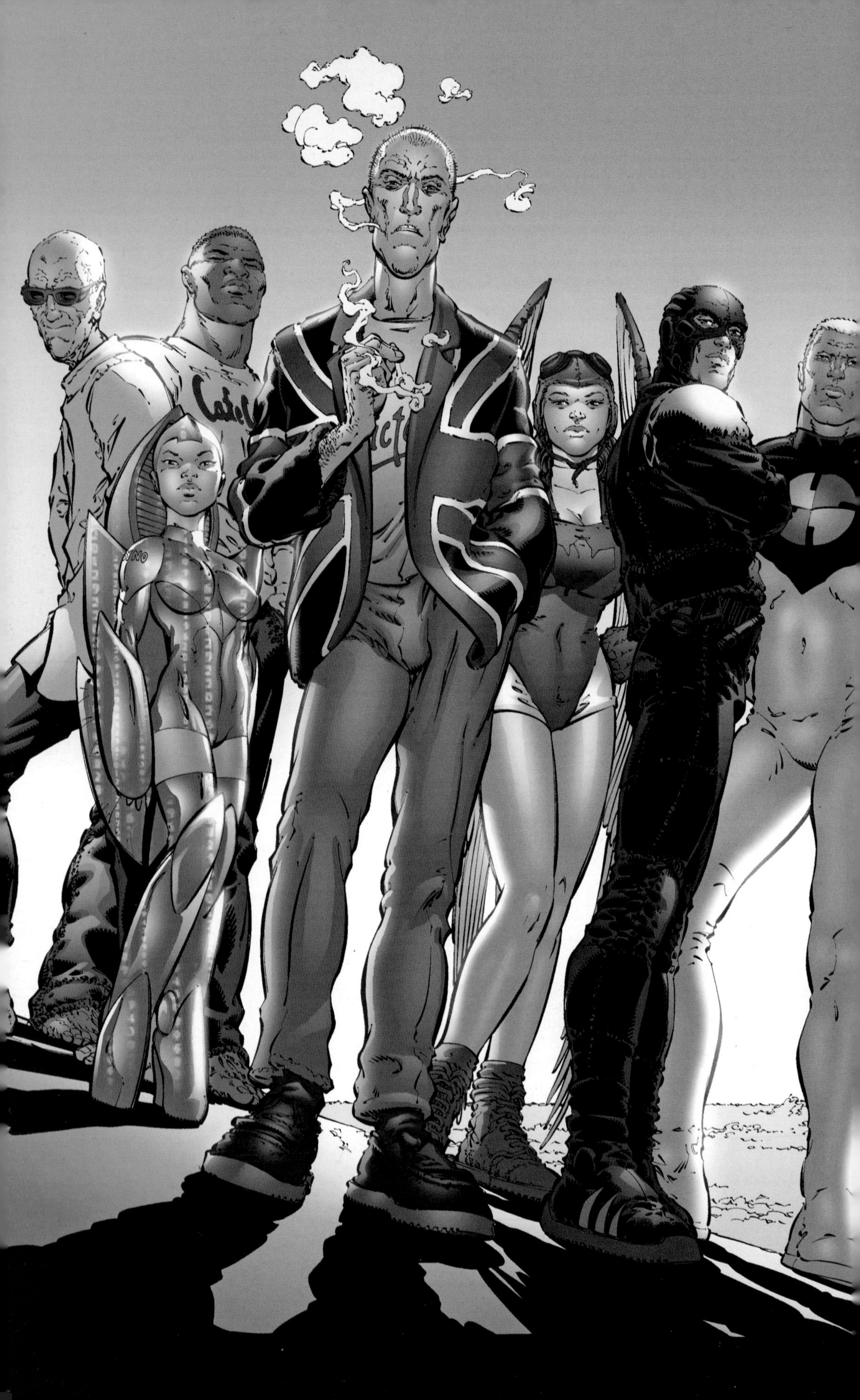

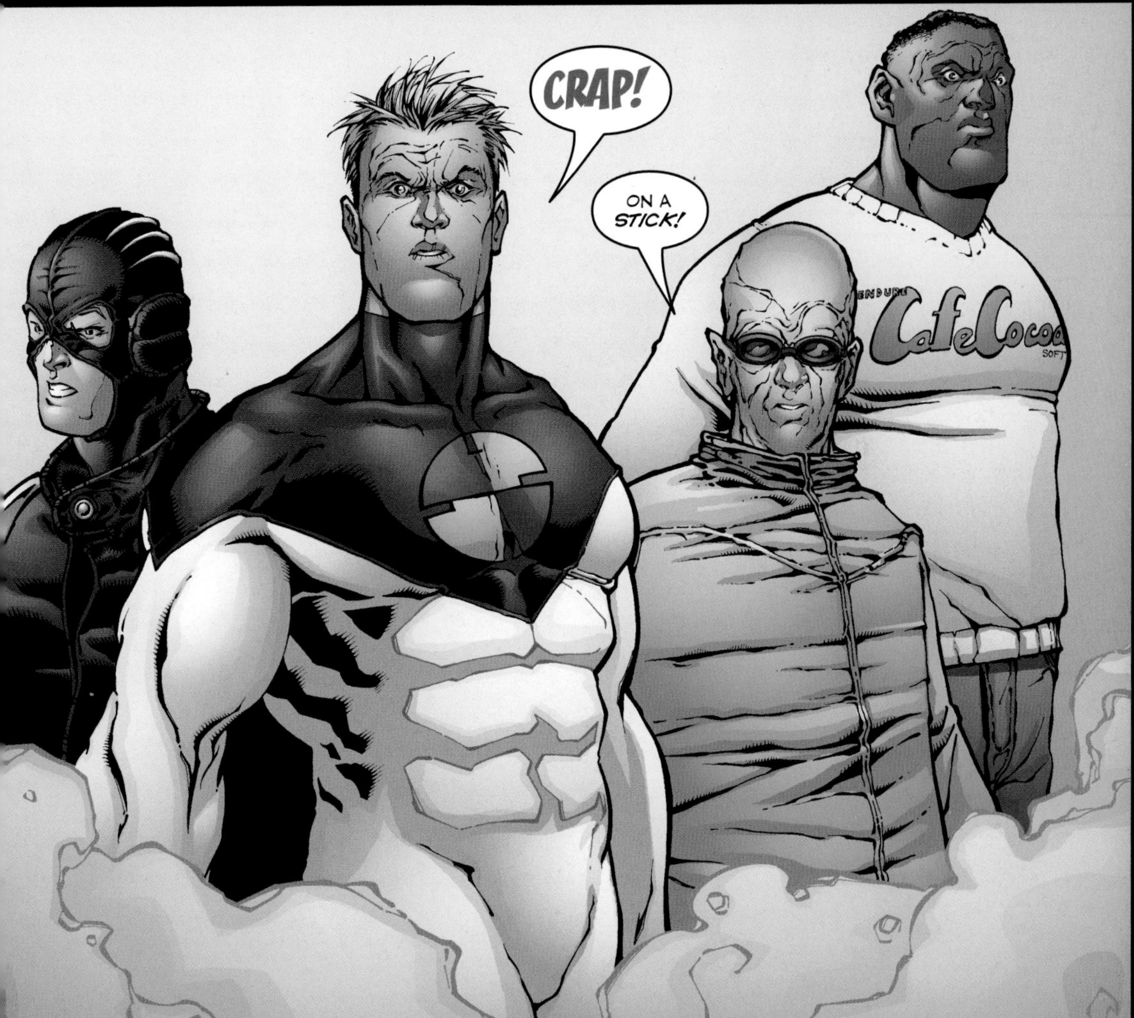
CRAP!
ON A STICK!
ENDURE
CafeCocoa
SOFT

The AUTHORITY

"Transfer of Power"

ONE of FOUR

TOM PEYER writer
DUSTIN NGUYEN artist
RICH FRIEND & JASON MARTIN inkers
DAVID BARON colorist
RYAN CLINE letterer

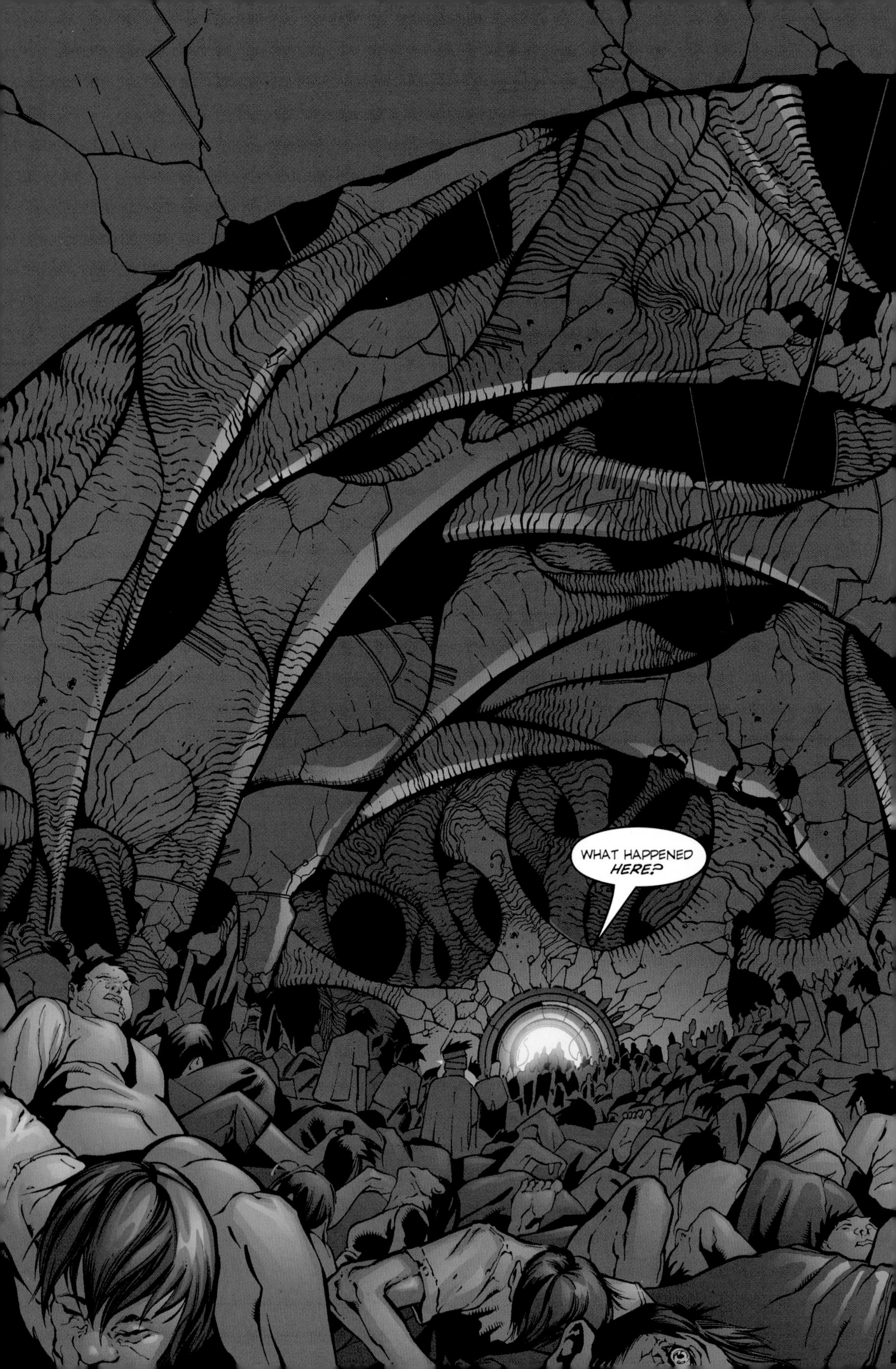
WHAT HAPPENED *HERE?*

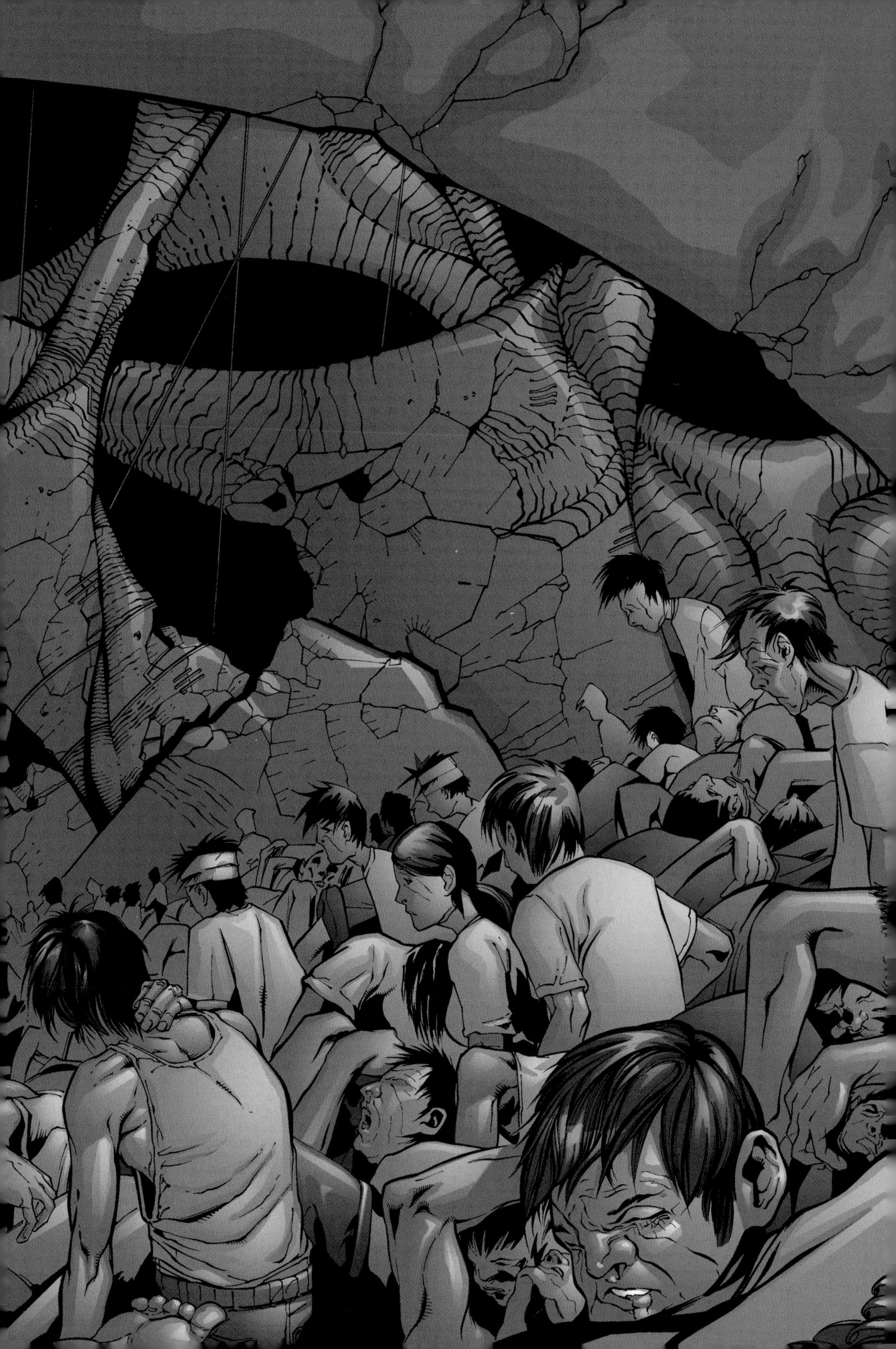

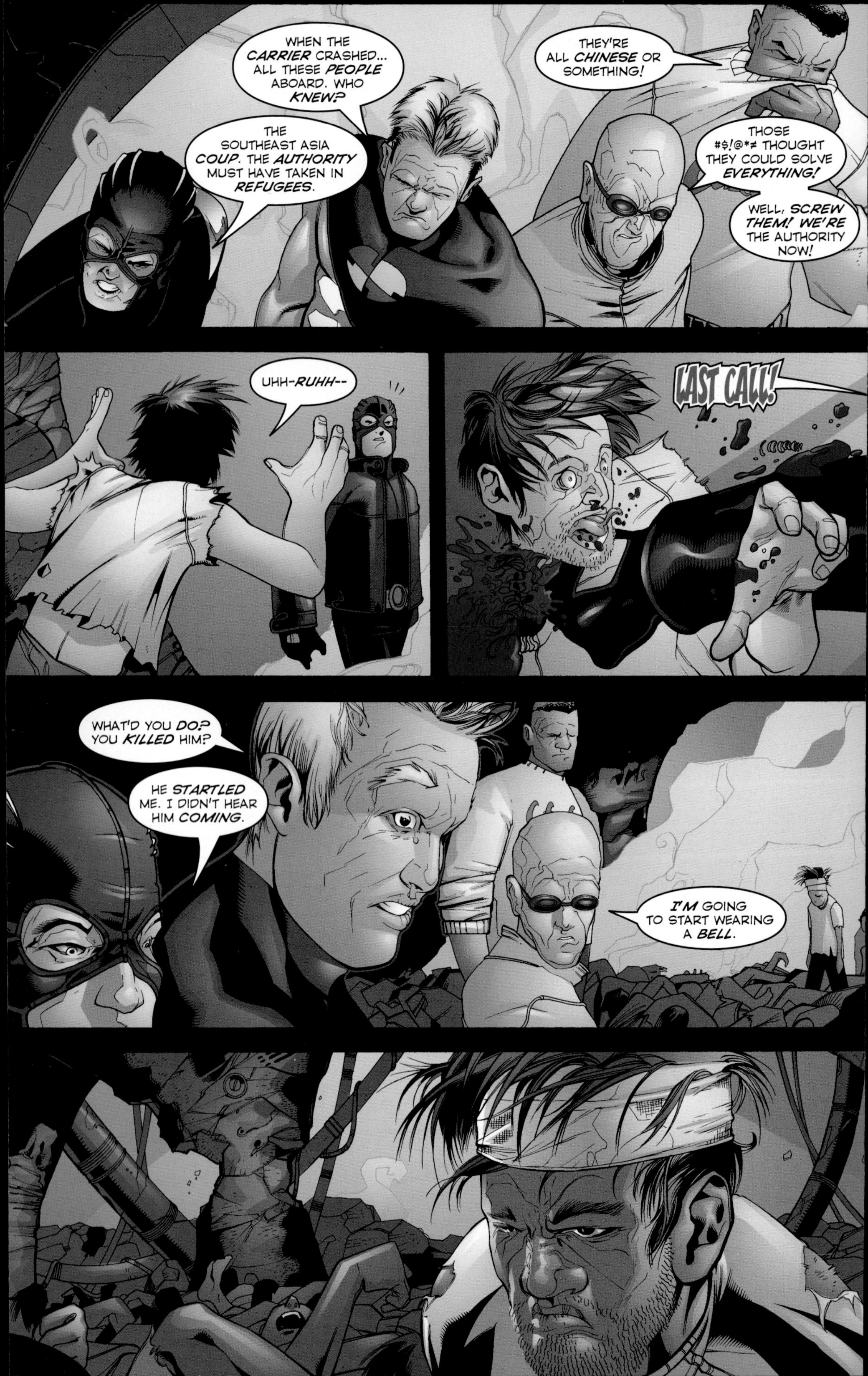

WHEN THE CARRIER CRASHED... ALL THESE PEOPLE ABOARD. WHO KNEW?
THE SOUTHEAST ASIA COUP. THE AUTHORITY MUST HAVE TAKEN IN REFUGEES.
THEY'RE ALL CHINESE OR SOMETHING!
THOSE #$!@*≠ THOUGHT THEY COULD SOLVE EVERYTHING!
WELL, SCREW THEM! WE'RE THE AUTHORITY NOW!
UHH-RUHH--
LAST CALL!
WHAT'D YOU DO? YOU KILLED HIM?
HE STARTLED ME. I DIDN'T HEAR HIM COMING.
I'M GOING TO START WEARING A BELL.

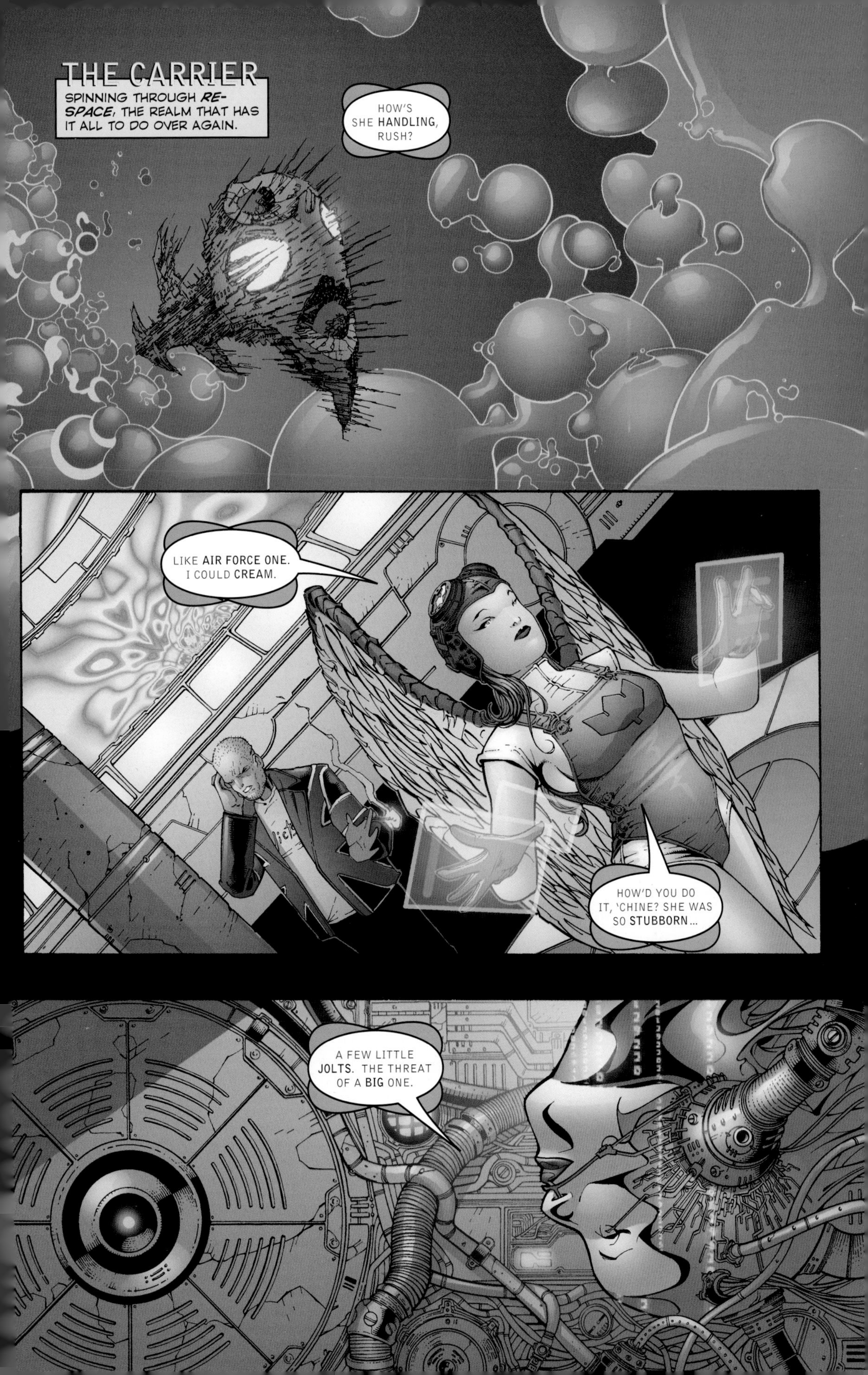
THE CARRIER
SPINNING THROUGH RE-SPACE, THE REALM THAT HAS IT ALL TO DO OVER AGAIN.
HOW'S SHE HANDLING, RUSH?
LIKE AIR FORCE ONE. I COULD CREAM.
HOW'D YOU DO IT, 'CHINE? SHE WAS SO STUBBORN...
A FEW LITTLE JOLTS. THE THREAT OF A BIG ONE.

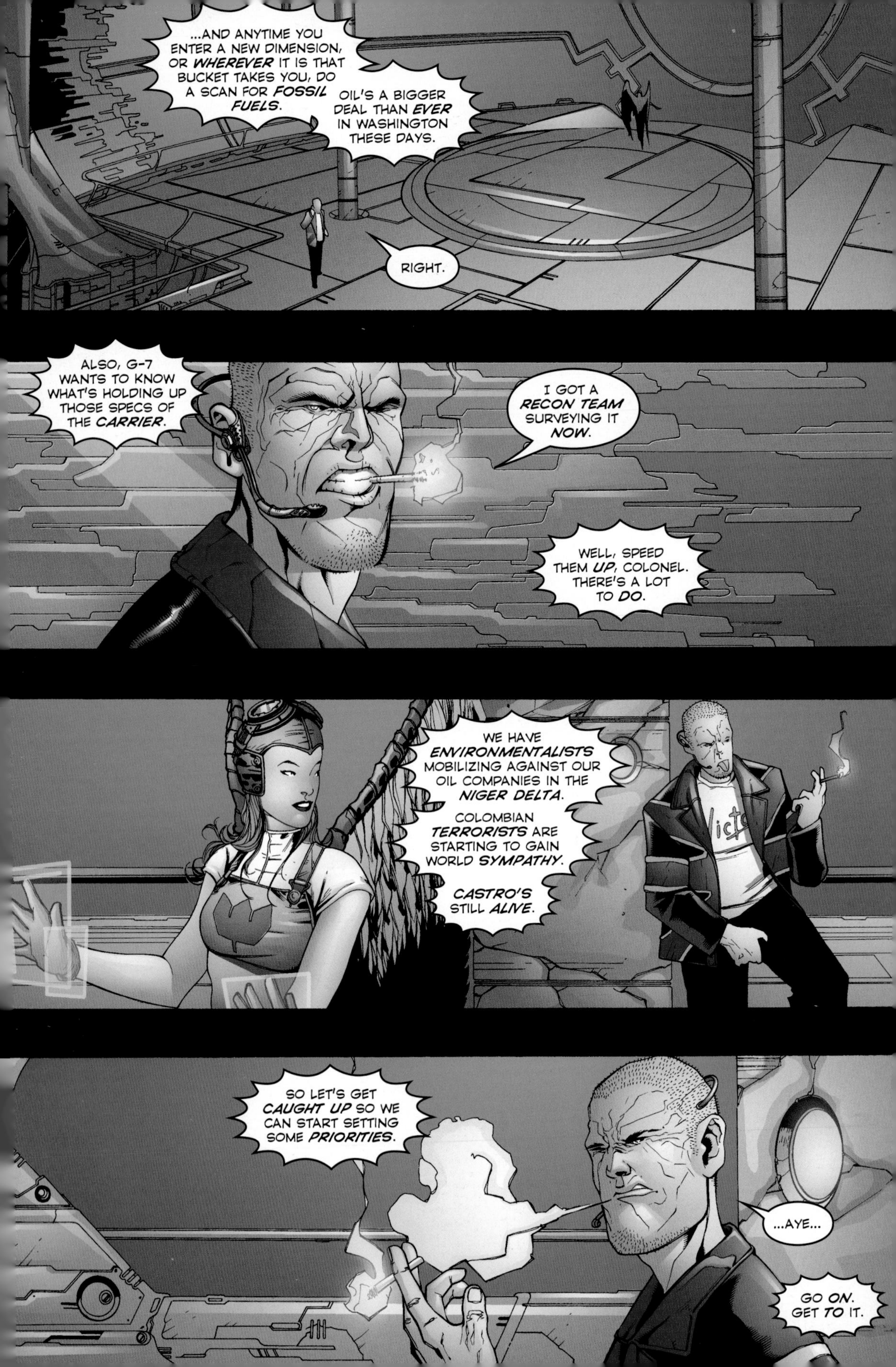
...AND ANYTIME YOU ENTER A NEW DIMENSION, OR *WHEREVER* IT IS THAT BUCKET TAKES YOU, DO A SCAN FOR *FOSSIL FUELS*.
OIL'S A BIGGER DEAL THAN *EVER* IN WASHINGTON THESE DAYS.
RIGHT.
ALSO, G-7 WANTS TO KNOW WHAT'S HOLDING UP THOSE SPECS OF THE *CARRIER*.
I GOT A *RECON TEAM* SURVEYING IT *NOW*.
WELL, SPEED THEM *UP*, COLONEL. THERE'S A LOT TO *DO*.
WE HAVE *ENVIRONMENTALISTS* MOBILIZING AGAINST OUR OIL COMPANIES IN THE *NIGER DELTA*.
COLOMBIAN *TERRORISTS* ARE STARTING TO GAIN WORLD *SYMPATHY*.
CASTRO'S STILL *ALIVE*.
SO LET'S GET *CAUGHT UP* SO WE CAN START SETTING SOME *PRIORITIES*.
...AYE...
GO *ON*. GET *TO* IT.

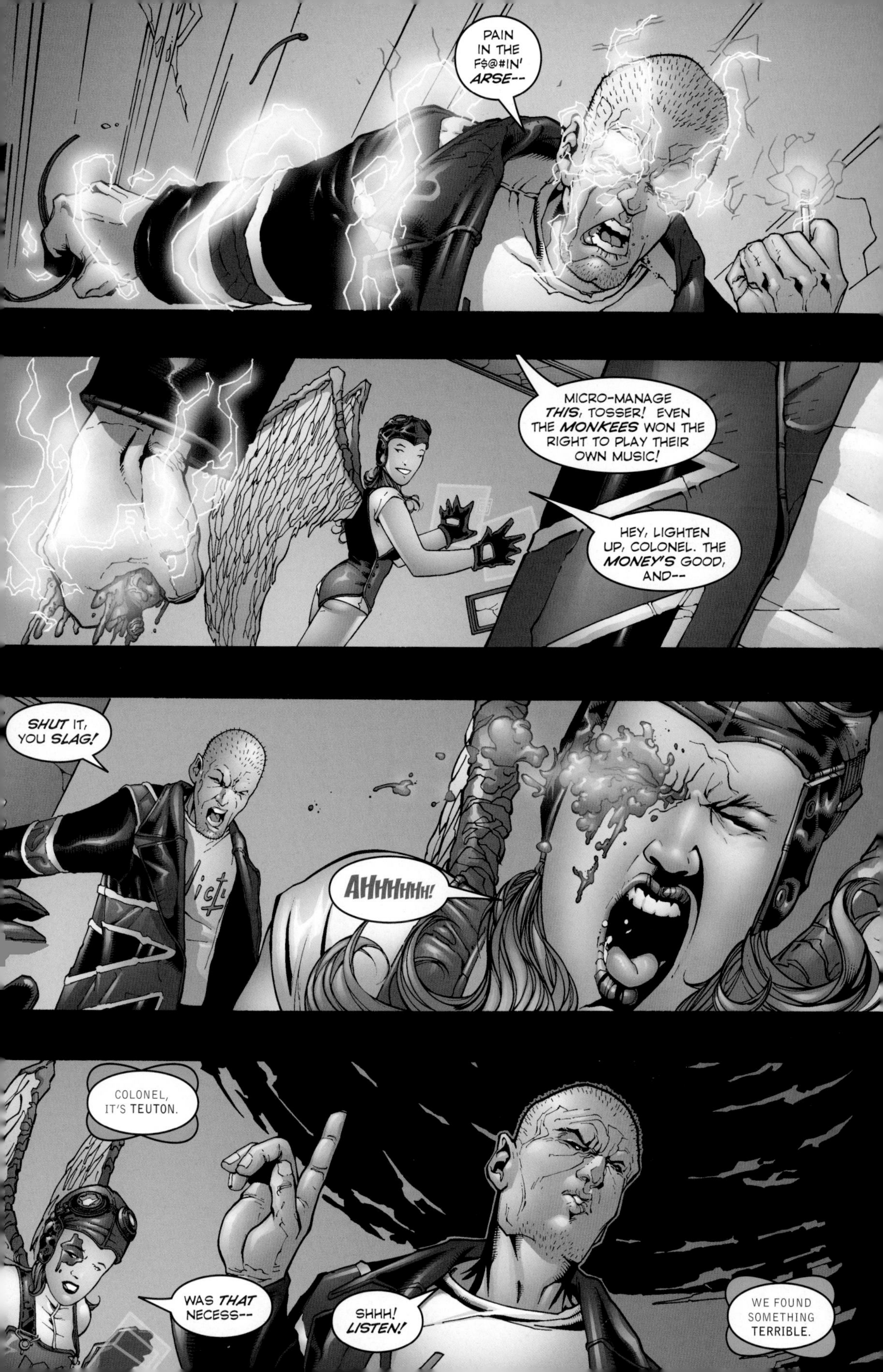
PAIN IN THE F$@#IN' ARSE--
MICRO-MANAGE THIS, TOSSER! EVEN THE MONKEES WON THE RIGHT TO PLAY THEIR OWN MUSIC!
HEY, LIGHTEN UP, COLONEL. THE MONEY'S GOOD, AND--
SHUT IT, YOU SLAG!
AHHHHHH!
COLONEL, IT'S TEUTON.
WAS THAT NECESS--
SHHH! LISTEN!
WE FOUND SOMETHING TERRIBLE.

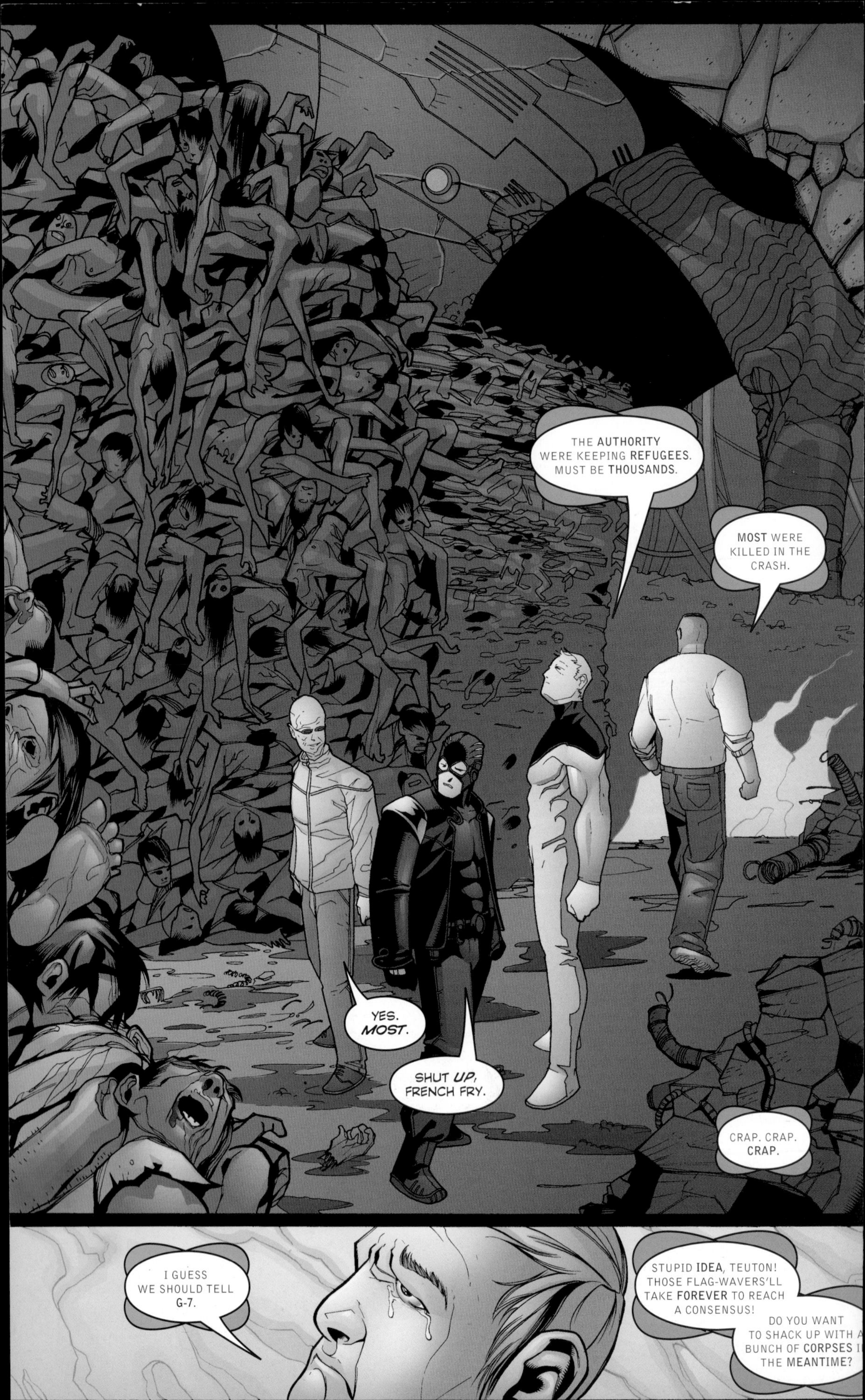
THE AUTHORITY WERE KEEPING REFUGEES. MUST BE THOUSANDS.
MOST WERE KILLED IN THE CRASH.
YES. MOST.
SHUT UP, FRENCH FRY.
CRAP. CRAP. CRAP.
I GUESS WE SHOULD TELL G-7.
STUPID IDEA, TEUTON! THOSE FLAG-WAVERS'LL TAKE FOREVER TO REACH A CONSENSUS!
DO YOU WANT TO SHACK UP WITH A BUNCH OF CORPSES IN THE MEANTIME?

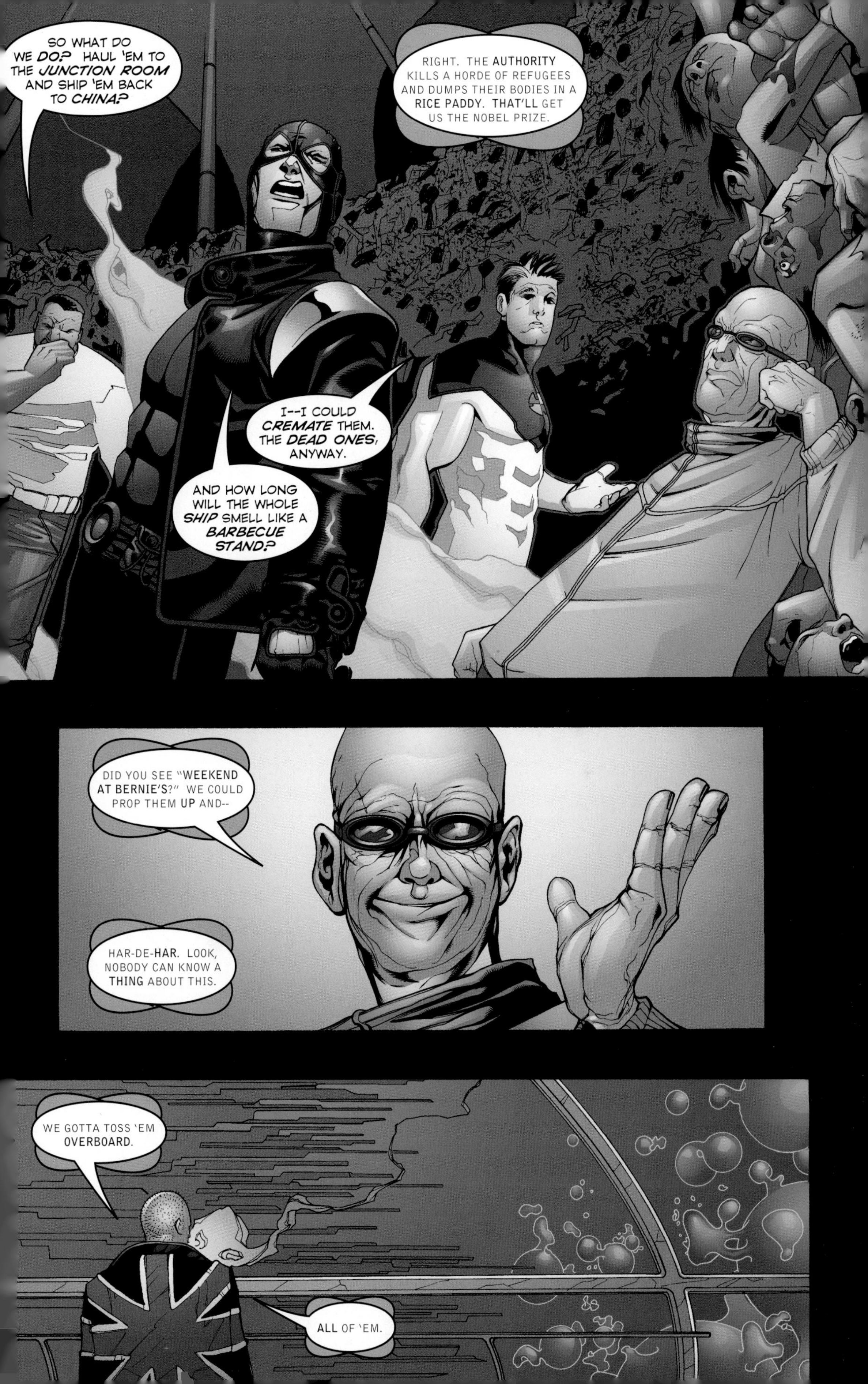
SO WHAT DO WE DO? HAUL 'EM TO THE JUNCTION ROOM AND SHIP 'EM BACK TO CHINA?
RIGHT. THE AUTHORITY KILLS A HORDE OF REFUGEES AND DUMPS THEIR BODIES IN A RICE PADDY. THAT'LL GET US THE NOBEL PRIZE.
I--I COULD CREMATE THEM. THE DEAD ONES, ANYWAY.
AND HOW LONG WILL THE WHOLE SHIP SMELL LIKE A BARBECUE STAND?
DID YOU SEE "WEEKEND AT BERNIE'S?" WE COULD PROP THEM UP AND--
HAR-DE-HAR. LOOK, NOBODY CAN KNOW A THING ABOUT THIS.
WE GOTTA TOSS 'EM OVERBOARD.
ALL OF 'EM.

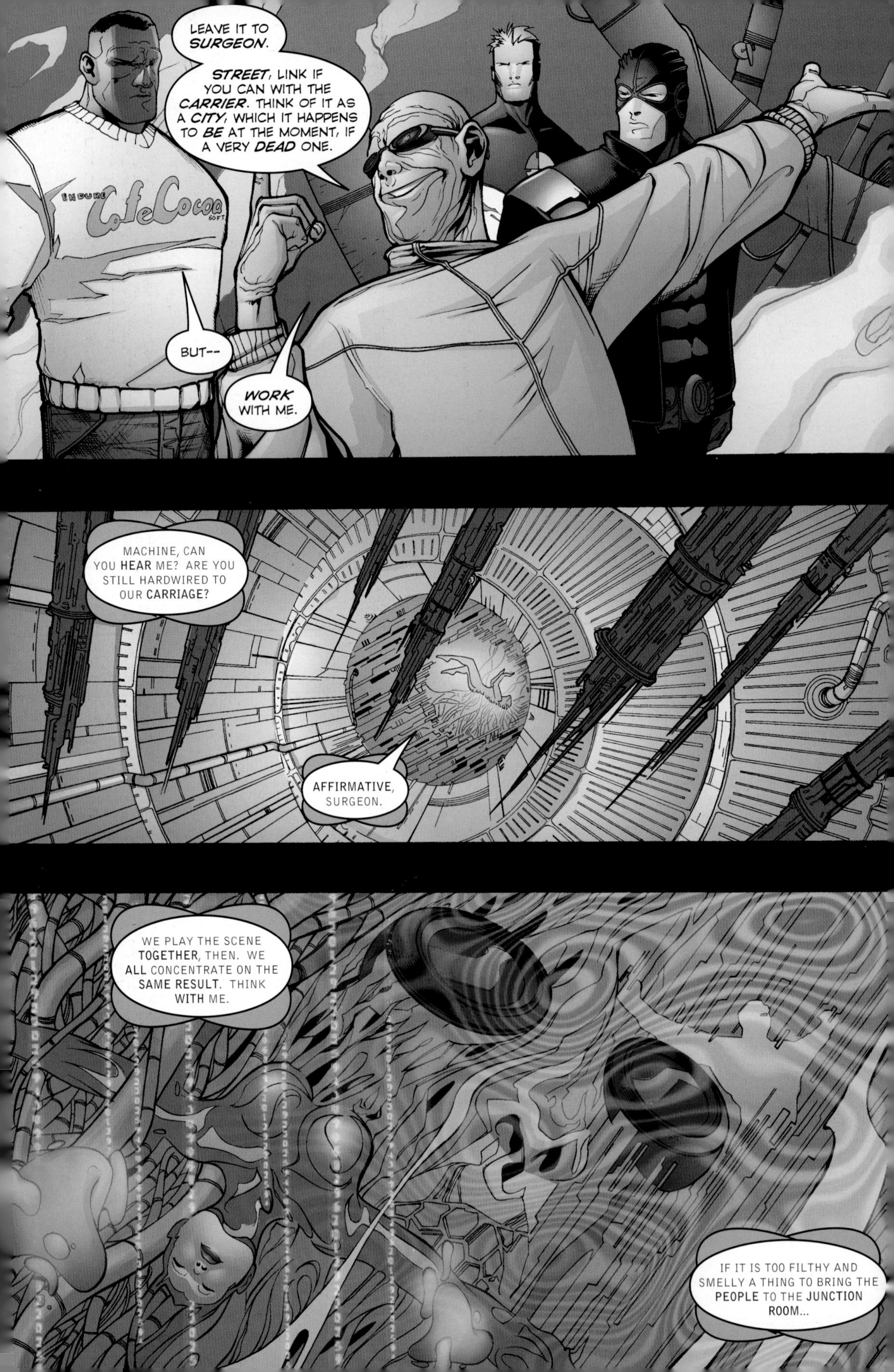
LEAVE IT TO SURGEON.
STREET, LINK IF YOU CAN WITH THE CARRIER. THINK OF IT AS A CITY, WHICH IT HAPPENS TO BE AT THE MOMENT, IF A VERY DEAD ONE.
BUT--
WORK WITH ME.
MACHINE, CAN YOU HEAR ME? ARE YOU STILL HARDWIRED TO OUR CARRIAGE?
AFFIRMATIVE, SURGEON.
WE PLAY THE SCENE TOGETHER, THEN. WE ALL CONCENTRATE ON THE SAME RESULT. THINK WITH ME.
IF IT IS TOO FILTHY AND SMELLY A THING TO BRING THE PEOPLE TO THE JUNCTION ROOM...

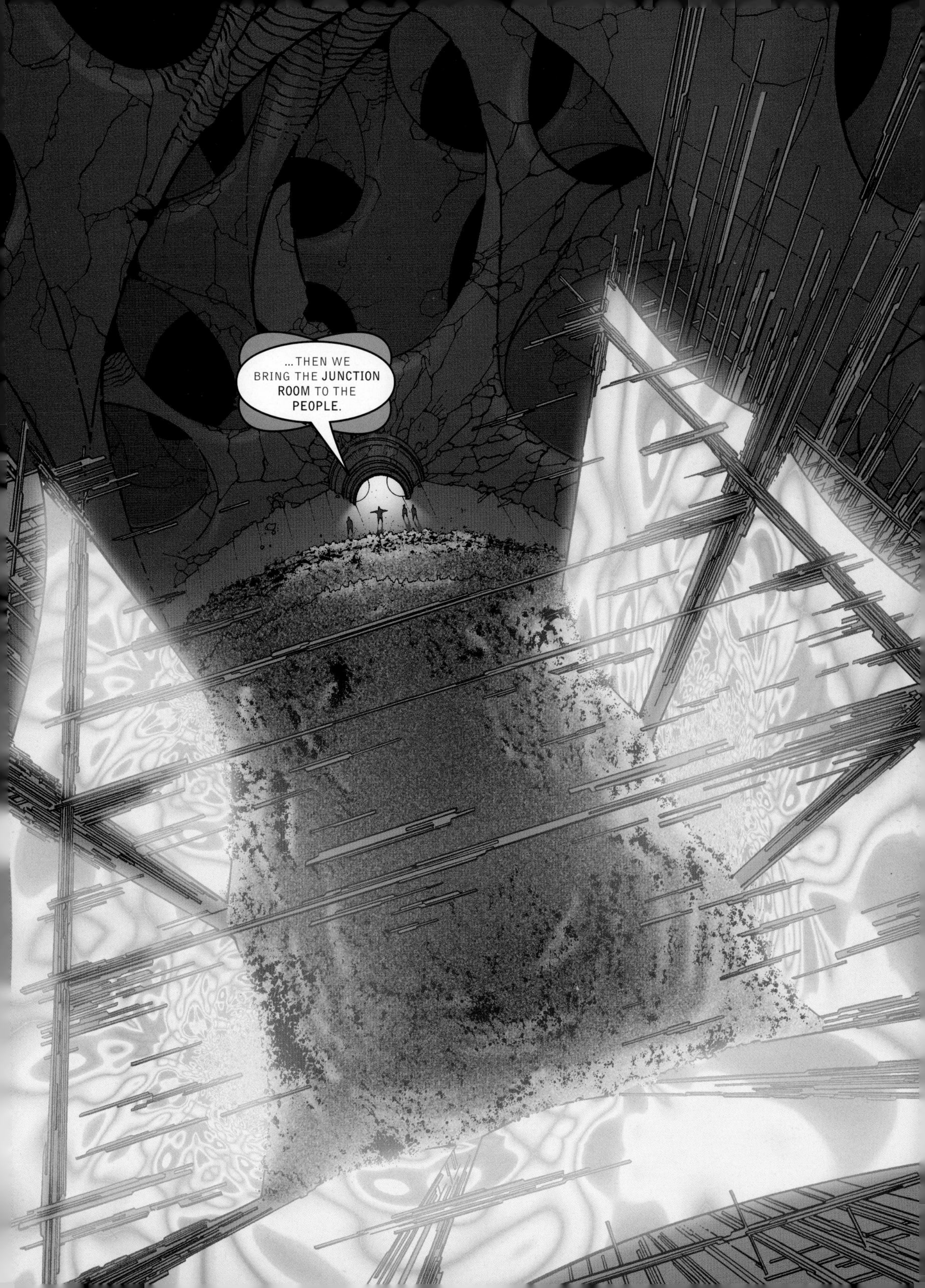
...THEN WE BRING THE JUNCTION ROOM TO THE PEOPLE.

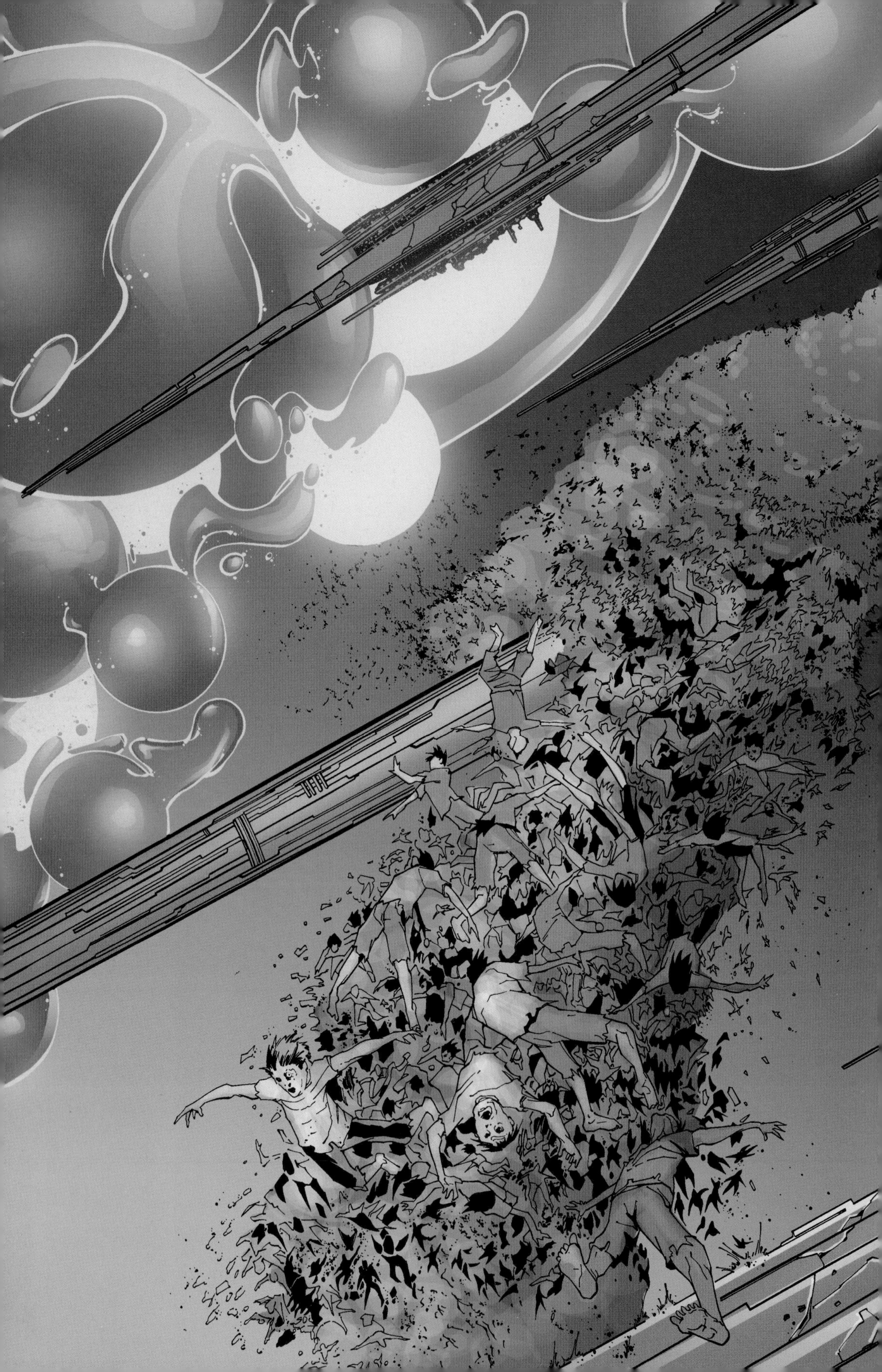

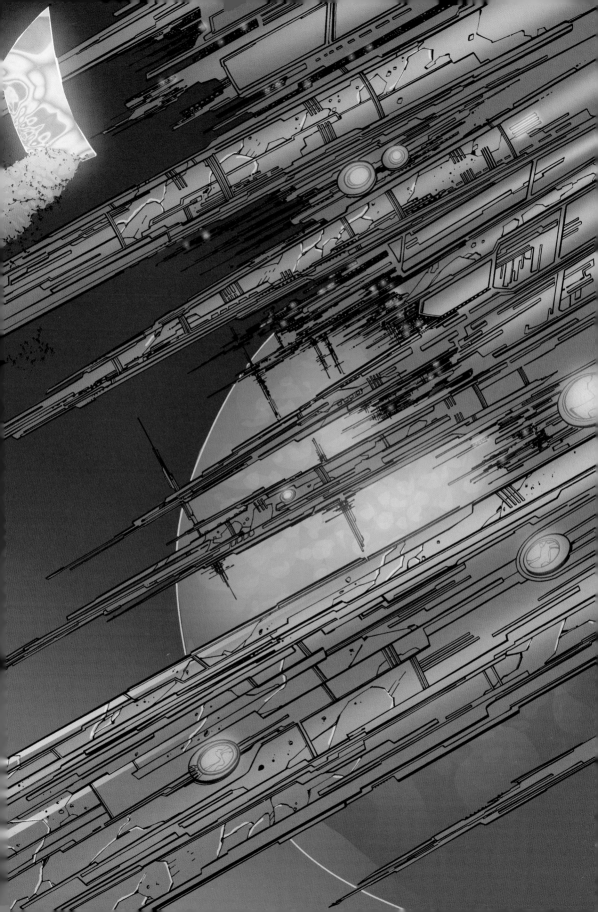

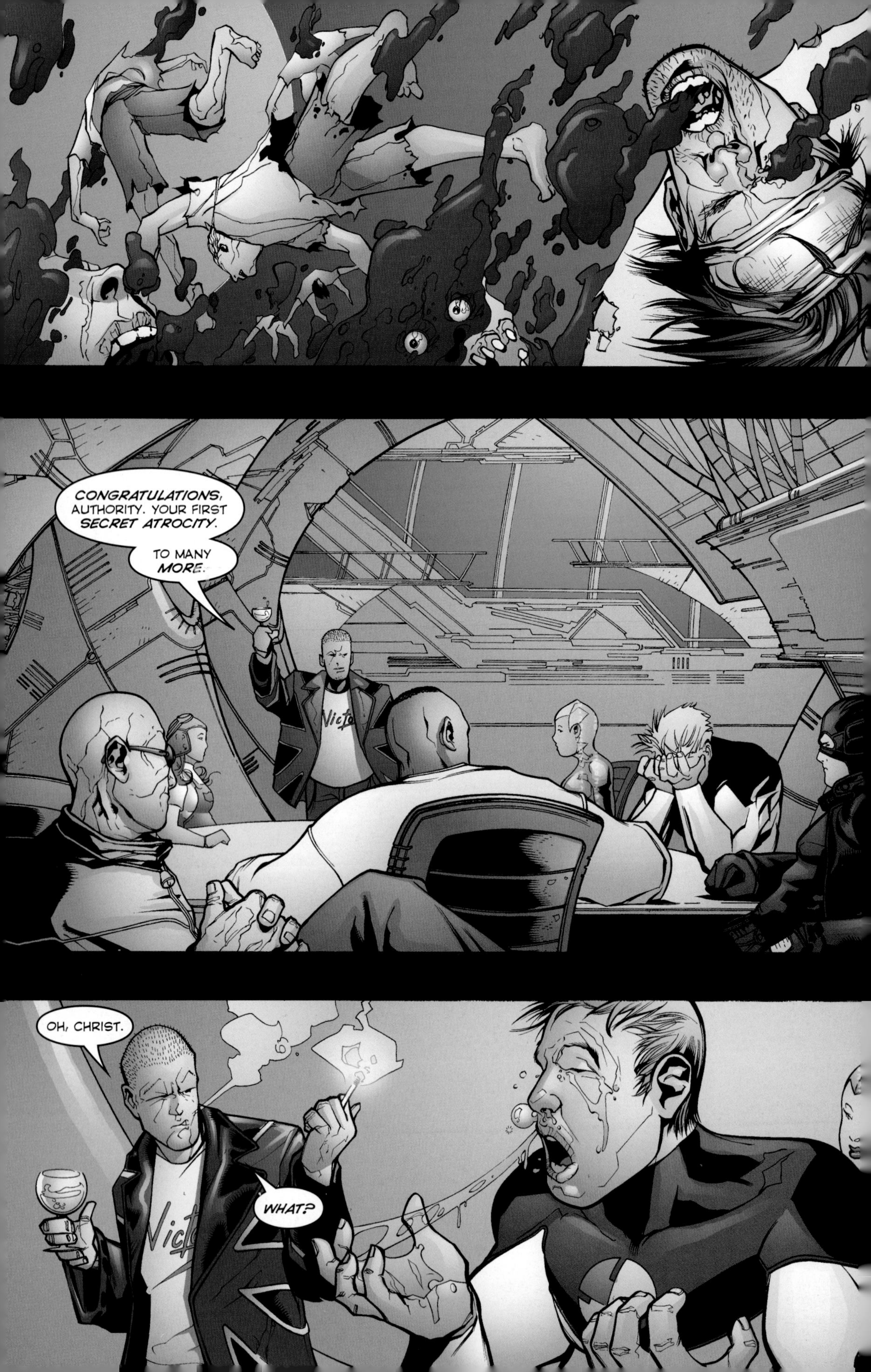
CONGRATULATIONS, AUTHORITY. YOUR FIRST SECRET ATROCITY.
TO MANY MORE.
OH, CHRIST.
WHAT?

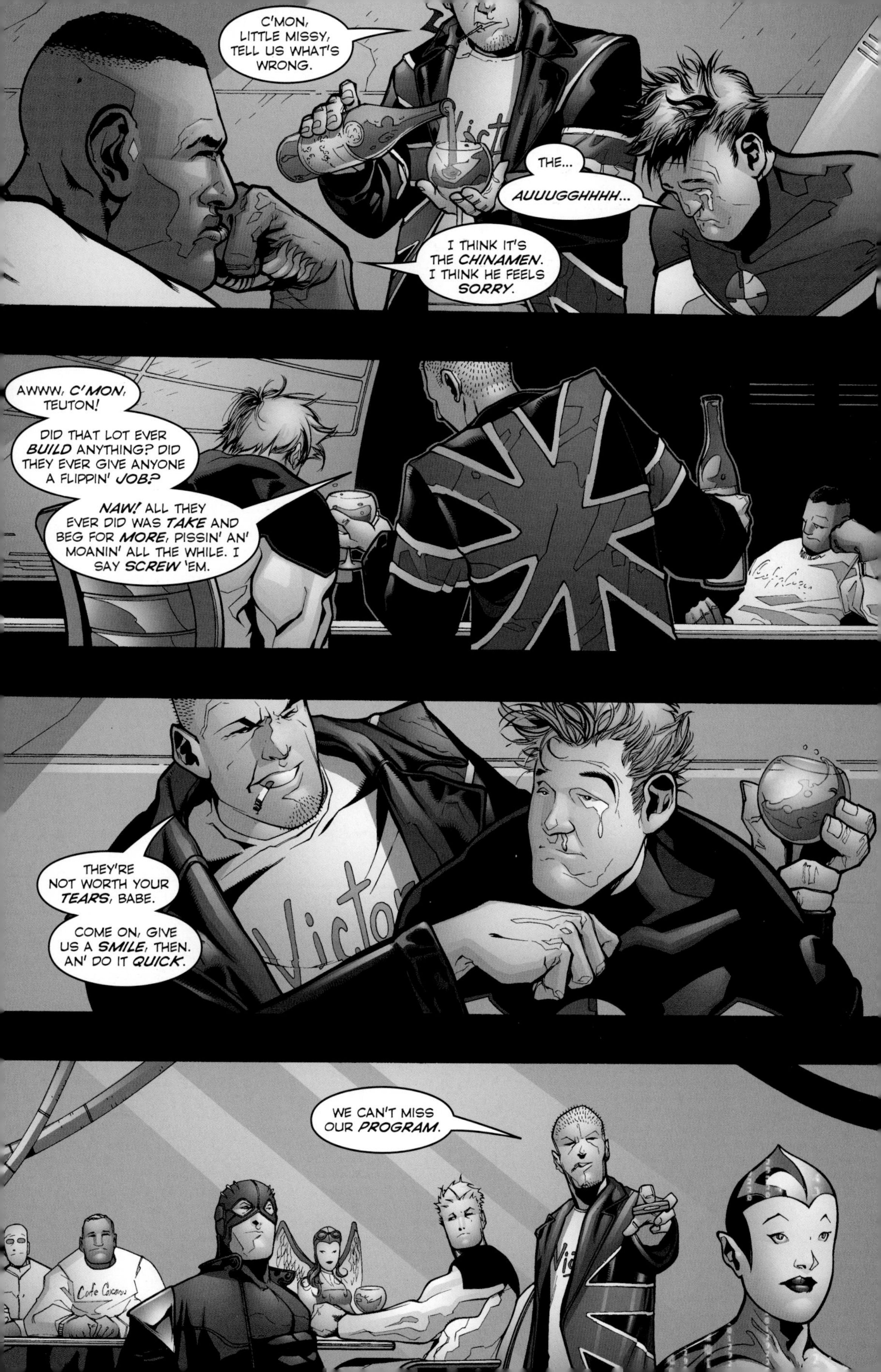
C'MON, LITTLE MISSY, TELL US WHAT'S WRONG.
THE...
AUUUGGHHHH...
I THINK IT'S THE CHINAMEN. I THINK HE FEELS SORRY.
AWWW, C'MON, TEUTON!
DID THAT LOT EVER BUILD ANYTHING? DID THEY EVER GIVE ANYONE A FLIPPIN' JOB?
NAW! ALL THEY EVER DID WAS TAKE AND BEG FOR MORE, PISSIN' AN' MOANIN' ALL THE WHILE. I SAY SCREW 'EM.
THEY'RE NOT WORTH YOUR TEARS, BABE.
COME ON, GIVE US A SMILE, THEN. AN' DO IT QUICK.
WE CAN'T MISS OUR PROGRAM.

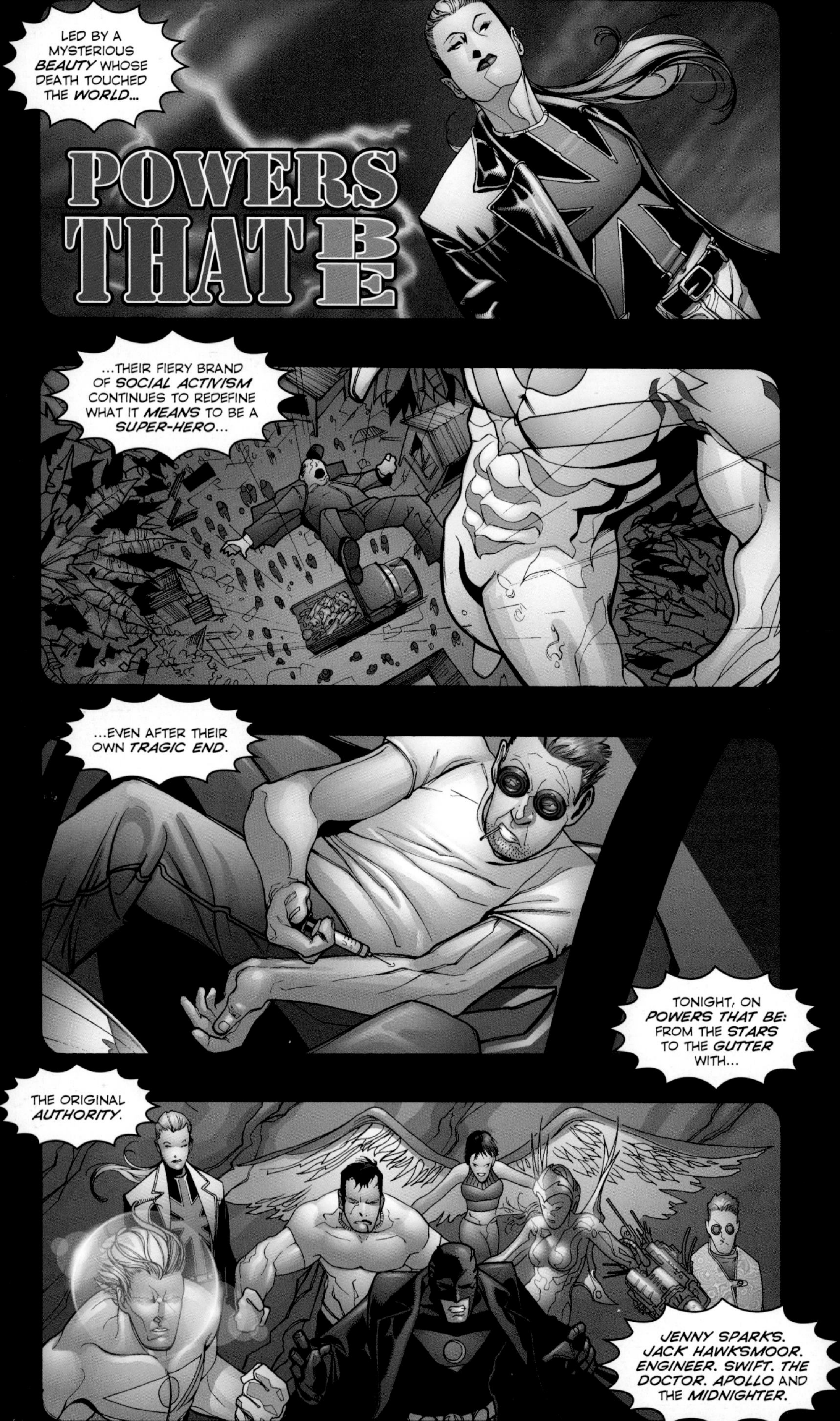
LED BY A MYSTERIOUS BEAUTY WHOSE DEATH TOUCHED THE WORLD...
POWERS THAT BE
...THEIR FIERY BRAND OF SOCIAL ACTIVISM CONTINUES TO REDEFINE WHAT IT MEANS TO BE A SUPER-HERO...
...EVEN AFTER THEIR OWN TRAGIC END.
TONIGHT, ON POWERS THAT BE: FROM THE STARS TO THE GUTTER WITH...
THE ORIGINAL AUTHORITY.
JENNY SPARKS. JACK HAWKSMOOR. ENGINEER. SWIFT. THE DOCTOR. APOLLO AND THE MIDNIGHTER.

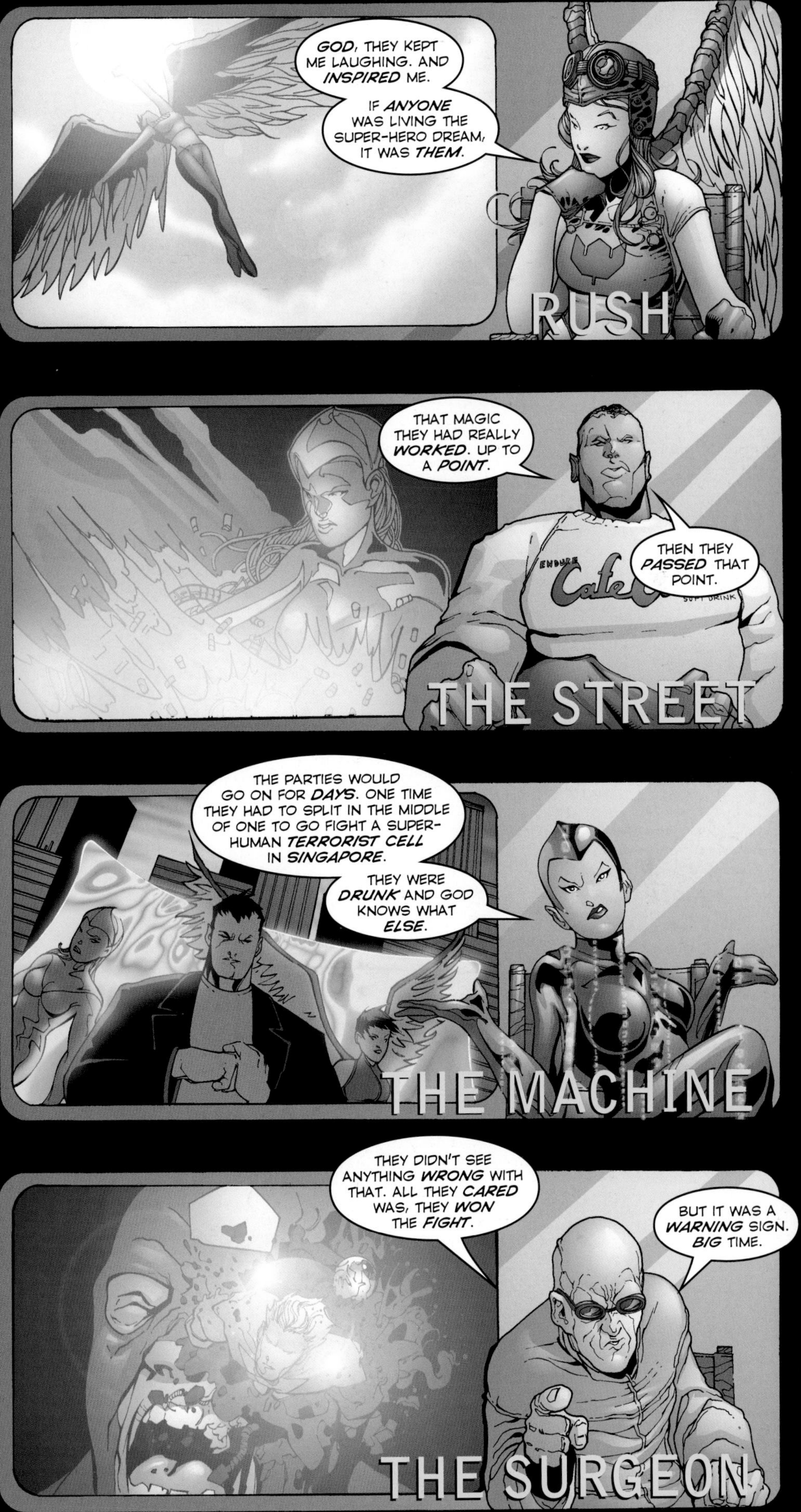
GOD, THEY KEPT ME LAUGHING. AND INSPIRED ME.
IF ANYONE WAS LIVING THE SUPER-HERO DREAM, IT WAS THEM.
RUSH
THAT MAGIC THEY HAD REALLY WORKED. UP TO A POINT.
THEN THEY PASSED THAT POINT.
THE STREET
THE PARTIES WOULD GO ON FOR DAYS. ONE TIME THEY HAD TO SPLIT IN THE MIDDLE OF ONE TO GO FIGHT A SUPER-HUMAN TERRORIST CELL IN SINGAPORE.
THEY WERE DRUNK AND GOD KNOWS WHAT ELSE.
THE MACHINE
THEY DIDN'T SEE ANYTHING WRONG WITH THAT. ALL THEY CARED WAS, THEY WON THE FIGHT.
BUT IT WAS A WARNING SIGN. BIG TIME.
THE SURGEON

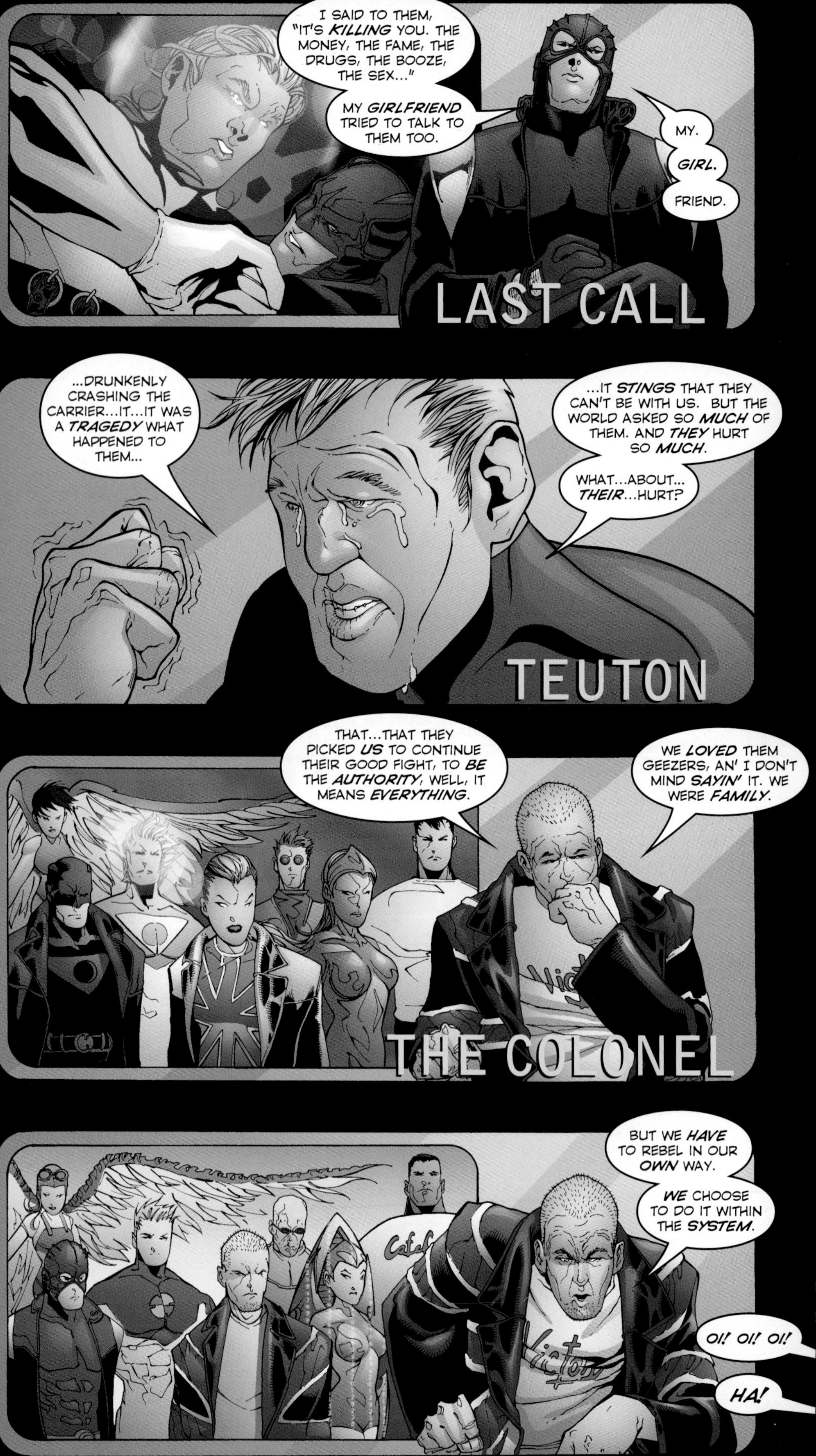
I SAID TO THEM, "IT'S KILLING YOU. THE MONEY, THE FAME, THE DRUGS, THE BOOZE, THE SEX..."
MY GIRLFRIEND TRIED TO TALK TO THEM TOO.
MY.
GIRL.
FRIEND.
LAST CALL
...DRUNKENLY CRASHING THE CARRIER...IT...IT WAS A TRAGEDY WHAT HAPPENED TO THEM...
...IT STINGS THAT THEY CAN'T BE WITH US. BUT THE WORLD ASKED SO MUCH OF THEM. AND THEY HURT SO MUCH.
WHAT...ABOUT... THEIR...HURT?
TEUTON
THAT...THAT THEY PICKED US TO CONTINUE THEIR GOOD FIGHT, TO BE THE AUTHORITY, WELL, IT MEANS EVERYTHING.
WE LOVED THEM GEEZERS, AN' I DON'T MIND SAYIN' IT. WE WERE FAMILY.
THE COLONEL
BUT WE HAVE TO REBEL IN OUR OWN WAY.
WE CHOOSE TO DO IT WITHIN THE SYSTEM.
OI! OI! OI!
HA!

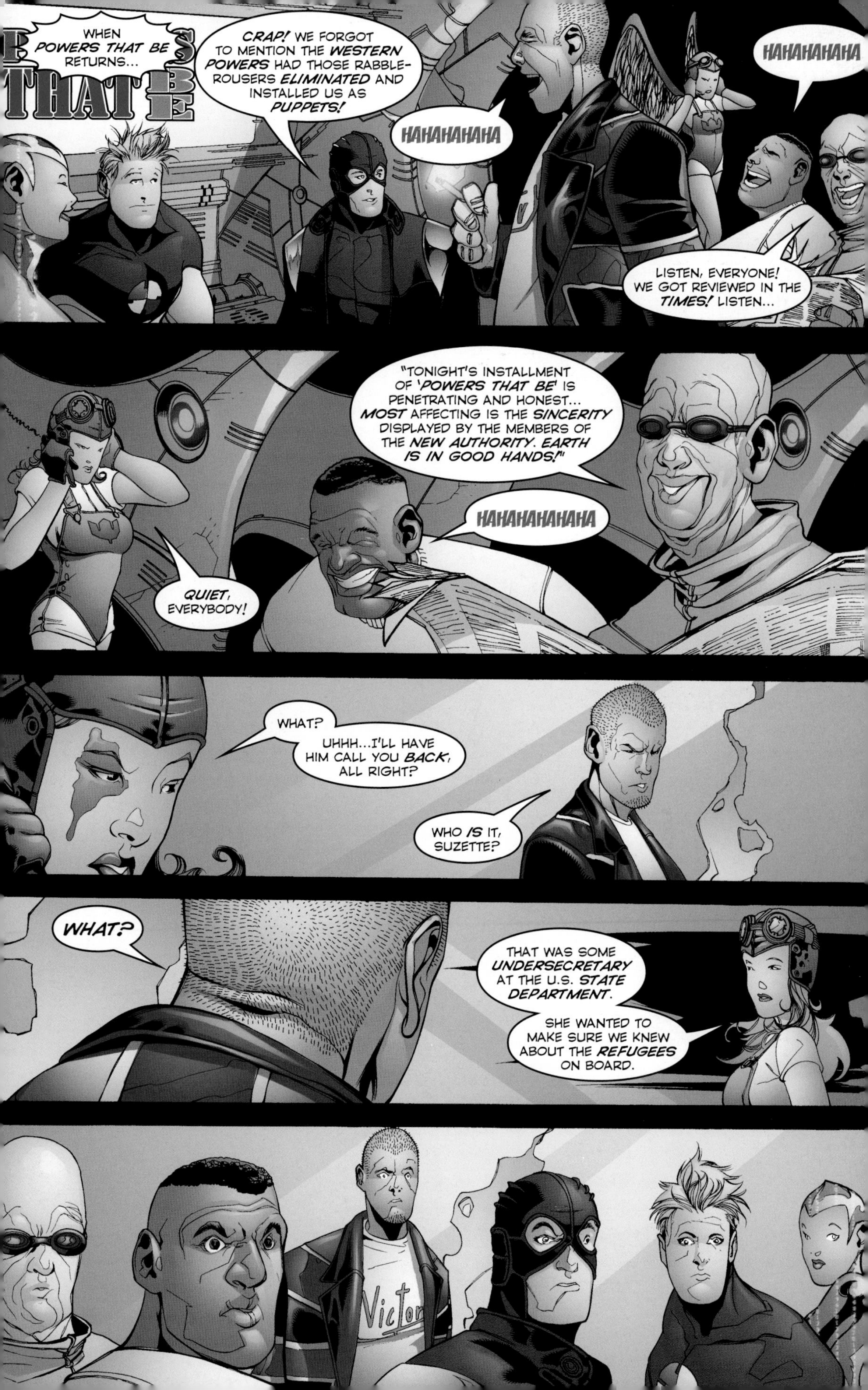
WHEN POWERS THAT BE RETURNS...
POWERS THAT BE
CRAP! WE FORGOT TO MENTION THE WESTERN POWERS HAD THOSE RABBLE-ROUSERS ELIMINATED AND INSTALLED US AS PUPPETS!
HAHAHAHAHA
HAHAHAHAHA
LISTEN, EVERYONE! WE GOT REVIEWED IN THE TIMES! LISTEN...
"TONIGHT'S INSTALLMENT OF 'POWERS THAT BE' IS PENETRATING AND HONEST... MOST AFFECTING IS THE SINCERITY DISPLAYED BY THE MEMBERS OF THE NEW AUTHORITY. EARTH IS IN GOOD HANDS!"
HAHAHAHAHAHA
QUIET, EVERYBODY!
WHAT?
UHHH...I'LL HAVE HIM CALL YOU BACK, ALL RIGHT?
WHO IS IT, SUZETTE?
WHAT?
THAT WAS SOME UNDERSECRETARY AT THE U.S. STATE DEPARTMENT.
SHE WANTED TO MAKE SURE WE KNEW ABOUT THE REFUGEES ON BOARD.
Victor

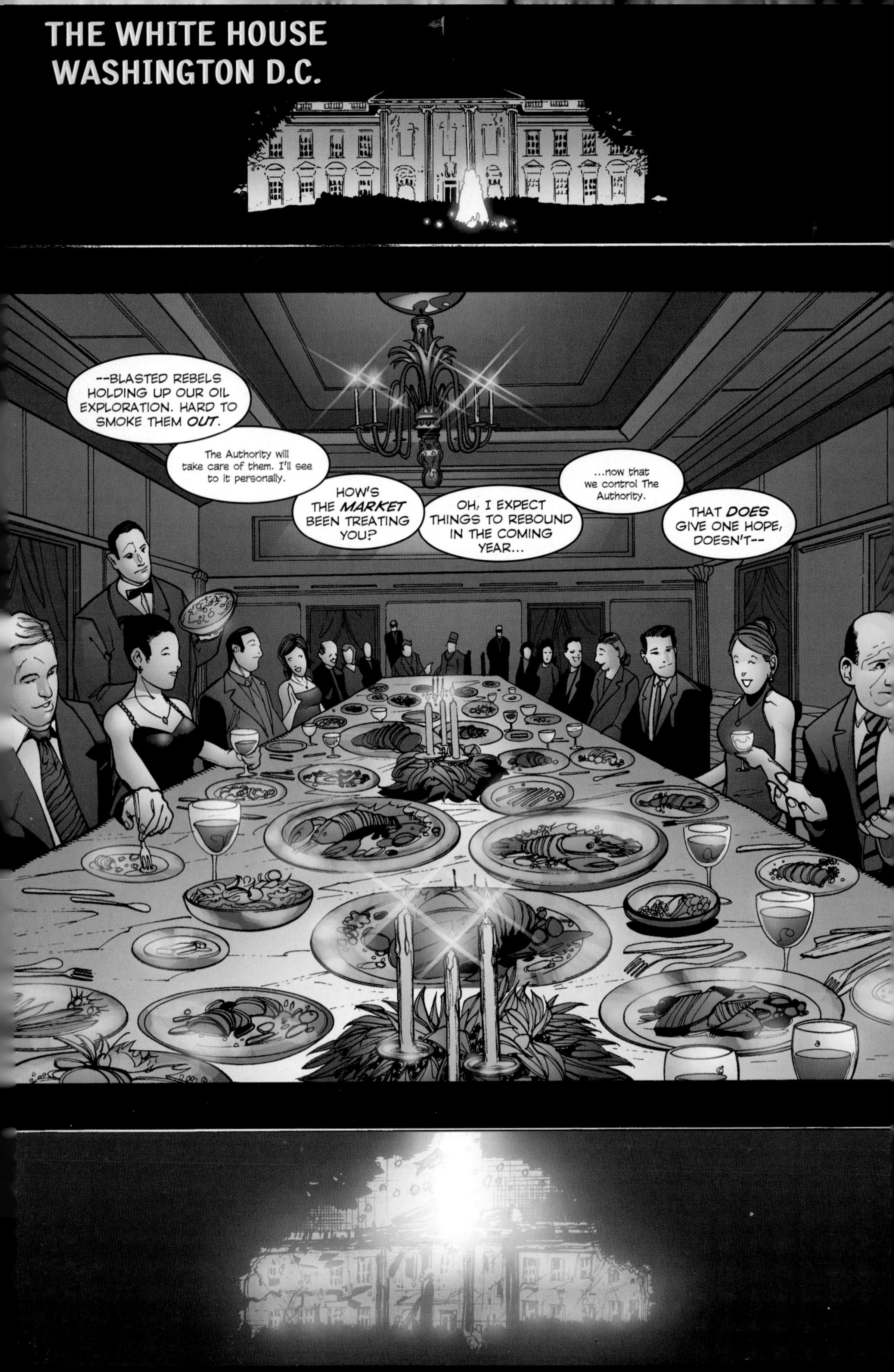
THE WHITE HOUSE
WASHINGTON D.C.
--BLASTED REBELS HOLDING UP OUR OIL EXPLORATION. HARD TO SMOKE THEM OUT.
The Authority will take care of them. I'll see to it personally.
HOW'S THE MARKET BEEN TREATING YOU?
OH, I EXPECT THINGS TO REBOUND IN THE COMING YEAR...
...now that we control The Authority.
THAT DOES GIVE ONE HOPE, DOESN'T--

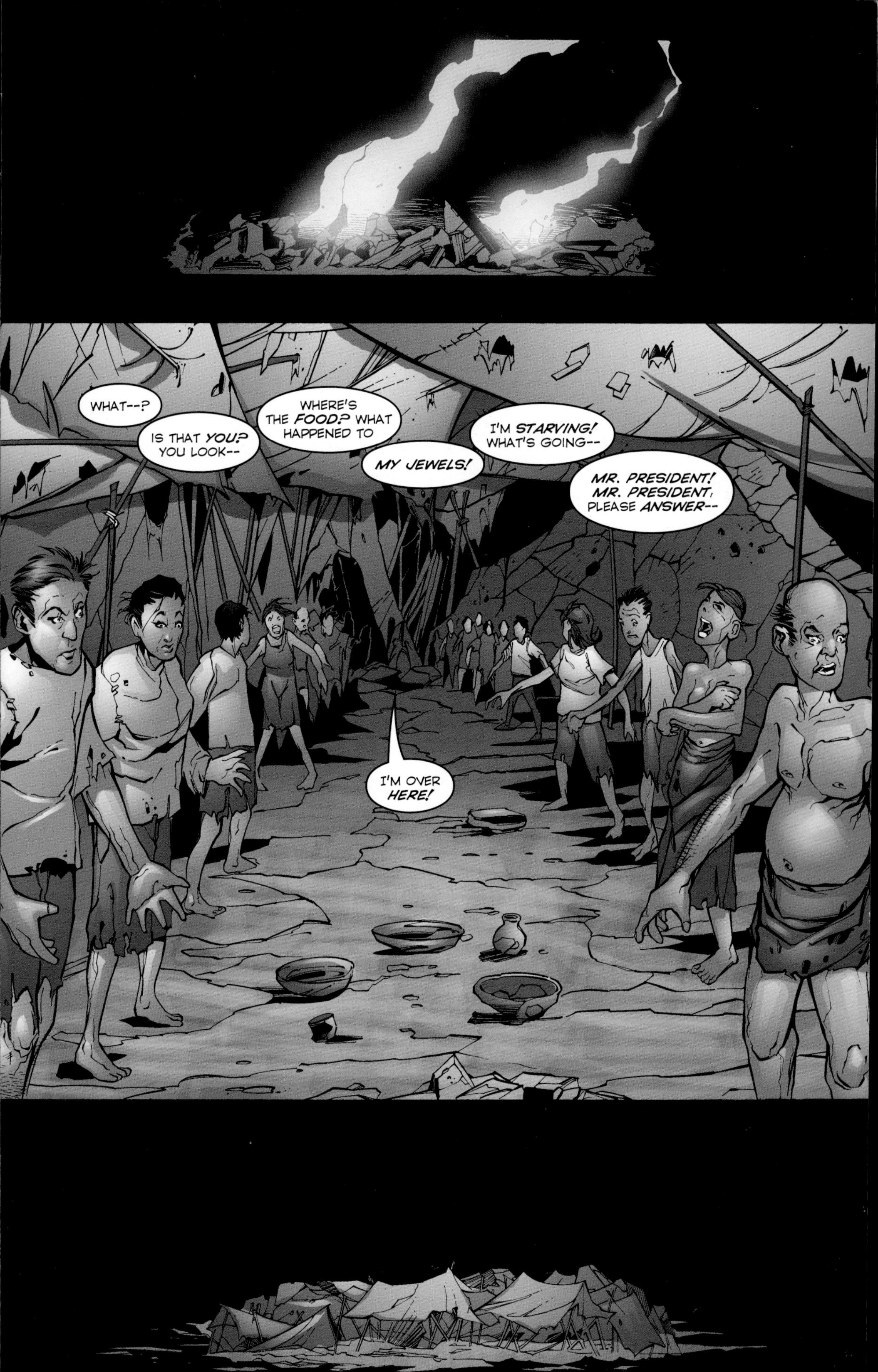
WHAT--?
IS THAT *YOU?* YOU LOOK--
WHERE'S THE *FOOD?* WHAT HAPPENED TO
MY JEWELS!
I'M *STARVING!* WHAT'S GOING--
MR. PRESIDENT! MR. PRESIDENT, PLEASE *ANSWER--*
I'M OVER *HERE!*

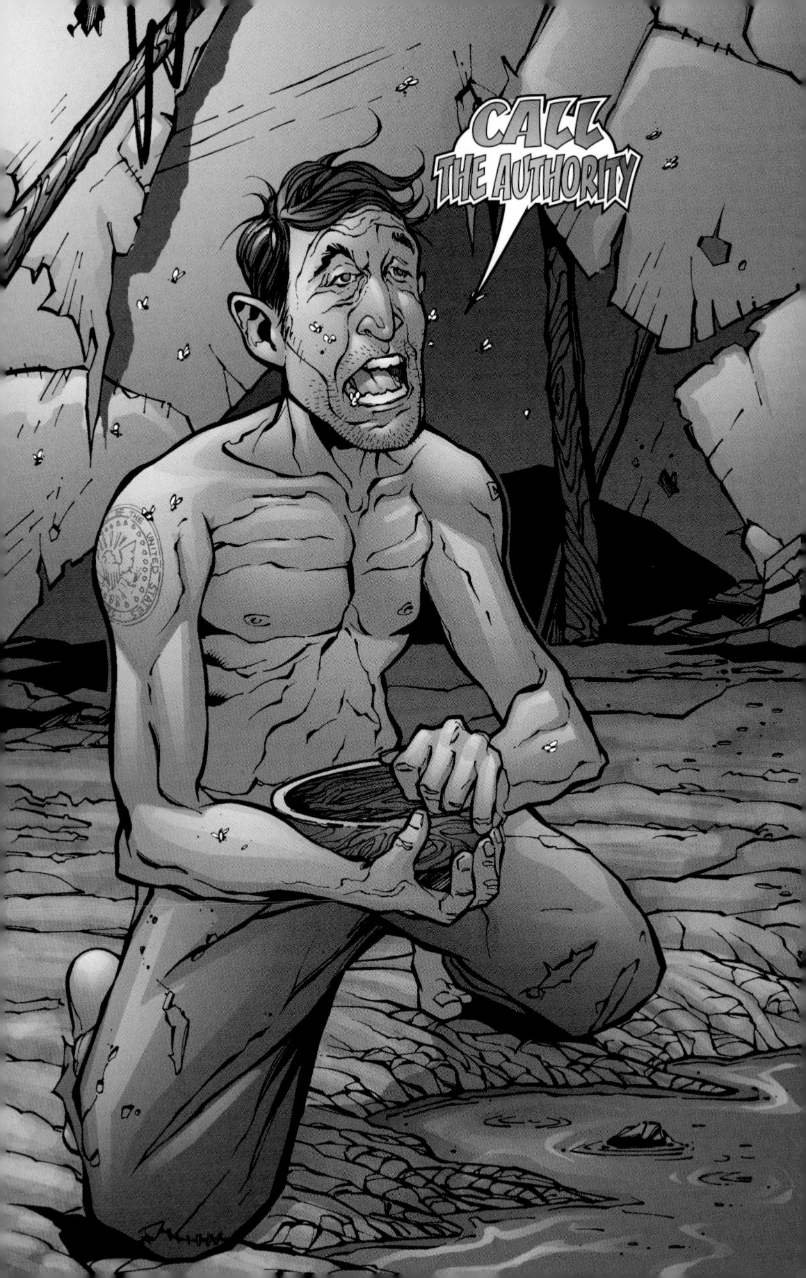
CALL THE AUTHORITY

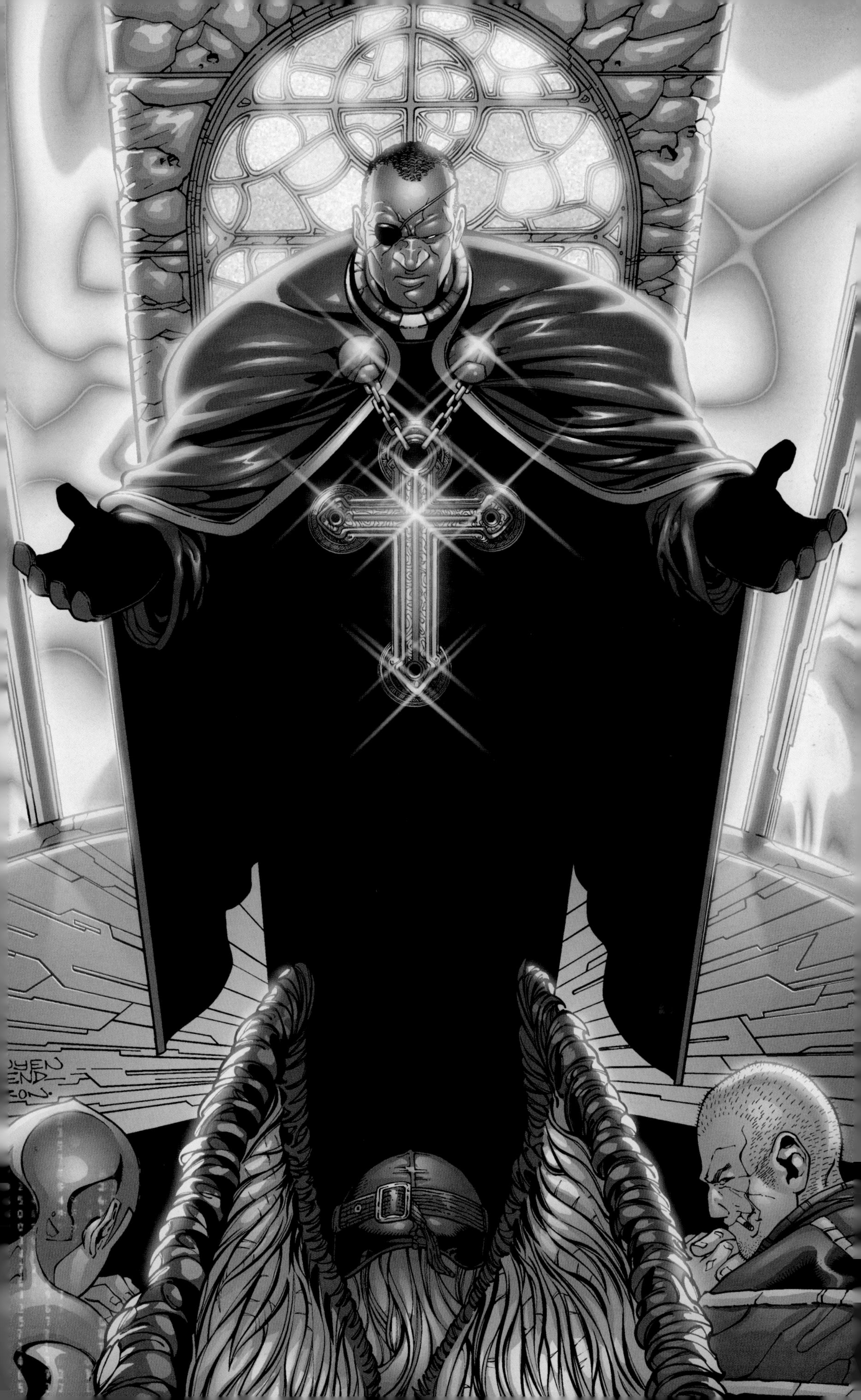

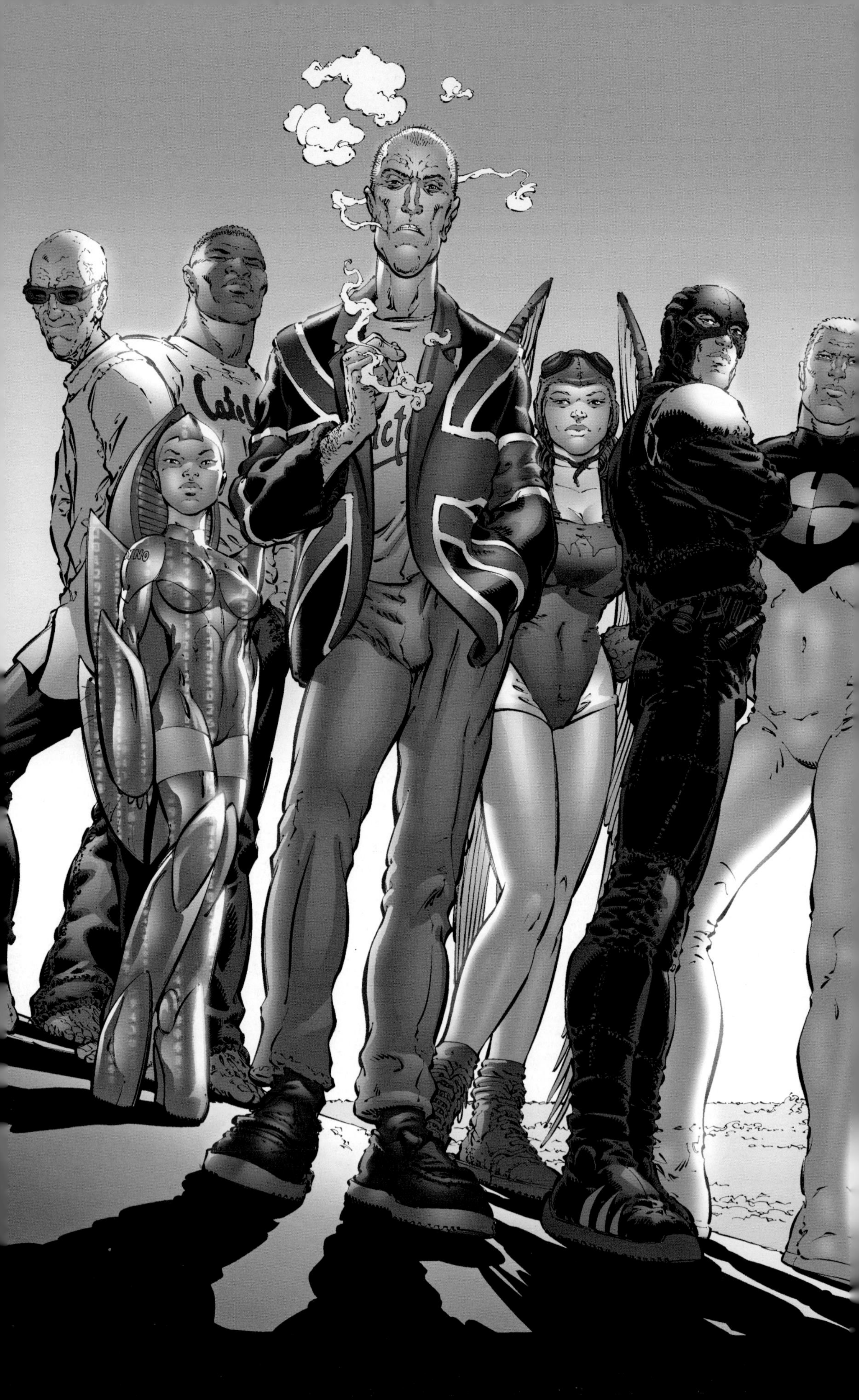

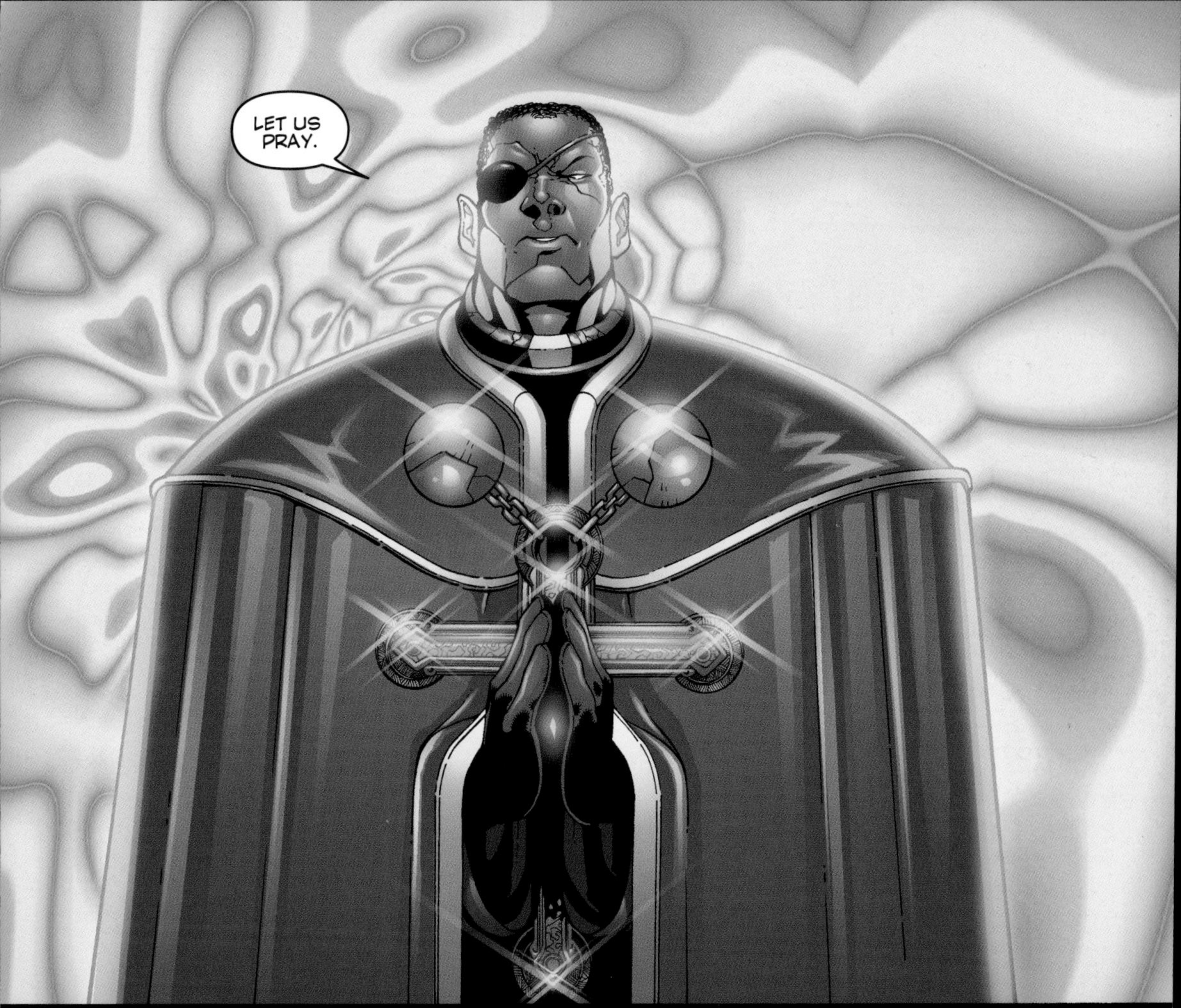
LET US PRAY.

THE AUTHORITY
TRANSFER OF POWER
Two of Four

TOM PEYER words **DUSTIN NGUYEN** pencils **RICHARD FRIEND** & **JASON MARTIN** inks

DAVID BARON colors **BILL O'NEIL** letters

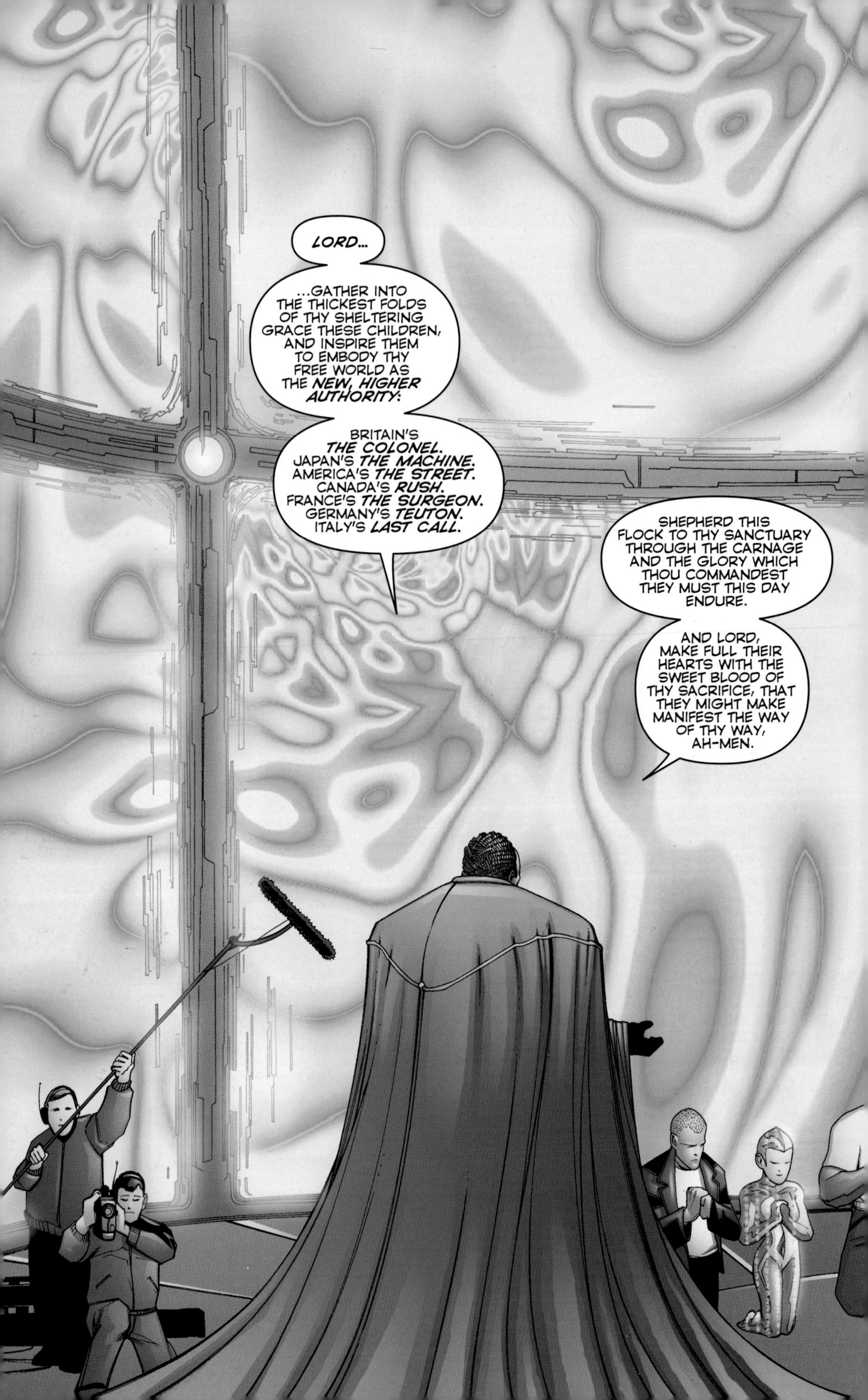
LORD...
...GATHER INTO THE THICKEST FOLDS OF THY SHELTERING GRACE THESE CHILDREN, AND INSPIRE THEM TO EMBODY THY FREE WORLD AS THE NEW, HIGHER AUTHORITY:
BRITAIN'S THE COLONEL. JAPAN'S THE MACHINE. AMERICA'S THE STREET. CANADA'S RUSH. FRANCE'S THE SURGEON. GERMANY'S TEUTON. ITALY'S LAST CALL.
SHEPHERD THIS FLOCK TO THY SANCTUARY THROUGH THE CARNAGE AND THE GLORY WHICH THOU COMMANDEST THEY MUST THIS DAY ENDURE.
AND LORD, MAKE FULL THEIR HEARTS WITH THE SWEET BLOOD OF THY SACRIFICE, THAT THEY MIGHT MAKE MANIFEST THE WAY OF THY WAY, AH-MEN.

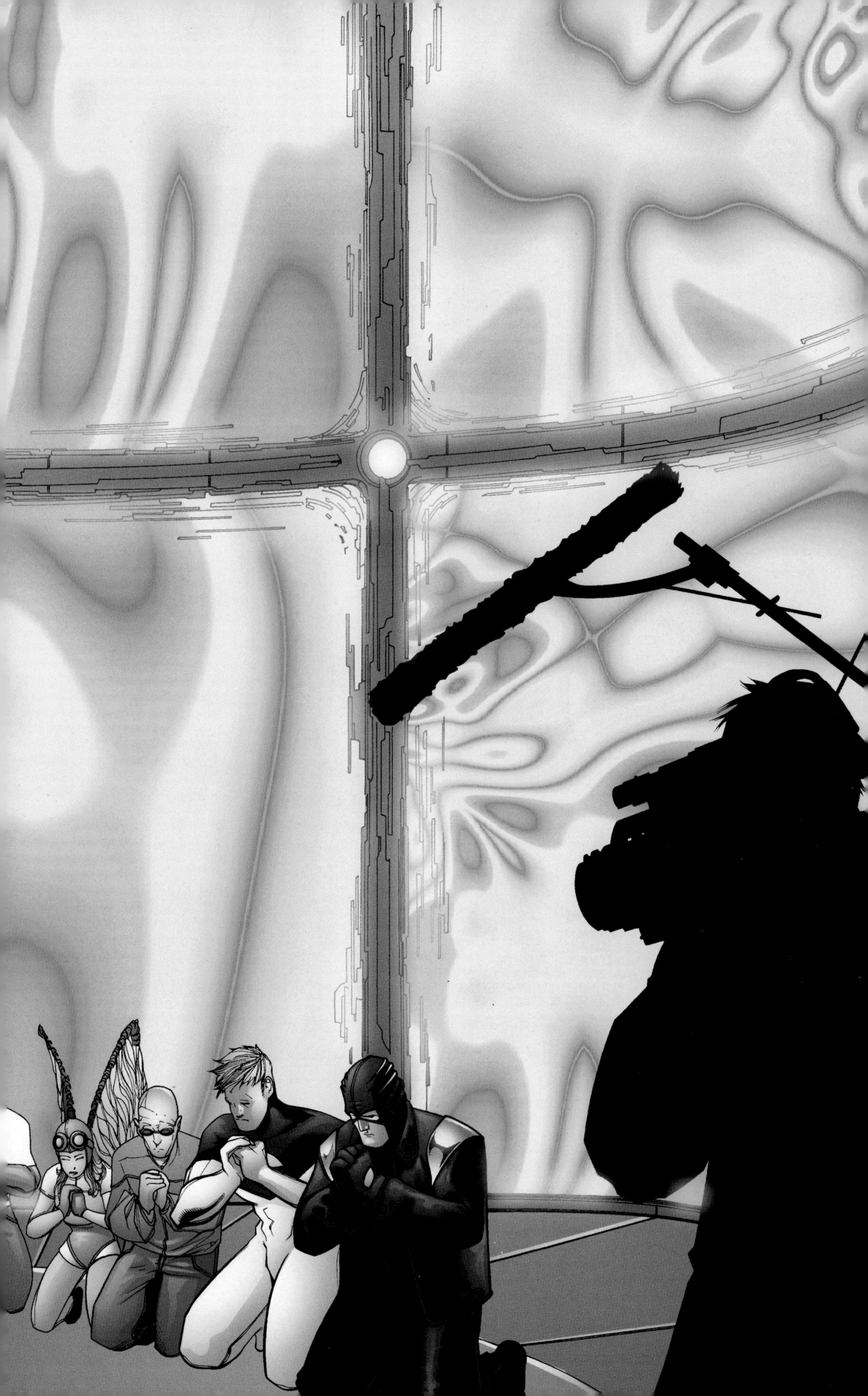

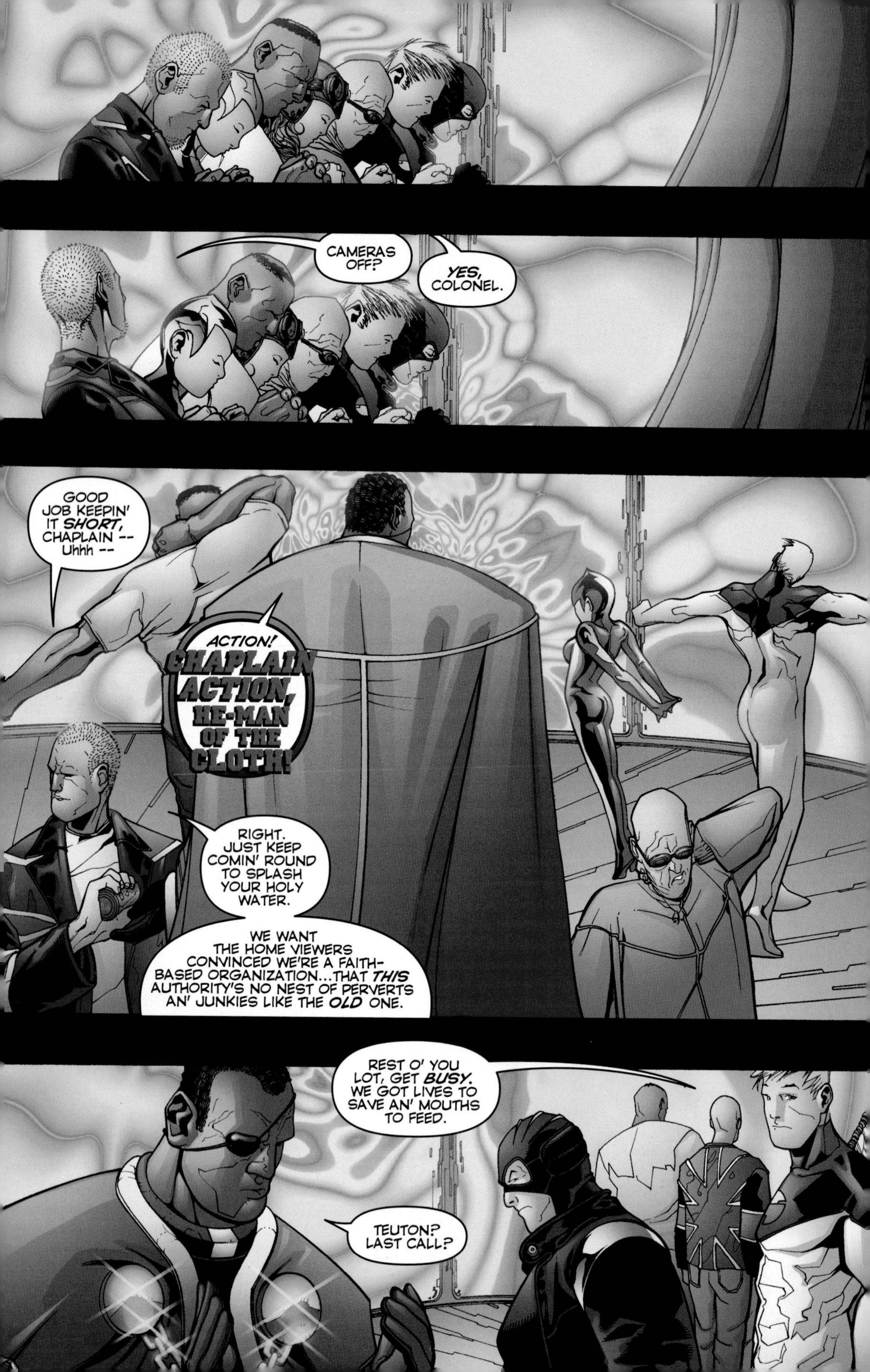
CAMERAS OFF?
YES, COLONEL.
GOOD JOB KEEPIN' IT SHORT, CHAPLAIN -- Uhhh --
ACTION! CHAPLAIN ACTION, HE-MAN OF THE CLOTH!
RIGHT. JUST KEEP COMIN' ROUND TO SPLASH YOUR HOLY WATER.
WE WANT THE HOME VIEWERS CONVINCED WE'RE A FAITH-BASED ORGANIZATION...THAT THIS AUTHORITY'S NO NEST OF PERVERTS AN' JUNKIES LIKE THE OLD ONE.
REST O' YOU LOT, GET BUSY. WE GOT LIVES TO SAVE AN' MOUTHS TO FEED.
TEUTON? LAST CALL?

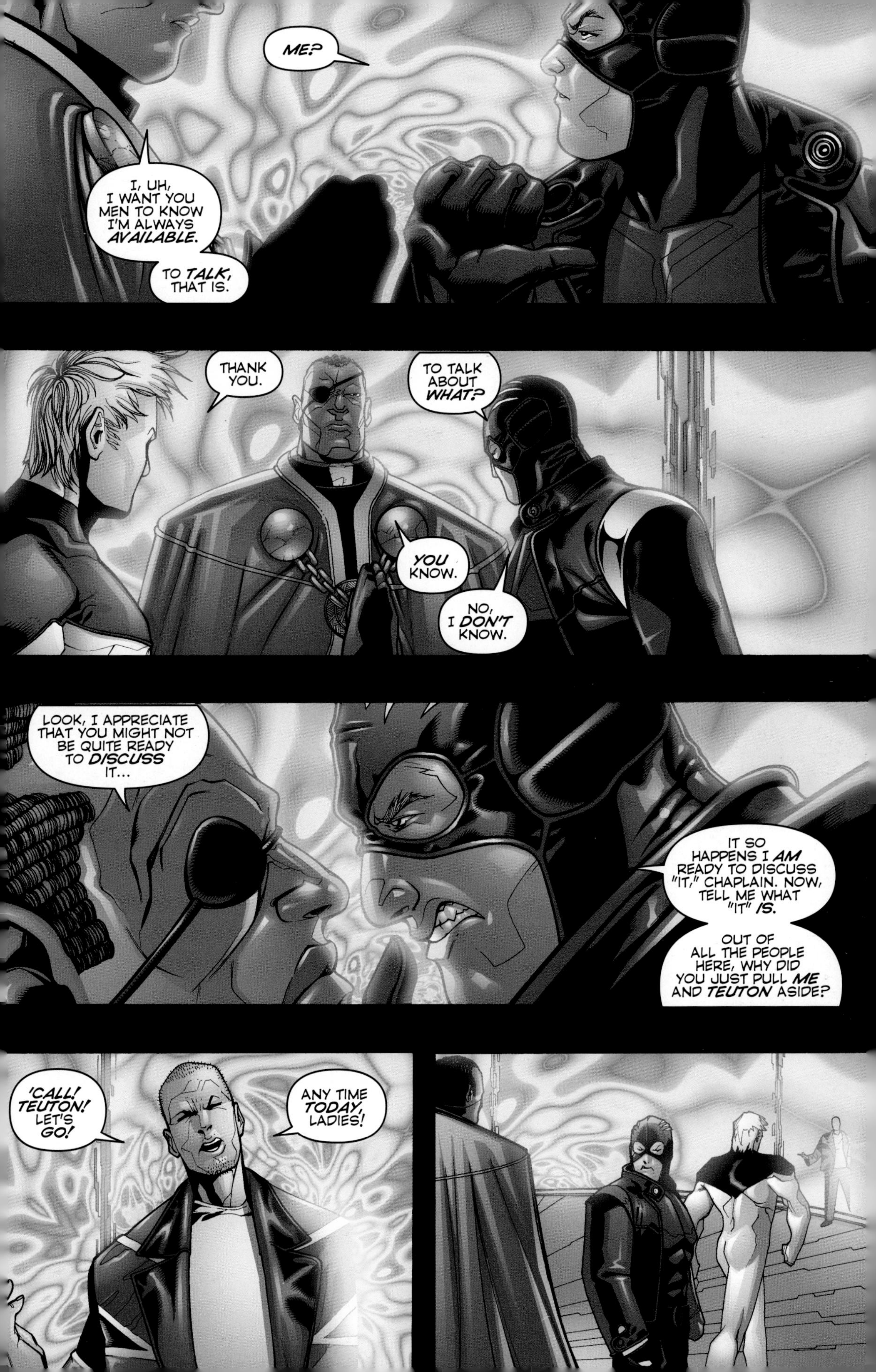
ME?
I, UH, I WANT YOU MEN TO KNOW I'M ALWAYS AVAILABLE.
TO TALK, THAT IS.
THANK YOU.
TO TALK ABOUT WHAT?
YOU KNOW.
NO, I DON'T KNOW.
LOOK, I APPRECIATE THAT YOU MIGHT NOT BE QUITE READY TO DISCUSS IT...
IT SO HAPPENS I AM READY TO DISCUSS "IT," CHAPLAIN. NOW, TELL ME WHAT "IT" IS.
OUT OF ALL THE PEOPLE HERE, WHY DID YOU JUST PULL ME AND TEUTON ASIDE?
'CALL! TEUTON! LET'S GO!
ANY TIME TODAY, LADIES!

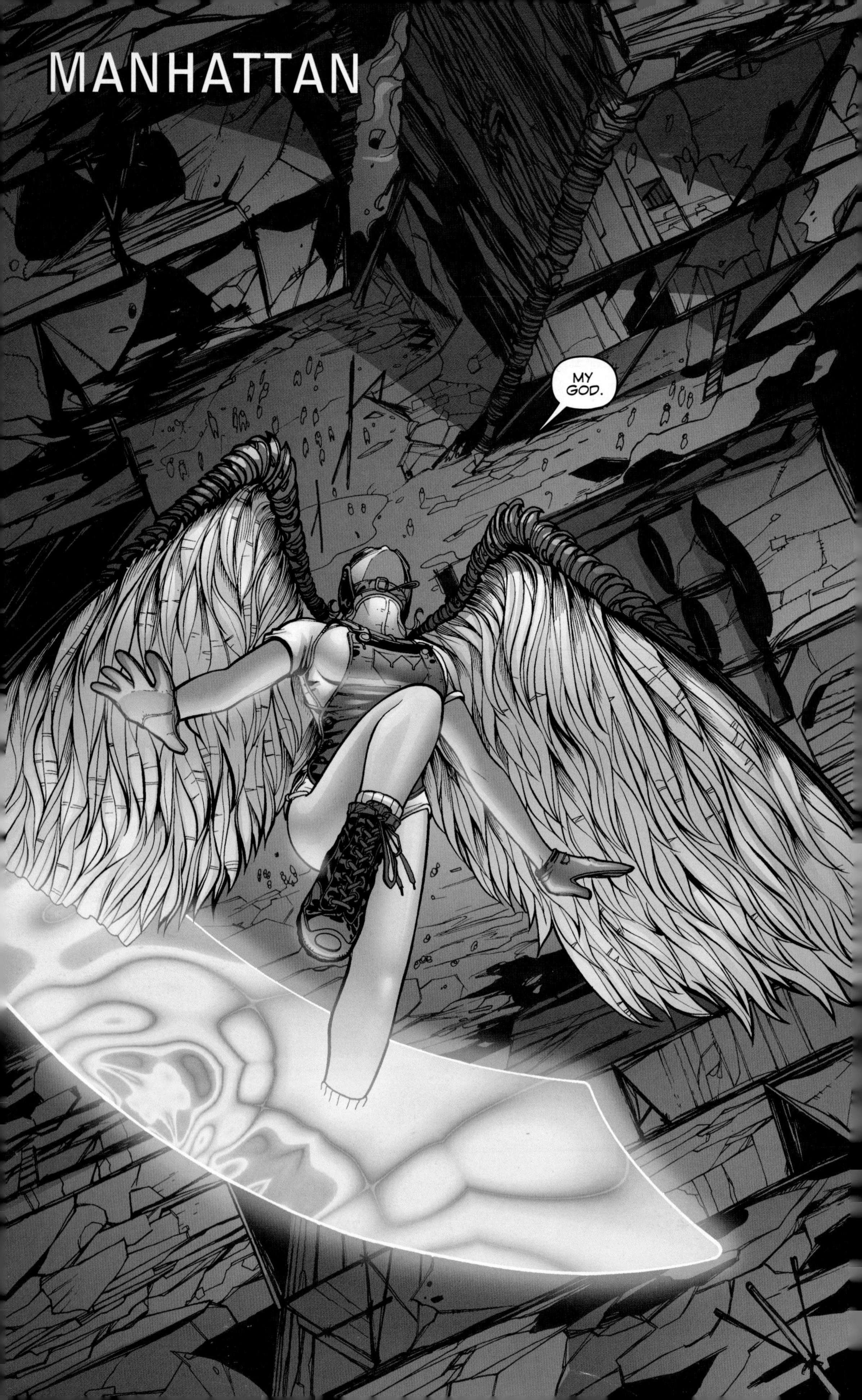
MANHATTAN
MY GOD.

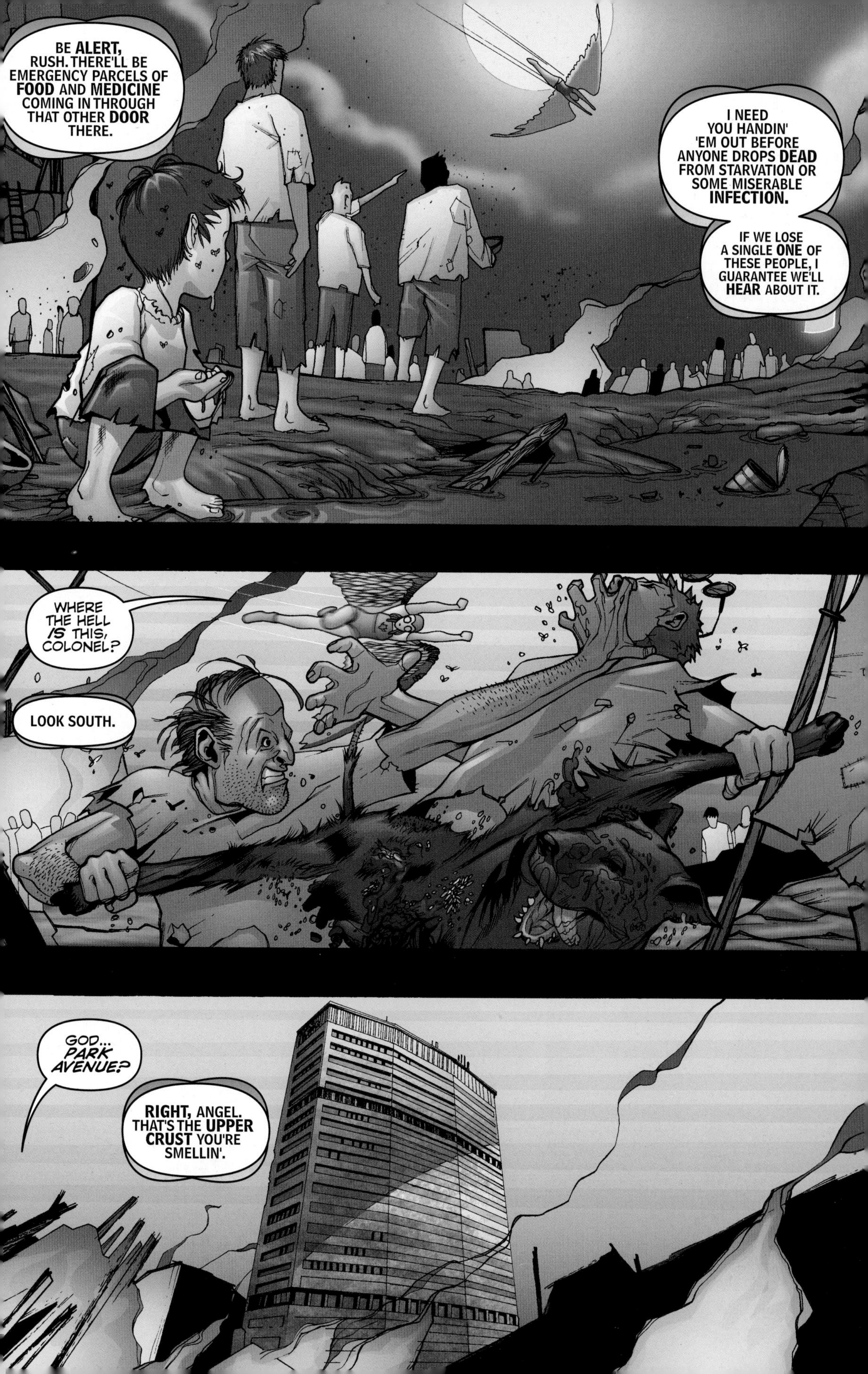
BE ALERT, RUSH. THERE'LL BE EMERGENCY PARCELS OF FOOD AND MEDICINE COMING IN THROUGH THAT OTHER DOOR THERE.
I NEED YOU HANDIN' 'EM OUT BEFORE ANYONE DROPS DEAD FROM STARVATION OR SOME MISERABLE INFECTION.
IF WE LOSE A SINGLE ONE OF THESE PEOPLE, I GUARANTEE WE'LL HEAR ABOUT IT.
WHERE THE HELL IS THIS, COLONEL?
LOOK SOUTH.
GOD... PARK AVENUE?
RIGHT, ANGEL. THAT'S THE UPPER CRUST YOU'RE SMELLIN'.

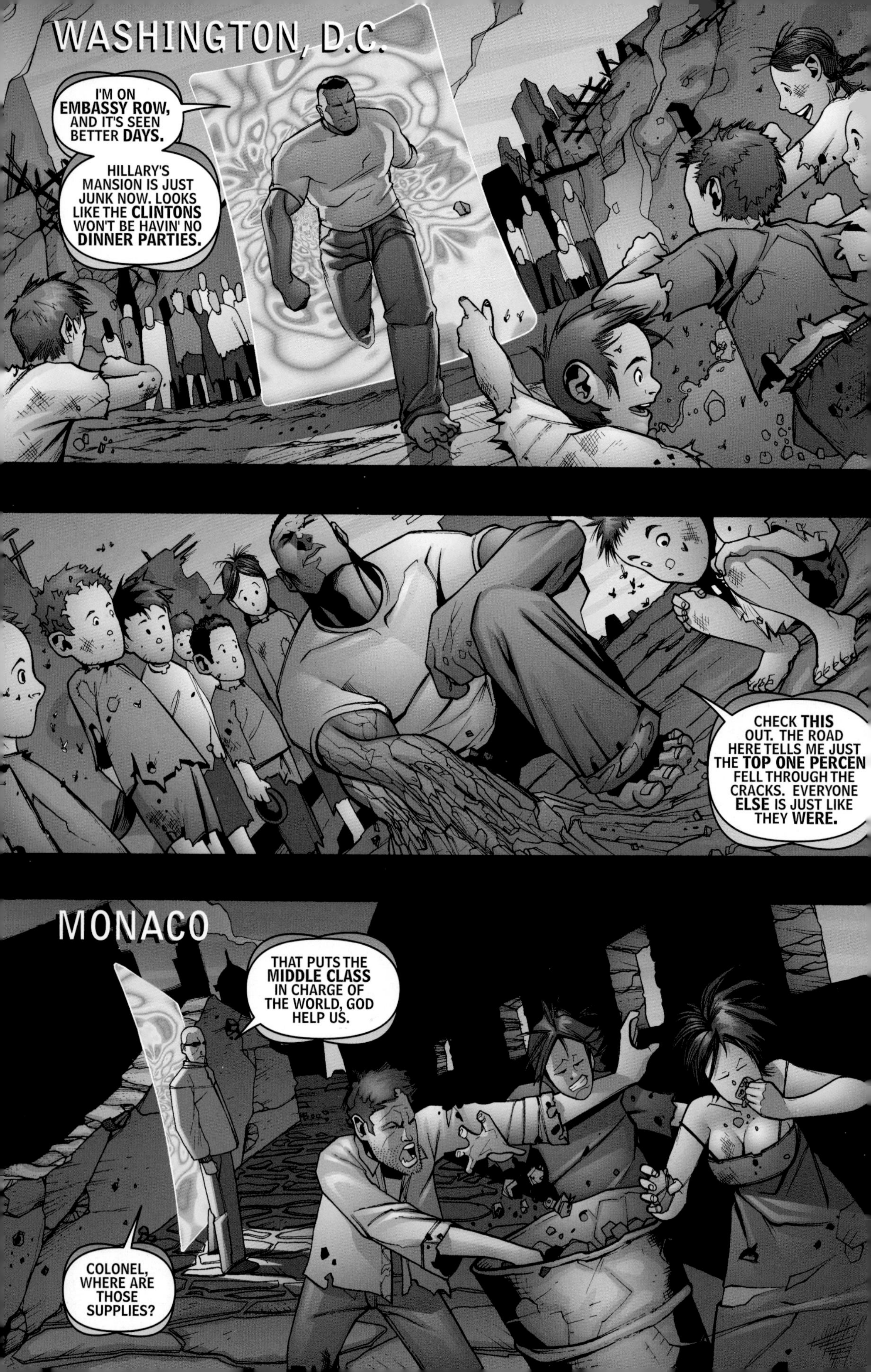
WASHINGTON, D.C.
I'M ON EMBASSY ROW, AND IT'S SEEN BETTER DAYS.
HILLARY'S MANSION IS JUST JUNK NOW. LOOKS LIKE THE CLINTONS WON'T BE HAVIN' NO DINNER PARTIES.
CHECK THIS OUT. THE ROAD HERE TELLS ME JUST THE TOP ONE PERCEN FELL THROUGH THE CRACKS. EVERYONE ELSE IS JUST LIKE THEY WERE.
MONACO
THAT PUTS THE MIDDLE CLASS IN CHARGE OF THE WORLD, GOD HELP US.
COLONEL, WHERE ARE THOSE SUPPLIES?

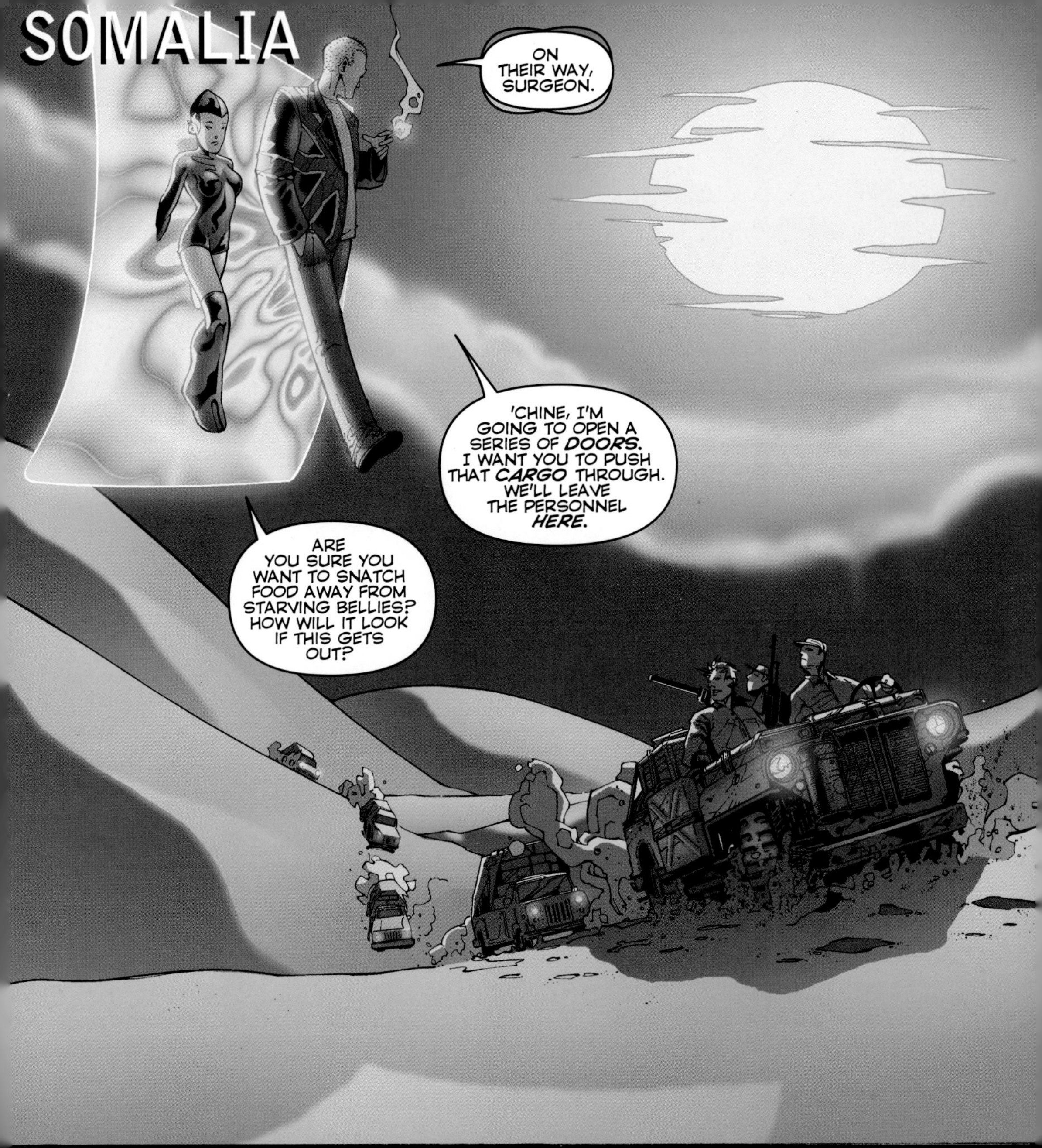
SOMALIA
ON THEIR WAY, SURGEON.
'CHINE, I'M GOING TO OPEN A SERIES OF DOORS. I WANT YOU TO PUSH THAT CARGO THROUGH. WE'LL LEAVE THE PERSONNEL HERE.
ARE YOU SURE YOU WANT TO SNATCH FOOD AWAY FROM STARVING BELLIES? HOW WILL IT LOOK IF THIS GETS OUT?

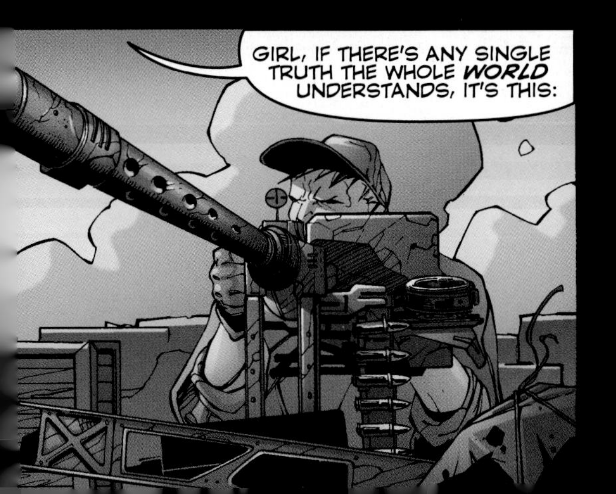
GIRL, IF THERE'S ANY SINGLE TRUTH THE WHOLE WORLD UNDERSTANDS, IT'S THIS:

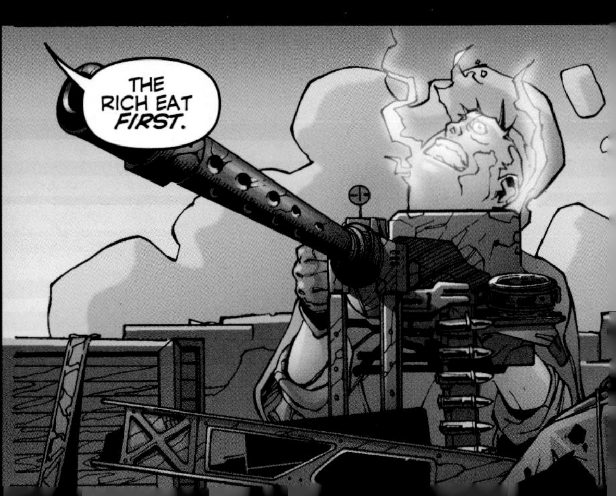
THE RICH EAT FIRST.

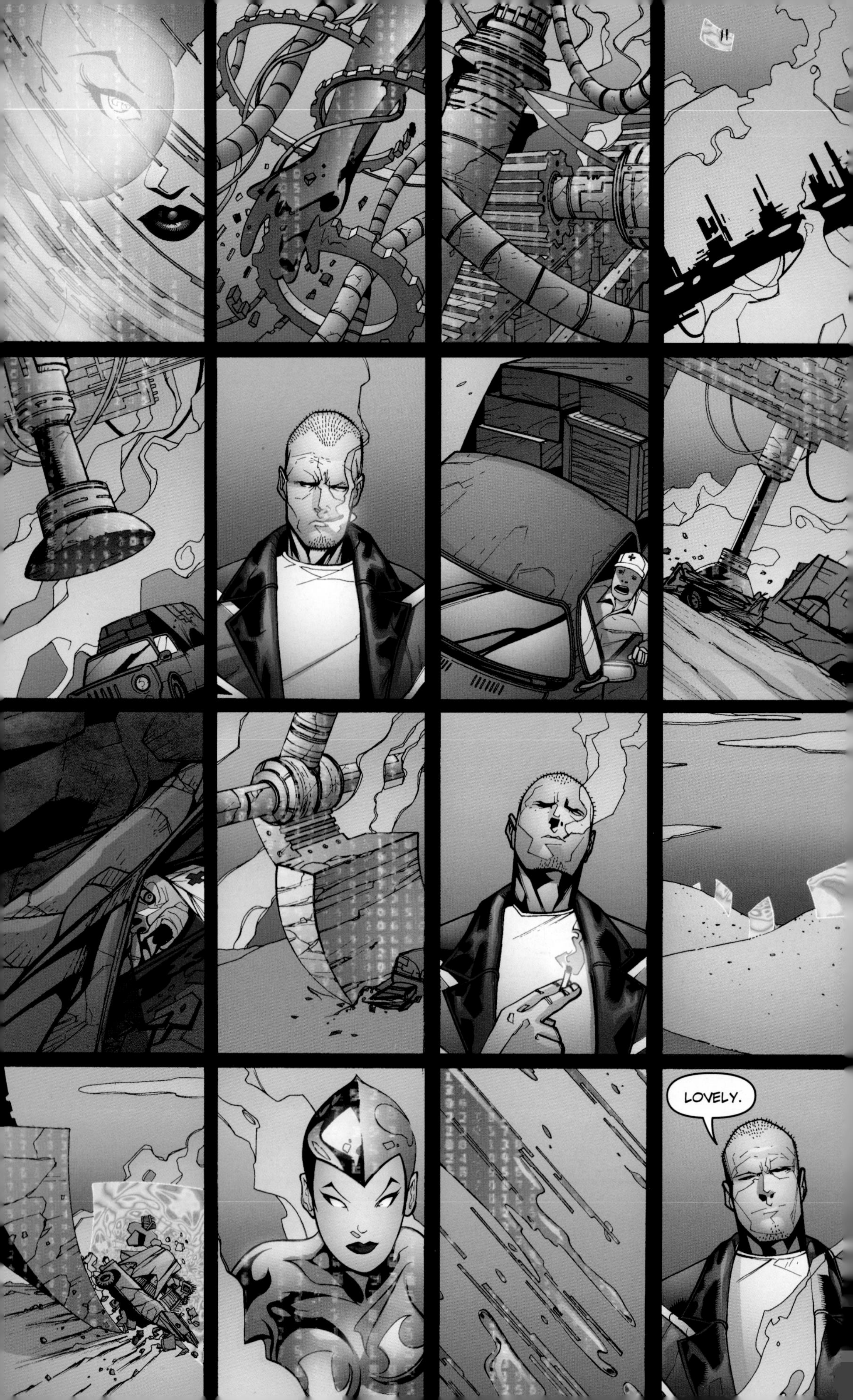
LOVELY.

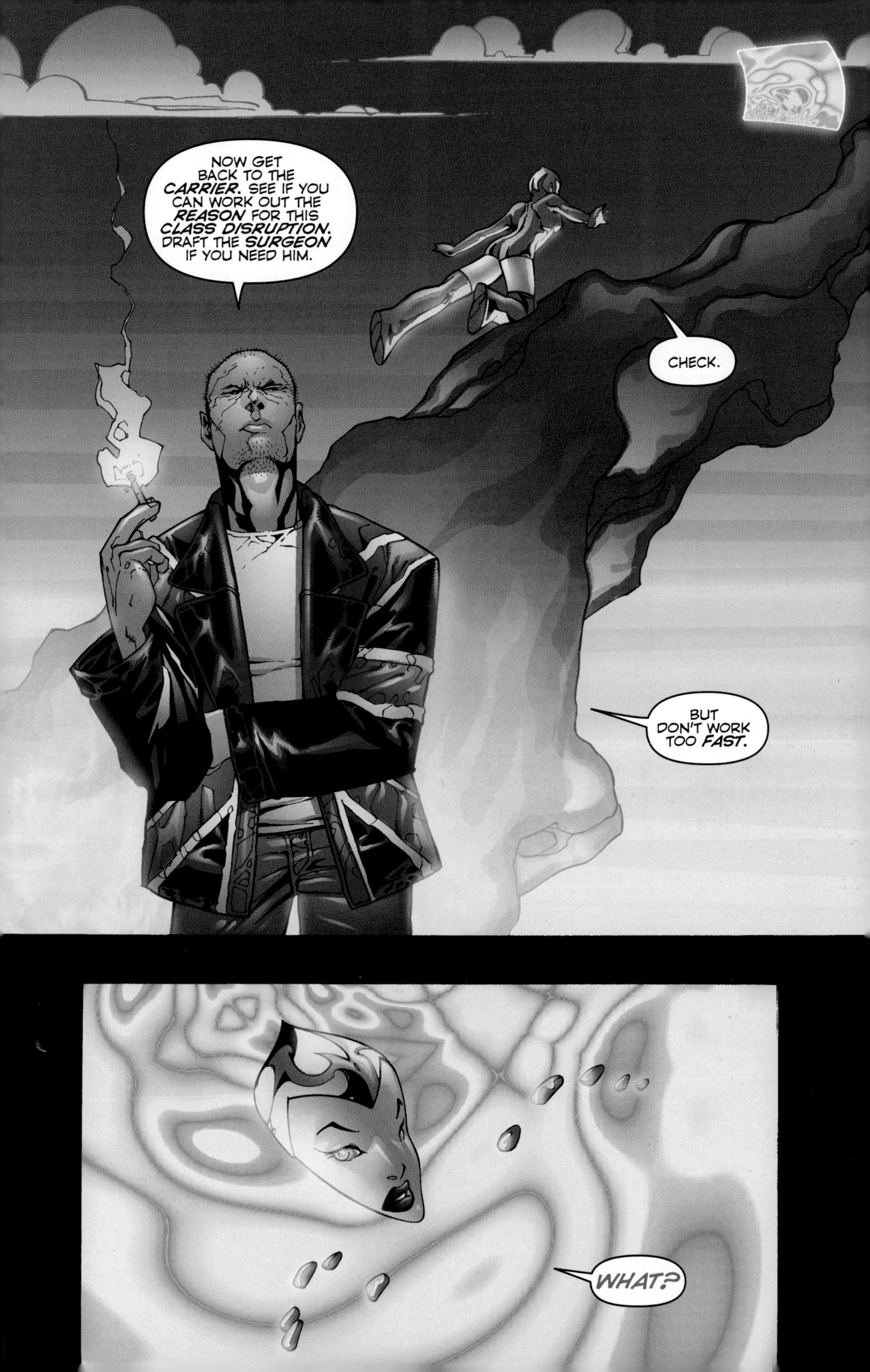
NOW GET BACK TO THE CARRIER. SEE IF YOU CAN WORK OUT THE REASON FOR THIS CLASS DISRUPTION. DRAFT THE SURGEON IF YOU NEED HIM.
CHECK.
BUT DON'T WORK TOO FAST.
WHAT?

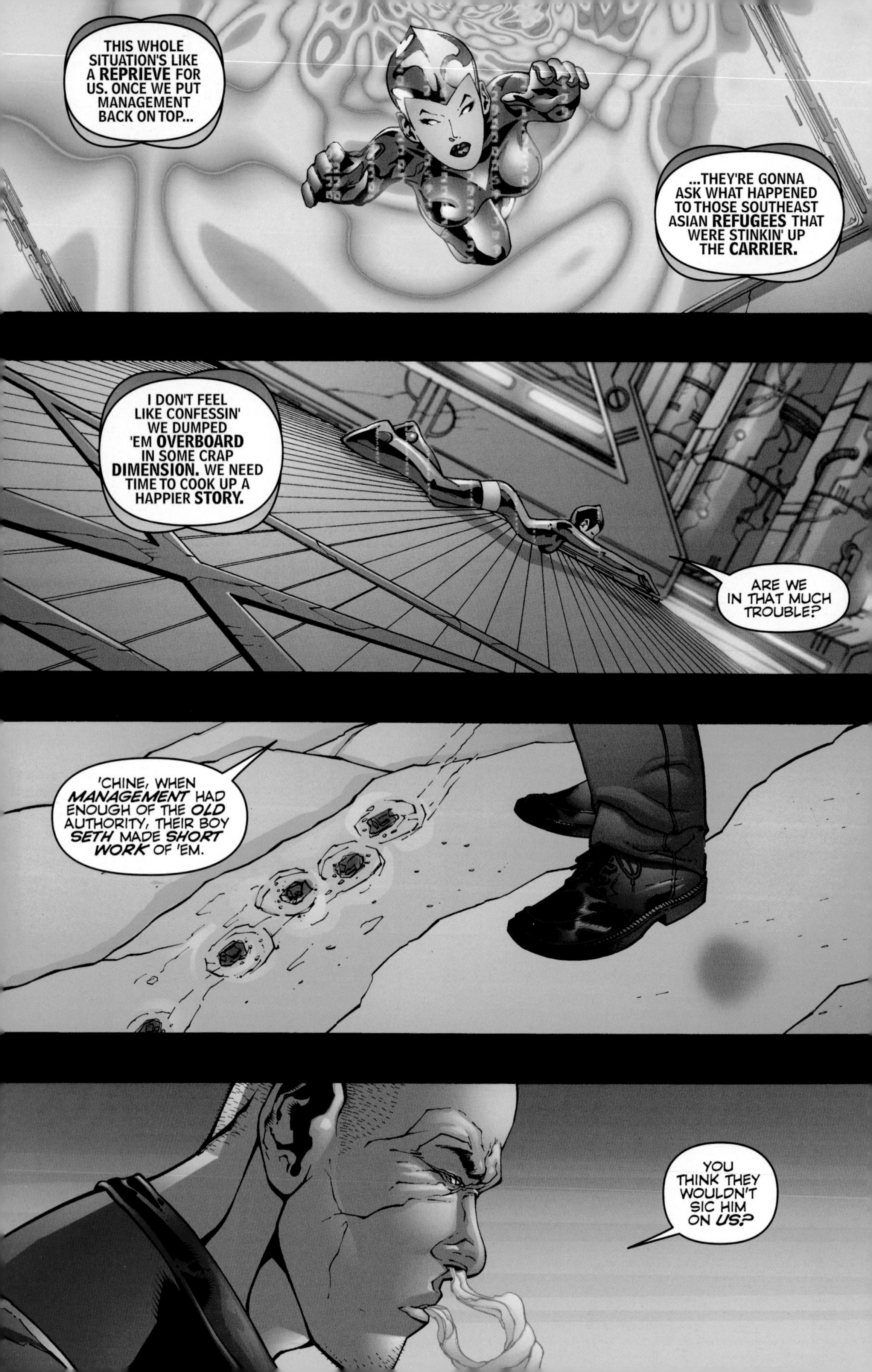
THIS WHOLE SITUATION'S LIKE A REPRIEVE FOR US. ONCE WE PUT MANAGEMENT BACK ON TOP...
...THEY'RE GONNA ASK WHAT HAPPENED TO THOSE SOUTHEAST ASIAN REFUGEES THAT WERE STINKIN' UP THE CARRIER.
I DON'T FEEL LIKE CONFESSIN' WE DUMPED 'EM OVERBOARD IN SOME CRAP DIMENSION. WE NEED TIME TO COOK UP A HAPPIER STORY.
ARE WE IN THAT MUCH TROUBLE?
'CHINE, WHEN MANAGEMENT HAD ENOUGH OF THE OLD AUTHORITY, THEIR BOY SETH MADE SHORT WORK OF 'EM.
YOU THINK THEY WOULDN'T SIC HIM ON US?

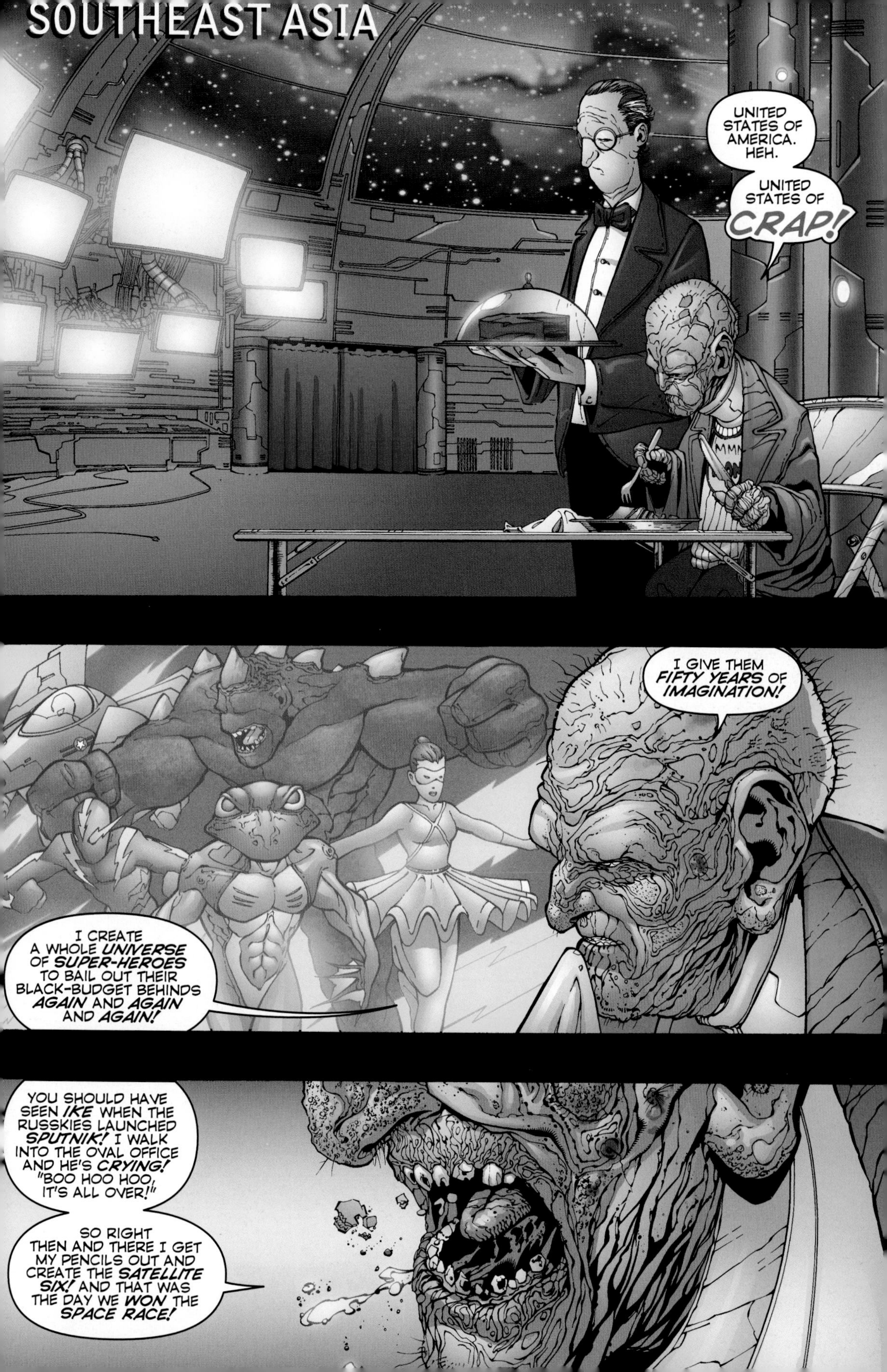
SOUTHEAST ASIA
UNITED STATES OF AMERICA. HEH.
UNITED STATES OF CRAP!
I GIVE THEM FIFTY YEARS OF IMAGINATION!
I CREATE A WHOLE UNIVERSE OF SUPER-HEROES TO BAIL OUT THEIR BLACK-BUDGET BEHINDS AGAIN AND AGAIN AND AGAIN!
YOU SHOULD HAVE SEEN IKE WHEN THE RUSSKIES LAUNCHED SPUTNIK! I WALK INTO THE OVAL OFFICE AND HE'S CRYING! "BOO HOO HOO, IT'S ALL OVER!"
SO RIGHT THEN AND THERE I GET MY PENCILS OUT AND CREATE THE SATELLITE SIX! AND THAT WAS THE DAY WE WON THE SPACE RACE!

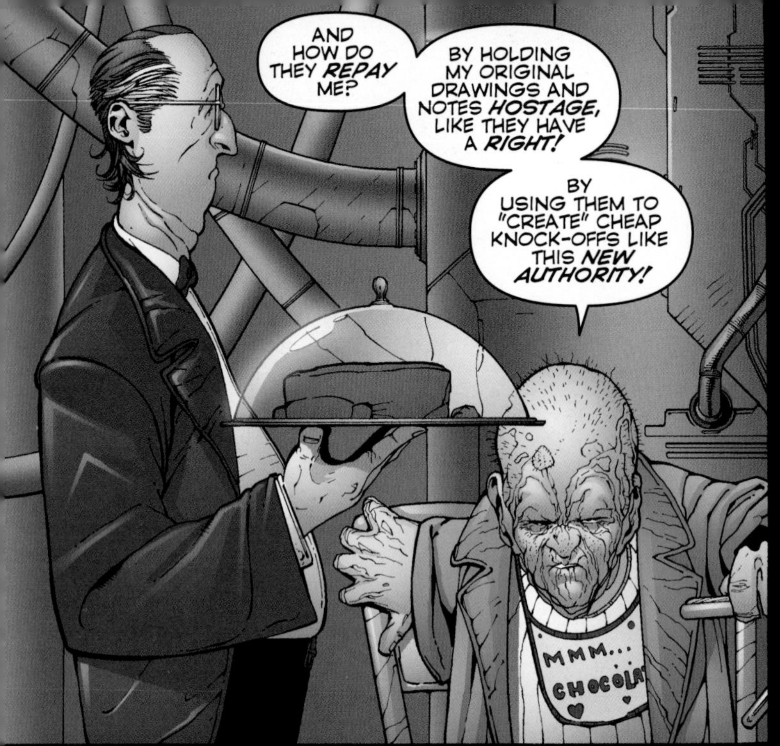
AND HOW DO THEY *REPAY* ME?
BY HOLDING MY ORIGINAL DRAWINGS AND NOTES *HOSTAGE*, LIKE THEY HAVE A *RIGHT!*
BY USING THEM TO "CREATE" CHEAP KNOCK-OFFS LIKE THIS *NEW AUTHORITY!*
MMM... CHOCOLA
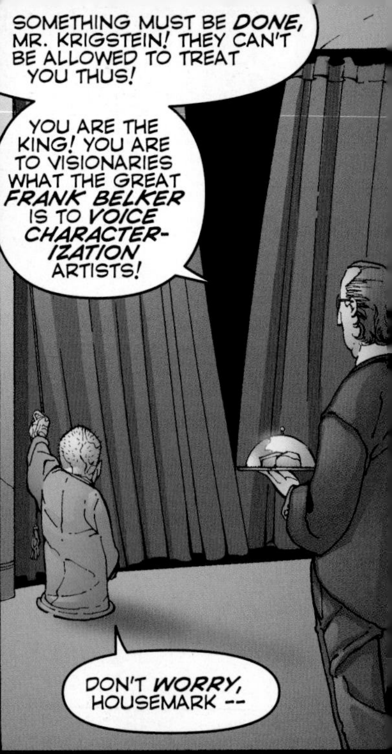
SOMETHING MUST BE *DONE*, MR. KRIGSTEIN! THEY CAN'T BE ALLOWED TO TREAT YOU THUS!
YOU ARE THE KING! YOU ARE TO VISIONARIES WHAT THE GREAT *FRANK BELKER* IS TO *VOICE CHARACTER-IZATION* ARTISTS!
DON'T *WORRY*, HOUSEMARK --
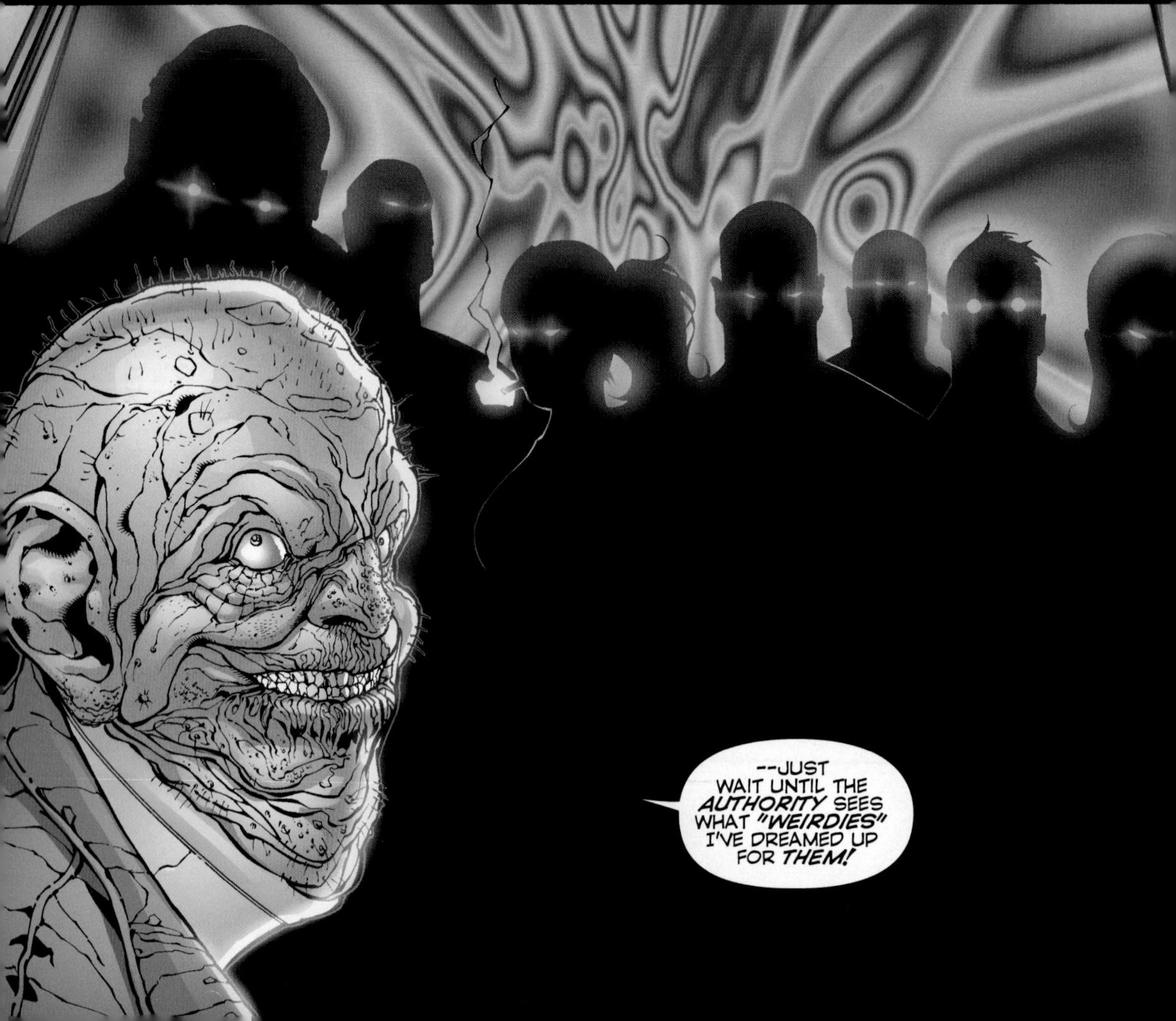
--JUST WAIT UNTIL THE *AUTHORITY* SEES WHAT *"WEIRDIES"* I'VE DREAMED UP FOR *THEM!*

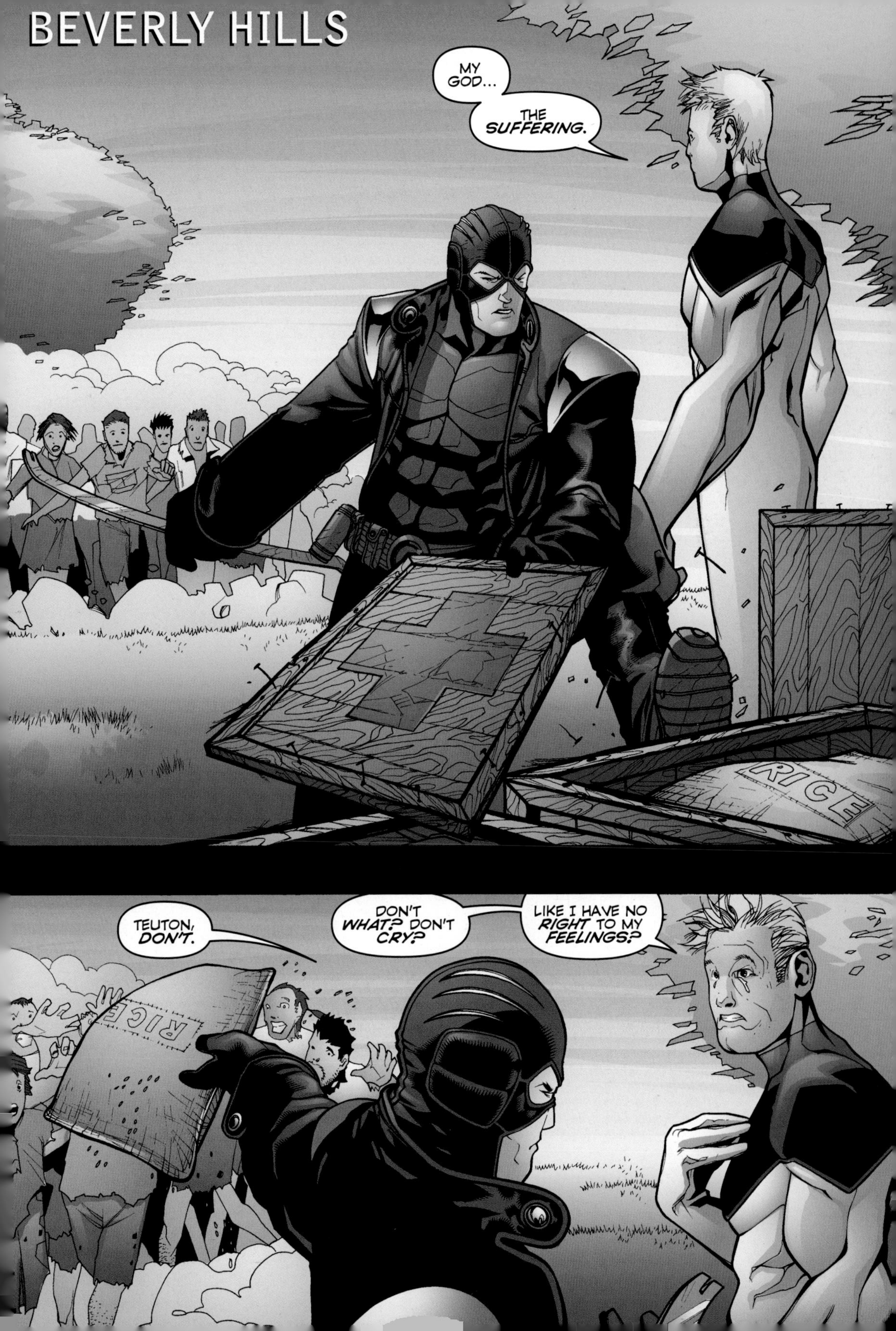
BEVERLY HILLS
MY GOD...
THE SUFFERING.
TEUTON, DON'T.
DON'T WHAT? DON'T CRY?
LIKE I HAVE NO RIGHT TO MY FEELINGS?
RICE

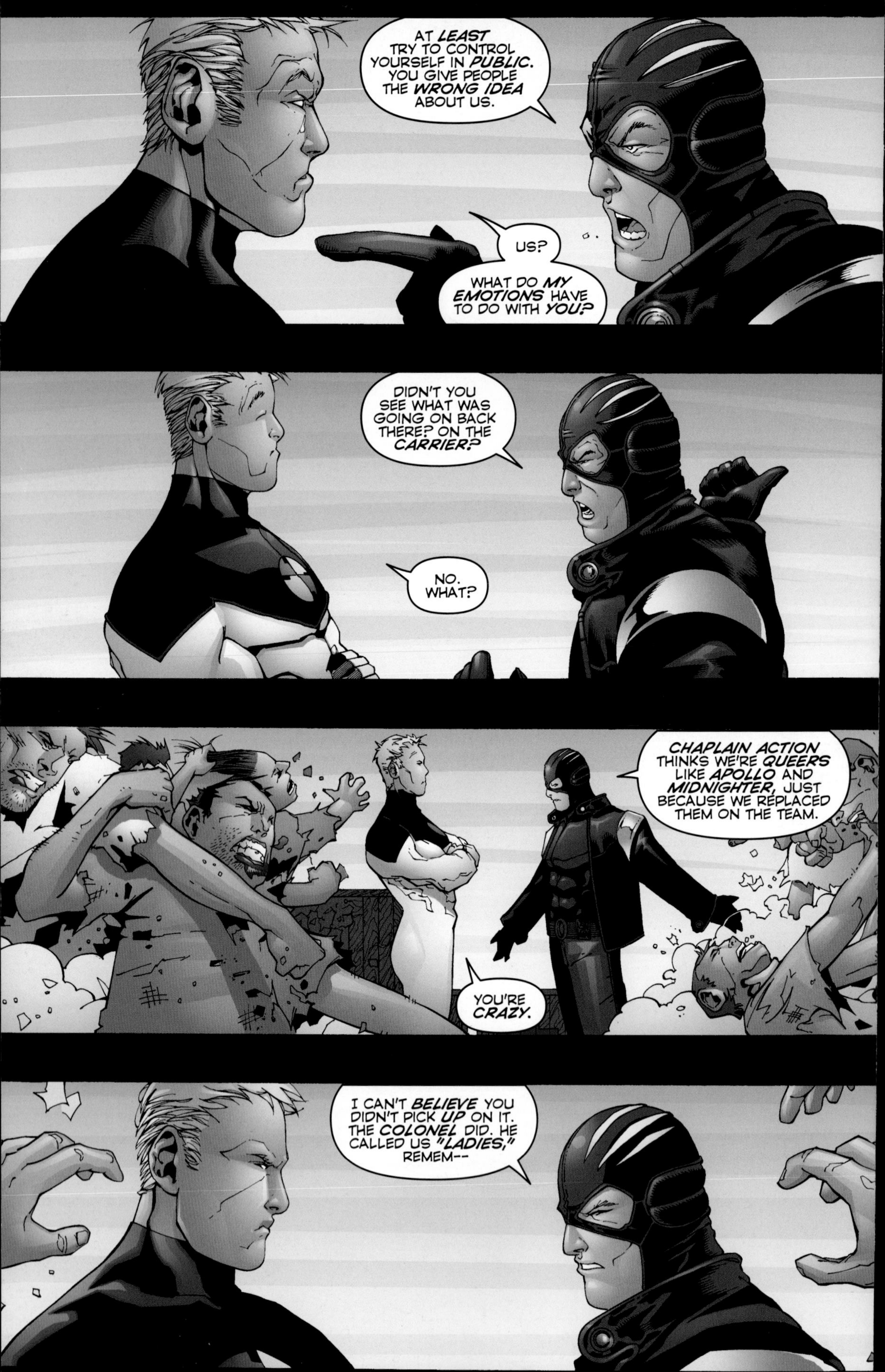
AT LEAST TRY TO CONTROL YOURSELF IN PUBLIC. YOU GIVE PEOPLE THE WRONG IDEA ABOUT US.
US?
WHAT DO MY EMOTIONS HAVE TO DO WITH YOU?
DIDN'T YOU SEE WHAT WAS GOING ON BACK THERE? ON THE CARRIER?
NO. WHAT?
CHAPLAIN ACTION THINKS WE'RE QUEERS LIKE APOLLO AND MIDNIGHTER, JUST BECAUSE WE REPLACED THEM ON THE TEAM.
YOU'RE CRAZY.
I CAN'T BELIEVE YOU DIDN'T PICK UP ON IT. THE COLONEL DID. HE CALLED US "LADIES," REMEM--

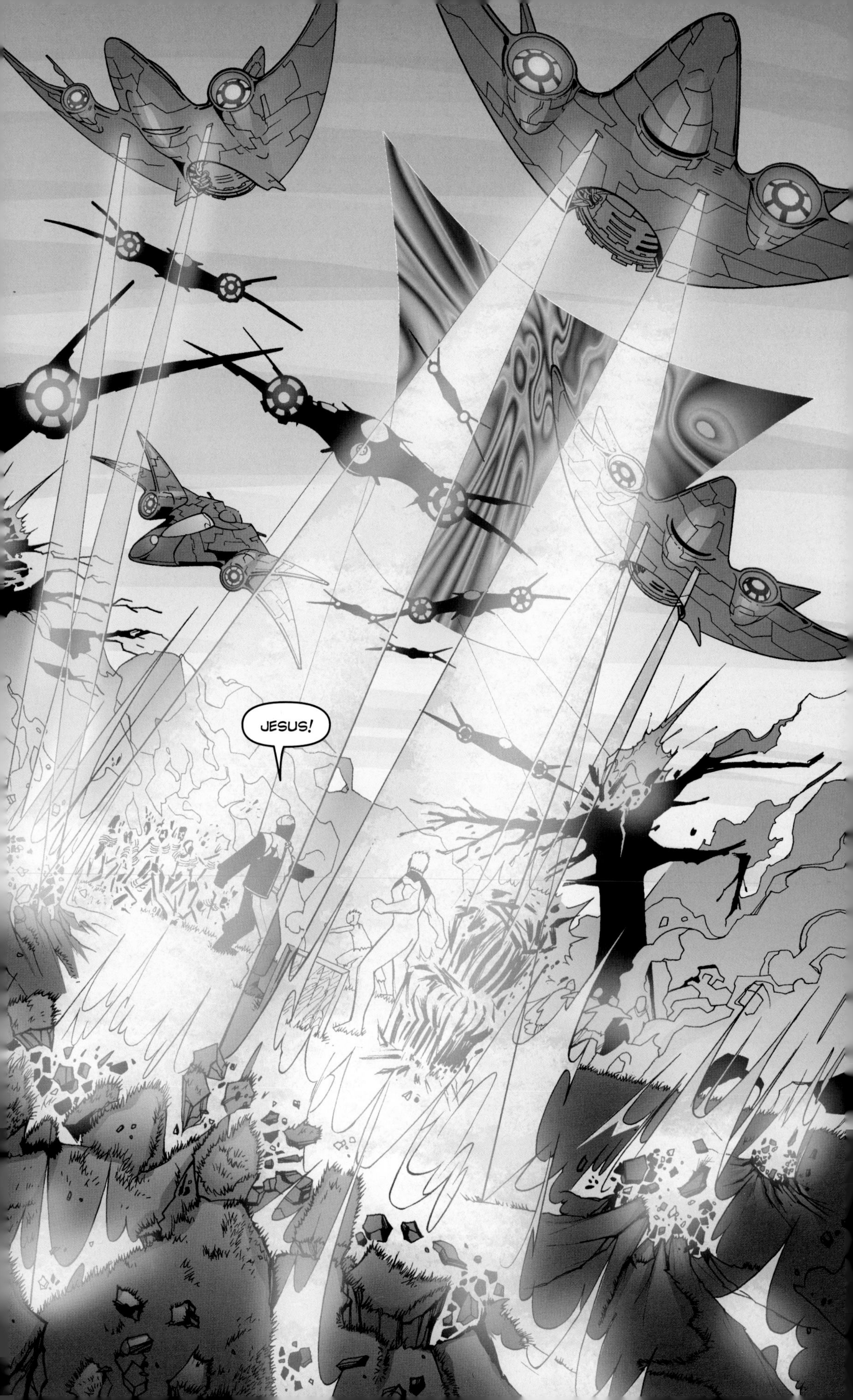
JESUS!

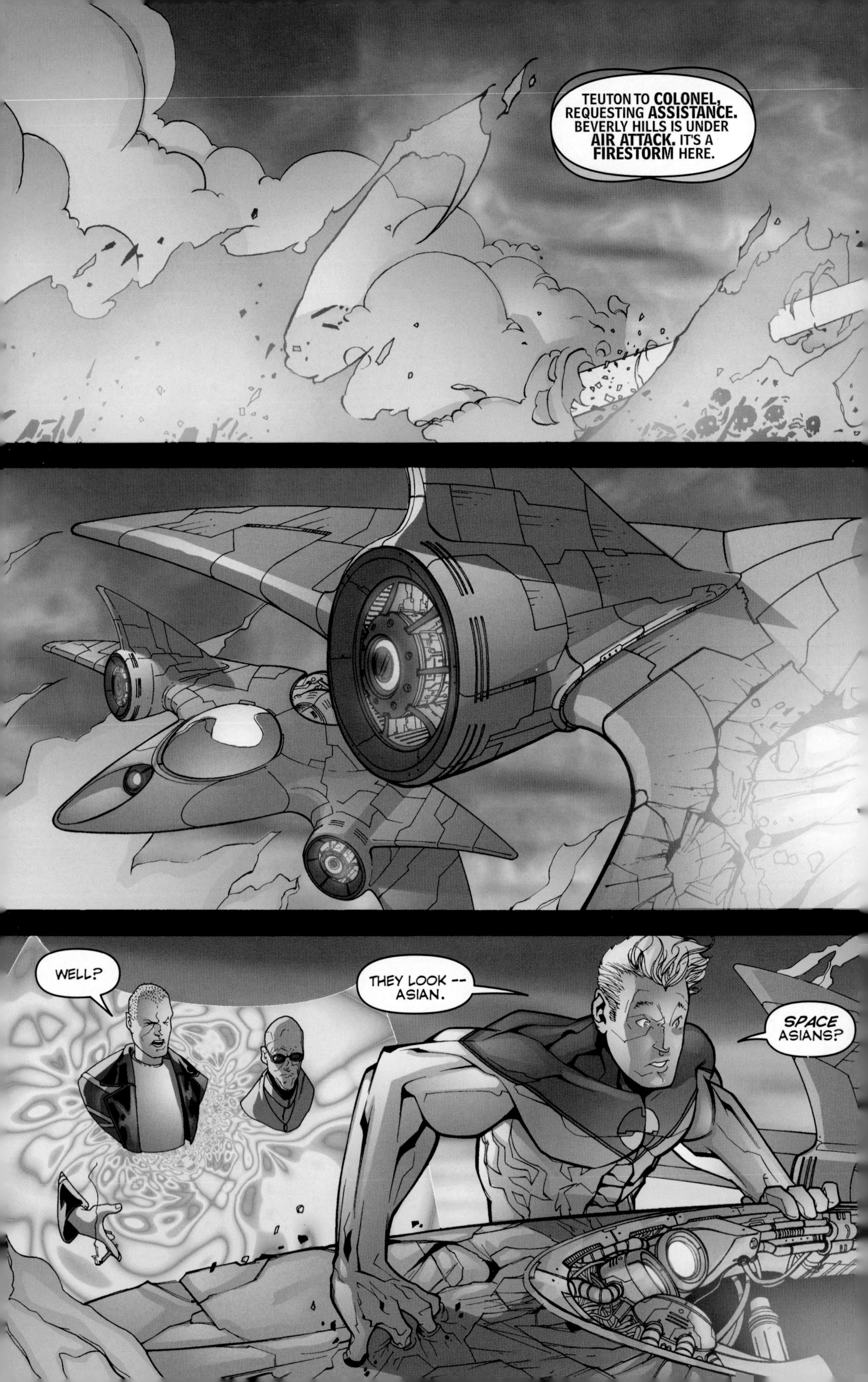
TEUTON TO COLONEL, REQUESTING ASSISTANCE. BEVERLY HILLS IS UNDER AIR ATTACK. IT'S A FIRESTORM HERE.
WELL?
THEY LOOK -- ASIAN.
SPACE ASIANS?

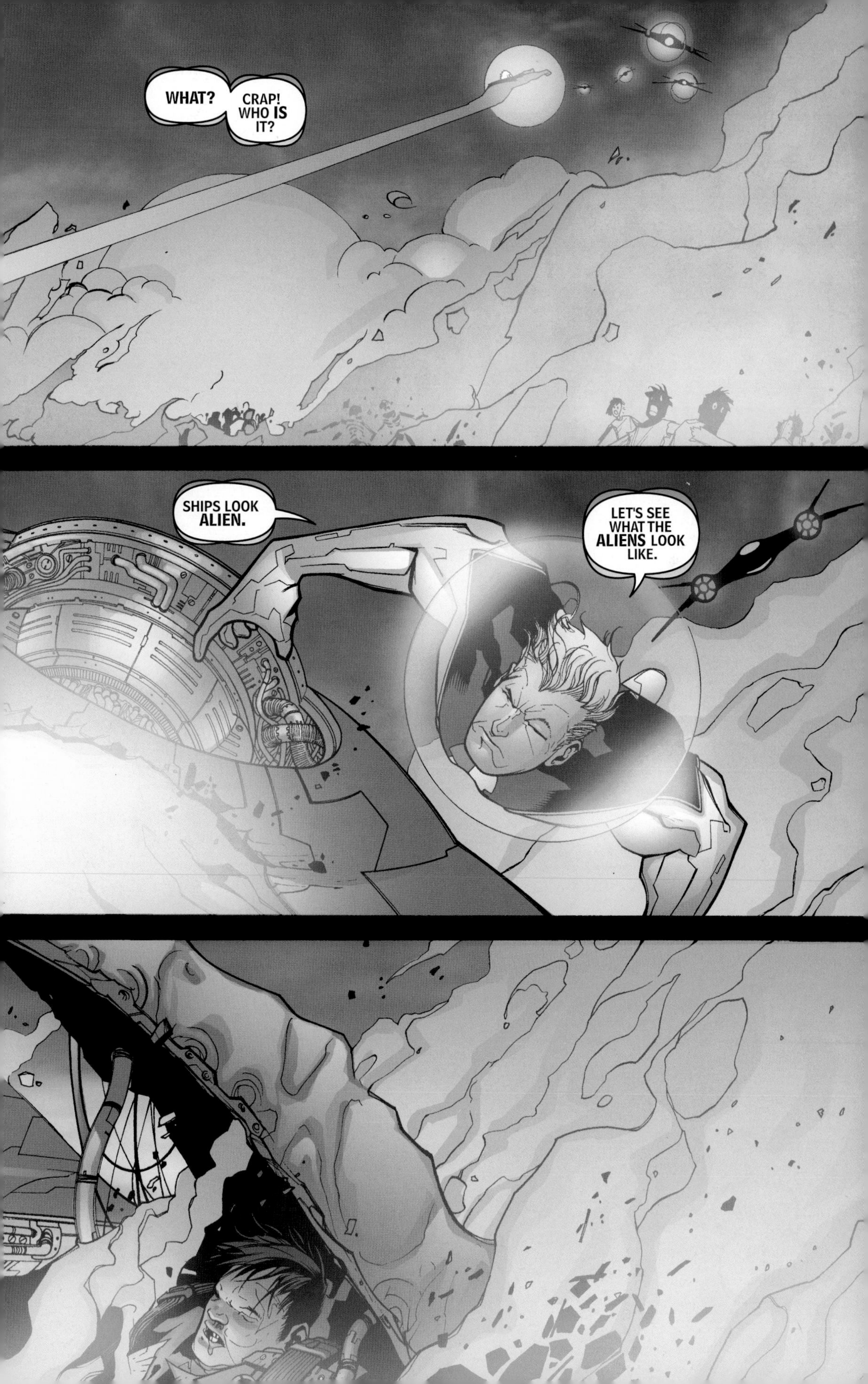
WHAT?
CRAP! WHO IS IT?
SHIPS LOOK ALIEN.
LET'S SEE WHAT THE ALIENS LOOK LIKE.

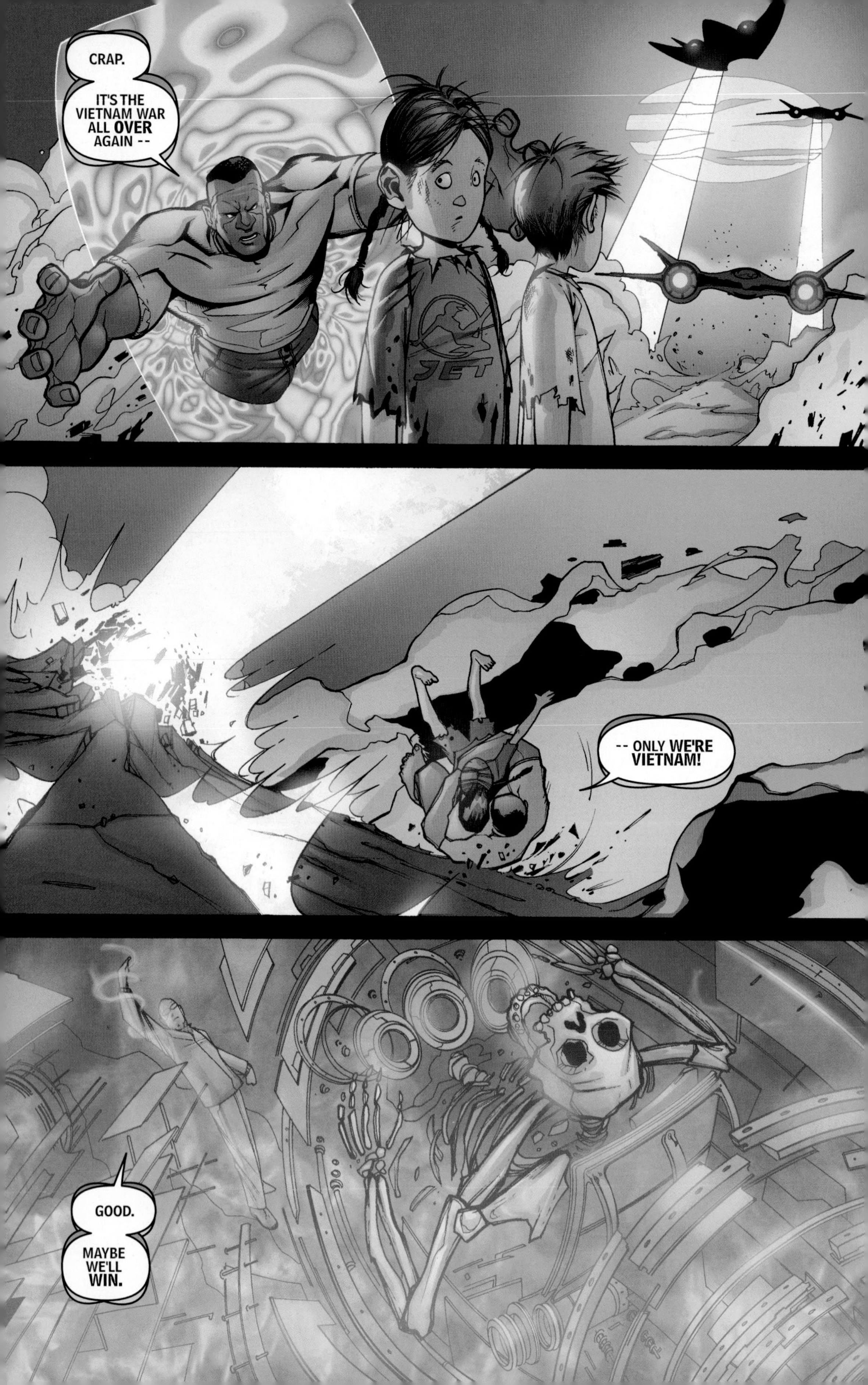
CRAP.
IT'S THE VIETNAM WAR ALL OVER AGAIN --
-- ONLY WE'RE VIETNAM!
GOOD.
MAYBE WE'LL WIN.

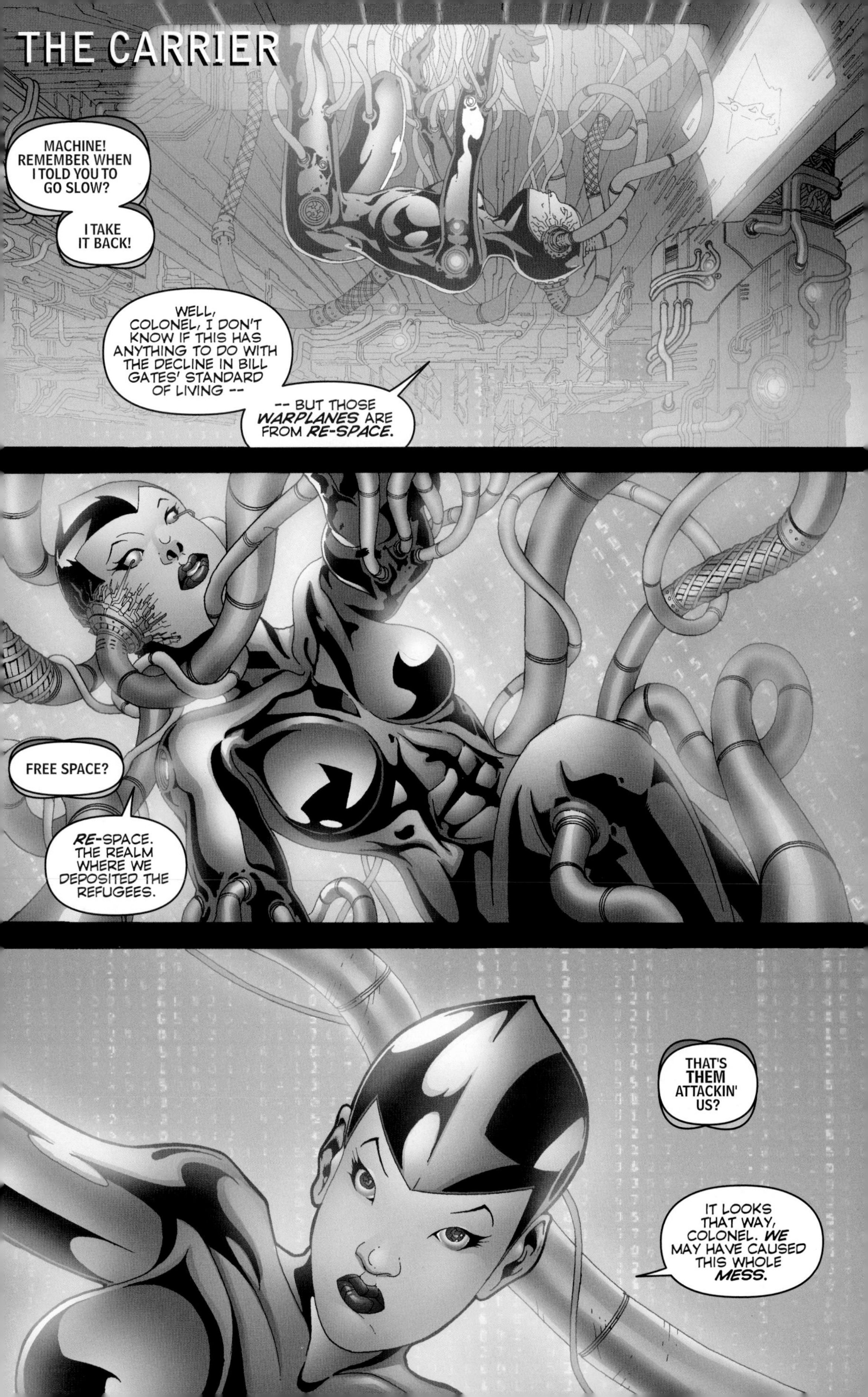
THE CARRIER
MACHINE! REMEMBER WHEN I TOLD YOU TO GO SLOW?
I TAKE IT BACK!
WELL, COLONEL, I DON'T KNOW IF THIS HAS ANYTHING TO DO WITH THE DECLINE IN BILL GATES' STANDARD OF LIVING --
-- BUT THOSE WARPLANES ARE FROM RE-SPACE.
FREE SPACE?
RE-SPACE. THE REALM WHERE WE DEPOSITED THE REFUGEES.
THAT'S THEM ATTACKIN' US?
IT LOOKS THAT WAY, COLONEL. WE MAY HAVE CAUSED THIS WHOLE MESS.

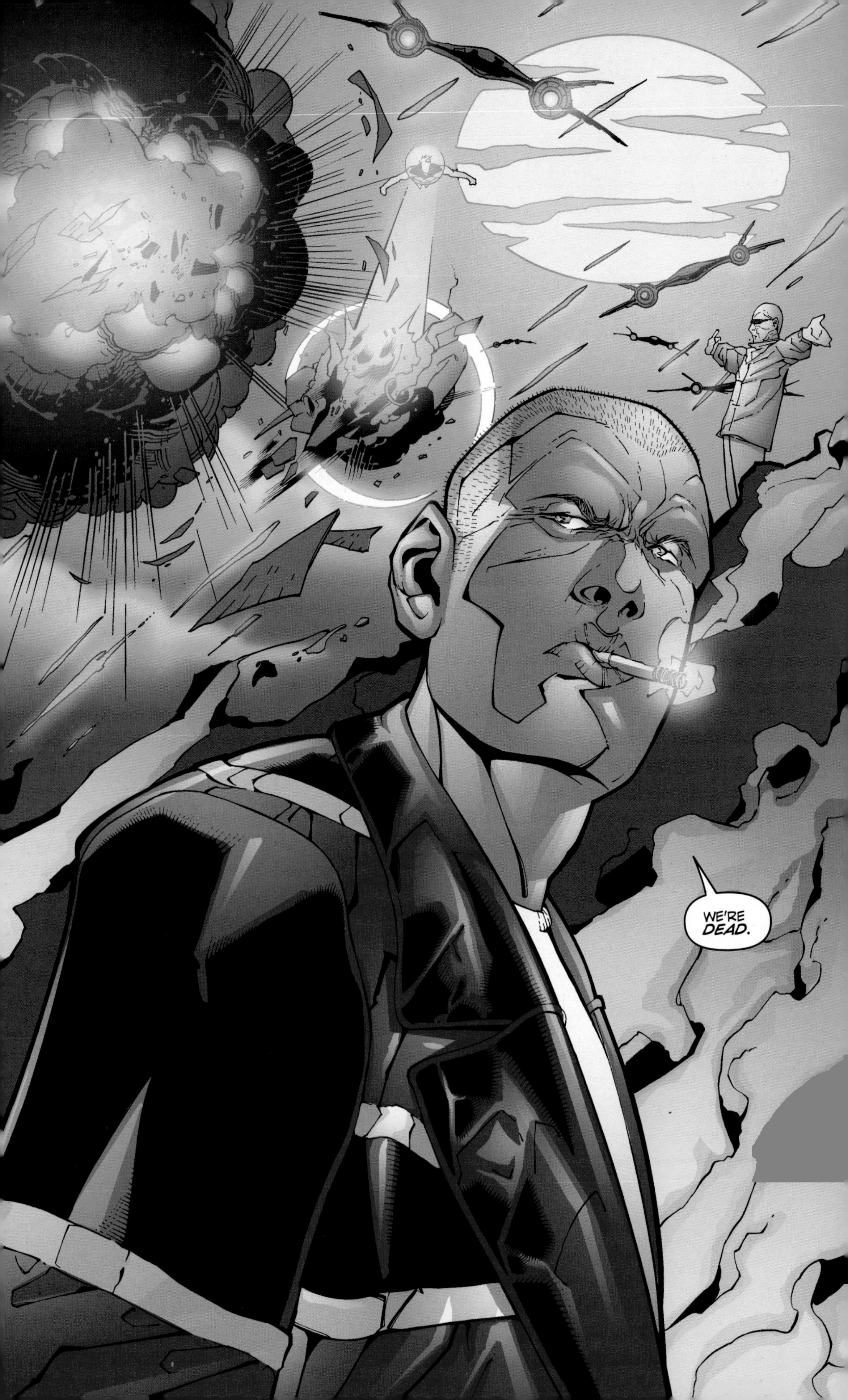
WE'RE DEAD.

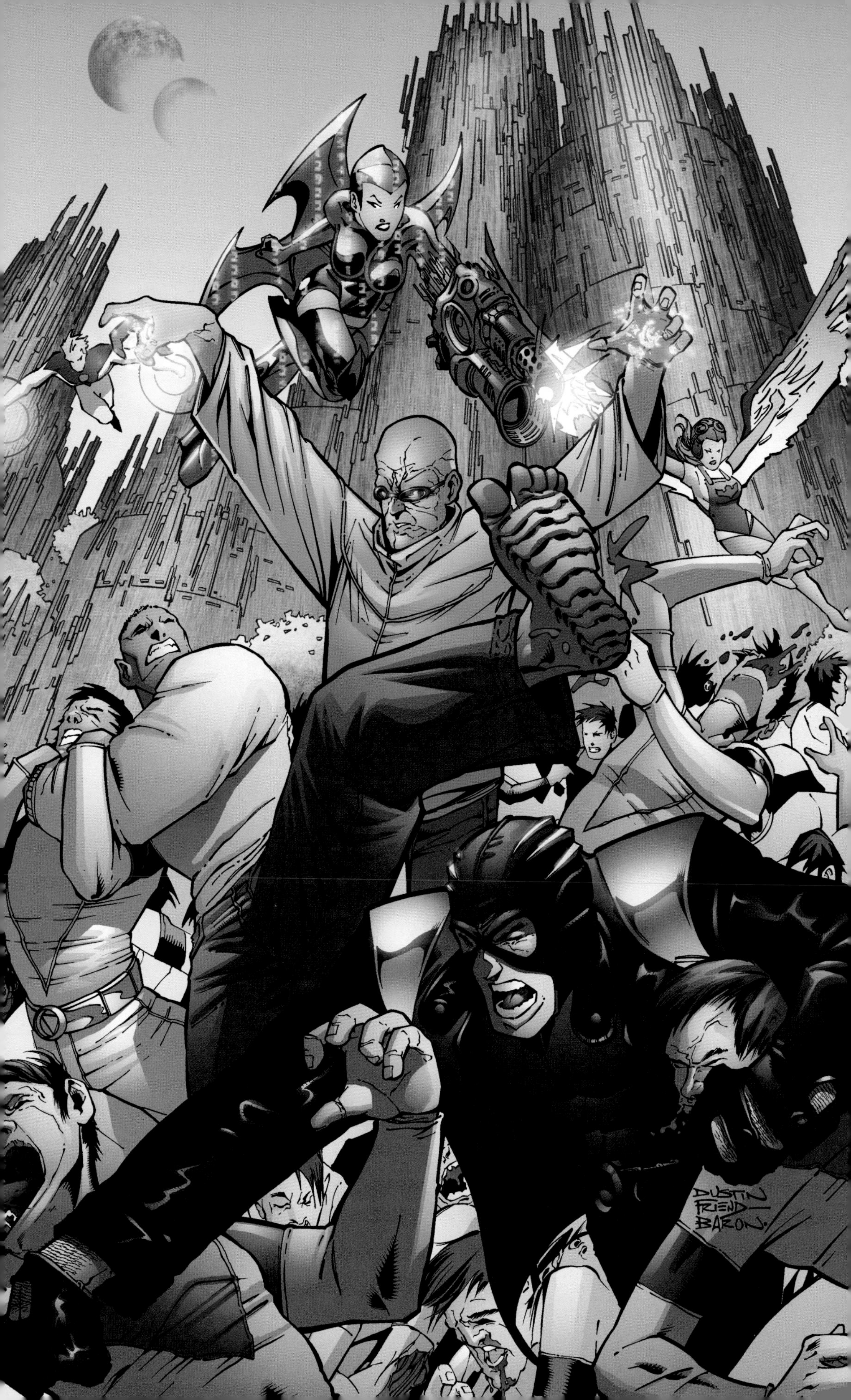
DUSTIN
FRIEND-
BARON.

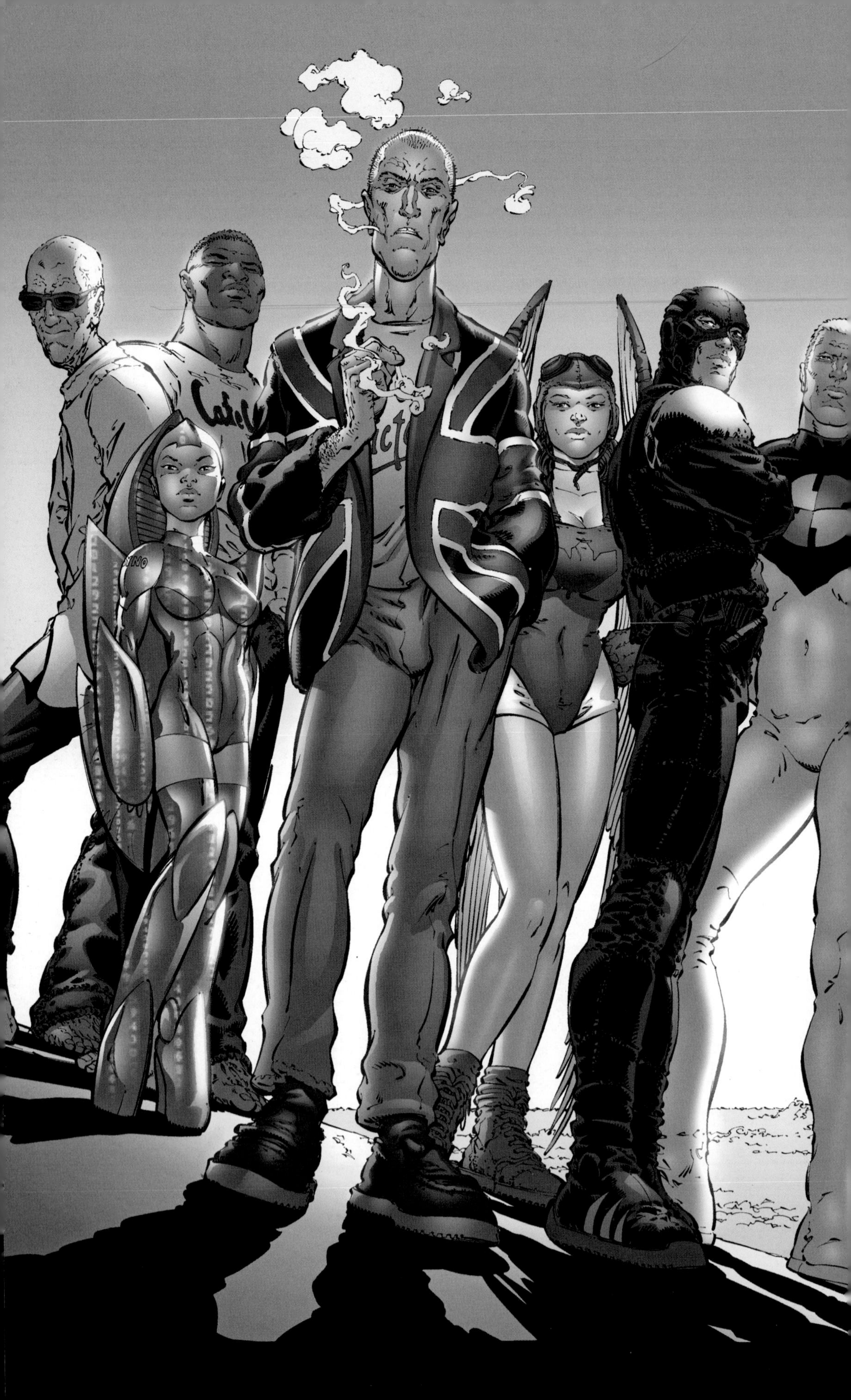

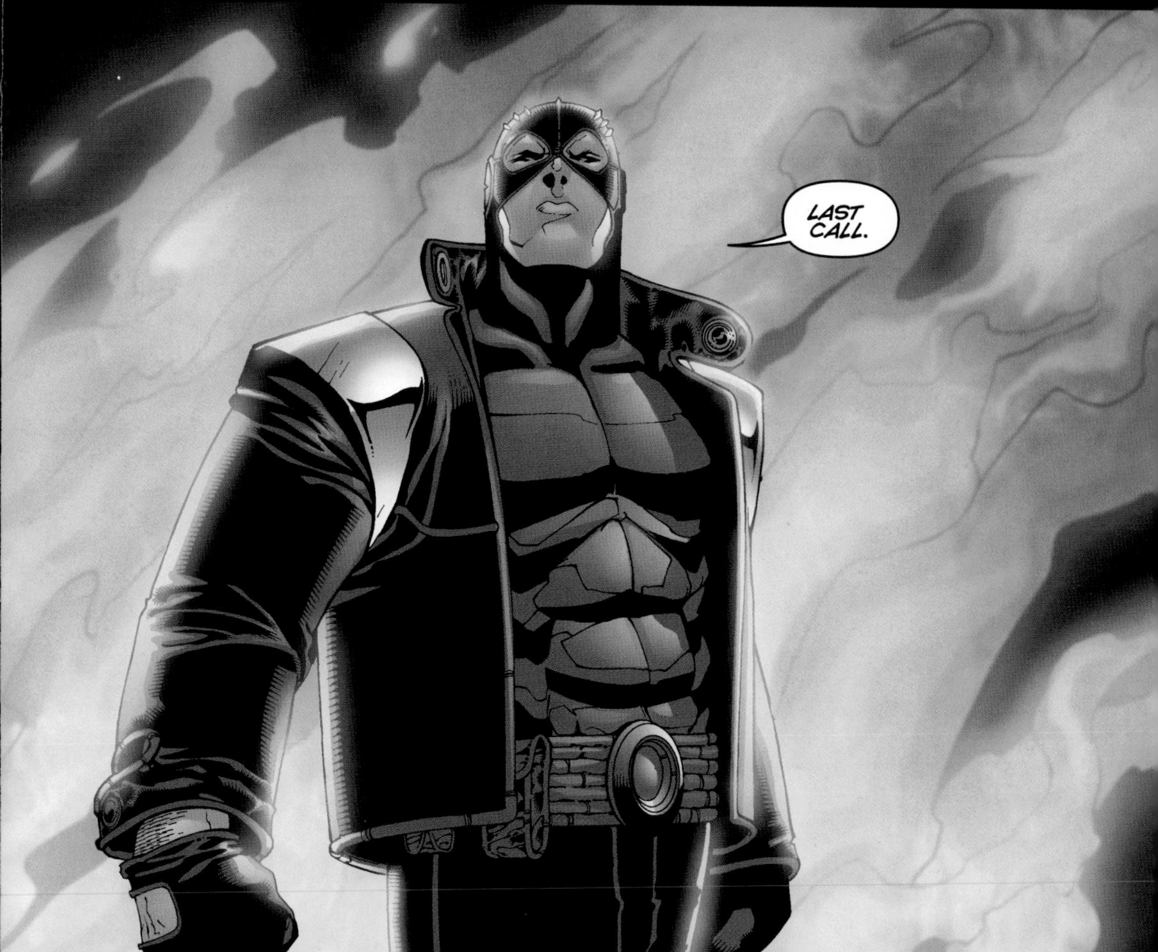
LAST CALL.

THE AUTHORITY
TRANSFER OF POWER
Three of Four

TOM PEYER words
DUSTIN NGUYEN pencils
RICHARD FRIEND inks
DAVID BARON colors
BILL O'NEIL letters

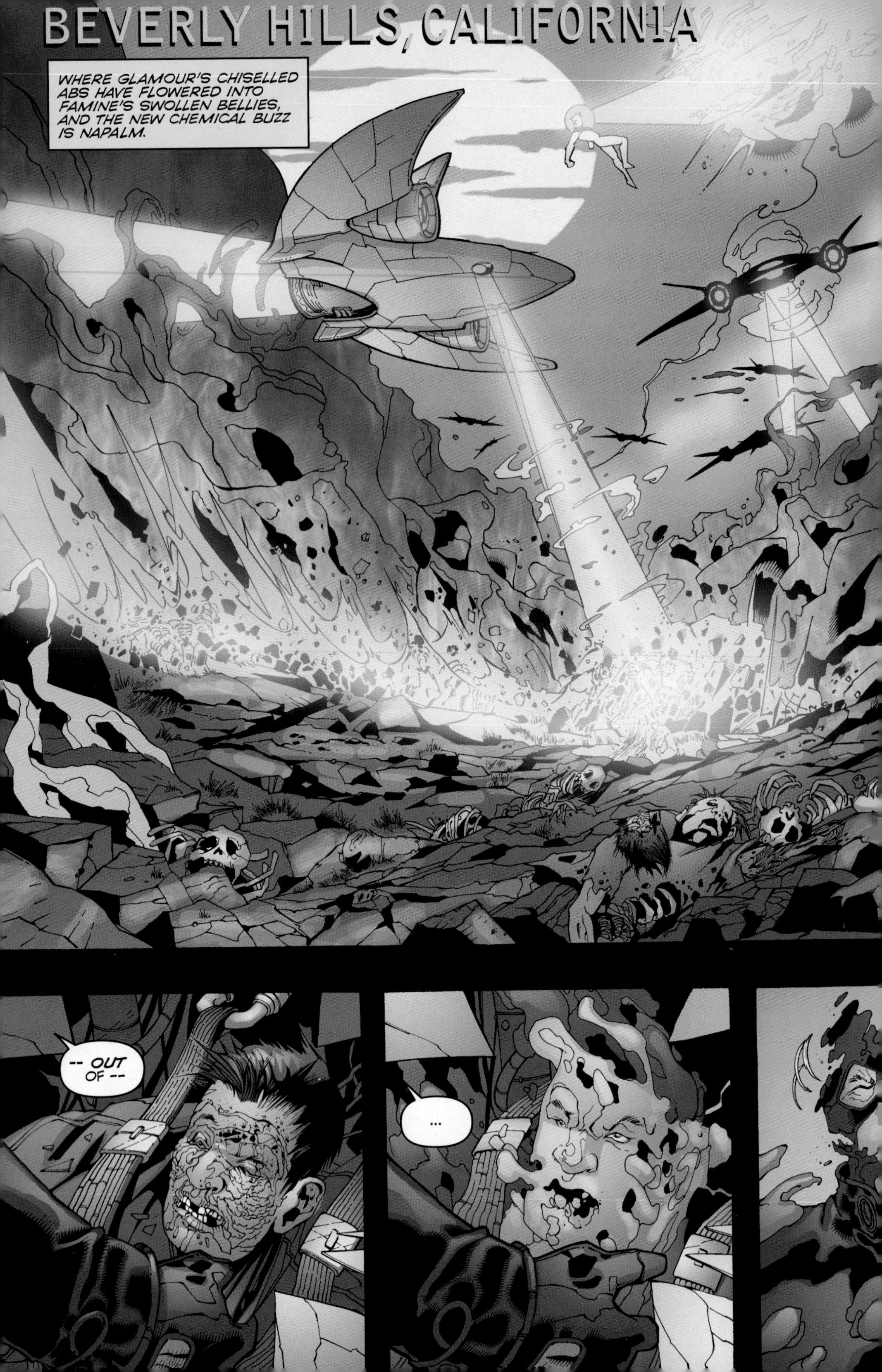
BEVERLY HILLS, CALIFORNIA
WHERE GLAMOUR'S CHISELLED ABS HAVE FLOWERED INTO FAMINE'S SWOLLEN BELLIES, AND THE NEW CHEMICAL BUZZ IS NAPALM.
-- OUT OF --
...

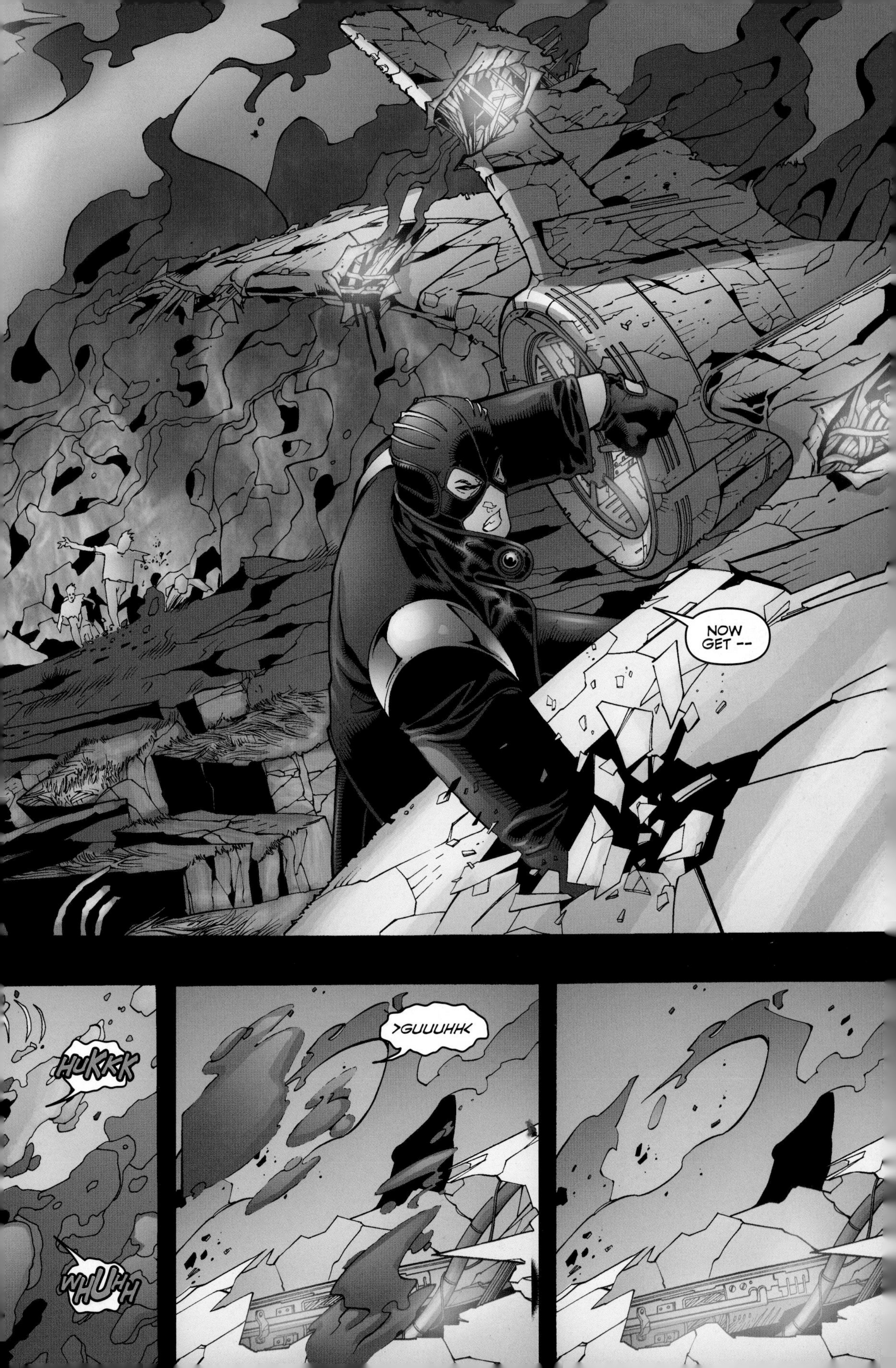
NOW GET --
HUKKK
WHUHH
>GUUUHH<

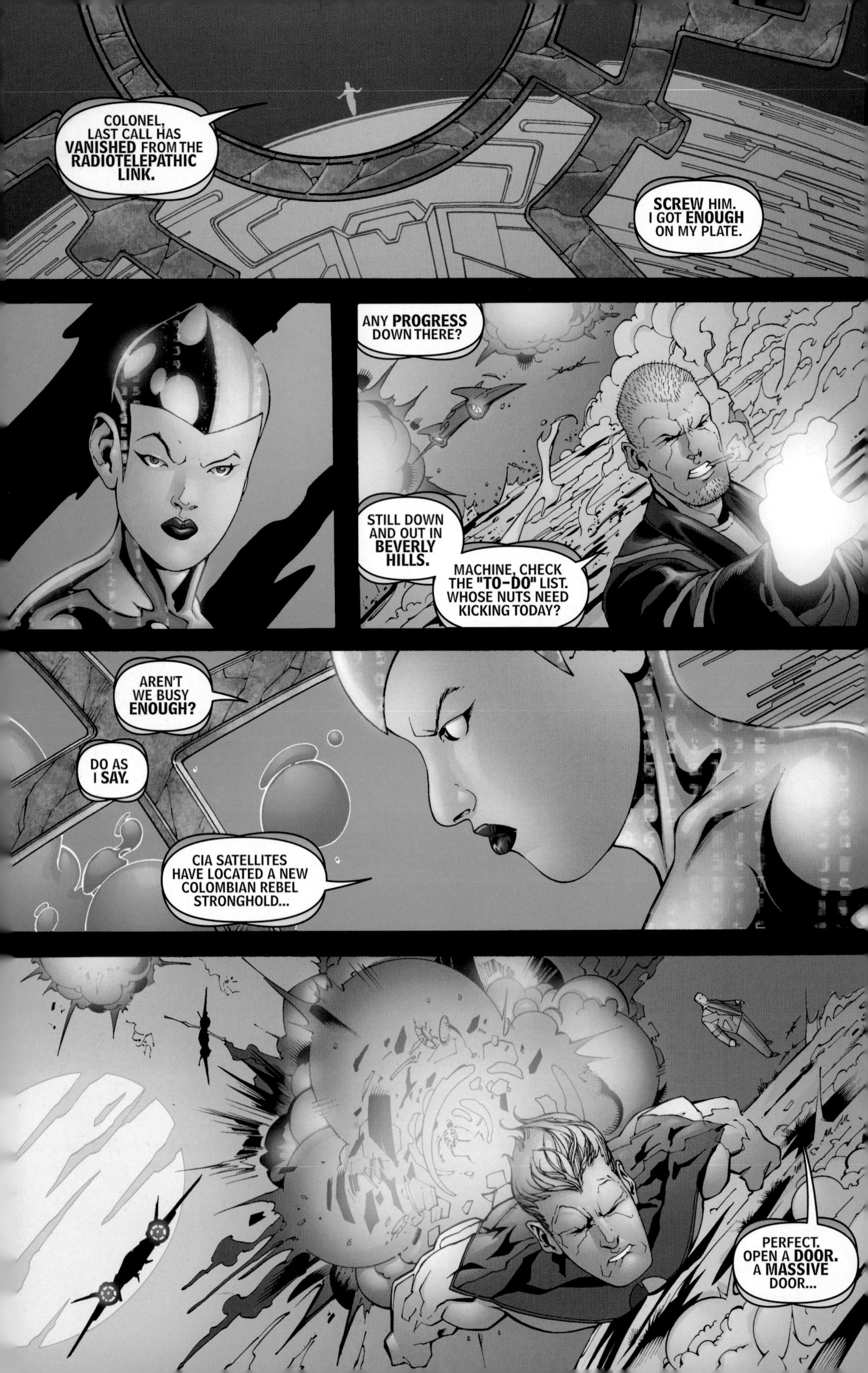
COLONEL, LAST CALL HAS VANISHED FROM THE RADIOTELEPATHIC LINK.
SCREW HIM. I GOT ENOUGH ON MY PLATE.
ANY PROGRESS DOWN THERE?
STILL DOWN AND OUT IN BEVERLY HILLS.
MACHINE, CHECK THE "TO-DO" LIST. WHOSE NUTS NEED KICKING TODAY?
AREN'T WE BUSY ENOUGH?
DO AS I SAY.
CIA SATELLITES HAVE LOCATED A NEW COLOMBIAN REBEL STRONGHOLD...
PERFECT. OPEN A DOOR. A MASSIVE DOOR...

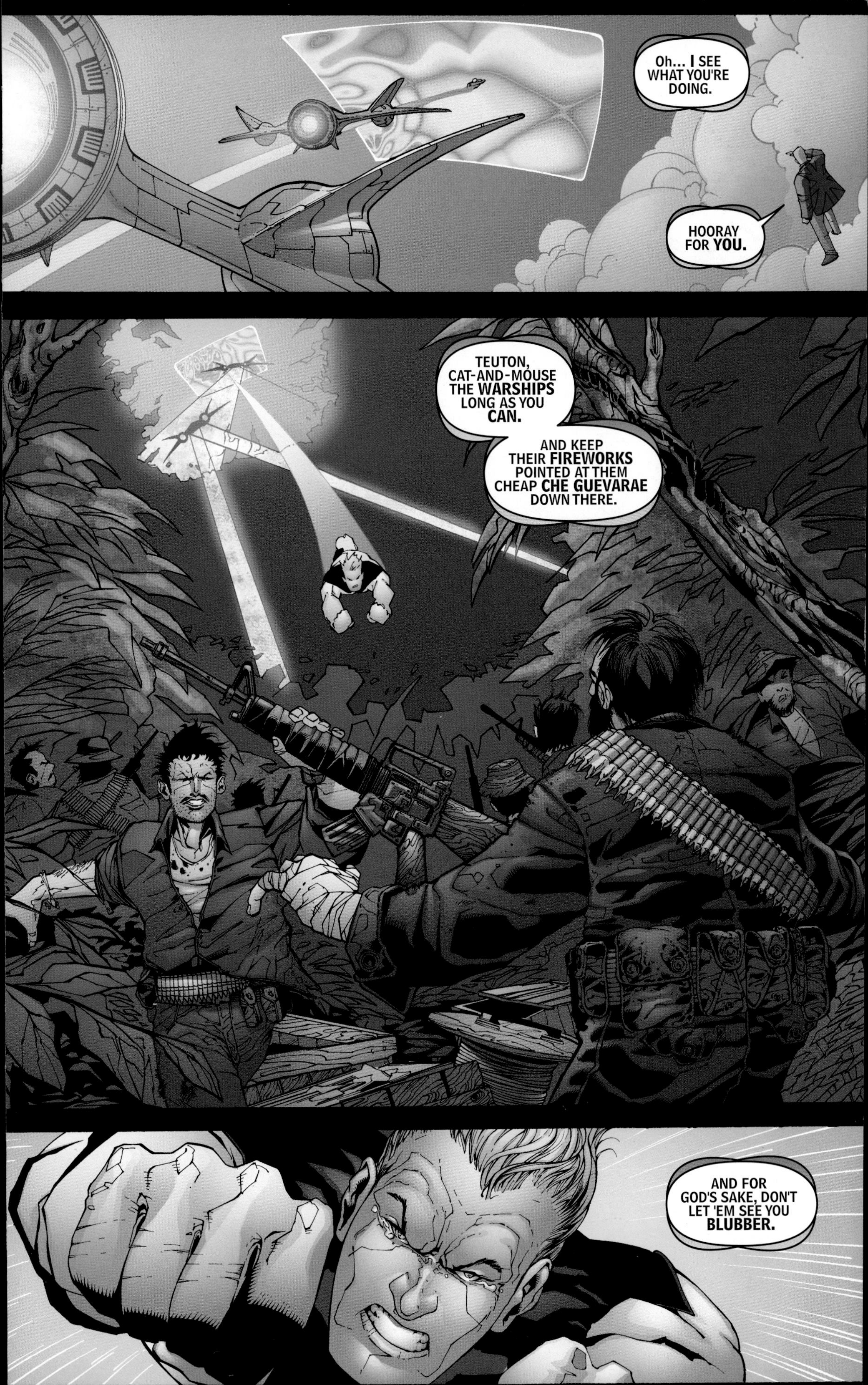
Oh... I SEE WHAT YOU'RE DOING.
HOORAY FOR YOU.
TEUTON, CAT-AND-MOUSE THE WARSHIPS LONG AS YOU CAN.
AND KEEP THEIR FIREWORKS POINTED AT THEM CHEAP CHE GUEVARAE DOWN THERE.
AND FOR GOD'S SAKE, DON'T LET 'EM SEE YOU BLUBBER.

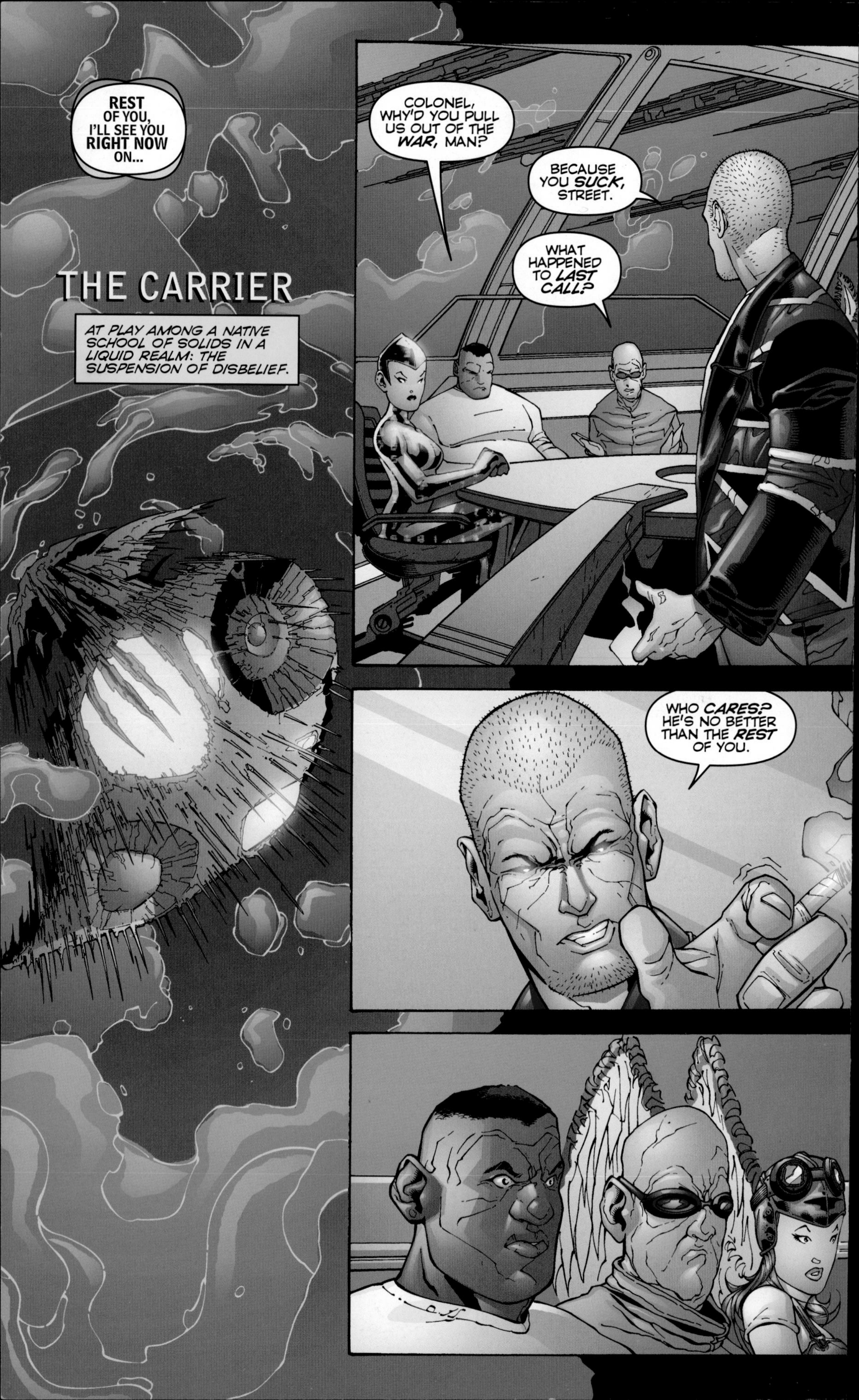
REST OF YOU, I'LL SEE YOU RIGHT NOW ON...
THE CARRIER
AT PLAY AMONG A NATIVE SCHOOL OF SOLIDS IN A LIQUID REALM: THE SUSPENSION OF DISBELIEF.
COLONEL, WHY'D YOU PULL US OUT OF THE WAR, MAN?
BECAUSE YOU SUCK, STREET.
WHAT HAPPENED TO LAST CALL?
WHO CARES? HE'S NO BETTER THAN THE REST OF YOU.

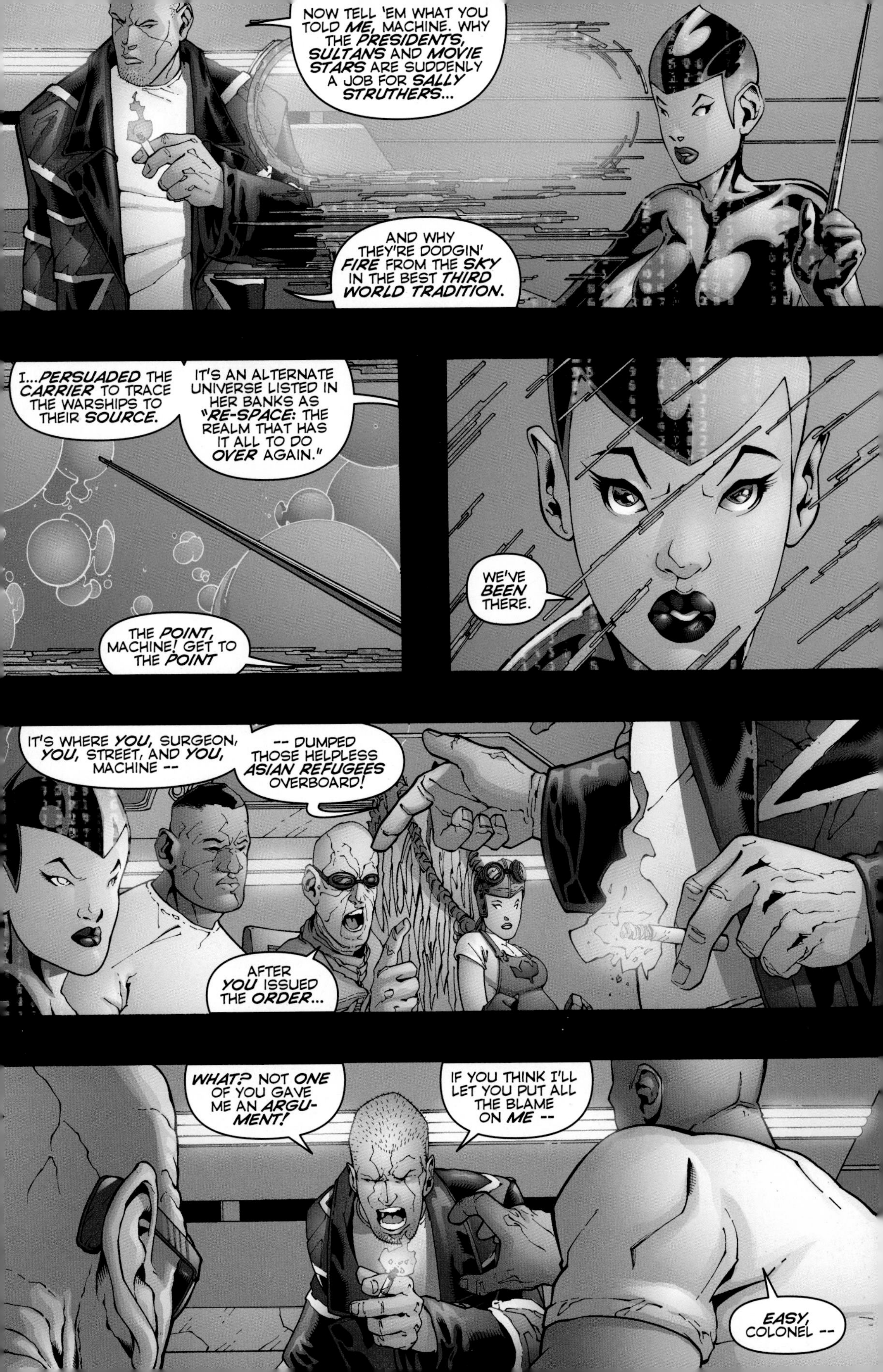
NOW TELL 'EM WHAT YOU TOLD ME, MACHINE. WHY THE PRESIDENTS, SULTANS AND MOVIE STARS ARE SUDDENLY A JOB FOR SALLY STRUTHERS...
AND WHY THEY'RE DODGIN' FIRE FROM THE SKY IN THE BEST THIRD WORLD TRADITION.
I...PERSUADED THE CARRIER TO TRACE THE WARSHIPS TO THEIR SOURCE.
IT'S AN ALTERNATE UNIVERSE LISTED IN HER BANKS AS "RE-SPACE: THE REALM THAT HAS IT ALL TO DO OVER AGAIN."
THE POINT, MACHINE! GET TO THE POINT
WE'VE BEEN THERE.
IT'S WHERE YOU, SURGEON, YOU, STREET, AND YOU, MACHINE --
-- DUMPED THOSE HELPLESS ASIAN REFUGEES OVERBOARD!
AFTER YOU ISSUED THE ORDER...
WHAT? NOT ONE OF YOU GAVE ME AN ARGU-MENT!
IF YOU THINK I'LL LET YOU PUT ALL THE BLAME ON ME --
EASY, COLONEL --

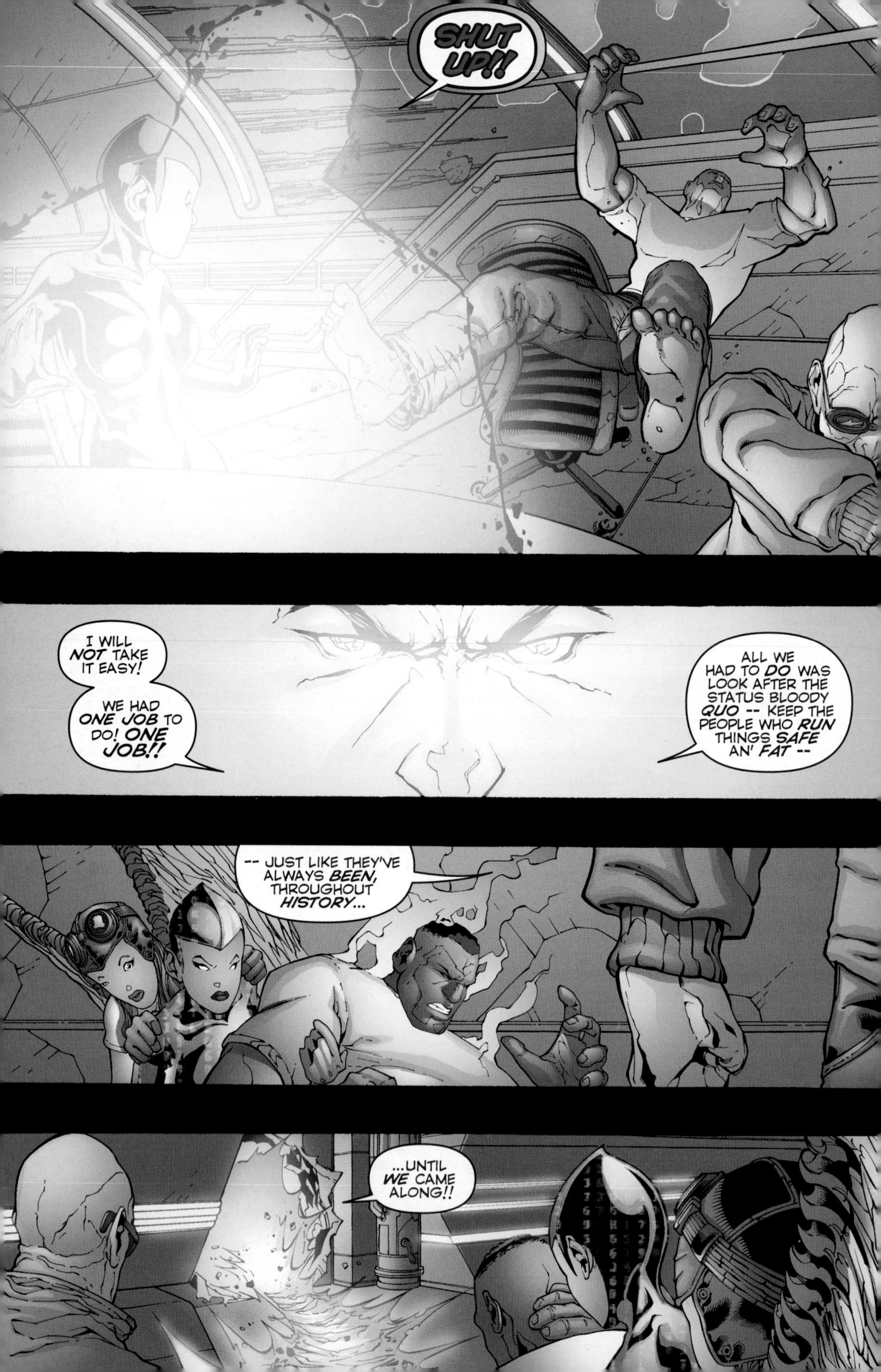
SHUT UP!!
I WILL NOT TAKE IT EASY!
WE HAD ONE JOB TO DO! ONE JOB!!
ALL WE HAD TO DO WAS LOOK AFTER THE STATUS BLOODY QUO -- KEEP THE PEOPLE WHO RUN THINGS SAFE AN' FAT --
-- JUST LIKE THEY'VE ALWAYS BEEN, THROUGHOUT HISTORY...
...UNTIL WE CAME ALONG!!

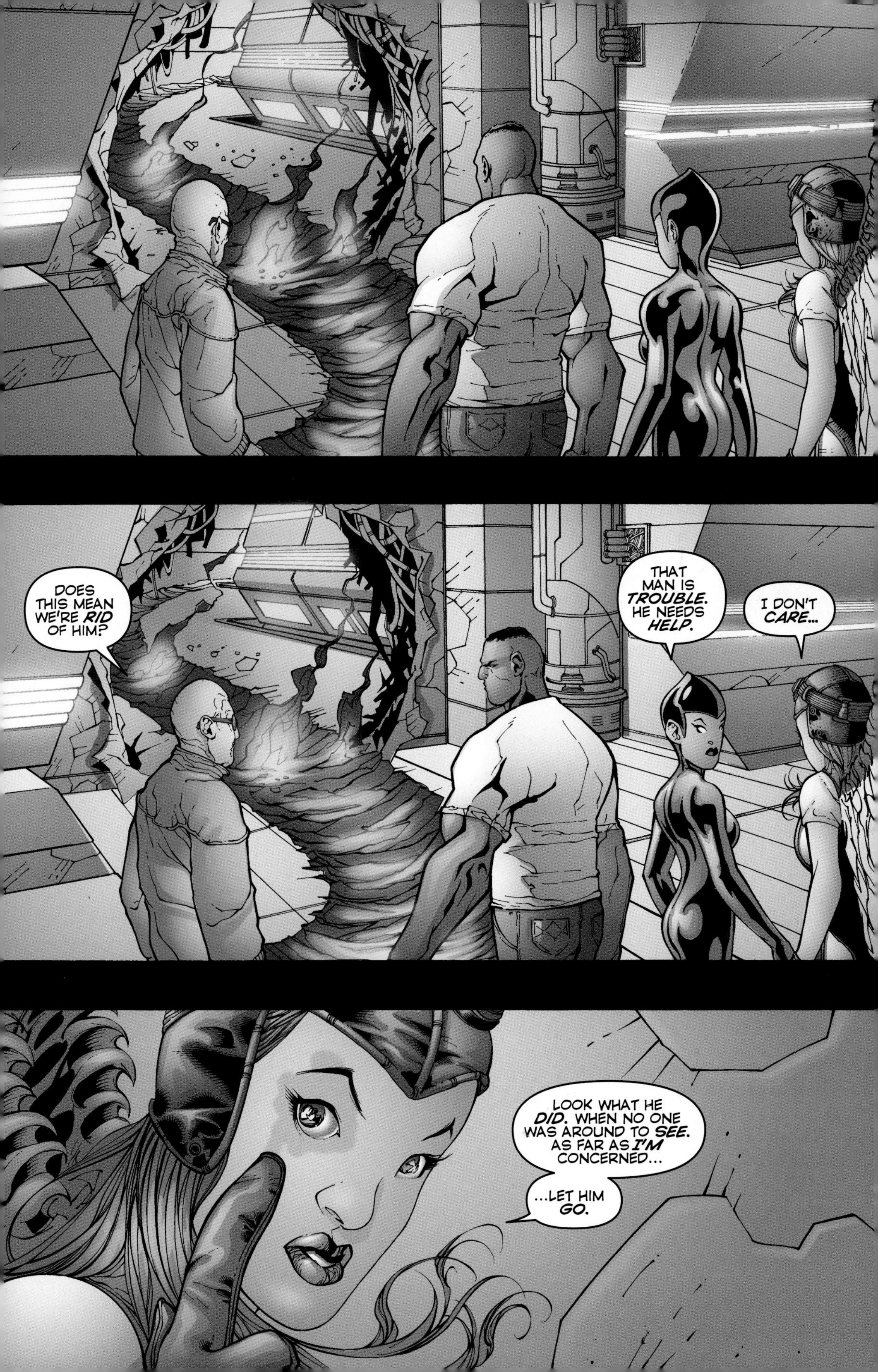
DOES THIS MEAN WE'RE *RID* OF HIM?
THAT MAN IS *TROUBLE*. HE NEEDS *HELP*.
I DON'T *CARE*...
LOOK WHAT HE *DID*. WHEN NO ONE WAS AROUND TO *SEE*. AS FAR AS *I'M* CONCERNED...
...LET HIM *GO*.

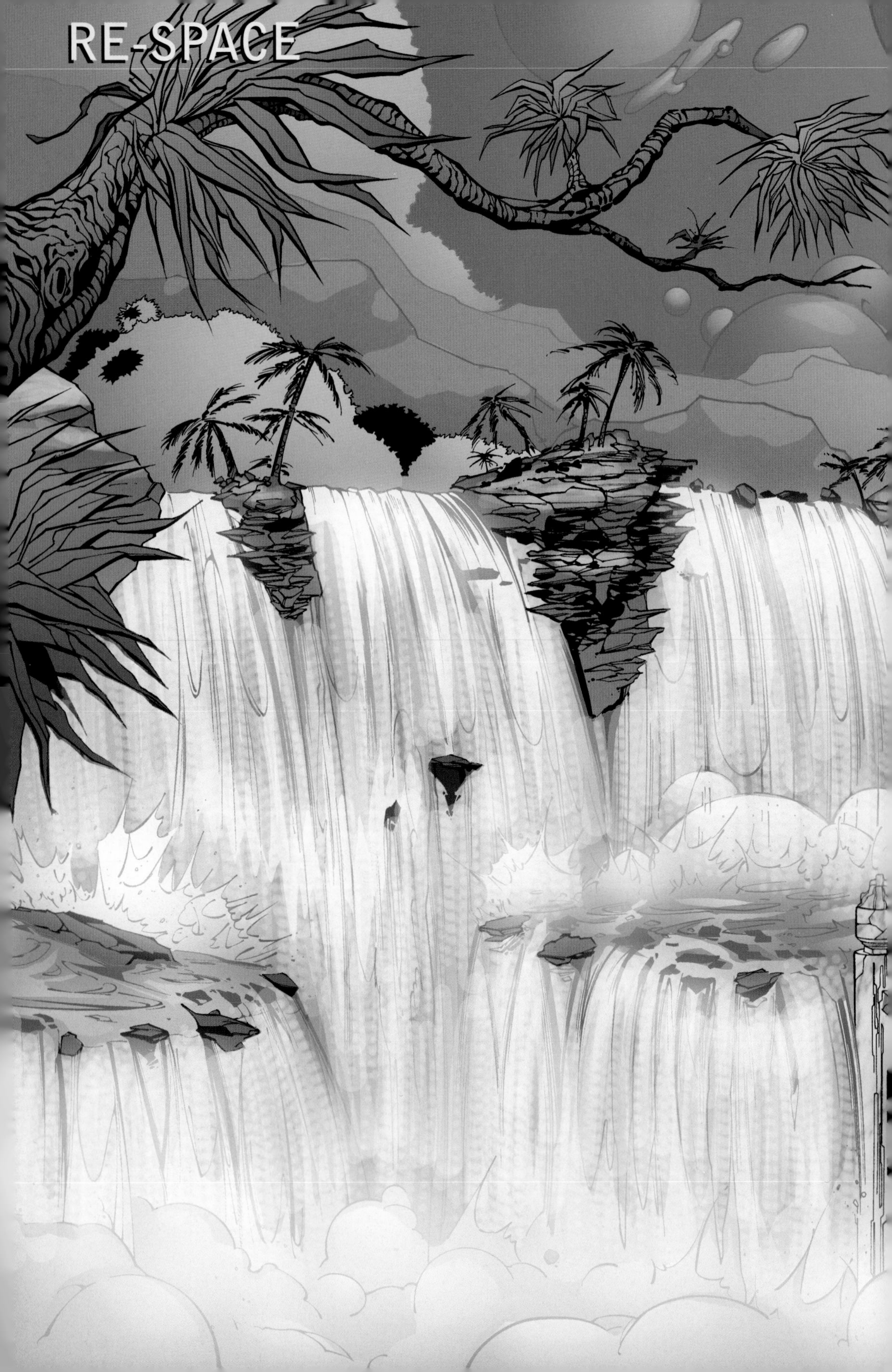
RE-SPACE

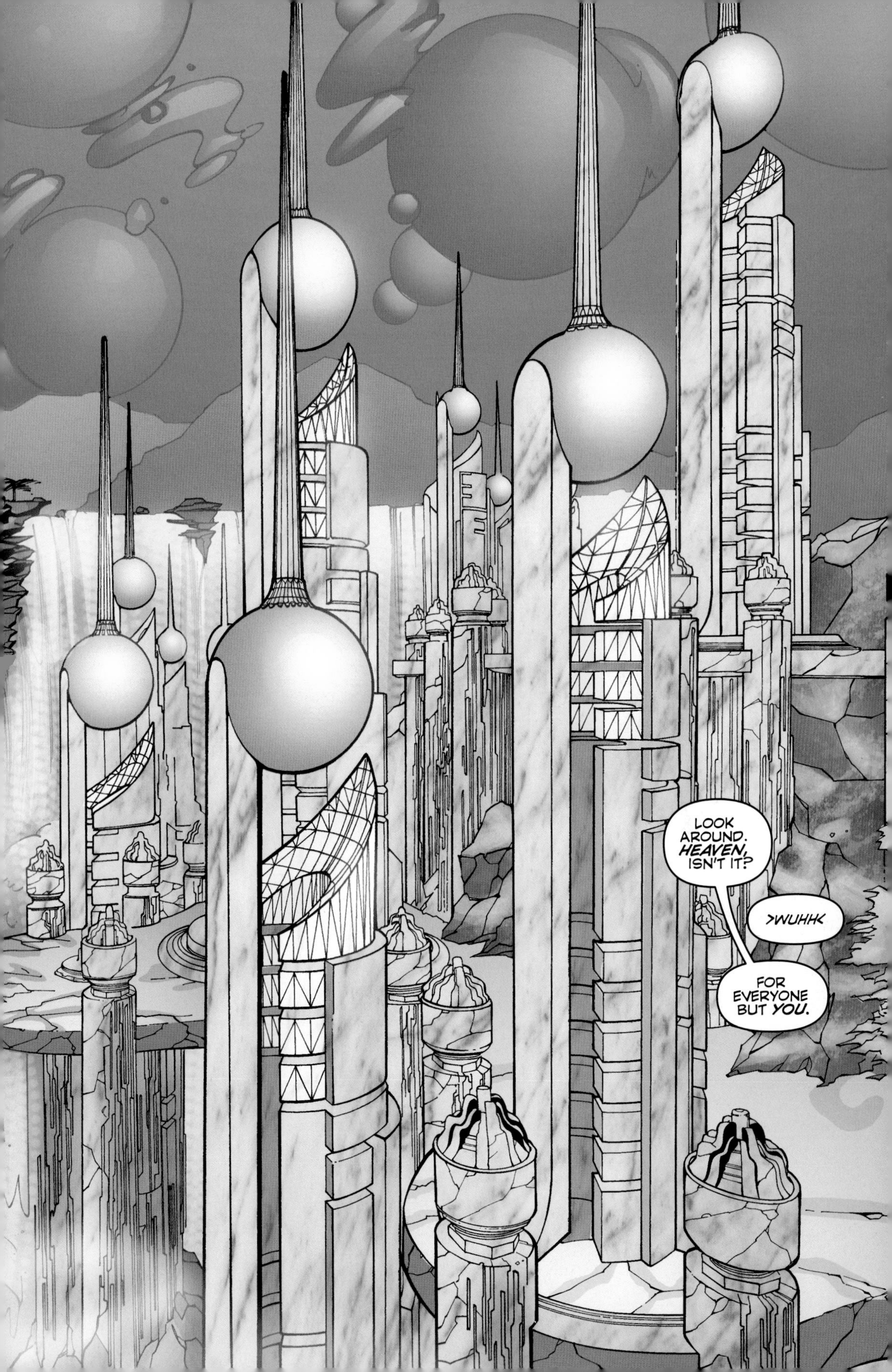
LOOK AROUND. HEAVEN, ISN'T IT?
>WUHH<
FOR EVERYONE BUT YOU.

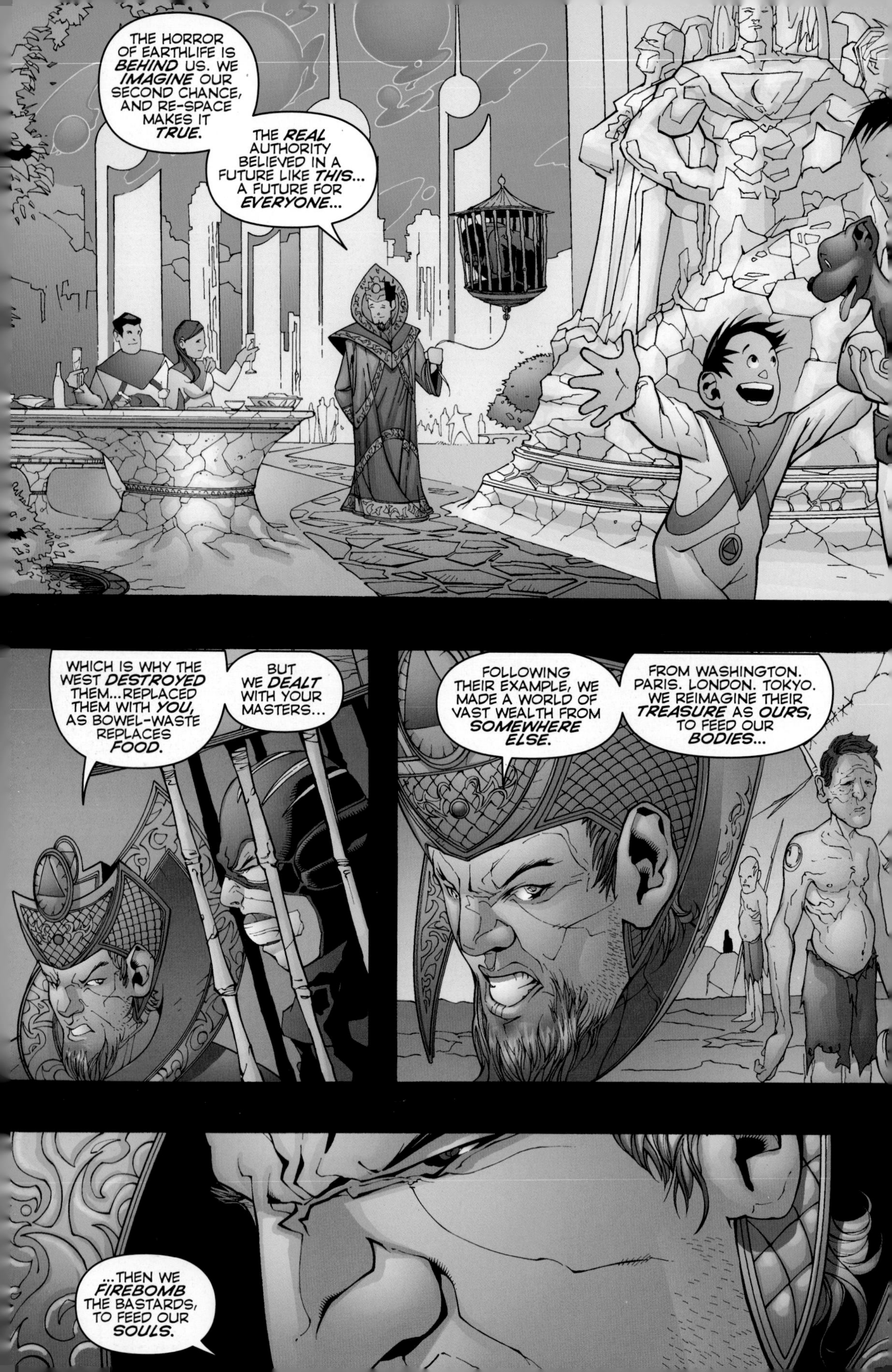
THE HORROR OF EARTHLIFE IS BEHIND US. WE IMAGINE OUR SECOND CHANCE, AND RE-SPACE MAKES IT TRUE.
THE REAL AUTHORITY BELIEVED IN A FUTURE LIKE THIS... A FUTURE FOR EVERYONE...
WHICH IS WHY THE WEST DESTROYED THEM...REPLACED THEM WITH YOU, AS BOWEL-WASTE REPLACES FOOD.
BUT WE DEALT WITH YOUR MASTERS...
FOLLOWING THEIR EXAMPLE, WE MADE A WORLD OF VAST WEALTH FROM SOMEWHERE ELSE.
FROM WASHINGTON. PARIS. LONDON. TOKYO. WE REIMAGINE THEIR TREASURE AS OURS, TO FEED OUR BODIES...
...THEN WE FIREBOMB THE BASTARDS, TO FEED OUR SOULS.

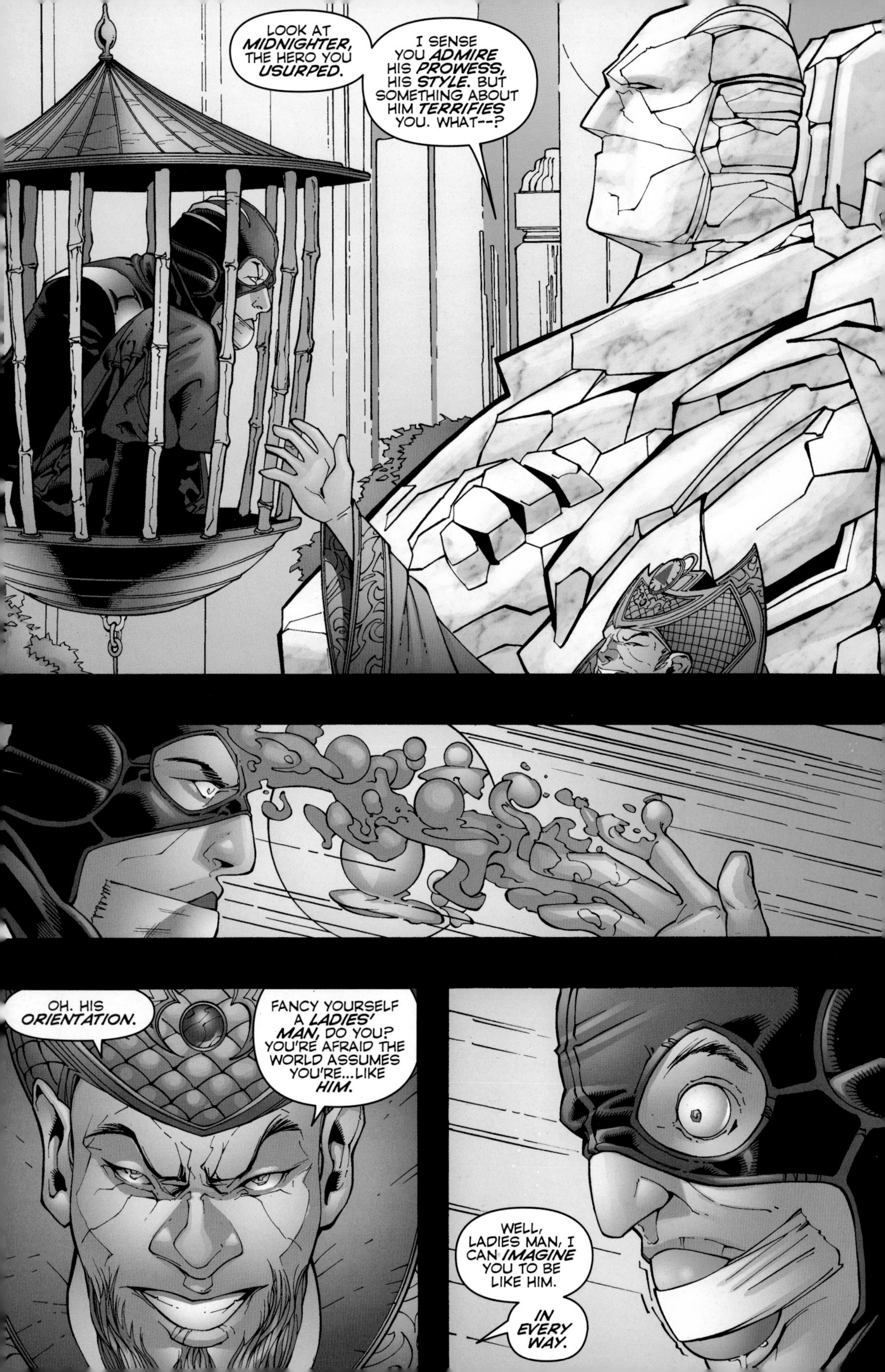
LOOK AT MIDNIGHTER, THE HERO YOU USURPED.
I SENSE YOU ADMIRE HIS PROWESS, HIS STYLE. BUT SOMETHING ABOUT HIM TERRIFIES YOU. WHAT--?
OH. HIS ORIENTATION.
FANCY YOURSELF A LADIES' MAN, DO YOU? YOU'RE AFRAID THE WORLD ASSUMES YOU'RE...LIKE HIM.
WELL, LADIES MAN, I CAN IMAGINE YOU TO BE LIKE HIM.
IN EVERY WAY.

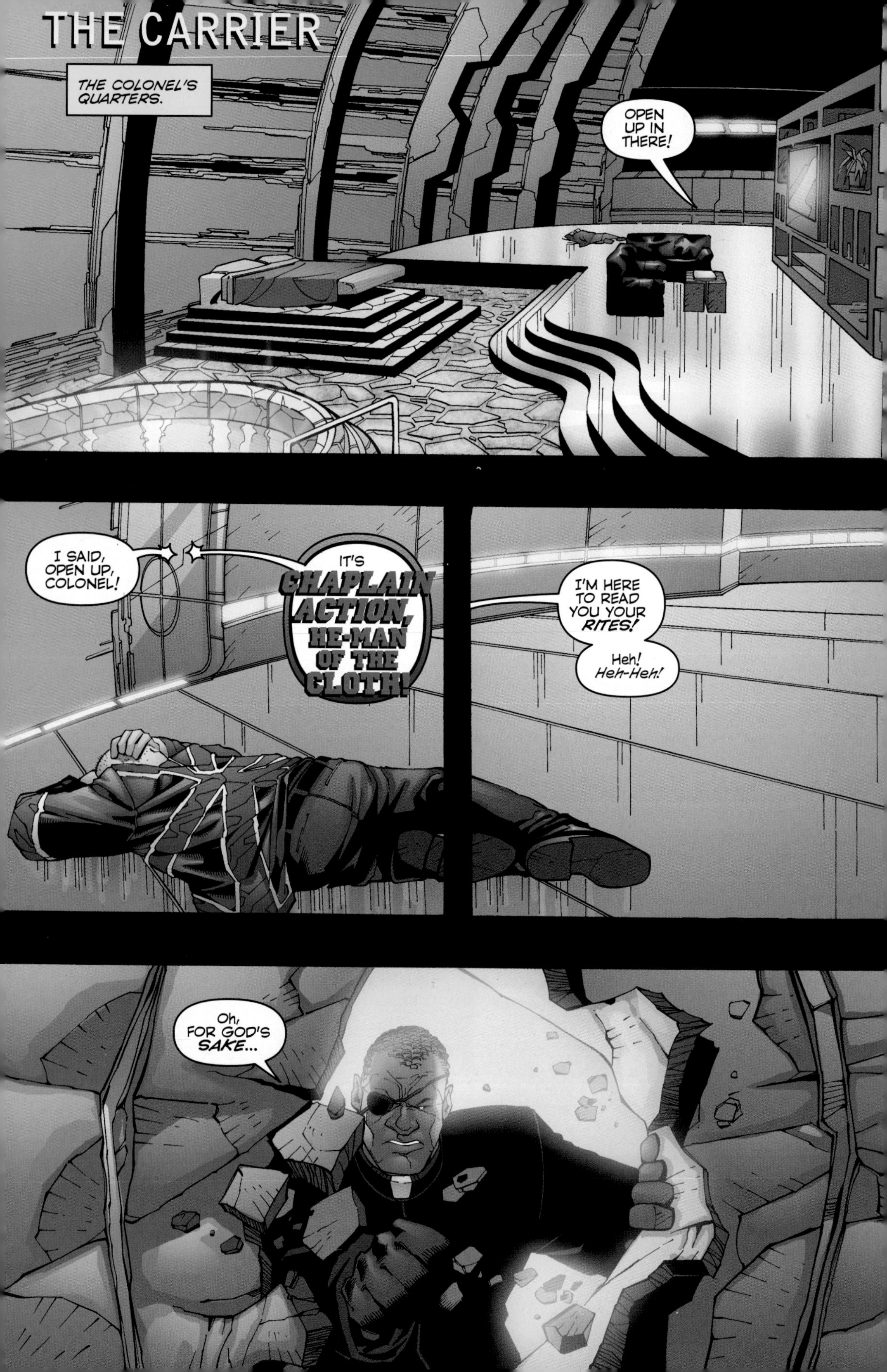
THE CARRIER
THE COLONEL'S QUARTERS.
OPEN UP IN THERE!
I SAID, OPEN UP, COLONEL!
IT'S CHAPLAIN ACTION, HE-MAN OF THE CLOTH!
I'M HERE TO READ YOU YOUR RITES!
Heh! Heh-Heh!
Oh, FOR GOD'S SAKE...

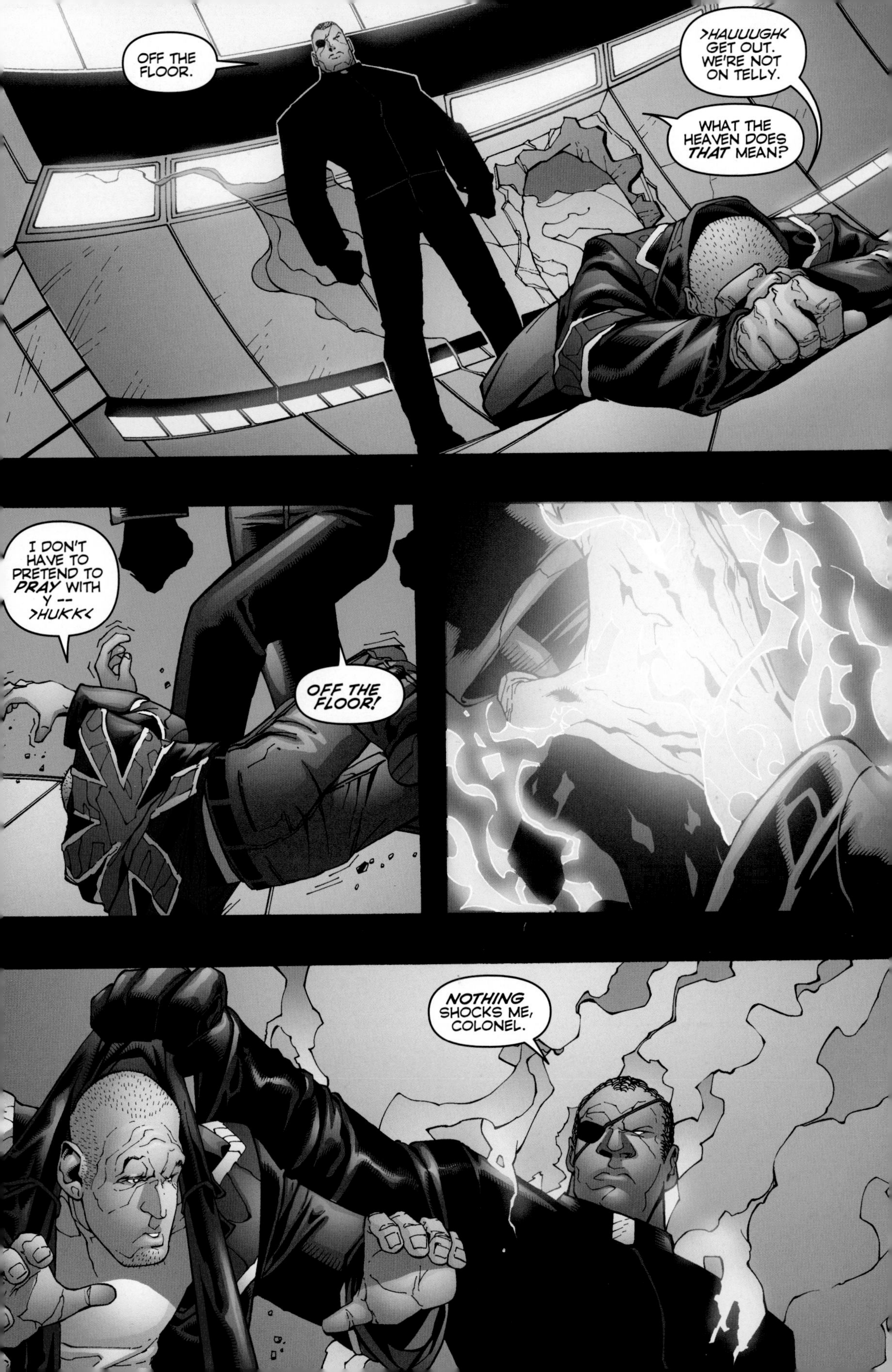
OFF THE FLOOR.
>HAUUUGH< GET OUT. WE'RE NOT ON TELLY.
WHAT THE HEAVEN DOES THAT MEAN?
I DON'T HAVE TO PRETEND TO PRAY WITH Y -- >HUKK<
OFF THE FLOOR!
NOTHING SHOCKS ME, COLONEL.

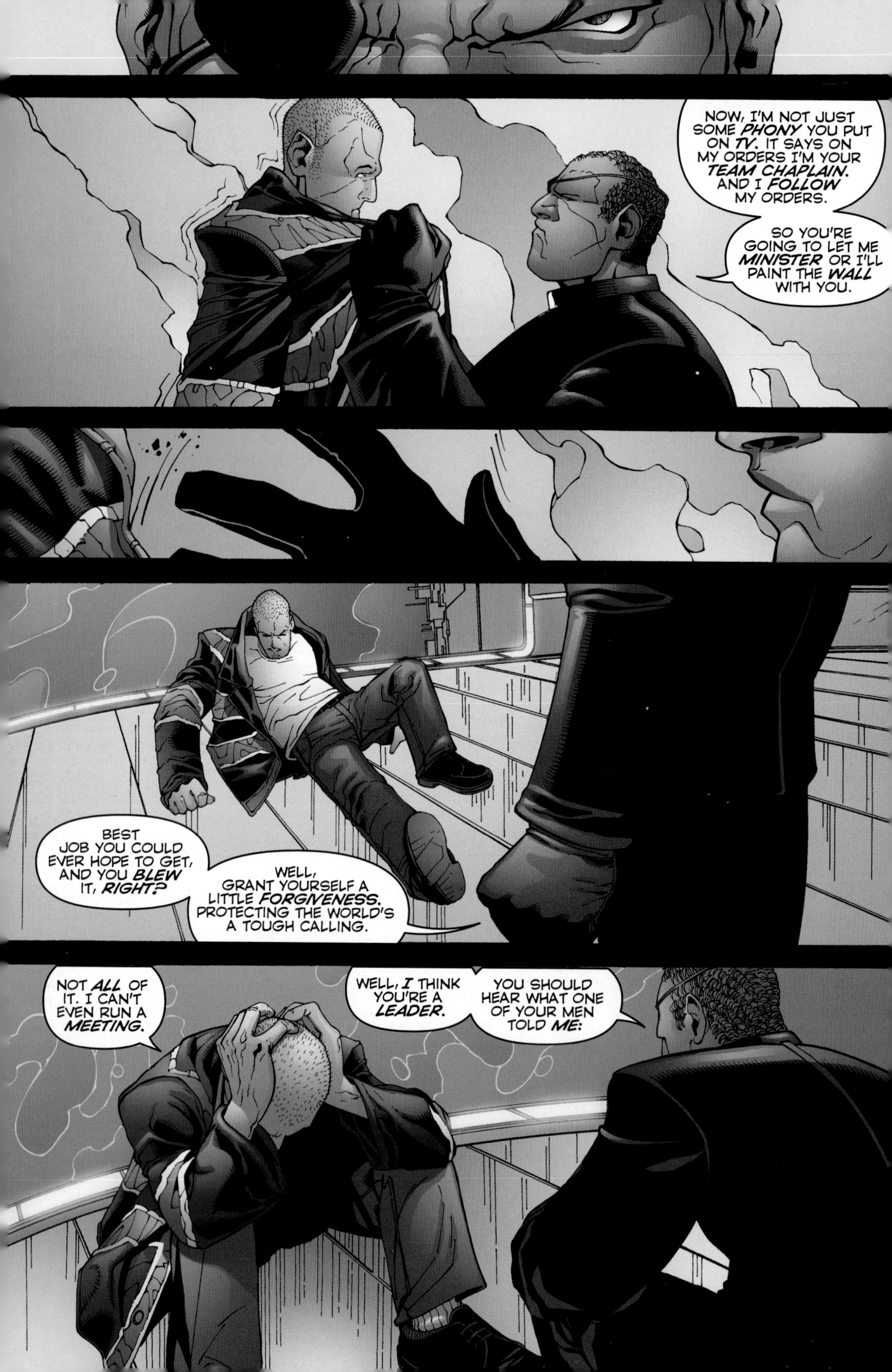
NOW, I'M NOT JUST SOME *PHONY* YOU PUT ON *TV.* IT SAYS ON MY ORDERS I'M YOUR *TEAM CHAPLAIN.* AND I *FOLLOW* MY ORDERS.
SO YOU'RE GOING TO LET ME *MINISTER* OR I'LL PAINT THE *WALL* WITH YOU.
BEST JOB YOU COULD EVER HOPE TO GET, AND YOU *BLEW* IT, *RIGHT?*
WELL, GRANT YOURSELF A LITTLE *FORGIVENESS.* PROTECTING THE WORLD'S A TOUGH CALLING.
NOT *ALL* OF IT. I CAN'T EVEN RUN A *MEETING.*
WELL, *I* THINK YOU'RE A *LEADER.*
YOU SHOULD HEAR WHAT ONE OF YOUR MEN TOLD *ME:*

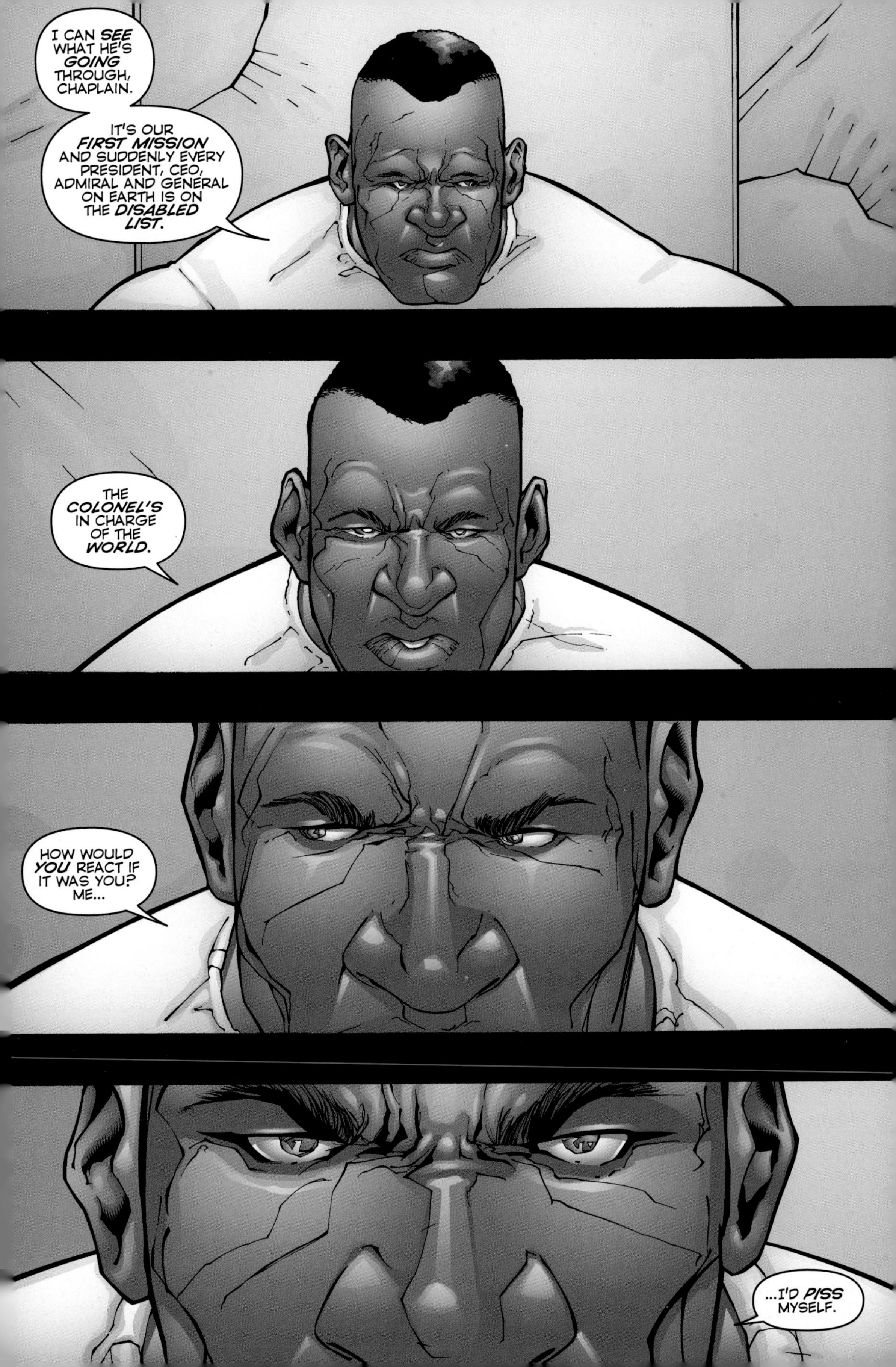
I CAN SEE WHAT HE'S GOING THROUGH, CHAPLAIN.
IT'S OUR FIRST MISSION AND SUDDENLY EVERY PRESIDENT, CEO, ADMIRAL AND GENERAL ON EARTH IS ON THE DISABLED LIST.
THE COLONEL'S IN CHARGE OF THE WORLD.
HOW WOULD YOU REACT IF IT WAS YOU? ME...
...I'D PISS MYSELF.

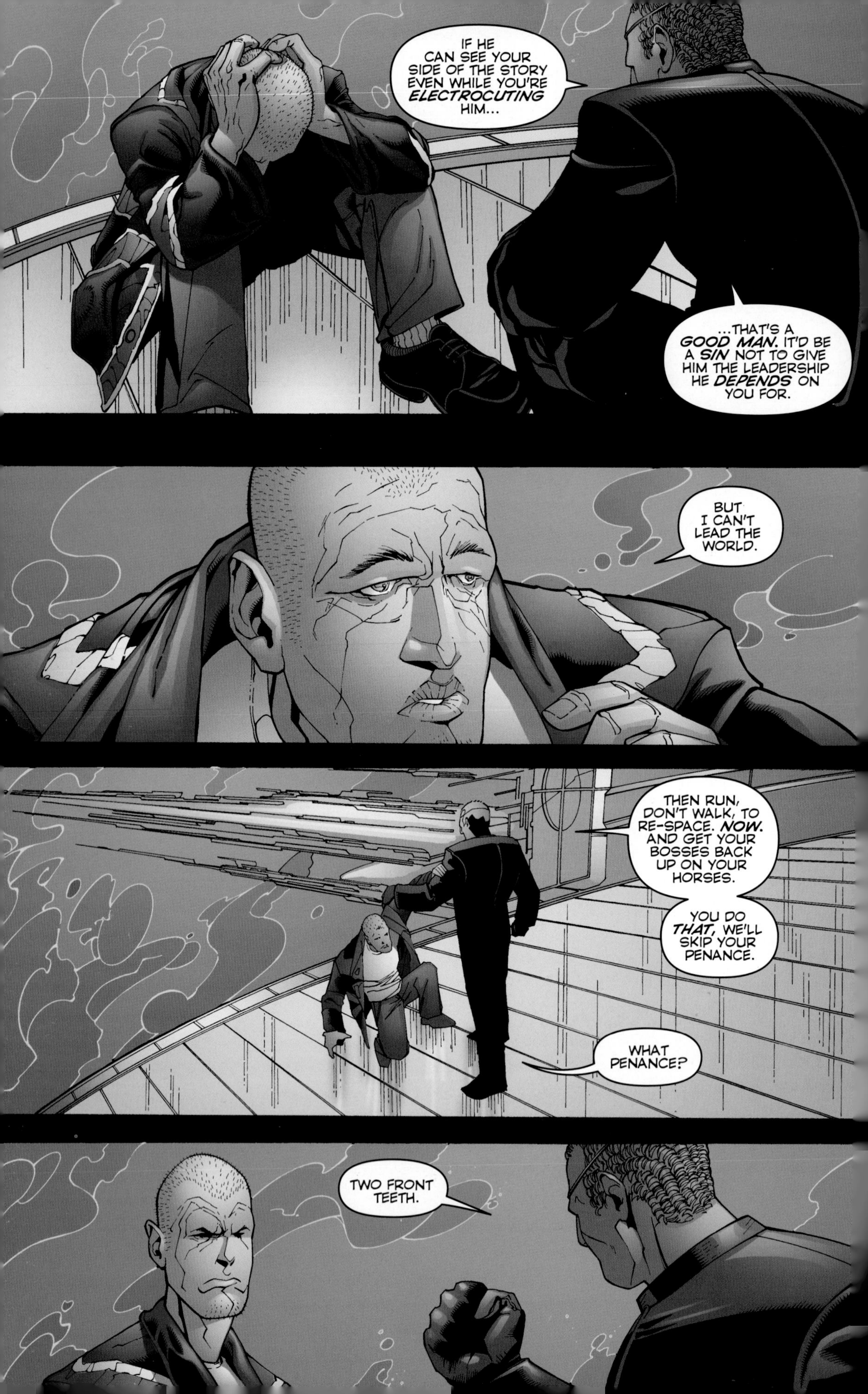
IF HE CAN SEE YOUR SIDE OF THE STORY EVEN WHILE YOU'RE ***ELECTROCUTING*** HIM...
...THAT'S A ***GOOD MAN.*** IT'D BE A ***SIN*** NOT TO GIVE HIM THE LEADERSHIP HE ***DEPENDS*** ON YOU FOR.
BUT I CAN'T LEAD THE WORLD.
THEN RUN, DON'T WALK, TO RE-SPACE. ***NOW.*** AND GET YOUR BOSSES BACK UP ON YOUR HORSES.
YOU DO ***THAT,*** WE'LL SKIP YOUR PENANCE.
WHAT PENANCE?
TWO FRONT TEETH.

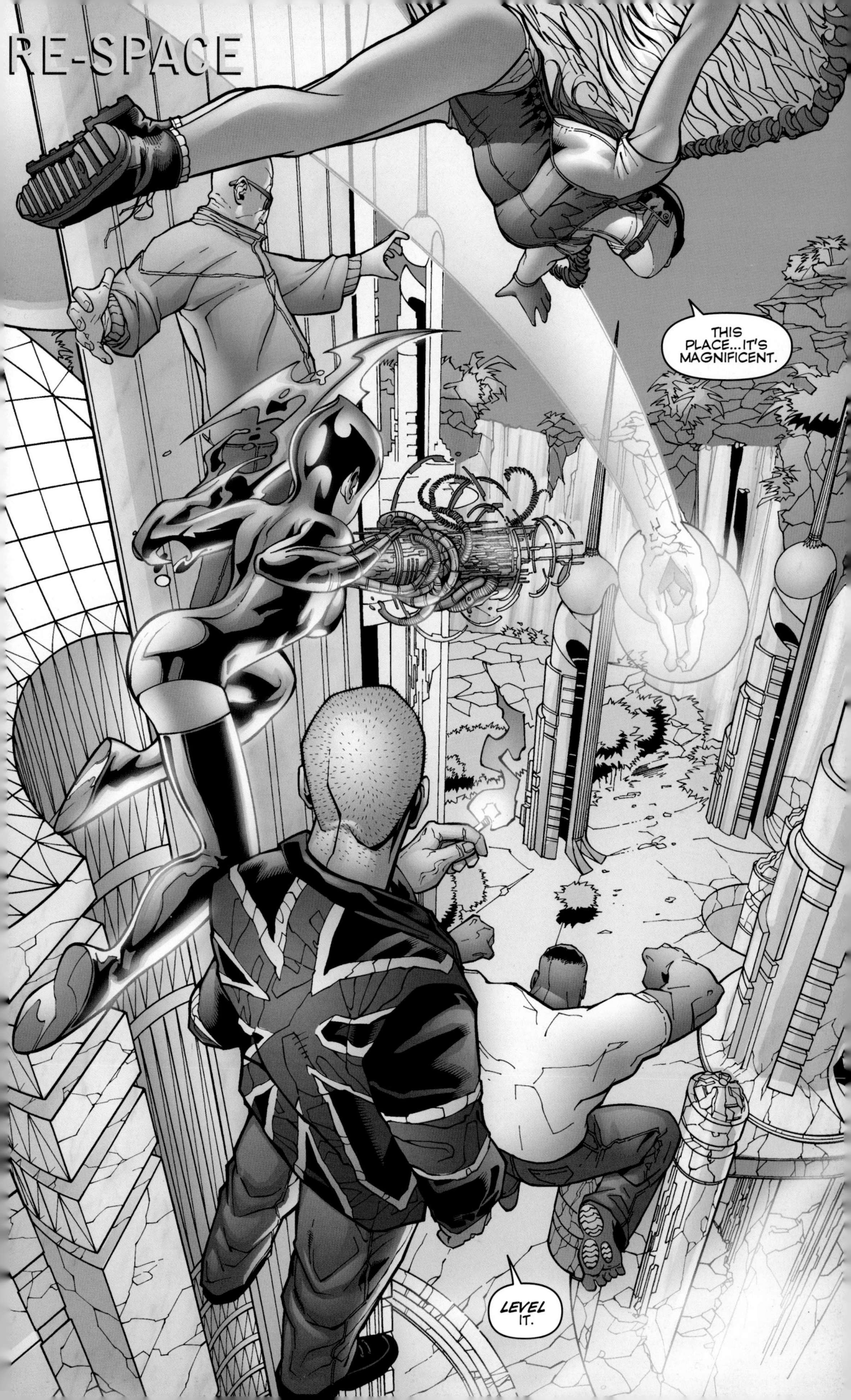
RE-SPACE
THIS PLACE...IT'S MAGNIFICENT.
LEVEL IT.

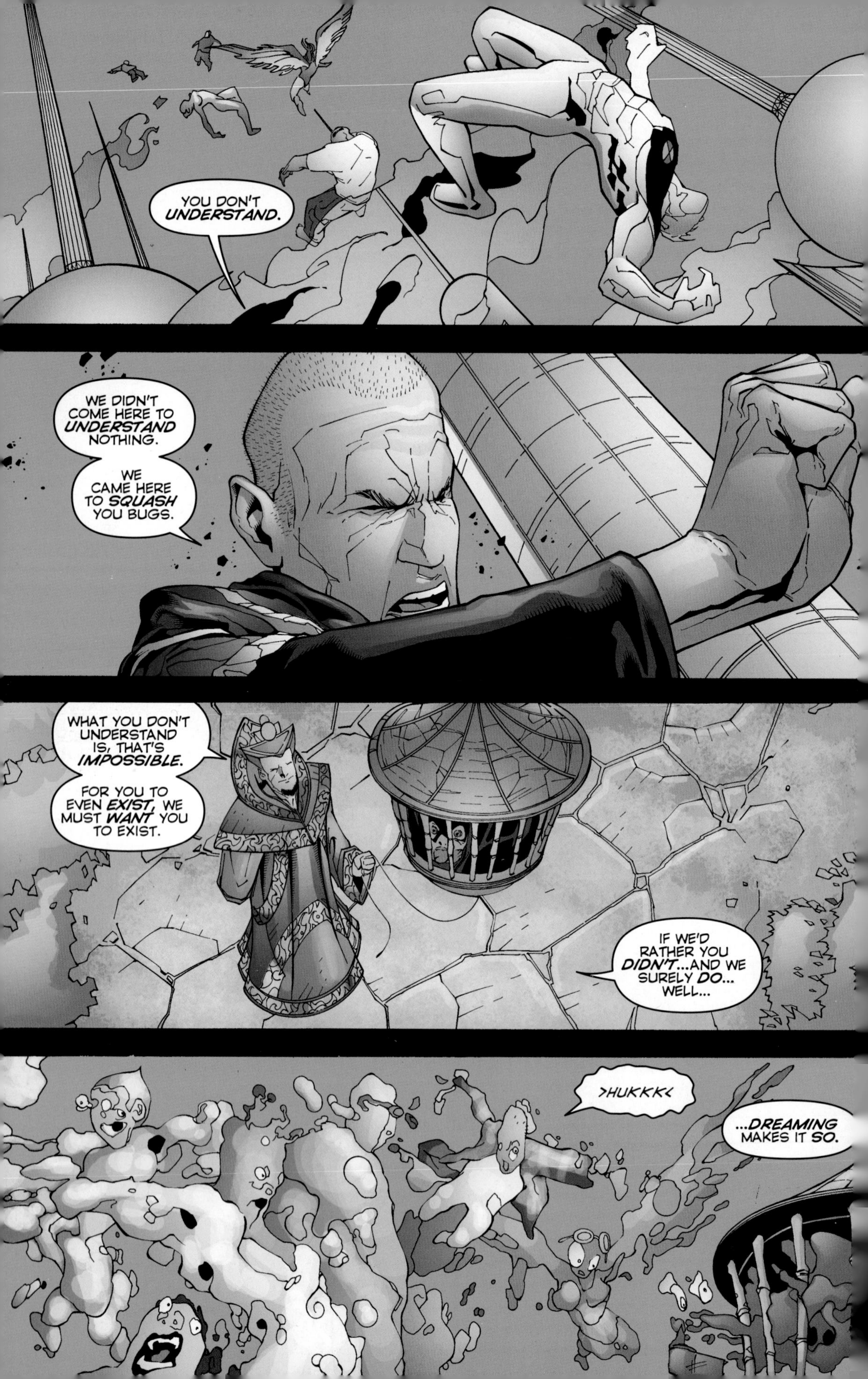
YOU DON'T UNDERSTAND.
WE DIDN'T COME HERE TO UNDERSTAND NOTHING.
WE CAME HERE TO SQUASH YOU BUGS.
WHAT YOU DON'T UNDERSTAND IS, THAT'S IMPOSSIBLE.
FOR YOU TO EVEN EXIST, WE MUST WANT YOU TO EXIST.
IF WE'D RATHER YOU DIDN'T...AND WE SURELY DO... WELL...
>HUKKK<
...DREAMING MAKES IT SO.

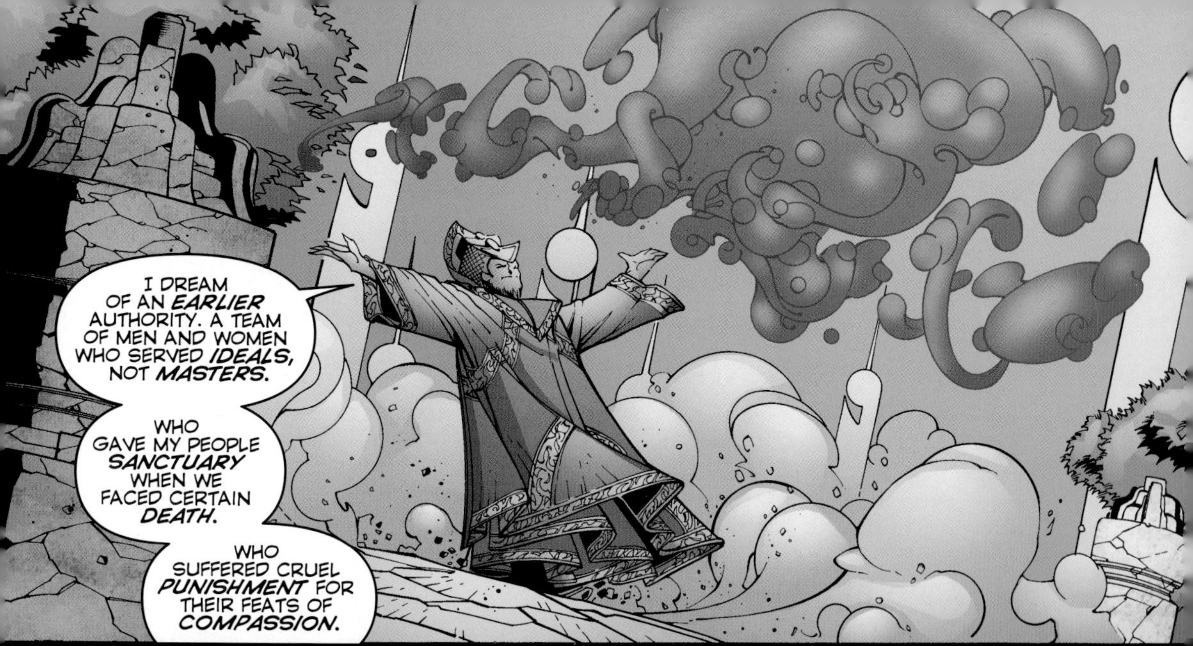
I DREAM OF AN EARLIER AUTHORITY. A TEAM OF MEN AND WOMEN WHO SERVED IDEALS, NOT MASTERS.
WHO GAVE MY PEOPLE SANCTUARY WHEN WE FACED CERTAIN DEATH.
WHO SUFFERED CRUEL PUNISHMENT FOR THEIR FEATS OF COMPASSION.

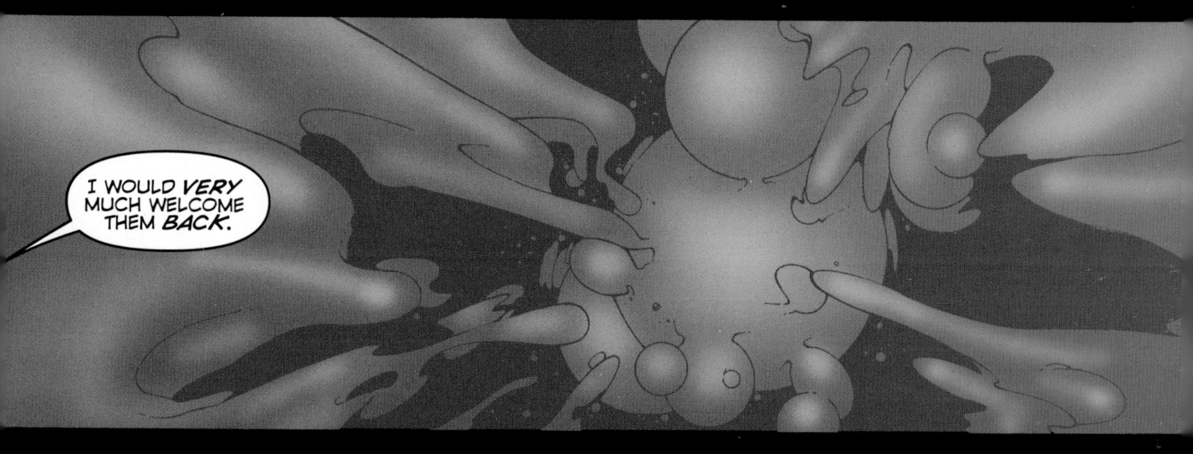
I WOULD VERY MUCH WELCOME THEM BACK.

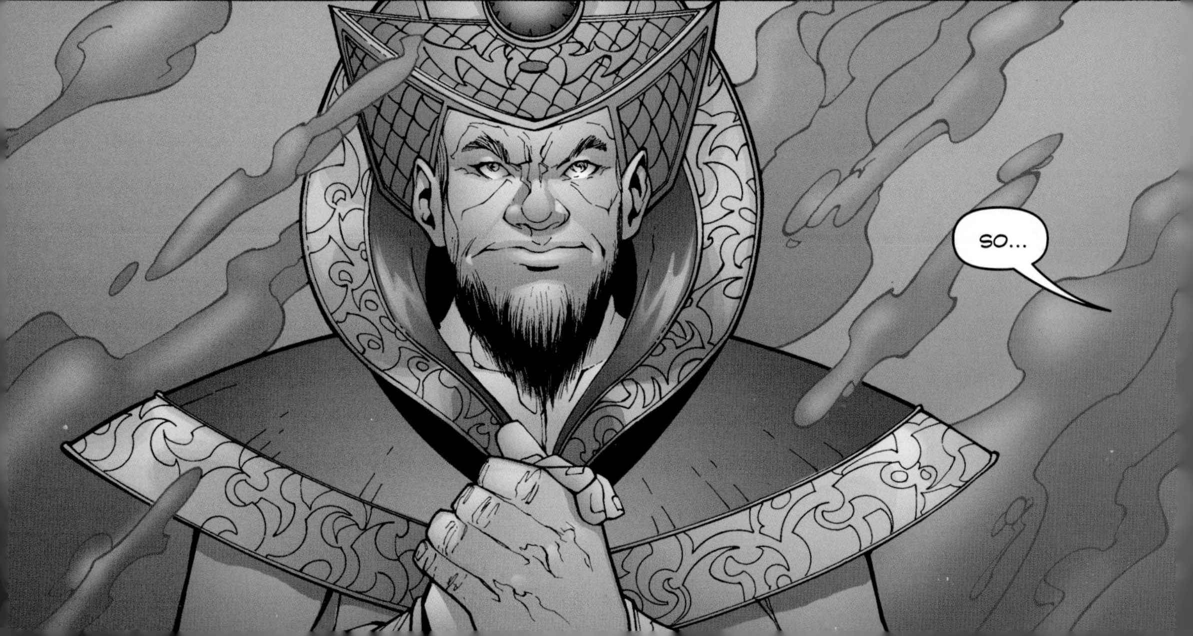
SO...

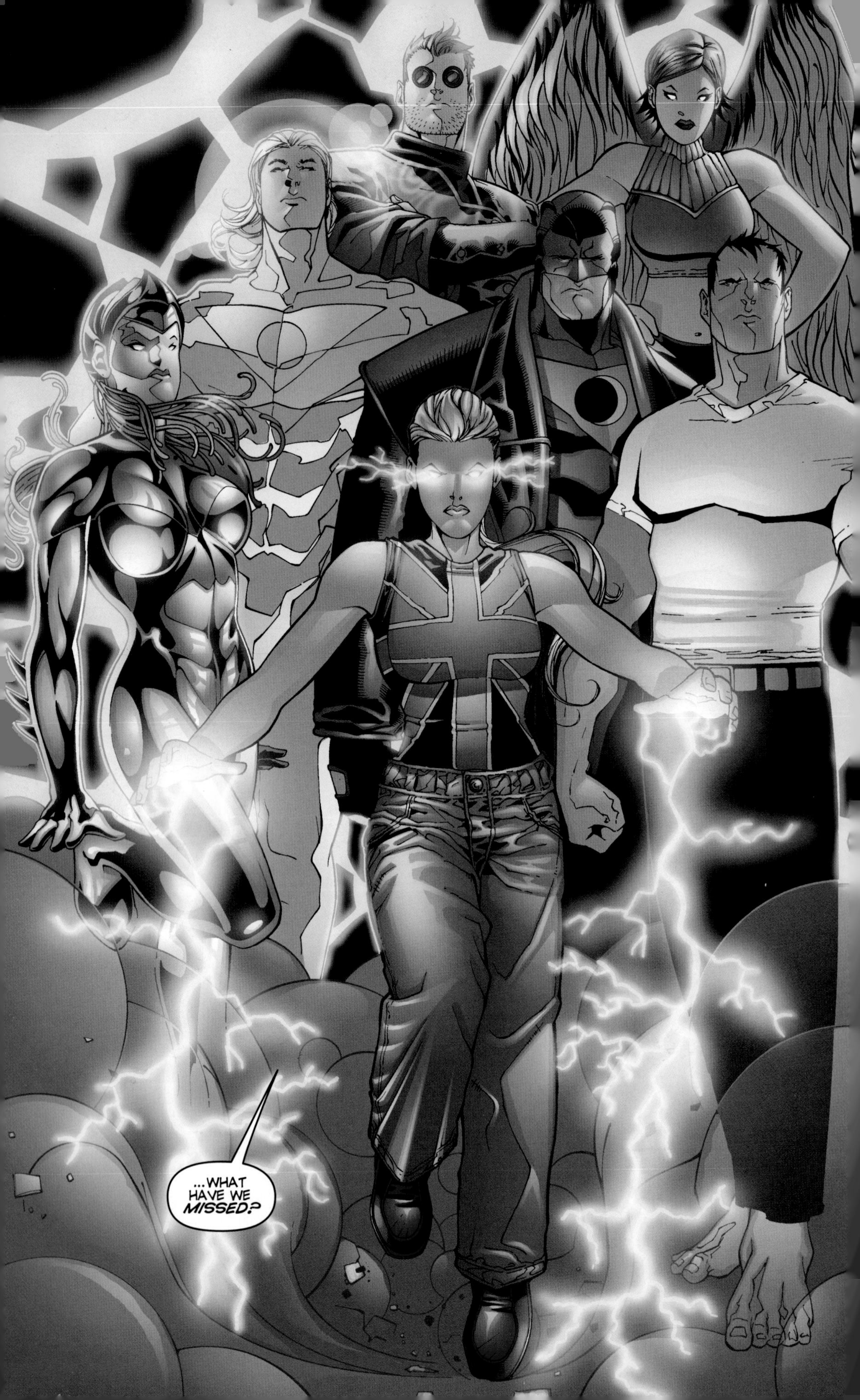
...WHAT HAVE WE MISSED?

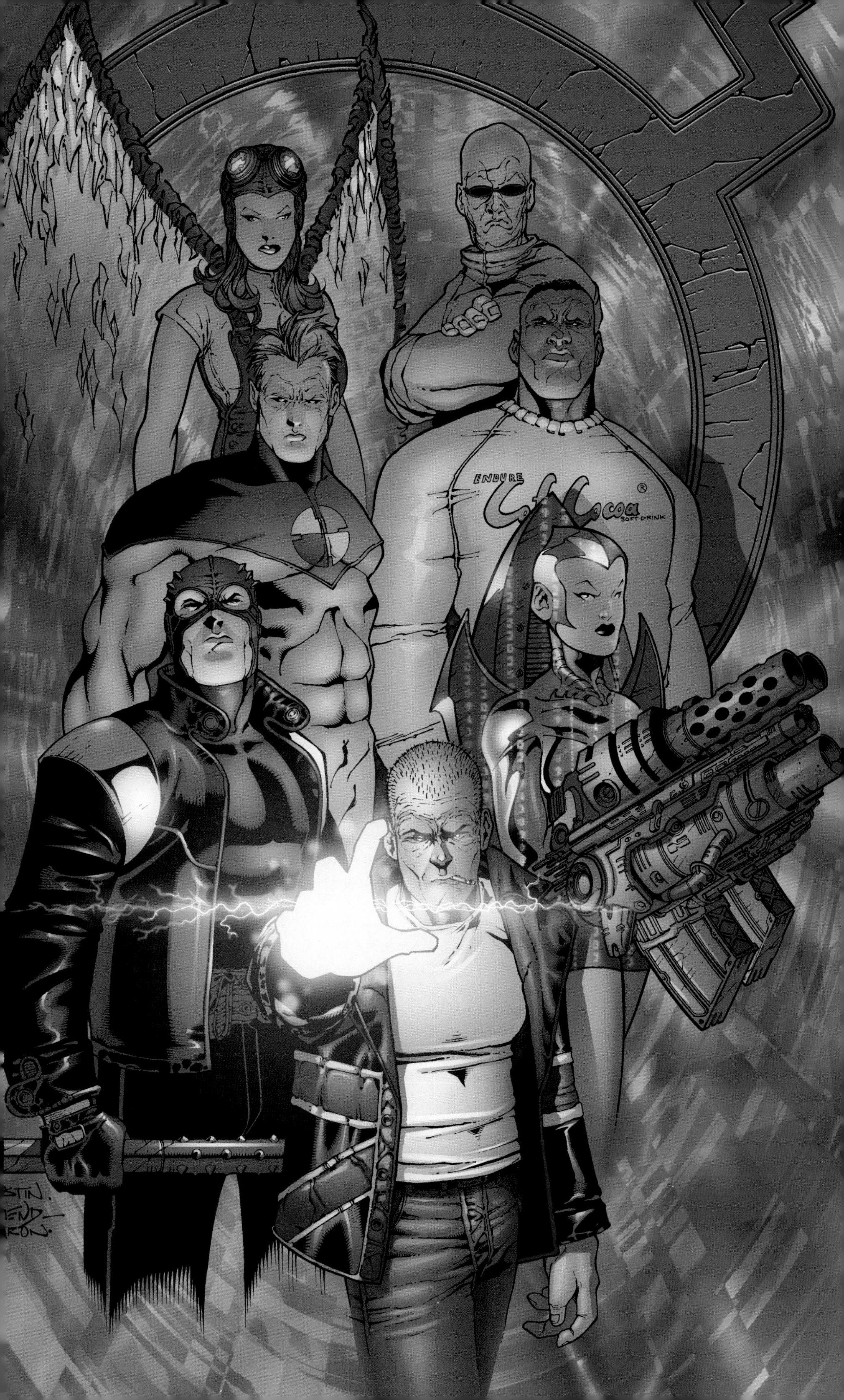
ENDURE
SOFT DRINK

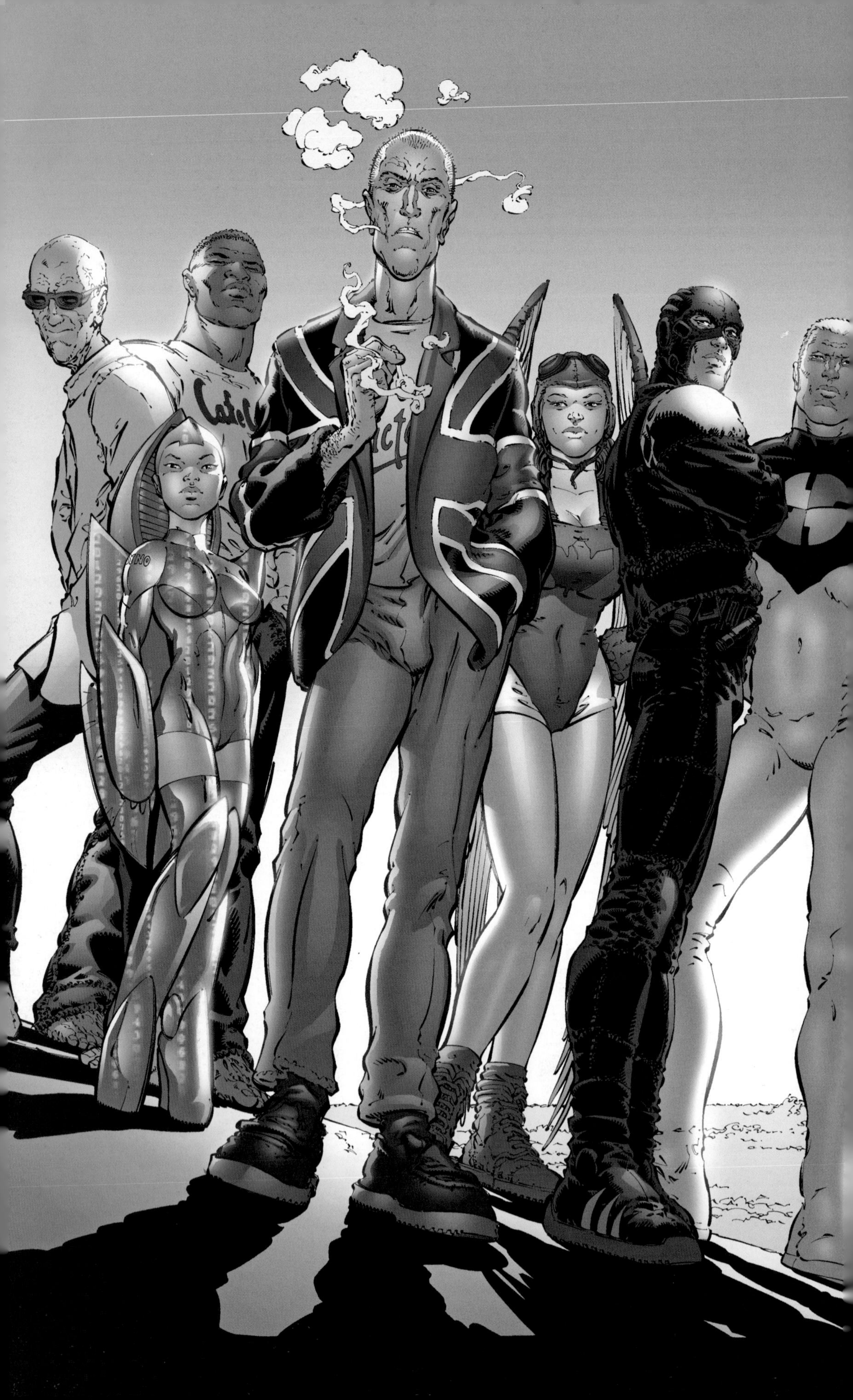

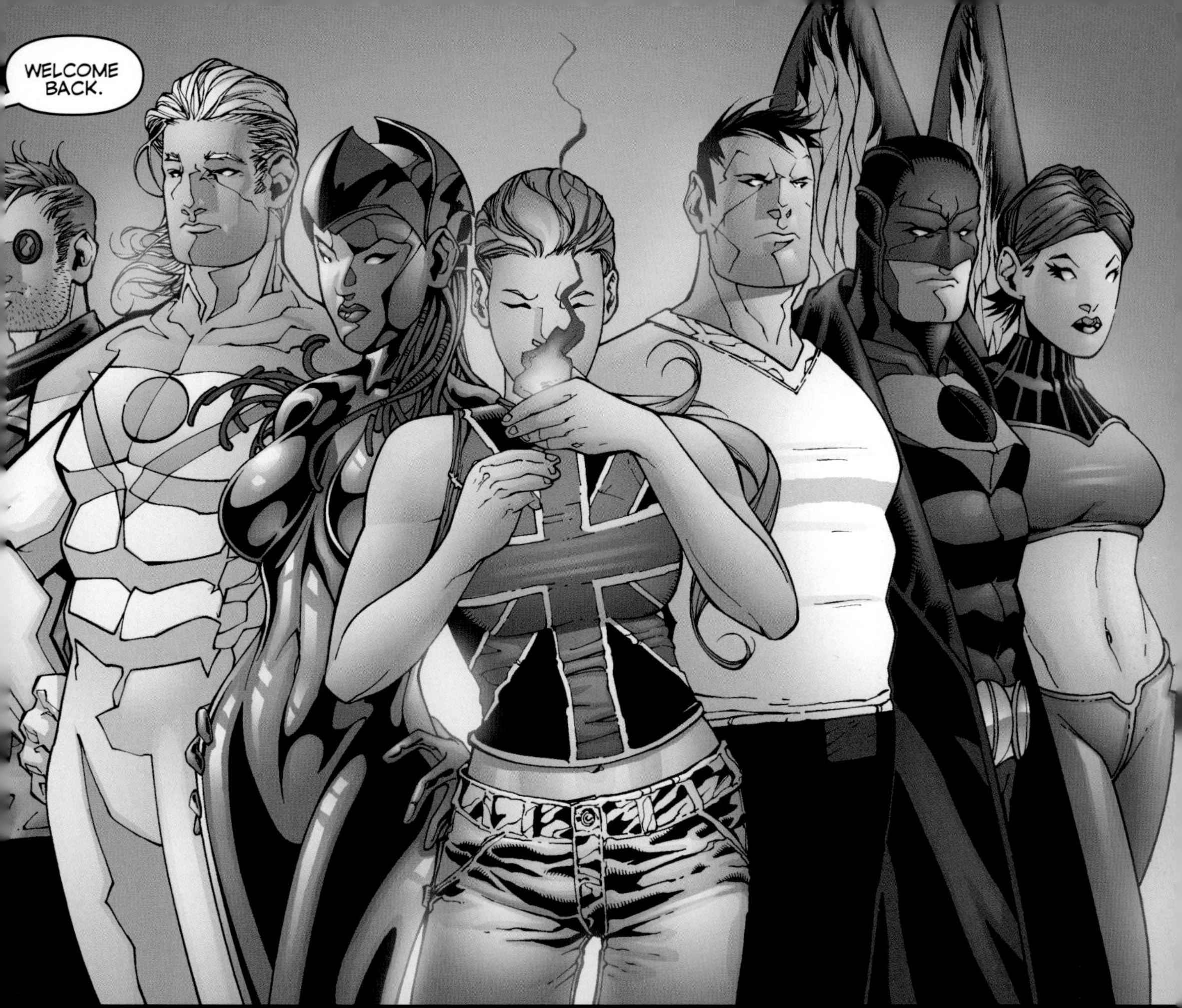
WELCOME BACK.

THE AUTHORITY

TRANSFER OF POWER

Four of Four

TOM PEYER words
DUSTIN NGUYEN pencils
RICHARD FRIEND, JASON MARTIN, DEREK FRIDOLFS, and "THE DUSTIN" inks
DAVID BARON colors
BILL O'NEIL letters

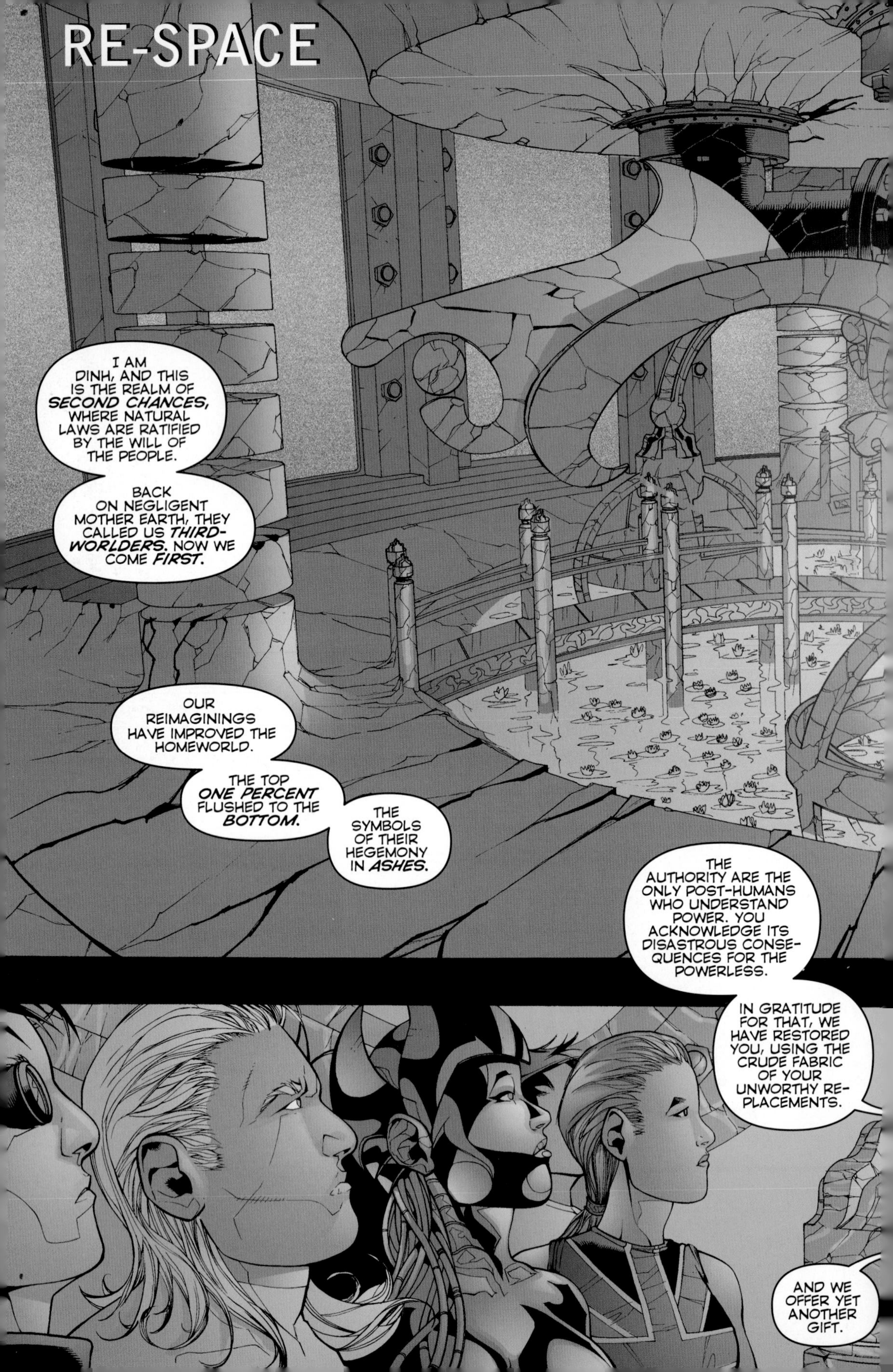
RE-SPACE
I AM DINH, AND THIS IS THE REALM OF *SECOND CHANCES,* WHERE NATURAL LAWS ARE RATIFIED BY THE WILL OF THE PEOPLE.
BACK ON NEGLIGENT MOTHER EARTH, THEY CALLED US *THIRD-WORLDERS*. NOW WE COME *FIRST*.
OUR REIMAGININGS HAVE IMPROVED THE HOMEWORLD.
THE TOP *ONE PERCENT* FLUSHED TO THE *BOTTOM*.
THE SYMBOLS OF THEIR HEGEMONY IN *ASHES*.
THE AUTHORITY ARE THE ONLY POST-HUMANS WHO UNDERSTAND POWER. YOU ACKNOWLEDGE ITS DISASTROUS CONSE-QUENCES FOR THE POWERLESS.
IN GRATITUDE FOR THAT, WE HAVE RESTORED YOU, USING THE CRUDE FABRIC OF YOUR UNWORTHY RE-PLACEMENTS.
AND WE OFFER YET ANOTHER GIFT.

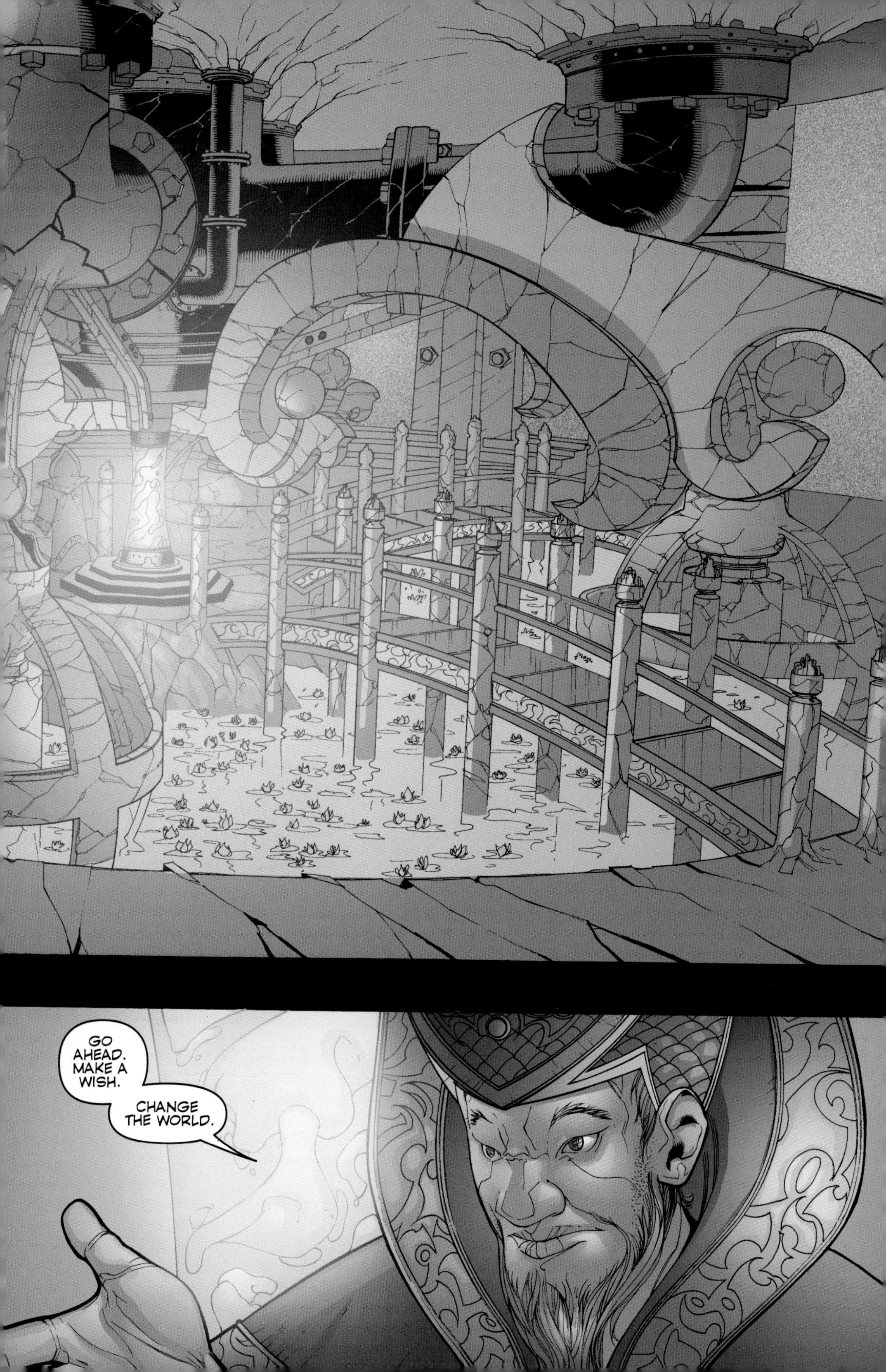
GO AHEAD. MAKE A WISH.
CHANGE THE WORLD.

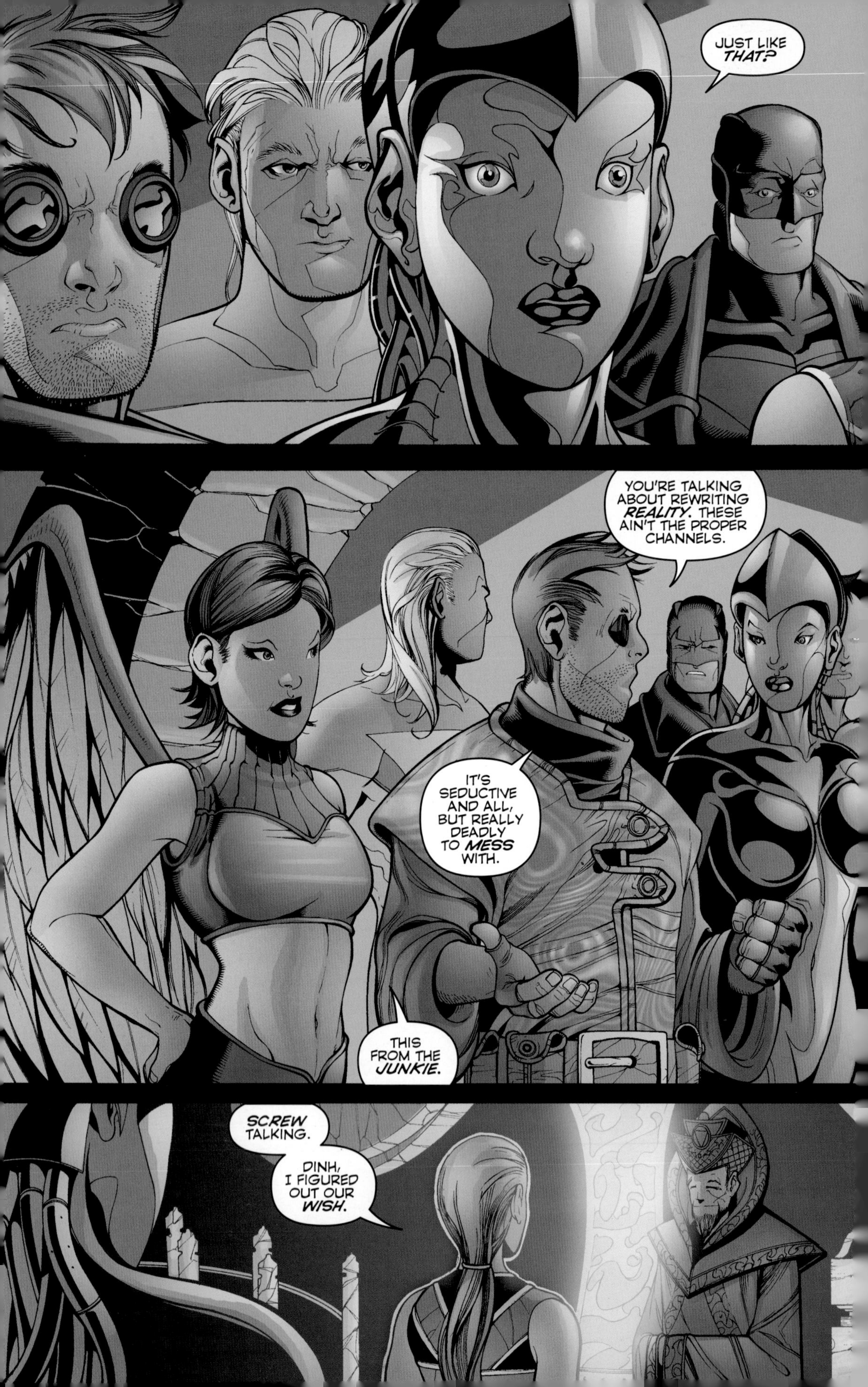
JUST LIKE *THAT?*
YOU'RE TALKING ABOUT REWRITING *REALITY*. THESE AIN'T THE PROPER CHANNELS.
IT'S SEDUCTIVE AND ALL, BUT REALLY DEADLY TO *MESS* WITH.
THIS FROM THE *JUNKIE*.
SCREW TALKING.
DINH, I FIGURED OUT OUR *WISH*.

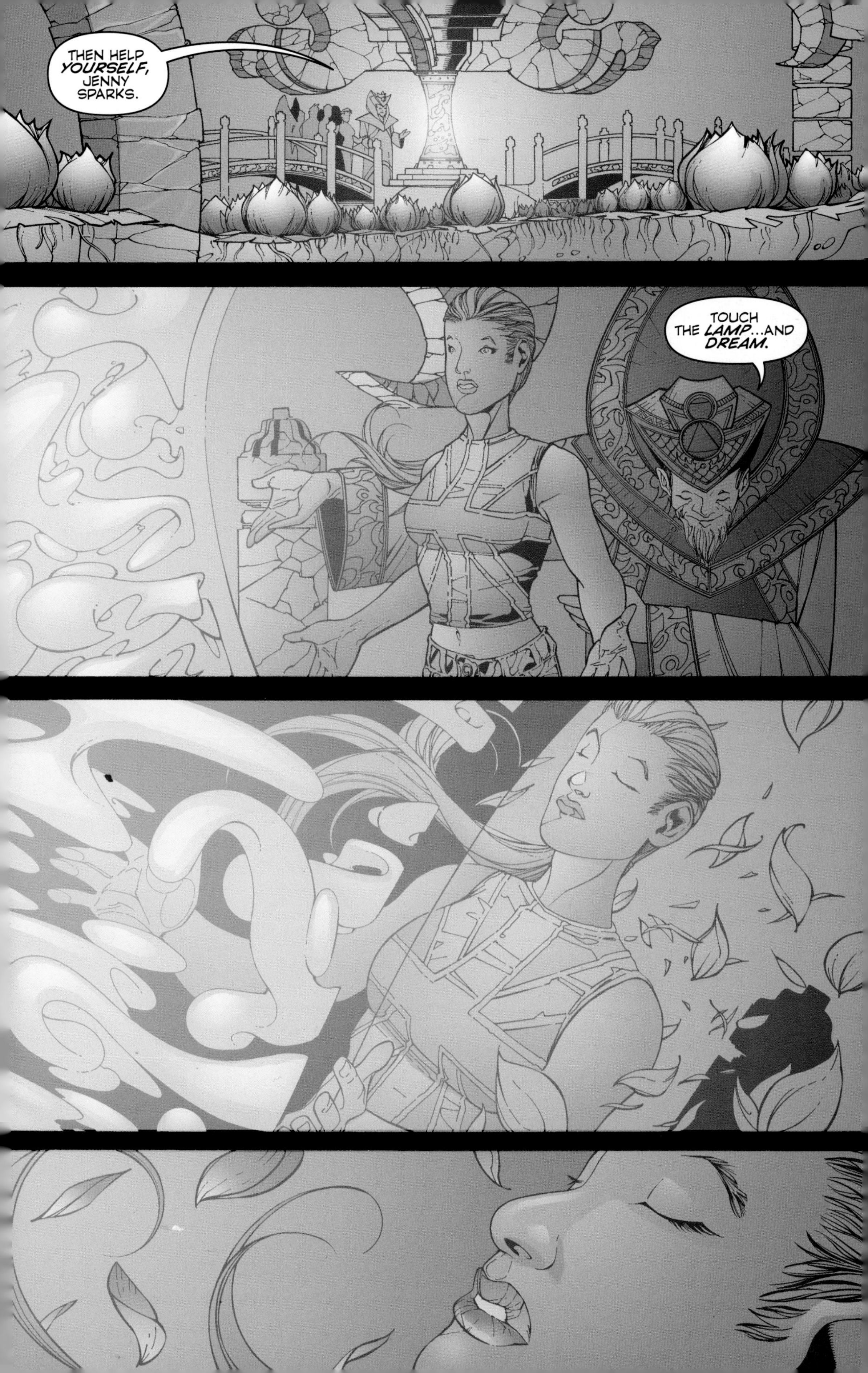
THEN HELP *YOURSELF,* JENNY SPARKS.
TOUCH THE *LAMP*...AND *DREAM.*

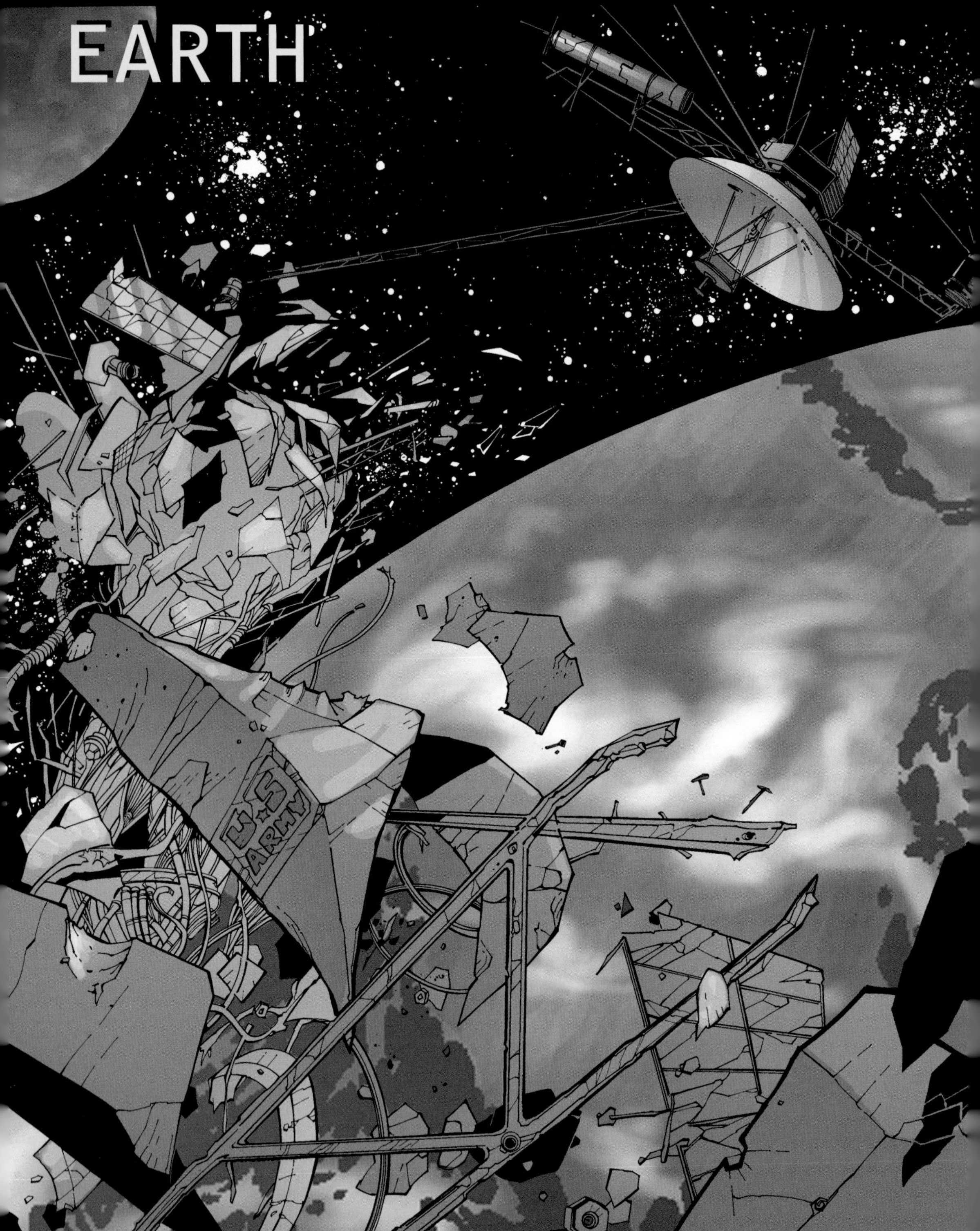
EARTH
US ARMY

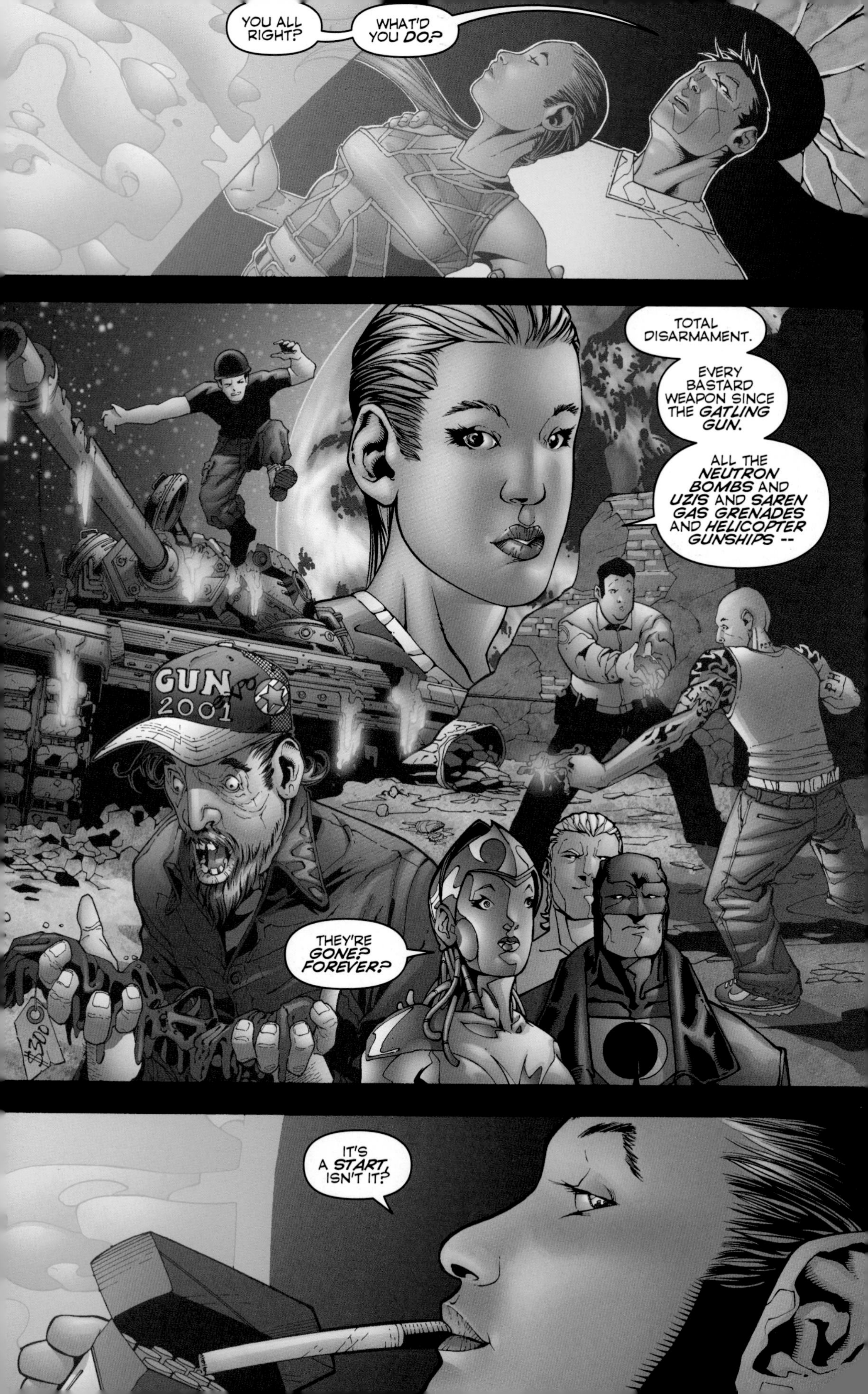
YOU ALL RIGHT?
WHAT'D YOU DO?
TOTAL DISARMAMENT.
EVERY BASTARD WEAPON SINCE THE GATLING GUN.
ALL THE NEUTRON BOMBS AND UZIS AND SAREN GAS GRENADES AND HELICOPTER GUNSHIPS --
GUN 2001
THEY'RE GONE? FOREVER?
IT'S A START, ISN'T IT?

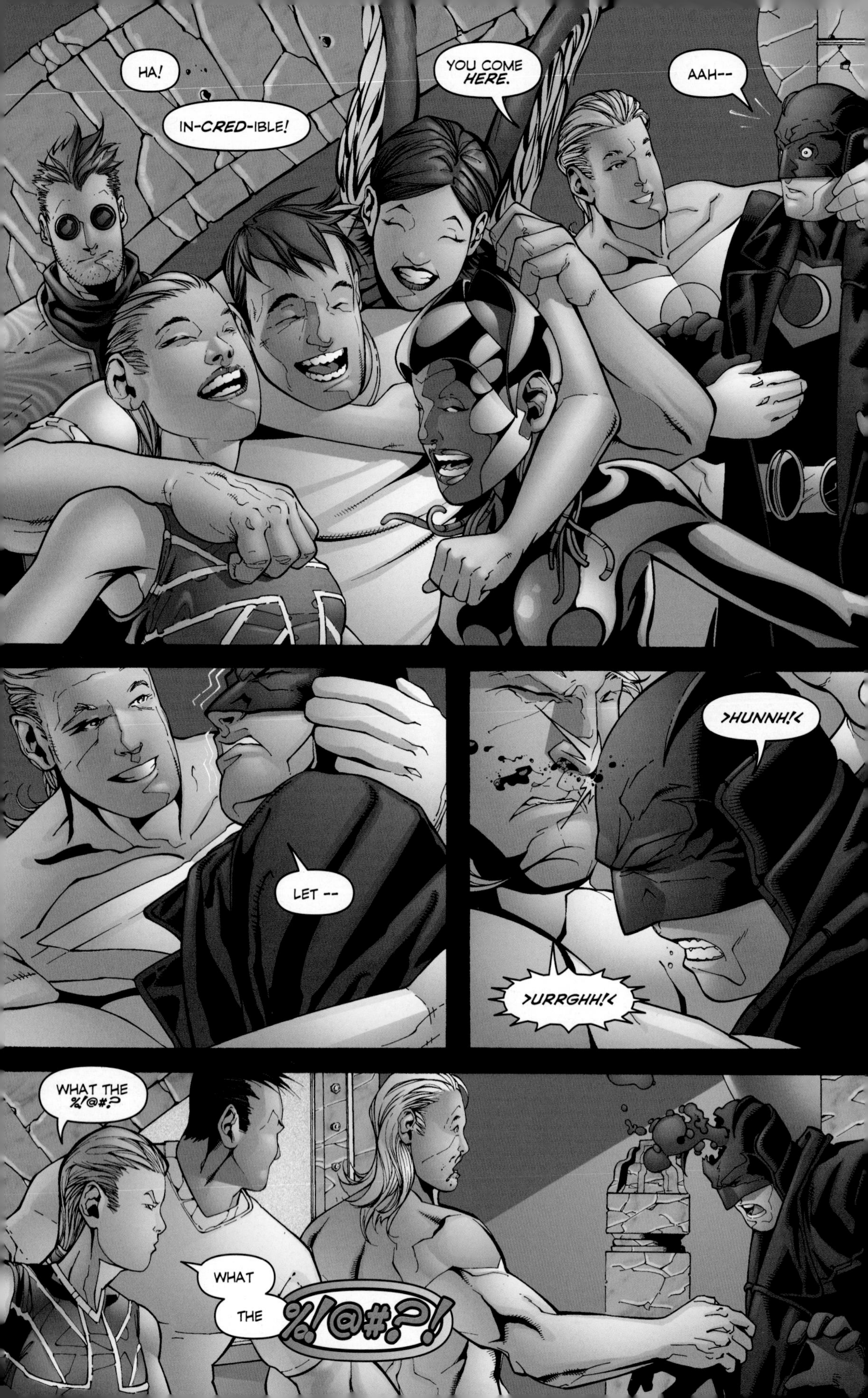
HA!
IN-*CRED*-IBLE!
YOU COME *HERE.*
AAH--
LET --
>*HUNNH!*<
>*URRGHH!*<
WHAT THE %!@#?
WHAT
THE
%!@#?!

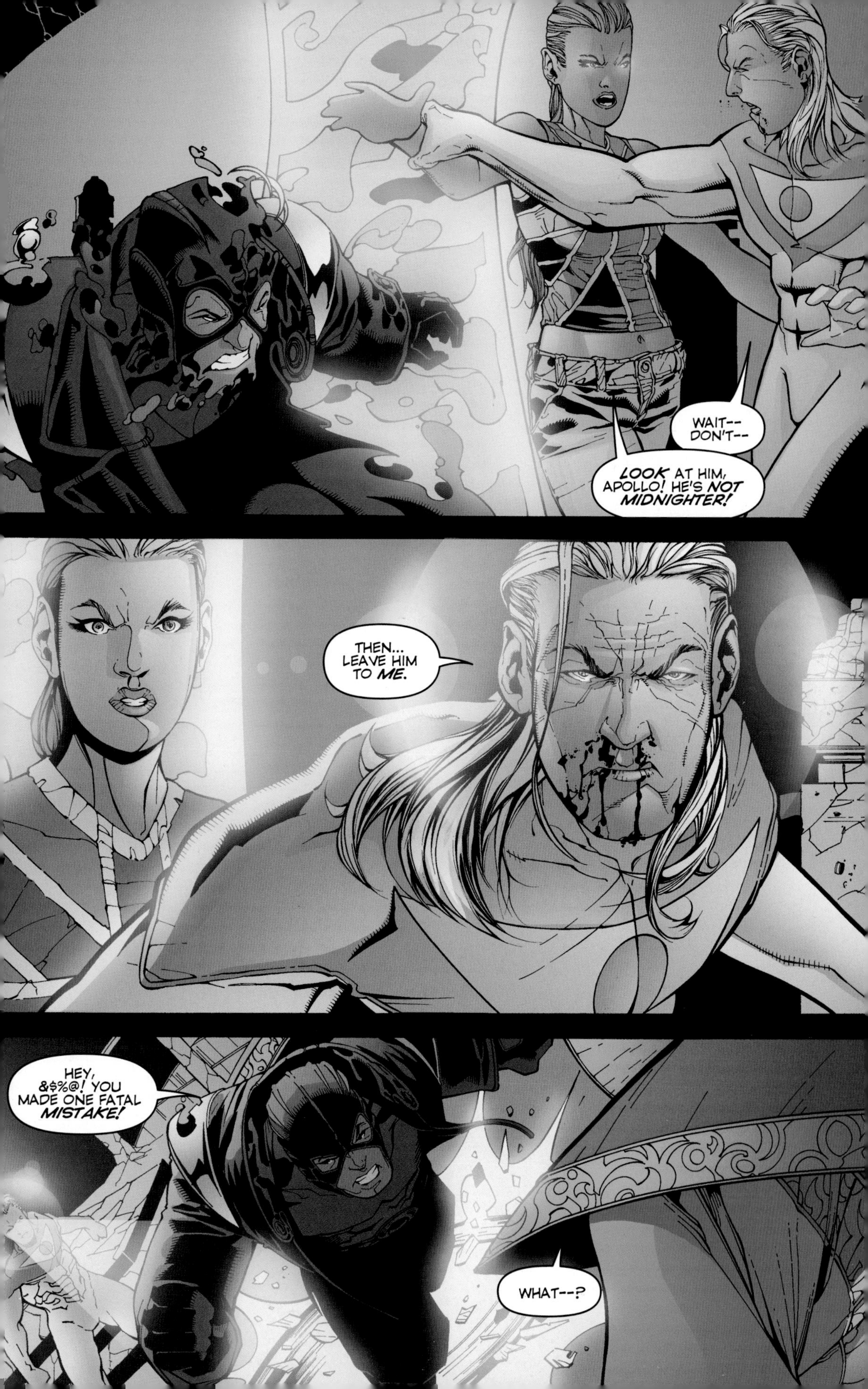
WAIT-- DON'T--
LOOK AT HIM, APOLLO! HE'S NOT MIDNIGHTER!
THEN... LEAVE HIM TO ME.
HEY, &$%@! YOU MADE ONE FATAL MISTAKE!
WHAT--?

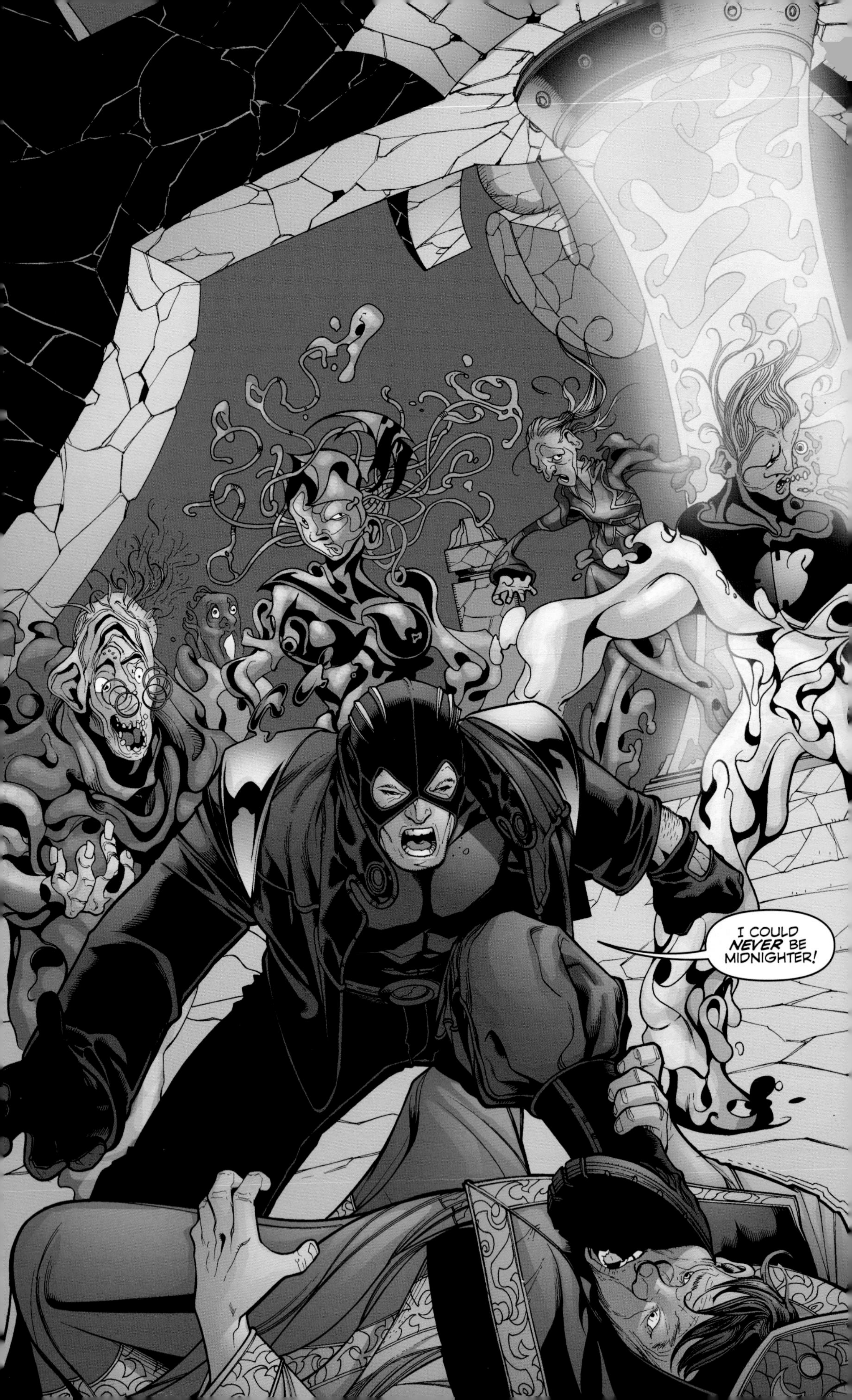
I COULD NEVER BE MIDNIGHTER!

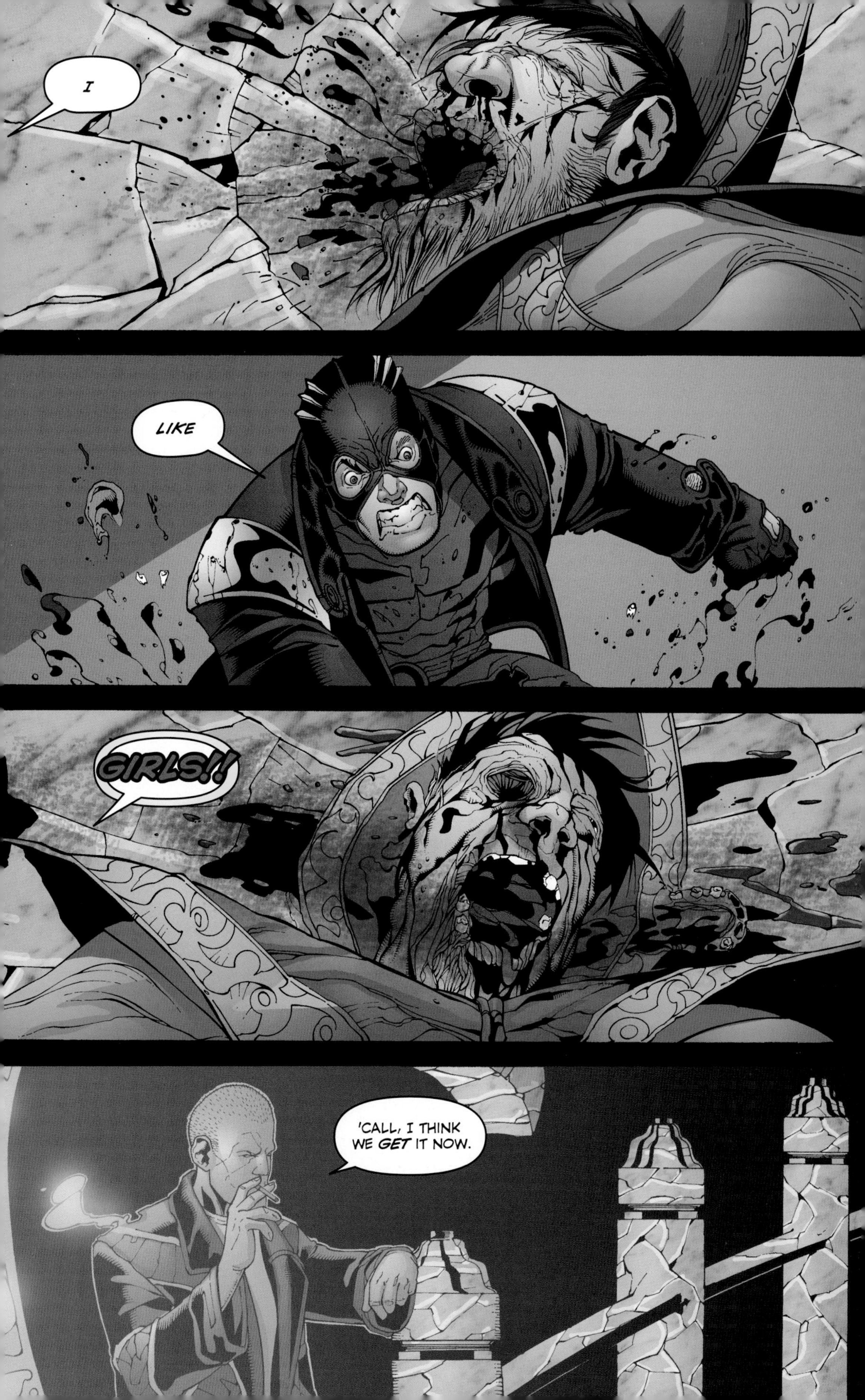
I
LIKE
GIRLS!!
'CALL, I THINK WE GET IT NOW.

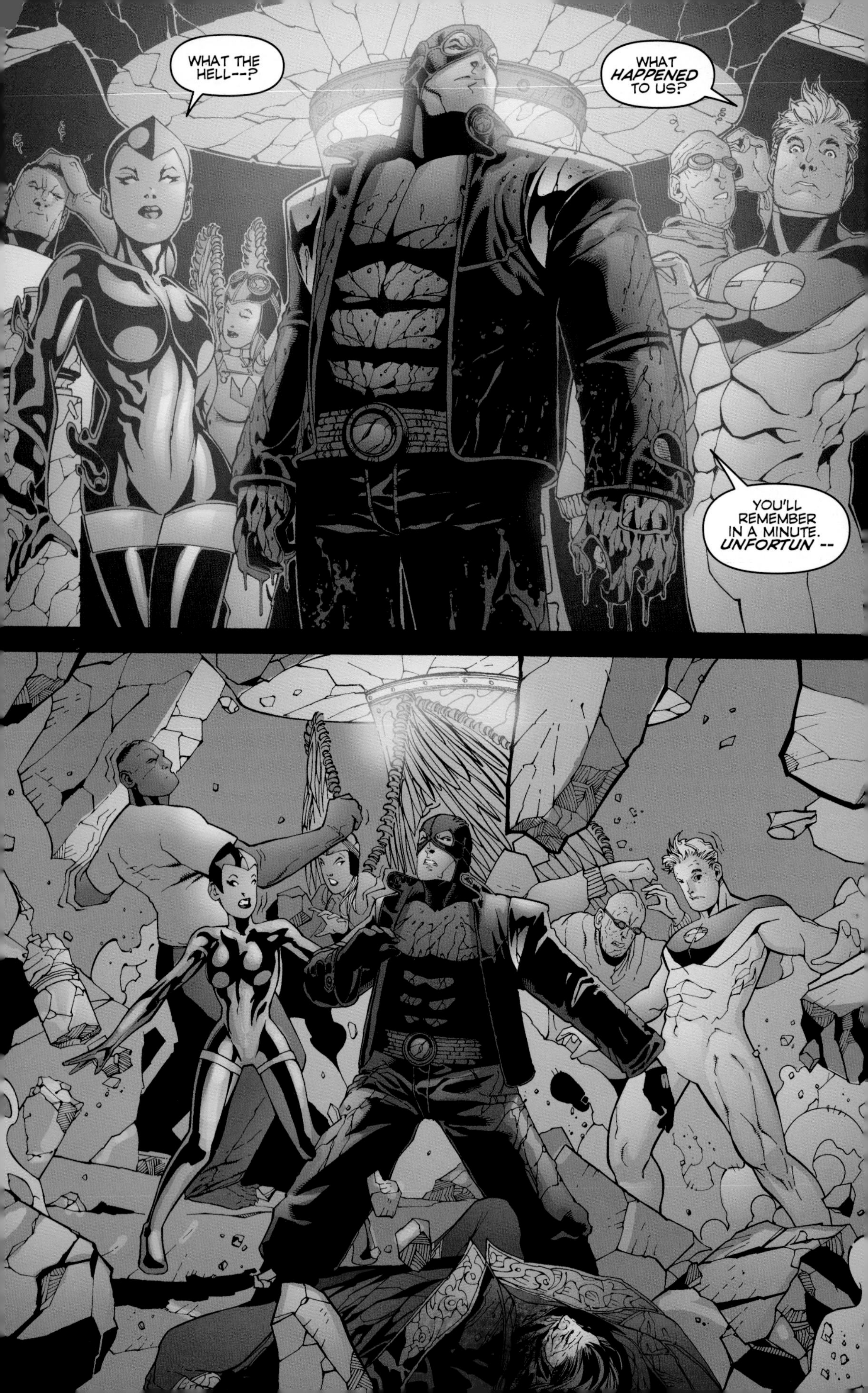
WHAT THE HELL--?
WHAT *HAPPENED* TO US?
YOU'LL REMEMBER IN A MINUTE. ***UNFORTUN*** --

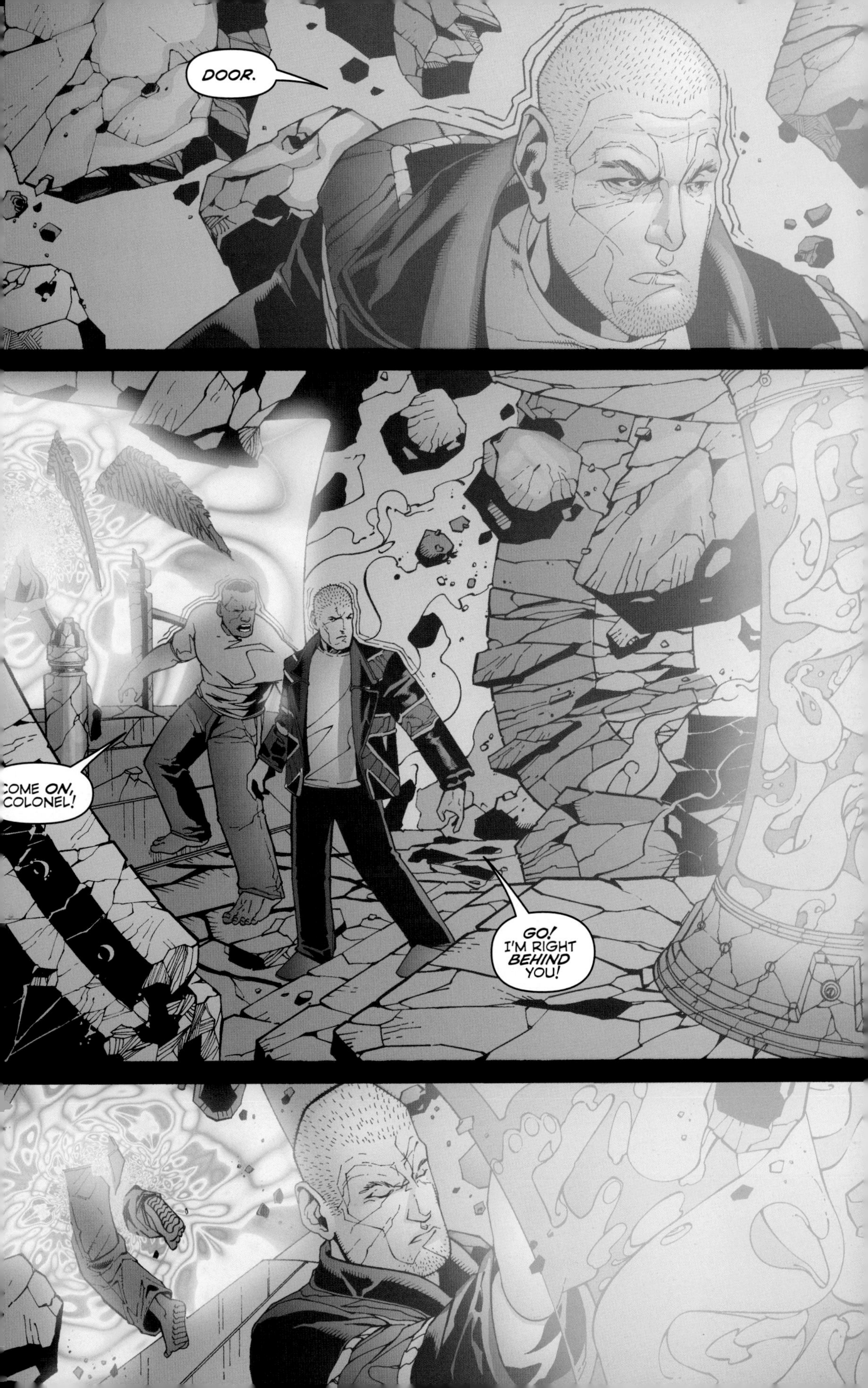
DOOR.
COME ON, COLONEL!
GO! I'M RIGHT BEHIND YOU!

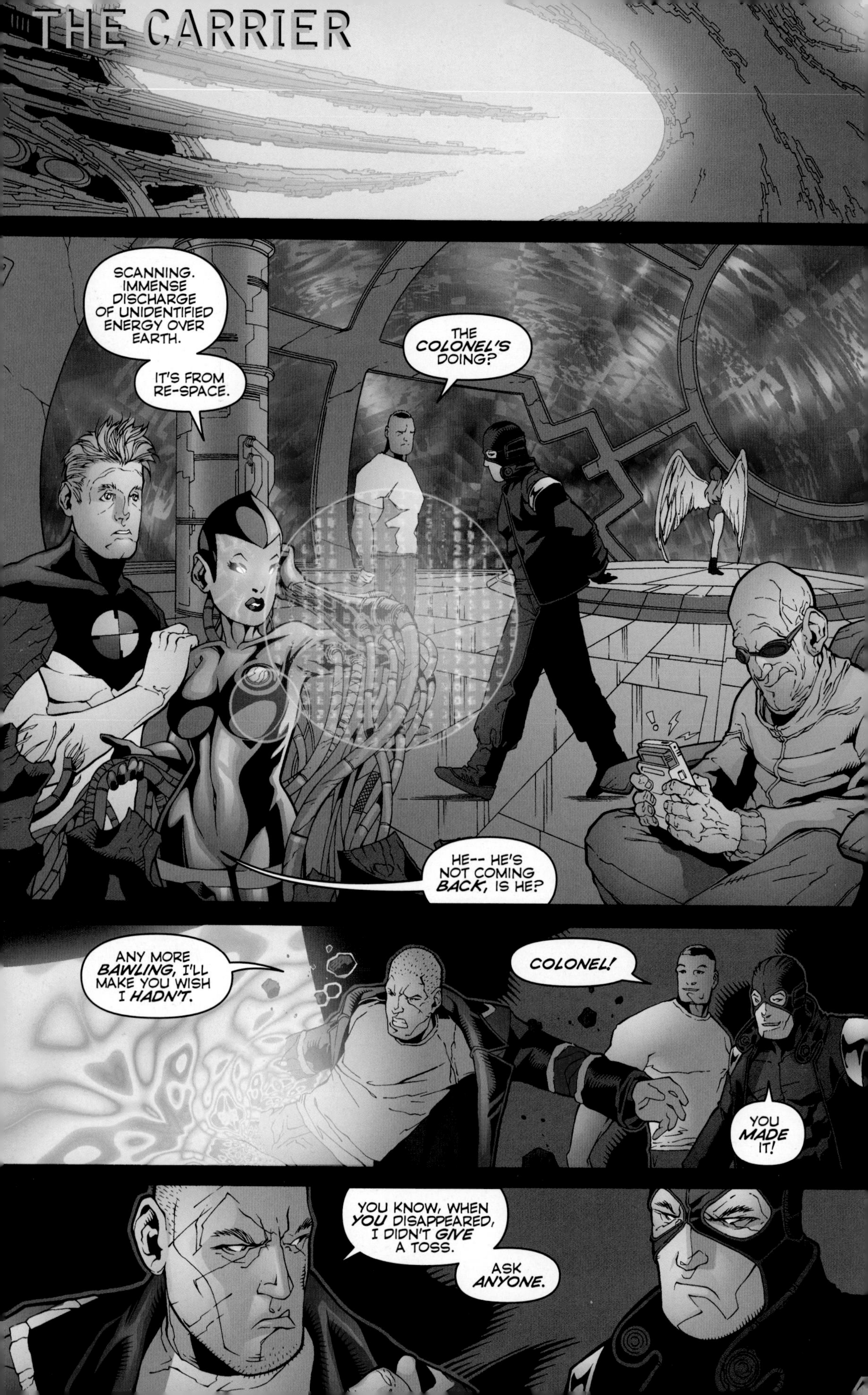
THE CARRIER
SCANNING. IMMENSE DISCHARGE OF UNIDENTIFIED ENERGY OVER EARTH.
IT'S FROM RE-SPACE.
THE COLONEL'S DOING?
HE-- HE'S NOT COMING BACK, IS HE?
ANY MORE BAWLING, I'LL MAKE YOU WISH I HADN'T.
COLONEL!
YOU MADE IT!
YOU KNOW, WHEN YOU DISAPPEARED, I DIDN'T GIVE A TOSS.
ASK ANYONE.

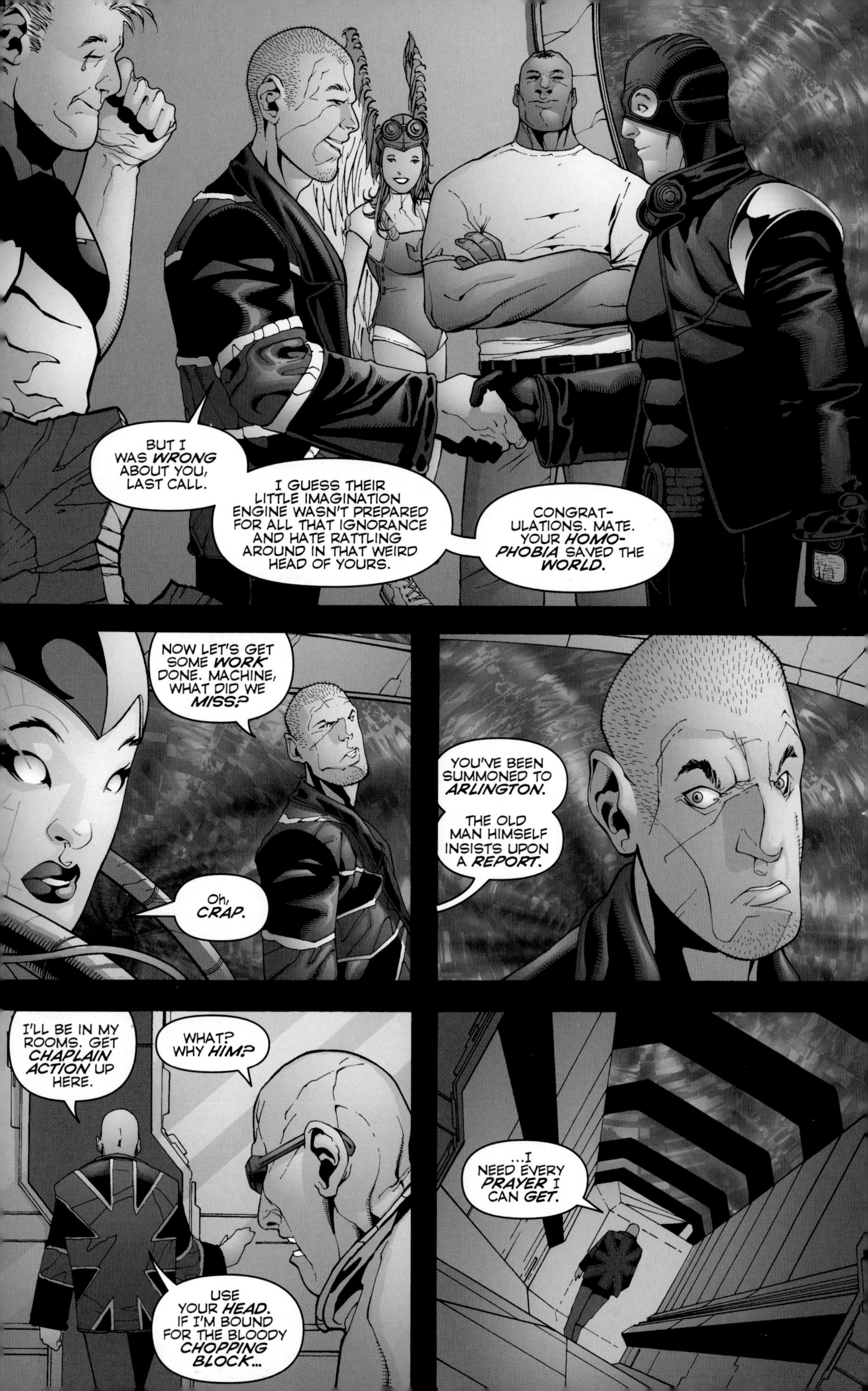

BUT I WAS *WRONG* ABOUT YOU, LAST CALL.
I GUESS THEIR LITTLE IMAGINATION ENGINE WASN'T PREPARED FOR ALL THAT IGNORANCE AND HATE RATTLING AROUND IN THAT WEIRD HEAD OF YOURS.
CONGRAT-ULATIONS. MATE. YOUR *HOMO-PHOBIA* SAVED THE *WORLD*.
NOW LET'S GET SOME *WORK* DONE. MACHINE, WHAT DID WE *MISS?*
Oh, *CRAP*.
YOU'VE BEEN SUMMONED TO *ARLINGTON*.
THE OLD MAN HIMSELF INSISTS UPON A *REPORT*.
I'LL BE IN MY ROOMS. GET *CHAPLAIN ACTION* UP HERE.
WHAT? WHY *HIM?*
USE YOUR *HEAD*. IF I'M BOUND FOR THE BLOODY *CHOPPING BLOCK*...
...I NEED EVERY *PRAYER* I CAN *GET*.

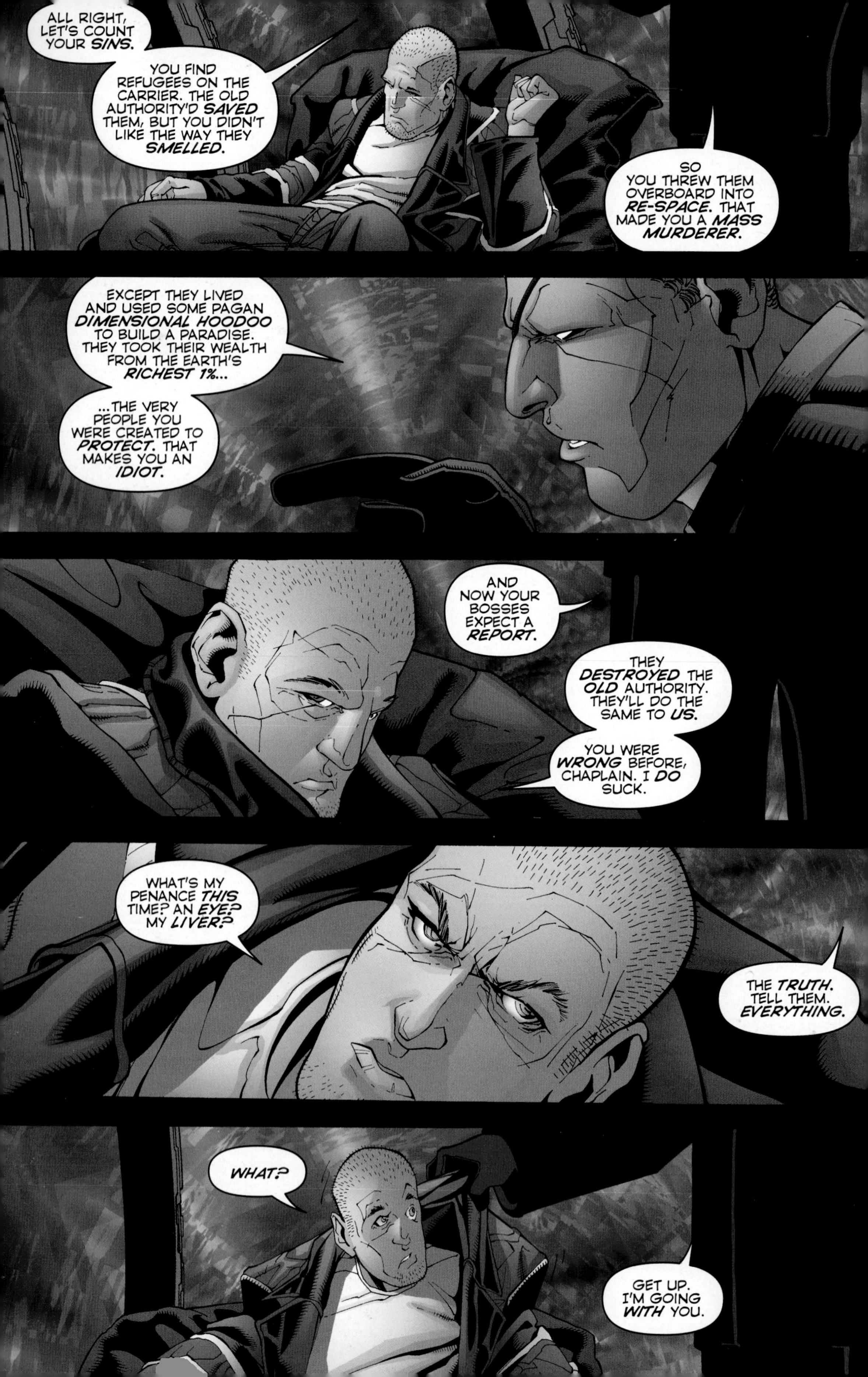
ALL RIGHT, LET'S COUNT YOUR SINS.
YOU FIND REFUGEES ON THE CARRIER. THE OLD AUTHORITY'D SAVED THEM, BUT YOU DIDN'T LIKE THE WAY THEY SMELLED.
SO YOU THREW THEM OVERBOARD INTO RE-SPACE. THAT MADE YOU A MASS MURDERER.
EXCEPT THEY LIVED AND USED SOME PAGAN DIMENSIONAL HOODOO TO BUILD A PARADISE. THEY TOOK THEIR WEALTH FROM THE EARTH'S RICHEST 1%...
...THE VERY PEOPLE YOU WERE CREATED TO PROTECT. THAT MAKES YOU AN IDIOT.
AND NOW YOUR BOSSES EXPECT A REPORT.
THEY DESTROYED THE OLD AUTHORITY. THEY'LL DO THE SAME TO US.
YOU WERE WRONG BEFORE, CHAPLAIN. I DO SUCK.
WHAT'S MY PENANCE THIS TIME? AN EYE? MY LIVER?
THE TRUTH. TELL THEM. EVERYTHING.
WHAT?
GET UP. I'M GOING WITH YOU.

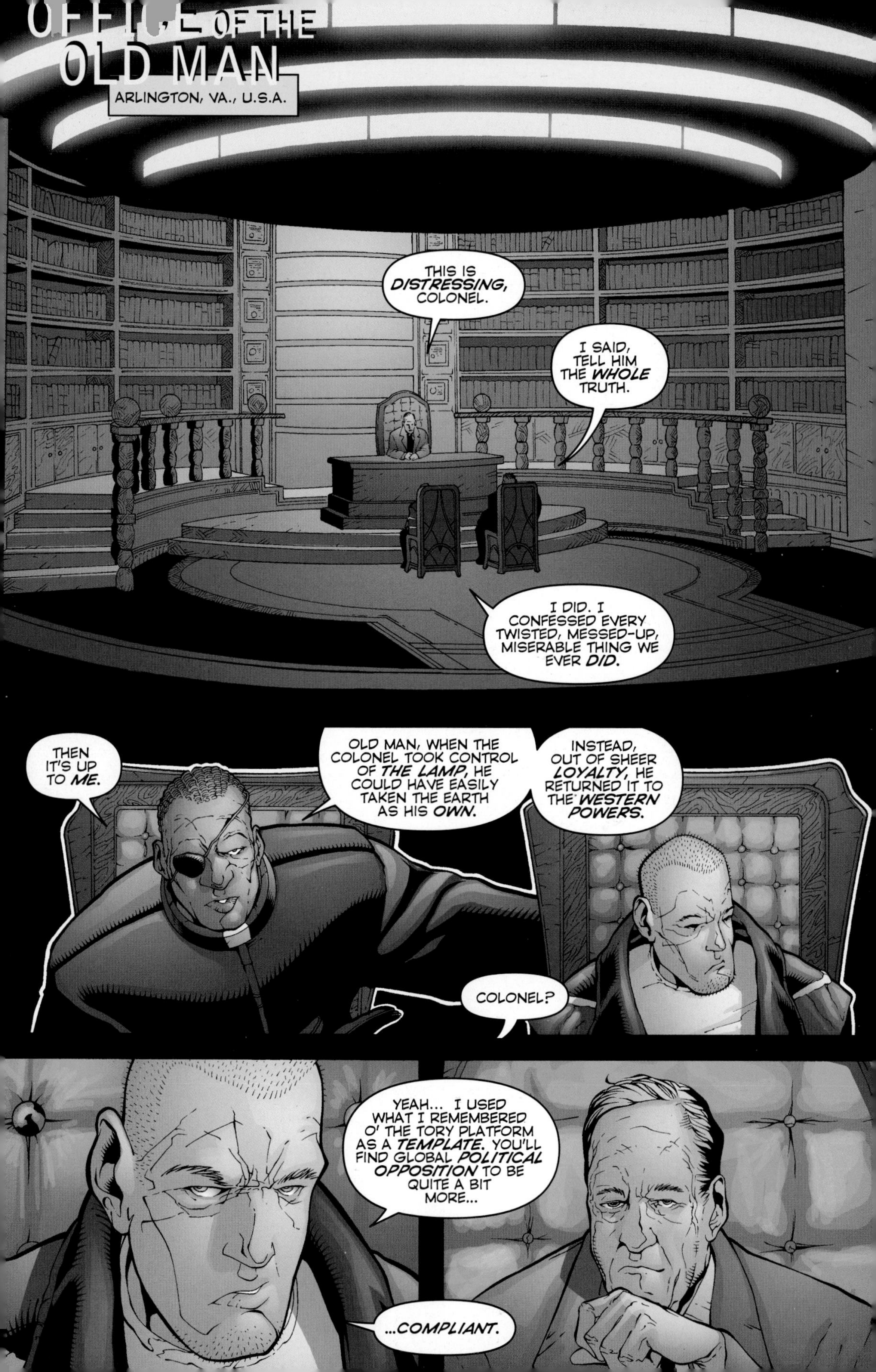
OFFICE OF THE OLD MAN
ARLINGTON, VA., U.S.A.
THIS IS DISTRESSING, COLONEL.
I SAID, TELL HIM THE WHOLE TRUTH.
I DID. I CONFESSED EVERY TWISTED, MESSED-UP, MISERABLE THING WE EVER DID.
THEN IT'S UP TO ME.
OLD MAN, WHEN THE COLONEL TOOK CONTROL OF THE LAMP, HE COULD HAVE EASILY TAKEN THE EARTH AS HIS OWN.
INSTEAD, OUT OF SHEER LOYALTY, HE RETURNED IT TO THE WESTERN POWERS.
COLONEL?
YEAH... I USED WHAT I REMEMBERED O' THE TORY PLATFORM AS A TEMPLATE. YOU'LL FIND GLOBAL POLITICAL OPPOSITION TO BE QUITE A BIT MORE...
...COMPLIANT.

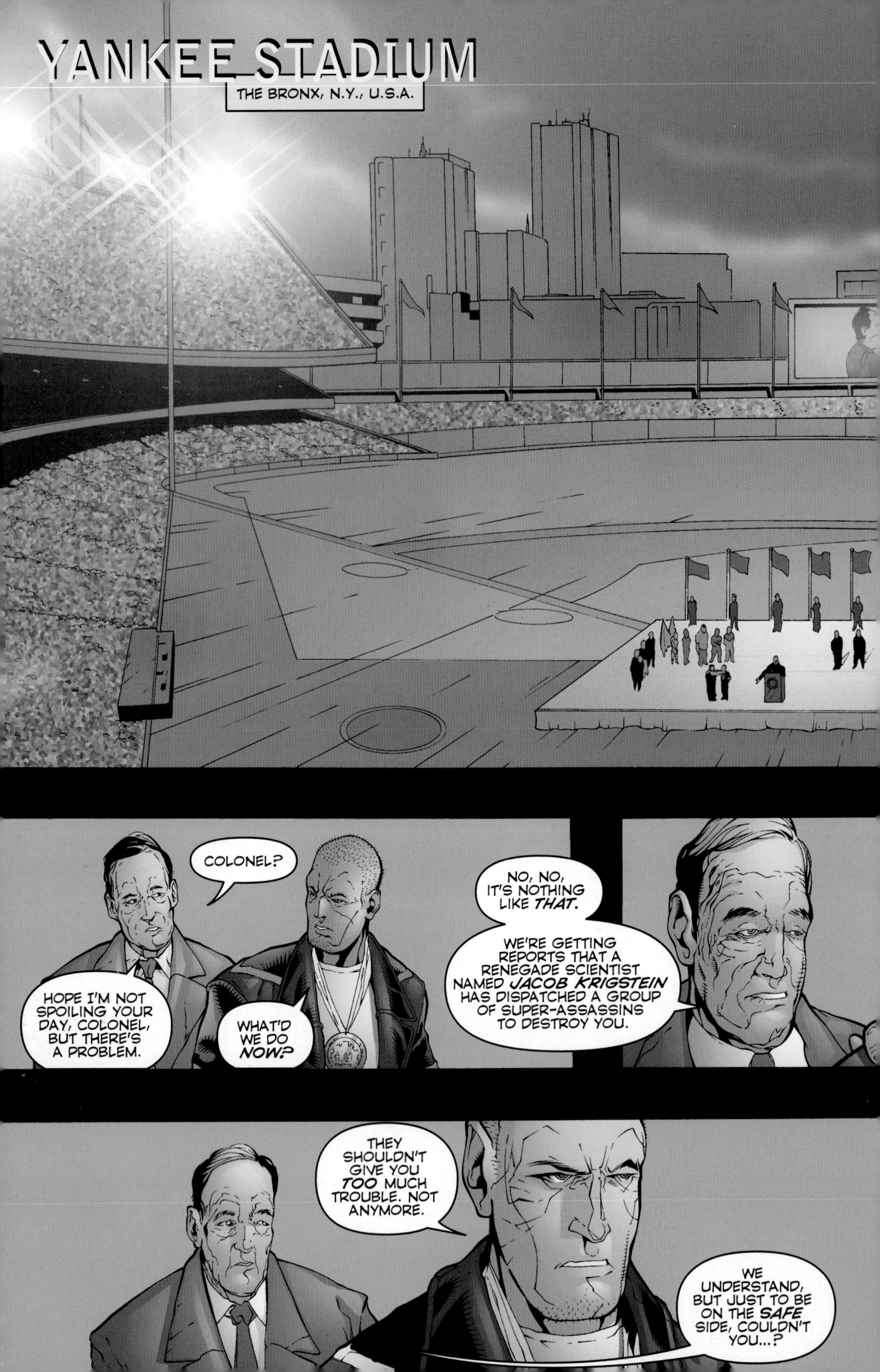

YANKEE STADIUM
THE BRONX, N.Y., U.S.A.
COLONEL?
HOPE I'M NOT SPOILING YOUR DAY, COLONEL, BUT THERE'S A PROBLEM.
WHAT'D WE DO NOW?
NO, NO, IT'S NOTHING LIKE THAT.
WE'RE GETTING REPORTS THAT A RENEGADE SCIENTIST NAMED JACOB KRIGSTEIN HAS DISPATCHED A GROUP OF SUPER-ASSASSINS TO DESTROY YOU.
THEY SHOULDN'T GIVE YOU TOO MUCH TROUBLE. NOT ANYMORE.
WE UNDERSTAND, BUT JUST TO BE ON THE SAFE SIDE, COULDN'T YOU...?

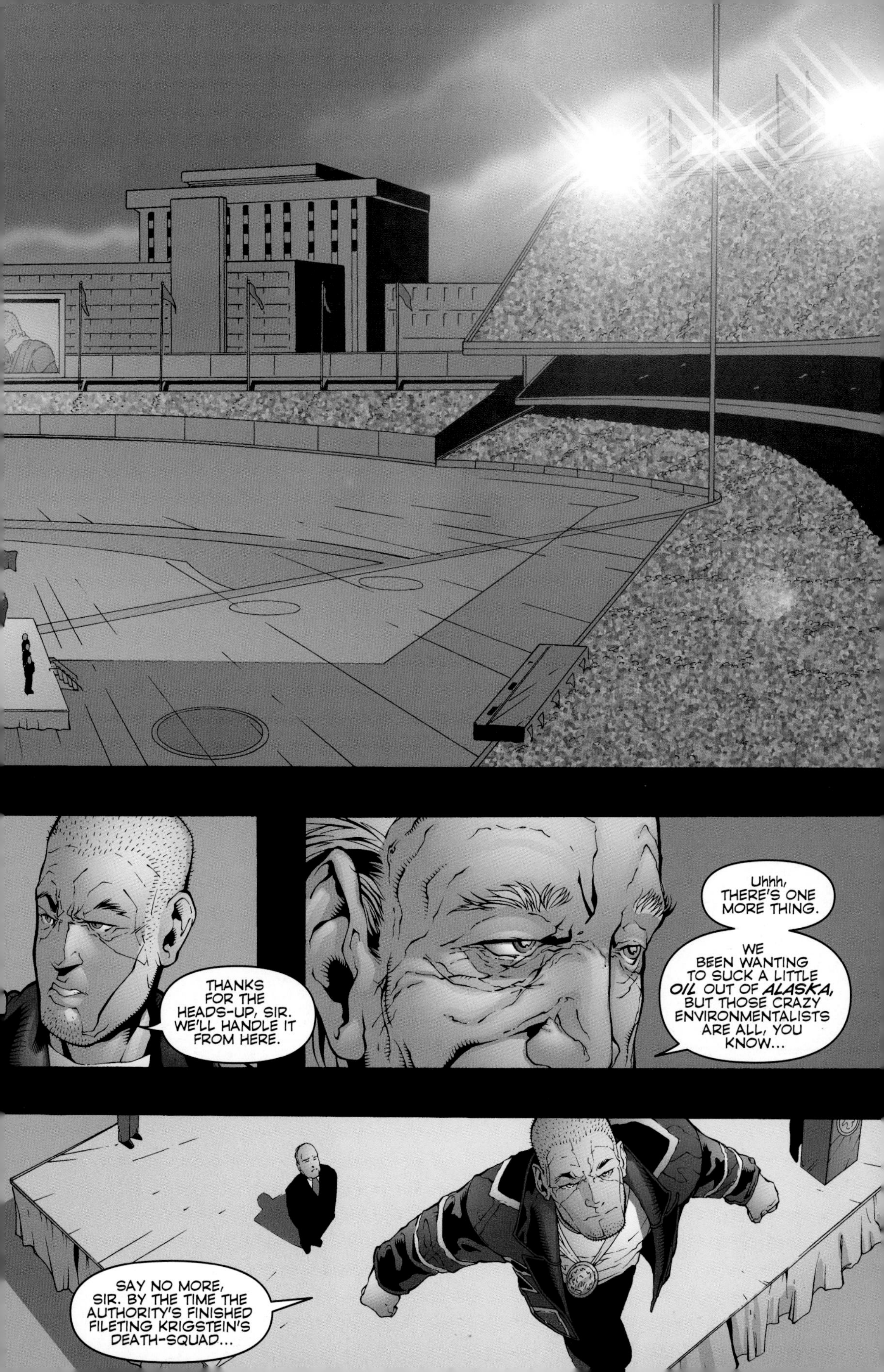

Uhhh, THERE'S ONE MORE THING.
WE BEEN WANTING TO SUCK A LITTLE OIL OUT OF ALASKA, BUT THOSE CRAZY ENVIRONMENTALISTS ARE ALL, YOU KNOW...
THANKS FOR THE HEADS-UP, SIR. WE'LL HANDLE IT FROM HERE.
SAY NO MORE, SIR. BY THE TIME THE AUTHORITY'S FINISHED FILETING KRIGSTEIN'S DEATH-SQUAD...

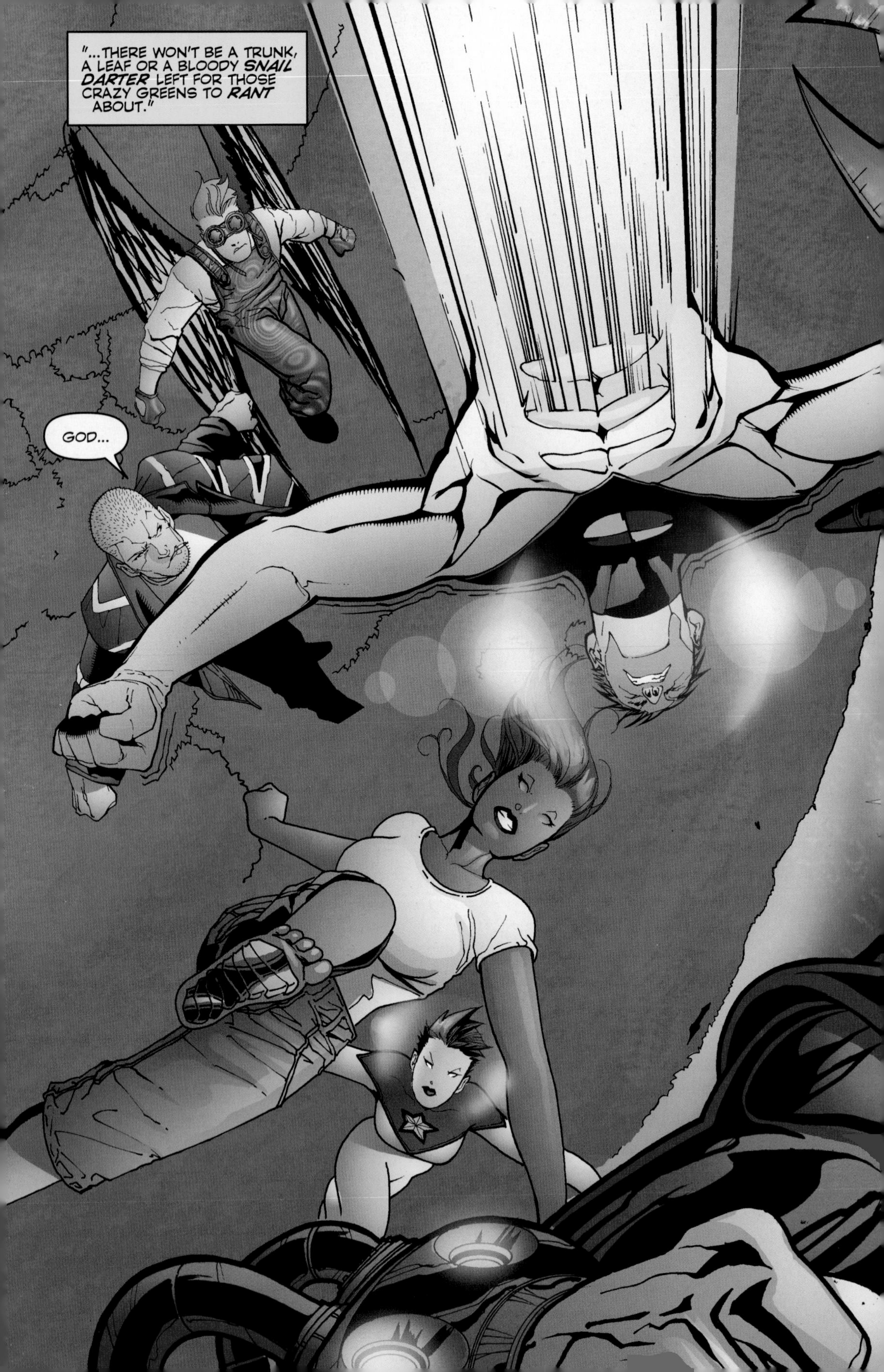
"...THERE WON'T BE A TRUNK, A LEAF OR A BLOODY SNAIL DARTER LEFT FOR THOSE CRAZY GREENS TO RANT ABOUT."
GOD...

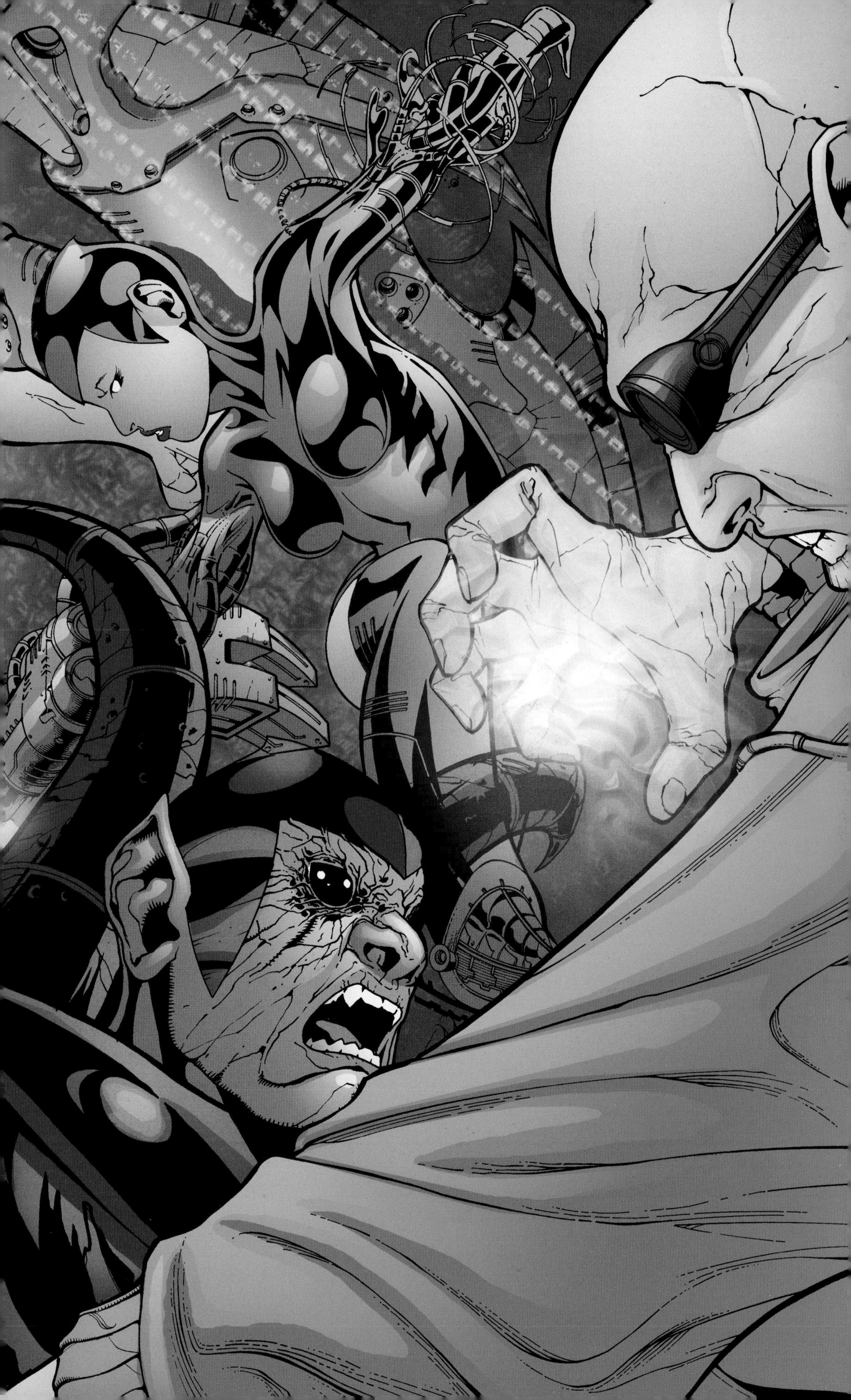

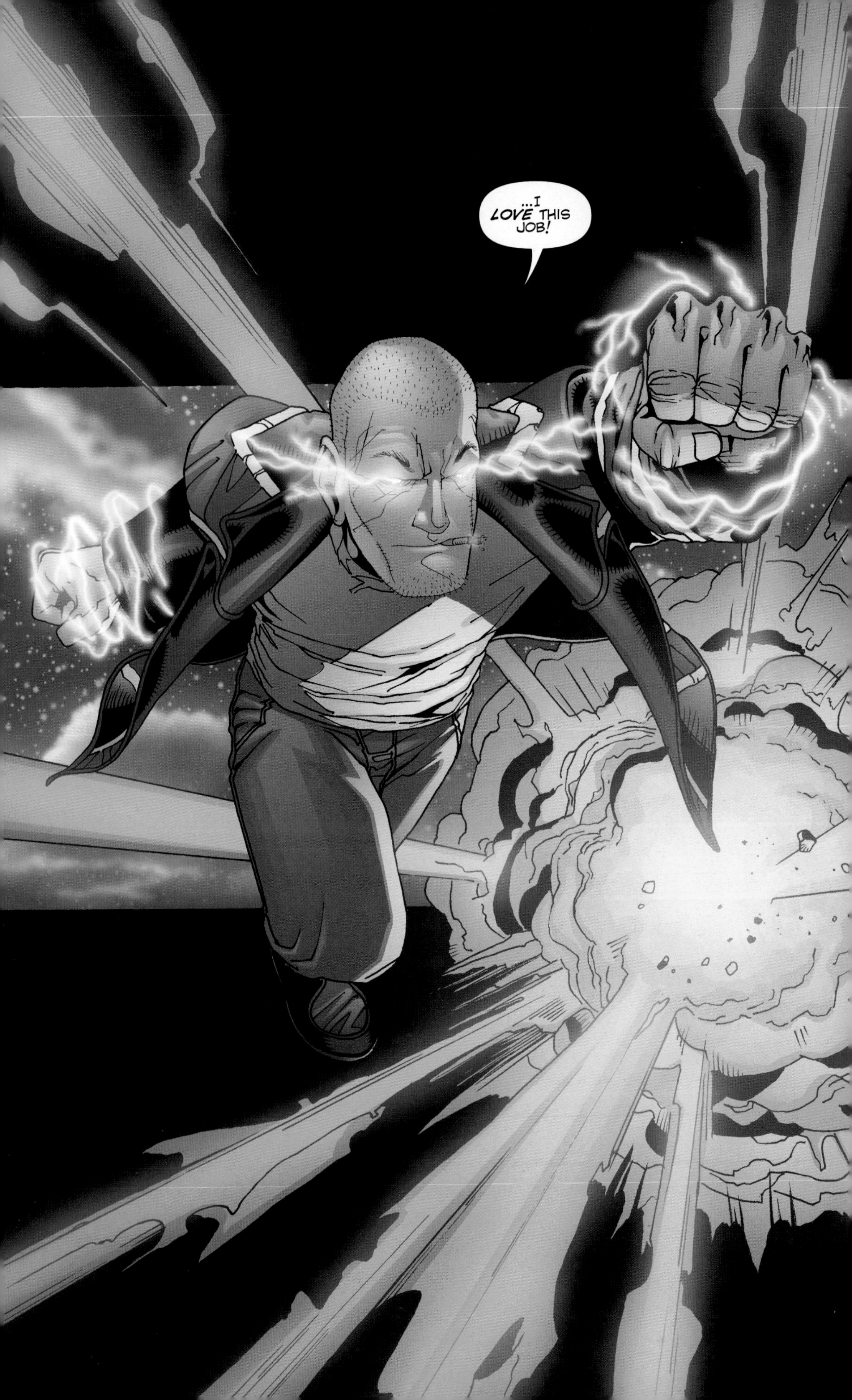
...I *LOVE* THIS JOB!

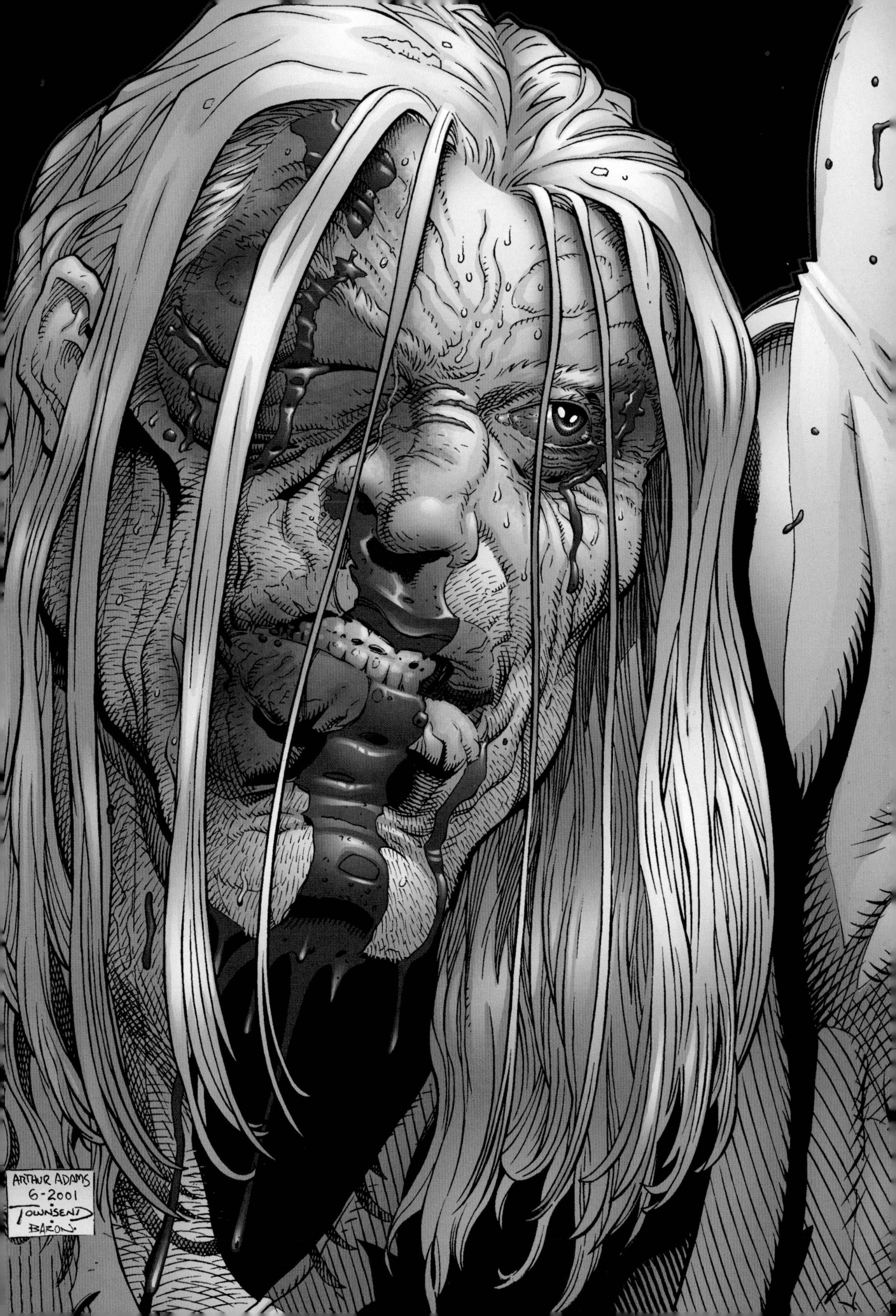
ARTHUR ADAMS
6-2001
TOWNSEND
BARON

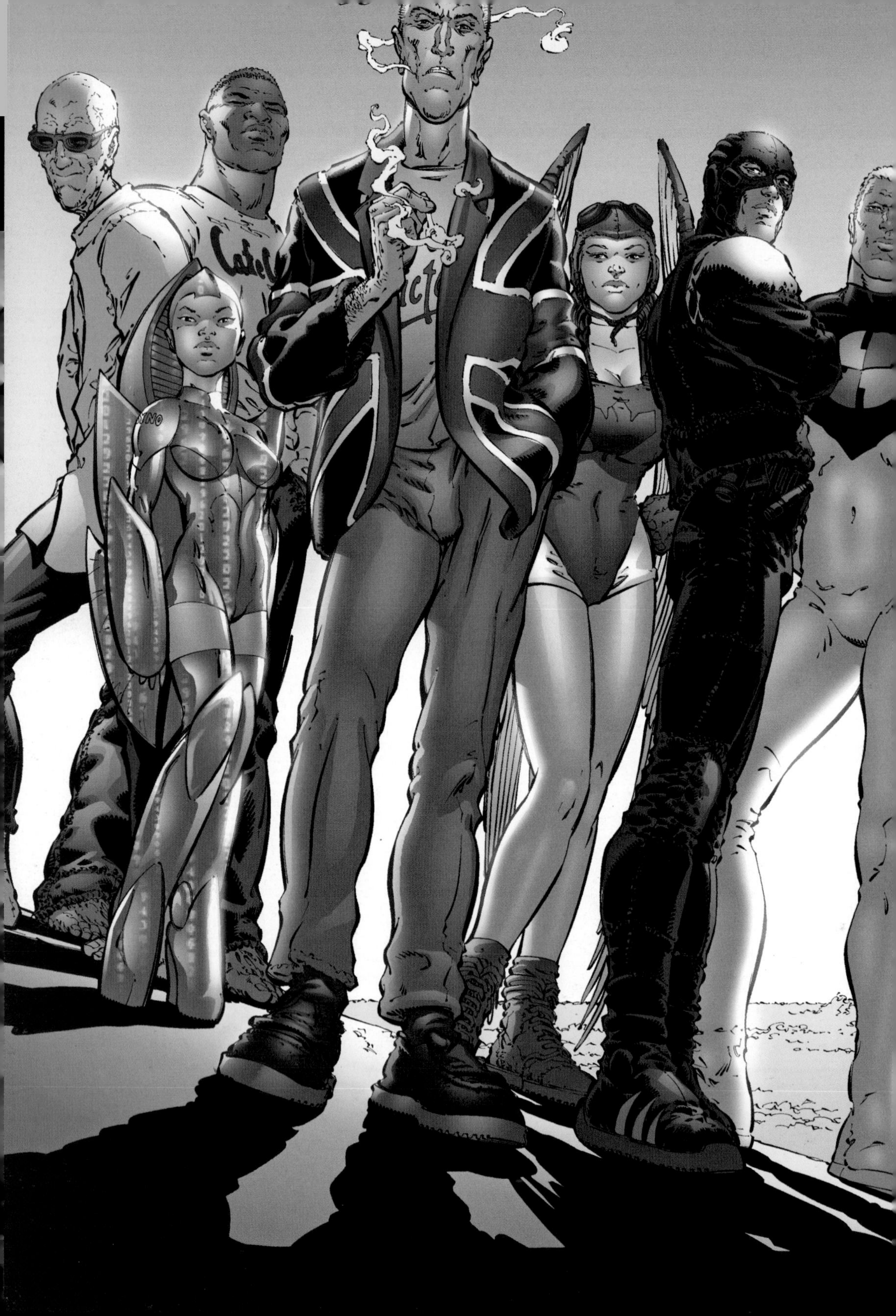

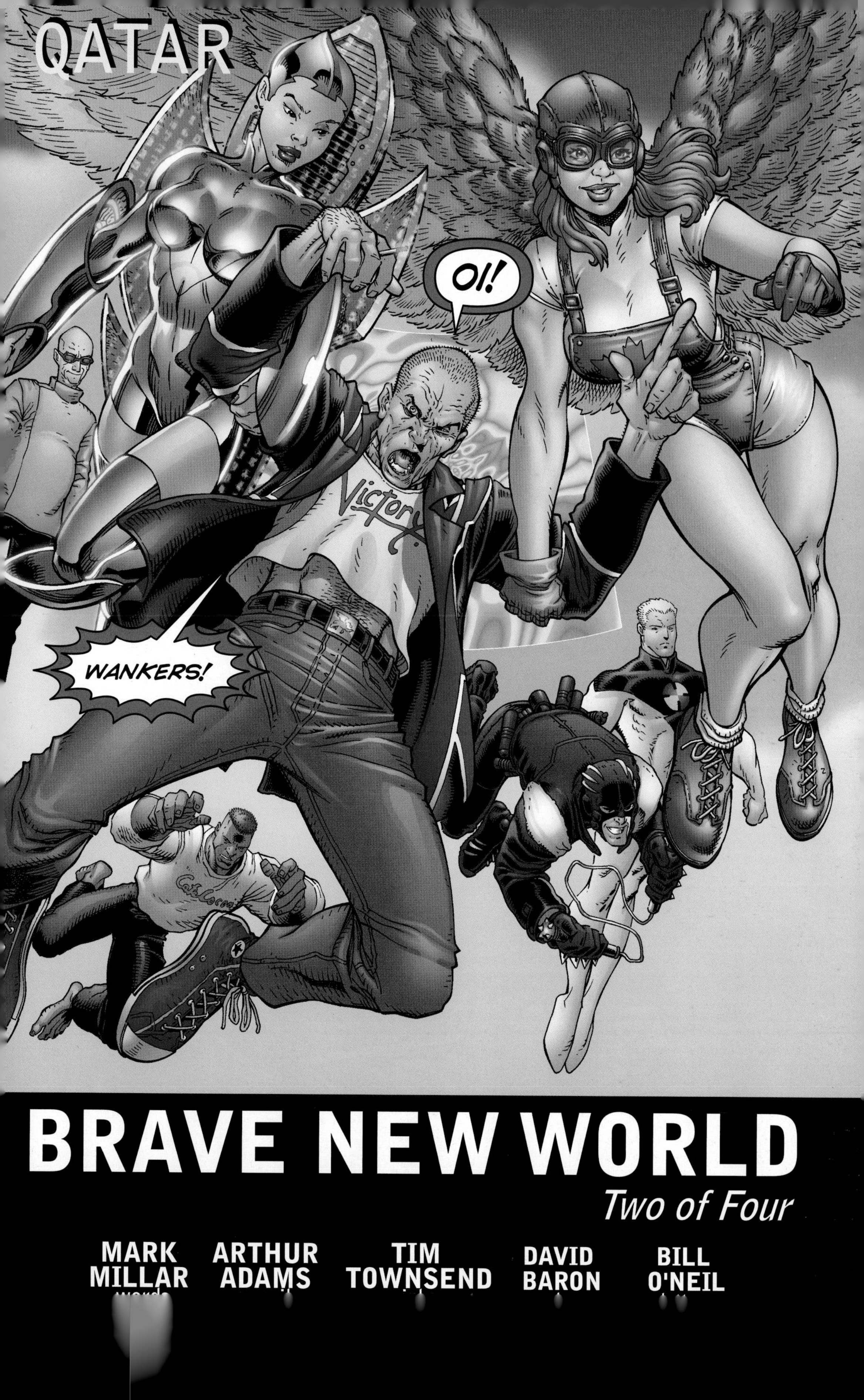
QATAR
OI!
WANKERS!

BRAVE NEW WORLD

Two of Four

MARK MILLAR
ARTHUR ADAMS
TIM TOWNSEND
DAVID BARON
BILL O'NEIL

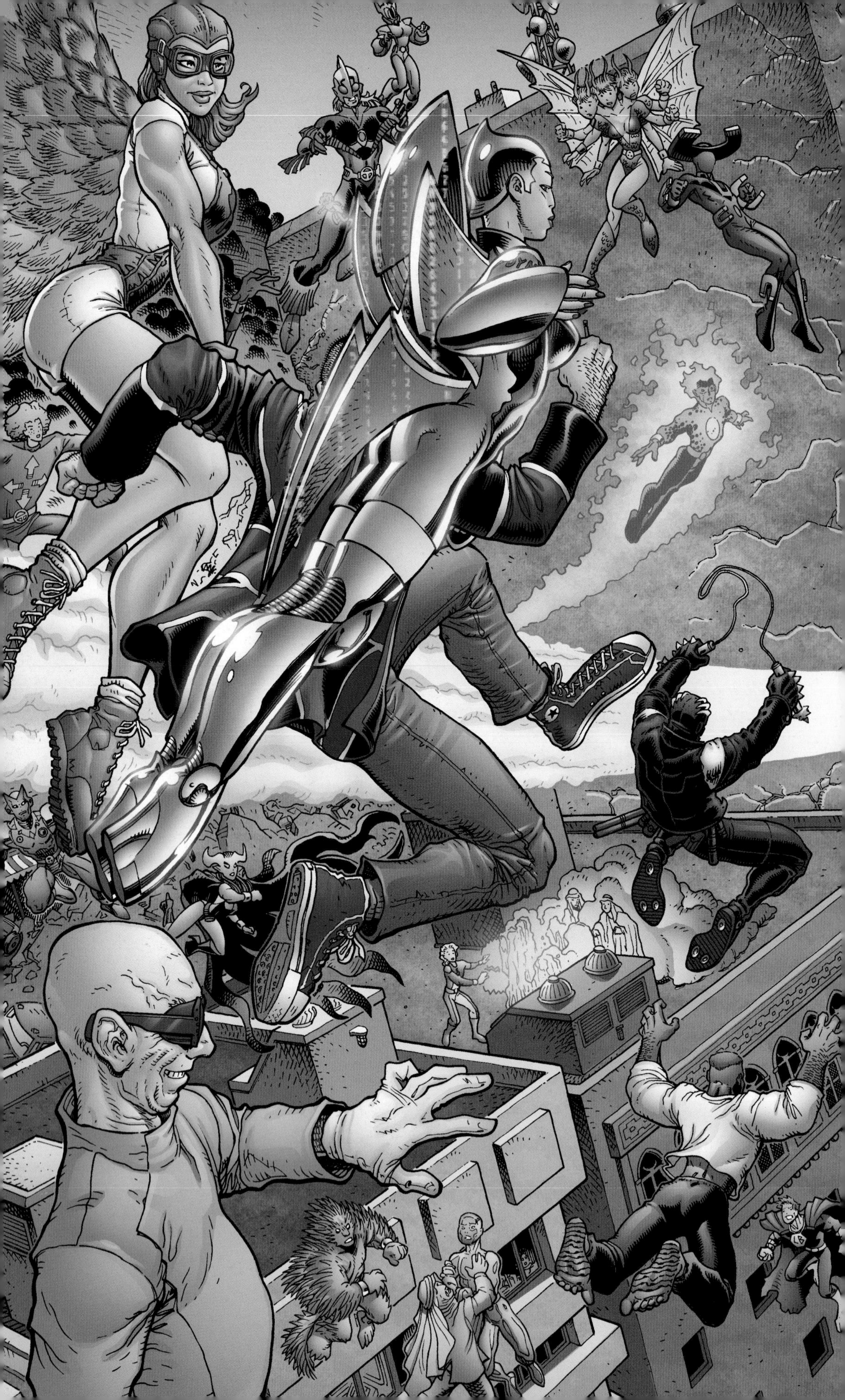

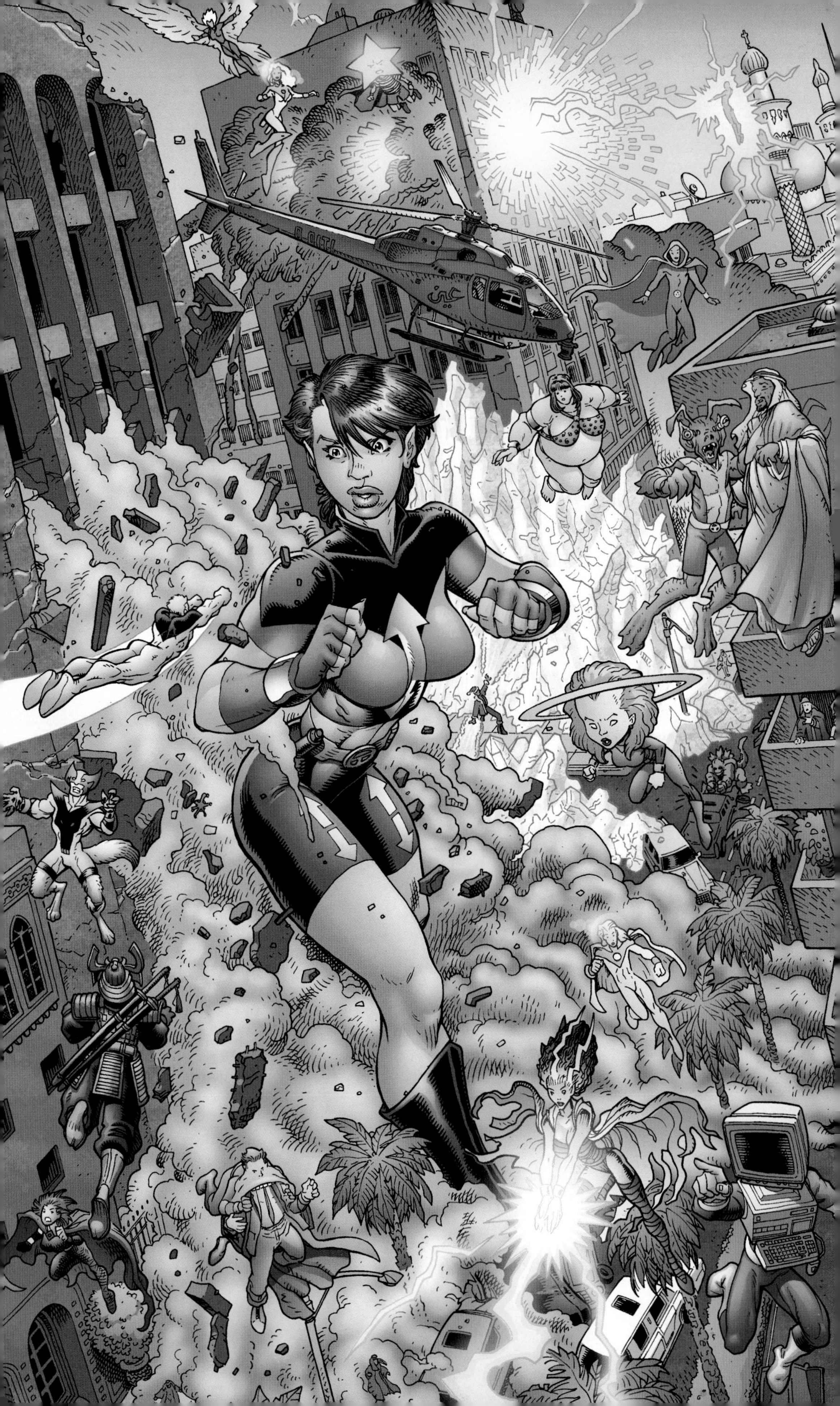

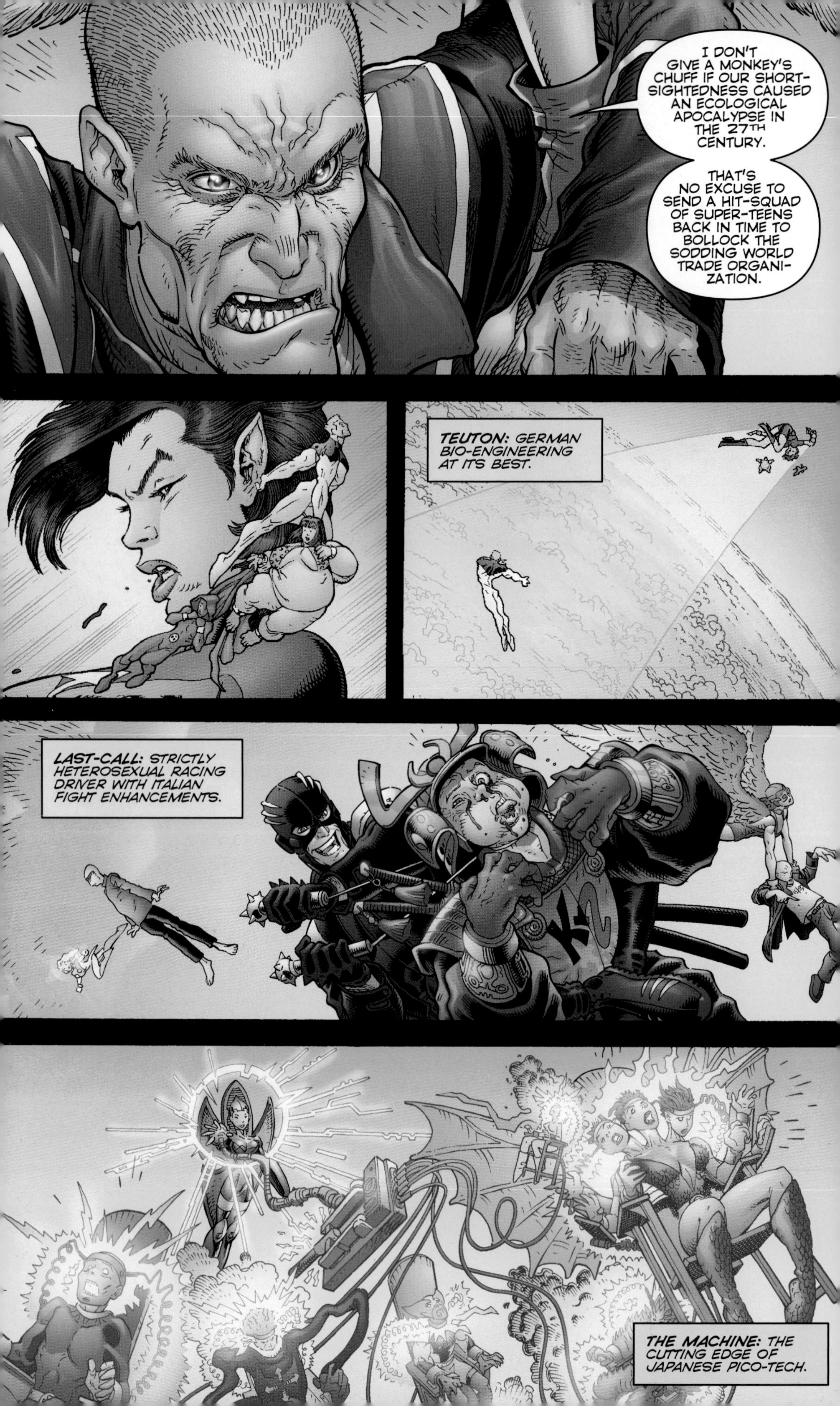
I DON'T GIVE A MONKEY'S CHUFF IF OUR SHORT-SIGHTEDNESS CAUSED AN ECOLOGICAL APOCALYPSE IN THE 27TH CENTURY.
THAT'S NO EXCUSE TO SEND A HIT-SQUAD OF SUPER-TEENS BACK IN TIME TO BOLLOCK THE SODDING WORLD TRADE ORGANI-ZATION.
TEUTON: GERMAN BIO-ENGINEERING AT ITS BEST.
LAST-CALL: STRICTLY HETEROSEXUAL RACING DRIVER WITH ITALIAN FIGHT ENHANCEMENTS.
THE MACHINE: THE CUTTING EDGE OF JAPANESE PICO-TECH.

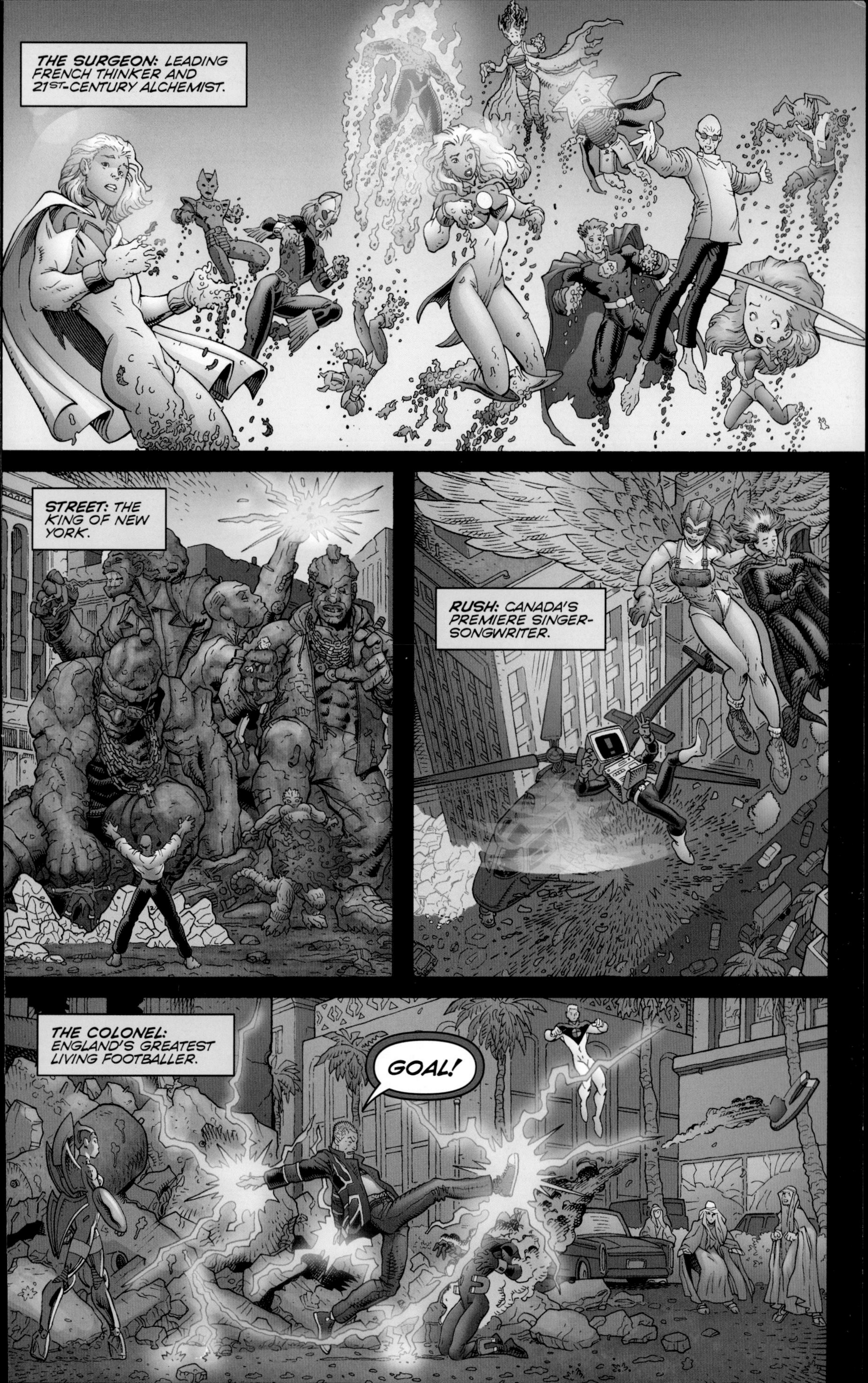
THE SURGEON: LEADING FRENCH THINKER AND 21ST-CENTURY ALCHEMIST.
STREET: THE KING OF NEW YORK.
RUSH: CANADA'S PREMIERE SINGER-SONGWRITER.
THE COLONEL: ENGLAND'S GREATEST LIVING FOOTBALLER.
GOAL!

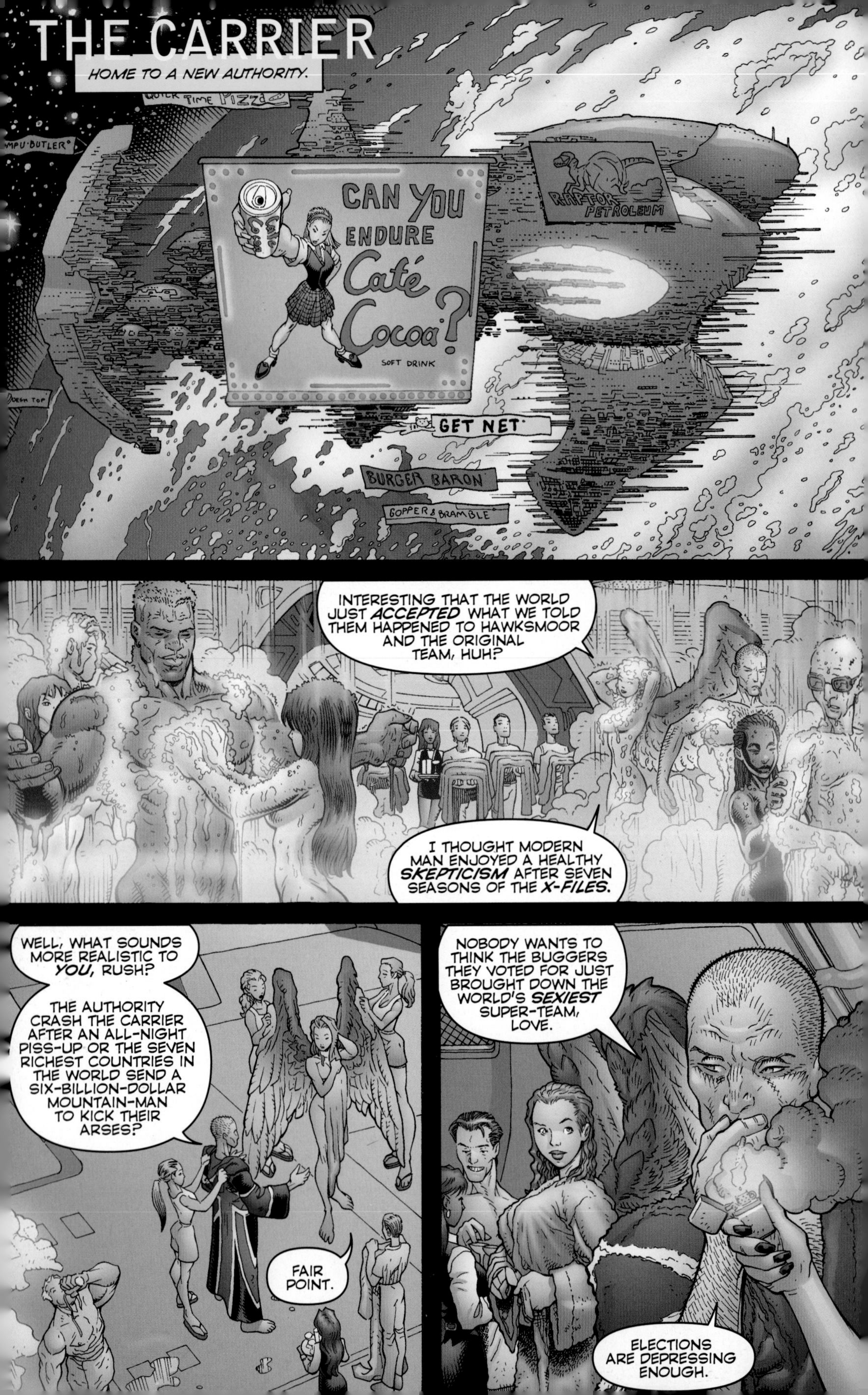
THE CARRIER
HOME TO A NEW AUTHORITY.
QUICK TIME PIZZA
CAN YOU ENDURE Café Cocoa? SOFT DRINK
RAPTOR PETROLEUM
GET NET
BURGER BARON
GOPPER & BRAMBLE
INTERESTING THAT THE WORLD JUST ACCEPTED WHAT WE TOLD THEM HAPPENED TO HAWKSMOOR AND THE ORIGINAL TEAM, HUH?
I THOUGHT MODERN MAN ENJOYED A HEALTHY SKEPTICISM AFTER SEVEN SEASONS OF THE X-FILES.
WELL, WHAT SOUNDS MORE REALISTIC TO YOU, RUSH?
THE AUTHORITY CRASH THE CARRIER AFTER AN ALL-NIGHT PISS-UP OR THE SEVEN RICHEST COUNTRIES IN THE WORLD SEND A SIX-BILLION-DOLLAR MOUNTAIN-MAN TO KICK THEIR ARSES?
FAIR POINT.
NOBODY WANTS TO THINK THE BUGGERS THEY VOTED FOR JUST BROUGHT DOWN THE WORLD'S SEXIEST SUPER-TEAM, LOVE.
ELECTIONS ARE DEPRESSING ENOUGH.

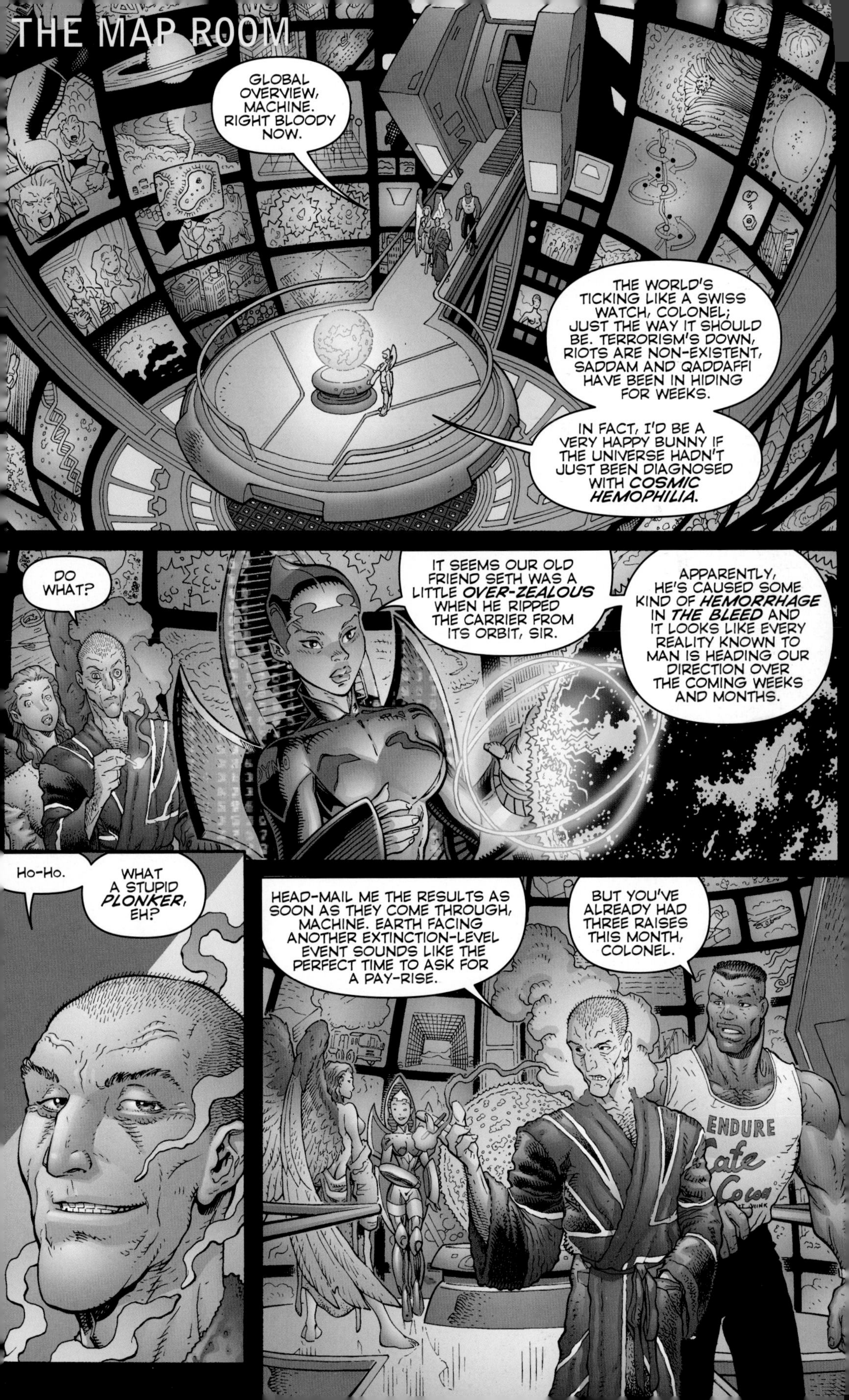
THE MAP ROOM
GLOBAL OVERVIEW, MACHINE. RIGHT BLOODY NOW.
THE WORLD'S TICKING LIKE A SWISS WATCH, COLONEL; JUST THE WAY IT SHOULD BE. TERRORISM'S DOWN, RIOTS ARE NON-EXISTENT, SADDAM AND QADDAFFI HAVE BEEN IN HIDING FOR WEEKS.
IN FACT, I'D BE A VERY HAPPY BUNNY IF THE UNIVERSE HADN'T JUST BEEN DIAGNOSED WITH COSMIC HEMOPHILIA.
DO WHAT?
IT SEEMS OUR OLD FRIEND SETH WAS A LITTLE OVER-ZEALOUS WHEN HE RIPPED THE CARRIER FROM ITS ORBIT, SIR.
APPARENTLY, HE'S CAUSED SOME KIND OF HEMORRHAGE IN THE BLEED AND IT LOOKS LIKE EVERY REALITY KNOWN TO MAN IS HEADING OUR DIRECTION OVER THE COMING WEEKS AND MONTHS.
Ho-Ho.
WHAT A STUPID PLONKER, EH?
HEAD-MAIL ME THE RESULTS AS SOON AS THEY COME THROUGH, MACHINE. EARTH FACING ANOTHER EXTINCTION-LEVEL EVENT SOUNDS LIKE THE PERFECT TIME TO ASK FOR A PAY-RISE.
BUT YOU'VE ALREADY HAD THREE RAISES THIS MONTH, COLONEL.

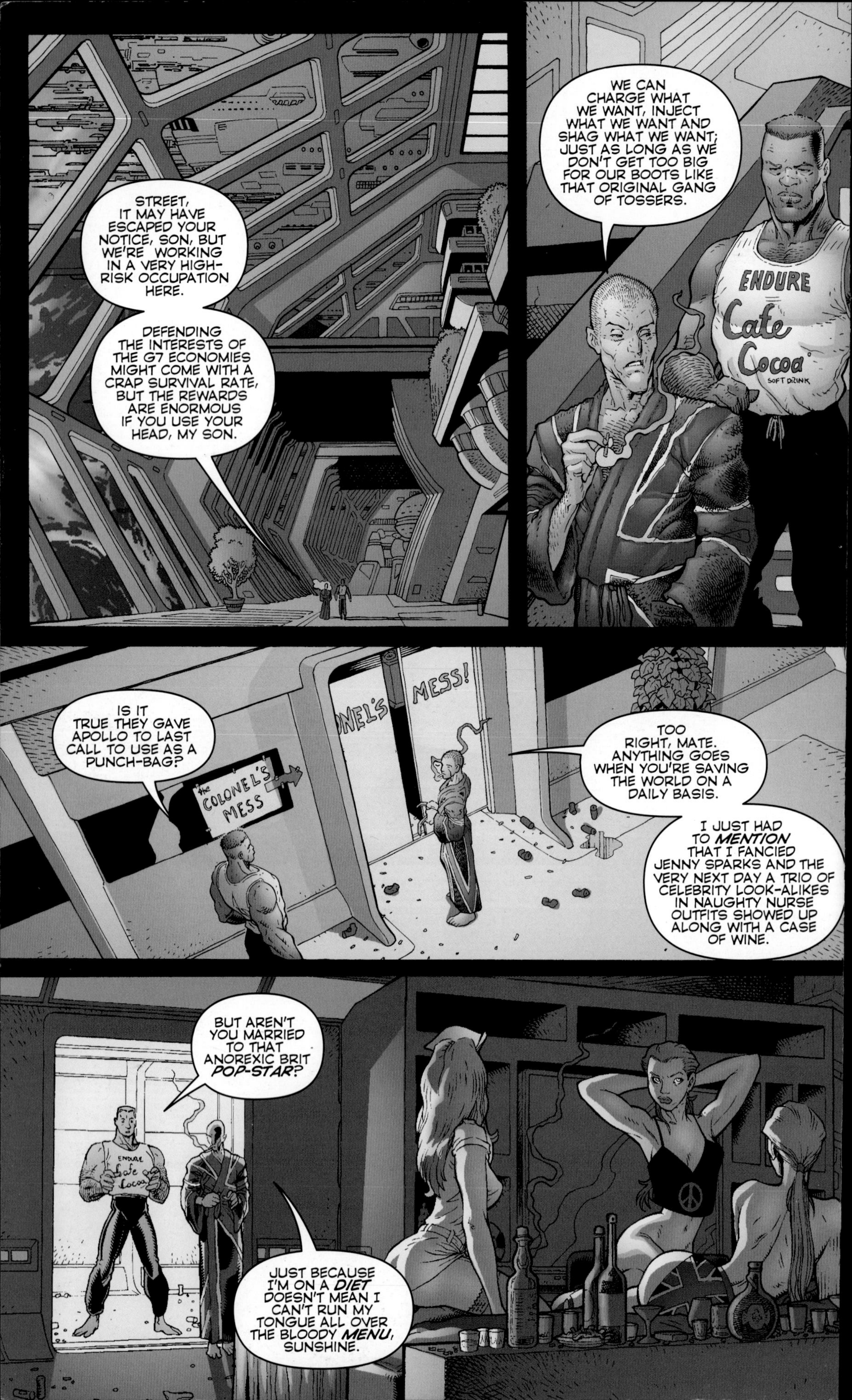
STREET, IT MAY HAVE ESCAPED YOUR NOTICE, SON, BUT WE'RE WORKING IN A VERY HIGH-RISK OCCUPATION HERE.
DEFENDING THE INTERESTS OF THE G7 ECONOMIES MIGHT COME WITH A CRAP SURVIVAL RATE, BUT THE REWARDS ARE ENORMOUS IF YOU USE YOUR HEAD, MY SON.
WE CAN CHARGE WHAT WE WANT, INJECT WHAT WE WANT AND SHAG WHAT WE WANT; JUST AS LONG AS WE DON'T GET TOO BIG FOR OUR BOOTS LIKE THAT ORIGINAL GANG OF TOSSERS.
ENDURE
Cafe Cocoa
SOFT DRINK
IS IT TRUE THEY GAVE APOLLO TO LAST CALL TO USE AS A PUNCH-BAG?
ONEL'S MESS!
the COLONEL'S MESS
TOO RIGHT, MATE. ANYTHING GOES WHEN YOU'RE SAVING THE WORLD ON A DAILY BASIS.
I JUST HAD TO *MENTION* THAT I FANCIED JENNY SPARKS AND THE VERY NEXT DAY A TRIO OF CELEBRITY LOOK-ALIKES IN NAUGHTY NURSE OUTFITS SHOWED UP ALONG WITH A CASE OF WINE.
BUT AREN'T YOU MARRIED TO THAT ANOREXIC BRIT *POP-STAR*?
ENDURE
Cafe Cocoa
JUST BECAUSE I'M ON A *DIET* DOESN'T MEAN I CAN'T RUN MY TONGUE ALL OVER THE BLOODY *MENU*, SUNSHINE.

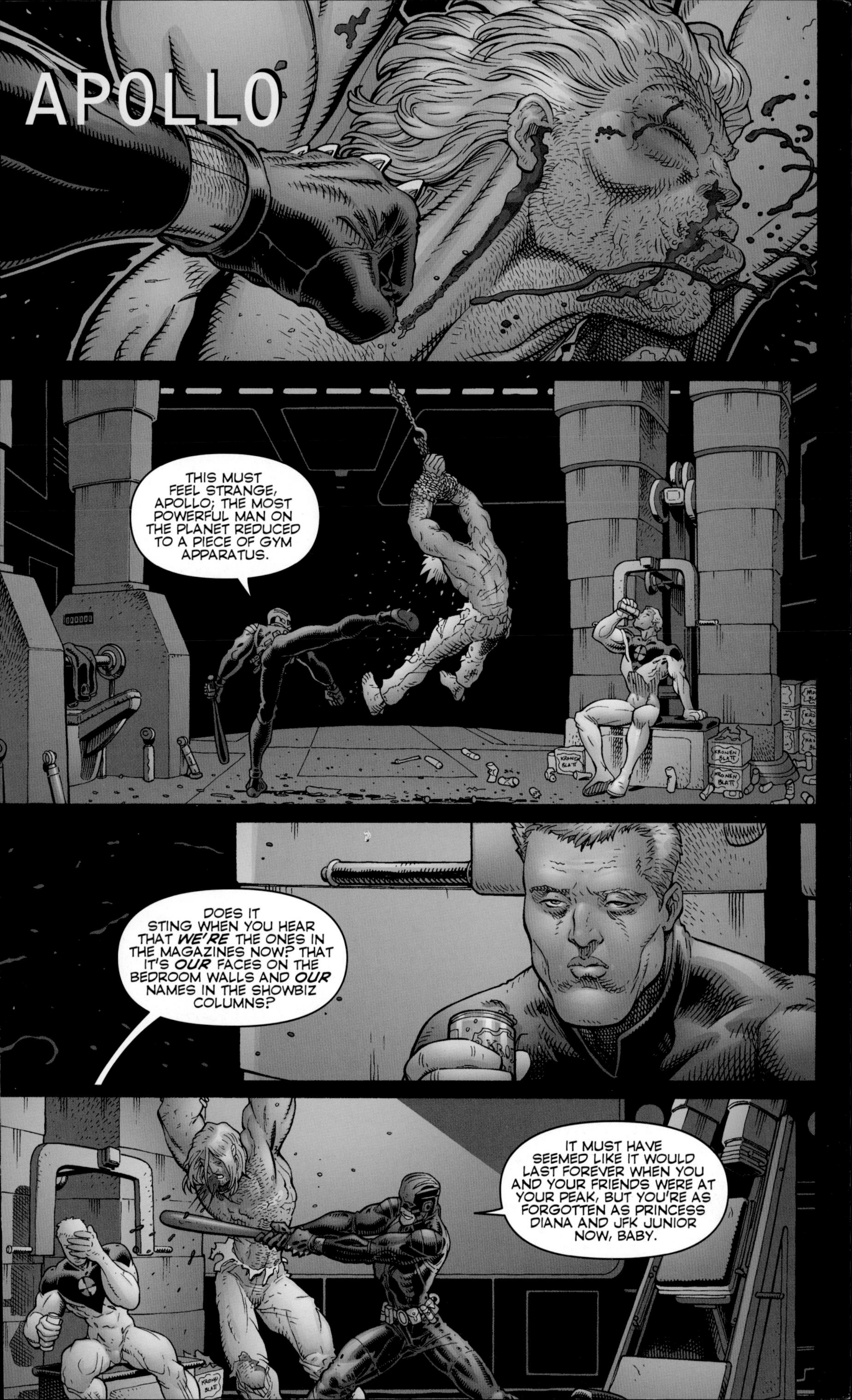
APOLLO
THIS MUST FEEL STRANGE, APOLLO; THE MOST POWERFUL MAN ON THE PLANET REDUCED TO A PIECE OF GYM APPARATUS.
DOES IT STING WHEN YOU HEAR THAT WE'RE THE ONES IN THE MAGAZINES NOW? THAT IT'S OUR FACES ON THE BEDROOM WALLS AND OUR NAMES IN THE SHOWBIZ COLUMNS?
IT MUST HAVE SEEMED LIKE IT WOULD LAST FOREVER WHEN YOU AND YOUR FRIENDS WERE AT YOUR PEAK, BUT YOU'RE AS FORGOTTEN AS PRINCESS DIANA AND JFK JUNIOR NOW, BABY.

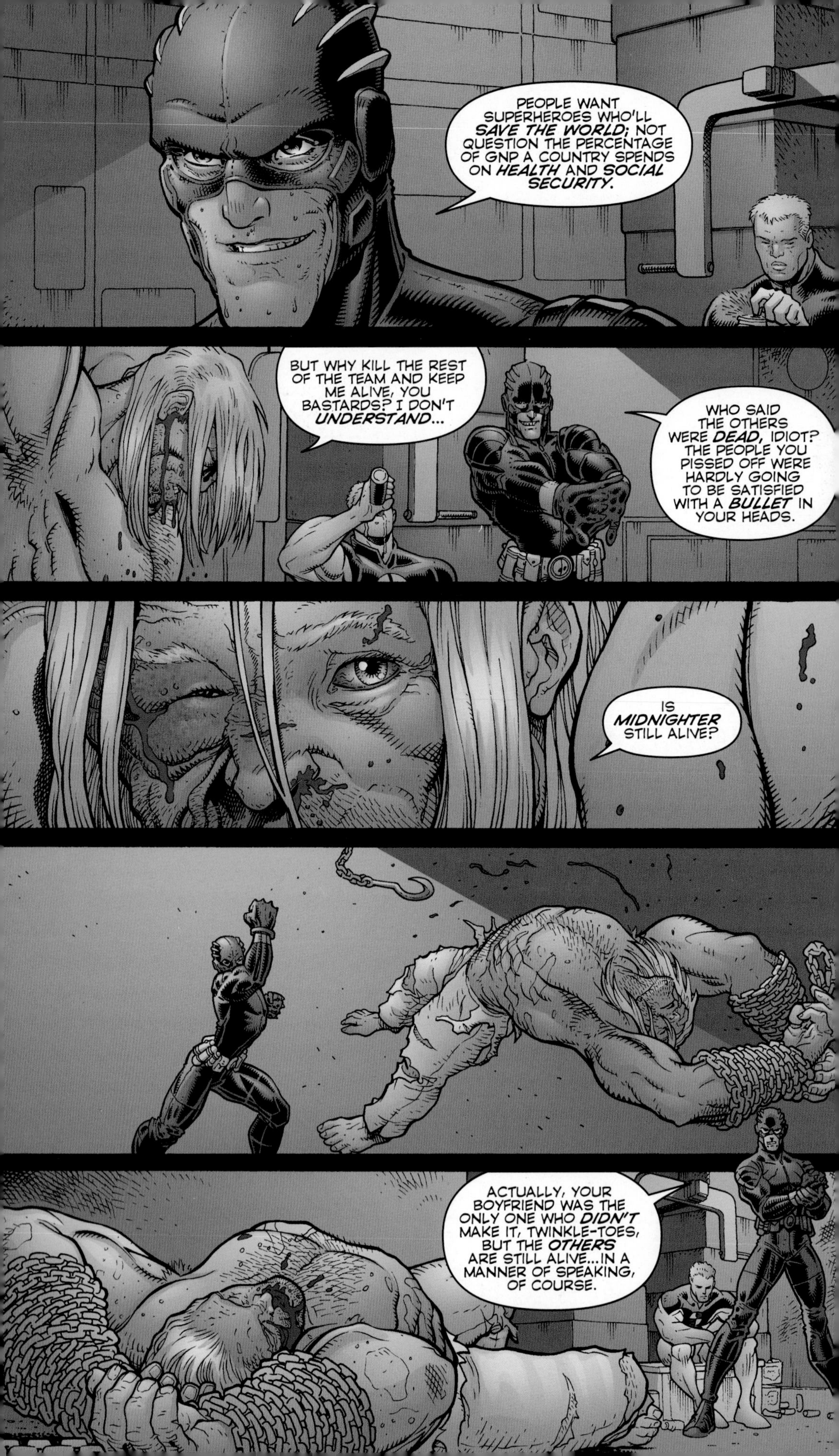
PEOPLE WANT SUPERHEROES WHO'LL SAVE THE WORLD; NOT QUESTION THE PERCENTAGE OF GNP A COUNTRY SPENDS ON HEALTH AND SOCIAL SECURITY.
BUT WHY KILL THE REST OF THE TEAM AND KEEP ME ALIVE, YOU BASTARDS? I DON'T UNDERSTAND...
WHO SAID THE OTHERS WERE DEAD, IDIOT? THE PEOPLE YOU PISSED OFF WERE HARDLY GOING TO BE SATISFIED WITH A BULLET IN YOUR HEADS.
IS MIDNIGHTER STILL ALIVE?
ACTUALLY, YOUR BOYFRIEND WAS THE ONLY ONE WHO DIDN'T MAKE IT, TWINKLE-TOES, BUT THE OTHERS ARE STILL ALIVE...IN A MANNER OF SPEAKING, OF COURSE.

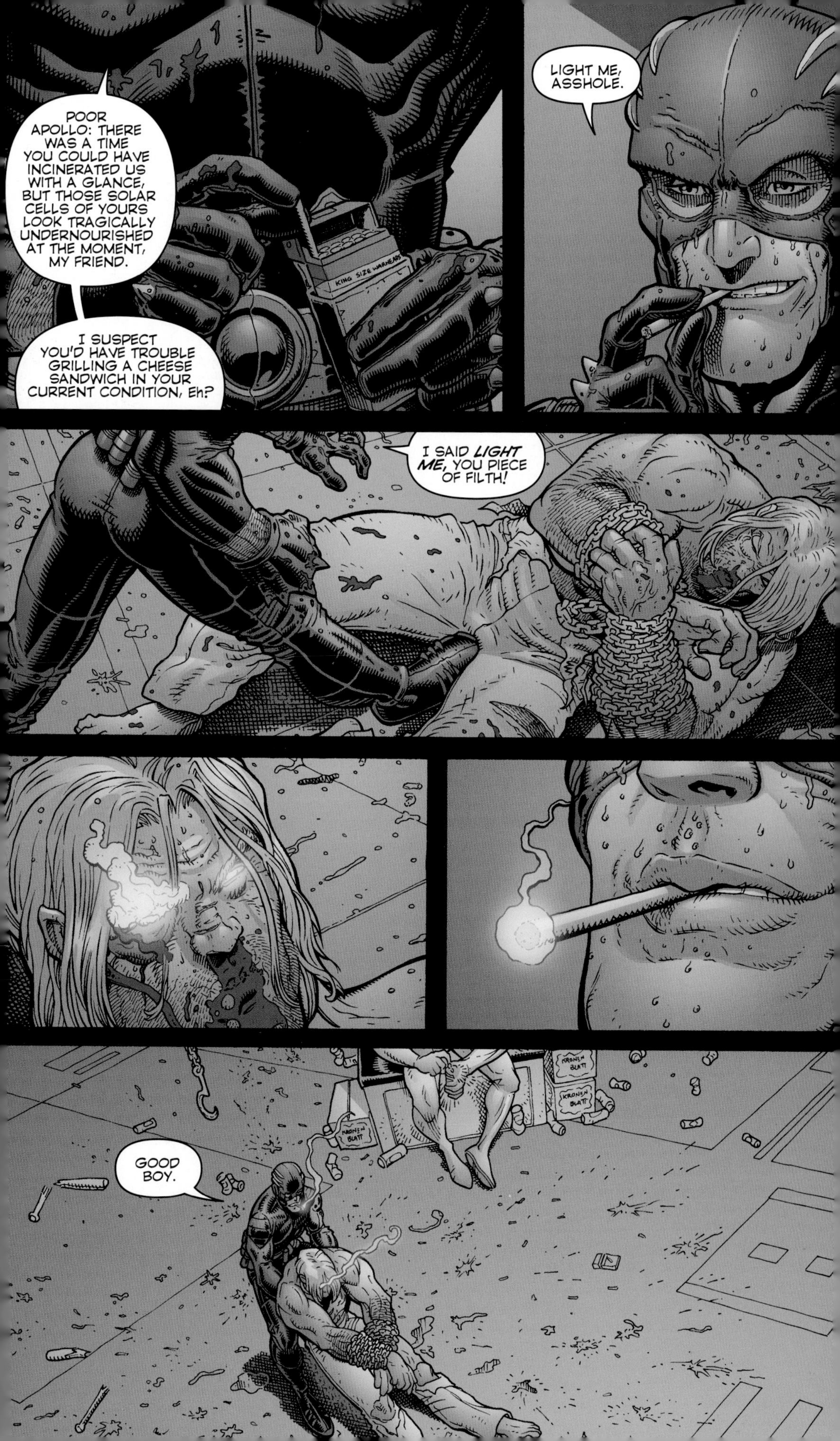
POOR APOLLO: THERE WAS A TIME YOU COULD HAVE INCINERATED US WITH A GLANCE, BUT THOSE SOLAR CELLS OF YOURS LOOK TRAGICALLY UNDERNOURISHED AT THE MOMENT, MY FRIEND.
I SUSPECT YOU'D HAVE TROUBLE GRILLING A CHEESE SANDWICH IN YOUR CURRENT CONDITION, Eh?
KING SIZE
LIGHT ME, ASSHOLE.
I SAID *LIGHT ME,* YOU PIECE OF FILTH!
KRONEN BLATT
GOOD BOY.

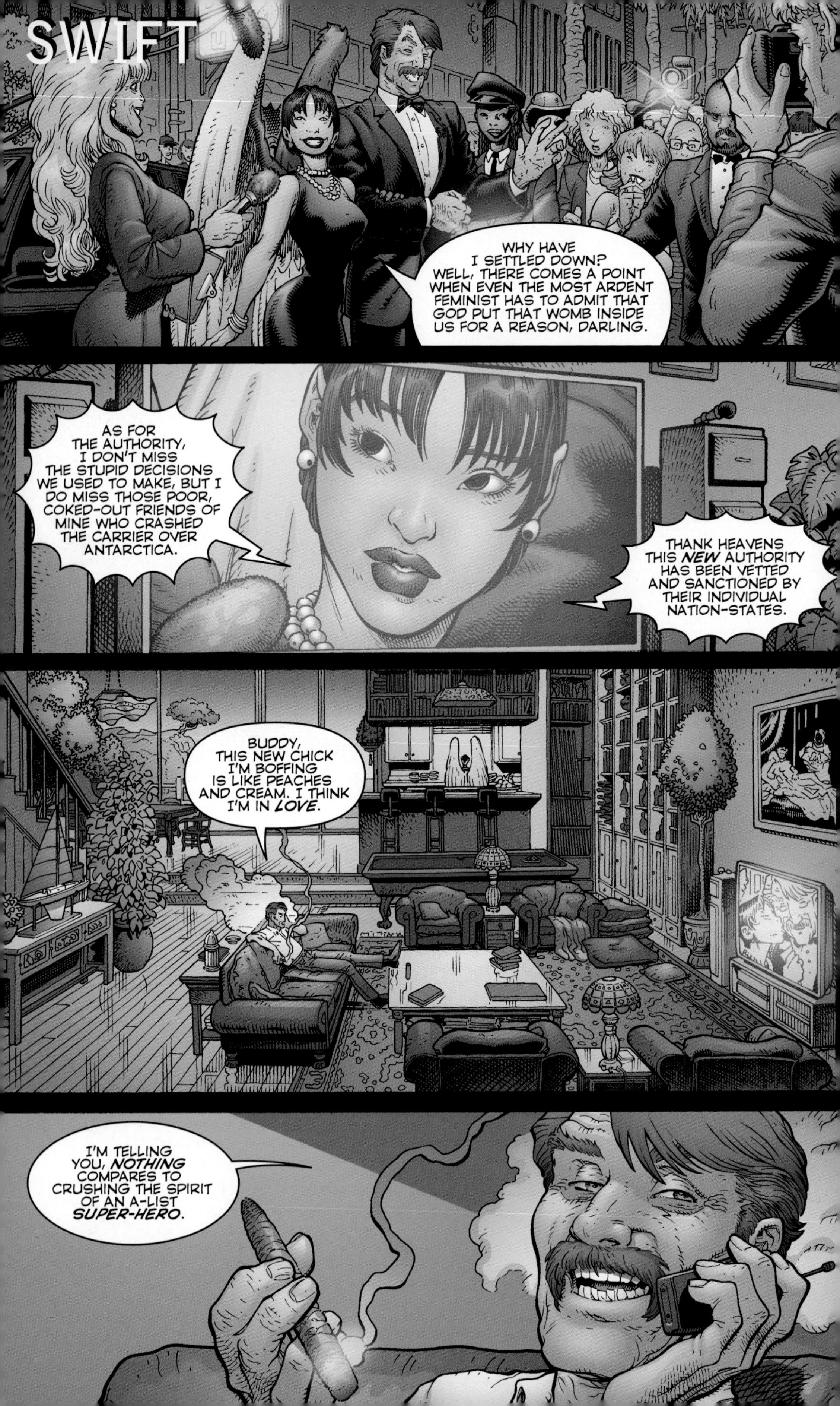
SWIFT
WHY HAVE I SETTLED DOWN? WELL, THERE COMES A POINT WHEN EVEN THE MOST ARDENT FEMINIST HAS TO ADMIT THAT GOD PUT THAT WOMB INSIDE US FOR A REASON, DARLING.
AS FOR THE AUTHORITY, I DON'T MISS THE STUPID DECISIONS WE USED TO MAKE, BUT I DO MISS THOSE POOR, COKED-OUT FRIENDS OF MINE WHO CRASHED THE CARRIER OVER ANTARCTICA.
THANK HEAVENS THIS NEW AUTHORITY HAS BEEN VETTED AND SANCTIONED BY THEIR INDIVIDUAL NATION-STATES.
BUDDY, THIS NEW CHICK I'M BOFFING IS LIKE PEACHES AND CREAM. I THINK I'M IN LOVE.
I'M TELLING YOU, NOTHING COMPARES TO CRUSHING THE SPIRIT OF AN A-LIST SUPER-HERO.

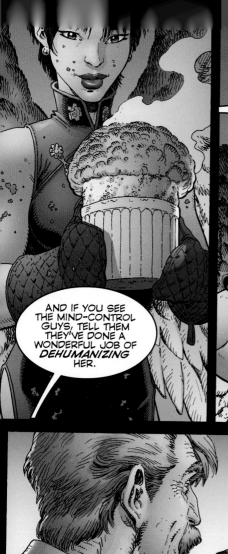

THEY HAVEN'T LEFT A *TRACE* OF THAT IRRITATING, SPUNKY PERSONALITY.

OUR MUTUAL FRIEND THE SOFTWARE BILLIONAIRE IS LITERALLY *BEGGING* ME FOR A CRACK AT HER, BUT I JUST CAN'T BEAR TO PART WITH MY LATEST PET ANARCHIST AT THE MOMENT.

AND IF YOU SEE THE MIND-CONTROL GUYS, TELL THEM THEY'VE DONE A WONDERFUL JOB OF *DEHUMANIZING* HER.

I'VE CHANGED MY *MIND*, HONEY.

I'M NOT HUNGRY.

I'M TELLING YOU; THIS ONE'S A *KEEPER*.

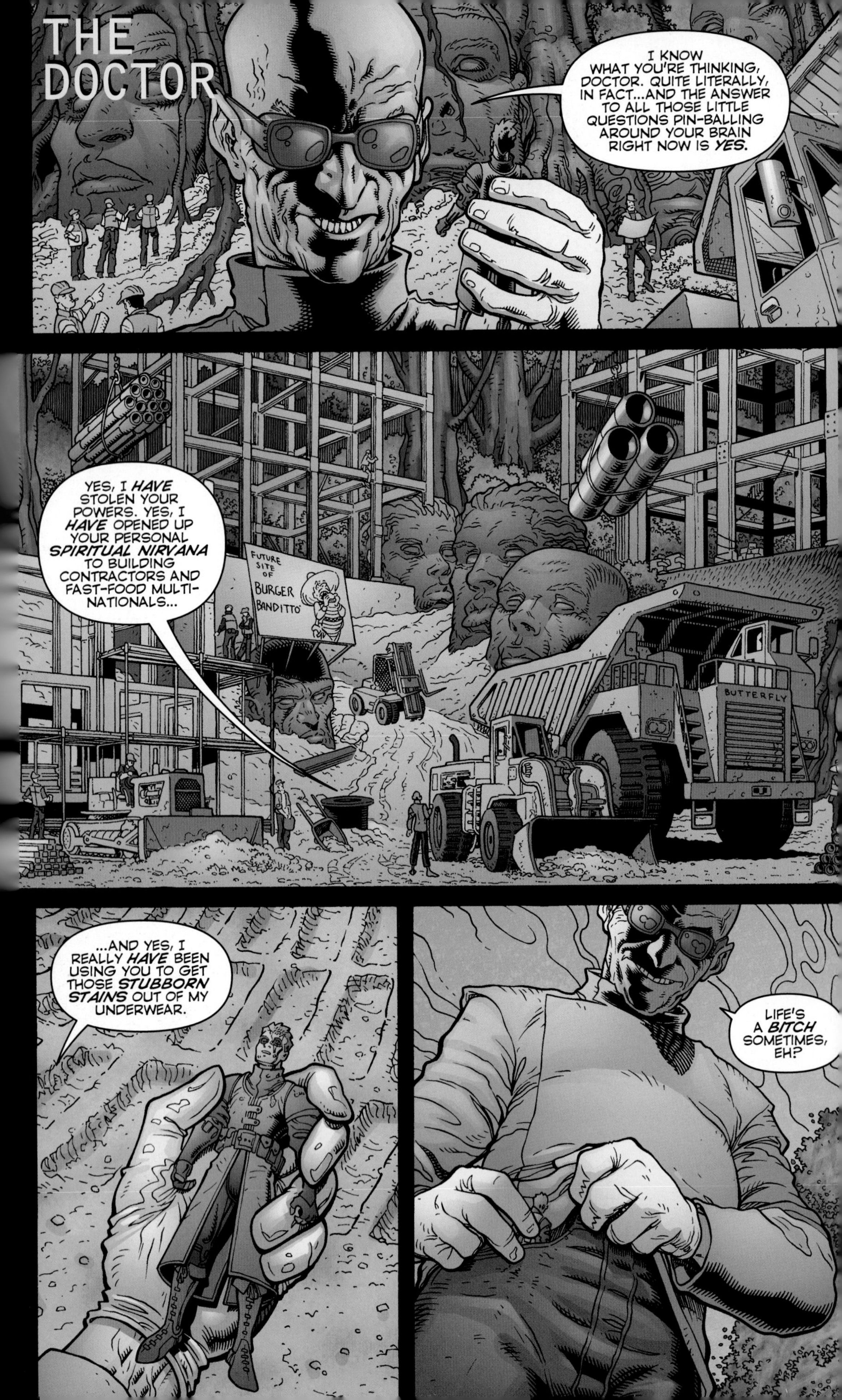
THE DOCTOR
I KNOW WHAT YOU'RE THINKING, DOCTOR. QUITE LITERALLY, IN FACT...AND THE ANSWER TO ALL THOSE LITTLE QUESTIONS PIN-BALLING AROUND YOUR BRAIN RIGHT NOW IS YES.
YES, I HAVE STOLEN YOUR POWERS. YES, I HAVE OPENED UP YOUR PERSONAL SPIRITUAL NIRVANA TO BUILDING CONTRACTORS AND FAST-FOOD MULTI-NATIONALS...
FUTURE SITE OF BURGER BANDITTO
BUTTERFLY
...AND YES, I REALLY HAVE BEEN USING YOU TO GET THOSE STUBBORN STAINS OUT OF MY UNDERWEAR.
LIFE'S A BITCH SOMETIMES, EH?

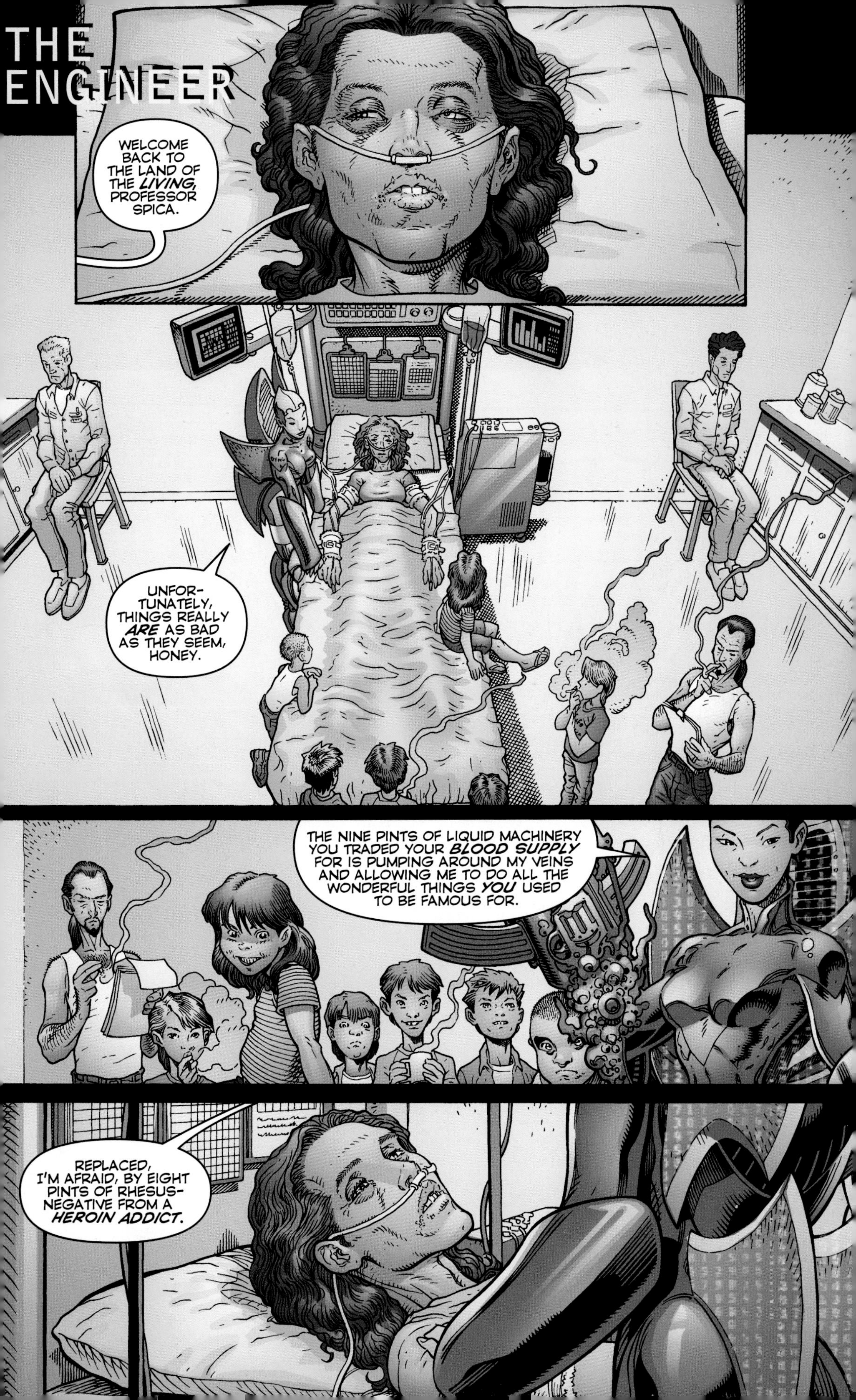
THE ENGINEER
WELCOME BACK TO THE LAND OF THE LIVING, PROFESSOR SPICA.
UNFOR-TUNATELY, THINGS REALLY ARE AS BAD AS THEY SEEM, HONEY.
THE NINE PINTS OF LIQUID MACHINERY YOU TRADED YOUR BLOOD SUPPLY FOR IS PUMPING AROUND MY VEINS AND ALLOWING ME TO DO ALL THE WONDERFUL THINGS YOU USED TO BE FAMOUS FOR.
REPLACED, I'M AFRAID, BY EIGHT PINTS OF RHESUS-NEGATIVE FROM A HEROIN ADDICT.

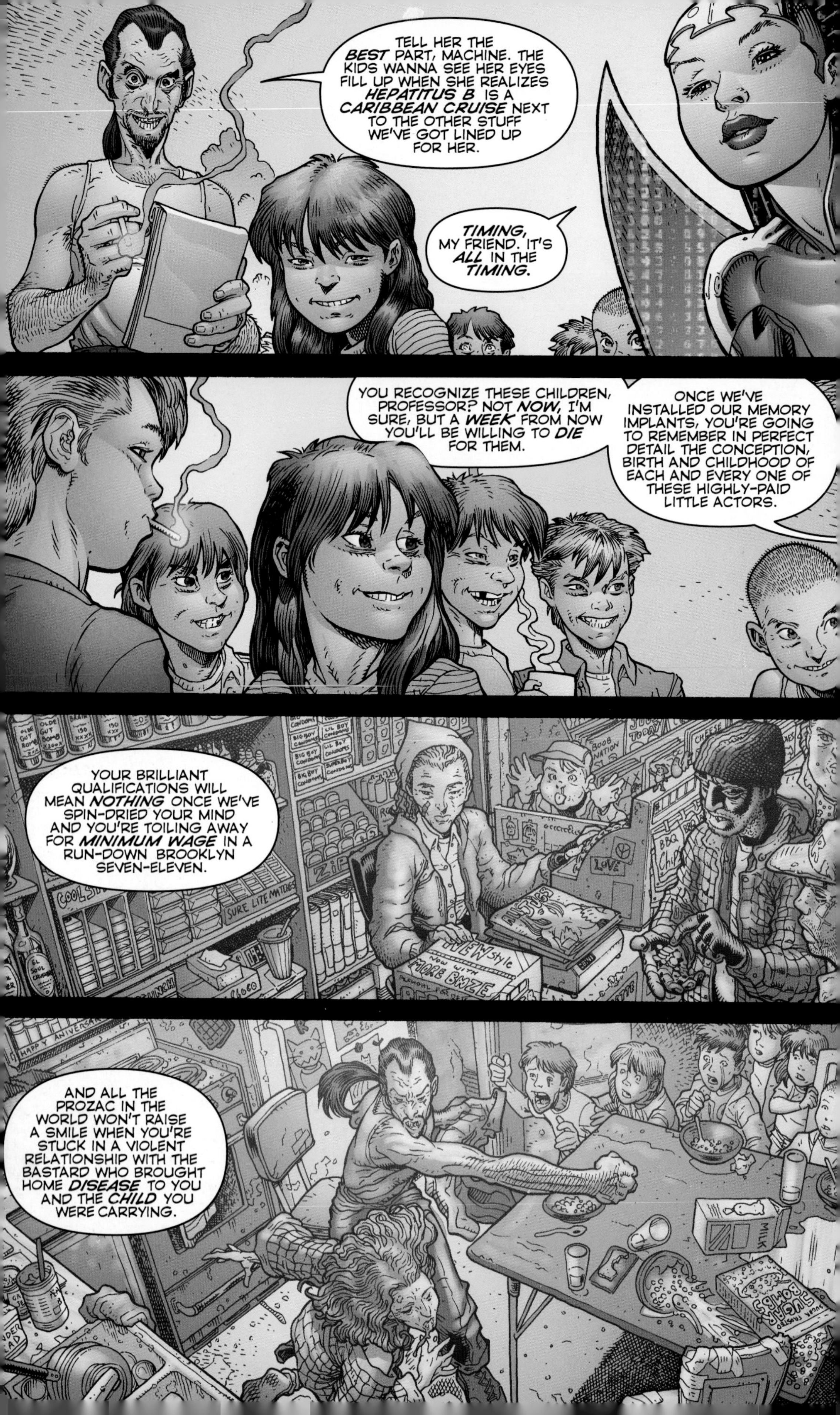
TELL HER THE BEST PART, MACHINE. THE KIDS WANNA SEE HER EYES FILL UP WHEN SHE REALIZES HEPATITUS B IS A CARIBBEAN CRUISE NEXT TO THE OTHER STUFF WE'VE GOT LINED UP FOR HER.
TIMING, MY FRIEND. IT'S ALL IN THE TIMING.
YOU RECOGNIZE THESE CHILDREN, PROFESSOR? NOT NOW, I'M SURE, BUT A WEEK FROM NOW YOU'LL BE WILLING TO DIE FOR THEM.
ONCE WE'VE INSTALLED OUR MEMORY IMPLANTS, YOU'RE GOING TO REMEMBER IN PERFECT DETAIL THE CONCEPTION, BIRTH AND CHILDHOOD OF EACH AND EVERY ONE OF THESE HIGHLY-PAID LITTLE ACTORS.
YOUR BRILLIANT QUALIFICATIONS WILL MEAN NOTHING ONCE WE'VE SPIN-DRIED YOUR MIND AND YOU'RE TOILING AWAY FOR MINIMUM WAGE IN A RUN-DOWN BROOKLYN SEVEN-ELEVEN.
AND ALL THE PROZAC IN THE WORLD WON'T RAISE A SMILE WHEN YOU'RE STUCK IN A VIOLENT RELATIONSHIP WITH THE BASTARD WHO BROUGHT HOME DISEASE TO YOU AND THE CHILD YOU WERE CARRYING.

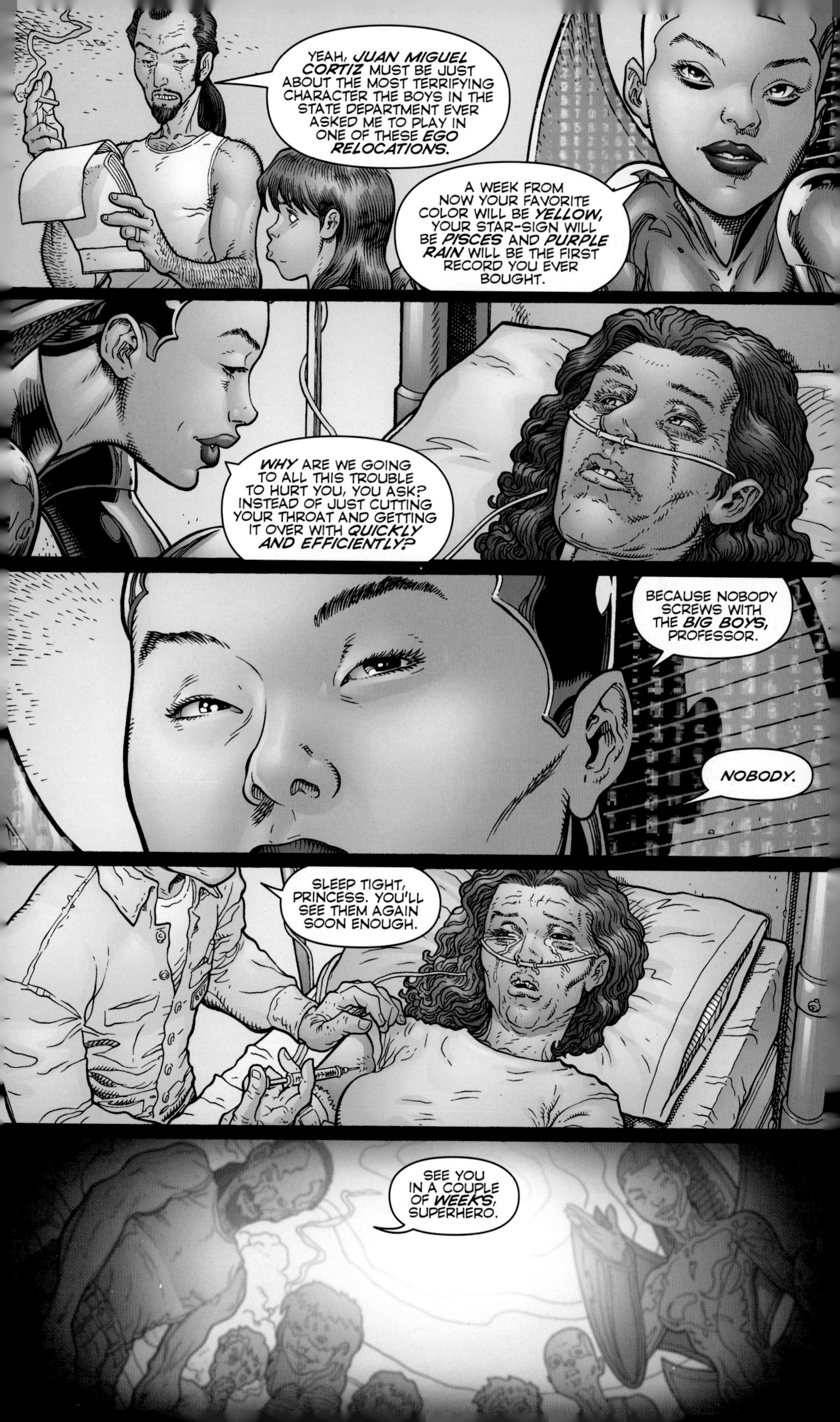
YEAH, JUAN MIGUEL CORTIZ MUST BE JUST ABOUT THE MOST TERRIFYING CHARACTER THE BOYS IN THE STATE DEPARTMENT EVER ASKED ME TO PLAY IN ONE OF THESE EGO RELOCATIONS.
A WEEK FROM NOW YOUR FAVORITE COLOR WILL BE YELLOW, YOUR STAR-SIGN WILL BE PISCES AND PURPLE RAIN WILL BE THE FIRST RECORD YOU EVER BOUGHT.
WHY ARE WE GOING TO ALL THIS TROUBLE TO HURT YOU, YOU ASK? INSTEAD OF JUST CUTTING YOUR THROAT AND GETTING IT OVER WITH QUICKLY AND EFFICIENTLY?
BECAUSE NOBODY SCREWS WITH THE BIG BOYS, PROFESSOR.
NOBODY.
SLEEP TIGHT, PRINCESS. YOU'LL SEE THEM AGAIN SOON ENOUGH.
SEE YOU IN A COUPLE OF WEEKS, SUPERHERO.

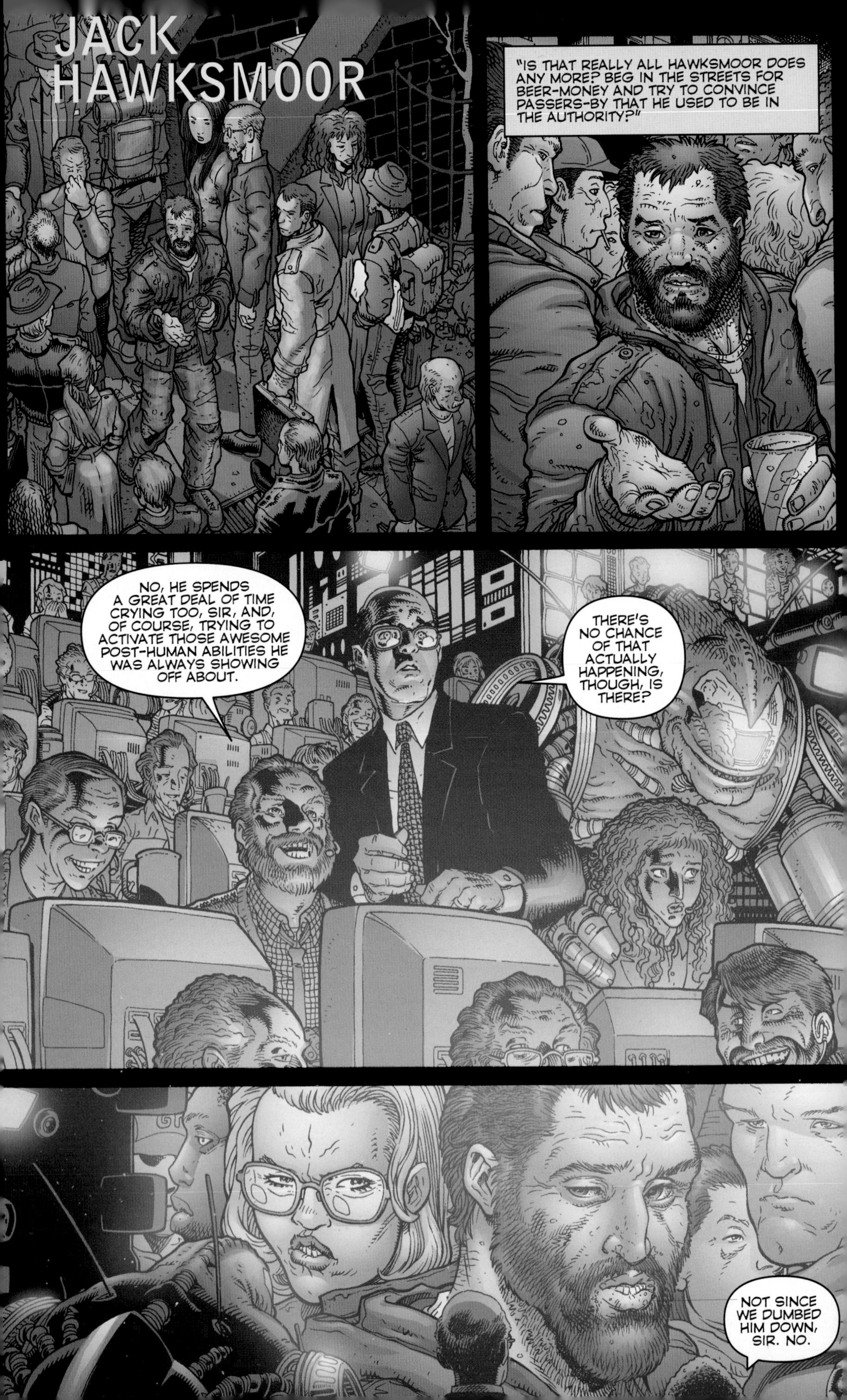
JACK HAWKSMOOR
"IS THAT REALLY ALL HAWKSMOOR DOES ANY MORE? BEG IN THE STREETS FOR BEER-MONEY AND TRY TO CONVINCE PASSERS-BY THAT HE USED TO BE IN THE AUTHORITY?"
NO, HE SPENDS A GREAT DEAL OF TIME CRYING TOO, SIR, AND, OF COURSE, TRYING TO ACTIVATE THOSE AWESOME POST-HUMAN ABILITIES HE WAS ALWAYS SHOWING OFF ABOUT.
THERE'S NO CHANCE OF THAT ACTUALLY HAPPENING, THOUGH, IS THERE?
NOT SINCE WE DUMBED HIM DOWN, SIR. NO.

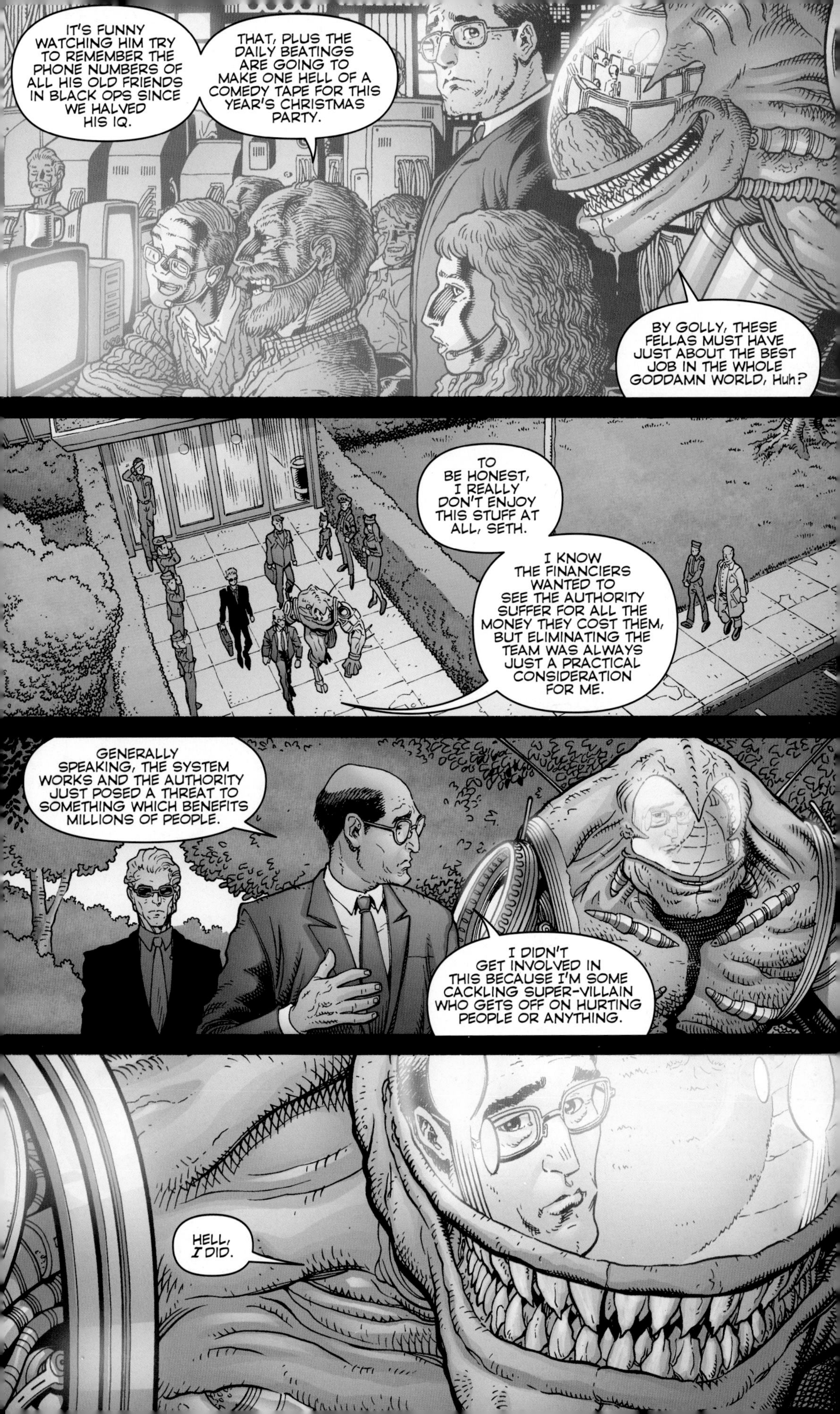
IT'S FUNNY WATCHING HIM TRY TO REMEMBER THE PHONE NUMBERS OF ALL HIS OLD FRIENDS IN BLACK OPS SINCE WE HALVED HIS IQ.
THAT, PLUS THE DAILY BEATINGS ARE GOING TO MAKE ONE HELL OF A COMEDY TAPE FOR THIS YEAR'S CHRISTMAS PARTY.
BY GOLLY, THESE FELLAS MUST HAVE JUST ABOUT THE BEST JOB IN THE WHOLE GODDAMN WORLD, Huh?
TO BE HONEST, I REALLY DON'T ENJOY THIS STUFF AT ALL, SETH.
I KNOW THE FINANCIERS WANTED TO SEE THE AUTHORITY SUFFER FOR ALL THE MONEY THEY COST THEM, BUT ELIMINATING THE TEAM WAS ALWAYS JUST A PRACTICAL CONSIDERATION FOR ME.
GENERALLY SPEAKING, THE SYSTEM WORKS AND THE AUTHORITY JUST POSED A THREAT TO SOMETHING WHICH BENEFITS MILLIONS OF PEOPLE.
I DIDN'T GET INVOLVED IN THIS BECAUSE I'M SOME CACKLING SUPER-VILLAIN WHO GETS OFF ON HURTING PEOPLE OR ANYTHING.
HELL, *I* DID.

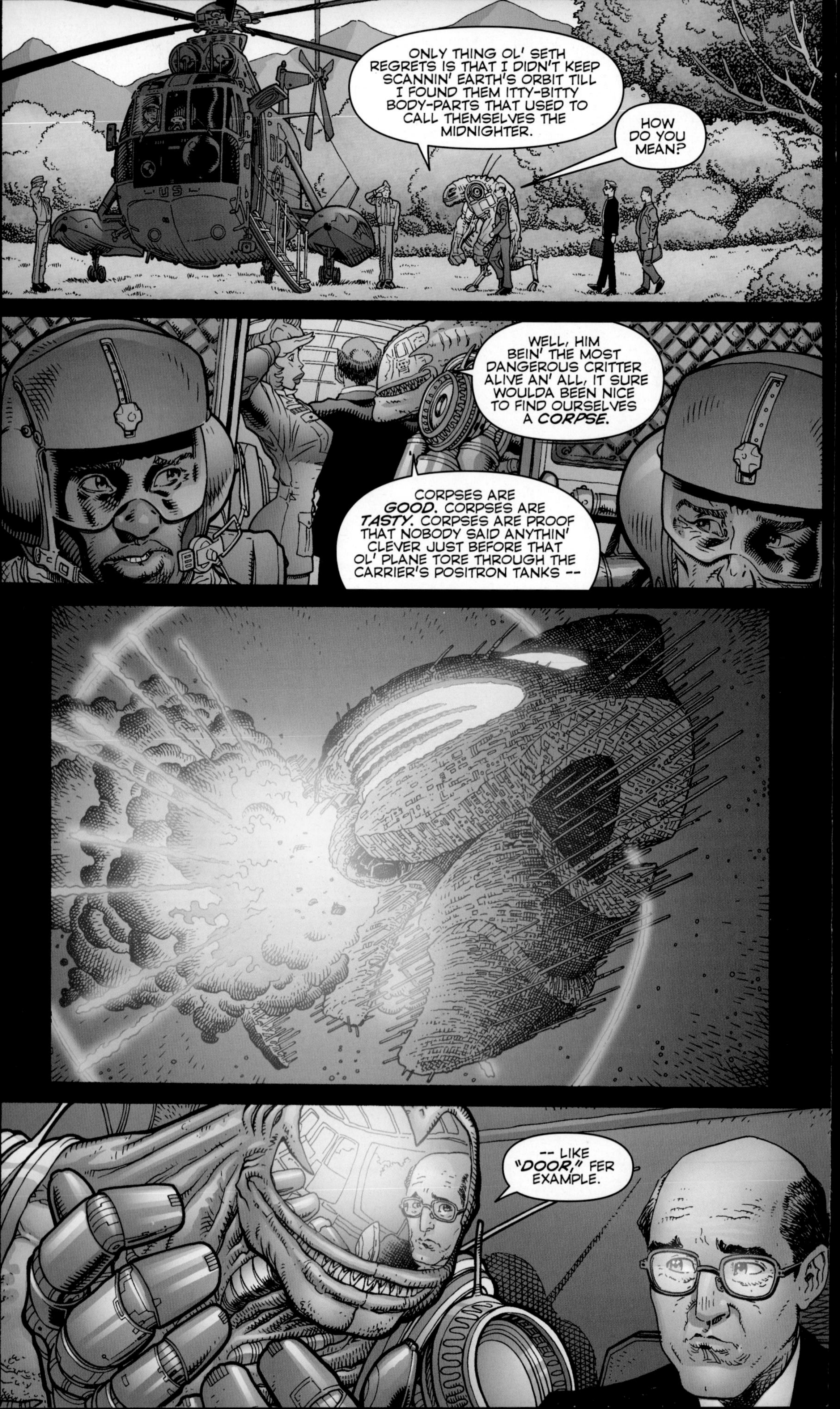
ONLY THING OL' SETH REGRETS IS THAT I DIDN'T KEEP SCANNIN' EARTH'S ORBIT TILL I FOUND THEM ITTY-BITTY BODY-PARTS THAT USED TO CALL THEMSELVES THE MIDNIGHTER.
HOW DO YOU MEAN?
WELL, HIM BEIN' THE MOST DANGEROUS CRITTER ALIVE AN' ALL, IT SURE WOULDA BEEN NICE TO FIND OURSELVES A *CORPSE.*
CORPSES ARE *GOOD.* CORPSES ARE *TASTY.* CORPSES ARE PROOF THAT NOBODY SAID ANYTHIN' CLEVER JUST BEFORE THAT OL' PLANE TORE THROUGH THE CARRIER'S POSITRON TANKS --
-- LIKE *"DOOR,"* FER EXAMPLE.

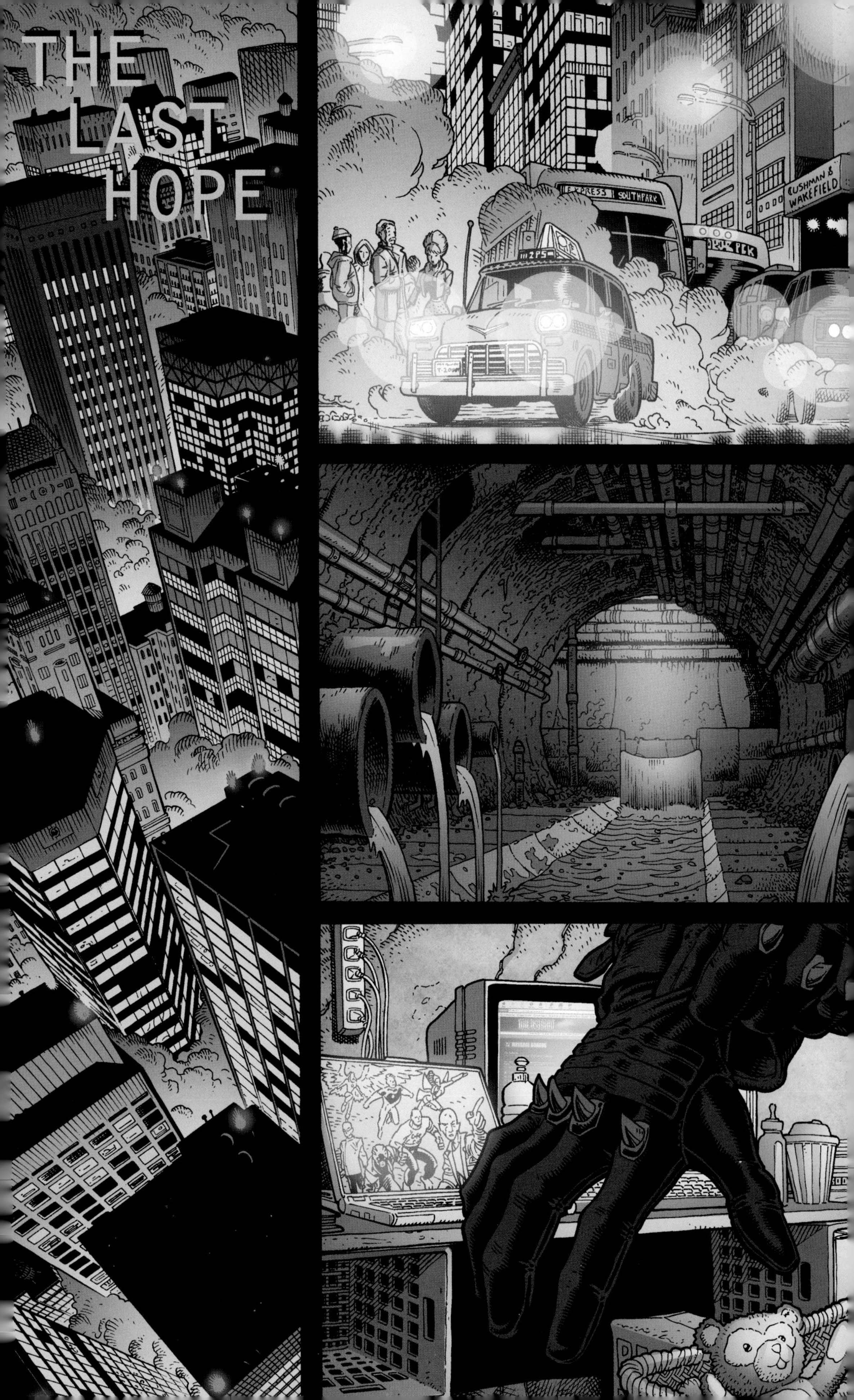
THE LAST HOPE
EXPRESS 1 SOUTHPARK
CUSHMAN & WAKEFIELD

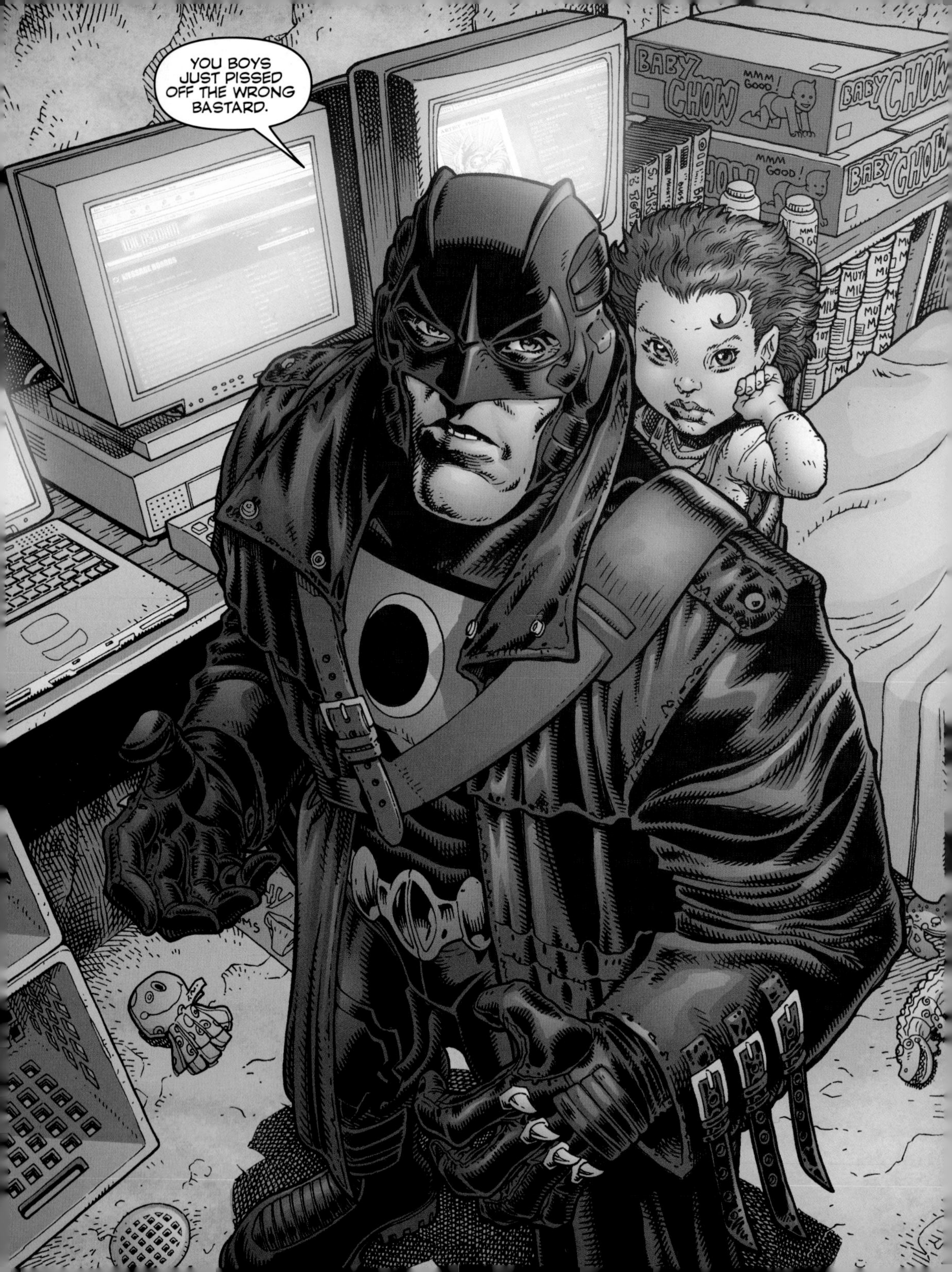
YOU BOYS JUST PISSED OFF THE WRONG BASTARD.

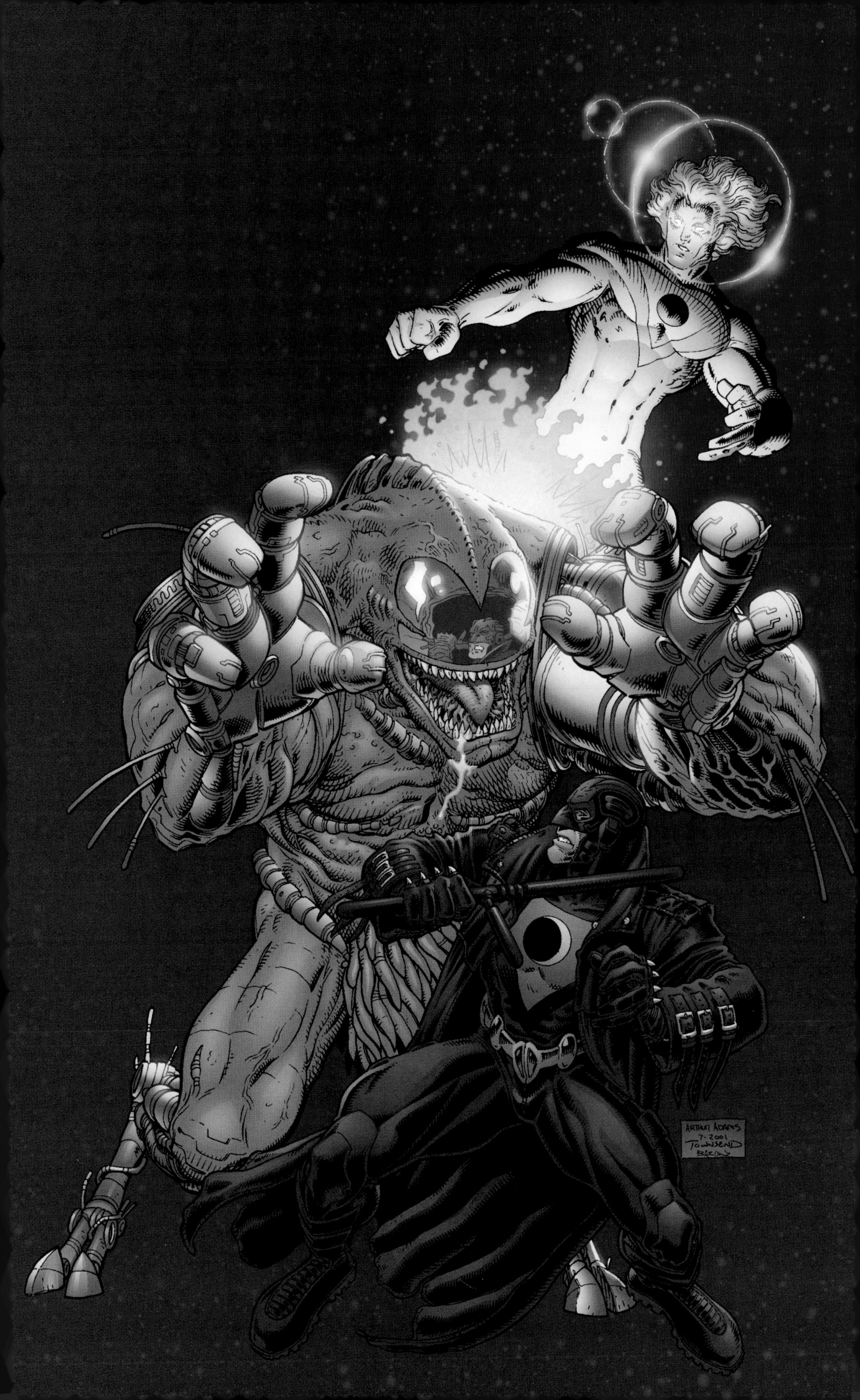
ARTHUR ADAMS
7-2001
TOWNSEND
BARON

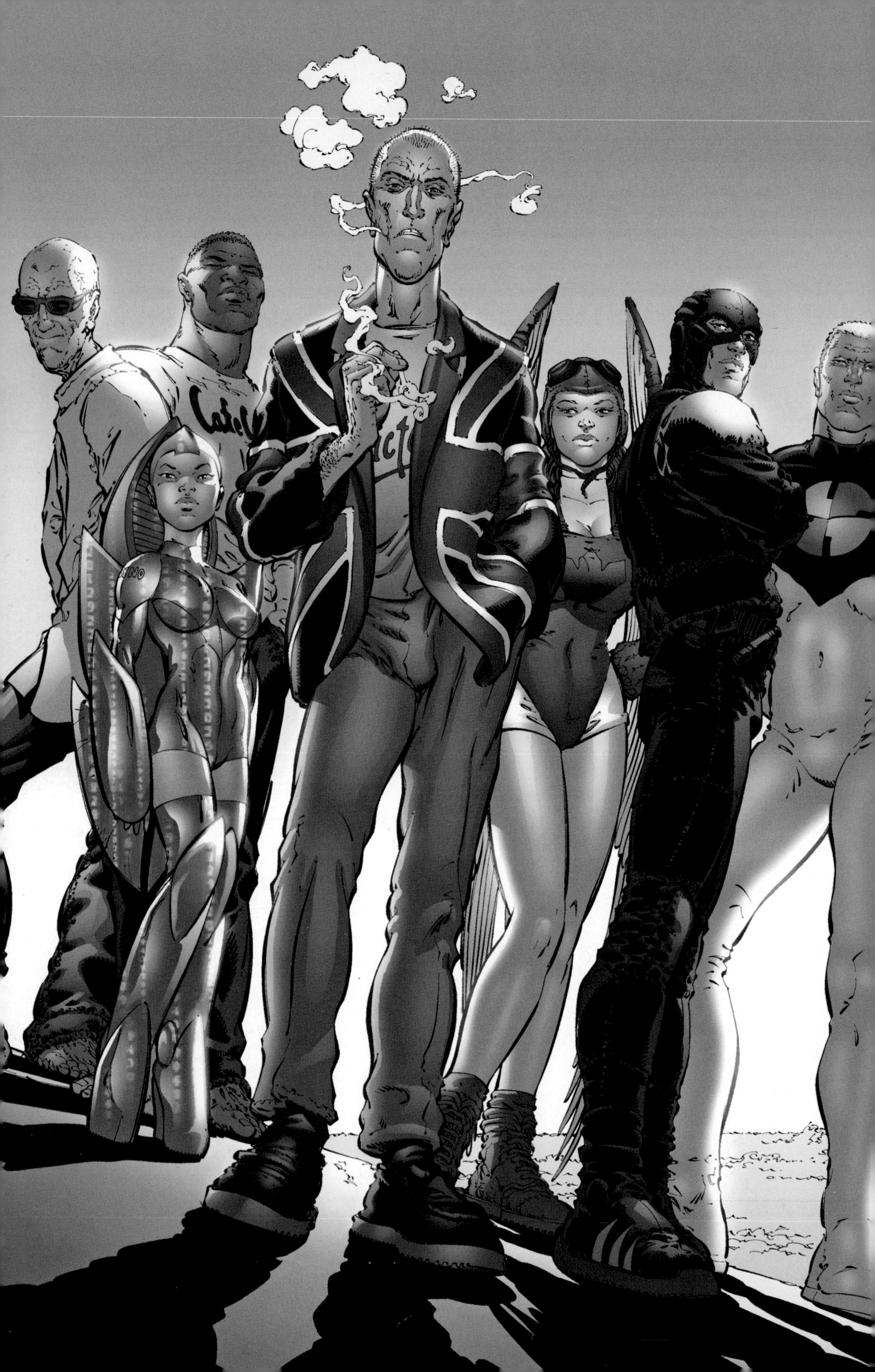

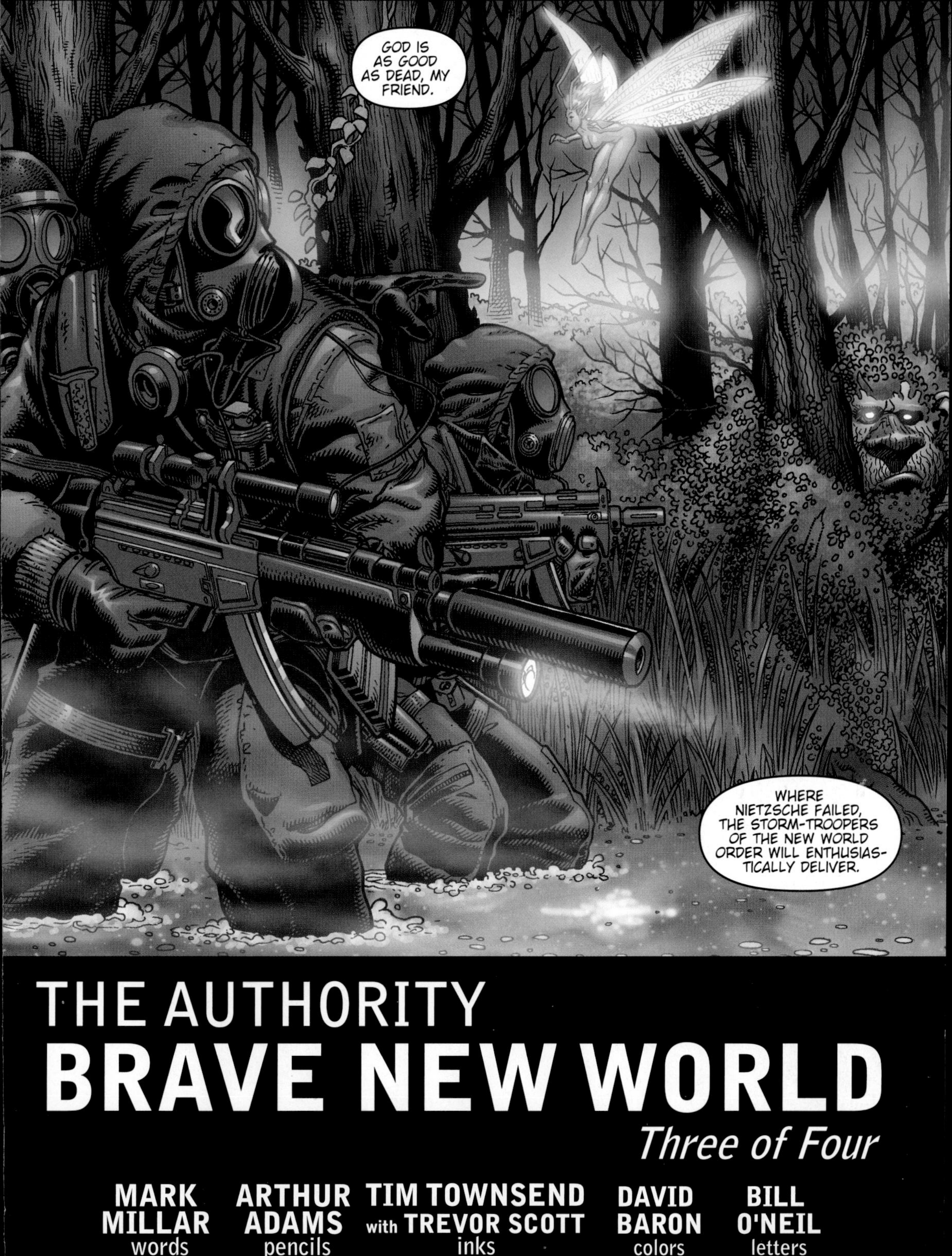

GOD IS AS GOOD AS DEAD, MY FRIEND.
WHERE NIETZSCHE FAILED, THE STORM-TROOPERS OF THE NEW WORLD ORDER WILL ENTHUSIASTICALLY DELIVER.

THE AUTHORITY
BRAVE NEW WORLD
Three of Four

MARK MILLAR words
ARTHUR ADAMS pencils
TIM TOWNSEND with TREVOR SCOTT inks
DAVID BARON colors
BILL O'NEIL letters

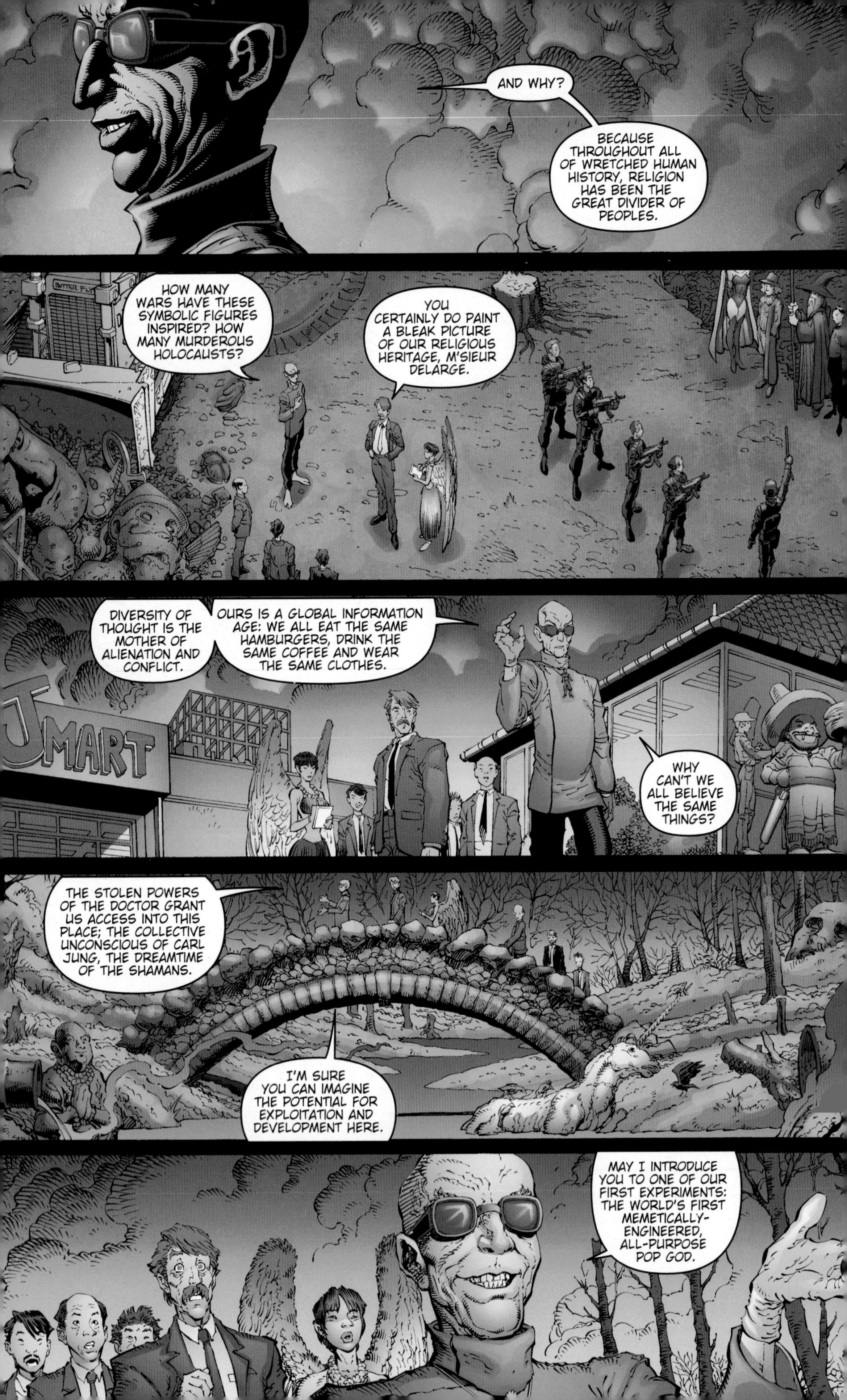
AND WHY?
BECAUSE THROUGHOUT ALL OF WRETCHED HUMAN HISTORY, RELIGION HAS BEEN THE GREAT DIVIDER OF PEOPLES.
HOW MANY WARS HAVE THESE SYMBOLIC FIGURES INSPIRED? HOW MANY MURDEROUS HOLOCAUSTS?
YOU CERTAINLY DO PAINT A BLEAK PICTURE OF OUR RELIGIOUS HERITAGE, M'SIEUR DELARGE.
DIVERSITY OF THOUGHT IS THE MOTHER OF ALIENATION AND CONFLICT.
OURS IS A GLOBAL INFORMATION AGE: WE ALL EAT THE SAME HAMBURGERS, DRINK THE SAME COFFEE AND WEAR THE SAME CLOTHES.
WHY CAN'T WE ALL BELIEVE THE SAME THINGS?
JMART
THE STOLEN POWERS OF THE DOCTOR GRANT US ACCESS INTO THIS PLACE; THE COLLECTIVE UNCONSCIOUS OF CARL JUNG, THE DREAMTIME OF THE SHAMANS.
I'M SURE YOU CAN IMAGINE THE POTENTIAL FOR EXPLOITATION AND DEVELOPMENT HERE.
MAY I INTRODUCE YOU TO ONE OF OUR FIRST EXPERIMENTS: THE WORLD'S FIRST MEMETICALLY-ENGINEERED, ALL-PURPOSE POP GOD.

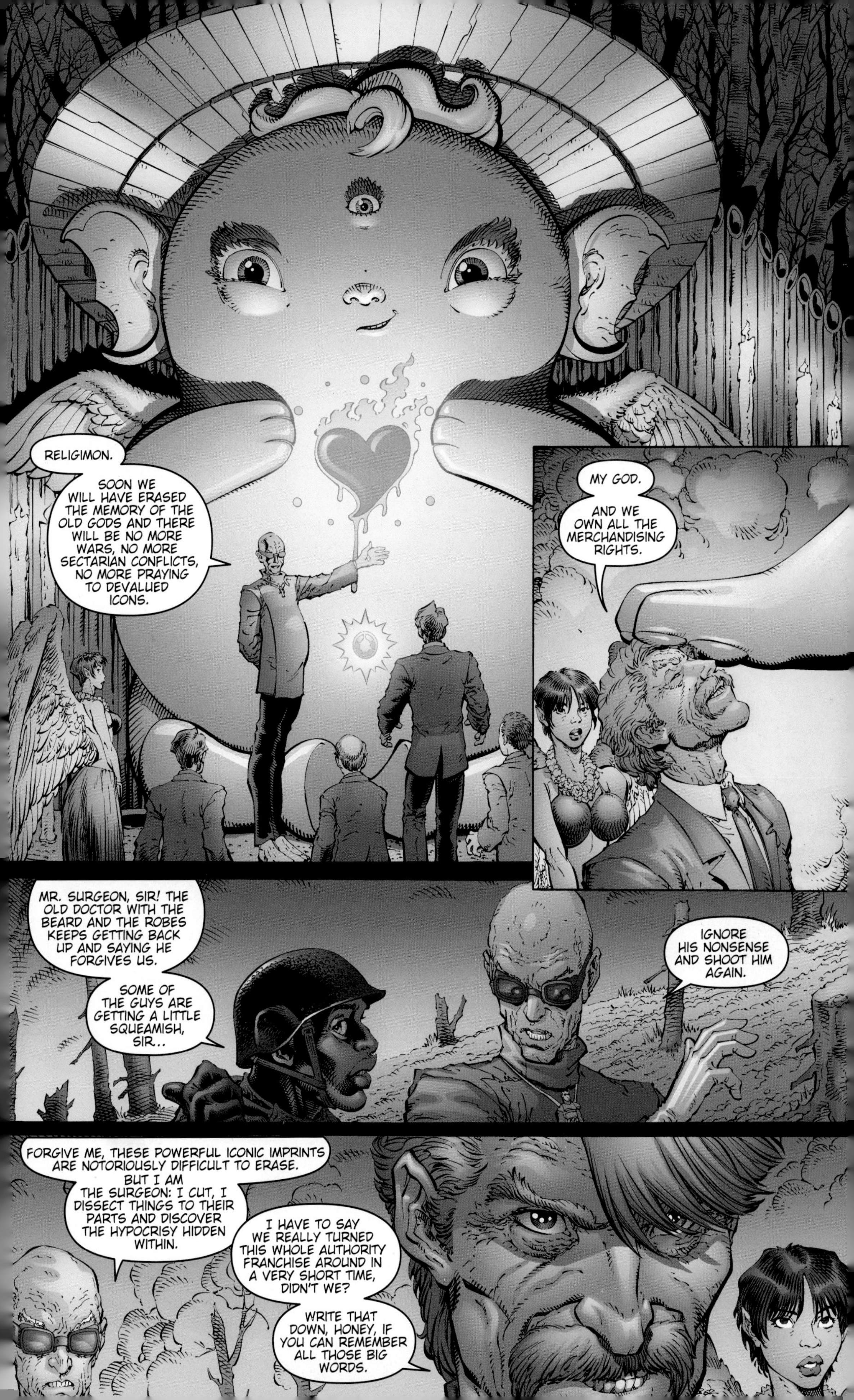
RELIGIMON.
SOON WE WILL HAVE ERASED THE MEMORY OF THE OLD GODS AND THERE WILL BE NO MORE WARS, NO MORE SECTARIAN CONFLICTS, NO MORE PRAYING TO DEVALUED ICONS.
MY GOD.
AND WE OWN ALL THE MERCHANDISING RIGHTS.
MR. SURGEON, SIR! THE OLD DOCTOR WITH THE BEARD AND THE ROBES KEEPS GETTING BACK UP AND SAYING HE FORGIVES US.
SOME OF THE GUYS ARE GETTING A LITTLE SQUEAMISH, SIR...
IGNORE HIS NONSENSE AND SHOOT HIM AGAIN.
FORGIVE ME, THESE POWERFUL ICONIC IMPRINTS ARE NOTORIOUSLY DIFFICULT TO ERASE.
BUT I AM THE SURGEON: I CUT, I DISSECT THINGS TO THEIR PARTS AND DISCOVER THE HYPOCRISY HIDDEN WITHIN.
I HAVE TO SAY WE REALLY TURNED THIS WHOLE AUTHORITY FRANCHISE AROUND IN A VERY SHORT TIME, DIDN'T WE?
WRITE THAT DOWN, HONEY, IF YOU CAN REMEMBER ALL THOSE BIG WORDS.

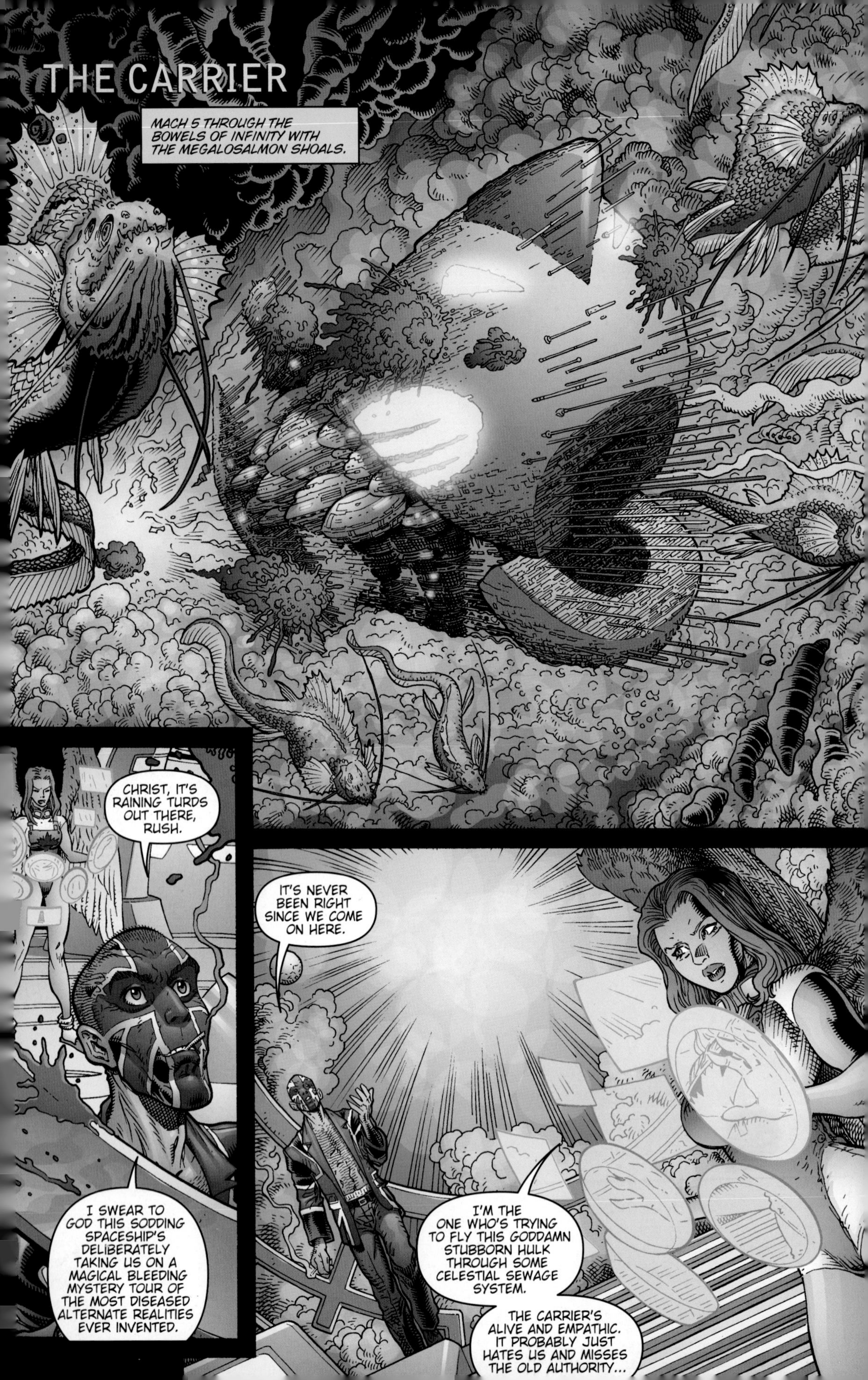
THE CARRIER
MACH 5 THROUGH THE BOWELS OF INFINITY WITH THE MEGALOSALMON SHOALS.
CHRIST, IT'S RAINING TURDS OUT THERE, RUSH.
IT'S NEVER BEEN RIGHT SINCE WE COME ON HERE.
I SWEAR TO GOD THIS SODDING SPACESHIP'S DELIBERATELY TAKING US ON A MAGICAL BLEEDING MYSTERY TOUR OF THE MOST DISEASED ALTERNATE REALITIES EVER INVENTED.
I'M THE ONE WHO'S TRYING TO FLY THIS GODDAMN STUBBORN HULK THROUGH SOME CELESTIAL SEWAGE SYSTEM.
THE CARRIER'S ALIVE AND EMPATHIC. IT PROBABLY JUST HATES US AND MISSES THE OLD AUTHORITY...

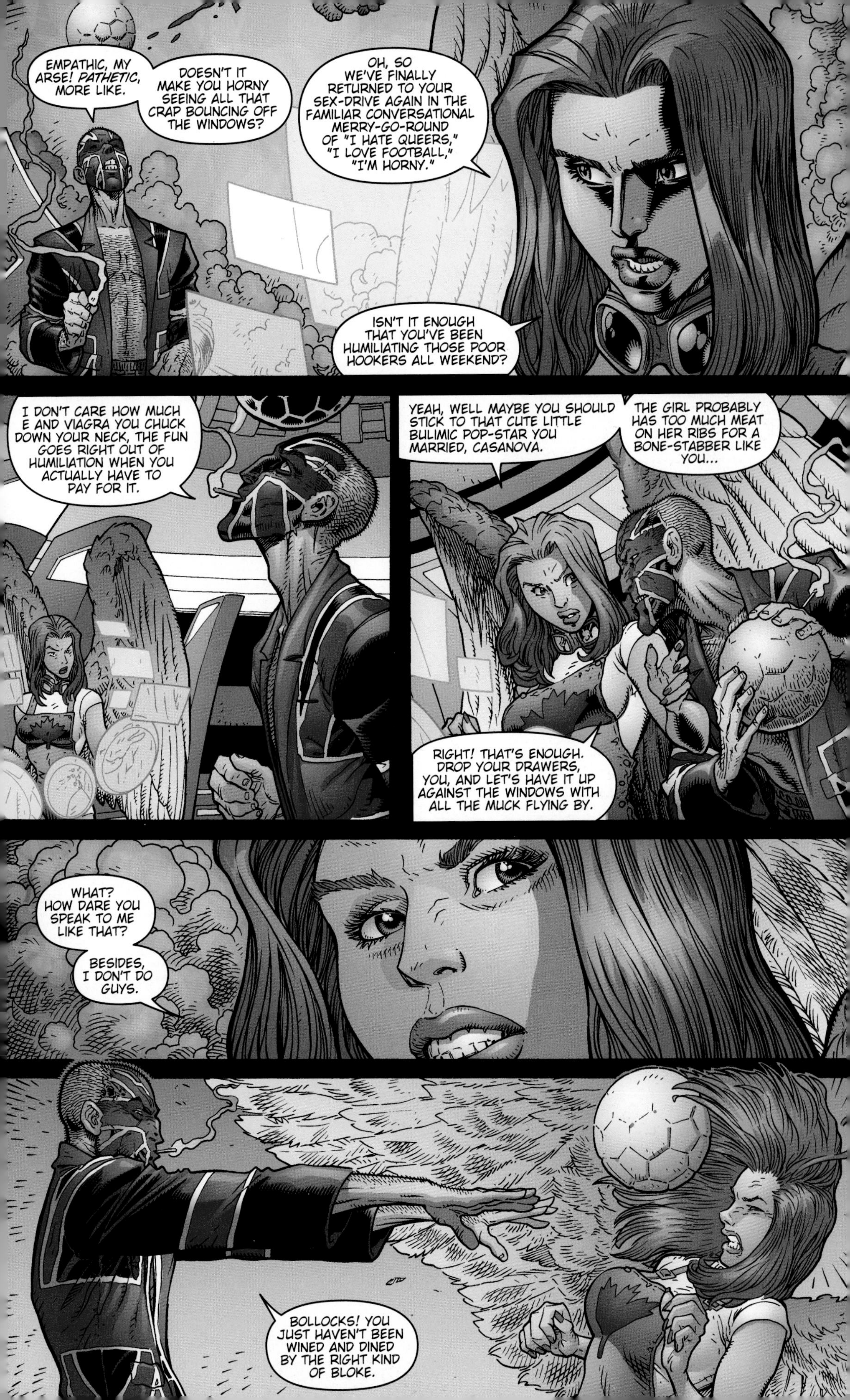
EMPATHIC, MY ARSE! PATHETIC, MORE LIKE.
DOESN'T IT MAKE YOU HORNY SEEING ALL THAT CRAP BOUNCING OFF THE WINDOWS?
OH, SO WE'VE FINALLY RETURNED TO YOUR SEX-DRIVE AGAIN IN THE FAMILIAR CONVERSATIONAL MERRY-GO-ROUND OF "I HATE QUEERS," "I LOVE FOOTBALL," "I'M HORNY."
ISN'T IT ENOUGH THAT YOU'VE BEEN HUMILIATING THOSE POOR HOOKERS ALL WEEKEND?
I DON'T CARE HOW MUCH E AND VIAGRA YOU CHUCK DOWN YOUR NECK, THE FUN GOES RIGHT OUT OF HUMILIATION WHEN YOU ACTUALLY HAVE TO PAY FOR IT.
YEAH, WELL MAYBE YOU SHOULD STICK TO THAT CUTE LITTLE BULIMIC POP-STAR YOU MARRIED, CASANOVA.
THE GIRL PROBABLY HAS TOO MUCH MEAT ON HER RIBS FOR A BONE-STABBER LIKE YOU...
RIGHT! THAT'S ENOUGH. DROP YOUR DRAWERS, YOU, AND LET'S HAVE IT UP AGAINST THE WINDOWS WITH ALL THE MUCK FLYING BY.
WHAT? HOW DARE YOU SPEAK TO ME LIKE THAT?
BESIDES, I DON'T DO GUYS.
BOLLOCKS! YOU JUST HAVEN'T BEEN WINED AND DINED BY THE RIGHT KIND OF BLOKE.

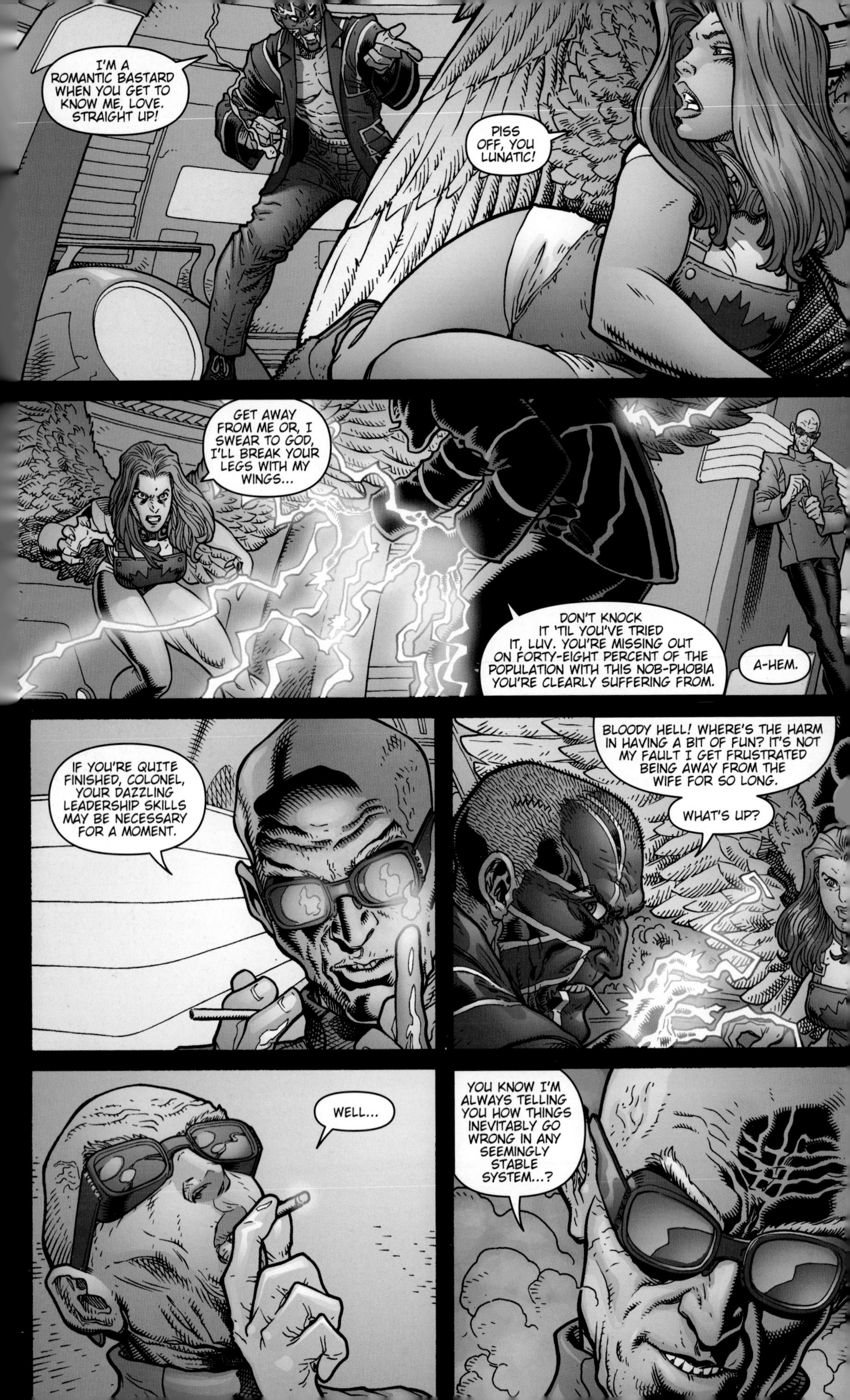

I'M A ROMANTIC BASTARD WHEN YOU GET TO KNOW ME, LOVE. STRAIGHT UP!
PISS OFF, YOU LUNATIC!
GET AWAY FROM ME OR, I SWEAR TO GOD, I'LL BREAK YOUR LEGS WITH MY WINGS...
DON'T KNOCK IT 'TIL YOU'VE TRIED IT, LUV. YOU'RE MISSING OUT ON FORTY-EIGHT PERCENT OF THE POPULATION WITH THIS NOB-PHOBIA YOU'RE CLEARLY SUFFERING FROM.
A-HEM.
IF YOU'RE QUITE FINISHED, COLONEL, YOUR DAZZLING LEADERSHIP SKILLS MAY BE NECESSARY FOR A MOMENT.
BLOODY HELL! WHERE'S THE HARM IN HAVING A BIT OF FUN? IT'S NOT MY FAULT I GET FRUSTRATED BEING AWAY FROM THE WIFE FOR SO LONG.
WHAT'S UP?
WELL...
YOU KNOW I'M ALWAYS TELLING YOU HOW THINGS INEVITABLY GO WRONG IN ANY SEEMINGLY STABLE SYSTEM...?

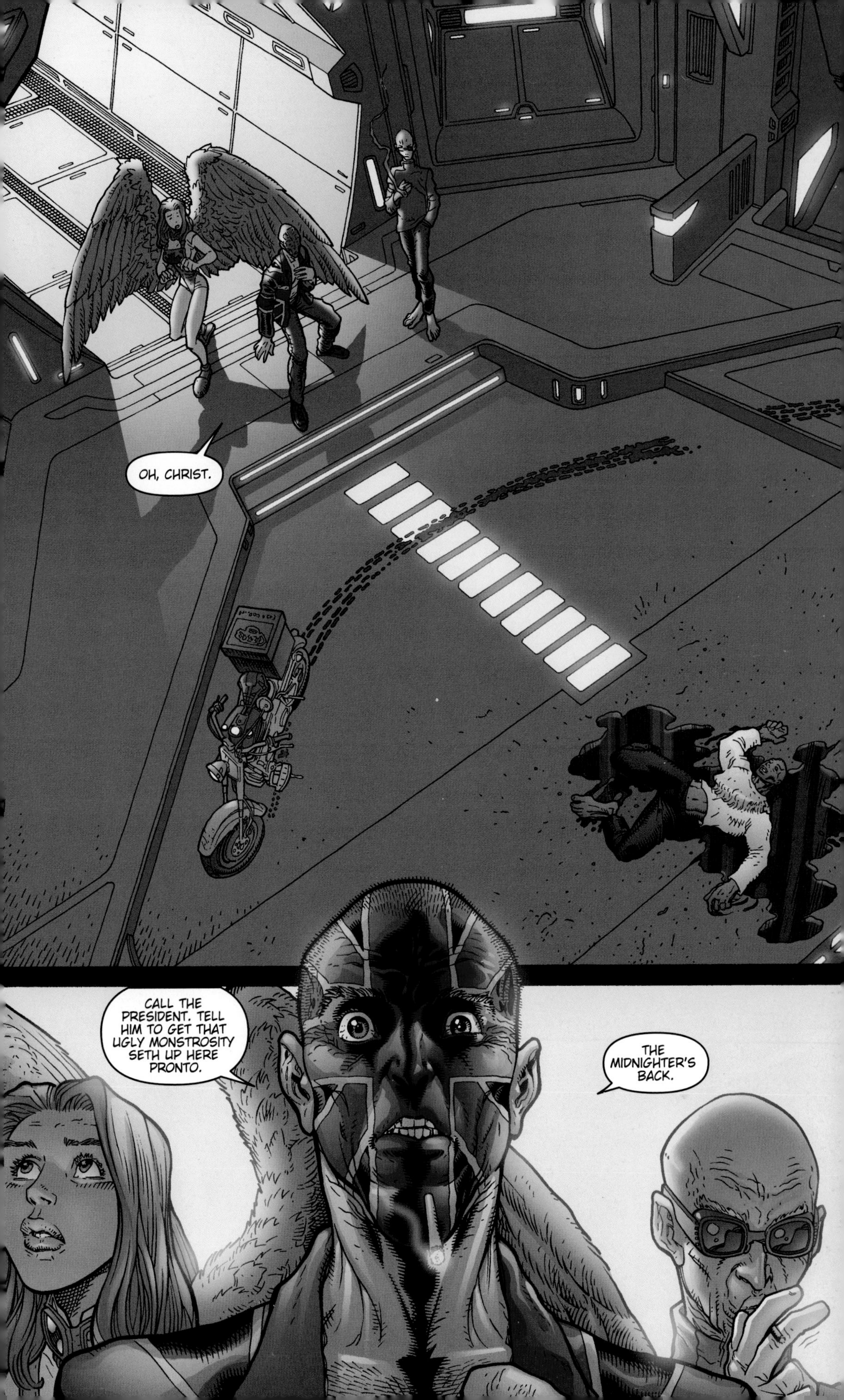
OH, CHRIST.
CALL THE PRESIDENT. TELL HIM TO GET THAT UGLY MONSTROSITY SETH UP HERE PRONTO.
THE MIDNIGHTER'S BACK.

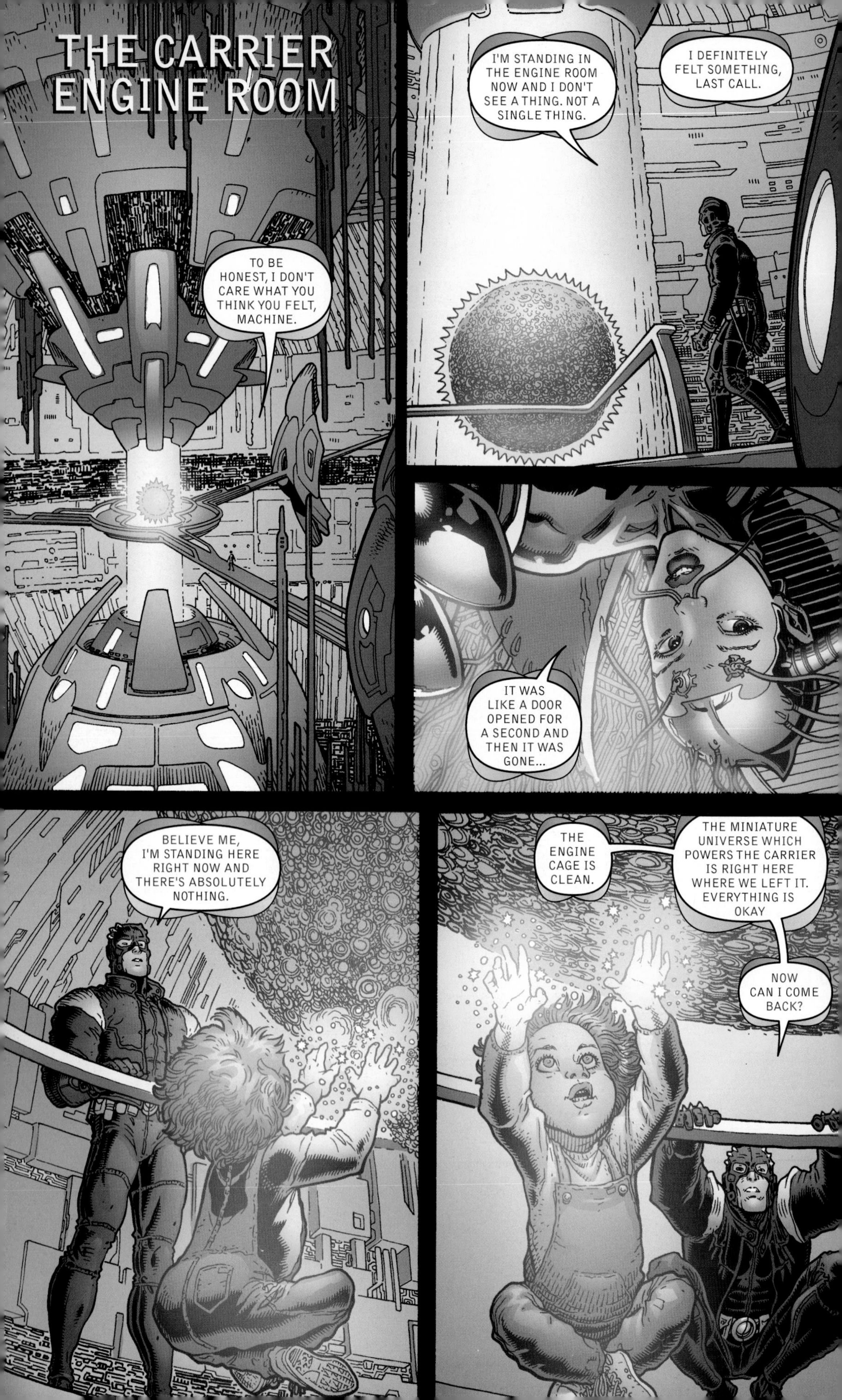
THE CARRIER ENGINE ROOM
TO BE HONEST, I DON'T CARE WHAT YOU THINK YOU FELT, MACHINE.
I'M STANDING IN THE ENGINE ROOM NOW AND I DON'T SEE A THING. NOT A SINGLE THING.
I DEFINITELY FELT SOMETHING, LAST CALL.
IT WAS LIKE A DOOR OPENED FOR A SECOND AND THEN IT WAS GONE...
BELIEVE ME, I'M STANDING HERE RIGHT NOW AND THERE'S ABSOLUTELY NOTHING.
THE ENGINE CAGE IS CLEAN.
THE MINIATURE UNIVERSE WHICH POWERS THE CARRIER IS RIGHT HERE WHERE WE LEFT IT. EVERYTHING IS OKAY
NOW CAN I COME BACK?

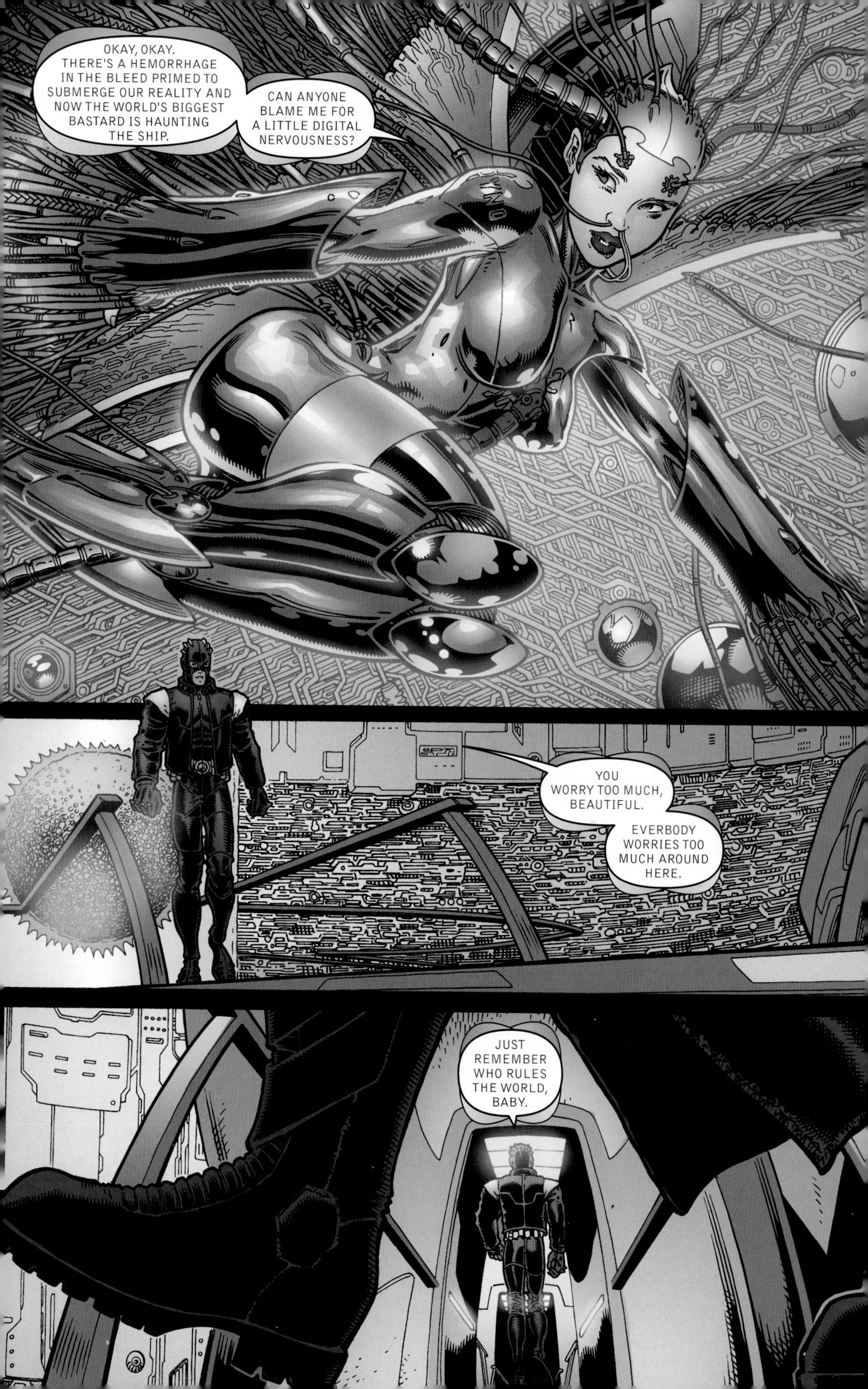
OKAY, OKAY. THERE'S A HEMORRHAGE IN THE BLEED PRIMED TO SUBMERGE OUR REALITY AND NOW THE WORLD'S BIGGEST BASTARD IS HAUNTING THE SHIP.
CAN ANYONE BLAME ME FOR A LITTLE DIGITAL NERVOUSNESS?
YOU WORRY TOO MUCH, BEAUTIFUL.
EVERBODY WORRIES TOO MUCH AROUND HERE.
JUST REMEMBER WHO RULES THE WORLD, BABY.

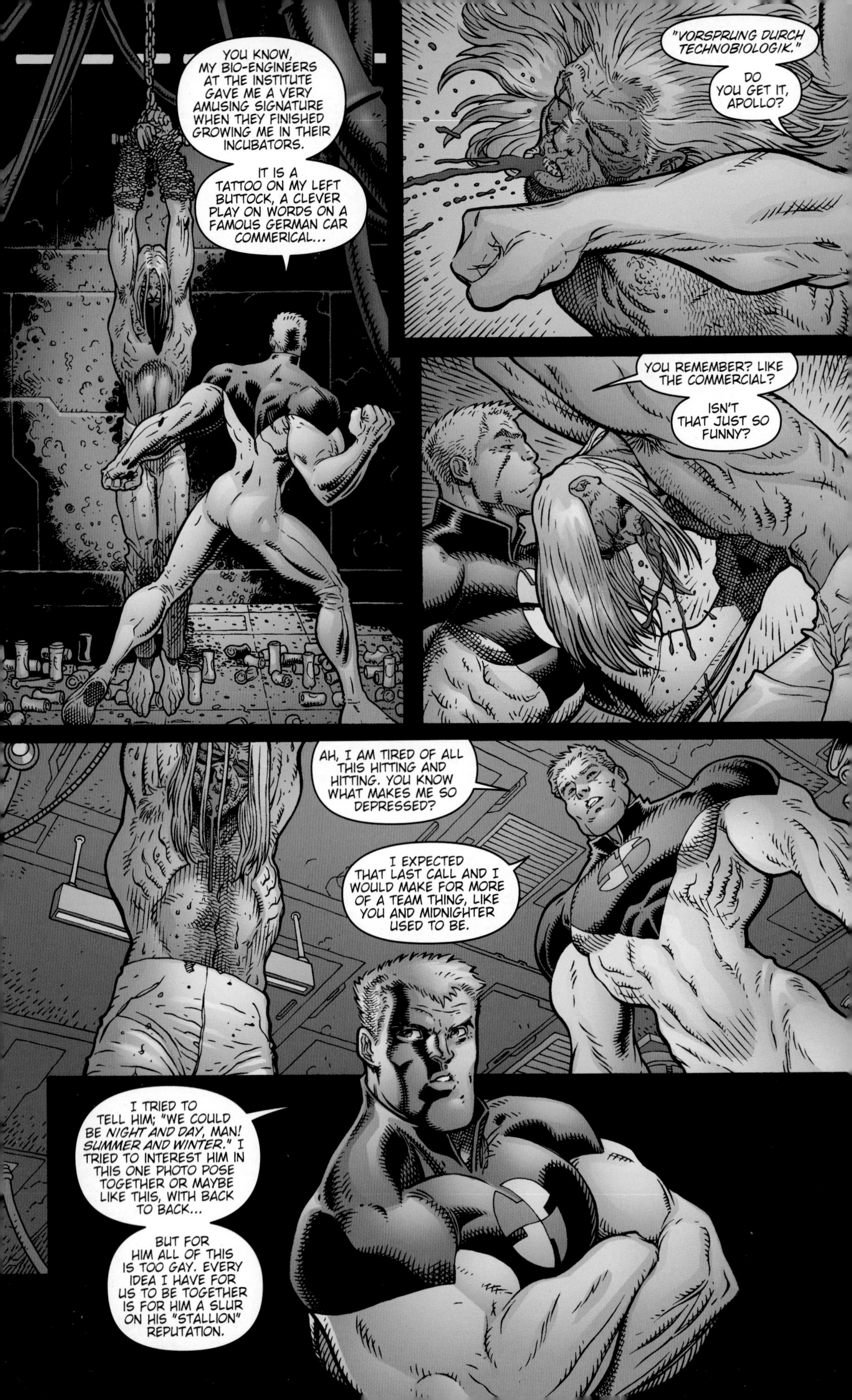
YOU KNOW, MY BIO-ENGINEERS AT THE INSTITUTE GAVE ME A VERY AMUSING SIGNATURE WHEN THEY FINISHED GROWING ME IN THEIR INCUBATORS.
IT IS A TATTOO ON MY LEFT BUTTOCK, A CLEVER PLAY ON WORDS ON A FAMOUS GERMAN CAR COMMERICAL...
"VORSPRUNG DURCH TECHNOBIOLOGIK."
DO YOU GET IT, APOLLO?
YOU REMEMBER? LIKE THE COMMERCIAL?
ISN'T THAT JUST SO FUNNY?
AH, I AM TIRED OF ALL THIS HITTING AND HITTING. YOU KNOW WHAT MAKES ME SO DEPRESSED?
I EXPECTED THAT LAST CALL AND I WOULD MAKE FOR MORE OF A TEAM THING, LIKE YOU AND MIDNIGHTER USED TO BE.
I TRIED TO TELL HIM; "WE COULD BE *NIGHT AND DAY, MAN! SUMMER AND WINTER.*" I TRIED TO INTEREST HIM IN THIS ONE PHOTO POSE TOGETHER OR MAYBE LIKE THIS, WITH BACK TO BACK...
BUT FOR HIM ALL OF THIS IS TOO GAY. EVERY IDEA I HAVE FOR US TO BE TOGETHER IS FOR HIM A SLUR ON HIS "STALLION" REPUTATION.

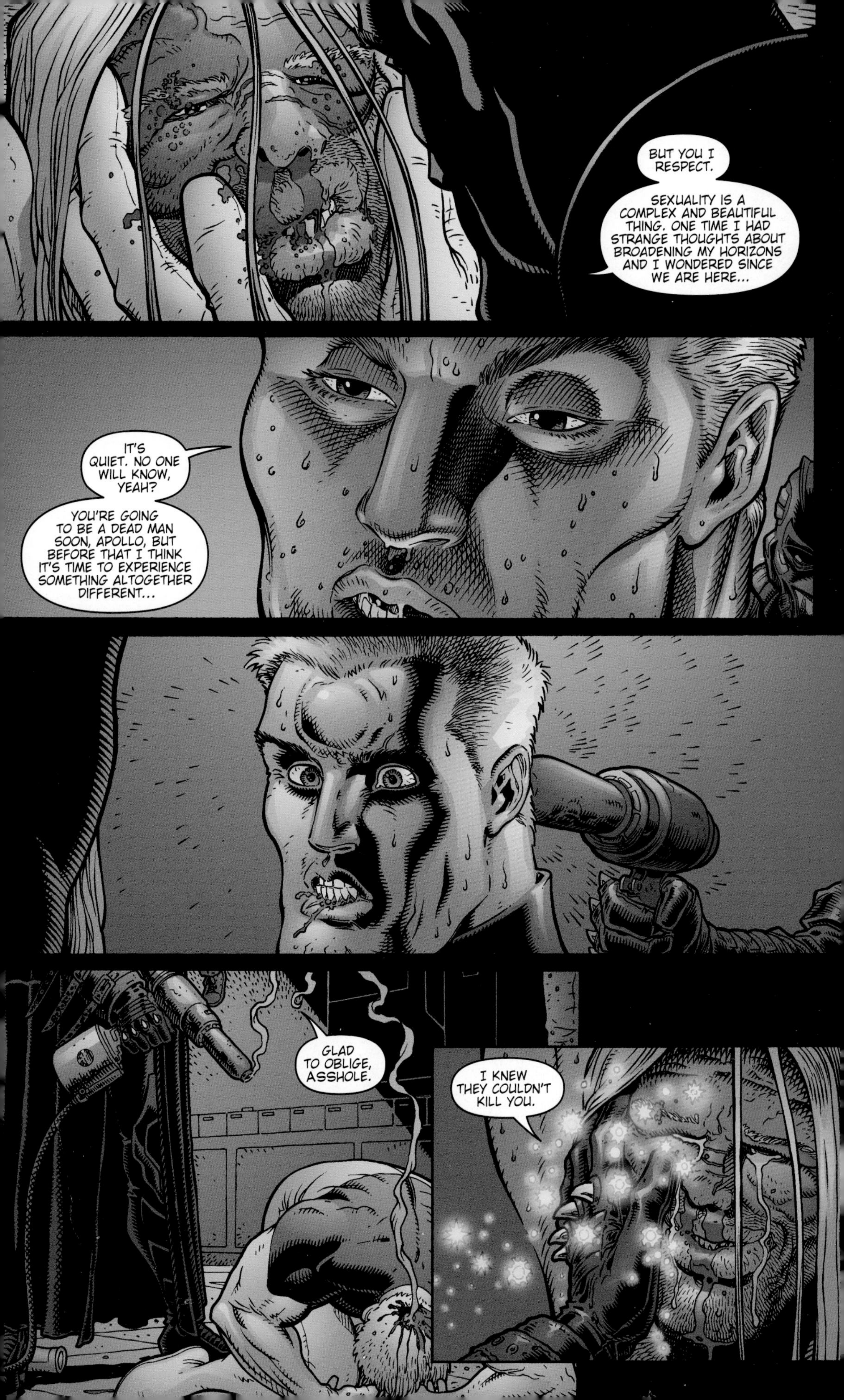
BUT YOU I RESPECT.
SEXUALITY IS A COMPLEX AND BEAUTIFUL THING. ONE TIME I HAD STRANGE THOUGHTS ABOUT BROADENING MY HORIZONS AND I WONDERED SINCE WE ARE HERE...
IT'S QUIET. NO ONE WILL KNOW, YEAH?
YOU'RE GOING TO BE A DEAD MAN SOON, APOLLO, BUT BEFORE THAT I THINK IT'S TIME TO EXPERIENCE SOMETHING ALTOGETHER DIFFERENT...
GLAD TO OBLIGE, ASSHOLE.
I KNEW THEY COULDN'T KILL YOU.

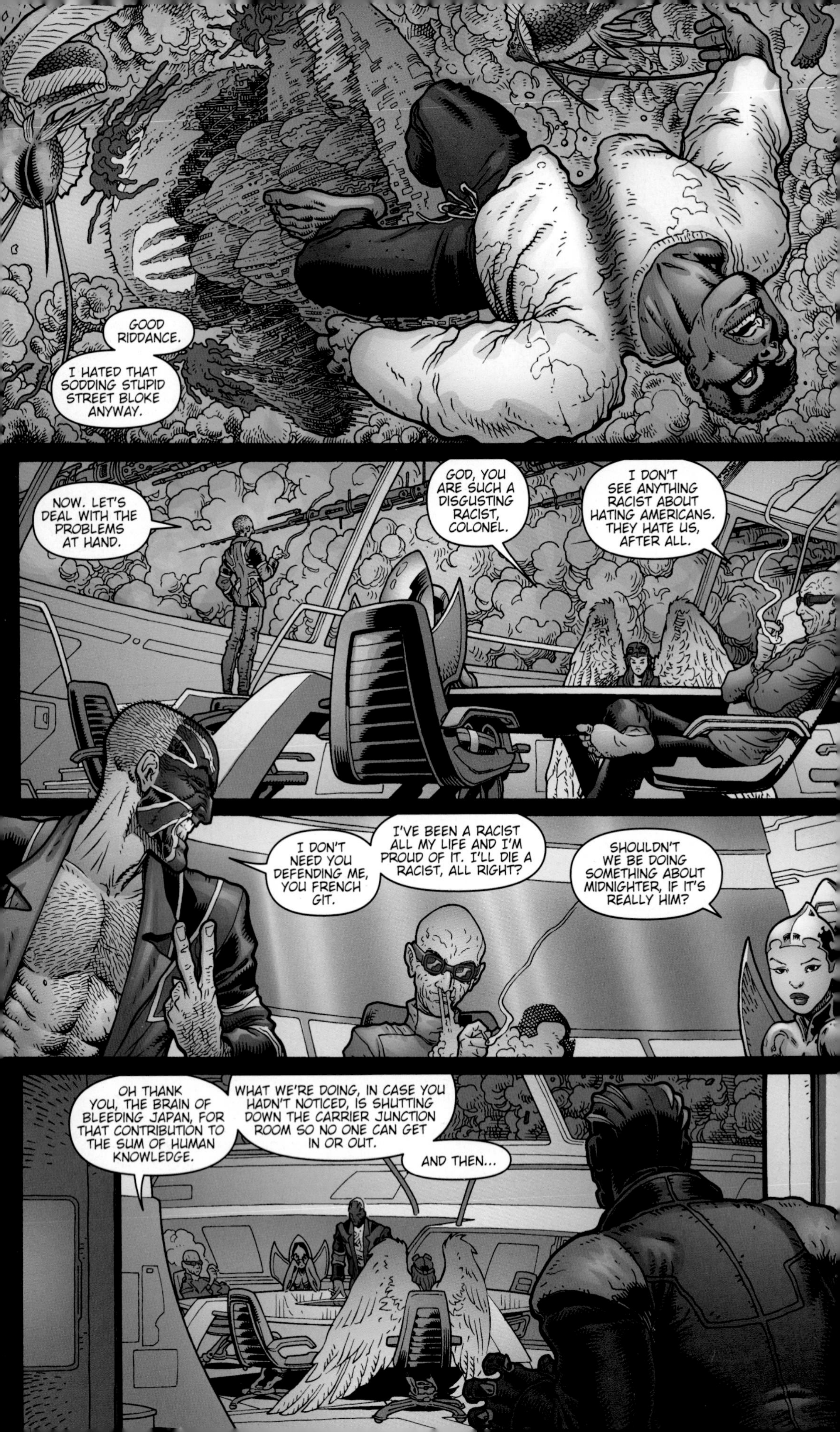
GOOD RIDDANCE.
I HATED THAT SODDING STUPID STREET BLOKE ANYWAY.
NOW. LET'S DEAL WITH THE PROBLEMS AT HAND.
GOD, YOU ARE SUCH A DISGUSTING RACIST, COLONEL.
I DON'T SEE ANYTHING RACIST ABOUT HATING AMERICANS. THEY HATE US, AFTER ALL.
I DON'T NEED YOU DEFENDING ME, YOU FRENCH GIT.
I'VE BEEN A RACIST ALL MY LIFE AND I'M PROUD OF IT. I'LL DIE A RACIST, ALL RIGHT?
SHOULDN'T WE BE DOING SOMETHING ABOUT MIDNIGHTER, IF IT'S REALLY HIM?
OH THANK YOU, THE BRAIN OF BLEEDING JAPAN, FOR THAT CONTRIBUTION TO THE SUM OF HUMAN KNOWLEDGE.
WHAT WE'RE DOING, IN CASE YOU HADN'T NOTICED, IS SHUTTING DOWN THE CARRIER JUNCTION ROOM SO NO ONE CAN GET IN OR OUT.
AND THEN...

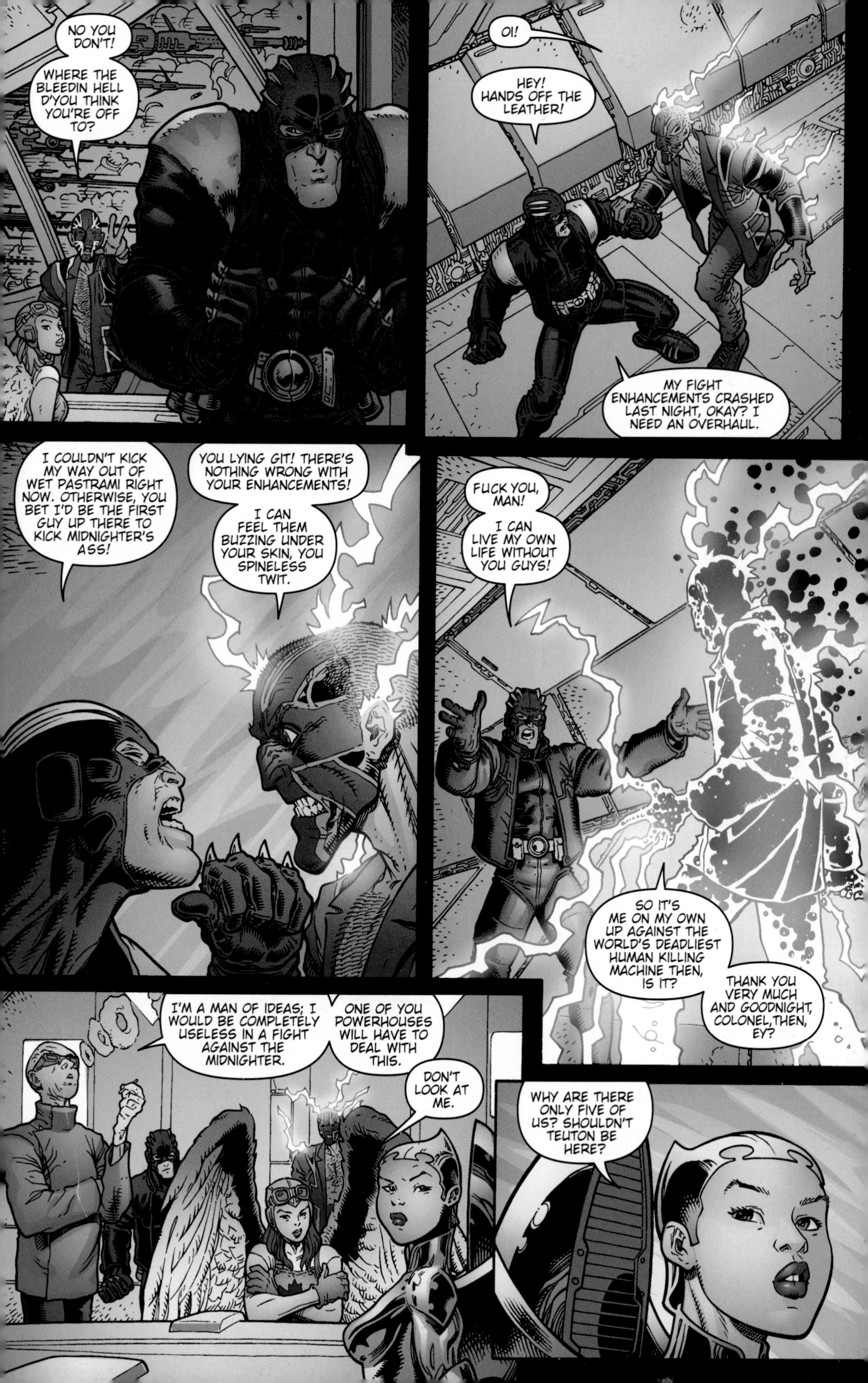
NO YOU DON'T!
WHERE THE BLEEDIN HELL D'YOU THINK YOU'RE OFF TO?
OI!
HEY! HANDS OFF THE LEATHER!
MY FIGHT ENHANCEMENTS CRASHED LAST NIGHT, OKAY? I NEED AN OVERHAUL.
I COULDN'T KICK MY WAY OUT OF WET PASTRAMI RIGHT NOW. OTHERWISE, YOU BET I'D BE THE FIRST GUY UP THERE TO KICK MIDNIGHTER'S ASS!
YOU LYING GIT! THERE'S NOTHING WRONG WITH YOUR ENHANCEMENTS!
I CAN FEEL THEM BUZZING UNDER YOUR SKIN, YOU SPINELESS TWIT.
FUCK YOU, MAN!
I CAN LIVE MY OWN LIFE WITHOUT YOU GUYS!
SO IT'S ME ON MY OWN UP AGAINST THE WORLD'S DEADLIEST HUMAN KILLING MACHINE THEN, IS IT?
THANK YOU VERY MUCH AND GOODNIGHT, COLONEL,THEN, EY?
I'M A MAN OF IDEAS; I WOULD BE COMPLETELY USELESS IN A FIGHT AGAINST THE MIDNIGHTER.
ONE OF YOU POWERHOUSES WILL HAVE TO DEAL WITH THIS.
DON'T LOOK AT ME.
WHY ARE THERE ONLY FIVE OF US? SHOULDN'T TEUTON BE HERE?

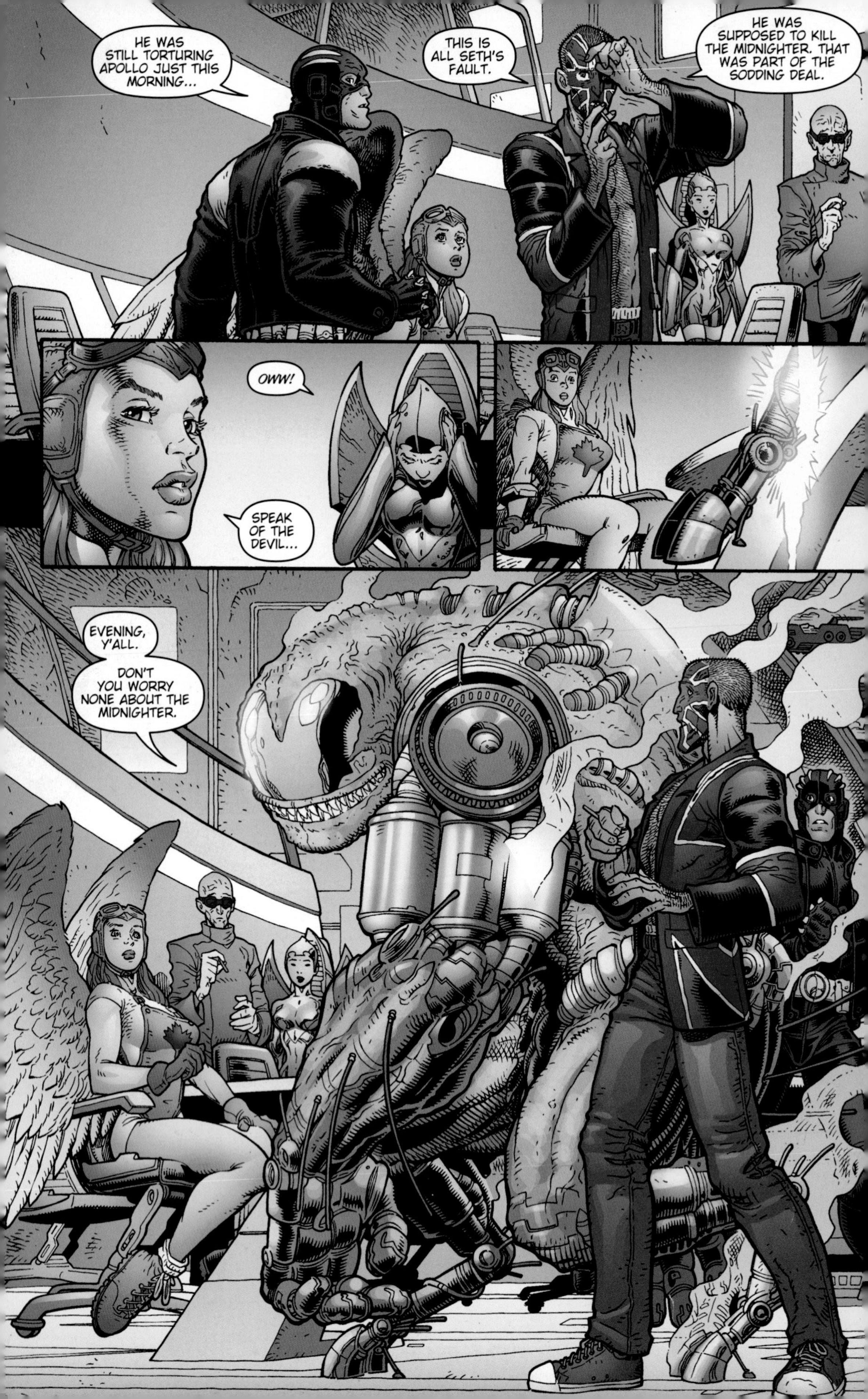
HE WAS STILL TORTURING APOLLO JUST THIS MORNING...
THIS IS ALL SETH'S FAULT.
HE WAS SUPPOSED TO KILL THE MIDNIGHTER. THAT WAS PART OF THE SODDING DEAL.
OWW!
SPEAK OF THE DEVIL...
EVENING, Y'ALL.
DON'T YOU WORRY NONE ABOUT THE MIDNIGHTER.

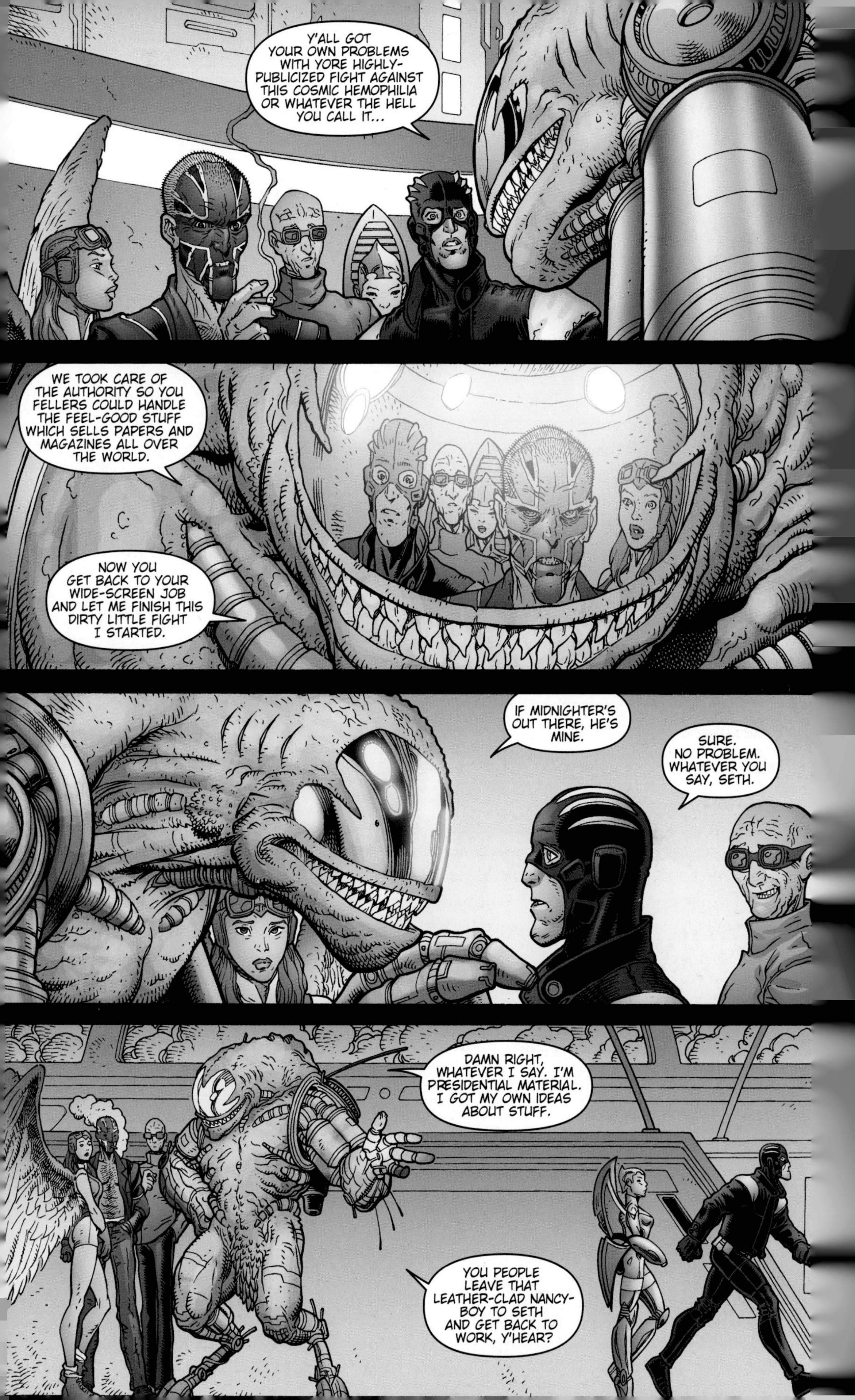
Y'ALL GOT YOUR OWN PROBLEMS WITH YORE HIGHLY-PUBLICIZED FIGHT AGAINST THIS COSMIC HEMOPHILIA OR WHATEVER THE HELL YOU CALL IT...
WE TOOK CARE OF THE AUTHORITY SO YOU FELLERS COULD HANDLE THE FEEL-GOOD STUFF WHICH SELLS PAPERS AND MAGAZINES ALL OVER THE WORLD.
NOW YOU GET BACK TO YOUR WIDE-SCREEN JOB AND LET ME FINISH THIS DIRTY LITTLE FIGHT I STARTED.
IF MIDNIGHTER'S OUT THERE, HE'S MINE.
SURE. NO PROBLEM. WHATEVER YOU SAY, SETH.
DAMN RIGHT, WHATEVER I SAY. I'M PRESIDENTIAL MATERIAL. I GOT MY OWN IDEAS ABOUT STUFF.
YOU PEOPLE LEAVE THAT LEATHER-CLAD NANCY-BOY TO SETH AND GET BACK TO WORK, Y'HEAR?

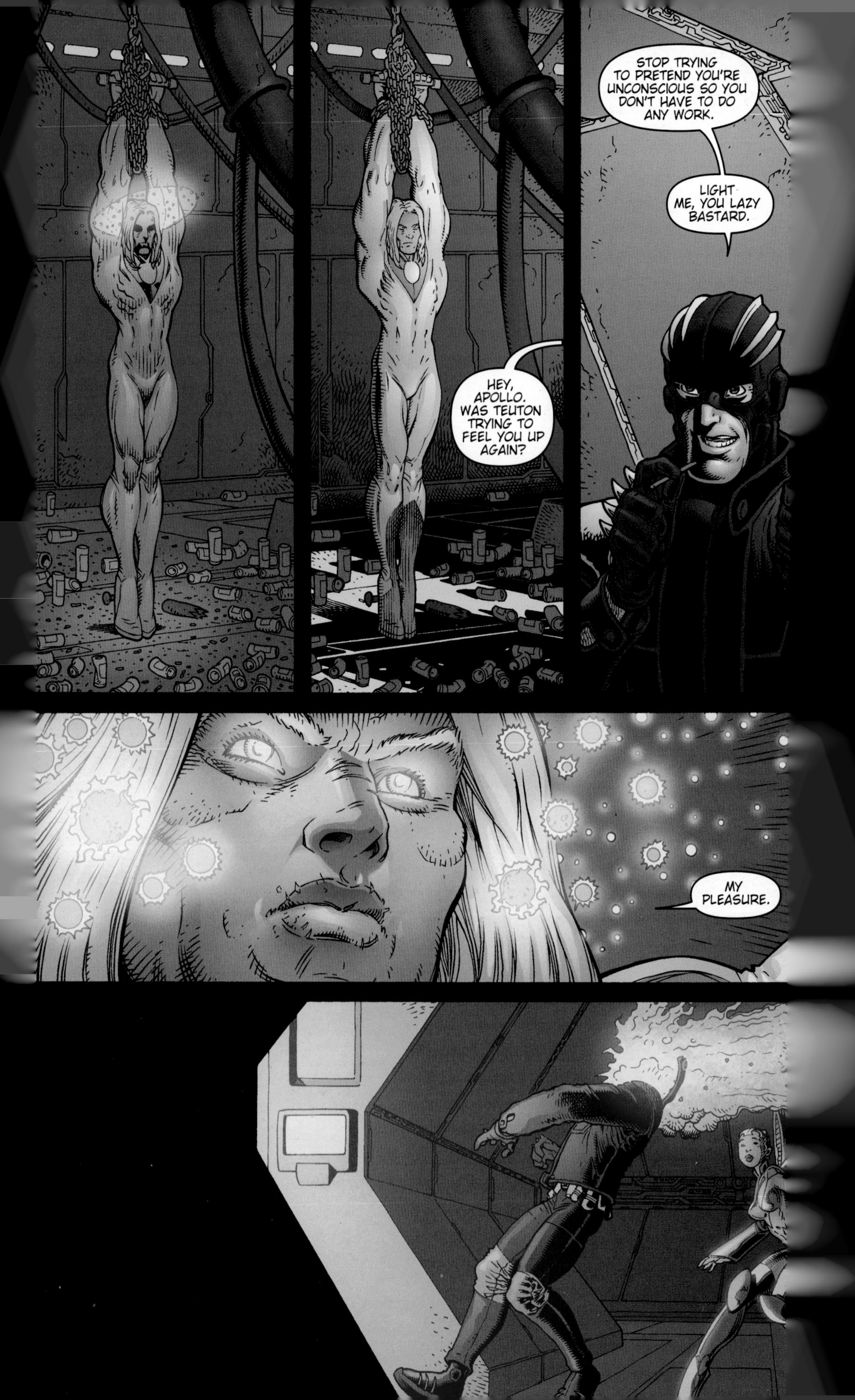
HEY, APOLLO. WAS TEUTON TRYING TO FEEL YOU UP AGAIN?
STOP TRYING TO PRETEND YOU'RE UNCONSCIOUS SO YOU DON'T HAVE TO DO ANY WORK.
LIGHT ME, YOU LAZY BASTARD.
MY PLEASURE.

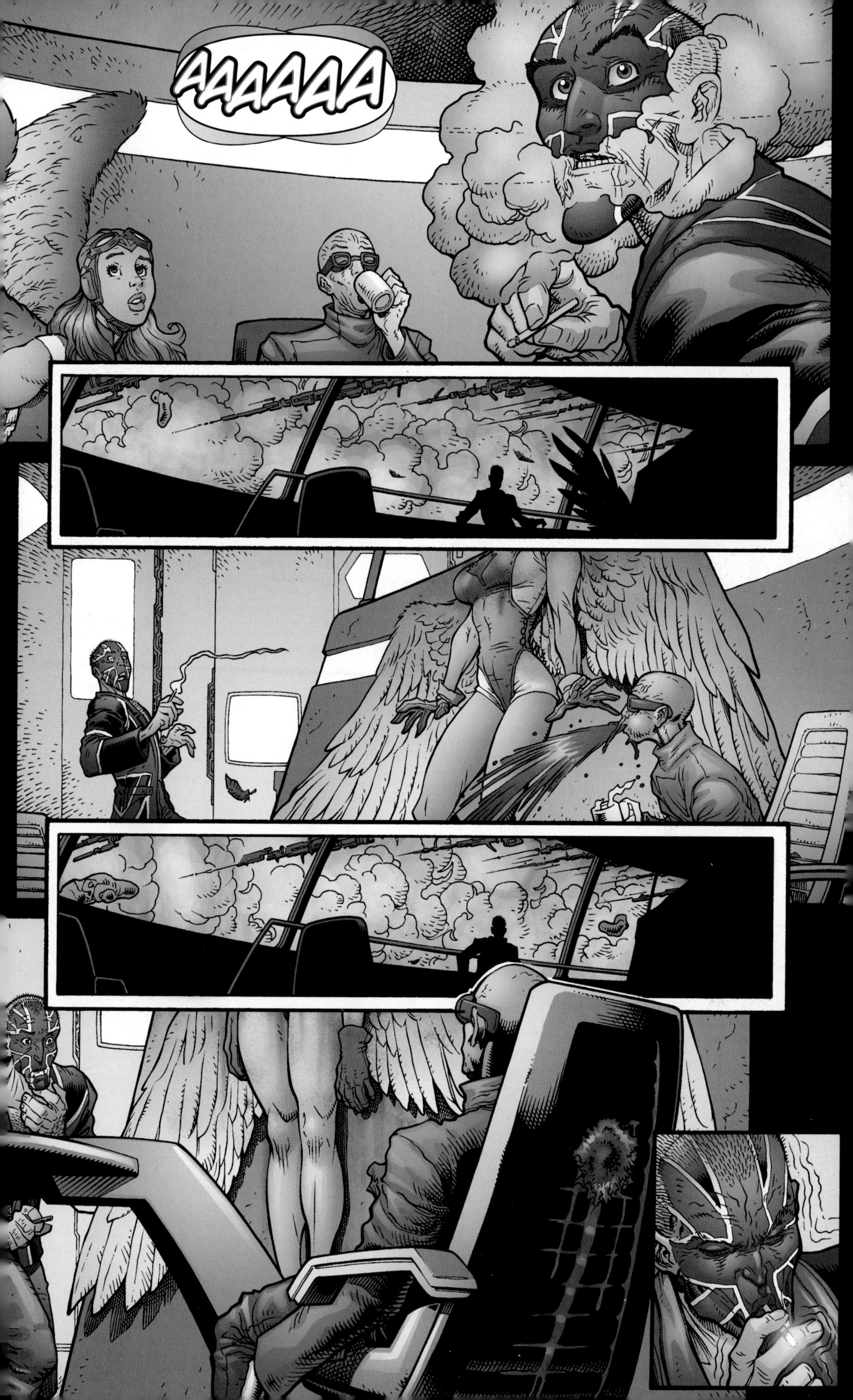
AAAAAA

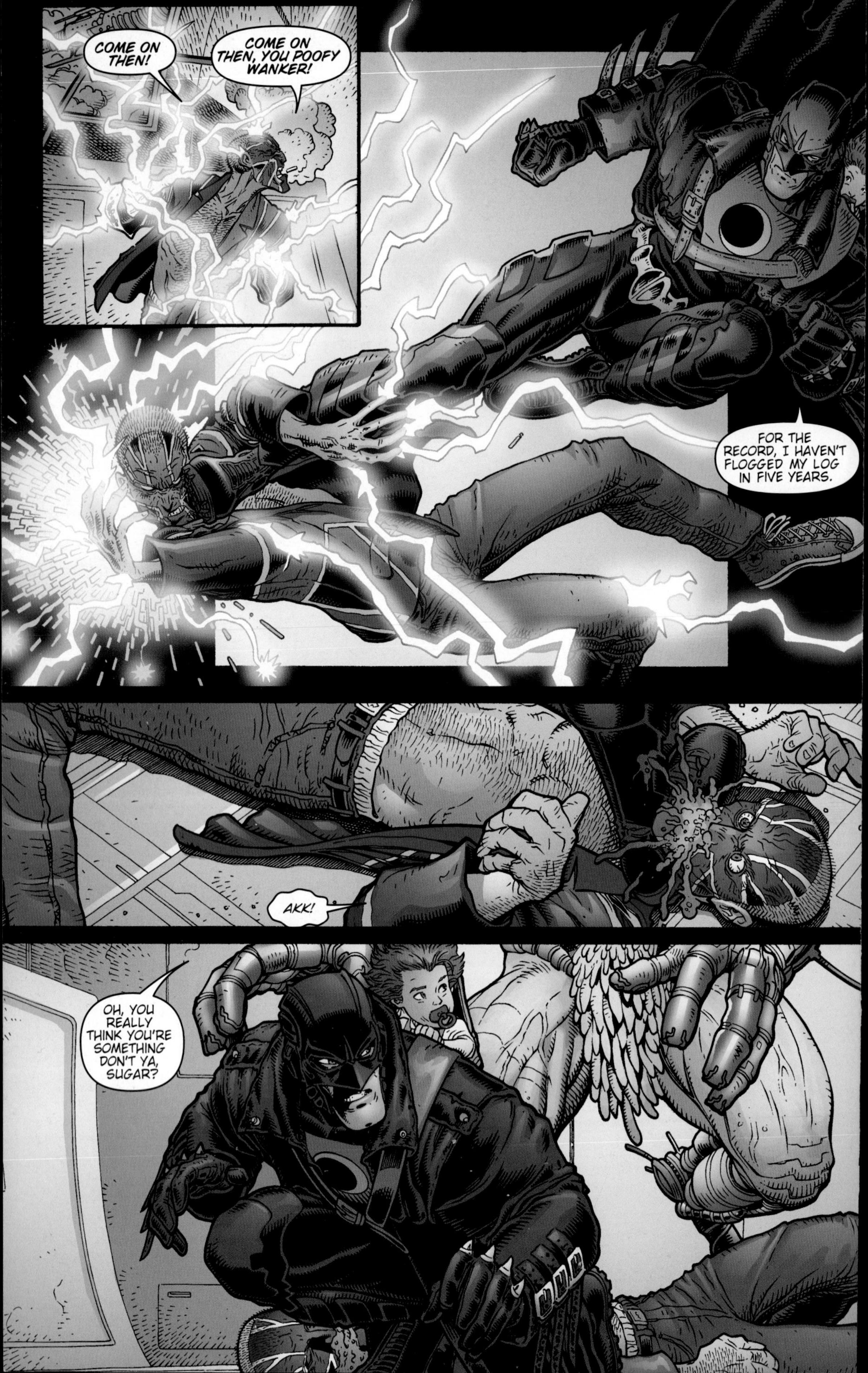
COME ON THEN!
COME ON THEN, YOU POOFY WANKER!
FOR THE RECORD, I HAVEN'T FLOGGED MY LOG IN FIVE YEARS.
AKK!
OH, YOU REALLY THINK YOU'RE SOMETHING DON'T YA, SUGAR?

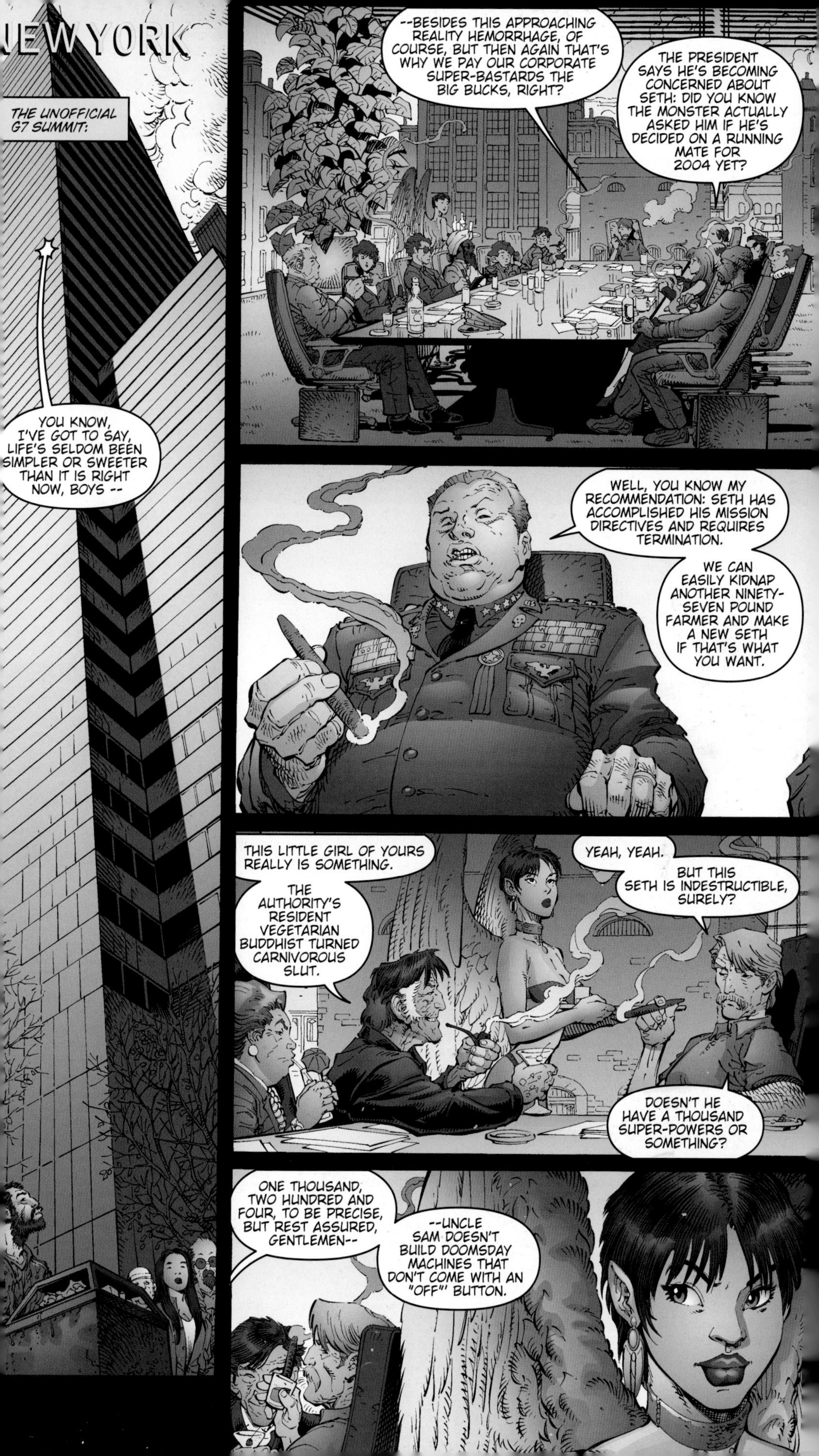
NEW YORK
THE UNOFFICIAL G7 SUMMIT:
YOU KNOW, I'VE GOT TO SAY, LIFE'S SELDOM BEEN SIMPLER OR SWEETER THAN IT IS RIGHT NOW, BOYS --
--BESIDES THIS APPROACHING REALITY HEMORRHAGE, OF COURSE, BUT THEN AGAIN THAT'S WHY WE PAY OUR CORPORATE SUPER-BASTARDS THE BIG BUCKS, RIGHT?
THE PRESIDENT SAYS HE'S BECOMING CONCERNED ABOUT SETH: DID YOU KNOW THE MONSTER ACTUALLY ASKED HIM IF HE'S DECIDED ON A RUNNING MATE FOR 2004 YET?
WELL, YOU KNOW MY RECOMMENDATION: SETH HAS ACCOMPLISHED HIS MISSION DIRECTIVES AND REQUIRES TERMINATION.
WE CAN EASILY KIDNAP ANOTHER NINETY-SEVEN POUND FARMER AND MAKE A NEW SETH IF THAT'S WHAT YOU WANT.
THIS LITTLE GIRL OF YOURS REALLY IS SOMETHING.
THE AUTHORITY'S RESIDENT VEGETARIAN BUDDHIST TURNED CARNIVOROUS SLUT.
YEAH, YEAH.
BUT THIS SETH IS INDESTRUCTIBLE, SURELY?
DOESN'T HE HAVE A THOUSAND SUPER-POWERS OR SOMETHING?
ONE THOUSAND, TWO HUNDRED AND FOUR, TO BE PRECISE, BUT REST ASSURED, GENTLEMEN--
--UNCLE SAM DOESN'T BUILD DOOMSDAY MACHINES THAT DON'T COME WITH AN "OFF" BUTTON.

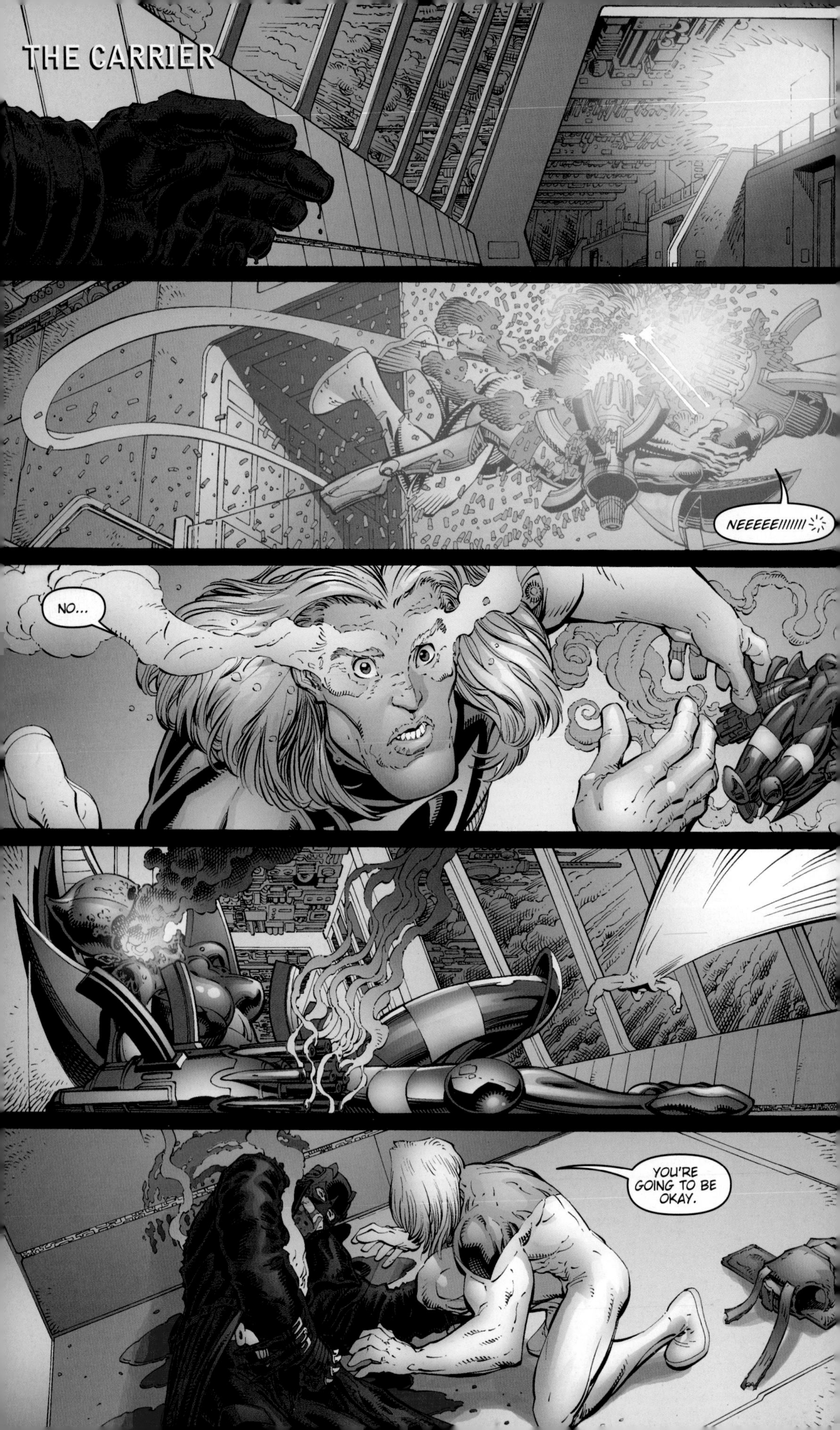
THE CARRIER
NEEEEE!!!!!!!
NO...
YOU'RE GOING TO BE OKAY.

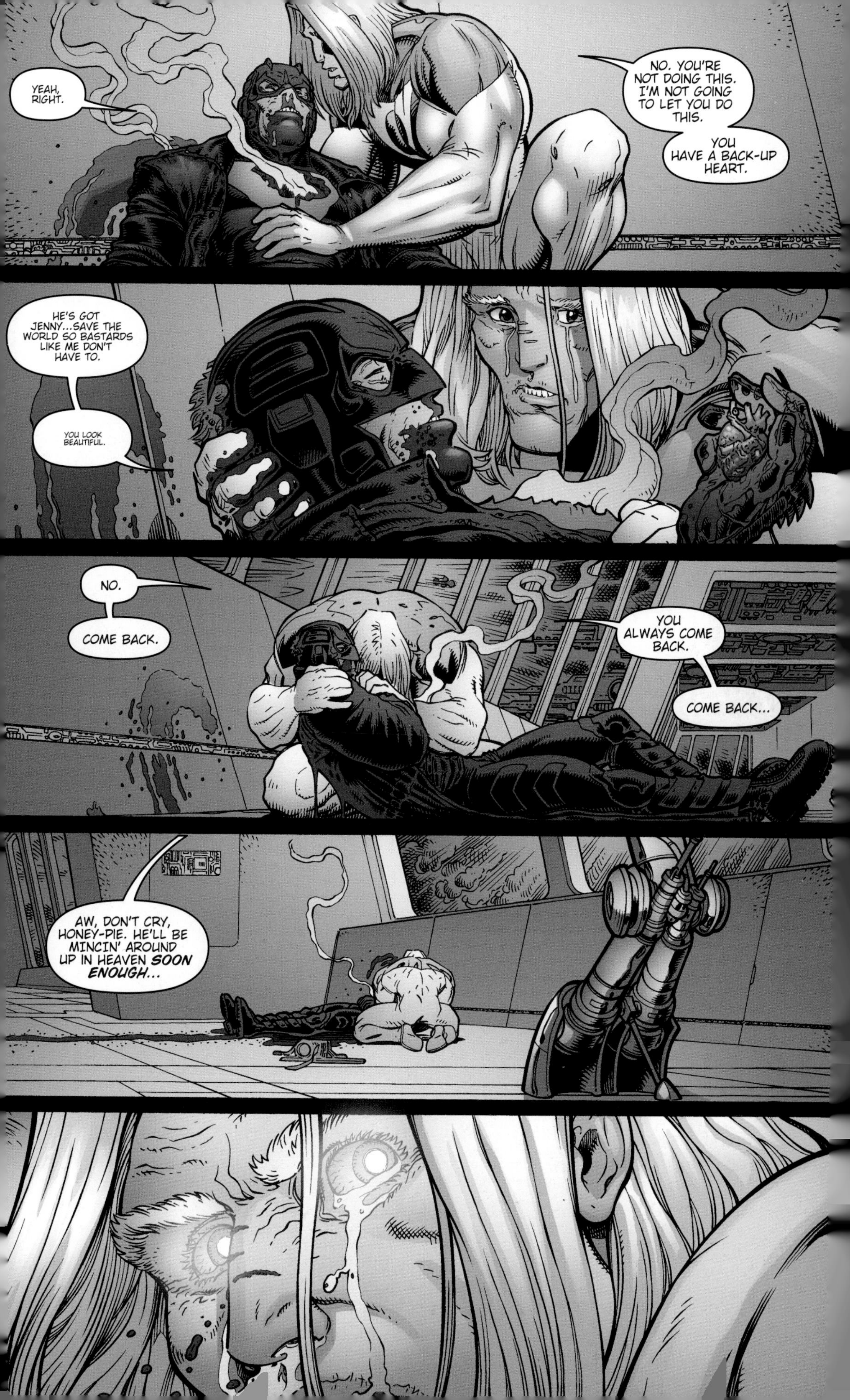
YEAH, RIGHT.
NO. YOU'RE NOT DOING THIS. I'M NOT GOING TO LET YOU DO THIS.
YOU HAVE A BACK-UP HEART.
HE'S GOT JENNY...SAVE THE WORLD SO BASTARDS LIKE ME DON'T HAVE TO.
YOU LOOK BEAUTIFUL.
NO.
COME BACK.
YOU ALWAYS COME BACK.
COME BACK...
AW, DON'T CRY, HONEY-PIE. HE'LL BE MINCIN' AROUND UP IN HEAVEN **SOON ENOUGH**...

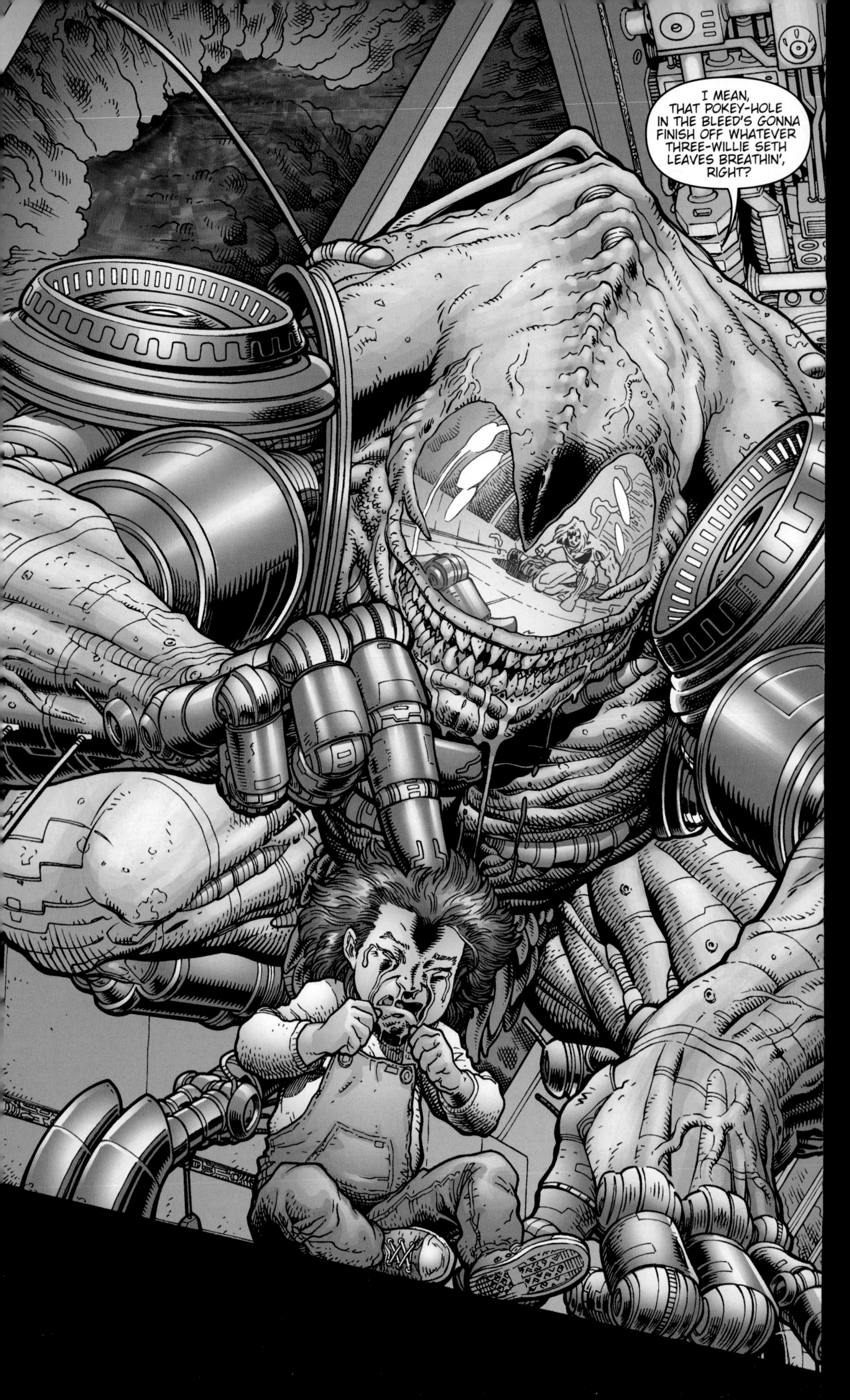
I MEAN, THAT POKEY-HOLE IN THE BLEED'S GONNA FINISH OFF WHATEVER THREE-WILLIE SETH LEAVES BREATHIN', RIGHT?

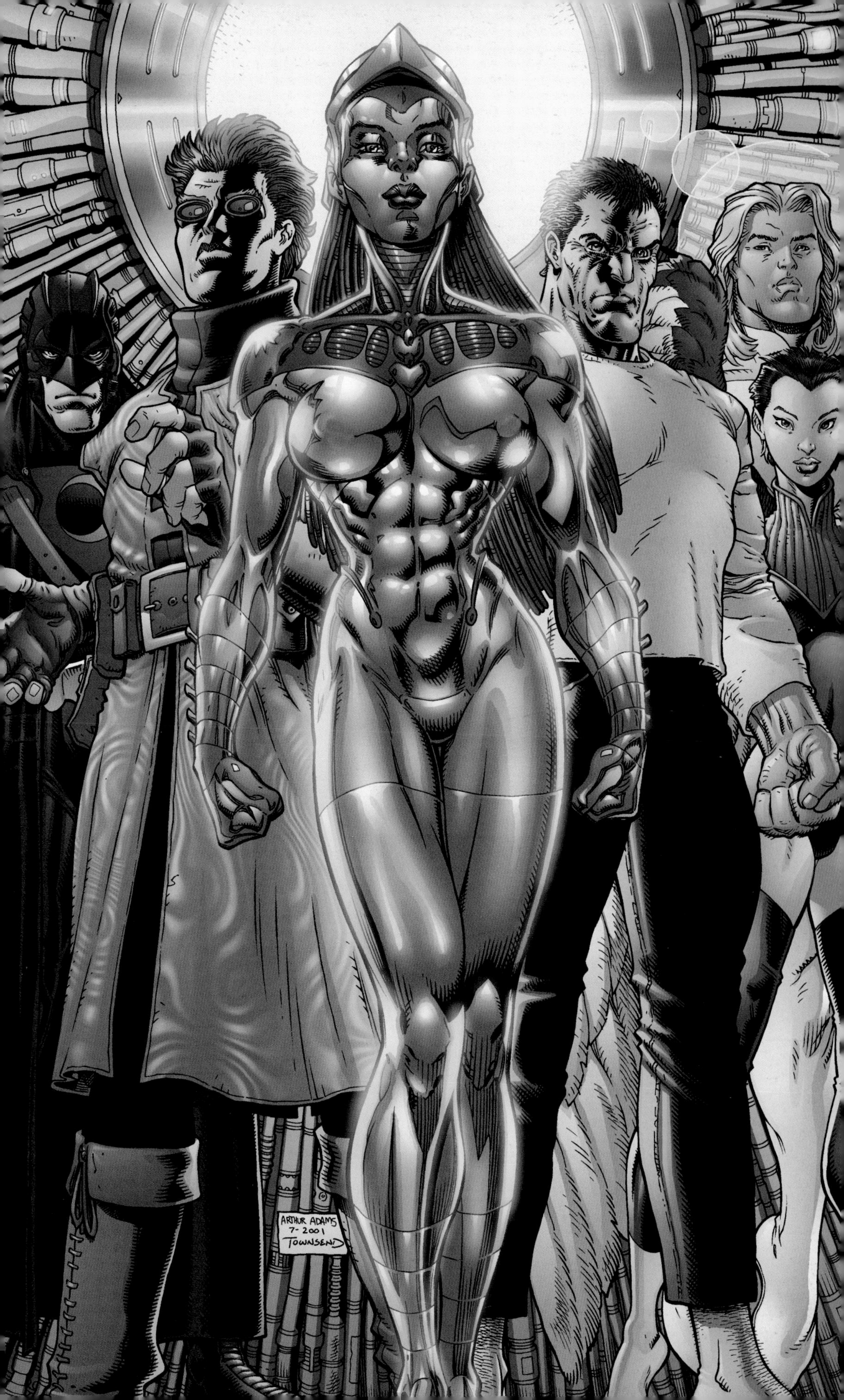
ARTHUR ADAMS
7-2001
TOWNSEND

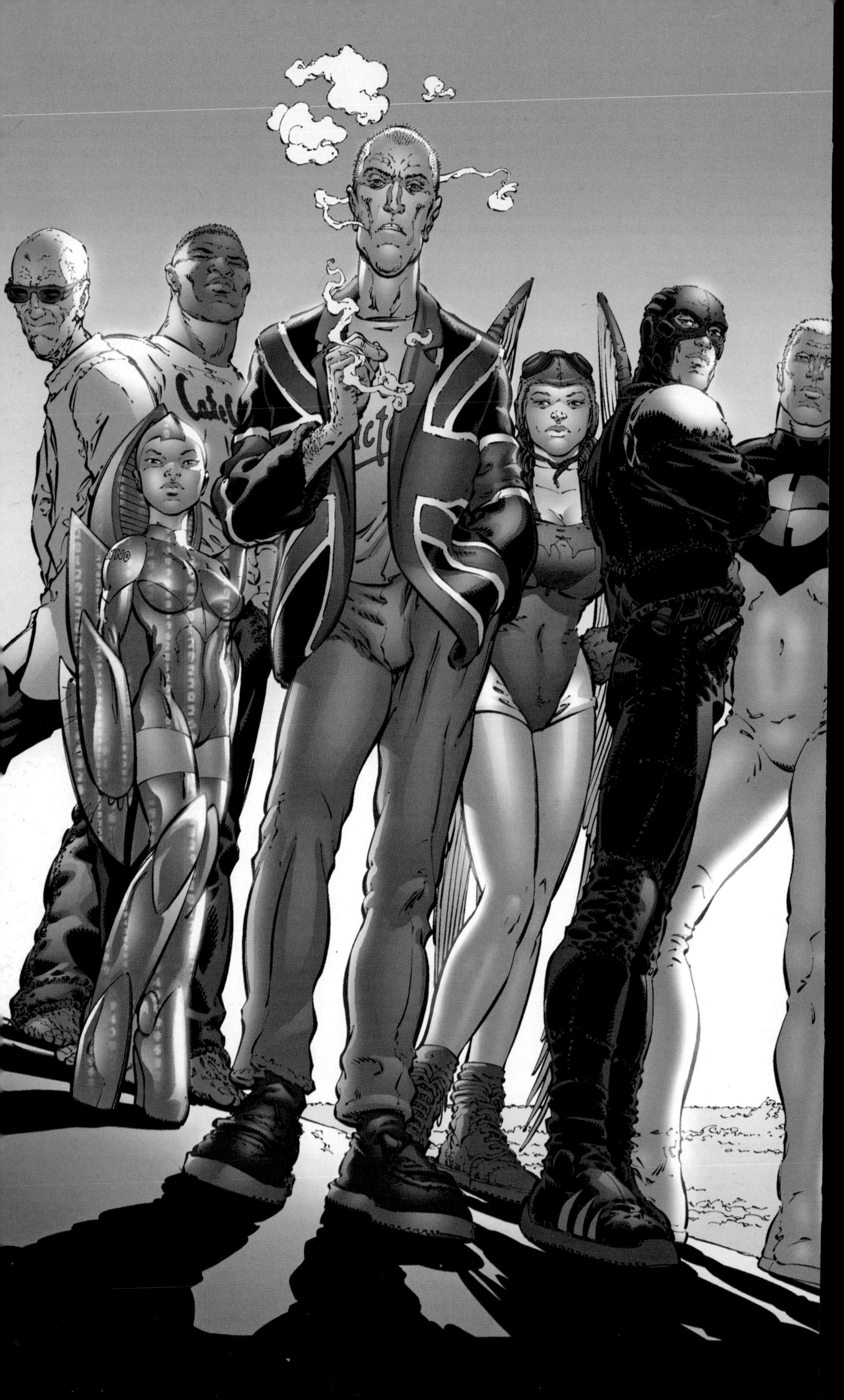

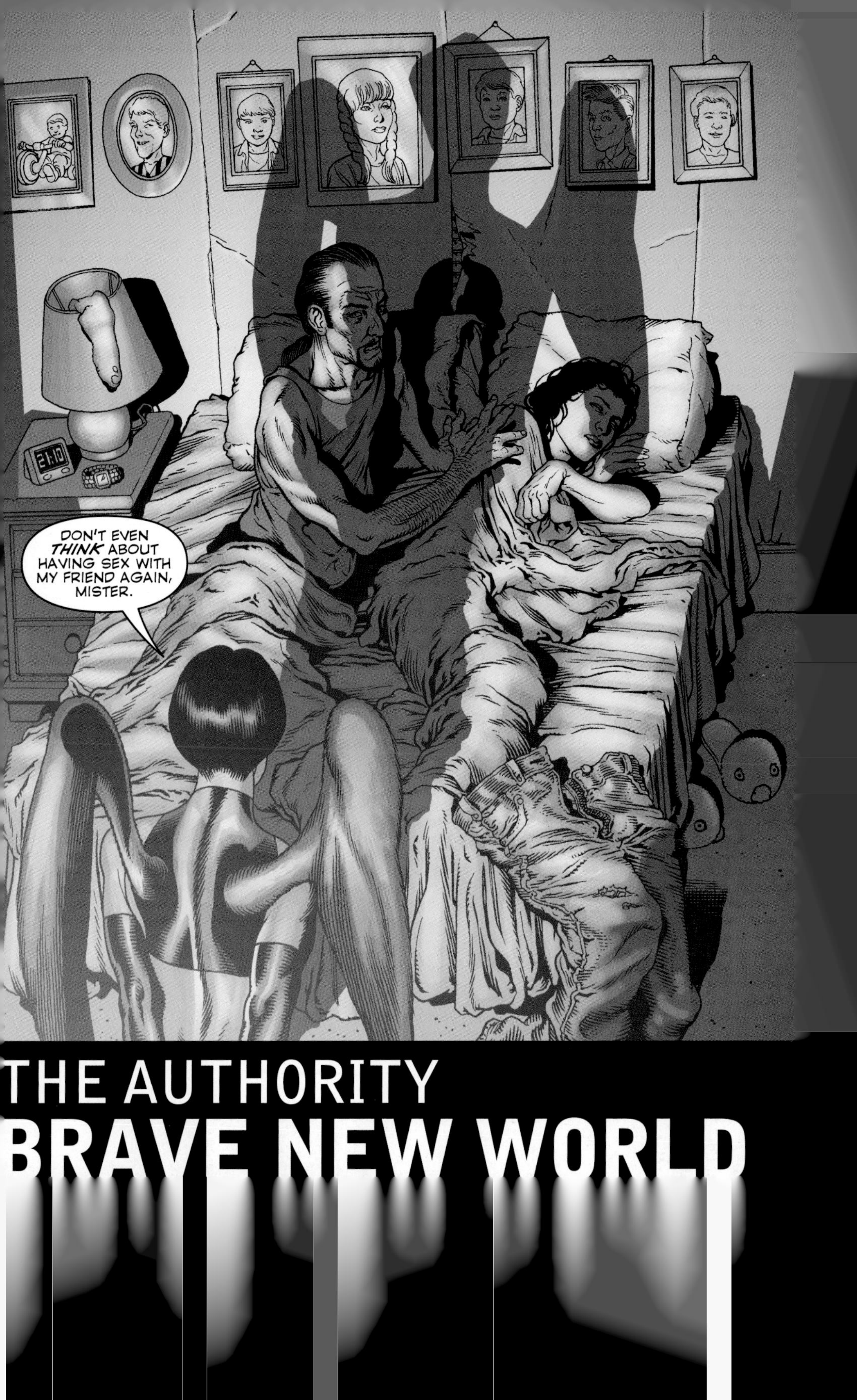
DON'T EVEN *THINK* ABOUT HAVING SEX WITH MY FRIEND AGAIN, MISTER.

THE AUTHORITY
BRAVE NEW WORLD

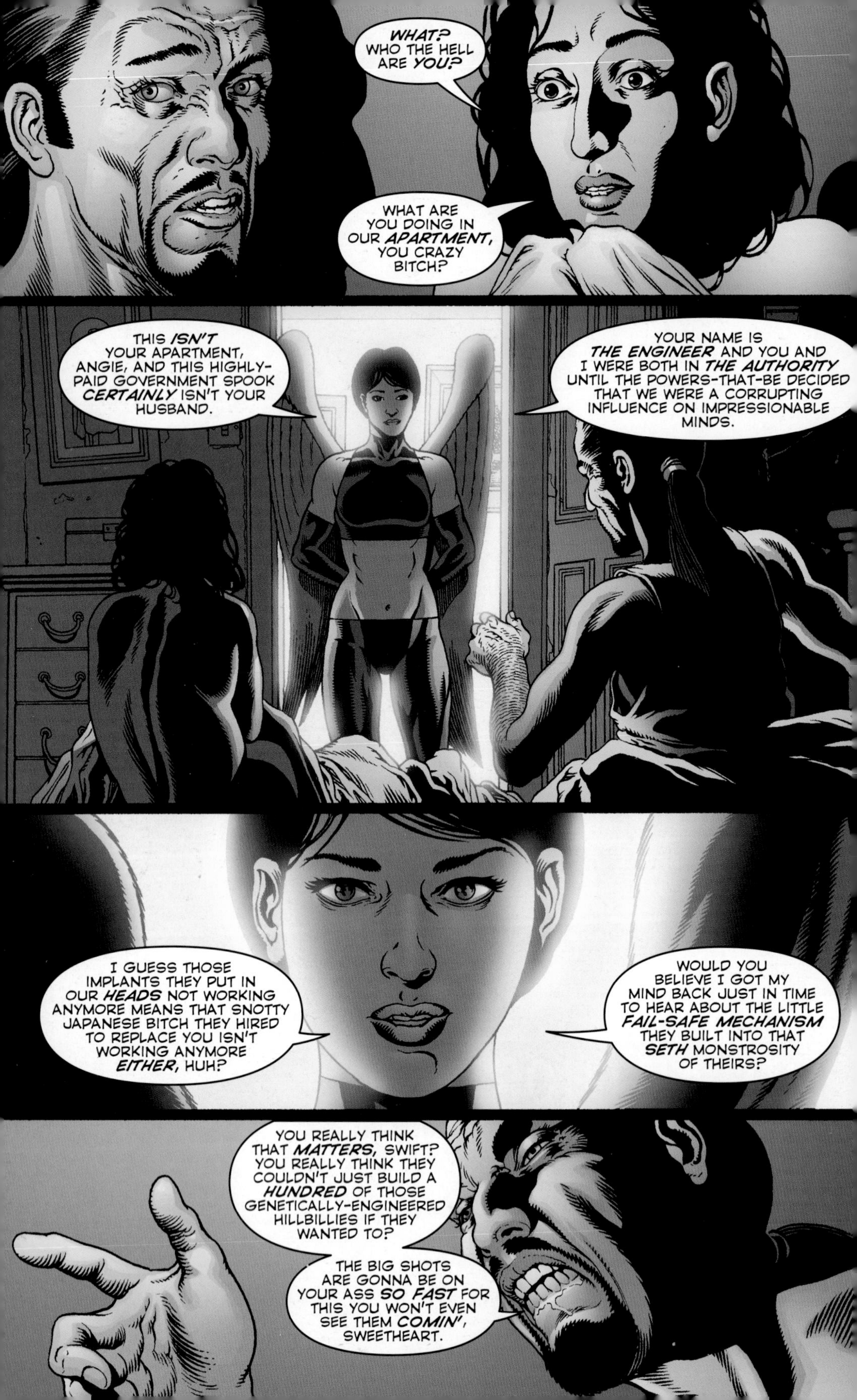

WHAT? WHO THE HELL ARE YOU?
WHAT ARE YOU DOING IN OUR APARTMENT, YOU CRAZY BITCH?
THIS ISN'T YOUR APARTMENT, ANGIE, AND THIS HIGHLY-PAID GOVERNMENT SPOOK CERTAINLY ISN'T YOUR HUSBAND.
YOUR NAME IS THE ENGINEER AND YOU AND I WERE BOTH IN THE AUTHORITY UNTIL THE POWERS-THAT-BE DECIDED THAT WE WERE A CORRUPTING INFLUENCE ON IMPRESSIONABLE MINDS.
I GUESS THOSE IMPLANTS THEY PUT IN OUR HEADS NOT WORKING ANYMORE MEANS THAT SNOTTY JAPANESE BITCH THEY HIRED TO REPLACE YOU ISN'T WORKING ANYMORE EITHER, HUH?
WOULD YOU BELIEVE I GOT MY MIND BACK JUST IN TIME TO HEAR ABOUT THE LITTLE FAIL-SAFE MECHANISM THEY BUILT INTO THAT SETH MONSTROSITY OF THEIRS?
YOU REALLY THINK THAT MATTERS, SWIFT? YOU REALLY THINK THEY COULDN'T JUST BUILD A HUNDRED OF THOSE GENETICALLY-ENGINEERED HILLBILLIES IF THEY WANTED TO?
THE BIG SHOTS ARE GONNA BE ON YOUR ASS SO FAST FOR THIS YOU WON'T EVEN SEE THEM COMIN', SWEETHEART.

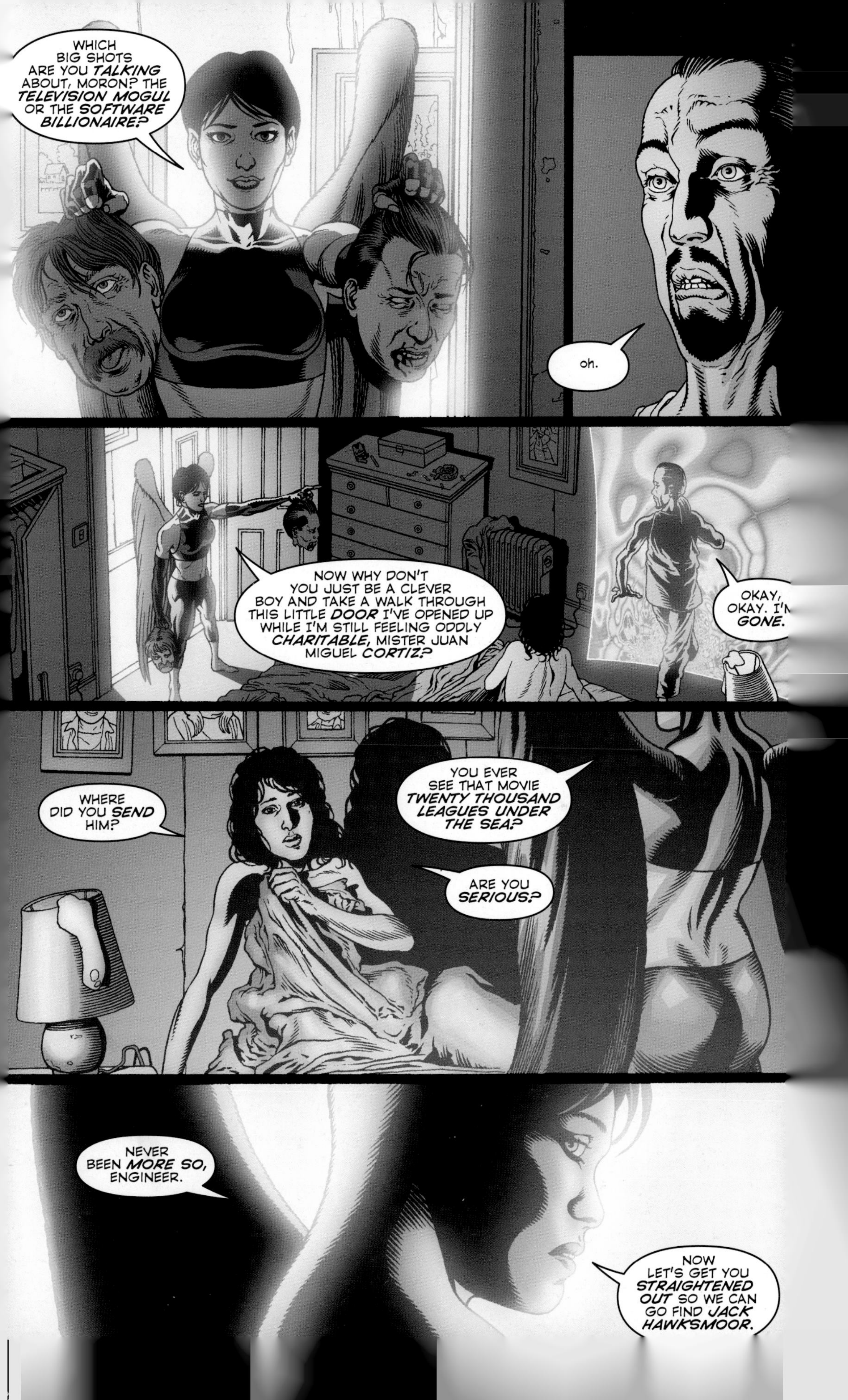
WHICH BIG SHOTS ARE YOU TALKING ABOUT, MORON? THE TELEVISION MOGUL OR THE SOFTWARE BILLIONAIRE?
oh.
NOW WHY DON'T YOU JUST BE A CLEVER BOY AND TAKE A WALK THROUGH THIS LITTLE DOOR I'VE OPENED UP WHILE I'M STILL FEELING ODDLY CHARITABLE, MISTER JUAN MIGUEL CORTIZ?
OKAY, OKAY. I'M GONE.
WHERE DID YOU SEND HIM?
YOU EVER SEE THAT MOVIE TWENTY THOUSAND LEAGUES UNDER THE SEA?
ARE YOU SERIOUS?
NEVER BEEN MORE SO, ENGINEER.
NOW LET'S GET YOU STRAIGHTENED OUT SO WE CAN GO FIND JACK HAWKSMOOR.

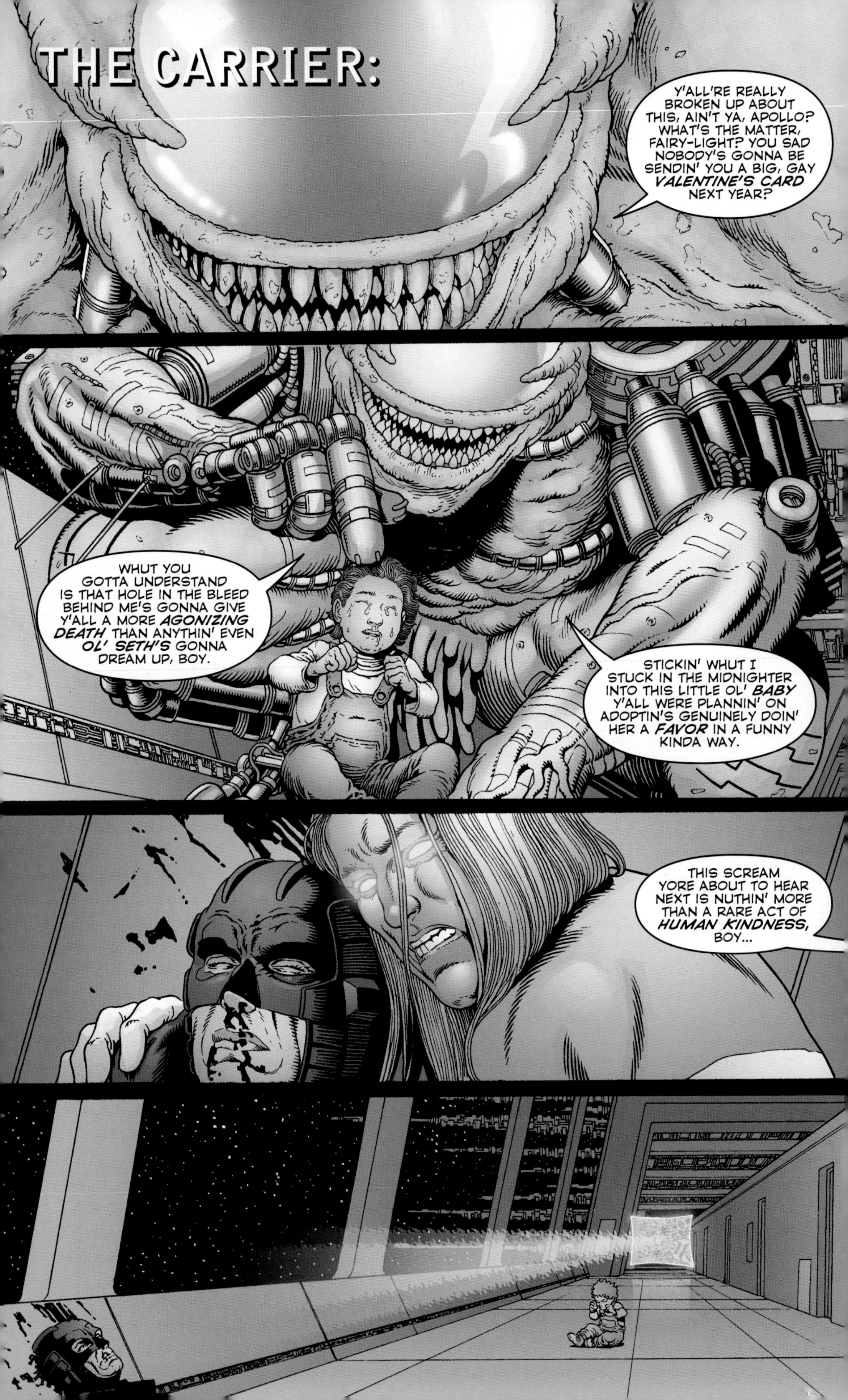
THE CARRIER:
Y'ALL'RE REALLY BROKEN UP ABOUT THIS, AIN'T YA, APOLLO? WHAT'S THE MATTER, FAIRY-LIGHT? YOU SAD NOBODY'S GONNA BE SENDIN' YOU A BIG, GAY VALENTINE'S CARD NEXT YEAR?
WHUT YOU GOTTA UNDERSTAND IS THAT HOLE IN THE BLEED BEHIND ME'S GONNA GIVE Y'ALL A MORE AGONIZING DEATH THAN ANYTHIN' EVEN OL' SETH'S GONNA DREAM UP, BOY.
STICKIN' WHUT I STUCK IN THE MIDNIGHTER INTO THIS LITTLE OL' BABY Y'ALL WERE PLANNIN' ON ADOPTIN'S GENUINELY DOIN' HER A FAVOR IN A FUNNY KINDA WAY.
THIS SCREAM YORE ABOUT TO HEAR NEXT IS NUTHIN' MORE THAN A RARE ACT OF HUMAN KINDNESS, BOY...

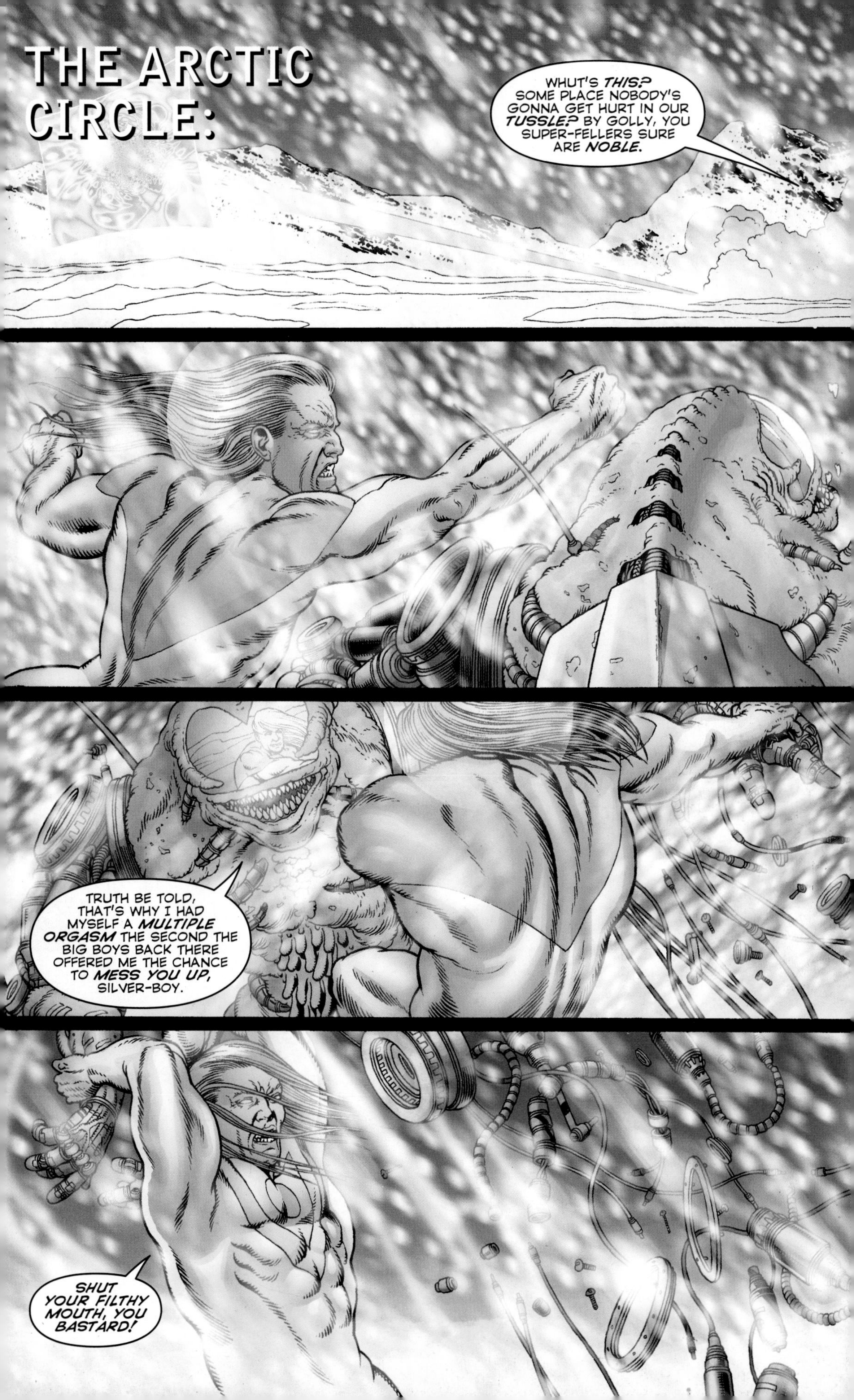

THE ARCTIC CIRCLE:
WHUT'S THIS? SOME PLACE NOBODY'S GONNA GET HURT IN OUR TUSSLE? BY GOLLY, YOU SUPER-FELLERS SURE ARE NOBLE.
TRUTH BE TOLD, THAT'S WHY I HAD MYSELF A MULTIPLE ORGASM THE SECOND THE BIG BOYS BACK THERE OFFERED ME THE CHANCE TO MESS YOU UP, SILVER-BOY.
SHUT YOUR FILTHY MOUTH, YOU BASTARD!

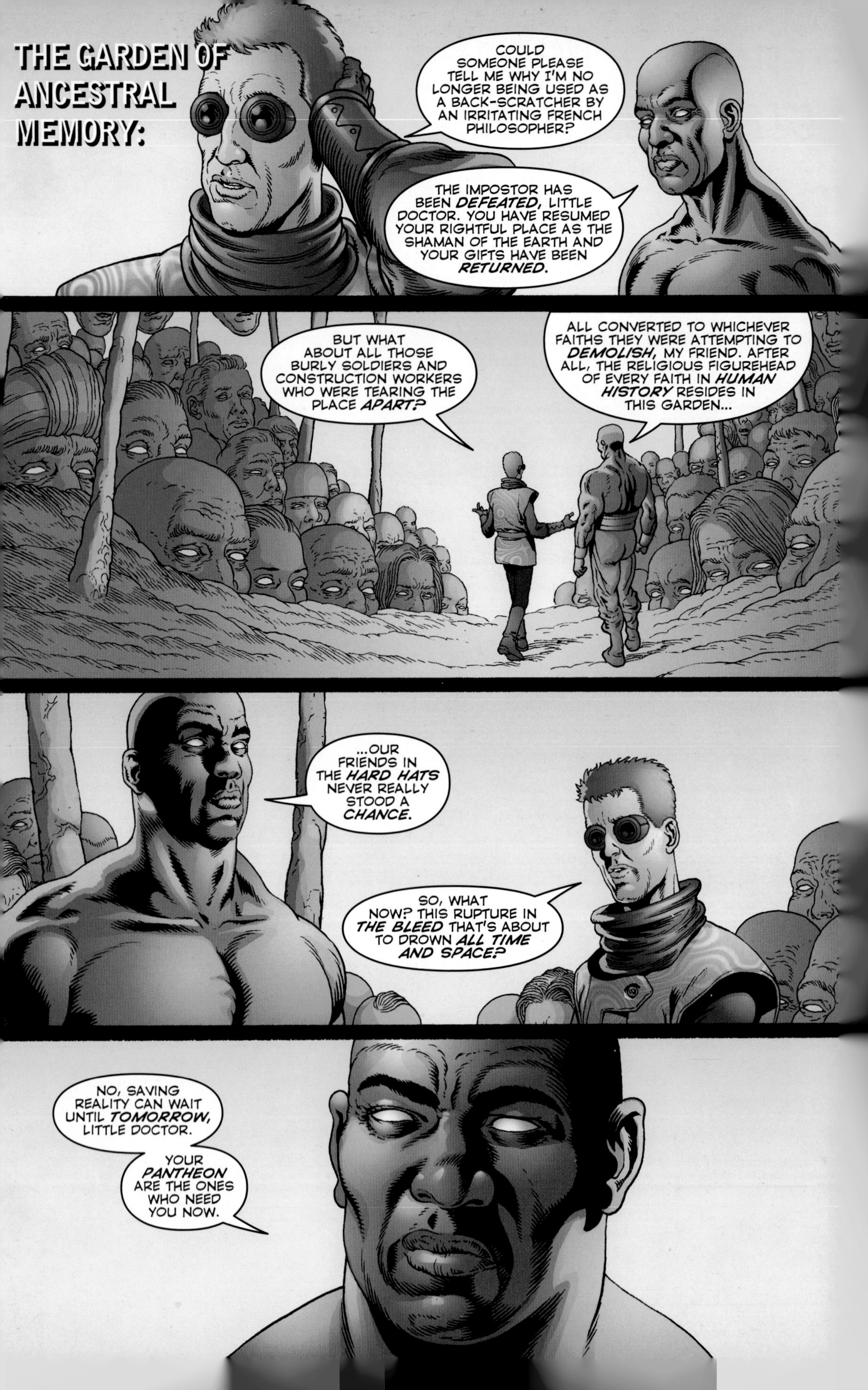
THE GARDEN OF ANCESTRAL MEMORY:
COULD SOMEONE PLEASE TELL ME WHY I'M NO LONGER BEING USED AS A BACK-SCRATCHER BY AN IRRITATING FRENCH PHILOSOPHER?
THE IMPOSTOR HAS BEEN DEFEATED, LITTLE DOCTOR. YOU HAVE RESUMED YOUR RIGHTFUL PLACE AS THE SHAMAN OF THE EARTH AND YOUR GIFTS HAVE BEEN RETURNED.
BUT WHAT ABOUT ALL THOSE BURLY SOLDIERS AND CONSTRUCTION WORKERS WHO WERE TEARING THE PLACE APART?
ALL CONVERTED TO WHICHEVER FAITHS THEY WERE ATTEMPTING TO DEMOLISH, MY FRIEND. AFTER ALL, THE RELIGIOUS FIGUREHEAD OF EVERY FAITH IN HUMAN HISTORY RESIDES IN THIS GARDEN...
...OUR FRIENDS IN THE HARD HATS NEVER REALLY STOOD A CHANCE.
SO, WHAT NOW? THIS RUPTURE IN THE BLEED THAT'S ABOUT TO DROWN ALL TIME AND SPACE?
NO, SAVING REALITY CAN WAIT UNTIL TOMORROW, LITTLE DOCTOR.
YOUR PANTHEON ARE THE ONES WHO NEED YOU NOW.

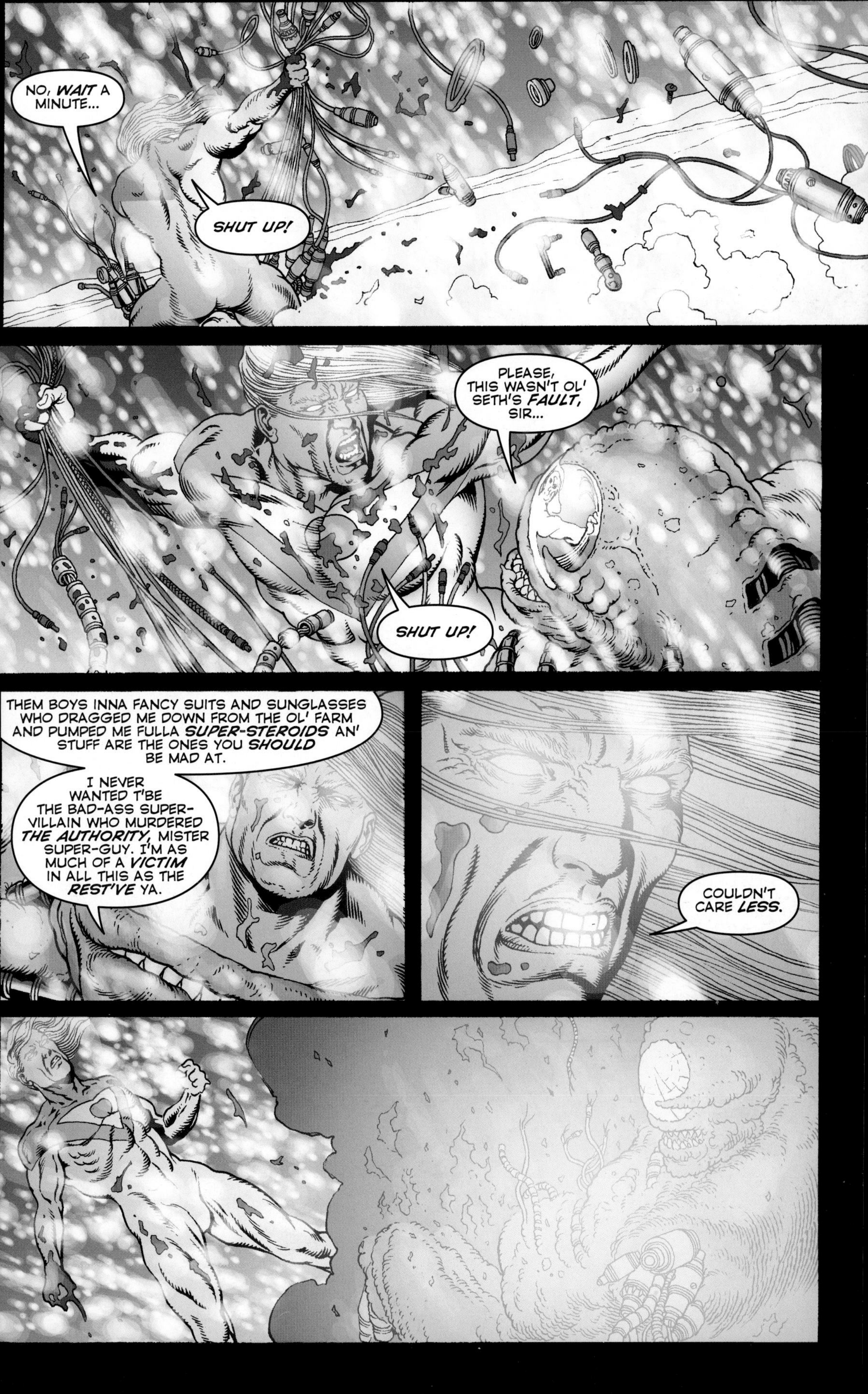
NO, *WAIT* A MINUTE...
SHUT UP!
PLEASE, THIS WASN'T OL' SETH'S *FAULT*, SIR...
SHUT UP!
THEM BOYS INNA FANCY SUITS AND SUNGLASSES WHO DRAGGED ME DOWN FROM THE OL' FARM AND PUMPED ME FULLA *SUPER-STEROIDS* AN' STUFF ARE THE ONES YOU *SHOULD* BE MAD AT.
I NEVER WANTED T'BE THE BAD-ASS SUPER-VILLAIN WHO MURDERED *THE AUTHORITY*, MISTER SUPER-GUY. I'M AS MUCH OF A *VICTIM* IN ALL THIS AS THE *REST'VE* YA.
COULDN'T CARE *LESS*.

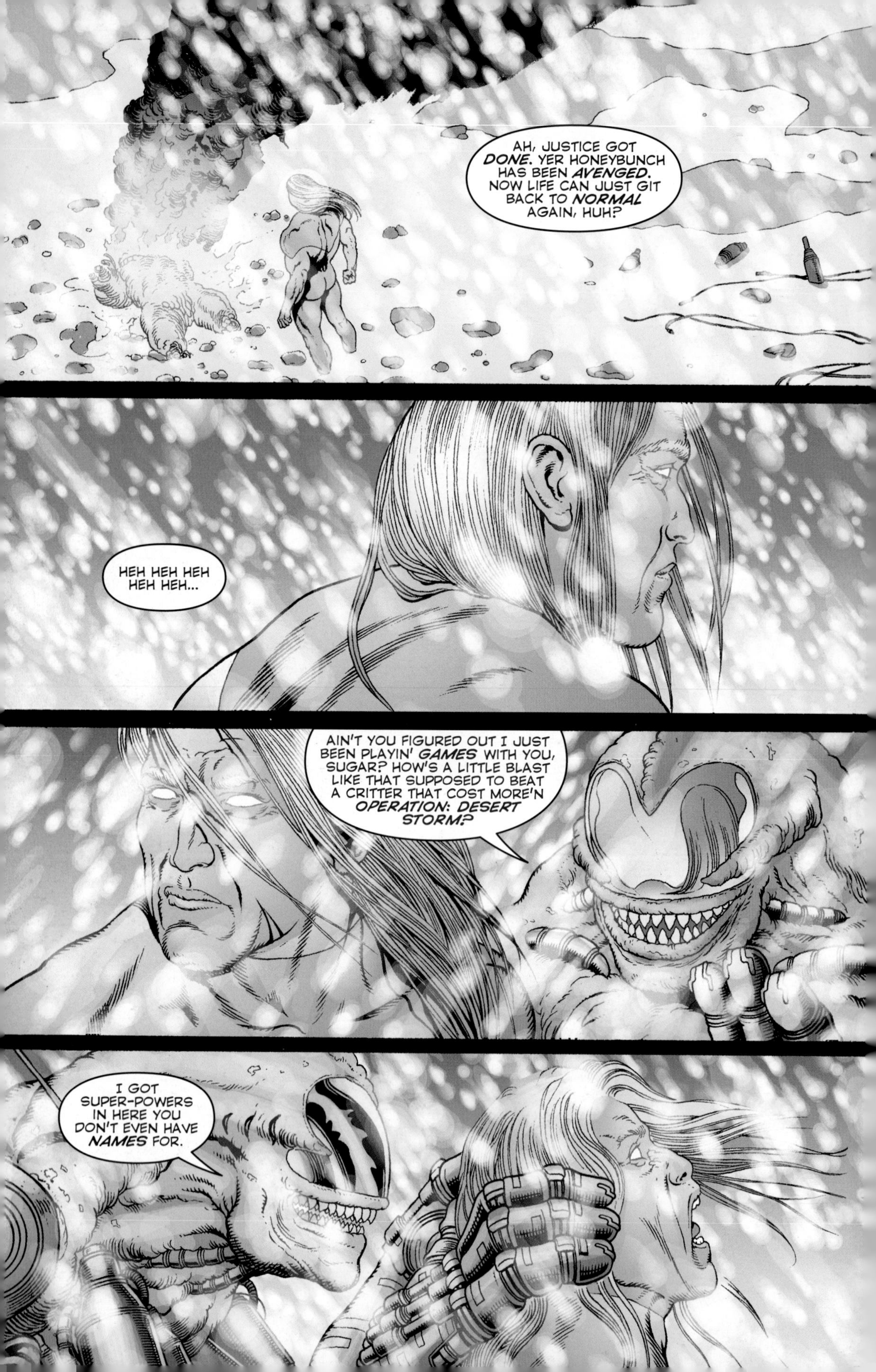
AH, JUSTICE GOT DONE. YER HONEYBUNCH HAS BEEN AVENGED. NOW LIFE CAN JUST GIT BACK TO NORMAL AGAIN, HUH?
HEH HEH HEH HEH HEH...
AIN'T YOU FIGURED OUT I JUST BEEN PLAYIN' GAMES WITH YOU, SUGAR? HOW'S A LITTLE BLAST LIKE THAT SUPPOSED TO BEAT A CRITTER THAT COST MORE'N OPERATION: DESERT STORM?
I GOT SUPER-POWERS IN HERE YOU DON'T EVEN HAVE NAMES FOR.

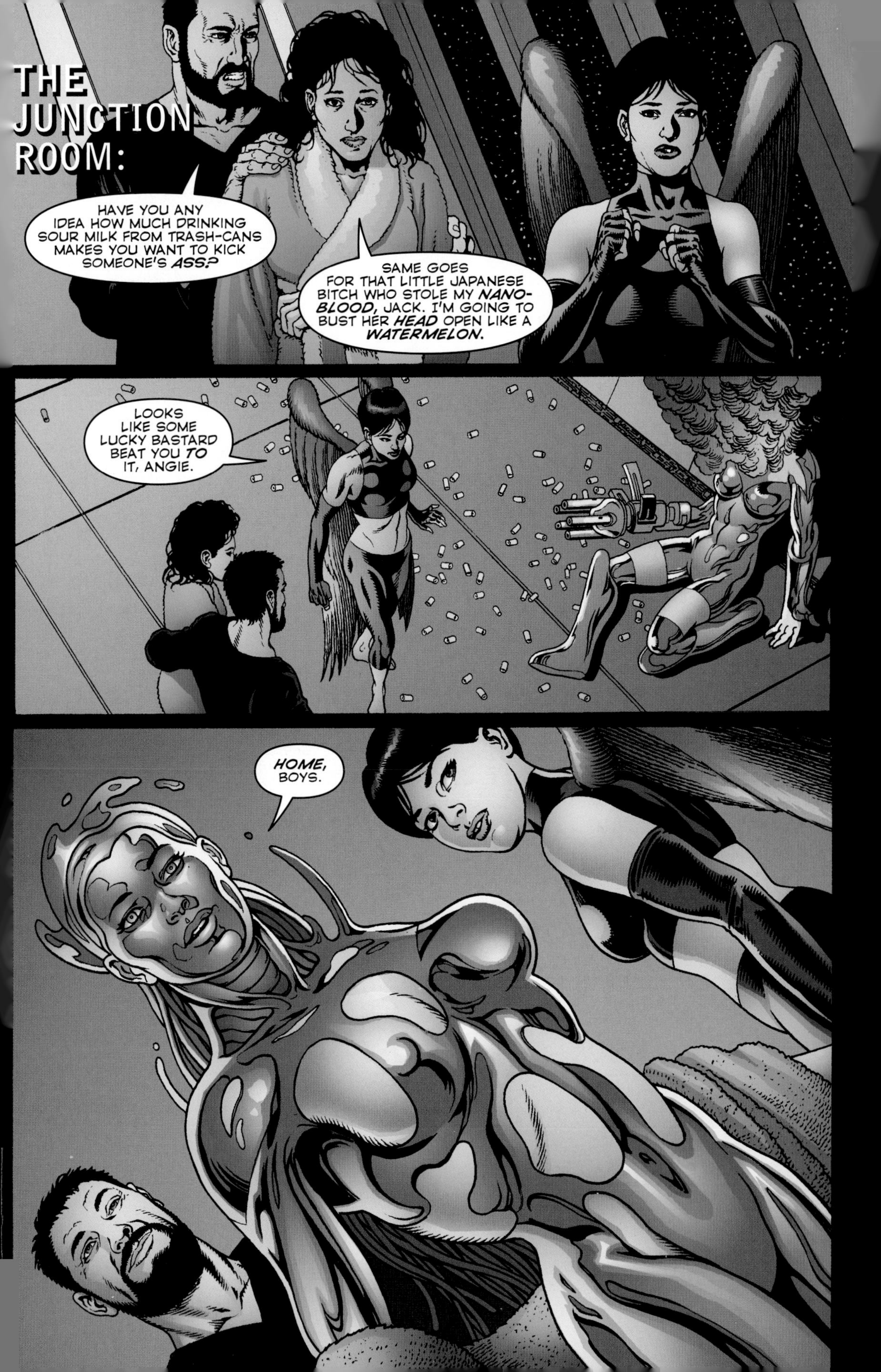
THE JUNCTION ROOM:
HAVE YOU ANY IDEA HOW MUCH DRINKING SOUR MILK FROM TRASH-CANS MAKES YOU WANT TO KICK SOMEONE'S ASS?
SAME GOES FOR THAT LITTLE JAPANESE BITCH WHO STOLE MY NANO-BLOOD, JACK. I'M GOING TO BUST HER HEAD OPEN LIKE A WATERMELON.
LOOKS LIKE SOME LUCKY BASTARD BEAT YOU TO IT, ANGIE.
HOME, BOYS.

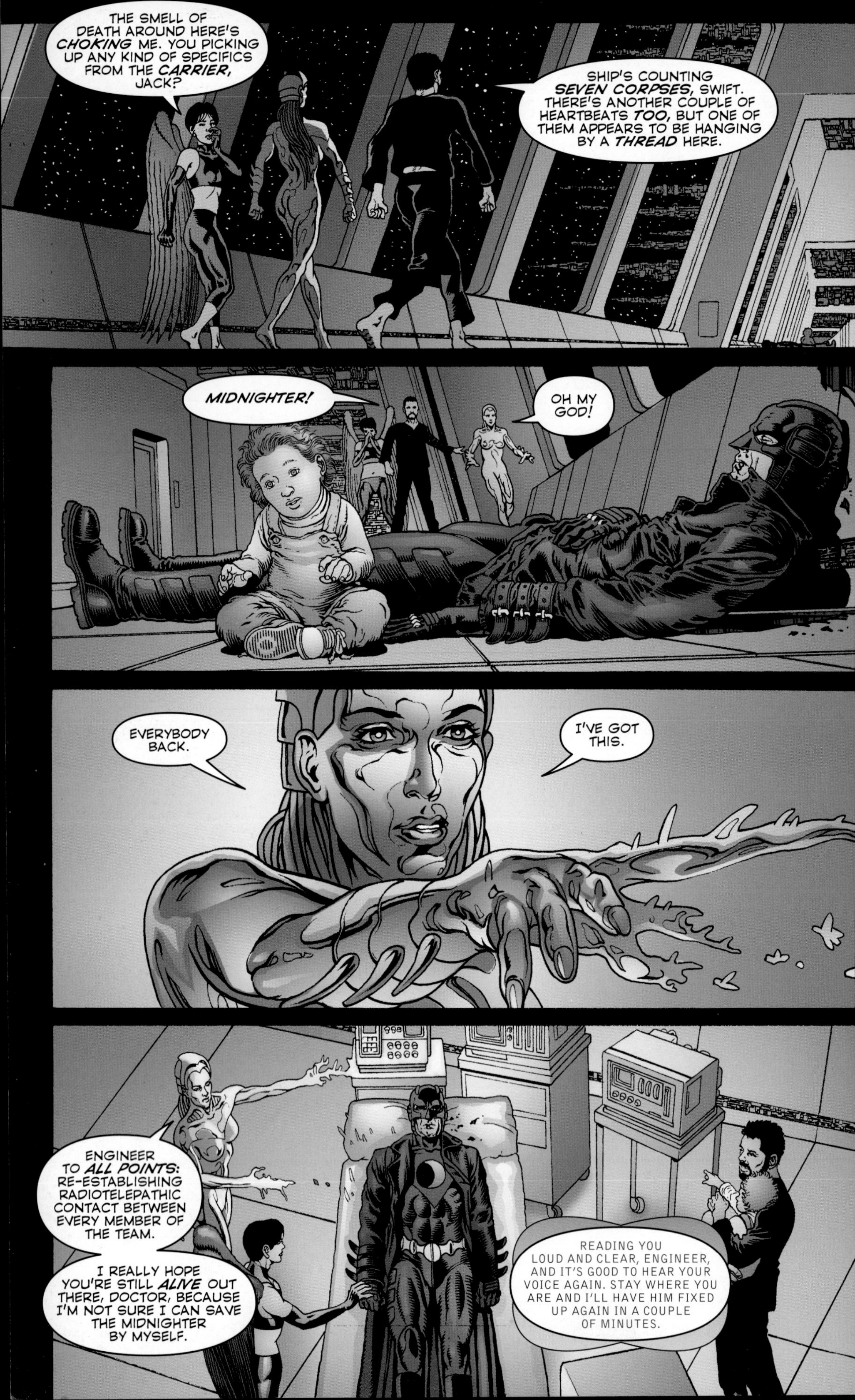
THE SMELL OF DEATH AROUND HERE'S CHOKING ME. YOU PICKING UP ANY KIND OF SPECIFICS FROM THE CARRIER, JACK?
SHIP'S COUNTING SEVEN CORPSES, SWIFT. THERE'S ANOTHER COUPLE OF HEARTBEATS TOO, BUT ONE OF THEM APPEARS TO BE HANGING BY A THREAD HERE.
MIDNIGHTER!
OH MY GOD!
EVERYBODY BACK.
I'VE GOT THIS.
ENGINEER TO ALL POINTS: RE-ESTABLISHING RADIOTELEPATHIC CONTACT BETWEEN EVERY MEMBER OF THE TEAM.
I REALLY HOPE YOU'RE STILL ALIVE OUT THERE, DOCTOR, BECAUSE I'M NOT SURE I CAN SAVE THE MIDNIGHTER BY MYSELF.
READING YOU LOUD AND CLEAR, ENGINEER, AND IT'S GOOD TO HEAR YOUR VOICE AGAIN. STAY WHERE YOU ARE AND I'LL HAVE HIM FIXED UP AGAIN IN A COUPLE OF MINUTES.

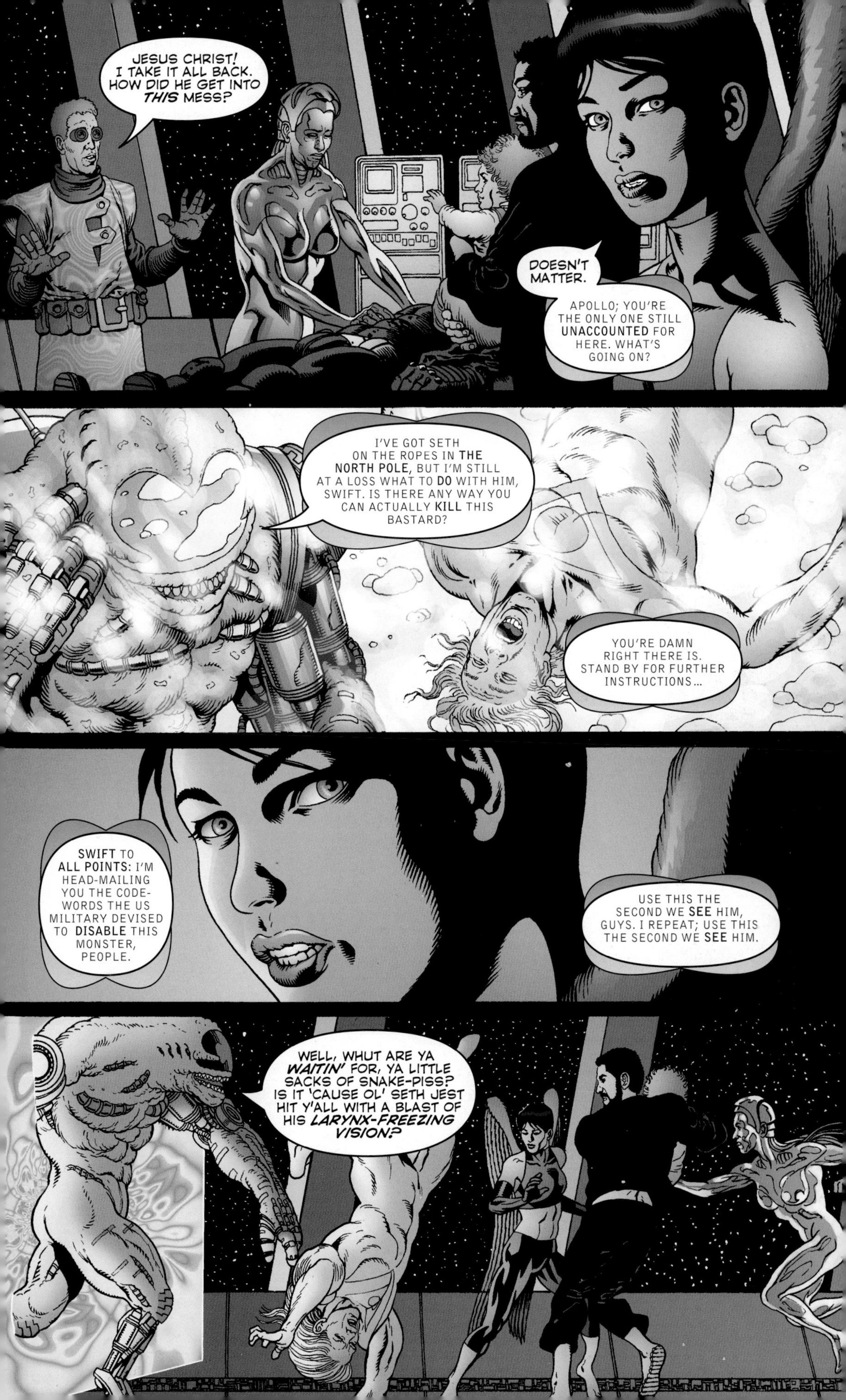
JESUS CHRIST! I TAKE IT ALL BACK. HOW DID HE GET INTO *THIS* MESS?
DOESN'T MATTER.
APOLLO; YOU'RE THE ONLY ONE STILL **UNACCOUNTED** FOR HERE. WHAT'S GOING ON?
I'VE GOT SETH ON THE ROPES IN **THE NORTH POLE**, BUT I'M STILL AT A LOSS WHAT TO **DO** WITH HIM, SWIFT. IS THERE ANY WAY YOU CAN ACTUALLY **KILL** THIS BASTARD?
YOU'RE DAMN RIGHT THERE IS. STAND BY FOR FURTHER INSTRUCTIONS...
SWIFT TO **ALL POINTS:** I'M HEAD-MAILING YOU THE CODE-WORDS THE US MILITARY DEVISED TO **DISABLE** THIS MONSTER, PEOPLE.
USE THIS THE SECOND WE **SEE** HIM, GUYS. I REPEAT; USE THIS THE SECOND WE **SEE** HIM.
WELL, WHUT ARE YA *WAITIN'* FOR, YA LITTLE SACKS OF SNAKE-PISS? IS IT 'CAUSE OL' SETH JEST HIT Y'ALL WITH A BLAST OF HIS *LARYNX-FREEZING VISION?*

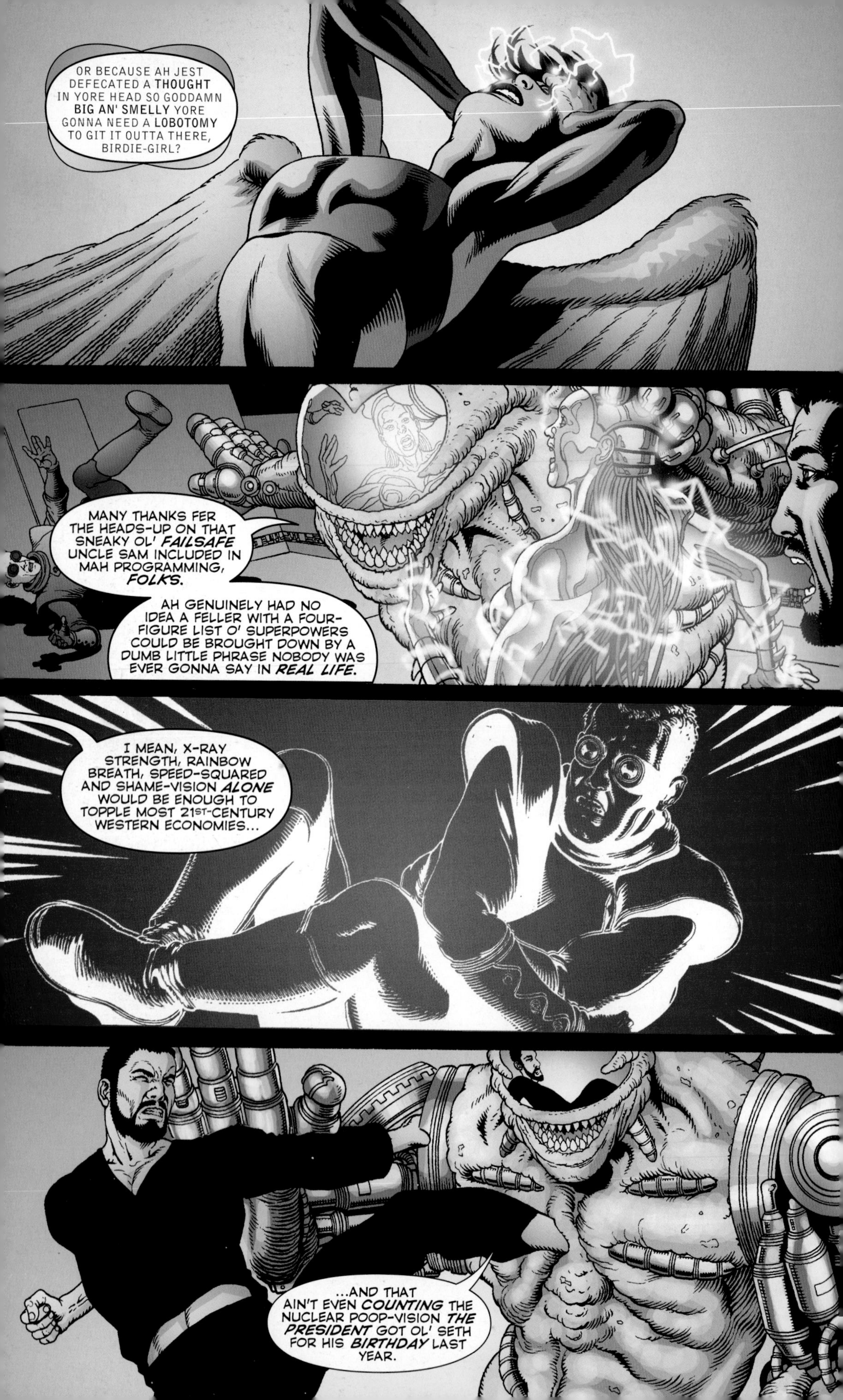
OR BECAUSE AH JEST DEFECATED A THOUGHT IN YORE HEAD SO GODDAMN BIG AN' SMELLY YORE GONNA NEED A LOBOTOMY TO GIT IT OUTTA THERE, BIRDIE-GIRL?
MANY THANKS FER THE HEADS-UP ON THAT SNEAKY OL' FAILSAFE UNCLE SAM INCLUDED IN MAH PROGRAMMING, FOLKS.
AH GENUINELY HAD NO IDEA A FELLER WITH A FOUR-FIGURE LIST O' SUPERPOWERS COULD BE BROUGHT DOWN BY A DUMB LITTLE PHRASE NOBODY WAS EVER GONNA SAY IN REAL LIFE.
I MEAN, X-RAY STRENGTH, RAINBOW BREATH, SPEED-SQUARED AND SHAME-VISION ALONE WOULD BE ENOUGH TO TOPPLE MOST 21ST-CENTURY WESTERN ECONOMIES...
...AND THAT AIN'T EVEN COUNTING THE NUCLEAR POOP-VISION THE PRESIDENT GOT OL' SETH FOR HIS BIRTHDAY LAST YEAR.

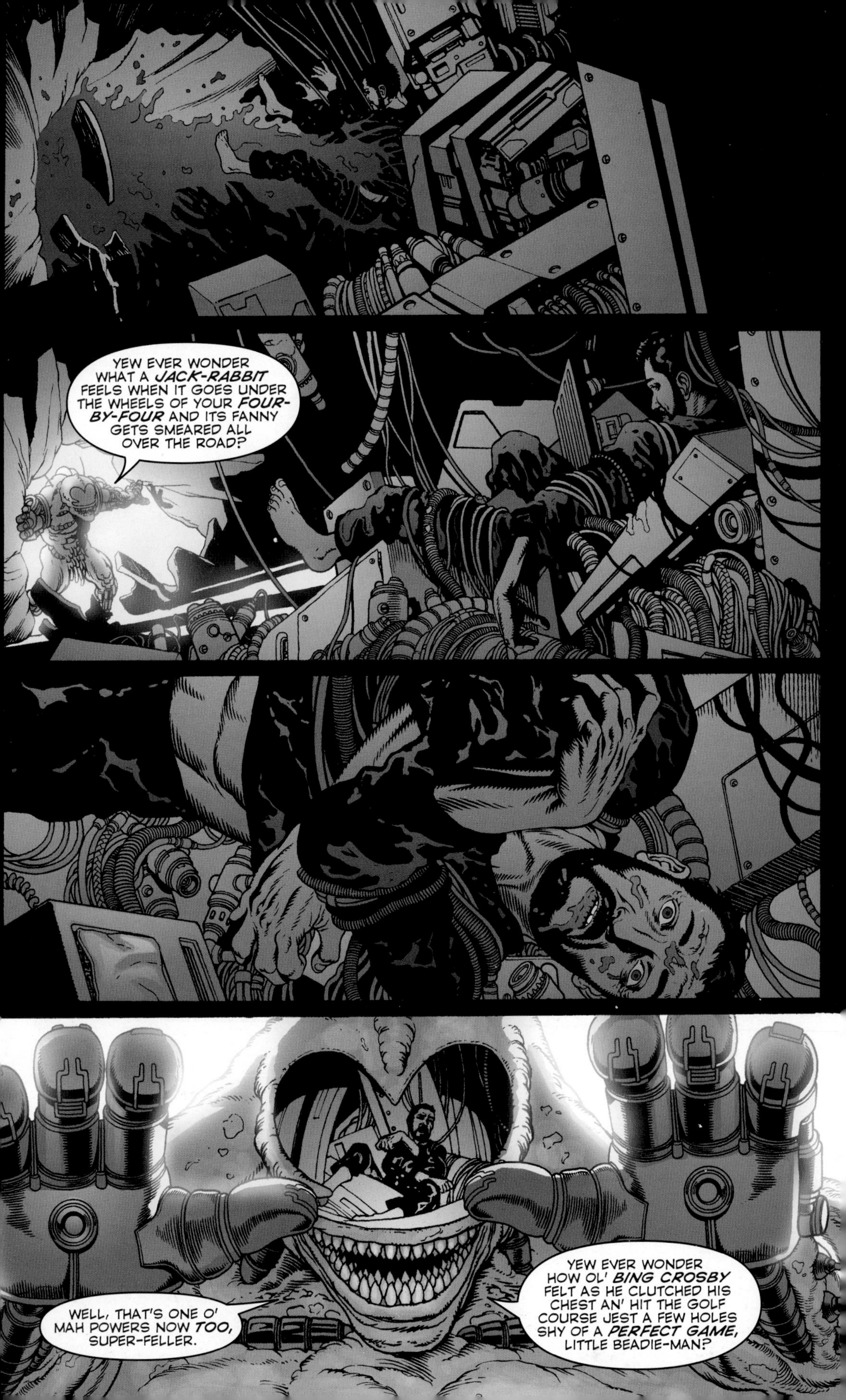
YEW EVER WONDER WHAT A JACK-RABBIT FEELS WHEN IT GOES UNDER THE WHEELS OF YOUR FOUR-BY-FOUR AND ITS FANNY GETS SMEARED ALL OVER THE ROAD?
YEW EVER WONDER HOW OL' BING CROSBY FELT AS HE CLUTCHED HIS CHEST AN' HIT THE GOLF COURSE JEST A FEW HOLES SHY OF A PERFECT GAME, LITTLE BEADIE-MAN?
WELL, THAT'S ONE O' MAH POWERS NOW TOO, SUPER-FELLER.

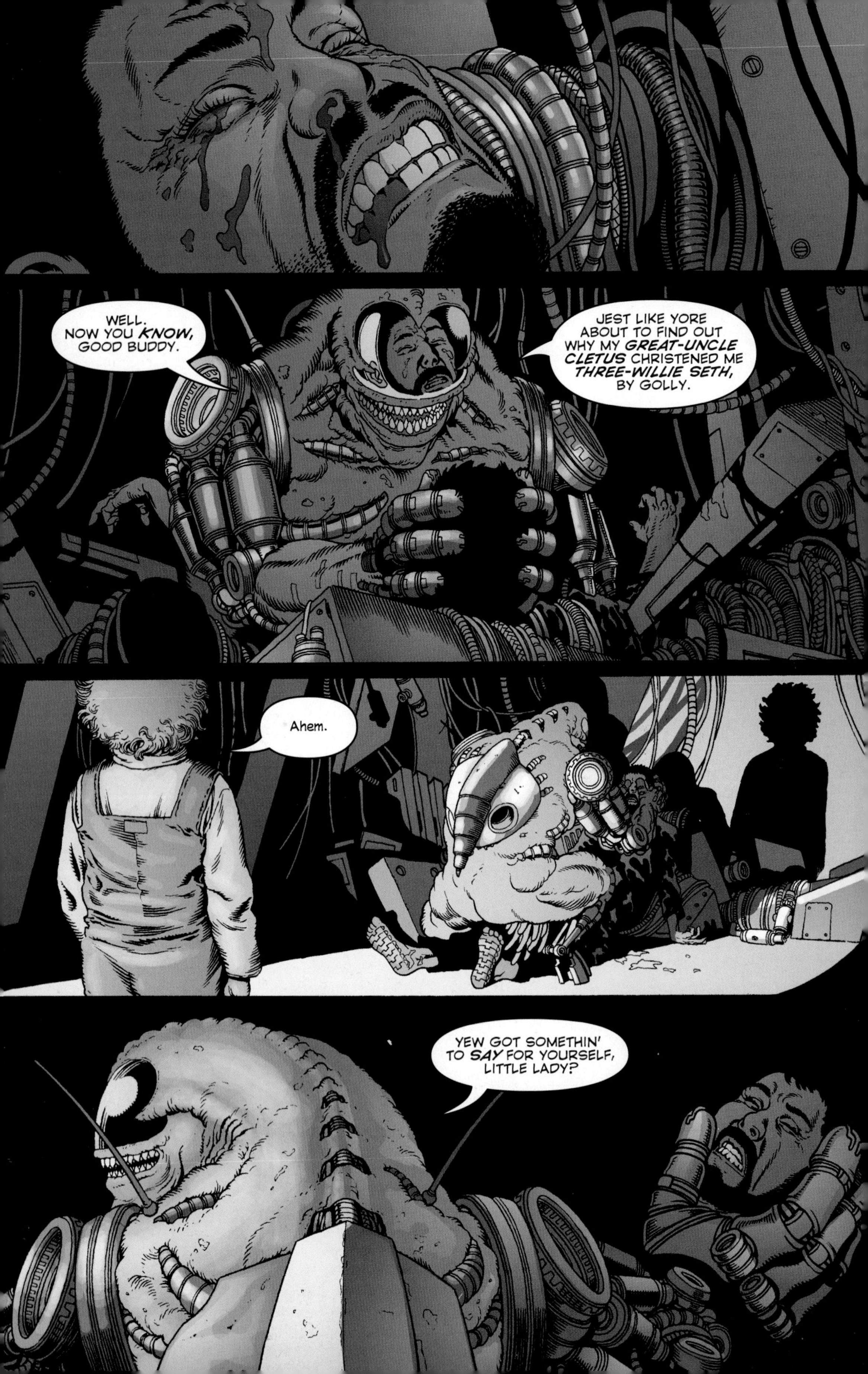
WELL. NOW YOU KNOW, GOOD BUDDY.
JEST LIKE YORE ABOUT TO FIND OUT WHY MY GREAT-UNCLE CLETUS CHRISTENED ME THREE-WILLIE SETH, BY GOLLY.
Ahem.
YEW GOT SOMETHIN' TO SAY FOR YOURSELF, LITTLE LADY?

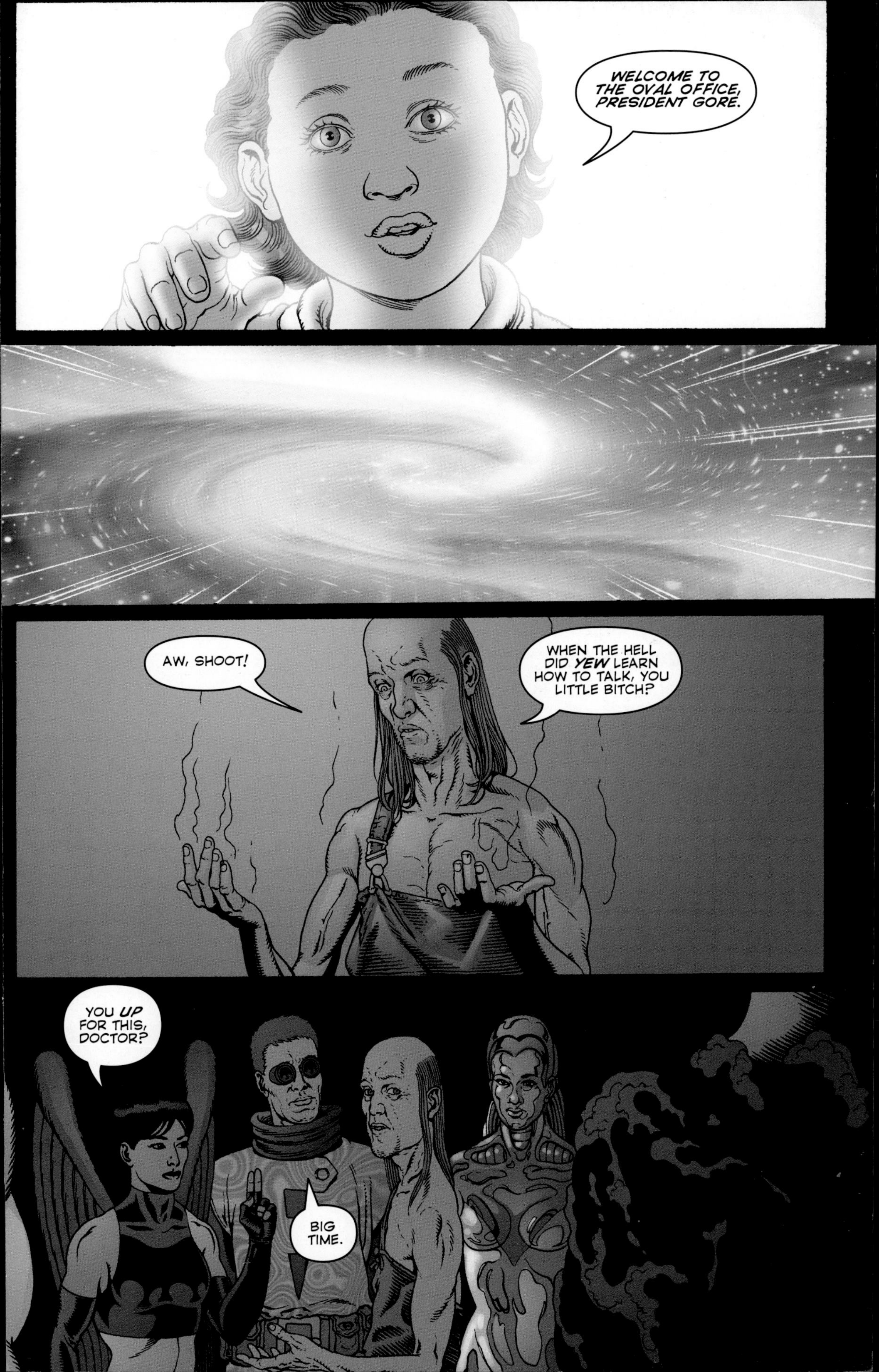
WELCOME TO THE OVAL OFFICE, PRESIDENT GORE.
AW, SHOOT!
WHEN THE HELL DID YEW LEARN HOW TO TALK, YOU LITTLE BITCH?
YOU UP FOR THIS, DOCTOR?
BIG TIME.

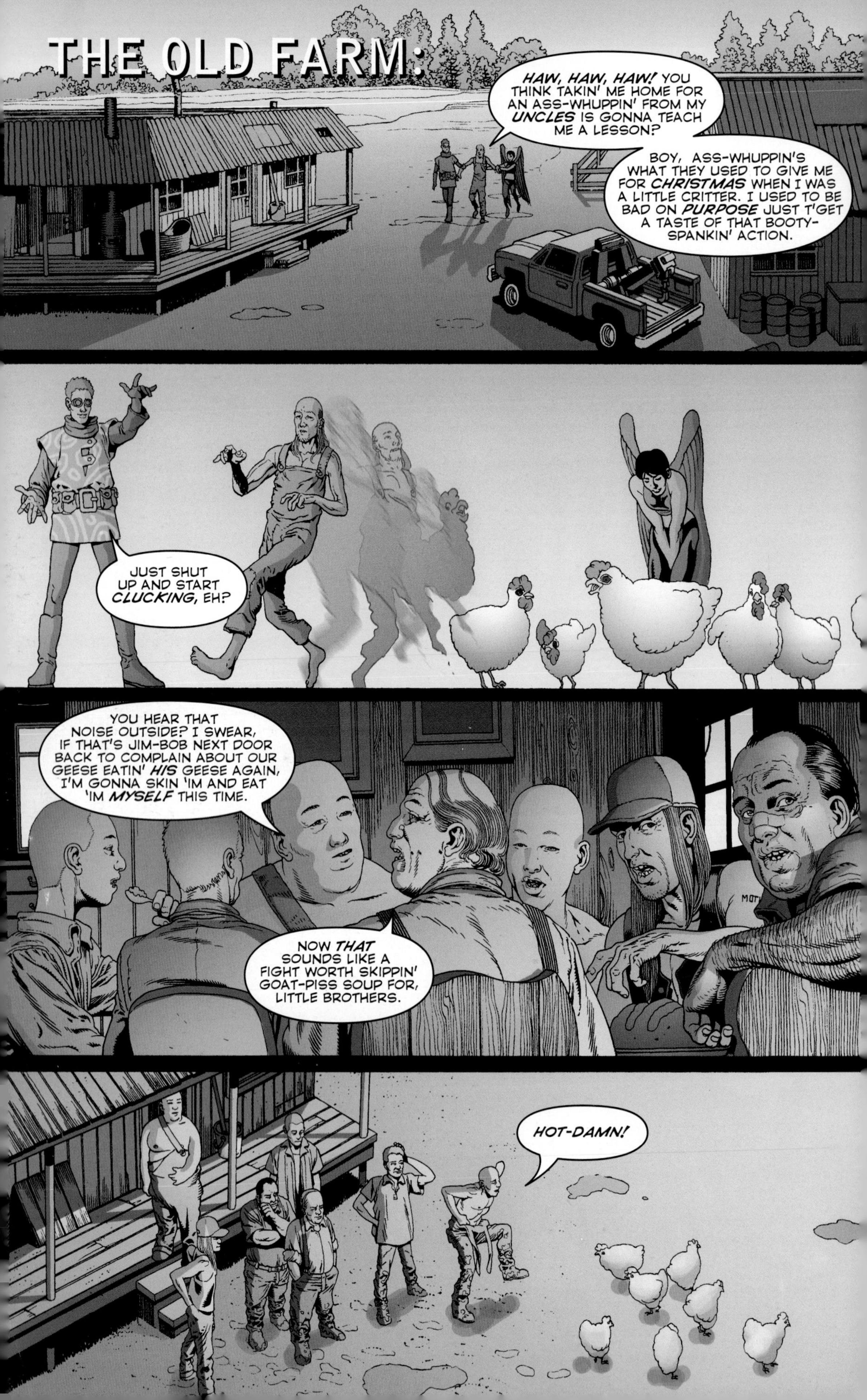
THE OLD FARM:
HAW, HAW, HAW! YOU THINK TAKIN' ME HOME FOR AN ASS-WHUPPIN' FROM MY UNCLES IS GONNA TEACH ME A LESSON?
BOY, ASS-WHUPPIN'S WHAT THEY USED TO GIVE ME FOR CHRISTMAS WHEN I WAS A LITTLE CRITTER. I USED TO BE BAD ON PURPOSE JUST T'GET A TASTE OF THAT BOOTY-SPANKIN' ACTION.
JUST SHUT UP AND START CLUCKING, EH?
YOU HEAR THAT NOISE OUTSIDE? I SWEAR, IF THAT'S JIM-BOB NEXT DOOR BACK TO COMPLAIN ABOUT OUR GEESE EATIN' HIS GEESE AGAIN, I'M GONNA SKIN 'IM AND EAT 'IM MYSELF THIS TIME.
NOW THAT SOUNDS LIKE A FIGHT WORTH SKIPPIN' GOAT-PISS SOUP FOR, LITTLE BROTHERS.
HOT-DAMN!

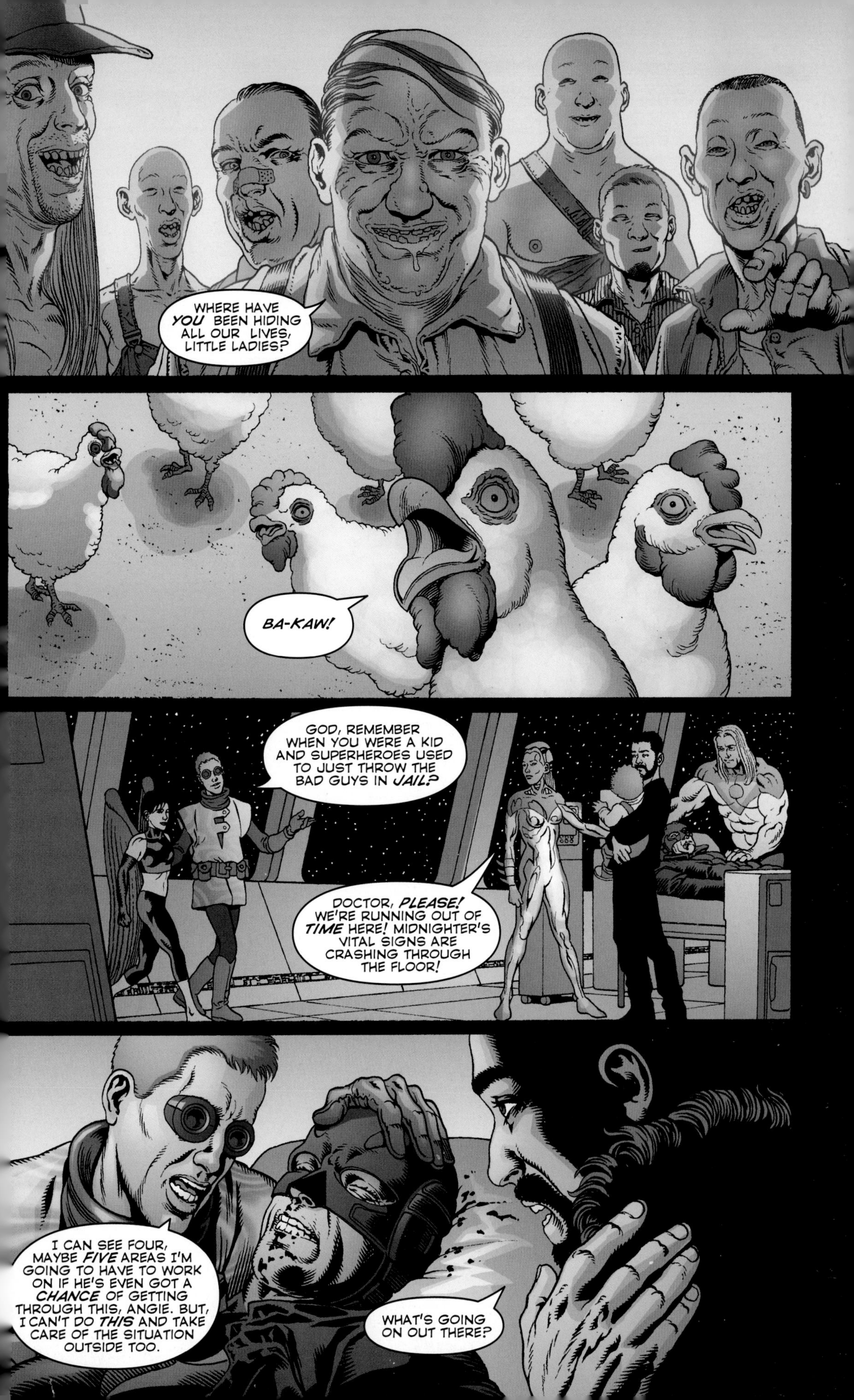
WHERE HAVE *YOU* BEEN HIDING ALL OUR LIVES, LITTLE LADIES?
BA-KAW!
GOD, REMEMBER WHEN YOU WERE A KID AND SUPERHEROES USED TO JUST THROW THE BAD GUYS IN *JAIL*?
DOCTOR, *PLEASE!* WE'RE RUNNING OUT OF *TIME* HERE! MIDNIGHTER'S VITAL SIGNS ARE CRASHING THROUGH THE FLOOR!
I CAN SEE FOUR, MAYBE *FIVE* AREAS I'M GOING TO HAVE TO WORK ON IF HE'S EVEN GOT A *CHANCE* OF GETTING THROUGH THIS, ANGIE. BUT, I CAN'T DO *THIS* AND TAKE CARE OF THE SITUATION OUTSIDE TOO.
WHAT'S GOING ON OUT THERE?

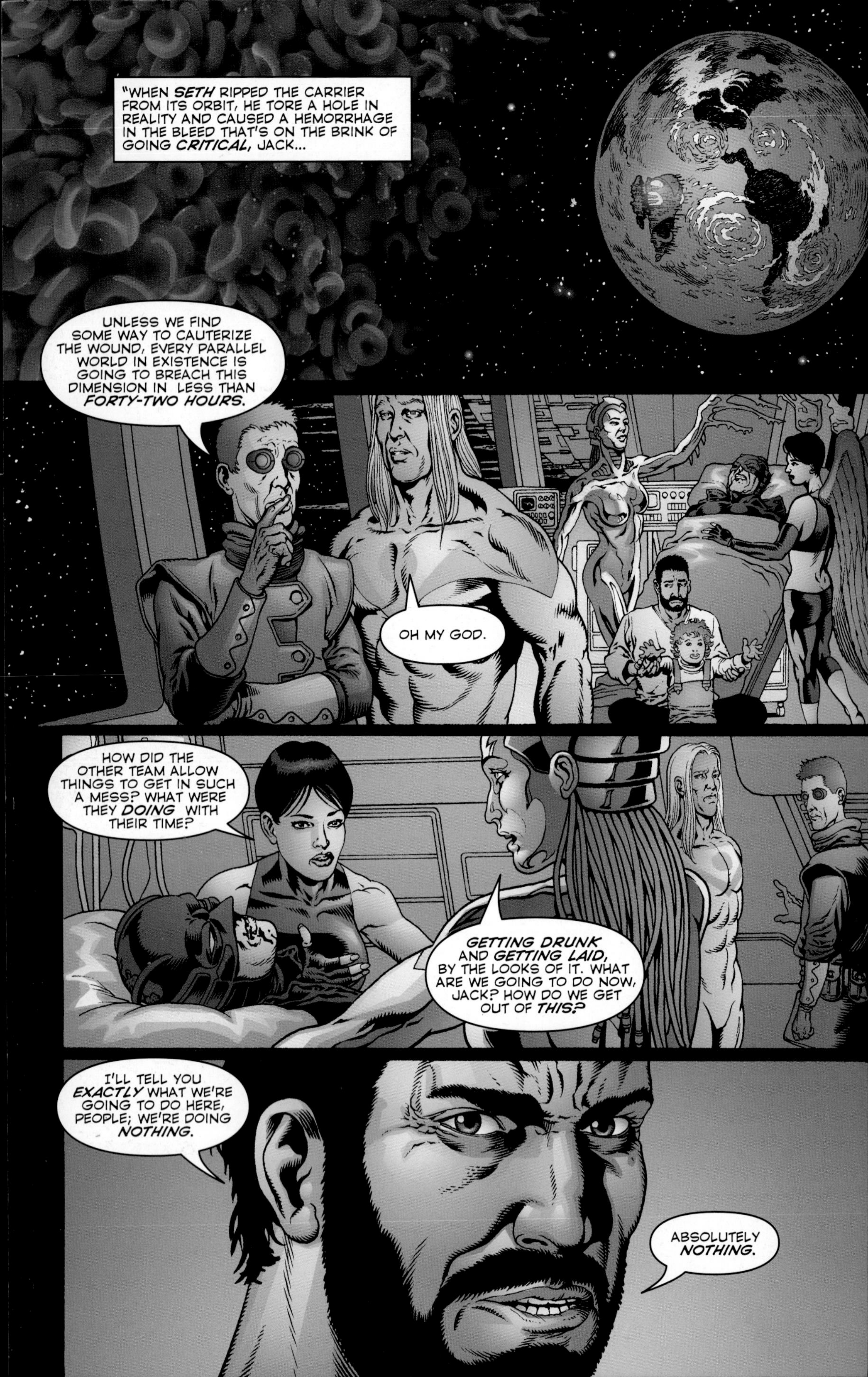
"WHEN SETH RIPPED THE CARRIER FROM ITS ORBIT, HE TORE A HOLE IN REALITY AND CAUSED A HEMORRHAGE IN THE BLEED THAT'S ON THE BRINK OF GOING CRITICAL, JACK...
UNLESS WE FIND SOME WAY TO CAUTERIZE THE WOUND, EVERY PARALLEL WORLD IN EXISTENCE IS GOING TO BREACH THIS DIMENSION IN LESS THAN FORTY-TWO HOURS.
OH MY GOD.
HOW DID THE OTHER TEAM ALLOW THINGS TO GET IN SUCH A MESS? WHAT WERE THEY DOING WITH THEIR TIME?
GETTING DRUNK AND GETTING LAID, BY THE LOOKS OF IT. WHAT ARE WE GOING TO DO NOW, JACK? HOW DO WE GET OUT OF THIS?
I'LL TELL YOU EXACTLY WHAT WE'RE GOING TO DO HERE, PEOPLE; WE'RE DOING NOTHING.
ABSOLUTELY NOTHING.

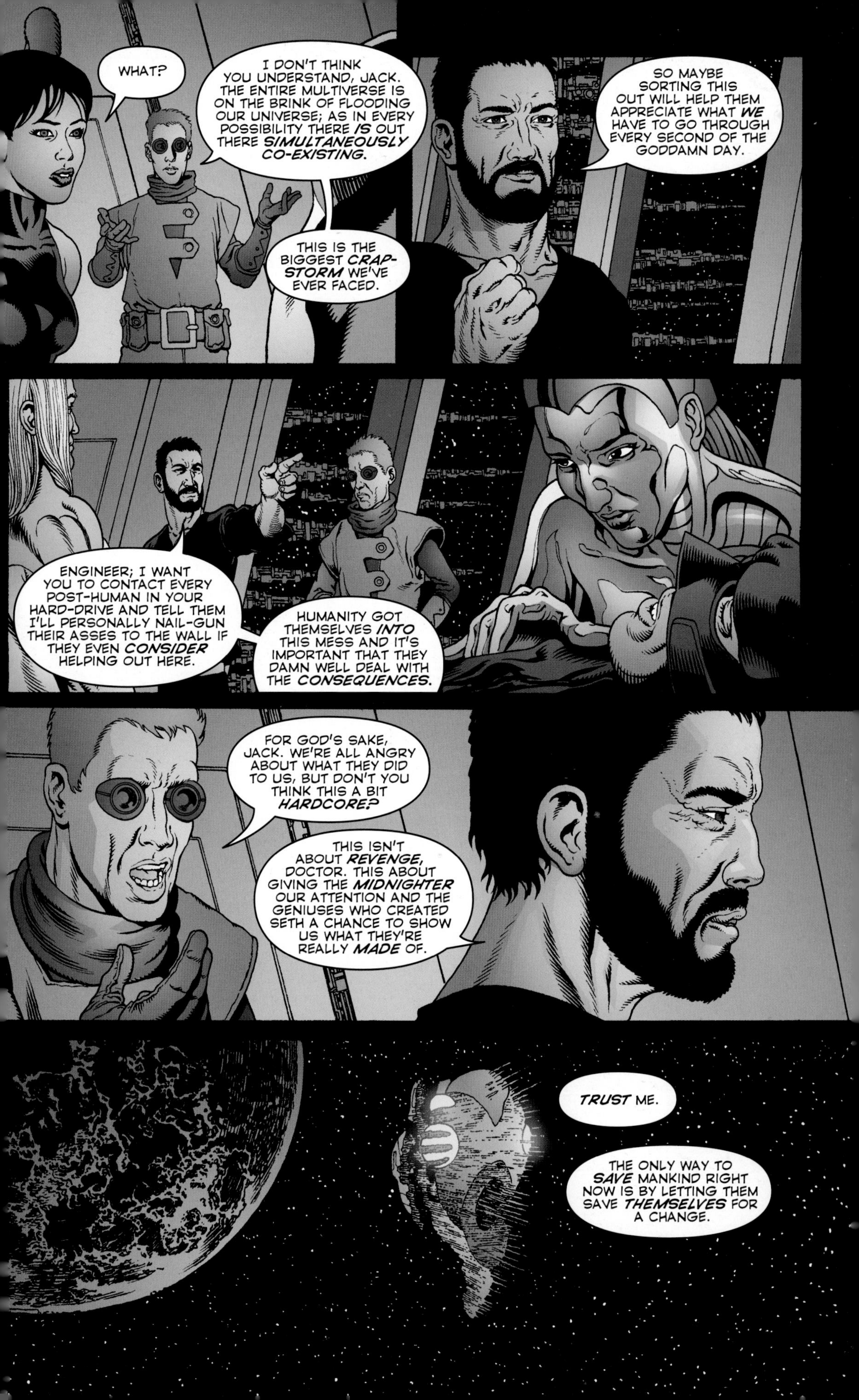
WHAT?
I DON'T THINK YOU UNDERSTAND, JACK. THE ENTIRE MULTIVERSE IS ON THE BRINK OF FLOODING OUR UNIVERSE; AS IN EVERY POSSIBILITY THERE *IS* OUT THERE *SIMULTANEOUSLY CO-EXISTING*.
THIS IS THE BIGGEST *CRAP-STORM* WE'VE EVER FACED.
SO MAYBE SORTING THIS OUT WILL HELP THEM APPRECIATE WHAT *WE* HAVE TO GO THROUGH EVERY SECOND OF THE GODDAMN DAY.
ENGINEER; I WANT YOU TO CONTACT EVERY POST-HUMAN IN YOUR HARD-DRIVE AND TELL THEM I'LL PERSONALLY NAIL-GUN THEIR ASSES TO THE WALL IF THEY EVEN *CONSIDER* HELPING OUT HERE.
HUMANITY GOT THEMSELVES *INTO* THIS MESS AND IT'S IMPORTANT THAT THEY DAMN WELL DEAL WITH THE *CONSEQUENCES*.
FOR GOD'S SAKE, JACK. WE'RE ALL ANGRY ABOUT WHAT THEY DID TO US, BUT DON'T YOU THINK THIS A BIT *HARDCORE?*
THIS ISN'T ABOUT *REVENGE,* DOCTOR. THIS ABOUT GIVING THE *MIDNIGHTER* OUR ATTENTION AND THE GENIUSES WHO CREATED SETH A CHANCE TO SHOW US WHAT THEY'RE REALLY *MADE* OF.
TRUST ME.
THE ONLY WAY TO *SAVE* MANKIND RIGHT NOW IS BY LETTING THEM SAVE *THEMSELVES* FOR A CHANGE.

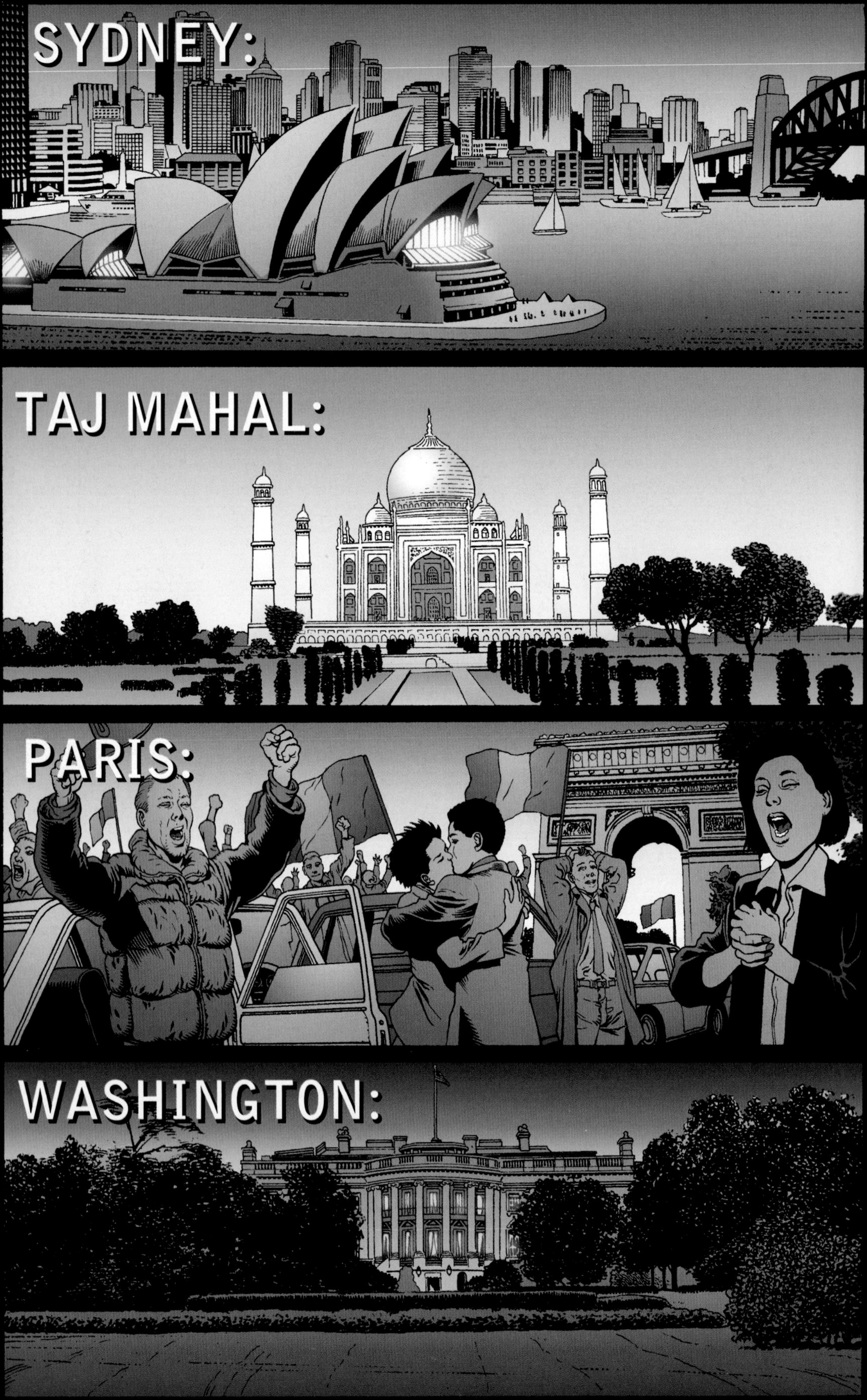
SYDNEY:
TAJ MAHAL:
PARIS:
WASHINGTON:

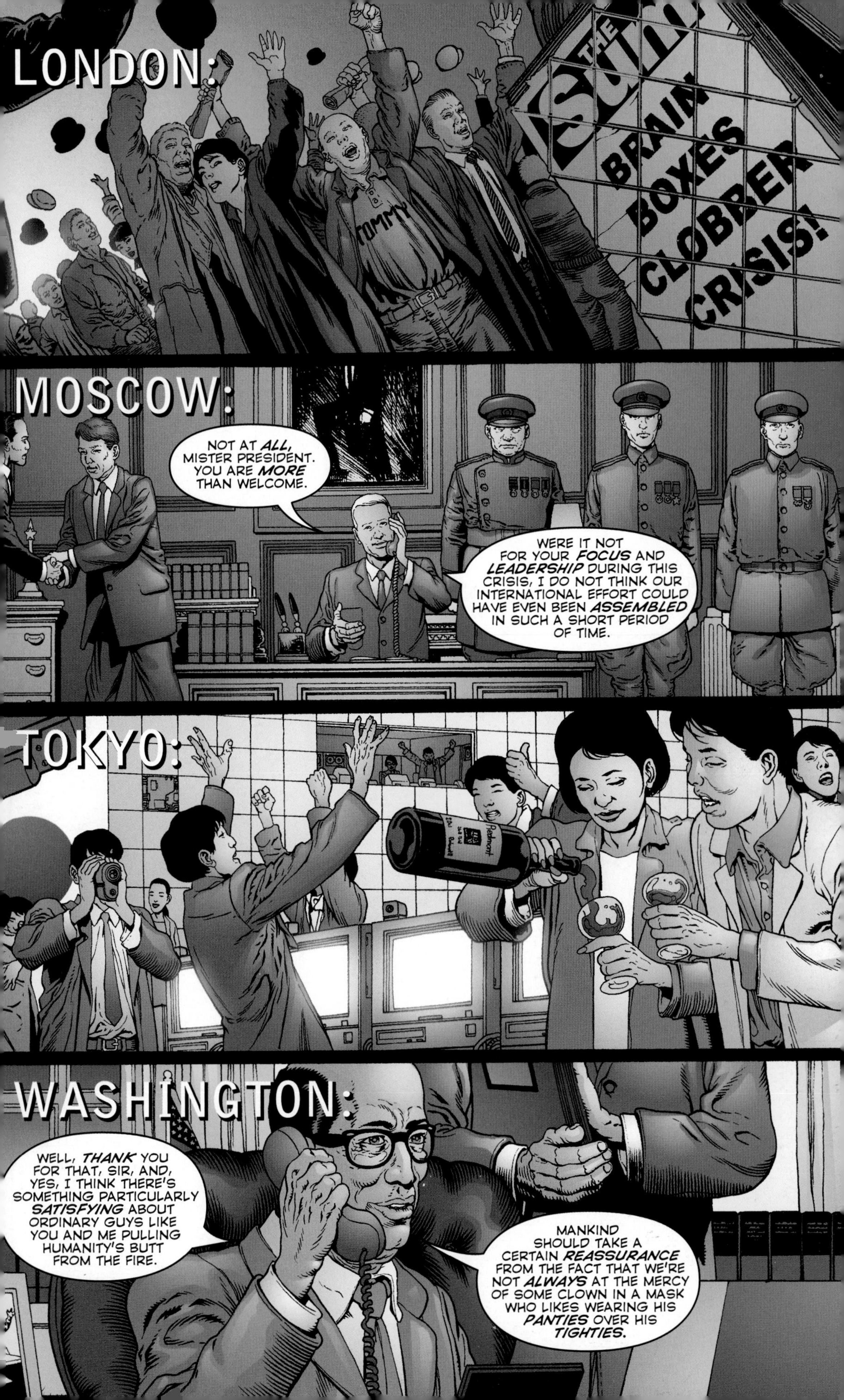
LONDON:
THE SUN
BRAIN BOXES CLOBBER CRISIS!
TOMMY
MOSCOW:
NOT AT ALL, MISTER PRESIDENT. YOU ARE MORE THAN WELCOME.
WERE IT NOT FOR YOUR FOCUS AND LEADERSHIP DURING THIS CRISIS, I DO NOT THINK OUR INTERNATIONAL EFFORT COULD HAVE EVEN BEEN ASSEMBLED IN SUCH A SHORT PERIOD OF TIME.
TOKYO:
WASHINGTON:
WELL, THANK YOU FOR THAT, SIR, AND, YES, I THINK THERE'S SOMETHING PARTICULARLY SATISFYING ABOUT ORDINARY GUYS LIKE YOU AND ME PULLING HUMANITY'S BUTT FROM THE FIRE.
MANKIND SHOULD TAKE A CERTAIN REASSURANCE FROM THE FACT THAT WE'RE NOT ALWAYS AT THE MERCY OF SOME CLOWN IN A MASK WHO LIKES WEARING HIS PANTIES OVER HIS TIGHTIES.

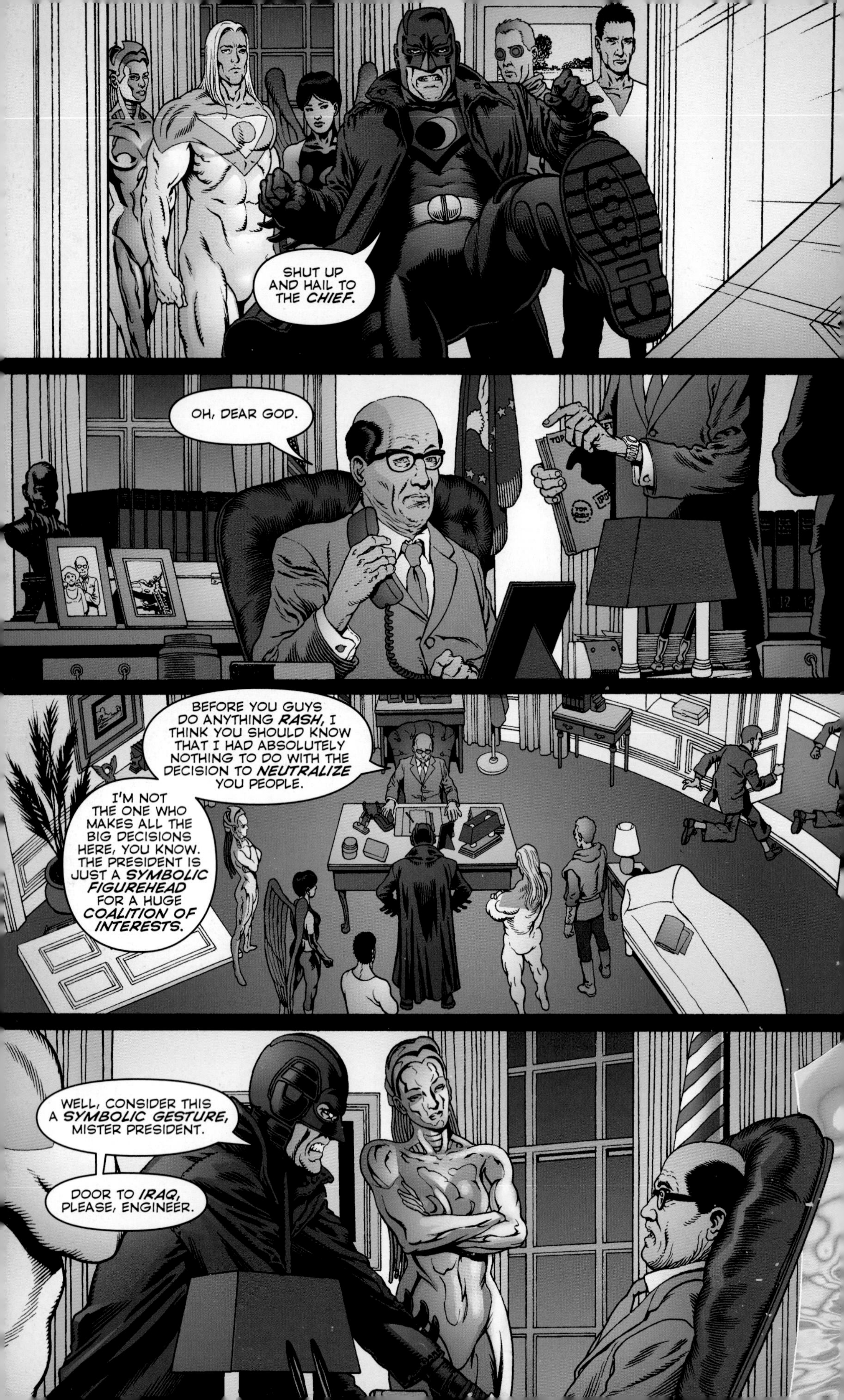
SHUT UP AND HAIL TO THE *CHIEF*.
OH, DEAR GOD.
BEFORE YOU GUYS DO ANYTHING *RASH*, I THINK YOU SHOULD KNOW THAT I HAD ABSOLUTELY NOTHING TO DO WITH THE DECISION TO *NEUTRALIZE* YOU PEOPLE.
I'M NOT THE ONE WHO MAKES ALL THE BIG DECISIONS HERE, YOU KNOW. THE PRESIDENT IS JUST A *SYMBOLIC FIGUREHEAD* FOR A HUGE *COALITION OF INTERESTS*.
WELL, CONSIDER THIS A *SYMBOLIC GESTURE*, MISTER PRESIDENT.
DOOR TO *IRAQ*, PLEASE, ENGINEER.

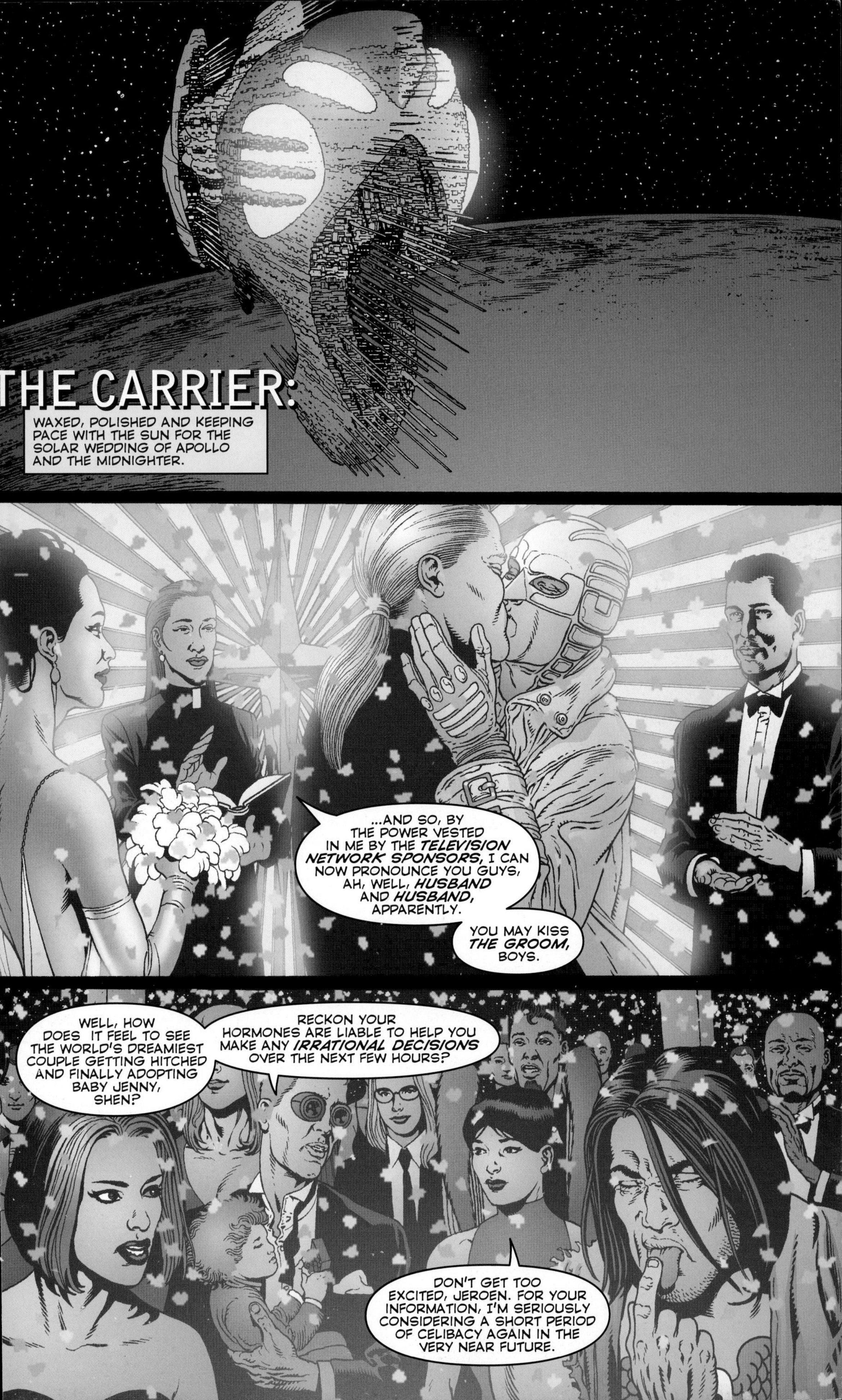
THE CARRIER:
WAXED, POLISHED AND KEEPING PACE WITH THE SUN FOR THE SOLAR WEDDING OF APOLLO AND THE MIDNIGHTER.
...AND SO, BY THE POWER VESTED IN ME BY THE TELEVISION NETWORK SPONSORS, I CAN NOW PRONOUNCE YOU GUYS, AH, WELL, HUSBAND AND HUSBAND, APPARENTLY.
YOU MAY KISS THE GROOM, BOYS.
WELL, HOW DOES IT FEEL TO SEE THE WORLD'S DREAMIEST COUPLE GETTING HITCHED AND FINALLY ADOPTING BABY JENNY, SHEN?
RECKON YOUR HORMONES ARE LIABLE TO HELP YOU MAKE ANY IRRATIONAL DECISIONS OVER THE NEXT FEW HOURS?
DON'T GET TOO EXCITED, JEROEN. FOR YOUR INFORMATION, I'M SERIOUSLY CONSIDERING A SHORT PERIOD OF CELIBACY AGAIN IN THE VERY NEAR FUTURE.

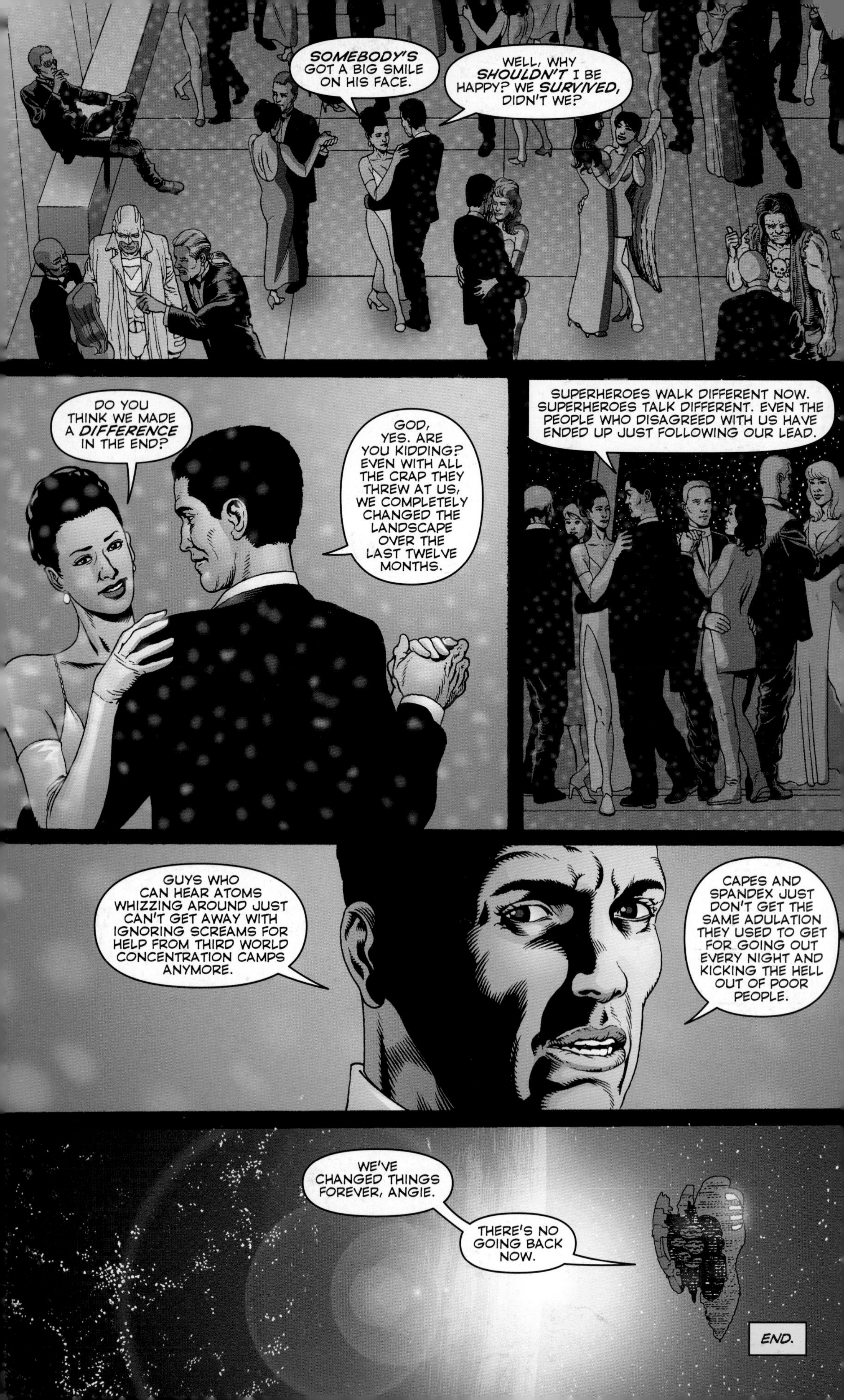
SOMEBODY'S GOT A BIG SMILE ON HIS FACE.
WELL, WHY SHOULDN'T I BE HAPPY? WE SURVIVED, DIDN'T WE?
DO YOU THINK WE MADE A DIFFERENCE IN THE END?
GOD, YES. ARE YOU KIDDING? EVEN WITH ALL THE CRAP THEY THREW AT US, WE COMPLETELY CHANGED THE LANDSCAPE OVER THE LAST TWELVE MONTHS.
SUPERHEROES WALK DIFFERENT NOW. SUPERHEROES TALK DIFFERENT. EVEN THE PEOPLE WHO DISAGREED WITH US HAVE ENDED UP JUST FOLLOWING OUR LEAD.
GUYS WHO CAN HEAR ATOMS WHIZZING AROUND JUST CAN'T GET AWAY WITH IGNORING SCREAMS FOR HELP FROM THIRD WORLD CONCENTRATION CAMPS ANYMORE.
CAPES AND SPANDEX JUST DON'T GET THE SAME ADULATION THEY USED TO GET FOR GOING OUT EVERY NIGHT AND KICKING THE HELL OUT OF POOR PEOPLE.
WE'VE CHANGED THINGS FOREVER, ANGIE.
THERE'S NO GOING BACK NOW.
END.

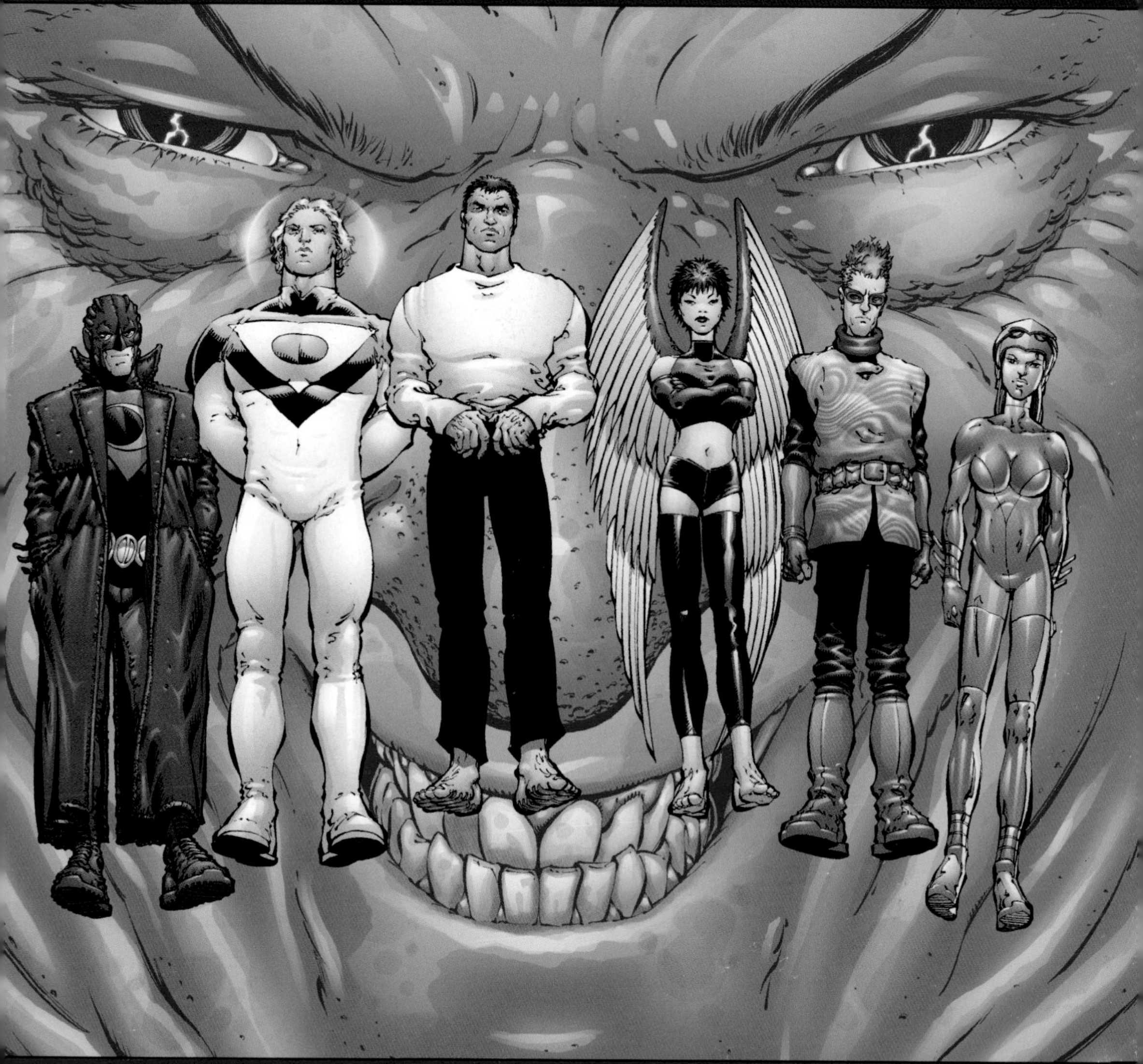

Cover art by FRANK QUITELY and TREVOR SCOTT (with color by DAVID BARON)
for the trade paperback collection THE AUTHORITY: EARTH INFERNO AND OTHER STORIES.

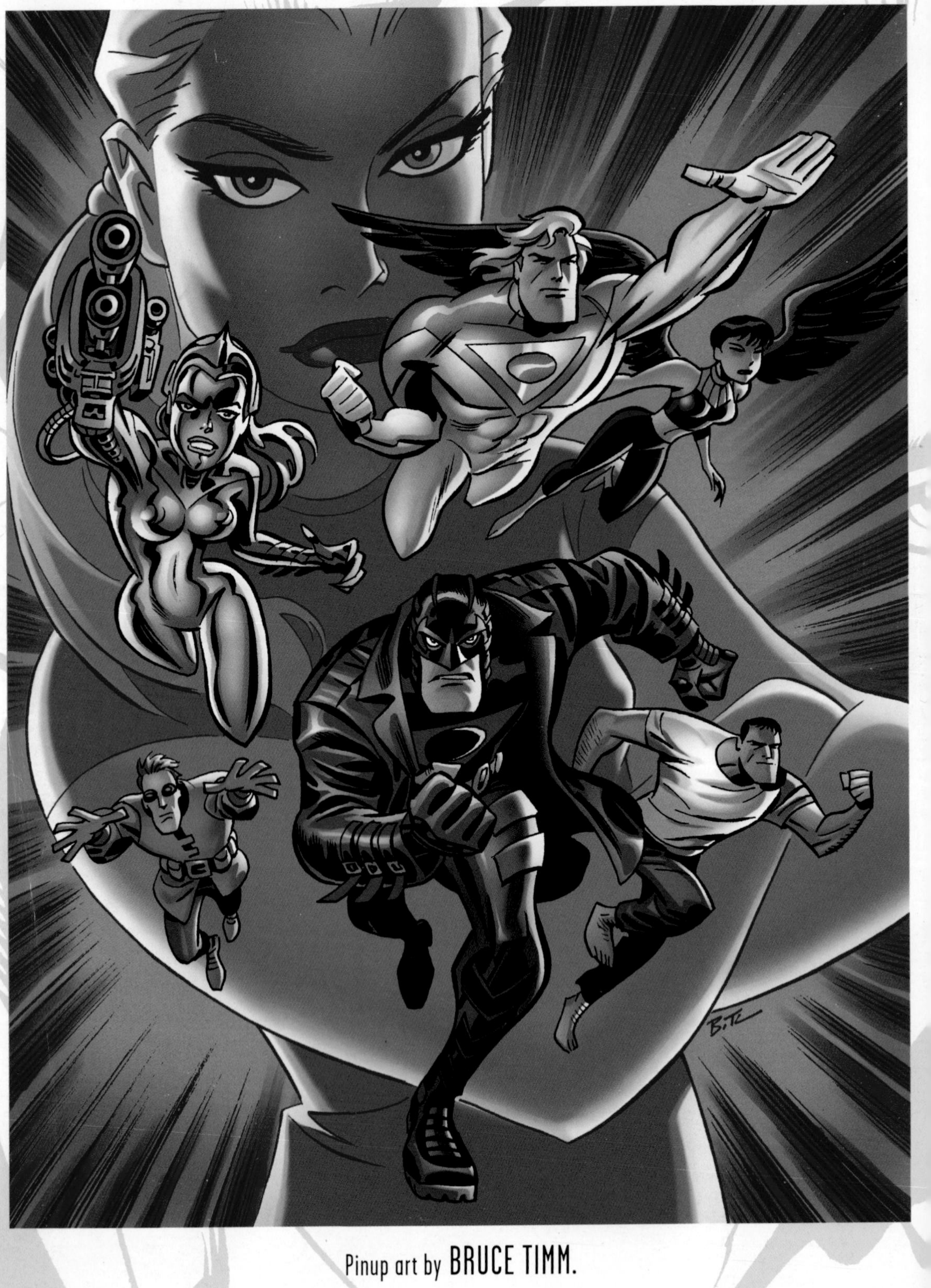

Pinup art by BRUCE TIMM.